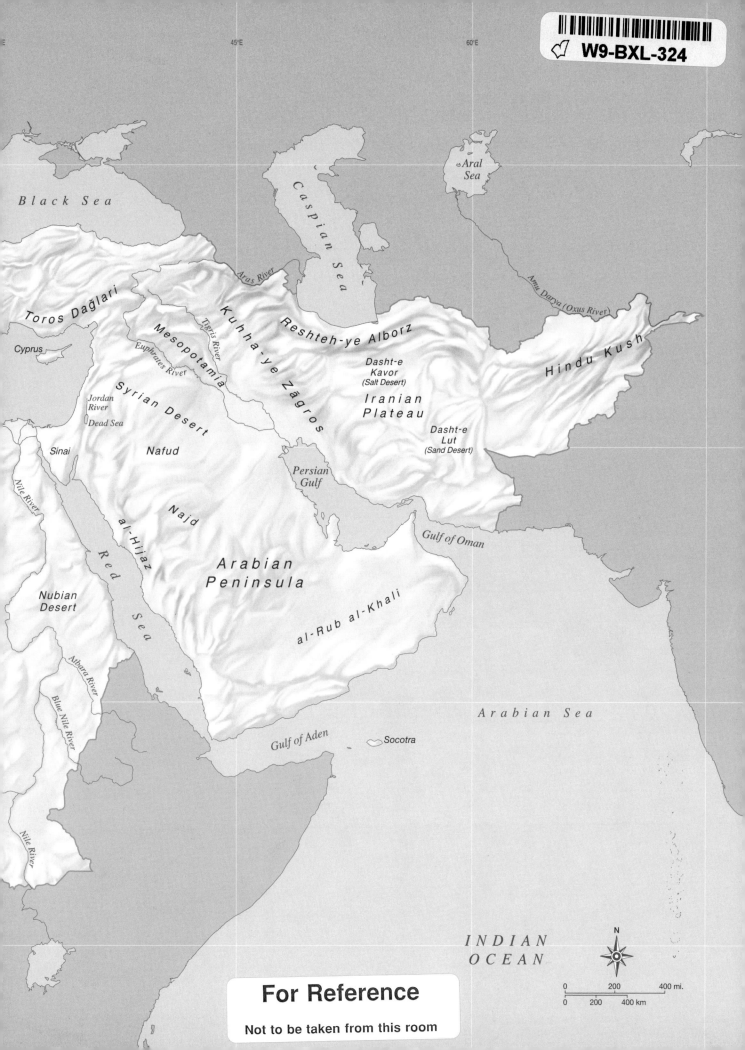

Black Sea

Toros Dağlari

Cyprus

Mesopotamia

Euphrates River

Tigris River

Kuhha-ye Zagros

Reshteh-ye Alborz

Caspian Sea

Aras River

Amu Darya (Oxus River)

Hindu Kush

Aral Sea

Dasht-e
Kavor
(Salt Desert)

Iranian
Plateau

Dasht-e
Lut
(Sand Desert)

Jordan
River

Dead Sea

Sinai

Syrian Desert

Nafud

al-Hijaz

Najd

Arabian
Peninsula

Persian
Gulf

Gulf of Oman

al-Rub al-Khali

Nile River

Red
Sea

Nubian
Desert

Atbara River

Blue Nile River

Nile River

Gulf of Aden

Socotra

Arabian Sea

INDIAN
OCEAN

N

For Reference

Not to be taken from this room

45°E   60°E

0   200   400 mi.

0   200   400 km

ENCYCLOPEDIA OF THE
MODERN
MIDDLE EAST &
NORTH AFRICA
SECOND EDITION

ENCYCLOPEDIA OF THE
MODERN
MIDDLE EAST &
NORTH AFRICA
SECOND EDITION

VOLUME I

Aaronsohn – Cyril VI

Philip Mattar

EDITOR IN CHIEF

MACMILLAN REFERENCE USA

An imprint of Thomson Gale, a part of The Thomson Corporation

Detroit • New York • San Francisco • San Diego • New Haven, Conn. • Waterville, Maine • London • Munich

The Encyclopedia of the Modern Middle East and North Africa, 2nd Edition

Philip Mattar

For permission to use material from this product, submit your request via Web at http://www.gale-edit.com/permissions, or you may download our Permissions Request form and sumbit your request by fax or mail to:

Thomson Gale
27500 Drake Rd.
Farmington Hills, MI 48331-3535
Permissions Hotline:
248-699-8006 or 800-877-4253, ext. 8006
Fax: 248-699-8074 or 800-762-4058

Cover photographs reproduced by permission of Corbis, and AP/Wide World Photos.

Since this page cannot legibly accommodate all copyright notices, the acknowledgements constitute an extension of the copyright notice.

While every effort has been made to ensure the reliability of the information presented in this publication, Thomson Gale does not guarantee the accuracy of the data contained herein. Thomson Gale accepts no payment for listing; and inclusion in the publication of any organization, agency, institution, publication, service, or individual does not imply endorsement of the editors or publisher. Errors brought to the attention of the publisher and verified to the satisfaction of the publisher will be corrected in future editions.

LIBRARY OF CONGRESS CATALOGING-IN-PUBLICATION DATA

Encyclopedia of the modern Middle East and North Africa / edited by Philip Mattar.— 2nd ed.
 p. cm.
  Includes bibliographical references and index.
  ISBN 0-02-865769-1 (set : alk. paper) — ISBN 0-02-865770-5 (v. 1 : alk. paper) — ISBN 0-02-865771-3 (v. 2 : alk. paper) — ISBN 0-02-865772-1 (v. 3 : alk. paper) — ISBN 0-02-865773-X (v. 4 : alk. paper)
  1. Middle East—Encyclopedias. 2. Africa, North—Encyclopedias. I. Mattar, Philip, 1944-

DS43.E53 2004
956'.003—dc22   2004005650

This title is also avalable as an e-book.
ISBN 0-02-865987-2 (set)
Contact your Gale sales representative for ordering information.

Printed in the United States of America
10 9 8 7 6 5 4 3

To Evelyn.

EDITORIAL & PRODUCTION STAFF

TABLE OF CONTENTS

INTRODUCTION

The purpose of this new edition of the encyclopedia is to respond to the growing need for an up-to-date, comprehensive compendium of knowledge about the Middle East and North Africa, from 1800 to the present. Indeed, much has changed in the Middle East since the first edition was published in 1996. The then leaders of Jordan, Morocco, and Syria have died and their sons have come to power. There have been two new prime ministers in Israel. Israeli–Palestinian negotiations failed at the Camp David summit in 2000 and were followed by the al-Aqsa Intifada. The events of 11 September 2001 triggered the United States' invasion of Afghanistan and Iraq, which resulted in the downfall of the Taliban and Saddam Hussein, and in the dispersion of Osama bin Ladin's al-Qaʿida.

The encyclopedia is as timely as ever. During the United States–Iranian crisis in 1979, a *Washington Post* editor, Meg Greenfield, pointed out in her 26 March *Newsweek* column (p. 116) that there are two things to say about American involvement in the Middle East: "One is that no part of the world is more important to our well being at the moment—and probably for the foreseeable future. The other is that no part of the world is more hopelessly and systematically and stubbornly misunderstood by us." In the wake of the tragedy of September 11, and the misunderstanding and hostility it generated towards Islam and the Muslim world among some groups, primarily in the United States, Greenfield's comment is as relevant and prescient now as it was then.

Coverage

This encyclopedia seeks to summarize and organize the most significant factual and analytical knowledge available on the subject and to present it in a readable style that is accessible to high school students, college students, and general readers. The four-volume encyclopedia contains one million words in some 3,000 entries written by approximately 400 scholars of diverse backgrounds and specialization. Entries range in length from 200 to 5,000 words, and about a third of them are biographies. One half of the 3,000 entries are new or have been partly or substantially updated. The revised articles are signed by the original authors, with the new authors' names preceded by the phrase "Updated by." Such entries include chronological data or other information that did not appear in the first edition.

A number of techniques have been employed to make the work as "user friendly" as possible. The articles are alphabetically ordered, although the *al-* prefix (which is the equivalent of the English word *the*) in some words should be disregarded. For example, al-Qaʿida would be found under Q, not A. Each entry is introduced by a brief summary. Articles are cross-referenced to related entries in two ways. First, at the end of most entries, the reader is guided to a list of other, related articles. Second, throughout the work, alternative words or phrases for subjects are listed as "blind entries" within the alphabetical sequence, and are followed by directions that will send the reader to the appropriate essay. For example, a researcher seeking information on census data would encounter the following: "Census: See Population."

A selected bibliography follows the longer essays. These bibliographies direct the reader to additional works in English that the interested reader might profitably consult for further information on the topic. The appendices include a glossary, genealogies, a list of the contributors to the encyclopedia, a list of all the entries, and a conceptual index of some 300 pages, one of the most thorough and useful in any work of this kind. Maps accompany country articles, and hundreds of newly acquired photographs of ordinary people, leaders, sites, and events enrich the text.

The articles cover a wide variety of topics in the fields of politics, history, economics, religion, sociology, geography, literature, fine arts, and many others. They also review twenty-three countries—all but one (Israel) predominantly Muslim. Coverage extends from Afghanistan, Iran, and Turkey to the Fertile Crescent (including Iraq, Syria, Lebanon, Israel, Palestinian territories, and Egypt) and to North African states such as Libya, Algeria, and Morocco. While each country is presented in depth, the Editorial Board decided that Western readers are likely to require more information on some countries than on others because of their historic significance or contemporary role in the region. For example, the entries covering Israel, Egypt, Iran, Turkey (including the Ottoman Empire), Iraq, historic Palestine, Lebanon, Saudi Arabia, Jordan, and the countries of North Africa have been allocated longer and more entries, whereas Cyprus and Mauritania have been given less space in these volumes.

Besides allowing us to update the factual data of the original edition, revising the encyclopedia has provided the opportunity to include new articles on topics that were previously neglected or underrepresented. For example, we have added approximately 200 biographies of women and their organizations, and a number of long articles on gender, such as gender and education, law, politics, and economy. In addition, we have added dozens of profiles of Islamic scholars, organizations, theologians, and activists that had been overlooked in the first edition.

This edition of the encyclopedia has also squarely addressed certain sensitive topics and terms, such as terrorism. This edition calls "terrorism" by its name, not just "military action," and the ritual sexual maiming of women is called "female genital mutilation," rather than employing the coldly clinical term, "circumcision." Sensitive topics, such as the war in Iraq (2003) and the Palestinian al-Nakba ("the disaster"), are explained and discussed openly, as are the Armenian genocide and anti-Semitism in the Arab world.

As editor, I have tried neither to reconcile inconsistencies nor to arbitrate between differing interpretations that have been offered by my colleagues, the contributors to this work. The reader will find a variety of quantitative references and data sets—populations, casualties, refugees—invoked in support of the arguments presented in each article. At times, the interpretations of events, treaties, concepts, and personalities offered by individual contributing authors diverge from or even conflict with one another. This diversity of voices and interpretations not only reflects the state of modern Middle Eastern scholarship, it enriches it and helps to stimulate further research.

I have tried to follow two simple guidelines in selecting the scholars who would write the entries. First, I recognized that a reference work is a forum for knowledge based on consensus, not a forum for new ideas and theories, for which there are many journals. Of course, a new emerging consensus must be reflected in any reference work, and this edition of the encyclopedia provides as wide a view of the field as is supported by rigorous scholarship. Second, I have favored scholars who base their research and analysis on primary material and original languages, and who have a proven record of adhering to high scholarly standards. I have also favored non-partisan scholars who were critical yet empathetic with the people about whom they were writing.

However, some topics are difficult to treat in a non-partisan way, even by scholars. For instance, the encyclopedia includes a considerable amount of coverage on the Palestine problem and Arab–Israeli conflict. In my view, many scholars on these topics are overwhelmed by ideology and emotion, which leads them, at times, to offer the (respective) national narratives rather than the historical record. Although this tendency began to change in the late 1980s, when mainly Israeli historians began to challenge the national myths and distortions present in the history of the conflict, it is nonetheless unavoidable in much Middle Eastern scholarship, even today.

Though comprehensive, this encyclopedia cannot be considered complete, nor is it immune from errors. We welcome readers to send their comments and corrections to Macmillan, for possible use in future editions. Of course, as with all reference works, this encyclopedia should be used as a gateway to knowledge that is found in more detailed books, such as those suggested in the bibliographies that accompany the articles.

Transliteration

The Editorial Board has preferred precision and consistency in the representation of non-English terms, and has generally tried to follow the modified system of the *International Journal of Middle East Studies* and *Encyclopedia Judaica*. However, we have chosen not to apply these systems universally, for a number of reasons. Many place-names and historical personalities are familiar to the Western reader by their English or French forms rather than by the more technically correct transliteration of their Arabic, Hebrew, Turkish, or Persian names. Thus, we have used the familiar English form, *Beirut*, rather than the more correct transliteration of *Bayrut*. Similarly, we have chosen to use the more familiar

Boumedienne to refer to the Algerian leader more properly called *Abu Midyan*. Further complicating the transliteration problem is the fact that people from the region often ignore generally accepted practices in spelling the names of places, persons, and things. In such cases we have often adopted local usage. When the correct spelling is not known, we have spelled it according to the generally accepted standard. Where possible, we have provided alternative spellings, either within individual essays or as blind entries.

We have, thus, favored ease of use over scholarly consistency in our presentation of transliterated words, because this work is for the general reader rather than for the specialist. This editorial choice is also evident in our treatment of diacritical marks in Arabic words. Dots under consonants and lines over vowels (macrons) have not been used, because they mean little to anyone not familiar with Arabic. For the same reason, we have excluded the "ayn" (pronounced in the back of the throat) and "hamza" (a glottal stop) symbols from the beginning and end of words, although we have generally retained these two marks in the middle of words in order to distinguish clearly between the letters on either side of the symbols.

Acknowledgments

There are several groups of people without whom this encyclopedia could not have been accomplished successfully and on time. First and foremost are the authors who invested their time and scholarship in this project. They followed the scopes and guidelines, submitted their entries in a timely manner, and revised according to the comments of the editors, readers, and the copyeditor. Some wrote many entries. To all of them, the Editorial Board and I are most appreciative.

I am also grateful to the Editorial Board, whose broad background and knowledge were of enormous benefit at every stage of this project. They reviewed the entire first edition, compiled the article list, wrote the scopes for entries in their areas of expertise, suggested the authors, read the entries and offered revisions, and contributed some of the entries themselves. Charles E. Butterworth, a specialist of Islamic and Arab culture, provided the encyclopedia with missing entries on Islam and the Muslim world. Neil Caplan, a nonpartisan and leading scholar of Zionism, Israel, the Palestine problem, and the Arab–Israel conflict, reviewed, edited, and wrote many articles. Michael R. Fischbach, an authority on Jordan, Palestine, and the general Middle East, proofread the entire manuscript for transliteration and style, and wrote more than one hundred entries. Eric Hooglund, a foremost expert on Iran, used his broad knowledge and contacts to enhance hundreds of entries, besides writing dozens of articles. Laurie King-Irani, a scholar and prolific writer, designed hundreds of entries on women and gender, and also wrote some fine entries. John Ruedy, one of the leading scholars of North Africa, brought his extensive knowledge to bear on the project. We also benefited from the wise advice of our consultant, Don Peretz, a preeminent scholar whose nonpartisan scholarship on the Arab–Israeli conflict preceded all others' by at least two decades.

I want to also thank my colleagues of the first edition, Reeva S. Simon and Richard Bulliet, both of Columbia University. Although the second edition is thoroughly revised, it would not have been possible without their work on the first. They contributed to the entry list and to hundreds of articles that have remained intact or were only slightly revised. In addition, I wish to thank James Keary, my research assistant, who intelligently and diligently helped me revise the entry list of 3000 articles for the second edition.

I am very grateful to the people at Macmillan Reference USA. Of the dozen publishing houses with which I have worked over two decades, Macmil-

lan provided an editorial team, headed by Hélène Potter, director of development, that is undoubtedly the most professional, efficient, and friendly. They made a complex and intense project seem easy and pleasant. Potter, who commissioned the project, provided us with guidance, encouragement, and, at critical junctures, judicious advice. I am most grateful for her support and friendship.

Potter's team of extraordinarily talented staff deserves special thanks. Corrina Moss, the assistant editor, with whom I was in frequent contact, was very well organized, and she handled relations with authors and associate editors with the skills of a seasoned diplomat. She was followed by an equally competent, organized, and friendly production editor, Kate Millson, who led the project to fruition. Kate and the project benefited from additional support: Editor Nancy Matuszak carefully and cheerfully developed the complex art program; the demanding typesetting program with its proliferation of details was made manageable by senior editor Carol Schwartz; and editor Erin Bealmear provided thorough, valuable support at a moment's notice wherever she was needed.

Finally, I am deeply grateful to my companion and friend—my wife Evelyn—for her loving support and patience from the inception of the project in the early 1990s, through two long periods of gestations and successful completions.

PHILIP MATTAR
WASHINGTON, DC, APRIL 2004

AARONSOHN FAMILY

Early Jewish settlers who founded Zikhron Ya'acov and the NILI spy ring.

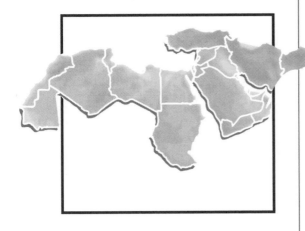

Ephraim Fishel Aaronsohn (1849–1939) and his wife, Malka, immigrated to Palestine from Bacau, Romania, in 1882 together with their son, Aaron (1876–1919), in order to fulfill their dream of returning to the land. Fishel was a founder of a new settlement, Zikhron Ya'acov, and became a farmer. Aaron was educated in the settlement and in France, and became a prominent agronomist. The parents subsequently bore another son, Alexander (1888–1948), and a daughter, Sarah (1890–1917).

Aaron and Sarah are the best known of the family. Aaron's reputation as an agronomist won him an invitation from the United States Department of Agriculture to meet with U.S. agricultural experts. During his visit to the United States in 1909 he also met with prominent Jewish leaders, with whom he discussed his ideas for agricultural experimentation and cultivating Palestine. The outbreak of World War I convinced Aaron that his ideas would never be realized under the Turks, and in 1915 he recruited a number of close friends and family members to found a Jewish espionage group whose objective was to spy on the Turks and provide secret information to British officials of the Arab Bureau in Cairo. The name of the group was NILI, which is an acronym for the text of 1 Samuel 15:29: "The eternity (or 'victory' or 'strength') of Israel will not lie." When Sarah learned that the network had been uncovered by the Turks, she disbanded the group. She was arrested in her home in Zikhron Ya'acov on 1 October 1917 and was tortured for four days, but rather than disclose the names of her comrades, she committed suicide.

NILI was shunned by Chaim Weizmann and many in the leadership of the Zionist Organization (later known as the World Zionist Organization). On the other hand, the significance of the information uncovered by NILI has been attested to by various British military officers, including General George Macdonogh, Field Marshall Edmund Henry Allenby, and Colonel Richard Meinertzhagen.

Aaron was a passenger in a Royal Air Force mail delivery airplane that went down in the English Channel on 15 May 1919. For years afterward there were rumors that he had been purposely killed by the British, but no evidence to support the allegations was ever found; on the contrary, extensive investigations concluded that his death was accidental.

See also WEIZMANN, CHAIM.

Bibliography

Engle, Anita. *The NILI Spies.* Portland, OR; London: Frank Cass, 1997.

Gribbon, Walter. *Agents of Empire: Anglo-Zionist Intelligence Operations 1915–1919: Brigadier Walter Gribbon, Aaron Aaronsohn, and the NILI Ring,* edited by Anthony Verrier. Washington, DC; London: Brassey's, 1995.

Katz, Shmuel. *The Aaronsohn Saga.* Tel Aviv: Ministry of Defense Publishing House, 2000.

Livneh, Eliezer. *Aaron Aaronsohn: His Life and Times.* Jerusalem: Bialik Institute, 1969.

Winstone, H. V. F. *The Illicit Adventure: The Story of Political amd Military Intelligence in the Middle East from 1898 to 1926.* London: Jonathan Cape, 1982.

CHAIM I. WAXMAN

ABADAN

A city with large oil refineries and an island in the province of Khuzistan in southwest Iran.

The island of Abadan is 40 miles long and from 2 to 12 miles wide. The island is bounded by the Shatt al-Arab River on the west, the Karun River on the north, and the Persian Gulf on the south. The city, 9 miles from the northwestern tip of the island, was first mentioned by Muslim geographers during in the mid-ninth century. In medieval times it was of importance to travelers and navigators as a source of woven straw mats, supplier of salt, and center of shipping and navigation.

The modern city that developed after 1910 was due to the oil industry. The first oil refinery, which was opened by the Anglo-Persian Oil Company in 1912 with an annual capacity of 120,000 tons, grew into one of the world's largest refineries by the 1960s. Abadan's population grew with its economic development. In 1948 refinery employees formed one-third of the city population of about 100,000.

By the 1950s the city's population reached about 220,000, and in 1976 it was 296,000, making Abadan the fifth largest city in the country. In August 1978 more than 400 persons burned to death in a fire at an Abadan cinema. This incident became a precursor to the 1979 revolution.

The Iran–Iraq War (1980–1988) heavily damaged the refinery as well as the city. Most of the population fled during the war, but some returned during the 1990s, when most of the city was reconstructed.

Because it is an industrial islet heavily influenced by foreign capitalist enterprise that uses the country's unskilled labor and raw material, Abadan's social structure is strongly segregated ethnically and economically. According to the 1996 census, the population of the reconstructed city was 206,073.

See also KHUZISTAN.

PARVANEH POURSHARIATI

ABANE, RAMDANE

See FRONT DE LIBÉRATION NATIONALE (FLN)

ABASIYANIK, SAIT SAIK

See LITERATURE: TURKISH

ABASSI, MADANI

See MADANI, ABASSI AL-

ABAYA

See CLOTHING

ABBAS, FERHAT
[1899–1985]

Leading Algerian nationalist and statesman.

Ferhat Abbas was born in Taher to a family identified with French colonial rule. His father was a member of the Legion of Honor and served as a Qaʾid or *caid* (administrator under the French). In 1909, Abbas entered the *lycée* at Philippeville (now Skikda) in Algeria. Following three years in the French army medical service, he enrolled in the pharmacy school at the University of Algiers.

Abbas's political career evolved from an earnest assimilationist to a reluctant revolutionary. In his first book, *Le jeune Algérien: De la colonie vers la province* (1931), he criticized the failure of French colonialism to live up to its assimilationist ideals. Along with Dr. Mohammed Saleh Bendjelloul, Abbas led the Fédération des Elus indigènes (founded in 1927), which continued to espouse the moderate reforms called for by the Jeunes Algériens (Young Algerians). Abbas embraced the ill-fated Blum-Viollette Plan, which would have granted full French citizenship to 20,000 to 30,000 assimilated Algerians. The failure of the Blum-Viollette Plan split the moderates as Bendjelloul founded the Rassemblement Franco-Musulman Algérien (Assembly of French-Muslim Algerians), while Abbas organized the Union Populaire Algérien (Algerian People's Union, UPA), a party that began to affirm a separate Algerian identity while calling for full citizenship for all Muslims. This marked the redefinition of Abbas's position that he had presented in the federation's newspaper, *Entente,* where he wrote that he was unable to locate a historical Algerian nation and therefore tied Algeria's future to France.

Abbas volunteered at the beginning of World War II, but he was alienated by the Nazi occupation of France, Vichy government administration, and then by Free French general Henri Giraud's disinterest in reform while concurrently exhorting Muslims to enlist (though not on an equal basis) and sacrifice their lives. Abbas reacted by presenting the "Manifeste du peuple algérien" (Manifesto of the Algerian People) in February 1943, followed by a more explicit supplement called the "Projet de réformes faisant suite au Manifeste" (Project of Reforms Made Following the Manifesto) in May. These documents called for an autonomous Algerian state that was still closely associated with France.

Charles de Gaulle's ordinance of 7 March 1944 went beyond the provisions of the Blum-Viollette Plan, but it no longer corresponded to the aspirations of the nationalist elite. In March 1944, Abbas organized the Association des Amis du Manifeste et de la Liberté (Friends of the Manifesto and of Liberty, AML), which briefly unified the Muslim nationalist movements under the leadership of Messali al-Hadj. Under Messalist pressures, the AML took a more radical position, calling for an Algerian government that reduced the attachment with France.

Ferhat Abbas was named on 18 September 1958 to serve as the first president of the Algerian Constituent Assembly. He held this position until 1961. Abbas's political career reflected his interests for political reforms, middle-class moderation, and the assimilation of Algerians and the French. © HULTON-DEUTSCH COLLECTION/CORBIS. REPRODUCED BY PERMISSION.

The deportation of Messali in April 1945 contributed to the bloody uprising at Setif and Guelma in May. Abbas was placed under house arrest. After being freed, he founded the Union Démocratique du Manifeste Algérien (Democratic Union of the Algerian Manifesto, UDMA) in 1946. The UDMA sought a sovereign Algerian state responsible for internal affairs while being a member of the French union. Abbas was also elected to the Second French Constituent Assembly. He served as a member of the Muslim College of the Algerian Assembly from 1947 to 1955.

During the first eighteen months of the Algerian War of Independence (1954–1962), Abbas attempted to act as an intermediary between the Front de Libération Nationale (National Liberation Front, FLN) and the French, but in April 1956 he joined the FLN with other moderates and declared that it was the only representative force for the liberation of the country.

Appreciating his international prestige, on 19 September 1958 the FLN appointed Abbas president of the Gouvernement Provisoire de la République Algérienne (Provisional Government of the Algerian Republic, GPRA). In January 1961, he participated in a continental conference to establish an African Charter. Abbas signed an agreement with King Hassan II of Morocco in July 1961 to settle border disputes after the end of the war of independence. In August, he was replaced by the more radical Ben Youssef Ben Khedda as president of the GPRA. The ouster of Abbas and the moderates signaled an important change in the FLN.

In fall 1962, Abbas was elected president of Algeria's National Constituent Assembly. He envisioned a democratic parliamentary form of government, which permitted political pluralism. His liberal democratic ideals were anachronistic compared to the revolutionary objectives of the younger elite (e.g., Premier Ahmed Ben Bella), which were based on those of Egypt's President Gamal Abdel Nasser. The construction of a constitution that ignored the Constituent Assembly and the growing authoritarianism of Ben Bella led to Abbas's resignation in August 1963. He was subsequently removed from the FLN. This was a symbolic repudiation of a revolutionary heritage that had aimed at liberal reform and close ties with France.

Abbas's opposition to Ben Bella led to his arrest in 1964. After Houari Boumédienne took over the government in June 1965, Abbas was released, but he refused to serve the military government. In March 1976, he joined Ben Khedda, Hocine Lahouel, and Mohamed Kheireddine in signing a manifesto entitled "New Appeal to the Algerian People." This courageous act condemned the lack of democratic institutions in Algeria, opposed the growing hostility between Algeria and Morocco over the decolonization of western Sahara and called for Maghrib (North African) unity. Abbas was again placed under house arrest.

Ferhat Abbas's contributions to the creation of the Algerian state were publicly acknowledged in the "enhanced" National Center of 1986, which was published about two weeks after his death. Besides *Le jeune Algérien* (1931), Abbas was the author of several important works: *Guerre de Révolution d'Algérie: La nuit coloniale* (1962) and *Autopsie d'une guerre: L'aurore* (1980) reflect upon the war years. In *L'indépendance confisquée, 1962–1978* (1984), Abbas expressed his disillusionment with postcolonial Algeria, but he also dedicated the book to the emerging new generation. In some ways, his call for youth to restore the true meaning of the revolution has been heard since the October 1988 riots.

See also ALGERIA; AMIS DU MANIFESTE ET DE LA LIBERTÉ; BEN BELLA, AHMED; BEN KHEDDA, BEN YOUSSEF; BLUM–VIOLLETTE PLAN; BOUMÉDIENNE, HOUARI; FRONT DE LIBÉRATION NATIONALE (FLN); HADJ, MESSALI AL-; HASSAN II; LAHOUEL, HOCINE; MAGHRIB; NASSER, GAMAL ABDEL; SETIF; UNION DÉMOCRATIQUE DU MANIFESTE ALGÉRIEN (UDMA); YOUNG ALGERIANS.

Bibliography

Naylor, Phillip C., and Heggoy, Alf A. *The Historical Dictionary of Algeria*, 2d edition. Metuchen, NJ: Scarecrow Press, 1994.

PHILLIP C. NAYLOR

ABBAS HILMI I
[1812–1854]

Viceroy of Egypt, 1848–1854.

Son of Tusun and grandson of Muhammad Ali, Hilmi Abbas was born in Alexandria (or, some sources say, Jidda) and reared in Cairo. A cavalry officer, he accompanied his uncle, Ibrahim Pasha, on his Syrian campaign, served as temporary governor-general of Egypt when Muhammad Ali went to the Sudan in 1839, and succeeded Ibrahim as viceroy upon his death in November 1848.

Abbas was viewed by many Europeans as a reactionary because he dismantled some of his grandfather's Westernizing reforms and dismissed most of the French advisers to the Egyptian government (his policies tended to be pro-British and anti-French), but he reduced taxes on the peasants. He awarded a concession to an English company to build Egypt's first railroad, connecting Cairo and Alexandria. The land route from Cairo to Suez was also improved. He sought the support of the Ulama (Islamic clergy) and the Sufi orders. He laid the cornerstone for the Sayyida Zaynab Mosque, a popular shrine, in Cairo. Abbas sent troops to fight on the side of the Ottoman Empire against Russia in the Crimea, where they suffered heavy casualties.

His policies antagonized many members of the Muhammad Ali dynasty, and he died in Banha in 1854 under mysterious circumstances.

See also IBRAHIM IBN MUHAMMAD ALI; MUHAMMAD ALI; *ULAMA*.

Bibliography

Toledano, Ehud R. *State and Society in Mid-Nineteenth Century Egypt.* Cambridge, U.K., and New York: Cambridge University Press, 1990.

ARTHUR GOLDSCHMIDT

ABBAS HILMI II
[1874–1944]

Egypt's khedive (viceroy), 1892–1914.

Born in Cairo, Abbas Hilmi was the seventh member of the Muhammad Ali dynasty to serve as viceroy of Egypt but the first whose whole term of office coincided with Britain's military occupation of the country. A high-spirited youth inclined to nationalism when he succeeded his father, Tawfiq, Abbas soon clashed with the British consul-general, Lord Cromer, over the appointment of Egypt's new prime minister. The two men agreed finally on a compromise premier, Mustafa al-Riyad, but Cromer had persuaded his government to enlarge the British occupation force.

In 1894 Abbas, while on an inspection tour of Upper Egypt, quarreled with the commander of the Egyptian army, Sir Herbert (later Lord) Kitchener, over what he viewed as the poor performance of the British-officered units. Kitchener offered to resign, but Cromer made Abbas issue a statement expressing his satisfaction with all the units of his army—a public admission of surrender. Unable to confront Britain directly, he formed a secret society that evolved into the National Party, which initially placed its hopes on French support.

Born on 14 July 1874, Abbas Hilmi II succeeded his father as ruler of Egypt from 7 January 1892 until 18 December 1914, following the declaration of a British Protectorate over Egypt. He abdicated all his powers in 1931. © BETTMANN/CORBIS. REPRODUCED BY PERMISSION.

When France's challenge to Britain's predominance in the Nile valley waned after the 1898 Fashoda incident, Khedive Abbas moved away from the Nationalists, who were turning to pan-Islam and to appeals for constitutional government. After the Dinshaway incident, he briefly resumed his opposition to the British by helping the Nationalists to publish daily newspapers in French and English. After Cromer retired, however, he was lured away from nationalism by the friendlier policies pursued by the new British consul, John Eldon Gorst. In 1908, he named a new cabinet headed by Boutros Ghali, a Copt (Christian) who favored the British. Abbas adopted a policy increasingly hostile to the Nationalists, reviving the 1881 Press Law, prosecuting the editor of al-Liwa, and promulgating the Exceptional Laws after the 1910 assassination of Boutros Ghali by a Nationalist. When Gorst died and was succeeded by Lord Kitchener, Abbas again broke with the British. His hope of using the 1913 Organic Law to bring his supporters into the new Legislative Assembly was only partly successful, since Sa'd Zaghlul, an old enemy, emerged as its leading spokesman.

When World War I broke out in 1914, he was in the Ottoman capital of Istanbul recovering from an assassination attempt. The British forbade him to return to Egypt, using the entry into war of the Ottoman Empire on their enemy's side as a pretext to depose him and sever Egypt's residual Ottoman ties. The former khedive spent most of the war years in Switzerland—plotting at first with the Nationalists to engineer an uprising in Egypt against the British; then with the Germans to buy shares in several Paris newspapers to influence their policies in a pacifist direction; and then with the British to secure the succession of his son to what had become the sultanate of Egypt.

After all these intrigues failed, Abbas returned to Istanbul and cooperated with the Central Powers (Germany, Austria-Hungary, and the Ottoman Empire) until their final defeat (1918). He tried for several years to regain control of his properties in Egypt, but finally accepted a cash settlement and went into business in Europe. He attempted to mediate the Palestine question and supported a Muslim organization. He then backed the Axis powers (Germany, Japan, and Italy) early in World War II (1939). Although energetic and patriotic, he failed to stem British moves to strengthen their military occupation of Egypt.

See also DINSHAWAY INCIDENT (1906); GORST, JOHN ELDON; MUHAMMAD ALI; RIYAD, MUSTAFA AL-; ZAGHLUL, SA'D.

Bibliography

Beaman, Ardern Hulme. *The Dethronement of the Khedive.* London: Allen and Unwin, 1929.

Cromer, Evelyn Baring, Earl of. *Abbas II.* London: Macmillan, 1915.

ARTHUR GOLDSCHMIDT

ABBAS, MAHMUD
[1937–]

A founder of al-Fatah; first Palestinian prime minister.

Mahmud Abbas (also called Abu Mazin or Abu Mazen) was born in Safed (in Hebrew, Zefat), now in northern Israel but then in the British mandate of Palestine. As a result of the Arab–Israel War of 1948, he became a refugee and ended up working in the Gulf oil states. He eventually obtained his doctorate in Israeli studies in the Soviet Union. During the late 1950s, Abbas began organizing Palestinians in Saudi Arabia and in Qatar. After suffering the disappointment of the Egyptian and Palestinian defeat by Israel in the Arab–Israel War of 1956, he joined Yasir Arafat, Khalil al-Wazir, Salah Khalaf, and others in forming the group al-Fatah.

He has remained one of the most senior al-Fatah members since then. After Israel's assassination of al-Wazir (known as Abu Jihad) in 1988, Abbas became Arafat's closest political strategist.

Abbas became the principal Palestinian architect of the 1993 peace accords concluded between Israel and the Palestine Liberation Organization. He, along with Israel's Foreign Minister Shimon Peres, signed the 13 September 1993 Oslo Accord in Washington, D.C. Although he expressed some dissatisfaction with the course of the peace process thereafter, Abbas remained committed to it. The al-Aqsa Intifada, which broke out in September 2000, all but destroyed the peace process and led the United States and others to exert tremendous pressure on Palestinian Authority (PA) president Arafat to create the office of prime minister within the PA, a position that would control the PA's security forces. In April 2003 Arafat appointed Abbas as prime minister. Abbas sought to control the security apparatus, while Arafat tried to keep as much control over events in the PA as possible. Tension mounted between the two over Abbas's candidate for the position of minister of the interior. Abbas's ultimate failure to dislodge the security apparatus from Arafat's control and thus assume meaningful powers as prime minister, along with Israel's continuing hard line toward the Palestinians in light of the suicide bombings it was sustaining, led Abbas to resign his position in September 2003 after serving only for a few months.

See also Aqsa Intifada, al-; Arab–Israel War (1948); Arafat, Yasir; Fatah, al-; Khalaf, Salah; Oslo Accord (1993); Palestine Liberation Organization (PLO); Palestinian Authority; Peres, Shimon; Wazir, Khalil al-.

Bibliography

Abbas, Mahmoud. *Through Secret Channels.* Reading, U.K.: Garnet, 1995.

Steve Tamari
Updated by Michael R. Fischbach

ABBAS MIRZA, NA'EB AL-SALTANEH
[1789–1833]

Crown prince of Iran and military leader of its forces against Russia.

Abbas Mirza was the son of Fath Ali Shah Qajar (r. 1797–1834). In 1799, Abbas Mirza was declared the crown prince and became the governor of Azerbaijan, with Mirza Bozorg Qa'em Maqam as his minister and mentor. Beginning in 1804, Iran became involved in a long, disastrous war with Russia in the Caucasus, which was under Iranian rule. The war ended in 1813 with defeat for Iran. Under the Treaty of Golestan, Iran ceded Georgia, Darband, Baku, Shirvan, Ganjeh, Karabagh, and Moghan to Russia. Boundaries were not well defined, which gave a pretext for the renewal of war by 1824. Abbas Mirza led the Iranian forces, which were no match for the better-equipped Russians. Iran was defeated in 1828, and Tabriz, Abbas Mirza's capital, was occupied.

The Treaty of Turkmanchai, which ended the war, had dire consequences for Iran: It agreed to cede all the areas north of the Aras River; accept indemnity and capitulatory clauses; and pay 5 million *tumans* (approximately $10 to $25 million) to Russia before Tabriz was evacuated. As a result, not only was Iran's economy undermined, but also the indemnity and capitulatory clauses served as a model for all future treaties with European nations.

In the years that followed the treaty, Abbas Mirza tried to pacify eastern Iran, where rebellion was undermining governmental authority. He also set out to reestablish Iranian rule over Herat, now in northwest Afghanistan. He died during the second expedition, and his father, Fath Ali Shah, declared Abbas Mirza's son, the future Mohammad Shah Qajar, the new crown prince.

During his years as crown prince, Abbas Mirza had come into contact with many European envoys because he often carried out diplomatic negotiations for the shah. He believed that Iran needed to modernize its army and governmental administration. He employed European military advisers toward this end, first from France, then from Britain. He also sent Iranian students to Britain to study such subjects as medicine, arms manufacture, languages, and the arts, and he subsidized the translation of several useful books. His untimely death ended any positive results from this pursuit.

See also Fath Ali Shah Qajar; Qajar Dynasty; Turkmanchai, Treaty of (1828).

Bibliography

Algar, Hamid. *Religion and State in Iran, 1785–1906: The Role of the Ulama in the Qajar Period.* Berkeley: University of California Press, 1969.

Pakravan, E. *Abbas Mirza.* Tehran: Institut Franco-Iranien, 1958.

Mansoureh Ettehadieh
Updated by Eric Hooglund

ABBUD, IBRAHIM
[1900–?]

Ruler of the Sudan, 1958–1964.

Born in a village on the Red Sea and educated in Khartoum at Gordon Memorial College (now

Khartoum University) and the military college, Ibrahim Abbud joined the Egyptian army in 1918 and later served with the Sudan Defense Force. During World War II he became the highest-ranking Sudanese officer. In 1956, he became commander-in-chief of the armed forces, when the Sudan became an independent republic.

After he engineered the coup d'état with the support of senior politicians in 1958, he headed the Supreme Council of the Armed Forces, which ruled the country for six years. Abbud suspended the constitution, closed parliament, and banned political parties and trade unions. He negotiated an accord with Egypt to reapportion the use of the Nile waters, but his hard-line policy toward the south, which included the forced Arabization of schools and government offices and the placement of restrictions on Christian institutions, led to an escalation in fighting in that region, an overall deterioration in the economy, and protests in northern cities. He was overthrown in 1964 during mass demonstrations, led by students, professionals, and trade unions, which sought a return to democracy and the undertaking of diplomatic efforts to resolve the civil war in the south. Abbud was not forced into exile or even arrested; he was allowed to resign and to receive his pension.

Bibliography

Lesch, Ann M. "Military Disengagement from Politics: The Sudan." In *Military Disengagement from Politics,* edited by Constantine P. Danopoulos. London and New York: Routledge, 1988.

ANN M. LESCH

ABD AL-AZIZ IBN AL-HASSAN

Sultan of Morocco, 1894–1908.

A young boy at the death of his father, Hassan I, in 1894, Abd al-Aziz assumed the powers of sultan in 1900 upon the death of the regent, Ahmad ibn Musa. Under Ibn Musa, the modernizing reforms of Hassan had been undermined by social and economic changes, and Morocco became increasingly vulnerable to European imperialist ambitions. In 1900, France annexed the Saharan oasis of In Salah, previously claimed by Morocco, as well as territory along the Algeria–Morocco frontier.

This inaugurated the Moroccan Question, a period of rising European imperialist ambitions (1900–1912). Abd al-Aziz's lack of experience and penchant for European ways permitted European speculators and business interests to take advantage of the situation. It also contributed to undermining his legitimacy. More important was the incompetent way a new universal tax on agriculture, the *tartib,* was introduced, which provoked revolts in several districts. The most important of these was the 1902 rebellion led by Abu Himara, whose victories enabled him to pose a long-term challenge to the regime. Following Moroccan attacks on Europeans, there were several important diplomatic crises.

The Moroccan crisis deepened in 1904 when, after complex French diplomatic maneuvers, Spain, Italy, and Britain renounced their claims to Morocco (although Spain's renunciation did not last). France sought rapidly to capitalize on the situation. It negotiated a major loan agreement with the bankrupt Moroccan government, thus gaining a dominant position in Moroccan finances. It also issued an ultimatum that Morocco adopt a French reform proposal, which would have amounted to it becoming a virtual protectorate. Seeking to stave off the French proposals, Abd al-Aziz referred them to an assembly of notables, or *majles,* in 1905, while seeking diplomatic support from Germany.

Despite German intervention and the convening of the international Algeciras Conference (1906), however, Morocco was forced to accept the substance of France's proposals. Eventually Abd al-Aziz was compelled to sign the Act of Algeciras (1906) over the vociferous objections of the Moroccan elite. By doing this, he fatally undermined his regime.

In the post-Algeciras period, a new French aggressiveness and the breakdown of rural security gave rise to attacks on French citizens. The landing of French troops at Oujda and Casablanca (1907) led to uprisings in both districts. More importantly, in August 1907, it provoked the rebellion of his brother, Abd al-Hafid, the governor of Marrakech, in alliance with Madani and Tuhami al-Glawi and other rural magnates of southern Morocco. Despite French support, Abd al-Aziz was eventually defeated after a yearlong civil war and compelled to abdicate his throne. Thereafter, he lived in retirement in Tangier.

See also ABD AL-HAFID IBN AL-HASSAN; ABU HIMARA; ALGECIRAS CONFERENCE (1906); HASSAN I; IBN MUSA, AHMAD; MOROCCAN QUESTION; TUHAMI AL-GLAWI.

Bibliography

Burke, Edmund, III. *Prelude to Protectorate in Morocco: Precolonial Protest and Resistance, 1860–1912.* Chicago: University of Chicago, 1976.

Harris, Walter Burton. *The Morocco That Was.* Edinburgh and London: W. Blackwood and Sons, 1921.

Pennell, C. R. *Morocco since 1830: A History.* New York: New York University Press, 2000.

EDMUND BURKE III

ABD AL-AZIZ IBN SAʿUD AL SAʿUD
[1880–1953]

Muslim leader and founder of Saudi Arabia.

Abd al-Aziz ibn Saʿud Al Saʿud (known as Ibn Saʿud) became the greatest of all Saudi rulers, restoring the Arabian empire of his ancestors in the early years of the twentieth century. In his reign of more than a half century he not only recovered the lost patrimony of the House of Saʿud but laid the foundations for the economically powerful Saudi Arabia, over which his sons continue to rule. Along with his ancestors Saʿud ibn Abd al-Aziz and Abd al-Aziz ibn Muhammad (rulers of the Saudi state at the turn of the nineteenth century), he was the only Arabian ruler since the early Islamic era to unify most of the Arabian Peninsula under a single political authority.

As he was growing up in Riyadh, the Saudi capital, where he received a traditional education centered on the memorization of the Qurʾan, he witnessed the last act in the decline of the second Saudi state and its submission to the Al Saʿud family's central Arabian rivals and former vassals, the Al Rashid of Haʾil, a town to the north of Riyadh. His father, Abd al-Rahman, failed in the attempt to reassert Saudi independence and the ten-year-old Abd al-Aziz fled into exile in Kuwait with the rest of the family. In 1902, he led a band of forty companions on a dramatic raid that seized Riyadh from its Rashidi overlords. Over the next quarter century bold military, political, and diplomatic initiatives

Abd al-Aziz ibn Saʿud Al Saʿud, the politically astute founder of the modern kingdom of Saudi Arabia. He unified most of the Arabian Peninsula under one political authority during the first three decades of the twentieth century. PUBLIC DOMAIN.

brought all of Arabia except for Yemen, Oman, and the Gulf shaykhdoms under his rule.

In reestablishing Saudi authority, Abd al-Aziz self-consciously re-created the religio-political state of his Wahhabi ancestors. It was based on adherence to the strict beliefs and practices of Muhammad ibn Abd al-Wahhab, the eighteenth-century Islamic reformer whose 1744 alliance with Muhammad ibn Saʿud had created the Saudi state of 1745. Indeed, he looked back to the first Islamic community under the prophet Muhammad in creating, from 1912 on, a series of communities called *hujar* (pl.; echoing the *hijra*—the migration of the prophet Muhammad and his early followers to Medina). Here unruly Bedouin tribesmen were settled as Ikhwan, brethren under the command of preacher/warriors who formed the core of Abd al-Aziz's military force. In addition to the crucial legitimacy provided by identification with Wahhabi Islam, he was able to draw on the established loyalty of many central Arabians, which derived from the significant history of rule by the House of Sa'ud. Moreover, Abd al-Aziz and the Saudi clan enjoyed the advantage of membership in the great Anaza tribal federation, conferring noble (sharifian) lineage, thus joining a critical aristocracy of blood to their religious credentials. Abd al-Aziz was brilliantly adept in his management of tribal relations, utilizing disbursement of material benefits, application of military force, and the establishment of marital ties to build the alliances necessary to secure his power. He made astute use of the bedouin magnanimity, for which he was famous, as when he carefully contrived to avoid casualties in his capture of Hail, last stronghold of the Al Rashid, then arranged for the comfortable confinement of his defeated rivals in Riyadh. Patient and generous treatment of his rebellious cousin Sa'ud al-Kabir served to deflect a challenge from within the Al Sa'ud and secured the line of succession for the direct descendants of Abd al-Rahman.

If mastery of traditional sources of power in Arabian statecraft carried Abd al-Aziz through the initial phases of reconquest, it was his capacity to utilize Western inventions and techniques as well as to adjust to new international realities that enabled him to establish a state that could endure. The source of this aptitude is not obvious and may be largely traceable simply to his superior intuitive abilities. It is likely, however, that it had something to do with his youthful exile in Kuwait, where the (by Arabian standards) cosmopolitan atmosphere meant exposure to information, ideas, and people not usually encountered in the xenophobic isolation of his native Najd. Early in his career of reconquest he met the British political resident in Kuwait, Captain William Shakespear, and developed an admiring friendship for him. Sir Percy Cox, senior British representative in the Gulf just before World War I, had a very strong influence on Abd al-Aziz, and Harry St. John Philby, a British civil servant who left his government's service to live in Saudi Arabia, provided Abd al-Aziz with advice (not always taken) and a window on the outside world. Abd al-Aziz also relied heavily on a coterie of advisers from Syria, Egypt, and other Arab countries. This awareness of the outside world helped to induce a certain pragmatism, evident early on in his search for British protection and in his 1915 treaty with Great Britain that recognized his independence and guaranteed him against aggression. Sim-

ilarly, after the 1924–1925 conquest of the Hejaz (western Arabia, with the holy cities of Mecca and Medina), he restrained his zealous warriors and assured his retention of that key province by demonstrating to the world Muslim community that he could provide a more efficient and secure administration of the territory than the Hashimite regime that he had defeated. In 1935, he granted generous terms to the imam of Yemen, whom he had defeated in a border war, doing so both to avert possible European intervention and to avoid inclusion in his kingdom of a population whose cultural distinctiveness would have made its assimilation very difficult.

In 1928, the pragmatic realism of Abd al-Aziz came into conflict with the tribal aggression and religious militancy of the Ikhwan forces he had unleashed. The Ikhwan's revolt followed his acceptance of the British-drawn borders of Transjordan and Iraq to the north—for the first time imposing the constraints of explicit state frontiers on a society to which such notions were alien. By 1930, Abd al-Aziz had surmounted this threat, the gravest to his rule, making effective use of automobiles, machine guns, and radio communications to crush the revolt. The passions that drove it, however, remained alive and shook the Saudi kingdom a half century later, in November 1979, when Islamic extremists and disaffected members of the Utaiba tribe, from which many Ikhwan rebels had come, seized the Great Mosque at Mecca in an effort to overthrow the rule of the Al Sa'ud.

With the Ikhwan revolt behind him, Abd al-Aziz moved to draw together the disparate parts of his extensive realm. Since Sharif Husayn ibn Ali had assumed the title King of the Hijaz, Abd al-Aziz adopted the same title after conquering that province; he coupled it somewhat incongruously with the title Sultan of Najd and Its Dependencies in 1926. In the following year, he elevated the second title as well to monarchical status, in effect creating a dual monarchy. In 1932, Abd al-Aziz abandoned this arrangement and explicitly identified the country with the Al Sa'ud family by naming it the Kingdom of Saudi Arabia. The two earlier Saudi states had been Wahhabi commonwealths, largely isolated from the outside world and ruled by a Saudi imam, the title emphasizing religious authority and obligations. The new kingdom, while remaining committed to its original religious purpose, was a nation-state that developed an expanding network of relations with other nations, including the establishment of close ties with secular states beyond the Arab-Islamic world.

To secure the future stability of the state he had created and to preserve the continued rule of his line, in 1933, Abd al-Aziz formally designated his eldest surviving son, Saʿud, to succeed him. This action, which senior princes, religious leaders, and tribal chiefs publicly endorsed, departed from the usual practice of Arabian tribal society. In addition to guaranteeing that future kings would come from Abd al-Aziz's branch of the Al Saud, it was doubtless also intended to avert the fratricidal conflict that had destroyed the second Saudi state at the end of the nineteenth century. It was understood that Faisal (Ibn Abd al-Aziz Al Saʿud), the next eldest brother, who possessed a much more impressive intellect and had, as foreign minister and viceroy for the Hijaz, exhibited a much greater capacity for public affairs, would succeed Saʿud. Abd al-Aziz may have had several reasons for favoring Saʿud as his immediate successor, but the establishment of seniority as the determining factor in succession was clearly preeminent. Saʿud and Faisal became rivals, but Saʿud's incompetence eventually drove the senior princes and religious leaders to depose him in favor of Faisal. Nevertheless, the principle that Abd al-Aziz established has, with certain qualifications, been preserved and served to maintain the stability of the kingdom.

The crucial economic and security relationships with the United States, a central pillar of the kingdom's foreign policy, grew from decisions that Abd al-Aziz took in the latter phase of his rule. In 1933, he granted the first oil concession to a U.S. company; he signed a petroleum exploration agreement with Standard Oil of California (SOCAL), choosing it over its British rival, the Iraq Petroleum Company. He did so largely because SOCAL could offer more money for his impoverished treasury but also because he saw an advantage in counterbalancing his close relationship with Great Britain with ties to a faraway country having no political involvement (as yet) in the Middle East. There followed the creation of the Arabian American Oil Company consortium and the exploitation of the world's largest oil reserves, bringing staggering wealth to the companies and the kingdom, and the

creation of an intimate alignment with U.S. industry that largely determined the course of Saudi Arabia's economic modernization and development. From this time on—especially on radio, in newsreels, and in newspapers—he became known as King Ibn Saʿud.

Equally significant for Saudi Arabia's future were the agreements that Ibn Saʿud made with the United States to assure his country's external security. The king's meeting with President Franklin D. Roosevelt on a U.S. Navy cruiser in Egypt's Great Bitter Lake, in February 1945, prefigured the close, if informal, U.S.–Saudi security alliance that developed after World War II, as British power declined. In 1947, the king waved aside the suggestion of his son Prince Faisal, the foreign minister, that Saudi Arabia break diplomatic relations with the United States over the Truman administration's support for the United Nations partition plan for Palestine—which paved the way for the creation of an independent Israel and contravened a pledge that Roosevelt had made to Ibn Saʿud. The king, however, expected the United States to offer him something in exchange and, between 1947 and 1950, secret U.S. undertakings gave the king the assurances he sought without a formal treaty. Thus the foundations were laid for the far-reaching security relationship—embracing arms sales, military training, and the massive defense infrastructure whose scope was revealed only forty years later, in the course of the Desert Shield/Desert Storm operation of the Gulf Crisis of 1990–1991.

The last years of the long rule of Ibn Saʿud, when his physical health was in decline, were an unhappy coda to an extraordinary career. As massive oil income began to flow in the early 1950s, the king displayed little understanding of the economic or social implications of vast wealth—and some of the ostentation that became the hallmark of his reign was apparent before his death. Politically, he was no longer able to master the novel and complex challenges of a very different world than the one he had earlier dominated. The government of Saudi Arabia remained the simple affair that suited a largely traditional desert monarchy, with a small retinue of advisers and a handful of rudimentary ministries that had been established in an ad hoc manner. Somewhat ironically, the last significant governmental act of the old king was to create the

Council of Ministers, until today the source of executive and legislative authority in the kingdom.

In November 1953, King Ibn Saʿud died at al-Taʾif in the Hijaz. He was buried with his ancestors in Riyadh.

See also AL RASHID FAMILY; ARABIAN AMERICAN OIL COMPANY (ARAMCO); COX, PERCY; FAISAL IBN ABD AL-AZIZ AL SAʿUD; HUSAYN IBN ALI; IKHWAN; PHILBY, HARRY ST. JOHN; ROOSEVELT, FRANKLIN DELANO.

Bibliography

Alangari, Haifa. *The Struggle for Power in Arabia: Ibn Saud, Hussein and Great Britain, 1914–1924.* Reading, U.K.: Ithaca Press, 1998.

Almana, Mohammed. *Arabia Unified: A Portrait of Ibn Saud.* London: Hutchinson Benham, 1980.

Armstrong, H. C. *Lord of Arabia: Ibn Saud.* New York: Kegan Paul International, 1998.

Besson, Yves. *Ibn Saud, roi bedouin: La naissance du royaume d'arabie saoudite.* Lausanne, Switzerland, 1980.

Bligh, Alexander. *From Prince to King: Royal Succession in the House of Saud in the Twentieth Century.* New York: New York University Press, 1984.

Holden, David, and Richard Johns. *The House of Saud: The Rise and Rule of the Most Powerful Dynasty in the Arab World.* New York: Holt, Rinehart, and Winston, 1981.

Lacey, Robert. *The Kingdom.* New York: Harcourt Brace Jovanovich, 1981.

Philby, H. St. J. B. *Arabian Jubilee.* London: Hale, 1952.

Philby, H. St. J. B. *Saʿudi Arabia.* London: Benn, 1955.

Rasheed, Madawi al-. *A History of Saudi Arabia.* Cambridge, U.K., and New York: Cambridge University Press, 2002.

Troeller, Gary. *The Birth of Saudi Arabia: The Rise of the House of Saud.* London: F. Cass, 1976.

MALCOLM C. PECK

ABD AL-GHANI, ABD AL-AZIZ

[c. late 1930s–]

Yemeni economist and politician.

Abd al-Aziz Abd al-Ghani was born in the late 1930s into a modest household in the Hujariyya, the Shafiʿi south of North Yemen. In 1958 he began studies in the United States, eventually earning his bachelor's and master's degrees in economics. A modernist and technocrat, Abd al-Aziz served as prime minister of the Yemen Arab Republic (YAR) under three presidents in all but three years in the period between early 1975 and Yemeni unification in 1990. He continued in that office after surviving the assassinations of two of those presidents; from 1980 to 1983, the years in which he did not head the government, he was YAR vice president. From the late 1960s to 1975, he was minister of economics twice and the founding head of the Central Bank of Yemen, one of the earliest and most important modern institutions. After Yemeni unification in 1990, he was for four years a member of the five-member presidential council of the new Republic of Yemen (ROY). He became prime minister of the ROY in 1994, after the civil war, and served in that capacity until he was appointed chairman of the newly created Consultative (Shura) Council in early 1997. In this office, he has over the years become something of an elder statesman.

Bibliography

Burrowes, Robert D. *Historical Dictionary of Yemen.* Lanham, MD: Scarecrow Press, 1995.

Burrowes, Robert D. *The Yemen Arab Republic: The Politics of Development, 1962–1986.* Boulder, CO: Westview Press; London: Croom Helm, 1987.

ROBERT D. BURROWES

ABD AL-HADI, AWNI

See ABD AL-HADI FAMILY

ABD AL-HADI FAMILY

Prominent Palestinian Arab family.

The Abd al-Hadis were a leading landowning family in the Palestinian districts of Afula, Baysan, Jenin, and Nablus. Already well established in the seventeenth century, in the 1830s the family supported the rule of Ibrahim Pasha. Family members were prominent in Ottoman political, diplomatic, and military circles, including the Ottoman parliament in 1908 and 1914. Ruhi Abd al-Hadi (1885–1954) served for fifteen years in the Ottoman foreign office, including consular and diplomatic posts in the Balkans, Greece, and Switzerland. Rushdi Abd al-Hadi fought for the Ottoman army in World War I and remained in Turkey to serve the new republic, whereas Ra'uf Abd al-Hadi was taken prisoner by the British forces and then joined Faisal's Arab army to fight the Ottomans.

The best-known member of the al-Hadi family is Awni Abd al-Hadi (1889–1970), a liberal Palestinian and Arab nationalist who was active in politics and diplomacy. He supported the Arab national movement and worked closely with Faisal in Damascus until his regime fell to the French in 1920. When Faisal's kingdom was destroyed, Awni returned to Palestine and soon became a leading Palestinian political figure. In spring 1930 he participated in the fourth Arab delegation to London, which requested the stoppage of Jewish immigration and land purchases until a national government could be formed. Two years later, Awni established the Hizb al-Istiqlal (Independence Party) as a branch of the pan-Arab party. The party called for complete independence and the strengthening of ties with Arab states. Awni became more militant in the early 1930s, arguing that the Palestinians should focus on opposing the British. Later in his life, Awni held various political posts such as ambassador to Cairo and foreign minister to Amman.

Members of the Abd al-Hadi family had divergent responses to the British mandate in Palestine. Ruhi Abd al-Hadi joined the British administrative service in 1921, initially as a district officer, then rising to become assistant senior secretary in 1944. Majid Abd al-Hadi was a supreme court judge, Amin Abd al-Hadi joined the Supreme Muslim Council in 1929, and Tahsin Abd al-Hadi was mayor of Jenin. Some family members secretly sold their shares of Zir'in village to the Jewish National Fund in July 1930 despite nationalist opposition to such land sales; other members sold land to the Development Department to resettle landless Arab peasants.

With the establishment of the state of Israel in 1948, the Abd al-Hadis lost substantial agricultural lands in lower Galilee, but retained important—although gradually diminishing—influence in Jenin and Nablus during Jordanian rule. Awni Abd al-Hadi joined the Jordanian diplomatic corps, serving as ambassador to Egypt.

Bibliography

Muslih, Muhammad Y. *The Origins of Palestinian Nationalism.* New York: Columbia University Press, 1988.

Porath, Yehoshua. *The Emergence of the Palestinian–Arab Nationalist Movement: 1918–1929.* London: Frank Cass, 1974.

Porath, Yehoshua. *The Palestinian–Arab National Movement: 1929–1939.* London and Totowa, NJ: Frank Cass, 1977.

Stein, Kenneth W. *The Land Question in Palestine, 1917–1939.* Chapel Hill: University of North Carolina Press, 1984.

ANN M. LESCH

ABD AL-HADI, TARAB

Political activist in Palestine in the first half of the twentieth century.

Tarab Abd al-Hadi (birth and death dates unknown) was a member of the Arab Women's Executive Committee (AWE), which convened the first Palestine Arab Women's Congress in Jerusalem in 1929. She was married to Awni Abd al-Hadi, who was a prominent Palestinian nationalist during the mandate period, and active in the Istiqlal Party, among other organizations. In 1933, after Matiel Mughannam, who was Christian, delivered a speech in the Dome of the Rock in Jerusalem during protests of the visit of Lord Edmund Allenby, Abd al-Hadi, a Muslim, delivered a speech before Christ's tomb in the Church of the Holy Sepulchre. Abd al-Hadi was also a member of the Palestinian delegation attending the Eastern Women's Conference on the Palestine Problem convened in Cairo in 1938. She delivered a speech at that conference and at the subsequent Arab Women's Conference, held in Cairo in 1944.

See also ADB AL-HADI FAMILY.

Bibliography

Mogannam, Matiel E. T. *The Arab Woman and the Palestine Problem.* London: Herbert Joseph, 1937.

ELLEN FLEISCHMAN

ABD AL-HAFID IBN AL-HASSAN
[1876–1937]
Sultan of Morocco, 1908–1912.

The fourth son of Sultan Hassan I, Abd al-Hafid served as *khalifa* (royal governor) of Tiznit (1897–1901) and Marrakech (1901–1907) under his younger brother, Abd al-Aziz ibn al-Hassan, who was the sultan of Morocco from 1894 to 1908. In the politically tense period of the Moroccan Question (1901–1912), Abd al-Hafid (also Abd al-Hafiz) found himself increasingly opposed to the policies of his brother. Following the latter's acceptance of the Act of Algeciras in 1906 and acquiescence in France's military landings at Oujda and Casablanca in 1907, Abd al-Hafid joined with Madani and Tuhami Glawi in a rebellion aimed at deposing Abd al-Aziz. A civil war between the two brothers lasted from August 1907 to August 1908. Despite French support for Abd al-Aziz, in 1908 Abd al-Hafid was able to defeat him and take the throne.

Abd al-Hafid was an intellectual, poet, and author of numerous books. He favored the introduction of the ideas of the Salafiyya Movement to the al-Qarawiyin mosque university in Fez. After becoming sultan in 1908, he appointed Abu Shuʿayb al-Dukkali (later known as "the Moroccan Abduh") to his Royal Learned Council. He sought to suppress heterodox Moroccan brotherhoods of Sufism, notably the Tijaniyya and the Kattaniya.

As sultan, Abd al-Hafid sought to recover Moroccan political and financial independence from France through a policy of alliances with the Ottoman Empire and Germany, and a program of governmental reforms. He cracked down on political dissidents, such as Muhammad ibn Abd al-Kabir al-Kattani and Abu Himara. In 1910, however, he was compelled to enter into a major loan agreement with France, the terms of which ended Moroccan financial independence. The loss of political independence came soon thereafter.

A rebellion of the tribes around Fez and Meknes in 1911 led to the occupation of the Moroccan interior by a French expeditionary force. On 28 March 1912, his authority weakened irreparably, Abd al-Hafid signed the Treaty of Fes, thereby establishing the French protectorate. On 12 August 1912, Abd al-Hafid abdicated as sultan and was succeeded by a French-imposed successor, his brother Yusuf (1912–1927). The protectorates of France and Spain were to last until 1956.

The last sultan of independent Morocco, Abd al-Hafid died in 1937 at Tangier. His legacy is a mixed one—he came to the throne on a program of opposition to the Act of Algeciras and a French protectorate; he faced an impossible task, however, and his defeat was most probable. His support of pan-Islam and of Salafiyya ideas for regenerating Morocco were undermined by the corruption and brutality of his rule, notably the actions of his close collaborators, the Glawi brothers. His shameless bargaining with the French over the terms of his abdication and his willingness to sign the Treaty of Fes earned him the enmity of a later generation of Moroccan nationalists.

See also ABD AL-AZIZ IBN AL-HASSAN; ABU HIMARA; FES, TREATY OF (1912); HASSAN I; KATTANI, MUHAMMAD IBN ABD AL-KABIR AL-; MOROCCAN QUESTION; SALAFIYYA MOVEMENT.

Bibliography

Burke, Edmund, III. *Prelude to Protectorate in Morocco: Precolonial Protest and Resistance, 1860–1912.* Chicago: University of Chicago Press, 1976.

Pennell, C. R. *Morocco since 1830.* New York: New York University Press, 2000.

EDMUND BURKE III

ABD AL-ILAH IBN ALI
[1913–1958]

Regent of Iraq for the child king Faisal II.

The son of Ali, king of the Hijaz, and grandson of the sharif of Mecca, Abd al-Ilah was brought up in Mecca. He came to Iraq at the age of thirteen, after his father lost the Hijazi throne in 1926. He had no strong roots in Iraq and was, or at least became, heavily dependent on British support. Abd al-Ilah came to prominence somewhat unexpectedly in 1939 following the accidental death of his cousin, King Ghazi (ibn Faisal) I. Ghazi's son, Faisal II, was only three years old, and Abd al-Ilah, who was also the child's maternal uncle, was made regent. He became crown prince in 1943, and although formally relinquishing the regency after Faisal reached his majority in 1953, he was always known in Iraq as "the regent" (al-Wasi).

His friend and mentor at the time of his rise to power was Nuri al-Saʿid, another faithful servant of Britain, who would eventually serve as prime minister fourteen times under the mandate and monarchy. It was Abd al-Ilah's misfortune to come to prominence at a time when the central institutions of the new Iraqi state were extremely weak, the result of a combination of several factors, including the premature death of his uncle Faisal I in 1933, the dominant role in politics being played by the officer corps, and the tide of anti-British sentiment flooding over Iraq and the rest of the Middle East at the end of the 1930s.

Although Iraq followed Britain's lead and declared war on Germany in September 1939, the Arab nationalist army officers, led by a group of four colonels known as the Golden Square, were soon able to make their influence felt, and an anti-British and more or less pro-Axis cabinet was formed under Rashid Ali al-Kaylani in March 1940. After a brief reversal of fortune in the early months of 1941, Rashid Ali returned to power on 12 April and he and the Golden Square set in motion a somewhat quixotic but immensely popular revolt against Britain. Although the outcome was a foregone conclusion, the episode showed how little support there was in Iraq for Britain or for Britain's Iraqi partners; Nuri and Abd al-Ilah fled to Jordan in April with British assistance and did not return until after the Iraqi army had been crushed in June. All four of the colonels were eventually tried by Iraqi authorities and hanged in public in Baghdad, apparently on the express instructions of the regent and Nuri.

In 1947 and 1948, the regent managed to alienate himself further from mainstream political sentiment by his support for the renegotiation of the terms of the Anglo–Iraqi Treaty. This time the opposition was more organized, and the demonstrations against the new treaty (signed in Portsmouth in January 1948) were so massive and so vehement that it had to be dropped. Over the next ten years there were frequent displays of mass discontent, which were usually countered by fierce repression and the imposition of martial law.

By the mid-1950s, the political situation in Iraq had deteriorated to the point that it was widely understood that it was a question of when, rather than

Former regent of Iraq Abd al-Ilah (1913–1958). In 1939, Abd al-Ilah was appointed regent for his four-year-old nephew, Faisal II, a position he held until 1953. © Hulton-Deutsch Collection/ Corbis. Reproduced by permission.

if, the regime would fall. Although not always on the best of terms during this time, Nuri and Abd al-Ilah were widely regarded as embodying many of the evils and shortcomings of the regime, especially its almost slavish dependence on the West. But if the end was long expected, the actual occasion was sudden; a group of Free Officers led by Abd al-Karim Qasim and Abd al-Salam Arif managed to take control of a number of key military units and staged a coup on 14 July 1958. The royal palace and Nuri's house were surrounded; Nuri evaded capture until the following day, but the king, the regent, and other members of the royal family were shot in the courtyard of the palace on the morning of the revolution, thus bringing the Iraqi monarchy to an abrupt, violent, and largely unlamented end.

See also Arif, Abd al-Salam; Faisal I ibn Hussein; Faisal II ibn Ghazi; Ghazi ibn Faisal; Golden Square; Kaylani, Rashid Ali al-; Qasim, Abd al-Karim; Sharif of Mecca.

Bibliography

Marr, Phebe. *The Modern History of Iraq,* 2d edition. Boulder, CO: Westview, 2004.

PETER SLUGLETT

ABD AL-MAGUID, ESMAT

[1924–]

Egyptian diplomat and statesman.

Born in Alexandria and educated there, Esmat Abd al-Maguid (also, Ismat Abd al-Majid) entered the Egyptian foreign service in 1950 and earned a doctorate from the University of Paris in 1951. He took part in the Anglo–Egyptian negotiations of 1954 and negotiated with France after the 1956 Suez War. In 1970 he served as Egypt's ambassador to that country. He headed Egypt's mission to the United Nations from 1972 to 1983 and was minister of foreign affairs from 1984 to 1991 and deputy prime minister from 1985. He was secretary-general of the League of Arab States from 1991 to 2001. An advocate of Arab unity, he worked closely with Mahmud Riyad. Shortly before his retirement Abd al-Maguid spoke at the Arab summit meeting of October 2000, calling on all Arabs to donate one day's pay as a gesture of support to the Palestinians. He was interviewed by the Yale United Nations Oral History Project.

See also RIYAD, MAHMUD.

Bibliography

Goldschmidt, Arthur. "Abd al-Majid, Dr. Ahmad Ismat." In *Biographical Dictionary of Modern Egypt,* edited by Arthur Goldschmit. Boulder, CO: Lynne Rienner, 2000.

ARTHUR GOLDSCHMIDT

ABD AL NASIR, JAMAL

See NASSER, GAMAL ABDEL

ABD AL-QADIR

[1807–1883]

Algerian leader who resisted initial French colonialism.

Abd al-Qadir (also spelled Abd el-Kader, Abdul Qader) was born in Guetna Oued al-Hammam, near Mascara, Western Algeria. His father, Muhyi al-Din, was spiritual head of the Qadiriyya order of Islam; his education was guided by Qadi Ahmad ibn Tahir of Azrou and Sidi Ahmad ibn Khoja of Oran. He pursued religious studies while traveling with his father within the Ottoman Empire, in Syria and Iraq and at al-Azhar in Egypt.

As the leader of Algerian tribal resistance to French colonialism between 1833 and 1847, Abd al-Qadir earned a reputation far beyond Algeria. It was only partly for military leadership, since his skill in founding alliances between hinterland tribes, especially in the western province of Oran and, for a time, as far east as Constantine, presented a political feat of no small consequence.

Abd al-Qadir's father had carried out several raids against the French in the Oran region in spring of 1832. The French had become enraged by the corsairs, pirates, and slave trade of the Barbary coast and wanted to end the taking and selling of Christian sailors from Mediterranean shipping. By this date two figures, neither Algerian, had played roles in reacting to the French presence in the former beylicate of Oran. The only serious previous attempt to defend Oran came between November 1830 and April 1832, when Ali ibn Sulayman of Morocco intervened unsuccessfully in Algeria. Meanwhile, between February and August 1831, a token Tunisian force had come and gone from Oran following an agreement between the bey of Tunis and the French government. According to its terms, the French promised to recognize ill-defined Tunisian responsibility to govern the Algerian west in their name.

By 1833, it was clear that the unorganized Algerian forces under Abd al-Qadir's father could do little more than harass the French in Oran. The decision was made to recognize Abd al-Qadir's leadership, both of the Qadiriyya order and of provincial tribal resistance. This decision proved fateful, since Abd al-Qadir clearly viewed his mission in terms that went beyond mere military leadership. An early sign of this was his insistence that his followers swear allegiance according to the *bayʿa* (the pledge) to the caliphs who succeeded the prophet Muhammad. A good portion of Abd al-Qadir's military and political career—beyond his relations with the French—involved attempts to impose legitimizing symbols of rule on neighboring tribes. Such struggles to command allegiance in Islamic as well as tribal terms were complicated by the fact that some key local tribes were traditionally *makhzanis* (mercenaries), which meant they were willing to receive pay from secular executive authorities. Before 1830, such tribes would have been in the service of the Algerian beys; after 1830, the French tried to recruit makhzanis to their service, thus creating a dilemma in them between Islamic and opportunistic loyalties.

In February 1834, soon after the French opened formal diplomatic contact with the Algerian resistance forces, two treaties, one containing essential French conditions, the second with additional Algerian conditions, were signed between France and Abd al-Qadir. These provided for mutual recognition of two different types of polities in the west: three French enclaves on the coast and Abd al-Qadir's emirate with its capital at Mascara. Thus he was recognized as dey of Mascara.

During this brief truce, Abd al-Qadir may have benefited from French help to defeat Mustafa ibn Isma'il, his primary rival for political and religious ascendancy over the western tribes. Another rival, Shaykh al-Ghumari, was also captured and hanged. Had Franco-Algerian peace continued, Abd al-Qadir might have succeeded in extending his unprecedented tax levy (the *mu'uwna*) to more and more subordinates of his emirate. As it was, hostilities resumed in 1835 (after the Ottomans had sent a new governor to Tripoli), and the French were repeatedly defeated by Abd al-Qadir. In 1837, the French signed the Treaty of Tafna, with Marshal Thomas-Robert Bugeaud de la Piconnerie granting most of the Algerian hinterland to Abd al-Qadir.

Perhaps the Tafna treaty was meant to keep Abd al-Qadir from objecting to French advances against the eastern beylicate of Constantine—which fell only four months after the Tafna accords. Once it fell, however, the French were never able to make deals with Abd al-Qadir again.

From late 1837 to 1847, intermittent hostilities with forces under Abd al-Qadir brought clashes as far east as Constantine and as far west as Morocco. It was only after Marshal Bugeaud led a large French expeditionary force into Algeria that systematic sub-

Abd al-Qadir led Algerian tribes against the French, succeeding his father Muhyi al-Din. By 1839 he had gained control of over two-thirds of Algeria and had established a Muslim state. © BETTMANN/CORBIS. REPRODUCED BY PERMISSION.

jugation of the interior began. At this point Abd al-Qadir's crossings into Morocco involved refuge rather than tactics; and the major battle of Isly in 1844 dissuaded the Moroccans from offering him refuge again. Although the Algerians tried to reverse the inevitable tide, his fate became as insecure in Morocco as it was in Algeria. After his decision to surrender in December 1847, Abd al-Qadir was promised exile but was sent as a prisoner to France. He was released in 1852 by Napoléon III and finally granted his requested exile in Syria. He died in Damascus in 1883. Some eighty-five years later and six years after Algeria's independence, Abd al-Qadir's remains were reinterred in his native land in 1968.

His contribution to the history of North Africa may be viewed from several perspectives. Within the closest political and cultural context, his leadership reflected intertribal dynamics in what was eventually to become the entity of Algeria. His efforts to unify disparate tribes included a certain number of institutional innovations, suggesting rudiments of governmental responsibility that surpassed anything that had preceded this key period. Among these, formal executive appointments, regular decision-making councils, and taxation figured most prominently. One cannot escape the fact, however, that hinterland submission to Abd al-Qadir's ascendancy, both military and political, often came only after successful imposition of his will by force.

By contrast, those who emphasize the nationalist implications of Algerian resistance to French colonialism would interpret Abd al-Qadir in ways that reflect more on the twentieth-century context of mass political movements than the highly fragmented setting of nineteenth-century Algeria. For the nationalist school, he represents a first stage in a process that became a model for the Algerian National Liberation Front at the end of the colonial era.

The third point of view combines speculation on what actual mid-nineteenth-century appraisals of Abd al-Qadir's leadership were with twentieth-century reflections on the living heritage of the past. This view would emphasize Islamic religious and cultural values embodied—then and thereafter—in resistance to foreign domination in any form. Seen from this perspective, a culturewide hero model like Abd al-Qadir represents a heritage that can be chronologically continuous and spatially all-encompassing. His actions not only had the effect of legitimizing his call to carry out a general jihad (holy war) against the French in the name of Islam but also gave him the assumed responsibility of overseeing the welfare of the entire *umma* (community of believers) in a responsible way that had not been effectively present in Algeria for centuries.

See also BUGEAUD DE LA PICONNERIE, THOMAS-ROBERT; CORSAIRS.

Bibliography

Danziger, Raphael. *Abd el Qadir and the Algerians: Resistance to the French and Internal Consolidation.* New York: Homes & Meier, 1977.

Ruedy, John. *Modern Algeria: The Origins and Development of a Nation.* Bloomington: Indiana University Press, 1992.

BYRON CANNON

ABD AL-QUDDUS, IHSAN
[1918–1990]

Egyptian journalist, novelist, and short-story writer.

Abd al-Quddus began his literary career as an editor and writer for the leading Egyptian weekly *Ruz al-Yusuf,* which was founded in 1925 by his mother, Fatima al-Yusuf, a former actress. These writings made him well known throughout the Arab world. In the 1960s and 1970s, he was the editor of the newspapers *Akhbar al-Yawm* and the influential *al-Ahram.* In his column, "At a Cafe on Politics Street," he created fictional dialogues between customers at a cafe to discuss contemporary issues.

Abd al-Quddus wrote more than sixty novels and collections of short stories, many of which were made into films. His works of Arabic literature were characterized by psychological studies of political and social behavior. Among his works translated into English are *I Am Free, The Bus Thief,* and *A Boy's Best Friend.*

See also NEWSPAPERS AND PRINT MEDIA: ARAB COUNTRIES.

DAVID WALDNER

ABD AL-RAHMAN, AISHA

See BINT AL-SHATI

ABD AL-RAHMAN AL-MAHDI
[1885–1959]

Leader in the Sudan after World War I.

Born after the death of his father, Muhammad Ahmad, in June 1885, Abd al-Rahman al-Mahdi was reared in Omdurman under the rule of the Khalifa Abdullahi. Upon the conquest of the Sudan by Anglo–Egyptian forces in 1898, he, as the eldest surviving son of the Mahdi (and consequently his spiritual and legal heir), was kept under close scrutiny by the British authorities until the outbreak of World War I, when they sought his assistance to counter any call for a jihad by the Ottoman Turks, who were allies of the Germans. Sayyid Abd al-Rahman unstintingly supported the British and in return received the freedom to enhance his wealth and his influence among the followers of his father, the Ansar; thus he emerged as the leading religious and political figure in the Anglo–Egyptian Sudan. Despite tensions between him and the British, who feared a revival of Muslim fanaticism in the guise of neo-Mahdism, the sayyid continued to prove his loyalty to the government. He used his abundant resources to acquire a loyal following among the Ansar, whom he converted into the Umma political party. After World War II he remained the most influential Sudanese in the emerging political system. Like his father, he frustrated Egyptian claims in the Sudan and for a time regarded himself as a possible king of an independent Sudan. This was unacceptable to the vast majority of Sudanese, who did not wish to be dominated by the Ansar as they had been in the last two decades of the nineteenth century. Until his death Abd al-Rahman continued to pursue his ambitions to ensure that the Ansar and the Umma would remain preeminent in an independent Sudan.

See also AHMAD, MUHAMMAD; UMMA PARTY.

Bibliography

Holt, P. M., and Daly, M. W. *A History of the Sudan: From the Coming of Islam to the Present Day,* 5th edition. Harlow, U.K., and New York: Longman, 2000.

Petterson, Donald. *Inside Sudan: Political Islam, Conflict, and Catastrophe,* revised edition. Boulder, CO: Westview, 2003.

ROBERT O. COLLINS

ABD AL-RAHMAN IBN HISHAM
[1789–1859]

Sultan of Morocco, 1822–1859.

During the reign of Abd al-Rahman, Morocco lost its international standing and suffered economic decline and social and political unrest.

A major problem was how to respond to the invasion of Algeria by France in 1830. Abd al-Rahman first tacitly supported Algerian resistance forces, then sought to avoid a confrontation. In August 1844, this policy failed when a Moroccan army was beaten at Isly by General Thomas-Robert Bugeaud de la Piconnerie and Moroccan ports were bombarded by the French navy. Morocco's defeat opened the door to increased European political and economic intervention.

The economic policies pursued by Abd al-Rahman became disastrous as well. The signing of an Anglo–Moroccan commercial agreement in 1856 gave most-favored-nation status to Britain, and its provisions were soon extended to other European powers.

Finally, a major conflict with Spain erupted into war in August 1859.

See also BUGEAUD DE LA PICONNERIE, THOMAS-ROBERT; MOROCCO.

Bibliography

Pennell, C. R. *Morocco since 1830.* New York: New York University Press, 2000.

Schroeter, Daniel. *Merchants of Essaouira: Urban Society and Imperialism in Southwestern Morocco, 1844–1886.* Cambridge, U.K., and New York: Cambridge University Press, 1988.

EDMUND BURKE III

ABD AL-RAHMAN KHAN
[1844–1910]

Ruler of Afghanistan.

Abd al-Rahman Khan Barakzai (also known as Abd er-Rahman) ascended the Afghan throne during the second British invasion of Afghanistan. Embarking on a relentless policy of centralization of power, he weathered four civil wars and a hundred rebellions during his reign (1880–1910).

He was the grandson of Dost Mohammad (ruled 1826–1839; 1842–1863), the founder of the Barakzai dynasty. At the age of thirteen, he was given his first appointment, and he showed his talent when assigned, later on, to command the army of the northern region, of which his father was governor. Playing an active role in the five-year war of succession, he twice won the throne for his father and an uncle before being defeated by yet another uncle, Sher Ali (ruled 1863–1866; 1869–1879). Forced to leave, Abd al-Rahman spent eleven years in exile in the Asiatic colonies of Russia. His opportunity came in 1880, when Britain's invading forces, shaken by the intensity of Afghan resistance, were casting for a candidate acceptable both to them and to the resistance. In return for British control over Afghanistan's foreign relations, he was recognized as the ruler, in July 1880, and assigned a subsidy by Britain.

In the wake of Britain's invasion, multiple centers of power had emerged in Afghanistan, with two of Abd al-Rahman's cousins controlling major portions of the country. He rejected offers to share power, defeating one cousin in 1880 and the other in 1885, and emerged as the undisputed ruler of the country. His next challenge was to overcome the clans, whom he subdued, in a series of campaigns between 1880 and 1896. He imposed taxation, conscription, and adjudication on the defeated clans. His policies encompassed all linguistic and religious groups but took a particularly brutal form in the case of the Hazaras.

To establish his centralizing policies, he transformed the state apparatus. The army, chief vehicle of his policies, was reorganized and expanded, and the bulk of the state revenue was spent on its upkeep. Administrative and judicial practices were bureaucratized, with emphasis on record keeping and the separation of home and office. He justified these policies on religious grounds, making *shari'a* (the law of Islam) the law of the land, and nonetheless turning all judges into paid servants of the state.

Abd al-Rahman was able to concentrate on consolidating his rule at home because of Britain's and Russia's desire to avoid direct confrontation with each other. Afghanistan became a buffer state between the two empires; they imposed its present boundaries. Playing on their rivalry, Abd al-Rahman refused to allow European railways, which were touching on his eastern, southern, and northern borders, to expand within Afghanistan, and he resisted British attempts to station European representatives in his country. Toward the end of his reign, he felt secure enough to inform the viceroy of India that treaty obligations did not allow British representatives even to comment on his internal affairs.

When he died, he was succeeded by his son and heir apparent, Habibollah Khan, who ruled until 1919.

See also BARAKZAI DYNASTY; DOST MOHAMMAD BARAKZAI; HABIBOLLAH KHAN.

Bibliography

Ghani, Ashraf. "Islam and State-Building in a Tribal Society: Afghanistan 1880–1901." *Modern Asian Studies* 12 (1978): 269–284.

Kakar, Hasan. *Afghanistan: A Study in International Political Developments, 1880–1896.* Kabul, 1971.

Kakar, Hasan. *Government and Society in Afghanistan: The Reign of Amir 'Abd al-Rahman Khan.* Austin: University of Texas Press, 1979.

ASHRAF GHANI

ABD AL-RAHMAN, UMAR
[1938–]

Religious Muslim leader sentenced to life in prison for his role in the attack on the World Trade Center in 1993.

An Egyptian Muslim militant and spritual leader of al-Gama'a al-Islamiyya, also known as the Islamic Group, Umar Abd al-Rahman was born in the Dakahliyyah province, south of Cairo, in 1938. He was educated at al-Azhar University, where he earned a doctorate in Islamic theology in 1965 and later became a lecturer. Abd al-Rahman's agitating religious sermons in which he challenged the legitimacy of Egypt's rulers (Nasser, Sadat, and Mubarak) provoked frequent arrest and imprisonment. He was critical of President Gamal Abdel Nasser and his ideology of Arab socialism. After Egypt's defeat in the 1967 Arab–Israel War, Abd al-Rahman became more bold in his attacks on Nasser and his socialist policies. Abd al-Rahman was briefly arrested in 1968 and dismissed from al-Azhar. He was arrested again after Nasser's death in 1970 but was released as part of the general amnesty President Anwar al-Sadat granted to a number of dissidents and opposition leaders.

Abd al-Rahman traveled and from 1971 to 1978 lived in Saudia Arabia, where he was able to work as a teacher of Islamic studies. He then returned to Egypt and became emphatically opposed to Sadat's signing of the 1978 Camp David Accords as well as his economic liberalization policies, which Abd al-Rahman viewed as moral and material corruption. After Sadat's assassination in October 1981, Abd al-Rahman was arrested and accused of issuing a *fatwa* for the assassination, but he was released due to insufficient evidence.

Shortly after his release, Abd al-Rahman published his book *Kalimat Haqq* (Word of truth), in which he openly attacked Sadat's successor, Husni Mubarak. Abd al-Rahman was arrested in 1984 and accused of instigating violence against the government, but was released, again for lack of direct and concrete evidence. He continued his antigovernment activities, including his demand that Egypt should be governed according to the *shariʿa*. From 1984 to 1989 Abd al-Rahman was actively involved in promoting militant Islam and traveled within Egypt, delivering speeches that inspired followers of several militant organizations. He was arrested and accused of ordering terrorist acts against Egyptian Copts and security forces, and he was prohibited from speaking in public. In response, he issued a *fatwa* instructing his followers to capture weapons from the police and the military and use them against Mubarak's regime.

In mid-1989 Abd al-Rahman fled Egypt to Sudan, where he was refused political asylum. He entered the United States in 1990 after he was erroneously issued a tourist visa by the American embassy in Sudan. In the United States, Abd al-Rahman was in charge of the operation of a mosque in Brooklyn that was frequently attended by Arab Muslim immigrants. In 1991 he was granted permanent residence status. He then moved to the adjoining state of New Jersey. Following the bombing of the World Trade Center in New York in 1993, Abd al-Rahman was arrested and tried for inspiring the terrorists who committed the act. In 1996 he was sentenced to life in prison.

Bibliography

Beinin, Joel, and Stork, Joe. *Political Islam: Essays from Middle East Report.* Berkeley: University of California Press, 1997.

Monterey Institute of International Studies. "Special Section: Terrorist Attacks on America." Available from <http://cns.miis.edu/research/wtc01/algamaa.htm>.

Sagiv, David. *Fundamentalism and Intellectuals in Egypt, 1973–1993.* Portland, OR: Frank Cass, 1995.

AHMED H. IBRAHIM

ABD AL-RAZIQ, ALI
[1888–1966]

Egyptian Islamic judge, writer, and politician.

Ali Abd al-Raziq, who came from a family of large landowners in southern Egypt, was educated at al-Azhar in Cairo and in England and became an Islamic court judge in Mansura. In 1925, he published a controversial book on the secularization of power in the Muslim state, *Al-Islam wa usul al-hukm* (Islam and the bases of rule), in which he argued for separating Islamic from political authority, on the grounds that the Qurʾan and biographies of Muhammad show that God called on the Prophet to be a religious counselor to his people, not a head of state, and that the caliphate as a political institution was a post-Qurʾanic innovation not essential to Islam. The publication of this book aroused controversy among Muslims, especially Egyptians, because in the new Republic of Turkey, Mustafa Kemal (Atatürk) had recently abolished the Islamic caliphate, because many Muslims wanted to elect or appoint a new caliph in a country other than Turkey, and because King Fuʾad I of Egypt had proposed himself as a candidate for the caliphate. Abd al-Raziq was accused of promoting atheism and was censured by the *ulama* (Islamic scholars) of al-Azhar, deprived of his title of shaykh, and relieved of his duties as a religious judge. He was, however, backed by many liberal writers, including Taha Husayn and Muhammad Husayn Haykal.

He continued to defend his ideas in articles written for *al-Siyasa,* the weekly journal of the Constitutional Liberal Party, and in lectures delivered in Cairo University's faculties of law and of letters. He later served twice as *waqf* (Muslim endowment) minister and was elected to membership in the Arabic Language Academy. Following the 1952 revolution, he practiced law and published a collection of writings by his brother, Mustafa Abd al-Raziq, including a detailed biography. He is often cited by Egyptian and foreign writers as a leading secularist thinker and an opponent of King Fuʾad's religious pretensions.

See also EGYPT; FUʾAD; HAYKAL, MUHAMMAD HUSAYN; HUSAYN, TAHA.

Bibliography

Adams, Charles C. *Islam and Modernism in Egypt: A Study of the Modern Reform Movement Inaugurated by Muhammad ʿAbduh.* London: Oxford University Press, 1933; New York: Russell and Russell, 1968.

Binder, Leonard. "Ali Abd al Raziq and Islamic Liberalism." *Asian and African Studies* 10 (March 1982): 31–67.

Rosenthal, Erwin I. J. *Islam in the Modern National State.* Cambridge, U.K.: Cambridge University Press, 1965.

ARTHUR GOLDSCHMIDT

ABD AL-SABUR, SALAH
[1931–1981]

Egyptian author, journalist, and poet.

Abd al-Sabur was born in the Egyptian countryside but grew up in Cairo. Originally writing poetry in traditional styles, Abd al-Sabur later wrote in free verse and is considered the leader of Egyptian modernists. In all of his works, Abd al-Sabur draws upon contemporary life for his subjects and his symbolism, expressing themes of existentialism, the search for new values, and the longing for youth and for rural life. Among his volumes of poetry are *Al-Nass fi Biladi* (The people of my country), published in 1957, and *Aqulu Lakum* (I say to you), published in 1961. Abd al-Sabur also wrote plays, including *Misafir Layl* (Nocturnal pilgrims) and *Layla wa Majnun,* and several volumes of literary criticism, including *Hayati fi al-Shi*'r (My life in poetry), published in 1969, and *Qira*'*a Jadida lil-Shi*'*rna al-Qadim* (A new reading of our old poetry), published in 1968. In addition, Abd al-Sabur translated the drama of Henrik Ibsen into Arabic, as well as articles and essays that covered a broad range of subjects from British politics to atomic submarines.

Bibliography

Allen, Roger, ed. *Modern Arabic Literature: A Library of Literary Criticism.* New York: Ungar, 1987, pp. 5–11.

Becka, Jiri, ed. *Dictionary of Oriental Literatures,* Vol. 3, *West Asia and North Africa.* New York: Basic, 1974, p. 2.

DAVID WALDNER

ABD AL-WAHHAB, MUHAMMAD IBN
[c. 1901–1991]

An illustrious name in twentieth-century Arab music.

An Egyptian with acknowledged talent and a long artistic career extending roughly from the early 1920s to the late 1980s, Muhammad ibn Abd al-Wahhab emerged as a leading singer, film star, and composer who wrote hundreds of songs that he and others sang and recorded. Through his mastery of traditional Arab singing and exposure to Western music, he developed a multi-faceted repertoire that combined local and European elements in ways that seemed to reflect both his own artistic outlooks and modern Egyptian taste. Growing up in a poor and conservative Cairo family, Abd al-Wahhab was exposed to Islamic religious music at an early age. After performing traditional vocal genres and taking roles in local musical plays, he composed distinctive works and acted and sang in seven feature films released between 1933 and 1946. Through his early association with the well-known poet Ahmad Shawqi, he gained access to Egypt's distinguished social, literary, and political circles and to the musical culture of the West. Among Abd al-Wahhab's recognized innovations are: the gradual enlargement of the performing ensemble; the introduction of European instruments and instrumentations; the creation of irregular forms, often with sections in strikingly contrastive styles; the quoting of melodic themes from Romantic and post-Romantic European composers; the occasional use of Western ballroom dance meters; and the composition of numerous descriptive, or programmatic, instrumental works. Muhammad Abd al-Wahhab represented both the mainstream and the vanguard in Arab music. Although at times his music was criticized by artistic purists, his legacy is highly acclaimed by musicians, critics, and government officials throughout the Arab world.

See also SHAWQI, AHMAD.

Bibliography

Azzam, Nabil S. "Muhammad Abd al-Wahhab in Modern Egyptian Music." Ph.D. diss., University of California at Los Angeles, 1990.

Racy, Ali Jihad. "Musical Aesthetics in Present-Day Cairo." *Ethnomusicology* 26 (1982): 391–406.

ALI JIHAD RACY

ABDELGHANI, MOHAMED BENAHMED
[1927–1996]

Algerian military officer; prime minister, 1979–1984.

Mohamed Benahmed Abdelghani was appointed commander of Algeria's first (1962), fourth (1965), and fifth (1967) military regions. In October 1973 he was charged with dispatching Algerian troops to the Arab-Israel War. Abdelghani supported Colonel Houari Boumédienne's coup against Ahmed Ben Bella's government (1965) and joined the council of the revolution. After the death of Ahmed Medeghri, Abdelghani was rewarded for his loyalty with the portfolio of minister of interior (1974–1979). He was dispatched by Houari Boumédienne on a sensitive diplomatic mission to Madrid in October 1975 in an unsuccessful attempt to dissuade the Spanish government from concluding an agreement with Morocco and Mauritania over the future disposition of Western Sahara. Algerian president Chadli Bendjedid selected Abdelghani as his first prime minister (1979–1984), a strategic political choice to satisfy the Boumédienne faction. Abdelghani served as a minister of state to the presidency (1984–1988) and then retired from political office.

See also BEN BELLA, AHMED; BOUMÉDIENNE, HOUARI.

PHILLIP C. NAYLOR

ABDESSELAM, BELAID
[1928–]

Algerian prime minister, 1992–1993; minister of industry and energy, 1965–1977.

Belaid Abdesselam was born in Kabylia. A founder of the Union Générale des Etudiants Musulmans Algériens (UGEMA) in 1953 while enrolled at the University of Grenoble, he joined the Front de Libération Nationale (FLN) and served in the Gouvernement Provisoire de la République Algérienne (GPRA) during the War of Independence. Under President Ahmed Ben Bella, in 1963 Abdesselam organized and inaugurated SONATRACH, the state hydrocarbons enterprise. After Colonel Houari Boumédienne seized power in 1965, Abdesselam received the minister of industry and energy portfolio. Under Abdesselam's direction, hydrocarbon revenues fueled impressive industrial capitalization, and Abdesselam became renowned as the "father of Algerian industrialization." He played an important role in the nationalization of French hydrocarbon concessions in February 1971. From 1977 to 1979 he was the minister of light industry, but he was removed from power and eventually was accused of mismanagement—a politically motivated charge.

Abdesselam resumed a public political role in 1989. He was particularly critical of the government's liberalized hydrocarbon policy and teamed with other ex-Boumédienne ministers in opposition to President Chadli Bendjedid. In July 1992 the Haut Comité d'Etat (HCE) appointed Abdesselam prime minister. His policies attempted to stop Islamist assaults and stabilize the collapsing economy. Escalating violence and economic deterioration led to his dismissal in August 1993. Abdesselam remained active in Algerian politics. He ran for the presidency in January 1999, but his candidacy attracted little support and he withdrew from the race.

See also SONATRACH.

Bibliography

Naylor, Phillip C. *Historical Dictionary of Algeria,* 3d edition. Lanham, MD: Scarecrow Press, 2005.

PHILLIP C. NAYLOR

ABDUH, MUHAMMAD
[1849–1905]

Islamic reformer and author.

Born in a village in Gharbiyya province, Egypt, Muhammad Abduh moved with his family to Mahallat Nasr in Buhayra province, where he was raised. Educated at the Ahmadi Mosque in Tanta and at al-Azhar University, Muhammad Abduh became interested in philosophy and Sufism. During the sojourn of Jamal al-Din al-Afghani in Cairo, Abduh came to know him and became his most loyal disciple. He taught for a while, then became editor of *al-Waqa'i al-Misriyya,* the Egyptian government newspaper, from 1880 to 1882. Although more moderate than his mentor, Abduh nevertheless backed the Urabi revolution. After its collapse he was imprisoned briefly and then was exiled to Beirut.

In 1884 Abduh went to Paris, where he collaborated with Afghani in forming a society called al-Urwa al-Wuthqa (the indissoluble bond), which published a journal by the same name. Although it lasted only eight months, the journal stimulated the rise of nationalism in many parts of the Muslim world. After it was banned, Abduh returned to Beirut to teach and write. He also translated into Arabic Afghani's *al-Radd ala al-dahriyyin* (Refutation of the materialists).

In 1889 he was allowed to return to Egypt, where he became a judge, then a chancellor in the appeals court, and in 1899 the chief mufti (canon lawyer) of Egypt. In 1894 he became a member of the governing council of al-Azhar, for which he proposed far-reaching reforms. He was named to the legislative council in 1899.

His best-known theological work, *Risalat al-Tawhid* (Treatise on unity), based on lectures he had given in Beirut, was published in 1897. He also wrote *al-Islam wa al-Nasraniyya ma'a al-ilm wa al-madaniyya*, published in 1902 in *al-Manar*, a journal edited by his disciple, Rashid Rida. Abduh also began writing a commentary on the Qur'an, completed by Rida after his death. He advocated reforming Islam by restoring it to what he believed had been its original condition, modernizing the Arabic language, and upholding people's rights in relation to their rulers. He was among the first *ulama* (Islamic scholars) to favor nationalism, and one of his political disciples was Sa'd Zaghlul. His efforts to reconcile Islam with modernization have not fully survived the test of time, but Abduh remains a towering figure in Egypt's intellectual history.

See also AFGHANI, JAMAL AL-DIN AL-; RIDA, RASHID; SUFISM AND THE SUFI ORDERS; ZAGHLUL, SA'D.

Bibliography

Adams, Charles C. *Islam and Modernism in Egypt: A Study of the Modern Reform Movement Inaugurated by Muhammad 'Abduh.* London: Oxford University Press, 1933; New York: Russell and Russell, 1968.

Ahmed, Jamal Mohammed. *The Intellectual Origins of Egyptian Nationalism.* London and New York: Oxford University Press, 1960.

Amin, Osman. *Muhammad 'Abduh,* translated by Charles Wendell. Washington, DC: American Council of Learned Societies, 1953.

Hourani, Albert. *Arabic Thought in the Liberal Age, 1798–1939.* London and New York: Oxford University Press, 1962.

Kerr, Malcolm H. *Islamic Reform: The Political and Legal Theories of Muhammad 'Abduh and Rashid Rida.* Berkeley: University of California Press, 1966.

ARTHUR GOLDSCHMIDT

ABDÜLAZIZ
[1830–1876]

Ottoman sultan, 1861–1876.

Administratively, the reign of Abdülaziz divides into two eras. During the first (1861–1871), real power was in the hands of the reformist ministers Ali and Fu'ad, protégés of the leader of the Tanzimat reforms, Mustafa Reşid Paşa. Although Abdülaziz was not a figurehead, his powers were limited by his ministers; the bureaucracy ruled. Reforms continued to centralize and rationalize the Ottoman administrative system. Provincial borders were redrawn, and provincial governments were reformed by the Vilayet Law of 1867. The General Education Law of 1869 set a national curriculum stressing "modern" subjects such as the sciences, engineering, and geography. Specialized higher schools were created in the provinces, and in Constantinople (now Istanbul) a university (at least in concept) was established.

The second era (1871–1876) began upon the death of Ali in 1871 (Fu'ad had died in 1869) when Abdülaziz took personal charge of the government. The centralization of power, one of the pillars of Tanzimat reform, was especially attractive to him; he planned to transfer power to himself. To avoid concentrating power in the hands of the bureaucracy, the sultan changed ministers of state often. Grand viziers (the most famous being Mahmud Nedim Paşa) averaged well under a year in office. Serving at the pleasure of the sultan, the bureaucrats adapted themselves to carrying out his wishes and protecting their own careers. Some reformist measures were passed, particularly improvements in central administration and taxation. The thrust of reform, however, was weakened.

The military was greatly improved after 1871. Under Grand Vizier Hüseyin Avni Paşa (1874–1876), the government invested in military hardware, including up-to-date rifles and artillery from Germany. It rebuilt and improved fortresses on the Asian border with Russia and reorganized the Ottoman army corps. Previously garrisoned to face a now-unlikely internal rebellion, they were shifted to meet foreign threats. The Anatolian army, for example, was transferred from Sivas to Erzurum. The Turkish Straits were fortified. Unfortunately, the Ottoman Empire could not support even these most necessary expenditures.

Militarily, Abdülaziz's reign was relatively quiet. He and his successor, Murat V, who reigned for three months, were the only nineteenth-century sultans who did not fight a major war with Russia. Bloody uprisings in Bosnia-Herzegovina and Bulgaria, which were to result in the Russo–Turkish War of 1877–1878, began in Abdülaziz's reign. A revolt in Crete (1866–1869) resulted in administrative reforms on the island.

Russia remained the primary enemy of the Ottomans. Balanced in international affairs by the generally pro-Ottoman diplomacy of Great Britain, Russia nevertheless managed to upset the Ottoman Empire. Most damaging was Russia's policy in the Caucasus. When it conquered Circassia in 1864 and Abkhazia in 1867, Russia forced approximately 1.2 million Muslims from their homes. Robbed of their belongings by the Russians, the refugees were herded to Black Sea ports. The Ottomans were forced either to transport them to the Ottoman Empire or to let them die. The Ottomans settled the refugees in Anatolia and the Balkans. There was little but land to give them, so thefts by the starving Caucasians were widespread. Conflicts between refugees and villagers disrupted the empire for a decade.

In the face of Russia's threat and despite a good record of military preparedness, the foreign policy of Abdülaziz's later years was more than odd. The government took Russia's ambassador, Count Nicholas Ignatiev, as adviser and accommodated Ottoman policy to Russian wishes. Mahmut Nedim, twice grand vizir and Abdülaziz's main counselor, was widely, and probably correctly, viewed as being in the pay of Ignatiev. If pro-Russia policies were designed to avoid war, they were surely misguided, as Russia's attack in 1877 demonstrated.

Finances were Abdülaziz's undoing. Since the Crimean War, the Ottoman government had existed on a series of European loans. Because of vast defense needs, the costs of reform—advisers, teachers, economic infrastructure—could be paid only through borrowing. The expectation that reform would lead to economic improvement, greater tax revenues, and easy repayment of loans was never realized. The bill came due under Abdülaziz. Famine in Anato-

A patron of public education, Abdülaziz was an Ottoman sultan from 1861 to 1876. This son of Mahmid II was the first sultan to visit Western Europe. © HULTON-DEUTSCH COLLECTION/CORBIS.

lia in 1873–1874 greatly reduced tax revenues, and the bureaucrats were not adept at collecting even what could be paid. Abdülaziz exacerbated the problem with personal expenditures on palaces and luxuries. By the end of his reign, debt payments theoretically took more than 40 percent of state income. European bankers, previously willing to cover Ottoman interest payments with further loans, had suffered from the general stock market crash of 1873 and were unwilling to oblige. The Ottoman government was forced to default on its loans.

Financial disaster turned European governments, always protective of bondholders, against Abdülaziz. Restive bureaucrats, reformers, and those who feared the effects of subservience to Russia already were against him. Popular resentment at weak Ottoman responses to the slaughter of Muslims by Serbian rebels in Bosnia added to the sultan's difficulties. On 30 May 1876, Abdülaziz was deposed in favor of Murat V. On 5 June he committed suicide.

See also CRIMEAN WAR; MUSTAFA REŞID;
TANZIMAT.

Bibliography

Brown, L. Carl. *Imperial Legacy: The Ottoman Imprint on the
Balkans and the Middle East.* New York: Columbia University Press, 1996.

Davison, Roderic H. *Essays in Ottoman and Turkish History,
1774–1923.* Austin: University of Texas Press, 1990.

Findley, Carter V. *Bureaucratic Reform in the Ottoman Empire:
The Sublime Porte, 1789–1922.* Princeton, NJ: Princeton
University Press, 1980.

Gershoni, Israel; Erdan, Hakam; and Woköck, Ursula,
eds. *Histories of the Modern Middle East: New Directions.*
Boulder, CO: Lynne Rienner Publishers, 2002.

Goffman, Daniel. *The Ottoman Empire and Early Modern Europe.*
Cambridge, U.K., and New York: Cambridge University Press, 2002.

Lewis, Bernard. *The Emergence of Modern Turkey,* 3d edition.
New York: Oxford University Press, 2002.

Shaw, Stanford, and Shaw, Ezel Kural. *History of the Ottoman Empire and Modern Turkey,* Vol. 2: *Reform, Revolution,
and Republic: The Rise of Modern Turkey, 1808–1975.* Cambridge, U.K., and New York: Cambridge University
Press, 1977.

JUSTIN MCCARTHY

ABDUL-AZIZ BIN BAZ, SHAYKH
[1912–1999]

Influential religious scholar and leader in Saudi Arabia.

Born in Riyadh in 1912, Abdul-Aziz Bin Baz (also
known as Ibn Baz and Ben Baz) began his religious
studies at an early age, memorizing the Qur'an and
taking tuition from members of the most notable
religious family in the country, the Al Shaykh, de-
scendents of Muhammad ibn Abd al-Wahhab. At
age 20 Bin Baz lost his eyesight due to illness, but
his rise through the religious establishment of Saudi
Arabia was steady. He was a religious judge in the
Kharj region beginning in 1949. He worked for
many years in Islamic higher education before being named, in 1975, chairman of the Saudi government's Department of Islamic Research, Guidance,
and Proselytizing with the rank of minister. He became the highest religious authority in the country
in 1993, when he was appointed grand mufti and
head of the High Council of Ulama.

Bin Baz was influential at home and abroad,
defining a strict, conservative interpretation of Islam;
supporting Muslims under threat in such places as
Palestine, Bosnia, and Kashmir; and issuing fatwas
on a variety of subjects, including a notable one that
declared that Earth was flat. Bin Baz played a prominent role as a defender of the Al Sa'ud during the
1990s against domestic Muslim opposition groups
such as the Committee for the Defense of Legitimate Rights. Bin Baz died in 1999.

Bibliography

Fandy, Mamoun. *Saudi Arabia and the Politics of Dissent.* New
York: St. Martin's Press, 1999.

Yassini, Ayman al-. *Religion and State in the Kingdom of Saudi
Arabia.* Boulder, CO: Westview, 1985.

ANTHONY B. TOTH

ABDÜLHAMIT II
[1842–1918]

Ottoman sultan, 1876–1909.

Abdülhamit II assumed the Ottoman throne in per-
ilous times. The two previous sultans, Abdülaziz and
Murat V, had been deposed—the former primarily
for financial incompetence, the latter for mental
incompetence. The Ottoman Empire was at war with
Serbia and Montenegro, and war with Russia threatened.

International Affairs

In international affairs, the main disaster of Abdülhamit's reign came at its beginning—the Russo–
Turkish War of 1877–1878. In addition to the loss
of more than 250,000 dead and the influx of more
than 500,000 refugees into the empire, the war resulted in the largest loss of Ottoman territory since
1699. Under the terms of the Treaty of Berlin of
1878, the Ottomans lost the Kars-Ardahan region
of northeastern Anatolia to the Russians, Serbia's
and Montenegro's borders were extended at Ottoman
expense, Romania and Serbia became independent,
northern Bulgaria was made an independent kingdom, southern Bulgaria (Eastern Rumelia) became
autonomous, and Austria's occupation of Bosnia-
Herzegovina was sanctioned.

Losses of territory and administrative control
over his empire might have been greater had Ab-

dülhamit and his ministers not acted resolutely. Ceding Cyprus to Britain ensured that the British supported the Ottomans at the Congress of Berlin. The congress overturned the terms of the Treaty of San Stefano, under which almost all of Ottoman Europe was to have been lost. Instead, the Ottomans retained Thrace, Macedonia, and Albania.

The only other war fought by Abdülhamit's army, in 1897 with Greece, was a success, although the European powers forced the Ottomans to renounce their territorial gains. The powers also obliged the Ottomans to make Crete autonomous under a high commissioner, Prince George of Greece, in effect putting the island under Greek control.

Abdülhamit accepted losses that were blows to Ottoman prestige while retaining the empire's core territory. France seized Tunisia in 1881; Britain, Egypt in 1882. Although neither territory had been under Ottoman control, the losses indicated the empire's weakness to both the Europeans and the Ottomans. In 1886 that weakness forced the Ottomans to accept the de facto unification of Bulgaria and Eastern Rumelia. The European powers also compelled administrative changes in Macedonia and eastern Anatolia.

In eastern Anatolia, the powers did not bring about significant changes, despite strong sentiment in the West in favor of Armenian independence. From 1894 to 1896, Armenians in eastern Anatolia rebelled, killing Muslims and Ottoman officials. Ottoman troops and local Muslims responded in kind. Diplomatic conflict, however, among Britain, France, and Russia, forestalled any European intervention, and Ottoman offers of administrative changes were accepted by the powers.

Domestic Affairs

Like the Tanzimat reformers, Abdülhamit was concerned with the centralization of authority, the regularization of the state system, and the development of the economy. He blended these goals with the traditional ideal of Ottoman rule—an Islamic state in which all power emanated from the sultan. Although at first he accepted limited democracy, a constitution (1876), and a parliament (1877), he prorogued the Parliament within a year and ruled

Abdülhamit II, son of Sultan Abdülmecit I, ascended the throne as ruler of the Ottoman Empire on 31 August 1876, and held this post for 33 years. He instituted a new constitution, and during his reign the empire saw economic growth through railroad development, creation of secular schools, and expanded telegraph service. © CORBIS. REPRODUCED BY PERMISSION.

personally. His concept of reform was improvement of finances, infrastructure, administration, and education, not a transition to democracy.

Abdülhamit was more financially adept than his predecessors. Upon taking power, he inherited the debts that had led the empire into bankruptcy under Abdülaziz. He persuaded the European bankers to accept partial payment, so nearly half of the Ottoman debt was forgiven (the Decree of Muharram, 1881). The price, however, was the loss of financial independence. Valuable sources of state revenue (taxes on silk, fishing, alcoholic spirits, official stamps needed for all legal documents, and tobacco, as well as the tribute from Eastern Rumelia, Cyprus, Greece, Bulgaria, and Montenegro) were ceded to the European-controlled Public Debt Administration. In effect, Europeans became tax collectors in the Ottoman Empire. The empire was left with too few financial resources, and as a result, borrowing resumed.

Economic development of the empire was a first priority of Abdülhamit's rule. Improved roads increased almost sixfold. Many government-sponsored enterprises thrived—such as mining and agricultural exports. Local industry developed as well, although European manufactures and the Ottomans' inability to levy protective tariffs slowed growth considerably. The telegraph and railroad systems experienced major growth. Fewer than 186 miles (300 km) of railroad track had been laid in Ottoman Asia before Abdülaziz's reign, and trackage grew threefold under Abdülhamit. By the end of Abdülhamit's reign, feeder lines ran to major ports, and trunk lines (the Baghdad Railway and the Hijaz Railroad) were under construction. The length of telegraph line nearly tripled. In education, the number of teachers and schools approximately doubled. The increase, however, was mainly in provincial capitals and, especially, Constantinople (now Istanbul).

Abdülhamit was vilified in the European and American press as the Red Sultan, an image primarily based on press accounts of events in eastern Anatolia, Crete, and Macedonia. He also was known as no friend of liberal democracy, an accurate assertion. In his concern for his personal rule and the continuation of a powerful sultanate, he took action against all manifestations of democratic reform. All publications were censored. His secret police spied on bureaucrats and intellectuals, on the lookout for revolution as well as malfeasance.

Abdülhamit was extremely concerned with his position (historically inaccurate) as caliph of the Muslims. Expenditures from his privy purse included donations to Islamic groups in Asia and Africa, as well as to Islamic revolutionaries against Christian rule. His view of the Ottoman Empire was traditional—a Muslim empire, not a Turkish state. This naturally put him at odds with the Turkish nationalism that developed during his reign.

A combination of economic pressures, foreign interference in the empire, and his own autocracy led to the demise of Abdülhamit's sultanate. In 1907, Bulgarian and Greek revolutionaries in Ottoman Macedonia were fighting guerrilla wars against Ottoman troops and each other. Russia and Austria had forced the sultan to accept European "controllers" over Macedonia. Officers of the Ottoman army in Macedonia felt, with justification, that Abdülhamit had placated the Europeans instead of punishing the guerrillas who were killing Muslim civilians, and that fear of the army had caused the sultan to keep needed support and supplies from them. Abdülhamit's fears were largely justified; army officers had been organized into revolutionary cells since their days at the military academy. They had opened communication with revolutionary groups in western Europe, and some had organized their own rebel bands. A poor harvest in 1907 reduced tax revenues, and salaries were in arrears, causing further disaffection.

Abdülhamit, however, defused the threat of revolution in 1908 by reinstating Parliament and calling elections, deciding to rule as a constitutional monarch. Those who opposed his rule, known as the Committee for Union and Progress, became a major force in the Parliament. Abdülhamit's mistake came in 1909. Conservative reaction against the new Parliament led to a revolt in Constantinople and the expulsion of the Committee for Union and Progress's parliamentary delegates and officials. Abdülhamit associated himself with the revolt to regain power. The Macedonian army, however, proved more powerful than the rebels. They converged on Constantinople, took control, and reinstated the Parliament. On 27 April 1909, Abdülhamit was deposed and exiled to Salonika. At the onset of the First Balkan War in 1912, he was moved to the Beylerbeyi Palace on the Bosporus, where he died in 1918.

See also ABDÜLAZIZ; BALKAN WARS (1912–1913); BERLIN, CONGRESS AND TREATY OF; COMMITTEE FOR UNION AND PROGRESS.

Bibliography

Brown, L. Carl. *Imperial Legacy: The Ottoman Imprint on the Balkans and the Middle East.* New York: Columbia University Press, 1996.

Davison, Roderic H. *Essays in Ottoman and Turkish History, 1774–1923.* Austin: University of Texas Press, 1990.

Findley, Carter V. *Bureaucratic Reform in the Ottoman Empire: The Sublime Porte, 1789–1922.* Princeton, NJ: Princeton University Press, 1980.

Lewis, Bernard. *The Emergence of Modern Turkey*, 3d edition. New York: Oxford University Press, 2002.

Quataert, Donald. *The Ottoman Empire, 1700–1922*. New York: Cambridge University Press, 2000.

Shaw, Stanford, and Shaw, Ezel Kural. *History of the Ottoman Empire and Modern Turkey*, Vol. 2: *Reform, Revolution, and Republic, 1808–1975*. Cambridge, U.K., 1977.

JUSTIN McCARTHY

ABDULLAH, CROWN PRINCE

See AL SAʿUD FAMILY

ABDULLAH I IBN HUSSEIN

[1882–1951]

King of Jordan, 1946–1951.

Abdullah ibn Hussein, born in Mecca, was a son of Husayn ibn Ali. On his eleventh birthday, he went to Constantinople (now Istanbul) to join his father, who had been summoned by the sultan. In 1908 Hussein was appointed Sharif of Mecca, over the objections of the Committee for Union and Progress (the Young Turks). Between 1910 and 1914, Abdullah represented Mecca in the Ottoman Parliament.

The Turkish authorities tried to strip Hussein of his administrative (but not religious) duties when the construction of railroad and telegraph lines made direct rule from Constantinople possible. Hussein resisted, and he was in danger of dismissal when the dispute was shelved due to the outbreak of World War I.

In February 1914, Abdullah met Lord Kitchener, then minister plenipotentiary to Egypt, and asked him if Britain would aid Sharif Hussein in case of a dispute with the Turks. Abdullah also met with Ronald Storrs, the Oriental secretary at Britain's consulate in Cairo. This meeting led to a subsequent correspondence between Storrs and Abdullah that later developed into the Husayn–McMahon Correspondence, an exchange in which certain pledges were made by Britain to the sharif concerning an independent Arab kingdom (with ambiguous boundaries) in the Fertile Crescent.

The Turks tried to persuade Hussein to endorse the call for jihad against the Allies, but he delayed

until 10 June 1916, when the Arab Revolt was declared. Abdullah was entrusted with the siege of the Turkish garrisons in al-Taʾif and Medina. His brother Faisal, meanwhile, scored quick victories in Syria. Faisal set up an independent Arab kingdom with its capital at Damascus toward the end of 1918; the French drove him out two years later. Meanwhile, Abdullah was defeated in an important battle with the Wahhabi followers of Ibn Saʿud. Britain placed Faisal on the throne of Iraq, which had been slated for Abdullah.

One key to understanding Abdullah is his deep loyalty to Islam, which in his mind was linked to the notion that God had favored the Arabs with a unique position as the carriers of culture and faith. For him, Arabism was inseparable from Islam and meaningless without it. His family, which claimed a direct line of descent from the prophet Muhammad, provided the crucial link between the two.

Another key to an understanding of Abdullah's personality is that, as a rule, he sought cooperation, even in the midst of conflict. He preferred bargaining to fighting, and he constantly formulated value-maximizing strategies in which he compromised with his adversaries so that all sides might stand to gain from the outcome.

Although Abdullah strove for unity, he engaged in nation-building on a limited scale when unity was unattainable. When he appeared with a small band of armed followers in Madaba, after the French had ousted his brother Faisal from the throne of Syria in 1920, he was intent on leading Syrian political refugees, members of the Istiqlal Party still loyal to Faisal, and the bedouins he could muster in a bid to wrest Arab rights in Syria from the French. With T. E. Lawrence acting as a go-between, he negotiated a deal with the new British colonial secretary, Winston Churchill, under which Abdullah agreed to administer Transjordan for six months, beginning on 1 April 1921, and was granted a subsidy by Britain. One consequence of this was to remove Transjordan from the sphere of applicability of the Balfour Declaration.

Abdullah took over the administration of an arid plateau with a population of about 235,000, largely bedouin, poor, and uneducated, a land with some two hundred villages, half a dozen towns, and

Abdullah I ibn Hussein ruled as king of Jordan from 1946 until 20 July 1951, when he was assassinated. He supported pro-British policies. © LIBRARY OF CONGRESS. REPRODUCED BY PERMISSION.

no major cities. Governmental services were virtually nonexistent. When he died, he left a nation-state comparable with others in the Middle East, although lacking in financial independence. The period from 1924 to 1940 was one in which central administration was developed, with Palestinians gradually replacing Syrians. An exemplary land program gave farmers property security unmatched in the Fertile Crescent. In 1925 the Maʿān and Aqaba regions were effectively incorporated into Transjordan (they had technically formed part of the Hijaz). In the same period, the bedouins, who had preyed on the sedentary population, were successfully integrated into the state, for which John Bagot Glubb, the organizer of the Desert Patrol, was largely responsible.

In 1928, Transjordan acquired an organic law under which Abdullah gained recognition in international law. It also provided for constitutional gov-

ernment and a legislative council, but Abdullah had wide authority to rule by decree, under the guidance of Britain. Although Transjordan remained militarily dependent on Britain, on 22 March 1946 a treaty was concluded whereby Britain recognized Transjordan "as a fully independent state and His Highness the Amir as the sovereign thereof." Following a name change, the Hashimite kingdom of Jordan concluded a new treaty with Britain in 1948.

Through years of dependency on Britain, Abdullah fell behind the times, continuing to reflect the Ottoman Empire in which he had grown up: dynastic and theocratic, Arabs accepting foreign suzerainty under compulsion. He was out of step with Palestinian and secular Arab nationalism as well as Zionism. He sought to use British influence to forge Arab unity rather than to get rid of the British as a first step toward unity. British residents, notably St. John Philby and Percy Cox, drove a wedge between him and Syrian members of the Istiqlal party, who had perceived the Hashimites as champions of Syria's independence from France. When Abd al-Rahman Shahbandar, a nationalist Syrian leader who had been a longtime supporter of Abdullah, was assassinated in July 1940, Abdullah's base of support in Syria died with him.

Abdullah could accept a Jewish homeland only in the context of the old millet system: as a minority with a large degree of autonomy within a kingdom that he ruled. Zionists found this totally unacceptable but valued his accommodating approach to the problem. Yet he was a pioneer of Arab–Jewish understanding. He accepted the Peel Commission Report of 1937, which recommended partition of Palestine, even if he did not embrace a Jewish state. He also publicly accepted the 1939 white paper on Palestine, which was favorable to the Arabs. It has been said that he was driven by personal ambition, hoping to incorporate the Arab portion of Palestine within his domain, yet it is clear that he saw himself as an Arab acting for the Arabs. As his grandson King Hussein pointed out, Abdullah realized that the Jewish community in Palestine was only the tip of the iceberg and that the balance of forces dictated compromise. Abdullah met with Golda Meir, who was acting on behalf of the political department of the Jewish Agency, on 17 November 1947, and it was agreed that Abdullah would annex the Arab part of Palestine under the UN partition plan but would not invade the Jewish part.

When the British mandate ended on 14 May 1948, the Jews declared the creation of a Jewish state, and war broke out with the Arabs. The Arab Legion (Jordanian army) occupied what came to be known as the West Bank; Britain accepted this as long as Abdullah kept out of the Jewish zone; when Jewish forces and the Arab Legion clashed over Jerusalem, which was to have been designated an international zone, Britain cut off arms supplies and spare parts, and ordered all of its officers to return to Amman. The Arabs held on to East Jerusalem, but the Arab Legion had to withdraw from the towns of Lydda and Ramla, which laid Abdullah open to charges of betrayal. In the final analysis, his strategy salvaged territory for the Arabs that may one day serve as the basis for a Palestinian state.

Abdullah initiated a conference in Jericho at which the Palestinian participants expressed a wish to join in one country with Jordan. Parliamentary elections were subsequently held in the west and east banks, with twenty seats assigned to each. Parliament convened on 24 April 1950, at which time Palestinian deputies tabled a motion to unite both banks of the Jordan. This was unanimously adopted. Abdullah became king of a country that now included the holy places in Palestine, with a population of 1.5 million, triple the population of Transjordan alone.

Abdullah was assassinated at the al-Aqsa Mosque on 20 July 1951 by a handful of disgruntled Palestinians believed to be working with Egypt's intelligence service.

See also ARAB REVOLT (1916); BALFOUR DECLARATION (1917); CHURCHILL, WINSTON S.; FAISAL I IBN HUSSEIN; GLUBB, JOHN BAGOT; HUSAYN IBN ALI; HUSAYN–MCMAHON CORRESPONDENCE (1915–1916); HUSSEIN IBN TALAL; ISTIQLAL PARTY: PALESTINE; ISTIQLAL PARTY: SYRIA; KITCHENER, HORATIO HERBERT; LAWRENCE, T. E.; MEIR, GOLDA; SHAHBANDAR, ABD AL-RAHMAN; STORRS, RONALD; WEST BANK.

Bibliography

Abdullah, King of Jordan. *My Memoirs Completed,* translated by Harold W. Glidden. London and New York: Longman, 1978.

Dann, Uriel. *Studies in the History of Transjordan, 1920–1949: The Making of a State.* Boulder, CO: Westview Press, 1984.

Kirkbride, Sir Alec. *From the Wings: Amman Memoirs 1947–1951.* London: F. Cass, 1976.

Shlaim, Avi. *Collusion across the Jordan: King Abdullah, the Zionist Movement, and the Partition of Palestine.* New York: Columbia University Press, 1988.

Wilson, Mary C. *King Abdullah, Britain, and the Making of Jordan.* Cambridge, U.K., and New York: Cambridge University Press, 1987.

JENAB TUTUNJI

ABDULLAH II IBN HUSSEIN
[1962–]

King of Jordan beginning in 1999.

Abdullah II ibn Hussein was born on 30 January 1962, the first-born son of Jordan's King Hussein (r. 1952–1999) and his English second wife, Princess Muna (née Antoinette Avril Gardiner). He briefly was Jordan's crown prince, from 1962 to 1965. Following primary studies in Jordan, Britain, and the United States, Abdullah entered Sandhurst, the Royal Military Academy in Britain, in 1980. He also did graduate work at Oxford University in 1984 and at Georgetown University in 1987. Abdullah became an officer in the Jordanian army in 1985, serving in armored units until 1993, when he became deputy commander of the Special Forces. He was promoted to brigadier-general and made head of the Special Forces in June 1994. By May 1998 he had been promoted to major-general.

Abdullah was catapulted from his quiet life as an army officer into the full glare of national and international attention when his dying father redesignated him crown prince on 25 January 1999. In so doing, Hussein demoted his brother, Hassan, who had been crown prince for thirty-four years. Abdullah became king two weeks later when his father died on 7 February 1999. Despite several drawbacks—his half-English parentage, weak command of formal Arabic, and lack of political and diplomatic experience—Abdullah rose to the occasion of ruling Jordan and carrying on his late father's immense legacy. Although he lacked Hussein's intimate knowledge of Jordan's tribes and traditions, as well as his flair for playing the role of "head shaykh" of the country,

Abdullah II ibn Hussein became the king of Jordan upon the death of his father in 1999. Since taking office, Abdullah II has worked to modernize his country, strengthen its ties with the United States, and bring some measure of accord between Israel and the Palestinians. PUBLIC DOMAIN. LIBRARY OF CONGRESS.

Abdullah's service in the East Bank–dominated military ensured him a degree of support and good will among key Hashimite constituencies. His Palestinian wife also helped him politically with Jordan's Palestinian population.

Abdullah ushered in his reign speaking of democracy, governmental efficiency, globalization, and technology. He was one of several young "Internet kings" who emerged in the Arab world at the turn of the twenty-first century. His habit of making unannounced inspection visits to government offices around the country, dressed as an ordinary citizen, demonstrated his zeal in improving bureaucratic efficiency, as did his interest in "e-government." Abdullah's "Jordan First" (al-Urdunn Awwalan) campaign also seemed to signal his attempt at promoting a unitary Jordanian national agenda. Although his father also spoke of "the one Jordanian" family, he also promoted a more personalized Hashimite rule than does Abdullah.

Abdullah escalated Jordan's traditional pro-Western orientation by identifying strongly with the United States and its regional policies. His embrace

of globalization and his support of President George W. Bush's "war on terrorism," including the permission he gave for U.S. forces to be based in Jordan during the 2003 U.S. invasion of Iraq, was a departure from his father's subtler policies. Like his father, however, he became a mediator in the ongoing Israeli–Palestinian dispute, and hosted a summit in Aqaba in 2003 that brought together Bush, Palestinian Authority prime minister Mahmud Abbas, and Israeli prime minister Ariel Sharon.

In June 1993 Abdullah married Rania al-Yasin (b. 1970), a Kuwaiti-born Palestinian whose family hails from the West Bank city of Tulkarm. In the tradition of Hashimite royal women's philanthropy, Rania established the Jordan River Foundation in 1995. She assumed the title "queen" following Abdullah's coronation in 1999 and quickly became a darling of the international media as well as an articulate spokesperson of the causes she champions. They have one son, Hussein (b. 1994), and two daughters, Iman (b. 1996) and Salma (b. 2000).

See also ABBAS, MAHMUD; BUSH, GEORGE WALKER; HUSSEIN IBN TALAL; PALESTINIAN AUTHORITY; RANIA AL-ABDULLAH (QUEEN RANIA); SHARON, ARIEL.

MICHAEL R. FISCHBACH

ABDULLAHI, MUHAMMAD TURSHAIN
[1846–1899]

Commander of the Mahdist forces and ruler of the Mahdist domains in the Sudan, 1885–1898.

Known in Western literature as Khalifa Abdullahi, Muhammad Turshain Abdullahi was born at Turdat in southwestern Darfur, one of four sons of a holy man of the Ta'ayshe Baqqara. Upon hearing of Muhammad Ahmad al-Mahdi, he went east to join him at Aba Island in the Bahr al-Abyad; he was the first to recognize him as the Mahdi. The Mahdi recognized his military abilities and made him a principal military commander. In 1881 Abdullahi was appointed a caliph, given the name Abu Bakr al-Siddiq, and placed in command of the prestigious black flag division of the Madhist army.

Abdullahi retired with the Mahdi to Kordofan and there organized a series of crushing defeats of the government forces that gave the Mahdist movement the reputation of invincibility. He fought in the Jazira and oversaw the siege of Khartoum, which, after long resistance, fell in January 1885. On the death of the Mahdi in June 1885, Abdullahi assumed the temporal functions of government as dictator of an empire that extended from Dar Mahas to the Upper Nile and from the Red Sea to Darfur. Except at Omdurman in 1898, when he was overthrown, he did not personally lead his armies, preferring to leave operational details to his field commanders.

Abdullahi ruled harshly and arbitrarily in order to maintain his large military establishment. His genius for organization was revealed in his system of taxation and his attempts to establish factories to manufacture steamers and ammunition, as well as mints to produce coins. He insisted on the strict observance of Islamic law. He was hostile to the religious brotherhoods, suppressing them where the Mahdi had only discountenanced them. His merciless rule at length aroused the opposition of most tribal peoples except his own *baqqara,* to whom he gave a privileged position in the state in return for their loyalty.

After the advance of the army of Egypt and Britain into Dongola in 1896, Abdullahi's prestige suffered. Numerous defeats of the incompetent general Amir al-Umara Mahmud Ahmad and Abdullahi's defeat at Atbara culminated in the battle of Omdurman in September 1898. Fleeing south, he and several companions were killed at Umm Dibaikarat in 1899. He was buried on the battlefield, several miles southeast of Tendelti on the Kordofan railway. His tomb is venerated.

See also AHMAD, MUHAMMAD.

Bibliography

Holt, P. M., and Daly, M. W. *A History of the Sudan: From the Coming of Islam to the Present Day,* 5th edition. Harlow, U.K., and New York: Longman, 2000.

Petterson, Donald. *Inside Sudan: Political Islam, Conflict, and Catastrophe,* revised edition. Boulder, CO: Westview, 2003.

ROBERT O. COLLINS

ABDÜLMECIT I

[1823–1861]

Thirty-first Ottoman sultan (r. 1839–1861); initiated Tanzimat reform program.

Abdülmecit I was the oldest surviving son of the Westernizing sultan Mahmud II. He had a good education, with a strong European component. He knew French well, subscribed to French publications, and admired European music. Abdülmecit was also well versed in Ottoman Islamic culture: His mother, Bezmialem, a formidable lady, had a great influence on his upbringing and may have encouraged him to follow the reformist (*müceddidî*) Naqshbandi teaching of her Sufi spiritual adviser.

When Abdülmecit succeeded to the throne on 1 July 1839, at age seventeen, the empire was in crisis: Its army was defeated and its navy had surrendered to the rebellious governor of Egypt, Muhammad Ali. The conflict was resolved only by the intervention of France and Great Britain, which imposed a settlement defining Muhammad Ali as hereditary viceroy and limiting his territories. Henceforth, the Ottoman Empire was forced to recognize that its internal affairs would remain a concern for the Concert of Europe in its aim to establish and protect an international balance of power.

Within a few months of his accession, Abdülmecit brought to power a group of young reformist ministers, who seem to have been motivated as much by the ideals of the Naqshbandi movement as by a strong commitment to Europeanization. The leader of this group, Mustafa Reşid, prepared and publicly proclaimed, in the form of an imperial decree, the Tanzimat reform program, limiting the sultan's arbitrary power and setting forth principles of fiscal, military, and religious reorganization. The young sultan held fast to this program and left political power in the hands of Mustafa Reşid and others of similar conviction, although factionalism among ministers continued among reformists as well.

The Crimean War (1853–1856) illustrates both the Great Powers' involvement in Ottoman affairs and a crucial occasion for Ottoman borrowing from Europe. The loans, obtained at unfavorable rates, were spent on the military as well as various features of material Europeanization that were economically unproductive but symbolically significant. British and French alliance with the Ottomans during the war was promoted in Europe as aiding valiant Ottoman attempts at Westernization. Queen Victoria made Abdülmecit an honorary Knight of the

Garter, while the sultan proclaimed a second reform decree (Islahat) to promote equality for his non-Muslim subjects, as requested by the Great Powers at the end of the war. In the long run, however, foreign loans led to financial distress and submission to European fiscal domination.

Hailed abroad as a sensitive and intelligent ruler, Abdülmecit's reforms were less popular among his Muslim subjects, who perceived little immediate benefit from them. Resentment culminated into violent uprisings in Jidda, Damascus, and Beirut, which occasioned only further European involvement. Neither were Tanzimat reforms sufficient to quell non-Muslim discontent in the Balkans, where various ethnic nationalisms were on the rise.

Abdülmecit died young, of tuberculosis. His Muslim subjects looked to his vigorous brother and successor Abdülaziz to champion their privileges. Among his many children were the last four sultans of the dynasty.

See also ABDÜLAZIZ; CRIMEAN WAR; MAHMUD II; MUHAMMAD ALI; MUSTAFA REŞID; NAQSHBANDI; OTTOMAN EMPIRE; TANZIMAT.

Bibliography

Davison, Roderic H. *Reform in the Ottoman Empire, 1856–1876.* Princeton, NJ: Princeton University Press, 1963.

İnalcık, Halil. *Application of the Tanzimat and Its Social Effects.* Lisse, Netherlands: Peter de Ridder Press, 1976.

Sakaoğlu, Necdet, and Akbayar, Nuri. *A Milestone on Turkey's Path of Westernization: Sultan Abdülmecid.* Istanbul: Creative Yayincilik, 2001.

I. METIN KUNT
UPDATED BY BURÇAK KESKIN-KOZAT

ABDÜLMECIT II
[1868–1944]

Last Ottoman caliph.

The son of Sultan Abdülaziz (r. 1861–1876) and cousin of Sultan Mehmed VI Vahideddin (r. 1918–1922), Abdülmecit II (also Abdülmecid) was known as a mild and scholarly man. He was elected caliph on 18 November 1922 by the Grand National Assembly in Ankara which, under the leadership of Mustafa Kemal (Atatürk), had abolished the Ottoman sultanate on 1 November. As caliph, Abdülmecit encouraged the loyalty of Muslims in Turkey and elsewhere, particularly India. His growing influence was seen as a threat to the new Turkish republic, and on 3 March 1924 the assembly abolished the Ottoman caliphate and sent Abdülmecit into exile aboard the Istanbul-to-Paris train known as the Orient Express.

See also ABDÜLAZIZ; ATATÜRK, MUSTAFA KEMAL.

Bibliography

Lewis, Bernard. *The Emergence of Modern Turkey,* 2d edition. New York; London: Oxford University Press, 1961.

Shaw, Stanford J., and Shaw, Ezel Kural. *History of the Ottoman Empire and Modern Turkey,* Vol. 2. *Reform, Revolution, and Republic: The Rise of Modern Turkey, 1808–1975.* New York; Cambridge, U.K.: Cambridge University Press, 1977.

ELIZABETH THOMPSON
UPDATED BY ERIC HOOGLUND

ABIDIN, DINO
[1913–]

Turkish painter.

Dino Abidin was born in the Ottoman Empire but spent most of his life in Paris. He was one of the founders of the New Group, an artistic movement of the 1940s that favored socially conscious art, often exhibiting the life of laborers, villagers, and fishermen. Abidin's art is characterized by efforts to forge compromise between seemingly contradictory elements. In addition, Abidin is a prolific author of articles on subjects from philosophy to contemporary cinema.

Bibliography

Renda, Günsel. "Modern Trends in Turkish Painting." In *The Transformation of Turkish Culture: The Ataturk Legacy,* edited by Günsel Renda and C. Max Kortepeter. Princeton, NJ: Kingston Press, 1986.

DAVID WALDNER

ABU

See GLOSSARY

ABU ALA

See QURAI, AHMAD SULAYMAN

ABU AL-HUDA, TAWFIQ
[1894–1956]

Prime minister of Jordan between 1938 and 1954.

Abu al-Huda formed Jordan's first cabinet of ministers in August 1949; until then, the government was an executive council under the terms of the British Mandate and the Anglo–Jordanian Treaty. He was part of the delegation that negotiated with Britain on amendments that led to new government structures, including a cabinet responsible to the head of state and a legislative council. He was leader of the Executive Council or prime minister twelve times between 1938 and 1954.

Abu al-Huda helped King Abdullah I ibn Hussein steer through the political maze during the Arab–Israel War of 1948 and the union between central Palestine and Transjordan. When King Abdullah was assassinated, Abu al-Huda was chosen by his peers, on 25 July 1951, to form the cabinet that saw Jordan through those troubled times. Paradoxically, he presided over the enactment of the very liberal constitution of 1952 under an impetus from King Talal ibn Abdullah. Yet, during this two-year period, which ended with King Hussein ibn Talal ascending the throne, there was a shift of power from the king to the prime minister. As a consequence, Abu al-Huda exercised more power than any other prime minister in the history of Jordan.

When Fawzi al-Mulqi's cabinet, the first under King Hussein, was shaken by disturbances following border clashes with Israel, the king turned to the veteran Abu al-Huda to form the new cabinet. He convinced the king to dissolve parliament on 22 June 1954 as an assertion of executive dominance over the legislature. He issued the Defense Regulations of 1954, empowering the cabinet to deny licenses to political parties, dissolve existing parties, prohibit public meetings, and censor the press. The opposition charged that the new elections were fixed, and Abu al-Huda's measures encouraged the opposition to seek extraparliamentary forms of dissent. Popular opposition forced his last cabinet to resign.

Bibliography

Satloff, Robert B. *From Abdullah to Hussein: Jordan in Transition.* New York: Oxford University Press, 1994.

JENAB TUTUNJI
UPDATED BY MICHAEL R. FISCHBACH

ABU AL-TIMMAN, JA'FAR
[1881–1945]

Iraqi nationalist leader.

Ja'far Abu al-Timman was born in Baghdad to a rich Shi'ite merchant family. He contributed generously to support troops of the Ottoman Empire who were fighting the British occupation of Iraq during World War I. After the war, he was instrumental in organizing the 1920 Iraqi armed uprising against the British, who had created for themselves a mandate through the League of Nations. By 1922, the British recognized Iraq as a kingdom, under their nominee for king, Faisal I ibn Hussein, but they continued controlling the country. They ended the mandate in 1932, and Iraq was then admitted into the League of Nations. A treaty of alliance, however, had been signed between the two countries in 1930.

Throughout his life, Abu al-Timman focused on two main goals: (1) forging a national union between the two largest Islamic communities, the Sunni and the Shi'ite; and (2) struggling to end British control. Upon his formation of the National Party in 1922, the British authorities exiled him to the island of Henjam in the Persian/Arabian Gulf for a year. In 1928, during the early years of the kingdom, he was elected a deputy of Baghdad in Iraq's parliament. He and the majority in the National Party boycotted the elections of both 1930 and 1933, objecting to the abuse of the democratic process by the governments in power. Abu al-Timman halted his political activities from 1933 to 1935; in late 1935, he started publishing the newspaper *al-Mabda* (The principle) and allied himself with the leftist group called al-Ahali (The people's group). From 1935 to 1939 he served as president of Baghdad's Chamber of Commerce and encouraged national industry as a way toward national independence. He supported the military coup led by Bakr Sidqi in October 1936 and served as minister of finance in the coup cabinet formed by Hikmat Sulayman. He worked for an egalitarian policy and for a larger role for the state in the economy of Iraq. Political infighting prompted him to resign this post in June 1937.

World War II began in 1939. In 1941, he supported the coup led by pro-Axis Premier Rashid Ali al-Kaylani, which attempted unsuccessfully to end the British presence in Iraq (based on the 1930 treaty of alliance).

See also AHALI GROUP; FAISAL I IBN HUSSEIN; IRAQ; KAYLANI, RASHID ALI AL-; SIDQI, BAKR; SULAYMAN, HIKMAT.

Bibliography

Batatu, Hanna. *The Old Social Classes and Revolutionary Movements of Iraq: A Study of Iraq's Old Landed and Commercial Classes and Its Communists, Ba'thists, and Free Officers.* Princeton, NJ: Princeton University Press, 1978.

MAHMOUD HADDAD

ABU AMMAR

See ARAFAT, YASIR

ABU DHABI

The largest, wealthiest, and most powerful of the seven shaykhdoms that make up the United Arab Emirates (UAE); also, the capital city.

Abu Dhabi's 28,000 square miles (75,520 square kilometers) make up 87 percent of the federation's area, and its 1.3 million inhabitants comprise about 40 percent of its population. Its terrain is mostly flat and rocky, with areas of dunes in the interior, and salt flats and numerous islands along the coast. Abu Dhabi City, the capital of the emirate and the country, occupies one of these islands. In the eastern part of the emirate lies its second most important city, al-Ayn, which grew from a small village within the Buraymi Oasis. In the western part of the emirate slight rainfall collects in depressions to create the arc of oases called al-Liwa. Abu Dhabi possesses 90 percent of the UAE's approximately 100 billion barrels of oil reserves and 60 percent of its significant gas reserves.

The al-Nahayyan section of the Banu Yas tribal confederation has dominated the political history of the region for more than 200 years. According to the founding legend of the emirate, a hunting party of the Bani Yas followed a gazelle across a shallow ford to an island in the Persian (Arabian) Gulf. After the discovery of water around 1761, a small settlement was established, which was named Abu Dhabi, "Land of the Gazelle." Shakhbut bin Diyab,

ruler of the Bani Yas, had a small fort built over the settlement's well, and he moved his seat of power to the island from al-Liwa. The coral block, adobe, and timber fort was the largest structure in Abu Dhabi for most of the town's history and was first mentioned in a written source in 1791. Because of its proximity to rich oyster banks in the Gulf, in the nineteenth century Abu Dhabi was host to many pearling ships. Before the discovery of oil, the principal means of livelihood for the emirate's inhabitants were diving for pearls in the summer and engaging in animal herding and oasis agriculture (mainly in al-Liwa and al-Ayn) during the rest of the year. The rulers of Abu Dhabi signed a series of treaties with Britain in the nineteenth century that put them under the Empire's protection.

The wholesale transformation of the emirate began in the 1960s with the advent of increasing revenues from oil exports. Under the rule of Zayid ibn Sultan al-Nahayyan, which began in 1966, a modern infrastructure and a large range of social services were established. Following the 1968 British announcement of impending withdrawal of military and political protection, Zayid convinced the rulers of the other emirates who were part of Trucial Oman, as the British protectorate was known, to form the UAE. Because of the prestige of its ruling family, and especially the magnitude of its oil and gas revenues, Abu Dhabi dominates the UAE politically and economically. These economic endowments helped to fund the construction of modern international airports, universities, hospitals, museums, towering hotels and office buildings, and a modern communications and transportation infrastructure where only fifty years earlier there were simple palm-frond huts and dusty paths.

See also AL NAHAYYAN FAMILY; AYN, AL-; BURAYMI OASIS DISPUTE; DUBAI; RA'S AL-KHAYMA; RUB AL-KHALI; SHARJAH.

Bibliography

Hoogland, Eric, and Toth, Anthony. "United Arab Emirates." In *Persian Gulf States: Country Studies,* 3d edition, edited by Helen Chapin Metz. Washington, DC: Library of Congress, 1994.

Peck, Malcolm C. *The United Arab Emirates: A Venture in Unity.* Boulder, CO: Westview Press; London: Croom Helm, 1986.

Zahlan, Rosemarie Said. *The Origins of the United Arab Emirates: A Political and Social History of the Trucial States.* New York: St. Martin's Press; London: Macmillan, 1978.

MALCOLM C. PECK
UPDATED BY ANTHONY B. TOTH

ABUHATZEIRA, AHARON

[1938–]

Israeli politician, member of the Knesset.

Born in Morocco, Aharon Abuhatzeira was elected to the Knesset (Israel's parliament) in 1974 and 1977 as a National Religious Party member and served as minister of religious affairs in the first government of Menachem Begin. In 1981, he founded and chaired TAMI, a party identified with Israel's Moroccan community. He was elected to the Knesset with TAMI in 1981 and 1984. He subsequently joined the Likud and served as minister of labor, welfare, and absorption.

See also ISRAEL: POLITICAL PARTIES IN; KNESSET; LIKUD.

MARTIN MALIN

ABU HIMARA

Arabic for "the man on the she-ass," a nickname of the leader of the 1902–1909 Moroccan rebellion that helped discredit the governments of the sultan Abd al-Aziz and his successor Abd al-Hafid.

Jilali ibn Idris al-Yusufi al-Zarhuni, the real name of Abu Himara, was a minor Moroccan official and former engineering student with a talent for mimicry and some skills as a thaumaturge. Following a 1902 incident, he declared himself to be the *mahdi* (legendary imam who returned to restore justice) and launched a rebellion among the tribes to the northeast of Fez. Subsequently he declared himself to be the sultan's elder brother Muhammad, a claim that, although false, was generally accepted by his supporters.

Between 1902 and his eventual defeat in 1909, Abu Himara (also called Bu or Bou Hmara) ruled much of northeastern Morocco from his base at Salwan, near Mellila. His rebellion derailed a 1901 British-sponsored reform program, and opened the way for the French colonial offensive. The in-

ability of Sultan Abd al-Aziz and his successor, Abd al-Hafid, to defeat him played a significant role in the Moroccan Question.

His unusual sobriquet derives from a precolonial Moroccan tradition, according to which recaptured army deserters would be paraded around camp mounted sitting backwards on a she-ass, to the jeers of the troops. The cultural referent is obscure, but may be a satiric inversion of the Maghribi (North African) tradition that states that the *mahdi* would appear from the west, mounted on a she-ass.

See also ABD AL-AZIZ IBN AL-HASSAN; ABD AL-HAFID IBN AL-HASSAN; FEZ, MOROCCO; *MAHDI*; MOROCCAN QUESTION.

Bibliography

Burke, Edmund, III. *Prelude to Protectorate in Morocco: Precolonial Protest and Resistance, 1860–1912.* Chicago: University of Chicago Press, 1976.

Dunn, Ross E. "The Bu Himara Rebellion in Northeast Morocco: Phase I." *Middle Eastern Studies* 17 (1981): 31–48.

Maldonado, Eduardo. *El Roghi.* Tétouan, Morocco, 1952.

EDMUND BURKE III

ABU IYAD

See KHALAF, SALAH

ABU JIHAD

See WAZIR, KHALIL AL-

ABU LUTF

See QADDUMI, FARUQ

ABU MAZIN

See ABBAS, MAHMUD

ABU MUSA ISLAND

Small island near the entrance to the Persian Gulf, claimed by both Iran and the United Arab Emirates.

Abu Musa is an island in the Persian (Arabian) Gulf located at 55° E longitude and between 25° 51′ N

and 25° 54′ N latitude. It is 31 miles (49 kilometers) east of Iran's island of Sirri, about 42 miles (68 kilometers) south of the Iranian mainland port of Bandar-e Lengeh, and 40 miles (64 kilometers) east of Sharjah in the United Arab Emirates. Abu Musa's total area is approximately 4 square miles (10 square kilometers). There are several fresh-water wells on the island, and these support a covering of dry grass.

Although Iran historically claimed ownership of all the islands in the Gulf, since the late nineteenth century the sovereignty of Abu Musa has been in dispute. The ruler of Sharjah, then a dependency of Britain, claimed jurisdiction over the island after tribesmen owing allegiance to him had begun to transport their domesticated animals by boat to Abu Musa for seasonal grazing there. Initially, Britain did not support the claim of its protectorate, but in 1903 British forces evicted Iranian customs officials on the island and claimed Abu Musa on behalf of Sharjah. At the time, Iran's military was virtually nonexistent and powerless to challenge Britain. Nevertheless, Iran lodged an official protest with the British government and in subsequent years periodically raised the issue.

After Britain in 1968 announced that Sharjah and its other dependencies in the Persian Gulf would become independent, Iran, which by then had reemerged as a regional power, insisted that its claims to Abu Musa be addressed. In 1971, on the eve of Sharjah's independence and admission to the new United Arab Emirates federation, the leaders of Sharjah and Iran signed a Memorandum of Understanding. This agreement left the question of ultimate sovereignty open but provided for Iranian jurisdiction in the northern half of the island and Sharjah's jurisdiction in the southern part. In addition, both parties agreed to divide the income from petroleum production in waters surrounding Abu Musa.

The agreement on shared sovereignty worked reasonably well for twenty years. In early 1992, however, the United Arab Emirates, with backing from the United States, accused Iran of violating the accord and interfering in Sharjah's administration of the southern half of Abu Musa. Although Iran and the United Arab Emirates subsequently worked out an informal arrangement to continue observing the terms of the 1971 Memorandum of Understanding pending a resolution of their dispute, the issue is one that continues to affect overall bilateral relations negatively. The position of the United Arab Emirates since 1992 has been that Iran should agree to permit the International Court to arbitrate their contending claims to sovereignty over Abu Musa; Iran rejects this position.

See also SHARJAH.

Bibliography

Amirahmadi, Hooshang, ed. *Small Islands, Big Politics: The Tonbs and Abu Musa in the Persian Gulf.* New York: St. Martin's Press, 1996.

Bavand, Davoud H. *The Historical, Political and Legal Bases of Iran's Sovereignty over the Islands of Tunb and Abu Musa.* New York: Internet Concepts, 1994.

Schofield, Richard. *Unfinished Business: Iran, UAE, Abu Musa and the Tunbs.* Washington, DC: Brookings Institution; London: Royal Institute of International Affairs, 2001.

ERIC HOOGLUND

ABU NADDARA

See SANU, YA'QUB

ABU NIDAL

See BANNA, SABRI AL-

ABU NUWWAR, ALI
[1925–1991]
Jordanian army officer.

Ali Abu Nuwwar was born in al-Salt. After the Arab–Israel War of 1948, he studied for one year at Sandhurst, the British military academy, returning to Jordan in 1950. Attracted to the ideology of the Ba'th party, he was sent to the Jordanian embassy in Paris by John Glubb, head of the Arab Legion, shortly thereafter to preclude his involvement in any political activities against the monarchy. Abu Nuwwar was also close to a group of anti-British, nationalist army officers who called themselves the Jordanian Free Officers and even advised the young King Hussein ibn Talal of the group's existence. Hussein eventually returned Abu Nuwwar to Jordan in late 1955, against Glubb's wishes, whereupon he became Hussein's protégé. The king eventually deposed Glubb in March 1956.

In May 1956 Abu Nuwwar was appointed chief of staff of the army and represented Jordan in the Israel–Jordan Mixed Armistice Commission under the United Nations Truce Supervisory Organization. As political turmoil mounted in Jordan from 1956 to 1957, he became involved in a conspiracy to overthrow the king. The attempted coup occurred at the same time that Sulayman al-Nabulsi, who was prime minister at the head of a leftist cabinet, was purging government officials loyal to the king. As a result, suspicions arose that Abu Nuwwar and Nabulsi were coconspirators, although both denied this. Abu Nuwwar was not tried for his actions but was allowed to flee to Syria after Hussein thwarted the coup. He remained in self-imposed exile in Egypt, was eventually pardoned by the king, and returned to Jordan.

> *See also* ARAB LEGION; ARAB–ISRAEL WAR (1948); BA'TH, AL-; GLUBB, JOHN BAGOT; HUSSEIN IBN TALAL; NABULSI, SULAYMAN AL-.

Bibliography

Dann, Uriel. *King Hussein and the Challenge of Arab Radicalism: Jordan, 1955–1967.* New York: Oxford University Press, 1989.

Massad, Joseph A. *Colonial Effects: The Making of National Identity in Jordan.* New York: Columbia University Press, 2001.

JENAB TUTUNJI
UPDATED BY MICHAEL R. FISCHBACH

ABU QIR, BATTLE OF (1798)

Naval battle in which the English destroyed the French fleet in Egyptian waters.

Abu Qir is a bay located between the Rosetta branch of the Nile River and Alexandria, Egypt. After capturing the island of Malta in the Mediterranean Sea in April 1798, the fleet of Napoléon, then commander of the army of France, avoided the swifter fleet of Britain, commanded by Admiral Horatio Nelson. After French troops landed in Alexandria on 1 July 1798, the French fleet took shelter in Abu Qir bay. On 1 August, Nelson's fleet located and destroyed the French fleet.

Bibliography

Goldschmidt, Arthur, Jr. *Modern Egypt: The Formation of a Nation-State.* Boulder, CO: Westview Press, 1988.

DAVID WALDNER

ABU RISHA, UMAR

Syrian poet.

One of the most influential literary figures in the Arab world, Umar Abu Risha was born in Aleppo. He studied at the American University of Beirut. He held several senior positions, including director of the National Library in Aleppo and ambassador of Syria to Brazil, India, and the United States. His literary talent earned him numerous orders of merit from Syria, Brazil, Argentina, Lebanon, and Vienna. Abu Risha's exquisite poetry echoes the beauty of nature and expresses a passion for freedom.

MUHAMMAD MUSLIH

ABU SA'ID

See HASAN, KHALID AL-

ABU ZAYD, HIKMAT

First Egyptian woman appointed to a cabinet-level position.

Originally from a village in Assiut, Hikmat Abu Zayd completed her education and began a career as a teacher at the Hilwan Secondary School in the 1940s. She then studied in England, receiving her doctorate in educational psychology in 1955. She taught at Ain Shams University and published two books before Gamal Abdel Nasser appointed her minister of social affairs in 1962. This achievement was significant in the history of Egyptian women, within the regime itself, and politically, because of Nasser's desire to co-opt female-run charitable organizations into the purview of the Arab Socialist Union.

In the nineteenth century, elite women took the lead in running many of the country's charitable organizations. They sponsored social and welfare programs that the government was unable or unwilling to support, particularly after the British occupation of 1882. Nevertheless, the 1952 revolution sought to dismantle the *ancien régime* and all vestiges of its power, including women's organizations. Abu Zayd's appointment in 1962 must be viewed in light of these circumstances as well as Nasser's reforms of 1961 and 1962, which included wide-ranging nationalization of industry, income redistribution, land reform, educational expansion, and family planning. Under Abu Zayd's leadership from 1962 to 1965 many charitable organizations came under state control and women's literacy programs expanded. In 1963 she presided over the first national congress convened to study issues related to women and work, which published its findings in 1964 in *Characteristics of the Path Facing the Working Woman* (Arabic).

See also NASSER, GAMAL ABDEL.

Bibliography

Badran, Margot. *Feminists, Islam, and Nation: Gender and the Making of Egypt.* Princeton, NJ: Princeton University Press, 1995.

Marsot, Afaf Lutfi al-Sayyid. "The Revolutionary Gentlewomen in Egypt." In *Women in the Muslim World*, edited by Lois Beck and Nikki Keddie. Cambridge, MA: Harvard University Press, 1978.

Sullivan, Earl. *Women in Egyptian Public Life.* Syracuse, NY: Syracuse University Press, 1986.

MONA RUSSELL

ABU ZEID, LAYLA
[1950–]

Moroccan fiction writer.

Raised and educated in French and Arabic in Rabat, Layla Abu Zeid (or Leila Abouzeid) was working as a radio and television journalist and presenter when she began to publish short stories. She followed these with a novel, *Am al-fil* (1983; *Year of the Elephant*), which received critical acclaim and was the first Arabic-language novel by a Moroccan woman to be translated into English. It treats the coming of age and adult struggle of an abandoned Moroccan woman in the context of the fight for national independence. This themes is echoed in her 1993 memoir of childhood, *Ruju ila al-tufula* (1993; *Return to Childhood*) and in her more subsequent fiction, in which she experiments with multiple viewpoints and narrative voices. Her works offer a subtle commentary on nationalist and misogynist misappropriations of Islam and especially of *shariʿa*.

Daughter of a prominent opponent of the colonial regime who was imprisoned for his activism, Abu Zeid grew up with a consciousness of the relationship between language and power. Even as a child, Abu Zeid has said, she resisted reading and writing in French, the language of the colonial administration in the Morocco of her earliest childhood. This resistant stance ensured that she would choose Arabic as her language of literary expression, she notes, rather than being one of many francophone writers in her country.

See also GENDER: GENDER AND EDUCATION; GENDER: GENDER AND LAW; GENDER: GENDER AND POLITICS; LITERATURE: ARABIC; MOROCCO; MOUDAWANA, AL-.

Bibliography

Abouzeid, Leila. *The Last Chapter: A Novel,* translated by Leila Abouzeid and John Liechety. New York and Cairo: American University in Cairo Press, 2000.

Abouzeid, Leila. *Return to Childhood: The Memoir of a Modern Moroccan Woman,* translated by Leila Abouzeid and Heather Logan Taylor. Austin: University of Texas Press, 1998.

Abouzeid, Leila. *Year of the Elephant: A Moroccan Woman's Journey Toward Independence, and Other Stories,* translated by Barbara Parmenter. Austin: University of Texas Press, 1989.

MARILYN BOOTH

ACHESON, DEAN
[1893–1971]

U.S. statesman.

As undersecretary of state (1945–1947), Acheson was one of the main proponents of the Truman Doctrine (1947), aiding Greece and Turkey. He is often associated with the U.S. containment policy for communism and promoted the foundation of NATO (1949). As secretary of state (1949–1953), he was concerned primarily with the USSR and Korea, although he had been involved in the early negotiations with Iran's prime minister (1951–1953) Mohammad Mossadegh. He won a Pulitzer Prize in 1969 for *Present at the Creation: My Years in the State Department.*

See also TRUMAN, HARRY S.

Bibliography

Findling, John, ed. *Dictionary of American Diplomatic History*, 2d edition. New York: Greenwood Press, 1989.

Spiegel, Steven. *The Other Arab-Israeli Conflict*. Chicago: University of Chicago Press, 1985.

ZACHARY KARABELL

ACHOUR, HABIB
[1913–1999]

Tunisian labor leader.

A native of the Kerkenna islands, off the coast of central Tunisia, Habib Achour founded the Tunisian General Labor Union, which merged with the General Union of Tunisian Workers (Union Générale des Travailleurs Tunisiens, UGTT) in 1957. Achour worked closely with Ferhat Hached, father of the Tunisian labor movement, until Hached's assassination in 1952. His adherence to nationalist ideologies led to his imprisonment and deportation in 1947 and 1952. Achour's appointment to the political bureau of the Destour Party in 1964 reflected broad cooperation between the union and the Destour Party, but he was arrested in 1966 because of political differences. During the mid-1970s, this cooperation gave way to tension as the union leadership grew critical of state policies and Achour reasserted the labor movement's autonomy from the government in the context of an unpopular agrarian reform. In January 1978 Achour resigned from the Destour Party political bureau and following the events of Black Thursday he and other leaders of the UGTT were arrested. Achour was pardoned by Tunisian president Habib Bourguiba in 1981 and elected president of the union, a newly created post. In 1984, in a successful power play, he wrested control of the post of secretary-general. The next year, with tensions high between the union and the government of Mohammed Mzali, Achour and other labor leaders were again imprisoned, but he was later released. Achour died in March 1999.

See also BLACK THURSDAY (1978); BOURGUIBA, HABIB.

Bibliography

Nelson, Harold D. *Tunisia: A Country Study*. Washington, DC: U.S. Government Printing Office, 1988.

Perkins, Kenneth J. *Tunisia: Crossroads of the Islamic and European Worlds*. Boulder, CO: Westview Press; London: Croon Helm, 1986.

MATTHEW S. GORDON
UPDATED BY VANESA CASANOVA-FERNANDEZ

ADALAT PARTY

An Iranian political party that unsuccessfully planned a Communist takeover of Iran.

The Adalat party was established in Iran by veteran Social Democrats, sympathetic to the Russian Bolsheviks, almost immediately after the Russian Revolution of 1917. The leadership of the party consisted mainly of Iranian intellectuals from Azerbaijan who were closely tied to the Bolsheviks. The Adalat founded a bilingual Azeri-Persian newspaper called *Hürriyet* (or Freedom) and was very active among the Iranian workers in the Baku oil fields. The party's membership, according to the party's own estimate, was primarily composed of workers and apprentices, but also included office employees, craftsmen, and tradesmen. After its first major congress at Baku in June 1920, the party changed its name to the Communist Party of Iran (Firqeh-ye Komunist-e Iran) and created a program that included land reforms, formation of trade unions, and self-determination for minorities. Clergymen, landowners, and merchants were barred from its ranks. Most importantly, together with the Jangali in Gilan, the party announced the formation of a Soviet Socialist Republic of Iran, based in Rasht. By the end of 1920, the party, together with the Red Army, was preparing a march into Tehran. The activities of the party at this time greatly contributed to the crisis that paved the way for the emergence of Colonel Reza Khan, who became Iran's ruler as Reza Shah Pahlavi and founded the Pahlavi dynasty.

See also HÜRRIYET; JANGALI; PAHLAVI, REZA.

Bibliography

Abrahamian, E. *Iran between Two Revolutions*. Princeton, NJ: Princeton University Press, 1982.

PARVANEH POURSHARIATI

ADAMIYAT, ABBASQULI
[1861–1939]

A pioneer of the constitutional and freedom movement in Iran.

Mirza Abbasquli Khan Qazvini, later surnamed Adamiyat (humanity), was born in Qazvin, Iran. His political activism started about 1885, in cooperation with Mirza Malkom Khan and Mirza Yousuf Khan Mostashar al-Dowleh. He was involved in the publication of the underground *Qanun* (Law) that was sent to his country from Europe, and he was one of the organizers of the Majma-el Adamiyat (Society of humanity). The society was the organizational expression of liberal and humanist thought in turn-of-the-century Iran; it fought for the formation of a parliamentary government (which was actually drawn up in 1906—but political events intervened until the Constitutional Revolution of 1909).

Adamiyat is the author of several articles, including "Farizeh-ye Adam" (Precept of the human being) and "Bung-i Bidari" (The sound of awakening).

See also CONSTITUTIONAL REVOLUTION; MALKOM KHAN, MIRZA.

MANSOOR MOADDEL

ADAMIYAT, FEREYDUN
[1920–]

A leading social historian of contemporary Iran.

Fereydun Adamiyat was born in Tehran in 1920; he is the son of Abbasquli Adamiyat, a pioneer of the constitutional movement. Fereydun Adamiyat received his B.A. from the University of Tehran and his Ph.D. in diplomatic history from the University of London. He is known for his original works on various aspects of the social and political history of Persia (Iran from 1935), most of them dealing with the ideological foundations of the Constitutional Revolution—the movement and reform in turn-of-the-century Persia. Although predominantly published in Persian, he is often cited by Western academicians. Adamiyat has also been a diplomat and has served, inter alia, as Iran's ambassador to the Netherlands and India. He has worked as well for the United Nations in various capacities.

See also ADAMIYAT, ABBASQULI; CONSTITUTIONAL REVOLUTION.

MANSOOR MOADDEL

ADANA

Capital of Adana province, Turkey.

Adana is the leading cotton-, cotton-textile-, and citrus-producing region of Turkey. Known since Hittite times, it was a minor town until the U.S. Civil War (1861–1865), when worldwide cotton shortages induced a boom in Adana's region. Nearby Incirlik Air Base is the largest NATO facility in the eastern Mediterranean. Adana, Turkey's fourth-largest city, had a 2002 population of 1.7 million.

See also COTTON.

JOHN R. CLARK

ADANA CONFERENCE

Meeting of Turkish president and British prime minister, 1943.

During World War II, Turkey was faced with a dilemma; for reasons of security, it remained officially neutral for much of the war, but its sympathies lay with the Allies. In the early stages of the war, Turkey stayed out of the conflict and even signed a nonaggression pact with Germany (1941), to forestall a German attack. Turkish neutrality, however, was assailed by the USSR as opportunistic and hypocritical.

On 30 and 31 January 1943, Britain's Prime Minister Winston Churchill met with Turkey's President Ismet İnönü in Adana, Turkey. Churchill assured İnönü that the Allies, under the Anglo-Turkish agreement of 1939, would continue to guarantee Turkish security. In addition, Churchill agreed to supply Turkey with supplies necessary for self-defense; henceforth, Turkey was eligible for the U.S. Lend-Lease Program and received significant amounts of such aid until 1945. Although Churchill did not extract any binding commitment from İnönü, he was assured that Turkey would do all it could to aid the Allies without violating its neutrality.

See also İNÖNÜ, İSMET; LEND-LEASE PROGRAM.

Bibliography

Shaw, Stanford, and Shaw, Ezel Kural. *History of the Ottoman Empire and Modern Turkey.* Cambridge, U.K., and New York: Cambridge University Press, 1976–1977.

ZACHARY KARABELL

ADEN

Seaport city in the Republic of Yemen.

Located on the southeastern tip of the Arabian Peninsula, Aden is the second-largest city in the Republic of Yemen and one of the best natural ports on the Arabian Sea. From 1839 to 1967, Aden was a British colony; from 1967 to 1990, it was the capital of the People's Democratic Republic of Yemen.

F. GREGORY GAUSE III

ADENAUER, KONRAD
[1876–1967]

German statesman and first chancellor of the Federal Republic of Germany (West Germany), 1949–1963.

Adenauer began his political career during the Weimar Republic but was dismissed from his several political posts by the Nazis to live in seclusion until 1944, when he was sent to a concentration camp in a political purge. After the Allied occupation of a defeated Germany in 1945, Adenauer became a founder of the Christian Democratic Union, a supradenominational party aimed at a centrist position and a rebuilding of Germany in the "Christian spirit." He became party leader (1946–1966), president of the parliamentary council (1949) that drafted the new constitution for the Federal Republic of Germany (West Germany), and first chancellor (1949–1963). He tied his country to the Christian West and encouraged German business development away from political controls.

From 1953 to 1965, he oversaw collective indemnification to the State of Israel and the Jewish people for property stolen under the Nazi administration (1933–1945); he admitted Germany's guilt without pressure from the West, and his Federal Republic assumed responsibility for the crimes of the Third Reich. In Israel, reparations became controversial, since they were seen as a political means for Germany to rejoin the West, by buying off Jewish survivors. After a vote in the Knesset, Adenauer and Israel's foreign minister Moshe Sharett signed the Reparations Agreement in 1952, by which Germany agreed to provide $845 million in reparations, in addition to $110 million to Jews outside Israel. Until 1964, payment was made by Adenauer's government in goods and monies; the agreement was carried out fully and Israel's economy received a firm financial base for the development of water resources, a merchant fleet, and the mechanization of agriculture and industry.

Bibliography

Balabkins, Nicholas. *West German Reparations to Israel.* New Brunswick, NJ: Rutgers University Press, 1971.

Sagi, Nana. *German Reparations: A History of the Negotiations,* translated by Dafna Alon. New York: St. Martin's Press; Jerusalem: Magnes Press, Hebrew University, 1986.

ZACHARY KARABELL
UPDATED BY MICHAEL R. FISCHBACH

ADHAM, SORAYA
[1926–]

Egyptian feminist and nationalist activist.

Born into a large family in Cairo, Soraya Adham was encouraged to pursue learning by her father, who strongly believed in education for girls. She attended Arabic schools and in 1948 graduated from Cairo University with a degree in English literature. As a university student she was drawn to the left wing and became a leader in the youth movement, and later was recruited by the Communist movement. She was one of approximately fifty women activists in the Egyptian Communist Party. Although Communists in Egypt were primarily men, the women activists are noteworthy because their participation involved a rebellion against both colonial society and gender conventions, which restricted interaction between men and women.

Because of ideological differences, Communist women did not take part in Huda al-Shaʿrawi's Feminist Union or Fatma Niʿmat Rashid's Feminist Party. In 1944–1945 Communist women established the League of Women Students and Graduates from the University and Egyptian Institutes (Rabitat Fatayat al-Jamiʿa wa al-Maʿahid al-Misriyya). The League sought to create a forum where women could discuss women's rights and envision Egypt free of colonial influence. It was closed down in 1946 by Prime Minister Sidqi Pasha as part of his attempt to wipe out all opposition.

Adham lived alone, which was unusual for women of this time, in a one-room furnished apartment in the Bulaq neighborhood of Cairo. In 1948 she was beaten by a group of Muslim fundamentalists for participating in political activity. She spent two months in prison in 1948 and another ten months in 1949.

The Egyptian Communist movement was never cohesive but instead fraught with internal dissension. Government opposition required it to remain clandestine and hindered any party unification. Nonetheless, various groups of individuals, motivated by British occupation, widespread poverty, and the rise of fascism in Europe, did form a number of Communist-oriented organizations that encouraged trade unions, strikes, political protests, and political journalism. Male members of the Communist Party generally were reluctant to put women in harm's way and also feared that giving women any prominent role would repel potential male participation. Thus radical women activists eventually took their feminist endeavors outside the party. They formed small feminist societies in institutions of higher learning and tried to establish contact with women working in factories to organize trade unions.

In the 1950s, when the nationalist movement was resurrected to fight British influence in the Suez Canal, women Communists served the nationalist cause and joined the Women's Committee for Popular Resistance (Lajnat al-Nisaʾiyya li al-Muqawama al-Shaʿbiyya), which included women from across the political spectrum. Its members gained access to the Canal Zone by telling the British they were visiting wounded Egyptians in the hospitals and tending to their families. They then established ties with Egyptian women living in the area. Later they informed the domestic and international press of living conditions there. The Women's Committee was reestablished in 1956 to protest the invasion of Egypt by Britain, France, and Israel.

Although the number of women in the Egyptian Communist movement was relatively small, their commitment to feminism made important contributions to improving gender equality for Egyptian women.

See also COMMUNISM IN THE MIDDLE EAST; EFFLATOUN, INJI; EGYPTIAN FEMINIST UNION; GENDER: GENDER AND POLITICS; RATEB, AISHA; SHAʿRAWI, HUDA AL-; SUEZ CANAL; ZAYYAT, LATIFA.

Bibliography

Ahmed, Leila. *Women and Gender in Islam: Historical Roots of a Modern Debate.* New Haven, CT: Yale University Press, 1992.

Badran, Margot. *Feminists, Islam, and Nation: Gender and the Making of Modern Egypt.* Princeton, NJ: Princeton University Press, 1995.

Botman, Selma. *Egypt from Independence to Revolution, 1919–1952.* Syracuse, NY: Syracuse University Press, 1991.

Botman, Selma. *Engendering Citizenship in Egypt.* New York: Columbia University Press, 1999.

Botman, Selma. "The Experience of Women in the Egyptian Communist Movement, 1939–1954." *Women's Studies International Forum* 2, no. 5 (1988): 117–126.

Botman, Selma. "Oppositional Politics in Egypt: The Communist Movement, 1936–1954." Ph.D. diss., Harvard University, 1984.

MARIA F. CURTIS

ADIVAR, ABDULHAK ADNAN
[1881–1955]

Turkish doctor, historian, and writer.

Born in Gallipoli to a prominent family of Ottoman *ulama* (Islamic clergy), Abdulhak Adnan Adivar was graduated from the Imperial School of Medicine in 1905. Suspected of working against the regime, he left for Europe and became an assistant at the Berlin Faculty of Medicine. Returning to Constantinople (now Istanbul) upon the restoration of the constitution, he taught at and became dean of the School of Medicine (1909–1911). He worked with the Red Crescent Society during the Tripoli War and with the Ottoman Department of Public Health in World War I, being credited with contributing substantially to the reorganization of both institutions.

At the armistice, Adivar became a member of the last Ottoman parliament but avoided British arrest and deportation, escaping to Anatolia with his wife Halide Edib Adivar and becoming one of Atatürk's inner circle. During the war of independence, he served in various ministerial positions and was vice-president of the Turkish Grand National Assembly. After the armistice, he served in the national government's delegation in Istanbul. He supported the short-lived Progressive Republican Party but was in Europe when news broke of a conspiracy against Atatürk (June 1926).

Tried in absentia for complicity, he was acquitted but chose to remain in exile until 1939, at first in England, then Paris, teaching at the École des Langues Orientales and engaged in scholarly research and writing. Upon his return, Adivar fostered the teaching and practice of science and was a founder and first president of the International Society for Oriental Research.

He directed publication of the Turkish edition of the *Encyclopaedia of Islam,* contributing its introduction and a number of articles. His other works include *La science chez les Turks Ottomans* (Paris, 1939), a Turkish translation of Bertrand Russell's *Philosophical Matters* (1936), a two-volume work in Turkish on science and religion through history, and many essays and articles on cultural and scientific topics. He served a final period as deputy for Istanbul (1946–1950).

See also ADIVAR, HALIDE EDIB; ATATÜRK, MUSTAFA KEMAL; TURKISH GRAND NATIONAL ASSEMBLY.

Bibliography

Shaw, Stanford, and Shaw, Ezel Kural. *History of the Ottoman Empire and Modern Turkey,* Vol. 2: *Reform, Revolution, and Republic: The Rise of Modern Turkey, 1808–1975.* Cambridge, U.K., and New York: Cambridge University Press, 1977.

Toynbee, Arnold S. *Acquaintances.* London: Oxford University Press, 1967.

KATHLEEN R. F. BURRILL

ADIVAR, HALIDE EDIB
[1884–1964]

Prolific Turkish author (best known as a novelist), journalist, pioneer feminist, nationalist, and educator.

Born in Constantinople (now Istanbul), Halide Edib Adivar lost her mother early in life. Her father (a first secretary to the sultan's privy purse) remarried, and she spent much of her childhood in her maternal grandmother's traditional Muslim household, where she learned to read, write, and recite the Qur'an. She also came in touch with Christianity and learned Greek (attending a Greek-run kindergarten), and her Anglophile father provided her with English governesses and later with various private tutors. She had spent a year at the American College for Girls when she was eleven but withdrew on orders of the sultan. Reentering in

1899, she was the first Turk to graduate from the college (1901). The same year, she married one of her tutors, mathematician Salih Zeki. They had two sons but were divorced in 1910 when he took a second wife. She later married Dr. Abdulhak Adnan Adivar.

Halide Edib Adivar began writing at the time of the Second Constitution (1908), contributing articles to Tanin that urged educational and social reforms. Vulnerable as a progressive, she left the country during the 1909 counterrevolution. On her return, she taught for a while then served as inspector of schools under the Ministry of Religious Foundations. Believing in democracy and the social responsibilities of the educated toward the people at large, she was a member of the first Women's Club in Turkey, addressing protest meetings on the treatment of women, and was active in relief and nursing activities during the Balkan War. Like other prominent intellectuals, she fell under the influence of Ziya Gökalp and participated in the activities of the Turkish Hearth Association, addressing public demonstrations after the Greek landing at İzmir in particular that of 23 May 1919, in Sultan Ahmet Square. First advocating an American mandate for Turkey, when the British started to deport members of the last Ottoman parliament to Malta, she and Adnan Adivar escaped to Anatolia to join the nationalists (March 1920).

She played an important role during the war of independence in Ankara as one of Atatürk's inner circle and as "Corporal Halide" at the front. Disillusioned after the founding of the republic, she left Turkey with her husband (1926) and, apart from one short visit, returned only after Atatürk's death. She spent the intervening period mainly in London and Paris but also toured India and visited the United States to lecture. Back in Turkey, she held the chair of English language and literature at Istanbul University and served as deputy in the Grand National Assembly (1950–1954).

Halide Edib Adivar's novels fall into three main categories: psychological novels, sagas of the war of independence, and panoramas of city life or period novels. She denied that she herself is the woman behind her heroines—whom she subjects to keen psychological analysis. Their experiences, however, frequently reflect her own, as in *Yeni Turan* (New

Turan, 1912) in which the heroine sacrifices herself for pan-Turkism, a cause then espoused by the author. Her most famous war of independence novel is *Ateşten Gömlek* (Shirt of fire). Serialized in the press before publication in book form (1923), it portrays the popular support for the national movement. *Sinekli Bakkal* (1923), a panorama of Constantinople life in the Abdülhamit II period is a highpoint of her novel writing. Published first in English as *The Clown and His Daughter* (London, 1935), it received the Turkish Republican People's Party Prize for Best Novel (1943). Also serialized, it became a best-seller and was made into a film.

In addition to novels and many articles, she produced translations (including Orwell's *Animal Farm*), a three-volume history of English literature, numerous short stories, and three works in English containing her impressions of India and lectures delivered in India and the United States. Her language and style (influenced by her English-American education) have been criticized by Turks. Nevertheless, she proved popular with the reading public, her Turkish being close to the spoken word of her day. Moreover, her works, which reflect her acute powers of observation and understanding of people, are extremely strong in descriptive passages and bring the Turkish scene alive in a manner not previously achieved.

See also ADIVAR, ABDULHAK ADNAN; ATATÜRK, MUSTAFA KEMAL; GÖKALP, ZIYA; LITERATURE: TURKISH; PAN-TURKISM.

Bibliography

Adivar, Halide Edib. *Memoirs of Halidé Edib.* New York: Arno Press, 1972.

Adivar, Halide Edib. *The Turkish Ordeal: Being the Further Memoirs of Halidé Edib.* Westport, CT: Hyperion Press, 1981.

Woodsmall, Ruth Francis. *Moslem Women Enter a New World.* New York: AMS Press, 1975.

KATHLEEN R. F. BURRILL

ADLI

[1864–1933]

Egyptian official, cabinet minister, and politician who served as prime minister three times between 1919 and 1930.

Descended from a family of large landowners and related to the Muhammad Ali royal family, Adli split from the popular Wafdist movement, led by Saʿd Zaghlul, beginning in 1919. Adli became prime minister in 1921, but the Wafd undercut his efforts to negotiate an independence treaty with Britain. After Britain unilaterally declared Egypt independent (but with significant restrictions) in 1922, Adli's supporters—large landlords and a handful of reformist intellectuals—formed the Liberal Constitutionalist Party. The Wafd won the parliamentary elections in 1926, but the British regarded Zaghlul as an extremist and refused to let him return to the prime ministry. Adli therefore headed a coalition cabinet with the Wafd. Forced to maneuver between the Wafd, the British, and the palace, neither Adli nor his party ever felt at home in the world of mass politics.

See also LIBERAL CONSTITUTIONALIST PARTY.

Bibliography

Deeb, Marius. *Party Politics in Egypt: The Wafd and Its Rivals, 1919–1939.* London: Ithaca Press, 1979.

DONALD MALCOLM REID

ADL WA AL-IHSAN, AL-

Moroccan Islamic movement.

Al-Adl wa al-Ihsan (Justice and Benevolence) is modern Morocco's largest Islamic movement, with a membership estimated at about 30,000. Its official foundation dates from 1987, though the organization started to take shape under different names as early as 1981. The structural and ideological nature of al-Adl wa al-Ihsan largely stems from the writings of its founder and charismatic Supreme Guide, Abdessalam Yacine. The movement, which is especially popular on university campuses, is based upon a pyramidal framework whose lowest unit is called *usra* (family). Each *usra* consists of two to ten individuals. Its function is to provide the members with a new familial environment where they may find the Islamic guidance and moral support necessary for their spiritual reeducation. Promoting the re-Islamization of Moroccan society, such small groups meet three times a week to pray, to study Yacine's teachings, and to cultivate the values of benevolence and communal responsibility. Members also benefit from social, recreational, and financial services. The movement provides medical services, offers funds for marriage, plans field trips, and organizes sporting events to build strong bonds between its members. At the top of this structure is a General Council presided over by the Supreme Guide, who retains strong discretionary powers. Although al-Adl wa'l Ihsan remains officially illegal, the Moroccan government tolerates its activities. This is due in part to the movement's quietism: It does not claim the right to partake in politics, nor does it advocate armed struggle against the state. Yacine often makes political statements, but he has so far eschewed direct political involvement.

See also YACINE, ABDESSALAME.

HENRI LAUZIÈRE

ADNAN, ETEL
[1925–]

A Lebanese artist.

Poet, novelist, writer, and visual artist Etel Adnan's work achieved recognition during the Lebanese Civil War (1975–1990). Her gripping novel *Sitt Marie Rose* (1978), based on the real life and murder of a pro-Palestinian Lebanese woman by Christian Phalangists, is a brilliant discursive collage of monologues, news bulletins, interviews, and film clips. It depicts the trial of the woman character and angrily lashes out against a violent, macho culture. Originally written in French, it has been translated into more than ten languages and remains a popular choice in women's studies, comparative literature, and Middle East studies curricula.

Born in Beirut in 1925 to a Muslim Syrian father and a Christian Greek mother, Adnan grew up speaking Greek and Turkish and learned French in school. Although she also spoke Arabic, it was like a "forbidden paradise" to her; she later learned English. Her many languages, she wrote in her autobiographical 1996 essay "To Write in a Foreign Language," posed a dilemma for her. Indeed painting, she writes, proved to be an important outlet: "Abstract art was the equivalent of poetic expression; I didn't need to use words, but colors and lines. I didn't need to belong to a language-oriented culture but to an open form of expression."

Etel Adnan established herself in the 1970s and 1980s as an avant-garde artist in multiple mediums. She experimented openly with joint expressions in poetry and drawing, as in her groundbreaking *The Arab Apocalypse* (1989). Although she writes primarily in English and French, she strongly identifies with an Arabic poetic tradition. In an article on the acclaimed Arab poet Adonis, Adnan defends contemporary Arab poets who choose not to write in Arabic. Indeed, she identifies herself as an Arab-American poet and has argued for the importance of including these Arab "foreign" voices in Arabic curricula and scholarship: "Until this is done, no judgment of any worth can be passed on contemporary Arab poetry."

See also ART; GENDER: GENDER AND EDUCATION; GENDER: GENDER AND LAW; GENDER: GENDER AND POLITICS; LEBANESE CIVIL WAR (1958); LEBANESE CIVIL WAR (1975–1990); LEBANON; LITERATURE: ARABIC.

Bibliography

Accad, E. "Of Cities and Women By Etel Adnan/Paris, When It's Naked By Etel Adnan." *World Literature Today* 68 (1994): 421–422.

Adnan, Etel. "Growing Up to Be a Woman Writer in Lebanon." In *Opening the Gates: A Century of Arab Feminist Writing*, edited by Margot Badran and Miriam Cooke. Bloomington: Indiana University Press, 1990.

ELISE SALEM

ADONIS
[1930–]

Pen name of Ali Ahmad Sa'id, Syrian-Lebanese modernist poet.

Born in Qassabin, Syria, Adonis was educated at Damascus University and St. Joseph University in Beirut, Lebanon. His critiques of orthodoxy in Islam and of conventional writing made him highly controversial. In poetry and prose, he opposes what he sees as the static and conservative tradition of Arabic literature and culture. His revolutionary ideas were shaped by involvement in the Parti Populaire Syrien, which resulted in his imprisonment in 1956. On release, he escaped to Lebanon, later becoming a Lebanese citizen.

In 1957, his *Qasa'id Ula* (First poems) was published, and he cofounded *Shi'r* (Poetry) magazine, later starting his own magazine, *Mawaqif* (Attitudes).

Adonis taught Arabic literature at Lebanese University until 1985 when he moved to France, where he held teaching and research posts; he now teaches in Geneva, Switzerland. *Orbits of Desire*, a selection of his poetry translated by Kamal Abu-Deeb, was published in London in 1992.

See also SYRIAN SOCIAL NATIONALIST PARTY.

Bibliography

Adonis. "This Is My Name," translated by Kamal Abu-Deeb. *Grand Street* (1992): 40.

Boullata, Issa, ed. *Modern Arab Poets, 1950–1975.* Washington, DC: Three Continents Press; London: Heinemann, 1976.

Jayyusi, Salma Khadra, ed. *Modern Arabic Poetry: An Anthology.* New York: Columbia University Press, 1987.

KAMAL ABU-DEEB

ADOT HA-MIZRAH

The popular term used in Israel for Oriental Jews—those who came from the Islamic countries—now known as Middle Eastern Jews.

The Jewish population that emigrated to Israel from the Middle East, North Africa, India, and Central Asia were considered Oriental by those who had emigrated from northern Europe. The term is problematic, since it lumps Sephardim (Jews expelled from Spain in 1492 to live in Christian Europe and the Islamic Middle East) with Jews who had lived among Muslims since the dispersal in Roman times. These two populations had, in 1,400 years, developed different languages, rituals, and social customs.

The term *Sephardim* had also been employed in Israel for all other Jews but the Ashkenazim (who had lived in and around medieval Germany); consequently another term was needed. In both popular and social science discourse, the accepted term is becoming *mizrahim* (literally, Orientals), while the term *adot ha-mizrah* is falling out of use. The customary English meaning of the term *Oriental* leads to another problem as it has the connotation of East

Asia, where very few Jews lived and from where even fewer had immigrated to Israel. In English-language discourse, then, social scientists increasingly use the term *Middle Easterners* (which includes immigrants from India—so a problem remains).

Until the late nineteenth century in Palestine, Middle Easterners dominated Jewish society both politically and demographically. Thereafter, as a result of Zionism and the vigorous pioneer settlement movement of northern European Jewry, the Middle Easterners faltered. Some immigrated, others became absorbed among the Ashkenazim, and over all, they lost political predominance. In 1948, when the State of Israel was established, mass immigration from Islamic nations changed the demography; by about 1970, some 50 percent of Israeli Jews were of Middle Eastern background. Since then, the rate of increase of Middle Easterners has lessened, but the inflow from the former Soviet Union has increased and will probably continue to increase as the new republics strike an economic and social balance in the new Europe. The former Soviet Jews are mostly Ashkenazim. In the long run, the reproduction rates of these two categories of Israeli Jews will probably equalize their populations.

It is notable that the marriages that link Israelis of Middle Eastern and European background amount to about 25 percent. Given the approximately even numbers of these two populations in Israel as of the 1990s, the data imply that the intermarriage rate is about 50 percent of the theoretical optimum, indicating social acceptance, at least on the individual level. In the 1950s and 1960s, both institutional and social discrimination had descended on Middle Eastern Jews to burden the economic plight of impoverished refugees, in many cases. The new state was struggling economically to cope with the flow of immigration, so many were housed in the tents and shacks of transit camps or taken to new settlements far from the cities and population centers—to the Galilee and Negev desert towns, to live in homogeneous settlements. Consequently, many acculturated only slowly to their emerging society.

In the 1970s, Middle Eastern Jews regained important political positions in an electoral shift that led to the ascendance of a Likud-led coalition government of right-wing and religious parties. The support of Middle Easterners for Likud is linked to their positive view of that party's long-time opposition to the Maʿarakh (Alignment) party. Maʿarakh had formerly dominated them; they are not necessarily in favor of Likud's right-wing politics.

Despite Israel's recent demographic and political developments, the Middle Easterners remain prominent in some of the problem areas of Israeli life. They are overrepresented among the poor, the undereducated, and the criminal fringe. These social problems are rooted partly in the handling of Israel's mass immigration of Middle Easterners in the early 1950s. Like most traditional Jews in the Diaspora, Middle Easterners had filled middleman positions in the economies of their host societies. Those who moved to Western countries soon filled their old economic roles; they did well. These who moved to Israel, however, encountered European immigrants of their own economic type who had arrived earlier, who were politically well connected, and who—crucially—already filled the few available middleman niches in Israel's small, underdeveloped economy; consequently, many Middle Eastern immigrants of the 1950s fell into social, economic, and cultural crises.

Israel's Middle Easterners are composed of ten major populations (listed here according to size): Morocco, Iraq, Yemen, Iran, Tunisia, Turkey, Libya, Egypt, Georgia, and India. According to 1988 figures, more than 600,000 Israelis originate (directly or through their parents) from North Africa; about 260,000 from Iraq; and 160,000 from Yemen. North Africans, the major groups of Middle Easterners, suffered most from the aforementioned travails of immigration. Since the 1950s, the North Africans have evolved certain ways to contend with their depressed condition, particularly through politics and through religio-cultural creativity. The Moroccans in particular have mobilized politically and captured positions within existing political parties dominated by European Israelis (but only secondarily are they engaging in political mobilization on a separatist base). On the religio-cultural plane, Moroccan Israelis have created new holy places to which mass pilgrimages converge, and they engage in the publication of religio-subethnic writings. In the pilgrimages, there figure motifs that enhance various depressed localities, linking them with general Israeli society; there has been a resurgence of interest in traditional religion and in Moroccan origins.

The other two major Middle Eastern groups have taken different paths in Israel. The Iraqis and Yemenis have kept a much lower profile than the Moroccans, both in politics and in religion. The Iraqis had a background of widespread modern education in Iraq, long before emigration. Consequently, once in Israel, the immigrants were better equipped to cope with the limited economic opportunities. Many moved into the professions. In fact, the Israeli Iraqis have done well socially and economically, in comparison with the Moroccans. The Yemenites, in contrast, were relatively less involved in trade but more in crafts in Yemen. Upon arrival in Israel they did not compete to enter trade niches but adapted themselves to opportunities, becoming skilled workers and craftsmen.

Since the 1970s, people of Middle Eastern background have attained many notable positions in Israel. There has been a state president (Yizhak Navon), two army chiefs-of-staff (David Elazar and Moshe Levy), and several cabinet ministers. Also in academics, there has been a Tel Aviv University president (Moshe Many) and several recipients of the prestigious Israel Prize for arts and science. No Middle Easterner has yet attained the pinnacle positions of prime minister or of minister of defense, although one did fill the crucial position of finance minister (Moshe Nissim). Typically, the single Middle Eastern figure who for several years was considered a serious contender for the position of prime minister is David Levy, whose main base of power is the Moroccan ethnic constituency. Although in the early 1990s the Middle Easterners did not succeed in attaining the ultimate political prizes, two fundamental sociopolitical factors operated in their favor. One was the long, slow resolution of the Palestinian problem (which has provided cheap labor for the Israeli market). The second was the early 1990s mass migration from the former Soviet Union, which has had a similar effect on the economic sector. The result is that Middle Easterners have become positioned well above the lowest rungs of the Israeli socioeconomic order—in contrast to conditions that existed before the 1970s.

See also ASHKENAZIM; DIASPORA; LEVY, DAVID; LIKUD; NAVON, YIZHAK; ZIONISM.

Bibliography

Ben-Rafael, E., and Sharot, S. *Ethnicity, Religion and Class in Israeli Society*. Cambridge, U.K., and New York: Cambridge University Press, 1991.

Deshen, S., and Shokeid, M., eds. *Jews of the Middle East: Anthropological Perspectives on Past and Present*. Jerusalem: Shoken, 1984.

Inbar, M., and Adler, C. *Ethnic Integration in Israel: A Comparative Study of Moroccan Brothers Who Settled in France and Israel*. New Brunswick, NJ: Transaction Books, 1977.

Schmelz, Uziel O.; DellaPergola, S.; and Avner, U. *Ethnic Differences among Israeli Jews*. Jerusalem: Institute of Contemporary Jewry, Hebrew University of Jerusalem, 1991.

Weingrod, Alex. *The Saint of Beersheba*. Albany, NY: State University of New York Press, 1990.

SHLOMO DESHEN

ADRIANOPLE

See EDIRNE

ADVISORY COUNCIL (PALESTINE)

An advisory body in Palestine to the British high commissioner during the British Mandate.

Shortly after taking office as the first British high commissioner of Palestine on 1 July 1920, Sir Herbert Samuel set up a nominated advisory council (AC) pending the establishment of a legislative body. The AC was composed of twenty-one members: the high commissioner, ten British officials, and ten nominated nonofficials, of whom seven were Palestinians (four Muslims and three Christians), and three were Jews. In August 1922 Samuel proposed, as a first step to self-government in Palestine, a constitution that called for the replacement of the AC with a Legislative Council (LC), which would consist of twenty-three members: the high commissioner, ten selected officials, two elected Jews, and ten elected Palestinians.

The Zionist Organization reluctantly accepted the offer, but the Palestinians rejected it and boycotted the elections for the LC in 1923 because acceptance of the LC implied endorsement of the Mandate, whose preamble and articles promoted a Jewish national home in Palestine. Also, the Palestinians, who had been seeking a proportionally representative government, were being offered only 43 percent representation in the proposed LC, even though they were 88 percent of the population. Samuel therefore returned to the 1920 system of an AC, which was to be composed now of twenty-three members, eleven of whom would be officials (including the high commissioner); of the rest, ten would be Palestinians (eight Muslims and two Christians) and two would be Jews.

The Palestinians had not objected to the AC in 1920 because it was considered a temporary measure until a legislative body could be established and because the appointees, who were prominent individuals, did not claim to represent the community. But in May 1923, although they had accepted the government's invitation to join the new council, all but three representatives withdrew when the high commissioner associated it with the LC, which had been repudiated by the Palestinians. Consequently, the high commissioner abandoned the idea of nonofficial participation in the Palestine government, and Palestine was run, from 1923 until the end of the Mandate in 1948, by the high commissioner in consultation with an AC composed only of officials.

See also LEGISLATIVE COUNCIL (PALESTINE); MANDATE SYSTEM; SAMUEL, HERBERT LOUIS.

Bibliography

Caplan, Neil. *Futile Diplomacy: Early Arab-Zionist Negotiation Attempts, 1913–1931*, Vol. 2. London: Frank Cass, 1983.

Government of Palestine. *A Survey of Palestine for the Information of the Anglo-American Committee of Inquiry* (1946), 2 vols. Washington, DC: Institute for Palestine Studies, 1991.

Great Britain and Palestine, 1915–1945. Information Papers 20. London: Royal Institute of International Affairs, 1946.

Lesch, Ann Mosely. *Arab Politics in Palestine, 1917–1939: The Frustrations of a Nationalist Movement*. Ithaca, NY: Cornell University Press, 1979.

Wasserstein, Bernard. *The British in Palestine: The Mandatory Government and the Arab-Jewish Conflict, 1917–1929*. London: Royal Historical Society, 1978.

PHILIP MATTAR

AEGEAN SEA

Arm of the Mediterranean between Greece and Turkey.

The Aegean Sea contains more than three thousand islands and is considered the home of the earliest European civilization (formerly the Mycenean-Minoan, now called the Aegean), from about 3000 to 1100 B.C.E. Crete is the largest island, lying almost equidistant from both Greece and Turkey, at the southern end of the Aegean, with the Ionian Sea to its west. Since the Aegean is the only breach in the mountainous belt to the north of the Mediterranean, it has been extremely important as a trading area and trade route; control of this sea has been the cause of wars since early Near Eastern civilization clashed with early European.

In 1820, all the shores and islands of the Aegean belonged to the Ottoman Empire, but the western shore and practically all the islands have since gradually gone to Greece, a cause of Turkish resentment. Two islands, İmroz (Greek, Im bros) and Bozca (Greek, Tenedos), are still Turkish. Greece claims the Aegean as a territorial sea, which Turkey disputes, in hopes of sharing benthic minerals. Petroleum was discovered on the sea bottom east of Thasos in 1970, which has sharpened the dispute.

Bibliography

Drysdale, Alasdair, and Blake, Gerald H. *The Middle East and North Africa: A Political Geography.* New York: Oxford University Press, 1985.

JOHN R. CLARK

AFAF, AL-

See NEWSPAPERS AND PRINT MEDIA: ARAB COUNTRIES

AFGHANI, JAMAL AL-DIN AL-

[c. 1838–1896]

Influential and charismatic Muslim leader.

One of the most seminal figures of the nineteenth-century Islamic world, Jamal al-Din al-Afghani, although not a major philosophical thinker, spoke and wrote effectively on such subjects as anti-imperialism and the strengthening of the self; these themes were to become increasingly central to the Muslim world. Much of what Afghani and his followers said about his life was myth, and many myths about him persist, even now when a more accurate picture can be drawn.

Ample evidence now indicates that Jamal al-Din was born and raised in northwest Iran (not in Afghanistan, as he usually claimed). It also appears that he got his higher education in the Shi'ite shrine cities of Iraq, where treatises in his possession show that he was attracted to the innovative, philosophical Shaykhi school of Shi'ism. From Iraq he went to India (c. 1857), and it seems likely that in India (and possibly in Bushehr in south Iran, which was under British wartime occupation around the time of his stop there) he developed his lifelong hatred for the British. After travels, apparently to Mecca and the Levant, he went across Iran to Afghanistan, where documents show he claimed to be a Turk from Anatolia. He soon entered into the counsels of the Afghan amir, whom he advised to fight the British, but he lost favor and was expelled when a new pro-British amir assumed power. After a brief stop in India, he went to Istanbul (1869–1871).

In Istanbul, he showed the reformist, self-strengthening part of his persona by entering the Council of Higher Education and signing up to give a public lecture at the new university. This lecture in which Afghani said that philosophy and prophecy were both crafts got him and the university and its director (the real targets of the *ulama*) in trouble. (This view accords with the teachings of the medieval philosophers, who are still taught in Iran today, although they are anathema in western Islam.) Afghani was expelled and went to Cairo, where he had stopped briefly on his way to Istanbul.

In Cairo, Afghani did his most important work (1871–1879), educating and inspiring a group of young thinkers and activists, many of whom (such as Muhammad Abduh, Sa'd Zaghlul, Abdullah Naqim, and Ibrahim al-Laqqani) continued to be important influences in later Egyptian political and intellectual life. The Muslim philosophers constituted the subject of Afghani's teachings; he stressed their belief in natural law, in reason, and in speaking one way to the religious masses and a different way to the intellectual elite. In the late 1870s, when government debt thrust Egypt into an international crisis, Afghani and many of his followers ventured more openly into politics. He encouraged his followers, who included Syrian immigrants as well as

Egyptians, to found newspapers, some of which published his lectures. He also gave talks to, secretly joined, and became the leader of a Masonic lodge, which he used as a political vehicle.

He and his chief disciple Abduh favored the deposition of Khedive Isma'il and the accession of his son Tawfiq, whom he expected to influence. When Tawfiq became khedive (1879), however, the deposition and accession were accomplished by the British and French, to whom Tawfiq was beholden. Tawfiq opposed Afghani's fiery anti-British speeches and activities, and soon had Afghani deported. There is no evidence that the British had a hand in this deportation.

Afghani went back to India, via Iran, and from 1880 to 1882 he chose to stay in the south-central Indian state of Hyderabad, which was ruled by a Muslim prince. During these years, Afghani wrote his most important articles and the short treatise known in English as "Refutation of the Materialists." In 1883, Afghani went to Paris, where Abduh rejoined him. Using funds that probably came from the Briton Wilfrid Blunt and a Tunisian general, they founded the newspaper *al-Urwa al-Wuthqa* (The firmest bond), which was sent free throughout the Muslim world. The paper, which primarily printed theoretical articles and critiques of British policy in Egypt, Sudan, and elsewhere, was one of the chief sources of fame for its two editors.

In Paris, Afghani also wrote a response to an article by Joseph Ernest Renan in which Renan had asserted that religion, and particularly the Semitic Muslim religion, was hostile to science. Afghani's response, frequently misrepresented as a defense of Islam, in fact agreed that all religions were hostile to science; it differed only in saying that Islam was no more hostile to science than Christianity, and that since Islam was several hundred years younger, it might evolve, as had Christianity. Renan then voiced his essential agreement with Afghani, who, he noted, was not a Semite.

After stopping publication of *al-Urwa al-Wuthqa*, probably for financial reasons, Afghani went to London (1885), where he joined Blunt in the latter's schemes to negotiate British withdrawal from Egypt and Sudan. There is no evidence for Afghani's claim that he was at the time an envoy of the Su-

danese Mahdi. Although it was the only occasion when he cooperated with the British (and even then it was with the goal of removing them from Egypt and Sudan), this period and Blunt's books about it accounted for the reputation Afghani acquired in some quarters of being a British agent.

Afghani then accepted an invitation from the anti-British Russian publicist Mikhail Katkov to go to Russia, but on the way he stopped in Tehran for several months. His plotting against the British in Russia came to nothing, but both in Iran and Russia, as usual, he won contacts with men in high places by dint of his personality. When the shah's party came to St. Petersburg on its way west, Afghani was snubbed, but he caught up with them in Europe and believed he had been given a mission in Russia by the prime minister. He returned first to Russia and then to Iran, but the prime minister, Ali-Asghar Amin al-Soltan, refused to see him. Amin al-Soltan planned to expel him, but Afghani avoided banishment by going to a shrine south of Tehran, where he continued to see his followers. A letter attacking concessions to Europeans, including the tobacco concession to the British, was attributed to Afghani, and he was forced to leave Iran for Iraq in midwinter.

From Iraq and then also from Britain, Afghani helped influence the movement against the tobacco concession (1891–1892). An invitation from the Ottoman sultan, Abdülhamit II, brought him to Istanbul, where he soon was forbidden to write or speak publicly. When one of his Iranian followers killed Naser al-Din Shah in 1896, the Iranians tried unsuccessfully to gain Afghani's extradition, but his death from cancer (1897) made the issue moot.

Although Afghani is known mainly as a pan-Islamist, the characterization applies to him only from the year 1883 or so. He was primarily concerned with awakening and strengthening the Muslim world, especially against the encroachment by the British, and for this purpose he sometimes stressed political reform, sometimes local nationalism, and sometimes a pan-Islamic approach. He was a charismatic speaker and teacher, but his writings do not measure up to the standard set by the writings of many of his contemporaries. Despite many facets of his life that underscore his unorthodoxy, he remains for many a model figure of modern Islam. Because he voiced so many of the ideas then in the air among politically minded Muslims, the potency of his influence and especially the myths surrounding him have remained strong.

See also ABDUH, MUHAMMAD; ABDÜLHAMIT II; AMIN AL-SOLTAN, ALI-ASGHAR; ISMAʿIL IBN IBRAHIM; NASER AL-DIN SHAH; URWA AL-WUTHQA, AL-; ZAGHLUL, SAʿD.

Bibliography

Hourani, Albert. *Arabic Thought in the Liberal Age, 1798–1939.* New York and London: Oxford University Press, 1962.

Kedouri, Elie. *Afghani and Abduh: An Essay on Religious Unbelief and Political Activism in Modern Islam.* London and Portland, OR: Frank Cass, 1997.

Tamimi, Azzam S. "The Renaissance of Islam." *Daedalus* 132, no. 3 (Summer 2003):51.

NIKKI KEDDIE

AFGHANISTAN

This entry consists of the following articles:

AFGHANISTAN: OVERVIEW
AFGHANISTAN: ISLAMIC MOVEMENTS IN
AFGHANISTAN: POLITICAL PARTIES IN
AFGHANISTAN: SOVIET INTERVENTION IN
AFGHANISTAN: U.S. INTERVENTION IN

AFGHANISTAN: OVERVIEW

Central Asian country that has been a republic since 1973.

As of July 2003, Afghanistan had an estimated population of 28.7 million, although no census had been conducted in the country since 1979. In addition, between 1.2 and 1.8 million Afghan refugees lived in Iran, 2 million in Pakistan, and 100,000 elsewhere. After the fall of the Taliban government in the wake of the U.S. invasion in late 2001, an Afghan Interim Authority was established to administer the country. This was reconfigured as the Transitional Authority in June 2002, and it is supposed to remain in place until elections for a representative government are held by June 2004.

Afghanistan has been troubled by political conflict since April 1978, when the Afghan Communist Party came to power in a violent coup. The new government was divided into two factions, and their competition for influence and power led to a splintering of the army and a breakdown of internal security in various parts of the country. The situation prompted the Soviet Union to send troops into Afghanistan in late in December 1979, in order to support the more moderate faction of the Afghan Communist Party. The Soviet intervention, in turn, sparked a revolt that was led by religious and tribal leaders opposed to the policies that Kabul was trying to implement. These leaders and their militias became known as Mujahedin, and they engaged in guerrilla warfare against Soviet troops until the latter withdrew from the country in early 1989. Following the Soviet withdrawal, the Mujahedin fought against the communist regime in Kabul until it fell (April 1992), then fought among themselves for control of the capital and government. As the country became engulfed by civil war, a new movement, the Taliban, arose with the aim of restoring order in accordance with its particular interpretation of Islam. Between 1994 and 1996, the Taliban consolidated its control over 85 percent of the country, the area to the northwest of Kabul being the main region it could not subdue.

Geography

Afghanistan is landlocked, comprising some 251,773 square miles (647,500 sq km). It shares borders with Iran, Pakistan, the Xinjiang province of China, and the newly independent successor Central Asian states of Turkmenistan, Uzbekistan, and Tajikistan. Kabul remains Afghanistan's capital and its largest city, with more than 1.5 million, including internal refugees. Cities of 50,000 to 200,000 people include Qandahar, Herat, Mazar-i-Sharif, Jalalabad, and Kunduz.

The Hindu Kush Mountains (rising to 24,000 feet [7,315 m]) stretch diagonally from the northeast, through the center, to the Herat region in the west, dominating the country's topography, ecology, and economy. Deep narrow valleys, many of them impenetrable, cover much of the central, northeastern, eastern, and south-central areas, surrounded by the fertile Turkistan plain and foothills in the north and northwest, the Herat-Farah lowlands, the Sistan basin and Helmand valley in the west, and the deserts of the southwest. Four major river systems drain the Hindu Kush—the Amu Darya (Oxus) drains the northern slopes and marks much of the former Afghan-Soviet border; the Hari Rud drains the northwest; the Helmand-Arghandab, the southwest; and the Kabul, the east. Communications and road systems between these valleys are poor, although a few difficult passes connect them with Central Asia and the subcontinent of India. Temperatures and the amount and form of precipitation are directly dependent on altitude. Summers are very hot and dry, the temperatures reaching 120° F (49° C) in the desert south and southwest. Winters are bitterly cold, the temperatures falling to -15° F (-26° C), with heavy snow cover in the mountains. Precipitation is low, two to six inches (50–150 mm) in the south and southwest, and

twelve to fourteen inches (300–350 mm) in the north.

Economy

Afghanistan has thirty provinces (wilayat), divided into districts (woluswali) and subdistricts (alaqadari). According to government figures, the per-capita income in 1986/87 was US$160. Although rich in natural resources, mineral extractions benefit investors or remain undeveloped. For example, in 1985/86, of the annual production of natural gas (estimated reserves of over 100,000 million cubic meters), 97 percent was exported to the Soviet Union at a rate of 2.6 billion cubic meters a year. Deposits of petroleum, coal, copper, high-grade iron ore, talc,

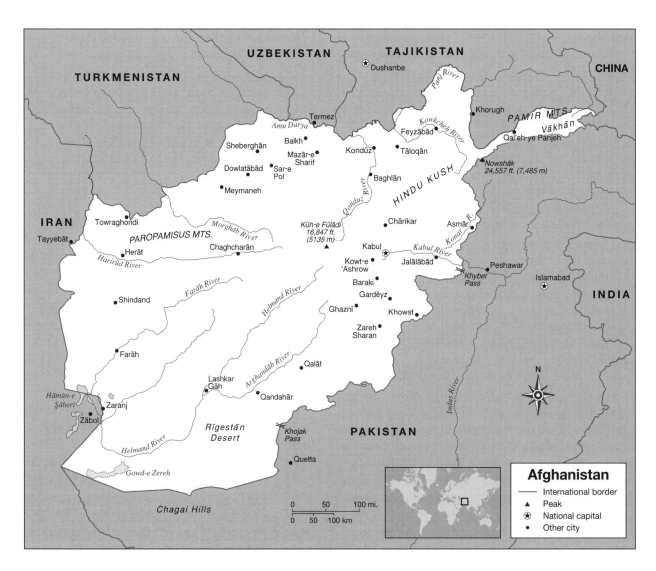

MAP BY XNR PRODUCTIONS, INC. THE GALE GROUP.

barite, sulphur, lead, zinc, salt, lapis lazuli, and other semiprecious and precious gemstones exist; some are extracted.

Before 1978, 85 percent of the population lived in 22,000 villages; they farmed or were Nomads. Their major subsistence crops are wheat, maize, barley, and rice; major cash crops are cotton, sugar beet, oilseeds, fruits, nuts, and vegetables. Sheep (including Karakul/Persian lamb), goats, and cattle are the main sources of milk, meat, wool, hides, and pelts, while camels, horses, and donkeys serve as means of transportation in the difficult terrain. Livestock become the vital buffer during poor harvests. Since 1978, the civil war has seriously damaged more than half the villages and much of the agriculture infrastructure. Reports show that 1987 wheat production was reduced by 50 percent, sheep and goats to 30 percent, and cattle to 52 percent of 1978 levels.

Industries include rugs, carpets, and textiles, chemical fertilizers, sugar, plastics, leather goods, soap, cement, natural gas, oil, coal, and hydroelectric power. Government figures for 1986/87 show industrial production accounted for 23.87 percent of gross domestic product. Exports, primarily to the former Soviet Union and Eastern Europe, India, and Pakistan, included natural gas, cotton, livestock products, rugs, medicinal herbs, fruits, and nuts, with reported earnings in 1988 of US$512 million. Imports of wheat, foods, textiles, vehicles, machinery, and petroleum products, at a cost of US$996 million in 1988, came mostly from the Soviet Union and Japan.

Language and Ethnic Groups

Two major ethnolinguistic communities, Indo-Iranian and Turko-Mongol, live in Afghanistan. The Indo-Iranians include the dominant Pushtu-speaking Pushtun (usually estimated at 45%); the Afghan-Persian or Dari-speaking Tajik (25–30%); and minority Nuristani, Gujar, Baluch, Wakhi, Sheghni, and Zebaki. The Hazara, who have a Mongol appearance, speak Hazaragi, a Persian dialect, and are estimated at 12 to 15 percent of the population. The Turkic speakers include the Uzbeks (about 10%), Turkmen, Kazakh, and Kirghiz. Persian (most widely spoken) and Pushtu are the official government languages. Islam is the religion of more than 99 percent of Afghans—about 80 percent are Hanafi Sunni and about 20 percent Shi'ite (mostly Imami and some Isma'ili). Also present are very small numbers of Hindus, Sikhs, Jews, and Christians.

Education

Primary education, grades one through eight, is compulsory for ages seven to fifteen. Secondary school continues for an additional four years (voluntary). Most schools in rural areas were destroyed during the early years of the civil war. International aid agencies since 2002 have been trying to reestablish schools throughout the country. Some poorly equipped and poorly run schools for Afghan refugee children in host countries also exist. Between 1979 and 2001, the execution, imprisonment, and departure of many teachers badly disrupted institutions of higher education. In 1987, an estimated fifteen thousand Afghans received training and education in the Soviet Union, but the collapse of the Soviet Union in December 1990 led to a sharp decline in the number of Afghan students studying in what became Soviet successor states. In 1988, the Kabul government claimed eight vocational colleges, fifteen technical colleges, and five universities in operation. Losses of previously trained manpower, along with the damage to educational, health-care, and cultural facilities and the lack of training opportunities for the new generation of Afghans during the 1980s and 1990s left a challenging legacy for post-2001 reconstruction efforts.

Government

The Afghan political leaders who met in Bonn, Germany, in December 2001, agreed to the creation of an Afghan Interim Authority to manage the country's day-to-day affairs. A special assembly, the Loya Jirga, subsequently met in Kabul in June 2002, and created a government, the Transitional Authority, headed by a president and a cabinet of ministers. The Transitional Authority organized a Loya Jirga for December 2003, and it was charged with drafting and approving a new constitution.

History

The emergence of Afghanistan in 1747 as a separate political entity is credited to Ahmad Shah Durrani,

Afghan resistance forces set out on a raid against Soviet positions near Herat, Afghanistan, 25 January 1980. © BETTMANN/CORBIS. REPRODUCED BY PERMISSION.

who made the city of Qandahar his capital and created a great empire stretching from Khurasan to Kashmir and Punjab; and from the Oxus River (Amu Darya) to the Indian Ocean. His son Timur Shah (1773–1793) shifted the capital to Kabul and held his patrimony together. By the turn of the nineteenth century, the Durrani empire had declined because of fraternal feuds over royal succession. Between 1800 and 1880, Afghanistan became a battleground during the rivalry between Britain and Russia for control of Central Asia. Afghanistan emerged as a buffer state, with its present boundaries demarcated entirely by Britain and Russia—and with Britain in control of Afghanistan's foreign affairs. The Afghan wars fought against the British by Dost Mohammad Barakzai, his son, and his grandson (1838–1842; 1878–1880) had ended in defeat.

With British military and financial help, a member of the Barakzai Pushtun clan—Amir Abd al-Rahman, the so-called Iron Amir—consolidated direct central government rule by brutally suppressing tribal and rural leaders to lay the foundation of a modern state (1880–1901). His son, Habibollah Khan, who ruled from 1901 to 1919, relaxed some of the harsher measures of the previous rule and in 1903 established the first modern school, Habibia. Later, the first significant newspaper, *Siraj al-Akhbar,* was published in Kabul (1911–1918). When Habibullah was assassinated, his son Amanollah took the title of king (1919–1929) and declared Afghanistan's independence from Britain, which was granted after a brief war in 1919. King Amanullah, impressed by the secular sociopolitical experiments of Mustafa Kemal Atatürk in the new Republic of Turkey, launched a series of secular, liberal constitutional reforms and modernization programs, which led to a rebellion—justified as jihad (religious war) against his rule—forcing his abdication. After nine months of rule by a non-

The Afghan city of Mazar-e Sharif is home to the shrine for Hazrat Ali, cousin and son-in-law of the prophet Mohammad, the fourth caliph of Islam. Most Muslims, however, believe that Ali's tomb is at Najaf in Iraq. The shrine was founded in the twelfth century and rebuilt in 1481, with blue mosaic tiling added in the nineteenth century. © CORBIS. REPRODUCED BY PERMISSION.

Pashtun (Amir Habibullah II), a member of the Musahiban family of the Barakzai clan, Muhammad Nadir (r. 1929–1933), reclaimed the monarchy. Following Nadir's assassination, his son of nineteen, Mohammad Zahir (r. 1933–1973), became king.

From 1933 to 1963, Zahir reigned while two of his uncles and a cousin ruled as prime ministers. Concerned primarily with preserving their family's position, the Musahiban adopted a cautious approach toward modernization, with highly autocratic domestic and xenophobic foreign policies until about 1935. During Sardar (Prince) Muhammad Daud's term as prime minister (1953–1963), with substantial military and economic aid, initially from the Soviet Union and later from the West, a series of five-year modernization plans was begun, focusing on the expansion of educational and communications systems. In 1963, Daud resigned because of disagreements over his hostile policies toward Pakistan and his favoring of greater depen-

dence on the Soviet Union. King Zahir then appointed Dr. Muhammad Yusuf, a commoner, as prime minister.

King Zahir's last decade (1963–1973) was a period of experimentation in democracy that failed—mostly due to his reluctance to sign legislation legalizing political parties and his unwillingness to curb interference in democratic processes by his family and friends. The Afghan Communist Party and Islamist-opposition movements were formed during this period; they agitated against both the government and each other. In July 1973, Daud, the former prime minister (and king's cousin and brother-in-law), overthrew the monarchy in a military coup, with assistance from the pro-Soviet Parcham wing of the Afghan Communist Party; he became the president of the Republic of Afghanistan (1973–1978). Daud returned autocratic rule and persecuted his perceived enemies, especially members of the Islamist movements. He relied heavily

An Afghan woman with her children. © CAROLINE PENN/CORBIS. REPRODUCED BY PERMISSION.

on his old networks and began to distance himself from the pro-Soviet Communists whom he had protected and nurtured. In an environment of growing discontent, in April 1978, a Communist coup ousted and killed Daud.

Nur Muhammad Taraki, the head of the People's Democratic party of Afghanistan (PDPA), was installed as president of the revolutionary council and prime minister (1978/79). He renamed the country the Democratic Republic of Afghanistan (DRA), abolished the constitution, and banned all opposition movements. Less than two months later, the coalition of two rival factions of PDPA—Khalq (People) and Parcham (Banner)—that had joined to gain power began to fall apart. Khalq monopolized all power, offering Parcham leaders ambassadorial posts overseas, and began purging Parcham members from military and civilian posts. Supported by the Soviets, Taraki attempted to create a Marxist state, but by the spring of 1979 resistance to these efforts was widespread. Brutal retaliation by government in rural areas forced the flight of thousands

of refugees to Iran and Pakistan. In September 1979, Hafizullah Amin, then deputy prime minister, minister of foreign affairs, and an advocate of extreme Marxist policies, suspecting a plot against himself, killed President Taraki and assumed his duties. During Christmas 1979, the Soviet army invaded Afghanistan with eighty thousand troops. They killed Amin and installed Babrak Karmal, leader of the Parcham, as the new head of state. Soviet intervention intensified factionalism between the Parcham and Khalq and also led to riots and strikes in the major cities. It turned anti-government resistance into a jihad for the cause of Islam and national liberation.

From 1980 to 1986, Karmal tried but failed to consolidate his power, reduce factional strife, and promote national unity. In 1986, Dr. Najibullah Ahmadzai, the former head of the state security forces (KHAD) and a member of Parcham, assumed power, relieving Karmal of all party and government duties. He adopted a shrewd policy of unilateral cease-fires, offers of negotiation and power sharing with his opponents, and the formation of a coalition government of national unity. He also adopted a new constitution in 1987, allowing the formation of a multiparty political system and a bicameral legislature. He won some support from his internal leftist opponents, but the seven-party alliance of Mojahedin (Islamic Unity of Afghan Mojahedin) remained defiant, calling for unconditional Soviet withdrawal and the abolition of communist rule.

The failure to achieve a Soviet military victory and the ever-increasing outside military and financial support for the Mojahedin (from 1984 to 1988) led to the signing of the Geneva Accords on 14 April 1988, under United Nations auspices. The accords called for the withdrawal of 120,000 Soviet troops, which was completed on 15 February 1989. After Soviet troop withdrawal, the continuing civil war in Afghanistan was overshadowed by events such as the democratization of Eastern Europe (1989) and what became the former Soviet Union (1991). The collapse of the Soviet Union, the end of its military and financial support to Dr. Najibullah's government, and the desertion of his militia forces to the resistance all contributed to Najibullah's ouster from power on 16 April 1992. A coalition of Islamist forces from northern Afghanistan led by Commander Ahmad Shah Mas'ud surrounded Kabul. In Peshawar, a fifty-member Interim Council of the Islamist resistance groups was formed and dispatched to assume power in Kabul. Following two days of factional fighting that resulted in dislodging Golbuddin Hekmatyar's forces from Kabul, Sebghatullah Mujaddedi, the president of the Interim Council—later called Shura-i qiyadi (Leadership Council)—took power on 28 April 1992, as the Head of the Islamic State of Afghanistan for a period of two months. Professor Burhanuddin Rabbani succeeded him as the interim president of the country on 28 June 1992, for four months. During his tenure Rabbani and the Leadership Council were to organize and convene the Loya Jirgah (the Council of Resolution and Settlement or the Grand National Assembly) representing all the peoples of Afghanistan, including those living in exile, to choose the next president for a term of eighteen months. The new president would then oversee the drafting of a new constitution and the first general election.

In opposition to Rabbani's government, Golbuddin Hekmatyar's forces launched a rocket attack

Afghans in the city of Herat dance in celebration after opposition forces captured the city from Taliban forces in November 2001. © AFP/CORBIS. REPRODUCED BY PERMISSION.

in late August 1992 destroying much of Kabul. Other forms of factional fighting along sectarian, ethnic, and regional lines plagued the new Islamist regime, seriously hampering repatriation of the refugees, reconstruction, and the return of law and order in the war-ravaged country. At the end of December 1992, a *shura* (assembly) of some 1,335 members convened and elected the sole candidate, Burhanuddin Rabbani, the interim president for two years. Five of the nine Islamist factions boycotted the assembly, disputing the validity of Rabbani's election. By 1993, all-out civil war had broken out, and much of the countryside was controlled by warlords. It was in this situation that groups of religious scholars and students in the Kandahar area and the nearby Pushtun-populated region of Pakistan began to organize with the aim of providing people with security. The new movement called itself the Taliban; by 1994, the Taliban had captured control of Kandahar and during the next two years extended its control over most of the country, including the capital, Kabul.

See also AMANOLLAH KHAN; AMIN, HAFIZULLAH; AMU DARYA; ATATÜRK, MUSTAFA KEMAL; BARAKZAI DYNASTY; DAUD, MUHAMMAD; DURRANI DYNASTY; HABIBOLLAH KHAN; HEKMATYAR, GOLBUDDIN; HINDU KUSH MOUNTAINS; KABUL; KARMAL, BABRAK; NADIR BARAKZAI, MOHAMMAD;

PARCHAM; RABBANI, BURHANUDDIN; ZAHIR SHAH.

Bibliography

Arnold, Anthony. *Afghanistan's Two-Party Communism: Parcham and Khalq.* Stanford, CA: Hoover Institution Press, 1983.

Bradsher, Henry S. *Afghanistan and the Soviet Union.* Durham, NC: Duke University Press, 1985.

Gregorian, Vartan. *The Emergence of Modern Afghanistan: Politics of Reform and Modernization, 1880–1946.* Stanford, CA: Stanford University Press, 1969.

Rashid, Ahmed. *Taliban: Militant Islam, Oil and Fundamentalism in Central Asia.* New Haven, CT: Yale University Press, 2001.

Roy, Olivier. *Islam and Resistance in Afghanistan,* 2d ed. Cambridge, MA: Cambridge University Press, 1991.

Rubin, Barnett. *The Fragmentation of Afghanistan: State Formation and the Collapse of the International System,* 2d edition. New Haven, CT: Yale University Press, 2002.

Shahrani, M. Nazif, and Canfield, Robert L., eds. *Revolutions & Rebellions in Afghanistan: Anthropological Perspectives.* Berkeley, CA: Institute of International Studies, 1984.

M. NAZIF SHAHRANI
UPDATED BY ERIC HOOGLUND

AFGHANISTAN: ISLAMIC MOVEMENTS IN

Ideologically based, politically motivated, organized Islamic movements.

Islamic movements were formed when Afghanistan established official *madrasas* (Muslim colleges) and the faculty of *shariʿyat* (Islamic law) at Kabul University to train modern Islamic scholars and functionaries during the 1940s and 1950s. The government sent a group of young faculty to al-Azhar in Egypt for graduate training in Islamic studies and law. In the early 1960s they returned home impressed by the Islamist ideals and political goals of Egypt's al-Ikhwan al-Muslimun (Muslim Brotherhood) and its struggles against Egypt's president Gamal Abdel Nasser. This small group of *ustazan* (professors) met clandestinely, translating, disseminating, and discussing the writings of Hasan al-Banna, Sayyid Qutb, Abu al-Aʿla al-Mawdudi, and other Islamist thinkers. The patron and guide of this emergent movement was Ghulam Muham-

mad Niyazi, who later became dean of the faculty of *shariʿyat* in Kabul. Led by Islamic intellectuals and reformist *ulama* (Minhajuddin Gahiz, Mowlana Khalis, Mowlawi Faizani, and others), groups also formed outside the university.

After the adoption of Afghanistan's 1964 liberal constitution and the unsanctioned establishment of the Khalq communist party on 1 January 1965, the pace of political activities quickened. Agitation and demonstrations against the government and violent confrontations among members of the Islamic movements and the communist parties marked the years from 1965 to 1972. The student branch of the Islamic movement Sazman-i Javanani Musalman (Organization of Muslim Youth), nicknamed the *Ikhwan-i-ha* (the Brothers), became increasingly active. In 1972 the "professors" also formally, but secretly, organized themselves as Jamiʿat-e Islami Afghanistan (Islamic Association of Afghanistan). Its fifteen-member executive council (shura-i ali), which was composed of students and faculty, primarily of rural and provincial origins, recognized Niyazi as founder and unofficial leader and appointed Burhanuddin Rabbani "amir" of the movement.

The movement's declared goal was the establishment of a completely Islamic political order that would oppose communism, atheism, corruption,

Gulbuddin Hekmatyer, *mojahedin* leader, and Abdul Gadser, eastern Nangarhar province governor, listen to speeches at a Jalalabad rally. The fatwa, or religious legal opinion, plays a critical role in Islamic movements and is used to take public opinion into political reality. © REUTERS NEWMEDIA INC./CORBIS. REPRODUCED BY PERMISSION.

and all forms of social and economic discrimination, internal oppression, external domination, and exploitation. Its initial strategy was to work methodically and peacefully against the government and the communists. After the overthrow of the monarchy (17 July 1973) Muhammad Daud and Parcham, the pro-Soviet communist party, Niyazi and 180 members of the movement were jailed; they were executed (29 May 1978) soon after the Khalq and Parcham parties overthrew Daud and took power.

Only a few leaders, including Rabbani and Golbuddin Hekmatyar, managed to escape to Pakistan during Daud's regime. In 1975 they failed at a revolt against Daud. Their efforts proved more effective when they organized the *jihad* (religious war) against the Khalq/Parcham communist coalition following the coup. Four of the seven major *mojahedin* parties that participated in the 1979 to 1989 struggle against the Soviets and the subsequent civil war after the Soviet withdrawal were splinter groups from the original Jami'at-e Islami movement. Their objectives are similar, although their strategies and organizational styles differ. Several Afghan Shi'ite Islamic organizations and three traditionalist Islamic groups were also formed after the 1978 communist coup.

The Islamist opposition fought effectively, defeated the communist regime in April 1992, and assumed power to establish the Islamic State of Afghanistan. The Islamists were unable to reconcile their political differences, however, and their factional fighting plagued the new government headed by Rabbani and contributed to its overthrow in 1996 by a very different kind of Islamic movement—the Taliban.

The Islamic Movement of the Taliban was created by Muhammad (Mullah) Omar and other religious teachers and students in response to the political insecurity that spread throughout much of Afghanistan following the establishment of the Rabbani government. Most of the Taliban leaders received part or all of their religious education in the *madrasas* of the conservative Deobandi movement, which is strong in the rural Pushtun areas of Afghanistan and Pakistan. The Deobandi approach to Islam derives from the religious ideas of an eighteenth-century Indian Muslim who was influenced by his contemporary, Muhammad

Afghan schoolgirls clad in burqas walk the streets of Faizabad. The burqa is an Afghan version of *hijab*, a term used by religious Muslims to mean that women ought to cover their hair or entire bodies when in public places where men can gaze at them. © REUTERS NEWMEDIA INC./CORBIS. REPRODUCED BY PERMISSION.

ibn Abdul Wahhab of Arabia. Like the followers of Wahhab in Saudi Arabia (the Muwahhidun), Muslims trained in Deobandi Islam reject liberal interpretation of sacred texts, insisting upon a literal reading. The affinity between the Muwahhidun and Deobandi approaches to Islam predisposed the Taliban to be receptive to Saudis such as Osama bin Ladin, who took up permanent residence in Afghanistan in 1995 or 1996.

The Taliban disliked most *mojahedin* leaders, who were viewed as warlords who violate true Islamic codes of conduct in order to further their personal interests. Thus, in 1994 the Taliban began a campaign to reclaim the country by capturing Kandahar, the country's second-largest city. By summer 1996 most of eastern, southern, and western Afghanistan had fallen under Taliban control. Then Kabul was captured, although the Rabbani government escaped to northern Afghanistan, where it organized resistance. The Taliban set up a government in which Mullah Omar became the "amir of the faithful" assisted by a *shura* (council). In August 1998 Taliban forces captured most of the north, reducing the territory held by the Rabbani government to a small strip of land in the northeast. This situation prevailed for three years until the terrorist attacks of 11 September 2001 in the United States.

Persuaded that bin Ladin's al-Qaʿida network had organized these sensational attacks from his sanctuary in Afghanistan, the United States sent an ultimatum to the Taliban government warning of severe consequences if bin Ladin were not extradited. The Taliban temporized, and was overthrown in the subsequent U.S. air and ground assaults on Afghanistan.

See also AZHAR, AL-; BANNA, HASAN AL-; BIN LADIN, OSAMA; DAUD, MUHAMMAD; HEKMATYAR, GOLBUDDIN; JAMIʿAT-E ISLAMI; JIHAD; MAWDUDI, ABU AL-AʿLA AL-; MUSLIM BROTHERHOOD; OMAR, MUHAMMAD (MULLAH); PARCHAM; QUTB, SAYYID; RABBANI, BURHANUDDIN; *SHARIʿA*; TALIBAN.

Bibliography

Roy, Oliver. *Islam and Resistance in Afghanistan.* Cambridge, U.K.: Cambridge University Press, 1986.

Rubin, Barnett. "Afghanistan Under the Taliban," *Current History* 98, no. 625 (February 1999): 79–91.

Shahrani, M. Nazif. "Introduction: Marxist 'Revolution' and Islamic Resistance in Afghanistan." In *Revolutions and Rebellions in Afghanistan: Anthropological Perspectives,* edited by M. Nazif Shahrani and Robert Canfield. Berkeley: University of California Press, 1984.

M. NAZIF SHAHRANI
UPDATED BY ERIC HOOGLUND

AFGHANISTAN: POLITICAL PARTIES IN

The development of mature political parties in Afghanistan did not occur until the 1960s, and they grew particularly upon the reforms of King Zahir Shah beginning in 1963.

Strong ties to tribal, regional, religious, or ethnic identities, the lack of class awareness, and the very small size of the intelligentsia limited the formation of political parties in Afghanistan. There were political societies as early as 1911, including the Young Afghan Party, which was centered on the personality of Mahmud Tarzi and his weekly journal *Siraj al-Akhbar,* and in 1947 the Awakened Youth (*Wish Zalmayan* in Pakhtun) was formed in Kandahar by members of the Pakhtun upper class.

Political parties arose in earnest during the constitutional reforms under King Zahir Shah (1933–1973) in 1963, especially with the liberalization of the press laws in 1964. By the mid-1970s

three types of political parties had emerged, each representing the sentiments of a relatively small educated class. One type was based on the European socialist-nationalist model and included the Jamʿiat-e Social Demokrat (the Social Democratic Society), usually called *Afghan Millat* (Afghan Nation), led by Ghulam Mohammad Farhad. This strong Pakhtun-oriented party led to several spin-offs, the most important of which was the *Millat* (Nation). The other major party of this type was the *Jamʿiat Demokrate-ye Mottaraqi* (Progressive Democratic Party), founded by the popular prime minister Mohammad Hashim Maiwandwal (1965–1967). It advocated evolutionary socialism and parliamentary democracy. By the 1980s these parties had ceased to play a major role in Afghan politics, even though remnants exist today.

Socialist parties also emerged in the mid-1960s. The most prominent was the People's Democratic Party of Afghanistan (PDPA), founded in 1965 by Babrak Karmal, Hafizullah Amin, and Mohammad Taraki. It was pro-Soviet and had a Marxist-Leninist ideology. In 1967, this party split into two factions, the *Khalq* (People's) faction, led by Taraki and Amin, and the *Parcham* (Banner), led by Karmal. In April 1978, the factions temporarily united and the PDPA led a successful coup. This party ruled Afghanistan until 1992.

Other parties on the left included the *Setem-e Melli* (National Oppression), led by Taher Badakhshi, which was Marxist-Leninist and strongly anti-Pakhtun. *Sholay-e Jawid* (Eternal Flame), another popular Marxist party, was led by Rahim Mahmudi. Both were popular among minorities (non-Pakhtun), especially the Shiʿa and the ethnic groups in northern Afghanistan. The leftist parties dominated campus politics at Kabul University and were influential in the government of Muhammad Daud that took over Afghanistan in 1973.

Islamic parties also appeared in Afghanistan in the late 1960s, partly as a reaction to the increased secularization of Afghan society and the government's growing friendship with the Soviet Union. Islam had played an important role in national politics in earlier periods, often as a means of mobilizing national sentiment against an outside force, usually the British. The Islamic parties were of two types: those of the traditional *ulama,* or religious scholars, and those that were hostile to the *ulama* and advocated a new and more radical Islam. The new and more radical parties sprung up on the campus of Kabul University, where a number of professors had studied at al-Azhar University in Cairo and had established contacts with the Muslim Brotherhood (*al-Ikhwan al-Muslimin*). Those professors brought the Islamic fundamentalist message back to Afghanistan, and in 1970 they established the *Javanan-e Muslimin* (Islamic Youth) movement on campus. That year, Javanan-e Muslimin won the university student elections, ending several years of leftist control of student government. In 1971 the Islamist movement became a party called *Jami'at-e Islami* (Islamic Society) led by Burhanuddin Rabbani and Abdul Rasul Sayyaf.

In 1973 Muhammad Daud Khan took over Afghanistan in a political coup, ending the democratic experiment. He incorporated many of the leftist parties into his government, but the Islamic parties were forced underground or into exile. Rabbani and Sayyaf fled to Peshawar, Pakistan, and began an armed insurrection against the government in Kabul. By 1980 the Islamic movement had split into four factions, including the original *Jami'at-e Islami*; the *Hezb-e Islami* (Islamic Party), led by Golbuddin Hekmatyar; another *Hezb-e Islami*, led by Mohammad Unis Khalis; and *Ittihad-e Islami* (Islamic Union), led by Sayyaf. These political groups were more regional militias than political parties, and each of their leaders had been allied with Jami'at-e Islami at one time.

The traditional clergy also fled to Pakistan in the late 1970s and formed resistance parties to fight against the Marxist government in Kabul and, after 1980, the Soviet Union. These parties included *Harakat-e Inqilab-e Islami* (Islamic Revolutionary Movement), led by Maulawi Mohammad Nabi Mohammadi; *Jebhe-ye Nejat Milli* (National Liberation Front), led by Sufi Pir Sebghatullah Mojaddedi; and *Mahaz-e Islami* (Islamic Front), led by Sufi Pir Sayyid Ahmad Gailani.

The seven Islamic parties formed a loose coalition in Peshawar, Pakistan, during the 1980s to coordinate their war effort and to attempt to form an Afghan government in exile. In February 1989 they formed an Afghan Interim Government (AIG) in Pakistan and elected Mojaddedi president. Very

Royalist Pushtun Hamid Karzai was endorsed as Afghanistan's head of state by the country's Loya Jerga (Grand Assembly) in July 2002. Karzai, a native of Kandahar, previously served as deputy foreign minister in Afghanistan's post-Soviet *mojahedin* government from 1992 to 1994. © AFP/CORBIS. REPRODUCED BY PERMISSION.

soon, however, conflicts arose, and the Hezb-e Islami led by Hekmatyar withdrew from the AIG.

Other religious parties, primarily the Shi'ite parties, were excluded from the AIG. Shi'a make up between 15 and 20 percent of the population of Afghanistan and are mostly Hazara. They have several political parties, most with ties to Iran. The first Shi'ite parties, founded in 1979, were the *Shura-ye Ittifagh-e Islami* (Islamic Council), led by Sayyed Beheshti, and the *Harakat-e Islami* (Islamic Union), led by Shaykh Asaf Mohseni. The *Shura* was formed as a quasi-government of the Hazarajat, and in the early 1980s it operated as such. However, by the mid-1980s the Shi'ite areas of Afghanistan, primarily the

Hazarajat, were taken over by Iranian-based parties, especially the *Nasr* (Victory) and the *Pasdaran* (Revolutionary Guards). These parties, imbued with Islamic fervor resulting from the Iranian revolution, ruthlessly pushed out the more moderate Shi'ite parties. In the late 1980s, these Iranian-based parties united in a political front called the *Wahadat* (Unity), which represents most of the Shi'ite parties and is led by Ustad Karim Khalili.

In 1992, the Islamic political parties returned to Kabul to form a government, but by late 1993, any unity that might have existed among them had disappeared, and there was bitter fighting between rival Islamic parties in Kabul and other major cities for control of Afghanistan. In the chaos a new political force emerged called the *Taliban,* a Persianized Arabic word meaning "religious students." The Taliban movement arose among the Afghan refugee population living in Pakistan in the early 1990s, the Taliban movement also received support from elements within the Pakistan government. The Taliban preached a puritanical form of Islam that combined Wahabi-style Islamic practices with strict tribal customs regarding the proper role of women and public behavior in general. Most of its followers were from southern Pushtun tribes in the Kandahar area. The Taliban seized control of Kandahar in 1994, and although opposed at first by most non-Pushtun groups, they were able to exert their control over most of Afghanistan by 1998. The leader of the Taliban government was Muhammad (Mullah) Omar.

In the aftermath of the terrorist attacks on 11 September 2001 in New York City, the United States began a military campaign to drive the Taliban out of Afghanistan. By December 2001 the Taliban had been forced from power, and on 21 December 2001 a new government, led by Hamid Karzai, took control in Kabul. The government was originally formed as an interim government at a conference in Bonn in November 2001, then was reaffirmed, albeit in a somewhat different form, by a national council, Loya Jerga, held in Kabul in July 2002. This new Afghan government is composed of several political factions, which can be divided into three major groups: the Northern Alliance, the Rome Group, and the Peshawar parties. The Northern Alliance holds the majority of the important cabinet positions in the interim government, except for the presidency. It includes the *Jami'at-i-Islami*, a predominantly ethnic Tajik group officially led by former president Burhanuddin Rabbani; the *Shura-i-Nizar,* composed of Panjshiri Tajiks who were followers of the late Ahmad Shah Mas'ud; *Jambish-i-Melli,* a predominantly ethnic Uzbek militia led by General Rashid Dostum; and *Hezb-i-Wahadat,* a predominantly Hazara militia led by Mohammad Karim Khalili. The Rome Group is composed primarily of followers of the king, who was in exile in Rome. The Peshawar parties consist of those resistance groups that fought against the Soviet occupation in the 1980s out of the Pakistani city of Peshawar.

As many of the older parties that orignallly had been organized essentially as military militias were attempting in early 2003 to reinvent themselves as electoral parties, new parties were emerging to vie for seats in the new parliament. These parties included the National Council of Peace and Democracy of Afghanistan, which was composed of students, university professors, liberal republicans, and nongovernmental agency (NGO) workers; and the *Nizat-i-Milli,* formed by Younus Qanooni, the former interior minister, and Wali Mas'ud, the brother of the assassinated leader Ahmad Shah Mas'ud.

See also AMIN, HAFIZULLAH; AWAKENED YOUTH; GAILANI, AHMAD; HAZARA; HEKMATYAR, GOLBUDDIN; HEZB-E ISLAMI; JAMI'AT-E ISLAMI; KARMAL, BABRAK; KHALIS, MOHAMMAD UNIS; MOHAMMADI, MAULAWI MOHAMMAD NABI; MOJADDEDI, SEBGHATULLAH; PARCHAM; PEOPLE'S DEMOCRATIC PARTY OF AFGHANISTAN; RABBANI, BURHANUDDIN; REVOLUTIONARY GUARDS.

Bibliography

Arnold, Anthony. *Afghanistan's Two-Party Communism: Parcham and Khalq.* Stanford, CA: Hoover Institution Press, 1983.

Ewans, Martin. Afghanistan: A New History. Richmond, U.K.: Curzon, 2001.

Farr, Grant. "The New Middle Class as Refugees and Insurgents." In *Afghan Resistance: The Politics of Survival,* edited by Grant Farr and John Merriam. Boulder, CO: Westview Press, 1987.

Roy, Olivier. *Islam and Resistance in Afghanistan.* New York; Cambridge, U.K.: Cambridge University Press, 1986.

GRANT FARR

AFGHANISTAN: SOVIET INTERVENTION IN

Soviet troops invaded Afghanistan in December 1979 to preserve a shaky Communist government, but after failing to quell guerrilla resistance, they withdrew in February 1989. A cutoff of military and economic aid from the collapsing Soviet Union led to the Afghan government's fall to a resistance coalition in April 1992.

The Union of Soviet Socialist Republics (USSR) secretly encouraged and financed Afghan communists from before the formation of the People's Democratic Party of Afghanistan (PDPA) in 1965 until the party unexpectedly came to power through a military coup d'état on 27 April 1978. There was no evidence that the USSR organized or controlled the coup, but it rushed advisers to Kabul to help consolidate the new regime under the PDPA leader, Nur Muhammad Taraki. When popular opposition to the regime's economic and social changes provoked armed resistance, Moscow supplied weapons and military advisers who took unofficial command of the Afghan armed forces. In mid-1979, the Soviets sought the removal of Taraki's deputy, Hafizullah Amin. They blamed Amin for antagonizing the Afghan people into rebellion.

Soviet President Leonid I. Brezhnev was angered by Amin's overthrow of Taraki on 14 September 1979 and Amin's later order to murder Taraki. Brezhnev and other Soviet officials also feared that Afghanistan's communist regime might be defeated by strengthening Muslim guerrillas, that such a defeat would damage Soviet prestige worldwide, and that the adjacent Muslim areas of the USSR would be destabilized. Brezhnev decided on 12 December 1979 to send the Soviet army into Afghanistan.

The Soviet army seized control of Kabul on 27 December, killing Amin and installing Babrak Karmal as president. Moscow claimed its army had been officially invited into Afghanistan. Through advisers, the USSR ran Karmal's government until Moscow decided he was a failure and replaced him in May 1986 with Mohammed Najibullah.

The Soviet invasion turned what had been a civil war into a defense of nationalism and the Islamic religion against foreign atheists and their Afghan puppets. A Soviet force that reached about 118,000 men fought an estimated 200,000 or more *mojahedin* (Islamic holy warriors). The Soviet army was

The Soviet occupation of Afghanistan became a contest of endurance and—primarily in the case of the Afghans—national pride. The Soviets found themselves outmaneuvered by *mojahedin* fighters, like these in Kunar, who knew the rocky terrain intimately and used this knowledge to their advantage. © AP/WIDE WORLD PHOTOS. REPRODUCED BY PERMISSION.

not trained or equipped for counterinsurgency warfare, and it never mastered the situation. Although it could mount offensives that temporarily seized control of any desired part of the Texas-sized country, it and the weak Afghan army were unable to maintain lasting control of much more than main towns and key communications lines. Soviet military operations drove some 5 million Afghans into refuge in Pakistan and Iran, and another 2 million sought shelter in towns from Soviet devastation of rural areas. Soviet soldiers slaughtered unarmed civilians in retaliation for guerrilla attacks—unproven reports said they used poison gas on unprotected villagers—and they spread millions of land mines that continued to kill and maim long after the war ended.

The *mojahedin,* armed by the United States and its allies, and trained and directed by Pakistan's military intelligence service, ambushed roads and harassed garrisons. Soviet adaptations for more mobile warfare, including sending raiding teams into guerrilla territory to interrupt supply lines, had only limited success. The guerrillas' introduction in September 1986 of U.S.-supplied Stinger antiaircraft missiles curtailed the Soviet advantage of air power to attack guerrillas and move troops over the rugged terrain. The military advantage began shifting to the resistance as the Soviets lost heart. Nonaligned nations voted in the United Nations against the Soviet troop presence in Afghanistan, and Western countries restricted ties with the USSR.

After becoming the Soviet leader in March 1985, Mikhail Gorbachev decided that the economically staggering USSR needed to improve relations with the West to reduce its military spending burden and obtain technical aid. He recognized the Afghanistan war as an obstacle to better Western relations as well as a source of Soviet public malaise. Therefore, Moscow coerced Afghanistan into signing agreements—under UN auspices in Geneva 14 April 1988—that the Soviet army would withdraw from Afghanistan. (Pakistan was also a signatory.) After the withdrawal was completed on 15 February 1989, the USSR said 14,453 of its personnel had been killed in Afghanistan and 11,600 had been rendered invalids. The number of Afghans killed—among the regime, *mojahedin,* and noncombatants—was estimated between 1 and 1.5 million, with tens of thousands of others crippled.

The Soviet Union continued to arm and finance the Najibullah regime after the withdrawal, enabling its survival against disunited *mojahedin* groups. The USSR and the United States had agreed in 1988 to terminate their support of their respective clients in the ongoing civil war on or before 31 December 1991. As it happened, the USSR was formally disbanded a few days before that. Deprived of aid, Najibullah's regime lost support and collapsed. The *mojahedin* who had fought the Soviet Union took control of Kabul on 28 April 1992.

The USSR's bitter Afghanistan experience created an "Afghan syndrome" that Moscow commentators compared with the "Vietnam syndrome" of U.S. wariness about foreign commitments after 1975. As a result, the Soviet Union was unwilling to get involved in the Gulf Crisis in 1991, and later

some Russian soldiers wanted to avoid commitment to regional conflicts in republics of the former USSR.

See also AMIN, HAFIZULLAH; BREZHNEV, LEONID ILYICH; GULF CRISIS (1990–1991); KARMAL, BABRAK; NAJIBULLAH.

HENRY S. BRADSHER
UPDATED BY ROBERT L. CANFIELD

AFGHANISTAN: U.S. INTERVENTION IN

The involvement of the United States in Afghanistan, from the 1950s through the period following the events of 11 September 2001.

The United States was actively involved in Afghanistan during the 1950s through the 1970s. The U.S. presence in Afghanistan ended in 1979 with the assassination of the U.S. ambassador Adolph Dubs in Kabul on 14 February 1979 and with the Soviet invasion the following December. Subsequently, U.S. involvement was indirect, primarily the provision of military aid to the Afghan resistance through the 1980s. After 11 September 2001, U.S. interest in Afghanistan was renewed as it became apparent that al-Qaʿida, the group responsible for the terrorist attack on the United States, was based in Afghanistan and was supported by the Taliban government in Kabul. On 14 September 2001 the U.S. Congress passed a joint resolution authorizing President George W. Bush to engage in a military response to the 11 September attacks. Following unsuccessful political attempts to force the Taliban government to expel Osama bin Ladin and his group, the United States began a bombing campaign on 7 October 2001, directed at Taliban military and political installations. By 13 November 2001 the Taliban government had fallen, and a U.S.–backed Afghan interim government was formed in December at a meeting sponsored by the United Nations in Bonn, Germany.

By early 2002 the United States had moved to restore political, military, and economic ties with Afghanistan. The U.S. Embassy in Kabul reopened on 17 January 2002, and the Afghan Embassy in Washington, D.C., opened that same month. U.S. military forces in Afghanistan grew to more than 8,000 troops as the U.S. military undertook the major task of finding and eliminating remnants of the Taliban and al-Qaʿida. The U.S. military re-built the former Soviet air base at Bagram, north of Kabul, as its headquarters and established smaller military bases in Kandahar, Mazar-e Sharif, and Farah.

U.S. reconstruction efforts in Afghanistan were led by the U.S. Agency for International Develop-ment (USAID), which focused on rebuilding Afghanistan's infrastructure and dealing with im-mediate emergency needs. In addition to providing food and shelter for displaced persons, returning refugees, and widows, the U.S. reconstruction ef-fort aimed to rebuild the Afghan educational sys-tem, restore agricultural productivity, and rebuild the Afghan transportation system, especially the in-terurban highways. The Kabul-Kandahar road, which was originally constructed by Americans dur-ing the 1950s and 1960s, became an important sym-bol of U.S. involvement in the reconstruction of Afghanistan.

On the political side, U.S. involvement in Afghanistan since 11 September 2001 has focused on providing support to the Afghan Transitional Administration, particularly to President Hamid Karzai, and on supporting the process of constitu-tional reform aimed at creating a representative government in a parliamentary system. The United States supported and financed the Emergency Loya Jerga in June of 2002 and exerted pressure on the ex-king, Zahir Shah, to withdraw from active polit-ical leadership. U.S. officials have been placed in the major Afghan ministries to oversee daily oper-ations of the Afghan government.

Despite political, military, and financial sup-port from the United States, a number of problems remain. The Afghan Transitional Administration has been slow to gain credibility in Afghanistan, in part because many Afghans believe this government to have been externally imposed by the Americans without a natural constituency in Afghanistan. Weaknesses of the Afghan government are blamed on the United States; for example, the United States has received criticism over the ethnic composition of the Karzai government, since ethnic Tajiks dom-inate major cabinet positions, alienating the Pushtun tribes. Human rights groups have cited widespread extortion, lawlessness, and kidnapping by Afghan

Afghanistan's Northern Alliance, a multi-ethnic, non-Pushtun opposition group, provided intelligence and military support to the United States during the American invasion of the country in 2001. Prior to the military operation, the Northern Alliance controlled approximately 5 percent of Afghanistan and relied on a core group of fifteen thousand armed fighters. © AFP/CORBIS. REPRODUCED BY PERMISSION.

police and intelligence officials. These groups ac-cuse the United States of supporting some of the worst offenders and for not doing more to stop the abuses. U.S. involvement in Afghanistan is also complicated by Afghanistan's large opium produc-tion. Afghanistan grows more than 70 percent of the world's opium, and the U.S.–backed govern-ment has had little success in stopping its cultiva-tion or halting its illegal smuggling to neighboring countries.

U.S. military efforts in Afghanistan also have faced problems. In attempting to capture or kill al-Qaʿida or Taliban forces, the U.S. military inad-vertently has caused a number of civilian deaths and dropped bombs on the wrong targets, including as a Red Cross warehouse and a United Nations mine-removal office. It is estimated that as many as 20,000 Afghans have died as the direct or indirect results of U.S. bombing, creating animosity toward the U.S. presence. The U.S. military also has been inadvertently involved in regional conflicts between contentious warlords, some of whom have induced the U.S. military to attack rival warlords by claim-ing that they are Taliban members.

After several years, the U.S. military has largely failed to accomplish its major goals: The United States has been unable to pacify or bring security to much of Afghanistan; it has been unable to find bin Ladin or Muhammad (Mullah) Omar, head of the Taliban; it has been unable to eliminate the Taliban, which is regrouping; and it has alienated a growing number of Afghans, who are becoming impatient with the U.S. military presence. U.S. reconstruction efforts also have come under criticism. Despite some progress, poverty remains, many children are still not able to go to school, and women still find their lives constrained and must veil when they are in public.

See also AFGHANISTAN; BIN LADIN, OSAMA; KARZAI, HAMID; PUSHTUN; TAJIKS; TALIBAN.

Bibliography

Human Rights Watch. *World Report 2003: Afghanistan.* New York: Human Rights Watch, 2003.

International Crisis Group. *Disarmament and Reintegration in Afghanistan.* Brussels: International Crisis Group, 2003.

U.S. Agency for International Development. *Afghanistan.* Washington, DC: USAID, 2003.

GRANT FARR

AFGHAN WOMEN'S COUNCIL

Humanitarian women's organization.

The Afghan Women's Council (AWC) is a nonprofit organization that provides humanitarian relief to Afghan women refugees in Pakistan. It was founded in 1986 in Peshawar, Pakistan, by Fatana Gailani, who belongs to a prominent Afghan clerical family. The AWC provides education and medical care for newly arrived Afghan women refugees. It also publishes a monthly journal, *Zan-i-Afghan* (Afghan women), which promotes women's rights, children's rights, and peace-building in Afghanistan. The AWC has received several international awards, including the U.S. Women's Commission for Refugee Women and Children Award in 1992 and the United Nations Association of Spain's Peace Award in 1999.

See also AFGHANISTAN: OVERVIEW; GENDER: GENDER AND POLITICS; REVOLUTIONARY ASSOCIATION OF THE WOMEN OF AFGHANISTAN (RAWA).

Bibliography

Amnesty International. "Voice of Afghan Women." Updated March 2002. Available from <http://web.amnesty.org/web/wire.nsf/March2002/Afghanistan>.

SENZIL NAWID

AFLAQ, MICHEL
[1910–1989]

Syrian Christian pan-Arab nationalist; intellectual, teacher, journalist, and politician; one of the founders of the Ba'th party.

Michel (also Mishayl) Aflaq was born the son of a Greek Orthodox grain merchant in the Maydan quarter of Damascus. During the French mandate over Syria, he began his secondary education in the Greek Orthodox lyceneum in Damascus (1922–1926), but after long-standing disagreements with students and teachers, he transferred in his final year to the Damascus state secondary school (*al-tajhiz*). He studied at the University of Paris (1928–1934), where he took the licentiate in law. After returning to Damascus, he taught history in the state secondary school and in the French lay secondary school. He participated in Arab nationalism in Damascus and Paris, but after returning to Damascus devoted himself to literary activities, writing short stories, a novel, and a play. Social reform was his preoccupation in his earliest political action—articles published in *al-Tali,* a weekly that he and Salah al-Din al-Bitar, a fellow student and friend in Paris, and others published for six months in 1935 to 1936. Aflaq and Bitar were attracted by Marxism and were friendly with communists in Paris and in Syria, but they never joined the party. The French author André Gide (1869–1951) was their greatest influence; the two friends became disillusioned by communist support for the 1936 Franco–Syrian treaty and the denunciation of the communists by intellectuals such as Gide.

With the start of World War II, Aflaq and Bitar organized a group of pan-Arab students, but the group's principal activity before 1943 was the distribution of occasional handbills. These circulars were identified simply as from al-Ihya al-Arabi (the Arab Awakening) or, from the later half of 1941 on, al-Ba'th al-Arabi (the Arab Resurrection), a term that Zaki al-Arsuzi had used to designate a similar group of students formed by him in 1940. Meanwhile, in May 1941, Aflaq and Bitar organized a group to send arms and volunteers to assist Rashid Ali al-Kaylani against the British.

Aflaq's literary activity won him a substantial reputation, and his teaching had a great impact on some students. Aflaq and Bitar were of middle economic status, but their families were considered notable and aristocratic. Nevertheless, with fewer than ten members in 1943, growth was slow and organization weak until two better positioned notables, Jalal al-Sayyid of Dayr al-Zawr and Midhat al-Bitar of Damascus, joined the leadership during 1942 to 1943. Thereafter, the undefined group without a fixed name became in 1943 the movement (haraka), in 1944 the party of the Arab Resurrection (al-Ba'th al-Arabi), with a permanent office, and in 1946 a newspaper. The followers of Arsuzi—now led by Wahib Ghanim—then joined, and a congress of 247 members met in Damascus to adopt a constitution on 4 April 1947.

Aflaq was elected the first amid (dean) and thereafter held, at least nominally, the leading position in the Ba'th party, as well as the editorship of the newspaper. Yet he was soon the focus of unending controversy. The most detailed information is provided by self-interested sources other than Aflaq, but these are consistent with each other and the public actions of the party. Aflaq possessed both ambition and envy. He ran without success for the Syrian parliament in 1943 and 1947. He was minister of education during the Hinnawi period but resigned when he failed to be elected to the constituent assembly; then when al-Sayyid was offered a place in the cabinet, Aflaq and Bitar foreclosed the appointment by demanding two positions. Unlike al-Sayyid, Aflaq had no power base of his own. Consequently, he was neither willing nor able to prevent the appropriation of the party by Akram al-Hawrani (also spelled Hurani, Hourani). Although party rules forbade membership by the military, Aflaq cooperated with Hawrani, whose greatest strength was a following in the officers corps. Despite the opposition of al-Sayyid, the Ba'th and Hawrani's Arab Socialist party cooperated and merged in November 1952 to form the Arab Socialist Ba'th party. Aflaq and Hawrani became political exiles from January to October of 1953, but

in 1954 their party numbered 2,500, in contrast to the 500 of premerger Ba'th in 1952. Hawrani's military friends and his political strength and skill kept the party at the center of power until Syria's union with Egypt in 1958—the formation of the United Arab Republic (UAR). Aflaq and Hawrani had been instrumental in this, but they defected at the end of 1959 and moved to Beirut (Lebanon). The party organization had been amended in 1954 to reflect its pan-Arab character, which was based on its growth outside Syria. Aflaq had been reelected secretary general and a member of the National Command (the executive body composed of representatives from the various regions [countries]), and he had retained these positions even though the party had been dissolved in Syria. As a strong pan-Arab, he broke with Hawrani, who took a Syrianist line, especially after Syria's secession from the UAR in 1961.

Aflaq's position in the party enabled him to take an active part in both Iraqi and Syrian politics after their Ba'thist coups in early 1963, but as the military Ba'thists gained control in Syria, Aflaq's influence waned until finally, following the coup of 23 February 1966, he fled Syria and was expelled from the party. During the rivalry between the Syria Ba'th and the Iraqi Ba'th, which came to power in 1968, the Iraqis continued to recognize Aflaq as secretary general of the party. In Syria, he was sentenced to death in absentia in 1971, and Arsuzi was accorded the honor of being the true founder of the Ba'th. Aflaq moved to Baghdad around 1980 and died there in 1989. At his death the Iraqi Ba'th announced that he had long been a secret convert to Islam.

Aflaq's version of Arabism is idealistic and metaphysical; it presents the ideology that became standard by the 1930s—Islamic modernism is combined with the historical vision of the Arab nation that holds that from the time of the earliest-known Arabs, the ancient Semitic peoples, they have been in perpetual conflict with aggressive neighbors—notably the Aryans—including the Europeans. Periods of Arab power and glory have been followed by corruption and disunion due to foreign influences and abasement by imperialism, from which the nation has recovered by returning to its true culture. The greatest of these awakenings was engendered by the gift of Islam, which, in Aflaq's version, was induced or earned by the prophet Muhammad's acting for the nation. To regain the lost greatness, according to Aflaq, every Arab must act as Muhammad did.

Amidst the chaos in Baghdad that accompanied the fall of the Ba'thist government in Iraq at the hands of invading U.S. troops in the spring of 2003, the tomb and mosque complex built over Aflaq's grave was looted (including by a Western journalist, who openly wrote about his act). The American-selected provisional government of Iraq later reportedly ordered the destruction of the tomb as part of the "de-Ba'thification" program in Iraq. Before this could occur, the tomb complex was found to conceal a secret Ba'th party archive containing over three million documents.

See also ARSUZI, ZAKI AL-; BA'TH, AL-; BITAR, SALAH AL-DIN AL-; HAWRANI, AKRAM AL-; HINNAWI, SAMI AL-.

Bibliography

Aflaq, Michel. *Fi sabil al-ba'th* (In the path of resurrection). Beirut, 1959; 2d edition, 1963.

Aflaq, Michel. *Ma'raka al-masir al-wahid* (The battle of the sole destiny). Beirut, 1958; 2d edition, 1963.

Aflaq, Michel. *Nuqtat al-bidaya: Ahadith ba'd al-khamis min haziran* (The beginning point: Talks after the fifth of June). Beirut, 1971.

Devlin, John F. *The Ba'th Party: A History from Its Origins to 1966.* Stanford, CA: Hoover Institution Press, 1976.

Salem-Babikian, Norma. "A Partial Reconstruction of Michel Aflaq's Thought." *Muslim World* 67 (October 1977): 280–294.

C. ERNEST DAWN

AGADIR CRISIS

Known as the second Moroccan crisis.

The Agadir crisis erupted as the almost inevitable outgrowth on the 1906 Algeciras Conference, which allowed for Spanish and French control over nominally independent Morocco. In 1911, local opposition culminated in revolts against the French. France responded by sending an occupation force to Fez (Morocco) in May 1911, and Germany concluded it

would not permit any revision of the Algeciras Act without some compensation. In July, under the pretext of protecting German citizens, the Germans then ordered the gunboat *Panther* to proceed to Agadir (Morocco) to pressure the French to negotiate. In November, after a brief war scare amid Britain's promises of support for France (Prime Minister Lloyd George's Mansion House speech), a Franco–German accord was signed, granting a French protectorate over Morocco in return for some French sub-Saharan territories to be ceded to Germany. This end to Morocco's nominal independence contributed directly to the outbreak of the 1911 Tripolitanian War and, thus, the Balkan Wars (1912–1913).

See also ALGECIRAS CONFERENCE (1906); BALKAN WARS (1912–1913).

Bibliography

Taylor, A. J. P. *The Struggle for Mastery in Europe, 1848–1918.* Oxford: Clarendon Press, 1954.

JON JUCOVY

AGAL

See CLOTHING

AGAM, YAACOV
[1928–]

Israeli artist and sculptor.

The son of a rabbi, Yaacov Agam was born in Rishon le-Zion and studied at the Bezalel Academy of Arts and Design in Jerusalem, at the Johannes Ittan School in Zurich, and at the Academy of Abstract Art in Paris. Since 1951, he has spent most of his time in Paris, where he became widely recognized for his optic and kinetic art and sculpture. Agam achieves motion in his works by endowing his creations with mobile segments or by giving the impression of movement through the viewer's changing position. His works also include religious objects such as the menorah, mezuzah, or Star of David. President Georges Pompidou of France commissioned him to decorate a room in the Elysée Palace. Agam's works are displayed in many public buildings and areas including the president's house in Jerusalem, the Juilliard School of Music in New

York, the Elysée Palace, and the Defense Quarters in Paris.

ANN KAHN

AGNON, SHMUEL YOSEF
[1888–1970]

Hebrew writer who won the Nobel Prize for literature in 1966.

Born in Buczacz (Buchach), Galicia, Shmuel Yosef Agnon emigrated to Palestine in 1907. In 1913 he went to Germany, where he married Ester Marx and started a family. In 1924 he returned to Palestine and settled in Jerusalem.

Agnon was influenced by a variety of social, cultural, and literary sources. The pious milieu of the small Jewish town where he grew up and the Jewish scholarly traditions in which he was steeped from an early age had a deep and lasting effect on his writing. The development of Hebrew literature at the end of the nineteenth century and the beginning of the twentieth also had a formative influence on him. In 1908, after his arrival in Palestine, Agnon became involved with the literary world of the Zionist pioneers, whose ideals and way of life remained important to him throughout his life. The horrors of World War I, which Agnon witnessed in Germany, were influential for his development as a writer. He saw the world he knew disappear before his eyes.

In his works Agnon examines the psychological and philosophical repercussions of the great historical changes that occurred during his lifetime. In particular, he writes about the demise of traditional Jewish culture in Eastern Europe after World War I and the development of a new Jewish center in Palestine. Although he uses the archaic language and pious style of earlier generations, Agnon gives full expression to the vicissitudes of modern human existence: the disintegration of traditional ways of life, the loss of faith, and the loss of identity.

Agnon published four novels, each of which represents a stage in his literary development. The first, *The Bridal Canopy,* was written in Germany between 1920 and 1921. The novel tells about a pious Jew who travels across Galicia to collect money for his daughter's wedding. The novel evokes a bygone world of faith and superstition through a complex

Israeli author Shmuel Yosef Agnon, born in 1888, began at age 15 to publish his stories and poems in the Hebrew and Yiddish languages. His works relay Hassidic folklore and Jewish traditional life from the eighteenth century to the present. He received the Nobel Prize for literature in 1966. © DAVID RUBINGER/CORBIS. REPRODUCED BY PERMISSION.

blend of nostalgia and irony. The second novel, *A Guest for the Night,* is an account of a writer's visit to his hometown shortly after the end of World War I. The account is an attempt to grapple with the devastating impact the war had on traditional Jewish life in Eastern Europe and with the responsibility of the artist as witness. Written in the 1930s, the novel eerily foreshadows the destruction of European Jewry during the Holocaust. The third novel, published in 1945, is called *Only Yesterday* and takes place in Palestine during the 1920s. It revolves around the unsuccessful attempt of its hero, an idealistic pioneer who came to settle the land, to live up to his ideals. The novel is a harsh account of one of the most important periods in the development of Zionism. The fourth novel, *Shira,* explores the social forces in Palestine during the 1920s and 1940s through the life of a Jerusalem academic who is torn between his petit bourgeois world and his desire to live his life to the fullest.

In addition to his novels, Agnon published many parables, short stories, novellas, and other works in varying genres, including psychological love stories (*The Doctor's Divorce, Fahrenheim*), social satires (*Young and Old*), grotesque tales (*The Frogs, Pisces*), and pious fables about Hassidic sages (*The Story of Rabbi Gadiel the Baby*). Their polished exterior and detached tone hide a deep sense of pathos and pervasive irony. Agnon's frequent use of ancient Jewish sources, and the new ways in which he interprets them, create a tension between style and content that enhances the meaning of both.

Agnon had greatly influenced several generations of Hebrew writers, who found in his works a link between the Jewish world that vanished after the world wars and the existential concerns of their own time. Admired by readers and critics alike, he is one of the most acclaimed Hebrew writers and among the most widely translated. *The Collected Works of S. Y. Agnon,* which includes twenty-four volumes of his fiction, was published in eight volumes between 1953 and 1962. Many of his works have been published posthumously.

Bibliography

Agnon, Shmuel Yosef. *The Collected Works of S. Y. Agnon.* 8 vols. 1953–1962. In Hebrew.

Band, Arnold. *Nostalgia and Nightmare: A Study in the Fiction of S. Y. Agnon.* Berkeley: University of California Press, 1968.

Mintz, Alan, and Hoffman, Anne Golomb, eds. *A Book That Was Lost and Other Stories by S. Y. Agnon.* New York: Schocken, 1995.

Shaked, Gershon. *Hebrew Narrative Fiction, 1880–1980,* vol. 2. Tel Aviv, 1988. In Hebrew.

Shaked, Gershon. *Shmuel Yosef Agnon: A Revolutionary Traditionalist,* translated by Jeffrey M. Green. New York: New York University Press, 1989.

YAROM PELEG

AGOP, GULLU

[1840–1891]

Early Turkish theater director and actor.

Gullu Agop was born in Constantinople as Gulluyan Hagop Vartovyan, to Armenian parents. He began working in theater in 1862 and, in 1867, founded the first Turkish language theater in the Ottoman Empire, called the Ottoman Theater. In 1870, he obtained a government monopoly on Turkish-language theater for fifteen years. He was known for innovation, producing in 1873 the first modern play written originally in Turkish: *Vatan Yahut Silistre* (The motherland silistre [a Bulgarian province and city on the Danube that was part of the Ottoman Empire from 1420 to 1878]) by Namik Kemal.

In 1884, Sultan Abdülhamit II labeled the theater subversive and had it burned down in 1885. Ironically, Agop then spent his last years as state director at the sultan's palace.

See also ABDÜLHAMIT II; NAMIK KEMAL.

Bibliography

Shaw, Stanford, and Shaw, Ezel Kural. *History of the Ottoman Empire and Modern Turkey.* Cambridge, U.K., and New York: Cambridge University Press, 1976–1977.

ELIZABETH THOMPSON

AGRICULTURE

The cultivation and harvesting of food in the Middle East, and how it has responded to the pressures of local and global demand and available environmental resources.

Soil cultivation for the production of crops began in the ancient Near East around 10,000 B.C.E. (the Neolithic Revolution), and agriculture is the base of the past and current civilizations of the region. In 1996, 50 percent of the Middle East's population still lived in rural areas. Through the centuries, various rural cultures have developed, and they have balanced environmental and social factors. For example, they have introduced various collective water-management systems. Nevertheless, in terms of food, the Middle East and North Africa (MENA) has become the least self-sufficient of the world's major populated regions.

Increasing Demand

In 2000, values for the agricultural exports for the entire MENA region were about US$11 billion, whereas the value of agricultural imports totalled

Camels, such as the one shown here turning a water wheel, are used by farmers in the Middle East to perform many types of labor. The camel is uniquely adapted to the dry desert climate, possessing many physical attributes that allow it to withstand the often harsh environment. © OWEN FRANKEN/CORBIS. REPRODUCED BY PERMISSION.

about US$33 billion. Although the differences among Middle Eastern countries are great (for example, Turkey is an occasional exporter of wheat, but Sudan repeatedly experienced famine during the 1980s and early 1990s), some regional generalizations can be made. Rapidly increasing demand for food has outpaced the domestic supply, because of population increase and considerable expansion of per capita incomes during the period of the petroleum boom (roughly 1973–1985). Supply response has been significant, although it has been constrained by nature, history, and public policy, but the agricultural systems of the region have undergone considerable transformation as a result of recent efforts to increase domestic food supplies.

During the period from 1980 to 1990, population in the MENA grew at 3.1 percent each year (only sub-Saharan African populations are growing more swiftly) but then slowed in the period from 1990 to 1999 to 2.2 percent, reaching a population of 301 million in 2001. From 1965 to 1988, per capita income was also growing at about 3 percent each year, but in the decade from 1991 to 2001 economic growth was slower in MENA than in any region except sub-Saharan Africa and the transition economies of Europe and Central Asia. From 2000 to 2001, the growth of output per capita was less than 1 percent.

Middle Easterners spend a substantial fraction of their additional income on food, especially on luxury foods such as meat and fresh produce. Accordingly, the demand for all food rose at about 4 to 5 percent each year, and the demand for meat, milk, vegetables, and fruits rose at roughly 6 percent each year in the same period.

Few of the world's agricultural sectors could have met this increased demand from domestic supply alone. The countries of the MENA could not, and they became increasingly dependent on food imports. Most countries in the region now import at least 290 pounds (130 kg) of grain per person per year, and many import far more. In 2001, Libya imported 885 pounds (402 kg), Jordan imported 764 pounds (347 kg), and the United Arab Emirates imported 1,852 pounds (841 kg). These are similar to the amounts needed by the nonagricultural city-state of Singapore. Over the decades, this increasing food dependency has led many national planners in the region to try to accelerate agricultural growth, but they have had to deal with significant natural and social issues.

Water

The scarcity of fresh water is the main natural obstacle to greater food production in the region. With only 1.847 cubic yards (1,413 cubic meters) of fresh water available per capita in 2000, the MENA ranks well below the average of other regions. Drought, a recurrent phenomenon in the region, seriously affects agricultural production. Many of the desert areas receive less than 20 inches (50 cm) of rain per year, making non-irrigated agriculture extremely risky or impossible. Seasonal rainfall patterns are highly variable; only the shores of the Caspian and Black seas receive rainfall year round. Elsewhere, precipitation follows one of two seasonal patterns: (1) a winter maximum along the Mediterranean shore, in the Fertile Crescent, and in central and southern Iran, or (2) a summer monsoonal maximum in Southern Arabia and Sudan. Precipitation within these areas often varies considerably, and rain may fall at the wrong time during the planting cycle.

From the early 1960s, the total irrigated land area increased from about 30 million acres (12 million ha), some 15 percent of arable land, to about 42 million acres (17 million ha), or about 17 percent of arable land, in 1985. Irrigation resources are unequally distributed across countries. Roughly 34 percent of all irrigated land in the region is in Iran. In descending order, the four countries with the largest amount of irrigated land are Iran, Egypt, Turkey, and Iraq. Likewise, irrigated land as a percentage of arable land varies widely by country. At one extreme, virtually all (97%) of Egypt's farmland is irrigated, as is 65 percent of Israel's. By contrast, only 8 percent of Turkey's and 7 percent of Mo-

rocco's arable land is irrigated. Iran and Iraq irrigate roughly 33 to 40 percent of their arable land. Since irrigated land produces much more per acre than nonirrigated land, and produces crops of higher value, such as fruits and vegetables (as opposed to grains), these numbers understate the economic contribution of irrigated farming in the Middle East. In the MENA, the proportion of irrigated land has increased from 25.8 percent of cropland in 1979 through 1981 to 35.5 percent in 1995 through 1997.

However, the development of irrigation has too often neglected long-term environmental issues, thereby jeopardizing the sustainability of the short-term gains from expanding irrigation. Two problems dominate: the neglect of drainage and the overexploitation of groundwater. Irrigation without drainage raises soil salinity, which reduces crop yields. Because irrigation raises output immediately, while neglect of drainage reduces it only after ten to twenty years, governments short of cash have often sacrificed the future by underinvesting in drainage. This problem has plagued most irrigation systems in the region as well as throughout the world. Overexploitation of groundwater is another example of heavily discounting the future. In many cases (Sahara, the Arabian Peninsula), this is fossil water, which is not renewable. In time, these ancient stores of water (similar to underground pools of petroleum) will be depleted and the farms and such ecosystems as oases that depend on such water will have to be abandoned.

It is often argued that since water is free to farmers they have no incentive to economize it. In fact, it is the giant irrigation projects, more than the farmers, that have overused this scarce resource. Two types of solutions were applied to this water problem: large-scale and small-scale infrastructure. Both are technical solutions and underestimate the social dimension of the problem. The large-scale solution is exemplified by such state projects as the Aswan High Dam (Egypt) and the Great Man-Made River (Libya). Drip irrigation is typical of the small-scale solution. Pioneered in Israel, it delivers precisely calibrated amounts of water to individual fruit trees or vegetables but costs at least three times as much to install as conventional flow irrigation. Drip techniques also require literature and trained technical personnel to operate them effectively. In addi-

Rice, one of Iran's most frequently consumed foods, is planted in the spring and harvested in September and October. Thanks to heavy annual rainfall, the Mazandaran and Gilan provinces alone produce 80 to 85 percent of the country's rice crop. © AP/WIDE WORLD PHOTOS. REPRODUCED BY PERMISSION.

tion, water conservation imperatives have an impact on the choice of crops, and may reduce the allocation of land to water-intensive crops such as alfalfa, rice, sugarcane, and cotton.

The region's rain-fed farming systems generally employ Mediterranean dry-farming techniques, in which winter wheat or barley alternates with fallow and the grazing of sheep, goats, cattle, or camels. Also found in the region are systems that employ the dry-farming techniques of Sudan. The Sudanese-type systems run up against the problems of desertification and the relationship between semi-migratory cattle herders and sedentary farmers.

Cereal grains are the dominant crop in the Middle East, occupying more than 40 percent of the arable land. Wheat (indigenous to the northern Fertile Crescent) is planted on about 25 percent of the farmed area in any year and constitutes more than 50 percent of all regional cereal production. It stabilized at 55 percent in the period between 1961

and 2001 in Middle East but grew from 55 percent to 73 percent during the same period in North Africa. Barley, which is also indigenous, is especially well suited to drier areas and is a distant second. About one-third of all the land planted in wheat in less developed countries is found in the Middle East. Because of natural and social constraints, grain production has grown less rapidly than population in the region. Increasingly, greater output of grains and all other foodstuffs will require a shift from bringing additional land into cultivation to raising the output per unit of land. The only country with significant unexploited or underexploited areas of land is Sudan. Such intensive agricultural growth, however, is constrained not merely by water resources but by social conditions and economic policies.

Land Ownership

The principal social constraints to agricultural development have been unequal access to land and other problems concerning property rights; unfavorable terms of trade facing farmers (local but also international trade with Western countries); low levels of investment; and technical difficulties, such as those involved with irrigation.

Despite considerable differences between countries and regions, certain generalizations on land tenure may be made. Prior to land reform, land tenure was generally bimodal, with a small number of farmers owning large areas of land and a large number of others holding small parcels or working on the large ones as sharecroppers. In addition, states were and are active in shaping land-tenure patterns. Land reform has reduced but not eliminated unequal distributions of land. Governments have usually intervened in land-tenure patterns largely for political reasons, specifically to ruin their enemies. However, states often have had development strategies or programs that involved transferring resources from agriculture to industry and urban areas. Thus, states have tried to monopolize the distribution of farm inputs (fertilizer, equipment, and other resources necessary for agricultural production) and farm outputs (the actual agricultural products). Under injunctions from international organizations (the World Bank, the International Monetary Fund), states throughout the region have retreated from land reform as part of a general regional economic trend giving an expanded scope to the private sector.

Governments often created state marketing monopolies as part of land reform programs, eventually allowing them to tax farmers by reducing the price of agricultural products below world market levels and raising the cost of inputs above world market levels. Such price policies, combined with macroeconomic and trade policies that distorted foreign exchange rates, weakened the incentives for farmers to produce the taxed crops. Not all crops were taxed, but grains and major export goods (e.g., cotton) usually were. These unfavorable pricing policies help explain the sluggish growth of grain output until the early 1980s. After that, governments increasingly recognized the need to offer farmers adequate incentives if the goal of food security was to be met. Taxes on farming have been reduced in many countries, and price policies have been improved. Less success has been achieved in improving life for small farmers (current policies

bankrupt the family economy) and in improving macroeconomic policies that affect agriculture, such as inflation control and exchange-rate management.

Increased output per land unit is usually associated with greater use of higher yielding crop varieties (HYVs), which have been bred to be more responsive to fertilizer. The adoption rate for HYV wheat has been constrained by both limited water supplies and pricing policies. Only about 30 percent of Middle Eastern wheat fields are planted with HYVs, compared with nearly 80 percent in Latin America and Asia. By contrast, farm mechanization, especially tractor use, has spread rapidly, especially for such power-intensive tasks as land preparation. From 1979 through 1981, there were twelve tractors per thousand agricultural workers in the region, and from 1995 through 1997, 25 per thousand, which is higher than the world average. In 1960, there were some 2,470 acres (1,000 ha) for every tractor in Iran, but only some 247 acres (100 ha) per tractor in 1985. The use of harvesting machinery, such as combines, has spread more slowly than the use of tractors. The pattern of mechanization indicates that machines were substituted for animal labor as opposed to being substituted for human labor; animals had become far more valuable as producers of meat and milk than as work animals, and governments in the region often subsidized fuel.

However, mechanized techniques are also important as a way to economize on human labor, since recent emigration from the countryside has negatively affected the agricultural sector in many MENA countries. Everywhere, the proportion of agricultural laborers has declined. From 1960 to 1985, the number of farm workers fell in Algeria, Jordan, and Syria, though it remained roughly stable in Egypt, Iraq, Tunisia, and Turkey. Labor migration, both from rural areas to cities and from non-oil to oil-exporting countries within the region, accounts for most of the decline in rural population figures. Education in the countryside has raised skill levels and expectations, leading many young people to abandon farming. Only if the educated youth are given the technology and incentives to succeed in agriculture will the MENA be able to mitigate water scarcity and even partially meet the growing demand for food.

See also FOOD; WATER.

Bibliography

Bessaoud, O.; Bourbouze, A.; Campagne, P.; et al. *Problems of Rural Development in Dry Land Areas in the MENA Region (Middle East and North Africa).* Montpellier, VT: Mediterranean Agronomic Institute of Montpellier, 2000.

Craig, G. M. *The Agriculture of Egypt.* New York: Oxford University Press, Centre for Agricultural Strategy series, vol. 3, 1993.

Food and Agriculture Organization of the United Nations. *The State of Food and Agriculture 2002.* Rome: FAO, 2002.

Tuijl, Willem van. *Improving Water Use in Agriculture, Experiences in the Middle East and North Africa.* World Bank Technical Paper no. 201. Washington, DC: World Bank, 1993.

World Bank. *Reaching the Rural Poor, A Rural Development Strategy for the Middle East and North Africa Region.* World Bank Departmental Working Paper. Washington, DC: World Bank Publications & Research, 2002.

World Bank. *2003 World Development Indicators Database.* Washington, DC: World Bank, 2003.

World Bank. *The World Bank Annual Report 2003, volume 1, Year in Review.* Washington, DC: World Bank, 2003.

World Bank. *World Development Report 2003, Sustainable Development in a Dynamic World, Transforming Institutions, Growth, and Quality of Life.* Oxford: Oxford University Press, 2003.

ALAN R. RICHARDS
UPDATED BY VINCENT BATTESTI

AGUDAT ISRAEL

Organization of Orthodox Jewry; political party of Orthodox Jews in Israel.

The organization was founded in Katowice (Upper Silesia, now in the southwestern part of Poland), in 1912, as a worldwide movement of Orthodox Jews. It established the Council of Torah Sages as its religious authority on all political matters. Opposed to secular Zionism and the World Zionist Organization (the settlement of Jews in Palestine; a return to Palestine), it consisted of three major groups: German Orthodox followers of Rabbi Samson Raphael Hirsch; the Lithuanian yeshiva (religious school) community; and Polish Hasidic rabbis and their followers—especially the Gur Hasidic group.

The major objective was to provide a range of religion-based communal services to strengthen the Orthodox community.

In Palestine, Agudat Israel was established to be independent of the organized Jewish community (the Yishuv). Despite its ideological opposition to secular Zionism, in 1933 it entered into an agreement with the Jewish Agency there (which represented the Yishuv to the British mandate authority), according to which Agudat Israel would receive 6.5 percent of the immigration permits. In 1947, just before Israel's independence, it entered into an even more comprehensive agreement, which has come to be known as the status quo letter. This purported to guarantee basic religious interests in Israel and served to legitimize Agudat Israel's joining the government-in-formation and the initial 1949–1951 government coalition. At this point, it bolted—opposing the government's decision to draft women into the military. In 1977, Agudat Israel supported the Likud-led coalition; it joined Israel's national unity government in 1984 and has since remained part of the government, although it has refused a ministry.

Agudat Israel experienced a number of internal rifts that came to a head in the 1980s and have resulted in the emergence of a group of ultra-Orthodox, or *haredi*, parties. In 1983, due to long-simmering anger over the absence of Sephardic leadership in the party, the Jerusalem *sephardi* members of Agudat Israel broke away and established the Sephardi Torah Guardians party, SHAS; it was so successful in the municipal elections in Jerusalem during October 1983 that it ran a national slate of candidates in 1984 and became an impressive force. At the same time, an old conflict between the Hasidic and Lithuanian-type yeshiva elements within Agudat Israel—represented by the Hasidic rabbis of Gur and Vizhnitz, on one side, and the head of the Ponevez yeshiva in B'nei Brak, Rabbi Eliezer Shach, on the other—reached new heights and culminated in the formation of Shach's Degel HaTorah (Torah Flag) party for the 1988 national elections.

Agudat Israel, like the other *haredi* parties, is generally moderate on foreign-policy issues, including the administered territories; but it is concerned with all matters of domestic policy, those it perceives as affecting religion, in general, and especially its own educational institutions.

See also ISRAEL, POLITICAL PARTIES IN.

Bibliography

Don-Yehiya, Eliezer. "Origin and Development of the Aguda and Mafdal Parties." *Jerusalem Quarterly* 20 (1981): 49–64.

Friedman, Menachem. *Dat ve-hevrah. Religion and Society: Non-Zionist Orthodoxy in Eretz Israel, 1918–1936.* Jerusalem, 1977.

Fund, Yosef. "Agudat Israel Confronting Zionism and the State of Israel—Theology and Policy." Ph.D. diss., Bar-Ilan University, 1989 (Hebrew with English summary).

Greilsammer, Ilan. "The Religious Parties." In *Israel's Odd Couple: The 1984 Knesset Elections and the National Unity Government,* edited by Daniel J. Elazar and Shmuel Sandler. Detroit, MI: Wayne State University Press, 1990.

CHAIM I. WAXMAN

AHAD HA-AM
[1856–1927]

Early Zionist author; pen name of Asher Ginzberg.

Born in Skvire in the Ukraine, Ahad Ha-Am (in Hebrew, One of the People) was moved to a rural estate in 1868, rented by his wealthy father, a follower of the mystical Hasidic movement. There he was educated in Jewish topics by private tutors, while teaching himself Russian, German, French, and English. Ginzberg broke with traditional Judaism and, in 1886, settled in Odessa, a center of progressive Jewish life. There he quickly rose to prominence in the emerging Zionist movement, then spearheaded by the Odessa-based Hovevei Zion. He worked as an editor of several periodicals and founded *Ha-Shiloah,* a pioneering Hebrew-language journal. In 1908, he moved to London, where became a close adviser to Chaim Weizmann during the negotiations leading to the Balfour Declaration of 1917. Ginzberg settled in Palestine in 1922; he died there at the age of seventy.

For several decades after 1889, when he first published his major article "Lo zeh ha-derekh" (This is not the way), Ahad Ha-Am became prominent in Hebrew letters. His ironic spare prose set new standards for the Hebrew essay. His stand on Jewish nationalism was based on two interlinked themes—the perils of Jewish assimilation and the role of Palestine as a spiritual center. He saw not mounting antisemitism but the threat of assimilation as the spur for Zionism. He saw the return of Jews to their homeland accompanied by a return to their original language and by a rebirth of political institutions—which had been supplanted by adherence to theology and ritual after the Roman conquest of Palestine in the first century C.E. In his view, before the Haskalah (enlightenment) movement of the late eighteenth century, Jewry had been sustained by commitment to community, to collective life—but modernism and citizenship or the prospect of citizenship in European states was isolating Jews from their natural community and from each other. He championed the Russian-based Hovevei Zion (Hibbat Zion) movement as the natural heir to the Jewish people's legacy of exile and the focal point of Jewish identity in a world where both the refusal to assimilate outside influences and an unchecked eagerness to do so could result in the disappearance of Jewry. Herzlian Zionism, which came to dominate Jewish nationalist circles following the First Zionist Congress in 1897, was, he contended, shortsighted in its stress on diplomacy and politics—and its indifference to the colonizing efforts of the Hovevei Zion.

As an alternative both to philanthropic and to diplomatic Zionism, Ahad Ha-Am promoted his concept of "spiritual center"—since, in the past, Jewry had owed its collective existence to an ability to concentrate its spiritual resources on the rebuilding of its future. Martin Buber, Mordecai Kaplan, Judah Magnes, and Zionist socialists read his work and respected his views, in part, while at the same time others criticized his politics as elitist, apolitical, and impractical.

He was the first Zionist to see the darker side to the Arab-Jewish relationship in Palestine, insisting that there were threats to the Jewish national enterprise. As early as 1891, in his essay "Emet me-eretz yisrael" (The truth from the land of Israel), he argued that the brutal recent treatment of Arabs by some Jews was a tragic reaction to a history of Jewish subjugation in the Diaspora. The weight he gave to the issue of Arab retaliation to Jewish settlement activity placed it, however tenuously, on the Zion-

Bibliography

Hertzberg, Arthur. *The Zionist Idea: A Historical Analysis and Reader.* Garden City, NY: Doubleday, 1959.

Luz, Ehud. *Parallels Meet: Religion and Nationalism in the Early Zionist Movement (1882–1904).* Philadelphia: Jewish Publication Society, 1988.

Simon, Leon. *Ahad Ha-am, Asher Ginzberg: A Biography.* Philadelphia: Jewish Publication Society, 1960.

Zipperstein, Steven J. *Elusive Prophet: Ahad Ha'am and the Origins of Zionism.* Berkeley: University of California Press, 1993.

STEVEN ZIPPERSTEIN

AHALI GROUP

Political group in Iraq, 1930–1958.

At the Ahali group's forefront in early 1930 were several young intellectuals imbued with liberal ideals and a strong desire to reform the economic, political, and social conditions of Iraq. Four of them stand out: Husayn Jamil, Abd al-Qadir Isma'il, Muhammad Hadid, and Fatah Ibrahim. The first two were Sunni Muslims from Baghdad who were classmates in high school and briefly at Baghdad Law College. Both were active in the opposition politics of the 1920s and were suspended from school. Muhammad Hadid was a Sunni Muslim who belonged to a wealthy conservative family from Mosul. He studied at the American University of Beirut and did a year of graduate work at Columbia University. Both Hadid and Ibrahim were influenced by liberal and socialist thought while studying abroad.

These four young men and other individuals decided to publish a newspaper to express their ideas and philosophy. They chose the name *Ahali* to stress their ties and unity with the people—this name has since been applied to the whole group. The first issue of the newspaper, dated 2 January 1932, appeared under the slogan "People's Benefit Is Above All Benefits." *Al-Ahali* quickly gained popularity and became the most influential paper in Baghdad. It served as a mouthpiece for the most constructive, the most modern, and the most progressive minds in Iraq. *Al-Ahali* was distinguished for its coverage and analysis of the social and economic conditions of the country and for its sharp attack on government policies. Consequently, it had difficulties with

Russian-born author Ahad Ha-Am was born Asher Ginzberg. He specialized in Talmudic and Hassidic literature, and he was a proponent of political Zionism and proposed a Jewish center of learning to strengthen cultural and national solidarity among the Diaspora Jewry. His pseudonym Ahad Ha-Am means "one of the people." © LIBRARY OF CONGRESS. REPRODUCED BY PERMISSION.

ist agenda. In the last years of his life he argued that Palestine would face its greatest test in how it treated the "strangers" in its midst.

Ahad Ha-Am's reputation declined after the establishment of the state of Israel in 1948. His caution appeared misguided, his pessimism idiosyncratic rather than prescient. After the election of Menachem Begin in 1977, however, he was put to use by some intellectuals on Israel's liberal-left who were frustrated by the ability of the right-wing Revisionist Zionists to win not only control of the government but to usurp classical Jewish nationalism as well.

See also BALFOUR DECLARATION (1917); BEGIN, MENACHEM; BUBER, MARTIN; HASKALAH; HIBBAT ZION; MAGNES, JUDAH; WEIZMANN, CHAIM.

government officials and publication was repeatedly suspended.

Initially, the members of the Ahali Group were united by their anti-British sentiment, their critical stand against the government, and their desire for reform. They advocated ideas of the French Revolution and called for a strengthening of the parliamentary system. In 1933, Kamil Chadirchi, a young liberal lawyer from an aristocratic family in Baghdad, joined the group. Chadirchi was a member of the opposition group who in the 1920s became disenchanted with the Ikha al-Watani Party headed by Yasin al-Hashimi. In 1934, the Ahali Group adopted a more socialist agenda. They called their new emphasis "Sha 'biyya" (populism) to avoid the misunderstanding surrounding the word *Ishti-rakiyya* (socialism). *Sha 'biyya,* a doctrine that seeks welfare for all people regardless of gender, class, race, or religion, stresses the importance of human rights, equal opportunity, and freedom from tyranny. It emphasizes the state as provider of health care and education for its people, and recognizes the importance of religion, family, and the parliamentary system.

In 1933 the Ahali Group established the Baghdad Club and the Campaign Against Illiteracy Association. Both organizations had cultural objectives but were designed to broaden popular support for the Ahali Group. In 1934, under the leadership of Chadirchi, the group was able to influence and recruit Ja'far Abu al-Timman to head the Campaign Against Illiteracy Association and later to join the Ahali Group. Al-Timman was formerly the leader of the national al-Watani Party. He was a well-respected national figure in Iraq and a believer in democratic institutions. His accession to Ahali enhanced the status of the group. Moreover, Chadirchi was able to recruit Hikmat Sulayman, a former member of the Ikha Party who left because of disagreements with its leader.

In 1935 the Ikha came to power and inspired the Ahali Group to work more actively toward achieving power. At this juncture it was decided to de-emphasize the Sha'biyya ideas and adopt a broader program of liberal reform to gain wider support. Through Sulayman's influence the Ahali Group recruited a few army officers; chief among

them was General Bakr Sidqi. Sulayman persuaded Sidqi to conduct a coup against the Ikha government. On 29 October 1936 the coup was successfully executed, the first in the modern history of Iraq and in the Arab world. The Ahali Group was a reluctant participant. Abu al-Timman, Chadirchi, and Hadid opposed the idea, fearing it could lead to tyranny and military dictatorship. However, Sulayman's opinion prevailed. Ahali received the lion's share of cabinet positions in the new government and organized the Popular Reform Society to propagate the group's reform ideals. The group, however, soon discovered that the real power was in the hands of Sidqi and Sulayman. Even though Sulayman was a member of Ahali, he abandoned its ideas in favor of "politics as usual." Unable to push for reform, the Ahali ministers resigned from the government on 19 June 1937. The Popular Reform Society and al-Ahali ceased to exist. The members of the group were scattered, exiled, or imprisoned.

In the 1940s and 1950s, Ahali's members and supporters continued to play an active role in Iraq's national politics. In 1946 three influential members of the group—Chadirchi, Hadid, Jamil—formed the National Democratic Party, which advocated democracy and moderate socialism. It functioned both openly and secretly, taking an active part in opposition politics of the 1940s and 1950s. It participated in the uprisings against the government in 1948, 1952, and 1956, and supported the revolution of 1958. The party eventually split into two factions because of internal disagreement over the regime of Abd al-Karim Qasim. In the 1960s and 1970s, Ahali's influence faded as other ideologies and groups, such as the Ba'th party, replaced it in the political spot-light.

See also ABU AL-TIMMAN, JA'FAR; BA'TH, AL-; HASHIMI, YASIN AL-; IKHA AL-WATANI PARTY; NATIONAL DEMOCRATIC PARTY (IRAQ); SIDQI, BAKR.

Bibliography

Batatu, Hanna. The Old Social Classes and Revolutionary Movements of Iraq. Princeton, NJ: Princeton University Press, 1982.

Khadduri, Majid. *Independent Iraq, 1932–1958: A Study in Iraqi Politics.* London and New York: Oxford University Press, 1960.

Khadduri, Majid. *Republican Iraq: A Study in Iraqi Politics Since the Revolution of 1958.* London and New York: Oxford University Press, 1969.

AYAD AL-QAZZAZ
UPDATED BY MICHAEL R. FISCHBACH

AHARDANE, MAJOUB
[1921–]

Moroccan political leader.

Born into a Middle Atlas Berber family, Majoub Ahardane served in the French army during World War II and then supported Moroccan nationalism. After independence in 1956, he led the effort to form the primarily Berber-based Popular Movement (Mouvement Populaire; MP) in 1957, which was recognized in 1959. As secretary-general of the MP (1962–1986), Ahardane remained closely tied to the throne, serving King Hassan II as minister of defense twice (1961–1964 and 1966–1967) and in other cabinet posts during the 1970s and 1980s. In 1991, after being ousted from the MP, he founded the Mouvement National Populaire, serving as its secretary general since that year.

See also BERBER; MOUVEMENT POPULAIRE (MP).

Bibliography

Waterbury, John. *The Commander of the Faithful: The Moroccan Political Elite—A Study in Segmented Politics.* New York: Columbia University Press; London: Weidenfeld & Nicolson, 1970.

MATTHEW S. GORDON
UPDATED BY ANA TORRES-GARCIA

AHD, AL-

A secret Arab nationalist society composed of Iraqi and Syrian officers in the Ottoman army in 1913.

Al-Ahd (literally, The Covenant) was headed by Aziz Ali al-Masri, an Egyptian officer. There is very little information on the society and how it was formed; it is significant, however, that it was formed after the Ottoman Empire lost Tripolitania to Italy (1911–1912) and was defeated in the first Balkan Wars (1912–1913). Apparently, member Arab officers were fearful that the Arab Ottoman Asiatic provinces were about to face a destiny similar to that of Tripolitania or the Balkans. The Arab officers may have had some grievances also against the ruling government of the Committee for Union and Progress (CUP). While al-Ahd called for Arab autonomy within a federated Ottoman state, it also spoke of Arab–Turkish cooperation to defend the East from the West and insisted on keeping the Islamic caliphate (religious leadership) under Ottoman control.

The most prominent members of al-Ahd were: Taha al-Hashimi, Yasin al-Hashimi, Nuri al-Sa'id, Mawlud Mukhlis, Ali Jawdat al-Ayyubi, Jamil Madfa'i, Abdallah al-Dulimi, Tahsin Ali, Muhammad Hilmi, Ali Rida al-Ghazali, Muwafaq Kamil, Abd al-Ghafur al-Badri (Iraqis); Salim al-Jazairi, Awni Qadamani, Muhammad Bek Ismail, Mustafa Wasfi, Yahya Kazim Abu al-Khair, Muhi al-Din al-Jabban, Ali al-Nashashibi, and Amin Lufti al-Hafiz (Syrians).

According to some sources, the society had some local branches. The Mosul branch in northern Iraq was said to have been led by Yasin al-Hashimi and included Mawlud Mukhlis, Ali Jawdat, Abd al-Rahman Sharaf, Abdullah al-Dulymi, Sharif al-Faruqi, Majid Hassun (Iraqis), and Tawfiq al-Mahmud, Hassan Fahmi, Sadiq al-Jundi, and Mukhtar al-Tarabulsi (Syrians).

See also AYYUBI, ALI JAWDAT AL-; COMMITTEE FOR UNION AND PROGRESS; HASHIMI, TAHA AL-; HASHIMI, YASIN AL-.

Bibliography

Khadduri, Majid. "Aziz Ali Misri and the Arab Nationalist Movement." In *St. Antony's Papers* 17, edited by Albert Hourani. London: Chatto and Windus, 1965.

MAHMOUD HADDAD

AHDUT HA-AVODAH

An Israeli socialist party founded in 1919 by veterans of the Jewish Legion and other Palestine pioneers.

With strong support in the Kibbutz ha-Me'uhad movement, Ahdut ha-Avodah (also Achdut Ha'-Avodah; The Unity of Labor) worked for the unification of Jewish labor movements and the development of new forms of settlement and labor units. It rejected Marxist doctrines of class warfare in favor of social democracy. In 1930, it joined with others in founding the MAPAI party. Becoming independent from that party in 1944, Ahdut ha-Avodah joined with ha-Shomer ha-Tzaʿir, a Zionist socialist youth movement, to found the more radical left-wing MAPAM in 1948. It split with MAPAM in 1954, formed an alignment with MAPAI in 1965, and in 1968 merged again with MAPAI and the Rafi Party to form the Israeli Labor Party. Among those closely associated with it were David Ben-Gurion, Yizhak Ben-Zvi, Yitzhak Tabenkin, Moshe David Remez, and Berl Katznelson.

See also BEN-GURION, DAVID; BEN-ZVI, YIZHAK; HA-SHOMER HA-TZAʿIR; ISRAEL: POLITICAL PARTIES IN; KATZNELSON, BERL.

Bibliography

Rolef, Susan Hattis, ed. *Political Dictionary of Israel,* 2d edition. New York: Macmillan, 1993.

WALTER F. WEIKER

AHL-E HAQQ

A heterodox sect of Shiʿite Islam based in Iranian and Iraqi Kurdistan.

Ahl-e Haqq (followers of truth) is an esoteric sect of around one million members, found primarily among the Kurds of Iran and Iraq; they are closely related to the Alevi and Bektashi of Turkey, and the Alawi and Nusayris of Syria. Popularly known as Alielahi (deifiers of Ali), the Ahl-e Haqq call their faith Din-e yari (religion of God) and themselves Yaresan (in Iran) or Kakaʾi (in Iraq). The sect dates from the fourteenth or fifteenth century C.E., a time of extreme proliferation of Sufi and Shiʿite religio-political groups in the Irano-Turkic world, which culminated in the establishment of the Safavi dynasty in Iran in 1501, with Shiʿism becoming the official religion.

Regarded as heretics by their Shiʿite and Sunni neighbors, the Ahl-e Haqq adopted a strict code of secrecy. They came to define their faith as a *sirr* (mystery), to be guarded from the outside world at any cost. The mystery was transmitted orally, in Gurani and other Kurdish languages, in the form of poetry known as *kalam,* which forms the sect's sacred narrative. Two cardinal dogmas are belief in transmi-

gration of souls and belief in manifestations of the divine essence in human form. There have been seven manifestations and in each the divine essence was accompanied by seven angels. Ali (the first Shiʿite imam) was the second manifestation; his position is overshadowed by the fourth, Sultan Sohak, the founder of the sect. The Ahl-e Haqq neither observe Muslim rites, such as daily prayers and fasting during the month of Ramadan, nor share Islamic theology and sacred space. Instead, they have their own sacred universe and their own rituals, centered on the *jam* (assembly), when they chant their *kalam,* play the sacred lute *(tanbur),* make offerings *(niyaz),* and share a sacrificial meal *(qorbani).* A primary feature of their religious organization is the division into two broad strata: *seyyeds* and commoners. *Seyyeds* are eleven holy families *(khandan),* descended from Sultan Sohak or one of the later manifestations. Each *khandan* is headed by a certain *seyyed* referred to as *pir,* who supervises the religious welfare of the commoners initiated into his following.

See also ALAWI; ALEVI; BEKTASHIS; KURDISTAN; KURDS; SHIʿISM; SUNNI ISLAM.

Bibliography

Hamzehʾee, M. Reza. *The Yaresan: Sociological, Historical, and Religo-Historical Study of a Kurdish Community.* Berlin: Klaus Schwarz, 1990.

Minorsky, Vladimir. "Ahl-i Hakk." In *Shorter Encyclopaedia of Islam,* edited by H. A. R. Gibb and J. H. Kramers. Leiden, Neth.: Brill; London: Luzac, 1961.

Mir-Hosseini, Ziba. "Faith, Ritual, and Culture among the Ahl-i Haqq." In *Kurdish Culture and Identity,* edited by Philip Kreyenbroek and Christine Allison. London: Zed Press, 1996.

Mir-Hosseini, Ziba. "Inner Truth and Outer History: The Two Worlds of Ahl-i Haqq of Kurdistan." *International Journal of Middle East Studies* 26 (1994): 267–285.

ZIBA MIR-HOSSEINI

AHMAD AL-JAZZAR

[1735–1804]

Mamluk governor of Acre, Syria, and Lebanon; known as the Butcher (Arabic, al-Jazzar) for his harshness.

Bosnian by birth, Ahmad Pasha al-Jazzar started his military and political career as part of a Mamluk household in Egypt. In 1768, he went to Syria and was appointed governor of Sidon (Lebanon) in 1775. Ahmad Pasha ruled southeastern Syria and Lebanon at a time when local forces posed serious threats to the Ottoman government. Although nominally subservient to the Ottoman Empire, Ahmad al-Jazzar, like Zahir al-Umar in Galilee, the Azm family of Damascus, the Chehab family of Mount Lebanon, and the Mamluks of Egypt, virtually ruled his territory independently.

Ahmad Pasha made concerted efforts to weaken the control of the Chehabs of Mount Lebanon and, by the end of his tenure, he had reduced them to subservience. Ahmad al-Jazzar's control over Lebanon interrupted economic ties between Beirut and Western Europe for a quarter century. He was appointed governor of Damascus in 1785, though Acre (in today's Israel) always remained the base of his power. With British help, he repulsed Napoléon Bonaparte, who invaded Palestine in 1799.

See also CHEHAB FAMILY; MAMLUKS.

Bibliography

Holt, P. M. *Egypt and the Fertile Crescent: 1516–1922: A Political History.* Ithaca, NY: Cornell University Press, 1966.

Salibi, Kamal. *House of Many Mansions: The History of Lebanon Reconsidered.* Berkeley: University of California Press, 1988.

STEVE TAMARI

AHMAD BEY HUSAYN
[1806–1855]

Bey, 1837–1855, who attempted to Westernize Tunisia and detach it from the Ottoman Empire.

Ahmad Bey's mother was a Sardinian slave captured in a raid on San Pietro in 1798; his father was Mustafa ibn Mahmud (bey of Tunis, 1835–1837). Ahmad was the tenth bey of the Husaynid dynasty. Ahmad Bey received a traditional education, learning the Qur'an by heart. Besides studying the traditional Qur'anic sciences and Turkish, Ahmad learned European history and geography. The latter knowledge influenced his efforts to modernize Tunisian society and turned his foreign policy orientation away from the Ottoman Empire and closer to Europe.

Ahmad Bey's upbringing introduced him to palace intrigues and political disputations. A month before his ascension to power, he participated in the execution of a prominent Mamluk official, Shakir Sahib al-Tabi, keeper of the seal. He had been the most powerful official in the bey's court. When Ahmad Bey assumed the throne in October 1837, he quickly consolidated his authority and built his own patron–client political machine. To do so, he appointed his own clique of friends, mamluks, and clients to key positions.

Ahmad had two primary goals: to maintain Tunisia's relative independence vis-à-vis the Ottoman Empire and France's colonial regime in Algeria, and to strengthen Tunisia's internal political order. To accomplish the first, he avoided implementing the Ottoman Tanzimat reform program that had begun in 1837. He also sought international legitimacy through recognition by nations of Europe (especially France). To placate the Ottomans, he continued to send the obligatory annual gift in exchange for the *firman* (decree) of investiture while avoiding implementation of the Tanzimat by pleading Tunisia's lack of resources to do so. Ahmad Bey maintained good relations with France, and continued to seek France's guarantees of Tunisian independence and to deny Ottoman claims of sovereignty. In the 1850s, he sent troops to the Crimea to show support for the Ottomans rather than to reject their sovereignty.

Ahmad Bey's goal of reforming the fabric of the state has been criticized for attempting too much and accomplishing too little. Inspiration for his reform efforts came from Napoléon's France, Muhammad Ali's Egypt, and the Tanzimat program. All of these taught him that military strength was paramount. Wedged between France's colonial regime in Algeria and a resurgent Ottoman Empire in Libya, Ahmad saw modernizing the military as one way to maintain Tunisia's territorial integrity against the aspirations of its powerful neighbors.

In 1831, Husayn Bey had begun reforming the military by inviting Europeans to train a *nizami* corps of infantry based on the latest European and Ottoman models. The term *nizami* was borrowed from the Ottoman designation *nizam-i cedit* (new order), applied by Sultan Mahmud II to Ottoman military modernization efforts. The Tunisian *nizamis* wore

European uniforms and Tunisian *shashiyas* (small red hats with tassels).

Mustafa Bey accelerated the expansion of the *nizami* corps by developing a conscription system. An informal system of recruiting troops (in exchange for returning an earlier batch to the same area as reserves) was developed in order to minimize friction between recruiters and the local populace. To avoid antagonizing the Turkish military elite, the bey maintained Turkish-Mamluk domination of the upper ranks. The army thus remained top-heavy in inefficient higher-rank officers who were traditional in outlook and ill-suited to the disciplinary codes of modern armies. The lower ranks and noncommissioned officers were reasonably motivated but poorly led. As a result, the reforms largely failed to produce the desired results.

From a small contingent of about 1,800 men at the beginning of his reign, by 1850 Ahmad Bey had expanded the *nizami* forces to between 26,000 and 36,000, with 16,000 actually in service at any one time. Seven regiments of infantry, two of artillery, and a partial one of cavalry comprised the corps. In the last two years of his reign, financial constraints forced Ahmad Bey to drastically reduce the size of the military.

A critical step in Ahmad Bey's military reform efforts was the establishment in 1840 of a military academy *(maktab harbi)* adjacent to the Bey's Palace at Bardo (a suburb of Tunis), to train young Mamluks, Turks, and sons of prestigious Arab families in the military arts. The school prepared an elite cadre of graduates who later led reform efforts in the 1870s, during the administration of Prime Minister Khayr al-Din al-Tunisi (1873–1877). It set the precedent for Sadiqi College (established in 1875), which trained Tunisians in modern subjects. Its graduates were members of the Young Tunisians in the 1890s and early 1900s. Most Tunisian nationalists who formed the Destour and Neo-Destour political movements studied at Sadiqi, including independent Tunisia's first president, Habib Bourguiba.

Seeking to make Tunisia self-sufficient in military-related goods, Ahmad ordered the construction of a cannon foundry, a small arms factory, powder mills, tanneries, saddle/leather factories, a textile factory, and other industries. He imported European technicians to train Tunisian workers in modern manufacturing techniques. These efforts provided the Tunisian elite and some workers with a rudimentary understanding of European industrialization practices.

Between 1841 and 1846, Ahmad Bey abolished slavery, initiated with the closing of the slave market in Tunis (the Suq al-Birka) and culminating with the January 1846 decree officially abolishing slavery in Tunisia. At al-Muhammadiya, about ten miles southwest of Tunis, he built a magnificent governmental complex, which he intended to serve as Tunisia's Versailles. Europeans designed and furnished this complex with the latest European gadgets.

The last five years of Ahmad's reign were a period of financial chaos, declining agricultural production, his poor health, and overall ruin of his accomplishments. His need for money to finance his military reforms led him to depend on a ruthless tax farmer, Mahmud ibn Ayad. Ahmad Bey tolerated the financial oppression of his subjects so long as ibn Ayad increased the state revenues. The decline of those state revenues between 1849 and 1852 culminated in the flight of ibn Ayad to Paris and his subsequent attempts to sue Tunisia's government. Khayr al-Din arbitrated the matter in Paris, but recovered none of the funds ibn Ayad had taken.

In July 1852, Ahmad Bey suffered a stroke, which impaired his ability to rule. In 1853, he was forced to disband his army due to financial problems. Ahmad Bey died in May 1855, at age forty-eight. He had sought to modernize a backward and traditional state and society through emphasis on military reforms. He established positive precedents in the Bardo military academy and the conscription of native Tunisians, and negative ones in the lack of accountability of his leading ministers and in his own financial irresponsibility.

See also BOURGUIBA, HABIB; KHAYR AL-DIN; MAHMUD II; MAMLUKS; SADIQI COLLEGE; TANZIMAT; YOUNG TUNISIANS.

Bibliography

Anderson, Lisa. *The State and Social Transformation in Tunisia and Libya, 1830–1980.* Princeton, NJ: Princeton University, 1986.

Brown, L. Carl. *The Tunisia of Ahmad Bey, 1837–1855.* Princeton, NJ: Princeton University Press, 1974.

Nelson, Harold D., ed. *Tunisia: A Country Study,* 3d ed. Washington, DC, 1986.

Perkins, Kenneth J. *Historical Dictionary of Tunisia,* 2d edition. Metuchen, NJ: Scarecrow, 1997.

LARRY A. BARRIE

AHMAD BEY OF CONSTANTINE
[c. 1784–1850]

Commander of the province of Constantine in eastern Algeria, 1826–1837.

When the French conquered Algiers in 1830, ending Ottoman rule, al-Hajj Ahmad assumed direct authority in the name of the sultan. The latter, however, was unable to provide support, and after an initial victory over the French (1836), Ahmad was forced to abandon Constantine (1837) and eventually to surrender (1848). Nationalists today consider him, together with Abd al-Qadir, one of the heroes of resistance.

PETER VON SIVERS

AHMAD DURRANI
[c. 1722–1772]

Ruler of Afghanistan; founder of the Durrani dynasty.

Ahmad Durrani was elected ruler by an assembly of Pakhtun elders in Kandahar in 1747, at a time when the Moghul empire in India was disintegrating and the recent Afshar dynasty in Persia was collapsing. He united the Pakhtun (Pushtun) clans and led them to create an empire that went from Meshed to Punjab. This Durrani empire did not outlast him by long, but Afghanistan did become a polity with Pakhtuns playing the dominant role in the country's politics.

Born in Herat around 1722, Ahmad belonged to the Saddozai lineage of the Abdali clan. His ancestors had led the clan since 1588. In 1717, the Abdalis proclaimed Herat an independent state but were defeated by Nadir Afshar in 1732 and relocated in Khorasan (in Persia). Then in 1736, they were permitted to go to Kandahar. That year Nadir became king of Persia and Ahmad joined Nadir's army, rising to prominence. When Nadir was assassinated in 1747, the Abdali contingent serving in his army returned to Kandahar. In a *loya jirga* (grand assembly) of clan elders, it was decided to create a Pakhtun kingdom, and Ahmad was elected leader.

Ahmad spent most of his reign campaigning in India and Persia (Iran). His most memorable encounter took place in the field of Panipat, near Delhi, on 14 January 1761, when he destroyed a Mahratta army and briefly became the master of Northern India. The Pakhtuns were unable to consolidate their hold, but the destruction of Mahratta power paved the way for the conquest of India by the British. Booty and revenue from the provinces of Punjab, Kashmir, and Sind provided the riches to consolidate Ahmad's rule at home and to keep content the Pakhtun, Baluchi, Uzbek, and Kizilbash clans that constituted his army. As his reign drew to a close, Sikh resistance in the Punjab made campaigning in India less and less profitable.

By then, an Afghan polity was already in place. To incorporate the various clans within the structure of the state, Ahmad systematically assigned to each clan a khan (leader) who was allowed to farm taxes *(iltizam)* in the newly conquered territories or was granted a regular stipend. Ahmad's own clansmen were given even more privileges—the khans among them controlled most key positions in the state, while the rest were exempted from taxation and paid salaries during their campaigns in India. Investing their newly found wealth in land, they became the dominant power in southern Afghanistan and acquired land elsewhere. To reflect their enhanced status, Ahmad changed their name from Abdali to Durrani (Persian, *dur,* or pearl).

A poet and a patron of Sufis (Muslim mystics and scholars of Islam), Ahmad justified his campaigns in India in Islamic terms. During his reign, Sunni Islam flourished in Afghanistan; mosques, shrines and Islamic schools enjoyed the financial support of the state. He died in the mountains east of Kandahar, and his son Timur Shah succeeded him (1772–1793).

See also HERAT; KANDAHAR; PUSHTUN; SUNNI ISLAM.

Bibliography

Dupree, Louis. *Afghanistan.* Oxford, U.K., and New York: Oxford University Press, 1997.

Rawlinson, H. "Report on the Durranis." In *Historical and Political Gazetteer of Afghanistan,* edited by Ludwig Adamec. Graz, Austria: Akadem. Druck- u. Verlagsanst, 1980.

ASHRAF GHANI

AHMAD HIBAT ALLAH
[c. 1870–c. 1920]

Moroccan resistance leader against the French, 1912–1920.

Ahmad Hibat Allah (also known as El Hiba) was the son of the noted scholar of Islam and patriot Ma al-Aynayn. He led an important millenarian movement in the Sous valley, which was able to capture Marrakech in August 1912, following the abdication of Abd al-Hafid as sultan. After his defeat in September 1912, he withdrew into southern Morocco and established his headquarters at Tiznit.

During World War I, Hibat Allah was a major beneficiary of a pan-Islamic Turco–German effort to support Moroccan resistance from Spain. Together with his brother Murabbih Rabbuh, who succeeded him upon his death about 1920, he sought with little success to organize attacks on the French positions in the Sous valley.

See also ABD AL-HAFID IBN AL-HASSAN; MA AL-AYNAYN.

Bibliography

Burke, Edmund, III. "Moroccan Resistance, Pan-Islam and German War Strategy, 1914–1918." *Francia* 3 (1975): 434–464.

Burke, Edmund, III. *Prelude to Protectorate in Morocco: Precolonial Protest and Resistance, 1860–1912.* Chicago: University of Chicago Press, 1976.

EDMUND BURKE III

AHMAD IBN MUHAMMAD AL-RAYSUNI
[?–1926]

Political figure in Morocco from 1900 until his death in 1926.

A descendant of the Sharifian lineage of Bani Arus and a charismatic personality, Ahmad ibn Muhammad al-Raysuni (also called al-Raysuli or El Raisuni) parlayed his position as a rural power broker in Mo-rocco and leader of local anti-European feelings to rise to prominence in the period 1903–1906. By organizing a series of political kidnappings, the most celebrated of which was of the American Ian Perdicaris, he helped to undermine the regime of Sultan Abd al-Aziz.

Following the establishment of the protectorates of France and Spain in 1912, al-Raysuni became an official in the Spanish protectorate. Following the rebellion of Abd al-Karim against the Spanish authorities (1921), al-Raysuni came briefly to prominence again by playing off the two sides and enhancing his own position. In this, his career resembles those of other Moroccan regional figures of the period.

See also KHATTABI, MUHAMMAD IBN ABD AL-KARIM AL-; MOROCCO; SHARIFIAN DYNASTIES.

Bibliography

Forbes, Rosita. *The Sultan of the Mountains: The Life Story of Raisuli.* New York: Holt, 1924.

Woolman, David. *Rebels in the Rif: Abd el Krim and the Rif Rebellion.* Stanford, CA: Stanford University Press, 1968.

EDMUND BURKE III

AHMAD IBN YAHYA HAMID AL-DIN
[1891–1962]

The second of the three Hamid al-Din imams to govern Yemen after independence in 1918, from 15 March 1948 to 18 September 1962.

During his father's tenure as imam, from 1904 to 1948, and as king of Yemen, from 1918 to 1948, Ahmad ibn Yahya Hamid al-Din was apprentice to and an important supporter of his father. Ahmad was also the governor of Ta'iz province, Yemen's primary military commander, and the designated successor to his father as both imam and king.

After Imam Yahya's assassination in 1948, and the effort at major reforms, Ahmad organized important tribal elements to overthrow the usurpers and became imam and king. Although he had earlier established some tenuous links with reform elements, he introduced very few changes to the autocratic and highly centralized system established by his father. By the early 1960s, the extent of opposition to his rule had resulted in numerous revolts and assassination attempts, even by some of the tribal elements that had earlier supported him. He died in September 1962, and was succeeded by his son Muhammad al-Badr who, however, was deposed one week later in the revolution that turned Yemen into a republic.

See also BADR, MUHAMMAD AL-; YAHYA IBN MUHAMMAD HAMID AL-DIN.

Bibliography

Dresch, Paul. *A History of Modern Yemen.* Cambridge, U.K., and New York: Cambridge University Press, 2000.

MANFRED W. WENNER

AHMAD, MUHAMMAD

[c. 1840–1885]

Islamic politico-religious leader, called al-Mahdi, known as the father of Sudanese nationalism.

Born Muhammad Ahmad ibn Abdullah, Muhammad Ahmad was the son of a boat builder on Labab island, in the Nile, south of Dongola, Sudan. His father claimed descent from the family of the Prophet. The family moved to Karari, north of Omdurman, and then Khartoum, while Muhammad Ahmad was a child. He was enrolled in Qur'anic schools and then pursued advanced studies under Shaykh Muhammad al-Dikar in Barbara and then under Shaykh al-Quashi wad al-Zayn in the Sammaniyya *tariqah* (religious order) school in Khartoum. An ascetic person, who sought a puritanic, meditative lifestyle, he broke with his religious teacher in 1881, soon after he moved to Aba island in the White Nile.

In June 1881, he dispatched letters to religious leaders throughout the Sudan, informing them that he was the "expected Mahdi," the divine leader chosen by God to fill the earth with justice and equity at the end of time. After emissaries from the Turko–Egyptian government tried to dissuade him, an armed force was dispatched to capture him and his small band of followers. His three hundred adherents, armed only with swords and spears, defeated the expedition on Aba island, 12 August 1881. Following that seemingly miraculous victory, the Mahdi led his followers to Qadir mountain in the region of Kurdufan. Their migration imitated the prophet Muhammad's *hijra* (holy flight) from Mecca to Medina. The move to Kurdufan also enabled him to recruit adherents from the Nuba and *baqqara* (cattle-herding Arab) tribes of the west, who had long defied the control of the central government. The Ansar (helpers or followers) defeated government expeditions in December 1881, June 1882, and November 1883.

By then, the Mahdi had flooded the country with letters that explained the politico-religious significance of his mission: his task was to reverse the socioreligious abuses of the Turko–Egyptian regime, which had departed from God's path, and to revive the simple and just practices of early Islam. Since his mission was divinely ordained, those who opposed him were termed infidels. Efforts by the government and established clergy to denounce him as an imposter had diminishing effect, as growing numbers of tribes and religious leaders rallied to his banner. By the time that the Mahdi besieged Khartoum in late 1884, some 100,000 Ansar were camped outside. The Mahdi captured Khartoum on 26 January 1885 and established his capital across the White Nile at Omdurman. Muhammad Ahmad al-Mahdi died of a sudden illness on 22 June 1885 and was succeeded by his principal *baqqara* follower, Abdullahi ibn Muhammad, who converted Mahdi's religious state into a military dictatorship and ruled until the Anglo–Egyptian conquest in 1898. Under the leadership of his son Abd al-Rahman al-Mahdi, the Mahdi's followers formed a brotherhood to continue his teachings.

Sudanese nationalists later viewed the Mahdi as "the father of independence," who united the tribes, drove out the foreign rulers, and founded the Sudanese nation-state; he saw himself, rather, as "a renewer of the Muslim Faith, come to purge Islam of faults and accretions" (Holt and Daly, p. 87). Moreover, as the successor to the prophet, he was restoring the community of the faithful: That belief justified his political role. Finally, his belief that he was the "expected Mahdi" emphasized the ecstatic dimension and the idea that his coming foretold the end of time. The combining of those elements—political, religious, and social—produced a powerful, popularly based movement that swept away the decaying Turko–Egyptian regime. The Mahdi's death, immediately after gaining control over almost all of northern Sudan, made it impossible to assess whether he had the ability to craft an Islamic polity on the basis of his charismatic authority.

Bibliography

Holt, P. M. *The Mahdist State in the Sudan, 1881–1898: A Study of Its Origins, Development, and Overthrow.* Oxford: Clarendon Press, 1970.

Holt, P. M., and Daly, M. W. *The History of the Sudan: From the Coming of Islam to the Present Day.* London: Weidenfeld and Nicolson, 1979.

Shibikah, Makki. *The Independent Sudan.* New York: R. Speller, 1959.

ANN M. LESCH

AHMAD QAJAR

[1869–1929]

Sixth and last monarch of Persia's Qajar dynasty.

Ahmad Qajar was the son of Mohammad Ali Shah and Malekeh Jahan (daughter of Kamran Mirza, a son of Naser al-Din Shah, the fourth Qajar monarch). Ahmad Shah (also called Soltan Ahmad Shah) ascended to the throne at age eleven, when his father was deposed in 1909. Care was taken with his education; besides the traditional studies, he had a French professor who taught him political science and administrative law. A regent was appointed until he reached his majority, and the second *majles* (assembly) was called by him.

Ahmad Shah's reign coincided with a change in rivalry between Britain and Russia. The Convention of 1907 had divided Persia into three zones: Russia in the north, Britain in the southeast, and a neutral zone. The old rivalry between Russia and Britain, which had guaranteed Persia's independence, became an alliance that threatened to control. Russia issued an ultimatum that they would occupy Tehran unless Persia dismissed Morgan Shuster, an American financier, employed with the approval of the *majles* to reform Persia's financial administration. This was done and the regent closed the *majles* for three years, until Ahmad Shah came of age in 1914 and had to take his oath of office in the *majles* before he could be crowned. The coronation actually preceded the opening, on the eve of World War I.

At the outbreak of war, Persia declared neutrality, but the belligerents disregarded it and soon turned the country into a battleground. Nationalists and the *majles* favored the Germans and Turks—who opposed Persia's traditional enemies, Britain and Russia. When the Russians threatened to advance on Tehran, Ahmad Shah was persuaded that were he to go he would forfeit his throne.

Until the Russian Revolution in 1917, the Allies controlled Persia, with financial aid and military occupation. The Russian Revolution left the British in sole control. They tried to take advantage of the new situation by negotiating a treaty to keep financial and military control—and Ahmad Shah signed it, reluctantly, since it was opposed by the nationalists, who eventually defeated it.

A succession of weak governments, civil war, and communist infiltration from the newly formed Soviet Union caused a coup d'état in 1921, partly planned and inspired by the British occupying forces, which were soon to evacuate the country. The coup was carried out by Reza Khan, commander of the Persian Cossack Brigade, and a pro-British journalist, Sayyid Ziya al-Din. Overcome by the turn of events, Ahmad Shah installed them in power—Sayyid Ziya as prime minister and Reza as minister of war. Reza ousted Sayyid Ziya and became prime minister, controlling the new army he had formed. His modernization policy also won him the support of the young nationalists.

In 1923, Ahmad Shah left Iran, appointing his brother to be in charge. A movement to establish a republic with Reza as president was defeated, especially by the *ulama* (body of mullahs), who feared secularization, as was established in Turkey. In 1925, the Qajar dynasty was deposed by the fifth *majles,* which voted to give the monarchy to the Pahlavi dynasty, with Reza Khan becoming Reza Shah Pahlavi, the founder. Ahmad Shah has been maligned by the historians of the Pahlavi era, shown as weak and vacillating; recent historians have emphasized his democratic nature, his wish to reign and not to rule. He lived and died in exile and was buried in Karbala, a holy Shi'ite city in southern Iraq.

See also NASER AL-DIN SHAH; PAHLAVI, REZA; QAJAR DYNASTY; SHUSTER, W. MORGAN.

Bibliography

Bayat, Mangol. *Mysticism and Dissent: Socioreligious Thought in Qajar Iran.* Syracuse, NY: Syracuse University Press, 1999.

Daniel, Elton L., ed. *Society and Culture in Qajar Iran: Studies in Honor of Hafez Farmayan.* Costa Mesa, CA: Mazda Publishers, 2002.

Documents on British Foreign Policy, 1919–1939. First series, vol. 13. London: H.M. Stationery Office, 1963.

Ghani, Cyrus. *Iran and the Rise of Reza Shah: From Qajar Collapse to Pahlavi Rule.* New York and London: Tauris, 1998.

Keddie, Nikki R., and Matthee, Rudi, eds. *Iran and the Surrounding World: Interactions in Culture and Cultural Politics.* Seattle: University of Washington Press, 2002.

Lambton, A. K. S. *Qajar Persia: Eleven Studies.* London: Tauris, 1987.

Van den Bos, Matthijs. *Mystic Regimes: Sufism and the State in Iran, from the Late Qajar Era to the Islamic Republic.* Leiden, Netherlands, and Boston, MA: Brill, 2002.

MANSOUREH ETTEHADIEH

AHMAD SHAH MAS'UD

[1953–2001]

Afghan resistance leader.

Ahmad Shah Mas'ud was a well-known Afghan resistance fighter and political figure. Born in the Panjshir valley in 1953, Mas'ud joined the Afghan Islamic group Jami'at-e Islami Afghanistan (the Islamic Society of Afghanistan) in 1973, as a student at the Kabul Polytechnic Institute for Engineering and Architecture. With the Soviet occupation of Afghanistan in 1979, Mas'ud retreated to the Panjshir Valley, where he led a guerrilla war first against the Soviet-supported government and later against the Taliban government. As an ethnic Tajik and one of the few non-Pushtun commanders in the resistance movement, he gained a large following in the northern areas of Afghanistan. He also attracted an international reputation and was sometimes referred to as the Lion of the Panjshir, or as Afghanistan's Che Guevara. When the Islamic resistance fighters captured Kabul in 1992, Mas'ud became defense minister under the Burhanuddin Rabbani government.

In 1996, he was forced to flee Kabul in the face of the advancing Taliban forces. Retreating to the north part of Afghanistan, he formed the Northern Alliance, also called the United Front, which continued its guerilla war against the Taliban. The Northern Alliance recaptured Kabul in November 2001. However, Mas'ud did not live to see the recapture of Kabul. He was assassinated on 9 September 2001 at his headquarters in northern Afghanistan. Because of the timing of his murder and the way in which it occurred, it is thought to be linked to the 11 September 2001 attack on the World Trade Center in New York City.

See also JAMI'AT-E ISLAMI; PUSHTUN; RABBANI, BURHANUDDIN; TALIBAN.

Bibliography

Ewans, Martin. *Afghanistan: A New History.* Richmond, U.K.: Curzon, 2001.

Roy, Olivier. *Islam and Resistance in Afghanistan.* New York; Cambridge, U.K.: Cambridge University Press, 1986.

BARNETT R. RUBIN
UPDATED BY GRANT FARR

AHMAR, ABDULLAH IBN HUSAYN, AL-

[1919–]

Yemeni politician and leader of the Hashid, one of the two most powerful tribes in North Yemen.

Abdullah ibn Husayn al-Ahmar's father, Shaykh Husayn al-Ahmar, was executed by Imam Ahmad ibn Yahya; as a result, during the Yemen Civil War Abdullah al-Ahmar sided with the republicans against the royalists and was appointed governor of Hajja, but he refused to join the Egyptian-backed government of Abdullah al-Sallal. After Egypt withdrew from Yemen, he helped topple the Sallal government and his tribes provided crucial support to the new regime of Abd al-Rahman al-Iryani against the royalists.

In 1970, the civil war ended with the abolition of the monarchy and al-Ahmar became the chairman of the new Consultative Council. When Colonel Ibrahim al-Hamdi seized power in 1974, he tried to limit the representation of the tribal leaders, which led to an open rebellion by the Hashid tribes. After the assassination of Hamdi in 1977, Saudi Arabia helped bring about a reconciliation between the tribes and the new government in

1978, first under Ahmad Husayn Ghashmi and then under Ali Abdullah al-Salih. Al-Ahmar was appointed to the Constituent People's Assembly. Although he opposed the government of South Yemen, he supported the 1990 unification of North and South Yemen and formed the Islah Party, which represents tribal as well as Islamic interests. The Islah Party won 62 seats out of 301 in the parliamentary elections of 1993, in which it ran in coalition with President Salih's People General Congress (PCG). In 1997, the party won 56 seats and al-Ahmar was elected speaker of parliament. Though his party won only 45 seats in the 2003 elections and is no longer in coalition with the PGC (which won a majority of 225 seats), al-Ahmar was re-elected speaker of parliament.

See also BAKIL TRIBAL CONFEDERATION; HAMDI, IBRAHIM AL-; IRYANI, ABD AL-RAHMAN AL-; ISLAH PARTY; SALIH, ALI ABDULLAH; SALLAL, ABDULLAH AL; YEMEN CIVIL WAR.

Bibliography

Dresch, Paul. *A History of Modern Yemen.* Cambridge, U.K.: Cambridge University Press, 2000.

MAYSAM J. AL FARUQI

AHMET İHSAN TO'KGOZ
[1868–1942]

Ottoman Turkish publisher.

Ahmet İhsan To'kgoz was born in Erzurum, where his father was a civil servant, and graduated from the Mülkiye civil service school in Istanbul, where he studied literature with Recaizade Mahmud Ekrem. Upon graduation, he began to work as a French translator in the foreign ministry and to publish a journal, *Ümran* (Prosperity). In 1891, he began to publish the journal *Servet-i Fünun* (The wealth of sciences), which was the main medium for the literary movement known as the new literature. Disputes between Ahmet İhsan To'kgoz and his editor, Tevfik Fikret, hastened the downfall of *Servet-i Fünun,* which was ordered closed in 1897. Ahmet İhsan To'kgoz joined the Committee for Union and Progress in 1907, and, following the revolution, began to publish *Servet-i Fünun* as a daily political paper. Tiring of politics, he turned it into a weekly literary digest, the organ of the Fecr-i Ati literary movement. In 1931, he became a member of parliament representing Ordu.

See also RECAIZADE MAHMUD EKREM; TEVFIK FIKRET.

Bibliography

Shaw, Stanford J., and Shaw, Ezel Kural. *History of the Ottoman Empire and Modern Turkey,* Vol. 2: *Reform, Revolution, and Republic: The Rise of Modern Turkey, 1808–1975.* Cambridge, U.K., and New York: Cambridge University Press, 1977.

DAVID WALDNER

AHMET İZZET
[1864–1937]

Ottoman general and grand vizier.

Ahmet İzzet rose to prominence in 1893 as an influential second scribe of Abdülhamit II. After the 1908 revolution, he became chief of general staff under the Young Turks and commander of the Caucasus front during World War I. During his brief tenure as grand vizier (October–November 1918), he negotiated the Mudros Armistice with the British, formally ending Ottoman participation in World War I. He closed his career as minister of war in the early years of the Turkish Republic.

Bibliography

Lewis, Bernard. *The Emergence of Modern Turkey,* 3d edition. New York: Oxford University Press, 2002.

Shaw, Stanford J., and Shaw, Ezel Kural. *History of the Ottoman Empire and Modern Turkey,* Vol. 2: *Reform, Revolution, and Republic: The Rise of Modern Turkey, 1808–1975.* Cambridge, U.K., and New York: Cambridge University Press, 1977.

ELIZABETH THOMPSON

AHMET RASIM
[1864?–1932]

Turkish journalist and short-story writer.

Born in Istanbul during the Ottoman Empire, Rasim grew up in poverty after his father, a Cypriot postal official, divorced his mother. Forced to attend school at an orphanage, he graduated at the head of his class. After a short period as a postal worker, he began to work as a journalist; for the next forty-eight years, he wrote in the major Istanbul newspapers. He was also an elected member of the Turkish Grand National Assembly from 1927 to 1932 in Atatürk's new Republic of Turkey.

Rasim's writings are characterized by his incorporation of the folklore and anecdotes of daily life in Istanbul. Using sparse language, he captured the vitality of the different neighborhoods of the city, making him an important source of information about the daily existence of Old Turkey. Rasim's contributions to Turkish literature also include memoirs, travelogues, historical accounts, and articles on various subjects.

See also ATATÜRK, MUSTAFA KEMAL.

Bibliography

Mitler, Louis. *Ottoman Turkish Writers: A Bibliographical Dictionary of Significant Figures in Pre-Republican Turkish Literature.* New York: P. Lang, 1988.

DAVID WALDNER

AHMET RIZA
[1859–1930]

Young Turk leader and educator.

Born in Istanbul to an Austrian mother and to a father who was an Anglophile Ottoman bureaucrat, Ahmet Riza grew up among the wealthy elite. He attended the prestigious Galatasaray Lycée in Istanbul and studied agriculture in France. As an idealistic young man, he sought to improve the condition of the Ottoman peasantry, first at the Ministry of Agriculture, then at the Ministry of Education, where he served as the director of education in the city of Bursa.

At the age of thirty, Ahmet Riza returned to France, where he became an early leader of the Young Turks. In 1894 he published a series of tracts demanding a constitutional regime in the Ottoman Empire based on Islamic and Ottoman traditions of consultation. In 1895, he began publishing a bimonthly newspaper, *Meşveret,* which soon became a locus of the exile Young Turk movement. The news-

paper was also smuggled into the empire and circulated among liberal intellectuals there. Ahmet Riza's chief rival was the more radical Prince Sabahettin, who founded a separate Young Turk group and newspaper in Paris. Ahmet Riza opposed the prince's calls for revolution and European intervention in the empire at the 1902 Congress of Ottoman Liberals in Paris. At the Second Young Turk Congress in 1907, Ahmet Riza at first reluctantly endorsed the use of violence to depose the sultan, but later reversed his position.

Ahmet Riza returned to Istanbul after the 1908 revolution and headed the Unionist Party, which was backed by the Committee for Union and Progress (CUP) and which opposed Prince Sabahettin's Ottoman Liberal Union Party and Islamist groups. The Unionists were successful in the elections, and Ahmet Riza became president of the Chamber of Deputies. In April 1909, however, leaders of a mass demonstration at the Sultan Ahmet mosque organized by the Society of Islamic Unity called for Ahmet Riza's resignation and for his replacement by a "true Muslim." Two deputies were killed, apparently mistaken for Ahmet Riza, when the crowd entered the Parliament buildings. Ahmet Riza was deposed, and Isma'il Kemal was elected the new president of the Chamber in the ensuing reorganization of government.

Ahmet Riza remained loyal to CUP during his years in government. But, in 1919 he founded a new party, the National Unity Party, and allied himself with Sultan Vahidettin against the Kemalists. He spent the years of the Independence War in Paris, then returned to Istanbul, where he was an instructor at the prestigious Dar al-Fonun school until his death.

Riza's contribution to the Young Turk movement went beyond his organizational abilities. As a follower of the French sociologist Auguste Comte, he first formulated the principles that would influence the development of secularist reform in Turkey. For example, the slogan heading his magazine *Meşveret,* "order and progress," was drawn from French positivist ideas and is probably linked to the simultaneous naming of an Istanbul opposition group, Union and Progress.

See also COMMITTEE FOR UNION AND PROGRESS; YOUNG TURKS.

Bibliography

Lewis, Bernard. *The Emergence of Modern Turkey*, 3d edition. New York: Oxford University Press, 2002.

Shaw, Stanford J., and Shaw, Ezel Kural. *History of the Ottoman Empire and Modern Turkey*, Vol. 2: *Reform, Revolution, and Republic: The Rise of Modern Turkey, 1808–1975*. Cambridge, U.K., and New York: Cambridge University Press, 1977.

ELIZABETH THOMPSON

AHMET VEFIK

[1823–1891]

Ottoman administrator and scholar.

Like his father and grandfather, Ahmet Vefik entered government service and soon rose to positions of great importance during the Tanzimat period of the Ottoman Empire. He served twice as minister of education (1872 and 1877) and helped to reform the Ottoman educational system. In 1877, Sultan Abdülhamit II appointed him president of the first Ottoman parliament, and when it was dissolved less than a year later, Ahmet Vefik served as the sultan's grand vizier for several months in early 1878, as governor of Bursa (1878–1882), and briefly as grand vizier once more at the end of 1882.

In spite of his illustrious political career, Ahmet Vefik is better remembered for his work as a writer, translator, and educator. Having served as ambassador to France, he translated Molière into Turkish. He also edited the first modern dictionary of the Turkish language, published in 1876, and he compiled a history of the Ottoman Empire that became the standard text in the Ottoman *ruşdiye* (adolescence) schools.

See also TANZIMAT.

Bibliography

Lewis, Bernard. *The Emergence of Modern Turkey*, 3d edition. New York: Oxford University Press, 2002.

Shaw, Stanford J., and Shaw, Ezel Kural. *History of the Ottoman Empire and Modern Turkey*, Vol. 2: *Reform, Revolution, and Republic: The Rise of Modern Turkey, 1808–1975*. Cambridge, U.K., and New York: Cambridge University Press, 1977.

ZACHARY KARABELL

AHRAM CENTER FOR POLITICAL AND STRATEGIC STUDIES, AL-

A policy research institute founded in Cairo in 1968.

Al-Ahram Center for Political and Strategic Studies is part of the publishing empire that Muhammad Hasanayn Haykal built up around the famous newspaper *al-Ahram*. It is showcased in a dazzling, steel and glass twelve-story building. The center's original name—Center for Zionist and Palestine Studies—is revealing. In the wake of Egypt's devastating defeat by Israel in the 1967 Arab–Israel War, Gamal Abdel Nasser and Haykal agreed that Egyptians could no longer afford to remain ignorant of Israeli social and political dynamics. As Nasser's closest journalist confidant, Haykal offered the center's researchers protection from outside interference. Boutros Boutros-Ghali, the respected academic who later served as secretary-general of the United Nations, became general supervisor of the center, and a son-in-law of Nasser served as director.

The center's privileged young social scientists set to work to analyze as dispassionately as possible such topics as the reasons for Egypt's defeat, the sources of Israel's strengths, and the nature of U.S.–Israel relations. Soon after its founding the center adopted its current name, which reflected its branching out into far-ranging social, economic, and political analyses, probing possible options as Egypt moved from the era of Nasser to that of Anwar Sadat, and then Husni Mubarak. The center also invited foreign scholars to make scholarly presentations.

Haykal fell out with Sadat and was dismissed from al-Ahram in 1974, and Nasser's son-in-law lost his post. The center drifted briefly, having lost its facile access to the top political elite. Sayyid Yasin, from the National Institute for Criminological Research, gave the center new direction. With the help of such talented social scientists as Ali al-Din Hilal Dessouki and Saadeddin Ibrahim, Yasin directed the center's efforts toward the educated elite in Egypt and the Arab world. The center's scholars often were able to make limited yet pointed criticisms of regime policies that would not have been tolerated in the regular press or other political forums. In place of Sadat's effusions about the new era of Egyptian–Israeli and Egyptian–U.S. relations, for example, the center's scholars offered hard-headed, detached analyses of Egyptian national interest.

See also HAYKAL, MUHAMMAD HASANAYN.

Bibliography

Baker, Raymond William. *Sadat and After: Struggles for Egypt's Political Soul.* Cambridge, MA: Harvard University Press, 1990.

DONALD MALCOLM REID

AHRAR, AL-

See NEWSPAPERS AND PRINT MEDIA: ARAB COUNTRIES

AHSA'I, AHMAD AL-
[1753–1826]

Innovative Shi'ite thinker.

Ahmad al-Ahsa'i was born in 1753 in al-Hasa or al-Ahsa, then nominally an Arabian/Persian Gulf province of the Ottoman Empire with a largely Shi'ite population. Ahmad may well have been from an artisan family, since he knew metalworking and carpentry, but a series of visions of the Shi'a imams led him to study the seminary subjects of Islam. Around 1792, he went to Iraq for higher studies, staying in Najaf and Karbala for four years, and afterward lived in Bahrain. From 1800 to 1806 he was based in Basra and journeyed in southern Iraq. From 1806 to 1814 he lived in Yazd, and from 1814 to 1824 in Kermanshah, although he continued to travel widely. He was in Karbala in 1825 and died in 1826 on his way to Medina.

His move to Persia (Iran) had come at the invitation of the shah and of Qajar princes who offered him patronage to adorn their cities. In 1808, Fath Ali Shah summoned Ahmad to Tehran and attempted to persuade him to stay in the capital, but the shaykh declined for fear that he would eventually come into conflict with the shah. Ahmad claimed authority not only as a trained jurisprudent (*mujtahid*) but also as the recipient of intuitive knowledge from the imams (the holy figures of Shi'ism); he emphasized the esoteric, gnostic heritage within Twelver Shi'ism, writing about letter/number symbolism (numerology) and other cabalistic subjects. He innovated in Shi'ite theology both in his doctrine of God's attributes and his positing of two sorts of body, the ethereal and the physical, allowing him to suggest that the resurrection would be of the ethereal type. He appears to have been influenced by the medieval Iranian illuminationist Suhravardi and wrote original commentaries on the metaphysical works of such Safavid thinkers as Mulla Sadra Shirazi and Mulla Muhsin Fayz, criticizing their monistic tendencies but accepting many of their other premises and technical terms. Only very late in life, from 1823, was Ahmad denounced by some of his colleagues as heterodox, and this appears to have been a minority position in his lifetime. His followers coalesced in the Shaykhi school, which for a time contended with the scholastic Usuli school for dominance of Twelver Shi'ism in the nineteenth century.

See also SHAYKHI; SHI'ISM; USULI.

JUAN R. I. COLE

AHVAZ

Capital of the province of Khuzistan in southwestern Iran.

Located on the Karun River, Ahvaz developed as a flourishing pre-Islamic city, and it became the capital of the province of Khuzistan in the late tenth century. Its silk textile and sugar production were very important. Ahvaz declined after the Mongol invasions. By the nineteenth century it had dwindled to a small town. But the opening of the Karun River in 1888 to international navigation, the beginning of oil exploration in 1908 at nearby Masjed Suleyman, and the construction of the Trans-Iranian railroad, which reached Ahvaz in 1929, all stimulated the growth of the city. By the 1950s the population of Ahvaz had reached more than 100,000. The primary causes of growth during this period were commerce and port activity. Beginning in the 1960s and continuing throughout and after the Iran–Iraq War (1980–1988), Ahvaz developed as a major industrial center. The population was 804,980 in the 1996 census.

See also IRAN.

PARVANEH POURSHARIATI

AICHA, LALLA
[1930–]

Eldest sister of King Hassan II of Morocco.

Lalla Aicha was born in the royal palace of Rabat in 1930. Her father, King Muhammed V, gave her the same primary education as he gave his sons. In 1942, she was one of the first women in Morocco to pass the exam allowing access to secondary schools. In 1947, she delivered a speech in Tangiers on behalf of her father without wearing a veil. It was a major political event in Morocco, which was at this time a French Protectorate, marking the accession of Moroccan women to modernity. Her gesture was intended to encourage fathers to send their daughters to school, and some did so, although others were critical. When Morocco gained independence in 1956, real change of the legal status of women was not forthcoming. The Moroccan code of personal status, al-Moudawana, is considered restrictive.

As king, Lalla Aicha's brother, Hassan II, appointed her ambassador to the United Kingdom (1965–1969), Greece (1969–1970), and Italy (1970–1973). Since 1973, she has remained active in charities and in the Red Crescent Society.

See also HASSAN II; MOUDAWANA, AL-.

RABIA BEKKAR

AIN SHAMS UNIVERSITY

The second largest university in Egypt.

Ain Shams (or Ayn Shams) University was established in Cairo in 1950 under the name Ibrahim Pasha University. In the wake of the 1952 revolution it was renamed Heliopolis University for about a year, then changed to an Arabic equivalent—Ain Shams. The founders evoked the tradition of learning associated with the ancient temple of the sun god Ra-Horakhty (who was depicted as a hawk) in the city of On (Heliopolis to the Greeks). The colleges of arts, science, commerce, education, engineering, and agriculture evolved from pre-existing higher institutes scattered around Cairo; the college of medicine had been a branch of Fuad I (Cairo) University. After the revolution, the administration, which had been located in the Munira district, was moved to the Za'afaran palace on the main campus in Abbasiyya. The university differed from the older universities of Cairo and Alexandria in maintaining a separate college for women, which had evolved out of a teacher-training institute and became almost a mini-university in itself.

The university consists of thirteen faculties and seven institutes and research centers covering a broad spectrum of specializations including law, arts, commerce, medicine, engineering, language, and agriculture. In 2002 it had about 127,000 students and a teaching staff of 6,450.

The university library consists of the central library and the faculty libraries, which contain valuable manuscripts, maps, drawings, encyclopedias, and collections of books. Full medical care is provided for its undergraduate and graduate students. The university has a central residential campus with various branches in different quarters. The main body of male residences, ten buildings, is situated at Khalifa al-Mamun Street near the university, whereas the main body of female dormitories, eight buildings, is situated at the faculty of women, some distance away from the main campus.

Each faculty has a student union that consists of elected members. Unions cooperate with the student welfare offices of the faculties in taking care of all student activities.

Bibliography

Ain Shams University web site. Available from <http://Asunet.shams.eun.eg/>.

Reid, Donald Malcolm. *Cairo University and the Making of Modern Egypt.* Cambridge, U.K.: Cambridge University Press, 1990.

The World of Learning 2004. London and New York: Europa Publications, 2004: 489–490.

DONALD MALCOLM REID

AIOC

See ANGLO–IRANIAN OIL COMPANY

AIPAC

See AMERICAN ISRAEL POLITICAL AFFAIRS COMMITTEE

AISHA: ARAB WOMEN'S FORUM

A network of progressive Arab women's organizations dedicated to promoting the rights of Arab women.

The Arab Women's Forum was founded by a group of Arab women's organizations in December 1992 in order to enhance collaboration and promote shared objectives. Members of the group include nongovernmental organizations from North Africa and the Levant. Objectives include the advancement of democratic principles, legal rights for Arab women, gender equality in all areas of society, and women's participation in the public sphere at the decision-making levels, as well as confronting all forms of discriminations against girls and women. It addresses such issues as violence against women, media portrayals of women, the promotion of human rights, and laws that discriminate against girls and women, and it works to educate women, especially on reproductive rights and on other health care and feminist concerns. It organizes panels, conferences, and presentations on these issues and on others that pertinent to women's lives. It also provides resources for research and awareness.

The forum also maintains a Web site, called NISAA (*women* in Arabic). This helps creates a network for Arab women and organizations, allowing them to make connections, exchange ideas, and share research and documentation on women's experiences. The Web site is maintained by the Women's Center, a legal aid and counseling center in Jerusalem, run by a Palestinian private organization. The forum relies heavily on the Internet to act as a central clearinghouse for ideas and research in its fight against injustices affecting women.

See also GENDER: GENDER AND EDUCATION; GENDER: GENDER AND LAW; GENDER: GENDER AND POLITICS.

Bibliography

Arab Women's Forum. NISAA: An Arab Women's Web Site. Available at <http://www.nisaa.org>.

"Discussing the Exclusion of Women in the Arab World from the Effective Protection of International Human Rights Law." Available from <http://bunian.org.jo>.

MIRNA LATTOUF

AIS (ISLAMIC SALVATION ARMY)

See ISLAMIC SALVATION ARMY (AIS)

AIT AHMED, HOCINE
[1926–]

Algerian revolutionary, opposition party, and Kabyle (Berber) leader.

Although his father served as a colonial magistrate (*caid,* or *qa'id*), Hocine Ait Ahmed joined Messali Hadj's nationalist Parti du Peuple Algérien (PPA) and its successor, the Mouvement pour le Triomphe des Libertés Démocratiques (MTLD). He headed the paramilitary Organisation Spéciale (OS) until accused of "Berberist" tendencies. He left Algeria in 1951 but became one of the cofounders of the revolutionary Front de Libération Nationale (FLN) in 1954. During the War of Independence he led the FLN delegation to the Bandung Conference in April 1955. French colonial authorities skyjacked an Air Maroc flight carrying Ait Ahmed in October 1956 along with other chief FLN leaders, including Ahmed Ben Bella, Mohamed Boudiaf, and Mohamed Khider. Ait Ahmed spent the rest of the war in prison. After his release, he helped to draft the Tripoli Programme of June 1962.

Opposed to Ben Bella and his ally, Colonel Houari Boumédienne, Ait Ahmed organized the Front des Forces Socialistes (FFS) in 1963 and led the Kabyles in revolt against the government. He was captured but escaped from prison in 1966 and fled to exile in France and then Switzerland. He denounced the National Charter of 1976 as an undemocratic document. Ait Ahmed blamed Algerian special services for the murder in April 1987 of André-Ali Mecili, an activist of Kabyle descent. After the destabilizing October 1988 riots, he returned to Algeria in December 1989. The FFS was legalized as an opposition party. He actively campaigned in the national parliamentary elections of December 1991 to January 1992 and organized a huge rally in Algiers in support of democracy. Although he had reservations regarding the Islamist Front Islamique du Salut (FIS), the expected winner of the elections, Ait Ahmed condemned the forced resignation of President Chadli Bendjedid and the cancellation of the elections by Haut Comité d'Etat in January 1992. In July 2002 he rebuked

General Khaled Nezzar, the chief architect of the overthrow of the government, calling the coup d'état "a catastrophe." Ait Ahmed supported the Sant Egidio Platform (national contract) of January 1995. The FFS has participated in national (1997) and local (2002) elections. Ait Ahmed was one of six presidential candidates who withdrew in protest over irregularities before the April 1999 presidential election. He reproached the government of President Abdelaziz Bouteflika after the killing of a Kabyle youth in police detention in April 2001 incited violent protest and severe suppression. Ait Ahmed is a fervent advocate of democracy, political pluralism, and human (especially Berber) rights. He authored *La Guerre et l'après guerre* (1964; The war and the aftermath) and *Mémoires d'un combattant* (1983; Memories of a combatant).

See also ALGERIA: POLITICAL PARTIES IN; ALGERIAN WAR OF INDEPENDENCE.

Bibliography

Agence France Presse. "Algerian Opposition Leader Accuses General of Election 'Coup.'" 4 July 2002.

Naylor, Phillip C. *The Historical Dictionary of Algeria,* 3d edition. Lanham, MD: Scarecrow Press, 2005.

PHILLIP C. NAYLOR

AJMAN

Smallest of the seven emirates comprising the United Arab Emirates.

Ajman extends over a distance of 10 miles (about 100 square miles) between the emirates of Sharjah and Umm al-Qaywayn, and covers about 0.3 percent of the total area of the United Arab Emirates (U.A.E.). The emirate is composed of three regions: the town of Ajman, which includes the commercial district; Masfut, an agricultural area in the southeastern mountainous portion of the emirate; and Manama in the eastern portion of the emirate. The population of Ajman was estimated to be 118,812 in 1995. The ruler of Ajman is Shaykh Humayd bin Rashid Al Nu'aymi.

The Ajman economy has traditionally relied on fishing and trade. In recent years the general economic development trend in the U.A.E. has extended to Ajman as well. The emirate has attracted numerous commercial and industrial enterprises due to its proximity to the commercial centers of Dubai and Sharjah and its relatively low rents. Especially prominent additions to the economy are the Free Zone, Ajman City Centre shopping complex, and several resort hotels, including the Ajman Kempinski, which is a popular destination for European and U.A.E. resident tourists. Ajman also hosts educational institutions: the Gulf Medical College Ajman and the Ajman University College of Science and Technology.

Ajman is perhaps best known for its cultural attractions. The Ajman Museum, which opened in 1981, is set in an eighteenth-century fort. The Dhow Yard is one of the most active boatbuilding yards in the country. Al Muwayhat was discovered in 1986 and is a major archaeological site on the outskirts of the city of Ajman.

See also ABU DHABI.

Bibliography

Camerapix, ed. *Spectrum Guide to the United Arab Emirates.* New York: Interlink Books, 2002.

KAREN HUNT AHMED

AKBULUT, AHMET ZIYA
[1869–1938]

Ottoman Turkish painter.

Born in Istanbul, Ahmet Ziya Akbulut was graduated from the Ottoman Empire's military academy in 1877 and spent the next fifteen years painting in the art studio of the General Staff. A student of Hoca Ali Riza, Akbulut was known for his close attention to perspective, about which he wrote articles. He taught painting at the Fine Arts Academy and at the military school.

DAVID WALDNER

AKÇURA, YUSUF
[1876–1935]

Turkish nationalist and writer.

Born Yusuf Akçurin in the Russian city of Simbirsk (Ulyanovsk), on the Volga river, Yusuf Akçura migrated to Istanbul, capital of the Ottoman Empire, with his family at an early age. He studied at a military school there and then at the Institut des Sciences Politiques in Paris, where he met several Young Turks. In 1904, Akçura wrote the first manifesto of Turkish nationalism, "Uç Tarz-i Siyaset" (Three Ways of Government), in which he considered Ottomanism and pan-Islam to be impractical routes for Turkish political development. Akçura soon became one of the most influential nationalists—promoting Pan-Turkism before World War I. He spent a number of years in Russia spreading Turkish nationalist ideas, returning to Istanbul after the Young Turk revolution of 1908.

Akçura was a cofounder of the Türk Yurdu Cemiyati (Turkish Homeland Society) in 1911, with Ziya Gökalp, publisher of its famous periodical *Türk Yurdu*. The group campaigned to simplify the Turkish language, to adopt the customs of Western civilization, and to promote the interests of Turks inside and outside the Ottoman Empire. He joined the Kemalist movement in 1921, but maintained that it was the embodiment of pan-Turkism, and continued to write on Turkism for Russian Turks.

See also GÖKALP, ZIYA; NEWSPAPERS AND PRINT MEDIA; PAN-TURKISM; YOUNG TURKS.

Bibliography

Arai, Masami. *Turkish Nationalism in the Young Turk Era.* New York: E. J. Brill, 1992.

ELIZABETH THOMPSON

AKHAVAN-SALESS, MEHDI
[1928–1991]

Iranian poet and literary critic who wrote under the pen name Mim Omid, or Omid.

Born in Mashhad, Mehdi Akhavan-Saless later lived in Khorramshahr and Tehran. During his youth, he was politically active and was imprisoned briefly after the coup d'état of 1953.

Akhavan's first published collection of verse, *Zemestan* (Winter; 1956), expresses a nostalgia for love by using nature imagery. His later verse at times reflects a deep cynicism and sarcasm, and at times is lively and witty. Akhavan is known for his long narrative poetry, which captures the reader's attention with its flowing dialogues. In addition to po-

etry, Akhavan has written a book for children, *Derakht-e Pir va Jangal* (The old tree and the jungle), and articles on literary criticism brought together as *Majmu'a-ye Maqalat* (Collection of articles).

Bibliography

Karimi-Hakkak, Ahmad, ed. and trans. *An Anthology of Modern Persian Poetry.* Boulder, CO: Westview Press, 1978.

PARDIS MINUCHEHR

AKHBAR, AL- (EGYPT)

See NEWSPAPERS AND PRINT MEDIA: ARAB COUNTRIES

AKHBAR, AL- (JORDAN)

See NEWSPAPERS AND PRINT MEDIA: ARAB COUNTRIES

AKHBAR AL-YAWM

See NEWSPAPERS AND PRINT MEDIA: ARAB COUNTRIES

AKHBARI

The school of Shi'ite jurisprudence.

Origins of the Akhbari can be traced to the twelfth century. It firmly rejected *ijtihad,* or the power of *ulama* to interpret the Qur'an and the teachings of the Prophet of Islam. Rather, it emphasized the supremacy of the teachings of God, the Prophet, and the infallible imams of Twelver Shi'ism, arguing that Islamic law can be derived directly from the *akhbar,* or traditions of the imams and the Prophet.

Akhbari traditionalism reemerged in the seventeenth and eighteenth centuries in Safavi Iran. Undermining the position of an independent clergy, the Akhbari school, at least by extension, advocated a fusion between government and religion by rejecting all forms of intercession between believers and the Prophet, plus his twelve infallible progeny. From the ascendancy of the Safavis to the nineteenth century, most Akhbari clerics resided in the shrine cities of Iraq. In Iran, the Akhbaris were eventually defeated by the rival Usuli camp, which favored a hegemonic clerical hierarchy. In Bahrain, however, Akhbarism triumphed by the end of the eighteenth century. During the Iranian constitutional revolution from 1905 to 1911, elements of Akhbari teachings were drawn upon by pro-constitutionalist *ulama* in refuting challenges by more conservative clergymen who objected to the un-Islamic nature of constitutionalism.

See also USULI.

Bibliography

Cole, Juan. *Sacred Space and Holy War: The Politics, Culture and History of Shi'ite Islam.* London: Tauris, 2002.

Gleave, Robert, and Kermeli, Eugenia. *Islamic Law: Theory and Practice.* London and New York: Tauris, 2001.

Hairi, Abdul Hadi. *Shi'ism and Constitutionalism in Iran: A Study of the Role Played by the Persian Residents of Iraq in Iranian politics.* Leiden, Netherlands: Brill, 1977.

Mazzaoui, Michel, ed. *Safavid Iran and Her Neighbors.* Salt Lake City: University of Utah Press, 2003.

NEGUIN YAVARI

AKHIR SA'A

See NEWSPAPERS AND PRINT MEDIA: ARAB COUNTRIES

AKHONDZADEH, MIRZA FATH ALI

[1812–1878]

Azerbaijani playwright, propagator of atheism, and proponent of alphabet reform.

After an early education in Azerbaijan along traditional lines, Mirza Fath Ali Akhondzadeh entered a Russian school in Tiflis (Tbilisi, Russian Georgia), where he swiftly mastered the Russian language and became acquainted with European literature and ideas. He was soon a pronounced Russophile, and from 1834 until the end of his life, he was continuously in the employ of the Russian government. His most important literary works were six satirical comedies, written in Azerbaijani Turkish (Azeri), intended to discredit the traditional classes of the Muslim world and their beliefs and to propagate a positivist worldview. Important for the development of modern Azerbaijani literature, these plays were also widely circulated in Persia (now Iran), in Persian translation.

Akhondzadeh expressed his hostility to Islam more systematically in a series of fictitious letters attributed to two princes, one Persian and the other Indian, in which the criticisms of Islam current in Christian nineteenth-century Europe were fully reflected. Among the Persian politicians and reformers with whom he was in contact, the most significant was Mirza Malkom Khan (Malkum Khan), with whom he shared not only a belief in the need for unconditional Westernization but also an enthusiasm for reforming the Arabic alphabet in its application to the Persian and Turkish languages by introducing letters to indicate vowels.

See also AZERI LANGUAGE AND LITERATURE; ISLAM; MALKOM KHAN, MIRZA.

HAMID ALGAR

AKKAD, MUSTAFA

[1935–]

Hollywood-trained Syrian-American filmmaker.

Mustafa Akkad was born in Aleppo, Syria, and moved to Los Angles in 1954 to study filmmaking. He worked as an assistant to the director Sam Peckinpah and then worked in American television, producing a public affairs show, *As Others See Us,* as well as documentaries and a syndicated travel show.

In 1976 Akkad directed his first feature film, *The Message,* which tells the story of the birth and early growth of Islam. Before filming, he submitted drafts of his script to Islamic scholars at al-Azhar University in Cairo for approval. Respecting Islamic injunctions against representing the Prophet, Akkad shot the film so that Muhammad is neither seen nor heard. Two versions were filmed, one in English with an international cast including Anthony Quinn and another in Arabic with an Arab cast.

In 1977, when the film was finally released in the United States, its first showing was delayed because of a hostage-taking incident in Washington, D.C., and the film faced protests from Muslim groups in both the United States and the Islamic world. Scholars at al-Azhar ended up condemning the film, and it was banned across the Arab world with the exception of Libya, where it had been filmed. Arab and Muslim audiences have nevertheless been able to view it on video, and in 2003 Egyptian authorities sought to lift the ban.

Akkad's second historical epic, *Lion of the Desert,* released in 1981, portrays the proto-nationalist struggle of Libyan resistance leader Umar al-Mukhtar, who used guerrilla tactics to fight Mussolini's Italian army in the early 1930s.

Although neither film met with commercial or critical success, they represent a form of transnational filmmaking in which narratives of Islamic and Arab history are told to global audiences within the conventions of Western film. Akkad's efforts to make other epic films, including ones on Gamal Abdel Nasser and Hannibal, faced financing difficulties, but in 2004 he began scouting locations in Jordan for a film about Saladin.

While making *Lion of the Desert,* Akkad agreed to finance a low-budget horror film, *Halloween* (1978), which became the highest-grossing independent film up to that time. It spawned a series of big-budget sequels and made Akkad one of the most successful Arab-American producers working in Hollywood.

See also FILM; MUKHTAR, UMAR AL-.

WALEED HAZBUN

AKP (JUSTICE AND DEVELOPMENT PARTY)

Political party with Islamic roots that was formed in 2001 and swept Turkey's 2002 parliamentary elections.

The Justice and Development Party (Adalet ve Kalkünma Partisi), known in Turkey by its Turkish acronym, AKP, was formed by a group of reformist politicians with roots in the Islamic movement. Its most prominent leaders are Abdullah Gül and Tayyip R. Erdoğan. After the Constitutional Court closed the Virtue Party, the successor to the banned Refah Partisi, its conservative faction founded the Felicity Party (Saadet Partisi) in 2001. The more moderate members broke away to form AKP in August 2001, thereby cementing a division in the Islamic political movement.

AKP defined itself not as a splinter group of the Virtue Party but as a dynamic new conservative-modern force for rebuilding the collapsing center

The leader of Turkey's Justice and Development Party, Recep Tayyip Erdogan, greets his supporters at a November 2002 rally in Bursa. © REUTERS NEWMEDIA INC./CORBIS. REPRODUCED BY PERMISSION.

of politics by redefining the political domain in terms of the needs of the populace. It is a socially conservative, Muslim-Turkish party that espouses economically liberal policies and integration with the European Union (EU). The charisma of Erdoğan, his conservative lifestyle, and his role as a generational bridge between younger and older voters gave the AKP broad appeal. The AKP capitalized on the public consensus about joining EU and curtailing the role of the Turkey's military-bureaucratic elite.

The AKP's success in the 2002 elections gave the socially Muslim party an opportunity to restructure the political landscape and expand civil rights. Of the eighteen political parties that competed for seats in the parliament, only two actually won any because parties are required to obtain 10 percent of the nationwide vote in order to seat representatives in the assembly. The AKP had the larger share, winning 34.26 percent of the popular vote and 363 of the 550 seats in parliament. The Republican People's Party won almost 19.40 percent of the votes, securing 178 seats. Independent candidates unaffiliated with any party on the other nine seats. The AKP formed the government under the leadership of Abdullah Gül because the party's leader, Erdoğan, was banned from being on the ballot in the elections. After AKP assumed control of the parliament, it passed legislation to annul the ban on Erdoğan; he subsequently won a seat in a by-election and in March 2003 became prime minister.

AKP's identity and ideology is a pragmatic form of Islamic politics, and for that reason the party has broad appeal. It is simultaneously Turkish, Muslim, and Western. This pluralist aspect has worked well politically, given the diverse lifestyles in Turkey. The AKP's Islamism has a very heavy Turkish accent, rooted in the Turko-Ottoman ethos of communal life and a sense of leadership that requires full obedience to the party "ruler," Erdoğan.

See also ERDOĞAN, TAYYIP; REFAH PARTISI; REPUBLICAN PEOPLE'S PARTY (RPP).

Bibliography

Yavuz, M. Hakan. *Islamic Political Identity in Turkey.* New York: Oxford University Press, 2003.

M. HAKAN YAVUZ

AKRAD, HAYY AL-

Kurdish quarter on the slopes of the mountain of Qasiyun, overlooking Damascus, Syria; the other two quarters are the Muhajirin and the Salihiyya.

The three quarters owe their existence to the water of the river Yazid, a tributary of the Barada River, which splits from it in the gorge of al-Rabwa. While al-Muhajirin was created by the municipality of Damascus, capital of Syria, and the Salihiyya is almost a replica of Damascus, Hayy al-Akrad has been described as a sheer fantasy. Its streets, though wide, are irregular and do not present a defensive aspect like those of Damascus because its inhabitants, the Kurds, were feared and not attacked.

Still inhabited mostly by Kurds, Hayy al-Akrad was originally a village for Kurds, starting in the time of Saladin in the twelfth century, and attracted a new wave of Kurdish immigrants in the nineteenth century. Engaged primarily in livestock trade and serving in the military and as aides in tax-farming, the Kurds polarized around their clan leaders, who

played major roles in the life of Damascus as notables, landowners, military chieftains, and also Communists. The head of the Communist Party since its early years has been the octogenarian Khalid Bakdash, who comes from Hayy al-Akrad and has the support of many of its Kurdish inhabitants.

See also KURDS.

ABDUL-KARIM RAFEQ

AKSARIYAT

See FEDA'IYAN-E KHALQ

AL-

See GLOSSARY

ALA, HOSEYN
[1883–1964]

Iranian statesman.

Hoseyn Ala, son of Mirza Mohammad Ali Khan Ala al-Saltaneh, was also known as the Mu'in al-Wizara. Similar to many political dignitaries of Pahlavi Iran, his father had served the Qajars as prime minister, minister, and ambassador, and was a main actor in the constitutional revolution from 1905 to 1911. Hoseyn Ala filled cabinet posts in the Ministries of Foreign Affairs, Finance, Agriculture, Trade, Court, and Public Welfare. He served as a delegate to the Paris Peace Conference following World War I, was Iran's chief delegate to the United Nations after World War II, and served as ambassador to the United States, Spain, and England.

Considered a royalist, Hoseyn Ala was appointed as prime minister by the monarch Mohammad Reza Pahlavi in 1951, following the assassination of Prime Minister Razmara by an Islamic group, the Feda'iyan-e Islam. During his tenure as prime minister, the Iranian Parliament passed the Oil Nationalization Bill of 1951. Unable to withstand public pressure in favor of nationalization, Ala resigned his position in 1952, and resumed his duties as Minister of Court. He was appointed as prime minister for a second time in 1955, and headed Iran's delegation to the first meeting of the Baghdad Pact, held in Iraq in 1955. Political dissatisfaction with the Baghdad Pact was manifested in an assassination attempt on Ala's life, before his departure to Baghdad, by a member of the Feda'iyan-e Islam. In 1957, Ala was reappointed as Minister of Court, retaining his position until 1963, when he was demoted to senator because of his opposition to the shah's policies in the quelling of the June 1963 uprisings.

See also PAHLAVI, MOHAMMAD REZA.

NEGUIN YAVARI

ALAINI, MUHSIN

See AYNI, MUHSIN AL-

AL AL-SHAYKH FAMILY

An important family or clan in Saudi Arabia; one of only two nonroyal families, the other being the Al Sudayri, with whom Al Sa'ud princes may marry.

The Al al-Shaykh (the family of the Shaykh) are descendants of Muhammad ibn Abd al-Wahhab, the Islamic reformer who formed an alliance with Muhammad ibn Sa'ud in the mid-eighteenth century. This association has shaped their families' fortunes and those of most of the Arabian peninsula since. Ibn Abd al-Wahhab was born in 1703 in the Najd, probably in the central Arabian town of al-Uyayna. Influenced by the strict teachings of Ibn Taymiya, a thirteenth-fourteenth century jurist of the conservative Hanbali Law School, he returned home from prolonged study to preach a simple, puritanical faith that eschewed theological innovations and aimed at countering the moral laxity of his Najdi contemporaries. Those who accepted his teaching and its emphasis on tawhid, the oneness of the Qur'anic god unchallenged and untainted by any earthly attributes, were Muwahhidun (unitarians), known outside Arabia as Wahhabis. Unwelcome in al-Uyayna, the preacher moved to al-Dir'iya, where Muhammad ibn Sa'ud was amir, ruler of a district in Najd. The latter's political leadership and the military abilities of his son, Abd al-Aziz, combined with the reformer's zeal, brought all of Najd under Saudi rule within thirty years. In 1803, the year of his death by assassination, Abd al-Aziz took Mecca, and his son Sa'ud expanded the first Saudi state over the course of the next decade to approximately its present limits.

During his lifetime, Ibn Abd al-Wahhab was the imam (Muslim spiritual leader) of the expanding Saudi state, a title conveying responsibility for enforcing norms of correct Islamic belief and behavior as well as carrying the Wahhabi interpretation of Islam to the rest of the Islamic world and beyond. When he died, the title passed to the Al Sa'ud rulers. The shaykh's descendants did not exercise direct political power in the decades that followed, although they were accorded special respect. The Al Sa'ud have continued the practice of intermarriage with members of the Al al-Shaykh, begun when Abd al-Aziz ibn Muhammad married a daughter of Muhammad ibn Abd al-Wahhab. The late King Faisal's mother was Tarfa bint Abdullah, daughter of a distinguished Al al-Shaykh scholar and jurist, making Faisal the great-great-great grandson of the original shaykh. Moreover, the family continued to produce religious leaders who exercised great influence on all decision-making in a state whose legitimacy depended on adherence to and propagation of Muwahhidin beliefs. Members of the Al al-Shaykh held the post of qadi (judge) of Riyadh, the Saudi capital, and later the position of grand mufti, highest judicial office in the state.

In recent years the position of the Al al-Shaykh has changed in significant ways. In 1969, as part of his effort to create a more efficient government securely under Al Sa'ud control, King Faisal ibn Abd al-Aziz abolished the office of grand mufti and replaced it with a ministry of justice. Although the first minister of justice deliberately was not an Al al-Shaykh, subsequent ministers have been. Moreover, from the early 1960s on, members of the Al al-Shaykh have held ministerial positions. The family's representation in the cabinet dropped from three to two members with the reshuffle of April 2003: minister of justice, Dr. Abdullah ibn Muhammad ibn Ibrahim Al al-Shaykh; and minister of Islamic affairs, waqf, *da'wa*, and *irshad*, Salih ibn Abd al-Aziz ibn Muhammad Al al-Shaykh. Other members of the family serve in important military and civilian capacities, as well as serving as qadis and other religious figures. Although the Al al-Shaykh domination of the religious establishment has diminished in recent decades, the family alliance is still crucial to the Al Sa'ud in maintaining their legitimacy. At the same time, the Al al-Shaykh wholeheartedly support the continued rule of the Al Sa'ud because of the exceedingly close ties between the two families.

See also AL SAʿUD FAMILY; MUWAHHIDUN; SHAYKH.

Bibliography

Helms, Christine Moss. *The Cohesion of Saudi Arabia: Evolution of Political Identity.* Baltimore, MD: Johns Hopkins University Press; London: Croom Helm, 1981.

Holden, David, and Johns, Richard. *The House of Saud: The Rise and Rule of the Most Powerful Dynasty in the Arab World.* New York: Holt, Rinehart, and Winston, 1981.

Kechichian, Joseph A. *Succession in Saudi Arabia.* New York: Palgrave, 2001.

MALCOLM C. PECK
UPDATED BY J. E. PETERSON

ALAM, AMIR ASADOLLAH

[1919–1978]

Iranian politician of the Pahlavi period.

Amir Asadollah Alam was the son of Showkat al-Molk Alam, who was governor of Birjand under Mozaffar al-Din Shah of the Qajars and also a member of Reza Shah Pahlavi's inner court. He was born in Birjand into a family that originally came from an Arab tribe of the southern region of Khuzistan. Patronized by Reza Shah from the start, Alam married Malektaj Qavam, the sister-in-law of Ashraf Pahlavi, the shah's daughter. His long-standing friendship with the crown prince was fostered in this period. Alam was one of the few members of Iran's traditional aristocracy who not only manifested his loyalty to the Pahlavi dynasty from the very start, but repeatedly did so in the course of an unusually long political career during which he held several gubernatorial and ministerial positions. A confidant of the new shah, Mohammad Reza Shah Pahlavi, he was ordered to found the Mardom (People's) Party, which was envisioned as the party of loyal opposition. In 1962, Alam was appointed prime minister, to facilitate the implementation of the White Revolution, launched in 1963 by the shah. He was also prime minister at the time of the uprisings engineered by Ayatollah Ruhollah Khomeini in Qom (1963), in protest against the White Revolution. In 1964, he was appointed president of the Pahlavi University in Shiraz, and under his leadership it became Iran's model university. In 1966, he was ap-

pointed minister of court, and in this capacity he allegedly was one of the strongest influences on the shah. He retained this position until 1977, when he was forced to resign because of illness. He died in 1978 of leukemia.

See also KHOMEINI, RUHOLLAH; MARDOM PARTY; PAHLAVI, MOHAMMAD REZA; PAHLAVI, REZA; WHITE REVOLUTION (1961–1963).

Bibliography

Alam, Amir Assadollah. *The Shah and I: The Confidential Diary of Iran's Royal Court, 1969–1977,* edited by Alinaghi Alikhani. New York: St. Martin's, 1991.

NEGUIN YAVARI

ALAMAYN, AL-

Village in northwest Egypt, on the Mediterranean, northeast of the Qattara depression, site of the battle of El Alamein, where the British drove back the Germans in a pivotal battle of World War II, 23 October–4 November 1942.

General Bernard Law Montgomery's British and Commonwealth Eighth Army met and overcame General Erwin Rommel's German–Italian Afrika Korps at al-Alamayn, approximately 80 miles (128.7 km) west of Alexandria. The retreat of Rommel's forces ended the Axis threat to conquer Egypt and seize the Suez Canal. Montgomery had some 195,000 men, 1,150 tanks, and 1,900 guns against Rommel's 100,000 men, 530 tanks, and 1,325 guns. Montgomery attacked at 9:30 P.M. on 23 October with an artillery barrage from 1,000 guns. The Afrika Korps held and counterattacked on 27 October. Montgomery resumed the offensive the next day, with a weeklong tank battle. British air superiority and force of numbers wore down the Afrika Korps, and Rommel withdrew a few miles to the west on 1 November. Another attack on 3 November resulted in Rommel's ordering another withdrawal, at first countermanded by Adolf Hitler, but finally approved. Montgomery's pursuit on 5 November stalled because of a rainstorm, and Rommel was able to disengage his force and retreat to the Libyan border by 7 November. The Afrika Korps had 59,000 men killed, wounded, and captured and lost some 500 tanks and 400 guns, against

Eighth Army losses of 13,500 men, 500 tanks, and 100 guns. Moreover, most of the British tanks were reparable while Rommel had only twenty operational tanks at the end of the fighting.

Bibliography

Pitt, Barrie. *The Crucible of War.* London: Cassell, 2001.

DANIEL E. SPECTOR

ALAMI FAMILY, AL-

A leading Arab family in Jerusalem that claimed direct descent from Hasan, a grandson of the prophet Muhammad.

The Alami ancestors migrated in the seventh century C.E. from Arabia to Morocco, where they adopted the name *Alam,* from Mount Alam. In the twelfth century Shaykh Muhammad al-Alami assisted Salah al-Din in expelling the Crusaders from Palestine and Lebanon and was granted substantial land, including most of the Mount of Olives in Jerusalem. The family played a prominent role in the civil and religious life of Jerusalem during the following centuries.

Faydi al-Alami (1865–1924) was the leading family member in the late Ottoman period. He worked in the finance department, as a tax assessor, as district officer of Bethlehem in 1902 and of Jerusalem in 1904, and as mayor of Jerusalem (1906–1909). He was then elected to the administrative council for the Jerusalem district and, in 1914, to the parliament in Istanbul. He returned to Palestine after World War I.

Musa al-Alami (1897–1984), Faydi's son, was born on 8 May 1897 in Jerusalem and was drafted into the Ottoman army during World War I. Musa studied law at Cambridge University from 1919 to 1924. The British administration appointed him junior legal adviser in 1925, assistant government advocate in 1929, private secretary to the high commissioner in 1932–1933, and then government advocate until 1937. Musa criticized the British tax policy that increased rural indebtedness and thereby encouraged land sales to Jewish land-purchasing organizations. He urged the British to balance the interests of the Arab and Jewish communities and to establish a legislative assembly. In June 1936 the high commissioner allowed him to circulate a petition that 137 senior Arab government officials signed, calling upon the government to suspend Jewish immigration as a precondition for ending the Arabs' general strike, which had begun in April.

Alami was fired in October 1937 after the Peel Commission report recommended his replacement by a British advocate. Forced into exile in Lebanon and then Iraq, he served in the Palestinian delegation to the London conference in 1939, then was allowed home to Palestine in 1941. In 1944 Alami represented the Palestinians at the Alexandria conference that established the League of Arab States. Alami had close relations with Arab leaders, notably his father-in-law, the Syrian nationalist Ihsan Jabri. Alami persuaded the conference participants to set up a fund to improve conditions in Palestinian villages and buy land from impoverished farmers, and also to establish information offices abroad to promote Arab perspectives on Palestine. Alami headed the London information office and organized the Constructive Scheme to help villages. In late 1945 the Arab League forced Alami to place these efforts under the Husayni-dominated Arab Higher Committee (AHC). By December 1947 Alami and his brother-in-law Jamal Husayni established rival information offices abroad.

Alami was in London during the Arab-Israel War of 1948–1949. Israel seized his property in Jerusalem and his agricultural land in the Baysan and Jaffa districts. Afterward, he established the Arab Development Society, which ran an orphanage for refugee boys on reclaimed land near Jericho. Despite the difficulty of growing produce, raising poultry, and promoting dairy products in that saline environment well below sea level, Alami turned the orphanage into a flourishing enterprise. During the 1967 war the Israeli army overran the farm; most of its residents fled to Jordan, but the farm continued, albeit at a sharply reduced level. After Alami's death in 1984, an international board of directors maintained the project.

Bibliography

Furlonge, Geoffrey. *Palestine Is My Country: The Story of Musa Alami.* New York: Praeger; London: Murray, 1969.

Muslih, Muhammad Y. *The Origins of Palestinian Nationalism.* New York: Columbia University Press, 1988.

Porath, Yehoshua. *The Palestinian Arab National Movement: From Riots to Rebellion*, Vol. 2: 1929–1939. London: Frank Cass, 1977.

ANN M. LESCH

ALAMI, MUSA AL-

See ALAMI FAMILY

ALAVI, BOZORG
[1904–1997]

One of Iran's most important twentieth-century writers.

Alavi was born in Tehran into a wealthy merchant family. Both his father and grandfather were active supporters the Constitutional Revolution. His father, Mortezar Alavi, opposed the British and Russian presence in Iran and during World War I fled to Germany, where he became one of the founders of the Iranian exile journal *Kaveh*. In 1921, Alavi and his older brother joined their father in Germany; he finished high school there and completed the equivalent of a B.A. at the University of Munich. Alavi returned to Iran in 1928 and initially taught at a technical school in Shiraz. He joined the faculty of a German technical high school in Tehran during 1931. At this school he became acquainted with several other foreign-educated Iranians, especially Dr. Taqi Arani, and he eventually joined Arani's weekly study circle, which read and discussed the works of European Marxists and socialists. The members of Arani's group gradually expanded, and in 1937 the police arrested fifty-three men, whom they charged with forming an illegal Communist party; all were tried and sentenced, with Alavi receiving a seven-year prison term. Arani died in prison, but Alavi and the others were freed in 1941, following the joint Anglo-Soviet invasion and occupation of Iran.

Alavi's first collection of short stories, *Chamedan* (Suitcase), was published in 1934. His prison experiences resulted in a second collection of short stories, *Varaq parehha-ye zendan* (Paper scraps of prison; Tehran: N.p., 1942), and a powerful account of his trial, *Panjah-o-seh nafar* (Fifty-three persons; Tehran: N.p., 1944). Although Alavi was among the founders of the Tudeh Party in 1941 and participated in party meetings, literary pursuits rather than

political activities seem to have occupied most of his time. He was a close friend of Sadegh Hedayat and regularly socialized with other prominent writers of the 1941 through 1953 period. He also continued to write, and his most famous work in Persian, the novel *Cheshmahayesh* (Her eyes), appeared in 1952. Alavi had left Iran for East Germany to take up a visiting appointment at Humboldt University when the 1953 coup d'état against the government of Mohammad Mossadegh took place. He decided not to return home, but remained in East Berlin, where he married a German woman and became a professor of Persian literature. He published several scholarly books about Iran in German during the 1950s and 1960s. After the Iranian Revolution, he made brief visits to Iran in 1979 and 1980.

See also CONSTITUTIONAL REVOLUTION; HEDAYAT, SADEGH; IRANIAN REVOLUTION (1979); MOSSADEGH, MOHAMMAD; TUDEH PARTY.

Bibliography

Raffat, Donné. *The Prison Papers of Bozorg Alavi: A Literary Odyssey.* Syracuse, NY: Syracuse University Press, 1985.

ERIC HOOGLUND

ALAWI

An offshoot of Isma'ilism.

Historically both the Druze and the Alawis are offshoots of Isma'ilism, which was an earlier split from the Shi'ite Imamis. The Shi'a are distinguishable in important respects from the majority of Muslims, namely the orthodox Sunnis, who believe and accept the *sunna* (sayings and doings) of the prophet Muhammad, side by side with the Qur'an, as their main source of inspiration. Although the Sunnis generally have endorsed the caliphate as the legitimate head of political and religious power, the Shi'ite Imamis have by and large rejected the caliph's claim to leadership, recognizing instead Ali ibn Abi Talib, who was the fourth caliph and cousin and son-in-law of the Prophet, as their first imam, or politicoreligious leader, and his two sons Hasan and Husayn as, respectively, the second and third imams. Starting with Ali, the Shi'a leadership progressed through a line of twelve imams, the last of which mysteriously vanished in 878. As such, the twelfth imam is known as the hidden imam.

The Isma'ilis broke with the Shi'ite Imamis over the issue of the succession to the sixth imam Isma'il (d. 760), from whom they claimed to be the legitimate descendants. What historically distinguished the Isma'ilis from the other more orthodox Shi'ia was their secrecy and their belief in the inner and allegorical meanings of the Qur'an. The mainstream Shi'ia, by contrast, held the view of the infallible imam who can guide the community to the right path and who possesses that unique power to interpret the scriptures. Both the Druze and Alawis maintain doctrines close to Isma'ilism.

The Alawis or, to use their more appropriate religious name, the Nusayris, are of an unknown origin, and there is much speculation as to their inner (hidden) beliefs. An accepted reference on their initial rites and doctrines was published in Aleppo in 1859 as *Kitab al-Majmu*. According to its author, Sulayman al-Adhani, the Nusayris, like other sects of the Syrian mountains on the Mediterranean, primarily believed in the transmigration of souls. He also argues that the term *Nusayri* is traceable to Abu Shu'ayb Muhammad (ibn Nusayr al-Abdi al-Bakri al-Namri), who in turn acted as the *bab* (communicator) of Hasan al-Askari (d. 874), the eleventh Shi'ite imam.

It remains uncertain, however, whether any of the historical genealogy and doctrine propounded in the *Kitab* is still held by the majority of Alawis today. Since the French mandate over Syria (1920–1946), the term *Nusayri* has been dropped in favor of the more common *Alawi*, and a doctrinal, if not political, rapprochement has been in the works with the majority of Shi'ias. In 1936 a body of Alawi *ulama* officially declared that "the Alawis are nothing but partisans of the imam Ali . . . the cousin, son-in-law, and executor (*wasi*) of the Messenger." That position was reiterated in a similar *ulama* declaration in 1973, three years after Syrian president Hafiz al-Asad (r. 1970–2000), himself an Alawi, came to power.

Today most Alawis are located in the southern Iskandarun region of Turkey (renamed Hatay by the Turks after its annexation in 1939, and still claimed by the Syrians) and the Syrian coastline. Only in Syria, however, where the Alawis comprise roughly 10 percent of the population, have they gained a political status. Although some had been members of the original Syrian army after the French mandate, and more took positions with al-Ba'th in 1963, it was only under President Asad that their power consolidated. Out of the thirty-one officers whom Asad handpicked between 1970 and 1997 as chief officers in the armed forces, for the élite military formations, and for the security and intelligence apparatus, no fewer than nineteen, or 61.3 percent, have been Alawis. The overall socioeconomic status of the Alawis within the Syrian community at large, however, does not seem to have improved much in the last few decades.

See also ASAD, HAFIZ AL-; ISMA'ILI SHI'ISM; SHI'ISM.

Bibliography

Batatu, Hanna. *Syria's Peasantry, the Descendants of Its Lesser Rural Notables, and Their Politics.* Princeton, NJ: Princeton University Press, 1999.

Seale, Patrick. *Asad of Syria: The Struggle for the Middle East.* Berkeley: University of California Press, 1988.

MAJED HALAWI
UPDATED BY ZOUHAIR GHAZZAL

ALAWITE DYNASTY

Moroccan rulers since 1666.

The Alawite Dynasty is part of the greater sharifian Arab sultanate whose origins are in the Middle East. The Sadi and Alawi (Alawite) sharifians migrated to Morocco from the Arabian Peninsula and settled there as early as the thirteenth century. They claim to be descendants of the prophet Muhammad. The Sadi sharifians gained control over Morocco in the first half of the sixteenth century, wresting it from the former Wattasid rulers.

In 1666, the Sadi family branch lost power to its Alawite counterpart when the latter gained possession of Fez, then the Sharifian capital. Under the Sadi sultans, the country suffered from internal turmoil owing to endless disputes among local petty rulers. When the Alawite dynasty took charge, they curbed the excessive powers of these local rulers and restored the country's political unity. The challenges and achievements of the Alawites can best be

Muhammad IV became king of Morocco upon the death of his father, Hassan II, in July 1999. The new ruler immediately introduced a more progressive and popular tone to the country's government, declaring war on bureaucratic corruption and expressing concern for human rights causes. © AP/WIDE WORLD PHOTOS. REPRODUCED BY PERMISSION.

discussed in two periods, from the onset of their rule to the French protectorate, and from independence in 1956 to the present.

The founders of the Alawite dynasty, Mawlay Rashid (d. 1672), who undertook the early conquests, and Mawlay Isma'il (d. 1727), who consolidated the empire and established a new capital at Meknès, set up a national administration and a workable taxation system to guarantee the trade routes and defend against Christian incursions. They also established an army that proved responsive to the sultanate, not to any local or tribal group. In response to these imperatives, Mawlay Isma'il established a centralized administration and a Janissary-like national army of slaves (abid) loyal to the person of the sultan. Muhammad III (d. 1790) emphasized the family's status as sharifs (nobles) and attempted to establish the regime's legitimacy on a religious basis as defenders of the Muslim community against the encroaching European infidels. Weaker successors eventually capitulated to European demands and, in 1912, France established a protectorate over Morocco and gave Spain control over the northern sector. Muhammad

V (d. 1961) played an instrumental role in the independence process.

Following Morocco's independence, the Alawite regime experienced a different set of challenges in building a postcolonial state. Muhammad V and his successor, Hassan II, inherited a unified nation (despite Spanish possession of Ifni, the Western [Spanish] Sahara, Ceuta, and Melilla), a coherent administration, and a strong popular sense of the regime's legitimacy based on their defense of Moroccan nationalism and the king's position as imam of the Moroccan Muslim community as well as head of state. Their task was to build a modern developed state, ensure the loyalty of divided political and regional groups, deliver social services, and stimulate employment and economic development for a population with heightened expectations. A war in the Western Sahara to reclaim territory considered part of historical Morocco proved popular.

The regime's greatest weaknesses since independence in 1956 have been administrative corruption, periodic disaffection of segments of the armed forces, a limited national resource base, drought, and most important, an expanding population. The regime has been challenged by popular discontent, due in part to the severe strain on state resources as the regime has tried to meet the needs of a rapidly expanding population while at the same time satis-

The Alawite Dynasty

Ruler	Reign
1. al-Rashid	1664–1672
2. Isma'il	1672–1727
3. Ahmad al-Dhahabi *and*	1727–1728
4. Abd al-Malik	[*contested*]
Second reign of Ahmad	1728–1729
5. Abd Allah	1729–1757
6. Muhammad III	1757–1790
7. Yazid	1790–1792
8. Sulayman	1792–1822
9. Abd al-Rahman	1822–1859
10. Muhammad IV	1859–1873
11. al-Hassan I	1873–1894
12. Abd al-Aziz	1894–1908
13. Abd al-Hafidh	1908–1912
14. Yusuf	1912–1927
15. Muhammad V	1927–1961
16. Hassan II	1961–1999
17. Muhammad VI	1999–present

TABLE BY GGS INFORMATION SERVICES, THE GALE GROUP.

fying vital interest groups. By 2003, the population of Morocco exceeded 30 million. Initially, Hassan II, who ruled the country with a firm hand from March 1961 until his death in July 1999, countered his political opponents by imposing stiff prison sentences or by forcing them into exile. It was only in the early and mid-1990s that Hassan turned serious attention to domestic reforms and the nation's chronic social and economic problems. He laid the groundwork for modernization, privatization of the economy, and the fostering of trade relations with the European Union and the United States, and he tolerated the proliferation of human rights and women's rights groups. He also maintained, since the early 1960s, clandestine intelligence and military ties with Israel and he helped bring the Egyptians and Israelis together in 1977, leading to the historic visit of Egyptian president Anwar al-Sadat to Jerusalem. Upon his death, Crown Prince Sidi Muhammad (b. 1963), now Muhammad VI, succeeded him to the throne. He has shown a predilection for western-style reforms and the notion of a civil society. He is seeking to expand his father's embryonic reforms.

See also HASSAN II; MOROCCO; MUHAMMAD V.

Bibliography

Abun-Nasr, Jamil M. *A History of the Maghrib,* 2d edition. Cambridge, U.K.: Cambridge University Press, 1975.

Cigar, Norman, ed. and trans. *Muhammad al-Qadiri's Nashr al Mathani: The Chronicles.* Oxford, U.K.: Oxford University Press, 1981.

Laroui, Abdallah. *The History of the Maghrib: An Interpretative Essay,* translated by Ralph Manheim. Princeton, NJ: Princeton University Press, 1977.

Laskier, Michael M. "A Difficult Inheritance: Moroccan Society under Muhammad VI." *Middle East Review of International Affairs* 7, no.3 (September 2003), 1–20.

Laskier, Michael M. *Israel and the Maghreb: From Statehood to Oslo.* Gainesville: University Press of Florida, 2004.

Pennell, C. R. *Morocco since 1830: A History.* New York: New York University Press, 2000.

Terasse, Henri. "Alawis." In *Encyclopedia of Islam,* 2d edition. Leiden: Brill, 1978.

DONNA LEE BOWEN
UPDATED BY MICHAEL M. LASKIER

ALBRIGHT INSTITUTE

See ARCHAEOLOGY IN THE MIDDLE EAST

AL BU SA'ID FAMILY AND TRIBE OF OMAN

One of the principal tribes of Oman.

A merchant from the tribe Ahmad ibn Sa'id rallied Omani forces against the invading troops of Nadir Shah in the 1740s and was elected Imam in gratitude. His descendants became the present ruling family of Oman, also known as the Al Bu Sa'id. Ahmad's grandson, Sa'id ibn Sultan, became ruler by assassinating his cousin in about 1807, and an alliance with the British enabled him to defeat threats from neighbors. Sa'id built up his maritime power and expanded his authority over the East African littoral, eventually moving his residence to Zanzibar and sending the first Arab envoy to the United States in 1840. On his death in 1856, his Arabian possessions, chiefly Oman, went to his eldest son, Thuwayni, and another son, Majid, received Zanzibar. The Al Bu Sa'id gradually evolved into separate ruling families and Omani fortunes subsequently declined under the Al Sa'id, as the descendants of Sa'id ibn Sultan are known (other members of the family are still known as Al Bu Sa'id). There were numerous struggles for power in the following decades until the accession of Faysal ibn Turki in 1888. Faysal's reign saw both the loss of the interior of Oman to tribal and religious forces and British domination of affairs in Muscat. He was succeeded on his death in 1913 by his son Taymur, who was forced in 1920 to give autonomy to the Omani interior. Taymur abdicated in 1931 in favor of his son Sa'id and died in 1965. Sa'id was overthrown by his son Qabus (also Qaboos) in 1970 and died in exile in 1972. Sa'id's half-brother Tariq ibn Taymur returned to Oman on Qabus's accession and served as prime minister for about a year.

See also AL BU SA'ID, QABUS IBN SA'ID; AL BU SA'ID, SA'ID IBN TAYMUR; OMAN.

Bibliography

Bhacker, M. Reda. *Trade and Empire in Muscat and Zanzibar: The Roots of British Domination.* New York; London: Routledge, 1992.

Landen, Robert G. *Oman Since 1856: Disruptive Modernization in a Traditional Arab Society.* Princeton, NJ: Princeton University Press, 1967.

Peterson, J. E. *Oman in the Twentieth Century: Political Foundations of an Emerging State.* New York: Barnes and Noble; London: Croom Helm, 1978.

Skeet, Ian. *Oman: Politics and Development.* New York: St. Martin's Press; London: Macmillan, 1992.

J. E. PETERSON

AL BU SA'ID, QABUS IBN SA'ID

Ruler of Oman.

Qabus ibn Sa'id ibn Taymur Al Bu Sa'id became sultan of Oman in 1970 and is the fourteenth member of the Al Bu Sa'id dynasty to rule Oman. Qabus (also Qaboos) was born in Salala, in the southern Omani province of Dhufar, on 18 November 1940. His father was Sultan Sa'id ibn Taymur (r. 1932–1970) and his mother came from the Bayt Ma'shani tribe of the Dhufari mountains. In 1958, Qabus was sent to England for schooling, and he subsequently attended the Royal Military Academy at Sandhurst. His return to Oman in 1964 was followed by years of enforced inactivity in Salala under his father's watchful eye.

The late 1960s saw increasing unrest in Oman due to Sultan Sa'id's apparent refusal to spend his new oil revenues and because of a rebellion in Dhufar against the sultan's paternalistic rule. By mid-1970, the situation had worsened and Qabus joined forces with his friends in Salala and British and Omani backers in Muscat to organize a coup d'état against his father on 23 July 1970.

In contrast to his father, Qabus threw the country open to development and welcomed back the thousands of Omanis working abroad. Within a week of his accession, the country's first true Council of Ministers was formed with Qabus's uncle, Tariq ibn Taymur, as prime minister. Two weeks after the coup, Sultan Qabus arrived in Muscat for the first time and took charge of the new government. Differences between the two men forced Tariq's resignation in 1971; Sultan Qabus has served as his own prime minister since then.

From the beginning of his reign, Qabus faced two primary challenges: economically transforming one of the world's most underdeveloped countries and dealing with the serious rebellion in Dhufar. In the early 1970s, development activity concentrated on providing education, healthcare, water, and electricity to the people and creating a modern infrastructure. At the same time, the course of the Dhufar rebellion was reversed with British, Jordanian, and Iranian assistance and through an intensive "hearts and minds" campaign. The sultan was able to declare the war over in 1975.

Sultan Qabus clearly stands at the apex of the political system of Oman. Decision-making tends to bypass the Council of Ministers and flow directly up to him. He also has steered the country to a moderate path in international affairs, establishing diplomatic relations with China and Russia while maintaining close political and security links with Britain and the United States. Sultan Qabus was one of the few Arab leaders not to break off relations with Egypt following the Camp David Accords. He was careful to keep channels open to both sides during the Iran–Iraq War (1988) and permitted Western powers to use Omani facilities during the hostilities against Iraq in 1990 and 1991. He also agreed to border treaties in the early 1990s with Yemen and Saudi Arabia.

Sultan Qabus has no direct heirs. A marriage arranged by his father to the daughter of an important tribal shaykh never was finalized. A marriage in 1976 to his cousin Kamila, a daughter of Tariq ibn Taymur, ended in divorce.

See also AL BU SA'ID FAMILY AND TRIBE OF OMAN.

Bibliography

Allen, Calvin H., and Rigsbee, W. Lynn, II. *Oman under Qaboos: From Coup to Constitution, 1970–1996.* Portland, OR, and London: Frank Cass, 2000.

Peterson, J. E. *Oman in the Twentieth Century: Political Foundations of an Emerging State.* New York and London: Croon Helm, 1978.

Peterson, J. E. "Qabus bin Said." In *Political Leaders of the Contemporary Middle East and North Africa: A Biographical Dictionary,* edited by Bernard Reich. New York: Greenwood Press, 1990.

Skeet, Ian. *Oman: Politics and Development.* New York: St. Martin's Press; London: Macmillan, 1992.

J. E. PETERSON

AL BU SAʿID, SAʿID IBN TAYMUR
[1910–1972]

Sultan of Oman from 1932 to 1970.

Saʿid ibn Taymur Al Bu Saʿid was born in Muscat to Sultan Taymur ibn Faysal Al Bu Saʿid and an Al Bu Saʿid mother. Like his father, Saʿid was sent to Baghdad and India for education. Upon his return to Muscat at the age of eighteen, Saʿid effectively was made regent in the absence of his father and succeeded his father in 1932. By the end of World War II, Sultan Saʿid had pulled Oman out of debt and reduced British influence in internal affairs. With British military assistance, he restored Al Bu Saʿid control over the interior in the 1950s. But his paternalistic rule led to growing discontent, especially after the discovery of oil in 1964. A rebellion in the southern province of Dhufar led to Saʿid's overthrow in July 1970 by his son Qabus ibn Saʿid Al Bu Saʿid. Saʿid died in exile in London in October 1972.

See also AL BU SAʿID FAMILY AND TRIBE OF OMAN; AL BU SAʿID, QABUS IBN SAʿID; MUSCAT; OMAN.

Bibliography

Joyce, Miriam. *Ruling Shaikhs and Her Majesty's Government, 1960–1969.* London: Frank Cass, 2003.

El-Solh, Raghid, ed. *The Sultanate of Oman 1914–1918.* Reading, U.K.: Ithaca Press, 2000.

Zahlan, Rosemarie Said. *The Ma king of the Modern Gulf States: Kuwait, Bahrain, Qatar, the United Arab Emirates, and Oman,* revised edition. Reading and Berkshire, U.K.: Ithaca Press, 1998.

J. E. PETERSON

ALCOHOL

An element of Middle Eastern life with a long and controversial history.

The drinking of alcoholic beverages has been a continuous feature of Middle Eastern life since the fourth millennium B.C.E. Beer played an important role in the Sumerian civilization of Mesopotamia, and the use of wild grapes to make wine originated in the region, where it became ritually important in Judaism and Christianity. In the medieval period, Muslim chemists pioneered the distillation process used to produce concentrated alcoholic beverages. Running counter to this historical tradition, however, are the clear strictures against wine drinking in Qurʾanic verses 4:43, 2:219, and 5:90–91. Yet the Qurʾan also visualizes paradise as containing rivers of wine "delicious to the drinkers" (47:15).

Since *khamr*, normally translated as "grape wine," is the only beverage specifically mentioned in the Qurʾan, Muslim legists long debated how broadly to interpret the prohibition against drinking it. All agreed to ban its sale to Muslims and to absolve anyone who destroyed wine in a Muslim's possession. They also held that the slightest taint of wine invalidated the ritual purity required for prayer. Shiʿite, Maliki, Shafiʿi, and Hanbali jurists further agreed that any intoxicating beverage should be considered as belonging to the category of *khamr*. The Hanafis, whose legal interpretations were favored by the Ottoman government, disagreed; they maintained that *khamr* denoted only the fermentation of uncooked fruit such as grapes, dates, raisins. They thereby permitted the use of certain beverages fermented from cooked juices and from uncooked materials like honey, wheat, barley, millet, and figs. These, however, could be consumed only in "non-intoxicating" amounts. The legists, who also debated this limitation, produced definitions of intoxication that ranged from "giddy" and "boisterous" to "blind drunk."

Islamic legal variations, local custom, and the acknowledged right of non-Muslims living under Muslim rule to make, sell, and consume alcoholic beverages resulted in an almost continual presence of alcohol in Middle Eastern society throughout the Islamic period. Drinking songs, royal and aristocratic drinking sessions, drunkenness as a metaphor for love of God, and the breaking of wine jars as an expression of moral outrage are commonplace in Islamic literature.

In the nineteenth century, alcoholic beverages were produced in many parts of the Middle East. Most of the vintners were non-Muslims, although some employed Muslims in their vineyards. In French-dominated Algeria, the alcoholic beverages produced were mostly designated for the European market. By World War I, Algerian grapes were yielding over 2 million metric tons (2.2 million tons) of wine per year. The yield from the Ottoman Empire was more modest and local. The region of Bursa, for example, produced some 12 metric tons (13.2 tons) of grapes in 1880, of which around one-third—from Christian growers—was made into wine or *raki,* an anise-flavored spirit distilled from grape pulp and allowed to ferment after pressing. (In Arab lands, *raki* is known as *araq.*)

The rise of secularism and socialism led to varying degrees of permissiveness and state control with respect to the production and sale of alcoholic beverages. In the Republic of Turkey, for example, a state monopoly *(tekel)* on tobacco and alcohol was established. After the Egyptian revolution of 1952, Greek-owned vineyards and European-owned breweries were nationalized, and the state became the primary producer. Algeria continued to produce wine for the French market after winning its war of independence in 1962. Regulations on importing alcohol in these countries varied according to the overall import policies of the country and its desire to protect profits from state enterprises.

Efforts to ban or sharply limit alcoholic beverages are often associated with states that favor a traditional way of life, often under an Islamic political ideology. Saudi Arabia and Libya strenuously enforce bans on both the production and importation of these beverages. Iran and Yemen strictly limit consumption to non-Muslims, although South Yemen (the former People's Democratic Republic of Yemen) once had a brewery that was destroyed by Muslim activists. Flogging (usually forty or eighty strikes) is the prescribed punishment for violating the religious proscription.

See also QUR'AN.

Bibliography

Hattox, Ralph S. *Coffee and Coffeehouses: The Origins of a Social Beverage in the Medieval Near East.* Seattle: University of Washington Press, 1985.

RICHARD W. BULLIET

AL-E AHMAD, JALAL
[1923–1969]

Iranian author; prominent nonestablishment intellectual.

The son of a Shi'ite Muslim cleric, Jalal Al-e Ahmad was educated at Tehran University and was the author of four volumes of short stories, four novels, and nearly a dozen volumes of essays. Al-e Ahmad focused on the present in his writing, concerned primarily with the negative influence of aspects of traditional Islam and of the modern West on Iran. His writings and life embody ongoing dilemmas for secular-minded Iranians, among them the values of the past versus the present, religion versus secularism, and West versus East. His strident attacks on historical Western imperialism and post–World War II U.S involvement in Iran, together with his recognition of the unifying capacity of Islam, persuaded some Iranians to consider him influential in the success of the Iranian revolution of 1979. Consequently, in Persian literature, this most-translated prose writer has suffered a loss of reputation among secular-minded Iranian intellectuals.

His best-known work of fiction is a realistic 1958 story about public education at the local elementary school level, *The School Principal,* available in two English translations (1974, 1986). Another of his longer fictions, a 1961 novel called *By the Pen,* available in a 1989 English translation featuring M. Hillmann's prefatory assessment of Al-e Ahmad's fiction in general, tells the story of an unsuccessful religious revolution.

Bibliography

Al-e Ahmad, Jalal. *Lost in the Crowd,* translated by John Green. Washington, DC: Three Continents Press, 1985.

Al-e Ahmad, Jalal. *Occidentosis: A Plague from the West,* edited by Hamid Algar, translated by R. Campbell. Berkeley, CA: Mizan Press, 1983.

Al-e Ahmad, Jalal. *Plagued by the West (Gharbzadegi),* translated by Paul Sprachman. Delmor, NY: Center for Iranian Studies, Columbia University, 1982.

Al-e Ahmad, Jalal. *Weststruckness (Gharbzadegi),* translated by John Green and Ahmad Alizadeh. Costa Mesa, CA: Mazda Publishers, 1997.

Hillmann, Michael C., ed. *Iranian Society: An Anthology of Writings by Jalal Al-e Ahmad.* Lexington, KY: Mazda Publishers, 1982.

MICHAEL C. HILLMANN

ALEMDAR

See BAYRAKDAR, MUSTAFA

ALEPPO

The principal city of northern Syria.

Syria's second-largest metropolis after Damascus, Aleppo has long been a prominent economic, cultural, and political center, and, with a population of 4.2 million (2002 estimate), it ranks among the leading cities of the Middle East. Located about 70 miles inland from the Mediterranean Sea, at an elevation of 1,280 feet (390 m), Aleppo has a moderate climate, with short, cool, wet winters and long, dry, hot summers. Its surrounding region, parts of which are semiarid, supports extensive agriculture as well as the raising of livestock.

The majority of Aleppo's townspeople are Sunni Muslims, but they live alongside substantial numbers of Christians affiliated with various churches. Tens of thousands of Armenian refugees from Anatolia settled in Aleppo during World War I and strengthened the traditionally prominent Christian presence. The local Jewish community, whose roots went back to pre-Islamic times, also grew during the modern period, but the Arab–Israeli hostilities caused most of its members to leave the country around 1948. The remaining Jewish presence, which continued to dwindle thereafter, came to a historic end with the departure of the last Jews in 1994.

During the period of Ottoman rule in Syria (1516–1918), Aleppo served as the administrative capital of a large province that extended over much of northern Syria as well as parts of southern Anatolia. Ottoman governors dispatched from Istanbul administered the affairs of the area with the cooperation of Aleppo's local Muslim elite. The city's politics were characterized by the competition for influence among local powerful figures and by periodic local clashes with the Ottoman authorities. The unusually troubled years from 1770 to 1850 witnessed violent factional strife, popular unrest, and occupation by the Egyptian army (1832–1840). In the calmer period that followed, more orderly Ottoman control was restored, and the community began to experience the benefits of European-inspired innovations, including modern schools, improved sanitation and health care, street lighting, printing, newspapers, and wheeled transport. The local notable families integrated themselves more

Located in Syria's large central plain, Aleppo is one of the country's two major population centers, along with Damascus. Aleppo, which includes a sizable community of Armenians who fled the Soviet Union in the mid-1940s, was also one of the centers of Syria's emerging independence movement beginning in the 1890s. K.M. WESTERMANN/CORBIS. REPRODUCED BY PERMISSION.

fully into the Ottoman provincial administration at this time and strengthened their power by acquiring large amounts of rural land.

With the establishment of modern Syria in 1920, Aleppo continued to serve as the seat of government for the surrounding region. Its Sunni landowning families, with their counterparts from Damascus, dominated national politics during the French mandate (1920–1946) and the first two decades of independence. As of the 1960s, however, the old landed notables began to be displaced by a new political elite composed of men of provincial and minority origins (particularly Alawi). Land-reform measures resulted in the expropriation of the great agricultural estates and helped to break the political back of the Sunni elite. In the 1970s and 1980s, opposition in Aleppo and other Sunni centers to the new political structure gave rise to clashes of Muslim organizations with Hafiz al-Asad's regime.

The modern period also transformed Aleppo's commercial role. Since the sixteenth century, the city had been a leading center of regional and international trade, with a network of markets that included cities in Anatolia, Iraq, Iran, Syria, Arabia, Egypt, Europe, and Asia. In the nineteenth century, however, much of the region's external trade, now oriented increasingly toward Europe, shifted from inland cities such as Aleppo to the Mediterranean coastal towns. The end of the Ottoman Empire (1918) cut Aleppo off from some of its traditional markets in the region and narrowed still further its commercial horizons. The city's manufacturing sector, however, remained strong, and today, as a major industrial center, Aleppo produces fine silk and cotton fabric, soaps and dyes, processed foods, leather goods, and articles of gold and silver.

Like other major Middle Eastern cities, Aleppo grew dramatically during the modern period, especially since around 1950, when the migration from rural regions to urban centers began to assume massive proportions. Its population, about 90,000 in 1800, had risen modestly to 110,000 in 1900 and to 320,000 in 1950, but it then increased sharply by 1.5 million in the next forty-five years.

With this population growth came a corresponding physical expansion. Beginning in the 1870s, vast new areas developed all around the old historic city, thereby giving birth to modern Aleppo. The new districts, built on a European model of apartment buildings and wide streets laid out in a regular grid pattern, contrasted sharply with the dense environment of courtyard houses and narrow, winding alleyways in the old parts. As the better-off townspeople gradually moved out of the old city, it deteriorated into an overcrowded habitat for the urban poor and for rural migrants. This exodus represented the rejection of an environment that had come to be regarded as backward and unsuited to modern living. The old city has nevertheless remained among the best preserved and most handsome of the traditional Middle Eastern cities, and since the 1970s a movement to conserve its historic monuments and urban fabric has taken hold, although with still unresolved debates over proposed rehabilitation plans.

Aleppo, which has remained one of Syria's leading centers of cultural life, is particularly renowned, in the country and wider region, for its role as a creative center of traditional music. The *muwashshah*, a song traced back to Muslim Spain, has been a local specialty; hundreds of these vocal pieces—now

known as *muwashshahat halabiyya*—were composed or preserved in the city and diffused from there throughout the region. Ottoman music has also been popular, and Turkish influences continue to distinguish local approaches to music theory. Many accomplished Arab musicians have hailed from Aleppo, among them the violin virtuosos Sami al-Shawwa (1887–1960) and Tawfiq al-Sabbagh (1890–1955) and the popular singer Sabah Fakhri (1933–). The most influential figure was Ali al-Darwish (1884–1952), whose encyclopedic knowledge of the Arab and Ottoman musical systems and repertoires, derived from thirty years of travel in the Middle East and North Africa, has profoundly marked the region's musical scene and scholarship.

See also SUNNI ISLAM.

Bibliography

Gaube, Heinz, and Wirth, Eugen. *Aleppo.* Wiesbaden, Germany: L. Reichert, 1984.

Marcus, Abraham. *The Middle East on the Eve of Modernity: Aleppo in the Eighteenth Century.* New York: Columbia University Press, 1989.

ABRAHAM MARCUS

ALEVI

A sect of Shiʿite Muslims in Turkey.

Alevis are the adherents of a belief system fitting loosely under a Shiʿite rubric; they constitute a significant minority in contemporary Turkey. Although no reliable statistics exist, estimates of their numbers run as high as 20 percent of Turkey's population, or somewhere between ten million and fifteen million people. Depending on the observer's political or social agenda, they have been understood to be a religious sect for some purposes and an ethnic minority group for others. Categorization ultimately proves futile, as the term *Alevi* refers to a number of diverse groups, all maintaining different levels of identification with Alevi-ness (in Turkish, *Alevilik*) and with each other. Scholars have posited numerous theories about Alevi influences and origins. Alevis are variously believed to be the descendants of Neoplatonists, gnostics, Manicheanists, Zoroastrians, pantheists, and early Anatolian Christian cults. Some of these lines of cultural descent would place them closer to Kurdish and Iranian elements than to Turkish. A popular theory, advocated by some nationalist politicians as well by as some Alevi leaders, links them with pre-Islamic Turkic belief systems (frequently mislabeled *shamanism*).

Language and Beliefs

Many Alevis living in the predominantly Kurdish regions of eastern Anatolia, particularly in the Dersim (Tunceli) region—the spiritual/historical heart of Kurdish Alevis—speak one of the indigenous Kurdish languages. Others, in southern Anatolia near the Syrian border, speak Arabic, while many in western Anatolia speak Turkish. Groups such as the Shabak Kurds of northern Iraq are also Alevis. By contrast, the Ahl-e Haqq of Iran, although they share some concepts and institutions with the Alevis, diverge historically and in their ritual practices and beliefs. However, most of these groups recognize a sacred hierarchy that includes a trinity consisting of Allah, the prophet Muhammad, and his cousin and son-in-law Ali; they also revere the twelve imams who are central to mainstream Shi'ism.

After these, the next most important figure in Alevi belief is the saint Haci Bektaş Veli, who settled with his followers in the Kir Şehir region of central Anatolia in the thirteenth century. A village bearing his name, Haci Bektaş Köyü, became the center of this group of dervishes, and a large *tekke* (local headquarters for Sufi orders) and a *medrese* (Ar. *Madrasa*; religious school)—still important today—were established there. Presumably Haci Bektaş Veli was part of a larger movement of Turkmen *babas* practicing a mystical tradition influenced by Ahmet Yesevi, the central Asian Sufi whose tomb remains an important pilgrimage site. Bektashis were associated with the Ottoman Janissary corps; Janissaries styled their headgear after the cloak said to have been worn by Haci Bektaş Veli. In the nineteenth and early twentieth centuries, the reformist Young Turks counted Bektashis among their members, as did the Freemasons.

History and Traditions

The history and traditions of the followers of Haci Bektaş Veli, the Bektashis, overlap with Alevis. However, in some respects Bektashis function much like many Sufi orders. Among the Bektashis, there has

been a distinction between Yol Evladi (children of the Path) and Bel Evladi (natural descendants). The former believe that Haci Bektaş was celibate, and membership in the order can only be accomplished through study with a *murşit*, or spiritual guide, and eventual initiation at an *ayin-i cem*. The *dedebaba*, the leader of the entire order, is elected by their *babas*. The Bel Evladi segment believe that Haci Bektaş married, begot a son, and that the order's leadership since that time should go to his descendants, the Çelebis. Çelebis need not go through initiation (although their followers, *talips*, must be initiated). Many Alevis concur with the Bel Evladi interpretation.

In the past, and to a lesser extent today, some village-based Alevis have been the *talips*, the client-disciples, of a Bektashi *effendi*, or Çelebi based in the *tekke* of Haci Bektaş Köyü, who might have visited them annually, collected tribute, officiated at an *ayin-i cem*, and mediated in disputes. Other Alevi villages have maintained the *talip* relationship with *pirs*, members of holy lineages not directly related to the Bektashis.

The central communal ritual for Alevis, as for Bektashis, is the *ayin-i cem*, held, if in a village, in a *cem evi*. Sites for the ritual exist in Turkish (and European) cities as well, often as part of Alevi cultural centers. The *pirs* officiate over the symbolic reenactment of the martyrdoms of Hasan and Hüseyin (Husayn), the second and third of the twelve imams, by dousing twelve candles, which is accompanied by impassioned wailing. Some groups of Alevis include wine or *raki* as part of the *cem*. Past and present *aşiks* or *ozans* (minstrels) are revered, and an essential component of the *cem* is the playing and singing of the poetry and songs of early Alevis such as Pir Sultan Abdal and Hata'i (pseudonym of Shah Isma'il Safavi). The songs sung in a *cem* are called *nefes* by Bektashis and *deyiş* by village Alevis. *Düvaz* (short for *Düvazdeh imam*, the twelve imams) are the most sacred of the songs sung at a *cem*. The poetry can be understood on multiple levels; ostensible love songs also refer to mystical aspects of the relationship between humans and God, for example. Music typically is played on the *saz*, a plucked instrument resembling a long-necked lute, sometimes said to be the embodiment of Ali. The strumming and fingering can be complex, demanding a high level of technical virtuosity; many of the rhythms are repetitive, conducive to the *semah*, trance-inducing dancing performed in the *ayin-i cem*.

Beliefs and Practices

Other beliefs and practices of many Alevis include fasting during the first twelve days of Muharram and the celebration of Nevruz. A well-known Alevi precept is *eline, diline, beline, sahip ol* (be the master of your hands, tongue, and loins). This guides behavior for Alevis, who avoid making an outward show of their piety at the expense of inner purity. This is consonant with the permitted practice of *taqiyya* (dissimulation). *Taqiyya* reflects the pervasive belief in esotericism, which emphasized the internal, the unseen, the purity of one's heart. Many Alevi beliefs have been codified and inscribed in Buyruk (decree), believed by some to be the collected sayings of Imam Cafer-i Sadik, the sixth of the twelve imams.

Other religious tenets include a belief in divine incarnations and in reincarnation. Spiritual guidance is manifested in the hierarchy of the four gates of *şeriat, tarikat, hakikat,* and *marifet.* Alevis are differentiated from Sunnis in their attitudes and practices surrounding the social and ritual status of women. An Alevi saying, *kadin, toplumun annesidir* (woman is the mother of society), summarizes the central role of women, who are integral to the *cem* ceremony and can take leading roles. It is uncommon to see Alevi women wearing headscarves in urban settings. In villages they may; however, their scarves do not cover all their hair. This is consistent with a belief system that values the inner aspects of life more highly than the external.

Politics and History

As a minority that explicitly opposed the hegemonic Sunni power of the Ottoman Empire, the Alevis have been seen as threatening and have long been subject to persecution. The pejorative sobriquet *kizilbaş* (redhead) derives from an implication that they were traitors, in league with the Iranian Safavi Empire and its founder, Shah Isma'il, who established a similar form of Shi'ism as the dominant religion of his realm; the terminology thus has its origins in the sixteenth and seventeenth centuries. In 1925, republican Turkey closed all Sufi orders,

tarikats, and *tekkes;* banned the use of related titles; and prohibited certain practices; the Alevis were driven underground in their religious practices.

A sense of victimization and martyrdom pervades the Alevi worldview. Subject to persecution and massacres throughout their history, Alevis revere and identify with ancestral martyrs. Twentieth-century massacres and oppression are conceptualized in mytho-historical terms, as part of the cultural logic of their understanding of history. Killings and attacks in Malatya, Kahraman Maraş, and Çorum in the late 1970s, and in Sivas in 1993, serve as proof for many Alevis of the persistence of persecution. The attacks in the 1970s, many perpetrated by right-wing Sunnis, were incited by the fascist National Movement Party and depended on the collusion of local police and the army, many of whom identified the Alevi not only with immorality and religious heresy but also with communism.

In the 1970s and 1980s many Alevi youth, particularly from the Dersim area, were attracted by Maoism; with the collapse of the left in Turkey, this was one of the few surviving outposts. Some of these activists moved away from the Turkish Maoists and developed an Alevi variant, proposing the ethnic basis of *Alevilik,* and advocating an Alevistan or Zazaistan as the rightful homeland of the Zazas. Such movements have been stronger in the European Alevi diaspora than in Turkey. One of the consequences was that the PKK, the dominant Kurdish nationalist group, vied for Alevi allegiance and in 1994 established a publication, *Zülfikar,* laden with Alevi symbolism and meant to attract Alevi adherents. The PKK also attempted to win Alevi followers by adopting an anti-Turkish-state stance, associating state oppression with Turkish Bektashi-ism. Ultimately many Dersim Alevis were forced through threats of violence to choose sides.

Beginning in the late 1980s, a resurgence of *Alevilik* emerged both in Turkey and in the European Alevi diaspora. In Turkey, numerous publications appeared in bookstores, *Alevilik* was discussed in the national press, and there were efforts to establish a special Alevi desk at the Directorate of Religion in Ankara. No longer associated exclusively with the political left, some Alevis have moved to the right. In the 1980s, the popular annual festival at Haci Bektaş Köyü began to be patronized by politicians of all persuasions, eager to win over the Alevi electorate; the state became a sponsor of the festival as sanctions against Alevi self-expression were lifted. Official support may have been meant "to counterbalance the growth of Sunni Islamism, but also to stop Kurdish nationalism making further inroads among Kurdish Alevis. There was some pressure to emphasize the Turkishness of Alevism." Since the 1990s, Alevi organizations and publications have proliferated in Turkey and Europe (predominantly in Germany). Internet technology has fostered new expressions of Alevilik, as it has facilitated transnational links.

See also AHL-E HAQQ; ALAWI; ALLAH; ANATOLIA; BEKTASHIS; JANISSARIES; KURDS; MADRASA; MUHAMMAD; MUHARRAM; SHIʿISM; SUFISM AND THE SUFI ORDERS; TEKKE; TURKEY; YOUNG TURKS.

Bibliography

Markoff, Irene. "Music, Saints, and Ritual: Sama and the Alevis of Turkey." In *Manifestations of Sainthood in Islam,* edited by Grace Martin Smith and Carl W. Ernst. Istanbul: The Isis Press, 1993.

Olsson, Tord; Özdalga, Elisabeth; and Raudvere, Catharina, eds. *Alevi Identity: Cultural, Religious and Social Perspectives: Papers Read at a Conference Held at the Swedish Research Institute in Istanbul, November 25–27, 1996.* Istanbul: Swedish Research Institute in Istanbul, 1998.

Van Bruinessen, Martin. "'Aslini inkar eden haramzadedir!' The debate on the Ethnic Identity of the Kurdish Alevis." In *Syncretistic Religious Communities in the Near East: Collected Papers of the International Symposium "Alevism in Turkey and Comparable Sycretistic Religious Communities in the Near East in the Past and Present": Berlin, 14–17 April 1995,* edited by Krisztina Kehl-Bodrogi, Barbara Kellner-Heinkele, and Anke Otter-Beaujean. New York; Leiden, Netherlands: Brill, 1997.

Van Bruinessen, Martin. "Kurds, Turks, and the Alevi Revival." *Middle East Report* 200 (summer 1996): 7–10.

Van Bruinessen, Martin. "The Shabak, a Kizilbash community in Iraqi Kurdistan." *Les annales de l'autre Islam* 5 (1998): 185–196.

RUTH MANDEL

ALEXANDRETTA

Mediterranean port city in Turkey, founded by Alexander the Great, 333 B.C.E.

Alexandretta (in Turkish, Iskenderun) is located in Turkey's Hatay province on the southeast shore of the Gulf of Iskenderun, just north of Syria. The ancient port city, noted for its fine harbor, was founded by Alexander the Great c. 333 B.C.E. It remained relatively small and unimportant in late Roman times, referred to as "Little Alexandria" (hence Alexandretta) in contrast to the much larger Alexandria in Egypt. It was captured by the Ottomans in 1515 under Selim I. Under Ottoman rule it became an important Mediterranean port and trade center. It developed into an outlet for trade during the 1590s due to its position as an overland trade route to the Persian Gulf. Because of rampant malaria, however, only its commercial functions kept it alive. Yet with the draining of its marshes, health improved—and thus so did commerce and production. With the agricultural boom that began around 1890, Alexandretta gained importance as an outlet for farm produce, but it was eventually eclipsed by Tripoli and Beirut, since the railroad came to it only in 1913.

During World War I, the *Sanjak* of Alexandretta was assigned to France under the Sykes–Picot Agreement. It became part of the French League of Nations mandate in Syria. Its population was an ethnic mix. In 1936, French authorities estimated that 39 percent were Turks, 28 percent Alawi Arab, 11 percent Armenian, 10 percent Sunni Arab, and 8 percent various other Christians. In December 1937 Turkey denounced its 1926 treaty of friendship with Syria, and France sent a military mission to Ankara threatening war. By July, France and Turkey came to an agreement to supervise elections in Alexandretta with 2,500 troops each. Fearing Italian expansionism, France had taken the Turkish side, arranging that twenty-two of the forty members of the new assembly would be Turkish. Alexandretta was ceded to Turkey in 1939.

Since annexation, Alexandretta has become strategically and commercially important to Turkey. During the Cold War, North Atlantic Treaty Organization planners assumed that the Turkish defense against a Soviet thrust into eastern Turkey could be supplied only through Alexandretta and Mersin. Consequently, a network of paved roads was built from the Gulf of Iskenderun into the eastern interior. Hostility between Iraq and Syria during the 1960s and 1970s threatened to close pipelines that brought Iraqi petroleum to Syrian ports. Iraq then arranged with Turkey to build pipelines from Iraq to the Gulf of Iskenderun, at Yumurtalik and near Dortyol, just north of Alexandretta. The first oil arrived in 1977. Alexandretta's tidewater location at the point in Turkey nearest its major Middle Eastern markets led to the construction of a large steel plant. These investments have made Alexandretta one of Turkey's fastest growing cities. As of 2003, the population was 171,700.

See also TURKEY.

Bibliography

Khoury, Philip S. *Syria and the French Mandate: The Politics of Arab Nationalism, 1920–1945.* Princeton, NJ: Princeton University Press, 1987.

JOHN R. CLARK
UPDATED BY NOAH BUTLER

ALEXANDRIA

Egypt's second largest city and main port.

Modern Alexandria stands on the site of the ancient city of the same name, founded by Alexander the Great in 331 B.C.E. It is located on a narrow spit of land with the Mediterranean Sea to the north and Lake Mariut to the south. The climate is temperate and averages 45°F during the winter months. Summer weather, although not as hot as in Cairo, is significantly affected by seaborne humidity and reaches 90°F.

Alexandria is bounded on the north by the Mediterranean Sea, and the city's white sand beaches are a popular recreation spot for tourists and natives alike. © SAMER MOHDAD/CORBIS. REPRODUCED BY PERMISSION.

Alexander the Great's general Ptolemy I made the new port city his capital, and his Greek-speaking dynasty ruled until Cleopatra VII's suicide in 30 B.C.E. as Octavian's Romans invaded the country. Famed for its lighthouse, museum (primarily a research institute), and library, Hellenistic Alexandria continued as a great Mediterranean center of commerce and learning through Roman times. Eratosthenes, Euclid, and Claudius Ptolemy were among its mathematical and scientific luminaries, and Callimachus, Theocritus, and Apollonius stood out as Greek poets. Alexandria declined in importance under Islamic rule as Egypt's center of gravity returned inland to the Cairo area, where it remains today.

Contemporary Alexandria is the site of oil refineries, food-processing plants, and car-assembly works. The port is the main point of export for cotton and other agricultural products and is one of Egypt's major venues for imports. Because of its significance to the commercial activity of the city, the harbor underwent major expansions in the first quarter of the twentieth century. Its size and position made it the headquarters of the British Royal Navy's Mediterranean squadron until the end of World War II.

The history of modern Alexandria begins in 1798 when the French occupied it until 1801 as part of Napoléon Bonaparte's Egyptian campaign. By then the city's population had shrunk to under 10,000. Alexandria experienced a remarkable revival in the early nineteenth century when Muhammad Ali connected it to the Nile River by the Mahmudiyya Canal, dredged its long-neglected harbor, and made it the site of his naval building program and arsenal. By 1824, because of Muhammad Ali's agricultural policies, Egypt was experiencing the first of two significant cotton exporting booms. Both booms led to the arrival of numerous European entrepreneurs involved with cotton, a combination that was to govern Alexandria's commercial and political fortunes until the advent of Gamal Abdel Nasser and the Suez Crisis of October 1956.

During the U.S. Civil War and the ensuing Union naval blockade of the Confederacy, Alexandria experienced a resurgence of its commercial and urban fortunes as well as a population explosion, reaching more than 180,000 inhabitants. With the

Sightseers float past the Bibliotheca Alexandria, an integrated cultural complex comprising libraries, museums, exhibition halls, educational centers, research institutes, and an international conference center. The Bibliotheca was built on the same site where the ancient library of Alexandria stood before it was destroyed by fire more than two thousand years ago. © AP/WIDE WORLD PHOTOS. REPRODUCED BY PERMISSION.

disappearance of cotton from the southern United States, European—especially British—mills turned to Egypt as the closest source of acceptable cotton. This in turn led to feverish economic activity aimed at improving agriculture and increasing urban development, manufacturing, and transport, and culminated in the opening of the Suez Canal in 1869. The Egyptian viceroy had embarked on an ambitious program of modernization, heavily indebting his country to Europe. European financiers and entrepreneurs settled in Alexandria, transforming it from a marginal seaside town into the major entrepôt of the eastern Mediterranean. The seaport also became the financial and political center of the country while Cairo remained the political capital of Egypt. By World War I, Alexandria's population had grown to nearly half a million and had reached a million when King Farouk abdicated in 1952.

Unable to repay or service its debt, in 1876 Egypt came under the supervision of Anglo-French finan-cial advisers. This helped fuel a nationalist reaction that culminated in the revolt led by Ahmad Urabi. In 1882 the British bombarded and then occupied Alexandria in order to crush the nationalist insurrection. The town was then rebuilt along European lines with clearly demarcated areas for business, industry, and residence. The new city grew into nearly separate European and indigenous sections reflecting, like much colonial urbanism, the demographic dichotomies of its population.

Thus from the middle of the nineteenth to the middle of the twentieth century, Alexandria was home to a polyglot population representing the Mediterranean littoral and comprising different national, ethnocultural, and religious backgrounds. The Greeks were the most numerous of the European communities, followed in number by Italians, British subjects (many of whom were actually Maltese), and Frenchmen. Poet Constantine Cavafy stood out in the vigorous Greek cultural scene; British residents gathered at the Sporting Club and in 1901 imported the English public school model for Victoria College. Today Alexandria still presents a unique mixture of architectural styles, blending Venetian rococo, turn-of-the-century Beaux Arts, Bauhaus, Mediterranean stucco, and, more recently, postmodernist high-tech, although it lacks Cairo's rich Islamic architectural heritage.

Extensive beaches and the moderate summer climate turned the city into a seaside resort where the well-to-do and a growing middle class escaped the heat of the interior. Ra's al-Tin and especially al-Muntaza Palace became the royal family's summer residences. In 1934 the construction of the fourteen-mile-long Corniche along the city's coast began.

The vast and disproportionate wealth and commercial influence of Egypt's foreign population was still particularly glaring in Alexandria when Nasser's Free Officers seized control in 1952. It was no coincidence that Nasser chose Alexandria, that most European of Egypt's cities, to deliver a speech in July 1956 announcing the nationalization of the Suez Canal Company. The Suez Crisis, the ensuing Arab–Israel War of 1956, and expropriation of foreign-owned property and businesses led to a mass exodus of Alexandria's foreign residents in the late 1950s and early 1960s. Those developments also encouraged Nasser to Arabize and Egyptianize the city's ethos.

Until the 1960s Pompey's Pillar (actually dating from the reign of Diocletian), the Roman-era Kom al-Shuqafa catacombs, the Mamluk Qaitbay Fort, and the Greco-Roman Museum attracted cursory attention from Western tourists passing on their way to the richer antiquities of the interior. The shift from steamship to air travel, however, put Alexandria off the beaten path as Western tourists flew directly into Cairo. This often reduced Alexandria to an optional day trip from Cairo for Westerners on a nostalgic quest for the lost (and highly imaginary) city of Lawrence Durrell's *Alexandria Quartet.* The UNESCO-sponsored Bibliotheca Alexandrina opened in 2002, an attempt by the city to regain something of its cosmopolitan glitter by invoking the glories of ancient Alexandria. With perhaps five million people today, greater Alexandria sprawls westward toward El Alamein and Marsa Ma-

truh, with beachside resorts devouring the once pristine desert coastline.

See also ARAB–ISRAEL WAR (1956); FREE OFFICERS, EGYPT; NASSER, GAMAL ABDEL; SUEZ CANAL; SUEZ CRISIS (1956–1957); VICTORIA COLLEGE.

Bibliography

Aciman, André. *Out of Egypt: A Memoir.* New York: Riverhead Books, 1995.

Forster, E. M. *Alexandria: A History and a Guide.* New York: Oxford University Press, 1987.

Owen, E. R. J. *Cotton and the Egyptian Economy, 1820–1914.* Oxford, U.K.: Oxford University Press, 1969.

Reimer, Michael J. *Colonial Bridgehead: Government and Society in Alexandria, 1807–1882.* Boulder, CO: Westview Press, 1997.

JEAN-MARC R. OPPENHEIM
UPDATED BY DONALD MALCOLM REID

ALEXANDRIA CONFERENCE OF ARAB STATES

See LEAGUE OF ARAB STATES

ALEXANDRIA CONVENTION

Agreement made between the British and Muhammad Ali of Egypt to end Egypt's territorial aggression.

By the London Convention of July 1840, Muhammad Ali Pasha, ruler of Egypt, was given an ultimatum by the Ottoman Empire and its allies, to evacuate his troops from Anatolia and Syria. He refused, and Britain sent a naval squadron under Admiral Charles Napier to aid Syria. After the defeat of Egypt's forces in Syria, the British sailed to Egypt's port of Alexandria. Muhammad Ali recognized the weakness of his position and the strength of the forces arrayed against him; he sued for peace and signed the Alexandria Convention with Napier on 27 November 1840.

Under its terms, Muhammad Ali renounced his claims to Syria and agreed to yield to the Ottoman sultan. In return, the sultan granted him hereditary possession of Egypt. When news of the Alexandria Convention reached Europe, there was some concern that the terms had been too light; it was months before the sultan fully endorsed the agreement, fearing additional empire-building on the part of Muhammad Ali. The convention was used to signify the end of Muhammad Ali as a threat to the integrity of the rest of the Ottoman Empire—an integrity that was thenceforth preserved with the aid of the European powers.

See also MUHAMMAD ALI.

Bibliography

Anderson, M. S. *The Eastern Question, 1774–1923: A Study in International Relations.* London and Melbourne: Macmillan; and New York: St. Martin's, 1966.

Hurewitz, J. C., ed. *The Middle East and North Africa in World Politics: A Documentary Record,* 2d edition. New Haven, CT: Yale University Press, 1975.

ZACHARY KARABELL

ALEXANDRIA PROTOCOL

See LEAGUE OF ARAB STATES

ALEXANDRIA UNIVERSITY

Egyptian institution of higher learning founded in 1942.

Originally named Farouk University after the country's ruling monarch, Alexandria University is Egypt's second oldest state university, after Cairo University, which was founded in 1925. It was renamed following the 1952 revolution that toppled the monarchy.

The university depicts itself as heir to ancient Greco-Roman Alexandria's tradition of learning centered in its famous library and museum. In the fall of 1942, only weeks after Britain's defeat of invading Axis forces a few miles outside the city, King Farouk opened the new university. At its opening the university had colleges of arts and law (founded as branches of the Egyptian—now Cairo—University in 1938) as well as colleges of commerce, science, medicine, agriculture, and engineering. Colleges of dentistry, pharmacy, nursing, education, and tourism were added later. The language of instruction is Arabic although English is used in classes in dentistry, medicine, science, and some branches of engineering. As of 2002, the university enrolled over 130,000 students and had a teaching staff of 5,550 in sixteen faculties and six institutes. As at other Egyptian institutions of higher education, Alexandria University faces difficulties in maintaining quality in the face of overcrowding, insufficient funding, and a hard-pressed teaching staff.

Bibliography

Alexandria University web site. Available from <http://www.alex.edu.eg/>.

Cochran, Judith. *Education in Egypt.* London: Croom Helm, 1986.

Reid, Donald Malcolm. *Cairo University and the Making of Modern Egypt.* Cambridge, U.K.: Cambridge University Press, 1990.

DONALD MALCOLM REID

ALGECIRAS CONFERENCE (1906)

Conference (16 January–7 April 1906) convened in Algeciras, Spain, to resolve the first Moroccan crisis over German attempts to break up the Anglo–French entente cordiale that dated from April 1904.

Anglo–French agreements recognized France's paramount interests in Morocco and Britain's special position in Egypt. They also secretly provided for the future partition of Morocco between France and Spain. In 1905, German chancellor Prince Bernhard von Bülow believed that Germany should demonstrate its great-power status and its right to be consulted over such issues. He pressed Germany's Kaiser Wilhelm II to undertake a trip to Tangier (March 1905) to assure the sultan of German support for Moroccan independence. French Premier Théophile Delcassé resigned, and Germany appeared to have achieved its goal of disrupting French–British ties. Nevertheless, von Bülow insisted on pressing his advantage and forced the convening of an international conference at Algeciras in Spain to discuss France's reform program for Morocco.

The conference was a disaster for the Germans. Their policy of threats had so alienated governments and public opinion throughout Europe that Germany found itself all but isolated, with only the Austro–Hungarian Empire and Morocco itself siding with the Germans. On the surface, Germany appeared to have gained its goal, for the conference reaffirmed Moroccan independence. But it also approved French and Spanish control over the Moroccan police and banks, and it paved the way for

France to further encroach on Moroccan independence. The first Moroccan crisis encouraged closer relations between France and Britain and revealed the weakness of Germany's diplomatic position. By permitting French penetration of Morocco, it practically guaranteed the rise of Moroccan nationalist opposition to the agreements. Such opposition was almost certain to lead to further French encroachments over Morocco's merely formal independence. The Algeciras Act was doomed from the outset, culminating in the Agadir Crisis of 1911.

See also AGADIR CRISIS.

Bibliography

Pennell, C. R. *Morocco since 1830.* New York: New York University Press, 2000.

Taylor, A. J. P. *The Struggle for the Mastery of Europe, 1848–1918.* Oxford: Clarendon Press, 1954.

JON JUCOVY

ALGERIA

This entry consists of the following articles:

ALGERIA: OVERVIEW
ALGERIA: CONSTITUTION
ALGERIA: POLITICAL PARTIES IN

ALGERIA: OVERVIEW

Arab republic situated in North Africa.

The second largest country in Africa, the Democratic and Popular Republic of Algeria comprises an area of some 920,000 square miles in the Maghreb (North Africa). It is bounded by the Mediterranean Sea on the north, Morocco on the west, Western Sahara and Mauritania on the southwest, Niger and Mali on the south, and Libya and Tunisia on the east. Its population at the end of 2002 totaled about 32 million. Major cities include the capital Algiers, Oran, Constantine, and Annaba.

Algeria is divided into the relatively moist and mountainous north, which is part of the Atlas Mountain system, and the Saharan south, which makes up roughly five-sixths of the country. The north consists of three major regions: the Tell Mountains near the sea, the steppe-like high plateaus to their south, and the Saharan Atlas farther down that abuts the desert. The Sahara, stretching south for 990 miles, is interrupted by several plateaus and in the farthest south by the great massif of the Ahaggar Mountains, whose highest point is about 10,000 feet and whose crystalline and volcanic peaks extend southwestward into Mali.

Climate

Northern Algeria, whose mountains are interspersed with agriculturally productive coastal plains and valleys, is subject to a Mediterranean subtropical climate. Most precipitation occurs between fall and spring; winter temperatures are cool. Summers are generally dry and can be subject to extremely hot winds from the south known as *chehili*. Some of the higher mountain areas to the center and east can receive annual rainfall of more than 39 inches, though averages in the north range between about 16 and 32 inches. Rainfall can vary greatly from year to year, however. A year of average and well-timed precipitation can be followed by one of extreme drought, which in turn can be succeeded by a winter of deluges, floods, and mudslides.

Average annual precipitation in most of the Sahara is less than 5 inches, and in some parts it is less than a half inch. Temperatures on many summer days can rise as high as 50°C and on some winter nights they can fall below freezing. Although rain-watered and irrigated agriculture are impossible in Saharan Algeria, the desert is sprinkled with a number of extremely productive oases. The region also contains most of the country's hydrocarbon reserves.

People and Culture

The 2003 Algerian population was estimated to contain 103 men for every 100 women. The fertility rate per woman was 2.79 and this, coupled with rapidly declining mortality rates, caused the population to grow at about 1.82 percent annually. In 2003 the percentage of Algerians under 15 years of age was 34.8, and the percentage over 65 was 4.1. Life expectancy for men was 68.7 years and for women, 71.8. Although the native population was overwhelmingly rural in the mid-twentieth century, by the beginning of the twenty-first it was slightly more than 60 percent urban. There was also a significant Algerian population living overseas, particularly in France, the former colonial power.

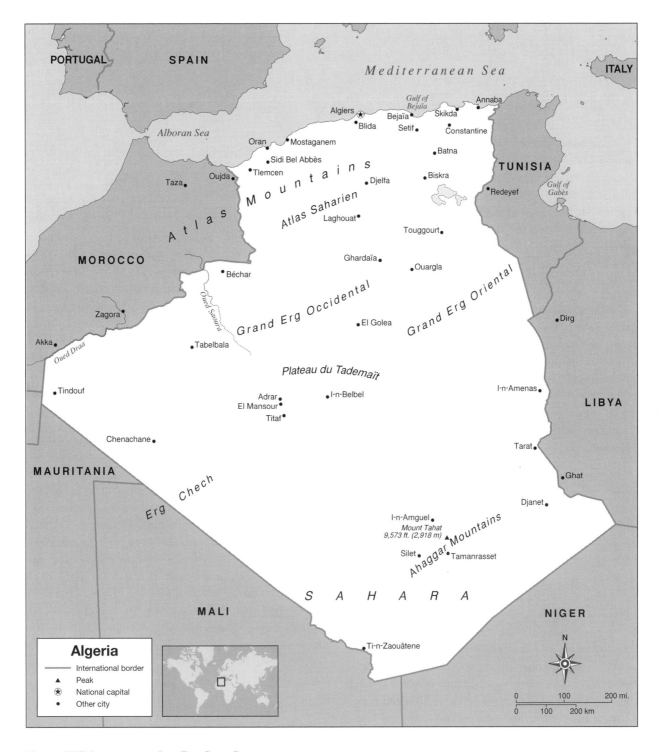

MAP BY XNR PRODUCTIONS, INC. THE GALE GROUP.

Arabs constitute the majority of Algeria's population, but Berbers are a significant minority. Since official censuses do not count ethnicity (the question has been politically charged since Algeria's independence), accurate determination of the percentages of each group is very difficult. Most esti-mates place the Arabic-speaking population at between 80 percent and 81 percent and Berber speakers at 19 percent to 20 percent. The majority of Berbers live in the mountainous Kabylia region east of Algiers and speak a variety of Berber known as Tamazight. Many of these Kabyles have moved to the cities over the decades, however, especially to Algiers, where they constitute a significant percentage of the capital's population. Other Berber speakers are Chaouias in the Aurès Mountains, Mzabis in the northern Sahara, and Twaregs in the far south.

The sole official language of Algeria after it gained independence in 1962 was Arabic, but a range of distinct Arabic dialects was and is spoken. In 2002, after decades of dissension, Tamazight, the Berber language of the Kabyles, was accepted as the second official language. Large numbers of Algerians, especially the better educated and the Kabyles, still speak, read, and write French, the official language of the colonial era.

Religiously, the overwhelming majority of Algerians are of Sunni Muslim heritage, though considerable numbers are nonobservant or only partially observant. A small number of Muslims are Ibadiyya, offshoots of the Kharijis, Islam's first splinter sect. Some rural Muslims still adhere to certain Maraboutic, populist, mystical traditions. There are also a few small Christian communities left from the colonial era.

Since independence, the Algerian state has greatly emphasized the importance of education. Adult literacy rates, which for native Algerians were calculated at about 10 percent at the outbreak of the Algerian War of Independence in 1954 had risen to 66.7 percent by 2002. While twelve years of education for boys and ten years for girls are compulsory, rates of compliance are difficult to assess. Access to schools can be difficult in some rural areas and in cities many schools are greatly overcrowded, detracting from the quality of the experience. Fearing attacks from Islamist insurgents during the 1990s, many parents in dangerous regions decided to keep their children home. Algeria has established a significant number of universities and technical institutes and it is estimated that 11 percent of the relative age group currently access postsecondary education at some level.

History

In the sixteenth century Ottoman Turks began establishing the political entity stretching along the coast from Morocco to Tunisia which came to be known until the French conquest as the Regency of Algiers. That regency was technically a part of the Ottoman Empire, but from the late seventeenth century it was effectively an independent state in which actual power was held by local Turkish military dominated by the elite Janissaries whose leaders were the *deep*. Beyond the Algiers region (Dar al Sultan), the country was divided into three *beyliks,* or provinces, centered respectively on Constantine, Oran, and Médéa. Beys (governors), who were usually Turks, controlled provinces. The *deys* and *beys* ruled directly in cities and in productive agricultural areas close to them. In much of the country, however, they depended on tribes. These extended family networks were the predominant sociopolitical formations of the indigenous Berber and Arab inhabitants, whether settled farmers, transhumants, or nomads. The regency would enlist some tribes as *makhzan* allies, whose role was to maintain control and extract taxes from other tribes known as *rayat* (subjects), a divide and conquer strategy. In more distant plains mountain tribes were largely independent, though control over some could be gained through periodic alliances.

In 1830 France, motivated by a complex mix of strategic, commercial, and domestic political concerns, invaded Algeria. The Turkish Janissaries were defeated and deported within weeks of the French landing, and France quickly occupied major coastal cities. As the occupation expanded into the interior, resistance devolved upon provincial Turks and especially upon Arab and Berber coalitions, the most prominent of which was led by the Amir Abdelkadir in the 1830s and 1840s. It was not until 1871 that the major wars of conquest in the north ended. Subsequently, due primarily to the late-nineteenth-century European scramble for Africa, France expanded its occupation to include what is now the Algerian Sahara.

During the first decades of colonial rule Algeria remained essentially under control of the French military, and during the 1848 revolution it was formally annexed to France, with the major administrative subdivisions of Constantine, Algiers, and Oran becoming *départements* of the French Republic. As French business interests invested increasingly in the Algerian economy and its infrastructure, and as others acquired through expropriation and other means more and more of the most productive farmland, tensions grew between them and the military,

An oasis town in the Algerian Sahara. Oases spring up in the rare areas of the desert where there is sufficient water supply to irrigate crops. Often home to Berbers who remain unassimilated to modern Arab culture and language, these oases are increasingly becoming popular attractions for tourists. © CORBIS.

who often felt compelled to make concessions to native Algerians in order to reduce the levels of resistance soldiers had to handle. With the collapse of the French military during the Franco-Prussian War of 1870, Paris inaugurated a process that effectively ceded power to the settlers. Although they were never more than one-ninth of the total population, the *colons* (settlers) created political, administrative, and judicial institutions that protected and enhanced their control over the means of production while assuring the subordination of native Algerians. Algerians were not citizens of the French Republic, but they were its subjects. A small minority of them were allowed to vote for members of local councils, the central *délégations financières,* effectively the Algerian parliament, but they were entitled to between one-fourth and one-third of the seats on the councils and twenty-one of sixty-nine in the central body. These arrangements assured the political dominance of the settlers and also their

control of tax revenues, the largest proportion of which always came from the native Algerians. The judicial system was totally European except in certain areas of religious and family law. With the imposition of such institutions, the tribal and clan systems, which had once determined access to land and the major means of production, and mediated internal and external disputes, lost their relevance. Algerian society was progressively proletarianized, with more and more peasants working on French-owned farms, gradually moving into services in French-controlled cities, and, toward the turn of the twentieth century, beginning a slow but accelerating process of emigration to France. At the same time, the traditional colonial establishment had dismantled most of the traditional Arab/Islamic educational system and created a secular system in which the language of education was French. Due to financial considerations and *colon* fears of the challenges an educated native elite might present,

Muslim access to education was severely limited. The result was that by 1954 only 397,000 (12.75%) of elementary-age Muslim children were enrolled in schools. Only 5,308 Muslims were enrolled in secondary schools, and 686 attended the University of Algiers.

Resistance to colonial rule in the first decades of the twentieth century came from two sources: the small French-educated elite who began demanding the rights of citizens, and a smaller group, mainly clerics, who were educated in Arabic and refused to accept the imposition of French culture. Between the two world wars various strains of Algerian nationalism began to emerge. One was an Islamic reformist movement that expressed its demands in mainly religious terms; another was a liberal movement headed by French-educated elites that, after failing to persuade the *colon* government to grant them the rights of Frenchmen, began pressing for an independent Algeria based upon secular democratic principles. A third movement, with roots amongst the working-class expatriates in France, was essentially Marxist. But within each of the major strains there always remained significant ideological, tactical, and personal differences. With the establishment's continuing refusal to allow major reform, elements of these opposition movements fused into the National Liberation Front (FLN), which launched the War of Independence on 1 November 1954. The war, which lasted until 1962, was extremely violent and bloody, eventually taking the lives of more than 500,000, causing the displacement of as many as 3,000,000 rural Algerians, and wreaking havoc upon the economy. Although the Evian Accords of March 1962, which led to Algeria's independence on 5 July, guaranteed the personal and property rights of French Algerians, at least 90 percent of them chose to leave the country before the end of that year. In anger, departing settlers methodically destroyed libraries, hospitals, government buildings, factories, machinery, communications facilities, and other valuable infrastructure. Their departure also deprived Algeria of the largest part of its professional, technical, and managerial expertise, and accelerated the flight of private capital that had begun several years earlier.

In addition to major economic challenges, independent Algeria faced challenges of national identity. The motto of the new state was "Islam is our religion, Arabic is our language, and Algeria is our nation." Yet the exact role of religion was (and has continued to be) a major source of debate, as was the question of language. The operative language of independent Algeria was French, but a range of Arab dialects was spoken in a majority of homes and Tamzight was spoken by the largest Berber minority. Regional, clan, and personal divisions among elites also divided the emerging nation.

Ahmed Ben Bella, one of the FLN's historic leaders who spent the last years of the war in French prisons, became the country's first president. He led the way to the drafting of the country's first constitution, which declared Algeria to be a socialist state, transformed the FLN into the sole legal political party, and created a strong executive in which Ben Bella was both head of state and head of government. Many opponents of Ben Bella's rule were imprisoned or forced into exile. He was overthrown in June 1965 in a military coup led by Colonel Houari Boumédienne, who sought to preserve the position of the military but also inaugurated a period of collegial leadership which, at least rhetorically, reached out more broadly to the Algerian masses. Under him Arabization of the educational system moved forward, and he sought to give the Algerian economy greater independence through a program of industrialization based on core industries that were state enterprises funded by rapidly increasing income from the petroleum and natural gas sectors. At the same time, neglect or mismanagement of the agricultural sector caused Algeria, which had been agriculturally self-sufficient at independence, to import 65 percent of its foods by 1978. A second constitution, approved in 1976, sought to give the system a more populist image, but it is clear that the country was run by a coalition of technocrats and military, and that the gap between these elites and the masses was growing both economically and culturally.

When Boumédienne died in 1978, he was succeeded by Colonel Chadli Bendjedid, who promised Algerians "a better life" and brought about a small degree of economic decentralization. But a plunge in global oil prices made Bendjedid's task much more difficult. During the 1980s, protest against

The Sahara desert covers about five-sixths of Algeria and sustains little life, but it contains vast oil and natural petroleum deposits, which make Algeria one of the wealthiest nations in Africa. © PHOTOWOOD INC./CORBIS.

the regime took on a more and more Islamic character, with major demonstrations and even some guerrilla activity in the countryside. Acceleration of Arabization policies was one of Bendjedid's responses to this problem, but this approach generated increasing opposition from the Kabyles, who felt more excluded than ever. Major strikes that led to riots broke out in Algeria's biggest cities in October 1988, and the army and other forces repressed them with great violence. In the wake of the riots, President Bendjedid announced a series of liberalizing reforms that led to the adoption in 1989 of Algeria's third constitution, which formally ended Algeria's socialist single party system. Civic organizations proliferated, Algeria's press became arguably the freest in the Arab world, and, by 1991, thirty-

three political parties had been formally recognized. The overwhelming majority of parties were secular, but the Front Islamique du Salut (FIS, or Islamic Salvation Front), a coalition of Islamists headed by Abassi al-Madani, a Muslim sociologist and educator, and Ali Belhadj, a popular preacher, became the most popular and far-reaching of them. In local and provincial elections held in June 1990, the FIS won 54 percent of the popular vote and gained control of 850 of 1,500 municipal councils. After much delay and contention, including the arrests of al-Madani and Belhadj, national parliamentary elections were held on 26 December 1991. FIS candidates won majorities in 188 of 430 electoral districts. It was clear that in runoffs for the remaining districts, which were scheduled for 16 January, FIS

A leading producer of leather, woolen, and linen goods, Constantine is the largest city in eastern Algeria and the oldest continually inhabited city in the country. Constantine is almost completely surrounded by the Rhumel Gorges, and access to the city is provided by several spectacular bridges. LIBRARY OF CONGRESS PRINTS AND PHOTOGRAPHS DIVISION WASHINGTON, D.C.

would win an absolute majority of parliamentary seats.

On 11 January the military, most of whom had opposed the elections, forced Bendjedid to resign the presidency. It then canceled the second round of elections and created a collective interim presidency, the Haut Comité d'Etat (HCS, or High State Council) to fill out the remainder of his term to 1994. The FIS was banned and more of its leaders were imprisoned. In response to this military takeover, many dedicated Islamists began moving toward violent opposition. Initial targets were security forces, bureaucrats, and government facilities, but as time went on, more and more ordinary civilians were targeted, including intellectuals, cultural figures, individuals noted for their secular views, foreigners, and ultimately anyone who refused to support the Islamist insurrection. The most violent

fighters came together as the Groupes Islamiques Armées (GIA, or Armed Islamic Groups), and a group closer to the FIS leadership, the Armée Islamique du Salut (AIS, or Islamic Salvation Army) fought in a somewhat more targeted way. The Algerian security forces used brutal measures in fighting the insurrection, including mass executions, torture, killing of prisoners, and encouragement of fights between local villagers and clans. By the end of the twentieth century, as violence began to taper off, estimates of the number of Algerians killed in the civil war ranged between 100,000 and 200,000. Surveys showed, however, that the overwhelming majority of Algerians, even those who had originally supported the FIS, opposed the tactics of the guerrillas, and also that secular liberals and Berbers would support the repressive military to whatever extent was necessary to suppress the violent fundamentalists.

The minister of defense, General Liamine Zeroual, was appointed to the presidency of the republic in January 1994, and was subsequently elected to that office by 61 percent of the vote in multiparty elections the next year. It was Zeroual's government that drafted and submitted to a referendum Algeria's fourth constitution, which was accepted by the voters in November 1996.

Government

Algeria's current government is based upon the constitution of 1996 which, in the Algerian tradition, establishes a strong presidency and provides for a considerably less powerful prime minister. Presidents are elected to five-year terms and are limited to two terms. Although the constitution provides for a multiparty political system, it prohibits parties based on religion, ethnicity, or regionalism. There are two houses of parliament. The lower house, or National Assembly, is elected by proportional representation (as opposed to the district system of the 1989 constitution), and this is the primary legislative body. In the upper house, or Council of the Nation, two-thirds of the seats are filled by indirect election and one-third are appointed by the president. To become law, bills must be approved by three-fourths of the members of the upper house, thus assuring veto power for the executive branch.

Algeria's central government is augmented by subnational units at the *wilaya* (provincial) level, of which there are presently forty-eight, and at the local level by communes, of which there are 1,540. Each has executive and legislative assemblies. In addition, an intermediate unit, the *daira*, facilitates a number of administrative and legal issues that neither the *wilaya* nor the commune engages.

The most important political parties in Algeria are the Rassemblement National Démocratique (RND, or National Democratic Rally), which was created by the government; the FLN, whose strength faded in the 1990s but which outplaced the RND in the 2002 elections; the Mouvement de la Société pour la Paix (MSP, or Movement of Society for Peace) and the Mouvement National pour la Réforme (MNR, or National Movement for Reform), both of which are have Islamic roots; the Front des Forces Socialistes (FFS, or Socialist Forces Front) and the Rassemblement pour la Culture et la Démocratie (RCD, or Rally for Culture and Democracy), both of which are based primarily on Kabyle populations. There are also several smaller parties.

President Zeroual stepped down before the end of his five-year term, reportedly because of disputes with more hard-line generals. He was succeeded in 1999 by Abdelaziz Bouteflika, a long-time supporter of Boumédienne, and the first nonmilitary man to hold the office since the overthrow of Ben Bella. Fearing that the military who had nominated Bouteflika were going to rig the elections, most of his opponents withdrew days before the 1999 elections took place. Consistent with a campaign pledge to try to end the violence afflicting the country, Bouteflika put forth a Civil Concord policy that called for amnesty for most who would lay down their arms. The amnesty was approved in a popular referendum in September 2000. As Algeria moved closer to a functioning democracy in the first decade of the new century, many believed that a group of generals and retired military known popularly as *le pouvoir* still maintained ultimate control of the system. Some also believed that President Bouteflika had fallen out with the military and that the presidential elections of 2004 might prove to be a major political turning point for the country.

Economy

With a gross domestic product (GDP) of $54.6 billion in 2001, Algeria is one of the richest countries in Africa. Industry constitutes 47.7 percent of GDP, of which manufacturing represents 4.3 percent. Services contribute 40.6 percent to GDP and agriculture, 11.7 percent. The most important portion of the manufacturing sector is petroleum and natural gas. Although Algeria exports some consumer products to neighboring North African countries, the majority of exports are from the hydrocarbon sector, which uses tankers for oil and a trans-Mediterranean pipeline and LNG (Liquefied Natural Gas) for exporting gas. Money transfers from expatriates also contribute significantly to income. Algeria imports many important consumer products, including about two-thirds of its foods and many household items. Its most important trading partners continue to be France and other countries of the European Union.

Beginning in the 1980s, with balance of payments worsening and foreign debt rising, the international community put Algeria under increasing pressure to restructure and privatize its economy. Important manufacturing sectors were privatized during the 1990s, but the government, led by the military, kept majority control of the hydrocarbon sector. During several of the tumultuous years of the 1990s annual growth of the economy was negative, but it had rebounded to 1.6 percent by 1999 to 2000. This growth rate is still lower than the rate of population increase, however. Roughly 25 percent of the workforce is employed in agriculture, 26 percent in industry, and 49 percent in services. The unemployment rate in 1997 had risen to 28 percent, and in 2000 GDP per capita was $1,750, with very large distributional inequities. As violence subsided in the first years of the new decade, domestic and foreign investment increased somewhat, raising hopes for accelerated economic growth.

> *See also* ALGERIAN FAMILY CODE (1984); ALGERIAN WAR OF INDEPENDENCE; ALGIERS; ALGIERS, BATTLE OF (1956–1957); ANNABA; BELHADJ, ALI; BEN BELLA, AHMED; BENDJEDID, CHADLI; BERBER; BOUMÉDIENNE, HOUARI; BOUTEFLIKA, ABDELAZIZ; CONSTANTINE; EVIAN ACCORDS (1962); FRONT ISLAMIQUE DU SALUT (FIS); GIA (ARMED ISLAMIC GROUPS); IBADIYYA; ISLAMIC SALVATION ARMY (AIS); KABYLIA; MADANI, ABASSI AL-; MZAB; ORAN; PARTI DU PEUPLE ALGÉRIEN (PPA); RASSEMBLEMENT NATIONAL DÉMOCRATIQUE (RND); RASSEMBLEMENT POUR LA CULTURE ET LA DÉMOCRATIE (RCD); TWAREG; ZEROUAL, LIAMINE.

Bibliography

Martinez, Luis. *The Algerian Civil War, 1990–1998.* New York: Columbia University Press, 1998.

Quandt, William B. *Between Ballots and Bullets: Algeria's Transition from Authoritarianism.* Washington, DC: Brookings Institute Press, 1998.

Roberts, Hugh. *The Battlefield: Algeria 1988–2002, Studies in a Broken Polity.* London: Verso, 2003.

Ruedy, John. *Modern Algeria: The Origins and Development of a Nation.* Bloomington: Indiana University Press, 1992.

Stora, Benjamin. *Algeria, 1830–2000: A Short History,* translated by Jane Marie Todd. Ithaca, NY: Cornell University Press, 2001.

JOHN RUEDY

ALGERIA: CONSTITUTION

Algeria has had four constitutions, in 1963, 1976, 1989, and 1996.

Algeria's four constitutions reflect its political development since attaining independence from France in 1962. The first two constitutions illustrated Algeria's commitment to socialism in its state-building. The third constitution responded to the turmoil wrought by the October 1988 riots. The civil war of the 1990s influenced the framing of the fourth and present constitution. Algeria's postcolonial constitutional history has in many ways been an existential project—an effort to define a nation. The four constitutions collectively indicate the evolution of that difficult process.

The Front de Libération Nationale (FLN) successfully led the political struggle against France, but it failed to present a complementary postcolonial political, economic, and social program. Roiling intraparty rivalries resulted in civil strife in the summer of 1962. Ahmed Ben Bella, supported by Houari Boumédienne, the commander of the external Armée de Libération Nationale (ALN), seized power from the wartime Gouvernement Provisioire de la République Algérienne (GPRA). Ben Bella was selected prime minister by the Assemblée Nationale, whose chief authority was constituent—the crafting of a constitution. But Ben Bella and his FLN supporters ignored the Assemblée, drafted a constitution themselves, and forced its acceptance.

The Constitution of 1963 expressed the fervor of Algerian revolutionary nationalism and the authoritarianism of the Ben Bella government, the FLN, and the ALN. Taking into account the FLN's Tripoli Programme of June 1962, the constitution defined Algeria as a socialist state committed to the anti-imperialist struggle internally and externally. It extolled *autogestion*—the spontaneous takeover by self-management committees of properties abandoned by colonial settlers *(pieds-noirs)*—as the model and means to assert socialism and egalitarianism. The FLN, described as "the revolutionary force of

Algerians wait to cast ballots in the 1996 constitutional election. Over 85 percent of voters approved the new constitution, which banned political parties based on religion or language, extended the president's powers, and affirmed Islam as the state religion. © CORBIS-SYGMA. REPRODUCED BY PERMISSION.

the nation" in the preamble, acquired a political monopoly as the only permissible legal party. The military was also to be politically engaged. The executive branch received great power at the expense of the legislative, as the Assemblée Nationale was reduced to a subordinate ratifying body. The constitution proclaimed Islam as the official religion and Arabic as the official language. After a national referendum approved the document, Ben Bella was elected Algeria's first president.

The rival ambitions of Ben Bella and Boumédienne produced political and personal hostility. In June 1965 Boumédienne successfully deposed Ben Bella's government in June 1965 and suspended the constitution in favor of a Conseil de la Révolution. Boumédienne was a fervent socialist who favored strong leadership and direction in state-building. He pursued state plans along with simultaneous industrial, agrarian, and cultural revolutions. In 1975

Boumédienne declared the need to assess the country's development. This resulted in remarkable public discussions that produced a National Charter, which also framed Algeria's second constitution.

The Constitution of 1976 introduced a 261-member Assemblée Populaire Nationale (APN). Its representatives were nominated and slated by the FLN, which retained its predominant constitutional privileges. The APN served as a ratifying body for legislation proposed by the FLN political bureau and central committee. Mirroring Boumédienne's domination, the constitution enormously empowered the executive branch. The president was commander in chief of the armed forces and secretary-general of the FLN. When the APN was not in session, the president could rule by decree. The cabinet was also responsible to the president rather than to the APN. Civil and political freedoms—including rights for women—were stipulated but not in fact exercised.

The constitution reaffirmed the official roles of socialism, Arabic, and Islam. The constitution also vested Boumédienne with a mantle of legitimacy after a decade of authoritarian rule. Ironically, it soon played an important role in ensuring a smooth transition after his untimely death in 1978.

Algeria underwent substantial changes during the presidency of Chadli Bendjedid. State-planning shifted greater attention to the first sector. The FLN also became increasingly inert and corrupt. A minor, though significant, Islamist insurgency also occurred. The Family Code of 1984 reinforced the *shariʿa* and contradicted the Constitution of 1976 regarding gender equality. The plunge in petroleum prices in the mid-1980s severely affected the economy and exacerbated chronic unemployment. These conditions deepened the distress of the educated but disillusioned youth. In October 1988 riots broke out throughout Algeria, destabilizing the government. After suppressing the violent protests, Bendjedid shifted some of his power to the prime minister and promised reform. This was the historical context for the Constitution of 1989.

The new constitution redefined the Algerian republic as "democratic and popular," but not "socialist." The FLN also lost its hegemonic position, as the constitution stipulated the freedom "to form associations of a political nature" (Article 40), thereby projecting a multiparty political system. Human and civil rights—including "freedom of expression, of association and of assembly" (Article 39)—were guaranteed, though women's rights were not specifically stated as in the Constitution of 1976. Significantly, the army's role was relegated to non-political responsibilities. Though the president still had predominant power—including rule by decree—the end of the FLN's political monopoly promised substantial reform and a greater role for the APN. The president could still select his prime minister and cabinet, but the APN had to approve his choices. Islam and Arabic retained their official status.

Subsequent legislation in July 1989 secured the right to organize political parties. By early 1990 Algeria was experiencing remarkable liberalization and freedom. Regional and local elections held in June 1990 astonished observers, as the recently or-

ganized Islamist Front Islamique du Salut (FIS) won most of the contests. Scheduled parliamentary elections in June 1991 had to be postponed after violent confrontations between the FIS and the government. After the FIS decisively won the first round of the rescheduled elections in December, alarmed military and civilian elites forced President Bendjedid's resignation in January 1992, suspended the constitution, and canceled the elections. A Haut Comité d'Etat (HCE) took control of the government. These events provoked the civil war chiefly between the government and alienated Islamists that resulted in an estimated 150,000 deaths. A cautious reinstitutionalization began in January 1994 when the HCE dissolved itself after announcing the appointment of Liamine Zeroual as president. In presidential elections that were remarkably free (though the officially disbanded FIS was not allowed to participate) Zeroual was elected to a full term in November 1995.

The Constitution of 1996 symbolized Algeria's deliberate "redemocratization." Approved by referendum that many considered rigged, the constitution prohibited parties based on religion, regionalism, gender, and language. This was meant to neutralize the political potential of Berbers (primarily Kabyles) and Islamists. The president was limited to two terms but preserved the power to dissolve parliament, choose a prime minister and cabinet, and rule by decree. The constitution inaugurated a bicameral legislature. It regenerated the APN as a lower house and introduced the Conseil de la Nation (CN) as an upper house. The president received the privilege of appointing one-third of the membership of the CN. Subsequent elections continued Algeria's redemocratization. Parliamentary and local elections in 2002 were marked by the remarkable renascence of the FLN. Concurrently, roiling events in Kabylia resulted in the recognition of the Berbers' Tamazight as an official national language in 2002. The question of whether the constitution needs to be amended to include Tamazight with Arabic remains controversial.

Algeria's constitutional history illustrates a country defining and redefining itself. That existential quest continues today as Algeria exercises an albeit limited democratic process. Most observers believe that for Algeria to have an authentic democracy, the military must withdraw from political affairs. In addition, accountability and transparency must be institutionalized. If pursued, this will probably mean more constitutional revision or reform.

See also ALGERIA: POLITICAL PARTIES IN; ALGERIAN WAR OF INDEPENDENCE; ARMÉE DE LIBÉRATION NATIONALE (ALN); BEN BELLA, AHMED; BENDJEDID, CHADLI; BERBER; BOUMÉDIENNE, HOUARI; FRONT DE LIBÉRATION NATIONALE (FLN); FRONT ISLAMIQUE DU SALUT (FIS); ZEROUAL, LIAMINE.

Bibliography

Quandt, William B. *Between Ballots and Bullets: Algeria's Transition from Authoritarianism.* Washington, DC: Brookings Institute Press, 1998.

Ruedy, John. *Modern Algeria: The Origins and Development of a Nation.* Bloomington: Indiana University Press, 1992.

PHILLIP C. NAYLOR

ALGERIA: POLITICAL PARTIES IN

Political parties have been an integral part of Algerian politics since the days of French colonial rule.

Until 1945, Algerian political parties included the Parti Social Français (PSF) and Parti Populaire Français (PPF), representing segments of the European settler population; the Parti Communiste Algérien (PCA), integrating educated Muslims, Jews, and Europeans; and the Reformist Ulama Movement, the Etoile Nord-Africaine (ENA), the Parti du Peuple Algérien (PPA) and the Mouvement pour le Triomphe des Libertés Démocratiques (MTLD), representing the parties and associations of Algerian nationalism.

When the Algerian War of Independence commenced in November 1954, one major movement-party, the Front de Libération Nationale (FLN), became dominant. It incorporated under its wings nationalist movements and leaders of different generations; it even developed its own liberation army—the Armée de Libération Nationale (ALN). Only one movement sought to challenge, albeit with little success, the nationalistic monopoly of the (FLN). It was the Mouvement Nationale Algérien (MNA), led by the veteran nationalist Messali al-Hadj.

The FLN as Ruling Party and the Absence of Real Political Opposition

Upon independence, Algeria became a republic under President Ahmed Ben Bella, a key figure within the FLN. Under the first constitution (1963) the FLN regime eliminated all political competition that posed a danger to its rule. Dissident forces led by former FLN revolutionaries, among them Mohamed Boudiaf's Parti de la Révolution Socialiste (PRS), Belkacem Krim's Mouvement Démocratique de Renouveau Algérien (Democratic Movement for Algerian Renewal—MDRA), and Hocine Ait Ahmed's Front des Forces Socialistes (Front of Socialist Forces—FFS), were either outlawed or neutralized by the FLN regime, and several of their leaders were exiled or assassinated. The parties that were tolerated, yet not officially recognized, could not participate in free elections, and served as mere adjuncts to the government. The justification given for the political monopoly of the FLN under Ben Bella was that it had obtained a national mandate as a "front" and, therefore, all groups needed to function as adjuncts to the FLN-dominated regime.

Because the FLN had been mandated as a "front," trade unions, women's groups, and civil associations came under FLN control and enjoyed scant autonomy. These included the FLN-formed Union Nationale des Etudiants Algériens (National Union of Algerian Students—UNEA) and the Union Générale des Travailleurs Algériens (General Union of Algerian Workers—UGTA). The UNEA was quite active throughout the 1960s despite government attempts to quell the movement. Strikes, boycotts, and other violent clashes between student groups and government officials continued to upset numerous university campuses until the UNEA was suppressed and dissolved in 1971. The student movement was subsequently integrated into the National Union of Algerian Youth (Union Nationale de la Jeunesse Algérienne—UNJA), a national conglomerate of youth organizations guided by the FLN.

The Algerian women's movement, which became institutionalized within the FLN's Union Nationale des Femmes Algériennes (National Union of Algerian Women—UNFA), subordinate to the FLN, had made few inroads since independence. Those who played a significant part in the War of Independence were relegated to marginal public roles. The only significant breakthrough for the women's movement was the Khemisti Law of 1963, which raised the minimum age of marriage. Although girls were still expected to marry earlier than boys, the minimum age was raised to sixteen for girls and eighteen for boys. This change facilitated women's pursuance of advanced education, but it fell short of the age-nineteen minimum specified in the original proposal.

Although the FLN was buttressed by the military and monopolized Algeria's public life under the presidencies of Ahmed Ben Bella (1962–1965), Houari Boumédienne (1965–1978), and Chadli Bendjedid (1978–1991), it lacked mass appeal. The central FLN leadership gradually lost touch with its regional branches and failed to mobilize the masses to endorse its domestic programs. The party's "self-management" socialist economy under Ben Bella, which intended to involve agricultural and industrial workers in the operation of state companies, soon gave way to an unpopular centralized socialist economy imposed from above. As the party branches on the local level became dormant, and bureaucratic inefficiency permeated the system, the FLN declined in popularity and was no longer regarded as a "front," as its name suggested.

By the 1980s, Algeria's economic polarization was such that 5 percent of the population earned 45 percent of the national income, and 50 percent earned less than 22 percent of the national income. Members of the party elite enjoyed privileged access to foreign capital and goods, were ensured positions in the helm of state-owned enterprises, and benefited from corrupt management of state-controlled goods and services. The masses, on the other hand, suffered from the increasing unemployment and inflation resulting from government reforms and economic austerity in the mid- to late 1980s. The riots of October 1988 indicated that the FLN had completely lost legitimacy in the eyes of the people.

Toward Reform: The Road to Free Elections and a Multiparty System

A new constitution in 1976 that was subsequently amended in 1979 was to sanction the proliferation of political parties and facilitate free elections. Yet, the articles referring to this matter were vague and, well into the 1980s, no real progress was made to enforce this policy. It was only under the new con-

stitution of 23 February 1989—modified in 1996—that changes finally could be implemented. These came in the wake of large-scale riots in October 1988 protesting food shortages. President Bendjedid and the FLN were pressured to surrender their monopoly on power and institute democratic reforms. During the riots, thousands of young protestors were wounded and at least 100 were killed.

According to the constitutional reforms, Algeria had universal suffrage. Unlike in past years, the president of the Algerian Republic would be elected as the head of state to a five-year term, renewable once. He would become the head of the Council of Ministers and of the High Security Council. He would appoint the prime minister, who also would serve as the head of government. The prime minister was to appoint the Council of Ministers. The Algerian parliament became bicameral, consisting of a lower chamber, the National People's Assembly with 380 members, and an upper chamber, the Council of Nation, with 144 members. The Council of Nation would thereafter be elected every five years. Regional and municipal authorities were to elect two-thirds of the Council of Nation; the president would appoint the rest. The Council of Nation members were to serve a six-year term with one-half of the seats up for election or reappointment every three years. As had been the case throughout much of Algeria's recent history, and not part of the new reforms, the country is divided into forty-eight *wilayas* (states or provinces) headed by *walis* (governors) who report to the minister of the interior. Each *wilaya* is further divided into communes. The *wilayas* and communes are each governed by an elected assembly.

Chadli Bendjedid's decision to engage in constitutional reform signaled the downfall of the FLN. The 1989 constitution not only eliminated the FLN's monopoly but also abolished all references to the FLN's unique posture as party of the avant-garde. The new constitution recognized the FLN's historical role, but the FLN was obliged to compete as any other political party. By mid-1989 the military had recognized the imminent divestiture of the FLN and had begun to distance itself from the party. The resignation of several senior army officers from party membership in March 1989, generally interpreted as a protest against the constitutional revisions, also reflected a strategic maneuver to preserve

This poster urged Algerian voters to support President Abdelaziz Bouteflika's "Civil Concord" policy to help end years of antigovernment violence, which began after the military canceled elections that seemed likely to favor fundamentalist Islamic parties. Approval of this referendum in September 2000 led to amnesty for most militants, but the military continued to resist the dominant moderate parties' attempts at total democratization. © AP/WIDE WORLD PHOTOS. REPRODUCED BY PERMISSION.

the military establishment's integrity as guardian of the revolution. In July 1991 Bendjedid himself resigned from the party leadership.

The legalization of political parties, further enunciated in the Law Relative to Political Associations of July 1989, was one of the major achievements of the revised constitution. More than thirty political parties emerged as a result of these reforms by the time of the first multiparty local and regional elections in June 1990; nearly sixty existed by the time of the first national multiparty elections in December 1991.

The Turning Point—Political Parties and Elections: 1990–2002

On 12 June 1990 the country's first free municipal elections took place. Chief among the numerous political parties contending for power were the ruling FLN; the Islamist fundamentalist Islamic Salvation Front (Front Islamique du Salut—FIS), founded in 1989 and led by Abassi al-Madani and Ali Belhadj; Hocine Ait Ahmed's pro-Berber Front of Socialist Forces (Front des Forces Socialistes—FFS); and another pro-Berber party—the Rally for Culture and Democracy (Rassemblement pour la Culture et la Démocratie—RCD). The results were stunning: The FIS won a majority of the municipal seats in the country's four largest cities—Algiers, Oran, Constantine, and Annaba—as well as 65 percent of the popular vote and 55 percent of 15,000 municipal posts throughout Algeria. It won representation in 32 of the 48 provinces.

Support for FIS was part of the growing admiration in the Arab-Muslim world for Islamic fundamentalist leaders in the wake of the Iranian Revolution of 1979 and the parliamentary victory achieved in 1989 by the Muslim Brotherhood in Jordan. Many of the voters used their votes to protest against low salaries, spiraling inflation, and limited economic choices for young people under the FLN regime. In fact, the vote for the fundamentalist party was not so much massive support for FIS as a reaction against the FLN's record of authoritarian rule and economic mismanagement and corruption.

Its electoral successes notwithstanding, FIS was somewhat vague from the outset about its objectives. It is known, however, that Madani struck an alliance with local merchants and espoused a free market economy in lieu of the FLN's state socialism. Both Madani and Belhadj described a woman's primary role as rearing a family, and limited women to such jobs as nursing and teaching. The local and provincial municipal councils, which serve five-year terms, have jurisdiction over such matters as renewal of liquor licenses, the type of activities allowed at cultural centers, and the issuance of permits to build mosques. Madani and Belhadj vehemently opposed public drinking, any form of dancing, and secular programming in the media.

At the time, in addition to the many secular parties that were newly created or had been revived after years of virtual clandestine existence, there also emerged Islamist parties who competed with the FIS. Among them two are noteworthy: the Mouvement de la Société pour la Paix (Society for Peace—MSP), also known at one time as Harakat al-Mujtama al-Islamiyya, or Hamas); and the Mouvement de la Réforme Nationale (Movement for National Reform—MRN). Both parties were moderate vis-à-vis central government control, sought to take part in the ruling cabinet, and opted for a gradual Islamization of society through religious education. The MSP and MRN shunned violence, unlike the FIS, which in the early 1990s developed the Islamic Salvation Army (Armée Islamique du Salut—AIS), a paramilitary force to struggle against the authorities.

The backing for FIS in 1990 and subsequently came primarily from the Arab population, which constituted at least 70 percent of the total Algerian

Sunni Muslim population of approximately 28 million. The Berber Muslims, as well as the ethnically mixed Arab-Berber population, were prone to support secular parties, including the Berber parties, especially the FFS and RCD. Both the FLN and the FIS were challenged in the June 1990 elections by the Kabyles, members of the largest, most important Berber group. The Berbers demanded then, as they still do, greater political freedom and the ability to expand their cultural heritage. The RCD is especially stubborn about the need to augment the influence of their Tamazight Berber dialect. Besides the FIS, the other major beneficiaries of the 1990 elections were the FFS and RCD. The latter gained 8 percent of the municipal vote.

The gains made by Islamist and Berber parties prompted these forces to pressure the authorities to call for general parliamentary elections, which were scheduled for 27 June 1991. The elections did not take place, however. Fearing an Islamist victory, the army declared martial law and arrested, on 30 June 1991, the top FIS leadership, including Madani and Belhadj.

Under relentless pressure from all political parties, the government rescheduled new parliamentary elections for December 1991, with second-round runoffs planned for January 1992. These elections were to provide a serious national test for the new multiparty system; they were open to all registered parties. Voting was by universal suffrage and secret ballots, and assembly seats were awarded based on a proportional representation system. Only 231 of the 430 seats were decided in the first round of elections, in which 59 percent of eligible voters participated, but a FIS victory seemed assured by the Islamist command of 80 percent of the contested seats. The second round of elections never took place following the coup d'état on 11 January 1992 because the military canceled them to avert a sweeping Islamist victory. The coup also marked a temporary end to FLN rule, and led to the resignation of President Bendjedid. From this point until the parliamentary elections of 1997, Algeria was guided by a five-member High State Council, which was backed and manipulated by the military.

The canceling of the second round of elections, coupled with political uncertainty and economic turmoil, led to a violent reaction on the part of FIS adherents and other Islamists. These elements organized themselves into the Islamic Salvation Army (AIS), the more extreme Armed Islamic Group (GIA), and a faction that seceded from it—the Salafist Group for Islamist Preaching. A campaign of assassinations, bombings, and massacres gained unprecedented strength. The High State Council officially dissolved and outlawed the FIS in 1992 and began a series of arrests and trials of FIS members that reportedly resulted in over 50,000 members being jailed. Despite efforts to restore the political process, violence and terrorism rocked Algeria throughout much of the 1990s and the early years of the twenty-first century. As many as 100,000 Algerians died as a result.

In November 1995 presidential elections took place despite the objection of some political parties to holding elections that excluded the FIS. Liamine Zeroual, who also headed the High State Council, was elected president by 75 percent of the vote. In an attempt to bring political stability to the nation, the Rassemblement Nationale Démocratique (National Democratic Rally—RND) was formed soon thereafter as the regime's new ruling party by Zeroual and a progressive group of FLN members. It was meant to constitute Algeria's major secular party alongside the declining FLN. Zeroual announced that presidential elections would be held in early 1999, nearly two years ahead of the scheduled time. In April 1999 the Algerian people elected Abdelaziz Bouteflika president with an official count of 70 percent of all votes cast. Bouteflika was the only presidential candidate that enjoyed the backing of the FLN and RND. His inauguration for a five-year term took place on 27 April 1999.

President Bouteflika's agenda focused initially on restoring security and stability to the country. Following his inauguration, he proposed an official amnesty for those who had fought against the government during the 1990s unless they had engaged in "blood crimes," such as rape or murder. This "Civil Concord" policy was widely approved in a nationwide referendum in September 2000. Government officials estimate that 85 percent of those fighting the regime during the 1990s, except for members of the GIA and the Salafists, accepted the amnesty offer and have been reintegrated into Algerian society. Bouteflika also launched national

commissions to study educational and judicial reform, and to restructure the state bureaucracy. His government has set ambitious targets for economic reform and attracting foreign investors.

In the 2002 parliamentary elections the tables turned in favor of the FLN, which won a majority of 199 seats in the 389-body parliament; the RND suffered a devastating defeat, with its representation reduced to 47 seats. The Islamist MRN and MSP won 43 and 38 seats, respectively. The FFS and the RCD had called for a boycott of the vote because they expected fraud and because of strained relations at the time between Berber leaders and the regime. With an absolute majority in the legislature and the support of the RND and the moderate Islamists, the FLN has an opportunity to push forward reforms, but the party and President Bouteflika face resistance from the army—the real power holders who often oppose genuine reforms.

See also ALGERIAN WAR OF INDEPENDENCE; ARMÉE DE LIBÉRATION NATIONALE (ALN); BELHADJ, ALI; BEN BELLA, AHMED; BENDJEDID, CHADLI; BOUDIAF, MOHAMED; BOUMÉDIENNE, HOUARI; FRONT DE LIBÉRATION NATIONALE (FLN); FRONT ISLAMIQUE DU SALUT (FIS); GIA (ARMED ISLAMIC GROUPS); HADJ, MESSALI AL-; HAMAS; HIGH STATE COUNCIL (ALGERIA); ISLAMIC SALVATION ARMY (AIS); MADANI, ABASSI AL-; MOUVEMENT NATIONAL ALGÉRIEN; MOUVEMENT POUR LE TRIOMPHE DES LIBERTÉS DÉMOCRATIQUES; PARTI DU PEUPLE ALGÉRIEN (PPA); RASSEMBLEMENT NATIONAL DÉMOCRATIQUE (RND); RASSEMBLEMENT POUR LA CULTURE ET LA DÉMOCRATIE (RCD); ZEROUAL, LIAMINE.

Bibliography

Global Security.org. "Algerian Insurgency." Available from <http://www.globalsecurity.org/military/world/war/algeria-90s.htm>.

Kapil, Arun. "Algeria's Elections Show Islamist Strength." *Middle East Report* (September–October 1990): 31–36.

Laskier, Michael M. "Algeria Holds its First Free Multiparty Elections." In *Great Events from History II: Human Rights Series,* edited by Frank N. Magill. Pasadena, CA, and Englewood Cliffs, NJ: Salem Press, 1992.

MICHAEL M. LASKIER

ALGERIAN FAMILY CODE (1984)

The Algerian Family Code of 1984 sanctions, after years of internal debates, a conservative model of family in which the male kin have privileges and power over women.

After Algerian independence in 1962, fundamental questions arose concerning the trajectory of Algerian society. The status of women was intrinsic to these concerns and ensuing debates. Some women, the *mujahidas,* contributed very actively in the struggle against the French, serving as liaison officers, nurses, and even combatants, sometimes carrying bombs or weapons, as did Hassiba Ben Bouali, Zohra Drif, Jamila Bouhired, and Zoulaika Boujemaʿa. The necessity to improve the legal condition of women was recognized in the "charte nationale" but the conservatism of some Front de Libération Nationale (FLN) leaders, especially those close to Islamist forces, led to demands for a stricter enforcement of the Islamic law and traditions.

The tensions and debates between these two tendencies lasted from 1962 to 1984. There were many attempts to modify family laws during this period, and some minor changes were introduced. The first comprehensive codification project emerged in 1981, and was considered very conservative. Leaked to the press, news of this project catalyzed many demonstrations by women. The project was withdrawn, making this one the few examples of this kind in Algeria.

But with the rising popularity of Islamist movements in the face of economic failures of Algerian policies during the 1970s, a new code, almost the same as the earlier project of 1981, was presented and passed virtually without any discussion at the National Assembly in June 1984. It is still in force today.

The main provisions of this code are the following:

- minimum ages for marriage are 21 years for men, 18 for women;

- the necessity of a matrimonial guardian (the father or a close agnatic man has to consent to the marriage, not the bride) for a woman to get married;

- up to four wives allowed per man, the consent of the other wives not being required;

- husband's privilege of repudiation.

See also ALGERIA: OVERVIEW; GENDER: GENDER AND LAW; GENDER: GENDER AND POLITICS.

Bibliography

Bekkar, Rabia. "Women in the City in Algeria: Change and Resistance." In *ISIM Newsletter,* no. 7 (March 2001): 27.

Charrad, Mounira. *States and Women's Rights: The Making of Postcolonial Tunisia, Algeria, and Morocco.* Berkeley: University of California Press, 2001.

Slyomovics, Susan. "'Hassiba Benbouali, If You Could See Our Algeria. . .': Women and Public Space in Algeria." *MERIP / Middle East Report* 192 (1995): 8–13.

RABIA BEKKAR

ALGERIAN PEOPLE'S PARTY

See PARTI DU PEUPLE ALGÉRIEN

ALGERIAN WAR OF INDEPENDENCE

This war ended more than 130 years of French colonial rule over Algeria.

The Algerian war of independence began in the early hours of 1 November 1954 and ended officially on 3 July 1962, when France's President Charles de Gaulle formally renounced his nation's sovereignty over Algeria and proclaimed its independence.

The French occupation of Algeria, begun in 1830, led to a colonial situation in which a minority of European settlers and their descendants dominated the Algerian economy. They maintained that domination through monopolies of political power and the means of coercion. During the first half of the twentieth century, a series of initiatives by various indigenous leaderships sought first to secure meaningful political participation for the Muslim majority within the colonial system and later to negotiate autonomy, confederation, or independence. When these efforts proved fruitless, a group of radical young nationalists founded the Comité Révolutionnaire d'Unité et d'Action (CRUA; Rev-

Police clear a street with tear gas after a demonstration by 20,000 French settlers turns into a riot in Algiers, 8 February 1956. The demonstration protested the arrival of French premier Guy Mollet, who was in Algeria to resolve French problems with Algerian nationalists. Mollet was pelted with tomatoes and rocks, and police had to use clubs to restore order. © BETTMANN/CORBIS. REPRODUCED BY PERMISSION.

olutionary Committee of Unity and Action), which began, in the spring or summer of 1952, to plan an insurrection. Six CRUA members, together with three political exiles, are considered the *chefs historiques* of the Algerian revolution. The CRUA chiefs, led by Mohamed Boudiaf of M'sila, included Moustafa Ben Boulaid, Mourad Didouche, Belkacem Krim, Rabah Bitat, and Larbi Ben M'hidi. The external leaders were Hocine Ait Ahmed, Mohamed Khider, and Ahmed Ben Bella, who later became Algeria's first president.

Estimates of the number of militants taking part in the initial insurrection range from nine hundred to about three thousand. It began with attacks on French installations in several parts of the country, but the most effective actions took place in the Au-

rès region of the southeast. During the ensuing winter, the French managed to contain the insurrection, limiting its manifestations to distant and inaccessible regions. In August 1955, the leadership, concerned that neither the bulk of Algerians nor the European community were taking the insurrection seriously, decided to begin targeting European civilians in some twenty-six localities in the eastern part of the country. As many as 123 people were killed in what were called the Philippeville massacres. In outraged reaction, French forces responded by taking a far larger number of Muslim lives. These events served to polarize the two communities in such a way that a narrowly based insurrection became a nationwide revolution; thousands of men joined guerrilla units, while France rapidly built its own forces into the hundreds of thousands.

Muslim girls celebrate Algerian independence, July 1962. The Algerian War of Independence (1954–1962) claimed over 300,000 French and Algerian lives. © BETTMANN/CORBIS. REPRODUCED BY PERMISSION.

In its initial proclamation, on 31 October 1954, the CRUA had announced the creation of a Front de Libération Nationale (FLN; National Liberation Front) to which it had invited Algerians of all political persuasions to rally. As a result of the polarization following the events of August 1955, Algerian political classes across a broad ideological spectrum gradually closed down their independent operations and joined the FLN in revolution. By the summer of 1956, only Messali Hadj, long leader of the most radical wing of the Algerian nationalist movement but now bypassed by events, remained outside of the FLN.

In order to accommodate the dramatically broadened movement, the revolutionaries organized a clandestine congress in the Soumamm valley of the Kabylia during August and September 1956. It created a broad Conseil National de la Révolution Algérienne (CNRA) to serve as a protoparliament and a Comité de Coordination et d'Éxécution (CCE; Committee of Coordination and Implementation) to bear the executive functions. One of the first decisions of the new executive was to initiate, at the end of September 1956, the urban warfare strategy that became known as the Battle of Algiers. A very visible phase of the war that

the French managed to win by the middle of 1957, the recourse to urban warfare brought the war home in a physical way to the majority of Colons, who were urban residents, and attracted the attention of metropolitan Frenchmen and the wider world for the first time to the Algerian situation. Another result of the Battle of Algiers was that the severe French repression drove the top FLN leadership out of the country to Tunis. This in turn generated problems in communications and orientation between the external leadership and the internal *mojahedin*. These problems caused troublesome divisions within the movement that lasted throughout the war and beyond.

Between the fall of 1957 and the spring of 1958, the French army, now grown to roughly 500,000 men, succeeded in bringing most of Algeria under its physical control and was concentrating on limiting cross-border raids by Algerian guerrillas from Morocco and Tunisia. But the military were apprehensive. They feared that their achievements might be undone by the divided political leadership at home, which was sensitive to the violence involved in pacification and to growing world pressure. Thus, the army, under the leadership of General Jacques Massu and with the enthusiastic support of the colons, proclaimed the creation on 13 May 1958 of a Committee of Public Safety at Algiers. This challenge to government authority brought down the Fourth French Republic and propelled de Gaulle to power as head of the Fifth Republic, pledging an early resolution of the Algerian conflict. By the autumn of 1958, de Gaulle offered Algerians the opportunity of total integration as equals into the French republic, inaugurated a massive plan of economic renewal, and invited the revolutionary troops to join their French compatriots in a "paix des braves."

The CCE and the CNRA rejected these terms and, instead, created a Provisional Government of the Algerian Republic (Gouvernement Provisoir de la République Algérienne; GPRA) at Tunis, with Ferhat Abbas at its head. From this point on, even though French forces remained in control of most of Algeria, the GPRA campaigned to win world support for Algerian independence. The campaign centered primarily on developing and eastern bloc countries and upon the United Nations. Within a year, de Gaulle began speaking of Algerian self-determination. The war of independence might have ended soon afterward, but there were obstacles. Principal among these was the fate of the Sahara, in which French companies had recently discovered oil. Even more important was the resistance of the colon community, which increasingly found more in common with the military. During 1960 they created a Front de l'Algérie Française in order to fight against independence and in January 1961 the Organisation Armée Secrète (OAS; Secret Army Organization), which eventually led an armed insurrection against French civil authority and launched a campaign of terror against Muslim Algerians.

After several abortive attempts at negotiations, the provisional government and France finally signed the Evian Agreement on 18 March 1962, which led to unequivocal independence in July. The war had caused the dislocation from their homes of about 3 million Algerians, the destruction of much social and economic infrastructure, and the deaths of several hundred thousand Algerians. The rebuilding tasks faced by independent Algeria would be formidable.

See also ABBAS, FERHAT; AIT AHMED, HOCINE; BEN BELLA, AHMED; BEN BOULAID, MOUSTAFA; BEN M'HIDI, MUHAMMAD LARBI; BITAT, RABAH; BOUDIAF, MOHAMED; COLONS; COMITÉ RÉVOLUTIONNAIRE D'UNITÉ ET D'ACTION (CRUA); CONSEIL NATIONAL DE LA RÉVOLUTION ALGÉRIENNE (CNRA); DIDOUCHE, MOURAD; FRONT DE LIBÉRATION NATIONALE (FLN); HADJ, MESSALI AL-; KABYLIA; KHIDER, MOHAMED; KRIM, BELKACEM; ORGANISATION ARMÉE SECRÈTE (OAS).

Bibliography

Horne, Alistair. *A Savage War of Peace: Algeria 1954–1962,* revised edition. New York: Penguin, 1987.

Ruedy, John. *Modern Algeria: The Origins and Development of a Nation.* Bloomington: Indiana University Press, 1992.

JOHN RUEDY

ALGIERS

Capital of the Democratic and Popular Republic of Algeria.

Algiers is located at the northwestern end of a large bay in the Mediterranean Sea. The city's industrial activity is concentrated to the south and east, on the plain of the Mitidja. The region contains 48 percent of the country's factories and 55 percent of its industrial workforce. In 2003, it had a population of 3 million.

The city's origins reach back to the Phoenicians and Romans (300 B.C.E.–100 C.E.). Berbers reestablished Algiers in the ninth century, naming it al-Jaza'ir (islands) because of rock outcroppings in the bay. In the early sixteenth century, Algiers was drawn into Castile's overseas expansion and the Ottoman reaction against it. After expelling the Spaniards in 1529, the Ottomans established a corsair principality. At its height in the 1600s, the city, with perhaps forty thousand inhabitants, held as many as twenty thousand Christians for ransom. In the eighteenth century, Western states forced an end to corsair activities and Algiers began to specialize in grain exports. A dispute over payment for grain deliveries to Napoleon led to the occupation of Algiers by the French (1830).

French army rule gave way to French civilian control in 1871. Both the military and the settlers initially erected their residential and commercial structures in the lower part of the Casbah (qasba, citadel), as the pre-1830 part of Algiers was called. In contrast to other areas of North Africa, no new European city center sprang up outside the existing one.

The end of the nineteenth century was a time of rapid population increase (by 41 percent from 1886 to 1896, and then to a total of 155,000 settlers and 45,000 Muslims by 1918) and considerable commercial wealth, particularly from wine exports. Public building included a central train depot and a new harbor (both completed by 1896), streetcar lines (begun in 1896), and municipal and educational infrastructures (water, gas, hospitals, a university). Ambitious plans to turn the entire lower Casbah into a city with wide boulevards were quashed by the military, but the incorporation of the suburb of Mustapha in 1904 opened the way for a more systematic southern expansion. Regional Algiers was born.

In the new city, the French rejected the Arab architecture of the Casbah for French bourgeois classicism, while the residents of the wealthier suburbs opted for imitations of Turkish gardens (jinan) architecture. After World War I, European monumental classicism took over, and in the 1930s functional modernism began to emerge. Construction of a new waterfront neighborhood pushed the Casbah into the hills, where it was greatly reduced in size. The former corsair city was finally cut off from the sea.

During the interwar period, Muslim agriculture in Algeria reached its productive limits on the less fertile lands that the colonists left for the indigenous population. The capital offered alternative employment in the port, shipyards, mechanical industries, and trucking firms. In addition, there were small-scale construction firms, an industry for the processing of agricultural products, and a large administrative sector. French settlers, however, held most of the skilled jobs. Muslim rural immigrants provided the unskilled labor. They crowded into shantytowns in the hills or into the Casbah, which had twice as many people as it had held in 1830, packed into one-quarter as many buildings.

In 1954, overwhelming agrarian inequality and misery triggered the Algerian War of Independence. The war hastened the rural exodus, and around 1956, for the first time, more Muslims than Europeans lived in Algiers. In 1957, the war extended to the city, where it was fought briefly in the Casbah's maze of cul-de-sacs. In 1962, France's President Charles de Gaulle grew weary of the political divisions the war was creating in France, and Algeria achieved its independence. Furious settlers scorched parts of downtown Algiers before leaving the city en masse (311,000 left between 1960 and 1962).

In a mad rush, many of the 550,000 Muslims in town occupied dwellings vacated by the settlers. The new independent government nationalized the vacated housing stock and introduced rent controls. The colonial pattern of urbanization continued: the central city of mixed business and residential structures; the decaying, overpopulated Casbah; the well-off (uphill) and poorer (downhill) suburbs; and the shantytowns in the hillside ravines. Free-market rents continued in the traditionally Muslim quarters, which were composed of mostly low-grade dwellings. Rural-urban migrants flowed into the shantytowns and slums, creating a total of 1 million inhabitants toward the end of the 1960s.

A state-led industrialization program that lasted from 1971 to 1985 provided Algiers with factories for mechanical and electrical machinery, processed agricultural goods, building materials, textiles, wood, and paper. These attracted new masses of migrants. At first, the government neglected to provide adequate housing for the new workers. Uncontrolled urban sprawl moved into Algiers's rich agricultural belt around the bay. When the population reached nearly 2 million in the early 1980s, the government finally began a program of urban renewal. Plans were made to move squatters to solid housing or back to their villages, to rehabilitate the Casbah, and to build subways and freeways to relieve urban gridlock.

Low world market prices for oil and gas from 1986 to 1992 triggered a severe financial crisis and brought the renewal program to a halt. The subsequent civil war (1992–2001) between the military, in control of the government, and Islamist challengers brought Algiers extortion rackets, bombings, shootouts, and abductions. Villagers fled from even worse carnage in the countryside, swelling the population of Algiers to over three million during the 1990s. At the same time, many middle-class professionals fled abroad, taking with them much of the city's previously flourishing intellectual and artistic culture. The civil war had abated considerably by 2001, but insecurity continued to a degree in the capital and country. Early in the twenty-first century, unemployment in the city was estimated at 35 percent.

See also ALGERIA: OVERVIEW; ALGERIAN WAR OF INDEPENDENCE; DE GAULLE, CHARLES.

Bibliography

Martinez, Luis. *The Algerian Civil War, 1990–1998,* translated by Jonathan Derrick. London: Hurst, 2000.

PETER VON SIVERS

ALGIERS AGREEMENT (1975)

Agreement between Iran and Iraq to settle border and political disputes.

On 6 March 1975 Iran and Iraq announced in Algeria that they had agreed to recognize the *thalweg* (middle) of the Shatt al-Arab River as their common border and to resolve other contentious issues.

Their riparian border had become a major issue in 1969 when Iran unilaterally abrogated a 1937 treaty that had reaffirmed, with the exception of a *thalweg* line at the Iranian port of Abadan, an Iran-Ottoman Empire treaty of 1913 establishing the common boundary along the Iranian shore of the Shatt al-Arab. Iran claimed that the 1937 treaty had been signed under British duress and that the principle of *thalweg* should be applied along the entire course of the river. Iran's action led to a series of border clashes beginning in 1971. Algeria mediated the 1975 agreement, which led to the signing of a bilateral border treaty at Baghdad in June.

Iraq renounced the Algiers Agreement and abrogated the Baghdad Treaty in September 1980 just before launching its invasion of Iran. Iran and Iraq accepted UN Security Council resolution number 598 establishing a cease-fire in 1988, but most of the graduated steps, including those pertaining to their common border, remained unimplemented in the early 2000s. However, even though the Algiers Agreement has not been reinstituted formally, Iran and Iraq have observed a de facto *thalweg* as their border in the Shatt al-Arab since the fall of 1990.

See also SHATT AL-ARAB.

Bibliography

Kaikobad, Kaiyan Homi. *The Shatt-al-Arab Boundary Question: A Legal Reappraisal.* New York: Oxford University Press; Oxford: Clarendon Press, 1988.

MIA BLOOM
UPDATED BY ERIC HOOGLUND

ALGIERS, BATTLE OF (1956–1957)

Events generally dated from September 1956 to May 1957 that marked an important turn in the 1954–1962 Algerian war for independence from France.

In Algeria, key developments led to the decision by the nationalist leadership of the Front de Libération National (FLN; National Liberation Front), which had largely concentrated on organizing rural opposition to French rule, to bring the war to the capital, Algiers, and other urban centers. These included an increasingly effective French military response to the nationalist insurgency in the countryside as well as the desire on the part of the FLN leadership to both demonstrate its standing in Al-

gerian society and to focus international attention on conditions in Algeria.

The decision to launch a coordinated campaign in Algiers was accompanied by the announcement by the FLN of an eight-day national strike. Organized by Muhammad Larbi Ben M'hidi, a founding member of the executive leadership of the FLN, and Saadi Yacef, the military commander of Algiers, the campaign itself was launched with a series of bombings and assassinations carried out against both the French official and civilian populations. Targets included cafés, restaurants, and offices as well as the French police, soldiers, and civil officials. These acts of urban violence capped a series of similar events carried out by parties on both sides in the summer of 1956.

France's response was harsh. The French commander-in-chief, Raoul Salan, assigned command of operations to General Jacques Massu, commander of the Tenth Paratroop Regiment. Massu turned ruthlessly to the task—his troops broke the back of the general strike by rounding up strike participants and forcing open shops and businesses. More violent still were the measures taken to suppress the FLN network under Yacef and his lieutenant, Ali la Pointe (né Ali Amara). Adopting tactics used in the rural areas, Massu isolated the Arab Muslim quarters and subjected them to massive searches and military assaults. "Most notably he instituted widespread and systematic use of torture as an aid to interrogation" (Ruedy, p. 168). Among the large numbers of victims of interrogation was Ben M'hidi. In 1958, publication of *La Question*, a firsthand account of torture by French Communist editor Henri Alleg, brought home to many in France the nature of French activities in Algeria.

Massu's measures were in the short term effective; by the summer of 1957, Yacef was in prison and la Pointe dead, their network largely silenced. The level of seemingly indiscriminate violence had soured popular support for the FLN, while continued French suppression led to the flight of the surviving FLN leadership to Tunisia—hence the weakening of its command and contact with the movement within Algeria. In the long term, however, French policies and the nine-month-long conflict in Algiers generated considerable world attention and sparked heated debate within France over Algeria and French colonialism. Negative press outside France and growing disillusionment within France contributed in a significant manner to the ultimate decision by the administration of Charles de Gaulle to accept Algerian independence.

The events in Algiers were the subject of an important film by Gillo Pontecorvo, an Italian director. Released in 1966, the documentary-style dramatic *La Battaglia di Algeri* contributed to the angry debate in France and, more significantly, brought home to a world audience sharp images of French policies in Algeria. Filmed in a grainy black and white and starring, among others, Saadi Yacef, the docudrama remains widely shown on university campuses in the United States and Europe.

See also BEN M'HIDI, MUHAMMAD LARBI; FRONT DE LIBÉRATION NATIONAL (FLN).

Bibliography

Heggoy, Alf Andrew. *Insurgency and Counterinsurgency in Algeria.* Bloomington: Indiana University Press, 1972.

Ruedy, John. *Modern Algeria: The Origins and Development of a Nation.* Bloomington: Indiana University Press, 1992.

Solinas, Pier Nico, ed. *Gillo Pontecorvo's "The Battle of Algiers."* New York: Scribner, 1973.

MATTHEW S. GORDON

ALGIERS CHARTER

The document that redefined the goals of Algeria's FLN after the country gained its independence.

The Algiers Charter is a 176-page document adopted by a congress of the Front de Libération Nationale (FLN; National Liberation Front) held in Algiers between 16 April and 21 April 1964. The processes of drafting and adoption were carefully managed by President Ahmed Ben Bella and his followers. The charter's aims were to reshape the FLN, a war-time organization that had led Algeria to independence, into an avant-garde party that would become the motor of social and economic revolution and to sharpen the ideologies and strategies of that revolution.

The charter formalized the organization of the FLN and defined, at least in theory, its relationship to government. Highly populist in tone, it reaffirmed Algeria's socialist option and laid out plans for agrarian reform and for nationalization of most major sectors of the economy. The Algiers Charter remained until 1976 the official statement of Algeria's political and ideological orientation.

See also BEN BELLA, AHMED; FRONT DE LIBÉRATION NATIONALE (FLN).

Bibliography

Ottaway, David, and Ottaway, Marina. *Algeria: The Politics of a Socialist Revolution.* Berkeley: University of California Press, 1970.

JOHN RUEDY

ALGIERS SUMMIT (1973)

See ARAB LEAGUE SUMMITS

ALI

See ISLAM

ALIA, QUEEN
[1948–1977]

Queen of Jordan, 1972–1977.

Alia Baha al-Din Tuqan was born a Palestinian in Cairo, 25 December 1948, the daughter of the Jordanian ambassador to Egypt, Baha al-Din Tuqan of Salt, and Hanan Hashim of Nablus. Ambassador Tuqan served in several other diplomatic posts, including Istanbul, London, and Rome, allowing Alia and her two brothers broad multicultural experience. Alia completed her undergraduate degree in political science at Loyola University's Rome Center and pursued graduate studies in business administration at Hunter College in New York. She then took a post in public relations for Alia Royal Jordanian Airlines. She married Jordan's King Hussein ibn Talal in 1972 and was named queen. They had two children, Haya (born in 1974) and Ali (born in 1975), and adopted a third, Abir (born in 1972). Known for her warm personality, intelligence, and wit, Queen Alia was devoted to her family and her country. She sponsored numerous charities and development programs and was particularly concerned with the welfare of children. Her active support for orphanages, schools for the deaf and blind, mobile medical units for the rural poor, and training centers for the physically and mentally handicapped established a model for women's participation in public affairs in Jordan as well as among her native Palestinians. Queen Alia died in a helicopter crash during a storm on 9 February 1977, returning from an inspection of an orphanage she had funded in southern Jordan. Her children carry on her charitable work through various foundations.

See also HUSSEIN IBN TALAL; TUQAN FAMILY.

TAMARA SONN

ALI NASIR MUHAMMAD AL-HASANI
[1939–]

A Yemeni politician and government official.

Born in 1939, Ali Nasir Muhammad al-Hasani is a member of the Dathina tribe from Abyan, in the rugged up-country northeast of Aden. An early activist in the National Liberation Front in the 1960s, Ali Nasir served as the South Yemen's prime minister throughout the 1970s. This forceful but moderate politician served as president of the People's Democratic Republic of Yemen and head of the ruling Yemeni Socialist Party from late 1980 until 1986. This period was distinguished by a pragmatic approach to domestic policy and by broadly cooperative external relations, most notably with the Yemen Arab Republic, Oman, and Saudi Arabia. Fearing an imminent coup by senior domestic opponents, Ali Nasir launched a bloody preemptive attack against his enemies in early 1986; it failed and he and many of his supporters were forced to flee abroad. Ali Nasir took up exile in Damascus, from where he was able to influence in Yemeni politics only indirectly and from a distance. Many of his civilian and military supporters who fled north soon aligned themselves with President Ali Abdullah Salih before Yemeni unification in 1990 and then sided with the Salih regime in the 1994 civil war; some of these supporters have attained high positions in that regime.

See also NATIONAL FRONT FOR THE LIBERATION OF SOUTH YEMEN; SALIH, ALI ABDULLAH; YEMENI SOCIALIST PARTY.

Bibliography

Halliday, Fred. "Catastrophe in South Yemen: A Preliminary Assessment." *MERIP Reports* (March–April 1986): 37–39.

Lackner, Helen. *P. D. R. Yemen: Outpost of Socialist Development in Arabia.* London: Ithaca, 1985.

Wenner, Manfred W. "The 1986 Civil War in South Yemen." In *The Arab Gulf and the Arab World,* edited by B. R. Pridham. London: Croom Helm, 1988.

ROBERT D. BURROWES

ALI, RASHID

See KAYLANI, RASHID ALI AL-

ALI RIZA
[1858–1930]

Ottoman Turkish landscape painter.

The son of an army officer, Ali Riza was born in Üsküdar, the district on the Asian shore of Istanbul. A pioneer of modern painting in Ottoman Turkey, Ali Riza was graduated from the Ottoman Empire's military academy and taught art there for many years. Like other nineteenth-century Ottoman artists, he used new brush techniques to create color effects, especially in his scenic watercolors and oils depicting Istanbul and Üsküdar.

Through his teaching and his detailed ornamental landscapes, Ali Riza was instrumental in the spread of secular concepts in painting in a culture long accustomed to nonrepresentational Islamic art forms.

See also ISTANBUL; OTTOMAN EMPIRE; ÜSKÜDAR.

Bibliography

Renda, Günsel. "Modern Trends in Turkish Painting." In *The Transformation of Turkish Culture: The Atatürk Legacy,* edited by Günsel Renda and C. Max Kortepeter. Princeton, NJ: Kingston Press, 1986.

DAVID WALDNER

ALI, SALIM RABBIYYA

See RABBIYYA ALI, SALIM

ALISHAN, GHEVOND
[1820–1901]

Armenian writer and historian.

Ghevond Alishan, baptized Kerovbe Alishanian, was born in Constantinople (now Istanbul) and attended an Armenian Catholic school before going to Venice to continue his education at the Mekhitarian monastery. He joined the Armenian Catholic order of monks known as the Mekhitarians in 1838 and later was ordained a priest. Although the author of a number of religious works, Alishan spent his adult years as an instructor in the educational institutions maintained by the Mekhitarians. Early on, he developed an interest in Armenian folklore and had turned to composing poetry. The last third of his life was devoted solely to scholarship.

Alishan gained fame as a prodigious writer of historical works. He published a twenty-two-volume series of Armenian primary sources from the manuscript collection in the Mekhitarian monastery. He also issued a set of large, illustrated volumes on various provinces of historical Armenia—*Shirak* (1881), *Sisvan* (1885), *Ayrarat* (1890), and *Sisakan* (1893)—containing therein all the geographical, topographical, historical, architectural, and other information culled from ancient and contemporary sources. These volumes provided the basis for the development of a strong sense of national identification with Armenia among Armenians in expatriate communities and among younger generations of Armenians. These people began to perceive of Armenia as a land imbued with history and creativity and not just desolation and oppression. In the last year of his life, on the occasion of the two-hundredth year of the founding of the Mekhitarian order, Alishan issued his culminating work, called *Hayapatum* (Armenian history), in which he arranged selections from Armenian historians into a comprehensive narrative history.

While most Armenian translators put works from French and German literature into Armenian, Alishan was one of the rare figures of the nineteenth-century Armenian cultural renaissance who also learned English. He traveled to England in 1852 and published that same year the translation, in Armenian, of a section of Milton's *Paradise Lost*. Subsequently he issued translations of Byron and Longfellow. In 1867 he published his *Armenian Popular Songs Translated into English,* believed to contain the first English renditions of Armenian poetry. Alishan died in Venice.

ROUBEN P. ADALIAN

ALI SUAVI
[1838–1878]

Ottoman intellectual.

Born into a working-class family in Istanbul, Ali Suavi became a teacher in *ruşdiye* schools (for adolescents) in Bursa and Filibe before being dismissed by an irate governor for his unorthodox ideas. He traveled to Paris and London and there joined such individuals as the poets Namik Kemal and Ziya Paşa, members of the Young Ottomans. In 1867, Ali Suavi became the editor of *Munbir,* a Young Ottoman newspaper devoted to issues of government reform.

Ali Suavi was deeply religious and passionately devoted to the unification of all Turkic-speaking peoples; he soon broke with the other Young Ottomans, who were more interested in the reform of the Ottoman Empire along the lines of European liberalism. After opposing Midhat Paşa, grand vizier of the empire, and the Constitution of 1876, Suavi gained the favor of the autocratic Sultan Abdülhamit II, and he was rewarded with an appointment as director of the Galatasaray Lycée. But Ali Suavi soon became dissatisfied with the new sultan, and after the ignominious defeat of the Ottomans in the Russo–Ottoman War of 1877–1878, Suavi led a coup attempt to restore the deposed Murat V to the throne. The coup failed, and Ali Suavi was executed.

See also ABDÜLHAMIT II; GALATASARAY LYCÉE; MIDHAT PAŞA; NAMIK KEMAL; RUSSIAN–OTTOMAN WARS; YOUNG OTTOMANS.

Bibliography

Lewis, Bernard. *The Emergence of Modern Turkey,* 3d edition. New York: Oxford University Press, 2002.

Shaw, Stanford, and Shaw, Ezel Kural. *History of the Ottoman Empire and Modern Turkey.* Cambridge, U.K., and New York: Cambridge University Press, 1976–1977.

ZACHARY KARABELL

ALI, WIJDAN
[1939–]

A Jordanian artist and art historian.

Princess Wijdan Ali, who often goes by the name "Wijdan," was born in 1939, in Baghdad. She is a former diplomat, a painter and art historian, the founder and director of the Jordan National Gallery of Fine Arts, a member of the Jordanian royal family, and the author of two major books on contemporary Islamic art. She holds a B.A. from the Lebanese American University (1961) and a Ph.D. in Islamic art history from the School of Oriental and African Studies, University of London (1993). She trained under Armando Bruno and Muhanna Durra. The latter influenced her early abstract works on the expressive properties of color. A second body of work includes landscape paintings of the Jordanian desert. She is best known for her recent contributions to the developing tradition of Islamic art, which experiments with the abstract and graphic elements of Arabic calligraphy. This foray into the aesthetics of the Arabic language as a vehicle for connecting with her roots and exploring issues of tragedy and injustice was especially motivated by the onset of the 1991 Gulf War. Both her art and her writings have contributed to the development of a recognized school of modern Islamic art in the Arab world and beyond.

See also ART; GENDER: GENDER AND EDUCATION.

Bibliography

Ali, Wijdan. *Contemporary Art from the Islamic World.* London: Scorpion, 1989.

Ali, Wijdan. *Modern Islamic Art: Development and Continuity.* Gainesville: University Press of Florida, 1997.

JESSICA WINEGAR

ALIYAH

Hebrew term for Jewish immigration to Palestine.

The Hebrew word for "ascent," *aliyah* (also *aliya*) is the term used in both religious tradition and secular Zionism to refer to Jewish immigration to Palestine. Within those ideological frameworks, emigration from Israel is called *yeridah* (descent).

During the almost two-thousand-year absence of Jewish sovereignty in the Holy Land, Palestine continued to play a significant role in traditional Jewish culture. Small Jewish communities persevered in Jerusalem, Safed, and a few other areas, aided by contributions from Jews in the Diaspora. Some Diaspora Jews visited Palestine, others actually managed to settle there on a more permanent basis, and others arranged to be buried there. Overall, the numbers who actually immigrated were small. During the nineteenth century, with the emergence of the Zionist movement, as well as a growing deterioration in the condition of Jews in Europe, Jewish immigration to Palestine increased. From that time until the establishment of the State of Israel in 1948, historians and demographers have categorized various waves of immigration, or *aliyot*.

The first *aliyah*, or wave, lasted from 1881 to 1903. It was comprised of 30,000 to 40,000 Jews, most of whom were from Eastern Europe. They were part of a much larger emigration of Jews out of Eastern Europe at the time, sparked by economic, political, and physical persecution, especially pogroms. The vast majority who fled went to the United States, but many of those who had been in the early Zionist movements went to Palestine and, with support from Baron Edmund de Rothschild, established agricultural communities, including Petah Tikvah,

Jewish refugees arrive in Haifa, Palestine. From 1881 until the creation of the state of Israel in 1948, five successive waves of Jews immigrated to Palestine, many fleeing poor economic conditions and political persecution in their home countries. © HULTON-DEUTSCH COLLECTION/CORBIS. REPRODUCED BY PERMISSION.

A ship bearing hundreds of Jewish immigrants steams into Haifa in 1946, flying a banner instructing Palestine to "keep the gates open, we are not the last." © Hulton-Deutsch Collection/Corbis. Reproduced by permission.

Zikhron Yaʿacov, Rehovot, Hadera, and Rishon le-Zion. During this period some 2,500 Jews from Yemen also emigrated to Palestine.

Another series of pogroms in Russia in 1903 and 1904 led to the next wave, the second *aliyah*, which numbered between 35,000 and 40,000 (mostly socialist-Zionists) and lasted until the outbreak of World War I in 1914. Among them were the pioneers of the kibbutz movement and the labor Zionist establishment in the Yishuv, the Jewish community in Palestine.

The Balfour Declaration as well as the Russian Revolution and its aftermath sparked the third *aliyah*. Between 1919 and 1924 another 35,000 Jews, mostly from Russia and Poland, immigrated and contributed to the early pioneering efforts in building up the Yishuv, including the establishment of the first cooperative settlements, *moshavim*.

The fourth *aliyah*, which lasted from 1924 to approximately 1930, differed from the previous waves in that it was sparked almost exclusively by economic conditions. As a result of a series of harsh taxation policies in Poland, some 80,000 Jews immigrated to Palestine, and the vast majority settled in the developing urban center, Tel Aviv. It may be assumed that a significant number of them would have preferred immigrating to the United States but were prevented from doing so by the restrictive immigration acts of 1921 and 1924, which brought immigration into the United States to a halt. That assumption is bolstered by the relatively high emigration rate among those of the fourth *aliyah* who settled only briefly in Palestine.

Approximately 225,000 Jews, primarily from Eastern Europe and also including a significant minority from Germany, arrived during the 1930s and were known as the fifth *aliyah*. Many of the immi-

Table 1: Aliyah, 1840–2000

Years	Numbers	Countries of Emigration	Motivation
1840–1881	20,000–30,000	Primarily Central and Eastern Europe	Religio-national
1882–1903	35,000	Primarily Eastern Europe—"First Aliyah"	Religio-national and "push" factors
1904–1914	40,000	Primarily Central and Eastern Europe—"Second Aliyah"	Religio-national and "push" factors
1919–1923	35,000	Primarily Eastern Europe - "Third Aliyah"	Religio-national and "push" factors
1924–1930	80,000	Primarily Poland—"Fourth Aliyah"	"Push" factors—Holocaust
1931–1939	225,000	Primarily Central and Eastern Europe—"Fifth Aliyah"	"Push" factors—Holocaust
1940–1948	143,000	Primarily Central and Eastern Europe	"Push" factors—Holocaust
1948–1951	667,613	About half North African and Asian	Mixed "push" and "pull" factors
1952–1967	582,653	About 65% North African and Asian	Mixed "push" and "pull" factors
1968–1988	532,744	More than 75% European and American, 43% of whom were from USSR	Religio-national and economic factors
1989–2000	1,039,821	Overwhelmingly FSU; about 56,000 Ethiopians	FSU—primarily economic; Ethiopians—religious and "push" factors

SOURCE: Courtesy of Chaim I. Waxman

TABLE BY GGS INFORMATION SERVICES, THE GALE GROUP.

grants from Germany had high educational and occupational status, and they played an important role in the economic development of the Yishuv.

World War II gave a critical impetus to *aliyah*. The numbers legally entitled to immigrate under the 1939 MacDonald White Paper quota were much too low for the hundreds of thousands who were fleeing the Holocaust in Europe. An illegal immigration movement known as Aliyah Bet was established by a branch of Yishuv's defense force, the Haganah, enabling approximately 70,000 Jews to reach Palestine.

With the establishment of Israel as a sovereign state, *aliyah* was accorded formal priority with the enactment of the Law of Return, which grants immediate citizenship to Jews who immigrate. Although the law initially had both ideological and self-interest components—it was widely perceived that the country was in need of population growth for its defense and survival—the resulting massive immigration, especially from North African countries, was viewed by some as threatening to Israel's economic stability and to the Ashkenazic or Western-ized character of the state, and they called for restrictions on immigration. Nevertheless, the government continued to encourage mass immigration, even though it was ill-equipped to manage it. The mass immigration during the years of early statehood dramatically altered the ethnic composition of

Israel, and continuing interplay between ethnicity and socioeconomic status has been an increasing source of tension and strain on the entire society.

Following the 1967 War there was a significant increase in *aliyah* from Western countries because of heightened nationalistic attachments as well as the pull of Israel's growing economy. By the end of the 1970s, those numbers receded to pre-1967 levels.

During the 1970s *aliyah* was boosted by emigrés from the Soviet Union, most of whom came for both ideological and persecution reasons. By contrast, the vast majority of the massive influx of close to one million immigrants from the Former Soviet Union (FSU) in the 1990s came for economic reasons. The Soviet immigrants in general, and especially those of the 1990s, retain strong identification with their former backgrounds and have forced Israeli society and politics to become much more multicultural. In addition, the relatively high rate of religious intermarriage among the FSU immigrants has created or heightened Jewish interreligious tensions in the country.

Finally, the immigration of some 60,000 "Beta Israel" or Falasha Jews from Ethiopia has created a whole set of new social, political, and religious issues that will probably increase before they recede, if indeed they ever do. This is a group that was cut off from contact with other Jewish communities for millennia. Their contemporary process of connection began with Christian missionary activities that brought them and world Jewry to mutual awareness. Since then, there had been only sporadic efforts to assist them. The mass immigration to Israel was sparked by deteriorating political and economic conditions after the Marxist overthrow of Ethiopia's Emperor Haile Selassie and the rescue efforts of the Israeli government. The radical and immediate changes experienced by the Ethiopian immigration are unique and make it a fascinating case study for students of migration and absorption.

See also ETHIOPIAN JEWS; LAW OF RETURN; ZIONISM.

Bibliography

Corinaldi, Michael. *Jewish Identity: The Case of Ethiopian Jewry.* Jerusalem: Magnes Press, Hebrew University, 1998.

Eisenstadt, S. N. *The Absorption of Immigrants: A Comparative Study Based Mainly on the Jewish Community in Palestine and the State of Israel.* New York: Free Press, 1955.

Eisenstadt, S. N. *Israeli Society.* New York: Basic Books; London: Weidenfeld and Nicolson, 1967.

Leshem, Elazar, and Shuval, Judith T., eds. *Immigration to Israel: Sociological Perspectives.* New Brunswick, NJ: Transaction Publishers, 1998.

Medoff, Rafael, and Waxman, Chaim I. *Historical Dictionary of Zionism.* Lanham, MD: Scarecrow Press, 2000.

Rebhun, Uzi, and Waxman, Chaim I., eds. *Jews in Israel: Contemporary Social and Cultural Patterns.* Hanover, NH: University Press of New England/ Brandeis University Press, 2004.

Waxman, Chaim I. *American Aliya: Portrait of an Innovative Migration Movement.* Detroit, MI: Wayne State University Press, 1989.

CHAIM I. WAXMAN

ALIYER, FATIMAH
[1862–1936]

Pioneer in the early Ottoman women's movement.

Fatimah Aliyer Hanoum, daughter of Ahmet Cevdet Paşa, the Western-minded Ottoman bureaucrat and codifier of Ottoman Civil Law (Mecelle), was a pioneer in early feminist writing, especially in *Kadinlara Mahsus Gazete* (Newspaper for women, 1895), and in the early Ottoman women's movement.

Fatimah Aliyer was brought up in an upperclass Ottoman household, receiving the *konak* (Ottoman mansion) education of the typical pasha's daughter of her time. She was taught at home, learning reading and writing in Arabic, Persian, and French, as well as geography, history, and literature. She first appeared in the Ottoman press as the "lady translator" of George Ohnet's *Volonte* (1888); her identity was only later revealed by Ahmed Midhat, and her competence as a writer was confirmed by him in the preface he wrote to her romantic novel, *Muhazarat* (Stories to remember, 1892).

Aliyer wrote within a moderate, modernist-Islamicist inspired framework, like male writers such as Namik Kemal, Ibrahim Sinasi, Şemseddin Sami, and Ahmed Midhat, who stressed the importance of women's roles as mothers and educators of the young and therefore promoted reform in women's education. The themes during this phase of Ottoman feminism were criticism of the Ottoman family system, arranged marriages and polygamy, the husband's one-sided right to divorce his wife, concubinage, and slavery.

Although Aliyer was against polygamy, she argued in her 1982 book, *Nisvan-I Islam* (Muslim women), that the West held a prejudiced view of Muslim women. She held that the situation of Ottoman women within a polygamic marriage was more secure than that of mistresses and their illegitimate children in Western societies.

See also ART; GENDER: GENDER AND EDUCATION; LITERATURE: TURKISH; NEWSPAPERS AND PRINT MEDIA: TURKEY.

Bibliography

Paker, Saliha. "Unmuffled Voices in the Shade and Beyond: Women's Writing in Turkish." In *Textual Liberation: European Feminist Writing in the Twentieth Century,* edited by Helena Forsås-Scott. New York, London: Routledge, 1991.

AYSE DURAKBASA TARHAN

ALIZADEH, GHAZALEH
[1946–1996]

Iranian writer, critic, and feminist.

Ghazaleh Alizadeh was born in Mashahd in 1946 and lived in Tehran, where she began a successful career as a writer of newspaper articles, novels, and short stories. Her stories represent the continuation of modernist genre inaugurated by Nima Yusij in the 1920s. Reminiscent of Hermann Hessse, they are best known for their allegorical realism laden with deep meanings that produce a surreal, distorted sense of fictional characters and places. Alizadeh's early collections of short stories, *Safar-e nagozashtani* (1976; The impossible journey), *Bad az tabestan* (1977; After summer), and *Do manzare* (1984; Two views) explore the individual's search for identity outside the restrictions of society. Likewise, her most famous novel, *Khaneh Edrisi* (1999; Edris house) continued the allegorical-realist approach in a narrative form, with fictional historical characters caught in a metaphorical clash between a decadent revolutionary state and a defiant emerging culture set in a male-dominated society. Alizadeh helped to reshape the permissible boundaries of gender representation in the modern Persian literature of postrevolutionary Iran; her works also helped to advance the critical feminist discourses of the woman's movement. Alizadeh's 1996 death was suspicious; her body was found hanged from a tree in a forest north of Iran.

See also LITERATURE: PERSIAN.

Bibliography

Hajibashi, Zjaleh. "The Fiction of the Postrevolution Woman." Ph.D. diss., University of Texas, 1998.

Khorrami, Mohammad Mehdi. *Modern Reflections of Classical Traditions in Persian Fiction.* Lewiston, NY: Edwin Mellen, 2003.

BABAK RAHIMI

ALKALAI, JUDAH BEN SOLOMON HAI
[1798–1878]

Precursor of modern Zionism.

Judah ben Solomon Hai Alkalai, a Sephardic rabbi who was born in Sarajevo and studied in Jerusalem, served as a rabbi in the Balkans and was influenced by Serbian Nationalism and the Damascus Affair (1840). Also, well-versed in the kabbalah, Alkalai believed that the era of messianic redemption was at hand. He asserted that redemption must be preceded by the return of the Jews to the land of Israel. In his books *Darkhei No'am* (1839) and *Shalom Yerushalayim* (1840), he called upon Jews to prepare

for the coming redemption and to donate money to those already residing in the Land of Israel. In *Minhat Yehudah* (1843), he advocated the formation of an Assembly of Jewish Notables to represent the Jewish people in their appeals to other nations to permit their return to their homeland. Alkalai wrote numerous pamphlets and articles and, in 1851 to 1852, toured several countries to spread his ideas. In 1871, he visited Palestine and founded a settlement society there, which was unsuccessful. In 1874, he settled in Palestine.

See also DAMASCUS AFFAIR (1840).

Bibliography

Hertzberg, Arthur, ed. *The Zionist Idea: A Historical Analysis and Reader.* Philadelphia: Jewish Publication Society, 1997.

MARTIN MALIN

AL KHALIFA FAMILY

Ruling family of the State of Bahrain, 1782–.

In 1782, the Al Khalifa, a prominent trading clan originally based in Kuwait, captured the Bahrain islands. The leader of the family, Shaykh Ahmad bin Khalifa, called "the Conqueror" by his allies, ruled the islands from Zubara, on the northwestern coast of Qatar, until his death in 1796. His sons Sulman, based first at Zubara and then at Manama on the main island of al-Awal, and Abdullah, based in Muharraq on al-Awal, then shared the rulership. They cosigned the pivotal 1820 treaty with Britain that recognized the Al Khalifa as the legitimate rulers of Bahrain. Abdullah outlived both Sulman and Sulman's son Khalifa, acting as sole ruler from 1834 to 1843. He was ousted by Sulman's grandson Muhammad, precipitating a quarter-century of fighting between the descendants of Sulman, based at Manama, and Abdullah, who formed alliances with powerful tribes in Qatar and al-Hasa. In 1869, British forces stepped in to end the fighting and appointed Shaykh Isa bin Ali, a great-grandson of Sulman, who had been in charge of the family's remaining holdings in Qatar, as ruler. Treaties in 1880 and 1892 confirmed Isa's undisputed position.

Around 1900, British officials demanded greater authority over Bahrain's internal affairs. Senior members of the Al Khalifa tried to buttress their deteriorating position by raising taxes on agricultural estates. This sparked riots on the islands in 1923, which prompted Britain to exile Isa and replace him with his son Hamad, who worked with British forces to restore order. Hamad acquiesced in the appointment of a British adviser, who took charge of all branches of the local administration. Hamad died in 1942 and was succeeded by his son Sulman, who preserved the family's prerogatives in the face of intense popular challenges during the mid-1950s. At the height of the unrest, tribes allied to the Al Khalifa formed a militia to protect the regime. These retainers were handsomely rewarded as oil revenues escalated, funding a dramatic expansion of state offices and business opportunities. Hamad named his son Isa heir apparent in 1958, ensuring a smooth transition upon his death three years later.

When Britain granted Bahrain independence in 1971, Shaykh Isa took the title *amir* and appointed his brother Khalifa prime minister and his son Hamad minister of defense. Other senior shaykhs of the Al Khalifa headed key ministries, particularly those of the interior, foreign affairs, and labor and social affairs. Matters of importance to the family but peripheral to governing the country were left to a council of elders, presided over by the ruler. This institution ensured the integrity of the Al Khalifa by controlling marriage choices, distributing allowances in proportion to each individual's power and status, and underwriting economic ventures undertaken by family members. Supported by plentiful oil revenues, along with an extensive security service, the Al Khalifa kept firm control over the country throughout the 1970s and 1980s.

In 1999, after four years of widespread popular unrest in the mid-1990s, Isa died and was succeeded by Hamad. The new ruler introduced a number of political reforms in an attempt to restore the regime's tarnished legitimacy. A 2001 referendum transformed Bahrain into a constitutional, hereditary monarchy, with Hamad as king. Hamad then repealed the draconian 1974 Penal Code, abolished the State Security Court, and reinstated public employees who had been fired for their political activities. He also appointed a committee to revise the 1973 constitution and prepare for elections to a new advisory council. Opposition organizations charged

that the proposals diluted the rights guaranteed by the earlier constitution but commended the king for entertaining a revival of popular participation in policy-making.

See also BAHRAIN; MANAMA.

Bibliography

Herb, Michael. *All in the Family: Absolutism, Revolution, and Monarchy in the Middle Eastern Monarchies.* Albany: State University of New York Press, 1999.

Khalaf, Abd al-Hadi. *Unfinished Business: Contentious Politics and State-Building in Bahrain.* Lund, Sweden: University of Lund, 2000.

Lawson, Fred H. *Bahrain: The Modernization of Autocracy.* Boulder, CO: Westview, 1989.

FRED H. LAWSON

ALLAH

The Arabic equivalent of the English word God.

A likely etymology of the term is that it is an ancient contraction of *al-ilah* (Arabic for "*the* god") and was probably first used in Arabian cosmologies before Islam to refer to some kind of high deity who may have been considered the progenitor of a number of lesser divinities. The word *Allah* is best known in the West as the name Muslims ascribe to the one and only God, whom they believe to be the transcendent and partnerless creator, lord, and judge of the universe. It is important to note that according to Muslim teaching, Allah is not only the God of the prophet Muhammad but also the God of Moses and Jesus—and is therefore identical to the divine being of Jewish and Christian sacred history.

While Muslim tradition recognizes Allah to be the comprehensive name of God encompassing all the divine attributes, it also ascribes to the deity an additional ninety-nine "beautiful names" (*al-asma al-husna*), each of which evoke a distinct characteristic of the godhead. The most famous and most frequently referenced of these are "the Merciful" (*al-rahman*) and "the Compassionate" (*al-rahim*).

See also ISLAM.

Bibliography

Guillaume, Alfred. *Islam.* London: Cassell, 1963.

SCOTT ALEXANDER

ALLENBY, EDMUND HENRY

[1861–1936]

British officer who commanded British forces in the Middle East during World War I; military governor of Palestine and high commissioner of Egypt.

Edmund Henry Allenby's early career included extensive service in Africa, including the Boer War (1899–1902). Posted to France at the start of World War I, he was sent to the Middle East in June 1917, where he led Britain's Egyptian Expeditionary Force and took Beersheba and Gaza (1917); with the help of Colonel T. E. Lawrence (of Arabia) and Prince Faisal I ibn Hussein, he occupied Jerusalem in December 1917. He launched his final offensive in 1918, taking Megiddo from 18 September to 21 September. This classic of military strategy led to the collapse of Ottoman Empire forces and the British occupation of Syria.

At the peace conference in Paris, Allenby argued, as military governor of Palestine, that Britain should support Faisal as king of Syria, but the League of Nations awarded the French a mandate over Syria; they occupied the new kingdom and ousted Faisal. Created a viscount in 1919, Allenby was appointed high commissioner for Egypt (1919–1925). There he advocated accommodation with rising Arab Nationalism, thus clashing over policy with British Colonial Secretary Winston Churchill. His threat to resign persuaded the British government to issue the Allenby Declaration on 28 February 1922, which granted formal independence to Egypt but retained enormous rights for the British over Egyptian affairs.

See also FAISAL I IBN HUSSEIN; LAWRENCE, T. E.

Bibliography

Wavell, Archibald P. *Allenby: A Study in Greatness.* 2 vols. London: G. G. Harrap, 1940–1943.

JON JUCOVY

ALLIANCE ISRAÉLITE UNIVERSELLE (AIU)

International Jewish organization created in Paris, 1860.

Until 1860 the Jews of France had been represented by the Consistoire Central des Israélites de France, headquartered in Paris, with branches throughout the country. The AIU was founded in Paris on 17 May 1860, by several idealistic French Jews—businesspeople, political activists, and members of the free professions. Certainly the most important older leader of the AIU was Adolphe Crémieux, who in 1870 became minister of justice while serving as AIU president.

The decision to create the AIU, a move to diversify and extend Jewish political activities outside France, was partly hastened by the controversy over the Mortara Case, concerning the abduction of a Jewish child by Roman Catholic conversionists. On the night of 23 June 1858, Edgardo Mortara, the six-year-old son of a Jewish family in Bologna, Italy, was abducted by the papal police and taken to Rome. The boy had been secretly and unlawfully baptized five years earlier by a Christian domestic servant, who thought he was about to die. The parents vainly attempted to get their child back, and the case caused a universal outcry. Young French Jews created the AIU two years later in the name of religious freedom.

The AIU's aim was to aid Jews and Judaism—mainly in the Ottoman, Sharifian (Morocco), and Qajar (Iran) empires—in three ways. The first was to "work toward the emancipation and moral progress of the Jews." While it did not state that education was the basic motivation behind emancipation and moral progress, the first aim defined the educational sphere. Moral progress meant combating disease, poverty, and ignorance, and acculturating Jews in the tradition of French education. Therefore, the AIU established schools that taught Jews in Mediterranean-basin countries the concepts of liberty, equality, and fraternity.

The most important schools were created between 1862 and 1914 in Morocco, Tunisia, Libya, Egypt, Syria, Turkey, Iran, and Iraq. The teachers dispatched to these countries were alumni of the AIU schools from the Ottoman Empire—Sephardim trained in Paris at the AIU teacher-training center, the École Normale Israélite Orientale (ENIO). Although the French language was used in AIU schools, the AIU did not advocate total emulation of French culture, attempting to strike a balance between secular learning, embodying Western ideas, and the sacred education of Jewish communities.

The second goal, "lending effective support to all those who suffer because of their membership in the Jewish faith," referred to allocating funds to help Jews in distress outside Europe. More importantly, it included forging contacts with European leaders and their diplomatic representatives in countries where Jews were harassed. Further, it meant that the AIU had to alert the leaders of both the Middle East and North Africa when such injustice occurred, possibly wresting concessions from them to remedy the situation.

The third aim was to awaken Europe to the Jews' plight. It called for "encouraging all proper publications to bring an end to Jewish sufferings." Whereas the second category called for quiet negotiations and diplomatic action, the third stressed the utilization of AIU and other periodicals to influence public opinion. For example, it published the *Bulletin de l'Alliance Israélite Universelle* (1860–1913) and *Paix et Droit* for this purpose, and utilized the French press and the London *Jewish Chronicle* to point out human rights violations, particularly in Iran and Morocco.

The AIU Central Committee in Paris obtained information on the abuses perpetrated against Jews in Muslim lands where it had schools through its personnel or regional committees. These forces also apprised local European consuls and plenipotentiaries about the abuses by regional governors and chieftains. The AIU Central Committee then brought the problems before the Foreign Office in London or the French Foreign Ministry in Paris, which in turn pressured the Ottoman Porte, the Qajar Shahs, and the Moroccan *Makhzan* to protect their Jewish subjects (*dhimmas*).

In terms of its educational influence, the AIU survived from the Ottoman and precolonial eras into the colonial period and beyond—well into the decolonization stage. In 1956 the AIU had 143 schools and approximately 51,000 students in Morocco, Iran, Tunisia, Israel, Syria, and Lebanon. In 2000 the AIU had 73 schools, mostly in Israel, France, Morocco, Canada, Belgium, and Spain; the total number of AIU schools, or AIU-affiliated ones, exceeded 29,000. Until the 1960s most AIU schools—primary, secondary, and vocational—were concentrated in the Muslim world; since then, school expansion has taken place in Israel, France,

Canada, Spain, and Belgium. In the wake of Jewish emigration from the former Soviet Union, the trend is to expand the schools in Europe and Israel. The AIU in France still helps to maintain the schools in the Muslim world—notably in Morocco and Iran—because Jewish communities continue to exist there despite attempted emigration to Europe, the Americas, or Israel. After 1997 plans were underway by the AIU, in conjunction with affluent Iranian Jews living in the United States, to open schools in the states of New York and California.

Since its inception, the AIU has been financed by membership fund-raising, conducted by the regional committees throughout the world. After World War I, however, as its school networks expanded in the Middle East, and especially in North Africa, a substantial portion of the AIU's budget was derived from the French government. Since the end of World War II, the AIU schools have also received subsidies from the American Jewish Joint Distribution Committee, which uses funds of the United Jewish Appeal.

Bibliography

Laskier, Michael M. *The Alliance Israélite Universelle and the Jewish Communities of Morocco: 1862–1962.* Albany: State University of New York Press, 1983.

Rodrigue, Aron. *French Jews, Turkish Jews: The Alliance Israélite Universelle and the Politics of Jewish Schooling in Turkey, 1860–1925.* Bloomington: University of Indiana Press, 1990.

Simon, Rachel. "Education." In *The Jews of the Middle East and North Africa in Modern Times,* edited by Reeva Spector Simon, Michael Menachem Laskier, and Sara Reguer. New York: Columbia University Press, 2003.

MICHAEL M. LASKIER

ALLIED MIDDLE EAST COMMAND

Military administrative command of the World War II era, headquartered in Cairo, Egypt, created by the British government in 1939 to organize the war effort in the Middle East.

General Sir Archibald Wavell was the first commander, taking charge in June 1939. At first encompassing Egypt, the Sudan, Cyprus, and Transjordan, the command spanned two continents and encompassed an area 1,700 by 2,000 miles (2,735 to

3,218 km). After the beginning of World War II, the command was expanded to include Aden, British Somaliland, and the Persian/Arabian Gulf. Under Wavell's command, the British were successful in operations against the Italians but failed when the Germans, under General Erwin Rommel, counterattacked. Command passed to General Sir Claude Auchinleck in July 1941, and then to General Sir Harold R. L. G. Alexander in August 1942. During this period, the British finally prevailed against German and Italian forces in North Africa. In August 1942, Iran and Iraq were detached from the command, and consideration was given by Prime Minister Winston S. Churchill to renaming it the Near Eastern Command. To preclude confusion, the Cabinet persuaded Churchill to retain the original name for the command in Cairo. After the successful American and British invasion of North Africa in November 1942, under the leadership of General Dwight D. Eisenhower, the Middle East Command was primarily concerned with administrative and logistic problems.

See also WAVELL, ARCHIBALD PERCIVAL.

Bibliography

Barnet, Correlli. *The Desert Generals,* 2d edition. Bloomington: Indiana University Press, 1982.

DANIEL E. SPECTOR

ALLON, YIGAL
[1918–1980]

Israeli politician; deputy prime minister, 1969–1974.

Born in Kfar Tabor, Palestine, Yigal Allon was originally named Yigal Paicovitch. He changed his name to Allon—which means oak, to symbolize his commitment to Israel—in 1948, at the time the state of Israel was proclaimed. Allon's early education took place in Palestine, at the Kadoorie Agricultural School and the Hebrew University, but he subsequently attended St. Anthony's College in Oxford. In 1937, he was one of the cofounders of Kibbutz Ginossar, on the western shore of Lake Tiberias.

From 1937 to 1939 he served in the Haganah; at the same time, he was working for the British as an officer in the Jewish Settlement Police. Along with Moshe Dayan, Allon was one of the leading forces in the creation of the Palmah, the commando unit of the Haganah, and in 1945 he attained the rank of commander in the unit. During World War II, he fought with Allied forces to liberate Vichyheld Syria and Lebanon and in 1948 was made brigadier general. A senior officer in the Israel Defense Forces at the time of the Arab–Israel War of 1948, he fought in a number of campaigns in that conflict.

Allon was a member of Knesset throughout Israel's early years. In 1960, he resigned his seat in order to attend Oxford University for a year, but in 1961 he was reelected and continued to serve. He was minister of labor from 1961 to 1967, deputy prime minister from 1966 to 1968, minister of education and culture from 1969 to 1974, and minister of foreign affairs from 1974 to 1977. From 26 February to 17 March 1969, he served as acting prime minister following the death of Prime Minister Levi Eshkol, until Golda Meir received a vote of confidence from the Knesset and took over the position of prime minister.

During Meir's term in office, Allon, who remained deputy prime minister, was an important adviser to the prime minister. The role he played during the period leading up to the Arab–Israel War of 1973, however, and his agreement with the position taken by Meir that Israel should never again engage in a preemptive strike against its Arab neighbors (even if they were threatening to attack) made him a nonviable candidate to succeed Meir when she resigned in 1974. Yitzhak Rabin, a war hero untainted with any part of the blame for the decision in 1973, was chosen by the Labor Party to succeed Meir, and Allon was appointed foreign minister. In 1975, during the era of Henry Kissinger's famous shuttle diplomacy, Allon actively participated in the peace talks, but his efforts were not repaid by substantive results.

Allon may best be remembered for suggesting, in discussions on Israeli defense, that since the Jewish people had a clear right to the lands on the West Bank of the Jordan River, it was necessary to act strategically to make sure Israel would be secure. The Allon Plan, as it became known, called for Israel to keep the Jordan River valley as its own territory (while returning about 70 percent of the West Bank to Jordan). In addition, Allon recommended that the Gaza Strip should also become part of Israel.

Although Allon did not reject the idea of a Palestinian state, he argued that it should not come about at the expense of Israel's security or its right to exist. His endorsement of the idea of a dense belt of Jewish villages along the Jordan River that would provide security for Israel continues to be cited to this day.

See also GAZA STRIP; HAGANAH; MEIR, GOLDA; PALMAH.

Bibliography

Allon, Yigal. *My Father's House,* translated by Reuven Ben-Yosef. New York: Norton, 1976.

Ben-Gurion, David. *Israel: A Personal History,* translated by Nechemia Meyers and Uzy Nystar. New York: Funk and Wagnalls, 1971.

Sachar, Howard M. *A History of Israel: From the Rise of Zionism to Our Time,* 2d edition. New York: Knopf, 1996.

GREGORY S. MAHLER

ALL-PALESTINE GOVERNMENT

Post–World War II concept for forming an Arab government for the whole of Palestine after the end of the British mandate, 14 May 1948.

The All-Palestine Government was the product of the complex relationship between the Palestinian national movement led by Hajj Amin al-Husayni, the Mufti of Jerusalem, and the Arab states loosely organized within the Arab League. After World War II, when the British mandate over Palestine was to expire and the struggle between the Arabs and the Jews was approaching its climax, the weakness of the Palestinian Arabs made them ever more dependent on the Arab League. Within the league, however, no one policy existed for the future of the region: The mufti's plan was maximalist, an independent Palestinian state throughout the whole of Palestine; King Abdullah of Transjordan's plan was to accept the partition of Palestine with the Jews and to incorporate the Arab part into his kingdom.

From December 1947, the mufti pleaded with the Arab League for the establishment of a Palestinian government to manage the affairs of the country and direct the struggle against the Jews, but his pleas fell on deaf ears. He and his colleagues on the Arab Higher Committee (AHC) were progressively marginalized. Thus, when the British mandate over Palestine expired and the State of Israel was proclaimed on 15 May 1948, the Arabs of Palestine had no government, no administrative regime, and no unified military command.

On 8 July 1948, the Arab League decided to set up a temporary civil administration in Palestine, to be directly responsible to the Arab League. This was a compromise proposal that failed to satisfy either of the two principal claimants. With strong opposition from King Abdullah, and only half-hearted support from the AHC, the new body was never properly established.

The Egyptian government, suspicious of King Abdullah's growing power in Palestine, put a proposal to the Arab League meeting that opened in Alexandria on 6 September 1948. The plan would turn the temporary civil administration, which had been agreed to in July, into an Arab government with a seat in Gaza for the whole of Palestine. The formal announcement of the Arab League's decision to form the Government of All-Palestine was issued on 20 September. In the eyes of its Egyptian sponsors, the immediate purpose of this government was to provide a focal point of opposition to King Abdullah's ambition to federate the Arab part of Palestine with Transjordan. The other Arab governments supported the Egyptian proposal at least partly because it furnished them with a means for withdrawing their armies from Palestine with some protection against popular outcry.

Despite the unpopularity of the Mufti of Jerusalem in most Arab capitals, the AHC played a major part in the formation of the new government, which was headed by Ahmad Hilmi Abd al-Baqi. Hilmi's cabinet consisted largely of followers of the mufti but also included representatives of the other factions of the Palestinian ruling class. Jamal al-Husayni became foreign minister, Raja al-Husayni became defense minister, Michael Abcarius was finance minister, and Anwar Nusayba was secretary of the cabinet. Twelve ministers in all, living in different Arab countries, headed for Gaza to take up their new positions.

During the first week of its life in Gaza, the All-Palestine Government revived the Holy War Army, with the declared aim of liberating Palestine; sought international recognition without much success;

A meeting of the Arab League, Cairo, Egypt, 1948. Established in 1945 between the countries of Egypt, Iraq, Syria, Lebanon, Jordan, Saudi Arabia, and Yemen, the Arab League was based on the notion of Pan-Arabism, which sought to unite all Arabs under one Arab state. The League also sought to further the collective interests of member countries and to protect their mutual security. © HULTON-DEUTSCH COLLECTION/CORBIS. REPRODUCED BY PERMISSION.

and issued several thousand Palestinian passports. To endow the government with legitimacy, a Palestinian National Council was convened in Gaza on 30 September 1948, under the chairmanship of the Mufti of Jerusalem. The council, in a mood of great elation, passed a series of resolutions culminating in a declaration of independence over the whole of Palestine. Although the new government claimed jurisdiction over the whole of Palestine, it had no administration, no civil service, no money, and no real army of its own. Even in the small enclave around the town of Gaza, its writ ran only by the grace of the Egyptian authorities. Taking advantage of the new government's dependence on them for funds and protection, the Egyptian paymasters manipulated it to undermine King Abdullah's claim to represent the Palestinians in the Arab League and international forums. Ostensibly the embryo for an independent Palestinian state, the new government

was thus reduced to the unhappy role of a shuttle-cock in the ongoing power struggle between Egypt and Jordan.

The Jordanian authorities were determined to stop the growth of the mufti's army. On 3 October, Jordan gave the order to the Arab Legion to surround, and forcibly disarm, various units of the Holy War Army. This move effectively neutralized the All-Palestine Government's military power and checked the growth of public sentiment in favor of an autonomous Palestinian state.

Shortly afterward, on 15 October 1948, Israel launched an offensive against the Egyptian army, forcing it to retreat down the coast to Gaza. Ironically, mid-October was also when the Arab governments got around to recognizing the All-Palestine Government. Nothing is more indicative of their half-hearted support than the lateness of their formal recognition. By the time it was granted, the game was over.

The Egyptian defeat deprived the All-Palestine Government of its last and exceedingly tenuous hold on Palestinian soil, forcing it to transfer its seat from Gaza to Cairo. Its weakness was exposed for all to see, its prestige slumped, and its authority was undermined. In Cairo, the Government of All-Palestine gradually fell apart because of its impotence, ending up four years later as a department of the Arab League. Thereafter, it continued to exist in name only until Egypt's President Gamal Abdel Nasser closed its offices in 1959.

Although the All-Palestine Government was projected as the nucleus of Palestinian self-government, it was an Egyptian-led phantom deliberately created by the Arab states to meet their publics' opposition to partition and to challenge Transjordan's claim to the rest of Arab Palestine. It was for selfish reasons that the Arab states created it, and it was for selfish reasons that they abandoned it. True, in the first three weeks of its short life, this fledgling government did represent a genuine attempt by the Palestinians to assert their independence from their dubious sponsors—to assume control over their own destiny; but the attempt was short-lived. Born of inter-Arab rivalries, the All-Palestine Government soon foundered on the rocks of inter-Arab rivalries. Consequently, if there is one lesson that stands, it is the need for Palestinian self-reliance, especially for defending the Palestinian cause against control and manipulation by the Arab states.

See also LEAGUE OF ARAB STATES.

Bibliography

Shlaim, Avi. "The Rise and Fall of the All-Palestine Government in Gaza." *Journal of Palestine Studies* 20, no. 1 (Autumn 1990).

Smith, Pamela Ann. *Palestine and the Palestinians, 1876–1983.* New York: St. Martin's, 1984.

AVI SHLAIM

AL NAHAYYAN FAMILY

Ruling family of Abu Dhabi emirate and the dominant family of the United Arab Emirates.

The history of Abu Dhabi, the largest emirate in the United Arab Emirates, is closely intertwined with that of the ruling Al Nahayyan family. The family originally presided over the tribes around the Liwa Oasis, but under Shakhbut ibn Dhiyab Al Nahayyan it ruled from a fort on Abu Dhabi Island beginning in the 1770s. The family's influence expanded to the al-Ayn Oasis under Shakhbut's grandson, Zayid ibn Khalifa. He also established friendly relations with the al-Maktum family of Dubai, the Qawasim in Sharjah, and the Al Bu Sa'id sultans of Muscat. The family presided over a period of economic growth fueled by the pearl trade, and its political influence became solidified as a result of its relations with British officials, who established a protectorate over the region.

Zayid's sons ruled until 1928, and his grandson, Shakhbut ibn Sultan, succeeded them and was in power when oil was discovered in 1958. Shakhbut's brother, Zayid ibn Sultan Al Nahayyan, became ruler in 1966 and was instrumental in establishing the United Arab Emirates in 1971.

See also ABU DHABI.

Bibliography

Kechichian, Joseph A., ed. *A Century in Thirty Years: Shaykh Zayed and the United Arab Emirates.* Washington, DC: Middle East Policy Council, 2000.

Lienhardt, Peter. *The Shaikhdoms of Eastern Arabia.* New York; Basingstoke, U.K.: Palgrave, 2001.

Metz, Helen Chapin, ed. *Persian Gulf States: Country Studies,* 3d edition. Washington, DC: Library of Congress, 1994.

M. MORSY ABDULLAH
UPDATED BY ANTHONY B. TOTH

ALONI, SHULAMIT

[1929–]

Israeli politician; civil rights, social affairs, and peace activist.

Born in Tel Aviv, Shulamit Aloni served in the 1948 Arab–Israel War, attended a teachers training seminar, and later studied law at the Hebrew University. In the 1950s and early 1960s, she earned a reputation as an advocate for social justice, civil and human rights, consumer protection, and above all the separation of religion from politics. She had a popular weekly radio program and a weekly column in which she propounded her antiestablishment views. In 1966, she established and headed the Israel Consumers' Council.

Elected to the Knesset in 1965, she served on various committees but was dropped from the Labor ticket in 1969 at the demand of Golda Meir. In 1973, she established the Civic Rights Movement (Ratz) and was elected to the Knesset, where she served until 1999. In 1974, she served briefly in the Yitzhak Rabin's first cabinet but resigned when the National Religious Party joined his cabinet. She was a prolific legislator, proposing scores of laws and serving mainly on the Knesset's Law and Constitution Committee. Rabin appointed her minister of education in 1992, after her party merged with Shinui to form Meretz. Pressure from the ultra-Orthodox Shas party forced her to give up some of her responsibilities. A well-known peace activist, she has advocated close ties with Israeli Arabs and the neighboring Palestinians and fought vehemently for the rights of the secular population and against what she considered undue religious coercion in Israel. She is the author of four books in Hebrew. Their titles, translated into English, are *The Citizen and His State, The Arrangement, Children's Rights in Israel,* and *Women as Human Beings.* In 2000 she was awarded the Israel Prize for lifetime achievements.

See also ARAB–ISRAEL WAR (1948); MEIR, GOLDA; RABIN, YITZHAK.

MERON MEDZINI

ALPHA, OPERATION

Code name for a major secret peace initiative in the mid-1950s.

Growing from British and U.S. concerns about the Near East conflict, Operation Alpha began as a shared initiative in October 1954 and eventually, after several stages, became a solely U.S. project a year later. Until March 1955, Francis Russell (U.S. State Department) and Evelyn Shuckburgh (British Foreign Office) made detailed plans for a peace settlement that involved financial aid for the resettlement of Arab refugees and security guarantees for Israel within agreed borders.

Subsequently, various efforts were made to "launch" Alpha: discussions with Israel's prime minister David Ben-Gurion and Egypt's President Gamal Abdel Nasser via normal diplomatic channels, a meticulously prepared speech by U.S. secretary of state John Foster Dulles in August 1955, and public proposals by British prime minister Anthony Eden in his November 1955 Guildhall speech. In a last-ditch attempt to save the initiative, U.S. president Dwight D. Eisenhower authorized the secret mission of a special envoy, Robert Anderson, a Texan lawyer and personal friend with ties to the U.S. Defense Department. From January to March 1956, Anderson engaged in CIA-supported shuttle diplomacy for negotiations with Ben-Gurion, Israel's foreign minister Moshe Sharett, and Nasser. In spite of the high-level support, Alpha failed. The question of blame remains controversial but the incompatibility of Israeli and Egyptian interests, insufficient willingness to make painful concessions, and inadequate U.S.-U.K. commitment all played a role. Instead of bringing peace, Alpha deepened mutual Israeli-Egyptian distrust and Anglo-American disillusionment with Nasser, thus contributing to developments that led to the Sinai War in 1956. In Washington, D.C., Alpha gave way to "Omega," a project to isolate and politically neutralize Nasser.

Bibliography

Caplan, Neil. *Futile Diplomacy,* Vol. 4: *Operation Alpha and the Failure of Anglo-American Coercive Diplomacy in the Arab-Israeli conflict, 1954–1956.* London: Frank Cass, 1997.

Touval, Saadia. *The Peace Brokers: Mediators in the Arab-Israeli Conflict, 1948–1979.* Princeton, NJ: Princeton University Press, 1982.

IRIS BOROWY

AL RASHID FAMILY

Rulers based in Ha'il, north central Arabia, from 1836 to 1921.

Although Abdullah ibn Rashid, the first of the Rashidi dynasty, was for a time allied with the Al Saud family, the two families were the principal political rivals in the region for a century. Abdullah came to power in 1836 by obtaining the support of Egyptian occupation forces. After the Egyptians left Arabia, Abdullah and his successors were able to consolidate their rule by winning the loyalty of the powerful Shammar tribal confederation and the residents of the important market town of Ha'il.

Talal ibn Abdullah ibn Rashid (r. 1848–1868) was responsible for increasing trade and commerce in Haʾil. In addition to treating Shiʿite merchants from Iraq with tolerance, he oversaw the construction of commercial buildings in his capital and the development of agriculture and rural settlement in the hinterland. The apogee of Rashidi rule in Arabia came under Muhammad ibn Rashid, who ruled the longest (1869–1897) and conquered the most territory. Rashidi influence extended across northern Arabia to northern Hijaz and the outskirts of Basra, Damascus, and Aleppo, and down as far as Oman. In 1891 the Rashidi capture of Riyadh forced the Al Saʿud into exile in Kuwait. Rashidi rule ended in 1921 with the Saudi capture of Haʾil.

See also SAUDI ARABIA.

Bibliography

Al Rasheed, Madawi. *A History of Saudi Arabia.* New York; Cambridge, U.K.: Cambridge University Press, 2002.

Al Rasheed, Madawi. *Politics in an Arabian Oasis: The Rashidi Tribal Dynasty.* New York; London: I. B. Tauris, 1991.

Vassiliev, Alexei. *The History of Saudi Arabia.* New York: New York University Press, 2000.

MALCOLM C. PECK
UPDATED BY ANTHONY B. TOTH

AL SABAH FAMILY

The ruling family of Kuwait.

"If the Al Sabah had not existed, it would have been necessary to invent them." This saying, reported by historian Alan Rush, reflects how deeply embedded the family is in the history of Kuwait. This clan has provided all the rulers of the small community since tribes from the Najd district of the Arabian Peninsula collected on the shores of the bay at the far northwest of the Persian Gulf early in the eighteenth century. The family also provided a rallying point for the community some 240 years later, after it was invaded and annexed by Iraq.

Within decades of the original settlement of what is now Kuwait, the Al Sabah were chosen as leaders by community consensus. The ruler was the local administrator of the community and the liaison between it and the shaykh of the Bani Kalid tribe

on which Kuwaitis depended for protection. He is chosen by consensus among senior family members rather than acceding through an automatic mechanism like primogeniture.

The first Kuwaiti ruler, Sabah, served from about 1752 to about 1756 and was succeeded by his youngest son, Abdullah, who ruled until 1814. Abdullah was reared to rule in consultation with his relatives and the leaders of the merchant clans who were the main beneficiaries of orderly governance. The primary crises of his reign were the migration of the Al Khalifa, the richest family of Kuwait, to Bahrain, where they became rulers in their own right, and the beginning of what would become a series of wars against the Wahhabi Ikhwan (followers of the family of Muhammad ibn Abd al-Wahhab, the "al-Shaykh," who ruled in tandem with the al-Saʿud).

Abdullah's son Jabir became amir following Abdullah's death in 1814. He was noted for his charity to the poor and for his political craft. He kept Kuwait on good terms but not aligned with the many rivals whose conflicts beset the region: Britain, the Ottomans, Egypt, and the Al Saʿud. His reign lasted until 1859 and is noted for the prosperity Kuwaitis enjoyed during that time.

Sabah II took power while in his seventies, having served for many years at his father's right hand and accepting most of the community's administrative responsibilities for some five years before his accession. Sabah maintained Kuwait's neutrality during tribal wars between the Al Saʿud and the Ajman and managed to keep the peace with Kuwaiti merchants who threatened to abandon Kuwait if his tax collector was not removed. Like his father, he was known for his charity.

Abdullah II, who ruled until 1892, was forced by Midhat Paşa to relinquish Kuwait's neutrality and become an ally of the Ottomans, thereby averting a war with Turkey and gaining an ally for himself and the merchants. He later accepted the title of *quaʾimmaqam* and a subvention from the Turkish government. Abdullah was assassinated in 1896, probably by a son of his successor, Mubarak.

Mubarak was the only Kuwaiti ruler to take power through a coup, having masterminded the assassination of two of his brothers, Abdullah II and his close adviser Jarrah. Mubarak's political base lay with the Bedouin tribesmen rather than the merchants, who disliked him for his high-handedness as much as for his high taxes. During Mubarak's rule, a group of merchants left Kuwait for Bahrain and, despite Mubarak's assurances, not all of them returned. Mubarak was a skilled diplomat, taking subventions from the Ottomans and also from the British, whom he persuaded to sign a series of secret agreements guaranteeing protection to Kuwait in exchange for surrender of its foreign policy autonomy and sovereignty over whatever oil reserves it might possess. Mubarak also got the British to agree that only his descendants would be allowed to rule Kuwait in the future, thereby denying the corporate rights of the sons of his brothers and impairing family solidarity.

Mubarak was succeeded by two of his sons, Jabir II (1915–1917) and Salim (1917–1921). Jabir was hearty and outgoing and presided over a short, warfueled economic boom. His untimely death brought his brother Salim, a devout Muslim, to power. Salim wanted the boundaries of Kuwait to be set according to the terms of the unratified Anglo–Turkish convention, signed in 1913 when his father's authority over neighboring tribes was at its height. The Al Saʿud objected and relations with them deteriorated. Kuwait was attacked by a Wahhabi army under Faysal al-Darwish in 1920. Defeated in the south, the Kuwaitis constructed a wall around Kuwait and Salim led an army to Jahra, successfully heading off the Wahhabi assault.

Jabir's son Ahmad became ruler upon Salim's death in 1921. He agreed to govern with the assistance of a council of notables but once installed never called it into being. Ahmad was ruler when the 1922 Treaty of Uqayr set the boundaries of Kuwait, Saudi Arabia, and Iraq. The only ruler who did not have a representative at the conference, he ended with a far smaller Kuwait than his grandfather had envisioned. Ahmad resisted merchant demands to share authority and also refused to provide even minimally for the welfare of the population, moving the merchants to establish newspapers, schools, and, after oil was discovered, a parliament elected from among themselves to write a constitution and pass laws that would force Ahmad to share the income. Ahmad closed the 1938 parliament and its 1939 successor, the latter in a showdown in which one Kuwaiti was killed and after which many went into exile.

Ahmad's successor was Abdullah al-Salim, his cousin, who had been his emissary in negotiations with the 1938 and 1939 parliaments. Abdullah al-Salim inaugurated many programs to distribute oil income, not only to his family and their merchant allies but also to the common people. He established hospitals, schools, and housing programs and placed a large, interest-free deposit in the nascent merchant-owned National Bank of Kuwait. Beset throughout his rule by economic corruption within his family, he was forced to borrow money from the merchants to cover state obligations, in return agreeing to keep his family members from competing against them. The most notable accomplishments of Abdullah al-Salim's rule were the writing and adoption of a modern constitution and the election of a parliament under its aegis.

Sabah al-Salim III succeeded his brother in 1965 and in 1976 suspended the constitution and the civil liberties it enshrined in an attempt to quash a growing merchant-led opposition from within the parliament to Al Sabah autocracy. Yet most Kuwaitis were satisfied with their social benefits and high living standard. During Sabah's rule, the Reserve Fund for Future Generations was launched. It receives 10 percent of the state's income for investment in blue-chip securities to provide for a post-oil future.

Upon Sabah's greatly mourned death in 1977, his nephew, Jabir al-Ahmad, became ruler of a country undergoing a crisis of legitimacy because of the constitution's suspension. Agreeing to hold elections, he attempted first to amend the constitution and then, when popular opinion turned against this plan, naturalized thousands of Bedouin tribesmen and redistricted the country to make it unlikely that a merchant-led opposition could dominate a reinstated parliament. A growing Islamist movement, encouraged by the ruling family, and candidates who were members of dominant clans and tribes, were heavily represented in the parliament elected in 1981, but its 1985 successor, in which these groups also were heavily represented, proved to be contentious. The amir dismissed the parliament and suspended civil liberties again in 1986, after a crash in oil prices and amid grave doubts that the government could continue to deliver social benefits at established levels. A broad-based movement demanding the restoration of constitutional government swept the country in 1989 and 1990. Jabir al-Ahmad responded by calling for the election of an interim national council that would recommend reforms. Two months after the election, on 2 August 1990, Iraq invaded Kuwait.

The senior Al Sabah fled into exile but others fought the invaders and served in the resistance. The amir became the focal point of efforts to reclaim the country and was reconciled with the leaders of the opposition, promising a new election for the constitutional National Assembly, not his extra-constitutional substitute, after liberation. That election took place in October 1992, returning a parliament ridden by dissension. Its successor proved even less able to legislate on pressing national issues. In 1999, Jabir al-Ahmad suspended the 1996 parliament but not the constitution, calling for new elections within the sixty days, as prescribed. Meanwhile, he issued more than sixty decrees, including one that would have enfranchised Kuwaiti women. The parliament elected in July 1999 voted down all but the budgetary decrees, leaving the country bemused by the spectacle of a liberal amir and a conservative parliament.

In 2003, Jabir al-Ahmad was frail and ill and his nominated successor, Crown Prince Abdullah al-Salim, was even less well. Despite his occasional ventures into querulous national politics, the amir is mostly a shadow of the vigorous man he was before an assassination attempt in 1985 initiated his gradual withdrawal from active public life. Still, following the 2003 elections, he initiated the separation of the post of crown prince and prime minister, offering at least the eventual possibility of empowering a parliamentary majority to bring down a government. Meanwhile, within the Al Sabah, barely veiled struggles over the succession were spilling over into national and international politics.

See also AL KHALIFA FAMILY; AL SABAH, MUBARAK; KUWAIT; MIDHAT PAŞA; MUWAHHIDUN.

Bibliography

Anscombe, Frederick F. *The Ottoman Gulf: The Creation of Kuwait, Saudi Arabia, and Qatar.* New York: Columbia University Press, 1997.

Crystal, Jill. *Oil and Politics in the Gulf: Rulers and Merchants in Kuwait and Qatar.* New York and Cambridge, U.K.: Cambridge University Press, 1990.

Herb, Michael. *All in the Family: Absolutism, Revolution, and Democracy in the Middle Eastern Monarchies.* Albany: State University of New York Press, 1999.

Kostiner, Joseph, ed. *Middle East Monarchies: The Challenge of Modernity.* Boulder, CO: Lynne Rienner, 2000.

Rush, Alan. *Al-Sabah: Genealogy and History of Kuwait's Ruling Family, 1752–1986.* Atlantic Highlands, NJ, and London: Ithaca Press, 1987.

Tétreault, Mary Ann. *Stories of Democracy: Politics and Society in Contemporary Kuwait.* New York: Columbia University Press, 2000.

MARY ANN TÉTREAULT

AL SABAH, MUBARAK

Ruler of Kuwait, 1896–1915.

Mubarak Al Sabah, often called "Mubarak the Great," has been called the most forceful ruler of Kuwait. He is the only ruler in Kuwait's history to achieve his position as the result of a coup; he killed one of his brothers, Muhammad, the ruler at the time, and one of his sons killed another of Mubarak's brothers, Jarrah, who was Muhammad's close adviser. Apologists excuse these actions by pointing to Muhammad's pro-Turkish proclivities. Critics agree that Mubarak prevented the absorption of Kuwait into the Ottoman Empire but note that he did this not by keeping Kuwait independent but by making it a British client. The result of Mubarak's several secret treaties with Britain was to relinquish Kuwait's autonomy in foreign policy. This amounted to a larger concession of sovereignty than had been made to the Ottomans by Mubarak's predecessor. More important for the political development of Kuwait in the twentieth century, however, was Mubarak's use of British economic and military resources to attenuate the power of local notables, a process that was continued by his successors, who relied on oil revenues to insulate themselves from popular checks on their power.

Kuwait's economy thrived during Mubarak's reign. His domestic power, however, rested on his close relationship to the bedouin tribes rather than to the urban merchants. Even after he became ruler,

Mubarak spent time camping with the bedouins in the desert. Unlike the tradition established by most previous amirs of Kuwait, however, Mubarak publicly enjoyed a lavish lifestyle. His income from taxes, British payments and annuities, and family investments (including date gardens located in Iraq) enabled Mubarak to live well and to employ armed guards to protect himself from his subjects. Resentment of his high taxes and military levies provoked several leading pearl merchants to leave Kuwait for Bahrain in 1910. A delegation from the ruler that carried Mubarak's promise to rescind the burdensome taxes encouraged only some to return.

Mubarak's military campaigns against the al-Rashid shaykhs of the Jabal Shammar were aimed at allies of the exiled relatives of Muhammad and Jarrah. In September 1902, British warships were sent against a force commanded by two of Mubarak's nephews who were seeking revenge for their fathers' deaths. But Mubarak's military adventures were also problematic for the British, who wanted to maintain their alliance with the Ottomans. Nevertheless, they continued to support him, and in 1905 the Turks abandoned their efforts to incorporate Kuwait into the *vilayet* of Basra.

Mubarak had confidence in the British as Kuwait's ultimate protectors against the Turks. But British rapprochement with the Sublime Porte prior to the outbreak of World War I produced the Anglo–Turkish Convention of 1913. This declared Kuwait to be a *kaza* (autonomous province) of the Ottoman Empire and recognized Turkey's right to have a political representative in Kuwait. Mubarak was shocked by what he saw as a betrayal of his interests. The convention, however, never went into effect. On 3 November 1914, it was repudiated, and two centuries of diplomatic ties between Kuwait and the Ottomans were broken. One year later, Mubarak died. True to their promise to a leader who had become a staunch ally, the British planned to honor another of their pledges to Mubarak: that they would ensure that the next ruler of Kuwait would be his designated heir rather than a descendant of the brothers he had killed in 1896. In the event, no external intervention was necessary. Subsequent rulers of Kuwait have also been direct descendants of Mubarak.

See also JABAL SHAMMAR; KUWAIT.

Bibliography

Rush, Alan De Lacy. *Al-Sabah: History and Genealogy of Kuwait's Ruling Family, 1752–1986.* London and Atlantic Highlands, NJ: Ithaca Press, 1987.

Rush, Alan De Lacy, ed. *Records of Kuwait, 1899–1961,* Vol. 1: *Internal Affairs, 1899–1921.* London, 1989.

Tétreault, Mary Ann. "Autonomy, Necessity, and the Small State: Ruling Kuwait in the Twentieth Century." *International Organization* 45 (Autumn 1991).

MARY ANN TÉTREAULT

AL SAQR FAMILY

Family prominent in the politics of Kuwait.

Members of the Al Saqr family were among the founders of Kuwait in the eighteenth century. They made their money in shipping and trade and were reputed to be among the toughest dealmakers in the country. They acquired the first stock ticker in Kuwait in the 1920s, and shortly afterward they cornered local coffee supplies after learning that a storm had destroyed much of the year's crop.

Like other prominent merchant families, the Al Saqr participated in the democratization movements that recurred throughout the twentieth century. In 1921 Hamid Al Saqr led an organization of notables who petitioned the ruling family for the right to advise on the succession to the amirship. After Ahmad al-Jabir became amir he refused to consult with the notables. Hamid Al Saqr became leader of the opposition and, upon his death in 1930, was succeeded by his son Abdullah Hamid.

The Al Saqr family founded the Ahliyya Library, where the opposition met to plan its strategy. Abdullah Hamid was a leader of the 1938 to 1939 majles movement. He was a member of both councils elected during this period and among those who refused to disband when the amir suspended the second council's activities. He was forced to flee the country when the movement failed. He died in India.

The merchants developed a close relationship with the amir's brother, Abdullah al-Salim, who had served as the president of the elected councils and attempted to mediate the many conflicts between the councils and the amir. After Abdullah al-Salim became amir in 1950, a group of five merchant families, including the Al Saqr, approached him about establishing a bank. He granted the National Bank of Kuwait a charter in 1952 and helped to capitalize the bank with a large interest-free deposit.

The Al Saqr family continued its political activities during the rule of Abdullah al-Salim. Abd al-Aziz, another of Hamid Al Saqr's sons, was a wealthy trader and shipyard owner. He was a member of the Constitutional Assembly that was convened in 1961 to prepare Kuwait's first constitution and was elected to the first National Assembly. He became its president and the minister of health in the first cabinet. Abd al-Aziz was one of the leaders of Kuwait's prodemocracy movement of 1989 to 1990 and, at the time, president of the Kuwait Chamber of Commerce and Industry. With Ahmad al-Sa'dun, the president of the 1985 National Assembly that had been suspended by the amir in 1986, Abd al-Aziz effected a reconciliation between the ruling family and the political opposition at an October 1990 meeting in Jidda, Saudi Arabia.

Another sibling, Jasim Hamid, served on the board of Kuwait University and was a private sector member of the board of the Kuwait National Petroleum Company before resigning, along with the other private members, in a 1960s dispute with the government representatives over selecting Hispanoil as a partner in an exploration concession. Jasim also served in the National Assembly and was its presiding officer when it was reorganized following the 1992 elections.

The Al Saqr family retains extensive business and financial interests in Kuwait and overseas and continues to be involved politically, both through its interests in the newspaper *Al-Qabbas* and in the person of Jasim's son Mohammad Jasim, who is the editor of *Al-Qabbas* and has been an elected member of the National Assembly since 1999.

See also BANKING; KUWAIT.

Bibliography

Crystal, Jill. *Oil and Politics in the Gulf: Rulers and Merchants in Kuwait and Qatar.* New York: Cambridge University Press, 1990.

Rush, Alan de Lacy, ed. *Records of Kuwait, 1899–1961.* Vol. 2: *Internal Affairs, 1921–1950.* Slough, U.K.: Archive Editions, 1989.

Tétreault, Mary Ann. *The Kuwait Petroleum Corporation and the Economics of the New World Order.* Westport, CT: Greenwood Press, 1995.

Tétreault, Mary Ann. *Stories of Democracy: Politics and Society in Contemporary Kuwait.* New York: Columbia Univeristy Press, 2000.

MARY ANN TÉTREAULT

AL SA'UD FAMILY

The ruling family of Saudi Arabia, the wealthiest and most powerful group in the country.

The king of Saudi Arabia, key government ministers, and other high officials are members of the Al Sa'ud family, who control the instruments of political power and the principal sources of wealth. In this patriarchal and conservative society, women are excluded from political office, but the Al Sa'ud consult with the religious establishment, wealthy merchants, and local and tribal leaders. Saudi domestic and foreign policy thus is greatly influenced by the interactions among these forces and is strongly stamped with the personalities of the king and top officials in the family. Because the family is so large, with several thousand "princes," and so diverse in outlook and interests, political divisions can be deep and struggles fierce within the ruling family, if oftentimes difficult to see from the outside. Still, it has managed to maintain its position on top of the Saudi political system by compromise, co-optation, and force.

The Foundation of the Kingdom

The ancestors of the Al Sa'ud ruled towns in the central Arabian region of Najd dating back to the fifteenth century. However, the family's influence and domains grew dramatically after the amir of the town of Dir'iyya, Muhammad ibn Sa'ud, made an alliance with the religious leader Muhammad ibn Abd al-Wahhab in 1744. During the nineteenth and early twentieth century, when the Al Sa'ud and their allies attempted to conquer lands beyond Najd, they clashed with local and foreign groups, including the Hashimites of Hijaz, the Rashids of Jabal Shammar, and the Banu Khalid in al-Hasa, as well as Ottoman and Egyptian forces. During the late nineteenth century, the power of the Al Sa'ud was eclipsed by the Rashids, who controlled most of Najd as well as

King Ibn Sa'ud (shown here with three sons and a grandson) returned from exile in Kuwait at the beginning of the twentieth century and reclaimed his family's historical domains, expanding them over the years to create the kingdom of Saudi Arabia in 1932. © BETTMANN/CORBIS. REPRODUCED BY PERMISSION.

Jabal Shammar. However, beginning in 1902, Abd al-Aziz ibn Abd al-Rahman Al Sa'ud, after living for years in exile in Kuwait, began a reconquest of his family's historical domains and those of its rivals. According to his contemporaries, the courage, intelligence, charisma, and occasional ruthlessness of Abd al-Aziz helped him win supporters and defeat opponents in his drive to expand his domains. In 1932 he proclaimed the Kingdom of Saudi Arabia.

Opposition, sometimes violent, on occasion arose to Abd al-Aziz from within the family, but the ruler managed to consolidate his preeminent role by eliminating threats from his other relatives while assuring the power of his sons, and keeping rival families such as the Rashid, the Al Shaykh, and the leading families of important tribes subordinate by marrying and divorcing many of their daughters in rapid and routine succession.

Abd al Aziz died in 1953 and was succeeded by his oldest son, Sa'ud (1902–1969), who had been designated crown prince in 1933. Sa'ud's reign has been described by analysts as exhibiting incompetence, greed, and self-indulgence, compounded by the ruler's serious medical problems. By 1958 debt and political crisis forced Sa'ud to yield power, but not the crown, to his brother and rival, Faisal ibn Abd al-Aziz Al Sa'ud. Once Faisal had restored the country's solvency and repaired foreign relations that Sa'ud had disrupted, Sa'ud thrust himself back into full power in alliance with Talal ibn Abd al-Aziz Al Sa'ud and other brothers identified as the Free Princes, who called for a constitutional monarchy. But once more a conclave of senior princes forced Sa'ud to yield power to Faisal. In 1964 Sa'ud tried for a final time to reclaim the powers of his office. The senior princes, backed by the *ulama,* forced Sa'ud's abdication on 2 November 1964.

The reign of Faisal (b. 1906) was shaped greatly by tremendous increases in oil revenues and his efforts to carry out previously neglected social and economic development projects using the framework of five-year plans. While overseeing these massive projects, Faisal tightened his grip on political power by assuming the title of prime minister as well as king and dividing key state positions among his half-brothers, thus removing any vestiges of his predecessor's influence. Some of Faisal's projects and social reforms, such as the introduction of education for girls and television broadcasting, were strongly opposed by conservative religious factions. In fact, he was assassinated in 1975 by the brother of a Saudi prince who had taken part in an antitelevision demonstration in 1965 and was shot dead by police.

Khalid ibn Abd al-Aziz (b. 1912) became king shortly after Faisal's death. The serious tensions caused by the influx of great wealth, technological and social change, royal family abuses, and a desire to maintain Islamic values that had begun to build during Faisal's reign exploded into open revolt during Khalid's. He used both force and compromise to deal with the takeover of the Grand Mosque and Shi'ite uprisings in the Eastern Province. Toward the end of his rule, failing health and competition from the crown prince, Fahd ibn Abd al-Aziz, forced him to become merely a figurehead.

Fahd (b. 1921) took over formal rule of the country after Khalid's death in 1982. Sharp drops in oil revenues during the 1980s forced Fahd to face dire economic and social questions, such as the role of the large foreign workforce, priorities for economic development, and the need to diversify the economy. In the late 1990s and early 2000s, ill health prevented him from carrying out his day-to-day responsibilities, and so his crown prince, Abdullah ibn Abd al-Aziz, became de facto ruler.

Abdullah and the Princes

Abdullah has had to contend with increased internal opposition to the ruling family's role in the country. While some groups merely have called for reform, others have called for a violent overthrow of the Al Sa'ud. Abdullah has responded by cracking down on these militant groups, incrementally increasing avenues for political participation, downplaying the kingdom's military and economic ties with the United States, and becoming an international advocate for issues important to Muslims around the world. The attacks of 11 September 2001 drew increased attention to the royal family and its complex relationship with militant Islam inside the country and worldwide. While Osama bin Ladin, has had support within Saudi Arabia, a series of deadly bomb attacks in 2003 attributed to his organization have drawn widespread popular condemnation and elicited a vigorous response from the government's security forces.

Besides the rulers, members of the Al Sa'ud have held key ministry positions and played other influential roles. For example, Muhammad ibn Abd al-Aziz Al Sa'ud (1910–1990), the sixth son of Abd al-Aziz, held no official positions in his later years, although he played a key role in the affairs of the kingdom as a strong-willed senior prince. When still in his twenties, Muhammad served as deputy to Faisal ibn Abd al-Aziz al Sa'ud, then viceroy of Hijaz (later king of Saudi Arabia). Muhammad, however, lacked a natural power base in the family and was notorious for his ungovernable rages, which led in late 1963 to his renunciation of a place in the royal succession. His younger full brother Khalid took his place. Khalid subsequently became king in 1975.

Muhammad strongly opposed his half brother Sa'ud ibn Abd al-Aziz Al Sa'ud, the successor to their father Ibn Sa'ud, as unfit to rule. He was the only son not to swear allegiance, and from 1955 on, he led efforts to depose Saʿud in favor of Faisal, playing a major role in pressing the case to its conclusion in 1964. He gained international notoriety from the television production "Death of a Princess," which was a dramatization of the execution—at his insistence—of his granddaughter, Princess Mishal, and her lover for adultery.

Sultan ibn Abd al-Aziz (b. 1924) has been deputy prime minister since 1982. Born in Riyadh, he is the next oldest full brother of King Fahd, a son of Hassa bint Ahmad Al Sudayri, the favorite wife of King Abd al-Aziz Al Saʿud. He is a key part of the Al Fahd—the king and his six full brothers—often referred to in the Western press as the Sudayri Seven—who began to consolidate their power within the Saudi royal family during the reign of Khalid.

Sultan and the other members of the Al Fahd are the first princes to build their careers through service in the bureaucracy. When Sultan was still in his early twenties, his father appointed him governor of the province of Riyadh. King Saʿud named him minister of agriculture in the first Council of Ministers in 1954. In 1960, Sultan replaced his half brother Talal, one of the Free Princes, as minister of communications. In 1962 Crown Prince Faisal, then serving as King Saʿud's prime minister, appointed Sultan defense minister—the position that he has held for thirty years. Faisal gave Sultan great authority in determining Saudi Arabia's military needs and in filling them. He also relied extensively on his advice in general matters, in part to balance the views of conservatives in the Al Saʿud family with Sultan's progressive perspectives. After 1975, during the reign of Faisal's successor, King Khalid, Sultan became part of the inner circle of senior princes who direct the nation's course. In 1982, when Fahd became king, Sultan was made second deputy prime minister, de facto successor after Crown Prince Abdullah—and likely will become king if he survives those two brothers.

Talal ibn Abd al-Aziz Al Saʿud (b. 1931), the twenty-third son of Abd al-Aziz, has been another influential member of the family. He reportedly lived an opulent lifestyle as a young man, and became comptroller of the royal household at age 19. He persuaded his father to permit him to establish a cement factory, one of the first princely ventures

King Ibn Saʿud (shown here with his eldest son Saud) proclaimed the kingdom of Saudi Arabia in 1932 and quickly consolidated his power. © AP/WIDE WORLD PHOTOS. REPRODUCED BY PERMISSION.

in entrepreneurship in Saudi Arabia. Talal also displayed early on a certain intellectual sophistication and, from a number of sources, drew ideas for liberal reforms that he intended to implement in Saudi Arabia. He may have assimilated some of these ideas from his first wife, the daughter of Lebanon's former premier, Riyad al-Sulh. When his ties to dissident army elements led in 1955 to his dismissal as minister of communications in King Saʿud's Council of Ministers, he went to Paris as ambassador (accredited both to France and Spain) and there further developed democratic constitutional concepts for Saudi Arabia.

In 1960 Saʿud named Talal minister of finance and economy. The king, though not in sympathy with Talal's ideas, saw him and his several reformist brothers as useful allies in his attempt to regain and consolidate power. Earlier, Saʿud had yielded most of his authority to Crown Prince Faisal in the monarchy's 1958 crisis. In this Talal saw an opportunity to implement his ideas for reform. Neither brother satisfied his expectations, and Sa'ud forced Talal out of the cabinet after less than a year.

Talal subsequently left Saudi Arabia for Beirut, Lebanon, where in the summer of 1962 he issued a manifesto titled "Letter to a Fellow Countryman." It called for a constitutional monarchy with a national assembly, two-thirds of its members to be elected, which could propose legislation, with the king retaining veto power. In the Saudi context, such notions were radical, and when Talal proceeded to criticize the Saudi government in public, to call for the freeing of slaves and concubines, and to introduce more extreme notions such as centralized "socialism," the king took his passport. Talal's full brother Nawwaf and his half brothers Badr and Fawwaz, collectively called the Free Princes outside Saudi Arabia but self-described as Young Najd (Najd al-Fatat), gave up their passports in sympathy and joined Talal in exile in Cairo. Egypt's President Gamal Abdel Nasser tried to use the situation to his advantage against Saudi Arabia, hoping that the defections by the princes could lead to the monarchy's collapse.

The episode shook the Saudi ruling family severely, especially as it immediately preceded a republican coup in neighboring Yemen and the defection of officers from the Saudi Air Force to Nasser's Egypt. It strengthened the resolve of the Al Sa'ud never again to permit family differences to be aired in public. The exiled princes all eventually returned, Talal doing so in 1964 and making an "admission of guilt." He has resumed a respected place in the royal family and, since 1979, has served as a special envoy to the United Nations Educational, Scientific, and Cultural Organization (UNESCO).

Nayif ibn Abd al-Aziz (b. 1933) is the twenty-sixth son of Abd al-Aziz, and is a full brother of King Fahd. He is one of the six brothers of the Sudayri Seven, or Al Fahd, to hold a senior government position. He was governor of Riyadh from 1953 to 1954, and in 1970 became deputy minister of the interior when Fahd headed that ministry. Since 1975, when Fahd became crown prince and relinquished the ministry, Nayif has been minister of the interior, and the youngest of the Al Fahd, Ahmad, has been his deputy.

Nayif is known as pious and austere, though he has amassed a considerable fortune, and has been sympathetic to conservative demands for more extensive restrictions on both Saudi and foreign conduct in public. He has a special interest in the Gulf Arab states, with which he has developed close internal security ties. Fahd places special trust in Nayif and, after the 1979 seizure of the Grand Mosque in Mecca, directed him to head a committee to draft plans for a consultative council (Majlis al-Shura) that was finally implemented in 1992.

Turki ibn Abd al-Aziz Al Sa'ud (b. 1934) is another brother of Fahd, and served as deputy defense minister from 1969 to 1978. The erratic behavior of his wife, which created unwelcome publicity, forced him to relinquish that post.

Fawwaz ibn Abd al-Aziz (b. 1934) was one of three Sa'ud princes who publicly called for a constitutional monarchy for Saudi Arabia in 1962. In 1971, King Faisal appointed him governor of Mecca. In November 1979 the leader of the seizure of the Grand Mosque of Mecca attacked Fawwaz for moral laxity; he resigned the governorship shortly afterward.

Sa'ud ibn Faisal Al Sa'ud (b. 1940) served as the country's foreign minister since 1975. The fourth son of King Faisal, Sa'ud is the eldest of the four born to the king's favorite wife, Iffat. Like his full brothers, he received a Western education, earning a bachelor's degree in economics at Princeton University. His father's influence was strong as was that of his maternal uncle Kamal Adham, former head of Saudi intelligence. Following King Faisal's assassination in 1975, Sa'ud assumed the position of foreign minister that was previously held by his father for over forty years. Both as crown prince and king, Fahd ibn Abd al-Aziz al Sa'ud has valued his nephew Sa'ud's intelligence and skill in handling foreign assignments, but their relationship is not particularly warm. Based on his strong belief in nationalism, Sa'ud has seen the U.S.-Saudi relationship as excessively one-way, in Washington's favor, and has argued for a nonaligned policy. He is probably the most likely candidate among the grandsons of King Abd al-Aziz Al Sa'ud to become king.

Turki ibn Faisal Al Sa'ud (b. 1945) is the youngest son of Faisal by Iffat. He received his college education in the United States and did graduate studies in Islamic law at London University. He became deputy to the head of the General Intelligence Directorate, Kamal Adham, his uncle. In early 1979 Turki replaced Adham, who had taken much of the blame for failure to foresee Egypt's peace initiative with Israel succeed in the agreement called the Camp David Accords.

In November 1979 Turki distinguished himself by taking charge of the operations to regain government control of the Grand Mosque in Mecca after Islamic extremists had seized it in an effort to promote the overthrow of the monarchy. Turki has acted as a polished spokesman for Saudi Arabia's international interests. Like his father, he combines a sophisticated knowledge of the contemporary world with genuine piety and a firm belief in his country's inherent moral superiority.

See also ABD AL-ʿAZIZ IBN SAʿUD AL SAʿUD; CAMP DAVID ACCORDS (1978); FAHD IBN ABD AL-AZIZ AL SAʿUD; FAISAL IBN ABD AL-AZIZ AL SAʿUD; KHALID IBN ABD AL-AZIZ AL SAʿUD; MAJLES AL-SHURA; SAUDI ARABIA.

Bibliography

Bligh, Alexander. *From Prince to King: Royal Succession in the House of Saʿud in the Twentieth Century.* New York: New York University Press, 1984.

Lees, Brian. *A Handbook of the Al Saʿud Ruling Family of Saudi Arabia.* London: Royal Genealogies, 1980.

Philby, H. St. J. B. *Arabia.* New York: Charles Scribner's Sons, 1930.

Philby, H. St. J. B. *Saʿudi Arabia.* London: Benn, 1955.

Al Rasheed, Madawi. *A History of Saudi Arabia.* New York; Cambridge, U.K.: Cambridge University Press, 2002.

Rush, Alan de Lacy. "The Monarchy of Saudi Arabia." In *Burke's Royal Families of the World,* Vol. 3: *Africa and the Middle East.* London: Burke's Peerage, 1980.

Vassiliev, Alexei. *The History of Saudi Arabia.* New York: New York University Press, 2000.

Winder, R. Bayly. *Saudi Arabia in the Nineteenth Century.* New York: St. Martin's Press, 1965.

ANTHONY B. TOTH

AL SAʿUD, SAʿUD IBN ABD AL-AZIZ
[1902–1969]

Succeeded his father, Ibn Saʿud, as king of Saudi Arabia, 1953–1964.

Saʿud ibn Abd al-Aziz Al Saʿud's life appeared to begin auspiciously, since he was born on 16 January 1902—the same day that his father Abd al-Aziz reconquered Riyadh. In 1919, the death of the eldest son, Turki, made Saʿud the eldest surviving son. He received the usual court education of memorizing the Qurʾan, formal instruction in practical subjects, and more relevant lessons in court business.

In 1921, Saʿud led troops in the final campaign against the Al Rashid, and in 1926, Abd al-Aziz appointed him viceroy of Najd, the Saudi heartland. In 1933 his father directed Saʿud's designation as crown prince. Ibn Saʿud was aware that Saʿud's abilities were greatly inferior to those of Faisal, his next son, or other potential candidates among the princes. What almost certainly led him to insist on Saʿud's designation as his successor was the memory of the family's internal rivalries, which shortly before had brought their fortunes to their lowest ebb: Also, there were potential challenges emerging to continued rule through Ibn Saʿud's line.

Despite a long tenure as viceroy and crown prince, Saʿud had never exercised meaningful authority before becoming king of Saudi Arabia in 1953, and he lacked any understanding of modern state administration and finance. Rather than relying on the council of ministers, Saʿud delegated authority to his sons and cronies. Self-indulgent and good-hearted, he regarded the country's oil wealth as his own, to be spent as he pleased. Serious physical infirmities were a major liability throughout his reign.

By 1958, debt and political crisis forced Saʿud to yield power to his brother Faisal. The precipitating factor was Saʿud's ill-considered attempt to challenge Egypt's President Gamal Abdel Nasser by acting as leader of the conservative Arab camp, supported by the United States. Once Faisal had restored the country's solvency and established a temporary modus vivendi with Nasser, Saʿud thrust himself back into full power in alliance with Talal ibn Abd al-Aziz Al Saʿud and other brothers identified as the Free Princes, who called for a constitutional monarchy. But once more a conclave of senior princes forced Saʿud to yield power to his brother Faisal.

In 1964, Saʿud tried for a final time to reclaim the powers of his office. The senior princes, backed by the *ulama,* forced Saʿud's abdication on 2 November 1964. The remainder of his life was passed in sybaritic exile, largely in Athens, Greece, where he died on 23 February 1969.

See also Abd al-Aziz ibn Saʿud Al Saʿud; Al Saʿud Family; Faisal ibn Abd al-Aziz Al Saʿud; Nasser, Gamal Abdel.

Bibliography

Bligh, Alexander. *From Prince to King: Royal Succession in the House of Saud in the Twentieth Century.* New York: New York University Press, 1984.

Holden, David, and Johns, Richard. *The House of Saud: The Rise and Rule of the Most Powerful Dynasty in the Arab World.* New York: Holt, Rinehart, and Winston, 1981.

Malcolm C. Peck

AL SUDAYRI FAMILY

Important family or clan in Saudi Arabia; part of a tribe of the same name.

The Al Sudayri (also spelled Al Sudairi or al-Sudairi) family's origins can be traced to a branch of the Dawasir tribe, which was a *sharifian,* or noble, tribe that lived on the edge of the Rub al-Khali desert in about 1400. By about 1550, the Al Sudayri were situated at the town of Ghat in Sudayr, an area in Najd, to the northwest of Riyadh, which took its name from the tribe. The main branch of the family, whose fortunes have been closely linked with the fortunes of the Al Saʿud family of Saudi Arabia, comes into view in the early eighteenth century.

First to achieve special prominence among the Sudayri was Ahmad al-Kabir, whose life spanned the first two-thirds of the nineteenth century. He served the Al Saʿud for fifty years in a number of civilian and military capacities, including the governorship of al-Hasa, the country's eastern province. His daughter Sara was the mother of King Abd al-Aziz (also known as Ibn Saʿud), and it was largely from her that he inherited his imposing physical stature. Ahmad al-Kabir's grandson and namesake, Ahmad bin Muhammad Al Sudayri (1869–1935), further cemented his family's ties to the Al Saʿud.

In the early twentieth century, he participated in the Al Saʿud's military campaigns against their Al Rashid rivals. His daughter Hassa was a favorite wife of Abd al-Aziz, who also married two of Ahmad's nieces, Haya and Jawhara. The extent and significance of the interrelationship between the Al Saʿud and Al Sudayri is evident in the fact that nearly two dozen of Abd al-Aziz's sons or grandsons were Sudayris in the maternal line. The first wife of his son Faisal (r. 1964–1975) was Sultana bint Ahmad Al Sudayri, younger sister of Hassa. Six of Ahmad's eight sons became governors of provinces. Other Sudayris have also served as governors, especially in strategic border areas of the kingdom, and in other high-level government positions.

The impact of the Al Sudayri on the ruling family is most apparent in the dominant position of the sons of Abd al-Aziz by Hassa bint Ahmad Al Sudayri. These constitute a grouping of senior princes known as the Al Fahd, the present king and his six full brothers. (The term *Sudayri Seven,* sometimes used in the West to refer to this grouping, is not used in Saudi Arabia.) The Al Fahd are the largest group of full brothers among the sons of Abd al-Aziz, and all but one, Prince Turki (who earlier served as deputy minister of defense and aviation), occupy key positions in the government. Sultan has been minister of defense and aviation for over three decades and Abd al Rahman has been the deputy minister, while Nayif is minister of the interior with Ahmad as his deputy. Salman has been governor of Riyadh since 1962 but exercises more influence than his official position suggests. Moreover, Sultan is second deputy prime minister and probably next after Crown Prince Abdullah to succeed Fahd as king.

While all the sons of Hassa bint Ahmad Al Sudayri are intelligent and ambitious, they differ significantly in character and in political and philosophical outlook. Fahd and Sultan are the most secular and the most pro-American, while Nayif and Ahmad most notably embody the traditional, conservative Islamic virtues. Ties of blood and a strong sense of self-interest, however, outweigh any differences. Moreover, their differences help to gain the family support from various constituencies within the Al Saʿud and in the country at large. It is likely that after Abdullah succession will continue through the Al Fahd. Should the Al Saʿud find themselves divided over the succession, Salman, who commands broad support, would be a likely compromise candidate. Other Sudayris have frequently served as governors of various provinces.

See also ABD AL-AZIZ IBN SAʿUD AL SAʿUD; AL SAʿUD FAMILY; HASA, AL-; NAJD.

Bibliography

Holden, David, and Johns, Richard. *The House of Saʿud: The Rise and Rule of the Most Powerful Dynasty in the Arab World.* New York: Holt, Rinehart, and Winston, 1981.

Kechichian, Joseph A. *Succession in Saudi Arabia.* New York: Palgrave, 2001.

Lees, Brian. *A Handbook of the Al Saʿud Ruling Family of Saʿudi Arabia.* London: Royal Genealogies, 1980.

Philby, H. St. J. B. *Arabian Jubilee.* London: Hale, 1952.

MALCOLM C. PECK
UPDATED BY J. E. PETERSON

AL SUDAYRI, HASSA BINT AHMAD

Wife of Ibn Saʿud, mother of Saudi kings.

Hassa bint Ahmad Al Sudayri was one of three Hassa cousins from a prominent clan in eastern Saudi Arabia who married King Abd al-Aziz ibn Saʿud Al Saʿud (known as Ibn Saʿud). Her sons include King Fahd ibn Abd al-Aziz Al Saʿud and Defense Minister Sultan ibn Abd al-Aziz and constitute the most important bloc of senior places among the Al Saʿud family.

See also ABD AL-AZIZ IBN SAʿUD AL SAʿUD; FAHD IBN ABD AL-AZIZ AL SAʿUD; SAUDI ARABIA.

Bibliography

Holden, David, and Johns, Richard. *The House of Saud: The Rise and Rule of the Most Powerful Dynasty in the Arab World.* New York: Holt, Rinehart, 1981.

Lacey, Robert. *The Kingdom: Arabia and the House of Saud.* New York: Harcourt Brace, 1981.

MALCOLM C. PECK

AL-SUSWA, AMAT AL-ALIM
[1958–]

Yemeni minister for human rights.

Amat al-Alim al-Suswa (b. 1958 in Taʿiz) is the second woman to act as a full cabinet member in the Yemeni cabinet, following Wahib Farʿa, the state minister for human rights. Al-Suswa is a journalist by education. She started her career early at age seven in Taʿiz as an announcer of children's programs on a local radio station. While working she completed her secondary education in Taʿiz and went on to Cairo University to complete a B.A. in mass communications (1980). She has an M.A. in international communications from the American University, Washington, D.C. (1984). In addition to her long career in Yemeni radio and television as an announcer and program director, Al-Suswa has also lectured at Sanʿa University in the faculty of political science and has published reports on women's issues (e.g., *Yemeni Women in Figures,* Sanʿa 1996). She joined the ruling People's General Congress prior to Yemeni unification and gained high posts in the party hierarchy, including as member of the Permanent Committee (1986–). She is a long-time activist in Yemen's women's movement and a founding member of the National Women's Committee (NWC). She has chaired both the NWC (1993) and the Yemeni Women's Union (1989–1990). In 1991 she was nominated assistant deputy minister of the ministry of information and in 1997 she became the deputy minister. After leaving the ministry, she served as the country's ambassador to the Netherlands from 2001 to 2003—the first woman in a high foreign ministry position since unification. In May 2003 al-Suswa was nominated as the state minister for human rights. She is particularly interested in questions of freedom of opinion and freedom of the press.

See also FARʾA, WAHIBA; GENDER: GENDER AND LAW; GENDER: GENDER AND POLITICS; NATIONAL WOMEN'S COMMITTEE (YEMEN); YEMEN; YEMENI WOMEN'S UNION.

Bibliography

Paluch, Marta, ed. *Yemeni Voices: Women Tell Their Stories.* Sanaa, Yemen: British Council, Yemen, 2001.

SUSANNE DAHLGREN

ALTALENA

Armed IZL ship sunk by the Israel Defense Force on 22 June 1948 on Tel Aviv's shore.

Purchased in America in 1947 by an official of the Irgun Zvaʾi Leʾumi (IZL) and renamed *Altalena,*

A cargo ship used by the Irgun extremist group burns in the waters off Tel Aviv-Yafo, Israel, 29 June 1948. The group, formed in 1931 to combat Arab and, later, British aggression in Palestine, was trying to run arms ashore, in violation of the Palestine truce. © HULTON-DEUTSCH COLLECTION/CORBIS. REPRODUCED BY PERMISSION.

Ze'ev Jabotinsky's Italian pen name, the 1,820-ton landing craft was at first used to carry European refugees to Palestine. It became a transporter of arms for the Irgunists following the United Nations's (UN) partition resolution on 29 November 1947, which set off the first Arab–Israel War (1947–1948). On 1 June 1948, Menachem Begin, a leader of the Irgun, met with official military leaders of the newly independent state of Israel to sign an agreement for the incorporation of the Irgun battalions into the Israel Defense Force (IDF) but did not let the government know of Irgun's negotiations with France, which had agreed to supply the Irgun with arms materiel from war overstock. The arms—including 5,000 British rifles, 4 million bullets, 300 Bren guns, 250 Stens, 150 Spandau rifles, and 50 eight-inch mortars—would be transported on the Altalena, also carrying 900 trained Irgun recruits from Europe.

The Altalena left Port du Bouc with its cargo of arms and men on 11 June 1948, the first day of a month-long UN-brokered peace that pledged Arabs and Jews not to import arms into Israel. In view of the truce and a newspaper article (10 June 1948) and a BBC broadcast (11 June 1948) that made Irgun's Altalena operation public, Begin notified the Israeli government of the ship's impending arrival.

Prime Minister Ben-Gurion considered the Irgun's actions a danger to the truce and a critical challenge to the authority of the state, but he conditionally permitted the ship to proceed because of the country's vital need for arms. In the ensuing negotiations between the Irgun high command and government representatives, which began on 16 June 1948, Irgunists agreed to hand over to the IDF half of the stock of arms, provided a considerable portion of the remaining supply would be apportioned to the incorporated Irgun units and that one-fifth would be allocated to the Irgun forces in Jerusalem (which, according to UN decree, had not become part of Israel). The Irgun leaders also agreed to dock the Altalena at Kfar Vitkin, a settlement north of Tel Aviv loyal to Ben-Gurion forces, to which the ship came on 19 June 1948. As a result of an unresolved difference as to where the arms would be warehoused, the government issued an ultimatum to Irgun to turn over the arms.

When the Irgun men ignored the ultimatum, government forces attacked disembarked Irgunists. Disregarding Begin's orders to stay and fight, the Irgunists removed the Altalena to Tel Aviv, where they believed the government would not hazard starting a civil war. In the port of Tel Aviv, on 22 June 1948, Ben-Gurion ordered government forces to take all measures necessary to put down Irgun's "revolt." An initial Irgun advantage was overcome by reinforced IDF units, which hit the ship with shells from a cannon ("a blessed gun," according to Ben-Gurion). In spite of a call for a truce from the mayor of Tel Aviv and the raising of a white flag by the Irgunists, government forces continued to hit the Altalena until the ammunition below deck caught fire and the burning ship had to be evacuated. It sank with bombs and ammunition detonating. In the fighting, a total of twenty Irgunists were killed and eighty-seven wounded.

In the aftermath of the sinking of the Altalena, the Irgun accused Ben-Gurion of conspiring to get rid of his opponents, and the government accused the Irgun of planning a revolt against it. The extended conflict, which increased the tension between the two groups, represented the last physical confrontation between the organized Yishuv and the dissenters. Two cabinet ministers resigned in protest of the government's handling of the situation, and for many years the events surrounding the *Altalena*'s sinking cast a pall over Israeli politics.

See also BEGIN, MENACHEM; BEN-GURION, DAVID; IRGUN ZVA'I LE'UMI (IZL); JABOTINSKY, VLADIMIR ZE'EV; YISHUV.

Bibliography

Dupuy, Trevor N. *Elusive Victory: The Arab–Israeli Wars, 1947–1974*, 3d edition. Dubuque, IA: Kendall/Hunt, 1992.

YAAKOV SHAVIT

ALTERMAN, NATAN
[1910–1970]

Israeli poet, playwright, essayist, and translator.

A central author of modern Hebrew poetry and an influential cultural and political figure of the first decades of the State of Israel, Natan Alterman immigrated to Palestine in 1925 from Warsaw via France, where he had studied agronomy. The five volumes of his collected poetry, his plays, his satirical works, and his children's books are noted for their wit, their creative use of traditional form in modernist variations, and their manipulation of the language. Alterman is considered the most prominent poet of Hebrew literature since Hayyim Nahman Bialik.

Alterman's affinity with the Russian and French avant-garde shaped his Hebrew poetry and, in turn, filtered into the mainstream of Israeli poetry. He was the leading imagist of his time and an exponent of the well-wrought poem that employed symmetry and balanced stanza, meter, and structured rhyme schemes. These poetic characteristics were turned against him in the 1950s, when Anglo–American literary tastes—with their preference for concrete poetry, free verse, irony, and colloquialism—replaced the neoromanticism of the previous generation.

Much of his work is enigmatic and hermetic. Autobiographic materials are coded into symbolic and abstract terms, personal experiences are suppressed, and historical events allegorized. Yet the tensions and drama of personal anguish are transmitted through a virtuoso use of language and intellectual structure. In *Stars Outside* (1938), his first collection, Alterman created a world in which troubadours and wandering minstrels roam roads and frequent taverns as they worship a symbolic merciless lady who represents the universe or earth. This poetry suggests that the role of the poet is to be the lyric transmitter of the world as he subjectively experiences it. Similarly, Alterman refrained from extensive employment of intertextual references to traditional Hebrew sources, an otherwise dominant characteristic of Hebrew literature. He thus maintained a universal, existential poetic perception.

In 1943 Alterman began to publish a weekly satirical column, "The Seventh Column," in which he reflected in verse on the turbulent circumstances of the Jewish population in Palestine on the road to independence and statehood. This column both expressed and formed the mood of the many people who read and quoted it weekly. One such column, "The Silver Platter" (November 1947), was a mythic poem of foresight and somber fortitude anticipating the war of independence. This poem soon reached the status of a national hymn and is still recited and performed annually in Memorial Day ceremonies.

Many of Alterman's poems have been set to music, in addition to the songs, ballads, and verse plays he composed for the stage. He translated into Hebrew the major works of Shakespeare, Racine, and Molière, among others, as well as classics of Russian and Yiddish literature. Only a few of his works have been translated into English (*Selected Poems* [1978]; *Little Tel Aviv* [1981]).

See also BIALIK, HAYYIM NAHMAN; LITERATURE: HEBREW.

Bibliography

Negev, Eilat. *Close Encounters with Twenty Israeli Writers.* London and Portland, OR: Vallentine Mitchell, 2003.

ZVIA GINOR

AL THANI FAMILY

Ruling family of Qatar since the late nineteenth century.

The founder of this dynasty was Muhammad ibn Thani (r. 1868–1876), whose political skills won British recognition of Qatar's independence from Bahrain. After 1868, political life in the country was dominated by conflict within the family. Because there were no rules of succession, the strongest and most aggressive family factions have tended to take power. The rule of Ahmad ibn Ali Al Thani (r. 1960–1972) was characterized by inefficiency and personal greed, which resulted in his being deposed by Khalifa ibn Hamad Al Thani (r. 1972–1995). Khalifa used oil revenues to develop the country, pay off an often fractious family, and fund an extravagant lifestyle. Hamad ibn Khalifa Al Thani became de facto ruler in 1992, when his father allowed him to appoint cabinet members, and in 1995 he led a bloodless coup to end his father's reign officially.

After taking power, Hamad retained his post as minister of defense and commander of the armed forces. Although he had taken the position of prime minister as well, he turned it over to Abdullah ibn Khalifa Al Thani in 1997. Hamad named his son Jassem heir apparent in 1996 and attempted to address the family's chronic succession struggles by amending the constitution to regularize the process. He survived a coup attempt in 1996 and oversaw national municipal elections in 1999. A controversy arose in 2002, when published reports noted that Interior Minister Abdullah ibn Kahlid Al Thani had supported al-Qaʿida, a sensitive issue for the United States because of newly established U.S. military facilities in the country.

See also QATAR.

Bibliography

Anscombe, Frederick F. *The Ottoman Gulf: The Creation of Kuwait, Saudi Arabia, and Qatar.* New York: Columbia University Press, 1997.

Crystal, Jill. *Oil and Politics in the Gulf: Rulers and Merchants in Kuwait and Qatar.* New York; Cambridge, U.K.: Cambridge University Press, 1990.

ANTHONY B. TOTH

AL THANI, HAMAD IBN KHALIFA
[1950–]

Amir of Qatar, 1995–.

Shaykh Hamad ibn Khalifa Al Thani became the amir of Qatar on 27 June 1995 when he ousted his father in a bloodless palace coup. The eldest son of his predecessor, Shaykh Khalifa, Hamad was born in Doha in 1950. He was graduated from the Royal Military College in Sandhurst, England, in 1971, and in 1977 he was named heir apparent and defense minister by his father. In 1992 he took control of the day-to-day governing of Qatar when his father allowed him to appoint a cabinet of his own choice. In his first cabinet, appointed in July 1995, he retained for himself the positions of defense minister and commander of the Qatari armed forces and, in addition, appointed himself prime minister, a position previously held by his father.

F. GREGORY GAUSE III

AL THUNAYYAN FAMILY

A branch of the Al Saʿud, the ruling family of Saudi Arabia.

The Al Thunayyan (also Al Thunayan, Al Thunaiyan) are descended from an eponymous ancestor who was the brother of the dynasty's founder, Muhammad ibn Saʿud. That Thunayyan joined his brother in support of the teachings of Muhammad ibn Abd al-Wahhab, the Islamic reformer whose teachings (known outside Arabia as Wahhabism) have provided the essential ideological legitimacy for the rule of the Al Saʿud family.

Abdullah ibn Thunayyan was briefly ruler of Najd (1841–1843), following the second Egyptian occupation of the Saudi state, then met defeat at the hands of Faysal ibn Turki Al Saʿud, who restored Saudi rule over both central and eastern Arabia. Subsequently, the family of Abdullah moved to Istanbul, acquiring there a certain cosmopolitanism that set them apart from their Najdi cousins. His great-grandson, Ahmad, returned to Arabia to serve as private secretary to Amir (later King) Abd al-Aziz, also known as Ibn Saʿud, from before World War I until his death in 1921. Ahmad accompanied the young Prince (later King) Faisal ibn Abd al-Aziz on the latter's diplomatic tour of Europe in 1919. Ahmad's intelligent and well-educated niece Iffat later became Faysal's very influential wife. A number of Al Thunayyan hold mid-level positions throughout the Saudi government and two are deputy ministers.

See also AL SAʿUD FAMILY; FAYSAL IBN TURKI AL SAʿUD; MUWAHHIDUN.

Bibliography

DeGaury, Gerald. *Faisal: King of Saudi Arabia.* London: Baker, 1966.

Kechichian, Joseph A. *Succession in Saudi Arabia.* New York: Palgrave, 2001.

MALCOLM C. PECK
UPDATED BY J. E. PETERSON

ALTINAY, AHMED REFIK
[c. 1879–c. 1935]

Turkish historian, journalist, and poet.

Born in Istanbul, Ahmed Refik Altinay was the son of an agha from Ürgüp who had migrated there to serve the government of the Ottoman Empire. Altinay joined the military in 1898 and later taught French and history at the war school. He worked as an official censor during the Balkan War and World War I, when he began writing history articles. Before and after the wars, he served on a government historical commission and in 1918 became a professor of Ottoman history at Istanbul University. He retired to his home on Büyük Ada Island in the 1930s.

His vast output of popular histories was written in simplified Turkish. He had a flair for storytelling. He wrote on many eras—from the period of Alexander the Great to the rise of the Prussian state—but is best remembered for his evocations of daily life in Constantinople through the centuries. Throughout his life, he contributed articles, sketches, and poems to newspapers, and he wrote several children's history books.

ELIZABETH THOMPSON

ALUSI, MAHMUD SHUKRI AL-
[1857–1924]

Iraqi historian, writer, and teacher; a Sunni reformer.

Mahmud Shukri al-Alusi was born in Baghdad to a well-known but impoverished family of clerics. Educated in Islam by his father and uncle, he taught in Madrasa (Islamic schools) attached to mosques, wrote, and occasionally engaged in politics.

In 1889, the Ottoman Empire's governor (*wali*) of Baghdad named Alusi to be Arabic-language ed-itor of the official journal *al-Zawra*; the next wali, however, persecuted Alusi for his pro-Wahhabi inclinations—Alusi had attacked Ottoman innovations and so-called superstitious religious practices. Around 1905, he was exiled for a short period when the wali accused him of incitement against the Ottoman sultan.

Due to Alusi's great popularity with the Sunni Muslims, in 1911 the Ottoman wali Cemal Paşa asked him to join the administrative council of Baghdad's province. In November 1914, he was sent to persuade the Saudi amir Ibn Saʿud to support the Ottoman Empire in World War I, but he failed.

In his writings, Alusi defends Islamic reformists, such as Jamal al-Din al-Afghani, Muhammad Abduh, and Rashid Rida; he attacks deviationist practices in Sunni Islam, which he saw as a return to polytheism. More ferocious were his attacks against the Shiʿites. He branded them *rafida* (renegades) and accused them of rejoicing in the Ottoman's defeat by the Russians; he also issued legal opinions (*fatwa*). His histories deal with Baghdad, its *ulama* (body of Islamic scholars), and mosques; Islamic Spain; the Najd; Arab markets, eating and drinking habits, and punishments in the Jahili period; Arab games; and Baghdadi proverbs. He also wrote essays on Arabic philology.

See also ABDUH, MUHAMMAD; AFGHANI, JAMAL AL-DIN AL-; RIDA, RASHID.

AMATZIA BARAM

AMAL

Resistance movement in Lebanon.

The AMAL movement was established in 1975 by Imam Musa Sadr. In Arabic the name means hope, but it is also the acronym for Afwaj al-Muqawama al-Lubnaniyya (Lebanese Resistance Detachments). The name was originally used for the military arm of the Movement of the Disinherited, which Sadr founded in 1974 to promote the Lebanese Shiʿite cause. Although Sadr established his own militia, he later opposed a military solution to the Lebanese Civil War, refusing to involve AMAL in the fighting during 1975 and 1976. This reluctance discredited the movement in the eyes of many Shiʿa, who chose instead to support the Palestine Liberation

Organization (PLO) and members of the Lebanese National Movement. AMAL was also unpopular for endorsing Syria's military intervention in Lebanon in 1976.

Several factors caused AMAL to make a dramatic resurgence during the late 1970s. First, Shiʿa became disillusioned with the conduct and policies of the PLO and its Lebanese allies. Second, the mysterious disappearance of Sadr while on a visit to Libya in 1978 made him a symbol of the Shiʿite heritage; the significance attached to his absence was not unlike the concealment/absence of the twelfth imam of the Shiʿite Twelvers. Third, the Iranian Revolution revived hope among Lebanese Shiʿa and instilled a sense of growing communal solidarity. Moreover, when the PLO feared AMAL's increased power, it tried to crack down on its cells using military force. This strategy backfired and rallied an even greater number of Shiʿites around AMAL.

Husayn al-Husayni, former speaker of parliament, headed AMAL from 1979 until April 1980, when Nabi Berri assumed the leadership and transformed the movement into one of the most powerful political and military forces in Lebanon. Although its charter expressed dedication to the Palestinian cause, the movement laid siege to Palestinian refugee camps in Lebanon and started the war of the camps, which lasted from 1985 until 1988. In 1994, Berri was speaker of parliament, and AMAL's role had been enhanced by the 1992 landslide victory of Berri's slate of candidates in the South. The disarming of militias during the late 1980s forced AMAL into the political arena, and it remains a major force. Its success has been aided by Berri's political subservience to Syria.

AMAL's broad support in predominantly Shiʿite areas notwithstanding, neither AMAL's rank and file nor its leadership is cohesive. The movement has become a political tool for Berri, who uses his influential position in government to advance the cause. Many members and leaders of AMAL have been appointed to key government positions. The movement's fortunes declined in the late 1990s; it barely managed to keep its seats in the parliament in the 2000 election. Hizbullah benefited from the reputation for corruption and insensitivity that surrounds AMAL leaders and deputies, but the Syrian government forced Hizbullah and AMAL to run on the same list in South Lebanon. In 2003 Nabi Berri revealed an internal crisis in AMAL when he forced the resignation of his two representatives in the cabinet, accusing them of corruption, although his motives were most likely political. Berri remained protected by strong Syrian support, although his popularity in South Lebanon suffered greatly.

See also BERRI, NABI; HUSAYNI, HUSAYN AL-; LEBANESE CIVIL WAR (1975–1990); LEBANESE NATIONAL MOVEMENT (LNM); PALESTINE LIBERATION ORGANIZATION (PLO); SHIʿISM.

Bibliography

Ajami, Fouad. *The Vanished Imam: Musa al Sadr and the Shia of Lebanon.* Ithaca, NY: Cornell University Press, 1986.

Norton, Augustus Richard. *Amal and the Shiʿa: The Struggle for the Soul of Lebanon.* Austin: University of Texas Press, 1987.

AS'AD ABUKHALIL

AMAL, AL-

See NEWSPAPERS AND PRINT MEDIA: ARAB COUNTRIES

AMANOLLAH KHAN
[1892–1960]

King of Afghanistan, 1919–1929.

Amanollah Khan (also called Amanullah Barakzai) launched a jihad (holy war) against Great Britain and declared Afghanistan's independence from Britain in 1919. He embarked on an ambitious program of modernization, introducing secular reforms and education.

He was the third son of Habibollah Khan (ruled 1901–1919), who was assassinated. Amanollah, then governor of Kabul, persuaded the army and power elite to prefer his claim to the throne over his brothers and uncle. In May 1919, he went to war against the British administration and, at the end of a one-month campaign, was able to negotiate control of his country's foreign policy (which his grandfather Abd al-Rahman Khan had surrendered). He welcomed recognition of his regime by the then new and revolutionary government of the Soviet Union; he soon turned, however, to countries without territorial designs on Central Asia, establishing ties with France, Germany, Italy, Japan, and the Ottoman Empire. He failed to initiate official relations with the United States.

Advised by Ottoman-educated Afghans and impressed by Ottoman Turkey's example, Amanollah embarked on his own scheme of development. First he promulgated a constitution and convened three *loya jirga* (grand assemblies, composed of various segments of the power elite) to ratify his important decisions. Second, he systematized the administrative divisions of the country into a territorial hierarchy of subdistricts, districts, and provinces. The centrally appointed administrators at each level were assisted by a locally elected consultative body. Third, he replaced *iltizam* (tax farming) with directly collected taxes in cash. Fourth, he tolerated a free press, entrusted the intelligentsia with responsible positions in the government, and spent a major portion of the revenue of the state on the expansion of education.

These reforms proved to be enduring. Nevertheless, he alienated his subjects with more symbolic policies such as the mandatory unveiling of Afghan women and the imposition of European attire on civil servants and schoolchildren. Simultaneously, he canceled the monetary and symbolic sinecures enjoyed by the leaders of the clans and the headmen of villages. Furthermore, his new tax policies weighed heavily on agricultural producers and were unpopular in the countryside. Opposition was organized under the symbolic defense of the values of Islam and spearheaded by leaders of the religious establishment. Leaders of clans and social bandits also played an important role. He might have overcome the challenge had he paid more attention to his army—but he had neglected its welfare and was unable to prevent soldiers from joining the several revolts that broke out simultaneously in 1928. He was forced to abdicate in May 1929 and went into exile in Italy.

See also AFGHANISTAN; HABIBOLLAH KHAN.

Bibliography

Adamec, Ludwig W. *Afghanistan 1900–1923: A Diplomatic History.* Berkeley: University of California Press, 1967.

Poullada, Leon B. *Reform and Rebellion in Afghanistan 1919–1929: King Amanullah's Failure to Modernize a Tribal Society.* Ithaca, NY: Cornell University Press, 1973.

ASHRAF GHANI

AMARI, RAJA
[1971–]

Tunisian film director.

Born in Tunis, Tunisia, Raja Amari trained as a dancer at the Conservatoire de Tunis (Tunis conservatory) and also received a degree in Romance languages with an emphasis on art history from the University of Tunis. After working as a film critic for *Cinécrit* (1992–1994), Amari moved on to film studies in Paris at the Institut de Formation et d'Enseignement pour les Métiers de l'Image et Son (National higher institute for audiovisual media studies) between 1994 and 1998. Her short films include *Le bouquet* (The bouquet; 1995), *Avril* (April; 1997), and *Un soir de juillet* (One evening in July; 2000). Her award-winning, full-length film *Satin rouge* (Red satin; 2002) is about the transformative powers of self-expression, which a middle-aged Tunisian widow, the seamstress Lilia, discovers through belly dancing. While it is common for Arab and Tunisian films to present women as being in conflict with society, Amari notes she was interested in how Lilia adapts to social hypocrisy, to the distance between individual desire and social mores, doing as she wishes while avoiding a frontal attack. Amari lists as her influences Pier Paolo Pasolini, François Truffaut, and the new French cinema, as well as actresses from Egyptian musicals from the 1940s and 1950s, such as Samia Gamal, whose freedom and ability to shift between oriental and occidental styles reflect Amari's own love of dance.

See also ART; FILM; GENDER: GENDER AND EDUCATION; TUNISIA.

Bibliography

Schultz, Kate. "Interview: Self-Empowerment by Way of the Midriff; Raja Amari's *Satin Rouge*." Indiewire. Available from <http://www.indiewire.com/people/int_Amari_Raja_020820.html>.

LAURA RICE

AMER, GHADA

[1963–]

New York–based multimedia artist from Egypt.

Ghada Amer was born in 1963, in Egypt. She trained in Paris and lives in New York and is one of the few Arab artists to be recognized in international avant-garde circles. She exhibited in the 2000 Whitney Biennial and won the UNESCO (United Nations Educational, Scientific, and Cultural Organization) prize at the 1999 Venice Biennial. Her work is primarily concerned with pleasure, the female body, and women's sexuality. She is best known for her two-dimensional stitchings of women in erotic poses, often taken from pornographic magazines. Observers have noted her reference in needlework to women's traditional labor, her reworking of the visual aspects of male-dominated abstract expressionism, and the ways in which her work reclaims women's sensual pleasure and challenges stereotypes about passive Muslim women. Amer describes her work as a series of ruminations on the problems of religious and feminist extremism, which she says are similar in their problematic views of the body and how it seduces. In 2000, she became the first Arab artist to receive a one-person show at the Tel Aviv Museum of Art, setting off a firestorm of controversy in her native Egypt, where most artists and intellectuals are against the normalization of cultural relations with Israel until it ends the occupation of Palestinian territories.

See also ART; GENDER: GENDER AND EDUCATION.

Bibliography

Auricchio, Laura. "Works in Translation: Ghada Amer's Hybrid Pleasures." *Art Journal* 60, no. 4 (2001): 26–37.

Knode, Marilu. "Interview with Ghada Amer." *New Art Examiner* 27, no. 4 (2001/2002): 38–39.

Oguibe, Olu. "Love and Desire: The Art of Ghada Amer." *Third Text* 55 (2002): 63–74.

JESSICA WINEGAR

AMERICAN COLLEGE FOR GIRLS

See RAMSES COLLEGE FOR GIRLS

AMERICAN COUNCIL FOR JUDAISM

Once formidable anti-Zionist campaigning body seeking to preserve the nonpolitical nature of liberal religious tradition in North American Judaism.

The American Council for Judaism (ACJ) was founded in 1942 by a group of prominent non-Zionist Reform rabbis opposed to the affirmation of political Zionism by the Central Conference of American Rabbis (CCAR). The ACJ initially sought to reaffirm the fundamentals of Classical North American Reform Judaism stated in the Pittsburgh Platform of 1885, which eliminated references to Jerusalem and Zion in prayer services and affirmed the absolute loyalty of Jews to the nation in which they lived. In 1942, CCAR support for a refuge in Palestine for Jews fleeing European antisemitism left non-Zionists concerned that their universalistic, liberal values and North American identity were in question. The ACJ initially had considerable impact on liberal Christians but was undermined by increasing sympathy toward Zionism within the North American establishment. The AJC's increasingly non-religious and anti-Zionist manifesto always attracted far smaller numbers of rabbis and laymen than Zionist organizations did (notably Women's International Zionist Organization, Hadassah, and the American Israel Political Affairs Committee). The largest secular Jewish bodies—notably the American Jewish Committee and American Jewish Congress—have identified firmly with the defense of Israeli interests, and religious Zionism has dominated mainstream Reform organizations since the 1970s. Some of the ACJ's most prominent spokespersons have been Louis Wolsey, William Fineshriber, Morris Lazaron, and Elmer Berger. The ACJ is sympathetic to Israeli critics of Zionism, religious traditionalism, and state policy, but has had weaker ties with Arabs in the Middle East.

See also AMERICAN JEWISH COMMITTEE; AMERICAN JEWISH CONGRESS; ZIONIST ORGANIZATION OF AMERICA.

Bibliography

American Council for Judaism. Available from <http://www.acjna.org/>.

Kolsky, Thomas. *Jews against Zionism: The American Council for Judaism, 1942–1948.* Philadelphia: Temple University Press, 1990.

Tekiner, Roselle; Abed-Rabbo, Samir; and Mezvinsky, Norton, eds. *Anti-Zionism: Analytical Reflections.* Brattleboro, VT: Amana Books, 1989.

GEORGE R. WILKES

AMERICAN ISRAEL PUBLIC AFFAIRS COMMITTEE

Umbrella organization, founded in 1954, to lobby the U.S. Congress in support of Israel.

The American Israel Public Affairs Committee (AIPAC; originally known as the American Zionist Public Affairs Committee) was established in 1954; the name of the organization was changed in 1959. Isaiah L. Kenen (1905–1988), the organization's executive director and chief lobbyist from 1959 to 1974, is credited with shaping AIPAC and overseeing its emergence as the leading Jewish-sponsored pro-Israel lobby in Washington, D.C. Kenen also served as chairman of AIPAC in 1974 and 1975 and as honorary chairman from 1975 to 1988. In these capacities, Kenen created the biweekly bulletin *Near East Report,* which he edited from 1957 to 1973, and introduced the widely distributed annual guidebook *Myths & Facts.* The latter was discontinued in 1992.

Thomas A. Dine, who served as AIPAC's executive director from 1980 to 1993, succeeded Kenen. Under Dine's tenure, AIPAC's membership rose from 11,000 to more than 50,000, and the organization's annual budget from $750,000 to more than $3 million. By 2003 AIPAC had 65,000 members nationwide and was regarded as one of the most effective and sophisticated lobbying groups in the United States.

In general, AIPAC serves as a watchdog group, tracking political, financial, and military attitudes and policies toward Israel in U.S. public life. AIPAC policy analysts regularly review hundreds of periodicals, journals, speeches, and reports and meet with foreign policy experts in order to track and analyze current events and trends related to Israel and the Middle East.

As a registered Washington lobby, AIPAC is prohibited from contributing funds to political candidates and elected officials. However, the organization does have a long-standing history of supplying U.S. politicians, elected officials, and government agencies with information and data on Israel and Middle East affairs. (In fact, during his tenure with AIPAC, Kenen drafted statements and speeches on Israel and U.S. policy in the Middle East for many politicians, including Harry S. Truman, Hubert H. Humphrey, and John F. Kennedy.) To this end, the organization conducts regular meetings with U.S. legislators and their support staff. AIPAC also promotes Israel on U.S. college campuses and maintains leadership development programs that educate and train young U.S. Jewish leaders in pro-Israel political advocacy.

See also AMERICAN COUNCIL FOR JUDAISM; AMERICAN JEWISH COMMITTEE; ZIONIST ORGANIZATION OF AMERICA.

MARK A. RAIDER

AMERICAN JEWISH COMMITTEE

Defense organization led by U.S. Jews and established in 1906.

The American Jewish Committee was established in 1906, after a series of pogroms in Eastern Europe convinced prominent U.S. Jews of the need to create a defense organization dedicated "to prevent the infraction of civil and religious rights of Jews in any part of the world." The present-day American Jewish Committee continues its focus on the welfare and security of world Jewry. In addition, it seeks to enhance the quality of Jewish life in the United States. The committee attempts to achieve these dual objectives by opposing antisemitism and attacks against Israel and by helping to strengthen Jewish identity through, among other things, deepening the ties between American Jews and Israel.

Although the American Jewish Committee was established by a small coterie of self-appointed and co-opted individuals rather than by elected leaders, the committee viewed itself as representing the needs and interests of the wider Jewish community. During World War I, a newly emerging U.S. Jewish leadership charged the committee with elitism and demanded a democratically elected American Jewish Congress to represent U.S. Jewry at a postwar peace conference. The American Jewish Committee first opposed and then negotiated an agreement whereby three-fourths of the delegates to such a congress would be elected and one-fourth appointed by the American Jewish Committee. The committee, perhaps in order to maintain its leadership position within the Jewish community, forged a relationship first with the Zionist movement and then later with the state of Israel.

In 1929 the chair of the American Jewish Committee, Louis Marshall, and the president of the World Zionist Organization, Chaim Weizmann, signed an accord establishing the Jewish Agency for Palestine, which would support Jewish development of Palestine and represent Jewish interests in Palestine. In 1950, two years after the state of Israel was established, Jacob Blaustein, the chair of the American Jewish Committee, and David Ben-Gurion, prime minister of Israel, signed an accord in which the prime minister recognized that "the Jews of the United States, as a community and as individuals, have one political attachment and that is to the United States of America." The chair of the American Jewish Committee, for his part, noted that "the vast majority of the American Jewry recognizes the necessity and the desirability of helping to make it [Israel] a strong, viable, self-supporting state. . . . The American Jewish Committee has been active. . . and will continue to be. . . in rendering. . . every possible support to Israel." The ideas and assurances expressed in the 1950 accord have served as the basis of the committee's subsequent approach to Israel and world Jewish affairs.

By 2003 the American Jewish Committee had a membership of 100,000 and was headquartered in New York City, with thirty-three regional offices in the United States and international offices in Israel, Germany, Switzerland, and Poland and partnership agreements with Jewish communal associations in nine different countries as well as with the European Council of Jewish Communities. The American Jewish Committee no longer claims to be the sole representative of U.S. Jewry. Rather, it supports the security and well-being of Israel and seeks to safeguard world Jewry and to enhance the continuity and quality of Jewish life in the United States and elsewhere.

See also AMERICAN COUNCIL FOR JUDAISM; AMERICAN JEWISH CONGRESS; ZIONIST ORGANIZATION OF AMERICA.

JERRY KUTNICK

AMERICAN JEWISH CONGRESS

Organization founded in 1917 to secure Jewish civil, political, and religious rights in Central and Eastern Europe and in Palestine.

The American Jewish Congress (AJC) is the second Jewish defense organization established in the United States. It was founded during World War I in order to fight antisemitism and help find a solution to the problems facing Jews in Europe. Its early history helped shape its present political perspective and its approach toward Jewish affairs.

Responding to the plight of millions of Jews caught in war-torn zones and suffering from antisemitic outbreaks during World War I, proponents of the idea of a congress sought to create a democratic institution that could represent the views and will of American Jewry. Supporters of the congress opposed what they considered the self-appointed leadership of the American Jewish Committee, which in their view represented mainly the wealthy and influential segments of the community. After much debate, the two sides reached an agreement allowing for the formation of a one-time-only congress in which one-quarter of the delegates would be appointed by the American Jewish Committee and three-quarters would be elected by U.S. Jews. In 1918, for the first and only time, some 330,000 Jews throughout the United States elected delegates to an American Jewish Congress. The AJC sent a delegation to the Paris Peace Congress. Once the conference was over and the delegation submitted its report, the congress, in accordance with its agreement with the American Jewish Committee, was dissolved.

In 1922, however, proponents of the congress idea formed a second American Jewish Congress, which was to become a permanent body within the organized Jewish community. Unlike its predecessor, this new AJC was a membership-based organization that did not purport to represent the views of all U.S. Jews. But, like its predecessor, the new AJC continued to seek support for its positions more through mass appeals and public protests than through the quiet intervention of well-connected individuals—the style that typified the American Jewish Committee.

Since the Holocaust, the U.S. Jewish community and the state of Israel have constituted the main centers of the Jewish people. The AJC is headquartered in New York and maintains an office in Jerusalem; it has 50,000 members. It continues to fight antisemitism throughout the world and to support liberal causes in the United States and Israel. On the U.S. scene, the AJC is an active supporter of civil rights and civil liberties and an advocate of church-state separation. A supporter of Zionism since its founding, the AJC seeks to ensure the security and prosperity of the state of Israel and supports Israel's quest for peace with the Palestinians and with her Arab neighbors. It took a lead in supporting the 1993 Oslo Accords. Although the AJC generally supports the Israeli government in power as the democratically elected representative of its citizenry and is wary of interfering in Israel's domestic affairs, the AJC's policies and positions are viewed as reflecting a liberal perspective in both the United States and Israel.

See also AMERICAN JEWISH COMMITTEE; PARIS PEACE SETTLEMENTS (1918–1923).

JERRY KUTNICK

AMERICAN UNIVERSITY IN CAIRO (AUC)

A small, international university founded in 1919 by U.S. educators.

The American University in Cairo (AUC) opened in 1920 under its founder and president Charles R. Watson, the Egyptian-born son of missionary parents from the United States. Although he had worked for the United Presbyterians' Board of Foreign Missions, Watson insisted that the university be independent of that organization; he wanted a Christian but nondenominational school.

The university opened modestly with a preparatory section (which closed in the early 1950s). Characteristic of colleges throughout the United States but then new to Egypt, there were also four other programs: an undergraduate College of Arts and Sciences; a noncredit Extension (now Public Service) Division; a Department of Education; and a School of Oriental Studies to serve missionaries, businessmen, diplomats, and other Westerners. AUC also featured physical education, coeducation, an open-stack library, a journalism major, and extracurricular clubs.

After twenty-five years, Watson was succeeded by John Badeau (1945–1953), who brought AUC into the postcolonial era. Arabic-speaking and affable, he cultivated Egypt's President Gamal Abdel Nasser and other influential Egyptians. As U.S. ambassador to Egypt (1961–1964), he kept a friendly eye on the university.

The students were drawn mainly from economic and cultural elites, including many foreigners and minorities—Jews, Greeks, and Armenians were numerous until their communities emigrated en masse during Nasser's regime. Egypt's Coptic Christians were part of the student mix, as were women. Muslims were few, especially during the 1930s, when it was charged that AUC was proselytizing them for Christianity. AUC dropped hymns and prayers from its assemblies, but it was not until the 1960s, when AUC began closing on the Muslim holy day, Friday, and hired some full-time Muslim academics, that Muslim students enrolled in great numbers. Today they outnumber Christians.

Tiny in comparison with other Egyptian universities, AUC has sought distinctive offerings for both its Egyptian and foreign students. In 1961 to 1962, when Cairo University had almost 30,000 students, AUC had only 360 enrolled; in 2002 AUC had about 5,000 students enrolled and a teaching staff of 396. Since 1950 graduate programs have been added, as well as the Social Research Center, English Language Institute, Center for Arabic Studies, Center for Arabic Studies Abroad (CASA), university press, Management Extension Services, and Desert Development Center. In the late 1950s the Ford Foundation and the U.S. government provided major funding to replace funding once provided by private U.S. donors with missionary ideals. In the 1980s a Saudi business alumnus was the largest private donor.

When the United States replaced Britain as the dominant foreign power in the Middle East, the highly visible AUC campus became the target of anti-American demonstrations. During the Arab-Israel War of 1967 the university was sequestered, but Nasser's personal interest (he had sent a daughter there) soon restored things to normal. Egypt's President Anwar Sadat (1970–1981) had pro-U.S. policies, which brought new opportunities to the university. Both President Husni Mubarak's wife

Suzanne and his politically prominent son Gamal are AUC alumni.

In 2007 the university is scheduled to move its main campus from Tahrir Square in the heart of downtown Cairo to the planned community of New Cairo being developed on the desert plateau east of the city. Its full-time enrollment is then planned to reach 5,500.

Bibliography

American University in Cairo web site. Available from <http://www.aucegypt.edu>.

Murphy, Lawrence R. *The American University in Cairo: 1919–1987.* Cairo: American University in Cairo Press, 1987.

DONALD MALCOLM REID

AMERICAN UNIVERSITY OF BEIRUT (AUB)

Prominent institution of higher education in Lebanon.

The American University of Beirut (AUB) was once the most famous university in the Middle East, if not in the entire African and Asian region. It was established as the Syrian Protestant College by the American Protestant Evangelical Mission to Syria in 1866. The AUB is run by a New York–based board of trustees, whose members are citizens of various countries. The university was incorporated under the laws of the State of New York.

The arts and sciences faculty awards bachelor's and master's degrees; the faculty of medicine awards bachelor's and master's degrees in science, master's degrees in public health, and certificates in undergraduate nursing and basic laboratory techniques; the faculty of engineering and architecture awards bachelor's and master's degrees in engineering and bachelor's degrees in architecture; the faculty of agriculture and food sciences awards master's degrees in all departments, as well as doctorates in agronomy. English is the language of instruction except in courses within the department of Arabic.

Initially, most of the students at the university came from elite Christian families. But the university's reputation soon eliminated any sectarian label, and it attracted Arabs from various countries. Its admissions standards and tuition made it, and continue to make it, inaccessible to most students from lower income groups. However, the student body has become somewhat diversified through scholarships and grants.

Although the university took its Christian message seriously in the early years, to the point of dismissing a popular professor for daring to teach Darwinism, its curricula became secularized during the twentieth century—perhaps to reflect the religious diversity of the Lebanese population.

AUB's medical school has been one of its most important divisions, training generations of physicians who practice throughout the Middle East. It was, and to a degree it remains, one of the most prestigious educational institutions in the region. The American University Hospital has become known as one of the best hospitals in the Middle East. The university has benefited from a relatively large endowment and from U.S. congressional support. The liberal atmosphere of Lebanon, at least before the Lebanese Civil War, allowed the university to attract scholars, faculty, and staff from the world's best educational institutions.

The AUB has been criticized by many thinkers and political activists, including such alumni as Dr. George Habash of the Popular Front for the Liberation of Palestine, for its U.S. associations. It was seen by some as a bastion of cultural pluralism, especially during the 1960s and 1970s, when the university administration responded firmly to student protests. For militant student leaders, the campus was considered no more than an espionage den and a recruiting center for the U.S. Central Intelligence Agency. Yet militants and moderates, secularists and fundamentalists, all wanted to be admitted. A degree from AUB provided the best financial prospects; in fact, until the 1970s it almost always guaranteed a job for its holder. Political and economic changes in Lebanon, however, decreased its value, especially when some Lebanese could afford to attend far more prestigious foreign universities.

The AUB underwent tremendous changes because of the civil war (1975–1990). Despite extensive damage, it continued to function, even during repeated interruptions due to intense fighting. Some of its professors were threatened or kidnapped, and its president, Malcolm Kerr, was assassinated in 1984 by unknown gunmen. Its main administrative building, College Hall, bombed in the early 1990s, has been reconstructed. The division of the city of Beirut into eastern and western zones affected the life of the campus community, which became more sharply divided along sectarian lines. The administration authorized the opening of an off-campus program in East Beirut during the war for those who could not reach predominantly Muslim West Beirut.

The quality and standards of the AUB have declined as a result of the war. Many foreign nationals on the faculty left, depriving students of some of the most qualified teachers. The flight of many Lebanese and Palestinian professors forced the administration to accept applicants who in previous times would have been considered underqualified. The shortage of professors in some departments led the administration to accept applicants with an M.A. as teachers, which was uncommon before the war.

The end of the civil war promised improvements at the university, and the restoration of peace and normalcy increased the number of professors returning from exile. The new president, Robert Haddad, formerly of Smith College, announced that his goal was to bring AUB back to its former level of excellence. Haddad was succeeded by John Waterbury in 1998, and he did much to improve the relationship between the administration and the faculty. Haddad had alienated the faculty by appearing to impose standards and procedures that many on the Beirut campus did not find suitable. Waterbury's tenure coincided with a deteriorating economic situation in Lebanon, and yet he remained committed to an ambitious fundraising campaign. Waterbury attracted professors from outside Lebanon, and from outside the Arab world, hoping to return AUB to its prewar days when faculty and students represented different cultures and religions. But the declining economic situation in Lebanon and the end of interest-free loans through the Hariri Foundation (formed in 1984 by Rafiq al-Hariri, who later became prime minister), has increased the percentage of upper-class students. Although financial aid exists, it is not sufficient to offset the higher cost of living and education in Lebanon. But AUB has benefited from the consequences of the 11

The American University of Beirut was incorporated in 1866 under a charter of the state of New York. The independent, coeducational university has five faculties and offers bachelor's and master's degrees. © CORBIS. REPRODUCED BY PERMISSION.

September 2001 attacks on the World Trade Center. Many Arab students from the Gulf region began to avoid higher education in the United States, long a favored destination for Middle Eastern students, and sought to study in Lebanese universities, especially AUB. The high cost of AUB education, however, still deters some applicants, and selectivity has been sacrificed across the board. AUB has also suffered from the proliferation of private universities in Lebanon (some forty-seven by one count). Gulf Arab countries have also competed with AUB by opening up their own versions of American universities. In 2003 the American University of Kuwait was added to the list of American universities in the Middle East.

See also BEIRUT; BLISS, HOWARD; HABASH, GEORGE; HARIRI, RAFIQ BAHA'UDDIN AL-; LEBANESE CIVIL WAR (1975–1990); POPULAR FRONT FOR THE LIBERATION OF PALESTINE; PROTESTANTISM AND PROTESTANT MISSIONS.

Bibliography

Coon, Carl, ed. *Daniel Bliss and the Founding of the American University of Beirut.* Washington, DC: Middle East Institute, 1989.

Penrose, Stephen. *That They May Have Life: The Story of the American University of Beirut 1866–1941.* Beirut: American University of Beirut, 1970.

AS'AD ABUKHALIL

AMICHAI, YEHUDA

[1924–2000]

Hebrew poet, playwright, and novelist.

Yehuda Amichai, born in Würzburg, Germany, emigrated with his family to Palestine in 1936. He grew up in an Orthodox Jewish home and was educated in religious schools, where he absorbed sacred texts, especially the prayer book. He served in the Jewish Brigade of the British army during World War II, in the Palmah in Israel's War of Independence, and later in the Israel Defense Force. Amichai studied Bible and literature at the Hebrew University of Jerusalem, then taught for decades, mostly in Jerusalem schools and colleges. He received the Israel Prize for poetry in 1982.

Amichai published his first poems in the late 1940s. His first book, *Akhshav Uvayamim Ha-aherim* (1955; Now and in other days), and his retrospective collection *Shirim 1948–1962* mark a major turning point in Hebrew poetry. Amichai's lyrics introduced new sensibilities, a new worldview, and new values, as well as a lower diction and style along with a whimsical irreverence toward central beliefs and texts of Judaism. His poetry was a quintessential expression of the "Generation of the State" literary revolution of Israel in the 1960s.

The individual's happiness is, for Amichai, the yardstick for all things. National, social, and religious commands are inferior to intimate human relationships; love (not God) is the only, yet fragile, shelter in a world of war. "I want to die in my bed," Amichai says, rejecting heroism and glory in one poem; he portrays God as responsible for the shortage of mercy in the world in another. Amichai achieves his unique, hallmark diction by absorbing and reworking prosaic materials (such as colloquialisms and technical, military, or legal terms), then combining them with fragments of prayers or biblical phrases. He has rejuvenated classical Hebrew, and dismembered and rebuilt idioms. His playful inventiveness is manifest in his surprising figurative, conceitlike compositions.

Love, war, father, God, childhood, time, and land—Amichai's main themes—form a pseudoautobiographical diary that, together with his blend of the modern and conventional, has contributed to his great popularity. His poetry is at once deeply personal and a universal expression of the human condition. The long lyrical epic "Travels of a Latter-Day Benjamin of Tudela" (1968) stands out for its account of specific events.

Landmark collections of the 1970s and 1980s are *Time, Great Tranquility: Questions and Answers,* and *Of Man Thou Art, and Unto Man Shalt Thou Return.* Amichai's late poetry is looser in form and less sure of its stand. The placard statements are replaced with understatement, even resignation. Metaphors are fewer but are carefully wrought, suggestive, and intertextually loaded. Experience is more intimate, yet Amichai's awareness of the role of camouflage in his poetry grows.

Although Amichai is known mainly for his poetry, his works of fiction have a significant place in modern Hebrew literature. His novel *Not of This Time, Not of This Place* (1963), with its complex structure and its protagonist's double existence, is a precursor of postmodernist works. Amichai's works have been translated into more than twenty languages.

See also LITERATURE: HEBREW.

Bibliography

Abramson, Glenda. *The Writing of Yehuda Amichai.* Albany: State University of New York Press, 1994.

Amichai, Yehuda. *Not of This Time, Not of This Place,* translated by Shlomo Katz. New York: Schocken Books, 1968.

Amichai, Yehuda. *Open Closed Open.* New York: Harcourt, 2000.

Amichai, Yehuda. *The Selected Poetry of Yehuda Amichai, Newly Revised and Expanded Edition,* translated by Chana Bloch and Stephen Mitchell. Berkeley: University of California Press, 1996.

NILI GOLD

AMIENS, TREATY OF

Treaty that brought peace to Europe under Napoléon, as signed by England and France, 27 March 1802.

The Napoleonic wars had reached a point where France and England concluded that further fighting was useless. Under the terms of the treaty, all of England's conquests were surrendered to France, but Napoléon Bonaparte delayed the signing because he still hoped to retain Egypt, which he had invaded in 1798; after his troops there capitulated to the British, however, he agreed to return Egypt to the Ottoman Empire and Malta to the Order of the Knights of Malta. Because of the treaty, peace was also concluded between France and the Ottomans. Napoléon became consul for life of the French Empire, with the right of appointing his successor, but his interlude was brief and Napoléon hinted at the possible reconquest of Egypt.

Britain, during this period, could not abide French control of Europe under Napoléon and refused to evacuate Malta. By 1803, war had resumed. Napoléon never managed to recover his position in the eastern Mediterranean.

See also BONAPARTE, NAPOLÉON.

Bibliography

Lefebvre, Georges. *Napoleon: From Tilsit to Waterloo, 1807–1815,* translated by J. E. Anderson. New York: Columbia University Press, 1969.

JON JUCOVY

AMIN, AHMAD
[1886–1954]

Egyptian Muslim educator and writer.

Ahmad Amin was born in Cairo, the son of a shaykh at al-Azhar. His early education was in *kuttabs,* at a government primary school, and then at al-Azhar. In 1907 he entered Madrasat al-Qada, a mosque school, spending four years as a student and some ten as assistant to the director, who introduced him to Western and particularly English scholarship. After a few years as a *shariʿa* judge, he joined the faculty of the Egyptian University (now University of Cairo) in 1926 and remained there until retirement in 1946. He was dean of the Faculty of Arts from 1939 to 1941. From 1914 until his death, he chaired the Committee on Authorship, Translation, and Publication (Lajnat al-Taʾlif wa al-Tarjama wa al-Nashr), editing its weekly literary magazine, *al-Thaqafa,* from 1939 to 1953. He was also a member of the Arabic Language Academy, founded the Popular University (later, Foundation for Popular Culture), and served as director of the Cultural Department of the Arab League. Through these and other activ-

ities, he was a prominent participant in the intellectual life of Egypt.

The best known of his writings are his eight-volume series on early Islamic cultural history, *Fajr al-Islam* (The dawn of Islam, 1929), *Duha al-Islam* (The forenoon of Islam, 1933–1936), and *Zuhr al-Islam* (The noon of Islam, 1945–1955), the first effort by an Arab Muslim writer to make use of Western scholarship in writing this history. He wrote over 600 articles on almost every conceivable topic except party politics for periodicals such as *al-Thaqafa, al-Risala,* and *al-Hilal;* most of these were republished in ten volumes of *Fayd al-Khatir* (Overflowing thoughts, 1938–1955) or in *Zuʿama al-Islah fi al-ʿAsr al-Hadith* (Leaders of reform in the modern age, 1948). He collaborated in editing a number of classical Islamic texts and wrote or cowrote books for schools and books on Western philosophy and literature. Other writings include *Yawm al-Islam* (The day of Islam, 1952), *al-Sharq wa al-Gharb* (The East and the West, 1955), and his autobiography, *Hayati* (My life, 1950, 1952).

He held opinions close to the secularist ones for which Ali Abd al-Raziq and Taha Husayn were criticized but stated them more cautiously; he was particularly known for questioning the authenticity of the *hadith* (legends and traditions surrounding the prophet Muhammad). He wanted his compatriots to learn from the West but at the same time affirm their own Arab–Islamic cultural personality. Thus, much of his work seeks to present the treasures of Islamic civilization to his readers. His series on Islamic cultural history uses Western scholarship to help make that history accessible to modern Muslims, while, by stressing the contribution of non-Muslim cultures to early Islamic culture, the series conveys the message that Muslims today can also learn from non-Muslims. Other writings also give a positive presentation of Western ideas and ways, although his criticism of Western colonialism and materialism could be harsh and angry, especially in some of his last writings.

See also ABD AL-RAZIQ, ALI; HUSAYN, TAHA.

Bibliography

Amin, Ahmad. *My Life: The Autobiography of an Egyptian Scholar, Writer, and Cultural Leader,* translated by Issa J. Boullata. Leiden, Netherlands: Brill, 1978.

Shepard, William. *The Faith of a Modern Muslim Intellectual: The Religious Aspects and Implications of the Writings of Ahmad Amin.* New Delhi: Indian Institute of Islamic Studies, 1982.

WILLIAM SHEPARD

AMIN AL-DOWLEH, MIRZA ALI KHAN
[1844–1904]

One of the most influential statesmen of the Qajar dynasty.

Born in Tehran (Persia) to an important court official, Mirza Ali Khan was a proponent of Westernization and modern education and an opponent of the *ulama* (Islamic clergy). He is regarded as a reformer who tried to centralize revenue collection and cut expenditures. He held a succession of high posts under the Qajar dynasty, under Naser al-Din Shah, serving for twenty years as his private secretary. He enriched himself by managing the mint and the postal system. His archrival was Ali-Asghar Amin al-Soltan.

In 1880, the shah granted him the title Amin al-Dowleh (Trusted of the State). In 1897, Mozaffar al-Din Qajar named him prime minister. To alleviate the fiscal crisis, he encouraged the shah to contract foreign loans, a disastrous policy that contributed to the downfall of the dynasty. After failing to obtain a large loan from the British-owned Imperial Bank of Persia, to which he had promised significant concessions, including control of the southern customs, rivals at court helped to engineer his dismissal from office on 5 June 1898. Amin al-Dowleh, although noted for his personal pessimism over the country's prospects for reform, was later (especially during Iran's Constitutional Revolution) admired for his progressive policies.

See also AMIN AL-SOLTAN, ALI-ASGHAR; MOZAFFAR AL-DIN QAJAR; NASER AL-DIN SHAH; QAJAR DYNASTY.

Bibliography

Farmayan, Hafez. "Portrait of a Nineteenth-Century Iranian Statesman: The Life and Times of Grand Vizier Amin ud-Dawlah, 1844–1904." *International Journal of Middle East Studies* 15 (1983): 337–351.

LAWRENCE G. POTTER

AMIN AL-SOLTAN, ALI-ASGHAR
[1858–1907]

One of the most influential politicians of late nineteenth-century Persia and prime minister to three Qajar shahs.

Ali-Asghar Amin al-Soltan was notorious for surrendering Persian sovereignty to foreign interests in order to raise money for the king (shah). His father was reportedly a slave boy of Christian Circassian origin who rose from a lowly position in the shah's household to become his most trusted adviser. Upon his father's death in 1883, Ali-Asghar inherited his title, *amin al-soltan* (Trusted of the Sovereign), and many of his duties.

During his first period in power, until 1896, he was regarded as pro-British. He supported the granting of a monopoly on Iran's tobacco crop to a British subject (1890), a key event in Persian history that led to mass protests and the cancellation of the concession. He retained the confidence of the king and his own power, however, and was able to maintain order in Tehran after the assassination of Naser al-Din Shah in 1896. He was briefly replaced by his archrival Mirza Ali Khan Amin al-Dowleh, after which he enjoyed a second period as prime minister (1898–1903). During this time he was regarded as pro-Russian, having secured two large loans with conditions compromising his country's sovereignty. In 1900, he was granted the exceptional title, *atabak-e aᶜzam.*

Before being forced to resign, he was supposedly excommunicated by the Shiᶜite *ulama* (Islamic clergy) living in Iraq. Following a world tour, he returned in 1907 to head briefly a new government under Mohammad Ali Shah. The details of his assassination are still disputed.

See also AMIN AL-DOWLEH, MIRZA ALI KHAN; MOHAMMAD ALI SHAH QAJAR; NASER AL-DIN SHAH.

Bibliography

Keddie, Nikki R. "The Assassination of the Amin as-Sultan (Atabak-i Aᶜzam), 31 August 1907." In *Iran and Islam,* edited by C. E. Bosworth. Edinburgh: Edinburgh University Press, 1971.

LAWRENCE G. POTTER

AMIN AL-ZARB, MOHAMMAD HASAN
[1837–1898]

Custodian of the state mint under Naser al-Din Shah and the most prominent entrepreneur in late nineteenth-century Persia.

Born in Isfahan, Persia, to a family of modest traders, Mohammad Hasan Amin al-Zarb had only an elementary education. He moved to Tehran in the 1860s and within two decades had achieved great success as a banker and as a leading trader with Western Europe.

In 1879, as master of the mint for the Qajar dynasty, he instituted currency reforms. In the 1880s and 1890s, he was widely, and probably erroneously, believed to have enriched himself while debasing the Persian currency. After a rapid drop in the value of copper coinage used in local transactions, he was arrested in 1896, imprisoned, and given a large fine. He later regained government favor. Mohammad Hasan was an advocate of reform and was closely associated with Ali-Asghar Amin al-Soltan.

See also AMIN AL-SOLTAN, ALI-ASGHAR; QAJAR DYNASTY.

Bibliography

Amin al-Zarb II, Haj Muhammad Husayn. "Memento of a Life." *Iran* 30 (1992): 107–121.

LAWRENCE G. POTTER

AMIN BEY, AL-

Head of the Husaynid beylicate of Tunisia, 1943–1957.

Al-Amin assumed power following the ouster by the Free French of Tayyib Brahim Munsif Bey. In 1942, Munsif Bey had acceded to power but was removed because of his nationalist stance against French control of Tunisia. Al-Amin, in his early sixties at the time of his accession, proved unable to rally nationalist support for the beylicate and to resist French demands on his government. The Neo-Destour movement headed by Habib Bourguiba and Salah Ben Yousouf dominated the movement for nationalism from that point forward. Following Tunisia's independence in March 1956 and the election of a constituent assembly, the beylicate was abolished. Al-Amin was formally deposed in August 1957.

See also BEN YOUSOUF, SALAH; BOURGUIBA, HABIB.

Bibliography

Abun-Nasr, Jamil. *A History of the Maghrib,* 2d edition. Cambridge, U.K., and New York: Cambridge University Press, 1975.

Perkins, Kenneth J. *Tunisia: Crossroads of the Islamic and European Worlds.* Boulder, CO: Westview Press, 1986.

MATTHEW S. GORDON

AMIN, HAFIZULLAH
[1929–1979]

Prime minister and president of Afghanistan, 1979.

Hafizullah Amin was born in the Afghan province of Paghman near Kabul to a Gilzai Pushtun family, the youngest son of seven children. His father was a low-ranking civil servant, and Amin attended the local village school. He continued his education as a boarder at the Dar al-Moʿallamin Teachers Training High School in Kabul and, after graduation, became a schoolteacher. His extensive connections with the United States included receiving a master's degree from the University of Wisconsin and serving as the cultural officer at the Embassy of the Royal Government of Afghanistan in Washington, D.C., from 1952 to 1953. He also worked for the United States Agency for International Development in Kabul from 1955 to 1958 and was a U.S. embassy translator in Kabul from May 1962 to September 1963. He was expelled from the United States in 1965 for his political activities among Afghan students while he was working on a doctorate at Teachers College, Columbia University.

Amin was a well-known teacher in Kabul and became active in leftist politics during the period of constitutional reforms by Zahir Shah (1963–1973). Amin was one of the founding members of the People's Democratic Party of Afghanistan (PDPA), a Marxist organization with strong Leninist leanings that was founded in 1965. In 1967, the PDPA split into rival factions over issues of personality and ideology. Amin became a leader of the Khalq, or people's faction of the PDPA, which had strong Pushtun and rural ties.

When the PDPA gained control of Afghanistan in the Saur Revolution in April 1978, Nur Mohammad Taraki became president and prime minister and Amin became foreign minister and deputy prime minister. Amin subsequently became prime minister in March 1979 and, after a power struggle with Taraki, became president in September of the same year. As president, Amin inherited a government that was near collapse after the Marxist reforms instigated by the PDPA had led to massive revolt in the countryside. Amin sought to bring the revolt under control by imposing increasingly harsh measures that included arresting thousands of people and imposing conscription for military service.

Amin also sought to develop a foreign policy that would move Afghanistan away from dependence upon the Soviet Union. He was unsuccessful, and on 23 and 24 December 1979, a large Soviet military contingent occupied Kabul. Amin and his family were killed in a barrage of gunfire in the Tapi Tajbek Palace, where they had taken refuge on 27 December 1979.

Opinion is divided on Amin's place in history. Some see him as a Soviet puppet who was responsible for numerous killings—including the killing of Adolph Dubs, the U.S. ambassador to Kabul—and who was ultimately responsible for the Soviet invasion that ironically led to his own death. Others liken him to Abd al-Rahman and consider him an Afghan nationalist with strong American sympathies who tried to steer Afghanistan away from its close reliance on the Soviet Union. His reign, either way it is viewed, was short and tragic.

See also AFGHANISTAN: POLITICAL PARTIES IN; PEOPLE'S DEMOCRATIC PARTY OF AFGHANISTAN.

Bibliography

Arnold, Anthony. *Afghanistan's Two-Party Communism: Parcham and Khalq.* Stanford, CA: Hoover Institution Press, 1983.

Male, Beverley. *Revolutionary Afghanistan: A Reappraisal.* New York: St. Martin's, 1982.

GRANT FARR

AMINI, ALI
[1905–1991]

Iranian statesman of the Pahlavi period.

Ali Amini was born in 1905 to Qajar aristocracy. His father was Amin al-Dowleh, prime minister in the Qajar period, and his mother was Fakhr al-Dowleh, daughter of Qajar monarch Mozaffar al-Din Shah.

After being educated in France, Ali Amini returned to Iran and entered government service. By 1947, he was a member of the Iranian parliament and was known as a pro-American liberal. The shah, Mohammad Reza Pahlavi, distrusted Amini primarily because of the latter's support for a limited constitutional monarchy. In 1950, after the nationalization of Iranian oil, Mohammad Mossadegh, the premier, appointed Amini minister of finance, but he was dismissed in 1952. He was reinstalled as minister of finance in the cabinet of General Fazlollah Zahedi, following the CIA-engineered coup against the government of Mossadegh.

Amini was the main Iranian statesman to negotiate the Consortium Oil Agreement of 1954, whose signatories were made up of a number of foreign oil companies (several American companies with 40 percent of the shares, several British ones with another 40 percent, and a host of French and Dutch companies with the remaining 20 percent). According to the agreement, the companies would produce and market Iranian oil for twenty-five years, and the Iranian government would receive 50 percent of the proceeds. The agreement in effect annulled the nationalization of Iranian oil achieved under Mossadegh.

In 1961, faced with popular unrest over the state of the economy and lack of political freedom, the shah reluctantly appointed Amini prime minister. In 1962, Amini was forced to resign because of the shah's refusal to curtail military expenditures in the national budget. As manifested in the tenets of the White Revolution of 1963 (renamed the Revolution of the Shah and the People after 1967), the shah appropriated Amini's pro-American, liberal, and land-reform policies. While not silent during the 1979 Islamic Revolution, Amini did not assume a prominent position in it. He left Iran shortly thereafter and died in Paris in 1991.

See also MOSSADEGH, MOHAMMAD; WHITE REVOLUTION (1961–1963).

Bibliography

Katouzian, Homa. *The Political Economy of Modern Iran: Despotism and Pseudo-Modernism, 1926–1979.* New York: New York University Press, 1981.

Zonis, Marvin. *The Political Elite of Iran*. Princeton, NJ: Princeton University Press, 1971.

NEGUIN YAVARI

AMINI, FATEMEH

[1933–]

Founder of first seminary for women in Iran.

Fatemeh Amini was born in 1933 to a traditional family in Qom, Iran. Her parents were against women's education and she obtained her high school diploma only after the 1979 Islamic Revolution at the age of 47. She was granted her divorce and the guardianship of her two young daughters in 1965, raised them alone, and supported herself and her children as a tailor. She taught sewing to the female relatives of religious authorities in Qom, regularly visited their homes, and came to be known as a pious woman. The late Grand Ayatollah Kazem Shariatmadari supported her in 1972 in establishing the first religious seminary for women in Qom, called Makteb-i Tawhid. She then founded three more seminaries, including Maktab-i Ali, for which she enjoyed the moral and financial support of Ayatollah Haeri-Shirazi, the Imam Jomeh in Shiraz. She also founded Maktab-i Zahra in Yazd with the support of the late Ayatollah Saddouqi. After the revolution, when Ayatollah Khomeini ordered all seminaries to unite and appointed a council of management, she moved to Tehran and founded an independent religious seminary called Fatemeh-ye Zahra in 1988. She believes that according to the Qur'an men and women are equal, and her aim is to train women *mujtahids* (doctors of jurisprudence) capable of finding solutions to women's problems. Women from religious backgrounds who seek advice in practical and spiritual matters consult her. The seminary, which in 1994 had 250 students, including high school and university students, also assists poor women in order to increase their self-esteem and to boost their activities in the public sphere.

Bibliography

Azadeh Kian-Thiébaut. "Women's Religious Seminaries in Iran." *ISIM Newsletter* 6 (2000): 23.

AZADEH KIAN-THIÉBAUT

AMIN, QASIM

[1865–1908]

One of the first modern Arab writers to treat women's issues.

Qasim (also Kassim) Amin was the son of Muhammad Bey Amin Khan, an official of the Ottoman Empire who at one point served as governor of Kurdistan. When Kurdistan revolted, the sultan retired him with a land grant near Damanhur in Egypt. Qasim's father married into the family of Ahmad Bey Khattab and became a brigadier in the military of Isma'il Khedive in Egypt. Qasim was born in Alexandria, and he attended the aristocratic primary school in Ra's al-Tin. The family then moved to Cairo, where Qasim studied French in the Khedivial primary school. In 1881, he received a bachelor's degree from the School of Law and Administration. From 1881 to 1885 he studied law in Montpelier, France; he then began a career in the Egyptian judicial system.

In 1894, he married a daughter of the Turkish admiral Amin Tawfiq, who had been raised by an English nanny. Thus, his own daughters were given European nannies. Amin's first book on women's issues, *Les Égyptiens,* published in 1894, defended the treatment of women by Islam in the Middle East. He reversed himself in 1899 with *Tahrir al-Mar'a* (Liberation of women), cowritten with Muhammad Abduh and Ahmad Lutfi al-Sayyid. This tract was rooted in Islam, but it argued for a reform of women's position. In a third book, *Al-Mar'a al-Jadida* (The new woman), Amin advanced an even more liberal, social Darwinist argument, jettisoning many of its Islamic arguments.

See also ABDUH, MUHAMMAD.

Bibliography

Ahmed, Leila. *Women and Gender in Islam: Historical Roots of a Modern Debate.* New Haven, CT: Yale University Press, 1992.

JUAN R. I. COLE

AMIR

See GLOSSARY

AMIR, ABD AL-HAKIM
[1919–1967]

Egypt's minister of war, 1954–1967.

General Abd al-Hakim Amir played a role in securing military support for Gamal Abdel Nasser as
president of Egypt. He was graduated from the military academy in 1938 and served in the Arab–Israel
War of 1948. In 1964 he was appointed first vice
president of Egypt but resigned after the Arab defeat in the Arab–Israel War of 1967. On 14 September 1967 Amir committed suicide after being
arrested for allegedly plotting a military coup against
President Nasser.

See also NASSER, GAMAL ABDEL.

KAREN A. THORNSVARD

AMIR, ELI
[1937–]

Israeli writer and civil servant.

Eli Amir was born in Baghdad and immigrated to
Israel in 1950 at the age of twelve. As part of the
systematic absorption process of the great immigration waves of the 1950s, Amir was separated from
his family and sent to be educated on a kibbutz. He
later studied the Arabic language and literature and
the history of the Middle East at the Hebrew University of Jerusalem. Following his studies he joined
the Israeli civil service and served in various immigration absorption and educational capacities.

In 1984 Amir published his first novel, *Scape-
goat.* Loosely based on his own life, the novel tells
the bittersweet story of an Iraqi immigrant boy who
is torn between the world he knew and loved in the
old country and the new one he must adopt. The
novel describes the clash between two different
Jewish cultures—European and Middle Eastern—
through the eyes of an innocent adolescent. Amir's
novel brought back into national consciousness one
of the most painful social conflicts in Israel's short
history: an internal conflict that marked the beginning of the momentous social and cultural
changes that shape Israeli society to this day. *Scape-
goat* was an immediate success and established Amir
as a promising writer and a keen critic of Israeli society.

Amir's second novel, *Farewell Baghdad,* is about the
Jewish community in Baghdad on the eve of its mass
immigration to Israel in the 1950s.

Bibliography

Shaked, Gershon, ed. *Hebrew Writers: A General Directory.* Israel: Institute for the Translation of Hebrew Literature, 1993. In Hebrew.

YAROM PELEG

AMIR-ENTEZAM, ABBAS
[1933–]

An Iranian political activist.

Abbas Amir-Entezam was born in Tehran into a
bazaar carpet-manufacturing family. As a student at
Tehran University in the early 1950s he became
politically active, eventually joining the National
Resistance Movement, a clandestine group formed
by religious nationalists following the 1953 coup
d'état against the government of Prime Minister
Mohammad Mossadegh. The National Resistance
Movement was a forerunner to the Freedom Movement, of which Amir-Entezam became a founding
member in 1961. From 1964 to 1969 he lived in the
United States, where he obtained a master's degree
in engineering from the University of California at
Berkeley (1966) and was active in the Muslim Student Association and the Confederation of Iranian
Students. Upon returning to Iran, he resumed his
participation in the Freedom Movement. In 1977,
the party selected him to be a contact with the U.S.
embassy in Tehran. Freedom Movement leader
Mehdi Bazargan chose Amir-Entezam to be his
deputy prime minister in the provisional government he formed in February 1979 to rule Iran in
the wake of the Iranian Revolution. Later that year
he went to Stockholm to serve as Iranian ambassador
to the Scandinavian countries.

After Iranian students seized the U.S. embassy
in Tehran (November 1979), they found documents
indicating several meetings between Amir-Entezam
and U.S. diplomatic personnel. Although Bazargan
insisted that Amir-Entezam had met with the Americans at the behest of the government, he was recalled to Iran, where a revolutionary court charged
him with being a spy. Amir-Entezam was convicted
of espionage in 1980 and sentenced to life impris-

onment. Beginning in 1996, however, he was permitted to have periodic weekend home visits. In December 1997, prison authorities failed to pick him up at the end of one such visit, but he was rearrested in September 1998 after criticizing his former prison warden in a radio interview. He was released on bail in early 2002 but rearrested again in April 2003, a few days after faxing to national and international media outlets an appeal for a referendum on the country's political system. Amir-Entezam is believed to be modern Iran's longest-serving political prisoner.

See also BAZARGAN, MEHDI; CONFEDERATION OF IRANIAN STUDENTS; FREEDOM MOVEMENT (*NEZHAT-E AZADI IRAN*); IRANIAN REVOLUTION (1979); MOSSADEGH, MOHAMMAD.

Bibliography

Chehabi, H. E. *Iranian Politics and Religious Modernism: The Liberation Movement of Iran under the Shah and Khomeini.* Ithaca, NY: Cornell University Press, 1990.

NEGUIN YAVARI
UPDATED BY ERIC HOOGLUND

AMIR KABIR, MIRZA TAQI KHAN
[1807–1852]

Prime minister and the most famous reformer of nineteenth-century Persia.

Born the son of a cook in the Farahan district in western Persia, Mirza Taqi Khan joined the staff of the crown prince, Abbas Mirza, at Tabriz. He later held several positions in the army of Azerbaijan. In 1848, he accompanied Naser al-Din to Tehran upon his accession, and the new Shah of Persia's Qajar dynasty gave him the titles *amir-e kabir* (the great amir) and *atabak-e aʿzam*, which referred to his function as the shah's tutor (who was then only sixteen years old).

Before he went to Tehran, Mirza Taqi Khan had participated in several diplomatic missions to Russia and the Ottoman Empire, and he sought to institute in Persia some reforms he had observed abroad. One key to reform, he believed, was reducing the power of the *ulama* (Islamic clergy). Amir Kabir suppressed the Babi insurrection, a major challenge to central authority, and executed Sayyid Ali Mohammad, the Bab, in 1850.

During his four years as prime minister, Amir Kabir instituted numerous administrative and economic reforms and built up-to-date factories, often with the aim of strengthening the military. He was also active in building public works throughout the country. Particularly significant was his founding of Iran's first technical school, the Dar al-Fonun (Abode of Sciences). In foreign affairs, he sought to avoid dependence on either of the predominant outside powers, England or Russia.

Amir Kabir made many enemies at court and alienated others because of his haughty manner and successful measures to extract revenue. Ultimately the shah turned against him, dismissed him from office in November 1851, and subsequently had him assassinated. By the twentieth century, Amir Kabir had become an idealized figure, regarded as the most enlightened statesman of his time who was regrettably prevented from modernizing the country. Modern critical scholars (Abbas Amanat, Hamid Algar, John Lorentz), however, regard his goal as improving the system to increase the power of the shah, not ushering in democratic government.

See also ABBAS MIRZA, NAʾEB AL-SALTANEH; BAB, AL-; DAR AL-FONUN; NASER AL-DIN SHAH.

Bibliography

Amanat, Abbas. "The Downfall of Mirza Taqi Khan Amir Kabir and the Problem of Ministerial Authority in Qajar Iran." *International Journal of Middle East Studies* 23 (1991): 577–599.

LAWRENCE G. POTTER

AMIS DU MANIFESTE ET DE LA LIBERTÉ

Algerian nationalist organization (usually called AML), 1944–1945 (in English, Friends of the Manifesto and of Liberty).

The AML represented a remarkable synthesis of Algerian groups dedicated to nationalism—moderates, followers of Messali al-Hadj (Messalists), and the *ulama* (Islamic scholars). It was chiefly organized by Ferhat Abbas, a moderate nationalist who was increasingly pessimistic over the prospects of genuine colonial reform; he had written the "Manifesto of the Algerian Muslim People" in February 1943. Messali al-Hadj, the most radical nationalist, was recognized as the AML's titular head. In addition, the Association of Algerian Muslim Ulama (or Reformist Ulama) supported the new nationalist front. The AML was blamed for the violence of the Setif Revolt in May 1945. Its fragile unity, fissured before this tragedy, fractured afterward as the nationalists resumed their separate paths toward independence.

See also ABBAS, FERHAT; ASSOCIATION OF ALGERIAN MUSLIM ULAMA (AUMA); HADJ, MESSALI AL-; SETIF REVOLT (1945).

PHILLIP C. NAYLOR

AMIT, MEIR
[1921–]

Israeli business executive, former director of Military Intelligence and head of the Mossad.

Born in Mandatory Palestine, Meir Amit joined the Haganah underground in 1936 and rose in its ranks. He commanded a regiment in the 1948 Arab–Israel War and made the army his career. From 1949 to 1951 he commanded the Golani Infantry Brigade, and later served as head of the Instruction and Southern Commands. During the 1956 Sinai–Suez War he served as chief of military operations of the Israel Defense Force (IDF) General Staff. In 1958 he commanded the Central Command, but a parachuting accident hospitalized him for a year. From 1959 to 1961 he studied economics and business at Columbia University and in May 1961 was appointed director of military intelligence. In March 1963, following the resignation of Isser Harel, he was appointed head of the Mossad, a position he held for five years. He was instrumental in strengthening ties with the Kurdish rebels in Iraq and with the Morocccan and Iranian intelligence services. He also modernized the Mossad.

On the eve of the Arab–Israel War of 1967 he was sent to Washington to ascertain America's intentions. In a meeting with U.S. defense secretary Robert McNamara, Amit realized the United States had no plan of action to relieve the seige of Israel and would not be averse to Israel's launch of a preemptive strike, a move he strongly urged the Israeli cabinet to adopt. When Amit asked MacNamara what he would do if he were in Amit's place, MacNamara said, "Go home, that's where you belong."

Israel launched its strike two days after Amit's return from the United States.

Amit retired from the Mossad in 1968 and headed Koor Industries until 1977. That year he was a founding member of the Democratic Movement for Change, a centrist party seeking electoral reform. Elected to the Knesset in 1977, he served briefly as transport minister in the first Menachem Begin government. He resigned his post in September 1978, claiming that Begin was not doing enough to bring about peace with Egypt. Later he realized his mistake, when Begin and Anwar al-Sadat signed a peace treaty in 1979. Since 1978 he has held managerial posts in various high-technology industries in Israel and has written two autobiographical books.

See also HAGANAH; MOSSAD.

Bibliography

Oren, Michael B. *Six Days of War: June 1967 and the Making of the Modern Middle East.* New York: Ballantine, 2003.

Raviv, Dan, and Melman, Yossi. *Every Spy a Prince: The Complete History of Israel's Intelligence Community.* Boston: Houghton Mifflin, 1990.

MARTIN MALIN
UPDATED BY MERON MEDZINI

AMMAN

Capital and largest city of Jordan.

Amman enjoys a special position in Jordan because of its size and population composition, as well as its importance as the capital and the center of communication, commerce, banking, industry, and cultural life. Unlike the ancient capitals of other Arab countries, Amman is a relatively new city. Before 1875, what is now Amman consisted solely of the site of the long-forgotten biblical town of Rabbath Ammon. That town later became the prosperous Roman city of Philadelphia, of which significant ruins, including an amphitheater, remain. Encouraged by the Ottoman Empire, the Circassians started settling the area in the 1870s, and the Circassian village of Amman developed with a minor reputation as a commercial center. In 1905 this role was considerably augmented by the construction of the Hijaz railroad, which reached the vicinity of the village, three miles (5 km) distant. This major communications link connected Amman with Damascus, Constantinople (Istanbul), and eventually the Hijaz—the western Arabian peninsula of Mecca and Medina. The official role of the budding town of Amman was established in 1921, when Amir Abdullah I ibn Hussein, the head of the newly formed Hashimite Emirate (princedom) of Transjordan, made it his residence and his capital.

Although the departments and institutions of government were centered in Amman, its population growth was slow. It reached only about 20,000 in the early 1940s. After 1948 the establishment of the State of Israel and the influx of Palestinians caused the town to experience very rapid growth: 108,000 in 1952; 848,587 in 1979; and 1,864,500 in 1999. While the impetus and sustaining cause for this population growth was the arrival of the Palestinians, refugees and nonrefugees alike, it was also increased by rural-to-urban migration and a rising birth rate. Still, Amman by the 1980s was called the "largest Palestinian city in the world" given its size and the preponderance of Palestinian inhabitants in the city.

By the early 1990s Amman possessed a well-developed infrastructure. From an original small town built on precipitous hills, called *jabal*s, it has spread to rolling plains in all directions from the city center. Throughout are found the royal palace, parliament, the courts, ministerial and government offices and institutions, numerous parks, sports facilities, schools, hospitals, colleges, and a major university (the University of Jordan). Banking and commerce are a vibrant part of the city, including a stock exchange and the Amman central vegetable market, which sells as far afield as the United Arab Emirates and Iraq. Amman is served by a major international airport, a railroad, and major trunk roads to all parts of the nation and to neighboring countries. Radio has long been present; television was introduced in the 1960s. Newspaper, magazine, and book publishing is part of the political and cultural life. Since the 1970s, with the increase in hotels and meeting facilities, Amman has become a much frequented center for both regional and international conferences.

Amman witnessed many changes in the 1990s. During and after the Gulf Crisis (1990–1991), it housed hundreds of foreign journalists and became the port of embarkation for those traveling overland

Jordan's capital city of Amman, home to almost two million inhabitants, is a busy commercial and administrative center and a major travel hub of the Middle East. Amman was originally built on seven hills, like Rome, but after a rapid population growth that started in the late 1970s, it has expanded to cover a much larger area. © ROBERT LANDAU/CORBIS. REPRODUCED BY PERMISSION.

to Iraq, the only way to reach the country. The city's population swelled; thousands of Palestinians holding Jordanian passports arrived, following their expulsion from Kuwait after its liberation from Iraqi occupation, in addition to large numbers of Iraqi refugees. Wealthy newcomers began constructing palatial new homes for themselves and investing money in construction projects in the city to replace their investments in Kuwait. The 1994 Israeli–Jordanian peace treaty later boosted hopes of increased tourism, leading to another building boom as many large hotels were constructed to accommodate large numbers of tourists (who did not come in the numbers hoped). These trends, combined with the construction of many new bridges and tunnels to ease traffic congestion, led to great changes in the western part of the city by the early twenty-first century, although this was not nearly the case in the poorer eastern quarters.

See also REFUGEES: PALESTINIAN; UNIVERSITY OF JORDAN.

Bibliography

Gubser, Peter. *Jordan: Crossroads of Middle Eastern Events.* Boulder, CO: Westview, 1983.

Hacker, Jane M. *Modern Amman: A Social Study.* Durham, England: Durham Colleges, 1960.

Hannoyer, Jean, and Shami, Seteney, eds. *Amman: The City and Its Society.* Beirut: CERMOC, 1996.

PETER GUBSER
UPDATED BY MICHAEL R. FISCHBACH

AMRI, HASAN AL-
[c.1920–1989]

North Yemen soldier and politician.

Hasan al-Amri was born around 1920 in the highlands of North Yemen. In 1936, along with Abdullah al-Sallal, he was among the first group of thirteen boys sent to Iraq by Imam Yahya for modern military training. As an army officer, he was deeply involved in Yemeni politics during the 1940s and 1950s. He participated in the 1962 revolution and was closely associated with President al-Sallal in the nascent Yemen Arab Republic. Nevertheless, he survived al-Sallal's overthrow in 1967 and became the military strongman during the first four years of the regime of President Abd al-Rahman al-Iryani, serving as either commander-in-chief of the armed forces or as prime minister, or as both together. Hailed as the "Sword of the Republic," al-Amri was revered for his military leadership in the field during the Yemen Civil War and especially during the siege of San'a in 1968. Volatile, if not unstable, he was called by some the General George C. Patton of Yemen. He was forced into permanent exile by President al-Iryani over a bizarre 1971 shooting incident involving a journalist who had angered him. He lived in exile in Egypt and was never again involved in Yemeni politics; he died in Egypt in 1989.

See also IRYANI, ABD AL-RAHMAN AL-; SALLAL, ABDULLAH AL-; YAHYA IBN MUHAMMAD HAMID AL-DIN; YEMEN CIVIL WAR.

Bibliography

Burrowes, Robert. D. *The Yemen Arab Republic: The Politics of Development, 1962–1986.* Boulder, CO: Westview; London: Croom Helm, 1987.

ROBERT D. BURROWES

AMROUCHE, FADHMA AT MANSOUR
[1882–1967]

Kabyle Berber writer and mother of Jean and Taos Amrouche.

Fadhma At Mansour was raised in a mission school for girls in Algeria's Kabyle Berber region, where she became one of the first Kabyle girls to learn to read and write French. She converted to Christianity in 1899 following her marriage to Belkacemou Amrouche. Facing a difficult economic situation, the couple moved to Tunis in 1906. She gave birth to eight children, two of whom (Jean and Taos) went on to become key figures in Algeria's Berber identity movement. In 1956 Amrouche returned to Kabylia. Three years later, following the death of her husband, she emigrated to France.

Fadhma Amrouche is best known for her autobiography *My Life Story,* the first published memoir by a Kabyle woman. The work recounts her difficult childhood in Kabylia and her experiences raising a family as an immigrant in Tunis. Although she wrote most of the narrative in 1946, in keeping with her wishes it was not published until after her husband's death. Amrouche's legacy also includes the transmission of dozens of Berber stories, poems, and songs, which she taught to her son Jean and her daughter Taos, who published and recorded them. Fadhma Amrouche is now revered by Berber activists for her documentation of Berber culture.

See also ALGERIA; AMROUCHE, JEAN; AMROUCHE, MARY LOUISE (A.K.A. MARGUERITE TAOS); BERBER.

Bibliography

Amrouche, Fadhma At Mansour. *My Life Story: The Autobiography of a Berber Woman,* translated by Dorothy S. Blair. London: The Women's Press, 1988.

JANE E. GOODMAN

AMROUCHE, JEAN
[1906–1962]

Algerian poet and essayist.

Jean Amrouche was the son of Kabyle Christian converts. Though assimilated into French culture, Amrouche was deeply drawn by his native roots, as he reflected: "France is the spirit of my soul, Algeria is the soul of my spirit." Among his poetic works are *Cendres* (1934) and *Étoile secrète* (1937); *L'éternel Jugurtha* (1943) is his renowned essay. He significantly influenced the Generation of 1954 writers (e.g., Mohammed Dib, Yacine Kateb, Malek Haddad, Moulaoud Mammeri, Mouloud Feraoun). During the war of independence, Amrouche attempted to serve as an intermediary between Ferhat Abbas and Charles de Gaulle. Taos (Marie-Louise) Amrouche (1913–1976), another prominent Algerian literary figure, was his sister.

See also DIB, MOHAMMED; FERAOUN, MOULOUD; HADDAD, MALEK; KATEB, YACINE.

PHILLIP C. NAYLOR

AMROUCHE, MARIE LOUISE (A.K.A. MARGUERITE TAOS)
[1913–1976]

Kabyle Berber singer and novelist.

Marie Louise Amrouche was an influential figure in the development of Berber cultural identity as well as an important novelist and singer in her own right. Born to an Algerian Berber Christian family and raised in Tunis, she traveled periodically to her parents' natal region of Kabylia, Algeria. She later emigrated to France, where she produced and hosted cultural programs for French national radio. The first female Algerian writer to publish under her own name, Amrouche wrote four autobiographically inspired novels set in Tunisia and France. These works highlight the identity conflicts stemming from the multiple allegiances Amrouche developed throughout her life: to her Berber heritage, her Tunisian childhood, and her Christian upbringing, as well as to French culture.

Amrouche was committed to preserving Berber oral traditions. Inspired by her mother Fadhma's singing, she recorded six albums of Berber folk songs and performed in concerts throughout Europe and Africa. She also published a collection of traditional Berber stories, proverbs, and poems. Her support for Berber culture was frowned upon by the Algerian government, however, and she was not permitted to sing at the 1969 PanAfrican Festival in Algiers.

The life and works of Amrouche have been commemorated at Berber cultural events in North Africa, Europe, and North America since the 1980s.

See also ALGERIA; AMROUCHE, FADHMA AT MANSOUR; AMROUCHE, JEAN; BERBER.

JANE E. GOODMAN

AMU DARYA

Afghan river.

The Amu Darya, also known in the past as the Oxus River, forms the principal boundary between Afghanistan and the Tajik and Uzbek republics, a distance of about 680 miles (1,094 km). The Amu Darya begins in the Pamir mountains, runs a total distance of about 1,500 miles (2,414 km), and eventually empties into the Aral Sea.

Bibliography

Dupree, Louis. *Afghanistan.* Oxford and New York: Oxford University Press, 1997.

GRANT FARR

ANATOLIA

The Asian region of Turkey, called Anadolu in Turkish.

Anatolia, also known as Asia Minor, is a large, mountainous peninsula of approximately 755,000 square kilometers (291,500 square miles) that extends from the Caucasus and Zagros mountains in the east and is bordered by the Black Sea on the north, the Aegean Sea on the west, and the Mediterranean Sea on the south. It comprises more than 95 percent of Turkey's total land area.

Central Anatolia consists of a series of semiarid basins, with average elevations of 600 to 1,200 meters (1,970 to 3,900 feet), surrounded by higher

Set amidst the hills of Aphrodisias in Turkey stand the ruins of what was once the preeminent temple to the Greek goddess Aphrodite in Asia Minor. The temple was constructed in the first century B.C.E., but excavations have shown the site was used as a place of religious worship as early as the fifth millennium B.C.E. © JONATHAN BLAIR/CORBIS. REPRODUCED BY PERMISSION.

mountains. This region is called the Anatolian Plateau and generally is considered to be the heartland of Turkey; it was here that the major events associated with the creation of the Republic of Turkey took place between 1919 and 1924. The Pontus Mountains separate the plateau from the Black Sea to the north, and the Taurus Mountains separate it from the Mediterranean Sea to the south. Although the plateau receives an average of only 200 to 300 millimeters of precipitation per year, most of this falls in the winter months and seeps into the soil as groundwater. Consequently, the Anatolian Plateau has sufficient water to support both rain-fed and irrigated agriculture. The most important urban center on the plateau is Ankara, historically a significant regional market town (ancient Angora) and since 1923 the capital of Turkey. Other large cities include Kayseri, Konya, Sivas, and Yozgut.

Western Anatolia has many bays and coves along the Aegean Sea and broad, fertile inland valleys that produce an extensive variety of crops. İzmir, Turkey's third largest city, is a major port, while the equally ancient inland city of Bursa is a major manufacturing center. Southern Anatolia, in contrast, has narrow coastal plains along the Mediterranean, with the Taurus Mountains coming right to the sea in some places. The major population centers of this area are Antalya in the west and Adana in the east.

Eastern Anatolia is not properly a peninsula because to its south is the landmass that forms part of Syria and Iraq. The Tigris and Euphrates rivers originate in the high mountains of eastern Anatolia. Other significant natural features include Mount Ararat, which at 5,166 meters (17,000 feet) in elevation is the highest point in Turkey, and Lake Van. The people, especially in the southeast, are predominantly Kurds.

See also ADANA; ANKARA; BURSA; İZMIR; KURDS; OTTOMAN EMPIRE; TAURUS MOUNTAINS; TIGRIS AND EUPHRATES RIVERS.

Bibliography

Hooglund, Eric J. "The Society and Its Environment." In *Turkey: A Country Study,* 5th edition, edited by Helen Chapin Metz. Washington, DC: U.S. Government Printing Office, 1996.

ERIC HOOGLUND

ANAWATI, GEORGES CHEHATA
[1905–1994]

Egyptian scholar and Dominican priest.

Georges Chehata Anawati was born in Alexandria, Egypt, in 1905 and died in Cairo in 1994. He was raised as a Greek Orthodox, joined the Roman Catholic Church in 1921, and entered the Dominican order in 1934. He studied Arabic language and literature, Islamic jurisprudence and theology, Arabic philosophy and science, and the history of the Arabic/Islamic world at the Institute of Oriental Languages of the University of Algiers. There he met Louis Gardet and began the intellectual and spiritual collaboration that resulted in their famous *Introduction to Muslim Theology* (1948).

In 1944 Anawati was sent to Cairo to found the Dominican Institute of Oriental Studies. It opened in 1953 as a center for Christian and Muslim dialogue where Western scholars interacted with Muslim scholars and teachers. Central to the institute were its library and journal, *Mélanges de l'Institut Dominicain d'Études Orientales (MIDEO).*

Anawati defended his Ph.D. dissertation on creation according to Avicenna and St. Thomas in 1956 at the Institute of Medieval Studies, University of Montreal. He was active in work on the editions of Avicenna's *Kitab al-Shifa* (Healing), prepared a bibliography for the millenary of Avicenna's birth, and translated his *Metaphysics* from the *Healing* into French. He also edited works by Averroes and Abd al-Jabbar in addition to composing about 350 scholarly articles on mysticism, pre-Islamic Arab Christian literature, political philosophy, fasting, Gnosticism, and Islamic science.

Indefatigable traveler to conferences around the world, constant contributor to improving interfaith relations and fostering informal meetings among religious leaders in Egypt, Anawati opened philosophical theology in French Catholic circles to Islam and attracted like-minded confreres and friends to Cairo where, with local Muslim and Christian supporters, they formed part of a unique research and faith-based institute. Moreover, his studies of Islamic and Christian philosophy and theology served to bring about greater dialogue on matters of faith and learning between Christians and Muslims.

Bibliography

Butterworth, Charles E.; Burrell, David, C. S. C.; and Gaffney, Patrick, C. S. C. "Georges Chehata Anawati (1905–1994)." In *Medieval Scholarship: Biographical Studies on the Formation of a Discipline*, Vol. 3: *Philosophy and the Arts*, edited by Helen Damico, with Donald Fennema and Karmen Lenz. New York: Garland, 2000.

Frank, Richard. "Georges C. Anawati." *Newsletter of the American Oriental Society* 17 (1994): 1–6.

CHARLES E. BUTTERWORTH

ANDRANIK OZANIAN

[1865–1927]

Leading figure in the Armenian resistance against Ottoman rule.

Andranik Ozanian is popularly known as General Andranik (Andranik Zoravar in Armenian). He was born in Shabin Karahisar in central Anatolia. He received only an elementary education and was trained as a carpenter. He became involved in revolutionary activities in 1888 and joined the Dashnak Party (ARF) in 1892. Soon after, he emerged as the leader of a band of guerrilla fighters involved in the defense of Armenian villages in the region of Sasun and Moush during the 1895–1896 mass killings instituted against the Armenians in the Ottoman Empire. He gained legendary stature among provincial Armenians after breaking out of the Arakelots Monastery in the Moush area, in which he had been trapped by Turkish troops. Andranik retreated with his men into Iran, resigned from the ARF, and thereafter traveled to Europe, where he participated in the First Balkan War in 1912 at the head of a small group of Armenian volunteers fighting in the Bulgarian army.

With the outbreak of World War I, Andranik went to Transcaucasia and took command of a contingent of Armenian volunteers supporting the Russian army in the campaigns against the Ottomans. He was promoted to the rank of major general, and eventually placed in charge of a division consisting of Armenians, who were left to defend the front as the Russian Army disintegrated in the wake of the Bolshevik Revolution. Forced to retreat against superior Ottoman forces, Andranik had a falling-out with the political leadership of the just-founded Republic of Armenia for submitting to Ottoman terms in the Treaty of Batum signed on 4 June 1918. Resigning his command, Andranik formed a new brigade consisting of Western Armenians. He took refuge in the Zangezur district of Eastern Armenia, where he continued fighting against local Muslim forces, and was about to march to relieve the Armenians of Karabagh when a telegram from General Thomson, the British commander in Baku, informed him of the end of the war and ordered him to cease hostilities. The moment proved fateful, as the British commander subsequently decided to place Karabagh under Azerbaijani jurisdiction. Forced by the British to disband his forces, Andranik left Transcaucasia in 1919 and traveled to Europe to plead the cause of the Western Armenians dispersed by the Ottomans. He eventually settled in the Armenian community of Fresno, California, where he spent his remaining years. Communist authorities in Armenia denied his remains entry while in transit; thus he was buried at Père Lachaise cemetery in Paris.

See also BALKAN WARS (1912–1913); DASHNAK PARTY.

Bibliography

Hovannisian, Richard. *Armenia on the Road to Independence, 1918.* Berkeley: University of California Press, 1967.

Walker, Christopher J. *Armenia: The Survival of a Nation,* 2d edition. New York: St. Martin's, 1990.

ROUBEN P. ADALIAN

ANGLO–AFGHAN TREATY (1855)

Peace treaty favoring the British.

Signed in 1855 in Peshawar for the British by Sir John Lawrence, chief commissioner of the Punjab, and for the Afghans by Ghulam Haider, the eldest son and heir apparent to Dost Mohammad, king of Afghanistan, the Anglo–Afghan peace treaty emphasized three points: mutual peace and friendship, respect for each other's territorial integrity, and a recognition that the enemies and friends of one country would be regarded as the enemies and friends of the other.

Most historians now believe that the treaty favored the British, who wanted to maintain the status quo in their relationship with the Afghans. Since the British defeat by the Afghans in the war of 1838–1842, the British had rapidly expanded their control over the Indian subcontinent and by 1855 their controlled area extended to the Afghan border. They wished, therefore, to reach an accommodation with the Afghans on potentially problematic border issues so that they would be left free to pursue military campaigns elsewhere.

Bibliography

Fletcher, Arnold. *Afghanistan: Highway of Conquest.* Ithaca, NY: Cornell University Press, 1965.

GRANT FARR

ANGLO–AFGHAN WARS

Three wars (1838–1842; 1879–1880; 1919–1920) that defined the northernmost limit of British expansion in Central Asia, determining the present boundaries of Afghanistan.

The first two wars took place in the context of the Great Game that pitted the empires of Britain and Russia against each other for the control of Central Asia and Persia (now Iran). The backdrop for the third war was an increasingly assertive Asian nationalism and a turbulent civil war in Russia following the revolution.

Interpreting a Persian attack on the city of Herat in 1837 as inspired by Russia, British officials decided to intervene in Afghanistan and restore a former ruler, Shah Shuja Durrani (ruled 1803–1809; 1839–1842). In November 1838, they assembled an army of 21,100 soldiers and 38,000 camp followers. The army entered Afghanistan on 14 April 1839. Kandahar fell without a struggle on 20 April. Shuja was proclaimed king on 8 May and marched toward Kabul on 27 June. The major confrontation took place in Ghazni on 23 July, when British forces swiftly overpowered the Afghan garrison. Abandoned by his followers, Dost Mohammad Barakzai (1826–1839; 1842–1863) the ruler of Kabul, fled to the northern region. Shuja entered Kabul on 8 August.

British and Afghan perceptions of the events differed considerably. The British officials attributed the initial absence of resistance to their military might. Afghans attributed Shuja's success to his legitimate claims and his skills at forging alliances. The British role was viewed as one of assistance rather than domination of Shuja; but it soon became evident that Shuja was no more than a tool for British power and that the British were keen to gain direct control of the affairs of the country. Armed resistance followed, reaching its peak in 1841. On 2 November 1841 Afghan forces attacked the British garrison in Kabul. On 6 January 1842 a British force of 16,500 evacuated the city but was attacked on the road to Jalalabad. Only one officer made it safely to tell the story of the army's destruction. Having spent 8 million pounds sterling on the conquest of Afghanistan, Britain judged the cost of conquest too high and decided to abandon its plans. To restore prestige, however, Britain sent a punitive expedition in 1842 that looted the city of Kabul, then returned to India at the end of December 1842. Dost Mohammad regained power.

By 1876, the Russian Empire had established itself as the paramount power in Central Asia. Alarmed at this expansion, Britain renewed plans to gain control of Afghanistan. Following a diplomatic squabble, British forces crossed into eastern Afghanistan on 21 November 1878, and in a treaty signed on 25 May 1878, gained their key objectives—one of which was the posting of British officials in Kabul. Afghan resentment grew at the increasing power of the British envoy, who was killed when his

A British camp in Afghanistan, December 1879. Britain had long sought influence in Afghanistan, and after a disastrous defeat there in 1842, it sent troops back to the country in 1878. This second occupation resulted in the deaths of over 4,000 British and Afghans. © HULTON-DEUTSCH COLLECTION/CORBIS. REPRODUCED BY PERMISSION.

embassy was burned down on 3 September 1879. British forces retaliated by taking over the city of Kabul on 5 October 1879, and unleashed a reign of terror in Kabul, Kandahar, and their surroundings. In December, the Afghan *ulama* (Islamic leaders) called for a jihad (holy war) against the British. By 14 December, the 10,281-strong British army in Kabul had been forced to withdraw to its cantonment. Afghan resistance in other locations was equally intense.

Shaken by the intensity of the opposition, British officials decided to withdraw from Afghanistan, but not before attempting to dismember the country into a number of principalities. Extensive campaigns against Afghans were undertaken. But the Afghan victory at the battle of Maiwand of 27 July 1880 shook the foundation of this policy.

British forces were withdrawn from Kabul and its surroundings on 7 September 1880, and from Kandahar and its surroundings on 27 April 1881.

To prepare for the evacuation of Afghanistan, British officials carried on intensive negotiations with Afghan leaders. On 22 July 1880 they recognized Abd al-Rahman Khan, a grandson of Dost Mohammad, as the ruler of Afghanistan. He agreed in return to cede control of his country's foreign relations to the British. Some districts were also annexed to British India.

Domestic and international conditions were quite different at the onset of the third Anglo–Afghan war. Internally, Abd al-Rahman had bequeathed his son and successor Habibollah Khan a centralized state in 1901. During his rule (to 1919) a group of Afghan nationalists had also forged a conception of Afghan nationalism, emphasizing the need for full sovereignty. Britain appeared exhausted by its travails in World War I, and nationalists were actively challenging Britain's domination of India. The Russian Empire had collapsed in revolution and was in the throes of civil war. And in Central Asia, independent Muslim governments were emerging.

Habibollah was assassinated on 19 February 1919. His son, Amanollah Khan (1919–1929), succeeded him, after thwarting an uncle's claim to the throne. On 13 April 1919 Amanollah officially declared his country independent. Britain, however, refused to accept the unilateral declaration of independence. On 4 May 1919 the undeclared third Anglo–Afghan War began when two Afghan columns crossed into the North-West Frontier province of British India. Afghan troops were initially victorious, but the British responded by using their air force to bomb Kabul and Jalalabad. The duration of the clashes was brief, as both parties agreed on 24 May to end the hostilities. The willingness of the Pakhtun tribes in the North-West Frontier province of India to join their Afghan kinsmen against the British troops was a major factor in driving British officials to the negotiating table.

Diplomatic negotiations started in earnest after the end of hostilities, but it took three conferences before an agreement could be reached. By 8 December 1921, Britain had agreed to recognize the full independence of Afghanistan. The brief war had cost the British Empire some 16.5 million pounds. Persia, Turkey, and the Soviet Union were the first countries to recognize the fully independent Afghan state in 1920.

See also ABD AL-RAHMAN KHAN; AFGHANISTAN; AMANOLLAH KHAN; BRITAIN AND THE MIDDLE EAST UP TO 1914; BRITAIN AND THE MIDDLE EAST FROM 1914 TO THE PRESENT; DOST MOHAMMAD BARAKZAI; GREAT GAME, THE; HABIBOLLAH KHAN; HERAT; IRAN; NATIONALISM; PUSHTUN; RUSSIA AND THE MIDDLE EAST.

Bibliography

Adamec, Ludwig W. *Afghanistan, 1900–1923: A Diplomatic History.* Berkeley: University of California Press, 1967.

Dupree, Louis. *Afghanistan.* Oxford and New York: Oxford University Press, 1997.

Norris, J. A. *The First Afghan War, 1838–1842.* Cambridge, U.K.: Cambridge University Press, 1967.

Yapp, M. E. *Strategies of British India: Britain, Iran, and Afghanistan, 1798–1850.* Oxford: Clarendon Press; New York: Oxford University Press, 1980.

ASHRAF GHANI

ANGLO–AMERICAN COMMITTEE OF INQUIRY (1946)

A collaboration of the United States and United Kingdom to create a solution for the Arab–Jewish conflict in Palestine and the Jewish refugees who survived the Holocaust.

With the termination of World War II in Europe in the spring of 1945, U.S. president Harry S. Truman sent special envoy Earl G. Harrison to Europe to report on the state and treatment of the European displaced persons (DPs) by U.S. troops. The Harrison report gave special attention to the Jewish survivors of the Holocaust among the DPs. It stated that "we appear to be treating the Jews as the Nazis treated them except that we do not exterminate them." To ameliorate the conditions of the Jewish DPs, Harrison recommended segregating them and granting them a favored status. His most crucial recommendation was to vacate 100,000 Jewish DPs from the DP camps and admit them into Palestine. A linkage was thus created between the plight of European Jewry and the future of Palestine. Soon after, the call for admission of the 100,000 Jews into Palestine became official U.S. policy, marking the beginning of active U.S. involvement in the conflict over Palestine.

The British government did not accept the U.S. demand, fearing vehement Arab resistance to an influx of Jewish DPs into Palestine. Instead Great Britain offered Washington to form an Anglo–American Committee of Inquiry (AAC) that would offer a solution to the Arab–Jewish conflict in Palestine and to the European Jewish refugees who filled the DP camps in Europe. Ernest Bevin, British foreign secretary at the time, was committed to the application of whatever solution the committee unanimously suggested, providing Washington joined forces with British troops if it became necessary to enforce the policy.

Early in January 1946 the AAC—composed of six Britons and six Americans (the "Twelve Apostles") headed by two high court judges—started its public hearings in Washington, applying judicial standards to an inherently political and religious conflict. From Washington the AAC moved to London, then to mainland Europe to inspect the ruins of European Jewry, visit the remains of concentration camps, and hear delegations of Jewish DPs. The AAC then moved to Cairo, conducting hearings with the high-ranking officials of the recently established Arab League and with the British military headquarters in the Middle East. It then moved to Palestine to confer with British civil and military administrators there, as well as with representatives of the Palestinian Arab and Jewish communities, and concluded its investigation by visiting Lebanon, Syria, Jordan, Iraq, and Saudi Arabia. Finally, the AAC moved to Lausanne, Switzerland, and in April 1946, after a month of deliberation, produced its unanimous report.

The report dealt with five subjects: immigration, land, form of government, development, and security. It recommended that the 100,000 Jewish DPs be authorized to enter Palestine as rapidly as possible. It also called for the annulment of the 1940 Land Transfer Regulations restricting Jewish purchasing of Arab land to specific zones in Palestine. Regarding future government in Palestine, the AAC recommended that the country be neither Arab nor Jewish; it also called for the indefinite extension of trusteeship in Palestine—practically the extension of the British Mandate system in that country. Reflecting Christian interests, the report also declared that Palestine was "a Holy Land . . . [that] can never become a land which any race or religion can claim as its very own" (*Report of the Anglo–American Committee of Enquiry*, p. 3). Based on the belief that the great disparity between the Jewish and Arab standards of living was one of the chief causes for friction in Palestine, other recommendations advocated equality of standards in economic, educational, agricultural, industrial, and social affairs between the Jewish and Arab communities. The tenth recommendation called for the suppression of any armed attempt—Arab or Jewish—that sought to prevent the adoption of the report.

Just a few months afterward, in early summer 1946, the report was shelved and the AAC became,

according to one count, the sixteenth commission to be asked to offer a solution to the Palestine problem. Britain backed away from adopting the report, and Washington was unwilling to assist in implementing it or quelling probable Arab or Jewish resistance to it. A year later, the United Nations Special Committee on Palestine (UNSCOP) devised a recommendation to partition the disputed land.

See also BEVIN, ERNEST; TRUMAN, HARRY S.; UNITED NATIONS SPECIAL COMMITTEE ON PALESTINE, 1947 (UNSCOP).

Bibliography

Cohen, Michael J. "The Genesis of the Anglo-American Committee on Palestine, November 1945: A Case Study in the Assertion of American Hegemony." *The Historical Journal* 22, no. 1 (March 1979): 185–207.

Crossman, Richard. *Palestine Mission: A Personal Record.* New York and London: Harper & Brothers; London: H. Hamilton, 1947.

McDonald, James G. *My Mission in Israel, 1948–1951.* New York: Simon and Schuster; London: Gollancz, 1951.

Nachmani, Amikam. *Great Power Discord in Palestine: The Anglo–American Committee of Inquiry into the Problems of European Jewry and Palestine, 1945–1946.* Totowa, NJ, and London: Frank Cass, 1987.

Report of the Anglo-American Committee of Enquiry regarding the Problems of European Jewry and Palestine. Lausanne, Switzerland; 20 April 1946. Cmd. 6808. London: His Majesty's Stationery Office, 1946.

STEVE TAMARI
UPDATED BY AMIKAM NACHMANI

ANGLO–EGYPTIAN TREATY (1954)

The 1954 Anglo–Egyptian Treaty terminated the British armed forces presence along the Suez Canal by June 1956.

The Anglo–Egyptian Treaty ("Heads of Agreement") was signed on 27 July 1954, ending more than seventy years of British occupation of the Suez Canal Zone. When Britain relinquished its military presence in other parts of Egypt after the end of the Second World War, it continued to keep its forces in scores of camps, a number of airfields, and other military installations along the Canal. Despite the British withdrawal from India and other colonies

"East of Suez" in the late 1940s, British and U.S. strategists continued to consider the installations along the Canal vital in case of war with the Soviet bloc.

The "Young Officers" who took power in Cairo in July 1952 persisted in the demand for total British withdrawal as one of the main items on their political agenda, and they resorted to guerrilla warfare using *fida'iyyun* (suicide attackers) against British troops in the Canal Zone. Given the urgent need to further curtail its financial burdens, and under some pressure from U.S. president Eisenhower's administration, Great Britain decided to quit the Canal. The treaty provided, however, for British civilian contractors to maintain some of the installations in peacetime, because Egypt agreed that British forces would be allowed to return and use the Canal base in the event of war. The last British troops left the Canal, according to treaty provisions, in June 1956, a few weeks before the eruption of the Suez Crisis sparked by President Nasser's July 26 announcement of the nationalization of the Suez Canal Company. The failed Suez–Sinai War at the end of October 1956 rendered the Anglo–Egyptian Treaty null and void. The civilian maintenance team did not return to the bases, and the last remnants of British presence along the Canal came to a final end.

See also SUEZ CANAL; SUEZ CRISIS (1956–1957).

Bibliography

Cohen, Michael. *Fighting World War Three from the Middle East: Allied Contingency Plans, 1945–1954.* London: Frank Cass, 1997.

Devereux, David. *British Defence Policy Towards the Middle East, 1948–1956.* London: Kings College, 1990.

Hahn, Peter. *The United States, Great Britain and Egypt, 1945–1956: Strategy and Diplomacy in the Early Cold War.* Chapel Hill: University of North Carolina Press, 1990.

MORDECHAI BAR-ON

ANGLO–IRANIAN AGREEMENT (1919)

Controversial agreement giving Britain extensive economic privileges in Iran.

Signed at Tehran on 9 August 1919, the Anglo–Iranian Agreement provided for Britain to supply, at a cost to Iran, administrative advisers, officers, munitions, and equipment for the formation of a uniform military force; to assist in the construction of railways and a revision of customs tariffs; to cooperate in the collection of war compensation from belligerent parties; and to lend Iran £2 million at 7 percent annual interest. In return, Britain obtained a monopoly in supplying administrative advisers as well as military experts and equipment, and Iran's customs' revenues were pledged to repay the loan. The agreement produced bitter controversy. The Iranian negotiators believed that it would finance administrative and military reforms, avert social revolution, and assist in maintaining order. The opposition and most foreign observers believed that the agreement would make Iran a virtual protectorate of Britain. Following the 1921 coup d'état, the new government of Seyid Ziya Tabataba'i and Reza Khan (the future Reza Shah Pahlavi) abrogated the agreement.

See also PAHLAVI, REZA; TABATABA'I, ZIYA.

Bibliography

Ramazani, Rouhollah K. *The Foreign Policy of Iran, 1500–1941: A Developing Nation in World Affairs.* Charlottesville: University of Virginia Press, 1966.

MANSOOR MOADDEL
UPDATED BY ERIC HOOGLUND

ANGLO–IRANIAN OIL COMPANY

British-organized oil company, based on a concession agreement with the shah of Persia, 1901; nationalized by Iran, 1951.

The history of the Anglo–Iranian Oil Company (AIOC) goes back to 1901 when a British engineer, William Knox D'Arcy, obtained a concession from Persia's shah giving him exclusive rights for the discovery, exploitation, and export of Petroleum in return for 16 percent of his annual profits and 20,000 pounds sterling in cash and another 20,000 pounds sterling in paid-up shares of stock in the venture enterprise. Oil was discovered in 1903. In 1905, D'Arcy became a part owner of the newly founded British Oil Company. In 1908, the British government bought D'Arcy's shares. In

An aerial photograph of the Anglo–Iranian Oil Company plant at Abadan, Iran, 28 June 1951. The company's headquarters were seized by Iranian officials after the British ordered 130 technicians out of the oil fields. © BETTMANN/CORBIS. REPRODUCED BY PERMISSION.

1909, the Anglo–Persian Oil Company (APOC) was formed.

Because of its bias, the 1901 concession was not ratified by the parliament of the Constitutional Revolution of 1905–1911. Moreover, APOC did not consistently follow the terms of the agreement. For example, during World War I from 1914 to 1920, oil output had increased from 274,000 to 1,385,000 tons (250,000 to 1,255,000 t) annually; by 1933, the company had made a profit of 200 million pounds sterling. By contrast, Persia had received only some 10 million of the 32 million pounds sterling due contractually—less than one-third of the share to which it was entitled by the concession.

In 1933, Reza Pahlavi terminated the concession of 1901 and concluded a new agreement with the British that reduced the area of concession from 400,000 to 100,000 square miles (1,036,000 to 260,000 sq. km), assured a minimum payment of 225,000 to 300,000 pounds sterling annually as a tax on the production of crude petroleum, and provided for a specific royalty of 4 shillings per ton of the oil sold. Iran was also to receive 20 percent of the net profit over and above a dividend guarantee of 671,250 pounds sterling. The agreement changed the company's name to the Anglo–Iranian Oil Company and, in 1935, Persia officially became Iran.

For Britain, the new agreement had certain advantages over the 1901 concession. It extended British control over Iranian oil for an additional thirty-two years, until 1993, while the previous concession was due to expire in 1961. Unlike the concession of 1901, the 1933 agreement was not a contract between a private individual and the shah of Iran, which could be terminated without much difficulty. The 1933 agreement had the character of public law because it had been ratified by the Iranian parliament; it could not be annulled without entailing political complications. The 1933 agreement, however, was not as beneficial to Iran, and some of its terms were particularly disadvantageous. For example, prices for refined petroleum products in Iran were based upon average Romanian or Gulf of Mexico f.o.b. (free on board) prices—whichever was lower—plus actual transportation and distribution costs, less a 10 percent discount. The bias of the agreement was argued based on the production cost of oil in the Middle East averaging only US $1.2 per ton compared to US$12.45 per ton in the United States. The AIOC's labor and housing policies were also less than satisfactory from the Iranian perspective.

The Anglo–Iranian oil disputes were not resolved amicably; they culminated in the nationalization of the British-run Iranian oil industry in 1951 under the premiership of Mohammad Mossadegh. AIOC then became the National Iranian Oil Company.

See also CONSTITUTIONAL REVOLUTION; IRAN; MOSSADEGH, MOHAMMAD; PAHLAVI, REZA; PETROLEUM, OIL, AND NATURAL GAS; WORLD WAR I.

Bibliography

Cable, James. *Intervention at Abadan: Plan Buccaneer.* New York: St. Martin's, 1991.

Elm, Mostafa. *Oil, Power, and Principle: Iran's Oil Nationalization and Its Aftermath.* Syracuse, NY: Syracuse University Press, 1992.

Moaddel, Mansoor. "State-Centered vs. Class-Centered Perspectives in International Politics: The Case of U.S. and British Participation in the 1953 Coup against Premiere Mosaddeq in Iran." *Studies in Comparative International Development* (Summer 1989): 3–22.

Painter, David S. *The United States, Great Britain, and Mossadegh.* Pittsburgh, PA: Pew Charitable Trusts; Washington, DC: Distributed by Institute for the Study of Diplomacy, School of Foreign Service, Georgetown University, 1993.

Walden, Jerrold L. "The International Petroleum Cartel in Iran—Private Power and the Public Interest." *Journal of Public Law* 11, no. 1 (Spring 1962): 64–121.

MANSOOR MOADDEL

ANGLO–IRAQI TREATIES

Four treaties between Britain and Iraq, signed in 1922, 1926, 1930, and 1948.

As a result of the dispositions between the victorious allies after World War I, Iraq became a mandated state of the newly formed League of Nations; in April 1920, under the terms of the Treaty of San Remo, Britain was awarded the mandate for Iraq. By the end of 1920, Britain had decided to set up an Iraqi monarchy and had selected Faisal, the third son of Husayn ibn Ali, the Sharif of Mecca, as king. In the summer of 1921, before Faisal's coronation on 23 August, Sir Percy Cox, the high commissioner in Baghdad, suggested that the mandate might be made more palatable if its terms were to be embodied in a treaty between Britain and Iraq. This was the genesis of the treaty of 1922.

A long period of bargaining followed, during which the British were intent on having their powers fully defined, and Faisal tried to convince them of the importance of his not being made to appear too blatant a British puppet. The treaty itself covered such matters as the framing of a constitution, the number and duties of British officials employed in Iraq, British supervision of the judicial system, Iraqi diplomatic representation abroad, equality of access to Iraq for all foreign states, and agreements governing the financial and military arrangements between the two states. Iraq was eventually to take responsibility to defend itself against external aggression; at the same time, British imperial interests in and around Iraq had to be secured.

What all this implied was a change in the form without any change in the substance; Britain would, ultimately, force the government of Iraq to comply with the terms, and the treaty was widely unpopular in Iraq. The opposition was so persistent that its leaders had to be arrested, and the prime minister eventually was coerced into signing the treaty, since Faisal had taken ill with appendicitis a few days before his signature was due. A protocol to the treaty was negotiated in 1923, reducing its operative period from twenty years to four years after the signature of the peace treaty with Turkey. Even so, ratification by the Chamber of Deputies in June 1924 was quite problematic; a bare quorum was obtained, with only 37 out of 59 deputies present (out of a chamber of 110) voting in favor.

The treaty of 1926 was less contentious, since its main function was to take account of the new circumstances that had come into being with the "final" settlement of the Turco–Iraqi frontier. Apart from guaranteeing a measure of local administration and Kurdish linguistic rights for the population of the area (mostly honored in the breach), this treaty extended the provisions of the 1922 treaty for twenty-five years, unless Iraq was admitted to the League of Nations before the end of that period.

The remaining six years of the mandate formed a period of general cooperation with Britain, in sharp contrast to the conflicts of earlier years. At the time of the first reconsideration of the treaty in 1927, it was suggested that Iraq should be considered for league membership in 1928; negotiations dragged on until September 1929 when the matter was dropped on the understanding that unreserved British support would be given for an application for 1932.

The Anglo–Iraqi Treaty of 1930 was concluded much more rapidly than its predecessors, largely because this time there was no real opposition. Apart from stipulations about the precedence to be given to the British representative, the employment of

British officials, and the employment of a British military mission, the treaty declared that "responsibility for the maintenance of internal order rests with the King of Iraq," while Britain was bound to go to the aid of her ally in the event of invasion from outside. Air bases were to be maintained rent-free in Iraq for the (British) Royal Air Force, and the treaty was to last until 1957, twenty-five years from Iraq's entry into the league in 1932.

It was not until the late 1940s that Iraqi opposition became sufficiently articulate or organized to oppose continued British control and influence. In 1946 and 1947, the British government expressed interest in extending the 1930 treaty under the guise of revising it. On the Iraqi side, the negotiations were masterminded by Nuri al-Sa'id and the regent, Abd al-Ilah, but actually carried out by the Shi'ite prime minister, Salih Jabr. Jabr and his colleagues spent late December 1947 and the first part of January 1948 in Britain working on a new Anglo–Iraqi treaty, the text of which was released on 15 January; it turned out to be almost identical with the treaty of 1930 and was rejected out of hand by crowds in the streets of Baghdad—so vehemently, in fact, that the regent was forced to disavow it. Relations between Britain and Iraq remained governed by the treaty of 1930 until 1958, when it was repudiated by the revolutionary government.

See also ABD AL-ILAH IBN ALI; COX, PERCY; FAISAL I IBN HUSSEIN; JABR, SALIH.

PETER SLUGLETT

ANGLO–OMANI TREATIES

Agreements concluded by Oman's rulers and British India's local representatives that successively expanded British involvement in Omani affairs and culminated in Oman becoming a virtual British protectorate.

British interest in Oman and the Persian/Arabian Gulf was based on the India trade. It became a political interest as the East India Company's focus shifted in the late eighteenth century from commerce to the administration of India as the British government's trustee. In addition, the gulf's strategic significance increased, since communications linking Britain to India skirted the region. The consequences became apparent in 1798 when, after Napoléon Bonaparte annexed Egypt, French plans to invade India were countered by a British diplomatic offensive to protect India's frontiers. Among this effort's fruit was the first formal treaty between an Arab state of the gulf and Britain, the Anglo–Omani Qawl-nama (agreement) signed 12 October 1798, by the Omani ruler, Sultan ibn Ahmad, and an East India Company representative. This excluded France and her allies, such as the Indian ruler, Tipu Sultan, from Omani territories and was amended in 1800 to permit stationing a British "agent" at Muscat. Since Oman was then a leading Indian Ocean maritime power, these engagements constituted an alliance between ostensible equals and implied no Omani dependency upon Britain.

Increased Omani subordination became apparent in the treaty of commerce signed 31 May 1839 by Omani and East India Company representatives. Concluded six years after the United States obtained a commercial agreement, and at a time when Muhammad Ali's Egypt seemingly threatened gulf peace, this treaty placed Anglo–Omani relations on firmer legal footing. It also significantly diminished Omani sovereignty, by limiting the duty Oman could levy on British goods, by formalizing British extraterritorial jurisdiction over its subjects resident in Oman, and by permitting British warships to detain Omani vessels suspected of slave trading, thereby expanding an 1822 anti-slave-trade engagement.

The 1839 treaty was superseded by one signed 19 March 1891 by Sultan Faysal of Oman and Britain's Political Resident Sir Edward Ross. Although this treaty barely increased Britain's formal privileges, an accompanying secret declaration issued 20 March 1891 bound Oman's ruler and his successors never to "cede, sell, mortgage, or otherwise give for occupation" any part of his possessions except to Britain. Actually, these engagements were reached in lieu of formally declaring a British protectorate over Oman, an idea shelved because it conflicted with an 1862 Anglo–French guarantee of Oman's independence. Nevertheless, the 1891 declaration initiated a fifty-year period when Oman, albeit legally independent, functioned as a veiled British protectorate. The legal regime founded on these undertakings began eroding in 1939, when the 1891 treaty was renegotiated and, especially in 1951, when the present Anglo–Omani treaty was concluded and Oman resumed formal control over its

foreign relations. It shattered completely between 1958—when the territorial nonalienation declaration of 1891 was mutually terminated—and 1967, when Britain's extraterritorial rights in Oman finally lapsed. Only an updated version of the original 1798 Anglo–Omani alliance endures.

See also PERSIAN (ARABIAN) GULF.

Bibliography

Aitcheson, C. U., compiler. *A Collection of Treaties, Documents, and Sanads Relating to India and Neighbouring Countries,* Vol. II, 5th edition. Delhi, 1933. Reprint, 1973.

Al-Baharna, Husain M. *The Arabian Gulf States: Their Legal and Political Status and Their International Problems,* 2d edition. Beirut: Librairie du Liban, 1975.

ROBERT G. LANDEN

ANGLO–PERSIAN WAR (1856)

War occasioned by Iran's seizure of Herat.

In March 1856, the government of Iran's Qajar monarch, Naser al-Din Shah (ruled 1848–1896), dispatched a military force to capture Herat, a city in western Afghanistan whose control had been a source of contention between the Afghans and Iranians since Afghanistan asserted its independence from Iran in the mid-eighteenth century. After a long siege, Herat surrendered to the Iranians in October 1856. The capture of Herat prompted Great Britain, which had long opposed Iran's claims to the city, to declare war. Actual hostilities between Iranian and British forces were limited, but Britain captured Kharg Island in the Persian Gulf and landed a military contingent at the port of Bushehr. Iran sued for peace, but the British captured the port of Khorramshahr before negotiations were completed. Under the terms of the Treaty of Paris of March 1857, Iran agreed to evacuate Herat, renounce all claims to the city, and recognize the independence of Afghanistan.

See also HERAT; KHARG ISLAND; NASER AL-DIN SHAH; PARIS, TREATY OF (1857).

Bibliography

Rawlinson, Sir Henry. *England and Russia in the East: A Series of Papers on the Political and Geographical Condition of Central Asia,* edited by Denis Sinor. New York: Praeger, 1970.

ERIC HOOGLUND

ANGLO–RUSSIAN AGREEMENT (1907)

Accord that divided Iran into spheres of influence.

During the last third of the nineteenth century, Russian imperial advances into Central Asia and the consolidation of British imperial domination in south Asia led to intense rivalry between the two European empires. The conflicting interests centered on Afghanistan, Iran, and Tibet, three states that constituted buffers between Britain's and Russia's colonial possessions in Asia. The emergence of Germany as a world power and the humiliating defeat in 1905 of Russia by a nascent Asian power, Japan, helped to persuade some British and Russian officials of a need to resolve their respective differences in Asia. Consequently, in 1907, Britain and Russia signed an agreement to regulate their economic and political interests. With respect to Iran, the Anglo–Russian Agreement recognized the country's strict independence and integrity, but then divided it into three separate zones.

The agreement designated all of northern Iran, which bordered Russia's possessions in Transcaucasia and Central Asia, as an exclusive sphere of influence for Russian interests. This northern zone was defined as beginning at Qasr-e Shirin in the west, on the border with the Ottoman Empire, and running through Tehran, Isfahan, and Yazd to the eastern border, where the frontiers of Afghanistan, Iran, and Russia intersected. A smaller zone in southeastern Iran, which bordered Britain India, was recognized as an exclusive sphere for Britain. The British zone extended west as far as Kerman in the north and Bandar Abbas in the south. The area separating these two spheres, including part of central Iran and the entire southwest, was designated a neutral zone where both countries and their respective private citizens could compete for influence and commercial privileges. For Britain and Russia, the agreement was important in establishing a diplomatic alliance that endured until World War I. The government of Iran, however, had not been consulted about the agreement; it was informed after the fact. Although not in a position to prevent Britain and Russia from implementing the Anglo–Russian Agreement, the Iranian government refused to recognize the accord's legitimacy, since from an Iranian perspective, it threatened the country's integrity and independence. Iranian nationalists, in particular, felt betrayed by Britain, a country they had idealized as a democratic beacon during the Constitutional Revolution (1905–1907). Thus, an important legacy of the agreement was the growth of anti-British sentiment specifically and anti-Western attitudes more generally as strong components of Iranian nationalism.

The Anglo–Russian Agreement did not eliminate all competition between the two powers with respect to their policies in Iran, but after 1907 it did foster broad cooperation, often to the detriment of Iranian interests. In particular, Britain and Russia intervened in Iran's domestic politics by supporting the royalists in their contest with the constitutionalists, and increasingly, their intervention assumed military dimensions. The agreement lapsed in 1918 after it was renounced by a new revolutionary government in Russia.

See also CONSTITUTIONAL REVOLUTION.

Bibliography

Kazemzadeh, Firuz. *Russia and Britain in Persia, 1864–1914: A Study in Imperialism.* New Haven, CT: Yale University Press, 1968.

Siegel, Jennifer. *Endgame: Britain, Russia, and the Final Struggle for Central Asia.* London and New York: Tauris, 2002.

White, John Albert. *Transition to Global Rivalry: Alliance Diplomacy and the Quadruple Entente, 1895–1907.* Cambridge, U.K., and New York: Cambridge University Press, 1995.

ERIC HOOGLUND

ANI, JANANNE AL-
[1966–]

A London-based multimedia artist of Iraqi-Irish descent.

Jananne Al-Ani was born in 1966, in Iraq. She is primarily a video and video installation artist and emigrated from northern Iraq to England in 1980, where she trained at the Byam Shaw School of Art and Royal College of Art. Her early works were photographic but in the late 1990s she began to work most frequently in video. Al-Ani's work is primarily concerned with the complexities, ambiguities, and power relationships that are part of the processes of cultural contact and mixing. She often draws on her own experience of moving from Iraq to Britain, and of being the child of an Iraqi father and Irish mother to explore these issues, but she intentionally disrupts the easy correlation between her work and her background. Al-Ani has done a series of pieces dealing with the male gaze and the female body, and the orientalist Western male gaze of Middle Eastern women in particular. A number of pieces that both confront and entice voyeurism exemplify her work on this theme, as do the works that deal with the politics and practices of veiling. Her video installations on the veil are part of the larger body of work being produced by women artists from the Middle East examining the complicated issue of the veil from their own diverse perspectives. Another theme running through Al-Ani's works is the relationship between memory and narrative, a topic motivated by her personal history. Like several other prominent artists of Arab descent, Al-Ani's artistic exploration of her mixed and diasporic identity was initially motivated by the 1991 Gulf War, which brought into focus the interwoven personal and political aspects of life in exile. Al-Ani is particularly interested in the ambiguities of personal histories as constructed through narratives of memory, and has created a series of works involving family members that explore the multiple layers of experience and identity. She has exhibited widely in the United States and Europe and is also active in curatorial projects.

See also ART; ATTAR, SUAD AL-; GENDER: GENDER AND EDUCATION; IRAQ.

Bibliography

Bailey, David A., and Tawadros, Gilane, eds. *Veil: Veiling, Representation, and Contemporary Art.* Cambridge, MA: MIT Blaisdell; London: INIVA, 2003.

Tohme, Christine, and Abu Rayyan, Mona, eds. *Home Works: A Forum on Cultural Practices in the Region—Egypt, Iran, Iraq, Lebanon, Palestine, and Syria.* Beirut: Ashkal Alwan, 2003.

JESSICA WINEGAR

ANIS AL-JALIS MAGAZINE

An Egyptian monthly that promoted women's rights; 1898 through 1907.

This Alexandria-based woman's monthly, whose title means *the intimate companion,* began publication in 1898 and continued for a decade. Its editor, Alexandra

Avierino (1872–1926), was a wealthy Greek Orthodox woman who had immigrated to Egypt from Beirut in 1886 and later married a wealthy transplanted European, Miltiades di Avierino.

While avowedly eschewing politics, Avierino used her magazine as a platform to call for girls' education, women's rights, and improved conditions for women. Although she used the topic of domesticity and household management to discuss such issues, her journal lacked the concrete household advice evident in journals targeting a less elite audience. The magazine had an extremely localized readership, as evidenced by the shops and service personnel advertising in the journal, which clustered around Sharif Street in Alexandria. Avierino optimistically projected her potential readership at over 31,000, a figure close to the literate female population of Egypt (including foreigners); however, actual numbers were but a tiny fraction of that figure. Although clearly a woman's magazine, its readership and contributors included men.

Avierino was a pioneer among Egypt's editors of the early twentieth century in her use of advertising to support for her publication. As much as a third of the journal might be dedicated to advertising. She even wrote an article touting the benefits of advertising as a means of promoting not only the exchange of goods but the exchange of ideas, because advertising would allow publications to proliferate. Despite Avierino's considerable talent and vision, she was forced to close the journal due to losses incurred after the 1907 recession.

See also EGYPTIAN FEMINIST UNION; GENDER: GENDER AND THE ECONOMY; GENDER: GENDER AND EDUCATION.

Bibliography

Baron, Beth. *The Women's Awakening in Egypt: Culture, Society, and the Press.* New Haven, CT: Yale University Press, 1994.

Booth, Marilyn. *May Her Likes Be Multiplied: Biography and Gender Politics in Egypt.* Berkeley: University of California Press, 2001.

MONA RUSSELL

ANJOMAN

Persian word for "assembly."

Used as far back as the eleventh century in Firdawsi's *Shah Namah* (Book of kings) in the sense of "assembly" or "meeting," the term *anjoman* had come to refer to cultural, religious, political, administrative, and professional "associations" by the late nineteenth century. During the Constitutional Revolution (1905–1912), a number of secret or open political groups that were often called *anjoman* played important roles. In the latter part of the twentieth century, a variety of Islamic associations, especially those formed among students in Iran and abroad, called themselves *anjoman*. Originally religious and cultural associations, these groups were politicized during the 1978–1979 Iranian revolution, when both Islamic and secular popular assemblies (called *shura,* or *anjoman*) appeared all over Iran, at all levels of society. With the consolidation of the new Islamic regime, however, these independent organizations were eliminated or else were turned into government organs. The notion of *anjoman,* or *shura,* as some ideal form of popular self-rule is nevertheless still current, especially in leftist political literature.

See also CONSTITUTIONAL REVOLUTION; IRANIAN REVOLUTION (1979); *SHURA.*

Bibliography

Bayat, Assef. *Workers and Revolution in Iran: A Third World Experience of Workers' Control.* Atlantic Highlands, NJ: Zed Books, 1987.

Lambton, A. K. S. "The Secret Societies and the Persian Revolution of 1905–1906." *St. Anthony's Papers* 4 (1958).

NIKKI KEDDIE

ANKARA

Capital of Ankara province and of the Republic of Turkey.

Ankara (formerly Angora) originally was a Hittite settlement and remained a provincial city throughout its history, except when it was made capital of the Celtic kingdom of Galatia (284 B.C.E.–17 C.E.). Subsequently, Romans, Persians, Byzantines, Seljuk Turks, and Crusaders conquered the city. The Ottoman Turks conquered it in 1360 and since then Ankara has been a Turkish city. However, it remained a minor provincial center of the Ottoman Empire until the late nineteenth century, when it received a spur of the Berlin-Baghdad Railway. In December 1919, after the Ottoman defeat in World War I, Mustafa Kemal Atatürk chose Ankara as headquarters of the nationalist resistance because of its transportation links with the capital, Istanbul, which was occupied by foreign forces. Subsequently, the new Turkish Grand National Assembly met in Ankara (1920) and voted to move the national capital there in 1923.

The modern city initially was built between the medieval citadel and the railroad station to its west. In 1932, architects began laying out a new city based on a plan by Austrian architect Hermann Jansen. The plan provided only for the upper and middle classes, not for the masses of villagers who came to Ankara to become tradesmen and artisans. To avoid the authorities, the migrants built houses, known as *gecekondu,* by night, which now ring the planned city and contain the majority of Ankara's inhabitants. The plan envisioned a population of 335,000 by 1985; in that year the population had reached 2,300,000, By 2000, Ankara's population was 3,540,522.

Ankara is the economic and transport center of Anatolia. Railroads were extended eastward to Kayseri, Sivas, Erzurum, and Diyarbakir in the 1920s and 1930s, and a network of paved roads connecting Ankara to all parts of the interior was built in the 1950s. The airport at Esenboğa has become the hub of Turkey's domestic air network. The government and the military are Ankara's major employers. Most service employment is directly related to government (education, legal services, support of the foreign community) or to the needs of running the metropolis (transportation, construction, and general services). Industry also is concentrated in the government sector (armaments, official publishing). The burgeoning of ministerial bureaucracies has fueled the city's rapid growth, which has led to problems other than *gecekondu* slums. These include serious air pollution from the burning of fossil fuels; severe traffic congestion; and respiratory ailments and other health conditions aggravated by the degraded urban environment.

See also ANATOLIA; ATATÜRK, MUSTAFA KEMAL; BERLIN–BAGHDAD RAILWAY; *GECEKONDU.*

Bibliography

Ahmad, Feroz. *The Making of Modern Turkey.* New York; London: Routledge, 1993.

JOHN R. CLARK
UPDATED BY ERIC HOOGLUND

ANKARA, TREATY OF (1930)

Treaty of friendship between Greece and Turkey, signed on 30 October 1930.

The Treaty of Ankara affirmed the boundaries between Turkey and Greece, settled the property claims of repatriated populations, and established naval parity in the eastern Mediterranean. The rapprochement was due particularly to the exceptional efforts of Greek prime minister Eleutherios Venizelos and Turkish president Mustafa Kemal Atatürk to normalize the historically problematic relations between the two countries. Turkish-Greek relations continued without any major conflict until the Cyprus Crisis (1954). The Ankara treaty also influenced Turkey's accession to the League of Nations (1932) and the establishment of the Balkan Pact (1934).

See also ATATÜRK, MUSTAFA KEMAL.

Bibliography

Bahceli, Tozun. *Greek-Turkish Relations since 1955.* Boulder, CO: Westview Press, 1990.

Hatzivassiliou, Evanthis. "The 1930 Greek-Turkish Naval Protocol." *Diplomacy and Statecraft* 9, no. 1 (1998): 89–111.

ELIZABETH THOMPSON
UPDATED BY BURÇAK KESKIN-KOZAT

ANKARA UNIVERSITY

A public university in the capital of Turkey.

Founded in 1946, Ankara University includes faculties of letters, pharmacy, education, science, law, divinity, political science, medicine, veterinary science, agriculture, and dentistry, as well as schools of home economics, journalism, justice, and health sciences, and vocational schools in neighboring Çankiri, Kastamonu, and Kirikkale provinces. In the 2002–2003 academic year, the university had about 2,600 teaching staff and 42,400 students (40 percent female).

Ankara University came into being with the incorporation of three existing colleges. The first to be established in Ankara, the new capital of the Republic of Turkey, was the Faculty of Law, founded in 1925. The Faculty of Language, History, and Geography was established in 1936. In the same year, the Faculty of Political Science, originally established in Istanbul in 1859 to train civil servants for the Ottoman Empire, was moved to Ankara. These were merged as Ankara University in 1946, and new faculties were subsequently added.

I. METIN KUNT
UPDATED BY ERIC HOOGLUND

ANNABA

Algerian seaport situated near the Tunisian border.

Called Bona (or Bône) before the independence of Algeria (1962), Annaba was one of North Africa's major trading posts prior to the French invasion in 1830. Bona itself, where France had obtained certain trading privileges prior to the invasion, was occupied in 1832. The city remained an important trading port throughout the nineteenth century. It was singled out by the French government in the 1950s for a number of major industrial projects, including Algeria's most important steel plant. These were part of the final effort by France—the so-called Constantine plan of 1958—to tie Algeria's postindependence economic development to the *métropole* (France itself).

After independence, Annaba emerged as an important harbor and industrial center. This was based in part on the earlier steel industry that had been started by the French and on heavy industries related to Algeria's socialist strategy adopted shortly after independence. Annaba's population is about 620,000 (2002).

Bibliography

Ruedy, John. *Modern Algeria: The Origins and Development of a Nation.* Bloomington: University of Indiana Press, 1992.

DIRK VANDEWALLE

ANNAN, KOFI A.

[1938–]

Seventh secretary-general of the United Nations.

Kofi A. Annan was born in Kumasi, Ghana. After studying at the University of Science and Technology in Kumasi, he completed his bachelor's degree in economics at Macalester College, in the United States, in 1961. He later was awarded an M.A. in management from the Massachusetts Institute of Technology in 1972. He began working for the United Nations' World Health Organization in Geneva in 1962. Annan later served with the UN Economic Commission for Africa in Ethiopia, the UN Emergency Force (UNEF) in Egypt, and the office of the UN High Commissioner for Refugees in Geneva, as well as in a number of positions at the UN Secretariat in New York beginning in 1987. These included assistant secretary-general for peacekeeping operations (1992–1993) and under-secretary-general (1993–1996). When Annan began his first term as UN secretary-general in January 1997, he became the first-ever UN staff member and the first non-Arab African to hold that position. In December 2001, Annan and the United Nations were awarded the Nobel Peace Prize.

Annan's UN service has involved him in Middle Eastern problems and issues. His first exposure to the region came during his service with UNEF II in Egypt. After the Iraqi invasion of Kuwait in 1990, he was the top UN official responsible for evacuating more than 900 Westerners and international staff workers from Iraq. He also led the first UN team that negotiated the terms of the oil-for-food program in Iraq. Later as secretary-general, he negotiated with Iraq over the ability of the UN Special Committee to search for banned weapons in Iraq. His biggest challenge as head of the UN came during and after the American invasion of Iraq in March 2003, when the low-key Annan tried to guide the UN through its biggest challenge since the first Gulf War of 1990. His task was made more difficult by a Security Council torn by bitter arguments, and by the subsequent need to ensure a UN role in the reconstruction of an American-controlled Iraq.

See also UNITED NATIONS EMERGENCY FORCE; WAR IN IRAQ (2003).

Bibliography

Annan, Kofi A. *Prevention of Armed Conflict: Report of the Secretary General.* New York: United Nations, 2003.

MICHAEL R. FISCHBACH

ANSAR, AL-

Disciples of Muhammad Ahmad ibn Abdallah, the self-declared Mahdi in the Sudan, who led the tribes to overthrow Turko–Egyptian rule in the early 1880s.

The Ansar (in Arabic, the Helpers or Followers) had three components during the Turko–Egyptian period in the Sudan: the religious disciples of the Mahdi, who joined him on Aba Island in 1881 and followed him on his *hijra* (holy flight) to Kurdufan that summer; the *baqqara* (cattle-herding Arab) nomads of Kurdufan and Darfur, who traditionally opposed the authority of the central government and one of whose members, Abdallahi ibn Muhammad, succeeded the Mahdi as ruler; and members of the Ja'aliyyin and Danaqla tribes of north Sudan who had been dispersed to the southwest where they became traders. Others also joined the Ansar from the Nuba tribe in southern Kurdufan and the Hadendowa (Beja) near the Red Sea. The Ansar thus joined the Mahdi for a combination of religious and material motives: the belief in him as the heir to the prophet Muhammad; and the benefit derived from him against government control and taxes.

When the Turko–Egyptian government was defeated in January 1885 and Abdallahi succeeded the Mahdi as ruler in June 1885, strains appeared among the Ansar. Those reflected tensions between the tribes that originated in the Nile valley (*awlad al-balad*) and those from the west (*awlad al-Arab*). Moreover, they reflected the tribes' resentment that the new government imposed taxes and control in a manner not dissimilar to the previous regime. Nonetheless, Abdallahi ruled the Sudan until 1898, when Anglo–Egyptian forces defeated the Ansar and Abdallahi died.

The Mahdi's posthumous son, Sayyid Abd al-Rahman, gradually regained authority in the traditional Mahdist areas during the 1920s and 1930s. Even in 1908, the Anglo–Egyptian government permitted him to cultivate land on Aba Island, the Mahdi's original stronghold. During World War I, he won contracts from the government to supply wood from the island for river steamers and, in the early 1920s, he won government contracts to supply materials to construct the Sennar Dam. The government also allowed him to cultivate substantial areas distant from Aba Island. Ansar from Kurdufan and Darfur worked on those projects, generally without pay. They received food and clothing from Sayyid Abd al-Rahman, who also conferred his blessing upon them. The economic and religious blessings were mutually reinforcing and helped provide the basis for his subsequent political strength.

The British authorities supported Sayyid Abd al-Rahman because he served as a counter to the nationalist politicians influenced by Egypt. He founded the Umma Party in 1945, which pressed for the separation of the Sudan from Egypt. The Ansar underlined his power: When the Egyptian president came on 1 March 1954, for example, to inaugurate the parliament in Khartoum, 40,000 Ansar demonstrated and the ceremony was postponed. When the Egyptians relinquished their claims to rule the Sudan, Umma participated in the first independent government (January 1956).

Sayyid Abd al-Rahman al-Mahdi died on 24 March 1959 and was succeeded by his son Sayyid Siddiq al-Mahdi as head of the Ansar and the Umma Party. When he died in September 1961, his brother Sayyid al-Hadi al-Mahdi became imam (leader) of the Ansar and his son Sayyid al-Sadiq al-Mahdi headed the Umma Party. That bifurcation weakened the movement, since al-Sadiq al-Mahdi challenged his uncle's authority. When Ja'far Muhammad al-Numiri seized power in a coup d'état in May 1969, he determined to destroy the power of the Ansar. After clashes between the army and the Ansar in Omdurman and Aba Island, Numiri launched an attack by the air force on Aba Island on 27 March 1970. Hundreds of Ansar died, Imam al-Hadi was killed as he attempted escape to Ethiopia, and al-Sadiq al-Mahdi fled into exile. Numiri confiscated the Mahdi family's holdings, to undermine their economic power.

Al-Sadiq al-Mahdi was a leader of the exiled opposition to Numiri and mounted a major attempt to overthrow the regime in July 1976. When he and Numiri reconciled in 1977, he returned to the Sudan and slowly rebuilt the economic and religious bases of the Ansar. When Numiri was overthrown, the Ansar-based Umma Party won 38 percent of the vote in April 1986, and al-Sadiq al-Mahdi became prime minister. He, in turn, was overthrown by a coup d'état on 30 June 1989. By then, Ansar was no longer a formidable paramilitary force. Its 1 to 2 million members provided guaranteed votes for the Umma Party but were not the cohesive movement that they had been in previous years.

See also ABD AL-RAHMAN AL-MAHDI; *MAHDI*.

Bibliography

Holt, P. M., and Daly, M. W. *The History of the Sudan, from the Coming of Islam to the Present Day*, 5th edition. Harlow, U.K., and New York: Longman, 2000.

Niblock, Tim. *Class and Power in Sudan: The Dynamics of Sudanese Politics, 1898–1985*. Albany: State University of New York Press, 1987.

Shebeika, Mekki. *The Independent Sudan*. New York: R. Speller, 1959.

ANN M. LESCH

ANSAR DETENTION CENTERS

See HUMAN RIGHTS

ANTAKYA

Ancient Antioch and capital of Hatay province, Turkey.

Antakya (Antioch in English) was the capital of Hellenistic and Roman Syria and remained an important commercial, cultural, manufacturing, political, and religious center for more than a thousand years, until it was looted and destroyed by Mamluk armies in 1268. The city never recovered from this devastation, although after it was incorporated into the Ottoman Empire in 1517 it reemerged as an important regional trade center. French forces occupied Antakya in 1918 and subsequently incorporated it as part of the French mandate of Syria on the grounds that its population was largely Arab Christian and Armenian rather than Turkish. The Republic of Turkey contested this action, and for several years the status of Antakya and nearby Alexandretta was a source of tension in Franco-Turkish relations. In 1939, France, against the wishes of Syrian nationalist politicians in Damascus, ceded Antakya back to Turkey, a move that prompted most of the city's Armenian population to depart.

Antakya has grown rapidly since 1950 and is a prosperous commercial center for Turkey's southernmost province of Hatay. It has a well-known archaeological museum and the extensive ruins of its ancient walls, as well as its old churches, are important tourist attractions. In 2000, the city's population of approximately 175,000 was diverse, both ethnically (Arabs, Kurds, and Turks) and religiously (Alevis, Christians, and Sunni Muslims).

See also ALEXANDRETTA.

Bibliography

Sansal, Burak. "Hatay (Antioch)." Available from <http://www.allaboutturkey.com/hatay.htm>.

ERIC HOOGLUND

ANTAR, ALI AHMAD NASIR
[ca. 1935–1986]

South Yemeni politician and government official.

Ali Ahmad Nasir Antar was a veteran of the Radfan Rebellion in the mid-1960s and a top leader in the People's Democratic Republic of Yemen (PDRY) from the late 1960s through the mid-1980s. He held high army, government, and party posts, among them longtime minister of defense, commander-in-chief of the armed forces, deputy prime minister, minister of local administration, and member of the politburo of the Yemeni Socialist Party. He came from al-Dhala region directly north of Aden and enjoyed up-country support; he also found much support in the military. Politically ambitious and fiercely competitive but non-ideological, Antar always seemed to be at the center of the political struggles. He was much involved in the armed fight that allowed Abd al-Fattah Isma'il to triumph over Salim Rabiyya Ali for control of the PDRY in 1978; he was also involved in the intrigues that first brought Ali Nasir Muhammad al-Hasani to the top position in the PDRY in 1980 and then sought to rein him in after 1983. Antar was killed in an intraparty blood bath in early 1986 when he tried to save himself by preemptively ambushing enemies who were allegedly planning a coup against him.

See also ALI NASIR MUHAMMAD AL-HASANI; PEOPLE'S DEMOCRATIC REPUBLIC OF YEMEN; RABIYYA ALI, SALIM; YEMENI SOCIALIST PARTY.

Bibliography

Dresch, Paul. *A History of Modern Yemen.* New York; Cambridge, U.K.: Cambridge University Press, 2000.

Lackner, Helen. *P.D.R. Yemen: Outpost of Socialist Development in Arabia.* London: Ithaca, 1985.

ROBERT D. BURROWES

ANTISEMITISM

Hatred of Jews, expressing itself in racist prejudice, discrimination, and sometimes violence.

The term *antisemitism* (also anti-Semitism), first coined by German pamphleteer Wilhelm Marr in 1879, denotes a modern form of Jew-hatred based on emerging theories of racial superiority and inferiority. Mistakenly appropriating terminology from linguistics (i.e., the "Semitic" language grouping), the term has become commonly understood to mean hatred of Jewish people, whether defined as a religious or as a racial group, and not hatred of "Semites."

Although the term *antisemitism* is relatively modern, the roots of Jew-hatred lie in folklore and popular prejudices dating back to antiquity. Perhaps the most serious contributions to antisemitism can be found in early Christian religious teachings. The first Christians blamed the Jews not only for rejecting Jesus Christ as the savior and messiah, but also—and more ominously—for killing him. Although not as widespread as it once was, the charge of deicide has persisted in some quarters in spite of the fact that Christ was crucified not by the Jews but by the Roman rulers of the Holy Land. Many, but not all, Catholics have accepted the 1965 Vatican ruling (*Nostra Aetate*) that the Jews neither then nor now should be blamed for Jesus' death.

A second Christian anti-Jewish motif introduced in medieval times was the "ritual murder" accusation, according to which Jews would supposedly kidnap an innocent Christian child so as to obtain drops of blood to bake unleavened bread (matza). This infamous "blood libel" has incited hatred and fear of Jews for centuries and has resurfaced in recent times even in Islamic societies, enjoying a resurgence thanks to racist Internet Web sites.

Apart from deep-seated theological rationalizations for despising Jews, situational factors such as political or economic rivalries and jealousies often help to account for overt expressions of antisemitism. Because of the Christian church's prohibition on usury, Jews—who were forced to live in ghettos and forbidden to own land in medieval Europe—became money-lenders who ended up wielding unexpected power over Christian borrowers, causing resentment and jealousy, and creating the long-enduring stereotype of all Jews being wealthy and greedy.

Many antisemites also believe in the existence of a Jewish conspiracy to dominate the world, directed by a secret council of which all Jews are agents. This myth, which first appeared toward the end of the eighteenth century, is fueled by the frequently republished hoax entitled *The Protocols of the Elders of Zion* (also *The Jewish Peril*). Despite the fact that the *Protocols* were shown in the 1920s to be a forgery (actually, a plagiarized version of a French anti-Freemason pamphlet), many antisemites continue to regard this text as an authentic document "proving" the evil intentions of the Jews. The *Protocols* and most other modern expressions of antisemitism were imported into the Middle East through European powers that came to dominate the region in the nineteenth and twentieth centuries. The ritual murder accusation was raised against Jews in Damascus (1840) and has resurfaced periodically ever since.

Anti-Jewish motifs were also present in early Islamic teachings, some originating in the tensions that existed between Muhammad and the Jewish tribes of Arabia. Early Muslims accused the Jews of having broken their covenant with God and of having corrupted the divine teachings. Along with positive references to Christians and Jews as the "people of the book," the Qur'an also contains a number of verses warning believers of the "wretchedness and baseness" of the Jews (Sura 2:61) and accusing the Jews of having "schemed" against Jesus (Sura 3:54). Despite such theological warrants and despite their status as *dhimmis* (minorities), Jews living under Islamic rule were never subjected to the same level of hateful and demonic stereotyping characteristic of Christian antisemitism.

Antisemitism has played a role in, and has been fueled by, the protracted Arab–Zionist and Israeli-Palestinian conflicts. Early Zionist thinkers saw the creation of an independent Jewish nation-state in the Middle East as a response to European antisemitism in the sense that this would normalize the Jewish people as having their own country instead of being strangers everywhere. On the other hand,

some Middle Easterners and Muslims have come to regard the establishment of the state of Israel, and the corresponding defeat of the Arabs and the Palestinians, as being connected to a Jewish conspiracy to dominate the world. In 2002 and 2003, major Egyptian and Lebanese television networks screened several historical-fiction series based on this theme as well as on the blood libel story.

The Palestinians' struggle to maintain the Arab character of their country against Jewish immigration, settlement, and political control has on occasion expressed itself in antisemitic terms. For example, Palestinian leaders Musa Kazim al-Husayni (addressing Winston Churchill in 1921) and Muhammad Amin al-Husayni (testifying before the Peel Commission in 1937) invoked the spectre of a world Jewish conspiracy when arguing their case against Zionism during the period of British mandatory rule over Palestine. Since the late 1940s, this view has been strengthened by the widespread perception throughout much of the Arab-Islamic world that Israel and U.S. Jews have wielded undue influence over the making of U.S. foreign policy.

The true extent and depth of antisemitism in the modern Middle East remain a matter of contemporary controversy. There is a tendency among some commentators to equate criticism of Israel's policies or military actions against the Palestinians with antisemitic intentions or beliefs, and this has the effect of inhibiting open discussion and debate. The unresolved Arab–Israeli and Israeli–Palestinian conflicts have elicited extreme antisemitic statements from some quarters, such as the resolutions of the Conference of the Academy of Islamic Research (Cairo 1969) or Syrian president Bashshar al-Asad's welcome address to the pope (Damascus 2001), both of which attacked world Jewry as an ominous force in the course of expressing their support for Palestinian rights. While some intellectuals and leaders are careful to distinguish between anti-Zionism and antisemitism, escalations of violence involving Israel, the Arabs, and the Palestinians are often accompanied by hostile press and public comment not only directed against Israel as a belligerent country but also fanning antisemitism through the demonization of its leaders and Jews in general as sinister and evil.

See also ASAD, BASHSHAR AL-; DAMASCUS AFFAIR (1840); DHIMMA; HUSAYNI, MUHAM-

MAD AMIN AL-; HUSAYNI, MUSA KAZIM AL-; JEWS IN THE MIDDLE EAST; PROTOCOLS OF THE ELDERS OF ZION.

Bibliography

Carroll, James. *Constantine's Sword: The Church and the Jews, a History.* Boston: Houghton Mifflin, 2002.

Cohen, Mark R. *Under Crescent and Cross: The Jews in the Middle Ages.* Princeton, NJ: Princeton University Press, 1994.

Lewis, Bernard. *Semites and Anti-Semites: An Enquiry into Conflict and Prejudice.* New York: Norton, 1986.

Wistrich, Robert S. *Antisemitism: The Longest Hatred.* New York: Pantheon, 1991.

NEIL CAPLAN

ANTONIUS, GEORGE
[1891–1942]

Egyptian-born Christian Arab; member of the British Palestine Administration; political mediator between the Arabs and the British.

George Antonius was an author, administrator, and sometime intermediary between the British and the Arabs, whose only book, *The Arab Awakening* (1938), generated an ongoing debate over such issues as the origins of Arab nationalism, the significance of the Arab Revolt of 1916, and the machinations behind the post–World War I political settlement in the Middle East.

Born in Alexandria to a Greek Orthodox family of Lebanese origin, Antonius was raised as a privileged member of his native city's commercial upper class. His father, Habib, had immigrated to Egypt from the Lebanese village of Dayr al-Qamr. He speculated on the Alexandria cotton exchange, served as a *wakil* (agent) for prominent absentee landlords, and may have become a landowner himself. His business success ensured that his four sons, Michael, George, Albert, and Constantine, could be educated at private schools and that he himself was able to retire to his native Lebanese village a prosperous man.

George Antonius attended Alexandria's elite Anglo-Arab public school, Victoria College, graduating as head of his class in 1910. He continued

his education at King's College, Cambridge, earning a degree in engineering in 1913. The influence that he was later to exercise stemmed from his ability to function in two cultural environments—that of the Oxbridge-trained British elite and that of the Arab notability. In circulating between these two elites, Antonius achieved the unique status of becoming recognized by each of them as its spokesman to the other. Despite his elegant use of the English language and his cultured manner, Antonius was never able completely to transcend the classification of "native" in the eyes of the British imperial administrators with whom he worked. Despite his command of Arabic and his disenchantment with British policy in Palestine, he was not regarded as a completely reliable colleague by Palestinian Arab Muslim leaders—who viewed him as something of an Anglophile.

During World War I, Antonius was employed in the censorship office of the British government in Egypt, stationed in Alexandria. As was to be the case throughout his life, his social and intellectual gifts enabled him to enjoy a diverse range of friendships, and he became a central figure in the literary and social circle that revolved around the British novelist E. M. Forster, the Greek poet Constantine Cavafy, and the bon vivants Demetrius Pericles and Robin Furness. Forster's published letters show that Antonius acted as his guide to Arab Alexandria, his traveling companion, and his confidant.

In 1921, Antonius accepted an appointment in the fledgling British Palestine Administration as assistant director of education. Jerusalem became his home for the rest of his life, and he came to regard himself as a Palestinian. Because of his administrative experience, his language abilities, and his interpersonal skills, however, Antonius was frequently ordered by British officials to undertake assignments outside Palestine. The most important of these required Antonius to spend much of the period from 1925 to 1928 on six arduous missions in Arabia and Yemen, five of them as first secretary to Sir Gilbert Clayton, the former head of the Arab Bureau. These missions found Antonius, the urbane Christian intellectual, serving as the principal negotiator between the British government and the Wahhabi tribal chieftain, Abd al-Aziz ibn Sa'ud (known later as King Ibn Sa'ud of Saudi Arabia). The missions achieved their objectives of satisfying

Ibn Saʿud's desire to be recognized as the ruler of Arabia and Britain's wish to obtain agreement on the demarcation of the frontiers between ibn al-Saʿud's domains and the British mandates in Iraq and Transjordan. In another instance of using his skills as a mediator, Antonius was called on by Lord Lloyd, the British high commissioner in Egypt, to play a crucial role in resolving the confrontation that became known as the Egyptian army crisis of 1927.

Although Antonius's service in Arabia earned him a commander of the British Empire, his lengthy absences from Jerusalem contributed to the ruin of his career in the Palestine government. Denied a promotion he thought he deserved and transferred against his will to the high commissioner's secretariat, he resigned in 1930.

From that point until shortly before his death, Antonius was employed as the Middle Eastern field representative of the Institute for Current World Affairs, a New York–based organization inspired and funded by the Chicago millionaire Charles Crane. In the course of his work for the institute, Antonius broadened his network of friends and acquaintances in high places and became a valued contact for many prominent foreigners visiting Jerusalem. His range of contacts was further expanded by his marriage in 1927 to Katy Nimr, the daughter of the wealthy Lebanese-Egyptian publisher and landowner, Faris Nimr. A vivacious and generous hostess, Katy Antonius made the Antonius home a focal point of Jerusalem social life, "a centre where people of all races could meet and talk and where a long succession of journalists, officials, officers and politicians were plunged, often for the first time, into a stimulating Arab intellectual milieu" ("Katy Antonius," obituary, The Times [London], 8 December 1984).

Once he resigned from government service, Antonius was able to associate freely with the Palestinian Arab community. He became an informal adviser to the Mufti of Jerusalem Hajj Amin al-Husayni, and he endeavored to mediate a simmering dispute between the Arab members of the Greek Orthodox clergy in Jerusalem and the patriarch in Alexandria. Antonius's major triumph within the Palestinian movement occurred during the London Conference of 1939, when he served as

a member and secretary of the Palestinian delegation as well as secretary general of the entire Arab delegation. Antonius's book, The Arab Awakening, figured in the proceedings of the conference. The book contained the previously undisclosed Husayn–McMahon Correspondence, copies of which Antonius had acquired from Amir Abdullah ibn Hussein of Transjordan. By publishing the correspondence, Antonius compelled the British government to acknowledge its secret wartime pledges to the Arabs, to print an official version of the documents, and to address the question of the existence of potential contradictions between the pledges and the reality of the postwar settlement.

In addition to its immediate impact in British official circles, The Arab Awakening exercised a considerable influence on scholarship for many years. Although several of Antonius's interpretations have now been successfully challenged, his book remains an eloquent statement of the Arab perspective on the events that led to the division and occupation of the Arab states after World War I.

Antonius was given little opportunity to bask in the acclaim accorded The Arab Awakening. He died in Jerusalem in 1942, during World War II, at the age of fifty-one, disillusioned by a warring world that had for the moment cast aside the need for mediators like himself.

See also ABD AL-AZIZ IBN SAʿUD AL SAʿUD; ABDULLAH I IBN HUSSEIN; ARAB NATIONALISM; ARAB REVOLT (1916); CLAYTON, GILBERT; HUSAYNI, MUHAMMAD AMIN AL-; HUSAYN–McMAHON CORRESPONDENCE (1915–1916); NIMR, FARIS.

Bibliography

Antonius, George. The Arab Awakening: The Story of the Arab National Movement. London: H. Hamilton, 1938.

Clayton, Gilbert. An Arabian Diary, edited by Robert O. Collins. Berkeley: University of California Press, 1969.

Hodgkin, Thomas. "Antonius, Palestine and the 1930s." Gazelle Review of Literature on the Middle East 10 (1982): 1–33.

Hourani, Albert. "The Arab Awakening Forty Years Later." In The Emergence of the Modern Middle East, by Albert Hourani. Berkeley: University of California Press, 1981.

Lago, Mary, and Furbank, P. N., eds. *Selected Letters of E. M. Forster,* Vol. 1. Cambridge, MA: Belknap Press, 1983.

Wasserstein, Bernard. *The British in Palestine: The Mandatory Government and the Arab–Jewish Conflict, 1917–1929,* 2d edition. Oxford, U.K., and Cambridge, MA: B. Blackwell, 1991.

WILLIAM L. CLEVELAND

ANTUN, FARAH
[1874–1922]

Lebanese intellectual.

Though originally from Tripoli in Lebanon, Antun spent much of his adult life in Cairo (Egypt) and in New York. He was the editor of the Arabic periodical *al-Jami*ʿ*a* and the author of several books, including the famous *Ibn Rushd wa Falsafatuhu* (Ibn Rushd and his philosophy). Antun was one of the pioneers of modern secular thought in the Middle East. As a Christian, and heavily influenced by the French orientalist Ernest Renan, Antun addressed the question of religion and science in Islam and the Middle East. He concluded that neither can claim to be more true than the other. In Antun's view, the only solution to the dichotomy is to allow each its sphere, although he was critical of religious law (what he termed the "inessential part of religion"). In the same vein, he believed in the separation of church and state. Only through such secularism, he argued, could the Middle East avoid being overtaken by Western civilization. Antun was sensitive about the capacity of Islam to tolerate other creeds, be they different religious faiths or alternative world models, such as the one posited by Western science. Though Antun was at odds with individuals such as the Islamic reformers Muhammad Abduh and Rashid Rida over these questions, he deeply respected Islamic culture and strove to defend it against the intellectual onslaught of the West.

See also ABDUH, MUHAMMAD; RIDA, RASHID.

Bibliography

Hourani, Albert. *Arabic Thought in the Liberal Age, 1798–1939.* New York: Oxford University Press, 1962.

ZACHARY KARABELL
UPDATED BY MICHAEL R. FISCHBACH

AOUN, MICHEL
[1935–]

Lebanese army officer.

Michel Aoun (also Awn) was born in 1935 in a suburb of Beirut to a lower middle class Maronite (Christian) family. He entered the military academy at Fayyadiyya in 1955 and graduated as a lieutenant in the artillery corps. He attended advanced courses in the United States and France and was promoted to commander of the artillery corps in 1976. Aoun, who rose through the ranks to general during the 1980s, sympathized with the Maronite-oriented militias during the Lebanese Civil War (1975–1990) and staunchly opposed the Palestinian presence in Lebanon. He supported the deployment of the army against the Palestine Liberation Organization and its Lebanese allies.

In 1977 Aoun persuaded enlisted men and officers from different religious sects to join him in forming an integrated brigade, known later as the Eighth Brigade. In June 1984 President Amin Jumayyil appointed him commander in chief of the Lebanese army. Just before the expiration of his term, and when deep divisions in the country prevented the emergence of a national consensus to elect a president, Jumayyil appointed Aoun head of an interim government (in effect, head of state). The appointment was rejected by many Lebanese. Aoun declared a "war of liberation" against the Syrian presence in Lebanon but wound up fighting Muslim militias, and later fought fiercely with the Maronite-oriented Lebanese forces. Aoun greatly alienated Muslims and others when he resorted to indiscriminate shelling of Muslim neighborhoods as a way of fighting the Syrian presence. Syrian forces intervened militarily and ousted him in October 1990. Aoun was forced into exile in France, where he remained as of 2003.

Aoun continued to challenge the Lebanese government and still commanded some following among Christian students on Lebanese university campuses in Christian areas. In 2003 Aoun reversed course and agreed to run a candidate in a Lebanese parliamentary by-election. This ran counter to his previous position, which was that no election in Lebanon was legitimate given the Syrian influence there. His candidate lost the election, and he further provoked his critics when he appeared before a U.S. congressional subcommittee to support the Syrian Accountability Act, which was designed by hawkish, pro-Israeli forces in Washington, D.C., to punish Syria's regional role.

See also Jumayyil, Amin; Lebanese Civil War (1975–1990); Maronites; Palestine Liberation Organization (PLO).

As'ad AbuKhalil

AOZOU STRIP

Disputed border land between Libya and Chad.

The Aozou Strip is disputed land along the common border between Libya and Chad some 310 miles (800 km) long and 40 miles (100 km) deep, encompassing at its northwestern end the Tibesti massif. The strip was ceded by France from French Equatorial Africa to Italian Libya under the Mussolini–Laval Treaty in 1935. Although the treaty itself was ratified by both France and Italy, the instruments of ratification were never exchanged and, under the 1955 Franco–Libyan Treaty and the 1956 Franco–Libyan exchange of letters, the previous border, stemming from the 1899 Anglo–French Agreement over their respective spheres of influence in Africa, was generally regarded as being the appropriate international border—although not by Libya. In November 1972, Libya occupied the Aozou Strip and administered it until forced out of most of the region in March 1987. The dispute over the strip between Libya and Chad is now before the International Court of Justice at The Hague.

Bibliography

Joffe, E. G. H. "Frontiers in North Africa." In *Boundaries and State Territory in the Middle East and North Africa,* edited by Gerald H. Blake and Richard N. Schofield. The Cottons, Cambridgeshire, U.K.: Middle East and North African Studies Press, 1987.

George Joffe

APPELFELD, AHARON

[1932–]

Hebrew writer and essayist.

Aharon Appelfeld, born near Czernowitz, Bukovina, grew up in a German-speaking, affluent, assimi-

Aharon Appelfeld. Photo by Frederick Brenner. Reproduced by permission.

lated Jewish home, close to Hasidic grandparents and Ukrainian caretakers. The Holocaust reached his family when he was eight: His mother and grandmother fell victim to it. Appelfeld spent the subsequent four years in constant flight, battling hunger and fear in forests or villages, often with other hunted Jewish children. When World War II ended, he made his way to a displaced persons camp in Italy and, in 1946, finally made his way to Palestine. There he went to agricultural boarding schools, joined the army, and attended the Hebrew University of Jerusalem where, at last, he filled the gaps in his education.

Continuously searching for his roots, Appelfeld delved into Hasidic, Yiddish, and mystical texts as well as into Kafka's works—all of these materials reverberate later in his own stories of uprootedness. Being a figure at the margins of the Israeli "generation of the state" writers, Appelfeld struggles with the Jewish, rather than the strictly Israeli, experience. With an idiosyncratic diction—attempting to forge silence with words, his memory's black hole with details—Appelfeld depicts the disintegrating prewar central European Jewish milieu and its dislocated, fragmented, post-Holocaust remnants, be they in Israel or elsewhere.

The 1983 Israel Prize laureate and author of nearly twenty books, Appelfeld published his first collection of short stories, *Ashan* (Smoke), in 1962 and a first novel, *The Skin and the Gown,* in 1970. These and other works such as *Badenheim, 1939* (1980), *The Healer* (1985), and *Katerina* (1989) situate him among the foremost chroniclers of the impact of the Holocaust on the human psyche. He is a dispossessed writer whose protagonists, tongueless and homeless, are forever in exile. Appelfeld teaches literature at the Ben-Gurion University of the Negev.

Bibliography

Ezrahi, Sidra DeKoven. *By Words Alone: The Holocaust in Literature.* Chicago: University of Chicago Press, 1980.

Ramras-Rauch, Gila. *Aharon Appelfeld: The Holocaust and Beyond.* Bloomington: Indiana University Press, 1994.

Roskies, David. *Against the Apocalypse: Responses to Catastrophe in Modern Jewish Culture.* Cambridge, MA: Harvard University Press, 1984.

Schwartz, Yigal. *Aharon Appelfeld: From Individual Lament to Tribal Eternity,* translated by Jeffrey M. Green. Hanover, NH: University Press of New England, 2001.

NILI GOLD

AQABA

Seaport at the head of the Gulf of Aqaba, on the Red Sea, and just across the border from Elat in Israel.

Aqaba was a small fishing village and site of an Ottoman fort when it became officially incorporated into the Emirate of Transjordan in 1924, giving Jordan its only outlet to the sea. In 1959, Aqaba's port became operational, and in 1976, a free trade zone was opened. The port experienced substantial development as a result of aid from Iraq, which needed safe access to a seaport during its war with Iran. Iraqi aid also helped develop the country's roads and overland transportation systems. Cargo handled through Aqaba increased steadily throughout the 1980s, peaking in 1988 at 20 million tons, and fell sharply to 10 million tons after the United

Nations embargo of Iraq in 1990. In 1999 Aqaba handled 12.8 million tons of cargo. Port facilities will require modernization to increase handling potential once the embargo is lifted. In addition to the port, Aqaba, with a population of 40,500 (1998), is a popular tourist resort known for its beaches, water sports, and spectacular coral reefs.

Bibliography

Nowar, Ma'an A. *The History of the Hashemite Kingdom of Jordan: The Creation and Development of Transjordan.* St. Paul, MN: Consortium Book Sales and Distribution, 1989.

JENAB TUTUNJI

AQABA, GULF OF

Jordan's only seaport, at the head of the Gulf of Aqaba, on the Red Sea.

Aqaba was a small fishing village and site of an Ottoman fort when it was incorporated into the Emirate of Transjordan in 1925, giving Jordan its only outlet to the sea. In 1959 Aqaba's port became operational, and in 1976 a free trade zone was opened. The port experienced substantial development as a result of aid from Iraq, which needed safe access to a seaport during its war with Iran from 1980 to 1988. By mid-1990, facilities at the port included twenty berths, one container terminal, two 40-ton gantry cranes, and 358,000 square yards of storage area. Iraqi aid also helped to develop the country's roads and overland transportation systems.

Cargo handled through Aqaba increased steadily throughout the 1980s, peaking in 1988 as trade with Iraq increased to 18.7 million tons of imports and exports handled in 1989. Cargo handling fell sharply to 10 million tons after the United Nations imposed sanctions against Iraq in 1990. The continuation of sanctions hurt Aqaba considerably. Jordanians complained that crews from warships from the United States and other countries boarded and searched their ships for illicit Iraq-bound cargo. The lifting of UN sanctions in 2003 boded well for Aqaba's economy. The city's population at that time was 95,000.

In addition to the port, Aqaba is a popular tourist resort known for its beaches and water

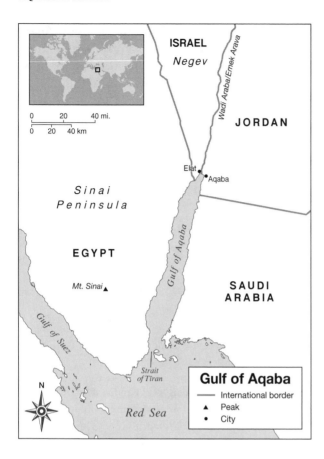

sports, and it is the site of some of the world's most spectacular coral reefs.

Bibliography

Gubser, Peter. *Jordan: Crossroads of Middle Eastern Events.* Boulder, CO: Westview Press, 1983.

JENAB TUTUNJI
UPDATED BY MICHAEL R. FISCHBACH

AQABA INCIDENT

Border crisis in 1906 in the Sinai peninsula, also known as the Taba incident.

In 1906, Ottoman troops occupied Taba, an Egyptian town in the Sinai peninsula west of Aqaba (in present-day Jordan), to enlarge Ottoman access to the Red Sea. The British, who occupied Egypt, forced them to withdraw. The two sides later agreed to cede to the Ottoman Empire a small area west of Aqaba, while retaining Taba in Egypt.

The Taba incident provoked a wave of secular nationalist agitation led by Mustafa Kamil and others who challenged Britain's right to negotiate Egyptian territory. Mustafa Kamil had started a newspaper, *al-Liwa,* to encourage nationalism.

See also AQABA; KAMIL, MUSTAFA; NEWSPAPERS AND PRINT MEDIA: ARAB COUNTRIES.

Bibliography

Holt, P. M. *Egypt and the Fertile Crescent 1516–1922: A Political History.* Ithaca, NY: Cornell University Press, 1966.

Vatikiotis, P. J. *The History of Modern Egypt: From Muhammad Ali to Mubarak,* 4th edition. Baltimore, MD: Johns Hopkins University Press, 1991.

ELIZABETH THOMPSON

AQL, SA'ID
[1912–]

One of Lebanon's most prominent poets and intellectuals, whose career spans the 1930s to the twenty-first century.

Born in Zahla, Lebanon, Aql is the foremost representative of the symbolist movement in Arabic poetry. He once noted that poetry's power derives from its ability to hint at and allude to something. His poems indeed are rarely explicit; instead they are characterized by images and a gifted use of words to convey emotions. A prolific writer, he is the author of some thirty books, plays, and anthologies, several written in French. Early in his career, he became the leading proponent of "Lebanonism," according to which modern-day Lebanese are viewed as the descendants of the ancient Phoenicians and thus as having a separate Lebanese identity that has little to do with Islam or Arabism. Aql has argued that the distinctiveness of the Lebanese people is also reflected in a separate language, Lebanese, which he regards as being more than merely a dialect of Arabic. He even developed a version of the Latin alphabet that he thought was better suited to the Lebanese language, and he has repeatedly contended that Lebanon's children should be taught this language instead of standard classical or modern Arabic.

In the 1930s his ideas found a favorable reception among Maronites who were trying to build a Lebanese Christian brand of nationalism that emphasized distinguishing Lebanon from its Arab Muslim environment. Although the appeal of Lebanonism declined after Lebanon became independent in 1943, Aql's ideas were revived in the 1970s, when they served to inspire the Guardians of the Cedars, a quasi-fascistic, violently anti-Palestinian Maronite militia whose proclaimed mission was to fight for the survival of a Christian Lebanon. Aql also founded The World's Most Beautiful Books publishing house in 1968 and the weekly *Lebnaan* in 1975.

See also MARONITES.

Bibliography

Allen, Roger, ed. *Modern Arabic Literature.* New York: Ungar, 1987.

Rabinovich, Itamar. *The War for Lebanon, 1970–1985.* Ithaca, NY: Cornell University Press, 1985.

GUILAIN P. DENOEUX
UPDATED BY MICHAEL R. FISCHBACH

AQQAD, UMAR ABD AL-FATTAH AL-
[1927–]

Palestinian-Saudi engineer and banker.

Umar Abd al-Fattah al-Aqqad began his career as a director of the Saudi British Bank. He has subsequently directed the Saudi Bank and the Arab Investment Company of Luxembourg and Switzerland. Aqqad has been a major supporter of Palestinian educational institutions such as Bir Zeit University.

STEVE TAMARI

AQSA INTIFADA, AL-

A Palestinian uprising against the Israeli occupation of the West Bank and Gaza Strip.

Al-Aqsa Intifada, or the Second Intifada, began after Ariel Sharon, a leader of Israel's right-wing Likud Party, visited al-Haram al-Sharif/Temple Mount in Jerusalem on 28 September 2000. Al-Haram, which contains al-Aqsa Mosque, is the third holiest shrine of Islam. The visit itself was provocative, especially because Sharon was accompanied by 1,000 riot police. But what triggered the Intifada the following day was the Israeli police's use of live ammunition and rubber bullets that killed 6 and injured 220 rock-throwing (but otherwise unarmed) Palestinian demonstrators.

The fundamental cause of the Intifada ("shaking off") was the continued Israeli occupation of the West Bank and Gaza Strip. Israeli–Palestinian negotiations at Camp David in July 2000 that were supposed to end the occupation had broken down. Palestinians had expected that the Palestine Liberation Organization's (PLO) recognition of Israel would lead to an end of the thirty-three-year Israeli occupation and to the establishment of a Palestine state. However, in the 1990s the number of Israeli settlers in the West Bank and Gaza had doubled to 200,000, for which Israel confiscated more Palestinian land for the settlements and their access roads. Israel extended its policy of closures, which restricted movements, and its network of checkpoints, where Palestinians were often humiliated. Israel also continued to demolish homes and to uproot and burn olive and fruit trees for security reasons and as a form of collective punishment for acts of terrorism. In short, Israeli repression and Palestinians' unmet expectations of freedom and independence had contributed to years of pent-up Palestinian frustration, despair, and rage.

As in the first Intifada (1987–1991), in October 2000 Palestinians began by using nonviolent methods. But after 144 Palestinians had been killed, Islamist groups such as HAMAS and Islamic Jihad began a campaign of suicide bombings against mostly civilians in occupied territories and Israel. Groups associated with al-Fatah such as al-Aqsa Martyr's Brigade focused on resisting Israeli army incursions and attacking settlers in the West Bank and Gaza. Starting in January 2002, al-Aqsa Brigade also began conducting suicide bombings against mostly Israeli civilians, a practice condemned by the international community. Although Yasir Arafat, head of al-Fatah and the Palestine Liberation Organization, and president of the Palestinian Authority (PA) since 1996, did not initiate the Intifada, he reportedly gave tacit approval to armed resistance and terrorism despite his promise made in the Oslo Accord in 1993 to Prime Minister Yitzhak Rabin to renounce "the use of terrorism and other acts of violence."

Palestinian violence contributed to the downfall of Israel's Labor prime minister Ehud Barak and to the rising popularity of Ariel Sharon, who became prime minister on 6 February 2001. Sharon—a proponent of Greater Israel, an architect of the settlements, and an opponent of the Oslo process—proceeded with broad public support to use harsh measures against the Palestinians in the West Bank and Gaza. In response to Palestinian violence he initiated a policy of assassinations—euphemistically called "targeted killings"—of suspected terrorist leaders, that sometimes included activists and innocent bystanders. He reoccupied major Palestinian cities, using helicopter gunships, warplanes, and tanks. Some of Sharon's methods were considered to be war crimes by human rights groups, and were condemned by the United States.

The Intifada was costly to the Palestinians, to Israel, and to the United States. Some Palestinian analysts considered the militarization of the Intifada to be a blunder. The Oslo process was destroyed, Arafat sidelined, the Palestinian economy damaged, and PA areas occupied, as Israeli settlement construction and a separation barrier (called wall by Palestinians and fence by Israelis) continued apace. By early 2004 Sharon's harsh measures had led to the deaths of about 3,000 Palestinians, of whom most were civilians, including about 500 children. In addition, the Palestinians lost much popular, moral, and diplomatic support around the world. The Intifada also cost the lives of about 900 Israelis, most of whom were civilians, and brought insecurity to the everyday lives of Israelis, who lost faith in the Palestinians as peace partners. It also contributed to Israel's worst economic recession, for which the government sought a large loan from the United States. President George W. Bush's neglect of the peace process and support for the hard-line policies of Sharon resulted in anger at the United States in much of the Muslim and Arab world, which has helped anti-American Muslim extremist groups to recruit members.

The Intifada also had unintended positive consequences. Pressure from Sharon and Bush prompted reform of the PA, which most Palestinians had sought for years because they viewed the PA as corrupt, inept, and autocratic. A new office of prime minister was created to assume many of the duties and much of the authority of the president of the PA. One diplomatic by-product of the Intifada was the Arab League's approval in March 2002 of a Saudi plan calling for Arab recognition and normalization of relations with Israel, provided that United Nations Resolution 242 is implemented and

an independent state of Palestine is created. Another was the United States's initiation of another peace effort, the Road Map, in 2003, The Intifada also increased support within Israel for the dismantling of most of the settlements and withdrawal from Gaza. Despite the violence, destruction, and insecurity, and despite the failed leadership of Arafat, Sharon, and Bush, most Israelis and Palestinians continued to support the concept of a two-state solution as the only viable solution to the Arab–Israel conflict.

See also ARAB–ISRAEL CONFLICT; ARAFAT, YASIR; BUSH, GEORGE WALKER; FATAH, AL-; GAZA (CITY); HAMAS; HARAM AL-SHARIF; INTIFADA (1987–1991); ISLAMIC JIHAD; ISRAELI SETTLEMENTS; WEST BANK.

Bibliography

Carey, Roane. *The New Intifada: Resisting Israel's Apartheid.* London: Verso, 2001.

Grossman, David. *Death as a Way of Life.* New York: Farrar, Straus, and Giroux, 2003.

Journalists of Reuters. *The Israeli–Palestinian Conflict: Crisis in the Middle East.* Upper Saddle River, NJ: Prentice Hall, 2003.

Reinhart, Tanya. *Israel/Palestine: How to End the War of 1948.* New York: Seven Stories Press, 2002.

PHILIP MATTAR

ARAB

A person who speaks Arabic as a first language and self-identifies as Arab.

Arabs comprise less than one-quarter of the world's 1.2 billion Muslims. Arabic is a Semitic language, as are Aramaic, Hebrew, Amharic, and some other languages. In its original Arabic meaning, an Arab is a pastoral nomad. Before the introduction of Islam in the seventh century C.E., Arabs participated in most ancient Near Eastern civilizations as traders, auxiliary warriors, and as providers of camels and other desert produce. They migrated with their extended kin and animals, following seasonal patterns of available water and vegetation, and made a sophisticated adaptation to arid environments. Poetry, their main artistic expression, presented their most strongly held beliefs and values:

bravery in battle, patience in misfortune, persistence in revenge, protection of the weak, defiance toward the strong, hospitality to the guest, generosity to the needy, loyalty to the kin grouping, and fidelity in keeping promises. Most early Arabs were animists or ancestor-worshipers, but some adopted Judaism or Christianity before the advent of Islam.

Islam came to humanity through the last Messenger of God, Muhammad, an Arab of the Quraysh tribe (570–632 C.E.) who profoundly affected not only the Arabs but world history. Arab clans took part in the early conquests to extend Islamic rule into the Fertile Crescent and across North Africa as far west as Morocco and Spain (711 C.E.) and eastward to the borders of India and China. The Arabic language and the Islamic religion were widely adopted by non-Arab conquered peoples, some of whom intermarried with Arabs.

Politically, the term "Arab" has been applied to all citizens of states in which Arabic is now the official language, whether or not they are native Arabic speakers. These "Arab" states, listed from west to east in North Africa and the Middle East, include: Morocco, Algeria, Tunisia, Libya, Egypt, Sudan, Saudi Arabia, Yemen, Lebanon, Syria, Jordan, Iraq, Kuwait, Bahrain, Qatar, the United Arab Emirates, and Oman. Culturally, the term has also been applied to persons of Arab descent living outside the Arab world.

Arab identity can mask linguistic and other ethnic identities in North Africa and the Middle East. Culturally and linguistically, Iranians (Farsi), Pakistanis (Urdu), and Afghanis (Pashtun) are not Arabs, although they employ Arabic script in writing their languages. The Turks, leaders of the Ottoman Empire since the fifteenth century, are not Arabs, and before the reforms of Mustafa Kemal Atatürk during the 1920s, they too wrote Turkish using Arabic calligraphy. The term "Arab" has also been used as a racial designation, in some cases used in racial profiling after 11 September 2001.

During the late 1800s Arab nationalism began to emerge in Beirut student societies. Some Arabs called for the restoration of Arab rule in the caliphate, as it was then claimed by the Ottoman sultans. In World War I, a family of Arabs (Hashimites) led by the Sharif of Mecca and Amir Husayn, a

Even those as far removed from the modern world as the nomadic Arabic Bedouin (desert dwellers) have found their simple and traditional lifestyles increasingly altered by the universal encroachment of technology. © MOSHE SHAI/CORBIS. REPRODUCED BY PERMISSION.

Sayyid and descendant of Muhammad, revolted against Ottoman rule and freed parts of the Hijaz (Arabia), Palestine, and Syria. Aided by Britain, these Arabs hoped that they might form a united Arab state in the Arabian peninsula and the Fertile Crescent, but Britain honored other promises it had made to its allies (especially France) and to the Zionist movement. Husayn took but later lost control of the Hijaz; his son Faisal I ibn Hussein briefly ruled in Syria (until the French mandate took over in 1920) but was then made king of Iraq; another son, Abdallah, was given an emirate called Transjordan (now the Hashimite Kingdom of Jordan). In the peace settlement that ended World War I, Arabs in Syria and Lebanon were placed under a League of Nations mandate administered by France;

Muslims at prayer. Muslims are followers of Islam, a monotheistic faith that has 1.2 billion followers, or one-fifth of the world's population. Although less than 20 percent of Muslims are Arabs, many Muslim believers can be found in the Middle East and North Africa. © PETER TURNLEY/CORBIS. REPRODUCED BY PERMISSION.

Britain held similar mandates in Palestine (initially including Transjordan) and Iraq. These mandates were intended to be temporary means for Arabs to govern themselves, but the winning of independence from European control between 1932 and 1946 did not facilitate Arab unification. Arab energies from 1900 to about 1950 were devoted mainly to achieving independence and to unifying the Arabic-speaking states. Continuing these efforts, the League of Arab States was created in 1945, with Egypt assuming a leadership role. In its first major test, the League failed to protect the Palestinians from the creation in 1948 of the state of Israel.

"Arab Nationalism" is a term used by anticolonial, nationalist leaders throughout the Middle East, especially recognized when Gamal Abdel Nasser, the first postindependence leader of Egypt, nationalized the Suez Canal and succeeded in gaining Egyptian control over the canal despite imper-

ial pressure from Britain and France, allied with Israel. Generally political efforts at Arab union and federations have not succeeded, but inter-Arab pacts to create customs and telecommunications unions have been implemented. Arab success in imposing an oil embargo on the United States during and after the October 1973 war with Israel raised hopes for Arab unity. However, Egypt's separate peace with Israel in 1979; the division of Arab countries over the Lebanese Civil War (1975–1990); the Iran–Iraq War (1980–1988); Iraq's invasion of Kuwait (Gulf Crisis, 1990–1991); and two Gulf wars all pointed to deep-seated divisions among Arab governments and peoples. Petroleum revenues have enriched some Arab regimes, but on the whole the Arab people have not prospered. In the second American war against Iraq in 2003, Arab nationalism was revived in the widespread response of the Arab world to what was described as an "invasion" and "occupation" of Arab territory. New Arab television networks, such as al-Jazeera and al-Arabiyya, have facilitated this revived solidarity.

Historically, appeals to the Arab Nation have come from Palestinian nationalists, whose lack of a territorial base makes Arab nationalism a matter of essential politics. The juxtaposition of "Arab" and "Israeli" in the usually hyphenated "Arab–Israeli conflict" adds to the sense of the Arabs being constituted as a single nation.

Arab nationalism has been a secular movement, with religion either irrelevant or kept separate from politics. Although people may still respond emotionally to the call for Arab unity, the political dynamic is shifting away from Arab nationalism to political alternatives framed by Islamic discourse, generally referred to as "Islamist," meaning the political use of the Islamic faith.

If Arabs have been deeply frustrated by their failure to unite, they still take pride in their historical achievements, their culture, notably their language and literature, their role in the development and spread of Islam, and their keen family loyalty, generosity, and hospitality.

Bibliography

Fluehr-Lobban, Carolyn. *Islamic Society in Practice*, 2d edition. Gainesville: University Press of Florida, 2004.

Goldschmidt, Arthur, Jr. *A Concise History of the Middle East*, 4th edition. Boulder, CO: Westview Press, 1991.

Hitti, Philip K. *History of the Arabs: From the Earliest Times to the Present*, revised 10th edition. New York: Palgrave Macmillan, 2002.

Hourani, Albert. *History of the Arab Peoples.* Cambridge, MA: Belknap Press of Harvard University, 2002.

Ibrahim, Saad Eddin, and Hopkins, Nicholas S., eds. *Arab Society: Social Science Perspectives.* Cairo: American University in Cairo Press, 1985.

Musallam, Basim. *The Arabs: A Living History.* London: Collins/Harvill, 1983.

Nydell, Margaret K. (Omar). *Understanding Arabs: A Guide for Westerners*, 3d edition. Yarmouth, ME: Intercultural Press, 2002.

Polk, William R. *The Arab World Today*, 5th edition. Cambridge, MA: Harvard University Press, 1991.

ARTHUR GOLDSCHMIDT
UPDATED BY CAROLYN FLUEHR-LOBBAN

ARAB ACADEMY OF DAMASCUS

Center for Arabic studies.

Modeled on the Académie Française, the Academy of Arab Learning in Damascus (al-Majma al-Ilmi al-Arabi bi Dimashq) was established in June 1919 as a center for Arabic linguistics and studies in literature and the humanities. It was part of a concerted effort by the government of the newly established Kingdom of Syria to make Arabic the language of administration, the armed forces, high culture, and education within its boundaries. Its founders included Amin Suwayd, Anis Sallum, Saʿid al-Karmi, Abd al-Qadir al-Maghribi, Isa al-Maʿluf, Dimitri Qandalaft, Izz al-Din al-Tanuhi, and Muhammad Kurd Ali (who was its president). Influential nationalists such as Abd al-Rahman Shahbandar, Rashid Baqdunis, and Faris al-Khuri were early members.

The academy, headquartered in the historic Adiliyya School (al-Madrasa al-Adiliyya), sponsored public lectures on a wide range of cultural subjects and supervised the editing of important Arabic-language texts. In addition, it was responsible for overseeing the extensive collection of manuscripts and books that had been gathered by Shaykh Tahir al-Jaza'iri during the final decades of the nineteenth century in the adjacent Zahiriyya School (al-Madrasa al-Zahiriyya), as well as for administering the Syrian National Museum. By the spring of 1920, growing fiscal difficulties forced the government of King Faisal to cut back funding for the organization, which disbanded later that summer.

In early September 1920, Kurd Ali proposed to the French mandatory authorities that the academy reopen. The high commissioner, who saw the proposal as an opportunity to split Damascus's intelligentsia, immediately approved the proposal. Successive mandatory governors provided generous financial support for the organization, severely limiting its ability to serve either as a forum for open political debate or as an incubator of Arab nationalist sentiment. Nevertheless, the academy's cultural activities flourished under French patronage. A journal (*Majalla al-Majma al-Ilmi al-Arabi*) appeared in January 1921, along with a series of critical editions of writings by prominent Arab authors. The academy merged with the Syrian University in June

1923, and was reincorporated as a research institute for the study of formal Arabic language (al-lugha al-fusha) three years later. Throughout the 1930s and 1940s, the academy organized international festivals celebrating the contributions of major Arab literary figures. By the 1950s the circle of corresponding members had expanded to include such influential Western scholars as Carl Brockelmann, Ignaz Goldziher, Snouck Hurgronje, and Louis Massignon.

See also KURD ALI, MUHAMMAD; SHAHBANDAR, ABD AL-RAHMAN.

FRED H. LAWSON

ARAB BOYCOTT

Various measures of economic warfare against Israel by the League of Arab States.

In an attempt to assist the Palestinians in their struggle against Zionism, the newly formed League of Arab States (Arab League) passed Resolution 16 on 2 December 1945, calling on its member states to prohibit the purchase of products made by the Jewish sector of Palestine. After the Arab defeat in the first Arab–Israel War (1948), the Arab League expanded the boycott to include three levels. The primary boycott barred Arab states, companies, and individuals from buying from or selling to Israel any goods or services, and prohibited other commercial or financial relationships with Israel. In 1950, a secondary boycott extended the prohibitions to dealings with companies anywhere in the world who themselves engaged in important economic relations with Israel. A subsequent tertiary boycott was aimed more broadly at individuals and organizations seen as supportive of Israel. An example of the secondary boycott concerned the giant Coca-Cola Company. Because of the company's activities in Israel, many Arab countries boycotted it and gave their business to the rival Pepsi Cola Company instead. An example of the tertiary boycott can be seen in the policies of Jordan, which boycotted entertainers it considered pro-Israel, including Danny Kaye and Frank Sinatra, and banned their films and recordings from entering the country.

In 1951, the Arab League set up the Central Office for the Boycott of Israel in Damascus, Syria,

operating under the league's secretary-general. It administered boycott activities and maintained a roster of blacklisted companies with which member states were not to trade. By the 1970s, the league had enacted over forty articles clarifying how the boycott was to work. By 1976, 6,300 firms from ninety-six countries had been blacklisted. However, rulings from the office were only advisory. Several Arab states, including Tunisia, Sudan, and Algeria, chose not to follow the secondary and tertiary boycotts or followed them only selectively. International reaction to the boycott ranged from repeated expressions of outrage and judicial counteractions by the United States and some European countries, to Japanese and Korean reluctance to engage in economic dealings with Israel for fear of offending Arab countries.

The boycott failed to throttle Israel's economic development, even though Israel's economy was weak in the years following the first Arab–Israeli War. Among other things, Israel benefited financially early on from its confiscation of the land left behind by the Palestinian refugees, which enabled it to settle new immigrants inexpensively. Israel also began demanding that the compensation it had pledged to pay the refugees for their property be reduced to account for the boycott's damage to its economy. Additionally, Israel benefited in the 1950s and 1960s from massive infusions of goods from West Germany in the form of reparations for Nazi crimes, as well as from funds donated by Jewish individuals and organizations around the world. In 1992, the Federation of Israeli Chambers of Commerce estimated that the boycott had reduced Israeli exports by 10 percent and investments by 15 percent for a cumulative loss of $45 billion. Yet by that point, Israel had defeated the Arabs in four major wars and had clearly thrived despite the boycott.

The boycott was dealt several further major blows when Egypt and Jordan signed peace treaties with Israel (1979 and 1994, respectively), and ended their participation in the boycott. The Palestine Liberation Organization also gave up the boycott as a result of the Israeli–Palestinian peace process, and in February 1995 joined Egypt and Jordan in pledging to support an end to boycott activities. Other Arab states, including Oman and Qatar, began establishing trade ties with Israel after the October 1991 Madrid Conference and the subsequent Israeli–Palestinian peace process. Countries outside the Arab League, including Japan, have also begun dropping their adherence to the boycott. Despite this, the Arab League has not formally rescinded the boycott, and the Central Office for the Boycott of Israel still exists. Although this office it did not hold its biannual conference for a number of years after 1993, it did convene its seventy-first conference in Damascus in October 2003, which even a delegation from American-occupied Iraq attended.

See also ARAB–ISRAEL WAR (1948); LEAGUE OF ARAB STATES; MADRID CONFERENCE (1991); REFUGEES: PALESTINIAN; WEST GERMAN REPARATIONS AGREEMENT.

Bibliography

Feiler, Gil. *From Boycott to Economic Cooperation: The Political Economy of the Arab Boycott of Israel.* London: Frank Cass, 1998.

Sarna, A.J. *Boycott and Blacklist: A History of Arab Economic Warfare against Israel.* Totowa, NJ: Rowman and Littlefield, 1986.

Sharif, Amer A. *A Statistical Study on the Arab Boycott of Israel.* Beirut: Institute for Palestine Studies, 1970.

GEORGE E. GRUEN
UPDATED BY MICHAEL R. FISCHBACH

ARAB BUREAU (CAIRO)

Intelligence and propaganda agency operated by the British in Cairo from 1916 to 1920.

From 1916 through 1920, to counter Muslim opposition arising from their war against the Turks, the British sought to ally themselves with the Arabs within and north of the Arabian peninsula. In 1916, when he returned to London from his tour of the area for Lord Kitchener, Mark Sykes established the Arab Bureau in Cairo. The Arab Bureau reported to the Foreign Office in London, and most of its expenses were met by Egyptian taxpayers. The Arab Bureau was housed in Cairo's Savoy-Continental Hotel, and its work included collecting intelligence, finding collaborators, and producing propaganda. With its officers posted in different parts of the Arabic-speaking world, this wartime improvisation produced the *Arab Bulletin*, which disseminated intelligence to British officialdom.

The Arab Bureau was more influential during World War I than T. E. Lawrence and the Arab Revolt, whose exploits were heroically depicted by postwar legend makers. Among the colorful British personalities involved with the bureau were Gertrude Bell, a wealthy spinster who believed that she cut a more imposing figure in the East than in the West; Gilbert Clayton, a tough-minded army intelligence officer who ran often ruthless operations; and Reginald Wingate, the chief British soldier in Sudan who continued his proconsular posturing in Cairo. The Arab Bureau saw collaboration with Sharif Husayn ibn Ali and his sons as a way of avoiding all the expensive trappings and personnel associated with the government of India and the British army. Because of its hostility to Zionist settlement in Palestine, those who ran the Arab Bureau have been depicted as romantic partisans of Sharif Husayn and his family, the Hashimites, but the Arab Bureau simply used the Arabs for its own ends, just as the British used the Zionists, the Armenians, and others in the Middle East during and immediately after World War I.

See also BELL, GERTRUDE; CLAYTON, GILBERT; HASHIMITE HOUSE (HOUSE OF HASHIM); KITCHENER, HORATIO HERBERT; SYKES, MARK; WINGATE, REGINALD.

Bibliography

Adelson, Roger. *London and the Invention of the Middle East: Money, Power, and War, 1902–1922.* New Haven, CT: Yale University Press, 1995.

Westrate, Bruce. *The Arab Bureau: British Policy in the Middle East, 1916–1920.* University Park: Pennsylvania State University Press, 1992.

ROGER ADELSON

ARAB CLUB

Early twentieth-century organization that promoted Palestinian nationalism.

The Arab Club (al-Nadi al-Arabi) was originally set up in Damascus as an offshoot of al-Fatat by Palestinian nationalists who moved to the city after it fell to the armies of Field Marshal Viscount Edmund Allenby and Faisal I, king of Iraq, toward the end of World War I. The same organization emerged in Jerusalem in June 1918 and was dominated by younger members of the al-Husayni family, most notably Hajj Amin, who became the president of the Palestine branch of the club. Real power rested in the hands of Damascus-based Palestinians from Nablus. Before the decline of its activities at the end of 1920, the club had over five hundred members, with branches in major Palestinian towns. Although al-Nadi was openly engaged in cultural and social activities, its overriding concerns were political. Under the direction of its Damascus central organization, the club opposed Zionism and called for the unification of Palestine with Syria. The club's principal instruments of mobilization were the mosques, the press, and political activists in Palestinian towns and villages. With the collapse of Faisal's Arab government in Syria in the summer of 1920 and the disintegration of its Arab nationalist lieutenants, the Arab Club lost the two most important sources of its support. It was eventually overtaken by the Arab Executive and the Muslim–Christian Association.

See also FATAT, AL-; HUSAYNI FAMILY, AL-; PALESTINE.

Bibliography

Porath, Yehoshua. *The Emergence of the Palestinian-Arab National Movement, 1918–1929.* London: Cass, 1974.

MUHAMMAD MUSLIH

ARAB COLLEGE OF JERUSALEM

One of the most important Arab educational institutions in Palestine during the British Mandate.

The Arab College of Jerusalem was officially established in 1926 in Bab al-Zahira (Herod's Gate) in Jerusalem, on the premises of the Teacher Training Academy (Dar al-Mu'allimin). In 1935, it was moved to Jabal al-Mukabbir in Jerusalem, where it remained until 1948, when its activities were suspended after the creation of the state of Israel.

The Teacher Training Academy was established by Britain, which conquered Palestine in the winter of 1917/1918. A number of Egyptian teachers were appointed to positions at the academy. In 1919, Khalil al-Sakakini, a Palestinian Christian and a well-known Arab literary figure, was named director. He remained in that office until 1922, when he resigned to protest British policy.

Soon after, Khalil Totah, another Palestinian Christian and an educator with a master's degree from Columbia University, was appointed director. In 1925, he too resigned when the students and teachers went on strike to protest the Balfour Declaration of 1917 (the strike coincided with the visit to Palestine of Britain's Arthur James Balfour). Ahmad al-Samih al-Khalidi then assumed the post of acting principal, and in 1926 he became principal. Al-Khalidi introduced important changes in the curriculum that made it necessary to change the name from Teacher Training Academy to Arab College of Jerusalem (al-Kulliyya al-Arabiyya fi al-Quds). Al-Khalidi remained principal until the college closed in 1948, when about 726,000 Palestinians fled or were expelled from historic Palestine and took refuge in the neighboring Arab countries, most never to return or be allowed to return again.

The Arab College of Jerusalem and its predecessor, the Teacher Training Academy, were open to both Arabs and Jews, but Jews refrained from enrolling; of the twenty-three students enrolled at the academy in 1918, only one was Jewish. As the years went by, only Arab students attended the college; but although the majority of Arab students were Muslim, they also included Christians and Baha'is.

The total number of students in the college rarely exceeded one hundred; most graduating classes numbered around twenty. With such small numbers, one would not expect the college to have a great impact on the cultural life of Palestine. In fact, however, it acquired wide fame in both Palestine and in neighboring Arab countries. This was due primarily to the quality of its students and of the education they received. It was a mark of outstanding performance for a student to be admitted to the college.

The principal of the college recruited his first-year students from the various Arab elementary schools in Palestine; he would choose good students who had finished elementary school, interview them, and then select the best from among them. (There were rare exceptions to this rule: Prince Nayef, of the ruling Hashimite family in Transjordan, and Prince Abd al-Ilah, a Hashimite who became regent during the early 1930s in Iraq, were admitted to the college on the basis of their social status.) Al-Khalidi was the first educator in the Arab world to apply intelligence tests to college applicants.

Once admitted, the students did not generally have to pay tuition. They were taken as boarders, for which they paid a modest stipend. This was necessary, since most students came from poor villages. The curriculum of the college was unique in the Arab countries; it was conceived on the pattern of modern British schools, with special emphasis on English language and literature, Arabic, Latin, and practical training in teaching, in addition to history, geography, science, and mathematics. Upon graduation, the students who proved themselves worthy were sent to continue their education at British universities or at the American University of Beirut. The remaining graduates continued their educations at Arab universities. The college's graduates distinguished themselves in the Arab world as doctors, professors, ambassadors, and ministers.

The teachers at the Arab College were outstanding in science, literature, and the arts; the English-language instructors were, in most cases, British. The college attracted numerous visitors from Arab countries and Britain, including Colonel Bertram Thomas, the explorer of Rub al-Khali in the Arabian Peninsula, and Rudyard Kipling, poet laureate of the British Empire.

See also AMERICAN UNIVERSITY OF BEIRUT (AUB); BALFOUR DECLARATION (1917); KHALIDI, AHMAD AL-SAMIH AL-; RUB AL-KHALI; SAKAKINI, KHALIL AL-.

Bibliography

Abidi, Mahmud. "The Arab College, Jerusalem." *Islamic Quarterly* 19, no. 1–2 (1975): 22–29.

Tibawi, A. L. *Arab Education in Mandatory Palestine.* London: Luzac, 1956.

HISHAM NASHABI

ARAB DEVELOPMENT SOCIETY (ADS)

See ALAMI FAMILY, AL-

ARAB FEMINIST UNION

Pan-Arab women's organization committed to Arab nationalism as well as to women's rights.

Huda al-Sha'rawi (1882–1947) was an early leader in Arab women's rights in Egypt. Her husband, Ali al-Sha'rawi, was the treasurer of the Wafd Party, and during his exile and after his death her interest in the nationalist cause continued. Frustrated with the Wafdist lack of commitment to the feminist cause, she and other women who had worked diligently in the nationalist struggle left the Wafdist Women's Central Committee to form the Egyptian Feminist Union (EFU; al-ittihad al-nisa'i al-misri). While women's rights had been a key component of nationalist and modernist rhetoric prior to independence from Britain, feminist issues were not a part of the Wafdists concern after they officially took office. Feminist groups certainly helped shape reform in Egypt, but their victories were hard fought and their activities sometimes seen as being contrary to national concerns. Efforts to improve the lives of women that had at first been rooted in the struggle against Britain now became a separate endeavor as the major focus shifted toward changing local Egyptian social conventions regarding the status of women.

After its establishment, the EFU sponsored schools, workshops, women's clubs, and training for women. Its goals were to make education available to girls, raise the minimum age of marriage to sixteen, ensure equal employment opportunities, abolish prostitution, and establish orphanages, women's centers, and workshops where unemployed women could earn a living. To familiarize women with the goals of the union, the EFU disseminated a magazine, *Egyptian Woman* (al-Misriyya), which was published in French and Arabic.

The EFU formed ties with the International Alliance of Women (IAW) while its goals were universal women's suffrage. The EFU eventually had difficulty justifying ties with the IAW, whose leadership bore traces of British imperialism. The IAW's refusal to take a stand for the women of Palestine against Zionism marked the end of the EFU–IAW collaboration. In 1944, the EFU was instrumental in establishing the All-Arab Federation of Women, which set an example for the Arab League, developed two years later.

Palestinian women nationalists called upon the EFU to help them in their struggle and in 1944, Sha'rawi and EFU members traveled to Lebanon, Syria, Palestine, and Trans-Jordan, discussing a confederation of Arab feminist unions, and the Arab Feminist Conference convened in Cairo later that year. The goal of consolidating Arab women's struggles led to the formation of the Arab Feminist Union in 1945. In addition to propounding nationalist causes, women from Arab countries challenged patriarchal values, practices, and institutions, and demanded the reform of personal status laws throughout the region.

See also GENDER: GENDER AND THE ECONOMY; GENDER: GENDER AND EDUCATION; GENDER: GENDER AND LAW; LEAGUE OF ARAB STATES; SHAʿRAWI, HUDA AL-.

Bibliography

Badran, Margot. *Feminists, Islam, and Nation: Gender and the Making of Modern Egypt.* Princeton, NJ: Princeton University Press, 1995.

Fernea, Elizabeth Warnock, and Bezirgan, Basima Qattan, eds. "Huda Shaʿrawi, Founder of the Egyptian Women's Movement: Biographical Sketch." In *Middle Eastern Muslim Women Speak,* edited by Elizabeth Warnock Fernea and Basima Qattan Bezirgan. Austin: University of Texas Press, 1977.

Hatem, Mervat. "Egyptian Upper- and Middle-Class Women's Early Nationalist Discourses on National Liberation and Peace in Palestine (1922–1944)." *Women and Politics* 9 no. 3 (1989): 49–69.

Kader, Soha Abdel. *Egyptian Women in a Changing Society, 1899–1987.* Boulder, CO: Lynne Rienner: 1987.

Shaarawi, Huda. *Harem Years: The Memoirs of an Egyptian Feminist,* translated by Margot Badran. New York: Feminist Press, 1987.

MARIA F. CURTIS

ARAB FILM

See FILM

ARAB HIGHER COMMITTEE (PALESTINE)

Umbrella organization formed in 1936 to represent the Palestinian Arabs.

The Arab Higher Committee (AHC) was formed on 25 April 1936 to present Palestinian demands to the British government during the general strike launched by local committees five days earlier. Chaired by Supreme Muslim Council President Hajj Amin al-Husayni, the AHC included the heads of six political parties—Palestine Arab, National Defense, Istiqlal (independence), Reform, National Bloc, and the Youth Congress—and two Christians. The AHC resolved to strike until the British stopped Jewish immigration. It also called for banning land sales to Jews and establishing a national government responsible to an elected assembly. The AHC did not control the local committees or militias, but it moderated their calls to stop paying taxes and to include Arab government officials in the strike. As Britain poured in troops and the strike caused increasing economic hardship, the AHC arranged for Arab rulers to ask the Palestinians to end the strike. The AHC endorsed that appeal on 10 October 1936.

Although not formally recognized by the British, the AHC presented the Palestinian position to the Peel Commission early in 1937. After the AHC rejected that commission's report in July 1937 and a British official was killed in September, the British banned the local committees and the AHC, deported five leaders to the Seychelles, and banned four others from returning to Palestine. Amin al-Husayni and his cousin Jamal al-Husayni fled abroad; they coordinated the subsequent revolt from exile.

Despite the ban, the British let the AHC participate in the London Conference in 1939, freeing the politicians held in the Seychelles but banning Amin al-Husayni. The AHC rejected the subsequent White Paper, fearing that its promise of independence was illusory, but tried to persuade Britain to improve its terms.

The AHC was moribund during World War II. In November 1945 and May 1946 the Arab League reorganized the AHC, giving disproportionate representation to the Husaynis. The AHC testified before the United Nations in spring 1947 but boycotted the United Nations Special Committee on Palestine, 1947 (UNSCOP) mission and was quoted in the *New York Times* as rejecting its partition plan as "impracticable and unjust" (9 Sept. 1947). After the United Nations endorsed partition, the AHC failed to design a Palestinian government or an effective military strategy. It tried to form an All-Palestine Government in Gaza in September 1948, but subsequently lost its leadership role. Amin al-Husayni remained the nominal head, living in exile.

See also ALL-PALESTINE GOVERNMENT; LONDON (ROUNDTABLE) CONFERENCE (1939).

Bibliography

Government of Palestine. *A Survey of Palestine,* Vol. 2. *Jerusalem Government Printer* (1946). Washington, DC: Institute for Palestine Studies, 1991.

Hurewitz, J. C. *The Struggle for Palestine* (1950). New York: Schocken Books, 1976.

Lesch, Ann M. *Arab Politics in Palestine, 1917–1939: The Frustration of a Nationalist Movement.* Ithaca, NY: Cornell University Press, 1979.

Mattar, Philip. *Mufti of Jerusalem: Al-Hajj Amin al-Husayni and the Palestinian National Movement,* rev. edition. New York: Columbia University Press, 1992.

Porath, Yehoshua. *The Palestinian Arab National Movement: From Riots to Rebellion,* Vol. 2, *1929–1939.* Totowa, NJ; London: Frank Cass, 1977.

ANN M. LESCH

ARABIAN AMERICAN OIL COMPANY (ARAMCO)

Petroleum partnership between U.S. firms and Saudi Arabia, 1933–1990.

The origins of the Arabian American Oil Company (ARAMCO) go back to the May 1933 signing of an oil concession agreement between Saudi Arabia's finance minister, Shaykh Abdullah Sulayman, and Lloyd N. Hamilton, an attorney representing Standard Oil of California (SOCAL, now Chevron). Oil exploration was begun three months later by CASOC, the SOCAL subsidiary established to operate the Saudi concession.

At that time, SOCAL was seeking a partner to market the oil it was producing in Bahrain and hoped to produce in Saudi Arabia. In 1936 it transferred 50 percent of the Bahrain Petroleum Company (BAPCO) and 50 percent of CASOC to the Texas Company (Texaco), receiving in return $21 million in cash and deferred payments, plus a half interest in Texaco's marketing facilities east of Suez, which were reorganized as a subsidiary of BAPCO and named CALTEX. On 3 March 1938 CASOC brought in its first commercial oil well, Dammam number 7. On 1 May 1939 King Abd al-Aziz was present when the first oil tanker was loaded with Saudi crude oil and sailed from Ras Tanura.

The development of Saudi Arabia's oil fields was hampered, but not halted, by World War II. In 1940 Italian aircraft bombed Dhahran, where CASOC was headquartered, and the war at sea limited shipping to and from the Perisan Gulf throughout the conflict. During the war, fears of oil depletion sparked U.S. government interest in the resources of Saudi Arabia. Although plans for the U.S. government to buy all or part of CASOC eventually were shelved, in late 1943 steel and other rationed materials were allocated to the company to construct a tank farm, refinery, and marine terminal at Ras Tanura, along with a submarine pipeline to the BAPCO refinery on Bahrain.

CASOC had an unusually close relationship with its host government and its personnel made great efforts to be good guests in the kingdom. CASOC also protected its conception of Saudi interests within its parent corporations, primarily by opposing any move that would restrict production. SOCAL and Texaco were equally committed to a long-term relationship with the kingdom. In January 1944, at the suggestion of State Department adviser Herbert Feis, who had taken part in the negotiations over government participation in CASOC, SOCAL and Texaco changed the name of the operating company to the Arabian American Oil Company (ARAMCO). ARAMCO became the chief conduit communicating Saudi Arabia's interests to its parent corporations and to the U.S. government.

ARAMCO's rapid growth was assured once the Red Line Agreement was canceled and the company was able to acquire two new partners, Standard Oil of New Jersey and Socony Vacuum, in December 1948. The infusion of capital fueled the rapid development of Ras Tanura and the construction of the Trans-Arabian Pipeline. That, along with continuing exploration and development efforts, transformed ARAMCO into the largest oil-producing company in the world. In 1978, forty years after oil was discovered in commercial quantities in Saudi Arabia, ARAMCO's cumulative total production exceeded 30 billion barrels.

The concern for and protection of one another's interests by Saudi Arabia and ARAMCO's parent companies were remarkable. A notable instance of efforts made on behalf of Saudi Arabia's government took place in 1973 when the parent companies mounted an intensive campaign in the United States to convince policymakers and the public that the continued failure of efforts to resolve the Arab-Israel conflict could lead to an oil embargo if another war broke out. The success of the oil embargo imposed by the Organization of Arab Petroleum Exporting Countries (OAPEC) during the Arab-Israel War of 1973 was underpinned by ARAMCO's decision to observe its conditions to the letter. The government of Saudi Arabia supported ARAMCO through its oil-pricing policy. In the early 1980s the government kept prices below the OPEC average, thus enabling the ARAMCO partners to earn huge profits through purchase of cheap Saudi oil, some of which was deliberately produced in excess of the OPEC-established quota.

Before the oil revolution of 1970 to 1973, the ARAMCO parents might have hoped to retain some of their equity in ARAMCO's operations, even though "participation" as a concept was developed by the oil minister of Saudi Arabia and a participation agreement was reached between the Persian Gulf producers and their concession holders in 1972. In June 1974 Saudi Arabia took over 60 percent of ARAMCO under that participation agreement. By the end of the year, the government told the unwilling ARAMCO parents that it wanted 100 percent of the company. In 1976 arrangements for the transfer were worked out; in 1980 the government acquired 100 percent participation interest and almost all of the company's assets.

Under Saudi ownership the company commissioned construction of east-west pipelines to carry crude oil and natural gas liquids from the Eastern Province to Yanbu, on the Red Sea, and in 1984 it acquired its first four supertankers. In 1988 the name of the company was changed to the Saudi Arabian Oil Company, or Saudi Aramco. During the 1990s Saudi Aramco took complete control of its domestic oil industry, expanded the capacity of its pipelines, and added to its transport fleet. It began acquiring overseas interests, including shares in the Ssang Yong Refining Company in South Korea and Petron, a Philippine refiner, and established an overseas marketing company, Star Enterprises, with Texaco.

Saudi Aramco has made every effort to train and employ Saudi nationals. Its first Saudi president,

Ali al-Naimi, took the company's helm in 1989. By 2000 more than 85 percent of its 54,500 workers were Saudi citizens, and most of its contracts went to Saudi-owned or joint venture businesses.

See also ORGANIZATION OF PETROLEUM EXPORTING COUNTRIES (OPEC); RED LINE AGREEMENT; TRANS-ARABIAN PIPELINE.

Bibliography

Anderson, Irvine H. *Aramco, the United States, and Saudi Arabia: A Study of the Dynamics of Foreign Oil Policy, 1933–1950.* Princeton, NJ: Princeton University Press, 1981.

Barger, Thomas C., and Barger, Timothy J. *Out in the Blue: Letters from Arabia, 1937–1940.* Vista, CA: Selwa Press, 2000.

Miller, Aaron David. *Search for Security: Saudi Arabian Oil and American Foreign Policy.* Chapel Hill: University of North Carolina Press, 1980.

Nawwab, Ismail I.; Speers, Peter C., and Hoye, Paul F. *ARAMCO and Its World: Arabia and the Middle East.* Dhahran, Saudi Arabia: ARAMCO, 1980.

Tétreault, Mary Ann. *Revolution in the World Petroleum Market.* Westport, CT: Greenwood Press, 1985.

Yergin, Daniel. *The Prize: The Epic Quest for Oil, Money, and Power.* New York: Simon and Schuster, 1991.

MARY ANN TÉTREAULT

ARABIAN GULF

See PERSIAN (ARABIAN) GULF

ARABIAN HORSES

The Arabian horse is a particular breed of horse that likely evolved during the prehistoric period from Central Asian regions, eventually finding its home in Arabia and Egypt, perhaps introduced into Egypt by the Hyksos.

The existence of the Arabian horse in early periods is indicated by inscriptions found on the walls of ancient Egyptian temples. Its type is evident in the concave head, refined features, and arched tail carriage.

The modern Arabian horse emerged from the Arabian Peninsula after the period of Islamic conquest in the seventh century. Arab tribes produced horses whose beauty evolved from traits acquired from life in an unforgiving desert: large eyes, strong bones, and great heart and lung capacity. These traits proved vital attributes in their use in military ventures and eventually in the founding of the modern English thoroughbred racehorse.

Arabian horse pedigrees were items of extreme importance to their Arab breeders. Oral transmission of a horse's history took place in front of witnesses who swore to its accuracy. The importance of Arabian horses held such high priority that they were used as gifts between tribal leaders, rulers of city-states, and later, heads of state, in diplomatic exchanges. Rulers such as Muhammad Ali of nineteenth-century Egypt sent expeditions into Arabia to acquire elite horses for his armies and his personal stables. Many travelers throughout the centuries noted the esteem in which Arabian horses were held.

Modern appreciation of the Arabian horse manifests itself in a worldwide network of Arabian horse breeders and owners who provide educational forums and exhibitions of their prized horses. They sometimes compete with one another in horse shows, or simply appreciate the unique heritage of their fine animals.

Bibliography

Bulliet, Richard W. *The Camel and the Wheel.* New York: Columbia University Press, 1990.

LISA M. LACY

ARABIAN MISSION

Mission for Protestant proselytization in Arabia; established in 1889.

The mission was founded by James Cantine and Samuel Zwemer, students at the New Brunswick Theological Seminary, under the guidance of Professor John G. Lansing. Initially independent, it came under the Reformed (Dutch) Church's Board of Foreign Missions in 1893 but remained nondenominational.

By 1902, missions had been established at Basra, Bahrain, and Muscat, and in 1910 another was started in Kuwait. Despite the distribution of a considerable amount of Christian literature, the missionaries' objective of winning converts made little headway against the conservative Islam of Arabia. Many people were reached, however, through the work of dedicated teachers and medical doctors and received modern education and health services for the first time. Between 1889 and 1938, eighty missionaries went to Arabia, and, in the years between the world wars, tens of thousands of patients were treated each year in the Arabian Mission's seven hospitals.

The missionaries' work left a legacy of goodwill that has persisted to this day, and the sons of missionaries later played a significant role as American diplomats in the Arab world.

Bibliography

Mason, Alfred De Witt, and Barny, Frederick J. *History of the Arabian Mission, 1855–1923.* New York: Board of Foreign Missions, Reformed Church in America, 1926.

Zwemer, Samuel M., and Cantine, James. *The Golden Milestone: Reminiscences of Pioneer Days Fifty Years Ago in Arabia.* New York: Fleming H. Revell, 1938.

MALCOLM C. PECK

ARABIAN PENINSULA

Great peninsula of southwest Asia bounded by the Persian/Arabian Gulf to the east and the Red Sea to the west.

The Arabian Peninsula is about 1,300 miles (2,090 km) wide at its maximum breadth and about 1,200 miles (1,900 km) in length along the Red Sea. It is bounded at the north by Jordan and Iraq. It is fertile in some of the coastal regions, but the center is an arid plateau, called in ancient times Arabia Deserta (not to be confused with the Arabian Desert of Egypt, east of the Nile River to the Gulf of Suez). No rivers exist in the peninsula's arid region, but there are many short wadis and a few oases. The Arabian Peninsula is an important region for petroleum production, and the Gulf states of the peninsula that produce petroleum include Bahrain (islands in the Gulf), Kuwait, Oman, Qatar, the United Arab Emirates (UAE), Yemen, and the large central kingdom of Saudi Arabia. The Arabian Sea is that part of the Indian Ocean between India on the east and the peninsula on the west.

The people of the peninsula belong to Semitic tribes; they are mainly Arab whose consolidation was begun by the prophet Muhammad. The consolidation was extended after his death in 632 C.E. but collapsed into tribal warfare during the 700s, after the disintegration of the Umayyad caliphate (661–750). Arabia was then generally dominated by the Mamluks until the early 1500s, then by the Ottoman Empire—but various parts were virtually independent—al-Hasa, Oman, Yemen, and Najd. The Wahhabi movement of Islam began in Arabia, centered in Najd, where resistance against the Ottoman Turks was organized in the eighteenth and nineteenth centuries. Reconquered for the Turks by Muhammad Ali Pasha of Egypt (1811–1820), the Wahhabi Empire was reestablished from 1843 to 1865, but internal strife continued between tribes and Islamic sects. During World War I, the British officer T. E. Lawrence (of Arabia) directed a resistance effort here with Amir Faisal and his followers against the Ottoman Empire. In the early 1920s and 1930s, a gradual consolidation was effected by Ibn Saʿud into the kingdom of Saudi Arabia.

See also ARAB; KUWAIT; MAMLUKS; MUHAMMAD; OMAN; PETROLEUM, OIL, AND NATURAL GAS; QATAR; SAUDI ARABIA; UNITED ARAB EMIRATES.

Bibliography

Netton, Ian Richard, ed. *Arabia and the Gulf: From Traditional Society to Modern States.* Totowa, NJ: Rowman and Littlefield, 1986.

MARTHA IMBER-GOLDSTEIN

ARABIAN PENINSULA: TRIBES

See TRIBES AND TRIBALISM: ARABIAN PENINSULA

ARABIC

Language of Islam, the Qur'an, and about 185 million people.

Arabic is a Semitic language and the major language of the modern Middle East; it is spoken by an estimated 185 million people. It spread throughout the region during the seventh century C.E., replacing in the Levant Aramaic—as well as non-Semitic languages—as Islam began its conquest and conversion. The Arabic language went as far east as Iran

and as far west as all of North Africa, crossing Gibraltar to the Iberian Peninsula in the early eighth century.

Arabic is related to two Semitic languages still used in the Middle East: chiefly Hebrew in its ancient liturgical and modern (nineteenth- and twentieth-century) revival forms, but also Amharic, the official language of Ethiopia. Arabic is classified as South Central Semitic, sharing features not only with Amharic but also with the ancient languages Geez and Akkadian. Some countries that are now home to predominantly Arabic speakers also have speakers of traditional, non-Semitic languages, such as Berber, Nubian, Kurdish, and Coptic.

Arabic has a special relationship to Islam; it is considered the divine language of Allah by Muslims. The language has therefore been constrained by reverence, with the liturgical or classical Arabic (called *Fusha,* the "purest" style) remaining basically unchanged since the revelation of the Qur'an in the seventh century. Today's spoken Arabic is, however, considered corrupt, with diverse local vernacular versions used throughout the region.

Arabic script is written in phonetic symbols similar to Hebrew letters in that each symbol represents a letter and words are written and read from right to left. A feature of Arabic script is its use as an Islamic art form, since there is a religious pronouncement against rendering figures in art. Such calligraphy decorates books, buildings, banners, and jewelry; most words are so stylized that they cannot be read, but as they are often taken from the Qur'an, their sources are recognized by most Muslims.

Arabic Dialects

The most noticeable linguistic situation in the Arab world is termed *diglossia,* which literally means "twin vocabularies," referring to the fact that every speaker of Arabic knows a local spoken vernacular and learns the formal *Fusha* in addition to it. Because of the historical spread of Islam and, with it, Arabic, the language has today been spoken for more than 1,300 years over a wide territory that includes parts of Europe, North Africa, and the Levant. Despite the freezing of the literary grammatical style of Arabic, the colloquial versions, like all spoken languages, changed unfettered by normalized rules or classical prescriptions of correctness. Often speakers from one end of the region cannot understand speakers from another without difficulty, although they can understand the versions spoken in adjacent areas.

At the same time, Arabic is said to be the uniting factor of the modern Arab world—the one institution all Arabs share regardless of the cultures or subcultures of the countries they now inhabit. Where Arabic is the nation's official language, the classical style is used for government, religion, and schooling. No pressure seems to exist for adopting a type of "Esperanto" Arabic, or even agreeing on one dialect as the standard for all sophisticated communication.

With the advent of radio, television, and the broadcasting of news in literary Arabic, comprehension of that form has increased. Knowledge of other dialects has also been spread by the motion picture industry. For example, Egyptian Arabic (Cairene) has been used in the scripts of many movies, and television soap operas produced in Cairo have helped to familiarize many non-Egyptians with that dialect.

Of the large number of Arabic dialects, only a few have been given names and studied in any detail: Egyptian and Iraqi Arabic refer to the colloquial dialects of the educated classes of Cairo and Baghdad, respectively. Media broadcasts from country capitals have also become comprehensible to rural and nomadic speakers with access to radios, televisions, and video- and audiocassette recorders. Uneducated or rural vernacular dialects differ, though, sometimes dramatically, because many have developed in relative isolation. Nevertheless, speakers of similar backgrounds understand one another over short geographic distances.

The differences between dialects are mostly confined to vocabulary and the shifting or loss of some sounds. The Egyptian use of *gim* for *jim* or even *djim* is one of the best examples of a sound shift. Greater shifts have affected the entire sound of a dialect; for example, in North Africa, most short vowels have been lost and the stress of most words moved from the medial to the last syllable. This produces many words that start with consonant clusters. In

contrast, the dialects of Cairo and those farther to the east have maintained most of the short vowels and lost mostly those at the end of the word, keeping the stress, as in *Fusha*, on the next-to-last syllable. Consonant clusters are generally limited to word-final positions and are no more than two consonants in length. In addition, word borrowing from other languages has occurred in both *Fusha* and the dialects. In some cases older Arabic words are used to meet the needs of modern life, but in others a borrowed word is used—the word for "telephone" might be written *hatif* ("one who calls out"), and it might be spoken as *telefon*.

Arabic-language academies exist—in Cairo, Damascus, and Baghdad—each attempting to minimize the use of borrowings. They publish lists of desired usages, but it is difficult to legislate language change.

Classical Arabic

Fusha, the high style, is characterized by a complicated system of conjugations that change the case of words, which are composed of three consonants (*s-l-m*, for example). Using prefixes, infixes, and suffixes, as well as a change of vocalization according to rules, is basic to all Semitic languages—and formal Arabic demonstrates this practice to a greater extent than any of the others. None of these case markings has survived in the dialects; however, the Qur'an and children's books are published with them written in place so that they will not be read aloud incorrectly. Nevertheless, even the pronunciation of *Fusha* varies with the colloquial background of the speaker. *Fusha* is used in all writing that does not attempt to represent casual speech. In most novels the characters speak in *Fusha*, but cartoon characters speak in vernacular Arabic, as do actors in most modern plays, and some modern novels are written in dialect. The Arabic version of *Sesame Street* uses *Fusha* because it is the language style that children must learn to read.

Rise and Development of Arabic

The early history of *Fusha* is not clear. Before the appearance of Islam there are few traces of Arabic in the Arabian Peninsula, but it is clear from the language of the Qur'an that an oral tradition of poetical style was well established before the revelation of that holy book. The language of the Qur'an is not just a reflection of the dialect of the Hijaz (western Arabia, the original center of Islam); it is a style reflecting the koine of the poets, used for sophisticated performances of oral poetry at the markets to which the nomads came at least once a year. It is probably a combination of both language usages, which is why it is said to have been unique and miraculous at the time of Muhammad's reception of it.

Arabic script was already in use before the codification of the Qur'an, but it was unified and provided with diacritical marks to resolve ambiguities in the holy text. As the Islamic conquests began in the seventh and eighth centuries, the language of formal usage was being standardized by grammarians in the towns of Basra and Kufa (Iraq). By the ninth and tenth centuries, this linguistic work was completed, and these rules became the standard by which to measure all future literary Arabic output. To this day, "correct" Arabic is measured by these rules, and they are maintained in the belief that to change them is to offend Allah, who produced them.

See also ARABIC SCRIPT; CALLIGRAPHY; HEBREW; ISLAM; QUR'AN; SEMITIC LANGUAGES.

Bibliography

Bateson, Mary C. *Arabic Language Handbook.* Washington, DC: Georgetown University Press, 1967.

Bergstrasser, Gotthelf. *Introduction to the Semitic Languages,* translated by Peter T. Daniels. Winona Lake, IN: Eisenbrauns, 1983.

Killean, Carolyn G. "Classical Arabic." In *Current Trends in Linguistics,* Vol. 6: *Linguistics in South West Asia and North Africa,* edited by Thomas A. Sebeok. The Hague, Netherlands: Mouton, 1971.

Omar, Margaret. *From Eastern to Western Arabic.* Washington, DC: Government Printing Office, 1974.

Wright, C. *Grammar of the Arabic Language,* 2 vols. Cambridge, U.K.: Cambridge University Press, 1971.

CAROLYN KILLEAN

ARABIC SCRIPT

Used to represent the Arabic language, as well as certain non-Arabic and non-Semitic languages.

The Arabic script is an alphabet in which each written symbol represents a single sound. It is Semitic and, thus, a near relative of the Hebrew alphabet but also historically related to the Roman alphabet. The Arabic alphabet is second only to the Roman in use today. It is used by over 185 million first-language speakers of Arabic. As the medium in which the Qur'an was revealed and much Islamic learning was recorded, Arabic is a second or liturgical language for Muslims worldwide. In addition, the Arabic alphabet has been adapted for use in other non-Arabic and non-Semitic languages, among them Persian, Urdu, and Ottoman Turkish.

The Arabic script is written from right to left. It is cursive, so that each letter in a word is joined to the following letter (exceptions to this rule are the letters *alif, dāl, dhāl, rā, zāy,* and *wāw*). The alphabet is consonantal, consisting of twenty-eight consonants and semivowels. Other signs or diacritical marks indicate short vowels and other sound changes, but these do not typically appear in written texts. In theory, at least, the lack of written vowels causes a certain ambiguity when it comes to deciphering the written word. To take one example, the word *ktb* can be read in several ways: *kataba,* "he

Arabic Alphabet

Name	Letter	Name	Letter
'alif	ع	t ā'	ط
bā'	ب	ẓā'	ظ
tā'	ت	'ayn	ع
tha'	ث	ghayn	غ
jīm	ج	fā'	ف
hā'	ح	qāf	ق
khā'	خ	kāf	ك
dāl	د	lām	ل
dhāl	ذ	mūm	م
rā'	ر	nūn	ن
zāy	ز	hā'	ه
sīn	س	wāw	و
shīn	ش	yā'	ى
ṣād	ص		
ḍād	ض		

TABLE BY GGS INFORMATION SERVICES, THE GALE GROUP

wrote"; *kutiba,* "it was written"; *kattaba,* "he dictated"; *kuttiba,* "he was made to take dictation"; *ktab,* "[the act of] writing"; *kutub,* "books." In practice, however, context plays a considerable role in clarifying meaning. In a sentence such as "he wrote five *ktb* on this topic, *ktb* could only mean "books." Where lack of ambiguity is necessary or desirable, as in the written text of the Qur'an, in classical Islamic or literary texts, and in writings for children, the diacritical marks are written as a matter of course.

The Arabic alphabet is not simply a vehicle for written communication but is the medium for one of the most highly developed art forms of the Arab and Islamic world, the art of calligraphy. For the Arabic language, calligraphy recognizes two principal types of Arabic script, *kufi* and *naskhi,* where the former is generally more square in shape and the latter more rounded. This binary division, however, hardly reflects the tremendous diversity of scripts, from the tiny Turkish *ghubari,* or "dust," script, to the large *jali* scripts that decorate the walls of certain mosques, from the severely "squared" *kufi,* with right angles rather than curves, to the elaborate "tied" scripts, in which the capitals are linked to form knotted arabesques.

In the Arab world and elsewhere, Arabic script is a powerful symbol of ethnic and religious affiliation. Its significance does not make it inviolable, however. The Arabic alphabet was replaced by the Roman alphabet in Turkey in 1928 and by the Cyrillic alphabet in a number of republics in the former Soviet Central Asia, to name two examples. Proposals to Romanize the Arabic alphabet in the Arab world have been advanced since the late nineteenth century. To date, however, only in Malta, which was conquered by the Sicilians in the eleventh century, is any variety of Arabic regularly written in other than the Arabic script.

ELIZABETH M. BERGMAN

ARAB–ISRAEL CONFLICT

Conflict over the post–World War I mandated territory of Palestine.

In Palestine, the conflict began at the end of the nineteenth century, more than fifty years before the state of Israel was established in 1948. The crux of the conflict has been between Jewish nationalism

(called Zionism) and Palestinian Arab nationalism for political control over the area that, in the peace settlement after World War I (1914–1918), became the League of Nations mandated territory of Palestine—held by Britain from 1922 to 1948. When Israel was established, the struggle became known as the Arab–Israel conflict.

Palestine before 1948

Soon after the first late-nineteenth-century Eastern European Jewish settlers arrived in Palestine (whose population in 1882 consisted of about 450,000 Arabs and 25,000 Jews), they clashed with local Arabs over Jewish-owned land and grazing rights. By the 1920s, Palestinian opposition to Jewish settlement and to the Zionist movement became widespread because Palestinians feared that continued Jewish immigration would lead to their domination or expulsion. During 1920, 1921, 1929, 1933, and from 1936 to 1939, Palestinian nationalist demonstrations led to violence. Palestinians demanded that the British authorities halt further Jewish immigration into Palestine; that sale of Arab and government lands to Jews cease; and that immediate steps be initiated toward granting Arab Palestinian independence.

The 1929 riots in Jerusalem arose over prayer rights at the Temple Mount, site of the sacred Western (or Wailing) Wall, which is believed by pious Jews to be the last remnant of the Second Temple (destroyed by the Romans in 70 C.E.). Because the wall adjoins the third most sacred site in Islam, the Haram al-Sharif (Sacred Enclosure, containing two important mosques), it has been a source of continuing conflict. Many Muslims believed then and continue to believe that Jews seek to destroy the mosques and replace them with a new temple.

By 1936 Palestine's Jewish community, the Yishuv, increased to 384,000, mainly from European immigration; the number of Jewish cities and towns, industries, and agricultural settlements extended widely through the country, raising fears among Palestinians that they would soon become a minority in their native land. The 1936 to 1939 uprising, called the Palestine Arab Revolt, galvanized most of the Palestinian community to oppose the British authorities, and the Yishuv Zionist attempts to assuage Palestinian fears were unsuccessful. Even proposals by a small group of Jewish intellectuals in favor of establishing a binational Arab–Jewish state based on political parity between the two communities received only a faint response from Arab leaders. Both Arabs and Jews rejected proposals by the 1937 British Royal Commission under Lord Peel (the so-called Peel Commission) to partition Palestine between its two communities, although many Zionist leaders accepted the partition principle, if not specific details of the Peel plan. Massive British force ended the Arab revolt in 1939, just as Britain became involved in World War II (1939–1945). Focus on Europe then kept the Arab–Jewish conflict quiescent until 1946.

Partition

With international postwar pressure on Britain to remove all restrictions on Jewish immigration and land purchases in Palestine—because of the Holocaust in Europe—and calls for for the establishment of a Jewish commonwealth, tensions between the Yishuv, the mandatory government, and the Arab community brought Palestine to the brink of civil war. Britain appealed to the United Nations, which recommended that Palestine be partitioned into Arab and Jewish states with an international enclave containing the Jerusalem area. The mainstream of the Zionist movement accepted the proposal (but a nationalist minority continued to insist on a Jewish state on both banks of the Jordan River). Palestinians, supported by leaders throughout the Arab world, rejected the principle of partition. Clashes that occurred between Palestinians demonstrating against violation of their right to self-determination and Jews celebrating their coming independence soon turned into a full-scale civil war. Since Britain's mandate was to end on 14 May 1948, a disorderly withdrawal of British troops began from disputed areas. By May 1948, as the Yishuv organized its military forces, many Palestinians retreated, fled, or were expelled from territory held by the new state of Israel despite military assistance from the Arab world, which continued until 1949. After Israel was established on 15 May 1948, the term *Palestinians* referred to members of the Arab community while Palestinian Jews were called *Israelis*.

Arab–Israel Wars

The first Arab–Israel war lasted until Egypt, Lebanon, Jordan, and Syria signed armistice agreements with Israel in 1949. As a result of that war, Israel was able to extend its frontiers approximately 2,000 square miles from the UN partition borders to those of the armistice agreements. More than 700,000 Palestinians became refugees, unable to return to their homes and lands, which were confiscated by Israel; most lived in refugee camps in the surrounding Arab countries, but some moved to North Africa, Europe, and North America. Territory intended as part of the Arab state in the UN partition plan became controlled by Israel, Jordan, and Egypt. Jerusalem was divided between Jordan and Israel.

Since the end of the first Arab–Israel war there has been continuing dispute between Israel and the surrounding countries over borders, refugee rights to return or to compensation, the status of Jerusalem, the equitable division of Jordan River waters, and Arab recognition of Israel. The United Nations dealt with these issues through several organizations. An armistice regime was established with the United Nations Truce Supervision Organization to oversee the 1949 agreements between Israel and Egypt, Lebanon, Jordan, and Syria. In 1948 the United Nations Conciliation Commission for Palestine was established to achieve a peaceful settlement by dealing with the refugee problem, Middle East economic development, and equitable distribution of water resources. But the Arab states refused to enter direct negotiations unless Israel withdrew to the UN partition borders and permitted the refugees to return. U.S. and UN proposals for refugee resettlement in the context of the broad economic development of the Middle East were also rejected without the resolution of the other key issues.

Opinion in the Arab world was so strongly anti-Israel that defeats sparked antigovernment uprisings in several countries and led to the assassination of several Arab political leaders. Egypt's setbacks in the 1948 war, for example, contributed to its 1952 revolution. In Israel, tensions heightened by 1955, when Egypt's new ruler Gamal Abdel Nasser (who had led the coup that overthrew Egypt's monarchy) was perceived as a growing threat, and relations with Egypt deteriorated with an increase of infiltrations and attacks into Israel by Palestinians from Egyptian-held Gaza. The situation sparked an arms race; Egypt acquired large amounts of military equipment from the USSR and the Eastern bloc, while Israel obtained advanced aircraft from France.

By 1956, uneasy relations between Egypt and Israel became part of the larger conflict between Egypt and the West over control of the Suez Canal. Israel formed a secret alliance with Britain and France to overthrow Nasser after Egypt nationalized the Suez Canal in July 1956. As Israel attacked Egypt in October, Britain and France occupied the northern Canal Zone. This tripartite scheme was stymied by U.S. and Soviet intervention at the United Nations and by Moscow's threat of military action to aid Egypt. In November 1956 the UN General Assembly established the United Nations Emergency Force (UNEF) to supervise the withdrawal of the invaders' troops and to act as a peacekeeping body between Egypt and Israel. Egypt–Israel frontiers were relatively quiet until the 1967 Arab–Israel War. But incidents also erupted along other Israeli borders. Continued Palestinian refugee infiltration and guerrilla attacks from Jordan plus clashes with Syria over Israeli projects to divert the Jordan River created obstacles to a peace settlement. In 1960, the Arab League (officially, the League of Arab States) called Israel's Jordan River diversion scheme "an act of aggression" and in 1963 adopted its own diversion blueprint, which would have greatly diminished Israel's access to water.

1967 Arab–Israel War

The tensions caused by the Jordan River dispute, the escalation of border incidents, the Middle East arms race, and increasingly bitter rhetoric led to several border clashes in 1967. When President Nasser threatened to blockade Israel's passage through the Strait of Tiran (at the southeast Sinai Peninsula), ordered UNEF to leave the Sinai, and massed his troops on the border, Israel's leaders responded with a preemptive strike in June 1967 against Egypt. After firing on Israel-controlled Jerusalem, Jordan also became involved, and Israel mounted an attack against Syrian positions on the Golan Heights several days later. After six days Israel emerged from the 1967 Arab–Israel War as the dominant power, with the Arab states thrown into disarray. Israel had conquered the Sinai Peninsula and the Gaza Strip from Egypt, the Golan Heights from Syria, and East Jerusalem and the West Bank from Jordan. The war intensified competition in the Middle East between the United States, which supported Israel, and the Soviet Union, which backed Egypt, Syria, and Iraq. It led to further escalation of the arms race, Egypt's closing of the Suez Canal, and an additional 300,000 West Bank and Golan Heights refugees, who fled to Jordan and to Syria.

Although defeated, the Arab states refused direct negotiations with Israel, demanding that Israel first withdraw to the 1967 armistice lines and permit the return of refugees. Efforts to end the conflict through the United Nations were blocked by disagreements between the United States and the Soviet Union. The Soviets supported resolutions condemning Israel and called for return of the territories. The United States supported Israel's insistence that territory be returned only through direct negotiations and the signing of a peace agreement.

The stalemate was somewhat eased by UN Security Council compromise Resolution 242 in November 1967, which called for "withdrawal of Israeli armed forces from territories" occupied in the war, termination of belligerency, "just settlement of the refugee problem," and "the need to work for a just and lasting peace." The parties disagreed over interpretation of Resolution 242. The Arab side insisted it meant Israel's withdrawal from all territory seized in 1967; Israel and its supporters insisted that the resolution did not mean total withdrawal. Most Arab states no longer demanded that Israel withdraw to the 1947 partition lines, only to the 1949 armistice frontiers; they also recognized that a just solution of the refugee problem would have to include alternatives to total repatriation of the Palestinians and their descendants to their original homes, since twenty years had passed.

After the 1967 war, Palestinian nationalists brought several guerrilla factions into the Palestine Liberation Organization (PLO), an umbrella group established in 1964. Israeli and Palestinian forces clashed along the borders, and Palestinian guerrillas attacked Israeli civilians at home and abroad. After King Hussein ibn Talal of Jordan put down a Palestinian-initiated civil war and drove guerrilla factions from the protection of his country in September 1970, several factions set up bases in south Lebanon to attack northern Israel.

1973 Arab–Israel War

With the failure of diplomacy, Egypt and Syria attempted to regain territories lost in 1967 through a two-front surprise attack on Israel in October 1973.

Initially, Egypt recaptured large sectors of the Sinai, and Syria retook the Golan but within a few days, Israel recovered the territory. Nevertheless, the 1973 Arab–Israel War shattered the myth of Israeli invincibility. Following a formalistic two-day conference in Geneva in December 1973, the United States initiated a step-by-step process that led to disengagement agreements in which Egypt regained parts of Sinai and Syria reoccupied al-Kuneitra in the Golan region.

In November 1977 the visit to Jerusalem by Egypt's President Anwar al-Sadat made direct negotiations possible—this marked a new phase in Arab–Israel relations. As the talks faltered, U.S. president Jimmy Carter convened a conference in September 1978 of Egypt's and Israel's leaders at the presidential retreat at Camp David, Maryland, where they eventually agreed on Israel's withdrawal from Sinai and autonomy for the Palestinians. After some communication difficulties, but the continued mediation of President Carter, a peace treaty was signed by Egypt and Israel in Washington, D.C., on 26 March 1979 that provided for mutual recognition and normalization of relations.

Relations remained strained by differing interpretations of the Camp David Accords and the treaty terms and by continued hostilities between other Arab states and Israel. Attempts to involve local Palestinian representatives in negotiations for autonomy led nowhere. In June 1982 Israel invaded Lebanon to uproot an entrenched PLO, force Lebanon into a peace agreement, and remove Syria's troops from the country. Only one of these objectives was realized: PLO headquarters and its infrastructure were uprooted (and relocated to other Arab states). After several months of Israeli occupation, Lebanese militia attacks forced Israel to withdraw to a narrow southern border strip—an Israeli "security zone"—that Israel continued to occupy until 2001.

Intifada and Negotiations in the 1980s and 1990s

Twenty years of Israeli occupation of Gaza and the West Bank caused increasing unrest among the Palestinian inhabitants, which led to a major uprising, or intifada, in December 1987. Unlike previous occasions, demonstrations did not die down but escalated into a full-scale civil resistance. Palestin-

ian demands to end the occupation galvanized the PLO to revise its political program, and in November 1988, it proclaimed an independent Palestinian state and for the first time accepted UN Resolution 242, recognized Israel, and renounced terrorism.

International attention on the intifada and the Palestine problem and the Persian Gulf crisis that led to war in 1990 and 1991 also led to the Middle East Peace Conference convened in Madrid, Spain, in October 1991 by the United States and the Soviet Union. The conference initiated a series of bilateral, direct negotiations between Israel and the Syrian, Lebanese, and Jordanian-Palestinian delegations, with multilateral discussions on Middle Eastern refugees, security, environment, economic development, and water. After secret negotiations in Oslo, Norway, in September 1993 Israel and the PLO signed an agreement providing for mutual recognition as well as Palestinian self-government to begin in Gaza and the town of Jericho in the West Bank during a five-year transition period.

Progress in negotiations between Israel and the PLO led to improvement of relations between Israel and Jordan, culminating in a peace treaty between them in October 1994. However, direct negotiations with Syria collapsed over differences on the border along the Lake Tiberias shore. The Oslo negotiation with the PLO was followed by agreements providing for redeployment of Israeli forces from parts of the West Bank and Gaza and establishing Palestinian self-government, but each side charged the other with violating the agreements, and violent clashes arose. An attempt by the United States to resolve the conflict at a tripartite summit at Camp David in July 2000 failed, leading to further violence. A clash at the Temple Mount in Jerusalem in September 2000 was followed by Palestinian suicide bombings in Israel and retaliations that caused thousands of Israeli and Palestinian casualties and reoccupation of Palestinian territory. Dispute continued over Israeli occupation of the West Bank and Gaza and Jewish settlement there, the refugee "right of return," the future of Jerusalem, borders, and security.

See also ARAB–ISRAEL WAR (1948); ARAB–ISRAEL WAR (1967); CAMP DAVID ACCORDS (1978); CARTER, JIMMY; GAZA STRIP; GOLAN

HEIGHTS; GULF CRISIS (1990–1991); HOLO-
CAUST; HUSSEIN IBN TALAL; INTIFADA
(1987–1991); ISLAM; ISRAEL: OVERVIEW;
JERUSALEM; JORDAN RIVER; LEAGUE OF ARAB
STATES; NASSER, GAMAL ABDEL; PALESTINE;
PALESTINE ARAB REVOLT (1936–1939);
PALESTINE LIBERATION ORGANIZATION
(PLO); PEEL COMMISSION REPORT (1937);
SADAT, ANWAR AL-; SINAI PENINSULA; SUEZ
CANAL; TIRAN, STRAIT OF; UNITED NATIONS
AND THE MIDDLE EAST; UNITED NATIONS
CONCILIATION COMMISSION FOR PALESTINE
(UNCCP); UNITED NATIONS EMERGENCY
FORCE; UNITED NATIONS TRUCE SUPERVI-
SION ORGANIZATION (UNTSO); WEST BANK;
YISHUV; ZIONISM.

Bibliography

Bickerton, Ian J., and Klausner, Carla L. *A Concise History
of the Arab–Israeli Conflict,* 4th edition. Upper Saddle
River, NJ: Prentice Hall, 2002.

Elmusa, Sharif S. *Water Conflict: Economics, Politics, Law, and
the Palestian-Israeli Water Resources.* Washington, DC: Institute for Palestine Studies, 1997.

Gerner, Deborah J. *One Land, Two Peoples: The Conflict over
Palestine,* 2d edition. Boulder, CO: Westview Press,
1994.

Laqueur, Walter, and Rubin, Barry, eds. *The Israel-Arab
Reader: A Documentary History of the Middle East Conflict,* 6th
revised edition. New York and London, Penguin
Books, 2001.

Lesch, Ann M., and Tschirgi, Dan. *Origins and Development
of the Arab–Israeli Conflict.* Westport, CT: Greenwoood
Press, 1998.

Morris, Benny. *Righteous Victims: A History of the Zionist–Arab
Conflict, 1881–1999.* New York: Alfred A. Knopf,
1999.

Shapira, Anita. *Land and Power: The Zionist Resort to Force,
1881–1948.* Stanford, CA: Stanford University
Press, 1999.

Shlaim, Avi. *The Iron Wall: Israel and the Arab World since 1948.*
New York: W. W. Norton, 1999.

DON PERETZ

ARAB–ISRAELI GENERAL ARMISTICE AGREEMENTS (1949)

*United Nations–sponsored armistice agreements con-
cluded in 1949 between the state of Israel and four Arab
states.*

Between February and July 1949, General Armistice
Agreements (GAAs) were signed between the state
of Israel and four Arab states: Egypt, Jordan,
Lebanon, and Syria. Iraq, which had participated in
the war with an expeditionary force, did not conclude an agreement since it did not have a common
border with Israel; its forces just left the arena.
All negotiations were mediated on behalf of the
United Nations (UN) by Ralph Bunche, whose
achievement earned him the 1949 Nobel Peace Prize.
These agreements put an end to the Arab–Israel War
of 1948. The failure of the UN Conciliation Commission for Palestine to achieve more comprehensive peace treaties created a de facto situation that
made the General Armistice Agreements into quasi-
permanent arrangements that regulated the relations between Israel and its Arab neighbors until the
1967 war.

The first GAA was signed by Col. Mohammad
Ibrahim Sayf el-Din for Egypt and Walter Eytan for
Israel on the Greek island of Rhodes on 24 February 1949. It provided, among other stipulations,
for large demilitarized zones in the Nitzana-Abu-
Agayla sector. On the other hand, it did not specify the rights of Israeli shipping through the Suez
Canal and the Straits of Tiran. Israel considered the
blocking of these waterways incompatible with international law and the armistice provisions and
brought the Suez blockade to the attention of the
UN Security Council on several occasions. But neither the support received in the form of UN Security Council resolution 95 (1951) nor the military
achievements of the Sinai campaign of 1956 were
successful in changing Egypt's view, and the blockade in the Canal persisted for thirty years.

The controversy over the demilitarized zones
caused much irritation and warfare, especially after
Israel decided to establish, on its side of the Nitzana
zone, settlements that the Egyptians considered
military strongholds. In the aftermath of the 1956
Suez–Sinai War, Israel considered annulling its
GAA with Egypt, but this failed to receive international recognition. The positioning of the UN
Emergency Force along the demarcation lines after
1957 introduced a new factor into Egypt–Israel relations, in effect superseding application of the
Egypt–Israel GAA. Israel's conquest of the Sinai
Peninsula in June 1967 rendered the GAA inoper-

With UN mediator Ralph Bunche (second from left at far side of table) and his associates in attendance, Israeli representative Rafael Eytan (at right) signed the armistice agreement between Israel and Egypt on 2 February 1949 on the Greek island of Rhodes. Three similar agreements between Israel and Lebanon, Jordan, and Syria were signed by July, ending their 1948–1949 war. © BETTMANN/CORBIS. REPRODUCED BY PERMISSION.

ative, while the return of Sinai to Egypt in 1982 in accordance with the 1979 Egypt–Israel peace treaty resulted in its final, legal termination.

The Israel–Lebanon GAA was signed by Lt. Col. Mordekhai Makleff for Israel and Lt. Col. Tawfiq Salim for Lebanon in Ra's Naqura on 23 March 1949. Israel's forces, having retreated from parts of southern Lebanon that they had occupied in the summer of 1948, agreed to fix the armistice demarcation lines along the old international borders and thus introduced greater stability to Israeli–Lebanese relations for more than twenty years. However, after "Black September" of 1970, the Palestine Liberation Organization (PLO) and the different Palestinian guerrilla groups transferred the locus of their operations from Jordan to the refugee camps in Lebanon, causing the Israel–Lebanon frontier to become a recurrent battlefield. Israel attacked and briefly occupied southern Lebanon in March 1978, and again in June 1982. Israel failed, in the wake of the 1982 invasion, to push Lebanon into a peace agreement, and the border region remained one of aggravated instability for almost two decades; the presence of a special UN force (UNIFIL) did little to change the situation. The final retreat of Israel's forces from southern Lebanon in 2000 marked the return of relative tranquillity to this zone. In the ab-

sence of an alternative binding arrangement, the 1949 Israel–Lebanon GAA remains the only legal instrument regulating relations between the two countries.

The Israel–Jordanian GAA was formally signed in Rhodes on 3 April 1949 by Col. Ahmad Sidqi Bey al-Jundi for the Hashimite kingdom of Jordan and by Reuven Shiloah and Col. Moshe Dayan on behalf of Israel. The real breakthrough and terms of agreement were actually concluded in secret talks between king Abdullah and Israeli representatives in the king's palace in Shuna. The Israel–Jordan GAA left a number of issues, such as the access of Jews to the Wailing Wall in Jerusalem's Old City and the access of Jordanians to the south through the Bethlehem road, to be resolved in later negotiations. But the failure of the secret peace negotiations between Israeli officials and Abdullah during 1949 and 1951, the assassination of the king in July 1951, and the ensuing rapid deterioration of Israeli–Jordanian relations served to block the resolution of those outstanding issues. Nevertheless, with many ups and downs, this agreement was maintained for almost twenty years as a more or less effective framework regulating relations between the two states.

The most difficult issue, one that triggered occasional violence, was the widespread infiltration of Palestinians (mostly 1948 refugees) across the armistice demarcation lines. These actions provoked Israeli retaliatory assaults and brought into question the viability of Article II of the agreement. Nevertheless, both sides were loath to destroy the foundations of their GAA and kept using its mechanisms for the exchange of mutual complaints and also for keeping the tenuous status quo alive. No-man's-lands designated by the GAA were divided by consent; the biweekly convoy to the Israeli enclave at the Hebrew University on Mount Scopus was permitted to supply the Israeli police force stationed there and replace the policemen regularly; the mutual vulnerability of citizens in Jerusalem induced both sides to keep the city's division lines quiet most of the time. The conquest of Jerusalem and the West Bank of Jordan in June 1967 by Israeli forces brought an end to the applicability of the Jordan–Israel GAA, since neither Jordanian civil government nor the Jordanian army ever returned to these areas. The peace treaty concluded between Jordan and Israel in 1994 brought about the termination of the Jordan–Israel GAA.

The last agreement, the Syria–Israel GAA, was concluded after prolonged bickering and many delays. It was signed on 20 July 1949 near the Banat Yaʿqub bridge on the Jordan River by Lt. Col. Makleff on behalf of Israel and Col. Fawzi Silo for the Syrians. Two main issues continued to obstruct the full implementation of this GAA: the status of the demilitarized zones and the use of the waters of the river Jordan and its tributaries. These issues eventually contributed to the main causes of the June 1967 Arab–Israel War and the conquest of the Golan Heights by Israeli forces. The Syria–Israel GAA provided for a number of stretches of land, previously held by the Syrian army, to be declared demilitarized zones. Sharp disagreement, often leading to violent measures, erupted from the outset regarding the status and disposition of these areas. Israel implemented several civilian projects in these zones without paying attention to the rights of the Arab landowners, while Syrian gunners shot at the operators of such projects, which they considered to be in violation of the GAA. Some of these clashes, especially in the 1960s, escalated into major flare-ups, including the engagement of artillery, armor, and air force.

Negotiations on the sharing of the Jordan's waters in the early 1950s failed to achieve results, leaving Israel to press ahead to execute its own plan to divert a big part of these waters to the south of the country. The attempt of Syria to divert the headwaters of the Banyas River in 1965 provoked Israeli threats and attacks that stopped the Syrian diversion efforts. These tensions climaxed in May 1967 when Egypt responded to a call from Syria for help and moved its army into positions along the Israel border in the Sinai, removing the UN Emergency Force from the frontier. Israel's response was a successful offensive that resulted in the total conquest of the Sinai Peninsula, the West Bank of Jordan, and the Syrian Golan Heights. This development rendered the 1949 Israel–Syria GAA irrelevant. The legal vacuum was eventually filled following the October 1973 war. The May 1974 "Separation of Forces" agreement mediated by U.S. secretary of state Henry Kissinger resulted in a new demarcation line, which returned the town of Qunaytra to Syrian control,

and has since then been supervised by UNDOF, a special UN disengagement observer force.

The text of all four GAAs includes some similarly worded clauses. Article I, clause 2, for example, reads: "No aggressive action by the armed forces—land, sea, or air—of either party shall be undertaken, planned, or threatened against the people or the armed forces of the other." Article II, clause 2, declares that: "No element of the land, sea or air military or para-military forces of either Party, including non-regular forces, shall commit any warlike or hostile act against the military or para-military force of the other Party, or against civilians in territory under the control of that Party." Other clauses specify the settlement of problems specific to the terrain and military situation of each of the different frontiers.

All four agreements also provided for a mechanism of supervision and settling of disputes. The UN operated a Truce Supervisory Organization (UNTSO), staffed by a corps of officers from different countries, headquartered in a piece of no-man's-land in Jerusalem, and empowered to investigate complaints of violations of the GAAs. Such complaints were also adjudicated by Mixed Armistice Commissions, each chaired by a senior UN officer. Complaints of major violations were referred by the parties to the UN Security Council, which based its discussions on reports prepared by the UNTSO chief of staff.

From the outset, the Arab–Israeli GAAs were plagued by discord and disagreement. One basic disagreement concerned the level of responsibility the contracting states had to shoulder for criminal and often violent activities of irregulars who crossed the demarcation lines. The scope of such infiltration during the early 1950s worried the Israelis, and the inability of the UNTSO and several Arab states to effectively curb them triggered severe Israel Defense Force (IDF) reprisal actions, which were themselves equally in breach of the GAAs. Perhaps the most serious disagreement was over the very nature of the agreements that had been signed. While Israel took them as giving permanence to the demarcation lines as finite borders, awaiting only the final stage of signing full peace treaties, the Arab states interpreted them only as long-term cease-fire arrangements that did not end their status as belligerents and did not give any permanence to their different provisions.

See also ARAB–ISRAEL WAR (1948); ARAB–ISRAEL WAR (1967); SUEZ CRISIS (1956–1957); UNITED NATIONS TRUCE SUPERVISION ORGANIZATION (UNTSO).

Bibliography

Bar-Yaacov, Nisan. *The Israeli-Syrian Armistice: Problems of Implementation 1949–1966.* Jerusalem: Magnes Press, 1968.

Burns, E. L. M. *Between Arab and Israeli.* New York: Ivan Obolensky, 1963.

Morris, Benny. *Israel's Border Wars, 1949–1956: Arab Infiltration, Israeli Retaliation, and the Countdown to the Suez War.* Oxford: Clarendon Press, 1993.

Rosenthal, Yemima, ed. *Documents on the Foreign Policy of Israel.*, Vol. 3: *Armistice Negotiations with the Arab States, December 1948–July 1949.* Jerusalem: Israel State Archives, 1983.

Shalev, Aryeh. *The Israel-Syria Armistice Regime, 1949–1955.* Boulder, CO: Westview Press, 1993.

Urquhart, Brian. *Hammarskjold.* New York: W. W. Norton, 1994.

Urquhart, Brian. *Ralph Bunche: An American Life.* New York: W. W. Norton, 1993.

MORDECHAI BAR-ON

ARAB–ISRAEL WAR (1948)

The first conflict between the Arabs and the new state of Israel.

The Arab–Israel war of 1948 culminated half a century of conflict between the Arab and Jewish populations in Palestine. It began as a civil conflict between Palestinian Jews and Arabs following announcement of the United Nations (UN) decision in November 1947 to partition the country into a Jewish state, an Arab state, and an international enclave encompassing the greater Jerusalem area. While the majority of the Jewish population approved the plan, Arabs in Palestine and surrounding countries vehemently objected, considering it a violation of Palestinian Arabs' self-determination. In Palestine, Arab demonstrations against the UN decision and Jewish celebrations welcoming it met head-on and quickly erupted into violent clashes between the two communities. Within a few days armed Arab and Jewish groups were battling each other throughout the country.

Palestinian Arab guerrillas received weapons and volunteers from the neighboring states and were assisted by unofficial paramilitary units from Syria and Egypt. The Arabs, however, were not as effectively organized as the Jewish forces. The latter consisted of three principal groups: the Haganah, the defense organization of the mainstream Jewish community; and two dissident factions, the Irgun Zva'i Le'umi (IZL or Etzel; National Military Organization) and Lohamei Herut Yisrael (Lehi; Fighters for the Freedom of Israel), also known as the Stern Gang. The latter two were associated with Revisionist Zionism.

Following the partition resolution, casualties mounted on both sides. Arabs attacked Jewish settlements and bombed such urban targets as the *Palestine Post* and the headquarters of the Jewish Agency. Retaliatory and preemptive Jewish attacks against the Arab population—such as the Etzel raid on Dayr Yasin, which has been viewed by some as an instance of ethnic cleansing—set off a mass flight and military expulsion of the Arab population from areas seized by the Jewish forces.

By the end of the mandate in May 1948, when the British army left Palestine, Jewish forces had seized most of the territory allocated to the Jewish state in the UN partition plan as well as land beyond the partition borders.

With departure of the British and Israel's declaration of independence on 15 May 1948, the struggle became an international conflict between the Jewish state and the regular armies of Egypt, Transjordan, Syria, Lebanon, and Iraq. Saudi Arabia sent a token unit, and Yemen was nominally involved.

Arab states other than Transjordan intervened to preempt the plans of Amir Abdullah, developed in accord with Israel, to take over the largely Arab-inhabited parts of Palestine. In an attempt to gain Transjordan's cooperation in the war against Israel, the other Arab combatants agreed to appoint Abdullah commander in chief of the invading forces. The Arab military plans called for Egypt's units to move north along the Mediterranean coast toward Tel Aviv; for Syria's, Lebanon's, and Iraq's troops

Palestinian refugees flee from the Galilee region during the Arab–Israel War of 1948. The war, which established Israel as an independent state, resulted in 726,000 Palestinian refugees. © AP/WIDE WORLD PHOTOS. REPRODUCED BY PERMISSION.

to come through Galilee and move to Haifa; and for Transjordan's Arab Legion to approach the coast after occupying central Palestine. The Arab Legion, however, did not cross the UN partition line, and the other Arab forces were blocked from their objectives. Despite appointment of a commander in chief, the Arab armies failed to coordinate their plans, each operating under its own generals without integrating its actions with those of its allies. Except for the Arab Legion, the Arab armies were poorly trained and badly equipped, and morale was low. By June 1948 their offensive lost its momentum. Both sides accepted a twenty-eight-day truce ordered by the UN Security Council that went into effect on 10 June.

With resumption of fighting on 8 July, Israel's forces, now consolidated and equipped with heavy weapons, took the offensive. Arab areas including Nazareth in Galilee were seized, although attempts to capture the Old City of Jerusalem failed. Efforts to break through Egypt's lines to reach Jewish settlements in the Negev also were unsuccessful.

A second truce, initiated on 19 July, was broken several times when Israel's forces attempted to break Egypt's blockade of the Negev; Israel captured Beersheba in October and isolated most of Egypt's units south of Jerus alem. By the end of the year, Egypt's forces were either driven from Palestine or besieged in the south. In the north, another offensive extended the area under Israel's control to Lebanon's territory adjoining upper Galilee.

On 5 January 1949, Egypt agreed to accept a Security Council call for a new truce and negotiations for an armistice. Negotiations opened on 13 January 1949, on the island of Rhodes, under the chairmanship of Ralph Bunche. The General Armistice Agreement signed on 24 February 1949 served as a model for similar armistices with Lebanon on 23 March, with Jordan on 3 April, and with Syria on 20 July. Iraq refused to participate in armistice negotiations.

The armistice agreements were considered preliminary to permanent peace settlements. They established frontiers between Israel and its neighbors that remained in effect until the Arab–Israel War of 1967. A UN Truce Supervisory Organization with four Mixed Armistice Commissions, comprised of Israel and of Egypt, Lebanon, Jordan, and Syria, was established to deal with disputes between the signatories.

Israel's casualties in the war, which it called the War of Independence, were heavy—over 4,500 soldiers and 2,000 civilians killed (about 1 percent of the Jewish population). The Arab regular armies lost 2,000; there were no reliable figures for Palestinian irregulars, although some estimates ran as high as 13,000.

Israel extended territory under its control from the 5,400 square miles (13,986 sq km) allocated to it in the partition plan to 8,000 square miles (20,720 sq km), including land allocated to the Arab state and to what became Jewish West Jerusalem; Jordan occupied the old city and Arab East Jerusalem and the West Bank. Israel emerged from the war as a regional power equal in strength to any of its Arab neighbors.

A major consequence of the war was the Palestine Arab refugee problem. Although there was no accurate census of the refugees, their number was estimated by the United Nations to be over 700,000—more than half the Arab population of mandatory Palestine. Failure to prevent establishment of the Jewish state was considered a major disaster in the Arab world; loss of the war, the flight of the Palestinians, and the establishment of Israel were called by many the *nakba*, a disaster that was to

intrude into inter-Arab politics, affect Arab relations with the West, and color Arab self-perceptions for decades to come.

See also ARAB–ISRAEL WAR (1967); BUNCHE, RALPH J.; HAGANAH; IRGUN ZVAʾI LEʾUMI (IZL); LOHAMEI HERUT YISRAEL; MIXED ARMISTICE COMMISSIONS.

Bibliography

Begin, Menachem. *The Revolt: Story of the Irgun.* New York: Schuman, 1951.

Khouri, Fred. *The Arab–Israeli Dilemma,* 3d edition. Syracuse, NY: Syracuse University Press, 1985.

Morris, Benny. *The Birth of the Palestinian Refugee Problem, 1947–1949.* Cambridge, U.K., and New York: Cambridge University Press, 1987.

Rogan, Eugene L., and Shlaim, Avi, eds. *The War for Palestine: Rewriting the History of 1948.* New York: Cambridge University Press, 2001.

Shlaim, Avi. *Collusion across the Jordan: King Abdullah, the Zionist Movement and the Partition of Palestine.* New York: Columbia University Press, 1988.

DON PERETZ

ARAB–ISRAEL WAR (1956)

A war that lasted from 29 October to 6 November 1956, waged by Britain, France, and Israel against Egypt.

Although Egyptian leader Gamal Abdel Nasser's accession to power in 1952 was initially viewed as a positive development by Israel and the West, his leadership of Arab nationalism and his growing military and political strength were viewed with apprehension by Great Britain, France, and Israel.

Preparations for War

Nasser's nonalignment policies, including recognition of the People's Republic of China and opposition to a Western-sponsored alliance in the Middle East, were seen as threats to British and French hegemony in the region. The French were alarmed at Egyptian support of Algerian (FLN) nationalists; the Israelis, by Egypt's support of Palestinian guerrillas located in the Gaza Strip and the Egyptian blockade of Elat and the Gulf of Aqaba. Egypt's formation of a joint command with Syria and Jordan, and increased Fidaʾiyyun incursions from Gaza into

Israel, were seen as signs that Egypt was preparing for war. In February 1955 Israel retaliated with a full-scale attack on military bases in Gaza; this prompted Egypt to negotiate an arms deal with the Soviet Union for the purchase of weapons from Czechoslovakia.

When the United States, angered by Egypt's growing ties with the Soviet Union, cancelled negotiations for a development loan to construct a new Nile dam at Aswan, Great Britain and the World Bank also cancelled loan negotiations. Nasser retaliated on 26 July 1956 by nationalizing the Suez Canal Company, in which the British government held the majority of shares. The headquarters and many shareholders of the company were in France. Both Great Britain and France regarded Egypt's action as reason for war.

Throughout the summer of 1956 Israel, England, and France planned for war along parallel but independent lines. Israel negotiated with France for arms and developed operations to open the Strait of Tiran to Israeli shipping (Operation Kadesh). The British moved ships to Cyprus and to Malta with the aim of seizing the canal and bringing down Nasser (Operation Musketeer). The French then made overtures to the Israelis for joint planning and participation in the operation against Egypt; exploratory meetings began in early September. In October (22–24), at the invitation of the French, David Ben-Gurion, Shimon Peres, and Moshe Dayan met with French prime minister Guy Mollet and British foreign minister Selwyn Lloyd at Sèvres to plan the joint campaign, in which Israeli forces were to cross the Sinai and link up with the British and the French in the area of Port Sa'id. It was understood that the Anglo-French intervention would be seen as an "impartial"; separation of combatants and that Israel would be able to withdraw its troops if England and France did not carry out their military missions. The allies relied on the assumption that the Soviet Union (involved in Poland and in Hungary) and the United States (in the midst of presidential elections) would be too busy to interfere. Tensions on the Israeli-Jordanian border gave the impression that Israel was preparing to invade Jordan rather than Egypt.

As British and French troops were massing on Cyprus and Malta in August, Nasser anticipated an attack on Egypt and redeployed much of the Egyptian Sinai garrison to the delta region, leaving only 30,000 men in the northeast triangle of al-Arish, Rafah, and Abu Aqayla under the eastern command of Major General Ali Amr, headquartered at Isma'iliyya. The troops consisted of one Egyptian division and one poorly trained and lightly armed Palestinian division commanded by Egyptian officers and supported by field artillery and antitank guns, three squadrons of Sherman tanks, and a motorized border patrol. In addition, Amr commanded two infantry divisions and an armored division just west of the canal that could be used in the Sinai. The garrison at Sharm al-Shaykh was directly under the control of headquarters at Cairo. Of Egypt's 255 aircraft, only 130 were operational. Despite intelligence reports of Israeli mobilization, Amr did not return to Egypt from an official visit to Syria and Jordan until the morning of 29 October.

By the evening of 28 October, Israel had mobilized 45,000 men assigned to the southern command and six brigades held in reserve in the north. Israel's objective was to threaten the canal by securing the Mitla Pass (30 miles from the canal) and to achieve the flexibility either to advance—if the British and French carried out their part of the agreement—or to withdraw if necessary.

Outbreak of War

On 29 October Israeli parachutists landed east of the Mitla Pass and encountered heavy Egyptian resistance. This action was followed by a high-speed mobile column dash that met up with the Israelis at the pass. The next day, the British and the French issued an ultimatum calling for the withdrawal of forces from both sides of the canal in order to allow their troops to establish themselves along its length. Israel accepted, but Nasser rejected the ultimatum and began to issue orders for an Egyptian withdrawal from the Sinai to the delta. The British and the French vetoed UN-sponsored cease-fire resolutions. They began air attacks on Egypt on 31 October. Nasser subsequently sank all ships in the Suez Canal (4 November) in order to block passage. By 2 November Israel had taken Abu Aqayla and opened up a supply route to the Mitla Pass, cutting the Egyptians off from Gaza. On 5 November Sharm al-Shaykh was taken and Israeli troops reached the canal. Speed and mechanized transport, combined with tank warfare and air superiority, enabled the Israelis to outmaneuver the Egyptian forces sent to defend Sinai, who had no air cover for their troops due to the destruction of more than two hundred aircraft on the ground.

The British, anticipating heavy opposition by the Egyptian forces, set sail from Malta only on 1 November, delaying their landing in Egypt. The delay permitted the buildup of negative reactions to the mission both at home and in the international community. The allies tried to speed up the process, landing paratroops at Port Saʿid on 5 November and taking the city on the next day just as hostilities ceased.

By then, both the United States and the Soviet Union threatened to intervene, and the newly reelected U.S. president Dwight D. Eisenhower ordered a global alert of U.S. armed forces. The British, in the midst of the biggest crisis in Anglo-American relations since World War II, fearful of Soviet intervention, and worried about the falling pound sterling (later shored up by a line of credit from the U.S. Export-Import Bank), accepted a cease-fire. France and Israel followed suit.

Aftermath

During the fighting Israel lost about 190 soldiers: an additional 20 were captured and 800 wounded. Egyptian casualties were several thousand killed and wounded and about 4,000 taken prisoner by Israel. Egypt also lost massive amounts of military equipment.

On 4 December United Nations Emergency Force (UNEF) troops moved into Sinai, and on 22 December Britain and France withdrew from Egypt. Israeli troops withdrew from the Gaza Strip and the Strait of Tiran on 7 and 8 March under heavy pressure from the United States and following the stationing of UN troops at the entrance of the Gulf of Aqaba and assurances from the United States that it would uphold the right of innocent passage of Israeli and all other shipping through international waters. The last Israeli forces left Sinai in January 1957; they evacuated Gaza and Sharm al-Shaykh in March 1957. Although Nasser did not acknowledge Israel's right of passage through Egyptian waters, he allowed UNEF forces to remain in Sinai until 1967.

The war marked the end of an active British role in the region and its replacement by U.S. influence. It resulted in the development of modern armed forces in Israel, the beginnings of large-scale U.S. support for Israel, and the emergence of Nasser as victor and hero not only of the Arab region but the Third World as well.

See also ARAB–ISRAEL CONFLICT; NASSER, GAMAL ABDEL.

Bibliography

Bar-On, Mordechai. *The Gates of Gaza: Israel's Road to Suez and Back, 1955–1957.* New York: St. Martin's Press, 1994.

Dupuy, Trevor N. *Elusive Victory: The Arab–Israeli Wars, 1947–1974.* McLean, VA: BDM, 1984.

Golani, Motti. *Israel in Search of War: The Sinai Campaign, 1955–1956.* Brighton, U.K.: Sussex Academic Press, 1998.

Haikal, Mohammad H. *Cutting the Lion's Tail: Suez through Egyptian Eyes.* London: André Deutsch, 1986.

Kyle, Keith. *Suez.* London: Weidenfeld and Nicolson, 1991.

Louis, William Roger, and Owen, Roger, eds. *Suez 1956: The Crisis and Its Consequences.* New York: Oxford University Press, 1989.

Love, Kennett. *Suez: The Twice-Fought War.* New York: McGraw-Hill, 1969.

Troen, Selwyn Ilan, and Shemesh, Moshe, eds. *The Suez-Sinai Crisis, 1956: Retrospective and Reappraisal.* London: Frank Cass, 1990.

REEVA S. SIMON
UPDATED BY DON PERETZ

ARAB–ISRAEL WAR (1967)

Rapid and decisive victory by Israel over the combined forces of Egypt, Syria, Jordan, and Iraq.

The third major military conflict between Israel and the Arab states, the Arab–Israel War of 1967 between Israel and Egypt, Syria, Jordan, and Iraq, continued the century-old confrontation by Zionists and Arab nationalists over Palestine. The war erupted because of the failure to settle issues left unresolved by the wars of 1948 and 1956 and by the establishment of Israel in 1948. These issues included the problem of Palestinian refugees, disputes over water rights and the borders between Israel and the

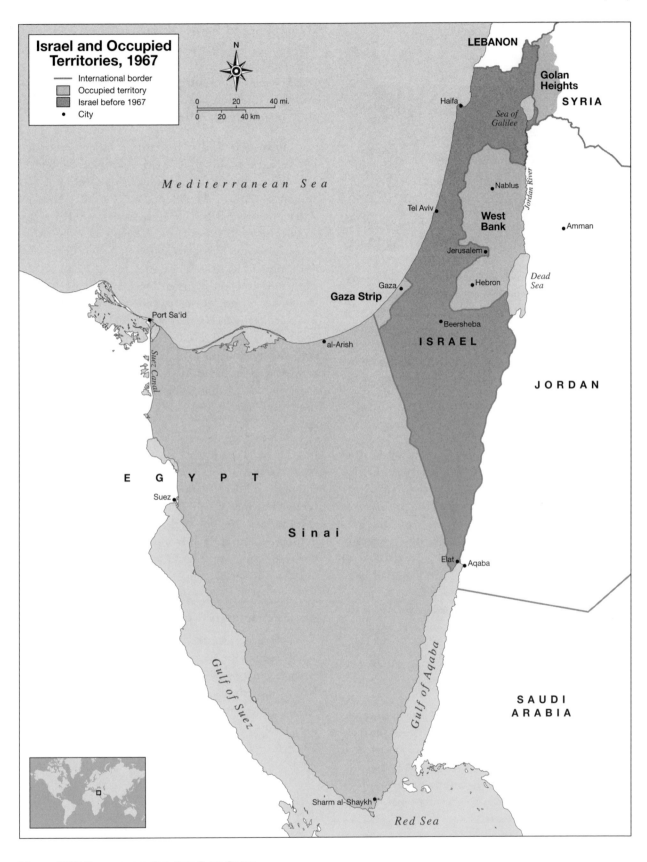

Israel and Occupied Territories, 1967

International border
Occupied territory
Israel before 1967
• City

N

0   20   40 mi.
0   20   40 km

LEBANON

Golan
Heights

SYRIA

Haifa

*Sea of
Galilee*

Mediterranean Sea

Jordan River

• Nablus

Tel Aviv

**West
Bank**

• Amman

Jerusalem

• Hebron

*Dead
Sea*

Gaza

Gaza Strip

• Beersheba

ISRAEL

Port Sa'id

• al-Arish

JORDAN

Suez Canal

E G Y P T

Suez

S i n a i

Elat • • Aqaba

Gulf of Suez

Gulf of Aqaba

SAUDI
ARABIA

Sharm al-Shaykh •

Red Sea

MAP BY XNR PRODUCTIONS, INC. THE GALE GROUP.

Triumphant Israeli soldiers in Old Jerusalem, which the country won from Jordan during the 1967 war. © BETTMANN/CORBIS. REPRODUCED BY PERMISSION.

Arab states, the Middle East arms race, the rising tide of Arab nationalism, and the question of Israel's right to exist.

Buildup to War

Efforts to peacefully resolve the Arab–Israel conflict had been unsuccessful since 1948; despite the defeat of the Arabs in 1948 and 1956, the state of war continued and intensified many of the problems it had caused. As the number of Palestine refugees increased, their infiltration from the Egyptian-occupied Gaza Strip and from the West Bank of Jordan created incidents that led to repeated border skirmishes. In retaliation for Fida'iyyun raids, Israel attacked Egyptian and Jordanian outposts. Disputes over the demilitarized zone (DMZ) between Israel and Syria erupted in battles that escalated into air warfare in which six Syrian MIGs were shot down in early 1967. Israel's insistence on proceeding with land development in the DMZ and its unilateral diversion of the Jordan River headwaters following the failure by the Arabs to ratify the Eric Johnson Jordan Valley Development project led to the decision by the Arab League to begin its own water-diversion scheme. The conflict over the Jordan River was a major cause of rising tensions and repeated border incidents.

The confrontation between Israel and the Arab states became a factor in the Cold War between the Soviet bloc and the West, with the Soviet Union pro-

viding arms to Egypt, Syria, and Iraq and with France and the United States helping to supply Israel. Israel continued to resist demands by the Arabs that it permit the return of the Palestinian refugees and that it withdraw to the borders established in 1947 by the UN partition plan.

Hostility to Israel, intensified by the Palestinian refugee problem, increased nationalist fervor throughout the Arab world, and this sentiment was rallied by Egypt's President Gamal Abdel Nasser. After the air battles between Syria and Israel in April, the Arab states (under Egyptian leadership) drew up a military pact to confront Israel. Egypt and Syria signed the agreement on 4 May, Jordan on 30 May, and Iraq on 4 June. The pact was backed by the Soviet Union, which supported Egypt's military buildup along the borders with Israel in Sinai, Gaza, and the Gulf of Aqaba. Border tensions between Israel and Egypt and Syria were intensified by false reports disseminated by the Soviet Union in Damascus and Cairo about an Israeli army buildup along the Syrian border and Israel's intent to attack Syria.

Responding to the challenge by Arab nationalists that he take a more confrontational position, in May Nasser ordered the withdrawal of the UN Emergency Force from its post along the Egyptian-Israeli border. Despite Egypt's heavy military involvement at the time in the Yemen civil war, Nasser deployed thousands of troops along the Israeli border and ordered a blockade of Israeli shipping in the Gulf of Aqaba.

The War and Its Aftermath

These actions created a sense of crisis in Israel, which led to the formation of a national unity government that for the first time included Menachem Begin and his right-wing Herut Party. Efforts to mediate the crisis through the United Nations and the Western nations failed, and proposals to form an international naval flotilla to test free passage in the Gulf of Aqaba were rejected. While negotiations to ease tensions were still being discussed in the United States, the Israel cabinet decided to initiate preemptive surprise strikes in Egypt, Syria, Jordan, and Iraq, and early on 5 June 1967 Israeli warplanes bombed airfields in these countries. Simultaneously, Israeli forces attacked Gaza and quickly advanced into Sinai. After three days, the Egyptian army was routed, and Israel seized the Gaza Strip, Sinai up to the Suez Canal, and Sharm al-Shaykh at the entrance to the Gulf of Aqaba.

Shortly after Israel attacked Egypt, Jordanian forces fired on the Jewish sector of Jerusalem, despite Israel's warnings to King Hussein not to intervene in the fighting. However, Hussein entered the war as a result of mass pressure to join forces with Egypt in expectation of a decisive victory. Within three days, Israel captured Jordanian East Jerusalem and most of the West Bank. On 7 June the UN Security Council called for a cease-fire, which Syria refused to accept. Shelling of Israeli settlements in northern Israel led Israel to attack and then capture the Golan region, and Syria to accept a cease-fire on 10 June. In the six days of combat, Israel destroyed over 400 Arab aircraft (mostly on 5 June), destroyed or captured more than 500 tanks, and demolished 70 percent of Egypt's, Syria's, and Jordan's military equipment. Egyptian casualties included more than 11,000 men killed and 5,600 prisoners of war; Jordan lost 6,000 men; and Syria about 1,000. Israel lost more than 20 planes and 60 tanks, and 700 of its soldiers were killed.

As a result of the war, Israel occupied territory equivalent to more than three times its pre-1967 area, including the Gaza Strip, the Sinai Peninsula, Jordan's West Bank and East Jerusalem, and the Golan Heights. The routing by Israeli forces and flight of some 300,000 Palestinian and Syrian civilians increased the refugee problem and further intensified Palestinian nationalism. The defeat led to the discrediting of most Arab leaders and to a new phase in the Palestine national movement, which ultimately resulted in the expansion of the Palestine Liberation Organization.

Immediately after the war, efforts to establish peace were renewed through the United Nations and passage of Security Council Resolution 242, which called for Israel's withdrawal from occupied territories and peaceful resolution of the conflict. Resolution 242 became the basis of most attempts to settle the conflict. Although the Arab states passed a resolution at a summit meeting in Khartoum in September 1967 that called for no peace, no negotiations, and no recognition of Israel, they eventually moderated their demands for a settlement from a return to the 1947 UN partition borders to an Israeli withdrawal from territories occupied in 1967—that is, to the 1949 armistice lines. They also no longer insisted on the repatriation of all refugees to their original homes within Israel.

In Israel, the war reinforced those militant nationalists who called for unification of the "whole land of Israel" and led to the formation of the Likud Party, which opposed withdrawal from territory acquired in June 1967. Arab East Jerusalem was for all practical purposes annexed by Israel soon after the war, and the Golan area was subjected to Israeli law in 1981. Israel's victory polarized politics between those who favored a peace settlement based on return of territory in exchange for secure borders and those who opposed any territorial concessions.

Victory in the 1967 War underscored Israel's position as the dominant military power in the region and strengthened the view of those who believed that territorial concessions were neither necessary nor advisable to resolve the Arab–Israeli conflict. This perception led to a program to establish a network of Jewish settlements in the West Bank, Gaza, and Sinai, and plans to integrate the economies of the conquered areas into Israel's economy. However, occupation and the imposition of military government in the territories stimulated Palestinian nationalist sentiment and led eventually to the Intifada in December 1987.

See also ARAB–ISRAEL CONFLICT; BEGIN, MENACHEM; FIDA'IYYUN; NASSER, GAMAL ABDEL; PALESTINE LIBERATION ORGANIZATION (PLO); UNITED NATIONS EMERGENCY FORCE.

Bibliography

Gawyrch, George W. *The Albatross of Decisive Victory: War and Policy Between Egypt and Israel in the 1967 and 1973 Arab–Israeli Wars.* Westport, CT: Greenwood Press, 2000.

Gordon, Haim, ed. *Looking Back at the June 1967 War.* Westport, CT: Praeger, 1999.

Haddad, William W.; Talhami, Ghada H.; and Terry, Janice L.; eds. *The June 1967 War after Three Decades.* Washington, DC: Association of Arab-American University Graduates, 1999.

Oren, Michael B. *Six Days of War; June 1967 and the Making of the Modern Middle East.* New York: Oxford University Press, 2002.

Parker, Richard B., ed. *The Six-Day War: A Retrospective.* Gainesville: University Press of Florida, 1996.

DON PERETZ

ARAB–ISRAEL WAR (1973)

War in October 1973 between Israel and Egypt and Syria; the fourth major military confrontation between Israel and the Arab states.

The 1973 Arab–Israel War resulted from failure to resolve the territorial disputes arising from the Arab–Israel War of 1967. Despite UN Resolution 242, which called for Israel to withdraw from territories occupied in June 1967, little progress was made in its implementation. President Anwar al-Sadat of Egypt sought to obtain the return of Sinai through diplomacy, and offered to reopen the Suez Canal if Israel would withdraw to the Mitla and Gidi passes in the Sinai Peninsula. He also offered to resume diplomatic relations with the United States and sign a peace pact with Israel, but Israel refused to withdraw to the armistice lines established before 5 June 1967.

While making diplomatic approaches to the conflict, Sadat was preparing for war. He contacted President Hafiz al-Asad of Syria to plan a two-front attack on Israel. Egypt, however, still depended on the Soviet Union for modern weapons. Angered by the Soviet Union's failure to respond to his demands for an assured supply, Sadat surprised the international community in July 1972 by expelling all 21,000 Soviet military advisers and personnel in Egypt. Although many in the West believed that the gesture would delay moves toward war, the Soviet Union responded by stepping up arms deliveries to both Egypt and Syria in an attempt to regain Sadat's favor.

In Israel, the governing Labor Party generally accepted the principle of "territory in exchange for peace," but it adamantly opposed return of all the occupied lands, asserting that for security reasons, Israel would have to continue occupation of substantial areas. Sadat's failure to follow through after his proclamations about the "year of decision" in 1971, and again in 1972, led Israel's general staff to conclude that the country was safe from an attack for the indefinite future and that the Bar-Lev line along the Suez Canal was impenetrable. Thus Israel's army commanders were unprepared for the October attack by Egypt and Syria. Israel's intelligence misinterpreted the buildup of Egyptian forces along the canal before the war as military exercises unlikely to escalate into a full-fledged attack.

The Two-Front War

The war began on two fronts on 6 October 1973, the Jewish Day of Atonement (Yom Kippur); hence, in Israel it was called the Yom Kippur War. It also was the Muslim month of fasting, Ramadan; thus, the conflict was called the Ramadan War by the Arabs. Egypt's forces quickly crossed the Suez Canal and overran the Bar-Lev line. In the north, Syria moved into the Golan Heights, nearly reaching the 1967 border with Israel. Because Israel had not fully mobilized, it was outnumbered almost twelve to one when the fighting began. Within the next few days, however, rapid mobilization of reserves redressed the balance.

The fighting was the heaviest since 1948, with major losses of manpower and material on both sides. The numbers of tanks, planes, and artillery pieces destroyed was larger than in any battle fought since World War II. Each side had to be rearmed in the midst of the fighting, Egypt and Syria by the Soviet Union, and Israel by the United States.

During the first days of the war, there was great consternation in Israel and fear that Arab forces, especially those of Syria in the north, might succeed in penetrating the pre-June 1967 borders. Within a week, however, Israel's counteroffensives turned the tide of battle. Syria was beaten back on the Golan Heights, and Israel's forces crossed the Suez Canal and began to push toward Cairo. The war precipitated an international crisis when the Soviet Union responded to an urgent appeal from Egypt to save its Third Army, which was surrounded by Israeli forces in Sinai. Despite the UN Security Council cease-fire orders, Israel's troops continued to attack. When the Soviet Union threatened to send troops to assist Egypt, the United States called a worldwide military alert. The crisis ended when all parties agreed to negotiate a safe retreat for the Egyptians.

When the combatants accepted a cease-fire on 22 October, Israel's forces had regained control of

Sinai and crossed to the west side of the Suez Canal. Most of the Golan was recaptured, and the IDF occupied some 240 square miles of Syrian territory beyond the Golan Heights. Both Egypt and Israel claimed victory: Egypt, because it drove Israel's forces back into Sinai; and Israel, because it defeated the Arab forces. However, the price of victory was steep. Nearly 3,000 of Israel's soldiers and more than 8,500 Arab soldiers were killed. Wounded numbered 8,800 for Israel and almost 20,000 for the Arabs. Israel lost 840 tanks; the Arabs, 2,550. The cost of the war equaled approximately one year's GNP for each combatant. Israel became more dependent on the United States for military and economic aid, and the Arabs turned to the Soviet Union to restock their arsenals.

The October War also emboldened the Organization of Petroleum Exporting Countries to double prices for its oil, and the Arab members to insist on tieing the sale of oil to support from consuming nations in the war against Israel. Saudi Arabia placed an embargo on shipments to the United States in retaliation for U.S. arms supplied to Israel. Gasoline shortages in the United States resulted, and the rise in oil prices began a spiral of worldwide inflation and a recession in 1974 and 1975.

Peace Negotiations

Attempts to resume the peace process began with Security Council Resolution 338, passed at the same time as the cease-fire ordered on 22 October 1973. It called for immediate termination of all military activity, implementation of Resolution 242, and the start of negotiations "aimed at establishing a just and durable peace." Resolution 338 subsequently became a companion piece to Resolution 242 as the basis for a peace settlement. In December a Middle East peace conference was convened in Geneva under the cochairmanship of the Soviet Union's foreign minister, the U.S. secretary of state, and the UN secretary-general. Egypt, Jordan, and Israel attended, but Syria refused to participate. After two days of wrangling over procedure, meetings were suspended; the conference failed to reconvene.

Its collapse provided U.S. secretary of state Henry Kissinger with the opportunity to bypass the United Nations and the Soviet Union in striving for

The town of Qunaytra in the Golan Heights was destroyed by Israeli forces during the Arab–Israel War of 1973, an act that later led to a United Nations accusation against Israel for violating the Geneva Convention. After the war, the Syrians refused to rebuild and reoccupy Qunaytra, insisting rather that the flattened remains stand as mute testimony to what they consider Israeli brutality. © AP/WIDE WORLD. REPRODUCED BY PERMISSION.

a settlement. The first step was a cease-fire agreement providing for relief of Egypt's besieged Third Army and return to the lines of 22 October. This was the first bilateral accord signed between Israel and Egypt since the 1949 armistice. In January 1974 Kissinger began another round of shuttle diplomacy, persuading Egypt and Israel to sign a disengagement agreement calling for Israel to withdraw its forces back across the Suez Canal. It was much more difficult to attain the disengagement agreement between Syria and Israel. After several trips between Damascus and Jerusalem, Kissinger finally persuaded Israel to withdraw from territory seized from Syria during October 1973 and from the town of Quneitra in the Golan region. A buffer zone patrolled by United Nations Deployment of Forces was established between forces of Israel and Syria in the Golan Heights, and Syria's President Asad agreed to prevent Palestinian guerrillas from using Syria as a base from which to attack Israel.

The disengagement agreements, which represented the diplomatic climax of the 1973 war, were the major accomplishment in Israel–Arab relations for the next several years. Egypt's military "accomplishments" opened the way for receptivity to Kissinger's diplomatic approaches, and they were a prelude to Sadat's startling peace initiative in 1977.

Israel's setback broke through a psychological barrier to territorial concessions and the belief in Israel's invincibility against any combination of Arab forces. While it enhanced Arab self-confidence, it shook Israel's belief that no concessions were necessary. But some of the long-term consequences of the war were disastrous for Israel. Israel's casualties exceeded those of the two previous wars, and military intelligence was discredited for not having predicted the attack. The Agranat Commission, established in November 1973 to probe the reasons for the setback, blamed the mistaken IDF assessment of Egypt's war prowess for Israel's failures and recommended removal of the chief of staff and other high-ranking officers. Its report led to a major shake-up of the Labor government, the resignation of Prime Minister Golda Meir, and a new cabinet led by Yitzhak Rabin in June 1974. The 1973 setback and the Agranat Report were among the major factors leading to Labor's defeat in the 1977 Knesset election.

See also ARAB–ISRAEL CONFLICT; ARAB–ISRAEL WAR (1967); ASAD, HAFIZ AL-; GOLAN HEIGHTS; KISSINGER, HENRY; ORGANIZATION OF PETROLEUM EXPORTING COUNTRIES (OPEC); SADAT, ANWAR AL-.

Bibliography

Amos, John W., II. *Arab Israeli Military/Political Relations: Arab Perceptions and the Politics of Escalation*. New York: Pergamon Press, 1979.

Aruri, Nasser H., ed. *Middle East Crucible: Studies on the Arab–Israeli War of October 1973*. Wilmette, IL: Medina University Press, 1975.

El-Badri, Hazzan, Taha El-Magdoub, and Mohammed Dia El-Din Zhody. *The Ramadan War: The Egyptian View*. Dunn Loring, VA: Dupuy Institute, 1978.

Gawrych, George W. *The Albatross of Decisive Victory: War and Policy Between Egypt and Israel in the 1967 and 1973 Arab–Israeli Wars*. Westport, CT: Greenwood Press, 2000.

Herzog, Chaim. *The War of Atonement, October 1973*. Boston: Little, Brown, 1975.

Parker, Richard B., ed. *The October War: A Retrospecitve*. Gainsville: University Press of Florida, 2001.

Raswamy, P. R. Kuma, ed. *Revisiting the Yom Kippur War*. London and Portland, OR: Frank Cass, 2000.

DON PERETZ

ARAB–ISRAEL WAR (1982)

War that began with Israel's invasion of Lebanon in June 1982.

Israel invaded Lebanon on 6 June 1982 in order to destroy the infrastructure and leadership of the Palestine Liberation Organization (PLO) and to install in Lebanon a Maronite-dominated government, led by the Phalange Party, which would ally itself with Israel. Israeli defense minister Ariel Sharon, Prime Minister Menachem Begin, Foreign Minister Yitzhak Shamir, and Chief of Staff Rafael Eitan believed that the elimination of the PLO would convince West Bank and Gaza Palestinians to seek an accommodation on Begin's terms of limited autonomy, thereby preempting the establishment of a Palestinian state, which was gaining international support.

The timing of the invasion favored Israel. The Arab world was in disarray. The most powerful Arab country, Egypt, had made peace with Israel in 1979 under the terms of the Camp David Accords. Support for Israel in the Reagan administration was strong. Israel's border with Lebanon had been quiet since July 1981, when U.S. emissary Philip Habib negotiated a cease-fire between Israel and the PLO. The invasion, however, was triggered not by a border incident, but by the attempted assassination on 3 June of the Israeli ambassador in London, Shlomo Argov. This was a pretext for invasion, though, because the attacker belonged to the anti-PLO Abu Nidal group, and PLO officials were also on the hit list.

The invasion might have been regarded in Israel and the United States as a necessary preemptive invasion (Israel called it "Operation Peace for Galilee") if it had been confined to "surgical" action against PLO forces within the 25-mile belt south of the Litani River, as Sharon had declared. However, once the invasion began on 6 June, Sharon ordered the Israel Defense Force (IDF) to proceed north to Beirut, defeated Syrian forces in the air and on the ground, and drove the PLO forces back to Beirut. The IDF reached Beirut in mid-June, laid siege to and shelled West Beirut for seven

Israeli troops moved into Damour, Lebanon, in June 1982, early in the invasion of that country. The Israeli attempt to destroy the entrenched Palestine Liberation Organization and place Lebanon under the control of Maronites ultimately proved costly not only to the Lebanese and Palestinians but also to Israel and its closest ally, the United States. © WEBISTAN/CORBIS. REPRODUCED BY PERMISSION.

weeks, and linked up with Israel's Lebanese allies, the Phalange.

Originally, Sharon had hoped that the Phalange forces (rather than the IDF) would enter PLO strongholds in West Beirut. Phalange leader Bashir Jumayyil and his aides had sought Israel's intervention and shared Sharon's goal of eliminating the PLO, especially from South Lebanon and West Beirut. Sharon's advisers, who lacked confidence in Phalange military ability, rejected such an operation; but fearing a high level of Israeli casualties, they also counseled against an Israeli assault. The result was a stalemate, and heavy Israeli bombardments and air strikes against West Beirut led to heavy civilian casualties. The nightly television pictures of death and destruction caused disquiet in the West. Although U.S. Secretary of State Alexander Haig seemed to acquiesce, the White House in fact disapproved of the bombing of civilians. Haig resigned

shortly thereafter, and the U.S. government sent Habib to Beirut to try to reach an agreement on PLO withdrawal.

An accord was reached wherein a multinational force, including U.S. Marines, would supervise an orderly PLO evacuation and safeguard civilians in the refugee camps. By 1 September, about 14,420 PLO fighters and officials had departed West Beirut for various Arab locales—particularly Tunis, which became PLO headquarters. About 3,000 Syrian troops were withdrawn from the city; U.S. troops were also removed. The same day, the United States announced the Reagan Plan, which opposed Israel's annexation of the West Bank and Gaza and called for a freeze on Israeli settlements there. The plan also declined to support the establishment of a Palestinian state. Instead, it supported Palestinian autonomy in association with Jordan, which the United States urged to begin negotiations with Israel. Some

Arab states, the PLO, and Israel rejected the plan.

Much of Sharon's grand design seemed to have been realized, including the election in late August of Bashir Jumayyil as president of Lebanon. However, Jumayyil resisted Begin and Sharon's demands for an immediate Lebanese–Israeli treaty and rejected Israeli insistence that their proxy in the South, Sa'd Haddad and his troops, remain under Israeli authority. Then, on 14 September, Jumayyil was assassinated—according to some, with Syrian help. Two days later, Sharon and Eitan ordered the IDF into West Beirut, in violation of the U.S.-brokered truce agreement.

Sharon approved the entry of Phalange forces into the Sabra and Shatila refugee camps, provided them with light at night, and extended their stay in the camps. The Phalange proceeded to kill between 800 and 1,500 Palestinian and Lebanese civilians from 16 to 18 September. An Israeli commission of inquiry, the Kahan Commission (1983), found that Israeli officials, in particular Sharon and Eitan, were indirectly responsible for the killings. An international commission chaired by Sean MacBride charged that Israel was directly responsible because it had been the occupying power and had facilitated the actions of its ally. In 2001 both Human Rights Watch and Amnesty International called for an investigation of Ariel Sharon's involvement into the Sabra and Shatila massacres.

In late September 1982 the IDF evacuated Beirut and were replaced by the multilateral force that included the U.S. Marines. The Arab–Israel War of 1982 was costly for all involved. According to Lebanese authorities, 17,825 Lebanese and Palestinians were killed, 84 percent of whom were civilians. Israel lost more than 1,000 soldiers by 2000, and spent $3 billion on the three-month operation. The war hurt Israel's international image and divided its own people; 400,000 Israelis (8 percent of the population) demonstrated against the war. Even the United States, which had sent the Marines to help fill the vacuum left by the Israeli departure from Beirut, got mired in Lebanese politics. The new secretary of state, George Shultz, engineered a security agreement between Israel and Lebanon that ignored Syria's interests in Lebanon, ratified Israel's control of South Lebanon, and hinted at U.S. support for Maronite primacy. Lebanese Muslims responded by bombing the U.S. embassy in Beirut,

and after the White House approved naval shelling of Druze villages, a suicide bomber attacked the Marine naval barracks, killing 241 Marines. U.S. forces were withdrawn four months later, and the Lebanese–Israeli agreement was aborted on 5 March 1984. Similar attacks took place against the French and the Israelis, who finally withdrew from Lebanon in 1985 after establishing a six-mile security zone patrolled by Haddad's army.

In 1999 a new Israeli prime minister, Ehud Barak, sensed the growing unpopularity of Israel's protracted involvement in southern Lebanon. In May 2000 Barak unilaterally and unconditionally withdrew all Israeli troops from Lebanon, except for those in a small disputed area called Sheba Farm.

See also BARAK, EHUD; BEGIN, MENACHEM; CAMP DAVID ACCORDS (1978); EITAN, RAFAEL; GAZA; HABIB, PHILIP CHARLES; HADDAD, SA'D; ISRAELI SETTLEMENTS; JUMAYYIL, BASHIR; KAHAN COMMISSION (1983); PALESTINE LIBERATION ORGANIZATION (PLO); PHALANGE; REAGAN PLAN (1982); SABRA AND SHATILA MASSACRES; SHAMIR, YITZHAK; SHARON, ARIEL; WEST BANK.

Bibliography

Fisk, Robert. *Pity the Nation: The Abduction of Lebanon.* New York: Atheneum, 1990.

Friedman, Thomas L. *From Beirut to Jerusalem.* New York: Farrar Straus and Giroux, 1989.

Khalidi, Rashid. *Under Siege: PLO Decisionmaking during the 1982 War.* New York: Columbia University Press, 1985.

Rabinovich, Itamar. *The War for Lebanon, 1970–1985.* New York: Cornell University Press, 1985.

Schiff, Ze'ev, and Ya'ari, Ehud. *Israel's Lebanon War.* New York: Simon and Schuster, 1984.

Smith, Charles D. *Palestine and the Arab–Israeli Conflict.* New York: St. Martin's Press, 2004.

Tessler, Mark. *A History of the Israeli–Palestinian Conflict.* Bloomington: Indiana University Press, 1994.

PHILIP MATTAR

ARABIZATION POLICIES

Maghrebian countries' (Algeria, Morocco, Tunisia) efforts to adopt the Arabic language following their independence.

After Morocco and Tunisia gained their independence in 1956 and Algeria in 1962, they decided, as an affirmation of their cultural identity against the former colonial power, to adopt Arabic as the official language instead of French. But the most common languages used by their citizens were Arabic dialects and Berber, not classical Arabic, which was known only in limited circles.

Algeria

By the time Algeria became independent in 1962, written communication, except in the religious sector, was almost exclusively conducted in French. Algeria's first constitution declared Arabic the only official language, although French remained the de facto language of government and industry.

Beginning in 1964, the gradual Arabization of the educational system was inaugurated. As there were few able teachers of Arabic in the country, many came from Egypt. By the 1970s, the secondary school system featured an Arabic track and a bilingual French-Arabic track. But the shortage of openings for non–French speakers in most scientific, technical, and managerial fields caused frustration among Arabized students and graduates and led to increasing unrest on university campuses. In response, in 1979 the government accelerated the Arabization of education and totally Arabized the judicial system, creating overnight significant new outlets for graduates of the Arabized track. By the end of the 1980s, most curricula, except in the physical sciences, had been Arabized and the parliament had passed a law calling for total Arabization of the administration.

In 1996, the National Council of Transition prohibited the use of any language other than Arabic after 1998 in government, commerce, and civil organizations, and after 2000 in the higher education system. Strong opposition appeared, especially in Kabilia, the heart of Berber country.

Morocco

Morocco had been a French protectorate, not a French colony, so some educational institutions had continued to use Arabic before independence, although most used French. Those using Arabic included the religious institutions connected to the Qarawiyyin Mosque of Fez just before its independence. Slightly more than 10 percent of Moroccan Muslim children attended French schools; most attended Qur'anic schools, where they memorized verses from the Qur'an and learned to write Arabic.

After it became independent in 1956, Morocco began a process of Arabization similar to Algeria's, but more human resources were available internally. Fewer than a hundred teachers were hired from Egypt and Syria. Arabic become the official language of political power, and French remained the vehicle of the governmental administration and economic sectors. Outside the main cities, Berber remained the most common language.

In 1962, an Egyptian high school was open in Rabat and a Iraqi college of science in Casablanca. Both were closed a year later as political tension arose between Rabat and Cairo, which was supporting Algeria in territorial disputes. In addition to public institutions, numerous French schools, supported by the French government, and bilingual French/Arabic schools continued to function. The former attracted mainly children from privileged backgrounds, because they were more able to open the doors to higher education.

Tunisia

After gaining independence in 1956, Tunisia, which had also been a French protectorate, was the most able of the three countries to shift to Arabic without outside help. It was only after 1970 that some teachers from the Middle East were invited to teach in Tunisian universities. With fewer Berber speakers than its neighbors, Arabization policies in Tunisia never gained the political attention they received in Algeria. The internal political debate focused more on curricula than on the language of instruction.

Under the Protectorate, some Arabic public schools functioned beside French schools: *les écoles franco-arabes*. An Arabic high school, Sadiki College, was created in Tunis as early as 1876. The influence and the prestige of the famous mosque of Zituna in Tunis was considerable, since most Arabic teachers received their training there.

In the first reform after independence, the bilingual system was not abrogated, but some courses about Islam and the history of the Arab world were introduced. After a short period between 1968 and 1971, where there was a clear attempt to separate citizen education (in French) from religious teaching (in Arabic) in secondary schools, Islam began to be taught in all public schools. Today, French remains widely used in business circles.

Cultural Identity in the Maghreb

A debate exists about the role foreign teachers played, especially in Algeria. Many of them came from small villages of Egypt and were criticized by their students' parents, who considered their methods old-fashioned and based too much on memorization. In return, some of these professors accused the families of non-Arabic, non-Muslim behavior.

Linguistic identity in the Maghreb is twofold: The language used within the family can be either local Arabic or Berber, and the language of the Qur'an is the link to Muslim identity. In Algeria, due to direct French rule and the violent struggle for independence, Arabization is a far more politically sensitive issue than it is in the neighboring countries.

See also ALGERIA: OVERVIEW; ARABIC; BERBER; MOROCCO: OVERVIEW; TUNISIA: OVERVIEW.

Bibliography

Entelis, John. *Algeria: The Revolution Institutionalized.* Boulder, CO: Westview Press; London: Croom Helm, 1986.

JOHN RUEDY
UPDATED BY RABIA BEKKAR

ARAB LEAGUE

See LEAGUE OF ARAB STATES

ARAB LEAGUE SUMMITS

Meetings of Arab heads of state since 1964.

Since 1964, heads of states (as opposed to foreign ministers) of member states of the Arab League have met periodically to deal with issues of regional and

---

Issues at Arab League summits

No.	Date and location	Resolutions, outcomes
1st	January 1964, Cairo	Agreed to oppose "the robbery of the waters of Jordan by Israel."
2nd	September 1964, Alexandria	Supported the establishment of the Palestine Liberation Organization (PLO) in its effort to liberate Palestine from the Zionists.
3rd	September 1965, Casablanca	Opposed "intra-Arab hostile propaganda."
4th	29 August–1 September 1967, Khartoum	Held post-1967 Arab-Israeli War, which ended with crushing Israeli victory; declared three "no's": "no negotiation with Israel, no treaty, no recognition of Israel."
5th	December 1969, Rabat	Called for the mobilization of member countries against Israel.
6th	November 1973, Algiers	Held in the wake of the 1973 Arab-Israeli War, it set strict guidelines for dialogue with Israel.
7th	30 October–2 November 1974, Rabat	Declared the PLO to be "the sole and legitimate representative of the Palestinian people," who had "the right to establish the independent state of Palestine on any liberated territory."
8th	October 1976, Cairo	Approved the establishment of a peacekeeping force (Arab Deterrent Force) for the Lebanese Civil War.
9th	November 1978, Baghdad	Condemned the Camp David Peace Accords between Egypt and Israel, and threatened Egypt with sanctions, including the suspension of its membership if Egypt signed a treaty with Israel.
10th	November 1979, Tunis	Held in the wake of Israel's invasion of Lebanon in 1978, it discussed Israel's occupation of southern Lebanon.
11th	November 1980, Amman	Formulated a strategy for economic development among League members until 2000.
12th	November 1981/September 1982, Fez	Meeting was suspended due to resistance to a peace plan drafted by Saudi crown prince Fahd, which implied de facto recognition of the Jewish state. In September 1982 at Fez, the meeting reconvened to adopt a modified version of the Fahd Plan, called the Fez Plan.
13th	August 1985, Casablanca	Failed to back a PLO-Jordanian agreement that envisaged talks with Israel about Palestinian rights. Summit boycotted by five member states.
14th	November 1987, Amman	Supported UN Security Council Resolution 598 regarding cease-fire in the Iran-Iraq War. Also declared that individual member states could decide to resume diplomatic ties with Egypt.
15th	June 1988, Casablanca	Decided to financially support the PLO in sustaining the Intifada in the occupied territories.
16th	May 1989, Casablanca	Readmitted Egypt into Arab League, and set up Tripartite Committee to secure a cease-fire in the Lebanese Civil War and re-establish a constitutional government in Lebanon.
17th	May 1990, Baghdad	Denounced recent increase of Soviet Jewish immigration to Israel.
18th	August 1990, Cairo	12 out of 20 members present condemned Iraq for invading and annexing Kuwait. Agreed to deploy troops to assist Saudi and other Gulf states' armed forces.
19th	June 1995, Cairo	Held after a hiatus of five years. Iraq not invited.
20th	October 2000, Cairo	Set up funds to help the Palestinians' Second Intifada against the Israeli occupation, and called on its members to freeze their relations with Israel. Iraq was invited.
21st	March 2001, Amman	Held after the election of Ariel Sharon as Israel's prime minister, it appointed Egypt's Amr Mousa as the Arab League's new secretary-general.
22nd	March 2002, Beirut	Adopted the Saudi Peace Plan of Crown Prince Abdullah, which offered Israel total peace in exchange for total Israeli withdrawal from Arab territories conquered in the 1967 war. Opposed the use of force against Iraq.
23rd	March 2003, Sharm al-Sheikh, Egypt	Agreed not to participate in the U.S.-led attack on Iraq, but allowed the United States to use military bases in some of their countries.

TABLE BY GGS INFORMATION SERVICES, THE GALE GROUP

Encyclopedia of THE MODERN MIDDLE EAST AND NORTH AFRICA

inter-Arab importance. The following chart summarizes the main issues discussed or approved at the various summit meetings.

Bibliography

Hiro, Dilip. *The Essential Middle East: A Comprehensive Guide.* New York: Carroll & Graf, 2003.

PHILIP MATTAR

ARAB LEGION

Transjordan/Jordan military.

In September 1923, after Britain created Transjordan, the Reserve Mobile Force, commanded by Capt. Frederick G. Peake, was reorganized and merged with all other forces in Transjordan, and given the name *al-Jaysh al-Arabi* (Arab Army), more commonly referred to as the Arab Legion. The Legion served initially as a force for British colonial rule in Transjordan. Just as importantly, the Arab Legion also served as the protectors of the regime of King Abdullah I ibn Hussein, and even played a central role in constructing Jordanian national identity itself, including tieing that sense of identity and nationhood to loyalty to the Hashimite monarchy. Like the modern Jordanian army, the Arab Legion was widely viewed as the best-trained and best-equipped army in the Arab world.

The Arab Legion began as a small, elite armed force of a little over a thousand men. Peake organized it to high efficiency, recruiting Arab volunteers from Transjordan, Palestine, Syria, Iraq, and Hijaz. Peake recruited mainly villagers rather than bedouin. By 1926 Peake had 1,500 men. Between 1923 and 1926 the Arab Legion fought bedouin raiders, repulsed incursions by the Wahhabi Ikhwan, established order, and extended the centralizing power of the Hashimite state. From its inception until 1957, the costs of the Arab Legion were subsidized entirely by Britain.

The creation of the Transjordan Frontier Force (TJFF) in April 1926, to protect the borders from Saudi Arabia's territorial ambitions, resulted in a reduction in the Arab Legion's strength. This changed, however, when Capt. John Bagot Glubb arrived from Iraq, in November 1930, to be second in command to Peake. Glubb created the Desert Mobile Force, composed mainly of bedouin, and provided it with fast transport and communications facilities. This force was able to shore up the Arab Legion's diminished functions and was the nucleus of the striking force of the future Jordan Arab Army.

The Arab Legion was further strengthened in the period from 1936 to 1939 with augmentation of manpower, arms, and equipment. Glubb succeeded Peake as commander of the Legion at the outbreak of World War II in 1939. Unlike Peake, who had seen the bedouin as the central challenge to Hashimite rule, Glubb shifted the emphasis completely toward bedouin recruitment, co-opting the tribes to be loyal bastions of support for the monarchy. During the war, the Arab Legion's main task was to support Britain by thwarting any attempt by the Axis powers to encroach on British or French interests in the mandated areas. In May 1941 the Legion reinforced British troops who had been rushed from Palestine to crush Rashid Ali al-Kaylani's rebellion in Iraq. The Desert Mobile Force won a battle at Falluja and, in cooperation with the Basra-based British-Indian military contingent, entered Baghdad at the end of May.

When Jordan gained full independence in 1946, the Arab Legion remained under Glubb's command but was transformed into a regular national army and renamed the Jordan Arab Army. It participated in the Arab–Israeli War of 1948, acquitting itself well despite its small size, and resisting Israeli assaults on East Jerusalem. At the end of hostilities, it was in complete control of the West Bank, which was formally incorporated into the Hashimite Kingdom of Jordan in April 1950. In the 1950s, demonstrations in Jordan protested the Baghdad Pact, the continuing presence of British troops in the kingdom and of British officers commanding the Jordanian army. In a hasty attempt to reassert legitimacy, King Hussein ibn Talal in 1956 dismissed and deported the long-serving Glubb. Although the incident caused a temporary diplomatic rift with Britain, British subsidies to the Arab Legion continued without interruption.

Under the command of General Ali Abu Nuwwar, the Jordanian Arab Army underwent a process of "Arabization," in which all British officers were dismissed and replaced by Jordanians. Abu Nuwwar also pursued a policy of modernization and profes-

The Camel Corps was one division of the Arab Legion in its heyday under Lt.-Gen. John Bagot Glubb. Others included a long range reconnaissance unit called the Desert Patrol and the Desert Mobile Force, a motorized strike force. © LIBRARY OF CONGRESS.

sionalization of the army, moving beyond Glubb's model of a bedouin-dominated force to one that represented Transjordanians of varied village, town, and tribal backgrounds. Palestinians too were recruited into the army, but the institution then and now remained nonetheless largely East Bank or Transjordanian, both in the enlisted ranks and even more so in the officer corps. In 1957 the last British troops left the kingdom but unrest nonetheless reached the ranks of the army itself, as the palace thwarted an attempted coup by nationalist officers (allegedly including Abu Nuwwar himself), purged the ranks of suspect officers, and reinforced the army as the most loyal base of Hashimite support. That same year, the Eisenhower administration in the United States declared Jordan "vital" to the U.S. interests, particularly as an anti-communist bulwark in the regional and global Cold War. In material terms, this increasingly close U.S.-Jordanian alliance resulted in a steady shift toward ever larger reliance on U.S. military aid and arms. This process accelerated further following Jordanian and Arab losses to Israel in the 1967 war.

Anticipating that war was imminent, King Hussein hastened to sign a military alliance with Egypt.

This placed the Jordanian army under direct Egyptian command as Israeli forces launched a surprise attack in June 1967. In the six days that followed, Jordanian forces fought tenaciously in the West Bank, and desperately attempted to retain control of East Jerusalem. The task proved too difficult, given the lengthy cease-fire lines demarcating the West Bank. Despite strong efforts, the outnumbered and outgunned Jordanians were ultimately defeated, losing the Holy city and indeed all of the West Bank to Israeli forces. After the war, the trend toward closer U.S.-Jordanian military cooperation continued, as Jordan relied heavily on U.S. arms, material, training, and financial assistance in reconstructing the Jordanian armed forces.

In the wake of the disastrous 1967 war, tensions within Jordan increased between the Jordanian army and guerrilla forces from the Palestine Liberation Organization. For a brief period in 1968, however, the two forces collaborated successfully in repelling an Israeli attack. Following Palestinian guerrilla attacks against Israeli forces routinely responded with massive retaliation. In March 1968, Israeli forces assaulted Karama, a town in the Jordan valley and base of Palestinian fighters. Unlike the 1967 war, this conflict proved more of a pitched battle, with heavy losses on all sides. Palestinian guerrillas and Jordanian soldiers, supported by artillery and tanks of the Jordanian army, eventually repelled the attack, and Karama quickly became legendary. The town's name, significantly, means "dignity." But despite the military success at Karama, the battle soon added to Palestinian-Jordanian tensions as each side claimed to have played the decisive role in the Arab victory. Ultimately, the episode fed into the tensions that culminated in the Jordanian Civil War. From "Black September" 1970 through the summer of 1971, Jordanian army units (particularly bedouin-dominated units) defeated Fida'iyyun forces and expelled them from the kingdom. The civil war was a particularly brutal affair, involving considerable urban warfare and the shelling of many Palestinian refugee camps. Given its losses in the 1967 war, and the trauma of the 1970–1971 civil war, Jordan refused to open up a third front in the Arab–Israel War of 1973. Instead, King Hussein sent a small contingent of Jordanian soldiers to Syria to bolster the Syrian front against the Israelis. Since that time, Jordan renounced its claims to the West Bank (1988) and signed a peace treaty with Israel (1994) formally ending hostilities between the two countries.

The Jordanian armed forces remain the heirs of the original Arab Legion. The Jordanian army continues to occupy a privileged position within Jordanian society as a central pillar of the Hashimite state, with close transnational ties (in both equipment and training) to military counterparts in the United Kingdom, the United States, and Pakistan. Especially since the 1999 succession to the throne of King Abdullah II ibn Hussein (former commander of the special forces units within the Jordanian army), Jordanian troops have played an increasingly large role in United Nations peacekeeping throughout the world.

See also ABU NUWWAR, ALI; ARAB–ISRAEL WAR (1948); BASRA; GLUBB, JOHN BAGOT; JORDANIAN CIVIL WAR (1970–1971); PEAKE, FREDERICK GERARD; TRANSJORDAN FRONTIER FORCE; WEST BANK.

Bibliography

Glubb, John Bagot. *The Story of the Arab Legion.* New York: Da Capo Press, 1976.

Lunt, James. *The Arab Legion, 1923–1957.* London: Constable, 1999.

Massad, Joseph A. *Colonial Effects: The Making of National Identity in Jordan.* New York: Columbia University Press, 2001.

Vatikiotis, P. J. *Politics and the Military in Jordan: A Study of the Arab Legion, 1921–1957.* New York: Praeger, 1967.

JENAB TUTUNJI
UPDATED BY CURTIS R. RYAN

ARAB LIBERATION ARMY

Military force of the Arab League in Palestine, 1947–1949.

After the United Nations voted to partition Palestine, in November 1947, the Arabs resisted the partition and went to war against Israel in the Arab–Israel War of 1948. The Arab League (also known as the League of Arab States) sponsored a military force after the 1947 vote, which was composed of Palestinians and non-Palestinian Arab volunteers, headed by a former Iraqi officer, Fawzi al-Qawuqji. This force was separate from the armies sent in by the five surrounding Arab states and the Palestinian forces under the command of Abd al-Qadir al-Husayni.

The first contingents of the Arab Liberation Army reached Palestine in January 1948. Between February and May, they suffered a string of defeats in northern Palestine. Between May and October, the Arab Liberation Army controlled parts of western Galilee but by October were completely defeated by Israel's forces.

See also ARAB–ISRAEL WAR (1948); HUSAYNI, ABD AL-QADIR AL-; LEAGUE OF ARAB STATES; PALESTINE; PALESTINIANS; QAWUQJI, FAWZI AL-; UNITED NATIONS AND THE MIDDLE EAST.

Bibliography

Hirst, David. *The Gun and the Olive Branch: The Roots of Violence in the Middle East,* 2d ed. London and Boston: Faber and Faber, 1984.

Lesch, Ann M. *Arab Politics in Palestine, 1917–1939: The Frustration of a Nationalist Movement.* Ithaca, NY: Cornell University Press, 1979.

Shlaim, Avi. *Collusion across the Jordan: King Abdullah, the Zionist Movement, and the Partition of Palestine.* New York: Columbia University Press, 1988.

STEVE TAMARI

ARAB LIBERATION FRONT

Faction of the Palestine Liberation Organization (PLO).

The Arab Liberation Front was established in 1969 in Baghdad, Iraq, by the Iraqi Ba'th party to counter the formation of the Syrian Ba'th party's al-Sa'iqa faction. The Front opposed a separate Palestinian state and in 1974 joined the Rejection Front against the al-Fatah faction's diplomatic initiatives. It also fought in the Lebanon war (Arab–Israel War, 1982). In the late 1980s, the Front's 400 members were led by Abd al-Rahim Ahmad, a member of the Palestine Liberation Organization's executive committee.

See also ARAB–ISRAEL WAR (1982); FATAH, AL-; REJECTION FRONT.

Bibliography

Cobban, Helena. *The Palestinian Liberation Organisation: People, Power, and Politics.* Cambridge, U.K., and New York: Cambridge University Press, 1984.

Fischbach, Michael R. "Arab Liberation Front." In *Encyclopedia of the Palestinians,* edited by Philip Mattar. New York: Facts On File, 2000.

Quandt, William B.; Jabber, Fuad; and Lesch, Ann Mosely. *The Politics of Palestinian Nationalism.* Berkeley: University of California Press, 1973.

ELIZABETH THOMPSON

ARAB MAGHREB UNION

Political body created 17 February 1989, consisting of Algeria, Libya, Mauritania, Morocco, and Tunisia.

Five North African states fashioned the Arab Maghreb Union (AMU; Union du Maghreb Arabe) in the image of the European Union (EU), originally intending to create a body through which members could negotiate trade relationships with the EU and improve relations among its member states. Specifically, the AMU sets out the conditions for an eventual free-trade zone among member states, a unified customs regime for extra-union trade, and a common market where people, products, and capital circulate freely.

The AMU is governed by a council made up of the heads of state of the five member states. The council meets biannually, with the chairmanship rotating annually. The union also includes a council of the ministers of foreign affairs from member states, a secretary general, and joint committees made up of the heads of various ministries, including the interior, finance, energy, tourism, and postal ministries. A judicial body made up of two magistrates from each member country serves to mediate issues between member states and advise AMU councils on matters of law.

Strained relations between Morocco and Algeria during most of the 1990s paralyzed the AMU, with Morocco claiming the Western Sahara as part of its territory while Algeria backed the Polisario Front in winning independence. The AMU's stance against Libya in the bombing of an airliner over Lockerbie, Scotland, in 1988 also prevented further collective agreements.

The AMU has become more active as relations between Algeria and Morocco have improved and as Libya has attempted to make amends for the Locker-

bie incident. Since 1999 it has established a number of joint bodies to address common concerns, including the International Organization for Migration, the Maghrebi Bank for Investment and External Trade, the Working Group on Fisheries, and the Maghrebi desertification observatory.

See also ALGERIA; LIBYA; MAURITANIA; MOROCCO; TUNISIA; WESTERN SAHARA.

Bibliography

Arab Maghreb Union. Available at <http://www.maghrebarabe.org>.

Zoubir, Yahia H. *North Africa in Transition: State, Society, and Economic Transformation in the 1990s.* Gainesville: University Press of Florida, 1999.

DAVID GUTELIUS

ARAB NATIONALISM

Ideology that Arabs are a nation.

The ideology that dominated the Arab world for most of the twentieth century, Arab nationalism, evolved, much as did other nationalisms in the developing world, out of a reaction to the prospect (and later the reality) of European domination and under the influence of European ideas about nationalism. The emerging ideology, whose core premise was that the Arabs are and have been a nation unified by language and a shared sense of history, but long divided and dominated by outside powers, drew on elements of the Arab and Islamic heritages. It incorporated them into a new narrative of Arab history and pride in the Arab past that was disseminated through the press and in novels, poetry, and popular histories.

By the 1920s, Arab nationalism was the hegemonic ideology of the eastern Arab world—the *mashriq*—and its influence continued to spread in succeeding decades. By the 1950s and 1960s, thanks to the espousal of Arab nationalism by the charismatic Egyptian leader Gamal Abdel Nasser, and the capacities for mobilization, organization, and clandestine action of parties such as the Ba'th and the Movement of Arab Nationalists, it appeared to be ascendant throughout most of the more than twenty independent states of the Arab world. Its decline in succeeding decades has been just as rapid, with nation-state nationalist tendencies and Islamic radicalism filling the apparent vacuum.

The first stirrings of Arab nationalism have been detected by some historians as early as the 1860s, but it is more commonly accepted that as a sustained political movement it began early in the twentieth century. This followed the reimposition of the Ottoman constitution in 1908, and the greater freedom of the press and of political expression that resulted throughout the Arab provinces of the Ottoman Empire. A tendency that has since come to be known as "Arabism" rapidly appeared: It stressed the ethnic identity of the Arabs and emphasized their common cultural roots. It also called for equality for Arabs with other national groups within the empire. As well as being influenced by European models and by reinterpretations of the Arab and Islamic past, Arabism was strongly affected by the rise of nationalism among the Turks, Armenians, and other peoples of the Ottoman Empire at this time.

The Arabist tendency built on the work of several groups of writers and thinkers, including the pioneers of the renaissance of the Arabic language, the Nahda. Starting in the mid-nineteenth century, this group produced new printed editions of the classics of Arabic literature, as well as encyclopedias, dictionaries, and works of history and literature, mainly in Beirut and Cairo. Another group, whose work was influential in a different way, was the Islamic reformers known as *salafis,* most of them from Syria and Lebanon, who argued for a return to the practices of the earliest days of Islam, and thus emphasized the period of Islamic history when the Arabs were dominant. Among them were the writers Rashid Rida, Abd al-Rahman al-Kawakibi, Tahir al-Jaza'iri, Jamal al-Din al-Qasimi, and Abd al-Razzaq al-Bitar. In addition, there were authors and publishers who traveled to Egypt to escape the censorship that increasingly afflicted the rest of the Ottoman Empire after 1876, and remained to publish newspapers, journals, and books. All these groups contributed to the growth of the Arabist idea.

The Arabist tendency identified politically with the liberal opposition to the ruling Committee for Union and Progress (CUP) in the Ottoman Empire. This was partly a response to strong Turkish nationalist tendencies in the CUP, and partly to its policy of tight centralization, which infringed on the autonomy of the Arab provinces. Although this Arab–Turkish tension did not erupt into open conflict until World War I, when the British helped to foment an Arab revolt in the Hijaz against the Ottoman state, it did have a lasting impact on the historiography of this and later periods. Some Arab writers reacted strongly against what they saw as Turkish suppression of Arab rights before the war, and the execution of some of the most prominent Arabist leaders during the war. This reaction engendered a version of Arab history that rendered the four centuries of Ottoman rule very negatively, in black and white, obliterating the nuances—and with them any understanding of the fruitful political and cultural symbiosis that characterized this lengthy period. This chauvinist version of modern Arab history—which ascribed the "backwardness" that afflicted the Arabs throughout much of their history to outsiders—is still influential in Arab schoolbooks and in much writing both within the Arab world and outside it.

In the wake of World War I, the Arabist aspiration to see an independent Arab state or federation of states stretching across the Fertile Crescent and the Arabian Peninsula was frustrated by Britain and France, which carved up the region into a series of mandates, protectorates, and nominally independent states, all of which were under the strong influence of their foreign patrons. The postwar response to European rule was a sequence of revolts in several Arab countries that impelled the granting of a measure of self-rule, and sometimes nominal independence, as in Egypt in 1922 and Iraq in 1932. The end result, however, was the perpetuation of the divisions that the European powers had imposed. Thereafter, within these new borders there gradually developed both a strong de facto attachment to the new states and the interests they represented, and a powerful, unrealized, and somewhat utopian aspiration for unity among them. Although these sentiments originated during the interwar years mainly in the newly created states of the Fertile Crescent—Syria, Lebanon, Jordan, Palestine, and Iraq—they were mirrored in other Arab regions in succeeding years, even in areas where the existing states had much older and more historically rooted foundations, such as Egypt, Tunisia, Morocco, Yemen, and Oman.

The tension between the contradictory sentiments of pan-Arabism and nation-state nationalism has characterized Arab politics since about 1945. On the one hand, most Arabs recognized that they had a common language, history, and culture, and that if these commonalities could find proper political expression, the Arab peoples might be able to rise above the fragmentation and weakness that have characterized their modern history. Such ideas were particularly appealing at the mass level, and long aroused the enthusiasm of the publics in many Arab countries. On the other hand, the states that existed in the Arab world for most of the twentieth century and on into the twenty-first century are in some cases rooted in long-standing entities with a strong, independent administrative tradition, have all engendered a powerful network of vested interests, and in recent decades have taken on an aura of permanence. The existence of these separate Arab states was reinforced by the Charter of the League of Arab States, established in March 1945, which reaffirmed the independence of the signatory states, provided that decisions had to be made unanimously in order to be binding, and forbade interference in the internal affairs of any Arab state by others.

In practice, most Arab governments have at most times been motivated by pragmatic varieties of *raison d'état* rather than any ideological vision. At the same time, their leaders have often clothed their actions in visionary Arabist rhetoric. Such ideological motivations were never entirely absent from the actions of most governments, if only because their respective public opinions resonated to such ideas. The result appeared to be hypocrisy, whereby governments did things for one reason while claiming an entirely different one as their real motivation. The paradoxical effect of all this was to discredit Arabism as an ideology when the failures of the various nominally Arab nationalist regimes finally exasperated their citizens and Arab public opinion generally. The ensuing bankruptcy of Arab nationalism as an ideology, and of the parties and regimes that still espouse it, would appear to be among the enduring features of modern Arab politics.

See also ARMENIANS IN THE MIDDLE EAST; BAʿTH, AL-; COMMITTEE FOR UNION AND PROGRESS; FERTILE CRESCENT; KAWAKIBI, ABD AL-RAHMAN AL-; LEAGUE OF ARAB STATES; NAHDA, AL-; NASSER, GAMAL ABDEL; RIDA, RASHID; TURKS.

Bibliography

Antonius, George. *The Arab Awakening: The Story of the Arab National Movement.* London: H. Hamilton, 1938.

Buheiry, Marwan, ed. *Intellectual Life in the Arab East, 1890–1939.* Beirut: Center for Arab and Middle East Studies, American University of Beirut, 1981.

Dawn, C. Ernest. *From Ottomanism to Arabism: Essays on the Origins of Arab Nationalism.* Urbana: University of Illinois Press, 1973.

Hourani, Albert. *Arabic Thought in the Liberal Age, 1798–1939,* 2d edition. Cambridge, U.K., and New York: Cambridge University Press, 1983.

Khalidi, Rashid; Anderson, Lisa; Muslih, Muhammad; et al., eds. *The Origins of Arab Nationalism.* New York: Columbia University Press, 1991.

Khoury, Philip S. *Urban Notables and Arab Nationalism: The Politics of Damascus, 1860–1920.* Cambridge, U.K., and New York: Cambridge University Press, 1983.

RASHID KHALIDI

ARAB NATIONAL MOVEMENT (ANM)

Organization dedicated to the unification of the Arab world.

The Arab National Movement (ANM) was established by Palestinian students at the American University of Beirut in the 1950s. In Kuwait it found a spokesman in Dr. Ahmad al-Khatib, a member of the National Assembly since 1963. The ANM also had some impact in Bahrain, but not elsewhere in the Gulf, and as of the mid-1990s was an almost wholly spent force.

Bibliography

Kelly, J. B. *Arabia, the Gulf and the West.* New York: Basic Books, 1980.

Peterson, J. E. *The Arab Gulf States: Steps toward Political Participation.* New York: Praeger, 1988.

MALCOLM C. PECK

ARAB REVOLT (1916)

Uprising of Arab nationalists against the Ottoman Empire during World War I.

Although many Arabs had reached the highest positions in the Ottoman government by the end of the nineteenth century, opposition to Turkish authority was spreading through the empire's Arabic-speaking provinces of the Ottoman Empire. A separatist nationalist movement had followers in many Arab towns and cities, including Damascus, Cairo, Baghdad, and Jerusalem by the early 1900s. Members formed secret cultural and political organizations, including groups of Arab officers in the Ottoman military. Prominent secret societies were al-Qahtaniya and al-Fatat; the former sought to establish a dual Arab–Turkish monarchy similar to the Austro–Hungarian Empire. Al-Fatat wanted to establish Arabic as the official language in the Arab provinces, where it would be taught in all schools.

Efforts by the Young Turk regime that seized power in 1908 to repress Arab nationalism intensified opposition to the government and increased demands for separation from the empire. The arrest for treason in 1914 of Major Aziz Ali al-Masri, an Ottoman staff officer of Arab origin, brought opposition to the regime among Arab officers to a head.

Among the ardent nationalists was the sharif of Mecca, Husayn ibn Ali, a Hashimite descendant of the prophet Muhammad, and his four sons, Ali, Abdullah, Faisal, and Zayd. Because the authorities suspected their loyalty, they were forced to live in Constantinople (now Istanbul) from 1893 until 1908. After they returned to Mecca, Husayn began to rally surrounding tribes against attempts to conscript Arabs into the Ottoman armed forces. Although the Turkish governor-general of Mecca backed down from the conscription order, Husayn sought an alliance with an outside power against further Ottoman attempts to undermine his authority.

In February 1914, Husayn sent one of his sons to negotiate with the British agent and consul general in Cairo, Lord Kitchener, but Great Britain was not yet ready to support an Arab uprising against the Ottomans. With Turkey's entry into World War I on the side of Germany (October 1914), the British authorities reconsidered the sharif's offer to revolt in return for guarantees of Arab independence after defeating the Turks.

Ottoman efforts to rally support among Muslims throughout Asia for a jihad against the Allies

British commander-in-chief Sir Edmund Allenby enters Jerusalem on 11 December 1917, days after capturing it on 9 December. The loss of the city, which fell in just one day, was a demoralizing blow to Turkish forces in World War I. © LIBRARY OF CONGRESS. REPRODUCED BY PERMISSION.

failed to win over many Arab subjects. Rather, most Arab notables were sympathetic to the growing demands for independence, and many looked to Husayn for leadership. As relations between the Arab provinces and Constantinople continued to deteriorate due to poor economic conditions, mass arrests of suspected Arab nationalists, and resentment of conscription, Husayn attempted to reestablish contact with the British.

In 1915 he reopened negotiations through Lord Kitchener's successor in Cairo, Sir Henry McMahon. In an exchange of ten letters known as the Husayn–McMahon Correspondence, the sharif offered assistance to Great Britain against the Turks in return for a British promise to recognize the independence of what was to become Syria, Lebanon, Palestine, Iraq, and most of the Arabian Peninsula, and to endorse proclamation of an Islamic Arab caliphate. The British, however, refused to accept so precise a definition of the area for Arab independence because of conflicting promises and obligations regarding the territory. McMahon eventually replied that Britain would recognize the territory demanded by the sharif except for certain areas "not purely Arab." The imprecision of British promises was the cause of postwar quarrels between Great Britain and Arab nationalists, particularly with regard to Palestine.

Following the exchange of correspondence with McMahon, Ottoman authorities initiated a massive crackdown on Arab nationalists. In May 1916, twenty-one leading Arab citizens of Damascus and Beirut were arrested and executed by public hanging. These events undermined what little loyalty remained among Arab subjects of the sultan, and sparked widespread support for open revolt against the Ottomans. Opposition to the government was further intensified by famine resulting from destruction of crops by a locust plague in 1916. In retaliation for Arab opposition, the Turkish authorities refused to permit outside relief supplies into the region; as a result, some 300,000 people died of starvation.

Sharif Husayn gave the order to tribes in the Hijaz to strike at Ottoman garrisons and proclaimed Arab independence in May 1916. After three weeks the Ottoman garrison in Mecca fell, followed shortly thereafter by most others in the main towns of the peninsula. Arab forces were supplied by Britain, and British officers served as military advisers. The most prominent was Colonel T. E. Lawrence, an adviser to Faisal.

The Arab revolt against the Turks ended in October 1919 when Faisal's armies captured Damascus, and an Arab regime was established with Faisal as king. At the end of the war, Husayn alienated many of his Arab neighbors when he proclaimed himself "king of the Arab countries." Although the British government refused to recognize him as more than "king of Hijaz," he persisted in the grander title, leading to confrontation with Ibn Saʿud and eventual defeat by the latter, followed by the annexation of the Hijaz into the Saudi kingdom.

The Arab revolt played an important and controversial role in postwar negotiations, and in the decisions taken by Great Britain and France about the territorial divisions of the former Arab provinces in the Ottoman Empire.

See also ABD AL-AZIZ IBN SAʿUD AL SAʿUD; ABDULLAH I IBN HUSSEIN; FAISAL I IBN HUSSEIN; FATAT, AL-; HUSAYN IBN ALI; HUSAYN–MCMAHON CORRESPONDENCE (1915–1916); KITCHENER, HORATIO HERBERT; LAWRENCE, T. E.; MCMAHON, HENRY; YOUNG TURKS.

Bibliography

Antonius, George. *The Arab Awakening: The Story of the Arab National Movement.* London: H. Hamilton, 1938.

Gershoni, Israel. "The Muslim Brothers and the Arab Revolt in Palestine, 1936–39." *Middle Eastern Studies* 22, 3 (July 1986): 367–397.

Haim, Y. "Zionist Policies and Attitudes towards the Arabs on the Eve of the Arab Revolt of 1936–39." *Middle Eastern Studies* 14 (1978): 211–231.

Hurewitz, J. C. *The Struggle for Palestine.* New York: Norton, 1950.

Kedourie, Elie. *In the Anglo–Arab Labyrinth: The McMahon–Husayn Correspondence and Its Interpretations, 1914–1939.* London and Portland, OR: Frank Cass, 2000.

Lawrence, T. E. *Seven Pillars of Wisdom: A Triumph.* London: J. Cape, 1935.

Marlowe, John. *The Seat of Pilate.* London: Cresset, 1961.

Sheffer, G. "British Colonial Policy Making towards Palestine 1929–1939." *Middle Eastern Studies* 14 (1978).

Silberstein, Laurence J., ed. *New Perspectives on Israeli History: The Early Years of the State.* New York: New York University Press, 1991.

Smith, Charles D. *Palestine and the Arab–Israeli Conflict,* 3d edition. London: Macmillan, 1996.

Swedenburg, Ted. *Memories of Revolt: The 1936–1939 Rebellion and the Palestinian National Past.* Minneapolis: University of Minnesota Press, 1995.

Swedenburg, Ted. "The Role of the Palestinian Peasantry in the Great Revolt 1936–1939." In *Islam, Politics, and Social Movements,* edited by Edmund Burke III and Ira Lapidus. Berkeley: University of California Press, 1988.

Sykes, Christopher. *Crossroads to Israel.* Bloomington: Indiana University Press, 1973.

Wasserstein, Bernard. *The British in Palestine: The Mandatory Government and Arab–Jewish Conflict, 1917–1929.* Oxford, U.K., and Cambridge, MA: B. Blackwell, 1991.

Zeine, Zeine N. *The Emergence of Arab Nationalism, with a Background Study of Arab–Turkish Relations in the Middle East,* 3d edition. Delmar, NY: Caravan Books, 1973.

DON PERETZ

ARAB REVOLTS (1936–1939)

See PALESTINE ARAB REVOLT (1936–1939)

ARAB SOCIALISM

Political philosophy advocating governmental and collective ownership of the means of production and distribution.

Arab socialism emerged as a result of colonialism in the Middle East coupled with the corruption and underdevelopment characteristic of Arab societies at the beginning of the twentieth century. It was not until the late 1940s that Arab thinkers began writing about the socialist option. Among the major parties and movements that emerged as a result of this effort were the Arab Renaissance Socialist party (al-Ba'th) and the movement called the Free Officers, led by President Gamal Abdel Nasser of Egypt. The aims of Arab socialism were to free the Arab world from Western colonial rule, to establish pride and social justice within Arab societies, and to unify the Arab world.

Arab socialism emerged at a time when liberation movements were sweeping developing countries, so self-determination and tight controls against multinational corporations and their exploitation of local resources became a major priority. Arab socialism rejected Marxism and class struggle as basic tenets; it promoted cooperation between classes for the welfare of the entire community, based on the principles of justice and the equal distribution of wealth, with government provisions for the poor and underprivileged.

Agrarian reform and land redistribution were important goals. The nationalization of industries provided the government with funds, but some forms of private property were retained if they were in the national interest. In Egypt, under the radical economic policies adopted by Nasser, nationalization hit French and British economic interests first. Then, in 1960, banks, newspapers, most foreign assets, industrial and mining industries, and export-import businesses were all nationalized. The land reform promulgated in 1952 had set limits on land ownership, and in 1960 these were cut in half, to 100 *feddan.* These same nationalization policies were also applied in Algeria, Libya, and Iraq, with tighter government control of the petroleum and gas industries. In the 1990s, several Arab regimes whose economic policies had been inspired by Arab socialism attempted to liberalize some sectors of their economies. These efforts were not always successful and faced stiff resistance from the bureaucracy.

In foreign policy, Arab socialism advocated a constant struggle against imperialism and Zionism. Support for the Palestinians' cause became a major issue, especially for Nasser. He and other Arab revolutionary leaders used the Palestinian issue to enhance their own power and legitimacy. Nonalignment and support for liberation movements were also goals of Arab socialist regimes. After the defeat of Arab armies by Israel in 1967, after Nasser's death in 1970, and after a bitter rivalry between the two sections of the Ba'th Party—one in Syria and the other in Iraq—Arab socialism lost much of its appeal. Lack of democracy, corrupt and huge bureaucracies, and the emergence of a new class composed of bureaucrats and army officers all contributed to the end of Arab socialism.

In the Middle East, a few political parties and regimes still claim inspiration by Arab socialism. These are the Arab Socialist Union in Egypt; the Sudanese Socialist Union in Sudan; the People's General Congress of the Socialist Jamahiriya of Libya; the National Liberation Front of Algeria; the Ba'th Party in Syria; the Revolutionary Socialist Party in Somalia; the socialist parties of Yemen, including the People's Socialist Party; and the Destour Party of Tunisia.

See also BA'TH, AL-; COLONIALISM IN THE MIDDLE EAST; FREE OFFICERS, EGYPT; IMPERIALISM IN THE MIDDLE EAST AND NORTH AFRICA; PALESTINE; NASSER, GAMAL ABDEL; ZIONISM.

Bibliography

Brynen, Rex; Korany, Bahgat; and Noble, Paul, eds. *Political Liberalization and Democratization in the Arab World,* 2 volumes. Boulder, CO: Lynne Rienner, 1995.

Goode, Stephen. *Prophet and the Revolutionary: Arab Socialism in the Modern Middle East.* New York: Watts, 1975.

Hopwood, Derek. *Egypt: Politics and Society 1945–1984.* Boston: Allen and Unwin, 1985.

El-Kikhia, Mansour O. *Libya's Qaddafi: The Politics of Contradiction.* Gainesville: University Press of Florida, 1997.

GEORGE E. IRANI

ARAB SOCIALIST RENAISSANCE PARTY

See BAʿTH, AL-

ARAB SOCIALIST UNION

Egypt's sole legal political organization, 1962–1977.

The Arab Socialist Union (ASU) was preceded by the Liberation Rally (1953–1956) and the National Union (1956–1962). All three organizations served President Gamal Abdel Nasser's regime as instruments of mass mobilization as Egypt shifted from capitalism to socialism and from a laissez-faire policy to a planned economy.

President Gamal Abdel Nasser (right) created Egypt's only legal political organization, the Arab Socialist Union (ASU), two years before this 1964 meeting with President Ahmed Ben Bella (left) of Algeria and Premier Nikita Khrushchev of the Soviet Union. The ASU, part of Nasser's plan to make Egypt a socialist country, lasted until 1977. © BETTMANN/CORBIS. REPRODUCED BY PERMISSION.

In May 1962 Nasser presented to the National Council of Popular Forces his Charter for National Action, an ideological document outlining a plan for the socialist transformation. It called for the creation of the ASU, which was to symbolize "the working forces of the people," defined as workers, peasants, intellectuals, national capitalists, and the armed forces. Because workers and peasants were to be the main beneficiaries of socialism, they were to occupy at least 50 percent of all elected posts in parliament and the ASU. Egyptians whose property had been nationalized or sequestered were declared "enemies of the people" and denied political rights. The National Council accepted the charter, with a few modifications, in July 1962.

The ASU's basic law was issued on 7 December 1962. Its organization was based on place of residence and profession, and branches (basic units) were established in villages, city quarters, schools, universities, and factories. They were organized on district, provincial, and national levels; the latter included a general committee, a supreme executive committee, a secretary-general, and a president.

In theory, the ASU was supposed to serve as the supreme authority of the state. Both parliament and the cabinet were to implement its policy decisions. In practice, however, the ASU's institutional development was confused and episodic. Its elections were not conducted on time, leaders were both elected and appointed, and for a while elected and appointed committees coexisted. In 1965 Nasser decided to establish a more radical "vanguard" organization consisting of cells whose members were appointed and whose activities were secret. In addition, the ASU created a Youth Organization as a means of recruiting and indoctrinating students and workers between the ages of fifteen and twenty-five (some of the leaders were as old as thirty-five) and set up an academic center called the Higher Institute for Socialist Studies to train future Youth Organization leaders in Nasser's doctrines and socialism.

As in many developing countries, the single party was an organization that claimed to represent the people's will. It was not intended to be an active institution with decision-making powers. Indeed, it was viewed more as a means of mobilizing political support than as a vehicle for popular participation. Lacking any real authority, the ASU served as an appendage of the executive.

Following Egypt's defeat in the 1967 Arab–Israel War, student and worker demonstrations revealed popular discontent with the organization. Nasser agreed on 30 March 1968 to hold new ASU elections, but no drastic changes took place. After Nasser died in 1970, his successor, Anwar al-Sadat, called for a reexamination of the ASU, which both Egypt's leaders and people had come to view as ineffective. In 1971 Sayyid Marʿi, who became the ASU secretary-general after the "Corrective Revolution" had purged the leftist elements from the Egyptian government, issued a "guide for political action" that hinted at some political liberalization for the organization.

After the 1973 Arab–Israel War, Sadat spearheaded a critique of the ASU by issuing a paper on the need to reform its structure and introduce diversity into Egypt's political life. Between 1974 and 1976, politically articulate Egyptians debated the ASU's future, leading to the regime's creation of three platforms (manabir) within the organization: the right (under Mustafa Kamal Murad), the center (headed by Mahmud Abu Wafiyya, acting for Sadat, his brother-in-law), and the left (led by Khalid Muhyi al-Din). Satisfied with their performance in the November 1976 parliamentary elections, Sadat announced that the platforms would become political parties. Once the Parties Law was issued in May 1977, the ASU faded away. It has never been revived.

While the ASU served the Egyptian government as a means of indoctrinating the people, it did not enable Egyptian citizens to influence their leaders. It failed to promote a rigorous analysis of Egypt's society or to solve any of the country's problems.

See also ARAB–ISRAEL WAR (1967); ARAB–ISRAEL WAR (1973); LIBERATION RALLY; NASSER, GAMAL ABDEL; NATIONAL UNION (EGYPT); SADAT, ANWAR AL-.

Bibliography

Baker, Raymond. *Egypt's Uncertain Revolution under Nasser and Sadat.* Cambridge, MA: Harvard University Press, 1978.

Beattie, Kirk J. *Egypt during the Nasser Years: Ideology, Politics, and Civil Society.* Boulder, CO: Westview, 1994.

Choueiri, Youssef M. *Arab Nationalism: A History: Nation and State in the Arab World.* Oxford and Malden, MA: Blackwell, 2000.

Hinnebusch, Raymond A., Jr. *Egyptian Politics under Sadat: The Post-Populist Development of an Authoritarian-Modernizing State,* revised edition. Boulder, CO: Lynne Rienner, 1988.

Said, Abdel Moghny. *Arab Socialism.* New York: Barnes and Noble, 1972.

Waterbury, John. *The Egypt of Nasser and Sadat: The Political Economy of Two Regimes.* Princeton, NJ: Princeton University Press, 1983.

ALI E. HILLAL DESSOUKI
UPDATED BY ARTHUR GOLDSCHMIDT

ARAB WOMEN'S ASSOCIATION OF PALESTINE

A women's organization founded in Jerusalem in 1929 after the Wailing Wall riots.

The Arab Women's Association of Palestine (AWA) was founded in Jerusalem at the first Palestine Arab Women's Congress on 26 October 1929. The impetus for its establishment was the 1929 Western (Wailing) Wall riots and the national mobilization that came in their wake. The goals of the AWA, according to its bylaws, were to "work for the development of the social and economic affairs of the Arab women in Palestine, to endeavor to secure the extension of educational facilities for girls, [and] to use every possible and lawful means to elevate the standing of women" (Mogannam, p. 77). The AWA subsequently formed branches in most of the major cities and towns in Palestine and became the leading organization of the Palestinian women's movement during the mandate period. Its members were particularly active from 1929 to 1939 in demonstrating against the mandate; in providing support for the prisoners and rebels of the 1936 through 1939 revolt; in meeting with, writing memoranda to, and protesting to British government authorities; and in rallying international and regional support for the Palestinian national movement. The organization subsequently split into two: the AWA and the Arab Women's Union, which emerged sometime after the convening of the Eastern Women's Conference on the Palestine problem, in Cairo in 1938. The AWA continued its work as a charitable association in Jerusalem after 1948.

See also ARAB WOMEN'S EXECUTIVE COMMITTEE; PALESTINE; ZIONISM.

Bibliography

Fleischmann, Ellen L. "The Emergence of the Palestinian Women's Movement, 1929–1939." *Journal of Palestine Studies* 29, no. 3 (2000): 16–32.

Mogannam, Matiel. *The Arab Woman and the Palestine Question.* London: Herbert Joseph, 1937.

ELLEN L. FLEISCHMANN

ARAB WOMEN'S CONGRESS

The first group of Palestinian women leaders, active during the British mandate.

Initiated in Palestine by elite Muslim and Christian women, the first Arab Women's Congress met in Jerusalem in 1929, marking the beginning of the modern Palestinian women's movement. The executive committee submitted frequent protests to British mandate authorities concerning the immigration of Jews and their land purchases, as well as general economic conditions. The congress focused on education and welfare activities.

Bibliography

Lesch, Ann M. *Arab Politics in Palestine, 1917–1939: The Frustration of a Nationalist Movement.* Ithaca, NY: Cornell University Press, 1979.

STEVE TAMARI

ARAB WOMEN'S EXECUTIVE COMMITTEE

The coordinating committee directing the women's groups that formed the Palestinian women's movement during the mandate period.

The Arab Women's Executive Committee (AWE) was formed in Jerusalem in 1929 with the aim of founding a women's movement in Palestine. The members of the committee were: Wahida al-Khalidi (president), Matiel Mogannam and Katrin Deeb (secretaries), Shahinda Duzdar (treasurer), Na'imiti al-Husayni, Tarab Abd al-Hadi, Mary Shihada, Anisa al-Khadra, Khadija al-Husayni, Diya al-Nashashibi, Melia Sakakini, Zlikha al-Shihabi, Mrs. Kamil Budayri, Fatima al-Husayni, Zahiya al-Nashashibi, and Sa'diyya al-Alami. Many of these women came from prominent nationalist families in Palestine, especially in the Jerusalem region. The committee planned and convened the first Palestine Arab Women's Congress in Jerusalem in 1929, during which it visited the High Commissioner of Palestine and presented its resolutions to him as a form of protest. According to the bylaws of the Arab Women's Association of Palestine (AWA), the umbrella organization for the local branches of the movement, the AWE was to be the coordinating and administrative committee for these affiliates. In actuality, the AWE was not active much beyond the early 1930s, after which the local chapters often behaved autonomously yet in cooperation with the Jerusalem AWA, which apparently took over the functions of the AWE, acting as the central coordinating body of the women's movement.

See also ARAB WOMEN'S ASSOCIATION OF PALESTINE; JERUSALEM; PALESTINE; ZIONISM.

Bibliography

Fleischmann, Ellen L. "The Emergence of the Palestinian Women's Movement, 1929–1939." *Journal of Palestine Studies* 29, no. 3 (2000): 16–32.

Mogannam, Matiel. *The Arab Woman and the Palestine Problem.* London: Herbert Joseph, 1937.

ELLEN L. FLEISCHMANN

ARAB WOMEN'S SOLIDARITY ASSOCIATION INTERNATIONAL

International Women's Rights organization that advocates liberation of Arab women.

The Arab Women's Solidarity Association International (AWSA) was founded in Egypt in 1982 by 120 women under the leadership of Dr. Nawal al Saadawi to promote Arab women's active participation in social, economic, cultural, and political life. Its aims were to link the struggle of Arabs for liberation and freedom from economic, cultural, and media domination to the liberation of Arab women. By 1985, AWSA International had 3,000 members and was granted consultative status with the Economic and Social Council of the United Nations. Between 1982 and 1991, AWSA International organized several international conferences, developed income-generating projects for economically underprivileged women, published literary magazines and books, and produced films about Arab women's lives. In 1991, AWSA International took a stance against the Gulf War and demanded that the UN takes a firm position against the war.

This action provoked the Egyptian government to close down *Noon*, the magazine published by the association and later to close down the association and turn its funds to an Islamic women organization. AWSA sued the government but lost the case. Egyptian government officials maintained that the banning was due to "irregularities" in AWSA's financial accounts. AWSA International's headquarters shifted to Algeria and then to Cairo by 1996.

In the United States, AWSA has two active chapters in Seattle and San Francisco with a board of directors of seven elected members. In 2001, AWSA San Francisco published a paper entitled "The Forgotten '-ism': An Arab American Women's Perspective on Zionism, Racism, and Sexism" that served as a training guide for activists. AWSA members have established Cyber AWSA in 1999, a web site and e-mail listserv that connects Arab women internationally. The Cyber AWSA listserv provides a space for Arab women and their allies to discuss and share information around issues relevant to their lives and experiences. It also serves as a springboard for activism related to Arab women's issues.

Bibliography

Arab Women Solidarity Association web site. Available from <http://www.awsa.net>.

Badran, Margot. "Competing Agenda: Feminists, Islam and the State in Nineteenth and Twentieth Century Egypt." In *Global Feminisms: A Survey of Issues and Controversies (Rewriting Histories)*, edited by Bonnie Smith. New York: Routledge, 2000.

Hitchcock, Peter. "The Eye and the Other: The Gaze and the Look in Egyptian Feminist Fiction." In *The Politics of (M)Othering: Womanhood, Identity, and Resistance in African Literature (Opening Out)*, edited by Obioma Nnaemeka. New York: Routledge, 1997.

Peteet, Julie, and Harlow, Barbara. "Gender and Political Change." *Middle East Report*, no. 173 (1991): 4–8.

"The Forgotten '-ism': An Arab American Women's Perspective on Zionism, Racism, and Sexism." Available from <http://www.awsa.net/forgottenism.pdf>.

RITA STEPHAN

ARAFAT, YASIR
[1929–]

Chairman of al-Fatah and the Palestine Liberation Organization, and president of the Palestinian Authority.

Between early 1969 and early 1994, Yasir Arafat (also Yasser Arafat) was transformed from a guerrilla leader advocating armed struggle for the liberation of Palestine to the president of the quasi-state of Palestine after negotiations with Israel, which had long denounced him as a terrorist. Despite frequent quarrels with rivals and subordinates, no other figure has been as closely identified with the Palestine Liberation Organization (PLO) or the Palestinian national struggle as Arafat. Born Muhammad Abd al-Ra'uf al-Arafat al-Qudwa, "Yasir" became Arafat's nickname during his early guerrilla days. He has since gone by Yasir Abd al-Ra'uf Arafat or just Yasir Arafat, except when using the nom de guerre Abu Ammar. Arafat and his family have always insisted that he was born 4 August 1929, in his mother's family home in Jerusalem. Nevertheless, an Egyptian birth registration exists, suggesting that he was born in Egypt on 24 August 1929. His father had been living in Egypt, but his mother may have returned to her home to give birth; others suspect that the record has been altered to give Arafat a Palestinian birthplace. He is, in any event, of old Palestinian lineage: The Qudwas (his father's line) are an offshoot of a Gaza branch of the Sunni Muslim al-Husayni (Husseini) family, whereas Arafat's mother came from the more prominent Jerusalem branch of the Husaynis. His father was a merchant trading in Gaza and Egypt; whether or not Arafat was born there, he spent many of his teenage years in Egypt and long had a detectable Egyptian accent. He was the sixth of seven children. In 1942, his father returned to Cairo, and Arafat continued his schooling there. He reportedly became an aide to the military leader of the Palestinian resistance, Abd al-Qadir al-Husayni, a kinsman on his mother's side. The young Yasir fought with the Muslim Brotherhood in Gaza during the Arab–Israel War of 1948. Following the war, the family returned to Gaza. In the 1950s, Arafat studied at Fu'ad I University in Cairo (now Cairo University), majoring in civil engineering. He was reportedly a member of the Muslim Brotherhood and also became active as a Palestinian student organizer, heading the Union of Palestinian Students from 1952 to 1957. He then served in the Egyptian army for about a year.

A master of survival, Yasir Arafat has fought for a Palestinian homeland for over forty years, finally winning the presidency of the Palestinian Authority in 1996. © AP/WIDE WORLD PHOTOS. REPRODUCED BY PERMISSION.

Al-Fatah and the PLO

Arafat and other Palestinian activists were in Prague in 1957 when some of their colleagues were arrested in Egypt, suspected of Muslim Brotherhood activities. Arafat and the two men who were to become his closest aides until their assassinations, Khalil al-Wazir and Salah Khalaf, remained in Europe. Arafat studied engineering further in Stuttgart and then went to Kuwait. While working for the public works department, he started his own contracting firm. This engineering firm prospered, and Arafat reportedly became quite wealthy. Some accounts suggest that his personal wealth helped fund the beginnings of al-Fatah. The nucleus of al-Fatah had already been formed in the late 1950s, by Arafat, al-Wazir, Khalaf, Khalid al-Hasan, and others in Kuwait, who would become lifelong colleagues. Ini-

tially, al-Fatah was one of many small Palestinian exile groups advocating armed struggle to free Palestine. Arafat received some training in Algeria, it is believed, and in Syria, where al-Fatah's armed wing, al-Asifa, was formed. He also was imprisoned in Syria for several weeks at this time.

After the 1967 war, al-Fatah's prominence increased greatly. The Palestine Liberation Organization (PLO), originally created under Egyptian auspices in January 1964, was overshadowed by the new guerrilla groups, which increasingly won control of the Palestine National Council (PNC). In 1968 al-Fatah fought off an Israeli attack on a base in Karama, Jordan, and its prestige increased further. In early 1969, al-Fatah and its allies won enough seats in the PNC to elect Arafat the new chairman of the PLO's executive committee. Arafat, now head of both al-Fatah and the PLO, set up his headquarters in Amman, Jordan. In 1970, the PLO was drawn into conflict with the government of Jordan when one of its member organizations, the Popular Front for the Liberation of Palestine (PFLP), hijacked several aircraft. In the ensuing Black September of 1970, the PLO was driven out of its Jordanian operational base. Arafat, who escaped from Amman, set up his new base in Beirut, while the PLO began operations against Israel from southern Lebanon. After the Arab–Israel War of 1973, some PLO leaders began discussing the possibility of a settlement short of the previously envisioned secular state in all of Palestine. On 14 November 1974, Arafat addressed the General Assembly of the United Nations, claiming that he held both "an olive branch and a freedom fighter's gun."

The UN speech marked a high point, but Arafat's career took another turn downward with the outbreak of the Lebanese Civil War in 1975. The PLO found itself fighting not only Maronite forces but eventually the Syrian army, though these alignments shifted as the war went on. The 1977 visit of Egypt's President Anwar Sadat to Jerusalem and the 1978 peace between Israel and Egypt were yet further blows, and then in 1982 Israel invaded Lebanon. Having been driven from Jordan more than a decade before and besieged in Lebanon by Syrians and others from time to time, the PLO had nevertheless managed to maintain its base in Lebanon. In June 1982 Israel not only occupied all of Lebanon up to Beirut but also (unsuccessfully) targeted Arafat personally. Arafat and ten thousand Palestinian fighters were evicted from Beirut in August. An attempt to form a new base in Tripoli, Lebanon, failed due to Syrian opposition and an intra-Fath mutiny, and Arafat and the PLO moved to Tunis, far from the zone of Israeli–Palestinian confrontation (although in 1985 Israel did bomb PLO headquarters there in 1985, including Arafat's compound).

In 1984, Arafat entered into negotiations with King Hussein ibn Talal of Jordan to seek a common ground for a joint Jordanian–Palestinian negotiating position—the so-called Jordanian Option. The effort failed, with Jordan blaming Arafat for the failure. In December 1987, the Intifada, or Palestinian uprising, began in the occupied territories. Although Arafat's al-Fatah was a major player in the Unified National Leadership of the Intifada, it was local cadres, not the Tunis leadership, who were in charge of the actual uprising. This led many analysts to once again predict that Arafat's days were numbered and that the central PLO leadership had lost its relevance. As in 1970, 1982, and 1984—when earlier political obituaries had been written—they were wrong. One of the strengths that had kept Arafat in his position for so long, despite squabbles, plots, and even fighting and assassinations among Palestinian factions, was his ability to forge a grand coalition of very differently oriented factions, left and right, communist and capitalist. Increasingly unable to hold such a broad umbrella group together, Arafat was finally willing to gamble on seizing a moderate, pronegotiation position despite the fact that this meant the more radical factions now considered him a curse.

Peace Negotiations

In 1988, the PLO leadership—now more and more Arafat and the old al-Fatah elite—agreed to recognize Israel's right to exist, the principle of negotiating with Israel on peace in exchange for territorial withdrawal, and a renunciation of terrorism. After some adjustment, the formula finally met the United States's preconditions for a direct dialogue with the PLO, and this dialogue began with the U.S. ambassador to Tunisia, Robert Pelletreau. It was subsequently suspended in June 1990 when Arafat failed to condemn an attack on Israeli territory by a PLO faction. When the Madrid Conference was held in October 1991 with U.S. president George H. W. Bush, the U.S.-PLO talks had been suspended and Israel's Likud government under Yitzhak Shamir adamantly refused to deal with the PLO, which was still seen as a terrorist organization. Therefore, the Palestinians were awkwardly represented in Madrid by a panel of moderate Palestinians, all of whom were acceptable to the PLO but none of whom had been formally members of it. As long as Likud was in power, they were also technically half of a "joint Jordanian–Palestinian delegation." Once again, despite the insistence by the delegation that they were in coordination with the PLO leadership in Tunis, many analysts declared that Arafat and the PLO were no longer relevant to the search for a Palestinian–Israeli solution. Meanwhile, in 1992, as Arafat was flying to Sudan in a private aircraft, his plane crashed in the Libyan desert, killing the pilots and several passengers. Arafat survived, but he was badly injured and required surgery to correct further problems. His friends later indicated that his survival, when so many others had died, convinced him that he had been providentially spared for some reason. The lifelong bachelor also married, further putting his guerrilla days behind him. These factors may have helped prepare him for the decision that he soon would have to make.

As long as Likud was in power, no breakthrough was possible, and the Palestinian side of the peace talks went nowhere. But Shamir was replaced by Yitzhak Rabin and the Labor Party in 1992. Frustrated with the difficulties of negotiating with a Palestinian delegation that had little real authority to offer compromise, a secret back-channel negotiation began via Norwegian intermediaries. Ultimately, the result was the Oslo Accord, signed on the White House lawn on 13 September 1993. For the first time, Arafat—once denounced as a terrorist by U.S. presidents and forbidden entrance into the United States after his 1974 UN speech—came to the White House to be greeted by a U.S. president. Even more dramatically, at the signing of the agreement he offered his hand to Yitzhak Rabin, and Rabin accepted it, albeit with apparent reluctance. That dramatic handshake on the White House lawn underscored the fact that Arafat had survived his enemies within the PLO as well as in Israel and the United States. Arafat became the provisional head of the Palestinian Authority (PA), which took over self-government in Jericho and Gaza in the summer of 1994 and, eventually, more of the West Bank as well. Arafat's entry into Jericho in June 1994 marked a personal vindication for Arafat, at least in his own view.

Palestinian Authority

Arafat formally was elected president of the Palestinian Authority during elections in January 1996. He oversaw the growth of a PA bureaucracy and a number of security and intelligence agencies. His leadership came under mounting criticism by Palestinians both inside and outside the PA. The most intractable were the Islamist movements HAMAS and Islamic Jihad, both of which vowed to continue attacks against Israel. These groups had the support of the Palestinian community, and Arafat had to balance the support extended by the Palestinian street with his needs both to placate his Israeli and U.S. peace partners and to maintain his tight grip on power in the PA. The failure of the peace process led to the violence of the al-Aqsa Intifada in October 2000, which in turn led to Israel's reoccupation of large parts of the PA, the destruction of its infrastructure, and the lengthy siege of Arafat's compound in Ramallah that began in 2002 and continued into 2004. Despite the efforts of Israeli prime minister Ariel Sharon to ignore and isolate him, and similar efforts by U.S. president George W. Bush, Arafat has remained head of al-Fatah, the PLO, the PA, and the Palestinian national movement generally, and no one of even remotely the same stature or power has emerged to take his place.

Arafat had never married during his long guerrilla years. In 1991 or early 1992, however, he married Suha Tawil (1963–), the daughter of a PLO activist father and a lawyer mother who often represented accused Palestinians in the territories. Tawil had served as Arafat's secretary. A Christian who reportedly converted to Islam, she is more than thirty years his junior. She has given a number of interviews to the Arab and Western press (and even to the Israeli press), providing for the first time an intimate view of Arafat. A daughter, Zahwa, was born to the couple in 1994. Arafat himself is a practicing Sunni Muslim and is believed to practice his faith. After the 1992 plane crash, his religious convictions were reportedly strengthened. In his younger

days he was a member of the Muslim Brotherhood, but in middle age he stands staunchly against the Islamist elements in the Palestinian movement. His health has deteriorated noticeably in recent years, but he remains a survivor in a region that recently has witnessed the passing of several long-standing Arab rulers.

See also ARAB–ISRAEL WAR (1948); BLACK SEPTEMBER; BUSH, GEORGE HERBERT WALKER; BUSH, GEORGE WALKER; CAIRO UNIVERSITY; FATAH, AL-; GAZA (CITY); HAMAS; HASAN, KHALID AL-; HUSAYNI, ABD AL-QADIR AL-; INTIFADA (1987–1991); ISLAMIC JIHAD; JORDANIAN OPTION; KHALAF, SALAH; LEBANESE CIVIL WAR (1975–1990); LIKUD; MADRID CONFERENCE (1991); MUSLIM BROTHERHOOD; OSLO ACCORD (1993); PALESTINE LIBERATION ORGANIZATION (PLO); PALESTINE NATIONAL COUNCIL (PNC); PALESTINIAN AUTHORITY (PA); POPULAR FRONT FOR THE LIBERATION OF PALESTINE; RABIN, YITZHAK; SADAT, ANWAR AL-; SHAMIR, YITZHAK; SHARON, ARIEL; WAZIR, KHALIL AL-; WEST BANK.

Bibliography

Aburish, Said K. *Arafat: From Defender to Dictator.* New York: Bloomsbury, 1998.

Cobban, Helena. *The Palestinian Liberation Organization: People, Power, and Politics.* Cambridge, U.K., and New York: Cambridge University Press, 1984.

Gowers, Andrew, and Walker, Tony. *Behind the Myth: Yasser Arafat and the Palestinian Revolution.* London: W. H. Allen, 1990.

Hart, Alan. *Arafat: A Political Biography.* Bloomington: Indiana University Press, 1989.

Iyad, Abou, with Rouleau, Eric. *My Home, My Land: A Narrative of the Palestinian Struggle.* New York: Times Books, 1981.

Kiernan, Thomas. *Arafat: The Man and the Myth.* New York: Norton, 1976.

Wallach, Janet, and Wallach, John. *Arafat: In the Eyes of the Beholder.* New York: Lyle Stuart, 1990.

MICHAEL DUNN
UPDATED BY MICHAEL R. FISCHBACH

A'RAJ, WASINI AL-
[1954–]

Algerian novelist and critic.

Wasini al-Aʿraj was born on 8 August 1954, in the village of Sidi-bou-Jnan, near Tlemcen, Algeria. He received his Ph.D. in Arabic literature from the University of Damascus, and he is a professor of Arabic literature at the University of Algiers.

Al-Aʿraj, who writes in Arabic, is one of the most prolific of the new generation of Algerian writers. He initiated a new trend in the structure of the novel and experimented with its language. The most striking aspect of his style is the explosion of the rigid traditional frame of the novel. The linear approach is abandoned for a more provocative and richer technique that depends on flashbacks, fragments of history, and childhood memories intermingled with folk traditions. His innovative technique has attracted the attention of critics to his novels, which include *Waqa'i, min Awja Rajulin Ghamara Sawba al-Bahr* (Facts from the sufferings of a man who ventured toward the sea [Algiers, 1983]), *Masra' Ahlam Mariam al-Wadiʿa* (The death of sweet Myriam's dreams [Beirut, 1984]), *Jughrafia al-Ajsad al-Muhtariqa* (The geography of the burned bodies [Algiers, 1979]), and *Nuwwar al-Luz* (Almond blossoms [Beirut, 1983]).

In his collection of short stories, *Alam al-Kitaba an Ahzan al-Manfa* (The pain of writing about the sadness of exile [Beirut, 1980]), al-Aʿraj presents a highly emotional text on the theme of love of homeland, which is personified as a woman. He often employs the soliloquy, a narrative form that is more an exercise in writing than in storytelling. Even in his romance novel, *Waq al-Ahdhiya al-Khashina* (The sound of the rough shoes [Beirut, 1981]), the narration is driven rather more by literary style than by events.

Al-Aʿraj's writings criticize the shortcomings of government and its failure to fulfill the promises made during the war of independence. Some of the problems he evokes are related to the struggle of the poor and hungry to survive, a struggle that is described in his collection of short stories, *Asmak al-Barr al-Mutawahhish* (The fish of the wild land [Algiers, 1986]).

Like other writers of his generation, al-Aʿraj treats the killing of Communists who fought during the war of independence in *Ma Tabaqqa min Sirat Lakhdar Hamrouche* (Whatever is left of the biography of Lakhdar Hamrouche [Damascus, 1986]). He often uses events and characters from Arab history to evoke the Algerian present, a common trend to be found among the writers of his generation. Al-Aʿraj's latest novel (as of 1995), *Faji'at al-Layla al-Sabiʿa Baʿda al-Alf* (The tragedy of the seventh night after the thousand, 2 vols. [Algiers, 1993]), conveys his interpretation of the events of the present on the basis of the characters and events of the *Thousand and One Nights*. The time frame of the novel is stretched to encompass fourteen centuries of Islamic religion, and the Qurʾanic story of the People of the Cave and the last years of the Andalusian political life are used to allude to the atrocities committed in Algeria in the name of Islam and democracy. It is clear that al-Aʿraj wants the Arab rulers of the present to learn from history in order that they might build a better future for their peoples. His pain reveals a confused man who is grappling to find a solution to a complex situation.

See also LITERATURE: ARABIC, NORTH AFRICAN.

Bibliography

Bamia, Aida. "Interview with al-Aʿraj Wasini." *CELFAN*, Review, no. 3 (1989): 23–26.

AIDA A. BAMIA

ARAL, OĞUZ
[1936–]

Turkish comedian and cartoonist.

Born in Istanbul and educated at the Istanbul Academy of Fine Arts, Aral first became known in the 1950s as a cartoonist. In the early 1960s, he made his name on the Turkish stage as a comic actor and pantomime artist. Aral became editor of the political comic-strip magazine *Girgir* in 1973. Under his direction, it became one of the top-selling humor magazines in the world, reaching a circulation of 450,000 in the late 1980s. In the 1990s he established his own humor magazine, *Avni*, and returned to producing plays.

ELIZABETH THOMPSON

ARARAT, MOUNT

Mountain in eastern Turkey that figures prominently in the Bible.

Mount Ararat (in Turkish Ağri Daği) is in the province of Ağri, eastern Turkey, near the border of Iran. First climbed in modern times in 1829, the mountain consists of two peaks—Great Ararat at 16,946 feet (5,165 m), and Little Ararat at 12,877 feet (3,927 m). According to the Book of Genesis in the Bible, Mount Ararat was the landing spot of Noah's Ark.

DAVID WALDNER

ARAZ, NEZIHE
[1922–]

Turkish journalist, biographer, and playwright.

Nezihe Araz is known for writing that is ideologically shaped by traditional Turkish and Islamic culture. Works such as *Anadolu evliyalari* (1959), *Dertli dolap—Yunus Emre'nin hayati* (1961), and *Ask Peygamberi Mevlana'nin romani* (1962) are structured around narratives about Anatolian Sufism and the two representatives of Sufi orders, Yunus Emre and Mevlana. Some of her plays have won national prizes; one of these, *Afife Jale* (1988), is based on the life of the first Muslim actress to appear on stage, who struggled with the established social mores of a society that did not allow women on stage. Other works concentrate on women's problems, including her first play, *Bozkir guzellemesi* (1975), about the struggle of women from Central Anatolia, and the later *Kuvayi milliye kadinlari,* about women in the Turkish War of Independence. *Kadin erenler* is based on the life stories of the twenty-eight women mystics in Islamic history. Araz also has written a biography and screenplay about Mustafa Kemal Atatürk's wife, Latife Hanim, whom he divorced in 1925 after only two years of marriage. The research that has inspired her plays and biographical writing is based on records collected through the family connections of her father, who was a member of parliament from the second Turkish Parliament until 1954.

See also ART; GENDER: GENDER AND EDUCATION; NEWSPAPERS AND PRINT MEDIA: TURKEY; THEATER; TURKEY.

AYSE DURAKBASA TARHAN

ARCH

Kabyle tribal structure.

The *arch* is a tribal structure founded on real or sometimes imagined family relationships that emerged in the Kabylic region of North Africa during the fif-

teenth century, when the dynastic system that had provided considerable central government control disintegrated. Free of external authority, different tribes needed to provide themselves with tools for dealing with conflict, land allocation, and other critical problems. In this context they developed relationships, and alliances merged within larger structures known as *arch* (plural, *arouch*). Under the Ottomans this sociopolitical form of organization was maintained largely intact for four centuries, but it faded away progressively during the colonial period as more and more power was assumed by the state.

In spring 2001 two events in the Kabylia, the killing by police of a high school student on 18 April and subsequent student demonstrations commemorating the 1980 Berber Spring, led to widespread demonstrations and violent repression by security forces that resulted in the deaths of more than fifty-one and injury to some 1,500. The period and its events came to be known as Black Spring. One local response was the creation of a populist movement known as the Coordination des Archs, which resurrected the traditional institution as a vehicle for expressing the social, cultural, and political demands of the Kabyles within an Algerian system dominated by Arabs. A laterally structured organization that reached decisions by consensus, it represented Kabyles from a broad range of communities and classes in seven *wilayas* (provinces)—Tizi Ouzou, Boujaia, Bouira, Setif, Bordj, Bou Arreridj, Boumerdes, and Algiers. In its platform, elaborated in the meeting of Illoula Oumalou on 17 May 2001, this essentially pacifistic organization affirmed its autonomy from state institutions and political parties. Its tactics included boycotts of national events and holidays, sit-ins, demonstrations, and celebrations of local culture. Because of its inclusive and populist approach, the Coordination encountered a considerable amount of internal dissidence and was criticized by Berber political parties. It did, however, achieve significant success as an interlocuter with the Algerian government.

See also BERBER SPRING; BLACK SPRING.

Bibliography

Brett, Michael, and Fentress, Elizabeth. *The Berbers.* Oxford, U.K.: Blackwell, 1997.

AZZEDINE G. MANSOUR

ARCHAEOLOGICAL MUSEUM (ISTANBUL)

A major museum complex of three pavilions.

The pavilions are the Çinili Köşk (Tiled Pavilion), which, as its name indicates, is where Turkish tiles and ceramics are displayed; the Museum of the Ancient Orient, which houses mostly Hittite and Mesopotamian antiquities; and the Archaeological Museum building, which displays classical artifacts.

The Archaeological Museum building, commissioned by the first museum director in Turkey, Osman Hadi Bey, was opened to the public in 1891. The Museum of the Ancient Orient had been first founded as the Academy for Fine Arts in 1883.

Originally the Çinili Köşk housed the Ottoman collection. The spectacular discovery of a large number of sarcophagi at the Royal Necropolis at Sidon, Lebanon, in 1887, however, together with the growing Ottoman interest in the empire's antiquity-rich hinterland, necessitated the creation of a new space. These factors led to construction of the Archaeological Museum, first named the Museum of Sarcophagi. Important architectural elements of the museum's design were inspired by two of its most famous sarcophagi—the Alexander Sarcophagus and the Sarcophagus of the Mourning Women.

The Archaeological Museum houses some 45,000 pieces: Of these, 9,000 are stone objects; 12,000 are pieces of pottery; 10,000 are terra-cotta figurines; 10,000 are metal objects; and 3,000 are glass objects. A shortage of space allows only a small portion of this collection to be displayed at any one time. The museum has a library that contains approximately 80,000 books covering a wide range of topics. The museum also has an enormous cuneiform tablet collection (about 75,000 pieces) and a rich coin collection (about 760,000 coins).

KAREN PINTO

ARCHAEOLOGY IN THE MIDDLE EAST

Serious archaeological inquiry in the Middle East began during the Renaissance when Europeans became interested in their Christian and classical roots.

The key sources for the Middle East's archaeological past, the Bible and Homer's *Iliad*, inspired gentlemen scholars, travelers, and, later, members of the various European diplomatic missions, to discover sites and decipher scripts that launched the newly developing discipline of archaeology. Their interest was the ancient world—the Islamic period was deemed too recent and not particularly relevant to European historical interests. Europeans collected statues, pottery, and tablets for the sake of knowledge and the glory of imperialism and shipped them back to European metropoles, often without permission of local authorities.

The Eighteenth and Nineteenth Centuries

Napoléon Bonaparte's Egyptian expedition (1798–1801) initiated the scramble for the acquisition of antiquities from the Middle East. The discovery of the trilingual Rosetta Stone enabled Jean-François Champollion to decipher ancient Egyptian hieroglyphics. French scholars continued to remain heavily involved in Egyptology on Egyptian soil until 1952. Auguste Mariette, dispatched to Egypt by the Louvre to collect papyri, received permission from Khedive Isma'il ibn Ibrahim to establish the Egyptian Antiquities Service (1858) and the Egyptian Museum in Cairo in 1863. His successor, Gaston Maspéro, encouraged excavation by other foreign scholars. The British established the Egyptian Exploration Fund and sent Flinders Petrie (1853–1942), who set new standards for exact recording, publishing, and the study of pottery, and founded the British School of Archaeology in Egypt.

Napoléon's short sojourn in Palestine sparked new interest in the land of the Bible, which, until then, was solely the destination of religious pilgrims. Travelers found significant sites. Johann Ludwig Burckhardt (1784–1817) located Petra, and Lady Hester Stanhope (1776–1831) visited Palmyra. The field of biblical archaeology was inaugurated by the work of Edward Robinson (1858–1931). Robinson was followed by groups of international sponsors: the American Oriental Society; the American Palestine Oriental Society; the British Palestine Exploration Fund, which began work on Jerusalem in 1867; the German Society for the Exploration of Palestine (Deutscher Palästina-Verein); the École Biblique; and the Deutsche Orient Gesellschaft, which excavated Megiddo from 1901 to 1905. Maps and surveys of Jerusalem and other sections of the Holy Land were produced during the formative period in

Wall painting from the tomb of Queen Nefertari in Egypt. Discovered in 1904, the tomb features many beautifully colored wall paintings that were restored in 1994 by the Egyptian Antiquities Organization and the Getty Conservation Institute. Admission to the tomb, which lies in Luxor's Valley of the Queens, is limited to 150 persons per day to aid in the preservation of the structure. © CORBIS. REPRODUCED BY PERMISSION.

biblical archaeology. Intense interest in the area by U.S. Protestant groups led to the establishment of various Catholic and Russian (Eastern) Orthodox institutions. Jewish archaeological work began with the formation of the Jewish Palestine Exploration Society shortly before World War I.

In Mesopotamia (Iraq) and Persia (Iran), the British, Germans, and French achieved the major breakthroughs. The British resident of the East India Company in Baghdad, Claudius James Rich (1787–1820), surveyed Babylon and published his findings in 1818. In the 1840s Paul Emile Botta (1802–1870), the French consular agent at Mosul,

worked at Assyrian Nineveh, while Austen Henry Layard (1817–1894) excavated ancient Nimrud, and the French explored areas around Basra. Most of the work was sponsored by the British Museum and ceased during the Crimean War, resuming in the 1870s.

Georg Friedrich Grotefend (1775–1853) and Sir Henry Creswicke Rawlinson (1810–1895) worked on Old Persian and deciphered cuneiform. This could not have been accomplished without the transcriptions of Karsten Niebuhr (1733–1815) at Persepolis and Rawlinson's own painstaking copy of the inscriptions on the Behistun Rock. Cracking the cuneiform code expanded human history to prebiblical eras, and enabled Sir Leonard Woolley (1880–1960) to work on Abraham's Ur and the pre-Akkadian Sumerians. U.S. interest in Mesopotamia was fostered by the American Oriental Society, which focused on Assyria and Babylonia in addition to its goal of cultivating learning in the "Asiatic, African, and Polynesian languages."

The secular underpinnings of modern archaeology, namely that human existence predated the biblical Flood, the theory of evolution, and the categorization of human existence into the Stone, Bronze, and Iron Ages, affected the secularly oriented countries of the Middle East less than the Islamic monarchies. For the religious Muslim, the period before Islam, the *jahiliyya,* was the age of ignorance, and they had no interest in it. Egyptians, both Copts and Muslims, became interested in Egypt's pre-Islamic past very early. Rifaʿa al-Rafi al-Tahtawi, intrigued by the work on the Rosetta Stone, published a history of Egypt from the Pharoanic period and encouraged Egyptians to become involved in archaeology. Ahmad Kamal (1851–1923) established Egyptology for the Egyptians.

The Twentieth Century

Excavations in Syria, Lebanon, Iraq, and Palestine, were directed by Europeans. The discoveries at Byblos, Ras Shamra (Ugarit, 1929), Tall al-Hariri (Mari) in Syria, and Ebla revealed the link between ancient Semitic cultures in the Bronze Age. As a result, history was worked into pan-Arab ideology and local nationalisms. Pan-Arabism stressed the unity of pre-Islamic Semites, and Maronites in Lebanon and the Syrian Social Nationalist Party in Syria looked to their Phoenician and Canaanite forbears. The governments of North African countries became interested in Carthaginians and the Romans who settled along the southern coast of the Mediterranean.

As Middle Eastern countries achieved independence or asserted their national identities, they began to control the study of their own pasts and to direct their own archaeological excavations. By 1936, Iraq, newly independent, placed legal restrictions on foreign excavations and in 1941, appointed Tahir Baqir curator of the Iraqi National Museum in Baghdad and editor of *Sumer* (founded in 1945), which was devoted to investigating the Mesopotamian past. This study was continued under the Baʿth Party. Saddam Hussein, president of Iraq, used archaeology to stress the unity of ancient Mesopotamia in a country beset by ethnic and religious strife and, in pan-Arab terms, to emphasize Iraq's glorious Semitic past as opposed to Iran's later development. In spite of almost constant war since 1980, Saddam renovated the National Museum, designated the State Organization for Antiquities and Heritage to control all excavations, renovations, and tours to sites, and began rebuilding Babylon, completing the Ishtar Gate, amphitheater, ziggurat, and Ishtar Temple, in order to stress the city's special significance in Mesopotamian history.

Until the early 1960s, archaeology in Iran was dominated by the French, who began to excavate at Susa in the nineteenth century. In 1961 the government established a department of archaeological services and the Iran Bastan Museum in Tehran. By then, under Shah Mohammad Reza Pahlavi, Iran's Persian past was stressed almost to the exclusion of its Islamic significance. The Islamic religious population was angered by the intensive linguistic study, additional excavations at Siyalk, Tepe Yahya, and Marlik, and the lauding of the Pahlavis as successors to a long line of Persian dynasties whose capital at Persepolis was used as the setting for the 2,500th anniversary party of ancient Persian rule. Since the overthrow of the shah in 1979 and the establishment of a theocratic regime in Iran, there has been little concern with the country's pre-Islamic roots.

Nestled in the mountains of Jordan lie the ruins of Petra (known in the Bible as Sela), a fortress city carved out of high sandstone cliffs that once controlled the main commercial routes in the region. The ruins were rediscovered in 1812 by the Europeans, but were not fully surveyed and classified until the beginning of the twentieth century. © JOSE FUSTE RAGA/CORBIS. REPRODUCED BY PERMISSION.

Biblical archaeological research continued during the British mandate for Palestine, on both sides of the Jordan River. William Foxwell Albright's work on ancient Moab in Transjordan (Jordan) and in the Dead Sea area complemented Kathleen Kenyon's excavations at Jericho. The Jewish Palestine Exploration Society, founded in 1914 by Nahum Slouschz, undertook its first excavations at Hammath-Tiberias in 1921, and by 1928, the archaeology department at the Hebrew University of Jerusalem was headed by noted Jewish scholar E. L. Sukenik. Noted Palestinian Arab archaeologists during the mandate included Tawfiq Canaan, Dmitri Baramki, and Stephen Hanna Stephan. The Rockefeller Museum (later called the Palestinian Archaeological Museum), situated in what became in Israeli-occupied East Jerusalem after 1967, became a major repository for biblical artifacts.

A sixth-century wall relief in ancient Persia's capital, Persepolis, depicts figures climbing a stone staircase with offerings to the king. Excavation and documentation at Persepolis began in earnest in the 1930s. © CORBIS. REPRODUCED BY PERMISSION.

Archaeology in Israel remains focused on religious history, primarily of the Jewish and early Christian periods. Politically, excavations at biblical sites of the Megiddo of King Solomon, patriarchal Tel-Sheva at Beersheba, and at Davidic and Second Temple Jerusalem serve to authenticate Zionist claims to the land. Yigael Yadin's finds at Masada proved the existence of the heroic Jew—a counterfoil to the Holocaust victim—and provided physical evidence for the histories of Jewish Roman historian Josephus Flavius. The Dead Sea Scrolls, housed in the Shrine of the Book at the Israel Museum, focus on the origins of Christianity.

Heinrich Schliemann's excavations at Hissarlik (thought to be Troy) and Hugo Winckler's identification of the Hittite capital Hattusas at Bogazköy in 1905 sparked interest in the multicultural antecedents of Anatolia, which only recently was inhabited by the Turks. Saudi Arabia had explored early sites on the pilgrimage routes to the Hijaz, and in the late 1960s become interested in the significance of the Arabian peninsula in the development of human civilization. In the mid-1970s the Saudi government sponsored surveys of pre-Islamic sites in the peninsula and scholarly work on the Nabateans

and early Semitic peoples. Kuwait, Oman, and some of the United Arab Emirates began collecting Islamic antiquities and opened museums, such as the Dar al-Athar al-Islamiyya in Kuwait.

Politics of Archaeology in the Middle East

Archaeological sites and finds have provoked controversy in the Middle East. Whereas governments and political movements in the region have used archaeology and archaeological artifacts to bolster their ideological claims, terrorists have targeted archaeological and cultural sites, sometimes in an effort to kill Western tourists and disrupt tourism. In November 1997 seventy-one people died in an attack on tourists at the Luxor temple site in Egypt. Islamic militants are assumed to have been the culprits. In late 1999 Jordanian officials uncovered a plot by the al-Qaʿida network to attack tourists at several biblical sites in the country.

The theft and/or destruction of archaeological artifacts and cultural heritage items, particularly during wartime, also has created political storms in the Middle East and Southwest Asia. The Hague Conventions of 1899 and 1907 and the Washington Pact of 1935 deal with the necessity of belligerent powers to protect one another's cultural property. The Hague Convention for the Protection of Cultural Property in the Event of Armed Conflict (14 May 1954; entered in effect 7 August 1956) also forbids the removal of cultural artifacts by an occupying power. The Arab–Israel conflict has been particularly fraught with violations of these policies. Both Israeli and Jordanian authorities failed to prevent the desecration or destruction of religious sites and cemeteries in Jerusalem (and elsewhere) after the first Arab–Israel War in 1948. After Israel's occupation of the West Bank, including the eastern half of Jerusalem, in June 1967, Israeli archaeologists carried out numerous digs in the territory; Palestinians claimed they were pillaging their cultural artifacts. So sensitive has the issue of ownership of these items become that the Israeli–Palestinian peace process that began in 1993 early on addressed continued Israeli digs in certain areas. The Department of Antiquities of the Palestinian Authority has expressed its desire to regain items excavated from the West Bank by the Israelis, if and when a final peace treaty is signed. Palestinians also have expressed fears that digs in Jerusalem could compromise the structural integrity of important Islamic shrines nearby. For example, Israel's opening of an ancient tunnel in the city near al-Haram al-Sharif prompted disturbances in September 1996. Archaeological digs have also provoked violent confrontations among Jews in Israel, particularly in Jerusalem, where religious Jews have battled Israeli police over archaeological digs in areas deemed by some to be ancient Jewish cemeteries. Finally, some have complained that Israeli and Western archaeological activity has ignored the Islamic and Ottoman periods in favor of Biblical excavations.

One related issue rose to the international level. When Israel took over the Rockefeller Museum in East Jerusalem in 1967, the museum and its artifacts were incorporated into the Israeli Department of Antiquities and administered by the Israel Museum. Israel confiscated the Rockefeller Museum on the grounds that it was the property of the conquered Jordanian government (Jordan nationalized the museum in November 1966). When the Israel Museum tried to include some items from the Rockefeller Museum in a 1985 exhibition in the United States titled "Treasures from the Holy Land: Ancient Art from the Israel Museum," the Metropolitan Museum of Art in New York challenged Israel's acquisition of some of the items. The United States's Smithsonian Institution then agreed to host the exhibit the following year, but objected to the inclusion of eleven artifacts from the Rockefeller Museum. Israel refused to change the exhibition, which consequently was canceled.

Other examples of the theft of cultural property or destruction of archaeological sites abound. In October 2000 during the al-Aqsa Intifada, Palestinians sacked Joseph's Tomb, the reputed tomb of the biblical figure Joseph, in the West Bank city of Nablus, completely destroying the shrine that was venerated by Jews. Following Iraq's invasion of Kuwait in August 1991, Iraqi museum officials carted away the contents of the Kuwait National Museum and Dar al-Athar al-Islamiyya to Baghdad. The collections were returned after the Gulf War by the United Nations Return of Property (UNRP) agency, although fifty-nine valuable items were missing. During the U.S. invasion of Iraq in Spring 2003 there was an international furor when Iraqi museums were looted after the collapse of Saddam Hussein's regime. As the occupying power, the United States was responsible for securing these storehouses of archaeological and cultural treasures dating back 5,000 years, but in April 2003 the National Museum in Baghdad was looted by common pilferers and professional art thieves who stole nearly 15,000 artifacts. Although some precious objects had been hidden by museum employees and were recovered, more than 10,000 items were still missing by September 2003. These included the world's oldest example of representational sculpture, the Sumerian Warka Mask (3500 B.C.E.), and the Akkadian Bassetki Statue (2300 B.C.E.). Not all examples of destruction or theft occurred during wartime. In March 2001 the Taliban regime in Afghanistan destroyed 1,500-year-old statues of the Buddha in its own city of Bamyan because they were deemed idols that were offensive to Islam.

Despite such setbacks, virtually every country in the Middle East has established its own department of antiquities, where local employees either undertake or supervise foreign work, and they have enacted strict legislation against the export of national historical treasures. Countries have also worked with international agencies to save cherished monuments, including in Iraq, where Interpol tracked down some of the items looted from the National Museum in Baghdad. By November 2003 more than 3,400 items from the museum had been recovered, including the Warka Mask and the Bassetki Statue.

See also AQSA INTIFADA, AL-; ARAB–ISRAEL CONFLICT; BAMYAN; BASRA; BEERSHEBA; BONAPARTE, NAPOLÉON; COPTS; CRIMEAN WAR; DEAD SEA; DEAD SEA SCROLLS; EGYPTIAN MUSEUM; HARAM AL-SHARIF; HEBREW UNIVERSITY OF JERUSALEM; HIJAZ; HUSSEIN, SADDAM; ISMAʿIL IBN IBRAHIM; JERICHO; JERUSALEM; LUXOR; MARIETTE, AUGUSTE; MARONITES; MASADA; MASPÉRO, GASTON; MOSUL; PAHLAVI, MOHAMMAD REZA; PALESTINIAN AUTHORITY; PALESTINIANS; PALMYRA; PETRA; ROCKEFELLER MUSEUM; SYRIAN SOCIAL NATIONALIST PARTY; TAHTAWI, RIFAʿA AL-RAFI AL-; TALIBAN; TIBERIAS; WEST BANK; YADIN, YIGAEL.

Bibliography

Glock, Albert. "Archaeology." In Encyclopedia of the Palestinians, edited by Philip Mattar. New York: Facts On File, 2000.

Lewis, Bernard. *History: Remembered, Recovered, Invented.* Princeton, NJ: Princeton University Press, 1971.

Reid, Donald M. "Egyptology: The Decolonization of a Profession?" *Journal of the American Oriental Society* 105 (1985): 233–246.

Silberman, Neil Asher. *Between Past and Present.* New York: Henry Holt, 1989.

REEVA S. SIMON
UPDATED BY MICHAEL R. FISCHBACH

ARCHITECTURE

An area of great cultural creativity.

The architecture and city planning of the countries of North Africa and the Middle East are steeped in a history that has been marked by the development of Arab and Islamic culture since the seventh century. The architectural and urban traditions generated by this culture produced a remarkable built environment—composed of beautiful monuments of the Islamic art—and spatial typologies. Since the nineteenth century, this architectural inheritance has cohabited with and contrasted with a contemporary architecture that was produced on the one hand by an endogenous dynamics of "Westernization" developed during the Ottoman imperial period, and on the other hand by different forms of colonial domination (mainly French and British).

Since the independence of the region's countries, architecture has been the product of essentially two tendencies. In the vernacular, "minor" architecture, age-old traditions rooted in the materials, climate, and social structure of the local environment mark buildings in both rural areas and in new urban districts, where the self-construction is encouraged. There, the population produces an architecture without architects, and old forms cohabit, harmoniously or in a disjointed way, with modern structures. By contrast, in official, "major" architecture, buildings whose construction relied on governmental or institutional patronage have undergone a metamorphosis that has altered dramatically historical traditions and reflects the increasing impact of international styles and construction methods.

In addition to this influence, during the last thirty years the rate of construction in this part of the world has been intense, so architectural development has been rapid and buildings production radically transformed. However, as Udo Kultermann explained in *Contemporary Architecture in the Arab States,* this "rapidity and gigantic dimension of the transformation caused problems, among them waste, inefficiency, and misstated priorities, [and] the focus of international architectural activity shifted from Europe and North America to the Arab states as the world elite of the architectural profession competed with each other and with the emerging generation of Arab architects" (p. 1).

The Islamic Legacy

In the contemporary architecture, the influence of the Islamic legacy and local traditions is apparent not only superficially, in building forms and ornaments; instead, it affects the very design process. It "became, as the Aga Khan said, an instinctive manner of expression for any architect designing anywhere in the Islamic world" (The Aga Khan, 1979, cited by Kultermann, p.4). Old principles that governed the organization of space and the Isalmic aesthetic are actualized according to modern building requirements and are reintroduced to satisfy the religious rules and the climate. In addition, new buildings are least likely to complement the existing buildings so changes to the city environment are generally made house by house, block by block, and not by urban overhaul. If planned buildings are close to cities' historic districts, architects and governments build with care and sensitivity, but in cities' peripheries, they often propose buildings that do not correspond to the population's needs or lifestyles.

The Colonial Legacy

Even before the establishment of colonial empires in the Middle East, economic decline had reduced the quantity and quality of official patronage of architecture. Simultaneously, European styles influenced the building of European embassies and commercial concerns and the way that official patronage relied upon architects and builders who had traveled or studied in Europe, European publications on architecture, and changing tastes in Islamic courts. In the Ottoman Empire, for example, the Balyan family provided three generations of official architects for the sultans beginning in 1822, producing mosques, palaces, and other official buildings that reflected a mixture of European styles.

The Shahid Motahari Mosque in the Iranian capital of Tehran was built in the thirteenth century during the Qajar period. The mosque and school consists of chambers, porticos, a palace for prayer, a reputable library, and eight minarets from which the city can be viewed. © PAUL ALMASY/CORBIS. REPRODUCED BY PERMISSION.

European governments, banks, commercial trading enterprises, and missionary institutions began to erect buildings in the European style. French styles prevailed in Algeria and later in the Maghrib; the style of the Balyans and later the Italian architect Montani gained currency in the Ottoman capital of Constantinople (now Istanbul); in Egypt, Muham-

mad Ali (r. 1805–1848) favored buildings in a Europeanized Ottoman style, and the Khedive Isma'il ibn Ibrahim (r. 1863–1879), who had studied in Europe, imported European architects to build his palaces and to make over modern Cairo in the image of Paris under the Second Empire. Elsewhere on the Mediterranean littoral, and to an extent in

Iran, French, Italian, and British architectural ideas left their stamp on museums and government buildings.

Nationalism and Architecture

By the end of the nineteenth century, European architectural ideas had provoked reactions from Middle Eastern architects and from Europeans who were sensitive to local traditions. Moreover, as the neo-Islamic building style gained popularity in Europe in the nineteenth century, it began to appear in the Middle East as well. In Egypt a substantial number of Islamic Revival buildings were erected by local and foreign architects in Cairo and in Alexandria; these used European construction methods and floor plans but were decorated with Islamic motifs. Examples include Alfonso Manescalo's Islamic Museum (1903–1904) and Mahmud Fahmi's Awqaf Ministry building (after 1898). In the Ottoman Empire a revival of governmental patronage in the late nineteenth century led to an early-twentieth-century Ottoman Revival style, whose chief practitioners were the architects Kemalettin Bey and Mehmet Vedat, and to a new-Islamic style that drew its inspiration from Spain and the Maghrib, exemplified by the Valide Mosque (1873) by Montani, and by the mid-nineteenth-century neo-Marinid gateway to what is now Istanbul University. In Casablanca, the Law Courts and other official buildings that were built under the French protectorate reflected an attempt to understand and to promote "appropriate" local styles.

Nationalist architecture in the Middle East emerged during the twentieth century. The Ottoman Revival under the Young Turks in the early twentieth century manifested a new Turkish nationalism and sparked a tradition reflected today in the neo-Ottoman contemporary buildings of Sedad Hakki Eldem, such as his many Bosporus villas (*yah*) and the massive central complex of Istanbul University. After the Atatürk revolution, German architects were invited to devise a city plan for modern Ankara; public monuments in European styles often drew upon what their designers believed were the pre-Islamic Hittite and Assyrian traditions of Anatolia.

Similar attention to the pre-Islamic past was seen in the architecture of Iran under the Pahlavis, where the monarchy stressed cultural continuity not only with the Safavid Islamic past but also with a Persian heritage stretching back to Cyrus the Great. The government of Reza Pahlavi spent vast sums on restoring monuments, especially those that had been built with earlier royal patronage, while largely adopting the modern international style in its new institutional buildings. The regime's Islamic successor has produced no significant architecture that indicates its own political and religious agenda, mostly because of the country's economic decline and the demands of its war with Iraq.

Morocco's independence from the French, gained in 1956, led to a pronounced nationalism in architecture, first expressed in the tomb complex of Muhammad V in Rabat, and in the 1990s in a series of laws that required that the construction budgets for all institutional and governmental buildings allot a substantial percentage of funds to strictly defined traditional Moroccan crafts.

In Egypt, by contrast, the revolution of the 1950s led to a socialist government whose official architecture often imitated the monumental style popular in the Soviet Union, best exemplified in the massive and forbidding Central Government Building in Cairo. National revolutions thus developed architectural patronage that reflected their own ideologies. For example, the secularist Ba'thist regime in Iraq, when it drew on the past for inspiration, typically looked to the neo-Babylonian period rather than to traditional Islam, a tendency that increased under the government of Saddam Hussein. In a parallel though far less pronounced tendency, Egypt has sought pharaonic inspiration for building styles and public monuments. In Central Asia, Russia first pushed its Stalinist architectural agenda, then later espoused the Soviet version of modernism. At the same time, the Soviet governments in Central Asia put significant effort into restoring Islamic monuments such as the giant mosque of Bibi Khanym in Samarkand, and religious monuments in Tashkent and Bukhara.

Contemporary Dilemmas

Middle Eastern attempts to adapt modern Western architecture often conflicts with the desire to bring about a renaissance of traditional architecture, or to produce a modern Islamic architecture that can

The Süleymaniye Mosque in Istanbul, Turkey, was commissioned in 1550 by Sultan Süleyman the Magnificent and completed seven years later. Sinan, the mosque's master architect, used four main columns to support the structure: one from Baʿalbak, one from Alexandria, and two from ancient Byzantine palaces. © LAWRENCE MANNING/CORBIS. REPRODUCED BY PERMISSION.

keep its distinctive local or regional style while drawing upon the best of the new technology. There have been several institutional attempts to deal with this dilemma, but none has been more influential than the Aga Khan Awards, established in the late 1970s by the leader of the world's Ismaʿili Muslims. Beginning in 1980 an international jury composed of architects and others from the Islamic world, Europe, and the United States has periodically awarded prizes for contemporary Middle Eastern architecture that best reflects Islamic traditions and values combined with artistic distinction. The honored styles have varied widely, from the neotraditionalist architecture of Hassan Fathy in Egypt, typified in his buildings for the Wissa Wassef Foundation in Harraniya, near Giza, to the technically and formally avant-garde water towers designed for Kuwait City by the Swedish firm VBB. In general, the juries have shown remarkable breadth of vision and have taken an inclusive and eclectic (rather than ideological and

purist) approach to the enormous range of distinctive modern Middle Eastern architectural styles. Awards have been given for domestic architecture, historical restoration, institutional buildings, adaptive reuse, and commercial buildings. The first awards were memorialized in 1983 in a publication edited by Renata Holod; subsequent years' awards, and other subjects of Middle Eastern architecture, have been featured in the periodical *Mimar: Architecture in Development* (up to 1994).

Three main issues confront governments, patrons, architects, and urban planners in the Middle East today. The first is how and whether there should be an ideology of architecture; the answer in Morocco has been an unequivocal yes, reflected in neotraditionalist building codes that emphasize traditional ornament and decorative crafts while utilizing modern technology to the fullest. For example, the mosque of Hassan II in Casablanca (thought of as a pendant to the impressive twelfth-century ruins of the Almohad mosque in Rabat), although constructed in classical Moroccan forms and proportions with classical decoration, is an outsized reinforced-concrete giant whose skyscraper minaret is surmounted by a huge laser that sends beams far into the sky. Its construction has been hailed for its Islamic symbolism and condemned for its extravagance during a time of financial difficulties. Similar ideology prevailed in the reconstruction of the two major pilgrimage shrines in Mecca and Medina by the Saudi government. Although they greatly facilitate the comfort and ease (if not the safety) of vastly increased numbers of pilgrims, these structures, lavish in size and decoration and traditional in style, raise more questions than they answer about the future of Middle Eastern religious architecture.

Examples of the opposite approach, which could be termed "creative pluralism," are found in Turkey and Tunisia, where many different styles, structures, and forms of decoration exist side by side in a creative mixture. The issue remains: Is appropriate architecture to consist of a traditional decorative veneer on what are essentially Western buildings in plan and construction, or is the new architecture of the Middle East going to be based from the ground up on the rich mosaic of social, environmental, and historical traditions? In fact, with few exceptions, local vernacular architecture is disappearing, replaced by undistinguished modern structures or by an equally alien homogenized national traditionalism that often consists of little more than employing the arch solely as a decorative device on building surfaces.

The second issue is curricula in architectural schools and colleges. The twentieth-century conflict about the role of teaching and learning the art and architecture of the past exists in the Middle East as it does elsewhere; the almost universal acceptance of Western-originated construction techniques and equipment (reinforced concrete, steel, glass, the tower crane, and so on) lends an almost surreal quality to some of these debates, and the issues often have been obscured as much as illumined by the polemics against the West exercised by individuals such as the late Isma'il Faruqi. The dialectic between historicism and artistic creativity is as old as art itself, however, and these debates are bound to survive as an essential part of the creative process.

The third issue is one that confronts architects and patrons everywhere. Even an examination of the record of the Aga Khan Awards demonstrates an impressive array of beautiful structures that are creative in design and impressive in sensitivity to tradition, but for the most part, whether they are private houses or public monuments, expensive to construct and affordable to few. Whether architecture in the Middle East can fulfill its implicit role—to provide decent housing and urban environments for exploding populations while reflecting its national and local traditions and remaining affordable—is a dilemma that will not easily be resolved.

See also Atatürk, Mustafa Kemal; Balyan Family; Ba'th, al-; Eldem, Sedad Hakki; Fahmi, Mahmud Pasha; Hussein, Saddam; Isma'il ibn Ibrahim; Istanbul University; Kemalettin Bey; Muhammad Ali; Pahlavi, Reza; Young Turks.

Bibliography

The Aga Khan. *Introduction of the Aga Khan Award for Architecture. Proceedings.* Instanbul: Aga Khan Award for Architecture, 1979.

Akbar, Jamel. *Crisis in the Built Environment: The Case of the Muslim City.* Singapore: Concept Media Pte Ltd., 1998.

Evin, Ahmed. *Architecture Education in the Islamic World.* Singapore: Concept Media Pte. Ltd./Aga Khan Award for Architecture 1986.

Faruqi, Ismail al-. "Islam and Architecture." In *Fine Arts in Islamic Civilization,* edited by M. A. J. Berg. Kuala Lumpur: Alif International, 1981.

Holod, Renata, and Rastorfer, Darl, eds. *Architecture and Community: Building in the Islamic World Today.* New York: Aperture, 1983.

Kultermann, Udo. *Contemporary Architecture in Arab States. Renaissance of a Region.* New York: McGraw-Hill, 1999.

Sakr, Tarek Mohamed Refaat. *Early Twentieth-Century Islamic Architecture in Cairo.* Cairo: American University in Cairo Press, 1993.

Walter Denny
Updated by Azzedine G. Mansour

ARD, AL-

A Palestinian political movement within Israel.

Al-Ard (Arabic, "the Land") was a pan-Arab nationalist movement supportive of Egyptian president Gamal Abdel Nasser that emerged in 1959 among Palestinian citizens in Israel. It not only challenged the legitimacy of Israel; it also opposed the traditional leadership of the Palestinian community in Israel, which it accused of cooperating with the Israelis. Al-Ard also presented an alternative to the communists, who had dominated Arab politics in Israel. Leading figures included Sabri Jiryis, Habib Qahwaji, Salih Baransi, Mansur Qardawsh (also Kardosh), and Muhammad Mi'ari.

Israeli authorities banned al-Ard in 1964. The following year, al-Ard tried to field a list of candidates for the Knesset elections of 1965 using the new name the Arab Socialist List, but the Israeli authorities banned it once again. Some of the leaders, like Mi'ari, went on to form the Progressive List for Peace in the early 1980s.

Bibliography

Fischbach, Michael R. "The Palestinians." In *Political Parties of the Middle East and North Africa*, edited by Frank Tachau. Westport, CT: Greenwood Press, 1994.

Jiryis, Sabri. *The Arabs in Israel, 1948–1966*, translated by Inea Bushnaq. New York: Monthly Review Press, 1976.

Lustick, Ian. *Arabs in the Jewish State: Israel's Control of a National Minority*. Austin: University of Texas Press, 1980.

BRYAN DAVES
UPDATED BY MICHAEL R. FISCHBACH

ARENS, MOSHE

[1925–]

Israeli politician and cabinet minister.

Born in Lithuania, Moshe Arens immigrated to the United States in 1939 and to Israel in 1948. Having received his academic training at the Massachusetts and California Institutes of Technology, he was professor of aeronautical engineering at Haifa University from 1958 to 1961. He was vice president of Israeli Aircraft Industries from 1962 until 1971. Arens was elected to the Knesset in 1977 and served as chair of the Herut central committee from 1977 to 1978. From 1977 to 1982, he was also chair of the Knesset Foreign Affairs and Security Committee. Hawkish in his security views, Arens opposed the 1978 Camp David Accords in the Knesset vote. During Israel's invasion of Lebanon (1982–1983),

he was ambassador to the United States. He returned to Israel to become minister of defense (1983–1984), replacing Ariel Sharon. In the National Unity Government (1984–1986) Arens was a minister without portfolio, and in 1986 was placed in charge of Arab affairs. From 1988 to 1990 he was foreign minister, and in 1990 once again was appointed minister of defense.

See also CAMP DAVID ACCORDS (1978); KNESSET.

MARTIN MALIN

ARFA, HASAN

[1895–1986]

An Iranian general; supporter of Pahlavi dynasty.

Born in Tbilisi, Georgia, of an Anglo-Russian mother and Iranian father, Hasan Arfa was a career military officer in the Iranian army and retired with the rank of general. His mother, Ludmilla Jervis, was the daughter of a British diplomat and a Russian woman of the aristocratic Demidov family. His father, Reza Khan Arfa al-Dowleh, was an Iranian diplomat serving as counsul-general in Tbilisi; he later served as ambassador to Turkey and Russia. Arfa's parents divorced in 1900, after Arfa and his mother had moved to Paris, but the senior Arfa al-Dowleh provided comfortable homes in Europe for them.

Arfa received his early education from tutors and later attended private schools in Switzerland, Paris, and Monaco. From 1912 to 1914, he attended the Military Academy in Istanbul. After arriving in Iran in 1914, he joined the Imperial Guards, and during the early part of World War I that organization sponsored his training as a cavalry officer with the Swiss army. He joined the Iranian gendarmerie in 1920, and later joined the army. As a cavalry officer, he campaigned against rebellious tribes in Azerbaijan, Kurdistan, Lorestan, and Turkoman Sahara during the 1920s and rose rapidly through the ranks.

The Pahlavis

Arfa first met Reza Shah Pahlavi (ruled 1926–1941), who was then minister of war, at the outset of the campaign against the Kurds in 1921. Reza Shah's forceful character left a deep impression on him, and Arfa remained a loyal supporter of the Pahlavis throughout his life. In 1923, Arfa married Hilda Bewicke, a British ballerina in Sergei Pavlovich Diaghilev's Russian Ballet whom he met in Monaco; they had one daughter, Leila. He subsequently served a brief tour in 1926 as military attaché in London and attended the Staff College in Paris from 1927 to 1929. After his training in France, he was promoted to the rank of lieutenant colonel and placed in command of the newly formed Pahlavi Guards Cavalry Regiment, which he turned into a highly disciplined and professional unit. Reza Shah made him commandant of the Military Academy and in 1932 promoted him to the rank of colonel. In 1934, Arfa accompanied Reza Shah on his official visit to Turkey. He was appointed inspector general of the cavalry and armed forces in 1936 and promoted to general in 1939. During the joint Anglo-Soviet invasion of Iran in August 1941, the shah appointed Arfa chief of staff in charge of the defenses for Tehran. After the British and Soviets defeated the Iranian army and forced Reza Shah to abdicate, his son and successor, Mohammad Reza Shah Pahlavi (r. 1941–1979), appointed Arfa chief of military intelligence.

Arfa became involved in national politics during the 1940s and 1950s. As chief of the general staff from 1944 to 1946, he authorized the supply of weapons to the Shahsavan tribesmen who opposed the autonomous government of Azerbaijan. In early 1946, Arfa was instrumental in gathering signatures of parliamentary deputies for a petition supporting Iran's complaint before the United Nations Security Council that Soviet forces continued to occupy northern Iran in contravention of an agreement to withdraw. Arfa's actions placed him in the camp of political leaders who tended to perceive malevolent intentions in Soviet policies but benign intentions in British policies. The pro-Soviet/anti-British politicians denounced Arfa in the parliament and the press, and consequently Prime Minister Ahmad Qavam insisted that Arfa be dismissed from his post as chief of the general staff. In 1946, Arfa was imprisoned for seven months. He was eventually exonerated, but he was retired summarily from active duty in March 1947.

Arfa blamed his successor, Gen. Ali Razmara, for his forced retirement and subsequently cooperated with his political rivals, especially after Razmara

was appointed prime minister in 1950. Nevertheless, Arfa genuinely was disturbed when Razmara was assassinated in 1951, because he believed the increasing level of political violence threatened the country. He served as minister of roads and communications in the brief government of Prime Minister Hosayn Ala during the month following Razmara's assassination, before the parliament voted in Mohammad Mossadegh as premier. Arfa distrusted Mossadegh and formed a political group, the National Movement, to disrupt gatherings of Mossadegh supporters, whom he considered to be extremists opposed to the continuation of the monarchy and a strong army. The National Movement's newspaper published many articles written by Arfa, supporting the shah and respect for Islam. Arfa maintained contact with a variety of political activists, including Mozaffar Baqai of the Toilers' party, the fiery preacher Ayatollah Sayyed Abu al-Qasem Kashani, and Shaban Jaafari, an organizer of street mobs. Arfa became a founding member of the secret committee of military officers, the Committee to Save the Fatherland, formed in 1952 with the objective of overthrowing Mossadegh. Following the 1953 military coup that restored the shah to power, he served as Iran's ambassador to Turkey (1958–1961) and Pakistan (1961–1962). Subsequently he retired from active government service. He left Iran at the time of the Iranian Revolution of 1979 and died in France in 1986.

See also AZERBAIJAN CRISIS; IRANIAN REVOLUTION (1979); KASHANI, ABU AL-QASEM; MOSSADEGH, MOHAMMAD; PAHLAVI, MOHAMMAD REZA; PAHLAVI, REZA.

Bibliography

Arfa, Hasan. *Under Five Shahs.* New York: Morrow; London: John Murray, 1964.

Arfa, Hasan. *The Kurds: An Historical and Political Study.* London: Oxford University Press, 1966.

ERIC HOOGLUND

ARFA, MUHAMMAD IBN
[1877–?]

Interim puppet ruler of Morocco, 1953–1955.

A relatively unknown member of the Alawi dynasty, Muhammad ibn Arfa was selected by Tuhami al-

Glawi and other supporters of French colonialism in Morocco to replace Sultan Muhammad V, who was forced to abdicate in 1953. Following several attempts on his life and amid the mounting pressures of Moroccan nationalism, ibn Arfa was removed in October 1955, to be replaced by the restored Muhammad V, who ruled as king until his death in 1961, when his son Hassan II assumed the throne.

See also HASSAN II; MUHAMMAD V; TUHAMI AL-GLAWI.

Bibliography

Abun-Nasr, Jamil. *A History of the Maghrib in the Islamic Period.* Cambridge, U.K., and New York: Cambridge University Press, 1987.

Hahn, Lorna. *North Africa: Nationalism to Nationhood.* Washington, DC: Public Affairs Press, 1960.

MATTHEW S. GORDON

ARGOUD, ANTOINE
[1914–]

French officer during Algerian War of Independence.

Antoine Argoud is a graduate of the prestigious Ecole Polytechnique and an outstanding staff officer who became politicized to the cause of French Algeria. He supported the January 1960 settler (*pied-noir*) revolt against President Charles de Gaulle and was one of the French planners and participants of the unsuccessful April 1961 putsch against the government. He then joined the Organisation de l'Armée Secrète (OAS). He escaped Algeria and reached West Germany. He was kidnapped by French agents in 1963, brought back to France, and received a life sentence. He was released as a result of the amnesty of 1968. He has authored *La décadence, l'imposture et la tragédie* (1974; Decadence, imposture, and tragedy) and *Les deux missions de Jeanne d'Arc* (1988; The two missions of Joan of Arc). Although he opposed clandestine summary executions during the war, Argoud remains a defender of most military actions in French Algeria. He regrets that the military did not receive clear governmental guidance and support.

Bibliography

Horne, Alistair. *A Savage War of Peace: Algeria, 1954–1962,* 2d edition. New York: Viking, 1987.

PHILLIP C. NAYLOR

ARIF, ABD AL-RAHMAN
[1916–]

President of Iraq, 1966–1968.

Abd al-Rahman Arif was born in Baghdad to a poor Sunni Arab rug merchant. Graduating from the military academy in 1937, he followed an undisturbed military career, both under the monarchy and the republic of Iraq. He joined a clandestine Free Officers organization before the revolution in 1958. After the Ramadan Revolution of 1963, he replaced his deceased younger brother Abd al-Salam Arif as president of the republic in April 1966. Under Abd al-Rahman, Iraq retained close ties with Gamal Abdel Nasser's Egypt, but carefully refrained from any unification steps (to join the United Arab Republic). A less capable leader than his brother, he lost power to the Ba'th party in July 1968; his downfall was accelerated by Iraq's ineffective participation in the Arab–Israel War of June 1967. He stayed in Ankara until 1980, when he was allowed to return to Baghdad, where he has lived in retirement.

See also ARAB–ISRAEL WAR (1967); ARIF, ABD AL-SALAM; BA'TH, AL-; IRAQ.

Bibliography

Batatu, Hanna. *The Old Social Classes and the Revolutionary Movements of Iraq: A Study of Iraq's Old Landed and Commercial Classes and of Its Communists, Ba'thists, and Free Officers.* Princeton, NJ: Princeton University Press, 1978.

Khadduri, Majid. *Republican Iraq: A Study in Iraqi Politics since the Revolution of 1958.* London and New York: Oxford University Press, 1969.

AMATZIA BARAM

ARIF, ABD AL-SALAM
[1921–1966]

President of Iraq, 1963–1966.

Abd al-Salam Arif was born in al-Karkh, Baghdad, to a poor Sunni Arab rug merchant. His family had strong tribal connections in the Ramadi province (west of Baghdad) of Iraq. From 1938 to 1941, he attended military college. While he was too junior to be held responsible for the Rashid Ali al-Kaylani pro-Axis revolt of 1941, Abd al-Salam strongly sympathized with the revolutionaries. He first met Abd al-Karim Qasim in 1942. In 1948, Arif participated in the Iraqi Expeditionary Force that fought in the first Arab–Israel war.

Because of Qasim's insistence, Arif was incorporated into the central organization of the Free Officers in 1957. Until the 1958 revolution, he was regarded as Qasim's protégé. On the eve of the revolution (14 July), Arif's brigade was ordered to move to Jordan through Baghdad, but in coordination with Qasim, he entered the city and took it during the early morning hours. In the revolutionary government, he became deputy prime minister of the interior, and deputy supreme commander of the armed forces. By September 1958, he was relieved of all his posts, since he supported Iraq's unification with the United Arab Republic. In November, he was arrested and sentenced to death for attempting to kill Qasim; but he was released in early 1961, to be made figurehead president by the Ba'th regime that toppled Qasim in the Ramadan Revolution of 8 February 1963. Later that year, he ousted the Ba'th from power and became sole leader. His power base was the loyalty of the Pan-Arabian army officers, most of whom came from his family's region, Ramadi.

In 1964, he signed a unification agreement with Egypt's President Gamal Abdel Nasser and introduced social and economic changes designed to create a similar system to that of Egypt; these included the establishment of a Nasserite political party and wide-ranging nationalizations. Actual unification with Egypt never materialized, however. His social policy caused an economic decline, and his attempt to crush the Kurdish revolt failed. Arif was killed in a helicopter crash on 13 April 1966. Despite his many failures, his charisma and devotion to Islam were highly regarded by many Sunni Arabs in Iraq. The Shi'ites feared him, but his religiosity and tolerance for their educational autonomy enabled the two Islamic sects to coexist. He was succeeded by his older brother Abd al-Rahman Arif.

See also ARIF, ABD AL-RAHMAN; KURDISH REVOLTS; PAN-ARABISM; QASIM, ABD AL-KARIM.

Bibliography

Batatu, Hanna. *The Old Social Classes and the Revolutionary Movements of Iraq: A Study of Iraq's Old Landed and Commercial Classes and of Its Communists, Ba'thists, and Free Officers.* Princeton, NJ: Princeton University Press, 1978.

Khadduri, Majid. *Republican Iraq: A Study in Iraqi Politics since the Revolution of 1958.* London and New York: Oxford University Press, 1969.

AMATZIA BARAM

ARIF, ARIF AL-
[1892–1973]

Palestinian historian, administrator, and journalist who became mayor of Arab Jerusalem in the 1950s.

Arif began his political career in his native Jerusalem as editor of the first Arab nationalist newspaper in Palestine, *Suriyya al-Janubiyya,* in 1919. He was a supporter of unity with Syria and of the Amir Faisal of the short-lived Arab Kingdom in Syria (later King Faisal I ibn Hussein of Iraq). He fled from British rule in Palestine to Syria with al-Hajj Muhammad Amin al-Husayni after political disturbances in 1920, although he was allowed to return and began a career as a civil administrator in Palestine. He served in a variety of posts in Jenin, Nablus, Baysan, Jaffa, Beersheba, Gaza, Ashkelon, and Ramallah. He served briefly in Transjordan from 1926 to 1928 and was mayor of Jordanian-controlled East Jerusalem from 1949 to 1955.

Al-Arif was also one of the most prominent Palestinian historians. Among his most important books are *Ta'rikh Bi'r al-Sab wa Qaba'iliha* (History of Beersheba and its tribes, 1934), *Ta'rikh Ghazza* (History of Gaza, 1934), *al-Mufassal fi Ta'rikh al-Quds* (History of Jerusalem, 1961), and the seven-volume *Ta'rikh al-Nakba* (History of the disaster, 1956–1962).

Bibliography

Porath, Yehoshua. *The Emergence of the Palestinian–Arab National Movement, 1918–1929.* London: Frank Cass, 1974.

STEVE TAMARI
UPDATED BY MICHAEL R. FISCHBACH

ARISH, CONVENTION OF AL- (1800)

Agreement between France and the Ottoman Empire, providing for the French retreat from Egypt.

Napoléon Bonaparte and his troops had invaded Egypt in 1798. Besieged by British and Ottoman forces, his successor, General Jean-Baptiste Kléber, negotiated the terms of French withdrawal. The Convention of al-Arish, signed by Kléber and the Ottoman grand vizier Yusuf on 24 January 1800, allowed for a dignified retreat of France from Egypt.

The convention was rejected by both Napoléon and Britain and, within a year, the French were completely defeated and evicted from Egypt.

See also KLÉBER, JEAN-BAPTISTE.

Bibliography

Hurewitz, J. C., ed. *The Middle East and North Africa in World Politics: A Documentary Record,* 2d edition. New Haven, CT: Yale University Press, 1975.

Vatikiotis, P. J. *The History of Egypt.* Baltimore, MD: Johns Hopkins University Press, 1985.

ZACHARY KARABELL

ARKOUN, MOHAMMED
[1928–]

French-Algerian Islamic teacher and writer.

Mohammed Arkoun was born in 1928 in Algeria. He received his doctorate in Islamic studies from the Sorbonne in Paris and joined its faculty in 1963, teaching courses in Islamic thought. His writing is greatly influenced by French philosophy, especially that of Michel Foucault, whose thinking he tries to apply to the study of Islamic legal and philosophical traditions. Arkoun's writings are varied and cover a wide array of Islamic subjects. He believes that the study of Islam should be freed from the monopoly of interpretations exercised by the state-sponsored clerical establishment, which promotes a particularly conservative interpretation of Islam, and he calls for an "audacious, free, productive" thinking on Islam. Arkoun argues for multiple interpretations of tradition and text, and he is a proponent of both multiculturalism and secularism (although he avoids using the Arabic word *ilmaniyya* because it is widely equated with unbelief).

In recent years Arkoun has traveled widely, teaching and lecturing in the United States and Europe and serving for a time as a leader of a Muslim center in the Netherlands. Arkoun was the only male Muslim member of the twenty-person presidential commission (Stasi Commission) appointed by French president Jacques Chirac in fall 2003 to recommend solutions regarding the protection of non-religious against the increasing presence of religious symbols in public schools and buildings. (The other Muslim was a woman sociologist, Hanifa Cherifi.) The commission recommended that the wearing of any conspicuous religious symbol (scarf or headress, skullcap, or large cross) be banned from public schools and buildings, and that there be state observance of a Jewish and a Muslim holy day. The commission's recommendations came under attack in Muslim countries, and Arkoun was singled out for blame as being insufficiently strong in his defense of Islam.

Bibliography

Lee, Robert D. *Overseeing Tradition and Modernity.* Boulder, CO: Westview Press, 1977.

AS'AD ABUKHALIL

ARLOSOROFF, CHAIM
[1899–1933]

Labor-Zionist intellectual and leader.

Chaim Arlosoroff was born in the Ukraine, and his parents moved to Berlin in 1905, following a pogrom. He received his doctorate in economic sociology from the University of Berlin. Arlosoroff opposed the Marxist doctrine of class conflict and developed a unique version of Zionist socialism, which he termed *Volksocialismus*—a Jewish national socialism that focused on the unity of the Jewish people historically and culturally as well as economically.

Arlosoroff became a leader of ha-Po'el ha-Tza'ir and in 1924 settled in Palestine, where he continued his political activity. He was critical of many in the Zionist leadership who, he felt, were blind to the reality of Arab nationalism. He was convinced of the need for reconciliation between the two nationalist movements. In 1926, he was appointed to the Zionist delegation to the League of Nations Permanent Mandates Commission. He was a staunch supporter of Chaim Weizmann, whom he accompanied on several visits to the United States. When Ahdut ha-Avodah and Ha-Po'el ha-Tza'ir merged to become MAPAI in 1930, Arlosoroff assumed a leadership position and in 1931 was elected to the Jewish Agency Executive to serve as head of its political department. In this capacity he met with some Palestinian leaders and encouraged economic contacts and cooperation with Transjordan's Amir Abdullah and members of his coterie. By June 1932, however, he reached the despairing conclusion that Zionism would be unable to proceed gradually and peacefully toward the achievement of a Jewish majority in Palestine.

After Adolf Hitler's rise to power, Arlosoroff negotiated with the Nazis for the emigration of the Jews and the transfer (ha'avara) of German Jewish assets to Palestine. The agreement was bitterly denounced by the Revisionists as a violation of the international Jewish boycott of Germany. In June 1933, shortly after his return from Germany, Arlosoroff was murdered while walking with his wife along Tel Aviv's beach. In the context of the bitter divisions between MAPAI and the Revisionists, many on the left were convinced that the Revisionists had assassinated Arlosoroff. Three Revisionists were arrested and charged with murder, two of whom were exonerated. The third, Avraham Stavsky, was found guilty and sentenced to death but was eventually freed on appeal on the grounds of insufficient evidence. Uncertainty as to the murderer(s) remains to this day, despite the report of an official commission of inquiry in 1982.

See also AHDUT HA-AVODAH; ISRAEL: POLITICAL PARTIES IN; ZIONIST REVISIONIST MOVEMENT.

Bibliography

Avineri, Shlomo. *Arlosoroff*. New York: Globe Weidenfeld, 1990; London: Peter Halban, 1989.

Laqueur, Walter. *A History of Zionism*. New York: Holt, 1972.

Shimoni, Gideon. *The Zionist Ideology*. Hanover, NH: University Press of New England, 1995.

CHAIM I. WAXMAN
NEIL CAPLAN

ARMÉE DE LIBÉRATION NATIONALE (ALN)

The fighting force mobilized to wage the Algerian war of independence.

Beginning in 1954, the Armée de Libération Nationale (ALN; National Liberation Army) was com-

posed of guerrilla units divided into five and later six *wilayas* (military districts within Algeria). From 1956 onward, standing armies began to emerge among expatriate Algerians in both Morocco and Tunisia, which, by 1960, came under a unified general staff.

Bibliography

Horne, Alistaire. *A Savage War of Peace: Algeria, 1954–1962*, revised edition. New York: Penguin, 1987.

JOHN RUEDY

ARMENIAN COMMUNITY OF JERUSALEM

Site of the Armenian patriarchate and center of the Armenian community in Israel, the West Bank, and Jordan.

The Armenian presence in Jerusalem had its beginnings in early Byzantine monasticism. Armenian inscriptions in mosaic floors from this era are found in and around Jerusalem, attesting to the existence of permanent settlements. The present boundaries of the Armenian quarter, covering nearly one-sixth of the Old City at the southwestern corner, appear to have been in place prior to the First Crusade (1099), with a patriarchate established during the sixth century.

History

After the defeat of the Crusaders, the Muslim rulers formed an alliance with the Armenians in Jerusalem, since both groups were persecuted by their common enemy, the Byzantines, because of religious differences. Likewise the Ottomans, during their rule, sided with the Armenians against the Greek Orthodox Church—and at times against the Roman Catholics—over ownership, control, or maintenance of sacred sites, especially within the Church of the Holy Sepulchre and the Church of the Nativity in Bethlehem. (In both churches, Armenians have nearly equal holdings with the other two denominations.) The Armenian community in Jerusalem traces its status to the original edicts issued on its behalf by several Muslim rulers, beginning with Umar ibn al-Khattab, affirming the rights of Armenians to their possessions in Jerusalem and elsewhere. The last of these rulers was Sultan Mahmud II, whose edict of 1813 settled a long dispute with the local Greek hierarchy over ownership of Saint James Monastery with its cathedral, the seat of the Armenian patriarchate. Rights to traditional holy places since then have remained unchanged by virtue of the famous *firman* (edict) issued by Sultan Abdülmecit I in 1852, establishing the status quo for the various churches' control over such sites, a decree honored by all successive administrations governing Jerusalem.

The prominence of the Armenian patriarchate of Jerusalem rests on the tradition that Saint James Cathedral marks the site where the apostle James, the brother of Jesus, had his residence. It is also where the Jerusalem Council was held under his leadership, as recorded in Acts of the Apostles, chapter 15. The Armenian patriarch of Jerusalem is deemed the successor of Saint James. His office is much coveted by the local hierarchies, who have schemed throughout history to possess the site and appropriate the office. Also within Saint James Cathedral is the traditional burial place of the head of Saint James, son of Zebedee and brother of the apostle John, whose martyrdom is also recorded in Acts of the Apostles, in chapter 12. Thus the Saint James compound, with its traditions surrounding the two apostles named James, is one of Jerusalem's most venerated sites as well as the largest monastic center in the country. The cathedral, built during the tenth century and expanded during the twelfth, is a prized monument of Eastern Christianity.

As head of the largest Monophysite church in the Holy Land, the Armenian patriarch traditionally champions the cause of the Syriac, Coptic, and Ethiopian churches.

Beginning in the seventeenth century, some patriarchs played significant roles, with lasting benefits for the Armenian community. Grigor V (1613–1645) expanded the community's estates beyond Jerusalem; Grigor VI (1715–1749) implemented financial reforms; Yesayi III (1865–1885) promoted publishing; and Yeghishe I (1921–1930) founded new schools. The insightful leadership of these and other patriarchs, especially during the seventeenth and eighteenth centuries, enabled the monastic community to stabilize its resources and to acquire additional properties in and around Jerusalem. These continue to provide a regular—albeit meager—income for the brotherhood.

Until recently 1931, the patriarch's jurisdiction extended over all Armenians in the Arab world. With the settlement at Antelias, near Beirut, of the displaced catholicosate of Cilicia (the ancient pontificate of Armenia domiciled in southern Turkey until 1921) during the French administration of Lebanon (1923–1943), the patriarch's jurisdiction over Lebanon, Syria, and Cyprus was ceded to Antelias. To help that fledgling establishment, Jerusalem provided clerical administrators and instructors. Until 1991, because of communism in Armenia, where the Catholicos of All Armenians resides, Jerusalem took the lead in providing parish priests for nearly all Armenian communities in the diaspora—a task now shared competitively with Antelias.

Manuscripts and Treasures

Unlike other ancient Armenian communities, whether in Armenia or in the diaspora, the Jerusalem community was rarely disturbed. Its continuity enabled it to flourish as a center of learning and religious worship. Over the centuries, the monastic community was enriched by a constant flow of pilgrims, including kings and other members of the Cilician Armenian royal family, prelates of the Armenian church, and scholiasts who took residence. Some of the accumulated treasures, and by no means the best, are on permanent display at the monastery.

The monastery holds the world's second largest collection of ancient Armenian manuscripts, which are housed in the Chapel of Saint T'oros. Four thousand medieval codices (manuscript books), including more than a hundred works of which only a single copy exists, are fully described in an eleven-volume catalogue. Some of these works were composed by local authors and many of the others are copies made by local scribes who, in personal comments at the end of the works, chronicled contemporary and near-contemporary events and encounters with other Christians, as well as with non-Christian entities. These manuscripts have not been sufficiently considered for their historical significance—especially their bearing on the medieval history of Jerusalem.

In addition to the library of ancient manuscripts and a few other chapels, the Saint James Monastery houses several academic establishments: a seminary largely supported by the Alex Manoogian Fund of Detroit; a modern library supported by the Calouste Gülbenkian Foundation of Lisbon; the Edward and Helen Mardigian Museum of Armenian Art and Culture; a printing press established in 1833, which published nearly 500 titles in the first hundred years of its operation (its earliest publications, including a complete concordance to the Armenian Bible, and the first issue of *Sion,* the scholarly journal of the patriarchate since 1866, are on display at the site); and a high school for the local community, built early during the twentieth century, when the Armenian population of Jerusalem more than doubled as a result of the Turkish persecutions of World War I. More Armenians moved into Saint James when their properties were confiscated by Israel during the Arab–Israel War of 1948. The sharp increase in the lay population brought a degree of secularism into the life of the monastic community.

The Late Twentieth and Early Twenty-First Centuries

The number of Armenians in Jerusalem decreased during the final forty years of the twentieth century, from about 4,000 in 1960 to about 1,500 in 2000; nearly two-thirds of them lived within the compound of Saint James and were increasingly dependent on the monastery for their livelihood. This was largely a result of the unification of Jerusalem under Israeli rule in 1967, which affected the population of East Jerusalem generally. The various partisan and political divisions among Armenians worldwide are represented in this small community, which until 1990 was further fragmented as a result of families taking sides with feuding bishops.

As one of the few minority groups with a presence for more than one millennium in the Holy Land, the Armenian community of Jerusalem maintains close ties with other such groups of various faiths. The current jurisdiction of the patriarchate includes Israel and Jordan, with an Armenian population of 3,000 and 8,000, respectively. While members of the older community continue to emigrate, mostly to Australia, Canada, and the United States, an influx of immigrants in mixed marriages arrived in Israel from Armenia during the 1990s. The consequences of the first Palestinian Intifada became evident in the near disappearance of Armenian merchants from Jerusalem's Old Market-

place, and the Israeli response to the al-Aqsa Intifada—building a security wall—has introduced new challenges to the Armenian community and the Armenian patriarchate, whose historic properties now straddle this new line. The solicitude of the government of the Republic of Armenia for the welfare of the Armenian patriarchate resulted in visits to the compound by presidents Levon Ter-Petrossian and Robert Kocharian. The Cathedral of Saint James and the other religious sites in the care of the patriarch remain the object of pilgrimage by Armenians the world over.

See also ABDÜLMECIT I; AQSA INTIFADA, AL-; ARAB–ISRAEL WAR (1948); HOLY LAND; INTIFADA (1987–1991); JERUSALEM; MAHMUD II.

Bibliography

Azarya, Victor. *The Armenian Quarter of Jerusalem: Urban Life behind Monastery Walls.* Berkeley: University of California Press, 1984.

Hintlian, Kevork. *History of the Armenians in the Holy Land,* 2d edition. Jerusalem: Armenian Patriarchate, 1989.

Narkiss, Bezalel, ed. *Armenian Art Treasures of Jerusalem.* New Rochelle, NY: Caratzas Brothers, 1979.

Prawer, Joshua. "The Armenians in Jerusalem under the Crusaders." In *Armenian and Biblical Studies,* edited by Michael E. Stone. Jerusalem: St. James Press, 1976.

Rose, John H. Melkon. *Armenians of Jerusalem: Memories of Life in Palestine.* New York; London: Radcliffe Press, 1993.

Sanjian, Avedis K. *The Armenian Communities in Syria under Ottoman Dominion.* Cambridge, MA: Harvard University Press, 1965.

ABRAHAM TERIAN
UPDATED BY ROUBEN P. ADALIAN

ARMENIAN GENOCIDE

The systematic expulsion and extermination of the Armenian population of historic West Armenia and Anatolia during and immediately after World War I.

In April 1915 the Ottoman government embarked upon policies designed to bring about the wholesale reduction of its civilian Armenian population. The persecutions continued with varying intensity until 1923 when the Ottoman Empire itself went out of existence and was replaced by the Republic of Turkey.

Armenians are hanged in Constantinople during the Armenian Genocide. The genocide began in 1915 with the arrest and deportation of seven hundred Constantinople Armenian public figures. Mass executions followed, and by 1923 between 0.8 and 1.1 million Armenians had lost their lives. DEUTSCHES LITERATURARCHIV, MARBACH. © WALLSTEIN VERLAG, GÖTTINGEN, FEDERAL REPUBLIC OF GERMANY. ALL RIGHTS RESERVED. REPRODUCED BY PERMISSION.

The Armenian population of the Ottoman state was reported at a little over two million in 1914. Nearly a million had already perished by 1918, while hundreds of thousands had become homeless and stateless refugees. By 1923 virtually the entire Armenian population of Anatolian Turkey had disappeared and total losses had reached up to 1.5 million.

The unraveling of Armenian society in the Ottoman Empire began with the crisis precipitated by the Balkan Wars and the 1913 coup staged by the Committee for Union and Progress (CUP, *Ittihad ve Tarraki*) which catapulted the triumvirate of Enver, Talaat, and Cemal to the head of government as minister of war, minister of the interior (and grand vizier in 1917), and minister of the marine, respectively. The coup effectively ended all hopes of se-

curing constitutional rule and liberal change in the Ottoman Empire as the clique in power, which concentrated all critical decision making in its hands, also represented the extremist wing of the Young Turk movement. Exponents of Turkism and Pan-Turanism, the CUP promotion of an exclusive Turkish nationalism, threatened the multi-ethnic fabric of the Ottoman state at a time when the Armenian minority's hopes for administrative reforms and participation in local self-government had been elevated with the overthrow of Hamidian autocracy.

World War I provided cover for the implementation of the plan to eliminate the Armenian population putatively from the flank of the Ottoman Empire exposed to Russia. The military debacle on the Russian front in December 1914 and January

1915, and the barricading of the Armenian population inside its quarter of the city of Van in April 1915, in fear of threatened massacre, provided a pretext to validate charges of sedition by Armenians and justification for their evacuation. The announced purpose of Young Turk policy aside, the facts of the matter proceeded by a different course. The Armenian population in the war zone along the Russian front was in the main slaughtered in situ and not subjected to deportation. The mass expulsion of the Armenian population stretched the entire length of the Anatolian Peninsula from Samsun and Trebizond in the north to Adana and Urfa in the south, from Bursa in the west and all other communities around the Sea of Marmara, including the European sector of Turkey, all the way to Erzerum and Harput in the east and everywhere in between, including Ankara, Konya, Sivas, and Malatia.

The beginning of the deportations actually represents the second phase of the annihilation plan. On 24 April 1915 two hundred prominent Armenian leaders in Istanbul were summarily arrested, exiled, and subsequently executed. The expulsions had been preceded since February 1915 by the disarming of Armenian draftees in the Ottoman army, who were then reassigned to labor battalions and were eventually executed. With the elimination of able-bodied men from the Armenian population, the deportation of the civilian population proceeded with little resistance.

The journey of the convoys of families on the open road for hundreds of miles from all across Anatolia toward Syria, through the primary concentration point of Aleppo, resulted in massive loss of human life. The deliberate exhaustion of the population through deprivation of access to water proved a particularly excruciating and effective means of reducing numbers quickly. Though guarded to prevent escape, the convoys were by no means protected. Their arrival at predetermined locations in remote areas turned out to be appointments with the killer units known as the *Teshkilati Mahsusa,* the Special Organization, under the direct command of CUP functionaries reporting to Talaat. These wholesale massacres were also occasions for the abduction of children and younger women. In places like Sivas, Harput, and Bitlis, massacres as much as deportation announced the implemention of the policy of genocide.

The survival rate of deportees entering Syria from the farthest distances were as low as 10 percent. Deportees from regions closer to Syria, such as Adana Aintab and Marash, stood a fairer chance because of the shorter distances traveled; yet on arrival they were herded into concentration camps at places like Islahiya, Katma, Meskene and Raqqa, which became the breeding ground of epidemics that easily wiped out tens of thousands of the exhausted and starving refugees. From these locations smaller groups were sent farther into the desert to killing centers such as Ra's al-Ayn and the infamous Dayr al-Zawr, where possibly more Armenians perished than at any other place on earth. The subterranean caves in some of these desert sites became the graveyard of thousands who were herded into them and burned alive. The deportees who were spared massacre were scattered from Syria as far as Ma'an and Petra in southern Jordan. To the east, deportees were sent all the way to Mosul and Kirkuk in northern Iraq. In all, only about 150,000 Armenians were found still living in Syria and Iraq at the end of the war.

The catastrophic loss of life and the violent and traumatic treatment of the deportees constituted only part of the larger scheme to reduce the Armenians. A second element was the total confiscation of their wealth; the government attempted to organize the transfer of title of their immovable properties to its cohorts, while the general population helped itself to all the movable property that deportees could not conceivably carry with them. More secure assets, such as bank accounts and corporate holdings, were seized by the government. Communal property, in the form of churches, schools, orphanages, and other institutions, was expropriated outright. It is presumed that much of the plunder was acquired by Young Turk party functionaries, with liquid assets deposited into party coffers. Since the genocide was implemented as much as a CUP scheme as government policy, the looting associated with the deportations constituted part of the payment system to the actual implementers of the genocide, effectively covering the expense of the mass deportation and murder of the Armenians with the plundered wealth of the victims, making the entire plan a highly profitable enterprise sanctioned by the allowances of martial law in wartime.

The plunder represented more than the loss of physical ownership by the Armenians, for in the process of looting, the cultural possessions of an entire people accumulated over the ages were turned into artless stone and metal. Centuries-old sanctuaries, from town chapels to pontifical cathedrals, were torched and demolished. Entire manuscript collections of monastic libraries vanished. Libraries went up in flames. The entire output of Armenian civilization since its beginnings was subjected to a policy of desecration and destruction.

The collapse of the Russian front ensuing the Bolshevik Revolution opened the way for Ottoman armies to advance through the Caucasus, creating additional opportunities for the slaughter of Armenian civilians in a campaign reaching Baku by September 1918. The end of the war prompted survivors to trek back to their former homes only to find them in possession of Turks, Kurds, and other Muslim refugees violently reluctant to return property to the Armenians. Under dire economic conditions, with so many Armenian refugees unable to resettle in their native towns, new tensions arose between the Armenians and the Turkish populace, who within a year began rallying to the Turkish Nationalist banner. Between 1920 and 1921 the Armenians of Anatolia were made refugees yet again, driven from their resettlements. The withdrawal of French occupation forces from Cilicia facilitated the uprooting of the Armenians through another series of massacres in Marash, Hadjin, and other towns in the area. The partition of the Republic of Armenia in the east in 1920 by Kemalist forces and the Sovietization of the Russian half had already been accomplished with the total excision of the Armenian population of Turkish-occupied Kars. The sweep through Smyrna in 1922 meant the utter and total eradication of the Armenians from all of Turkey in Asia.

Resistance to the deportations was infrequent. In only one instance were Armenians reasonably successful in avoiding certain death by taking flight up the mountain of Musa Dagh on the Mediterranean coast, where French naval vessels rescued them. The Armenians in the city of Van held out for a month until the arrival of the Russian army in May 1915, only to have to evacuate the city upon the retreat of the Russians in the face of an Ottoman counteroffensive. The mass flight to the Russian border proved no less a tragic affair than actual deportation. Of the more than 300,000 refugees

counted in the Armenian republic in 1918, more than half perished within a year. Armenians in Urfa and Shabin-Karahisar who suspected the true intentions of the government defied the deportation edict in a vain attempt by barricading themselves in their neighborhoods. In these rare instances where the gendarmerie was unable to abide by the deportation timetable, artillery was called in to simply exterminate the resistant population through bombardment.

During the armistice period nearly 400 of the key CUP officials implicated in the atrocities committed against the Armenians were arrested. A number of domestic military tribunals were convened by the postwar Ottoman government, which brought charges ranging from the unconstitutional seizure of power, the conduct of a war of aggression, and conspiring the decimation of the Armenian population to more explicit capital crimes, including massacre. Some of the accused were found guilty of the charges. Most significantly, the ruling triumvirate was condemned to death. They, however, eluded justice by fleeing abroad. Their escape left the matter of avenging the countless victims to a clandestine group of survivors who tracked down the CUP archconspirators. Talaat, the principal architect of the Armenian genocide, was gunned down in 1921 in Berlin where he had gone into hiding. His assassin was arrested and tried by a German court, which acquitted him.

The chapter on the Armenian Genocide, however, was more conclusively closed by the 1923 Treaty of Lausanne, which, in extending international recognition to the Republic of Turkey, also absolved it of all responsibilities for the rectification of the crimes committed against the Armenians or for the resettlement of the tens of thousands made homeless and stateless. With immunity assured by the Treaty of Lausanne, the Turkish government subsequently adopted a policy of categorically denying that crimes had been committed against Armenians of the Ottoman Empire. Still concentrated in their historic homeland in 1915, surviving Armenians were scattered across the entire Middle East by 1923. All that was left of a once prosperous community were deportees living in squalid refugee camps. Under such circumstances the modern Armenian diaspora took form.

See also ARMENIANS IN THE MIDDLE EAST; LAUSANNE, TREATY OF (1923); OTTOMAN EMPIRE.

Bibliography

Adalian, Rouben P., ed. *The Armenian Genocide in the U.S. Archives, 1915–1918.* Alexandria, VA: Chadwick-Healey, 1991–1993.

Dadrian, Vahakn N. *The History of the Armenian Genocide: Ethnic Conflict from the Balkans to Anatolia to the Caucasus.* Providence, RI: Berghahn Books, 1995.

Davis, Leslie A. *The Slaughterhouse Province: An American Diplomat's Report on the Armenian Genocide, 1915–1917,* edited by Susan Blair. New Rochelle, NY: A. D. Caratzas, 1989.

Hovannisian, Richard G., ed. *The Armenian Genocide in Perspective.* New Brunswick, NJ: Transaction Books, 1986.

ROUBEN P. ADALIAN

ARMENIAN MILLET

Armenian community or nation in the Ottoman Empire since the fifteenth century.

The Armenian millet (Turkish, Ermeni millet) existed in the Ottoman Empire as an institution devised by the sultans to govern the Christian population of the Monophysite churches. The millet system extended internal autonomy in religious and civil matters to the non-Muslim communities while introducing a mechanism for direct administrative responsibility to the state in matters of taxation. The reach of the Armenian millet expanded and contracted with the changing territorial dimensions of the Ottoman state. Originally the Armenian millet was defined as a broad religious group rather than narrowly as a denomination reinforcing ethnic distinction. Not only Armenians of all persuasions, which by the nineteenth century included Orthodox, Catholic, and Protestant, were treated by the Ottoman government as constituents of the Armenian millet; other Oriental Christian denominations, which were excluded from the Greek millet, also were included in the Armenian millet.

The evolution of parallel Armenian and Greek millets has led to the proposition that the Armen-

ian community was introduced by the Ottoman government as a way of denying the Greek millet, and its leadership in the form of the Orthodox patriarch, governance over the entire Christian community in the Ottoman state. Although Ottoman political theory divided the populace along the lines of the three principal religions—Islam, Christianity, and Judaism—the Christian community was further divided to differentiate between the two branches of Christianity, Monophysite and Duophysite, and to foster competition within the sizable Christian population of the empire. From the standpoint of the overall system, the Oriental Christian communities related to the Ottoman regime through the intermediary of the Armenian leadership in the capital city of Constantinople (now Istanbul). In practice, direct communication with local Ottoman governors as the intercessors with the central authorities was more common. Nor did the system necessarily encompass the entire Armenian population as its settlements entered the Ottoman Empire during the period of expansion. In the remoter parts of the empire, the reach of the millet system was tenuous, and communities operated on the basis of interrelations traditional to the region. Only in the nineteenth century did the purview of the Armenian millet attain influence comprehensive to the Armenian population of the Ottoman Empire. By that point, however, the Ottomans had agreed to the further fractionalization of the Armenian millet by extending formal recognition, in 1831 and 1847, respectively, to the Catholic and Protestant millets, both of which were predominantly Armenian.

The history of the Armenian millet as an imperial institution is more properly the history of the Armenian patriarchate of Constantinople. Though in the strictest sense an ecclesiastical office functioning within the framework of the Armenian church, the patriarchate was created by the Ottomans, and its occupant served at the pleasure of the Sublime Porte (the Ottoman government). There was no precedent of an Armenian bishopric in Constantinople predating Ottoman occupation of the city. The early history of the patriarchate is barely known. Armenian tradition attributes its origins to the settlement of the Armenians of Bursa in the city upon the command of Mehmet the Conqueror and of the designation in 1461 of the Ar-

Khorvirap, a twelfth-century Armenian Apostolic cathedral, is pictured in the foreground on Mount Ararat. In 2001 Armenian religious leaders celebrated the 1,700th anniversary of that country's conversion to Christianity. © AP/WIDE WORLD PHOTOS. REPRODUCED BY PERMISSION.

menian bishop of Bursa, named Hovakim, as head of this community by the sultan himself. During the first 150 years of its existence, the importance of the office was restricted to the city and its environs. The rapid turnover of bishops deprived the patriarchate of political or practical significance to Armenians at large.

The patriarchate emerged as an agency central to the Armenian millet structure in the eighteenth century. Three factors appear to have contributed to the consolidation of ecclesiastical and political control by the patriarchate: growth in the Armenian population in and around Constantinople, which had been an area at some distance from the centers of Armenian demographic concentration in the Ottoman Empire—mostly eastern and central Anatolia and northern Black Sea coast; the strengthening of the economic role of the growing community in local trade, international commerce,

and government finances; and finally the appearance of primates who commanded respect and expanded the role of the patriarchate in Armenian communal life. The key figure in this century was Hovhannes Kolot, whose tenure lasted from 1715 to 1741. Thereafter, the Armenian patriarch of Istanbul was regarded as the most important figure in the Armenian church despite the fact that within the hierarchy of the church itself other offices, such as that of the Catholicos at Echmiadsin in Persian (and subsequently Russian) Armenia or the Armenian patriarch of Jerusalem, could claim historical and moral seniority.

The commercial success of the Armenians was evidenced by the rise of the so-called *amira* class in Constantinople. Originally merchants, the *amiras* gained prominence mostly as *sarrafs* (bankers) who played a critical role in financing the empire's tax-farming system. For their services the Duzians, for example, were awarded management of the imperial mint. The Balyans held the post of chief architect to the sultan from 1750 to the end of the nineteenth century and were responsible for the construction of virtually all imperial residences and palaces. These Armenian notables put their stamp on the Armenian community of Constantinople when they also received license from their sovereign to establish educational centers, charitable institutions, hospitals, and churches.

Although their status was defined by their connection with the Ottoman system, the role of the *amiras* in the Armenian millet was determined by the influence they exercised over the patriarchate. A conservative oligarchy by nature, nevertheless the *amira* presence underscored the growth of secular forces in Armenian society, which soon derived their importance from their role in the economy of the city independent of the monarchy. Those very forces were further encouraged by the revival of interest in Armenian literature sponsored by *amiras*.

The Tanzimat reforms unraveled the system of government on which the *amiras* depended. It also provided additional impetus to the growth of an Armenian middle class increasingly composed of smaller merchants, called *esnaf*, who demanded a voice in the management of the millet and the election of the patriarch. Soon popular sentiment called for the regulation of the election process and the adoption of a formal document prescribing the function and responsibilities of the patriarchate. A long drawn-out debate among conservative clergy and amiras, liberal-minded *esnaf*, and the press through the 1840s and 1850s resulted in the drafting of a so-called constitution for the Armenian millet. The compromise document was adopted by an assembly composed of laymen and ecclesiastics on 24 May 1860. Its formal approval by the Ottoman authorities took three more years. The Armenians called it their national constitution, and the rights and responsibilities contained in the document became the framework by which Armenians throughout the empire reorganized their communities. Placing millet leadership in the Armenian church, the national constitution also guaranteed a role for the lay community and provided specific mechanisms for its participation at all levels of management.

The constitution also elevated the office of patriarch to that of national leader with immediate responsibility in representing the concerns of the Armenian millet with the Sublime Porte. That proved a heavier burden than intended as the flock in the distant corners of the empire began to appeal more and more to the patriarch for relief from their woes at the hands of corrupt administrators and officials prone to violence. The patriarchate cataloged these problems and appealed to the resident ministers of the great powers to plead the Armenian case with the sultan. This problem of enhanced responsibility in the face of increasing unrest in the provinces while being powerless to persuade the Sublime Porte in political matters seriously compromised the patriarchate. Segments of the Armenian millet felt disfranchised; adherents turned to the Catholic and Protestant millets for protection. The Sublime Porte, in turn, closely scrutinized elections and appointments to contain the rising tide of Armenian nationalism.

The millet system remained in place until the end of the empire. The patriarchate remained in place until its suspension in 1916 by the government of the Young Turks. And although many of the later patriarchs, such as Mkrtich Khrimian (1869–1873), Nerses Varzhapetian (1874–1884), Matteos Izmirlian (1894–1896), and Maghakia Ormanian (1896–1908), were very important figures, Armenian loyalties were already divided by the late nineteenth century. Political organizations vied for leadership in the Armenian community and the religious basis of national organization was facing serious competition from these and other sources. The patriarchate was restored in 1918 and its role reconfirmed by the Republic of Turkey. By that time, however, the Armenian bishop presided over a community whose congregants had been seriously reduced in numbers and mostly inhabited the city of Istanbul, much as when the millet system was first introduced among Armenians. As for the Armenian national constitution, it remains a living document. Armenian communities throughout the world rely on its principles of mixed representation under ecclesiastical leadership in the organization and management of their now dispersed communities.

See also KHRIMIAN, MKRTICH; ORMANIAN, MAGHAKIA; SUBLIME PORTE; TANZIMAT; YOUNG TURKS.

Bibliography

Bardakjian, Kevork B. "The Rise of the Armenian Patriarchate of Constantinople." In *Christians and Jews in the Ottoman Empire: The Functioning of a Plural Society,* edited by Benjamin Braude and Bernard Lewis. New York: Holmes and Meier, 1982.

Barsoumian, Hagop. "The Dual Role of the Armenian *Amira* Class within the Ottoman Government and the Armenian Millet (1750–1850)." In *Christians and Jews in the Ottoman Empire: The Functioning of a Plural Society,* edited by Benjamin Braude and Bernard Lewis. New York: Holmes and Meier, 1982.

Sanjian, Avedis K. *The Armenian Communities in Syria under Ottoman Dominion.* Cambridge, MA: Harvard University Press, 1965.

ROUBEN P. ADALIAN

ARMENIAN REVOLUTIONARY MOVEMENT

Nationalist movement among Armenians of the Ottoman Empire, which lasted from 1878 to 1921.

In the 1878 Treaty of Berlin, the Ottoman government agreed to undertake reforms in the so-called Armenian provinces of the empire. Based on a track record of reforms promulgated but seldom implemented, Armenian nationalists disbelieved that any meaningful changes would be made in the Ottoman administration of the Armenian-populated regions of the Turkish state. Moderate and conservative Armenians, on the other hand, placed much stock in an international treaty signed by the great powers containing an explicit Ottoman commitment to reform. The failure of the great powers to hold Abdülhamit II to his promise as they became embroiled in the competition to carve up Africa and Asia and the sultan's recalcitrance in introducing voluntary reforms left many Armenians disillusioned with the Ottoman regime. A rising national consciousness obstructed by an increasingly despotic administration under Abdülhamit II did not take long to prompt a revolutionary movement among Armenians of the Ottoman Empire.

Local self-defense units had already taken to resisting Ottoman authorities. Particularly egregious from the standpoint of rural inhabitants was the government's license and tolerance of Kurdish predation over Armenian towns and villages. In response to this predicament, the first formally organized Armenian political society made its appearance in 1885 in the city of Van. The group was quickly disbanded by Ottoman police.

The Armenian revolutionary movement acquired its real impetus in the Russian Empire. In an atmosphere of greater freedom, better education, and social advancement, the new intellectual class taking form in the Russian Caucasus spawned a group of political thinkers who began to articulate serious concern with the fate of Armenians in the Ottoman Empire. Influenced by Russian populism and radicalism, they organized two groups advocating Armenian national goals. The Armenian Social Democratic Party first appeared in Geneva among Russian-Armenians studying abroad. The husband and wife team of Avetis and Maro Nazerbekian led the group. The party soon was known by the name of its publication, *Hunchak* (Clarion), selected in imitation of the Russian-language publication by the same name issued by the Russian revolutionary Alexander Herzen.

The Hunchak Party subscribed to socialism and called for the restoration of Armenian statehood. Members focused their activities on the Ottoman Armenians whom they tried to propagandize and provide with arms. Though it found adherents among Armenians in both the Russian and Ottoman Empires, the Hunchak Party never garnered a large following. Its ideological positions were viewed as too radical and its program infeasible in the face of the overwhelming power of the state and the absence of real political consciousness among the rural masses.

The Armenian Revolutionary Federation (ARF) had better success. Organized in Tbilisi in 1890 by a trio of ideologues known as Kristapor, Rostom, and Zavarian, the organization became known less by its acronym than by the Armenian word for federation, *dashnaktsutyun*. Its members and supporters were thus called Dashnak. The Dashnak Party gained greater mass appeal as it sought to define a populist platform that was based not so much on ideological propositions as on the objective conditions of the Armenian population. In its early years it advocated reform, autonomy, and self-government, forsaking independent nationhood. The ARF emphasized the need for political organization and support for

Armenian women join the defense of Adana, Galicia, 19 November 1920. The women of the city, which was being besieged by Turkish forces, feared what would happen to them should Muslims overrun the city. Rather than watch from the sidelines, many of them took up arms alongside the men. © BETTMANN/CORBIS. REPRODUCED BY PERMISSION.

groups engaged in local struggles, which it tried to bring under one umbrella, hence the notion of federation. The object of their program remained the fate and status of Armenians in the Ottoman Empire.

After its formative years, three critical developments—the 1894–1896 violence and the 1905 and 1917 Russian revolutions—redirected the thrust of the Armenian nationalist movement. The destruction visited upon the Armenian population of the Ottoman Empire between 1894 and 1896 compelled Armenian society to rethink its condition and Armenian political organizations to reassess their course of action. The level of lethal violence unleashed by the Turkish state reached beyond any-

thing experienced by the Armenians to that point. With hundreds of thousands affected and tens of thousands dead, the revolutionaries were confronted with a very serious dilemma. The sultan's regime used the charge of revolutionary activism against the Armenians to justify its wholesale measures. Armenians in the provinces and in Istanbul were openly challenging the state and its representatives. Demonstrations, reprisals against corrupt officials, underground publications, and revolutionary cells frightened the sultan and provided evidence of the emerging nationalism of one more minority in the empire. From the standpoint of the ruling Ottoman class, Russian tolerance of Armenian organizations advocating political change in the Ottoman Empire appeared particularly seditious.

The havoc wreaked in Armenian society by the killings alienated a large segment of the masses from political involvement. It also destroyed a good part of the Hunchak and Dashnak organizations. Thereafter, the distrust between the Ottoman regime and the Armenians was never repaired. The ARF and the Committee for Union and Progress cooperated in their opposition to the sultan Abdülhamit, whom even progressive-minded Turks accused of preventing the modernization of the state. After the Young Turk revolution of 1908, Armenian political organizations were legalized in the Ottoman Empire. Nevertheless, the charge of sedition would be brought up again by the Unionist government during World War I, and once again measures taken against the Armenian population at large. Executions and mass deportations brought an end to the existence of Armenian society in the Ottoman Empire and with that also completely halted Armenian political and revolutionary activism in Turkey.

Events in the Russian Empire took a very different course. The 1905 revolution witnessed the intensification of radicalism all across society. Armenians were no less affected. In fact, Armenian society already had been galvanized by a measure introduced by the government that had seriously undermined Armenian loyalty to the regime. In 1903 the czar had issued an edict confiscating the properties of the Armenian church. Designed to undercut the strengthening of Armenian ethnic consciousness by depriving Armenian society of its principal means of support for its educational institutions, the edict energized the moribund revolutionary organizations and helped attract new interest and membership in them. It also compelled them to consider socialism more seriously and finally to oppose czarism as a repressive system of government. The igniting of racial animosity and virtual warfare between the Armenians and the Azeris to distract them from the revolution augmented the prestige of the ARF all the more as it took to the defense of the populace in the absence of Russian policing to contain communal violence. The repression that followed once again curbed the activities of the Armenian organizations. By that point, however, the ARF had gained mass appeal and clearly had emerged as the leading political organization in Armenian society. When the Russian Empire broke up after the 1917 revolution, the ARF was in a position to assume charge of the process resulting in the establishment of the Republic of Armenia. From 1918 to 1920 during the entire duration of the independent republic, the ARF was the dominant party.

Armenian socialists, who were members of Russian organizations and opposed to specifically Armenian nationalist parties, soon gained prominence after the Bolshevik revolution. Though they were only a single strand of the Armenian revolutionary movement, the sovietization of Armenia placed the Armenian Bolsheviks at the helm of Armenian society. Calling Dashnaks and others bourgeois nationalists, the Bolsheviks excluded them from the political process in Soviet Armenia and persecuted them as counterrevolutionaries. By 1921, the momentum of the movement was spent, leaving a legacy of catastrophe in the Ottoman Empire and of successful nation-building in the Russian state.

See also ABDÜLHAMIT II; COMMITTEE FOR UNION AND PROGRESS; DASHNAK PARTY; HUNCHAK PARTY.

Bibliography

Nalbandian, Louise. *The Armenian Revolutionary Movement: The Development of Armenian Political Parties through the Nineteenth Century.* Berkeley: University of California Press, 1967.

Ter Minassian, Anaide. *Nationalism and Socialism in the Armenian Revolutionary Movement,* translated by A. M. Berrett. Cambridge, MA: Zoryan Institute, 1984.

ROUBEN P. ADALIAN

ARMENIANS IN THE MIDDLE EAST

A people of Asia Minor, long ruled by others, who became independent in 1991.

The territory of historic Armenia covered the Armenian plateau. The Pontic range on the north, the Little Caucasus chain to the east, the Anti-Taurus range to the south, and the Euphrates River in the west defined its perimeter. Armenian settlement in the area dates back at least to the second half of the second millennium B.C.E. Armenian statehood emerged in the sixth century B.C.E. and was maintained or revived after periods of occupation until the eleventh century C.E. Turkish penetration and settlement from the eleventh century C.E. gradually eroded the Armenian presence in the plateau area. A new Armenian state took shape in and around Cilicia on the Mediterranean coast between the tenth and fourteenth centuries. Thereafter, Armenians concentrated in towns and cities stretching in a belt from the Aegean coast of Anatolia to the Caspian Sea. Further dispersion placed Armenians across much of Eastern Europe and Western Asia as far as India. Ottoman state policies during the 1915 to 1923 Armenian genocide eliminated the Armenians from Anatolia and historic West Armenia and drove many of them into East Armenia within the zone of Russian domination. Armenian-inhabited territory at the beginning of the twenty-first century is confined to the Caucasus region that includes the current Republic of Armenia; the territory of the self-proclaimed Republic of Nogorno, or Mountainous, Karabagh; and the districts of Akhalkalaki and Ninotsminda (formerly Bogdanovska) in southern Georgia. The remainder of the Armenian population inhabits what are known as diaspora communities throughout the temperate zone of the globe.

Language

A majority of Armenians speak Armenian, an independent branch of the Indo-European family of languages. Armenian is spoken only by Armenians. Because most Armenians are bilingual, over the centuries the language has absorbed a vast vocabulary of foreign words. First recorded in the early fifth century, Classical Armenian served as the principal medium of written communication until the mid-nineteenth century. By that time, the spoken tongue had evolved into numerous dialects. With the spread of literacy, the dialects spoken in the two foremost centers of Armenian cultural activity outside of historic Armenia, namely Tbilisi and Constantinople (now Istanbul), emerged as the standard modern vernaculars of Eastern and Western Armenian. The former was used in the Russian Empire and Iran and the latter in the Ottoman Empire. The boundary between the two dialects holds to this day. In the twentieth century, Eastern Armenian became the state language of the Republic of Armenia. Western Armenian is now spoken only in the diaspora communities.

Religion

Most Armenians belong to the Armenian Apostolic Church, a denomination of Eastern Orthodoxy. The church traces its origins to the evangelizing missions of the Apostles Thaddeus and Bartholomew in Armenia. Formal Christianization traditionally is dated to the year 301 with the conversion of the reigning monarch, Trdat (Tiridates) IV. Political and theological differences led to the break from the Greek Orthodox and Roman Catholic churches by the sixth century, and a series of Armenian ecclesiastical councils rejected the Chalcedonian Creed, which condemned portions of the Armenian beliefs. Thereafter, the Armenian church was defined by its national character and became the focal point of Armenian cultural development. Roman Catholicism returned with the Crusaders and the growth of Mediterranean trade beginning in the eleventh century. Protestant denominations appeared under the influence of U.S. missionary activities in the mid-nineteenth century. Although voluntary adherence to Islam is recorded, most Armenian conversion occurred under duress and mainly during the period of Ottoman rule. Official atheism during the Soviet period drove religion from the Republic of Armenia. The pontiff of the Armenian church, titled Catholicos of All Armenians, resides at Edjmiadsin in Armenia, but church attendance is mostly symbolic and sparse. Religion plays a larger role in Armenian diaspora communities as a marker of national identity.

Demographics

The global Armenian population is difficult to calculate because many states do not measure ethnic constituencies. It is estimated at 8 million. In the Republic of Armenia the 2001 census reported the population figure at 3 million, down from 3.7 million in 1993. The current population of Nagorno Karabagh is estimated at 150,000 Armenians. About 500,000 live in Georgia, and another million or more are spread throughout Russia and the former Soviet republics including Central Asia. Between 1988 and 1991 a forced population exchange resulted in the departure of 350,000 Armenians from Azerbaijan. Armenians in the diaspora are concentrated in cities throughout the Middle East, Europe, and North and South America. An estimated half million or more live in the Middle East, with the larger communities of about 100,000 found in Iran, Syria, and Lebanon. Smaller communities are located in Turkey (60,000), Cyprus (3,000), Israel (3,000), Jordan (5,500), Egypt (6,500), United Arab Emirates (3,000), and Iraq (3,000). The bulk of the estimated million Armenians in Europe are found in France (450,000), and smaller concentrations in England (18,000), Belgium (8,000), Switzerland (5,000), Italy (2,500), Austria (3,000), Germany (42,000), Czech Republic (10,000), Romania (10,000), Bulgaria (10,000), and Greece (20,000). The combined North and South American population is estimated at nearly two million, with the larger portion living in the United States. Other significant communities are located in Canada (80,000), Brazil (40,000), Uruguay (19,000), and Argentina (130,000). An estimated 60,000 live in Australia.

Livelihood

Agrarian life dominated traditional Armenian society until its complete displacement during World War I. Throughout centuries of dispersion, Armenians adapted economically. Most notably they formed a strong urban commercial class that eventually became involved in international trade. Armenians, especially in the Middle East, occupied the role of middlemen in virtually every city they inhabited. Between the seventeenth and twentieth centuries, in places such as Istanbul, Tbilisi, Isfahan, Tehran, Aleppo, Cairo, and Beirut, whether through official sponsorship or individual and communal ability, Armenians dominated various sectors of the local, and in some instances the national, economy. They tended to be traders, craftsmen, retailers, and shopkeepers in earlier centuries, but the twentieth century saw the rapid rise of an urban professional class in the fields of medicine, engineering, banking, electronics, and computers. In the Republic of Armenia, the Soviet period was marked by intensive industrialization that produced a country with a high density of factories involved in heavy manufacturing. The breakup of the Soviet Union placed the entire economy of Armenia in jeopardy. A crippling energy crisis, compounded by the blockade of the country by Turkey and Azerbaijan, led to a considerable shrinkage of the economy and serious hardships in the 1990s. By the start of the twenty-first century, Armenia had turned the corner on its economy and was steadily recovering through market reforms. Upon independence in 1991, Armenia proceeded rapidly toward privatization. Agricultural lands were distributed to farmers, dwellings were declared real estate and titles were transferred to residents, making them homeowners, and both small and large industries were progressively privatized.

Major Historical Figures

The 3,000-year span of Armenian history is mostly recalled in narratives recording the deeds, valor, and accomplishments of a multitude of figures. Certain kings, religious leaders, noblemen, and men of culture stand out. The extinction of the Armenian royal and princely families by the fifteenth century meant waiting until the early modern period for the reappearance of figures of national significance. In the absence of the men of the sword, men of the cloth and men of the pen—and often of both—began to lead the Armenian nation out of its dark ages. Mekhitar Sebastatsi founded an Armenian Catholic monastery in Venice in 1717 and guided the cultural recovery of the Armenians. Mikayel Chamchian, a member of the Mekhitarian order, resumed the writing of Armenian history and began shaping a modern national identity. Khachatur Abovian in Russian Armenia promoted modernism through the use of the vernacular by authoring the first Armenian novel in 1848. Mikayel Nalbandian in Russia advocated Armenian nationhood. Mkrtich Khrimian, writer, publisher, and priest, embodied the coalescing of Armenian consciousness by the end of the nineteenth century. As Armenian patriarch of Constantinople, in which capacity he was head of the Armenian Millet and subsequently Catholicos of All Armenians in Edjmiadsin, he allied the conservative Armenian church with the ad-

vocates of national emancipation. While repression and autocracy in the Ottoman and Russian empires were challenged by many locally, others took up arms, and the Armenian Revolutionary Movement found its leaders among intellectuals who formulated ideology and unschooled men who fought skirmishes with the police and militia of the tsar and the sultan. Andranik, the guerrilla fighter, entered national lore as he escaped every snare of the sultan's police while defending the Armenian rural population with his own brand of resistance against exploitation.

The founding of the Republic of Armenia in 1918 tested the mettle of men. Some, such as Aram Manukian and Simon Vratsian, defended its territories; others, such as President Avetis Aharonian and Prime Minister Alexander Khatisian, negotiated for its survival. The Soviet period reversed the roles of the hero and antihero. The dissident, more so than the Communist Party leader, captured the national imagination. In Soviet Armenia he came in the form of the poet, Yeghishe Charents or Paruyr Sevak, who spun with words an alternative consciousness to escape and defy totalitarian control. National sentiments that had been preserved underground resurfaced in a mass movement in 1988, finding a guiding figure in a scholar, Levon Ter-Petrossian, who, with independence restored in 1991, became the first democratically elected president of his country. Robert Kocharian, who led the struggle in Nagorno Karabagh in the early 1990s, succeeded him in 1998.

See also ANDRANIK OZANIAN; ARMENIAN COMMUNITY OF JERUSALEM; ARMENIAN GENOCIDE; ARMENIAN MILLET; ARMENIAN REVOLUTIONARY MOVEMENT; CHAMCHIAN, MIKAYEL; CILICIA; KHRIMIAN, MKRTICH.

Bibliography

Adalian, Rouben P. *Historical Dictionary of Armenia.* Lanham, MD: Scarecrow Press, 2002.

Bournoutian, George A. *A Concise History of the Armenian People: From Ancient Times to the Present.* Costa Mesa, CA: Mazda, 2002.

Der Nersessian, Sirarpie. *The Armenians.* London: Thames and Hudson, and New York: Praeger, 1969.

Hovannisian, Richard G., ed. *The Armenian People from Ancient to Modern Times.* 2 vols. New York: St. Martin's Press, 1997.

Nersessian, Vrej Nerses. *Armenia.* Santa Barbara, CA: Clio Press, 1993.

Walker, Christopher J. *Armenia: The Survival of a Nation.* New York: St. Martin's Press, 1990.

ROUBEN P. ADALIAN

ARMS AND ARMAMENTS IN THE MIDDLE EAST

Arms supply, imports, and control in the countries that comprise the modern Middle East.

The Arab–Israeli conflict has generated the most significant arms race in the Middle East, but rivalries involving Iran, Iraq, Saudi Arabia, Syria, and Turkey also have contributed heavily to regional instability. Attempts to control the supply of arms have been of limited duration and success.

During the Arab–Israel War in 1948, Israel bought arms from Czechoslovakia, a Soviet client state. The arms were obsolete, but with them Israel defeated several Arab states equipped with British and French arms. That war also brought the first attempts at arms control in the region. Britain and the United States withheld arms from the combatants, but the United Nations embargo, imposed in May 1948, prevented neither smuggling nor clandestine purchases.

In May 1950 the United States, Britain, and France announced the Tripartite Declaration and in June 1950 created the Near East Arms Coordinating Committee (NEACC), intending to regulate the sale of arms to the region. In fact, the United States left the Middle East arms markets to its allies, supplying few arms even to Iraq, with which in 1954 it signed a military aid agreement. Thus, in mid-1955, nearly all arms in the region were of Western European origin.

In 1955 the Soviet Union radically altered the Middle East balance with a deal that provided Egypt (through Czechoslovakia) with modern arms, including MiG-15 jets, worth $250 million. France's conflict with Egypt over its aid to the rebels in Algeria and the nationalization of the Suez Canal were the impetus for its sale in 1956 of seventy-two Mystère jets and other arms to Israel. France became Israel's main supplier until 1968, when it cited Is-

raeli preemption in the June 1967 Arab–Israel War as reason for an embargo.

After the 1956 Suez–Sinai crisis, the Soviet Union accelerated supply to its regional clients. From 1956 to 1967, the Soviet Union equipped Egypt with nearly 1,000 tanks and 360 jets, transferred 400 tanks and 125 jets to Iraq, and sold Syria 350 tanks and 125 jets. In 1964 the United States sold tanks to Jordan and in 1966 F-104 jets in order to preclude Soviet penetration. In 1966 the United States sold Israel A-4 Skyhawk jets, marking the first time it released combat aircraft to that country. Following the 1967 Arab–Israel War and during the 1969–1970 War of Attrition and the 1973 Arab–Israel War, the Soviet Union rearmed the Arab states, while the United States became Israel's principal supplier. The 1979 Israeli–Egyptian peace treaty was another turning point in arms supply to the region, after which the United States increased military aid to both Israel and Egypt. Israel continues to receive $1.8 billion annually in U.S. military assistance, and U.S. military aid to Egypt exceeds $1.3 billion. The United States sells Israel F-15I and F-16 multi-role jets; Egypt has purchased the latter model.

By the mid-1970s U.S. sales to Saudi Arabia, and Soviet transfers to Iraq and Syria, reached proportions similar to those of the Arab-Israeli context. Moreover, from 1977 to 1980, Iran purchased $3.4 billion in military equipment, mostly from the United States. In 1981, the United States sold Saudi Arabia an Airborne Warning and Command System (AWACS). Saudi expenditures on arms rose steadily and from 1987 to 1997 totaled $262 billion. Saudi Arabia's purchases have included U.S. M-1A2 Abrams tanks, F-15 jets, and Patriot surface-to-air missiles. Turkey's procurement has been more gradual but from 1981 to 1999 reached $11.55 billion worth of U.S. arms. The armaments levels of several states in the Middle East are comparable to those of the leading powers of Western Europe. Israel maintains some 1,300 high-quality main battle tanks and 350 high-quality jet aircraft. Syria has 1,600 first-line (T-72) tanks, purchased mainly from the Soviet Union and (after 1991) Russia, and 280 combat jets. Egypt's arsenal includes some 500 top-quality tanks of U.S. manufacture and 200 jets. Saudi Arabia has 200 such tanks and 170 jets.

Turkey fields medium-quality armor but maintains 225 high-quality jet aircraft.

Israel is the only state in the region with a sophisticated indigenous arms industry, producing the Merkava tank and Arrow surface-to-air missile. Israel is regarded as a nuclear power, but several other states in the Middle East possess non-conventional arms. Iraq has attempted to acquire a nuclear capability, and Libya and Syria have chemical weapons. All of the states of the region claim to support a Middle East Nuclear Weapons Free Zone, yet no agreements control the flow of arms to the Middle East.

See also MILITARY IN THE MIDDLE EAST.

Bibliography

Brom, Shlomo, and Shapir, Yiftah, eds. *The Middle East Military Balance, 2001–2002.* Cambridge, MA; London.: MIT Press, 2002.

Glassman, Jon D. *Arms for the Arabs: The Soviet Union and War in the Middle East.* Baltimore, MD: Johns Hopkins University Press, 1975.

Ilan, Amitzur. *The Origin of the Arab-Israeli Arms Race: Arms, Embargo, Military Power and Decision in the 1948 Palestine War.* New York: New York University Press; London: Macmillan, 1996.

Kemp, Geoffrey, with Shelley A. Stahl. *The Control of the Middle East Arms Race.* Washington, DC: Carnegie Endowment for International Peace, 1991.

Steinberg, Gerald M., with Aharon Etengoff. *Arms Control and Non-Proliferation Developments in the Middle East: 2000–1.* Ramat Gan: Begin-Sadat Center for Strategic Studies, Bar-Ilan University, 2002.

Stockholm International Peace Research Institute. *Arms Trade Registers: The Arms Trade with the Third World.* Cambridge, MA: MIT Press, 1975.

ZACH LEVEY

ARSEVEN, CELAL ESAT
[1876–1972]

Turkish art professor and historian.

Born the son of a pasha in Istanbul, Celal Esat Arseven was graduated from the Beşiktas Military School in 1888 and studied drawing at a fine arts school for a year before going to the war college. He continued writing and painting while in the army,

from which he resigned in 1908. In the years before World War I, he worked at the humor magazine *Kalem* with Cemil Cem, one of the great early caricaturists of Turkey.

Arseven was a writer and artist of diverse talents. In 1918, he wrote a libretto for one of the first Turkish operas and went on to write several musical plays performed at the Istanbul municipal and state theaters. In addition to being an accomplished watercolorist, he was also a professor of architecture and municipal planning at the Istanbul Fine Arts Academy from 1924 to 1941. He published a five-volume art encyclopedia between 1943 and 1954 and many books on Turkish painting and architecture during his lifetime. Before his death, he was awarded a doctoral degree by Istanbul University. He was also a delegate to the Turkish Grand National Assembly during its seventh and eighth sessions.

Bibliography

And, Metin. "Opera and Ballet in Modern Turkey." In *The Transformation of Turkish Culture: The Atatürk Legacy,* edited by Günsel Renda and C. Max Kortepeter. Princeton, NJ: Kingston Press, 1986.

ELIZABETH THOMPSON

ARSLAN, ADIL
[1880?–1954]

Syrian Arab nationalist politician.

Born in Shuwayfat (Lebanon), son of Amir Hamud, Adil Arslan was educated in the Maronite French Christian mission school, Madrasat al-Hikma, and at the Ottoman College in Beirut. He was also educated in France, then attended the Mülkiye (the Ottoman Empire's civil service school) but, according to one source, did not complete the course. He entered Ottoman political life under the wing of his paternal uncle, Amir Mustafa, whose tenure as leader of the Yazbaki Druze was just being successfully challenged by Amir Tawfiq Majid Arslan, and like his elder brother, Amir Shakib, Adil prospered as a member of the Union and Progress Party.

Adil Arslan became secretary, first grade, in the ministry of the interior in 1913, director of immigration in the *vilayet* of Syria in 1914, *qa'immaqam* of the Shuf in 1915, and representative from Mount Lebanon (*mutasarrifiyya*) from 1916 to 1918. According to some sources, he joined an Arab secret society before World War I, but older sources date his membership to the postwar period. Like many others who had served the Ottomans until the beginning or end of World War I, he joined up with Emir Faisal I ibn Hussein (who was promised a government by the British because of the effectiveness of his troops under T. E. Lawrence [of Arabia]). Arslan was appointed governor of the Lebanon in the fall of 1919, then aide to the military governor of Syria and, in 1920, political counselor to Faisal, who had become the new king of independent Syria. Despite Arslan's and his cousin Amin's efforts, most Druzes in Mount Lebanon followed Nasib Jumblatt or Tawfiq Majid Arslan and accepted the French mandate over Syria—hence Faisal's short-lived kingdom fell, and Adil Arslan fled to Transjordan, to Faisal's brother Amir Abdullah I ibn Hussein, where he served as chief of the *diwan* (court staff) from 1921 to 1923. When in response to the British, Abdullah exiled the Syrian Arab nationalist expatriates, Arslan took refuge in Saudi Arabia. In exile, he was closely associated with Shukri al-Quwatli and the Istiqlalists (independence movements). During the Syrian rebellion of 1925–1927, he was active as a fund-raiser and combat commander. Again condemned by the French, he continued his activities outside Syria, mainly in Egypt. When he was expelled from Egypt for anti-Italian activities in 1931, he went to Baghdad (since Faisal was then king of Iraq under British treaty protection). He was in Switzerland in 1937, continuing to participate in pan-Arab activities. After the Syrian National Bloc (to which Quwatli and the Istiqlalists adhered) reached agreement with France and formed a government, Arslan was appointed minister to Turkey, a post he held until 1938, when the Alexandretta territorial question reached a crisis (an Ottoman district that became a semiautonomous region of Syria in 1920, the Republic of Hatay in 1938, but was incorporated into Turkey in 1939 by agreement between France and Turkey). Arrested, then released by the French in 1940 and 1941, he fled in late 1941 to Turkey, where he spent the rest of World War II. Like other Arab nationalist politicians, he sought support for Arab causes from the Germans, but he opposed Rashid Ali al-Kaylani and Mufti of Jerusalem Hajj Amin al-Husayni, declining invitations to go to Germany.

Returning to an independent Syria after the war, he was minister of education in two National Party cabinets in 1946 and 1947 and was elected to parliament from al-Jawlan in 1947. He was a member of the Syrian delegation to the London round-table on Palestine in 1946 and 1947. He was a member and, after 19 April 1948, chief of Syria's United Nations delegation, but he resigned on 20 October, blaming the Syrian government for the Arab defeat in Palestine (Israel had declared independence in May 1948 and was fighting off invading Arab forces to remain a new state). In the volatile condition of Syrian politics, in December 1948 he twice failed to form a cabinet. Colonel Husni al-Za'im turned to him immediately after the coup of 30 March 1949 and made him his chief political aide. He served as foreign minister from 16 April to 26 June 1949. After Za'im's fall, Arslan was minister in Turkey from late 1949 to early 1952. He died at his home in Beirut on 23 January 1954. He was a writer and a poet, but his only books were *Dhikrayat al-Amir Adil Arslan an Husni al-Za'im* (Amir Adil Arslan's recollections concerning Husni al-Za'im [Beirut, 1962]) and *Mudhakkirat al-Amir Adil Arslan* (Memories of Amir Adil Arslan), edited by Yusuf Ibbish, in three volumes (Beirut, 1983).

> *See also* ABDULLAH I IBN HUSSEIN; ALEXAN-DRETTA; DRUZE; FAISAL I IBN HUSSEIN; HUSAYNI, MUHAMMAD AMIN AL-; LAWRENCE, T. E.; NATIONAL PARTY (SYRIA); QUWATLI, SHUKRI AL-; WORLD WAR II; ZA'IM, HUSNI AL-.

Bibliography

Cleveland, William L. *Islam against the West: Shakib Arslan and the Campaign for Islamic Nationalism.* Austin: University of Texas Press, 1985.

Hirszowicz, Lukasz. *The Third Reich and the Arab East.* London: Routledge and Kegan Paul, 1966.

Khoury, Philip S. *Syria and the French Mandate: The Politics of Arab Nationalism, 1920–1945.* Princeton, NJ: Princeton University Press, 1987.

Seale, Patrick. *The Struggle for Syria: A Study of Post-War Arab Politics, 1945–1958.* New Haven, CT: Yale University Press, 1987.

C. ERNEST DAWN

ARSLAN FAMILY

One of the two most important Druze families in Lebanon.

The Arslan family, in the Druze community for centuries, are now in competition with the Jumblatt Family to retain that position. Druze in Lebanon have historically been divided into Yazbakis and Jumblatts, and the Arslan family heads the Yazbaki confederation. Its head is now Amir Talal Arslan, who inherited the position from his father, Majid.

See also JUMBLATT FAMILY.

AS'AD ABUKHALIL

ARSLAN, SHAKIB

[1869–1946]

Lebanese poet, journalist, and political activist.

Shakib Arslan was a Druze notable from the Shuf region of Lebanon. He was dedicated to the preservation of the Ottoman Empire and to the social order of Islam. Between World War I and II, he became an anti-imperial activist and a relentless campaigner for the cause of Islamic solidarity. His voluminous writings, his well-connected network of associates, and his knack for attracting publicity made him one of the most visible Arab figures of this era.

The Arslans were a powerful Druze family whose members had the right to bear the title of amir (roughly equivalent to prince). Shakib's somewhat eclectic education—he studied at both the Maronite College and the Ottoman government school in Beirut—was designed to prepare him to carry on the family tradition of political leadership in changing times; his primary interest as a young man, however, was literature. He published his first volume of poetry at seventeen and continued to engage in literary pursuits for the next several years, earning for himself the honorific title "the prince of eloquence," by which he was known throughout his life. Eventually, he assumed the role expected of an Arslan amir by serving as qa'immaqam of the Shuf—in 1902 and from 1908 to 1911. He was elected to the Ottoman parliament in 1914 and spent the years of World War I defending the Ottoman cause—to hold the empire together. He disavowed the Arab Revolt of 1916, branded its leader Sharif Husayn ibn Ali a traitor to Islam, and predicted that an Allied victory

would lead to the division and occupation of the Arab provinces by the forces of European imperialism.

When this prediction was realized, Arslan became an exile, barred by British and French authorities from entering the Arab states that came under their control through League of Nations mandates. Instead of being marginalized by his changed circumstances, Arslan emerged as an international figure during the period between the world wars. His residence in Geneva, Switzerland, served as a gathering point for Arab and Muslim activists, and his position as the unofficial representative of the Syro-Palestinian delegation to the League of Nations afforded him opportunities to present the Arab case to the European community. His influence was expanded through the journal *La Nation Arabe* (1930–1938), which he founded and edited with Ihsan al-Jabiri. *La Nation Arabe* attacked all aspects of European imperialism but devoted special attention to French policies in the Maghrib (North Africa) and to Zionism in Palestine.

Notwithstanding his Druze origins, Arslan made his reputation as a staunch defender of mainstream Sunni Islam. He contributed frequent articles to such Islamic-oriented Egyptian journals as *al-Shura* and *al-Fath*; wrote biographies of his friends Rashid Rida and Ahmad Shawqi; compiled a history of Arab rule in Spain; and wrote other books on Islamic subjects. The purpose of his writing was to awaken among Muslims an awareness of their shared Islamic heritage and to summon them to action in the name of Islamic unity against the Western occupation. He believed in the primacy of an Islamic-inspired social order, and his interwar writings refuted all who challenged that belief, from the Egyptian liberal nationalists to Mustafa Kemal Atatürk, the founding president of the new secular Republic of Turkey.

More than any other figure of the era, Arslan endeavored to bring together the leaders of the North African and eastern Arab independence movements. He played an especially important role as political strategist and personal mentor to the group of young Moroccans associated with the Free School movement, and his orchestration of their international Islamic propaganda campaign against the French decree known as the Berber Dahir

(1930) was certainly one of the most successful Arab protest movements of this period.

Arslan's final reputation was diminished by his World War II association with the Axis powers; at the peak of his popularity, he endeavored to coordinate an Italo–German alliance with the Arab world in order to generate leverage against Britain and France. His pro-Axis stance during the war served to discredit him, and his death in Beirut in 1946 attracted little notice.

See also Arab Revolt (1916); Atatürk, Mustafa Kemal; Berber Dahir; Druze; Husayn ibn Ali; Sunni Islam; Zionism

Bibliography

Arslan, Shakib. *Our Decline and Its Causes,* translated by M. A. Shakoor. Lahore, Pakistan: Sh. Muhammad Ashraf, 1962.

Cleveland, William L. *Islam against the West: Shakib Arslan and the Campaign for Islamic Nationalism.* Austin: University of Texas Press, 1985.

WILLIAM L. CLEVELAND

ARSUZI, ZAKI AL-
[1900–1968]

Alawite Syrian Islamic pan-Arab intellectual and political activist; a founder of the Ba'th party.

Zaki al-Arsuzi was born in Latakia (north Syria) in or around 1900. His father, Muhammad Najib al-Arsuzi, originally from the Alexandretta district, was an Alawite Islamic landowner and the leading attorney for his coreligionists. Within the Ottoman Empire, his vehemence in the courtroom resulted in a transfer to Antioch (Turkey), and during World War I, the Ottomans banished him to Konya (Turkey). He is commonly said to have been of middling circumstances, but his official biography states that the family's material wealth in Alexandretta was great. Zaki attended the primary school in Antioch and completed his secondary education in Konya. He studied at the French lay mission school in Beirut (Lebanon) after World War I and the demise of the Ottoman Empire. He taught mathematics in the secondary school at Antioch (1920–1921), was director of the Arsuz *nahiya* (county; 1924–1925), and served as secretary of the department of education (1926–1927). After studying philosophy in

Paris from 1927 to 1930, he taught philosophy and history in the secondary schools, briefly in Antioch, and then in Aleppo and Dayr al-Zawr from 1930 to 1934. He built up a following among his students, in whom he instilled pan-Arabism, including the need for Arab resurrection (*ba'th*). He was an early member of the League of National Action (Asaba al-Amal al-Qawmi). He resigned or was forced out of his post in 1934 and returned to Antioch, where he was head of the Alexandretta province branch of the league. From 1936, his campaign to keep Alexandretta a part of Syria became violent and resulted in his expulsion in late 1938. He continued his protests from Damascus, but he broke with the league as well as the National Bloc. An agreement with Michel Aflaq, Salah al-Din al-Bitar, and three others to form a political party was fruitless, as was his own effort to organize a party that he called the Arab Nationalist Party (al-Hizb al-Qawmi al-Arabi). After experiencing disappointment as a teacher in Baghdad during 1939 and 1940, he resided in Damascus without employment, living with a group of students, fellow refugees from Alexandretta, but he continued to attract students from throughout Syria.

On 29 November 1940 he and six students formed al-Ba'th al-Arabi (which later became the ruling Ba'th party). The peak membership was twelve within the university, with a few more from the high school. Meanwhile, a similar group, calling itself at different times al-Ihya al-Arabi or al-Ba'th al-Arabi, gathered around Aflaq and Bitar. Most members of Arsuzi's group were students of Aflaq and Bitar, and members of their group frequently visited Arsuzi, but there was rivalry. Arsuzi disliked Aflaq intensely. Arsuzi was undeniably the more prominent. He had presided over the most successful branch of the League of National Action and won the acclaim of nationalist students throughout Syria. The head of the Italian Armistice Commission in Syria sought a meeting, but Arsuzi declined because he thought the British were about to occupy Syria. On similar grounds of military realism, he opposed Rashid Ali al-Kaylani's action in Iraq; his position was unpopular. Arsuzi became progressively unwilling to brook dissent; he was biting and sarcastic in his sessions with followers and opponents. His followers diminished, while Aflaq's group grew. The group dwindled, then broke up in

1944. In the same year, Arsuzi moved first to Latakia, then to Tartus, a Syrian coastal town. The members of his group, led by Wahib Ghanim, joined the Aflaq–Bitar organization in 1945–1946, but Arsuzi refused urgings to reenter politics. Accepting a teaching appointment secured through the intercession of his followers, he taught in Hama (1945–1948), Aleppo (1948–1952), and at the Dar al-Mu'allimin al-Ibtida'iyya in Damascus until retirement in 1959. He published books and articles on cultural and philosophical subjects and Arab nationalism and gave frequent lectures to army units. In the 1960s, as Alawite officers increased their influence in the Ba'th party and Syrian government, Arsuzi's reputation and influence rose as Aflaq's position declined.

Arsuzi died in Damascus on 2 July 1968. His collected works were published in six volumes by the Political Administration of the Army and the Armed Forces (al-Mu'allafat al-Kamila, Damascus, 1972–1976). His writings have received little attention in the published scholarship of Western languages, but his concept of the Arab nation, its mission, predicament, and future, is close to that of other writers of the 1920s and 1930s. His use of the Islamic theological term ba'th was not unprecedented, but he gave it unusual emphasis.

See also AFLAQ, MICHEL; BA'TH, AL-; BITAR, SALAH AL-DIN AL-; PAN-ARABISM.

Bibliography

Devlin, John F. The Ba'th Party: A History from Its Origins to 1966. Stanford, CA: Hoover Institution Press, 1976.

Olson, Robert W. The Ba'th and Syria, 1947 to 1982: The Evolution of Ideology, Party, and State, from the French Mandate to the Era of Hafiz al-Asad. Princeton, NJ: Kingston Press, 1982.

Rabinovich, Itamar. Syria under the Ba'th, 1963–66: The Army–Party Symbiosis. Jerusalem: Israel Universities Press, 1972.

C. ERNEST DAWN

ART

Art in the Middle East encompasses a broad range of cultural traditions and artistic ideologies.

The visual arts play an important role in cultural and political processes in the contemporary Middle East. The importance of visual art's relationship to politics and culture is largely due to how deeply embedded traditional art forms are, the tenuous relationship between figural art and Islamic theology, the ongoing entanglement between Western and Middle Eastern modern arts dating back to the colonial period, and significant governmental interest in the visual arts as an expression of political ideologies or cultural achievement. Most importantly, historical and contemporary arts together define concepts of local identity (e.g., national, religious, class) in relation to regional and global political and economic forces.

"Hanging Gardens," oil on canvas, by Syrian artist Madiha Umar. Umar graduated from a London university and taught art in Iraq in the 1930s before moving to the United States for further education. Umar pioneered the modern use of Arabic calligraphy in abstract painting, and her critically acclaimed work often appears in art history books. "HANGING GARDENS" BY MADIHA UMAR, OIL ON CANVAS, 1962. © MADIHA UMAR. REPRODUCED BY PERMISSION.

Jananne al-Ani's "Untitled I" and "Untitled II" photographs are always displayed as a pair. The Iraqi artist's work is influenced by her interest in the female form as depicted in Orientalist painting and photography. "UNTITLED I," BY JANANNE AL-ANI, 1996, SILVER GELATIN PRINTS, 180CM X 120CM, COLLECTION: SMITHSONIAN INSTITUTION/VICTORIA & ALBERT MUSEUM. © JANANNE AL-ANI. REPRODUCED BY PERMISSION OF THE ARTIST.

Since the nineteenth century, the visual arts have been produced in relationship to several historical and contemporary trends, which highlight the particular connections between art, culture, and politics in the region. First, artists, critics, collectors, and arts administrators have engaged with the styles, media, and ideologies of modern art from Europe, the Eastern bloc countries, and the United States. Beginning in the colonial period, Western European artists and teachers brought Western concepts, techniques, and styles of modern art to the Middle East. They were often instrumental in setting up arts institutions and East/West cultural hierarchies. Between the 1950s and 1970s, the Eastern bloc, with its socialist realism, replaced Western Europe as the main source of external cultural engagement, particularly in countries like Iraq and Egypt. Since at least the 1980s, classical and avant-garde Western European trends and cultural exchanges have again become influential, particularly with the advent of Western interest in opening up the canon of modern art to non-Westerners. In Egypt, Lebanon, and Israel especially, one finds intensified interest in American art forms, but in many cases this is complicated by dissatisfaction with American foreign policy.

The second major factor that has influenced the production of visual arts since the nineteenth century is recognition of the artistic achievements of the past, especially historical Islamic art, Pharaonic art, Assyrian art, and Phoenician art. Artworks from these traditions are seen not only as aesthetic accomplishments but also as emblems of a time when Middle Eastern countries were at the height of their political, economic, and cultural development. In many cases, these historical artworks have been incorporated into nationalism as artistic traditions, or

As of 2003, Jananne al-Ani was involved in the production of an exhibition dedicated to displaying contemporary works involving the veil. "UNTITLED II," BY JANANNE AL-ANI, 1996, SILVER GELATIN PRINTS, 180CM X 120CM, COLLECTION: SMITHSONIAN INSTITUTION/VICTORIA & ALBERT MUSEUM. © JANANNE AL-ANI. REPRODUCED BY PERMISSION OF THE ARTIST.

into broader ideologies of Arab or religious identity.

The same is true for folk arts and crafts, a third major influence on the production of modern art. Objects made by peasants or craftspeople, and the visual styles they developed, have also been made part of national canons and been used by modern artists seeking to legitimate themselves as part of local collectivities rather than elites who imitate the West—a common charge in the Arab world.

It would be a mistake to characterize this blending of historical and contemporary artistic trends as the degraded by-product of Western cultural imperialism, industrialization, socialist propaganda, or nationalist elitism. Rather, the arts of the Middle East (like arts everywhere) have always developed in relationship to cultural and political trends from within the region and to relationships between the region and the outside world. The situation of the

visual arts in the Middle East is complicated by the Western modernist notion of the strict separation and hierarchical ranking of fine art over craft or applied art—a separation which was introduced to the Middle East through the colonial encounter. It is further complicated by the history of European orientalist painting, which is criticized by many Middle Eastern and Western scholars for stereotypical portrayals of the Orient that assisted colonialism, but which greatly influenced the development of national subjects and styles within the Middle East itself.

Further complicating the situation of the visual arts is the unresolved debate over the acceptability of representational painting and sculpting (taswir) in Islam. Condemned as idolatrous by traditional theologians, works of art depicting people and animals nevertheless flourished from earliest Islamic times, especially under royal patronage. The efforts of some modern theological commentators to reinterpret or eliminate the theological ban on *taswir* through a revisionist view of the important *hadith* on the subject seem to have had an influence on the acceptance of such art among most Middle Eastern artists with the exception of many in the Gulf countries and in Iran, where there has been strict censorship of public art by the clerical regime. For the general population, the increasing acceptance of *taswir* owes much to the influence of television, film, and advertising, which provide public images that are highly figural, pervasive, and popular. Still, conventional Islamic mores concerning the image, and particularly the nude figure, still shape the choices that artists, curators, and collectors make, and are most noticeable in art education curricula.

All these factors have shaped the art worlds of Middle Eastern countries. In general, artistic production and the processes of evaluation, patronage, and consumption of the arts have been most marked by struggles to define cultural, national, and religious identity in relation to two poles: on the one hand, the achievements of historical art traditions and contemporary crafts, which are endangered by industrialization, and on the other, the influence and hegemony of Western modern art.

Arts Institutions

Arts institutions, including art colleges, museums, and galleries, exist in all Middle Eastern countries. While some date back to the colonial period, such as the first College of Fine Arts in the Arab world (Cairo, 1908), most were formed in the post-Independence period of nation-building. The 1990s also witnessed a growth in the number of arts institutions in both the public and private sectors. During this period, many private galleries opened in Cairo and Beirut, especially. Middle Eastern countries now have national collections, many housed in notable museums of national modern art, such as the Museum of Modern Egyptian Art in Cairo, the Jordan National Gallery of Fine Arts, and the Sursock Museum in Beirut. Many works from the Iraqi National Collection were destroyed during the 2003 war.

Artistic Trends

These specifics of modern Middle Eastern cultural production have produced a number of artistic trends and responses. One of the most popular trends is to take the spirit, principles, or forms (especially calligraphic and geometric) of historical Islamic art and put them into a contemporary artistic context through manipulation of form or material or by using them to address current political or cultural issues. This trend has been most influential in Jordan, Palestine, the Maghrib, the Gulf, and Iran. The creation of what has been called modern Islamic art challenges the common notion that Islamic art declined in the late nineteenth and early twentieth centuries as a direct result of the influence of Western techniques and styles. The changing economics of patronage, particularly after 1700, were the primary cause of the dramatic changes in Islamic art in the modern period. The talk of decline, it may be argued, comes from nostalgia for a premodern Muslim past. Not satisfied with being kept out of modernity, Muslim critics have engaged in significant attempts to develop Islamic aesthetic theories, and artists have produced some of the most original interpretations of the history of Islamic art. For example, calligraphy—the most distinctive, pervasive, and religiously embedded Islamic art form—has, due to the printing press, been less important in the media of pen and paper but has found expression in a host of new media, from oil on canvas and silk screen to neon-filled glass tubing and polymer or stone sculpture. In another example, geometric and vegetal arabesque forms, as well as the classic *muqarnas* architectural device (a honeycomb or stalactite vault), have been manipulated in new ways, often in combination with European or American abstraction devices. This innovation has occurred in both two- and three-dimensional art, including installation art. Faced with some resistance among those who see abstract art as an imitation of Western excesses, some art theorists have argued that abstraction actually originated in Islam (with its opposition to the image), and they have delved into the history of Islamic art theory in order to reinvigorate it. Sufi philosophy and practice, with its emphasis on experimentation and altered consciousness, has also been inspirational for many artists in the Middle East, although it is worth mentioning that Christian, and sometimes Muslim, artists also use traditional Christian motifs in their work. This is most apparent in Egypt, where Coptic history has been incorporated into the national artistic patrimony.

The most widespread trend among contemporary Middle Eastern artists is the visual search for and expression of cultural identity, which is usually defined in national terms but can also be formulated as Arab, Mediterranean, Mesopotamian, Maghribi, Kurdish, Berber, Nubian, Persian, Turkish, or a combination of any of these, depending on the context. The central importance of cultural identity in contemporary Middle Eastern art is related to several factors: the rich artistic sources found in the historical arts and in contemporary folklores, landscapes, and local materials (e.g., certain kinds of stone, plant dyes, found artifacts, local consumer goods, and industrial objects); the incorporation, through modern nationalist projects, of these sources into national traditions; state, local elite, and Western patronage, all searching for visual representations of cultural uniqueness; the anxiety, produced through colonialism, over Western influence and the desire to protect and develop what are seen as more authentic local traditions; and, often, secular artists' desires to create a nonreligious cultural identity through art. The art of cultural identity is found in most countries of the region and is especially dominant in Egypt, Iraq, Lebanon, Palestine, Tunisia, and Turkey. In Egypt, Iraq, and Turkey, in particular, it has had tremendous support from the secularist regimes. The most common themes in this trend are pastoral landscapes, premodern urban and rural architecture, peasants (especially rural women), the popular (sha'bi) urban classes, ancient civilizations (e.g., Pharaonic, Phoenician, Assyrian), and images from folk art. Popular styles include figurative primitivism and semi-impressionist realism in both painting and sculpture. Younger generations of artists in the Middle East, however, are engaging in their own searches for cultural identity, which sometimes draw on the past, the rural, and the folk but also try to account for the contemporary changes engulfing the region, particularly those related to consumer capitalism, technological globalization, and war and violence. They often explore their shifting, yet usually rooted, cultural identity in newer media, such as installation art, video art, and performance. Sometimes this art takes a completely conceptual and abstract, rather than literal and figurative, form.

Another major trend is the use of avant-garde media, styles, and art theory to launch critiques against the West or Israel and, less often, the artists' own governments. Many of these artists are concerned with such issues as the inequality of capitalist globalization, conspicuous consumerism, threats to morality (defined broadly) or cultural integrity, the oppression or commoditization of women, and violence.

Consumption and Patronage

Many governments of the region have put significant resources into supporting and reinvigorating traditional crafts, and into restoring historical monuments and architecture. These projects have often been connected to tourism planning, and to educating the population about the national artistic patrimony. Governmental and private sector attempts to market modern art to tourists, foreign curators, or the local population have been less successful for two primary reasons. First, foreigners often come to the region looking for objects that unambiguously reflect their preconception of a unique traditional culture, and modern art—particularly in its more experimental forms—does not fit these expectations easily. Second, the general population is often alienated by modern art forms and the institutions that display them.

That said, there has been a continuous growth in the consumption and patronage of contemporary art in several countries since 1985, which is due to several factors. One of the most important is the growth of capitalism and the effects of globalization generally, engendering increased exposure to contemporary avant-garde art from the United States and Europe and producing (in many countries) a local class of nouveaux riches (many of them under the age of forty-five) who are eager to support modern art and, it could be argued, display their cultural capital by purchasing it. These forces have also brought Western curators to the Middle East in unprecedented numbers. Having opened their canons to non-Western modern art, many of them are interested in finding Middle Eastern artists who challenge stereotypes of the region—particularly its women (though not its men). These Europeans and Americans have increased Western exposure to Middle Eastern art and artists, though sometimes their tactics have been criticized by local artists and governments. Not only do anxieties about Western influence and the effects of the colonial encounter still exist, in many cases they are heightened by the globalization of Middle Eastern art. A final factor contributing to increasing support for modern art is the attempt by government to raise the international status of the nation by developing the arts of the country and encouraging artistic expression as a counterweight to the rise of radical Islamism. In several countries, the state has become the primary collector of modern art as a result.

A major consequence of these global shifts has been the development of a significant body of art produced by the Middle Eastern diaspora in Europe and the United States. The themes of cultural identity, memory, political critique, and especially gender have been the most prominent.

See also ALI, WIJDAN; ATTAR, SUAD AL-; BAYA; CALAND, HUGUETTE; EFFLATOUN, INJI; FARAJ, MAYSALOUN; GHOUSSOUB, MAI; HATOUM, MONA; ISHAAQ, KAMALA IBRAHIM; JACIR, EMILY; KADRI, MUFIDE; KARNOUK, LILIANE; KHAL, HELEN; KHEMIR, SABIHA; NESHAT, SHIRIN; NIATI, HOURIA; SAUDI, MONA; SHAWA, LAILA; SIDERA, ZINEB; SIRRY, GAZBIA; TALLAL, CHAIBIA; UMAR, MADIHA; ZEID, FAHRALNISSA.

Bibliography

Ali, Wijdan. *Modern Islamic Art: Development and Continuity.* Gainesville: University Press of Florida, 1997.

Karnouk, Liliane. *Contemporary Egyptian Art.* Cairo: The American University Press, 1995.

Lloyd, Fran, ed. *Contemporary Arab Women's Art: Dialogues of the Present.* London: WAL, 1999.

Lloyd, Fran, ed. *Displacement and Difference: Contemporary Arab Visual Culture in the Diaspora.* London: Saffron Books, 2001.

Nashashibi, Salwa Makdisi, ed. *Forces of Change: Artists of the Arab World.* Lafayette, CA: International Council for Women in the Arts, 1994.

Tawadros, Gilane, and Campbell, Sarah. *Faultlines: Contemporary African Art and Shifting Landscapes.* London: inIVA, 2003.

Zuhur, Sherifa, ed. *Images of Enchantment: Visual and Performing Arts of the Middle East.* Cairo: The American University in Cairo Press, 1998.

WALTER DENNY
UPDATED BY JESSICA WINEGAR

AS'AD, AHMAD

Leader of the influential Shi'ite family of Jabal Amil.

The As'ad family (also spelled al-As'ad), which was descended from the Saghir family of Jabal Amil, traces its origins to Arab tribes in southern Arabia. This large landowning family has monopolized the political representation of the Shi'ites of south Lebanon for centuries. Ahmad As'ad, the leader of the family in the first half of the twentieth century, was elected to parliament from 1937 to 1960; was briefly speaker of parliament; and served in several cabinets. His popularity in south Lebanon was so strong that his entire list of candidates was assured victory. People in south Lebanon joked that a stick would win a parliamentary seat if included on Ahmad al-As'ad's list. He and his son Kamil were both in the 1953, 1957, and 1960 parliaments. After Ahmad's death, his wife, known as Umm Kamil, shared political responsibilities with her son.

See also AS'AD FAMILY; AS'AD, KAMIL.

AS'AD ABUKHALIL

ASAD, BASHSHAR AL-
[1965–]

Syrian army officer, ophthalmologist, president of the Syrian Arab Republic since 2000.

Born in Damascus on 11 September 1965, Bashshar al-Asad was the second son of the late president, Hafiz al-Asad. He attended the Franco-Arab al-Hurriyet school in Damascus and Damascus University, studying medicine and specializing in ophthalmology. He had three brothers and a sister, all of whom, at the insistence of their father, completed their education in Syria. The ethos of the Asad household was somewhat puritanical. While the children saw little of their father, they were intensely loyal to him. Bashshar al-Asad later continued his postgraduate education and specialization in the United Kingdom.

Asad entered the Homs Military Academy in 1994, graduating first in his class and rising quickly through the ranks to become a colonel in 1999. Immediately entrusted with heavier military and political responsibilities than would be justified by his junior rank, he later became commander in chief of the armed forces as well as secretary general of the Ba'th party. Also president of the Syrian Computer Society, an organization devoted to promoting the diffusion of information technology throughout the country, Asad's role there has often been cited as an indication of his interest in modernization.

After his father's death, Asad was elected to a seven-year presidential term on 10 July 2000, receiving 97.29 percent of the official vote tally. He was sworn in as the sixteenth president of the Syrian Arab Republic on 17 July 2000. In a speech immediately after the ceremony, he set the tone for the early years of his administration, emphasizing the dual themes of continuity and change that have characterized his presidency.

Asad immediately displayed political skill by gracefully eliminating potential political rivals and promoting younger officials dedicated to economic and technological modernization. He also made clear his distaste for the cult of personality, a prominent feature of his father's regime. Another sign of a more liberal inclination was his promise to activate the role of the Progressive National Front, a coalition of political groups established in 1972 and dominated by the Ba'th party. Asad also granted amnesty to several hundred political prisoners, including members of the Muslim Brotherhood and some communists. Another noteworthy step was to decree a 25 percent salary raise for public sector workers.

Growing regional conflict later diverted Asad's attention from domestic issues, dampening expectations of rapid economic and political change. Early liberalization measures, known as the Damascus Spring, were soon tarnished by steps taken to reassert the authority of the old regime, including a crackdown in 2001 on political discussion groups and the imprisonment of prodemocracy militants. Asad then reversed course in mid-2003, implementing a new round of minor reform measures, dismissed by some as cosmetic. Ba'th party officials were told to stay out of the day-to-day running of the bureaucracy, three private banks were licensed in an important step toward reforming the state-dominated economy, and two new private universities and four radio stations were approved. Broader economic reforms were delayed, in part out of fear of possible political destabilization; consequently,

the economy remained the primary long-term issue in Syrian domestic politics.

When compared with the domestic front, there was less immediate movement on regional and international levels. Syria remains committed to a just and comprehensive Middle East peace, including the recovery of every inch of Syrian territory. With this as the top national priority, Syrian foreign policy continues to revolve around three axes: Egypt–Saudi Arabia–Syria, Iran–Syria, and Lebanon–Syria. Departures in foreign policy under Asad include a dramatic opening to Iraq, better relations with Turkey, and support for the Palestinian intifada. The unresolved peace process with Israel continues to cloud development of healthy relations between Syria and the United States. In the process, the Israeli–Palestinian conflict, U.S. occupation of Iraq, and concerns that the war on terrorism could target Syria all reinforce the intransigence of the old guard in Syrian politics and become a pretext for obstructing change in both external and internal policies.

Bibliography

Hinnebusch, Raymond A. *Syria: Revolution from Above.* London: Taylor & Francis, 2002.

Seale, Patrick. *Asad: The Struggle for the Middle East.* Berkeley: University of California Press, 1995.

Van Dam, Nikolaos. *The Struggle for Power in Syria: Politics and Society Under Asad and the Ba'th Party.* New York; London: I. B. Tauris, 1996.

RONALD BRUCE ST JOHN

AS'AD FAMILY

A prominent family of southern Lebanon.

The As'ad family claims descent from the family confederation of al-Saghir, who in turn trace their lineage to tribes in Arabia. Ahmad al-As'ad and his son Kamil were dominant politicians in the twentieth century; both held ministerial positions and Kamil was speaker of Parliament for much of the 1970s and also in the 1960s and 1980s. His family leadership suffered from the rise of radical political parties among Shi'ites in the early phase of the civil war of 1975. In later years, the rise of AMAL and Hizbullah, eclipsed the influence of the family. Kamil al-As'ad failed to win a seat in the 1992 parliamentary elections.

See also AMAL; AsʿAD, AHMAD; AsʿAD, KAMIL; HIZBULLAH.

AsʿAD ABUKHALIL

ASAD, HAFIZ AL-
[1930–2000]

Syrian air force officer and statesman, late president of the Syrian Arab Republic.

Born in Qurdaha, near Latakia, Asad was the ninth of eleven children of Ali Sulayman, a peasant of Alawi origin whose strength, bravery, and chivalry made him a pillar of his village. Until his death in 1963, Ali carried on the family tradition of mediating quarrels and giving protection to the weak. Asad was one of a handful of boys in his village to receive formal education when the French opened primary schools in remote villages. From his father he acquired a lifelong determination not to submit when pressures mounted.

This family legacy offers an important clue to Asad's proud and vigorous personality. While a student, Asad joined the Baʿth party in 1947 and became one of its stalwarts in Latakia. After graduation from secondary school in 1951, he entered the military academy at Homs and later the flying school at Aleppo, graduating as a pilot officer in 1955. He then plunged into the intrigues of the highly politicized and faction-ridden officer corps, traveling to Egypt in 1955 and to the Soviet Union in 1958 for further military instruction. Asad returned to Egypt in 1959, having already joined the Baʿth party as a follower of Zaki al-Arsuzi, an Alawi from Alexandretta and one of the three founders of the Baʿth party. With four fellow officers who also followed al-Arsuzi, Asad founded in Cairo in early 1960 a secret organization they called the Military Committee. These young men had never admired the other two Baʿth party founders, Michel Aflaq and Salah al-Din al-Bitar, considering them to be middle-class Damascene theorists of the Baʿth, and believing that they had caused the party's demise by entering impulsively into an ill-fated union with Egypt in February 1958. Egypt's president, Gamal Abdel Nasser, distrusted political parties, and as a condition for accepting union with Syria, he had insisted on the dissolution of the Baʿth party.

Rise to Power

Being Baʿthists who aspired to positions of dominance in Syrian public life, Asad and his colleagues in the Military Committee were very careful not to reveal the existence of their organization to Egyptian intelligence. Following the breakup of the Egypt-Syria union in September 1961, Asad was jailed briefly in Egypt before returning to Syria, where he was granted indefinite leave from the air force and demoted to a low-paid clerk position in the Ministry of Economics. At times incarcerated in Lebanon as well as in Syria, he spent 1962 conspiring with his colleagues on the Military Committee to take power in Syria. In March 1963 he played a leading role in the coup that brought Baʿth officers to power. Following the coup, Asad was promoted to major general and made commander of the air force in 1964. From 1965, he was a member of the regional (*qutri*) and national (*qawmi*) Baʿth High Command.

During the seven years following the 1963 coup, Asad mastered the techniques of survival in the factional struggles that plagued Syria. Rejecting Aflaq and the social and economic order from which he came, Asad sided with the radical faction of Salah Jadid and Muhammad Umran, making in the process both lasting friendships and permanent enemies. Umran kept an eye on the government machine, Jadid ran the army, and Asad helped the Military Committee extend its networks in the armed forces by bringing every unit under its close control and by ensuring that Committee loyalists occupied the sensitive commands.

For ideological guidance, Asad sought the advice of Aflaq's early rival, the Alawite Zaki al-Arsuzi, who contributed editorials to the party and army press and provided Asad with insights until Arsuzi's death in 1968. In February 1966, following a bloody intraparty shootout, Asad was made Minister of Defense, thus moving very close to the top of the government. He was then promoted in 1968 to the rank of lieutenant general. To get to the top, he had to neutralize or purge the leftist team of Jadid and the officers who supported them. Asad believed the radicalism of the Jadid-led team caused Syria's isolation in the Arab world, and the army it tried to build was ill prepared to cope with Israel. In February 1969 he gained control of the government and party command but agreed to keep some of his adversaries in positions of power. In November 1970 Asad seized full control in what he termed a "corrective movement," purging and dismissing his opponents and detaining their leaders, including president and prime minister Nur al-Din al-Atasi.

With Asad's rise to power, a new chapter in the domestic and foreign policies of Syria began to unfold. On the domestic front, Asad sought to establish his rule on a firm footing, primarily by building stable state institutions and by wooing disenchanted social classes with measures of political and economic liberalization. Socialism, retained as a tenet in the rhetoric of the ruling party, became etatism or state capitalism. The Asad regime also relaxed restrictions on the private sector. Rapid economic growth, mostly through public expenditure, was the primary objective of both economic and development policies. In response, the Syrian economy grew at an annual rate exceeding 9 percent throughout the 1970s. After 1973 additional rounds of economic liberalization followed in 1979, 1987, and 1991.

Asad emphasized the need for reconciliation and national unity after the divisive years of the Jadid-led faction. To heighten the impression of a fresh start, he introduced a more liberal climate for writers and novelists and set about courting former Ba'thists who had been generally out of favor with the previous regime. Stable political structures also emerged after Asad's coup. A People's Council or parliament was established in 1971, and the following year, the Progressive National Front, an institutionalized coalition of the Ba'th party with a collection of smaller parties, was set up. In 1973, a new constitution was promulgated. On the other hand, Asad allowed no opposition to his rule. He ruthlessly suppressed the Muslim Brotherhood, virtually eliminating its resistance during the Hama uprising of February 1982.

Asad also neutralized or en ded factional struggles within the army and the Ba'th party. The institutional pillars of his rule were the army, a multilayered intelligence network, formal state structures, and revitalized party congresses. The People's Council in 1971 appointed Asad president following nomination by the Ba'th command; thereafter, plebiscites regularly endorsed his re-

A lifelong Ba'th Party member, Hafiz al-Asad was the president of Syria from 1970 until his death in 2000. © GETTY IMAGES. REPRODUCED BY PERMISSION.

election for seven-year terms. The consolidation of the state, accompanied by a concentration of power in Asad's hands, was accepted by the political elite as a necessary measure to confront the threat the country and regime faced following its defeat and occupation in the Arab-Israel War of June 1967. Asad's state-building was largely dependent on external resources, with the Soviet Union providing the arms to rebuild the military and Arab oil money funding an expansion of the bureaucracy and the co-opting of the bourgeoisie.

A Three-Stage Foreign Policy

In foreign policy, Asad called into question the radical policies of his predecessors, setting Syria on a new, more pragmatic course that took greater account of Israel's military superiority. Three stages of Syria's foreign policy in the Asad years can be identified. The first lasted from 1970 to 1974. During this stage, Asad moved quickly to improve relations with Egypt, which had been strained since the 1961 breakup of its union with Syria. He even joined the stillborn federation of Egypt, Libya, and the Sudan in November 1970. He also set about putting Syria's relations with Lebanon, Morocco, Saudi Arabia, and Tunisia on a friendly basis. To show good faith toward Saudi Arabia, he closed a Damascus-based, anti-Saudi radio station. The Arab-Israel War of October 1973, at least in part, was an efficiently coordinated Syrian-Egyptian-Saudi affair. While not a military success, it proved a political victory for Asad. Although Syria failed to regain the Golan Heights, he derived a high degree of legitimacy and considerable political leverage from a credible challenge to the Israeli status quo as well as from the Arab oil embargo initiated in response to the war.

Asad also moved very quickly to convince the Soviet Union that Syria was a reliable and valuable regional partner. This entailed facilitating a stable Soviet presence in the region to curtail American influence. Soviet arms deliveries proved vital to Syria's relative success in the 1973 war and were stimulated later by Egypt's separate peace with Israel and Israel's 1982 invasion of Lebanon. Soviet military power expanded steadily under Asad's rule in an effort to give Syria sufficient parity with Israel to constitute a credible deterrent and to give backing to Syrian diplomacy. The role of the Soviet Union as patron-protector also served as a deterrent to Israeli freedom of action against Syria. As for the United States, mutual hostility and mistrust kept the two countries diplomatically apart until the 1990s. In Asad's view, the United States biased the regional balance of power in Israel's favor by ensuring its military superiority and also by dividing the Arabs, notably by detaching Sadat's Egypt from the anti-Israeli coalition.

Stage Two

In the second stage, which lasted from 1974 to the end of the 1980s, there were three major modifications in Syria's foreign policy. The first was the revision of its alliance strategy with Egypt; it now sought to isolate Egypt in the Arab world. The aim was to discredit Anwar al-Sadat and eliminate any possibility of a Camp David–type agreement between Israel and other Arab states, especially Jordan and Lebanon. Asad worked to bring neighboring

Lebanon and Jordan, together with the Palestinians, into the Syrian orbit; and in 1983 and 1984, he struggled mightily to kill the May 1983 Israel-Lebanon accord, brokered by U.S. Secretary of State George Shultz. Soviet support was pivotal here in giving Asad the confidence necessary to challenge Israeli power and U.S. diplomacy in Lebanon following the 1982 Israeli invasion.

A second change concerned Asad's relations with the leader of Iraq, Saddam Hussein, who remained Asad's most implacable Arab adversary. Nonpersonal considerations notwithstanding, including the party schism and the geopolitical rivalry that divided the two countries, Asad swallowed his pride and went to Baghdad in 1978, following Egypt's entente with Israel. In June 1979 he again visited Iraq in an unsuccessful bid for a federation between the two countries. Suspecting that the federation scheme was intended to undermine his position of dominance in Iraq, Saddam did not bother to meet Asad at the airport and later accused Syria of hatching a plot to overthrow him. The following year, when the Iran-Iraq war broke out, Asad condemned Iraq and backed Iran. Asad denounced the Iraqi invasion of Iran as the wrong war at the wrong time with the wrong enemy, rightly predicting it would detract Arab attention from the Israeli threat. The alliance with Iran proved helpful in the aftermath of the 1982 Israeli invasion of Lebanon, when Iranian-sponsored Islamic resistance to Israel helped check a dangerous challenge to the Asad regime. Over time, Syria and Iran became increasingly close partners, to the displeasure of the rulers of Saudi Arabia and the Gulf states, who saw in Ayatollah Ruhollah Khomeini's revolution a potentially fatal threat to their regimes and to the territorial integrity of their countries.

The third change concerned Syria's relations with Israel. The process of change in this regard was relatively fast in getting under way. The first visible step was Syria's acceptance of UN Security Council Resolution 242 in March 1972. In the past, Asad had reiterated Syria's rejection of Resolution 242 on the grounds that without redressing the military and political balance with Israel, the Arabs could not force Israel to solve the Palestine question and withdraw from the Arab territories it had seized in June 1967.

A more tangible step was the May 1974 disengagement agreement between Syria and Israel, negotiated under the auspices of the U.S. government in the wake of the Arab-Israel War of 1973. The Soviet Union remained neutral except for hints in the Soviet press warning Asad not to be tricked into accepting half measures. One significant aspect of the agreement was the two sides' declaration that the disengagement of forces was only a step toward a just and durable peace based on UN Resolutions 242 and 338. Another was Asad's oral commitment not to allow any guerrilla raids from the Syrian side of the disengagement line.

Stage Three

The third stage in Syrian foreign policy, dating from the end of the 1980s, concerned its entente with Egypt, its participation in the U.S.–led alliance against Iraq, and its subsequent involvement in the U.S.–sponsored Middle East peace process that began with the Madrid Conference in October 1991. These events transpired in a milieu in which the negative impact of the decay of pan-Arabism in the 1980s was compounded by deteriorating domestic economic conditions as Syria wrestled with a prolonged economic crisis from 1985 to 1990. Triggered by a sudden decline in oil prices and foreign aid, the economic problems of the Asad regime were rooted in a history of excessive military spending, stifling economic regulations, and political corruption that combined to distort markets and drain resources.

Whereas in the previous stage Syria had been adamantly opposed to Egypt, it abandoned its policy of seeking "strategic parity" with Israel in 1988 and 1989 and entered into an alliance with the Egyptian government of Husni Mubarak, a pact involving de facto acceptance of the Camp David Accords. These moves led to Syria's entry, for the first time, into face-to-face negotiations with Israel. Not only did Syria drop its insistence on an international peace conference under UN sponsorship, but it helped to create the psychological climate for promising bilateral negotiations with Israel.

The end of the Cold War thus marked a period of transition for Asad. Faced with a hostile international environment, he adapted begrudgingly to the new power balance. The implosion of the Soviet Union, and its withdrawal as arms provider and reliable protector, exposed Syria to Western animosity for its long-time opposition to the Middle East peace process. Asad rightly concluded that the struggle with Israel would now have to take a diplomatic form and would require détente with the United States, which alone had leverage over Israel. The Gulf War coalition thus provided an opportunity for Asad to trade adhesion to the coalition for at least limited U.S. recognition of Syrian interests. In the process, Asad hoped to influence the new world order, as opposed to becoming its victim.

Syrian entry into the Madrid peace process marked not an abandonment of long-term goals, but their pursuit by other means. The containment of Israel remained center-stage in Syrian strategic thinking. Asad still hoped to maximize territorial recovery and minimize the concessions Israel expected in return. While Syria displayed newfound flexibility in the talks, negotiations eventually stalled over Israeli insistence on a surveillance station on Mount Hermon, which Asad saw as an affront to Syrian sovereignty, and the 1996 Likud election victory in Israel. Talks with Israel resumed after the 1999 election of Ehud Barak but later broke down over control of Golan water resources and Israeli insistence on modifying the pre-1967 border around Lake Tiberias.

As the transition from a state of belligerency to one of coexistence with Israel continued, Asad initiated a new round of economic reforms. The decade of the 1990s saw the slow dismantling of the public sector and the socialist measures associated with it. Private investment overtook public investment, and agriculture became almost exclusively the domain of the private sector. At the same time, resistance to additional economic reforms from members of the bureaucracy, the Ba'th party, and the military, together with widespread patronage, waste, and corruption, continued to constitute serious obstacles to rational economic policies. Moreover, while the continuation of economic reforms and the peace process generated pressures for greater political openness, political liberalization, especially democratization, remained anathema to the Asad regime.

The principles governing Asad's foreign and domestic policies have been compared to those that governed the policy of British statesman Lord Palmerston (1784–1865), who once said, "We have no eternal allies, and we have no perpetual enemies. Our interests are eternal and perpetual, and those interests it is our duty to follow." In the execution of these principles, Asad proved himself a cautious and calculating tactician as well as a master politician. President Hafiz al-Asad died on 10 June 2000. He was replaced by his second son, Bashshar al-Asad, on 17 July 2000.

See also ARSUZI, ZAKI AL-; BA'TH, AL-; GOLAN HEIGHTS; HAMA; IRAN–IRAQ WAR (1980–1988); MADRID CONFERENCE (1991); MUSLIM BROTHERHOOD.

Bibliography

Batatu, Hanna. *Syria's Peasantry, the Descendants of Its Lesser Rural Notables, and Their Politics.* Princeton, NJ: Princeton University Press, 1999.

Deeb, Marius. *Syria's Terrorist War on Lebanon and the Peace Process.* New York; Basingstoke, U.K.: Palgrave Macmillan, 2003.

Drysdale, Alasdair, and Hinnebusch, Raymond. *Syria and the Middle East Peace Process.* New York: Council on Foreign Relations Press, 1991.

Hinnebusch, Raymond A. *Authoritarian Power and State Formation in Ba'thist Syria: Army, Party and Peasant.* Boulder, CO: Westview Press, 1990.

Hinnebusch, Raymond A. "The Foreign Policy of Syria." In *The Foreign Policies of Middle East States,* edited by Raymond Hinnebusch and Anoushiravan Ehteshami. Boulder, CO: Lynne Rienner, 2002.

Hinnebusch, Raymond A. *Syria: Revolution from Above.* London: Taylor & Francis, 2002.

Kienle, Eberhard, ed. *Contemporary Syria: Liberalization between Cold War and Cold Peace.* London: British Academic Press, 1994.

Perthes, Volker. *The Political Economy of Syria under Asad.* New York; London: I. B. Tauris, 1995.

Sadowski, Yahya. "The Evolution of Political Identity in Syria." In *Identity and Foreign Policy in the Middle East,* edited by Shibley Telhami and Michael Barnett. Ithaca, NY: Cornell University Press, 2002.

Seale, Patrick. *Asad: The Struggle for the Middle East.* Berkeley: University of California Press, 1995.

Van Dam, Nikolaos. *The Struggle for Power in Syria: Politics and Society under Asad and the Ba'th Party.* New York; London: I. B. Tauris, 1996.

Wedeen, Lisa. *Ambiguities of Domination: Politics, Rhetoric, and Symbols in Contemporary Syria.* Chicago: University of Chicago Press, 1999.

MUHAMMAD MUSLIH
UPDATED BY RONALD BRUCE ST JOHN

AS'AD, KAMIL
[c. 1930–]

Lebanese political leader, son of Ahmad As'ad.

Kamil As'ad (also al-As'ad) was born in Tayba and educated in Beirut. He earned a law degree at Saint Joseph University in Beirut. As the only son of Ahmad al-As'ad, he was prepared for a political career from an early age. As'ad served in parliament from 1957 until 1992 (but lost the 1960 election), when he failed to win a seat in the highly controversial election. As'ad was speaker of parliament in 1964, 1968, and from 1970 until 1984, when he was replaced by Husayn al-Husayni. As'ad had a reputation for detesting the poor. The civil war brought an end to his political career as Shi'ites rebelled against "feudal" traditional families, who were seen as arrogant and insensitive. The rise of the left, the AMAL movement, and later Hizbullah brought a final end to the major role played by this family for centuries. As'ad heads the Democratic Socialist Party.

See also AMAL; AS'AD, AHMAD; AS'AD FAMILY; HIZBULLAH; HUSAYNI, HUSAYN AL-.

AS'AD ABUKHALIL

AS'AD WALI

Wali of the Vilayet of Sidon.

As'ad Wali is not to be confused with the As'ad Pasha who was a prominent Ottoman official in Istanbul. In 1843, under As'ad's rule, as *wali* of the *vilayet* (province) of Sidon, the Mount Lebanon region was divided into Druze and Maronite (Christian) sections in the wake of Druze–Maronite conflict. Some historians think that he sincerely tried to reconcile the various religious factions in Lebanon, but the intensity of conflict, not only between Maronites and Druzes but also between Maronites and Greek Orthodox, for example, prevented the establishment of a harmonious political arrangement in the mountains of Lebanon. The government of the Ottoman Empire accused him of bias in favor of Christians and replaced him in 1845. His replacement ushered in an era of more bloodshed and killing.

See also DRUZE; MARONITES.

AS'AD ABUKHALIL

ASH

See FOOD: ASH

ASHKENAZIM

European Jews whose daily language was Yiddish (often in addition to the languages of the countries and regions in which they lived during the Diaspora).

Ashkenazim is the plural of *Ashkenazi*, a term derived from the Hebrew name Ashkenaz, a great-grandson of the biblical Noah. The Ashkenazim are Jews whose Middle East ancestors migrated to Germany (called Ashkenaz by medieval Jews) and the surrounding areas, where they spoke Middle High German during the fourteenth and fifteenth centuries and that evolved into Jüdisch Diutsch, or Yiddish. Their liturgical Hebrew differs markedly in both rhythm and pronunciation from that of today's Middle Eastern Jews or of the Sephardic Jews of Southern Europe and North Africa.

In modern Israel, the Ashkenazim were, until recently, a minority, outnumbered by Sephardic and Middle Eastern Jews; as large numbers of refugees from the former Soviet Union arrive, however, the Ashkenazim may become the majority of the Jewish population.

Although the Hebrew language taught in Israel's public schools uses the Sephardic pronunciation, Ashkenazic Hebrew can be heard during services in East and Central European congregations. Small but strongly cohesive communities of Ashkenazic pietists—particularly in the United States, Jerusalem, and B'nei B'rak—speak Yiddish, regarding Hebrew as too sacred for secular matters and daily conversation. In the modern Middle East, outside Israel, only Turkey has a small but viable Ashkenazic community.

Bibliography

Avruch, Kevin, and Zenner, Walter P., eds. *Critical Essays on Israeli Society, Religion and Government.* Albany: State University of New York Press, 1997.

Baron, Salo Wittmayer. *A Social and Religious History of the Jews,* 2d edition. New York: Columbia University Press, 1952–.

Shafir, Gershon, and Peled, Yoav. *Being Israeli: The Dynamics of Multiple Citizenship.* Cambridge, U.K., and New York: Cambridge University Press, 2002.

ARNOLD BLUMBERG

ASHMAWI, MUHAMMAD ABD AL-RAHMAN SALIH, AL-
[1911–1983]

Ideologist of the Muslim Brotherhood.

Muhammad Abd al-Rahman Salih al-Ashmawi is one of the leading ideologists and journalists of the Muslim Brotherhood. He joined the Brotherhood in 1931 and graduated from the Faculty of Commerce, Cairo University, in 1932. He was appointed general secretary of the Brotherhood in 1936. He was the editor-in-chief of the main journals of the Brotherhood, *al-Nazir, al-Ikhwan al-Muslimun,* and others. Upon the request of Hasan al-Banna in the 1940s, Ashmawi founded and became the editor-in-chief of the Islamist journal *al-Da'wa,* which played a central and successful role in Islamic politics and organization. He became the head of the special apparatus in 1941 and was arrested in 1948. After al-Banna's assassination in 1949, Ashmawi led the Brotherhood for two and a half years. When judge Hasan al-Hudaybi became the supreme guide of the Muslim Brotherhood, Ashmawi joined the radical faction that opposed al-Hudaybi. It was Ashmawi who recruited Sayyid Qutb into the Brotherhood after his return from the United States. While President Gamal Abdel Nasser tried to convince Ashmawi to join his government, the supreme leader Hudaybi fired him from the organization. *Al-Da'wa* continued to be published independently by Ashmawi, who owned its license. When Umar al-Tilmisani assumed the leadership of the Brotherhood in 1973, Ashmawi joined again, and his journal was again published as its mouthpiece. President Anwar al-Sadat ordered his arrest along with other Muslim Brothers in 1981 in the aftermath of the Camp David Accords.

See also MUSLIM BROTHERHOOD.

Bibliography

Moussalli, Ahmad. *Historical Dictionary of Islamic Fundamentalist Movements in the Arab World, Iran, and Turkey.* Lanham, MD: Rowman and Littlefield, 1999.

AHMAD S. MOUSSALLI

ASHMAWI, MUHAMMAD SAʿID AL-
[1932–]

Egyptian jurist and writer.

Muhammad Saʿid al-Ashmawi graduated from Cairo University's law school in 1954. This retired Egyptian Supreme Court justice and former head of the Court of State Security has become one of the most influential liberal Islamic thinkers today. He is an effective polemicist against the Islamic fundamentalist trend in Egypt and elsewhere in the Arab world. He has published widely on the subject of Islamic law *(shariʿa)*, using his understanding of Islam combined with his reading of orientalist literature to undermine the conservative interpretation of Islam. He aims at distinguishing between Islam the religion and Islam as a political enterprise aimed at earning political legitimacy for the ruling regime. He tries to refute the myths about Islamic history held by Muslim fundamentalists and by students of state-sponsored Islamic education, arguing that Islamic history does not necessarily constitute the golden age that it is said to be. Al-Ashmawi's writing have been disseminated through state-sponsored publications in Egypt, perhaps in an effort to undermine the legitimacy of the fundamentalists, but he has had to rely on round-the-clock police protection due to death threats from Egyptian militants.

Bibliography

Fluehr-Lobban, Carolyn. *Against Islamic Extremism: The Writings of Muhammad Said Al-Ashmawy.* Gainesville: University Press of Florida, 2003.

AsʿAD ABUKHALIL

ASHOUR, RADWA
[1946–]

An Egyptian novelist.

Radwa Ashour (also Ashur) is a novelist, short-story writer, literary critic, and university professor from Egypt. She earned her M.A. in comparative literature from Cairo University (1972) and her Ph.D. in African-American literature from the University of Massachusetts (1975). She is professor of English literature at Ain Shams University, Cairo, and is active in the Committee for the Defense of National Culture. In addition to academic literary studies in both Arabic and English, Ashour has published prize-winning fiction: Her novel *Gharnata* (Grenada, 1994), first of a trilogy on the Muslim community in Spain during the period of the Spanish Inquisition, has garnered much praise for its subtle historical focus, beautiful descriptive writing, and rendering of gender and generational relations; the second and third parts were published as *Maryama, wa al-rahil* in 1995. She had already published three novels that differed widely in technique and theme— *Hajar dafi, Khadija wa-Sawsan,* and *Siraj*—and a travel memoir, *al-Rihla;* since then, she has published an autobiographical novel, *Atyaf,* that plays with conventions of authorship and the inside/outside of the text, and a volume of linked short stories in the form of reports by an elusive narrator, playing ironically with the notion of an authorial double and perhaps with the still-prevalent critical tendency to equate the characters created by female writers with the author herself *(Taqarir al-Sayyida Ra).* Ashour has published critical studies on West African literature, on the Palestinian writer Ghassan Kanafani, on Kahlil Gibran, and on William Blake; she has also published a collection of critical essays *(Sayyadu al-dhakira).* Several of her short stories have been translated into English *(My Grandmother's Cactus),* and in 2003 an English translation of *Gharnata* was in press.

See also BAKR, SALWA; GENDER: GENDER AND EDUCATION.

Bibliography

Ashur, Radwa. "My Experience with Writing," translated by Rebecca Porteous. In *The View from Within: Writers and Critics on Contemporary Arabic Literature,* edited by Ferial Ghazoul and Barbara Harlow. Cairo: American University in Cairo Press, 1994.

Booth, Marilyn. *Stories by Egyptian Women: My Grandmother's Cactus.* London: Quartet Books, 1991; Austin: University of Texas Press, 1993.

MARILYN BOOTH

ASHUR

See GLOSSARY

AS-IS AGREEMENT

Agreement establishing a cartel of Western oil companies, 1928.

Price wars among major oil companies in the 1920s, most significantly one in India between Standard Oil of New York and a subsidiary of Royal Dutch Shell, threatened major oil company profits, especially those from relatively high-cost production in the United States. At an August 1928 secret meeting at Achnacarry Castle in the Scottish Highlands, the As-Is Agreement was devised by the leaders of the Anglo-Persian Oil Company (later BP), Royal Dutch Shell, and Standard Oil of New Jersey (later Exxon). Together with the Red Line Agreement, the As-Is Agreement formed the basis of what a U.S. Senate subcommittee in 1952 called "the international petroleum cartel."

The As-Is Agreement consisted of seven "principles" to limit "excessive competition" that had led to enormous overproduction by dividing markets, fixing prices, and limiting the expansion of production capacity. The agreement affected the development of oil production capacity in the Middle East by limiting price competition in product markets and, as a result, supporting the prices of products made from high-cost, primarily American, crude oil. This strategy was implemented as a "basing-point" system under which all sellers calculated delivered prices as the sum of FOB prices at one or more specific locations—basing points—plus a standardized freight charge from that point to the point of delivery. Such a system is very effective because it ensures that all sellers quote the same prices and that producers with low costs cannot use that advantage to expand their market shares by passing on the low costs.

The impact of the As-Is Agreement on the position of Middle Eastern oil producers was profound. It was substantially responsible for the reluctance of concession holders to expand production in this low-cost region. In 1928, when it was adopted, more than a third of worldwide production capacity was shut down due to oversupply.

Owners feared that expanding low-cost capacity in the Persian Gulf would only add to their losses. The As-Is and Red Line agreements retarded the development of Middle Eastern oil resources until after World War II; at the same time they led to the depletion of reserves in what were later seen as politically "safe" areas, such as the United States and Canada. The resulting division of production shares between Middle Eastern countries and others aggravated anticolonial and anti-Western feelings among the populations of many Middle Eastern states, most notably Iraq and Iran. It also established a pattern for ensuring oil profits by exercising market control that the members of the Organization of Petroleum Exporting Countries later tried to emulate.

See also ARABIAN AMERICAN OIL COMPANY (ARAMCO); IRAN; IRAQ; ORGANIZATION OF PETROLEUM EXPORTING COUNTRIES (OPEC); PERSIAN (ARABIAN) GULF; RED LINE AGREEMENT; ROYAL DUTCH SHELL.

Bibliography

Penrose, Edith T. *The Large International Firm in Developing Countries: The International Petroleum Industry.* Westport, CT: Greenwood Press, 1976.

Sampson, Anthony. *The Seven Sisters: The Great Oil Companies and the World They Shaped.* New York: Bantam, 1991.

United States Congress. Senate. Select Committee on Small Business. Subcommittee on Monopoly. *The International Petroleum Cartel: Staff Report to the Federal Trade Commission.* 82nd Congress, 2nd session. Washington, DC: U.S. Government Printing Office, 1952.

MARY ANN TÉTREAULT

ASIYAN

See LITERATURE: TURKISH

ASKARI, JA'FAR AL-
[1887–1936]

Arab nationalist and military leader; friend of Faisal I ibn Hussein during the Arab revolt in World War I; political leader under Faisal as king of Syria, 1920, and as Faisal I of Iraq, 1921–1932.

Ja'far (also Ja'far) al-Askari was born in Baghdad, the son of a military leader for the Ottoman Empire. He was educated in both military and legal affairs, graduating from the Ottoman military academy in 1904. He served in the Ottoman army and was captured by the British in Egypt during World War I. Following a dramatic escape from an Egyptian fort, he later joined the Arab revolt against the Ottomans under T. E. Lawrence and Sharif Husayn ibn Ali of Mecca. Ja'far organized Husayn's army and led it, becoming the trusted friend of Husayn's son Faisal, who in 1920 became king of Syria (before he was removed by the French mandate).

When the British supported Faisal and made him king of Iraq in 1921, Ja'far was named first minister of defense (1920–1922) and assumed that position in 1930 and again in 1931 and 1932. He was also prime minister of Iraq (1923, 1926–1928) and Iraq's minister of foreign affairs (1926–1928 and 1931–1932).

See also ARAB REVOLT (1916); FAISAL I IBN HUSSEIN; HUSAYN IBN ALI; IRAQ; LAWRENCE, T. E.

Bibliography

Askari, Ja'far al-. *Memoirs.* London, 1988. In Arabic.

Batatu, Hanna. *The Old Social Classes and the Revolutionary Movements of Iraq: A Study of Iraq's Old Landed and Commercial Classes and of Its Communists.* Princeton, NJ: Princeton University Press, 1978.

AHMAD ABDUL A. R. SHIKARA

ASMAHAN
[1917?–1944]

Actress and singer.

Asmahan was a gifted singer known principally for her work in films. Her delicate and flexible high voice was clear, powerful, and brilliant, and she was frequently compared to Umm Kulthum (the Arab world's most famous female singer), although their voices and musical styles were very different. Many saw her as Umm Kulthum's only serious rival.

Asmahan was born Amal al-Atrash in Jabal al-Duruz (in Syria) to Fahd al-Atrash and Aliya Husayn. The mother and the children, Amal, Farid, and Fu'ad, moved to Cairo in about 1924, to escape the fighting in Syria during the French mandate. Amal began her performing career in the music hall

of Mary Mansur in Cairo around 1930 and adopted her stage name at the suggestion of one of her mentors, composer Dawud Husni. Asmahan's career was interrupted by marriage to her cousin Hasan al-Atrash in Jabal al-Duruz in 1933. They separated in 1939, and she returned to Cairo with her daughter. Asmahan subsequently appeared in two successful Egyptian films, *Intisar al-Shabab* and *Gharam wa Intiqam,* both with music composed by her brother Farid al-Atrash.

Asmahan performed at private parties, for radio broadcasts, and made commercial recordings. Her popular and financial success was limited, because she abhorred public concerts and preferred films. The film companies of the day typically released one film per singing star every two years; thus her performances were fewer than those of her principal competitors, notably Umm Kulthum and Layla Murad—both of whom performed extensively in public.

Asmahan's private life may have been too public: Her alleged affairs with a succession of prominent men, including journalist Muhammad al-Taba'i, banker Tal'at Harb, and royal aide Ahmad Hasanayn, were topics of public conversation. In 1941, she returned to Jabal al-Duruz, allegedly as a British spy, an activity that did little to enhance her popularity. She was, in many respects, her own worst enemy; her habits of cigarettes, alcohol, and late nights had a deleterious effect on her voice. Asmahan died in an automobile accident in Egypt in 1944. She was equally comfortable with Arab and European singing styles. Among her most famous songs were "Dakhalt marra fi al-jinayna," "Ya tuyur" (in which her skills in European virtuosic singing were aptly displayed), and "Alayk salat Allah wa salamuh."

See also ATRASH, FARID AL-; UMM KULTHUM.

Bibliography

Zuhur, Sherifa. *Asmahan's Secrets: Woman, War, and Song.* Austin: Center for Middle Eastern Studies, University of Texas at Austin, 2000.

VIRGINIA DANIELSON

ASMAR, FAWZI AL-
[1937–]

Palestinian journalist, activist, author, and poet.

Fawzi al-Asmar (or Fouzi El-Asmar) was born in Haifa, Palestine, and grew up in Israel. He studied history and political science in the United States and received his Ph.D. from the University of Exeter in Britain. He became a U.S. citizen in 1981. Asmar served as managing editor of the international Arabic-language daily *al-Sharq al-Awsat* and is bureau chief of the United Arab Emirates news agency in Washington, D.C.; he is also a columnist for the Saudi Arabian daily *al-Riyadh.*

Al-Asmar is best known for his book *To Be an Arab in Israel* (1975), in which he describes Israeli confiscation of his family's land, his arrest for political activity, and discrimination against Palestinian citizens of Israel between 1948 and 1970. The work has been translated into eight languages. Another of his books is *Through the Hebrew Looking-Glass: Arab Stereotypes in Children's Literature* (1986).

See also PALESTINIAN CITIZENS OF ISRAEL.

JENAB TUTUNJI
UPDATED BY PHILIP MATTAR

ASSOCIATION DES FEMMES TUNISIENNES POUR LA RECHERCHE ET LE DÉVELOPPEMENT (AFTURD)

Tunisian nongovernmental organization for research and outreach on women's legal rights.

The idea of establishing a Tunisian women's research group, Association des Femmes Tunisiennes pour la Recherche et le Développement (Association of Tunisian Women for Research and Development; AFTURD), which was to be affiliated with the larger women's research network, Association des Femmes Africaines pour la Recherche et le Développement (Association of African Women for Research and Development; AFARD), began with discussions among members of the Club Tahar Haddad in 1986. AFTURD was formalized in 1989. Proactive on national, regional, and international levels, AFTURD has participated in networks of exchange among women in the Arab and African region, such as the Collectif Maghreb Egalité 95 activities in preparation for the fourth UN-sponsored Women's conference (Beijing 1995). In addition to networking, AFTURD scholars have produced an important body of qualitative and quantitative research on the status of Tunisian women, including the two-volume *Tunisiennes en devenir* (Tunisian Women

on the Move). They have developed basic, accessible guides to women's legal rights and obligations (*La marriage* [Marriage] and *Le divorce* [Divorce]). Engaged also in activism to achieve effective emancipation for women, AFTURD participates in projects such as the Espace Tanassof, a women's shelter offering information, legal and psychological counseling, and training on specific themes concerning gendered approaches to social issues. AFTURD also sponsors forums on key women's issues such as inheritance, where ongoing research is presented and vigorously debated with an eye to developing culturally appropriate solutions to discrimination against women.

See also GENDER: GENDER AND THE ECONOMY; GENDER: GENDER AND LAW; TUNISIA; TUNISIA: POLITICAL PARTIES IN.

LAURA RICE

ASSOCIATION FOR THE PROTECTION OF WOMEN'S RIGHTS (AFGHANISTAN)

Afghan organization of the 1920s.

The Association for the Protection of Women's Rights (*Anjoman-i-Himayat-i-Niswan*) was founded in 1927 in Kabul, Afghanistan, under the direction of King Amanullah's (1919–1929) sister, Princess Kobra, its president, and Queen Soraya, Amanullah's wife, its main leader. Its main objectives were to help women become self-reliant and take part in the development of Afghanistan; to ensure women's right to education and to work outside the home; and to protect women against domestic abuse, including threats by male family members to prevent women from working outside the home. Cases of domestic abuse were heard and dealt with in special family tribunals presided over by the queen. The association offered courses in sewing, weaving, and other handicrafts, and it recruited women from low-income families to work in factories. In September 1928 several women participated in the *Loya-Jirga* (Grand Assembly) as representatives of the association to promote reforms to improve the status of women. The association had drafted a political platform and was ready to participate in upcoming parliamentary elections when its activities were interrupted by widespread opposition to Queen Soraya's campaign, begun in 1928, to unveil and emancipate women. The association was closed down shortly thereafter.

Bibliography

Nawid, Senzil K. *Religious Response to Social Change in Afghanistan, 1919–29: King Aman-Allah and the Afghan Ulama.* Costa Mesa, CA: Mazda Publishers, 1999.

SENZIL NAWID

ASSOCIATION OF ALGERIAN MUSLIM ULAMA (AUMA)

Islamic clergymen in Algeria organized to promote Muslim and Arab values during the French colonial period.

The Association of Algerian Muslim Ulama was formed in 1931 under the leadership of Shaykh Abd al-Hamid Ben Badis. In the Islamic reformist tradition, it affirmed Muslim values and the Arab identity of Algerians. In 1956 its leaders dissolved the organization and rallied to the Front de Libération Nationale (FLN; National Liberation Front).

See also BEN BADIS, ABD AL-HAMID; FRONT DE LIBÉRATION NATIONALE.

JOHN RUEDY

ASSYRIANS

A Semitic people indigenous to Mesopotamia, with a history spanning 4,700 years.

Contemporary Assyrians are the descendants of the Akkadian-speaking inhabitants of the Assyrian Empire, which ended in 612 B.C.E. Ancient Assyrians worshipped the god Assur until 256 C.E.; their descendants were among the first to accept Christianity, with the founding of the Assyrian Church of the East by the apostle Thomas in 33 C.E. By 1300, the modern culture's homeland included the territories of present-day northern Iraq, southeastern Turkey, northeastern Syria, and northwestern Iran. Contemporary Assyrians are ethnically distinct from Arabs and Jews and speak Neo-Syriac. Islam and Arab civilization engulfed the Assyrian Christians and some converted to Islam, but the Mongol invasions led by Tamerlane forced others into the Hakkari Mountains of eastern Turkey. Others continued to live in northern Iraq and Syria. Assyrian Christians of this period belonged to either the Assyrian Church of the East or the Syriac Orthodox Church. In 1550, a religious schism resulted in the creation of the Chaldean Church of Babylon and a Roman Catholic Uniate. The Assyrian Church of the East is Nestorian, but English speakers in the West classify Nestorian churches as belonging to the Oriental Orthodoxy. Contemporary religious divisions include the Chaldean, Syrian Catholic, Maronite (Uniate), and Jacobite churches, but Protestantism (Evangelical, Pentecostal, and Presbyterian) has also attracted converts.

Assyrians migrated to Europe and the United States by 1870, but the end of World War I witnessed genocides and dispersal throughout the world. From 1915 to 1918, approximately 750,000 Assyrians were massacred by Turkish and Kurdish forces. The French in Syria and the British in Iraq exacerbated the plight of the Assyrian survivors, who lost their ancestral lands and dispersed throughout the Middle East, Europe, and North America. Persecutions in Iran (1948), the Lebanese Civil War (1975–1990), unrest in Iraq (1970s), and the Gulf War (1991) resulted in increased immigration. By 2000, the Assyrian population was estimated at 3.5 million, with approximately one-third in a diaspora. Current demographic estimates are: Iraq, 1,500,000; Syria, 700,000; United States, 400,000; Sweden, 120,000; Lebanon, 100,000; Brazil, 80,000; Germany, 70,000; Russia, 70,000; Iran, 50,000; Jordan, 44,000; Australia, 30,000; Turkey, 24,000; Canada, 23,000; Holland, 20,000; and France, 20,000. Smaller numbers migrated to Belgium, Georgia, Armenia, Switzerland, Denmark, Greece, England, Austria, Italy, New Zealand, and Mexico. Chicago, Detroit, and Phoenix have substantial populations. Assyrians in the diaspora seek to maintain their language, culture, and religion, and financially support Assyrian refugees in the Middle East and other countries.

See also GULF WAR (1991); LEBANESE CIVIL WAR (1975–1990); MARONITES.

Bibliography

Andrews, F. David, ed. *The Lost Peoples of the Middle East: Documents of the Struggle for Survival and Independence of the Kurds, Assyrians, and Other Minority Races in the Middle East.* Salisbury, NC: Documentary Publications, 1982.

Brentjes, Burchard. *The Armenians, Assyrians, and Kurds: Three Nations, One Fate?* Campbell, CA: Rishi, 1997.

Macuch, R. "Assyrians." In *Encyclopedia Iranica.* London: Routledge & Kegan, 1992

Michael, John, and Jassim, Sheren. "The Assyrians of Chicago." Available from <http://www.aina.org/aol/ethnic.htm>.

CHARLES C. KOLB

ASWAN

Upper Egyptian province and its capital city, health resort, and industrial center.

Originally named Syene, the city was located on the east bank, at the first cataract of the Upper Nile River; it marked the southern border of pharaonic Egypt. About 3.5 miles (5.5 km) south of the city is the Aswan dam, erected by British and Egyptian engineers from 1899 to 1902 and enlarged in 1912 and 1934. The dam's construction facilitated the conversion of Middle Egypt and parts of Upper Egypt to perennial irrigation. From 1960 to 1971, this process was completed with the construction of the Aswan High Dam. One of the largest public works ever built, the High Dam has enabled Egypt to reclaim some desert land for cultivation (but not the 1.2 million acres [0.5 million ha] hoped for) and to generate hydroelectric power. It has cost dearly in soil erosion, the loss of fertile alluvium from the annual flood and of nutrients that used to support marine life, and the resettlement of Nubians who used to live in lands flooded by the waters of Lake Nasser, created by the dam. The province had some 801,400 inhabitants in 1986.

See also ASWAN HIGH DAM; EGYPT; NASSER, LAKE; NILE RIVER; NUBIANS.

Bibliography

Waterbury, John. *Hydropolitics of the Nile Valley.* Syracuse, NY: Syracuse University Press, 1979.

ARTHUR GOLDSCHMIDT

ASWAN HIGH DAM

Dam to control Nile River waters.

The first dam at Aswan, Egypt, on the Nile River, was completed in 1902 and heightened twice, in 1912 and 1934, to expand its capacity. This first dam, actually a barrage without the capability of holding multiyear water, proved insufficient for the growing water and power needs of Egypt, so a larger dam and reservoir, the Aswan High Dam, was constructed from 1960 to 1971. The High Dam is of embankment construction, 365 feet high and nearly 3,300 feet wide at its base. Lake Nasser, impounded behind the High Dam, is 300 miles long and 10 miles wide at the widest point. The power station at Aswan has a yearly capacity of 2.1 gigawatts at full pool.

In March 1953 the Free Officers of Egypt's army, which had overthrown King Farouk in a military coup, began planning for a high dam on the Nile some 5 miles south of the older British-built Aswan Dam. The U.S. and British governments and the World Bank agreed to finance construction conditional on Egypt's acceptance of Western government control of Egypt's economy, no new Egyptian arms purchases, and open bidding for the construction contract (excluding communist countries). Despite its reluctance, Egypt accepted these terms, but U.S. Secretary of State John Foster Dulles, alarmed by the ties to the Soviet Union of Gamal Abdel Nasser, Egypt's president, subsequently vetoed the deal. In response, Nasser nationalized the Suez Canal, intending to use canal tolls to pay for the dam's construction; this created an international incident.

In 1958 the Soviet Union financed the dam, providing the equivalent of $330 million, and work commenced in 1960. The hydroelectric power plant began operation in 1968. The reservoir formed by the dam created Lake Nasser, forcing the relocation of the Nubian people living upstream and generating an international effort by UNESCO to rescue antiquities within the soon-to-be-flooded valley. The temples at Philae and elsewhere upstream, dating from dynastic Egypt, were flooded. Ramses's Temple at Abu Simbel with its colossal statuary was raised to overlook the lake.

The dam's completion permitted downstream reclamation of 675,000 acres and the conversion of an additional one million acres to perennial irrigation. Twelve electric turbines initially provided 60 percent of Egypt's electrical needs, but economic growth has reduced this percentage. Increased use of irrigation without adequate drainage has caused waterlogging and salinization downstream. The dam has also been criticized for causing a variety of other adverse environmental consequences.

See also NILE RIVER.

Bibliography

Nyrop, Richard F., ed. *Egypt: A Country Study,* 4th edition. Washington, DC: Library of Congress, 1983.

Said, R. *The River Nile: Geology, Hydrology, and Utilization.* Oxford, U.K.: Pergamon, 1993.

Wucher King, Joan. *Historical Dictionary of Egypt.* Metuchen, NJ: Scarecrow Press, 1984.

DAVID WALDNER
UPDATED BY GREGORY B. BAECHER

ASYUT

See EGYPT

ATABAT

Shi'a holy places in Iraq.

Atabat, literally "thresholds," are Shi'ite holy places in Iraq, at Karbala, Qadimayn, Najaf, and Samarra, containing the tombs of six imams revered in Twelver Shi'ism, serving also as holy sites for pilgrimage. Ali ibn Abi Talib, the first imam of Shi'ism, is buried in Najaf. His son, Husayn ibn Ali, the third Shi'a imam; Husayn's half-brother Abbas; and Husayn's son Ali Akbar were martyred and buried in Karbala, fighting the Umayyads in 680. Qadimayn is the burial site of the seventh and ninth imams, Musa al-Kazim, who died in 802, and Muhammad al-Taqi, who died in 834. Samarra, which lies at a distance from the remainder of the Atabat, is the burial site of the tenth imam, Ali al-Naqi, who died in 868, and the eleventh imam, Hasan al-Askari, who died in 873.

The Atabat have historically served as centers of Shi'ite learning. During the Iranian constitutional revolution from 1905 to 1911, the Atabat, under Ottoman suzerainty, served as a safe haven for the revolutionaries. Ayatollah Hasan Shirazi, who engineered the retraction of the Regie tobacco concession in 1870, resided in Samarra. The Atabat also played a decisive role in fostering clerical opposition in the Pahlavi period, as Ayatollah Ruhollah Khomeini lived in exile in Najaf from 1965 to 1978.

See also KHOMEINI, RUHOLLAH.

NEGUIN YAVARI

ATASI, HASHIM AL-

[1876?–1960]

A prominent Syrian politician.

Hashim al-Atasi hailed from a Sunni Muslim family of landowning, scholarly Ashraf from Homs. In mandatory times this commercial city in west central Syria was commonly referred to as al-Atasi's fief. Atasi served three times as president of Syria (1936–1939, 1949–1951, and 1954–1955) and as prime minister for a short time in 1949.

Having received an advanced Ottoman education in Istanbul, he served as a district governor in the imperial bureaucracy of the Ottoman state. In 1920 he acted as chairman of the Syrian-Arab Congress. For a short time, he was also prime minister in Amir Faisal's government in Damascus. With the French occupying Syria, Atasi distinguished himself in Syria's struggle for independence. He was one of those who formed the core of the National Bloc (al-Kutla al-Wataniyya), a nationalist organization that steered the course of the independence struggle in Syria from 1927, when its seeds were planted at the Beirut conference (held in October of that year), until the completion of the fight for independence nineteen years later.

He belonged to an older generation of nationalists who subscribed to a policy of "honorable cooperation" with France—that is, a policy of collaboration based on reciprocity of interests and mutual obligations. Proponents of this policy believed that France supported the Syrian national cause and that establishing confidence through cooperation between the two nations would help the cause of independence. Nevertheless, French insensitivity to Syrian aspirations exposed the fallacy of the National Bloc's assumption and made Atasi increasingly frustrated by the bloc's failure to make any meaningful progress toward independence through the policy of "honorable cooperation." In 1931 and 1932 he assumed a more radical posture, which helped him attract to the bloc council more activist Syrian nationalists, most notably the Istiqlal Party leader Shukri al-Quwatli.

Atasi headed the Syrian delegation sent to Paris in March 1936 to negotiate Syria's independence with the government of Albert Sarraut. The inflexibility of the Sarraut government's bargaining position would have caused the complete breakdown of the negotiations had it not been for the victory of a left-wing coalition (known as the Popular Front) headed by the Socialist Party leader Leon Blum in the general French elections of April 1936. The advent of a new French government, together with the subsequent appointment of a second French negotiating team headed by the enlightened and forward-looking Pierre Vienot (who viewed the French mandate in the Levant as transitory) set the stage for the signing of the Franco–Syrian Treaty of 1936. The treaty, which was never ratified by France because the right-wing French forces were able to persuade the French parliament not to accept it, provided for peace, friendship, and alliance between France and Syria and defined France's military position in Syria as well as the relations of the Syrian state with Syrian minorities and with Lebanon.

With factionalism plaguing the National Bloc and other nationalist organizations, and with the French government suspending the Syrian constitution and instituting almost direct French control in the country, Atasi resigned his office as president in 1939 and adopted a less activist stance in Syrian politics until August 1949, after Colonel Sami al-Hinnawi's coup against Husni al-Za'im. In December of the same year Atasi became a titular president, with real power concentrated in the hands of Adib Shishakli, the tough pro-French colonel who overthrew Hinnawi on 19 December 1949, allegedly to save Syria from British influence and a union with the pro-British Hashimite monarchy of Iraq. It was convenient for both Hinnawi and Shishakli to have the veteran Atasi as president because he was the finest symbol of Syria's struggle against French imperialism. Differences with Shishakli, together with the chaotic Syrian politics, compelled Atasi to resign from the presidency in November 1951. He then began conspiring for the overthrow of Shishakli. In March 1954, Atasi returned to the presidency, and in September 1955 he retired from Syrian politics, disaffected by the internal struggles of officer cliques. Perhaps he was also bemused to see the door of Syria, whose allegiance remained with the West for much of the decade that followed independence, thrown open to Egyptian influence and to the flow of Soviet and East European arms and other blandishments.

See also HINNAWI, SAMI AL-; NATIONAL BLOC; QUWATLI, SHUKRI AL-; ZA'IM, HUSNI AL-.

MUHAMMAD MUSLIH

ATASI, JAMAL AL-
[1922–]

Syrian psychologist and politician.

Jamal al-Atasi was born in Homs, where he completed his primary and secondary studies. In 1947, he enrolled in the School of Medicine in Damascus, where he obtained a doctorate in psychology. He was then appointed doctor in the Ministry of Health. He is one of the founding and prominent members of the Syrian Ba'th party and editor of one of its newspapers, *Al-Jamahir*. In 1963, he was appointed minister of information in the cabinet headed by Salah al-Din al-Bitar. After a long fight with the Ba'th, he left the party and became general secretary of the Nasserist Arab Socialist Union. Atasi was also a member of the "Committee of Thirteen" which undertook the task of forming the National Progressive Front. During the regime of the late Hafiz al-Asad, Atasi was considered one of the president's main opponents.

See also ARAB SOCIALIST UNION; ASAD, HAFIZ AL-; BA'TH, AL-; BITAR, SALAH AL-DIN AL-; NATIONAL PROGRESSIVE FRONT (SYRIA).

GEORGE E. IRANI

ATASI, NUR AL-DIN AL
[1929–1994]

President of Syria, 1966–1970.

Atasi was a member of a Sunni landowning and scholarly family from Homs. A physician who had served as a medical volunteer in the Algerian revolution, he was a leader of the second civilian generation of the Ba'th party. Two other prominent leaders of this generation were Ibrahim Makhus and Yusuf Zu'ayyin. This generation, which was composed mainly of rural minorities—Alawis, Druzes, Isma'ilis, with a sprinkling of Sunnis like Atasi—imbued the Ba'th party in the early 1960s with vaguely argued ideas of class struggle and scientific socialism. Its members formed what came to be known as the neo-Ba'th. Their opponents believed them to have subordinated Arab unity to their program of revolutionary socialism. The neo-Ba'th was centered in Damascus, building up branches in other Arab countries; members of the old Ba'th (for example, Salah al-Din al-Bitar and Michel Aflaq) were either imprisoned or escaped to operate from Beirut or elsewhere. After the Ba'th officers' coup of March 1963, Atasi became minister of the interior (August 1963–May 1964), deputy prime minister (October 1964–September 1965), and a member of the Revolutionary Council and the Presidential Council in 1964. Atasi's political beliefs were consistent with those of the neo-Ba'thists: fearing communism, distrusting popular movements, endorsing economic reform along socialist lines, and subscribing to the theory of popular war, especially through the Palestinian resistance movement, which was developing around the mid-1960s.

In the internal power struggles that were buffeting Syria, Atasi sided with the hawkish faction of the group that came to power in the coup of 23 February 1966. This faction rejected the proposal of a peaceful solution with Israel and tried in vain to assert party authority over the army. Atasi's alliance with the faction of Salah Jadid put him on a collision course with the more powerful, army-supported faction of Lieutenant-General Hafiz al-Asad, whose position as defense minister and commander of the Syrian air force, together with his pragmatic and calculating approach, enabled him in February 1969 to occupy strategic points in the Syrian capital and to gain full control of the Syrian state in November 1970. After Asad's semi-coup of February 1969, Atasi retained his posts as president, prime minister, and secretary general of the party, due in part to the weakness of Asad within the party and in part to the intervention of Algeria, Egypt, and the Soviet Union. This created a duality of power in Syria, with Atasi and his colleagues in the Jadid faction controlling the regional (Syrian) Ba'th organization and its cadres—hence nominally the government; and Asad's faction controlling the army and intelligence—hence practically the government.

When Asad took full control in November 1970, Atasi was dismissed from all his posts and sent to jail, where he languished until his release in 1994. He died shortly thereafter.

Bibliography

Batatu, Hanna. *Syria's Peasantry, the Descendants of Its Lesser Rural Notables, and Their Politics.* Princeton, NJ: Princeton University Press, 1999.

Seale, Patrick. *Asad: The Struggle for Middle East.* Berkeley: University of California Press, 1990.

Van Dam, Nikolaos. *The Struggle for Power in Syria: Syria under Asad and the Ba'th Party.* New York; London: I. B. Tauris, 1996.

MUHAMMAD MUSLIH
UPDATED BY MICHAEL R. FISCHBACH

ATATÜRK, MUSTAFA KEMAL
[1881–1938]

Turkish soldier and nationalist leader; founder and first president of the Republic of Turkey, 1923–1938.

Born in Salonika, the eldest of the two surviving children of a lower-middle-class family, Mustafa Kemal Atatürk was given the name Mustafa at his birth. His father, Ali Riza Efendi, had been a minor officer in the Ottoman customs before trying his luck in trade. Although he died when his son was only seven, Ali Riza Efendi had a great influence on him through his adherence to secular values and his decision to send Mustafa to a secular elementary school. Like all Ottoman women in her situation, the mother, Zübeyde Hamm, had to be supported by relatives after her husband's death. It is during the years of refuge in the extended family that Mustafa seems to have developed the lifelong characteristics of both the ambitious, captivating loner and the resolute, charismatic leader.

It was his decision to pursue a military career. He was an outstanding student from the time he entered military middle school in Salonika (1893), where he was given his second name, Kemal, until the staff college from which he was graduated (1904) with the rank of captain. He also developed a strong interest in politics as well as literary and rhetorical pursuits during his school years. The command of late Ottoman Turkish with touches of pedantry that his writings disclose are the result of Mustafa Kemal's extensive readings in history and literature. Throughout his military and political career, his speeches and improvised harangues were marked by the eloquence and persuasiveness that he cultivated as early as his high-school years. His interest in politics developed somewhat later, when he attended the War Academy, and at a time when the negative aspects of Sultan Abdülhamit II's absolutism had become more offensive.

Mustafa Kemal served with the Fifth Army in Damascus (1905–1907), where he joined the revolutionary secret society Fatherland and Freedom. This society was soon subsumed in yet another secret society based in Salonika, the Ottoman Freedom Society, which subsequently took the name Committee for Union and Progress (CUP) after its merger with the Young Turk group that was active in Paris (1907). When Mustafa Kemal was transferred to the Third Army in his native city (late 1907), he joined the CUP, and for a long time thereafter he remained a frustrated member with minor influence in that society.

During the period between the Young Turk Revolution (23 July 1908) and the end of World War I, Mustafa Kemal emerged as an outstanding soldier with remarkable organizational skills, tenacious ambition, and a quarrelsome demeanor toward superiors with whom he disagreed. He distinguished himself in Libya, where he fought the Italians in the regions of Derna and Tobruk (1911–1912), but his political career was obstructed by the CUP leaders, who disliked his vocal criticism. After an unsuccessful bid for election to the Chamber of Deputies (1912), he was sent off as a military attaché to Sofia (1913–1914). He became a hero during World War I, thanks to his successes against the armies of the Triple Entente countries (France, Great Britain, Russia), which he checked twice in the Gallipoli Peninsula (1915). Promoted to brigadier general at the age of thirty-five, he was transferred to the eastern front, where he retook Bitlis and Muş from the Russians (1916). As the commander of the Seventh Army in Syria, he was in charge of the front north of Aleppo when the Mudros Armistice was signed (30 October 1918).

At the end of World War I, Mustafa Kemal organized a movement in Anatolia that consisted of both a constitutionalist rebellion against the sultan and resistance against the designs by Triple Entente countries to partition the Ottoman Empire. Mainly because of the support of local military authorities and of the notables whose provinces were threatened by partition, he managed to convene the Sivas Con-

Aerial view of the Boulevard Atatürk in Ankara, Turkey. Named after the title given to Turkish president Mustafa Kemal in 1933, the boulevard was modernized as part of a $100,000,000 program. © BETTMANN/CORBIS. REPRODUCED BY PERMISSION.

gress (4–11 September 1919), which forced the sultan to return to the parliamentarian rule the latter had suspended in November 1918. When the new Chamber of Deputies adopted the document known as the National Pact (28 January 1920), rejecting the dismemberment of the lands under Ottoman sovereignty at the conclusion of the armistice, the Triple Entente powers occupied Istanbul (16 March 1920). Subsequently, Mustafa Kemal called for the meeting of an extraordinary parliament in Ankara, thereby marking the beginning of the Turkish Revolution.

As the president of the Grand National Assembly (GNA), which opened on 23 April 1920, Mustafa Kemal successfully conducted a diplomatic and military campaign to defeat the stipulations of the Treaty of Sèvres imposed on the Ottoman government by the Triple Entente (10 August 1920). After he had succeeded in checking the Greek advance on Ankara in the battle of the Sakarya (August–September 1921), he was promoted to the rank of marshal and given the title ghazi (victorious) by the GNA. Under his command, the Turkish national forces launched an offensive (August 1922) that completed the liberation of practically all the territory considered Turkish homeland by the National Pact and forced the Allies to call for a new peace conference. The question of Turkish representation at the Lausanne Conference was given a radical solution by the GNA, which dissolved the

Former president of Turkey Mustafa Kemal. One of Kemal's innovations was the adoption of surnames. In 1933, he was given the honorific title Atatürk, meaning "Father of the Turks." © GETTY IMAGES. REPRODUCED BY PERMISSION.

Ottoman state after Mustafa Kemal's proposal to abolish the sultanate took effect on 1 November 1922.

The Treaty of Lausanne recognized an independent and fully sovereign Turkey (24 July 1923). Having gained complete control of the GNA through his newly founded People's Party, Mustafa Kemal embarked on a series of revolutionary changes. First he proclaimed the Republic of Turkey on 29 October 1923. The following year he instituted measures that set the republic on a secular path, including abolishing the caliphate and the ministry of shari'a and waqf, unifying education under state authority (3 March 1924), and abolishing the religious courts (8 April 1924). These developments prompted the growth of political opposition, which came out into the open with the founding of the Progressive Republican Party (November 1924). Seizing as a pretext the rebellion by Shaykh Sa'id (February 1925), Mustafa Kemal's republican regime quickly put an end to all political opposition in the

country by passing the Law on the Maintenance of Public Order (4 March 1925). In 1926, a plot to assassinate its leader gave the regime the opportunity to suppress the remnants of the CUP, whose leaders had posed a threat to Mustafa Kemal's power since the period of national resistance in Anatolia. By the time Mustafa Kemal read his famous speech in the GNA (October 1927), in which he gave his personal account of the recent history of Turkey, the country had entered the period of a de facto single-party regime, which, with the exception of the brief free party period (August–November 1930), lasted until after World War II.

In this political setting, Mustafa Kemal realized his far-reaching social-engineering program. Secularization was completed by the adoption of the Civil Code (4 April 1926) and the amendment of Article 2 and Article 26 of the Turkish constitution (10 April 1928), which, respectively, referred to Islam as the official religion and entrusted the GNA with enforcing the shari'a. Latin characters were adopted in 1928, thus putting an end to a long debate on the reform of the Turkish alphabet. Citizenship rights were extended to women in 1934 with a constitutional amendment that introduced universal suffrage. A new law, passed the same year, required all citizens to have a patronym in Turkish. The revolution also employed such symbolic measures as replacing the fez with Western-style hats (1925), obliging religious authorities to wear their particular garments only when officiating (1934), and banning the use of such honorific titles as pasha, bey, and effendi (1934).

In accord with the law on Turkish patronyms, Mustafa Kemal was named Atatürk (Father Turk) by the GNA (1934). Suggestive of the Roman *pater patriae*, the name reflected Mustafa Kemal's achievement and political status, but to its bearer, the connotations of "mentor" or "guide" that it had in old Turkish were probably more meaningful. The role of mentor, which his numerous remarks indicate he had assigned himself, was evidently accepted by Turks, as attested by the huge crowds that paid homage to his memory after his death in Istanbul (1938).

Mustafa Kemal's regard for modern science was conspicuous in many of his speeches but was only to a limited extent responsible for his comprehensive secularization campaign. Rather than being motivated by positivistic determinism, his policy grew out of his personal reading of the history of Islam and the vision of an astute politician. Two days before abolishing the caliphate, he told the GNA what amounted in fact to a secular rewording of the pious contention that the politics of humans tarnished Islam: "We see that the emancipation of Islam from the status of political tool that it has been constantly reduced to for centuries, and its exaltation, are really necessary" (*Parliamentary Minutes,* 2nd Session, vol. 7, pp. 3–6). Convinced of the autonomy and primacy of politics in the history of Islam in general, and of the Ottoman Empire in particular, Mustafa Kemal, in a way that was ahead of his time, was able to see that far from creating a dual society by introducing Western institutions into an Islamic polity, successive generations of Ottoman statesmen—from Sultan Selim III (1789–1807) to the Young Turks—had Westernized an age-old, secular state tradition. The perceived dualism was only an exacerbation of the secularity of the state. Under these circumstances, if what was sought was an organic relation between state and society (that is, democracy) the society must be synchronized with the state by strictly confining religion to the sphere of the individual. Hence, it would be more accurate to attribute Mustafa Kemal's secularizing measures to the radical anticlericalism of a standard-bearer of *raison d'état* than to interpret them as a reform of Islam or as the manifestations of anti-Islamic prejudice.

Although a nation builder, Mustafa Kemal was more of a patriot than a nationalist. His interest in the cultural and ideological aspects of nation building (as manifested by the founding of the Turkish Historical Society in 1931 and the Turkish Language Society in 1932) surfaced rather late in his life, and only after the economic and political upheavals of the Great Depression had revealed an ideological vacuum in the country. His first years as president of the republic were necessarily devoted to the strengthening of the new regime against an opposition that predated its founding. Even after establishing his de facto single-party system, however, he did not proceed in a nationalistic direction. His humorous references to the excesses associated with the "Turkish historical thesis" and the "Sun-language theory"—developed, under his guidance,

Turkish president Mustafa Kemal (foreground) and his officers, 6 March 1923. During his rule, Kemal was instrumental in bringing Turkey out of the ashes of the Ottoman Empire and transforming it into a modern state. © BETTMANN/CORBIS. REPRODUCED BY PERMISSION.

by the historical and language societies—also indicate his lighthearted approach to nationalist ideology and his view of such theories as a transient pedagogic device in the training of the common citizen.

Mustafa Kemal's aversion to ideological speculation is apparent in his reactions to the attempts to define his regime during his lifetime. Influenced by the proliferation of single-party dictatorships in Europe throughout the interwar period, zealous admirers tended to formulate a doctrine they called Kemalism to describe his government. Mustafa Kemal courteously discouraged such definitions, because he did not want anything to arrest the dynamism of the regime. For the same reason, he published his book *Civic Notions for the Citizens* (in Turkish; Istanbul, 1930) as the work of his adoptive daughter, Afet. This reluctance to associate his name with the actual politics of his time can best be explained by his view of his regime as being transitory and his ultimate vision of Turkey in the future as a liberal democracy.

Although his was a personal rule in which he went so far as to select individually all the candidates for the GNA, ample evidence shows he very much disliked such dictators as Adolf Hitler and Benito Mussolini and was genuinely offended by Western commentators and journalists who placed him in the same category as them. He rationalized that his role was exactly the opposite of theirs, in that he was trying to establish a democratic tradition in Turkey; that is why he took care to do everything through the legislature and did not envisage suspending the constitution of 1924 or altering its liberal spirit. He also refused life presidency; he preferred to be re-elected by the GNA at the beginning of each term. Mustafa Kemal's dictatorial rule was in effect an apprenticeship in democracy in the paradoxical tradition of Jacobinism, and he was aware of the tragic role he was playing in Turkish history. Very early on, he told a group of journalists how objective conditions prevail over ideas: "An individual would think in a particular manner in Ankara, in a different manner in Istanbul or Izmir, and in yet another different manner in Paris" (in Turkish, 1923; edited by Ari Inan, Ankara, 1982, p. 51).

Mustafa Kemal knew that the establishment of democracy was accompanied by legal, economic, social, and ideological prerequisites, and his regime was designed to prepare the country in these areas.

See also ABDÜLHAMIT II; ANKARA; COMMITTEE FOR UNION AND PROGRESS; KEMALISM; LAUSANNE, TREATY OF (1923); SELIM III; SÈVRES, TREATY OF (1920); *SHARI'A*; SIVAS CONFERENCE (1919); TURKISH GRAND NATIONAL ASSEMBLY; WAQF; YOUNG TURKS.

Bibliography

Ahmad, Feroz. *The Making of Modern Turkey.* London and New York: Routledge, 1993.

Kinross, Patrick Balfour, Baron. *Atatürk: The Rebirth of a Nation.* London: Weidenfeld and Nicolson, 1964.

Lewis, Bernard. *The Emergence of Modern Turkey,* 3d edition. New York: Oxford University Press, 2002.

A Speech Delivered by Mustafa Kemal Atatürk (1927). Istanbul: Ministry of Education, 1963.

Volkan, Vamik D., and Itzkowitz, Norman. *The Immortal Atatürk: A Psychobiography.* Chicago: University of Chicago Press, 1984.

Zürcher, Erik Jan. *The Unionist Factor: The Role of the Committee of Union and Progress in the Turkish National Movement, 1905–1926.* Leiden, Netherlands: Brill, 1984.

AHMET KUYAS

ATATÜRK UNIVERSITY

A public university in Erzurum, Turkey.

Founded in 1957, it comprises faculties of agriculture, medicine, arts and sciences, economics and administrative sciences, education, engineering, dentistry, theology, and veterinary science (the last located in Kars), as well as the College of Education (one in Agri and one in Erzincan), the School of Nursing in Erzurum, and the College of Vocational Education (one in Erzurum and one in Erzincan). In 1990, the university had about 850 teaching staff and about 18,000 students (about 4,500 were female). The state-funded budget of the university for 1991 was 200 billion Turkish lire, of which about 50 billion was for capital investment.

Named for Mustafa Kemal Atatürk, first president of Turkey (1923–1938), the university was founded in an era of increasing U.S. influence in Turkish politics and society. While older universities in Ankara, Istanbul, and İzmir were patterned after European models—mainly German and French—Atatürk University in Erzurum was modeled on an American land-grant college. Its original emphasis was on academic areas that would have a direct bearing on the needs of eastern Anatolia. From its inception, Atatürk University was aided by its association with the University of Nebraska; climatic similarity, especially in relation to the development of the region's agricultural potential, was an important consideration in this association. The university's teaching and research in the humanities, too, have been in harmony with the conservative and relatively traditional outlook of eastern Anatolian provincial society.

See also ANATOLIA; ATATÜRK, MUSTAFA KEMAL; ERZURUM.

Bibliography

Higher Education in Turkey. UNESCO, European Centre for Higher Education. December 1990.

I. METIN KUNT

ATAY, SALIH RIFKI
[1894–1971]

Turkish Kemalist politician and journalist.

Born in Istanbul, Salih Rifki Atay became a disciple of the Turkish nationalist Ziya Gökalp at an early age, joined the Committee for Union and Progress, and as a journalist wrote on nationalism during the final years of the Ottoman Empire. In the 1920s, he invested in the development of radio in the new Republic of Turkey and became a leading example of language reform, known for his beautiful style in the new Turkish language.

Atay became a close associate of Atatürk in the 1930s and 1940s and edited *Ulus* (Nation), the official newspaper of Turkey's ruling political party, the Progressive Republican. He was linked with the party's hard-line modernists, such as Recep Peker, prime minister from 1946 to 1947. He left *Ulus* in 1947 amid intraparty intrigue and was replaced by a more moderate editor. In the 1950s, he published the newspaper *Dünya* (World), opposing Democrat Party rule (Turkey's new second party, which became oppressive and was removed in the coup of 1960). Atay published several books on Atatürk and the nationalist struggle, as well as a number of travel books.

See also ATATÜRK, MUSTAFA KEMAL; COMMITTEE FOR UNION AND PROGRESS; DEMOCRAT PARTY; GÖKALP, ZIYA; NATIONALISM; TURKISH LANGUAGE.

Bibliography

Frey, Frederick W. *The Turkish Political Elite.* Cambridge, MA: MIT Press, 1965.

ELIZABETH THOMPSON

ATLAS MOUNTAINS

Mountain system in northwest Africa.

The Atlas Mountains extend approximately 1,300 miles (2,090 km) through the Maghrib countries of Morocco, Algeria, and Tunisia—from the Atlantic Ocean, south of Agadir, to the Mediterranean Sea near Tunis. This system comprises a series of roughly parallel ranges. From west to east, these include the Anti-Atlas, High Atlas, and Middle Atlas in Morocco; the Saharan Atlas, maritime Tell Atlas (itself formed of a series of distinct massifs such as the Ouarsenis, Grande Kabylie, and Petite Kabylie), and Aurès in Algeria; and the Kroumirie, Med-

jerda, and Tébessa Mountains in Tunisia, which are extensions of the Algerian ranges. Some authorities also include the Rif range (al-Rif), along Morocco's Mediterranean coast in the Atlas system.

The Atlas ranges dominate the landscapes of Morocco, Algeria, and Tunisia, differentiating them from the other North African countries, where desert lowlands prevail. These ranges serve as a barrier to the Sahara, sheltering the coastal lowlands of the three countries from the desert conditions to the south. They also function as orographic barriers to moisture-laden winter storms off the Atlantic and Mediterranean, causing rainfall in the coastal lowlands. Finally, they serve as vast water towers, capturing rain and snow and giving rise to numerous permanent rivers and streams. As a result, the northern portions of the three Maghrib countries are relatively well watered and have major agricultural potential. This potential has long fostered relatively dense settlement by the Berbers—indigenous Caucasoid tribal peoples—particularly in the mountains. The region's agricultural potential has attracted colonizers, beginning with the Phoenicians and Romans, then later the Arabs and French. Europeans have referred to the Maghrib highlands as the Atlas Mountains since classical times, because of the Greek legend that they were the home of the god Atlas; the Arabs have referred to the entire highland area as Jazirat al-Maghrib, the "Island of the

The Atlas Mountains stretch from Morocco to Algeria and Tunisia, contain many fertile valleys, and are rich in minerals. Jebel Toubkal, pictured here, is one of the mountain range's highest points, reaching 4,165 meters. © YANN ARTHUS-BETRAND/CORBIS. REPRODUCED BY PERMISSION.

West," because it represented a relatively lush mountainous island jutting out of the deserts.

The most impressive range within the Atlas system is the High Atlas, which extends for some 350 miles (560 km) through the center of Morocco and has an average elevation of around 10,000 feet (3,050 m). Many High Atlas peaks are snow-clad for much of the year. Jabal Toukal, south of Marrakech, reaches 13,665 feet (4,165 m) and is the highest peak in the High Atlas as well as in North Africa. The Middle Atlas range possesses the most luxuriant vegetation in the Atlas system, with extensive stands of fir and cedar at higher elevations. Forests of various species of oak are common on the more humid slopes throughout the Atlas system, with open stands of pine and juniper typical on drier slopes. Generally, the mountains diminish in elevation from west to east and become more barren of vegetation from north to south.

Historically, the Atlas Mountains have functioned as a refuge area for the indigenous Berber peoples, helping them to preserve their distinctive languages and customs. Portions of the Moroccan Atlas and the Kabylie in Algeria remain strong bastions of Berber culture. Tribal areas in the Atlas had autonomy in the precolonial period; only occasionally did they fall under the control of rulers in the lowland capitals. This tradition of dissidence continued during the colonial period: The Atlas Mountains figured prominently in the resistance and independence movements, serving as effective strongholds for rebel groups.

See also BERBER.

Bibliography

Gellner, Ernest. *Saints of the Atlas.* London: Weidenfeld and Nicolson, 1969.

Miller, James A. *Imlil: A Moroccan Mountain Community in Change.* Boulder, CO: Westview Press, 1984.

WILL D. SWEARINGEN

ATRASH, FARID AL-
[1915?–1974]

Composer, singer, and oud player.

Farid al-Atrash appeared in and composed music for numerous films and wrote songs for many other performers as well. His low-pitched voice was characterized by a poignant and evocative sadness (*huzn*), and he commanded vocal styles considered to be authentic (*asil*) in Egypt as well as in the Levant.

He was born in Jabal al-Duruz (Syria) to Aliya Husayn and Fahd al-Atrash. Aliya moved to Cairo with her children Fu'ad, Farid, and Amal (later the professional singer and film star known as Asmahan) in about 1924, to escape the fighting against the French mandate troops, in which her husband was involved. To sustain the family, Aliya sang for private radio stations in Cairo and appeared in music halls.

Farid began his performing career in the music halls of Mary Mansur and Badi'a Masabni. Ibrahim Hamuda, then a rising star in musical theater, encouraged Farid and hired him to play the *ud* (oud; a short-necked lute) in his accompanying ensemble. Soon thereafter, Farid enrolled in the Institute of Arabic Music and studied with oud virtuoso Riyad al-Sunbati. He also worked with Daud Husni and composer Farid Ghusn.

Farid's reputation spread via local radio stations. He was introduced to radio audiences by Medhat Assem, one of his mentors, who was then the director of music programming for Egyptian Radio. Farid's career as a composer blossomed in the late 1930s, and he flourished as a composer, singer, and oud player until his health began to deteriorate in the 1970s.

In his compositions, Farid, like Muhammad Abd al-Wahhab and many of his contemporaries, evinced interest in Western music and incorporated many Western instruments. He tried to modernize Arabic music while preserving its essential character. His efforts along these lines extended into harmonization, adoption of Western dance rhythms, and use of genres such as the operetta. In his vocal style, however, he cultivated local nuances, and his voice was believed to carry the flavor of authentically Egyptian and Arabic song.

He made over thirty films, for which he composed the music and appeared as the star; among them were *Bulbul Afandi, Matqulsh li-Hadd, Ayza At'jawwiz, Lahn al-Khulud,* and *Lahn Hubbi. Intisar al-Shabab,* with his sister Asmahan, was particularly successful. Several, such as *Wa-ja al-Rabi,* closely followed Western models. He also wrote hundreds of songs, sung by himself and others. Among the most famous are "Awwal Hamsa" and "al-Rabi."

See also ABD AL-WAHHAB, MUHAMMAD IBN; ASMAHAN.

VIRGINIA DANIELSON

ATRASH, SULTAN PASHA AL-

Prominent Syrian Druze chieftain.

Sultan Pasha was feared by the French because of his continued efforts to rally the Druzes against French interference in the Jabal Druze in Syria. He was the leader of the Jabal Druze revolt (1925–1927) against French administration in Syria, during which he called on all Syrians to fight for the complete independence of Syria. Although the revolt was under Druze leadership, it assumed a truly national character and became Syria-wide. Sultan Pasha's anti-French activities compelled him to live years of exile with many of his followers. Exile, which ended with the French amnesty of May 1937, allowed new rivals to Sultan Pasha to emerge in the Jabal Druze. Sultan Pasha remained close to the faction of Abd al-Rahman Shahbandar, a prominent Syrian politician who had British and Hashimite links.

See also JABAL DRUZE; SHAHBANDAR, ABD AL-RAHMAN.

MUHAMMAD MUSLIH

ATTAR, NEJAT AL-
[unknown]

Syria's first woman minister.

Nejat al-Attar was the longest-serving woman minister in the Arab world, and Syria's first woman minister. She was appointed minister of culture in 1976 and served in all the governments named by the Syrian president Hafiz al-Asad, until her retirement from government after the reshuffle of March 2000. Attar comes from a respected Damascene family. She received a Ph.D. from the University of Edinburgh in 1970. Her appointment in 1976 as a minister came during the Syrian regime's struggle with the Muslim Brotherhood, of which her brother, Isam al-Attar, had been the leader since 1957. Attar remained in her post even after the as-

sassination attempt on her brother in 1981, which led to the death of his wife. She is known for her strong character, and served in the 1980s and 1990s as the mouthpiece of Asad. After retiring from government, Attar assumed the post of chairman of the board of trustees of Syria's first private and virtual university.

See also ASAD, HAFIZ AL-; GENDER: GENDER AND EDUCATION; GENDER: GENDER AND LAW; GENDER: GENDER AND POLITICS; SYRIA.

Bibliography

Roberts, David. *The Ba'th and the Creation of Modern Syria.* London: Croom Helm, 1986.

Seale, Patrick. *Asad: The Struggle for the Middle East.* Berkeley: University of California Press, 1988.

KHALIL GEBARA

ATTAR, SUAD AL-
[1942 –]

An Iraqi painter and printmaker.

Suad (also Su'ad) al-Attar was the first Iraqi woman to hold a solo exhibition in Baghdad (1965). She was trained at California State University, at the University of Baghdad, and also at the Wimbledon School of Art and the Central School of Art in London. Al-Attar's work is rooted in the visual traditions of her native Iraq and makes use of elements of Islamic design, Assyrian art, and folk art in particular. Many of her works represent scenes from Arab legends and folklore, or detailed gardens filled with flora and fauna, both done in styles influenced by medieval Baghdadi painting and the broader tradition of miniature painting. Much of her work since the 1990s has been inspired by the tragic situation of Iraq and by the untimely death of her sister (also an artist as well as an influential curator) during the bombing of Baghdad during the 1991 Gulf War. Al-Attar has described her work as emotional archives that deal centrally with myths, sensuality, dreams, and taboos. She has exhibited in the Middle East, Europe, and the United States. She is the winner of the Miró Award and of several prizes at international biennials.

See also ANI, JANNANE AL-; GENDER: GENDER AND EDUCATION; IRAQ.

Bibliography

Ali, Wijdan. *Modern Islamic Art: Development and Continuity.* Gainesville: University Press of Florida, 1997.

JESSICA WINEGAR

ATTAS, HAYDAR ABU BAKR AL-

[c.1939–]

President, Democratic Republic of Yemen, and prime minister, Republic of Yemen.

Born in approximately 1939 in Wadi Hadramawt, Haydar Abu Bakr al-Attas is a member of a prestigious, highly respected, and learned family. After South Yemen gained independence from Britain in 1967, he was regarded as a loyal, hard-working technocrat and became a longtime second-level leader who despite, or possibly because of, a reputation for not being political, became prime minister of the People's Democratic Republic of Yemen (PDRY). He had been in that post for nearly a year at the time of an intraparty blood bath in 1986 that effectively decapitated the ruling Yemeni Socialist Party. He became PDRY president in the regime of survivors which followed that event and remained so until Yemeni unification in 1990. Al-Attas became prime minister of the united Republic of Yemen in 1990, remaining in that post until he was forced into exile in mid-1994 as a leader of a failed attempt at secession by southerners only two months earlier; during this brief period he was prime minister of the newly proclaimed Democratic Republic of Yemen. Subsequently, he and four other South Yemeni leaders were tried and sentenced to death in absentia; the five were granted amnesty by Republic of Yemen president Ali Abdullah Salih in 2003. Thereafter, al-Attas remained in exile in Saudi Arabia and was not actively involved in politics.

See also PEOPLE'S DEMOCRATIC REPUBLIC OF YEMEN; WADI HADRAMAWT; YEMENI SOCIALIST PARTY.

Bibliography

Burrowes, Robert D. *Historical Dictionary of Yemen.* Lanham, MD: Scarecrow Press, 1995.

Dresch, Paul. *A History of Modern Yemen.* New York and Cambridge, U.K.: Cambridge University Press, 2000.

ROBERT D. BURROWES

ATTLEE, CLEMENT

[1883–1967]

British Prime Minister (1945–1951) and leader of the Labour Party (1935–1955).

Clement Attlee was a member of Winston Churchill's war cabinet as Lord Privy Seal (1940–1942) and deputy Prime Minister (1942–1945). He resigned in May 1945 and won the general election in July of the same year. His premiership came at an important juncture in the Middle East, even though his government's Middle Eastern policy was conducted mainly by Foreign Secretary Ernest Bevin and Colonial Secretary Arthur Creech Jones.

Attlee initiated the formation of the Anglo-American Committee of Inquiry to make recommendations on the future of Palestine (1946), and won the consent of U.S. president Harry S. Truman. He was reluctant, however, to meet the latter's request to lift the barriers to Jewish immigration to Palestine. Under Attlee's premiership, an Anglo-Egyptian draft treaty was concluded in 1946, paving the way for the eventual British evacuation from Egypt. In the same year, Britain surrendered its mandate over Jordan and in 1948 its mandate over Palestine, which resulted in the establishment of the state of Israel.

See also ANGLO–AMERICAN COMMITTEE OF INQUIRY (1946); BEVIN, ERNEST; CREECH JONES, ARTHUR.

Bibliography

Attlee, Clement. *As It Happened.* New York: Viking Press; London: Heinemann, 1954.

Attlee, Clement. *A Prime Minister Remembers: The War and Post-War Memoirs of the Rt. Hon. Earl Attlee, Based on His Private Papers and on a Series of Recorded Conversations.* London: Heinemann, 1961.

Cohen, Michael J. *Palestine and the Great Powers, 1945–1948.* Princeton, NJ: Princeton University Press, 1982.

Louis, William Roger. *The British Empire in the Middle East, 1945–1951: Arab Nationalism, the United States, and Postwar Imperialism.* New York: Oxford University Press; Oxford, U.K.; Clarendon, 1984.

JENAB TUTUNJI
UPDATED BY JOSEPH NEVO

AUSTRIA-HUNGARY AND THE MIDDLE EAST

Austria and Hungary joined to form the Austro-Hungarian Empire in 1867, under Austrian Emperor Franz Joseph, a member of the Hapsburg dynasty that had ruled since 1278.

During the fourteenth through seventeenth centuries, before Hungary joined Austria, both countries had been repeatedly attacked, first by the Turks and then by the Ottoman Empire attempting to expand into Europe by way of the Balkan Peninsula. In the sixteenth century, western and northern Hungary accepted Austrian rule to escape Ottoman occupation. In 1683, the Ottoman armies were halted at Vienna, but fighting continued in the Balkans until a peace was signed in 1699, the Treaty of Karlowitz. After suppression of the 1848 revolt of Hungary against Austrian rule, the dual monarchy was formed in 1867, as a Christian empire, but one relatively tolerant of the religious and ethnic diversity that characterized its citizens.

Austro-Hungarian policy toward the Middle East was focused on two main concerns—preservation of the Ottoman Empire and containment of Balkan nationalism, which had emerged in the Serbian revolt of 1804 against Ottoman rule. The Balkan Peninsula was inhabited by both Christians and Muslims, most of them Slavs. Russia was in the process of instigating a pan-Slavic movement (in an attempt to link Russian Slavs with Poland and the Balkans and gain access to the warm-water ports of the eastern Mediterranean—crucial to Russian trade interests before aviation allowed a way around frozen northern ports). As a multinational empire encompassing several Slavic groups, Austria-Hungary was vulnerable to these same forces of Slavic nationalism and pan-Slavism that threatened the European possessions of the Ottoman Empire. Austro-Hungarian Slavs included Poles, Ukrainians, Czechs, Slovenes, Serbs, Croats, and Slavonized Bulgars. Nationalism in the Balkan Peninsula was seen as the beginning of the potential breakup of both the Austro-Hungarian and Ottoman Empires.

Even before the eruption of Balkan nationalism in the nineteenth century, Austrian statesmen had been concerned with the potential breakup of the Ottoman Empire and the resulting politics that would affect the Austrian Empire. Therefore, Austria-Hungary adopted a dual strategy: (1) help preserve Ottoman suzerainty over the Slavs where possible and (2) make sure that Austria, not Russia, gained when preservation of Ottoman authority was no longer possible. Toward this end, Austro-Hungarian bankers floated loans to the Ottomans and, to improve communications, sponsored the construction of the Vienna-Istanbul railroad. Under Klemens von Metternich, Austria's foreign minister from 1809 to 1848, and for the rest of the nineteenth century, Austria looked to expand its domain over the northwestern Balkan territories of Bosnia and Herzegovina. By the beginning of the great Eastern Crisis of 1875–1878, Austro-Hungarian Foreign Minister Julius Andrássy sent the Andrássy Note of 30 December 1875, calling for autonomy for Bosnia-Herzegovina and Ottoman reform of its administration of its Balkan provinces. Andrássy was simultaneously trying to curtail Russian pan-Slavism, which dictated Russian support for Serbian and Bulgarian expansion. The resulting crisis led to the defeat of the Ottomans by the Russians in the Russian–Ottoman War of 1877–1878 and the subsequent Treaty of San Stephano, which resulted in a vastly enlarged Bulgaria and a clear advantage for Russia in the Balkans. Andrássy sided with the British to attempt to force a revision of the treaty in Austria-Hungary's favor and, at the July 1878 Congress of Berlin, he prevailed, when a virtual protectorate over a technically autonomous Bosnia-Herzegovina was given to Austria-Hungary.

The following years saw increasing nationalist activity in the Balkans and increasingly complex alliances among the European powers. During the height of the Macedonian crisis at the turn of the twentieth century, Austria-Hungary at times supported Serbia and at times opposed it—all with the overall goal of obtaining Austrian influence on the northern Aegean. When the Albanians revolted against the Ottomans in 1912, Austro-Hungarian pressure on the Ottomans led to the creation of an independent state, which was advantageous from an Austrian perspective, because Albania provided a buffer against Serbian expansion to the Adriatic. The Ottoman defeat in the two Balkan wars, fought just prior to World War I, was disadvantageous to Austria-Hungary. Spurred by victories in the Balkan wars, Serbia overran northern Albania to the

Adriatic. Serbian ambitions in Bosnia-Herzegovina led to the assassination of the heir to the Austro-Hungarian throne, Archduke Franz Ferdinand, in July 1914; this was used as a symbolic outrage that allowed for the beginning of World War I in August.

Ultimately, both the Ottoman and Austro-Hungarian Empires were on the losing side of that war, and their territories were allowed to become independent states or protectorates of the winning European countries—mainly Britain and France—by the peace treaties and the League of Nations.

See also BALKANS; BALKAN WARS (1912–1913); BERLIN, CONGRESS AND TREATY OF; NATIONALISM; OTTOMAN EMPIRE; RUSSIAN–OTTOMAN WARS; WORLD WAR I.

Bibliography

Anderson, M. S. *The Eastern Question, 1774–1923: A Study in International Relations.* London: Macmillan; New York: St. Martin's, 1966.

Langer, William L. *European Alliance and Alignments, 1871–1890,* 2d edition. New York: Knopf, 1950.

Shaw, Stanford, and Shaw, Ezel Kural. *History of the Ottoman Empire and Modern Turkey.* Cambridge, U.K., and New York: Cambridge University Press, 1976–1977.

Taylor, A. J. P. *The Struggle for Mastery in Europe, 1848–1918.* Oxford: Clarendon Press, 1954.

ZACHARY KARABELL

AVNERY, URI

[1923–]

Israeli Journalist, writer, politician, and peace activist.

Born Helmut Ostermann in Beckum, Germany, Avnery immigrated to Palestine at the age of ten. As a youth he was close to the Canaanite movement, which advocated the creation of a new "Hebrew nation" by severing ties with the Jewish diaspora. Avnery also joined the Revisionist Irgun Zvaʾi Leʾumi in 1938, but left the dissident organization several years later because of its anti-Arab ideology.

Avnery recognized, early on, the right of the Palestinians to self-determination and advocated a "Semetic alliance" of both nations: Jews and Arabs.

In the Arab-Israel War of 1948 he fought and was wounded as a combat soldier; he later published his critical views of the war in two best-selling books. During the 1950s and 1960s Avnery owned and edited the controversial but successful weekly magazine *ha-Olam ha-Zeh,* which combined radically critical political editorials with socialite gossip and mild pornography. In 1965, cashing in on the popularity of his magazine, he established a party named after his journal and won two seats in the Knesset in which he served, with a one-term intermission, for ten years.

Ever since the Arab–Israel War of June 1967, Avnery has become one of the most outspoken radical leaders of Israel's peace movement, leading various groups and advocating both the recognition of the Palestine Liberation Organization (PLO) as the legitimate representative of the Palestinian people and the creation of a Palestinian state in the territories occupied by Israel in 1967. He was one of the first Israelis to establish contacts with PLO representatives, first with Saʿid Hamami in London and then with Issam Sartawi in Paris. Avnery was also one of the first Israelis to meet personally with Chairman Yasir Arafat, initially during the siege of Beirut and then at his headquarters in Tunis, in open defiance of Israel's ban on such meetings. After the Oslo Accords of 1993, Avnery founded a group called Gush Shalom (the Bloc for Peace) which advocated a total withdrawal of Israel from all occupied territories, total dismantling of all Jewish settlements in these territories, and the solution of the conflict by the creation of "two states for two nations" in historic Palestine. This message has been vigorously disseminated by vigils, demonstrations, clashes with the police, and paid advertisements, as well as through Avnery's regular newspaper columns and his personal web site "Avnery News."

See also SARTAWI, ISSAM.

Bibliography

Avnery, Uri. *Israel without Zionism: A Plea for Peace in the Middle East.* London: Macmillan, 1968.

Avnery, Uri. *My Friend the Enemy.* London: Zed Books, 1986.

"Avnery News." Available from <http://www.avnery-news.co.il/english/>.

Bar-On, Mordechai. *In Pursuit of Peace: A History of the Israeli Peace Movement.* Washington, DC: U.S. Institute of Peace, 1996.

MARTIN MALIN
UPDATED BY MORDECHAI BAR-ON

AWADHI, BADRIA A. AL-
[1943–]

Kuwaiti attorney, educator, author, and activist.

A noted attorney and women's rights activist, Badria al-Awadhi received her L.L.B. and L.L.M. from Cairo University and her Ph.D. in international law from University College London. She served as Dean of the Faculty of Law and Shari'a at Kuwait University from 1979 to 1982. Her international service includes membership on the Committee of Experts advising the International Labor Organization (1983–1996) and work with environmental and human rights groups. She has written extensively on family law and maritime environmental issues. A tireless advocate for women's rights, in 1992 she was the first woman to speak at a public campaign event sponsored by a candidate running for the Kuwaiti parliament. As of 2003 she directed the Arab Regional Center for Environmental Law and headed a private law practice, both in Kuwait City.

See also GENDER: GENDER AND LAW; GENDER: GENDER AND POLITICS; KUWAIT.

Bibliography

Tétreault, Mary Ann. "Civil Society in Kuwait: Protected Spaces and Women's Rights." *Middle East Journal* 47, no. 2 (Spring 1993): 275–91.

MARY ANN TÉTREAULT

AWAD, LOUIS
[1914/15–1991]

Egyptian scholar and essayist.

Louis Awad was born in the village of Sharuna in the district of Mina. He studied literature at the universities of Cairo, Oxford, and Princeton. As chairman of the faculty of letters at Cairo University, Awad inaugurated in Egypt the modern study of literary criticism based on scientific principles. From 1945 to 1950 he joined with other writers who drew from Marxism and other sources in a call for the total reform of Egyptian society. His novel *al-Anqa* (the Phoenix) expresses this orientation. In a volume of poetry, *Plutoland,* he introduced free verse forms to Egyptian literature and presented a scathing attack on traditionalism. Awad's unwavering critical stance continued after the 1952 revolution. As a consequence, he was forced to resign his position at Cairo University in 1954.

In 1960 Awad became the literary editor at the newspaper *al-Ahram.* He published a devastating critique of higher education in Egypt in 1964, arguing that students wished to be instructed, rather than to engage in independent study and research. Awad's writings in *al-Ahram* made him one of the leading opinion-makers in the Arab world. From the mid-1970s through the 1980s he served as a faculty adviser at the American Research Center in Egypt, developing a strong following among graduate students there.

See also LITERATURE: ARABIC.

Bibliography

Kilpatrick, Hilary. *The Modern Egyptian Novel: A Study in Social Criticism.* London: Ithaca Press, 1974.

DAVID WALDNER
UPDATED BY CHARLES E. BUTTERWORTH

AWAKENED YOUTH

Afghan political-literacy organization.

Awakened Youth was a political-literacy group formed in 1946 or 1947, in part as a reaction to the autocratic Afghan prime minister Shah Mahmoud. One of its founders was Muhammad Daud, a future prime minister and a member of the royal family. The party advocated social change and promoted the cause of Pushtunistan. Later it became more radicalized, and many members were arrested at the end of the Seventh Afghan National Assembly in 1952 when liberal laws allowing political activity expired.

See also DAUD, MUHAMMAD.

Bibliography

Arnold, Anthony. *Afghanistan's Two-Party Communism: Parcham and Khalq.* Stanford, CA: Hoover Institution Press, 1983.

GRANT FARR

AWALI, AL-

Town located in the middle of the island of Bahrain.

Situated atop Bahrain's oil field, Awali lies approximately 2 miles (3 km) south of Rifa, the town where the ruling family of Bahrain resides. Awali was built during the British protectorate by the Bahrain Petroleum Company (BAPCO), following the discovery of petroleum in 1932, to provide housing for the company's expatriate, especially European and American, personnel. The town consists primarily of small garden homes; it offers cultural and recreational facilities for its residents.

See also BAHRAIN; PETROLEUM, OIL, AND NATURAL GAS.

Bibliography

Nyrop, Richard F., ed. *Persian Gulf States: Country Studies.* Washington, DC: U.S. Government Printing Office, 1985.

EMILE A. NAKHLEH

AYAN

Plural of the Arabic word ayn, *meaning notable person.*

The term *ayan* was used in the Ottoman Empire to refer to a variety of elites, particularly landed notables in either cities or the countryside. *Ayan* were usually tax farmers from merchant, *ulama,* or Janissary families, although their origins differed in various regions of the empire. In the provinces of Egypt, Syria, and Iraq, the *ayan* were typically Mamluks or local Ottoman officials like governors. In eastern Anatolia, they were called *derebeys,* or valley lords affiliated with dominant clans.

In the late eighteenth and early nineteenth centuries, many provincial *ayan* amassed personal armies and control of local finances, challenging the influence of the central state. Particularly in the European provinces, the *ayan* were able to gain power in the late eighteenth century because they supplied crucial military support to the sultan in the several wars against Russia. Their power was formalized when the sultan granted them official status (*ayanlik*) as representatives of the people to the government in exchange for their support.

In the early nineteenth century, the *ayan* openly rebelled against the central state in the Serbian revolt (1803–1805) and in their refusal in the Balkans to cooperate in conscription to Selim III's new army, the Nizam-i Cedit. In 1807, *ayan* from the European provinces cooperated with opponents of reform to overthrow Selim. An attempt to negotiate a truce between Constantinople and provincial notables produced in 1808 the ineffective and largely ignored Sened-i Ittifak (Pact of Alliance). Mahmud II devoted the latter part of his reign to undermining the autonomy of the *ayan* and enlarging central power, reforms continued in the Tanzimat era.

See also ANATOLIA; MAMLUKS; OTTOMAN EMPIRE; TANZIMAT; *ULAMA.*

Bibliography

Karpat, Kemal H. "The Land Regime, Social Structure, and Modernization in the Ottoman Empire." In *The Beginnings of Modernization in the Middle East: The Nineteenth Century,* ed. by William R. Polk and Richard L. Chambers. Chicago: University of Chicago Press, 1966.

Shaw, Stanford, and Shaw, Ezel Kural. *The History of the Ottoman Empire and Modern Turkey.* Cambridge, U.K., and New York: Cambridge University Press, 1976–1977.

ELIZABETH THOMPSON

AYA SOFYA

Religious structure in Istanbul, now a museum.

The Aya Sofya (also known by its Greek name, Hagia Sophia) was built by the Roman emperor Constantine from 325 to 330 C.E. during his rebuilding of the city of Byzantium as his capital. It was built as a Christian church, the cathedral of Constantinople (now Istanbul), for the first Roman emperor to espouse that faith. The present structure dates from the sixth century, when the cathedral was rebuilt by the Byzantine emperor Justinian. In 1453, the Ottomans conquered the city and transformed the church into a mosque. In 1935, the new Republic of Turkey transformed it again, this time into a museum. The Aya Sofya served as the inspiration for several mosques built during the Ottoman Empire, including Süleymaniye Mosque, designed by Sinan, and the Sultan Ahmet Mosque (popularly known as the Blue mosque).

See also MOSQUE; OTTOMAN EMPIRE; SULTAN AHMET MOSQUE.

ZACHARY KARABELL

AYN, AL-

The second-largest city in the emirate of Abu Dhabi in the United Arab Emirates.

Originally one of nine oasis villages in the Buraymi region, the urban conglomeration of modern al-Ayn has enveloped the six villages that became part of the United Arab Emirates (UAE) after the resolution of the Buraymi Oasis dispute. The region around al-Ayn contains some of the most important archaeological sites in the UAE. For example, the country's oldest monumental sites are located at Jabal Hafit, south of al-Ayn, and include hundreds of tombs that date to 3200–2800 B.C.E. The ruler of Abu Dhabi has encouraged the study and promotion of the emirate's early history, much of which is showcased at al-Ayn's historical museum. Al-Ayn means "the spring" in Arabic, and in addition to having wells and springs, the oasis has been watered for centuries by a series of man-made underground channels (*aflaj* in Arabic; sing. *falaj*), a technique also found in Iran. Until the advent of oil revenues, al-Ayn's economy depended on oasis agriculture, links with pastoral nomads, trade, and migrating laborers who fished and pearled in the Persian Gulf. Modern al-Ayn continues to be an important agricultural region. In addition, the city hosts the Emirates University, Zayid Military Academy, a historical museum, and a world-class zoo.

See also BURAYMI OASIS DISPUTE.

Bibliography

Kay, Shirley. *Emirates Archaeological Heritage.* Dubai: Motivate Publishing, 1986.

Vine, Peter, and Casey, Paula. *United Arab Emirates: Profile of a Country's Heritage and Modern Development.* London: Immel Publishing, 1992.

ANTHONY B. TOTH

AYN AL-DOWLEH, ABD AL-MAJID MIRZA
[1845–1926]

Prominent Iranian political figure during Mozaffar al-Din Shah's reign, 1896–1907.

Ayn al-Dowleh, Sultan Abd al-Majid Mirza Atabak-e A'zam, was the son of Sultan Ahmad Mirza Azod al-Dowleh, Fath Ali Shah Qajar's forty-eighth son. After administering several governorates, he was given the title of Ayn al-Dowleh by Naser al-Din Shah in 1893. Shah Mozaffar al-Din appointed him chief minister in 1903, and he was promoted to prime minister the following year. His vociferous opposition to the constitutional movement brought about his dismissal in 1906. He was reinstated for brief intervals in 1915 and 1917, but British disapproval and the hostility of the parliament proved insurmountable. Following the coup d'état in 1921, he was arrested and heavily fined.

See also MOZAFFAR AL-DIN QAJAR; NASER AL-DIN SHAH.

Bibliography

Adamiyat, Fereydun. *The Idea of Freedom and the Origins of Constitutionalism in Iran.* Tehran, 1961. In Persian.

Algar, Hamid. *Religion and State in Iran, 1786–1906: The Role of the Ulama in the Qajar Period.* Berkeley: University of California Press, 1969.

NEGUIN YAVARI

AYNI, MUHSIN AL-
[1932–]

Yemeni politician.

A Yemeni nationalist identified with republican, progressive, and unionist policies, al-Ayni was exiled from North Yemen by Imam Ahmad in the 1950s. He then became involved in South Yemen's politics, associated with the Aden Trade Union Congress and its political wing, the Popular Socialist Party. With the military revolt and the fall of the imamate in North Yemen in 1962, he became the first foreign minister of the Yemen Arab Republic. He was also appointed prime minister four times, between 1968 and 1975. During his various tenures in that office he presided over the 1969 and 1970 reconciliation between republicans and royalists that ended the North Yemen civil war; he also negotiated the 1972 unity agreement with the People's Democratic Republic of Yemen (South Yemen; established 1967). Because he is a controversial political figure, al-Ayni's career after 1975 was limited to overseas diplomatic posts, including that of his

1990 appointment as the first ambassador of the Republic of Yemen to the United States.

See also YEMEN.

Bibliography

Burrowes, Robert. *The Yemen Arab Republic: The Politics of Development, 1962–1986.* Boulder, CO: Westview Press, 1987.

F. GREGORY GAUSE III

AYN, RAS AL-

Town in northeastern Syria near the border with Turkey.

This Syrian town has one of the world's largest karst springs, which are formed from Paleogenic (nummilitic) and marine Miocene limestone. The springs' average annual discharge is estimated at 1,056 gallons (4,000 liters per second) or 1,594 million cubic yards (1,219 million cu m). The springs form the Khabur River, which flows south into the Euphrates River near Dayr al-Zawr in Syria's province of Dayr al-Zawr. They have been called the "Queen of Springs" on account of their high, exceptionally steady discharge throughout the year.

ABDUL-KARIM RAFEQ

AYYUB, DHU AL-NUN
[1908?–1988]

Iraqi novelist of the 1930s and 1940s and social critic.

Born in Mosul to a Sunni Arab lower-middle-class merchant family, Ayyub was graduated from the Higher Teachers' College in Baghdad in 1928. For over a decade afterward, he worked as a high-school mathematics teacher in a number of places in Iraq. At the end of the 1930s, he became director of Baghdad's institute of Fine Arts, and between 1938 and 1944 he was chief editor of the cultural magazine *al-Majalla.* In 1941–1942, he was a member of the central committee of the Iraqi Communist Party from which he was expelled due to a controversy with its secretary general over Ayyub's demand for democratization in the party. Upon his expulsion, he established his own moderate left-wing party, the Congress (*al-mu'tamariyyun*). In 1944 he decided to

try his luck in agriculture and leased a plot of government land. This enterprise, however, failed miserably, and he lost his investment. In 1959, he was appointed by General Abd al-Karim Qasim as director general of guidance and broadcasts, but in June 1960 he was dismissed. For a while, he was a press attaché in the Iraqi Embassy in Vienna, but most of the time he lived off a small pension from the Iraqi government. He also tried unsuccessfully to run a restaurant. In the 1980s, due to the Iraq–Iran war, his pension was stopped. He died in Vienna.

Ayyub's first recognition as a writer resulted from a number of translations from Western prose, first published in 1933. His first, and most important novel, *Doctor Ibrahim,* was published about 1940 in his hometown. Until then, writing novels was regarded as a far less prestigious occupation than the writing of poetry. Ayyub contributed to this change in public opinion. His second book, a volume of short stories, *al-Yad wa al-Ard wa al-ma (The Hand and the Land and the Water),* reflecting his experience as a farmer, came out in 1948. Among his other writings were: *Burj Babil (The Tower of Babylon), al-Kadihun (The Toilers),* and *Rusul al-Thaqafa (The Messengers of Culture).* His novels and short stories are written in a naive, realistic style. They reflect the feeling that all good social values are the creation of simple working people, and they contain scathing criticism against the widespread corruption in Iraqi society, yet they lack a revolutionary message. *Doctor Ibrahim* portrays an ambitious and unscrupulous Iraqi politician, who some believed to be modeled after the Shi'ite politician Muhammad Fadhil al-Jamali. Ayyub's last novel was published in Beirut in the 1970s. Six volumes of his memoirs, still unpublished, are in the possession of Iraqi poet Buland al-Haydari, who lives in London.

See also COMMUNISM IN THE MIDDLE EAST; IRAQ; JAMALI, MUHAMMAD FADHIL AL-; QASIM, ABD AL-KARIM; SUNNI ISLAM.

Bibliography

Batatu, Hanna. *The Old Social Classes and the Revolutionary Movements of Iraq: A Study of Iraq's Old Landed and Commercial Classes and of Its Communists, Ba'thists, and Free Officers.* Princeton, NJ: Princeton University Press, 1978.

AMATZIA BARAM

AYYUBI, ALI JAWDAT AL-

[1885?–1969]

Friend and retainer of Faisal I ibn Hussein during the Arab revolt of World War I; politician in Iraq, 1920s–1958.

Ali Jawdat was born in Mosul (Iraq) during the Ottoman Empire, to a family who practiced Sunni Islam. His father was a military man, chief sergeant in the gendarmerie, and Ali's education was basically military. During World War I, he joined the Arab revolt against the Ottomans under Sharif Husayn ibn Ali and became a trusted friend of the sharif's son Faisal, who in 1920 became king of Syria (until the French mandate), then king of Iraq in 1921 under the British mandate.

Ali Jawdat was appointed military governor and head of several government ministries (finance, interior, and foreign affairs) during the early years, when Iraq tried to gain independence from the British. In 1932, the British mandate was ended, but Britain kept troops there until the mid-1950s. During the 1930s, Ali Jawdat became a chief administrative and diplomatic officer, representing Iraq in London, Paris, and Washington. He was made prime minister of Iraq in 1934 and 1935, 1949 and 1950, and during 1957 (just before the government was overthrown by a leftist military coup in 1958, headed by Abd al-Karim Qasim). In 1967, Ali Jawdat published his memoirs in Beirut, covering the years 1900 to 1958.

See also ARAB REVOLT (1916); FAISAL I IBN HUSSEIN; HUSAYN IBN ALI; IRAQ; OTTOMAN EMPIRE; QASIM, ABD AL-KARIM; SUNNI ISLAM; WORLD WAR I.

Bibliography

Ayyubi, Ali Jawdat al-. *Memoirs of Ali Jawdat, 1900–58.* Beirut, 1967. In Arabic.

Batatu, Hanna. *The Old Social Classes and the Revolutionary Movements of Iraq: A Study of Iraq's Old Landed and Commercial Classes and of Its Communists, Ba'thists, and Free Officers.* Princeton, NJ: Princeton University Press, 1978.

AHMAD ABDUL A. R. SHIKARA

AZERBAIJAN

Province in northwestern Iran; also, a republic (fully independent since 1991) along the western coast of the Caspian Sea, with Baku as capital.

An Iranian province with documented history going back to the Achaemenian period (700 to 330 B.C.E.), Azerbaijan was gradually Turkified by the end of the twelfth century through the migration of Turkic tribes from central Asia. Its spoken language, Azeri, is a Turkic language strongly influenced by Persian. Alongside the Turkish-speaking population, Azerbaijan is also home to a substantial Kurdish minority. Most Turkish-speaking Azerbaijanis are Shi'a Muslims, and the Kurds are mostly Sunni.

Iranian Azerbaijan is divided into three provinces: Western Azerbaijan, with its provincial seat in Urumia; Eastern Azerbaijan, the capital of which is Tabriz; and Ardebil, with its provincial capital at Ardebil. The independent Republic of Azerbaijan, formerly a republic within the Soviet Union until its dissolution in 1991, also had been a part of Iranian territory but was ceded to Czarist Russia under the provisions of the Treaties of Golestan (1813) and Turkamanchai (1828).

In 1945 a Soviet-backed autonomous republic, led by local Marxist leaders Ja'far Pishevari and Gholam Yahya, was declared in Iranian Azerbaijan. Opposition from the United States, combined with the shrewd diplomacy of Azerbaijan's prime minister, Ahmad Qavam, secured the withdrawal of the Soviet troops and led to the demise of the short-lived and self-styled Democratic Republic of Azerbaijan.

Iranian Azerbaijan has varied climatic conditions. It includes some of Iran's richest agricultural lands, producing barley, wheat, rice, and potatoes. Tabriz is the region's industrial center, where tractors, factory machinery, electrical equipment and turbines, motorcycles, clocks and watches, cement, textiles, processed foods, and agricultural implements are produced. In other parts of Azerbaijan sugar and textile mills and food-processing plants are in operation. There are copper, arsenic, coal, and salt mines in the province. According to the 1996 census, the total population of East Azerbaijan was 3,369,000, of which 64.8 percent lived in urban areas. West Azerbaijan's population was 2,496,320, of which 57.39 percent were urban dwellers. Of Ardebil's 1,197,364 inhabitants, 647,154 live in urban areas. According to the Statistical Center of Iran, in East Azerbaijan 75.4 percent of the population is literate; in West Azerbaijan, 69 percent; and in Ardebil, 73.3 percent.

See also AZERI LANGUAGE AND LITERATURE; IRAN; TABRIZ; TURKMANCHAI, TREATY OF (1828).

Bibliography

Atabaki, Touraj. *Azerbaijan: Ethnicity and Autonomy in Twentieth-Century Iran.* London and New York: British Academic Press, 1993.

Chehabi, H. E. "Ardabil Becomes a Province: Center-Periphery Relations in Iran." *International Journal of Middle East Studies* 29, no. 2 (1997): 235–253.

Fawcett, Louise L'Estrange. *Iran and the Cold War: The Azerbaijan Crisis of 1946.* Cambridge, U.K.: Cambridge University Press, 1992.

NEGUIN YAVARI

AZERBAIJAN CRISIS

A clash between the USSR and Iran that presaged the Cold War.

Considered by diplomatic historians to be one of the international political disputes that initiated the Cold War, the Azerbaijan crisis erupted in October 1945, when the newly formed Democratic Party of Azerbaijan in Iran's northwestern province began taking over local governments with the backing of the Soviet army, which had been occupying the area since the joint Anglo–Soviet invasion of Iran in 1941. By December 1945, the Democratic Party had established an autonomous government in Tabriz, the provincial capital of Iranian Azerbaijan, and this regime threatened to resist with force any effort by Tehran to restore central authority. A similar movement emerged in Mahabad, the main town in the Kurdish area of Iranian Azerbaijan. The Soviets prevented security forces of the central government from interfering with these takeovers, thus prompting fears in Tehran that Moscow intended to separate the province from Iran and possibly unite it with the neighboring Soviet Socialist Republic of Azerbaijan. These fears intensified when the Soviet Union declined to set a date for the withdrawal of its troops from the country, in contravention of the Tripartite Treaty of Alliance (1942) stipulating that all foreign military forces were to be withdrawn from Iran within six months of the end of World War II.

The Iranian government sought diplomatic support from the United States, which encouraged Iran to submit a formal complaint to the newly created United Nations. The Azerbaijan crisis thus became one of the first issues to be considered by the Security Council. Although the Security Council discussions about the Azerbaijan crisis were not substantive in nature, the publicized manifestation of tensions between the former wartime allies Britain, the Soviet Union, and the United States probably contributed to its resolution. While the situation in Iranian Azerbaijan remained on the Security Council's agenda during the first three months of 1946, Prime Minister Ahmad Qavam of Iran negotiated an agreement for the withdrawal of Soviet troops. The agreement provided for the evacuation of all Soviet forces from Iran by May 1946, in return for Tehran's promise to withdraw the complaint it had brought before the United Nations, to negotiate peacefully with the autonomous government of Azerbaijan, and to submit for parliamentary consideration a proposal for a joint Soviet–Iranian oil company with exclusive rights to exploit any petroleum resources in northern Iran.

Following the withdrawal of Soviet troops from the country, the central government discussed economic and linguistic grievances with the Azerbaijan autonomous government, but throughout the spring and summer of 1946 the two sides were unable to resolve their political differences. Finally, in December 1946, on the pretext that nationwide security had to be reestablished prior to holding elections for a new parliament that would consider the proposed Soviet–Iranian oil company, Qavam ordered the army into Azerbaijan, including the Kurdish area around Mahabad, and the autonomy movements were crushed. Parliamentary elections were held subsequently, but in June 1947, the new parliament rejected the prime minister's proposals for creating a joint Soviet–Iranian oil company.

See also DEMOCRATIC PARTY OF AZERBAIJAN; TRIPARTITE TREATY OF ALLIANCE.

Bibliography

Abrahamian, Ervand. *Iran between Two Revolutions.* Princeton, NJ: Princeton University Press, 1982.

Ramazani, Rouhollah K. *Iran's Foreign Policy, 1941–1973: A Study of Foreign Policy in Modernizing Nations.* Charlottesville: University Press of Virginia, 1975.

ERIC HOOGLUND

AZERI LANGUAGE AND LITERATURE

Language spoken in Azerbaijan and northwestern Iran by the Azeris.

Azeri is spoken by 6,770,000 Azeris (1989 census) in Azerbaijan and elsewhere in the former Soviet Union. Millions of additional speakers of Azeri live in northwestern Iran. Azeri (together with the closely related languages Turkish and Turkmen) belongs to the southwestern, or Oghuz, branch of the Turkic languages. Azeri was originally written using Arabic script (and in Iran is now written again in Arabic script); the Azeris of the former Soviet Union adopted Latin script in 1927 and a modified Cyrillic alphabet in 1939. There is a current move to adopt a Turkish-style Latin script.

Azeri literature enjoyed continuous close ties to Persian, Turkish, and Chaghatay literature since its beginnings in the thirteenth century. Major figures of classical Azeri literature include İsfaraini, Nesimi, Hatai, Habibi, Fuzuli, and Vakil. The founders of modern Azeri literature include Kasim Beg Zakir (1784–1857), who introduced satire, Abbas Kuh Agha Bakihani ("Kudsi," 1794–1848), İsmail Beg Kutkaşinli, and Mirza Şefi ("Vazeh," 1792–1852). Mirza Feth-Ali Ahundzade (1812–1878) first introduced drama and other prose genres, and Necef Beg Vezirli (1854–1926) was another notable playwright. Mirza Ali-Ekber Sabir (1862–1911) wrote fine satire, and Celil Mehmedkuhzade (1869–1932) wrote important prose.

See also ARABIC SCRIPT; AZERBAIJAN; LITERATURE: PERSIAN; LITERATURE: TURKISH; TURKISH LANGUAGE.

ULI SCHAMILOGLU

AZHAR, AL-

Official mosque and university at Cairo, the world center of Sunni Islamic learning.

Jawhar the Sicilian, the general of al-Muʿizz li-Din-Allah, established al-Azhar in 970; it was to be the official mosque of the new Fatimid regime and to serve as the center of the effort to bring the Egyptians into the Shiʿite fold. For this reason, it lost its official status under the Sunni Ayyubids but regained it under the Mamluks. The line of succession of its head, known as Shaykh al-Azhar, has been traced to Muhammad Abdullah al-Kurashi (d. 1690). Although the shaykh was always a member of a religious elite, the occupant of this position only gradually became the chief Muslim religious official in Egypt.

Al-Azhar is the world's oldest school of higher learning in continuous operation. Although the Islamic disciplines have dominated, it has a history of secular education as well. Moses Maimonides taught medicine there. By the middle of the nineteenth century, with over 7,000 students, it had achieved a preeminent position in Egypt and was attracting students from the entire Islamic world. In 1903 al-Azhar had 104 foreign students, mostly from Arab countries and Africa, but also from Afghanistan, India, Indonesia, and China. Although all four Sunni rites were represented there, the Maliki, Shafiʿi, and Hanafi rites, each with its own shaykh, dominated. The student residential sections were endowed for specific rites or geographical groups. The only organization to integrate this segmented structure was the office of the Shaykh al-Azhar, who sided with his own group when interests conflicted. There were no formal programs of study, no degrees, and no general examination system. Students sat in circles in the mosque, each group surrounding its teaching shaykh, who sat in front of one of the numerous columns. The teacher commented on a classical or postclassical text, which the students were to memorize. When a student was deemed to have mastered a text, the teacher wrote a note authorizing him to teach it. When a student had acquired a number of these certificates and a sufficient reputation, he could compete in the informal process by which teachers were given the right to teach in the mosque.

In the late nineteenth century al-Azhar came under sharp criticism for outmoded educational content and methods, not only from the secular elite but also from such Muslim reformers as Muhammad Abduh, himself an alumnus. The curriculum had almost no secular content, its religious content was more theoretical than applied, and student performance was very low. As early as 1812, the state intervened by appointing the Shaykh al-Azhar, and in 1895 to 1896 Abduh, representing the government, intervened by introducing a salary law, a government salary subsidy, the Azhar Administrative Council, and the Azhar Organization Law. A conservative reaction thwarted this effort, which was followed by a new organization law in 1911 that was designed to introduce a bureaucratic organization and modern programs of study, examinations, and degrees. In that year 62 percent of al-Azhar's budget came from the government (it reached 96 percent by 1959). In 1930, under Shaykh al-Azhar Muhammad al-Ahmadi al-Zawahiri, a major reform law established a true college program with three departments: theology, Islamic law, and Arabic. For the first time diploma programs roughly paralleled the Western bachelor's, master's, and doctorate system.

President Gamal Abdel Nasser promoted even more change. In 1961, under Shaykh al-Azhar Muhammad Shaltut, a secular campus was added at a different site; it had the various degree programs of a full university, including medicine and other sciences. The following year the government decreed the opening of the first of several al-Azhar colleges for women. In 2002 al-Azhar University had twelve colleges in Cairo, eight in Assiut, and twenty more in other parts of the country, with a total of 185,000 students and 9,000 teachers.

An extensive primary and secondary system of Azhar institutes had meanwhile been built throughout Egypt, with a core program of secular courses, but also including a significant number of courses in the Islamic disciplines. Thus al-Azhar established a viable, comprehensive Muslim alternative to the state education system, which Egypt's *ulama* tended to view as a secular threat to Islamic society and mores.

By virtue of the increased organizational differentiation and hierarchy, some positions began to enjoy a presumption of religious authority and cor-

The al-Azhar university and mosque in Cairo was established in 970 C.E. under the Fatimid regime. Though it focused mostly on Islamic religious subjects in its early years, course offerings have since expanded to include many secular studies. © OWEN FRANKEN/CORBIS. REPRODUCED BY PERMISSION.

rectness of opinion. The 1911 law created the Corps of High Ulama, which was partly an effort to coopt senior *ulama* who might otherwise have opposed the reform, and also a response to a perceived need to have a group to pronounce on Islamic issues. The 1961 organization law transformed this body into the Academy of Islamic Research, specifically to research and pronounce on Islamic issues. The academy holds conferences to bring together *ulama* from most Muslim countries to present and discuss studies. The academy, along with the non-Azhar positions of the *mufti* of Egypt, the minister of *awqaf* (religious properties), and the Supreme Council of Islamic Affairs, assists the state with important issues of control. All these positions, both in and outside al-Azhar, are filled by state appointees.

Since a number of Muslim countries have created their own centers of Muslim learning, it is a tribute to al-Azhar that it continues to enjoy the greatest prestige internationally, even if its dominance is somewhat eroded. However, both in Egypt and abroad, Muslims with differing views, including those who oppose current regimes in the Muslim world, criticize the Azharis as "official" or "government" *ulama*. It is true that most violent Muslim radicals in Egypt are neither Azhar *ulama* nor Azhar graduates, but the case of Umar Abd al-Rahman, a professor at al-Azhar's Asyut campus who associated with the jihad organization that killed Egyptian president Anwar al-Sadat, as well as well-known cases where Azharis oppose government policies (for example, in the realm of family planning), indicate that Azhari autonomy of opinion and action is far from totally compromised. Today, as in the past, al-Azhar performs an essential role in the accommodation of Muslim and secular institutions and maintains continuity in the face of rapid social and cultural change.

Bibliography

Crecelius, Daniel. "The Ulama and the State in Modern Egypt." Ph.D. diss., Princeton University, 1968.

Eccel, A. Chris. "Alim and Mujahid in Egypt: Orthodoxy Versus Subculture, or Division of Labor?" *The Muslim World* 78 (1988): 189–208.

Eccel, A. Chris. *Egypt, Islam, and Social Change: Al-Azhar in Conflict and Accommodation.* Berlin: K. Schwarz, 1984.

Reid, Donald Malcolm. *Cairo University and the Making of Modern Egypt.* Cambridge, U.K.: Cambridge University Press, 1990.

A. CHRIS ECCEL
UPDATED BY DONALD MALCOLM REID

AZHARI, ISMAʿIL
[1900–1969]

First prime minister of independent Sudan.

Ismaʿil Azhari, a descendant of the nineteenth-century religious leader Ismaʿil al-Wali and a grandson of the mufti of the Sudan, was educated at Gordon College in Khartoum and the American University of Beirut. After teaching mathematics in the Sudan Department of Education (1921–1946), he became a major figure in the Sudanese nationalism that favored union of the Nile Valley with Egypt. It remains unclear whether his support for this union was a sincere conviction or a device to eliminate Britain's control of the Sudan.

As he became increasingly absorbed in politics, Azhari was a founder of the Graduates Congress, whose members consisted of most of the educated elite. To promote his political aims, he founded the Ashigga (Brothers) Party; its principal goal was union of the Nile Valley with Egypt. In order to broaden his political base, he became the first president of the National Unionist Party (NUP), founded in 1952. The NUP dominated the elections for parliament.

Following his election as prime minister, Azhari continued his campaign for union with Egypt until he realized that the overwhelming majority of Sudanese wanted independence without Egypt. He then declared the independence of Sudan on 1 January 1956, creating a split in the NUP that led to the fall of his government. During the subsequent military regime of General Ibrahim Abbud, he held no political office and was active in the opposition to the government.

After the overthrow of the Abbud regime in 1964, Azhari again led the NUP, often in alliance with his former enemies, the Umma Party. He was elected permanent president of the Supreme Council, an office he held until the military revolution of Muhammad Jaʿfar Numeiri.

See also ABBUD, IBRAHIM; NUMEIRI, MUHAM-
MAD JAʿFAR; UMMA PARTY.

ROBERT O. COLLINS

AZIB

*Land ownership in precolonial Morocco in a system
similar to feudalism.*

In precolonial Morocco, *azib* was land property owned
by a sharif, for whom people called *azzaba* would
work. *Azib* land is usually conceded by the *makhzan*
(state) to some *shorfa*. *Azzaba* would work within a relationship of servitude toward the sharif to whom
they owed respect and obedience from father to son.
In case anyone wanted to leave the *azib,* they had to
seek permission from the landowner. The most important *azib* were to be found in the Gharb, such as
the *azib* of Ahl Wazzan.

See also GHARB; MOROCCO; SHARIF; SHORFA.

RAHMA BOURQIA

AZIZ, TARIQ
[1936–]

Iraqi politician.

Tariq Aziz was born Mikhaʾil Yuhanna to a lower-
middle-class Chaldean Christian family in the village of Baʾshiqa, near Mosul. He lost his father at
the age of seven. Joining the Baʿth party in the early
1950s, he became one of its first members in Iraq.
In 1958 he graduated from Baghdad University with
a degree in English and later received a master of
arts degree. From his first days in the party he was
one of its leading intellectuals. During most of the
1950s and 1960s, he edited the clandestine party
magazines *al-Ishtiraki* and *al-Jamahir.* After the Ramadan Revolution of 1963, Aziz supported the centrist faction in the party, under General Ahmad
Hasan al-Bakr.

During the mid-1960s Aziz became very close
to the Baʿthist figure Saddam Hussein. After Hussein became the strongman in Baghdad during the
early 1970s, Aziz served as his close confidant and
mouthpiece. Winning Hussein's trust may have
been easier for a Christian than for a Muslim, since
he posed no threat to the ruler. Under the Baʿthist
regime, Aziz served as chief editor of the party daily
newspaper and as minister of information. Begin-

ning in 1977 he was a member of the two highest
bodies: the Revolutionary Command Council and
the party's Regional (Iraqi) Leadership. Beginning in
1979 he served as a deputy prime minister. From
1983 to 1991 Aziz was Iraq's foreign minister, in which
capacity he managed to greatly improve Iraq's foreign relations during the Iran–Iraq War (1980–1988).

During the Gulf Crisis of 1990 to 1991, however, he did not dare to oppose Hussein, and thus
his contacts with the West were of no use to his
country. He traveled to the Soviet Union to seek Soviet help, which also was not forthcoming. Aziz finally met with U.S. secretary of state James A. Baker
in Geneva in January 1991 to discuss a negotiated
end to the crisis, once again to no avail. After the
Gulf War, he was relieved of his position as foreign
minister but retained his position as a deputy prime
minister. Because of his level of education and relations with the West, Aziz (along with Saʿdun Hammadi) remained an exceptional figure at the top of
the Baʿth hierarchy. It was he who served as the
regime's point man in Iraq's controversial dealings
with United Nations weapons inspectors from 1991
to 1998.

Following the U.S. invasion and occupation of
Iraq in March 2003, Aziz became a wanted man.
He surrendered to U.S. forces and was detained in
April 2003.

See also BAʿTH, AL-; GULF CRISIS (1990–1991);
GULF WAR (1991); HUSSEIN, SADDAM;
IRAN–IRAQ WAR (1980–1988); WAR IN IRAQ
(2003).

Bibliography

Baram, Amatzia. "The Ruling Political Elite in Baʿthi
Iraq, 1968–1986." *International Journal of Middle East
Studies* 21 (1989): 447–493.

Cockburn, Andrew, and Cockburn, Patrick. *Out of the
Ashes: the Resurrection of Saddam Hussein.* New York:
HarperCollins, 1999.

AMATZIA BARAM
UPDATED BY MICHAEL R. FISCHBACH

AZM, SADIQ AL-
[1937–]

Syrian Marxist intellectual and author.

Sadiq al-Azm (al-Adhm) was born in 1937 in Damascus to a family of Syrian notables. He studied at

the American University of Beirut (AUB) before leaving for the United States to study philosophy at Yale University. After finishing his Ph.D. (his dissertation on Immanuel Kant was subsequently published by Oxford University Press), he returned to Lebanon and joined the faculty of AUB. He flirted with several political ideologies in the region before settling on Marxism-Leninism. He was vocal in his criticisms of the United States and Israel, and often clashed with the administration of AUB. After 1967 he achieved great intellectual prominence with the publication of his *Self-Criticism After the Defeat,* in which he called for a thorough investigation of Arab social and political weaknesses and shortcomings. He believed that Arab leaders had deceived their people, and that Arab society's problems must be resolved before the political problems can be addressed. He called for a scientific approach to the Palestinian problem instead of the religious fatalistic outlook that was promoted by Arab leaders. Azm championed Palestinian guerrillas and was ideologically close to the Democratic Front for the Liberation of Palestine. His views got him fired from AUB, where he was quite active in the student movement, but he continued to teach, at the Lebanese University. Azm got into legal problems in 1969 when he published *Critique of Religious Thought;* his secular and materialist criticisms of religious thought stirred an uproar in Lebanon, especially among the Sunni clerical establishment. He was put on trial, but was exonerated. Azm was one of the best-known Arab Marxist intellectuals, and his contributions in journals and newspapers were hotly debated. After the 1982 Israeli invasion of Lebanon, Azm moved back to Damascus, where he joined the philosophy department. He kept a lower profile, and his views became more liberal. In the early 1990s Azm spent a few years as a visiting professor at Princeton University and at the Wilson Center for International Scholars in Washington, D.C. He also published a book in defense of the British novelist Salman Rushdie. He then moved back to Syria where, along with other Syrian intellectuals, he signed petitions in demand of political liberalization.

Bibliography

Ajami, Fouad. *The Arab Predicament.* New York: Cambridge University Press, 1981.

AS'AD ABUKHALIL

AZURI, NAJIB

[?–1916]

Ottoman official and Arab nationalist.

Najib Azuri, a Christian Arab born in Azur in south Lebanon, was an Ottoman official in Jerusalem. Through his Paris-based League of the Arab Homeland, in 1904 he issued manifestos appealing to the Arabs of Iraq and Syria to overthrow the sultan of the Ottoman Empire. In his book, which was published in Paris in 1905 under the title *Le réveil de la nation arabe* (The awakening of the Arab nation), he posited the existence of an Arab nation that was entitled to independence from Ottoman rule. He openly advocated the secession of the Arabs from the Ottoman Empire—this was the first open demand for complete detachment of the Arab provinces.

From the perspective of Azuri, the Ottomans were barbarous oppressors who inflicted much suffering on the Arabs. His accusations against the sultan and the governor of Jerusalem, Kazem Bey, were violent and bitter. Azuri directed his most violent attack against Abdülhamit II, whom he described as a pernicious "beast," running the empire through intrigue and espionage from his "cave" in Istanbul. Azuri also ridiculed Abdülhamit's claim to the caliphate because he did not know Arabic and because, at the age of sixty-five, he still had not performed the pilgrimage (Hajj) to Mecca.

Against this background, Azuri stated that the Arabs, with their national feelings now revived, would form an empire comprising Mesopotamia, Syria, Palestine, and the Arabian Peninsula. Within these boundaries, Azuri wanted to see the emergence of an Arab nation under the protection of a European power—France having a "better right" to rule the Arabs than the rest.

Azuri's preference for France stemmed from his anti-Russian stance and his apparent belief in the right of France to protect the Catholics and their establishments in the Ottoman Empire. In his book, Azuri warned that should Russia control the Turkish Straits and penetrate the Ottoman Empire, the people of the East would never attain their national independence.

Azuri had had close connections with French political figures in Paris and Cairo. Among them were René Pinon, Edmond Fazy, and Eugène Jung. In partnership with Jung, Azuri tried to create the impression, by means of articles and periodicals, that an Arab movement was under way in the Ottoman Empire. Both men, however, were rebuffed by the French, the Italians, and the British. Their ten-year partnership, which lasted roughly from 1905 to 1916, made no progress toward their goal of raising the Arabs against the Ottomans.

Azuri was also equally famous for his anti-Zionist position and for his prediction that the Zionist movement was destined to conflict with Arab nationalism. Beyond his contribution to Arab nationalist thought, one deduces in Azuri's work a European brand of antisemitism that was typical of other writings by Arab nationalists in this period. It is probable that Azuri had developed his antisemitic sentiments during the Dreyfus affair, at which time he was a student in Paris.

See also ABDÜLHAMIT II; DREYFUS AFFAIR.

MUHAMMAD MUSLIH

AZZAM, ABD AL-RAHMAN AL-
[1893–1976]

First secretary-general of the Arab League.

Abd al-Rahman al-Azzam started his political life as an anti-British Egyptian nationalist. Although he was a Wafdist in the first phase of his political life, he became associated with King Farouk and the anti-Wafdist prime minister Ali Mahir from the mid-1930s on. He was pan-Arabist and pan-Islamist at the same time. When Italy conquered Libya, then an Ottoman province in 1911, Azzam volunteered against the Italian invaders. During World War I, he left Egypt and fought alongside Sanusi forces in Cyrenaica (east Libya today) and the Egyptian western desert.

From 1934 on, Azzam called for the formation of an Arab bloc since, according to him, there was no place in the present age for small countries with limited resources. He also believed closer Arab ties would bring Egypt political, economic, and strategic advantages.

Azzam was appointed by the council of the League of Arab States in 1945 when the pact of the league was signed by member countries. He served as secretary-general until 1952, when he was replaced by Abd al-Khaliq Hassuna. Before becoming the league's secretary-general, Azzam served in a number of diplomatic positions and carried numerous diplomatic missions on behalf of Egypt to many Arab capitals.

See also FAROUK; LEAGUE OF ARAB STATES; PAN-ARABISM.

Bibliography

Gomaa, Ahmed. *The Foundation of the League of Arab States: Wartime Diplomacy and Inter-Arab Politics, 1941 to 1945.* London: Longman, 1977.

Macdonald, Robert. *The League of Arab States: A Study in the Dynamics of Regional Organization.* Princeton, NJ: Princeton University Press, 1965.

MAHMOUD HADDAD

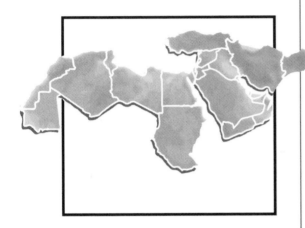

B

BAʿALBAK

City in Lebanon famous for its archaeological remains.

Located in the Biqa Valley some 53 miles (85 km) from Beirut, Baʿalbak (or Baʿalbek), is the foremost tourist site in Lebanon. Perhaps a center of the cult of the great Semitic god Baal, it owes its fame today to its Roman temples, which date to the late second century and the beginning of the third century. The Temple of Bacchus is the best-preserved Roman temple of its size in the world.

Prior to the Lebanese civil war (1975–1990), Baʿalbak was known for its annual international festivals, which offered a typical Lebanese blending of Eastern and Western cultures. The present city, the capital of one of the least Westernized districts of Lebanon, had an estimated 29,400 inhabitants in 2002, with a strong Shiʿite majority and a Christian minority. The political significance of the city was heightened in 1982–1983, when it became the base for a contingent of revolutionary guards sent by the Iranian regime to help build, organize, and train the militant group Islamic AMAL, which provided the nucleus for the better-known Hizbullah. In the early 1990s, Hizbullah's headquarters were in Baʿalbak.

See also AMAL; BIQA VALLEY; HIZBULLAH; REVOLUTIONARY GUARDS.

Bibliography

Alouf, Michel. *A History of Baʿalbek.* Beirut: Impr. des Belles-Lettres, 1905.

Ragette, Friedrich. *Baalbek.* Park Ridge, NJ: Noyes Press, 1980.

GUILAIN P. DENOEUX

BAʿALBAKKI, LAYLA
[1936–]

Lebanese novelist, short-story writer, and journalist.

Born to a Shiʿite family of modest means in south Lebanon, Layla Baʿalbakki pursued her postsecondary studies intermittently while working as a secretary at the Lebanese parliament. While still in her twenties she began publishing articles and short stories that were defiant in tone and focused on sensitive topics. Baʿalbakki's work sparked controversy by questioning the status quo, particularly gender roles and relations, and by discussing the body and sexuality in a frank and open manner. She published her first novel, *Ana Ahya* (I live), in 1958, when she was just twenty-two. It offered a bleak and uncompromising view of the world from the perspective of a rebellious, ultimately self-destructive young Arab woman. As a journalist and public speaker in the late 1950s, Baʿalbakki was a passionate advocate of self-criticism, social reform, equality between men and women, and freedom of expression. In 1960 she received a one-year scholarship to study in France. She returned to Lebanon in 1961, and in 1964 published a book of short stories entitled *Safinat hanan ila al-qamar* (A spaceship of tenderness to the moon). The title story of this collection is set in a young married couple's bedroom one morning. The husband is naked and the discussion is implicitly erotic. A line in the story, "he placed his hand on her stomach," was deemed obscene, and Baʿalbakki had to go to court to face charges that her writings were provocative and offensive to public morality. She won her case and in the following year went on to publish another novel, *Al-alihah al-mamsukha* (The monstrous gods), in which she broached the topic of virginity and hypocrisy surrounding the ideal of female purity in Arab society. Baʿalbakki married and raised a family in Lebanon during the war years (1975–1990). She has not published any novels or short stories since the 1960s.

See also LITERATURE: ARABIC.

Bibliography

Accad, Evelyne. "Rebellion, Maturity, and the Social Context: Arab Women's Special Contribution to Literature." In *Arab Women: Old Boundaries, New Frontiers,* edited by Judith Tucker. Bloomington: Indiana University Press, 1993.

Zeidan, Joseph. *Arab Women Novelists: The Formative Years and Beyond.* Albany: State University of New York Press, 1995.

LAURIE KING-IRANI

BAB, AL-

[1819–1850]

Charismatic leader of an Iranian religious movement that began in 1844.

Sayyid Ali Mohammad Shirazi was born on 20 October 1819 in Shiraz (southwestern Iran). His father, a clothier, had married into a clan of long-distance merchants. His family had adopted the Shaykhi school of Shiʿism, as had his elementary teacher, Shaykh Abid. Sayyid Ali Mohammad had an uneven education and rebelled against dry scholasticism and the minutiae of Arabic grammar. He engaged in the family trade, spending 1835 to 1840 in the Iranian port city of Bushehr on import–export affairs. But his real interests were religious devotions and Shaykhi-style dreams and visions of the imams (the holy figures of Shiʿism). He settled his accounts and left for the shrine cities of Iraq in 1841, in part to meet Sayyid Kazim Rashti, leader of the esoteric and millenarian Shaykhi school of Shiʿism. He spent eleven months there, but appears to have spent little time in seminary study, concentrating on devotions at the shrines. His family put pressure on him to return to Shiraz, which he did in 1842, where they married him off to Khadija Khanom and set him up once again in business. He continued to think and write about esoteric religious subjects and began to have a following as a charismatic figure.

When Rashti died in Karbala, in early 1844, a section of the Shaykhis, convinced that the appearance of the Muslim Mahdi (messiah) was near, set off in search of him. One of these, Molla Hosayn Bushru'i, stopped in Shiraz on his way to Kirman and accidentally met Sayyid Ali Mohammad, who put forward a charismatic claim. When Molla Hosayn became his disciple on 22 May 1844, followed by other Shaykhi seminarians in his circle, he was recognized as *al-Bab,* "the Gate"—an ambiguous term implying divine inspiration. Belief in his spiritual leadership spread rapidly among urban craftspeople and merchants, as well as some peasants.

The Bab went on pilgrimage later in 1844 to proclaim his mission to the sharif of Mecca but proved unable to get his attention. In the summer of 1845, he returned to Shiraz, but the municipal authorities, alarmed by his claims, put him under house arrest. In 1846 and 1847 he resided in Isfahan, gaining the protection of the Qajar governor there, who attempted to arrange an interview with the shah for him. The chief minister, however, thwarted this meeting, and ordered the Bab to be imprisoned in Maku, in Azerbaijan. There the Bab openly claimed to be the Mahdi and a manifestation of God and wrote his book of laws, the Bayan, intended to supplant the Qur'an. In July 1848, he was interrogated by a group of clerics and pronounced a heretic. He spent the last two years of his life imprisoned in the even more remote fort of Chihriq.

In 1849 and 1850, several outbreaks of violence occurred between Shi'ites and Babis, and the state began to feel the need to act decisively. On 8 July 1850, the government ordered the Bab executed in Tabriz. He was taken during a conversation with a disciple, then suspended against a wall with ropes. The first firing squad missed him, severing his ropes and allowing him to disappear, which many in the crowd took as a divine sign. He was found completing his words to the disciple. Another firing squad had to be commissioned to complete the execution.

The religion he founded was brutally persecuted in Iran and driven underground. From the late 1860s, most Babis became Baha'i, which remains Iran's largest non-Muslim religious community.

See also ARABIC; BAHA'I FAITH; QUR'AN; SHAYKHI; SHI'ISM.

Bibliography

Amanat, Abbas. *Resurrection and Renewal: The Making of the Babi Movement in Iran, 1844–1850.* Ithaca, NY: Cornell University Press, 1989.

JUAN R. I. COLE

BAB AL-MANDAB

The narrow waterway separating Asia and Africa.

Because of its place on the sea-lanes between Europe and the Indian Ocean and points east, the Bab al-Mandab straits have been assigned considerable strategic importance over the centuries, particularly with the building of the Suez Canal, the flowering of the British Empire, and the more recent dependence of Europe on oil from the Persian/Arabian Gulf. The two Yemens meet on the Asian side of the strait, and Ethiopia and Djibouti meet on the African side. This geography helps explain Yemeni interest in the politics of the Horn of Africa.

See also PERSIAN (ARABIAN) GULF; SUEZ CANAL.

ROBERT D. BURROWES

BABAN FAMILY

Prominent Iraqi family.

The oldest known ancestor of the Baban family is Mufti Ahmad, who was granted a huge lot of land by the Ottoman authorities in the north of Iraq. His son Sulayman Baba established himself as a powerful ruler and, in 1670, became the governor of the *sanjak* (an administrative unit smaller than a governorate) of Baban, from which the family derived its name. The most well-known ancestor of the family is Sulayman Pasha al-Kabir, who was called Abu Layla.

MAMOON A. ZAKI

BABIS

A millenarian religious movement developing out of Iranian Shi'ite Islam, begun by the Bab, Sayyid Ali Mohammad Shirazi, in 1844.

By 1849 there may have been 100,000 Babis in Iran and Iraq. The movement spread chiefly to cities, towns, and large villages, attracting the middle and lower-middle classes. Middle-ranking clerics, seminary students, urban artisans, laborers, and small landowners appear to have been its principal constituents, along with some influential merchants and retailers. The movement spread throughout Persia (Iran), with an especially strong showing in Khorasan to the northeast, as well as in Mazandaran, Fars, and Iraqi Ajam.

Between the beginning of the Bab's mission in 1844 and his execution in 1850, most Babis probably knew relatively little about his doctrines, and were attracted to him for charismatic and millenarian reasons. The Bab's works, many in Arabic, are abstruse and inaccessible except to the highly literate among his followers. The main emphases of mature Babi belief were that the Bab was the returned Mahdi (messiah), the hidden Twelfth Imam, and that the judgment day had symbolically occurred; that the Bab had the authority to reveal a new divine law; that he and his disciples possessed esoteric knowledge; that martyrdom was noble and that holy war could be declared by the Bab; and that a future messianic figure, "He whom God shall make manifest," would appear. The Bab allowed the taking of interest on loans and was favorable toward middle-class property; slightly improved the position of women by limiting polygamy; and admired what he had heard of Western science.

The rise of this new religion was attended by violence, as it was rejected by the Shiʿite clerics and by the state. The Babi movement often became implicated in the quarter-fighting that was typical of Qajar cities. A major clash took place in Mazandaran in 1848 and 1849, at the shrine of Shaykh Tabarsi, where several hundred Babis, including prominent disciples of the Bab, like Molla Hosayn, having raised the black banner of the Mahdi, were besieged by government troops and finally defeated, and killed or captured. In some small cities Babi quarters developed, with their own clerics and notables, and came into conflict with conservative neighborhoods. The Babis defended their quarters, withstanding sieges, until finally government troops intervened to crush them (Zanjan, 1850 and 1851, and Nayriz, 1850–1853).

In 1850, the Bab was executed in Tabriz; in 1852, a faction of about seventy notable Babis in Tehran plotted to assassinate the monarch, Naser al-Din Shah, in revenge for his execution of the Bab. The attempt failed, and in response the Qajar state ordered a nationwide pogrom against the Babis. By the middle 1850s perhaps five thousand had been killed, and most of the rest had gone underground.

Most Babis recognized Mirza Yahya Sobh-i Azal (1830–1912) as the successor to the Bab. After the failed attempt on the shah, he followed his elder half-brother, Hosayn Ali Bahaʾullah, into exile in Baghdad in 1853. From 1853 to 1864 he faced a number of regional challenges to his authority, but appears to have retained at least some loyalty among the furtive and much reduced Babi community. In the late 1860s, however, Bahaʾullah asserted that he was the messianic figure foretold by the Bab, and in the space of a decade most Babis had gone over to him, becoming Bahaʾi. The Babis who remained loyal to Azal were called Azalis, and by 1900 they numbered probably only two thousand to four thousand.

The small Babi community remained determinedly anti-Qajar and was open to Western ideas and culture. It produced radical intellectuals, such

as Aqa Khan Kermani and Shaykh Ahmad Ruhi (both became atheists and were executed in 1896 in connection with Naser al-Din Shah's assassination); and Yahya Dawlatabadi, Mirza Jahangir Khan, Malik al-Mutakallimin, and Sayyid Jamal al-Din Isfahani (all activists on the constitutionalist side in Iran's Constitutional Revolution that began in 1905). In the twentieth century, the Babi community shrank to negligible size and influence.

See also BAB, AL-; BAHAʾI FAITH; CONSTITUTIONAL REVOLUTION; NASER AL-DIN SHAH; QAJAR DYNASTY.

Bibliography

Amanat, Abbas. *Resurrection and Renewal: The Making of the Babi Movement in Iran, 1844–1850.* Ithaca, NY: Cornell University Press, 1989.

JUAN R. I. COLE

BACCOUCHE, HEDI
[1930–]

Prime minister of Tunisia, 1987–1989.

Hedi Baccouche holds a degree in political science from the Sorbonne in Paris. He was leader of the nationalist Neo-Destour Party, then party director of the Destourian Socialist Party during the 1980s, and a member of the political bureau of its successor after Zayn al-Abdine Ben Ali came to power. As ambassador, he served in Berne (1981), the Vatican (1981), and Algiers (1982).

Baccouche was chosen as prime minister by President Zayn al-Abidine Ben Ali in November 1987, following the latter's overthrow of thirty-year president of Tunisia Habib Bourguiba; he was charged with pursuing the platform of reforms promised by Ben Ali upon his accession to office. These included the lifting of restrictions on press freedoms, the introduction of political pluralism, and reforms of the judicial system. Shortly after taking office, Baccouche met with leaders from the Communist and Social Democratic parties and permitted the media to report the activities of these opposition parties. Moves toward a multiparty system continued through 1988 and included a loosening of restrictions on even the Islamic Tendency Movement (MTI); in May of that year, the head of the MTI, Rached Ghannouchi, was pardoned by the

Ben Ali government. It remained clear, however, that the dominant political institution was to remain the ruling party, the Destourian Socialist party, renamed the Constitutional Democratic Rally in 1987.

From the start of his tenure in office, Baccouche and his cabinet faced severe economic problems, including a mounting payments deficit, a faltering tourist industry, and high unemployment; little progress was made toward solving these problems. In September 1989, Baccouche was replaced by Dr. Hamed Karoui. According to rumors, Baccouche was too cautious for Ben Ali's tastes in pursuing political and economic reforms, since he reportedly disagreed with austerity measures proposed by other cabinet members.

During the late 1990s, Baccouche served as President Ben Ali's special envoy to Algeria on occasion, since as former ambassador to Algiers he kept close contact with the neighboring country.

See also BEN ALI, ZAYN AL-ABIDINE; BOURGUIBA, HABIB; GHANNOUCHI, RACHED.

Bibliography

Murphy, Emma C. *Economic and Political Change in Tunisia: From Bourguiba to Ben Ali.* New York: Macmillan Press; New York: St. Martin's Press in association with University of Durham, 1999.

MATTHEW S. GORDON
UPDATED BY ANA TORRES-GARCIA

BADRAN, MUDAR
[1934–]

Prime minister of Jordan 1976–1979, 1980–1984, and December 1989–June 1991.

Before becoming prime minister of Jordan in 1976, Mudar Badran had risen through the ranks as a public security (intelligence) officer. He was asked to form a government at a time when security was a high priority in the kingdom. He was known not to be on friendly terms with Syria, even supporting the Muslim Brotherhood rebellion in Syria in 1978 and 1979, and may have been the target of a Syrian-backed assassination attempt. During the 1980s, he supported the development of a close relationship with Iraq. During the Iran–Iraq War of 1980–1988,

Iraq was given access to the port of Aqaba, providing it with a vital supply line and providing Jordan with the economic benefits that ensued. In December 1989, Badran headed the cabinet formed after the first general elections to be held in Jordan in twenty-two years.

See also AQABA; IRAN–IRAQ WAR (1980–1988); MUSLIM BROTHERHOOD.

Bibliography

Gubser, Peter. *Jordan: Crossroads of Middle Eastern Events.* Boulder, CO: Westview Press, 1983.

JENAB TUTUNJI

BADR, LIANA
[1950–]

Acclaimed Palestinian author.

Born in Jerusalem, educated in Jericho, Amman, and Beirut, Liana Badr worked for a magazine and for refugee organizations in Jordan and Lebanon. Her first novel, *A Compass for the Sunflower* (1979), published in Beirut, was acclaimed for its lyrical style and broke the dominance of male characters in Palestinian writing. Upon the Israeli invasion of 1982, she fled to Damascus, marrying activist Yasir Abd Rabbo, future negotiator of the Oslo Accords, and moving with him to Tunis and Amman. During that time she published two novels (*The Eye of the Mirror* [1991] and *Stars of Jericho* [1993]), four collections of short stories and novellas (*Stories of Love and Pursuit* [1983], *Balcony over the Fakahani* [1983], *I Want the Day* [1991], and *Golden Hell* [1993]) and five children's books. Returning to Palestine in 1994, she published an interview-memoir (*Fadwa Tuqan* [1996]) and an anthology of poetry, directed three documentaries (*Fadwa, A Tale of a Palestinian Poetess* [1999], *Zaytunat* [2000], and *Green Bird* [2002]), and wrote the script for another film (*Rana's Wedding* [2002]). Badr's work focuses on Palestinians, particularly women, in war, in exile, and under military rule. She heads the Cinema and Audiovisual Department at the Palestinian Authority's Ministry of Culture, and is a founding editor of the ministry's periodical, *Dafatir Thaqafiyya*.

See also GENDER: GENDER AND EDUCATION; LITERATURE: ARABIC.

Bibliography

Jayyusi, Salma Khadra. *Anthology of Modern Palestinian Literature.* New York: Columbia University Press, 1992.

GEORGE R. WILKES

BADR, MUHAMMAD AL-
[1926–1978]

Ruler and 111th Zaydi imam of Yemen, 1962.

Muhammad al-Badr (also called Imam al-Badr) was the son of Imam Ahmad ibn Yahya Hamid al-Din, who ruled Yemen following his election to the imamate on 13 March 1948. In October 1961, Muhammad al-Badr was designated by his father as successor despite earlier disagreements. He became the ruler and the 111th imam after his father's death on 9 September 1962. Imam al-Badr was the last Zaydi imam of the Rassid dynasty to hold the title. This dynasty of Shiʿite Muslims was established in northern Yemen (Sanʿa) in the final decade of the ninth century. The Zaydi imams traced their origin to Ali ibn Abi Talib, the prophet Muhammad's cousin and fourth caliph. They base their absolute rule on their claim of descent from the Prophet and on the allegiance given them by individual tribes—who, at least in Yemen, were the mainstay of the imamate.

Imam al-Badr was educated in Egypt and in the 1950s presented himself as interested in nationalism and liberal reform. He admired Gamal Abdel Nasser during his presidency of Egypt; he also supported the nonalignment movement and advocated a neutral role for Yemen in world affairs. In the 1950s, al-Badr traveled to the Soviet Union and Eastern Europe and tried to establish friendly relations with the communist world. In Yemen, he consolidated tribal support for himself and supported the South Yemen (Aden) political struggle for independence from Britain.

Upon assuming power, Imam al-Badr proclaimed social and economic reform in Yemen. He announced the establishment of a forty-member advisory council, of which half would be elected, and he appointed himself prime minister. Egyptian, Soviet, and Chinese leaders believed he was implementing a policy of socialism and sent him their best wishes.

Nevertheless, dissatisfaction with al-Badr emerged immediately among the military and within the tribes seeking revenge for the execution of some of their leaders by al-Badr's father, Imam Ahmad. Within a week, a group of army officers formed the Free Officers movement and sought Egypt's support for a coup. Egypt encouraged them to move against al-Badr quickly, since he had not yet consolidated his power; the British were preoccupied with the problems of federating South Yemen, and the Saudi ruling family had its internal problems. Within a month, a republic was declared by General Abdullah al-Sallal.

On 27 September 1962, Radio Sanʿa announced that a coup was in progress; it also announced, erroneously, that al-Badr had been killed. The Yemen Civil War was under way; Imam al-Badr was overthrown and Egyptian forces entered Yemen in large numbers to support the new regime. Saudi Arabia, where Imam al-Badr had fled, and Jordan supported the royal forces. The civil war continued until 1970.

In 1968, however, a split developed within the royalist ranks that resulted in al-Badr relinquishing the imamate in favor of the new Imamate Council, headed by Muhammad ibn Husayn. Al-Badr died in 1978.

See also AHMAD IBN YAHYA HAMID AL-DIN; FREE OFFICERS, YEMEN; NASSER, GAMAL ABDEL; NATIONALISM; SALLAL, ABDULLAH AL-; YEMEN; YEMEN CIVIL WAR; ZAYDISM.

Bibliography

Burrowes, Robert D. *The Yemen Arab Republic: The Politics of Development, 1962–1986.* Boulder, CO: Westview Press, 1987.

Nyrop, Richard F. *The Yemens: Country Studies,* 2d edition. Washington, DC: American University, Foreign Area Studies; distributed by U.S. Government Printing Office, 1986.

Wenner, Manfred. *The Yemen Arab Republic: Development and Change in an Ancient Land.* Boulder, CO: Westview Press, 1991.

EMILE A. NAKHLEH

BAGHDAD

The largest city and capital of Iraq.

Al-Kazimayn Mosque was constructed in Baghdad during the Abbasid caliphate, which founded the city in the eighth century to serve as its administrative capital. For centuries, Baghdad was also a major commercial and cultural center of Islam, until invaders nearly destroyed it in the mid-thirteenth century and again 150 years later. © THE ART ARCHIVE. REPRODUCED BY PERMISSION.

Baghdad is the largest city in Iraq and is situated on both sides of the Tigris River at a point 40 miles from the Euphrates River. The city is approximately 300 miles from the northern, southern, and western borders of the country. It has a temperature range of 29°F (-1.6°C) to 31°F (-0.5°C) in the winter and 114°F (45.5°C) to 121°F (49°C) in the summer. The name and the site of Baghdad are pre-Islamic. The etymology of the name is not clear. It is not of Arabic origin; it may be a combination of two Persian words, *bad* and *dad,* which together mean gift of God. Others suggest that the name existed before the time of Hammurabi as the name *Bagh-*

dadu. Records of Baghdad's early history before Islam are sketchy. There are some indications that in the late period of the Sassanids and at the time of the Islamic conquest of Iraq, Baghdad was a small village next to major cities such as Ctesiphone of Sassanide.

Early History

Baghdad was founded on the west bank of the Tigris by al-Mansur, the second caliph of the Abbasid Empire, in 762 C.E. It was to be the administrative capital of the new empire. The construction of Baghdad was completed in 766 C.E. It cost more than 883,000 dirhams to build, and employed more that 100,000 architects, craftsmen, and workers drawn from all over the Muslim world. It was built in a circular form, in the Parthian Sassanid tradition. It had three concentric walls with four gates opening toward Basra, Syria, Kufah, and Khorasan. It was surrounded by a deep moat and had four highways radiating out from the four gates. Unlike the Greek, Roman, and Sassanid emperors, who named cities after themselves, al-Mansur chose the name Dar al-Salam, abode of peace, a name alluding to paradise. Furthermore, he did not object to the use of the ancient city name of Baghdad. The city later gained many more appellations, including al-Mudawara, meaning round city, because of its circular form, and al-Zawarh, meaning the winding city, because of its location on the winding banks of the Tigris.

The site for the city was chosen because of its strategic location in the middle of Mesopotamia. It was a meeting place for caravan routes on the road to Khorasan. It had a system of canals that provided water for cultivation and could be used as ramparts for the city. It also had an adequate water supply for the people of the city and provided an environment more or less free of malaria. The city was first built as an administrative center, but it grew into a veritable cosmopolis of the medieval world. It became a conglomerate of districts on both banks of the Tigris that gained fame and importance socially, economically, and culturally. Baghdad reached its Golden Age during the fourth and sixth reigns of Harun al-Rashid (786–809 C.E.) and his son al-Ma'mun (813–833 C.E.). In the ninth century, Baghdad, with a population of 300,000 to 500,000, was larger than any other Middle East city except Istanbul. The population included Arabs and non-Arabs, Muslims and non-Muslims who had come to Baghdad to work, to trade, and to study. Baghdad became an international trade center for textiles, leather, paper, and other goods from areas that ranged from the Baltic to China. Baghdad also became a center for scientific and intellectual achievements. The famous Bayt al-Hikma Academy, established in 830 C.E., had facilities for the translation of scientific and philosophical works from Greek, Aramaic, and Persian into Arabic.

Baghdad lost its splendor with the decline of the Abbassid Caliphate due to religious, ethnic, and re-

gional strife. In 1258 C.E. Hülegü Khan, the grandson of Chinggiz Khan (Jengis Khan), sacked Baghdad. He burned the schools and the libraries, destroyed the mosques and the palaces, and ruined the elaborate system of canals that made it possible to support agricultural production for a large population. The fall of Baghdad at the hands of Hülegü, and the subsequent destruction of Baghdad by Timur Lenk (Tamarlane) in 1401, were turning points in the history of the city, and the city never recovered. Successive Persian and Turkish dynasties controlled Baghdad. It was captured by Shah Isma'il of Persia in 1501 and later by the Ottomans under Süleiman the Magnificent in 1556. The city remained under Ottoman rule until the disintegration of the Ottoman Empire in 1918, except for a short period of Persian Safavid control in the seventeenth century (1623–1638). During the Ottoman's period, Baghdad lost its importance as a center for trade and learning. The heart of Islam had shifted to Istanbul, and Baghdad sank to the level of a decaying provincial town with doubtful authority, even over the neighboring country districts. Furthermore, a succession of plagues, famines, floods, and other disasters besieged Baghdad, destroying thousands of houses and killing thousands of people. The population was reduced, according to one report in the sixteenth century, to less than 50,000 people.

In the nineteenth century, Baghdad began to receive some attention from both the Ottoman rulers and Western powers. Two Ottoman governors, Da'ud Paşa (1816–1832) and Midhat Paşa (1869–1872), made some serious attempts to improve the conditions of the city. Da'ud tried to control the tribes and to restore order and security. He cleaned up the irrigation canals, established textile and arms factories, and encouraged local industries. He built three large mosques and founded *madrasas* (schools). He organized an army of 20,000 soldiers and had them trained by a French officer. Midhat Pasha laid telegraph lines, built a horse tramway to Kasimayn, and built several schools. He introduced a Turkish steamboat line between Baghdad and Basra. Western powers, particularly Britain, showed some interest in Baghdad for commercial reasons and as a land route to India. Britain established a consulate in Baghdad in 1802, and France followed soon after. Western countries introduced steam navigation on the Tigris in 1836 and telegraph lines in 1860s.

Twentieth Century

Late in the nineteenth century, Baghdad was chosen to be the terminal railroad station for the line that ran between Istanbul and Baghdad (later extended to Basra). In 1917 Baghdad was occupied by the British. In 1921 Baghdad became the capital of the new country of Iraq. Since 1921, Baghdad has grown by leaps and bounds both in size and in population. At the beginning of the twentieth century, Baghdad covered an area of less than 4 square miles that was surrounded by dikes in several directions to protect it from the unpredictable flooding of the Tigris. These dikes limited Baghdad's outward expansion, but thanks to flood-control projects in the 1950s, Baghdad's area increased from less than 30 square miles in 1950 to 312 square miles in 1965, and from 375 square miles in 1977 to more than 780 square miles in 1990. Modern Baghdad incorporates many of the surrounding areas and numerous suburbs.

The city's population increased from 200,000 in 1921 to 515,000, in 1947 and from 1,490,000 in 1965 to about five million in 1990. The huge increase was due in part to natural increases in population, but also to the large number of immigrants, particularly those from southern Iraq who had been driven north by the desperate economic conditions present in the south and by the lure of better employment opportunities. Baghdad was the headquarters of most government agencies, the center for most industrial establishments and economic activities, and the home to major educational facilities. It was also a center for health and social services, as well as a major site for recreational activities. The Iran–Iraq War (1980–1982) and the Gulf War of 1991 contributed to Baghdad's population as thousands of people fled the war zone searching for safety. Many of the early southern immigrants lived in temporary *sharaif* (mud houses) on the northern edge of the city.

In the early 1960s the regime of Abd al-Karim Qasim built numerous housing projects to improve the living conditions of these immigrants. Also, the area was renamed al-Thawra (Revolution) City, commemorating the revolution of 1958. This, in turn, attracted more immigrants. By the early twenty-first century, the city was home to more than one-third of Baghdad's population and was informally known as Saddam City.

Despite ongoing violence and shortages of many essential supplies since Baghdad was occupied by American military forces on 9 April 2003, the marketplace in Saddam City—a section of Baghdad renamed by its residents Sadr City, after a leading Shi'ite cleric assassinated in 1999—was bustling just eighteen days later, when this photograph was taken. © ANTOINE GYORI/FRANCE/REPORTAGE/CORBIS. REPRODUCED BY PERMISSION.

In 1980 the Iraqi government spent more than $7 billion to give Baghdad a facelift in preparation for hosting the Non-Aligned conference in 1982. The conference did not convene in Baghdad due to the Iran–Iraq War. The government constructed new freeways and wider streets across the city, opened several five-star hotels and a plethora of modern shopping centers and high rises, and built several new bridges. The government adorned the city with historical and modern monuments, as well as pictures and posters of Iraqi president Saddam Hussein. Names of some of the districts were changed to commemorate famous people and places in Islamic Arabic history and the contemporary Arab world; examples are Khalid ibn al-Walid, Tariq Ibn Ziyad, and Palestine.

Modern Baghdad, as in the past, is divided into two parts by the Tigris River; the eastern part is called al-Risafa and the western part is called al-Karkh. Al-Risafa is more historic and contains many of the historical monuments, popular markets, and al-Thawra City. Al-Karkh is more modern, with wealthy districts such as al-Mansur and al-Yarmuk, modern hotels, the international airport, government buildings, and many palaces housing high-ranking government officials.

Baghdad is the burial place of several important religious people, among them the seventh and ninth Shi'ite Imam, in the Kasimayn district; Abd al-Qadir al-Jilani, the great Muslim Sunni Sufi, in the Bab al-Shaykh district; Abu Hanifa, the founder of the Hanafi School of Law in the Sunni tradition, in the Asamiyad district. It also is the site of the tomb of the famous Sufi Ma'ruf al-Karkhi, who died in 815 C.E. Baghdad and its environs are home to a number of Jewish shrines, notably the reputed tomb of Joshua and those of Ezra and Ezekiel. Baghdad has several other historical sites, including the Arch of Ctesiphon, the Mustassriya School, the Abbasid Palace, and the Jami al-Khulafa and Mirjan mosques.

In the 1990s, and until it fell to the invading U.S. military forces on 9 April 2003, Baghdad suffered like the rest of the country from the sanctions imposed on it by the United Nations in the aftermath of Iraq's invasion of Kuwait and the Gulf War. The United States and the Allied Forces bombed Iraq, including Baghdad, relentlessly for forty-three days in the aftermath of Iraq's invasion of Kuwait in 1991. The bombing, in the words of a United Nations report, pushed Iraq into a preindustrial age. The Iraqi government repaired and restored some of the destroyed and damaged facilities, but it was unable to restore them to prewar levels due to the sanctions that limited Iraq's ability to sell its oil and import spare parts. Electricity, clean water, medicine, and food were in short supply, and many children, women, and elderly people died. United Nations documents reported that more than one million Iraqis (including Baghdadis) died as a result of the sanctions.

On 9 April 2003 Baghdad surrendered to the U.S. armed forces, and Iraq was occupied. During the invasion, Baghdad was relentlessly attacked by the U.S. forces, which bombed Baghdad on a daily basis for three weeks, destroying many major government buildings with one notable exception, the ministry of oil. Extensive looting and some burning took place in the aftermath of the fall of Baghdad, which lasted for more than a week. The looting took place in front of the occupying American forces, which did not intervene until later. Baghdad suffered from shortages in electricity, clean water, and other essential supplies. The city also lacked security and became a major center for the resis-

tance against the occupying U.S. forces. The residents of al-Thawra or Saddam City decided to change the name of their city to Sadr City to commemorate Ayatullah Sadiq al-Sadr, a leading Shi'ite cleric who was killed in southern Iraq presumably by government assassins in January of 1999.

See also DA'UD PASHA; GULF WAR (1991); HUSSEIN, SADDAM; IRAQ; IRAN–IRAQ WAR (1980–1988); MIDHAT PAŞA; WAR IN IRAQ (2003).

Bibliography

Ellis, William. "The New Face of Baghdad." *National Geographic* 167, no. 1 (1985): 80–109.

Hitti, Philip K. *Capital Cities of Arab Islam.* Minneapolis: University of Minnesota Press, 1973.

Mackey, Sandra. *The Reckoning: Iraq and the Legacy of Saddam Hussein.* New York: W. W. Norton, 2002.

Marr, Phebe. *The Modern History of Iraq,* 2d edition. Boulder, CO: Westview Press, 1985.

AYAD AL-QAZZAZ

BAGHDADI, ABD AL-LATIF AL-
[1917–]

Egyptian officer, politician, and cabinet minister.

A graduate of Egypt's military academy, Abd al-Latif al-Baghdadi joined the Free Officers, who plotted the 1952 revolution, and later the Revolutionary Command Council. He was the inspector general for the liberation rally in 1953 and defense minister under Muhammad Naguib in 1953 and 1954.

When Gamal Abdel Nasser took power of Egypt in 1956, Baghdadi transferred to municipal affairs and later became minister of planning. He became the first president of the National Assembly in 1957 and, after the formation of the United Arab Republic in 1958, he became vice president for economic affairs and minister of planning. After Syria seceded in 1961 Baghdadi became minister of finance and economic planning. In September 1962 Baghdadi became one of Egypt's five vice presidents and resumed the chair of the assembly.

Removed in 1964 from the vice presidency, Baghdadi also left the Assembly and has not been active in politics since then. Poor health and differences with Nasser over Yemen war policy and

Arab Socialism have been offered as reasons for his mysterious early retirement, but the deciding factor was probably the rise of his rival, General Abd al-Hakim Amir, to Egypt's second highest political post in March 1964. Baghdadi criticized Egypt's friendship treaty with the Soviet Union in 1971 and its peace treaty with Israel in 1979. His memoirs, *Mudhakkirat Abd al-Latif al-Baghdadi* (Memoirs of Abd al-Latif al-Baghdadi), were published in 1977.

See also AMIR, ABD AL-HAKIM; FREE OFFICERS, EGYPT; REVOLUTIONARY COMMAND COUNCIL (EGYPT).

ARTHUR GOLDSCHMIDT
UPDATED BY DONALD MALCOLM REID

BAGHDAD PACT (1955)

Anti-Soviet security pact sponsored by Britain and the United States.

The Baghdad Pact formally came into existence in 1955; it was an exemplary Cold War agreement reflecting the priority the Eisenhower administration gave to containment of the Soviet Union through collective security agreements. The member states—Turkey, Iraq, Iran, Pakistan, and Britain—formed a bulwark of the "northern tier" states against the Soviet Union. The pact's headquarters were in Baghdad.

The pact's most forceful Middle Eastern proponent, Nuri al-Saʿid of Iraq, championed the agreement because it tied Iraq more closely to the West and provided the Iraqi leader with potential leverage against his chief rival, Egypt's President Gamal Abdel Nasser. Nasser viewed the Baghdad Pact, with its British membership, as another manifestation of Western imperialism, and he used all the means at his disposal to persuade other Arab states not to join. In this he was successful—Lebanon, Syria, and Jordan refused offers of membership.

The United States, although heavily involved in the various security guarantees, did not become an official member. Nonetheless, the security agreement fit U.S. strategic interests in the region. Through Turkey, the Middle East was linked to NATO, and through Pakistan, to the Southeast Asia Treaty Organization (SEATO). U.S. influence continued through guarantees of military aid and diplomatic support.

The Iraqi revolution in July 1958 led to the deaths of the monarch and Nuri al-Saʿid. Iraq withdrew from the Baghdad Pact in 1959 and denounced it as a vestige of Western imperialism. The group was then renamed the Central Treaty Organization (CENTO).

See also NASSER, GAMAL ABDEL.

Bibliography

Jankowski, James. *Nasser's Egypt, Arab Nationalism, and the United Arab Republic.* Boulder, CO: Lynne Rienner Publishers, 2002.

Spiegel, Steven L. *The Other Arab-Israeli Conflict: Making America's Middle East Policy, from Truman to Reagan.* Chicago: University of Chicago Press, 1985.

ZACHARY KARABELL
UPDATED BY WILLIAM L. CLEVELAND

BAGHDAD SUMMIT (1978)

Arab summit held after the Camp David Accords.

Egypt's President Anwar al-Sadat's diplomatic overtures to Israel beginning in late 1977 came as a tremendous shock to the rest of the Arab world, which was concerned by the prospects of Egypt, Israel's strongest Arab enemy, splitting Arab ranks by signing a separate peace with the Jewish state. Iraq, emerging as a powerful force in intra-Arab politics, was instrumental in convening a summit meeting after the Camp David Accords, signed by Israel and Egypt in September 1978. Leaders from twenty Arab states and the Palestine Liberation Organization (PLO) met in Baghdad between 2 and 5 November 1978, to consider the Arab world's response.

The summit acted on several major issues. It rejected the Camp David Accords and offered its own peace proposal. Based on United Nations Security Council Resolution 242, it called for Israel's full withdrawal from occupied Arab territories, the establishment of a Palestinian state, and recognition of the right of all states within the region to exist.

Second, the summit threatened Egypt with severe penalties if it followed up on the Camp David Accords by signing a formal peace treaty with Israel. Although Saudi Arabia tried to prevent such drastic steps, these threats amounted to total isolation of Egypt from the rest of the Arab world. Specific measures included expelling Egypt from the League of Arab States, moving the league's headquarters from Cairo, breaking off diplomatic relations, and halting all economic and military aid.

Third, the summit adopted financial measures to bolster the remaining frontline states and prevent further defections from Arab ranks. Some Arab states were particularly concerned that Jordan, which had expressed guarded interest in President Sadat's diplomatic initiatives with Israel, might follow his lead. Responding to a proposal by Iraq, the summit created a $9 billion fund to provide financial assistance for Syria, Jordan, and the PLO. The action proved crucial in discouraging Jordan from going against Arab consensus.

The summit also was important in paving the way for collective action among Arab states after several years of tension. Iraq and Syria set aside their poor relations, at least temporarily, just as the summit and the financial aid it provided symbolized Jordan's improving relations with Iraq.

Representatives of the summit were dispatched to meet with Sadat on 4 November, but he refused to receive them. On 27 March 1979, the day after the peace treaty between Israel and Egypt was signed, the council of the League of Arab States met in Baghdad to follow through on the reprisals promised at the November summit; representatives of Sudan, Oman, and the PLO were not present. The sanctions were applied on 31 March, the final day of the meeting: All Arab states except Sudan, Oman, and Somalia terminated diplomatic relations with Egypt and halted all forms of assistance. Egypt was expelled from the League of Arab States, the headquarters of which were transferred from Cairo to Tunis.

See also CAMP DAVID ACCORDS (1978); LEAGUE OF ARAB STATES; PALESTINE LIBERATION ORGANIZATION (PLO); SADAT, ANWAR AL-.

MICHAEL R. FISCHBACH

BAGHDAD UNIVERSITY

Administrative unit, dating from 1957, which centralized ten of the twelve autonomous colleges in Iraq.

In Baghdad, the first institutions of modern higher education were the College of Law and the Higher Teachers' Training School. By the time steps for unification were taken, schools of medicine, pharmacy, dentistry, engineering, agriculture, commerce, arts and sciences, and veterinary science had been added. The Shariʿa College (of Islamic law) was incorporated into the university in 1960.

In 1992, there were twelve colleges and seven higher institutes under the Baghdad University administration, and the colleges in Basra and Mosul originally attached to Baghdad have developed into separate universities. Student enrollment in 1985 was 44,307, with 1,346 engaged in postgraduate studies. Iraq has been ranked second to Egypt in the region for producing university graduates in the sciences; it does, however, lose many trained scientists through emigration.

JOHN J. DONOHUE

BAHA'I FAITH

Baha'ism is a religion founded in the second half of the 1860s by an Iranian Babi, Mirza Hosayn Ali Nuri (1817–1892), known as Baha'ullah (the Glory of God).

Baha'ism grew out of the millenarian (messianic) Babi movement that began in the 1840s. Baha'ullah, a Babi nobleman, had been exiled for his beliefs to Baghdad in the Ottoman Empire in 1853. He declared himself in 1863 to a small group of close relatives and disciples as the messianic figure promised in Babism, "He whom God shall make manifest." He was exiled to Istanbul (1863), to Edirne (1864–1868), and finally to Acre in Ottoman Syria (1868–1892). From about 1864 he began sending letters back to Babis in Iran, announcing his station. He later asserted that he was the fulfillment of millenarian hopes, not only in Babism, but in Islam, Christianity, Zoroastrianism, and in other traditions as well. Within a decade or so the vast majority of Babis had become Baha'is.

Baha'ullah, in an age of Middle Eastern absolutism, advocated parliamentary democracy. His own religion lacked a formal clergy, and he put executive power in the hands of community-steering committees he called "houses of justice," which later became elective bodies. Baha'ullah preached the unity of religions, progressive revelation, and the unity of humankind. He urged peace, criticized states for engaging in arms races, and advocated a world government able to employ collective security to prevent aggression. He said all Baha'is should school their children, both boys and girls, and he improved the position of women, saying that in his religion women are as men. Baha'i women are not constrained to practice veiling or seclusion. The initial social base of the movement was the urban middle and lower-middle classes and small landowners who had been Babis. Merchant clans who claimed descent from the prophet Muhammad (Sayyids) emerged as especially important in the leadership of the Baha'i community in Iran. Substantial numbers of Shi'ites, Jews, and Zoroastrians also became Baha'is throughout Iran.

Baha'ullah was succeeded by his eldest son, Abdu'l-Baha, who presided over the religion from 1892 to 1921. By 1900, the community had recovered from the persecution of the 1850s and had reached from 50,000 to 100,000 out of a population of 9 million. Shi'ite clerics and notables agitated against the Baha'i faith, and major pogroms broke out in 1903 in Rasht, Isfahan, and Yazd. In 1905, the Constitutional Revolution broke out in Iran. Abdu'l-Baha at first supported it, but later declared his community's neutrality. Nonintervention in party politics then became a Baha'i policy. The religion spread internationally. Restricted to the Middle East and South Asia in Baha'ullah's lifetime, it now spread to Europe, North America, East Asia, Africa, and South America.

From 1921 to 1957, the Baha'i faith was led by Shoghi Effendi Rabbani, Abdu'l-Baha's grandson, from his headquarters in Haifa, Palestine/Israel. Thereafter, from 1963, the worldwide Baha'i community periodically elected a central body, the Universal House of Justice, as prescribed in Baha'ullah's writings. The religion developed close ties with the United Nations, and it is recognized as a nongovernmental observer. In Iran, the rise of the Pahlavi state from 1925 to 1978, and a more secular policy had both benefits and drawbacks for Baha'is in Iran. Greater security and a decreased clerical influence produced less violence toward them, although they continued to face harassment. The authoritarianism of the Pahlavi state also led to tight restrictions on Baha'i activities and publications, and occasional state persecution, as in 1955.

The Shrine of the Bab on Mount Carmel, near Haifa, Israel, is the second-most holy place for those of the Baha'i faith. © HANAN ISACHAR/CORBIS. REPRODUCED BY PERMISSION.

By an accident of history (Baha'ullah's Ottoman exile), the world headquarters of the religion since the nineteenth century, Haifa, are now in Israel, although less than a thousand Baha'is live in that country. Critics of the Baha'is in the region charge them with being Zionist agents, but Baha'is point to their principle of nonintervention in partisan politics. Israel has granted Baha'is freedom of religion, as it has other religious communities, and no evidence of political collusion has ever been produced. In the 1960s, the rise of authoritarian populist regimes stressing Arab nationalism led to the persecution of Baha'is in Egypt, Libya, Iraq, and elsewhere in the Arab world, a situation that continues to this day.

In Iran, by 1978, the Baha'i community numbered around 300,000 out of a population of 35 million. Most Baha'is were lower-middle and middle class, although they included a few prominent millionaires. The Islamic Republic of Iran launched an extensive campaign against the Baha'is from 1979 through 1988. Many Muslim clerics despised the Baha'is as heretics and apostates, whose beliefs posed a dire threat to traditional Islam. Iran executed nearly 200 prominent Baha'is for their beliefs and imprisoned hundreds more. Baha'i investments and philanthropies were confiscated. Baha'is were denied ration cards, excluded from state schools and universities, and often forced to recant their faith. After 1988, most were released from prison but still suffer widespread official discrimination in Iran.

As the religion has grown in India and the Americas, the often persecuted and constrained Middle Eastern communities have come to represent less than 10 percent of Baha'is worldwide—estimated in 2001 at 5 million.

See also ARAB NATIONALISM; BABIS; CONSTITUTIONAL REVOLUTION; MUHAMMAD; ZOROASTRIANISM.

Bibliography

Hartz, Paula. *Baha'i Faith.* New York: Facts on File, 2002.

Smith, Peter. *The Babi and Baha'i Religions: From Messianic Shi'ism to a World Religion.* Cambridge, U.K., and New York: Cambridge University Press, 1987.

JUAN R. I. COLE

BAHARINA

Ethnically Arab and mainly Shi'ite descendants of the original inhabitants of Bahrain Island; also refers to the Shi'a in al-Hasa and al-Qatif, Saudi Arabia.

Bahrain is the only Arab country on the Persian (Arabian) Gulf to have a population with a Shi'ite majority. While official census figures do not provide religious affiliation, estimates for the Shi'ite population range from 60 to 70 percent. In addition to its Baharina component, the Shi'ite population has been augmented by immigrants arriving from Iran. Because political power has been monopolized by the Sunni Khalifa family and its associates for more than two centuries, the Shi'ite population has suffered discrimination in employment, political rights, and social benefits. These and other grievances have been cited by Shi'ite and other opposition leaders as grounds for political protest and demands for reform. During the 1990s the Shi'ite opposition intensified, involving both peaceful and violent expressions of dissent. Prior to 2000, the government attempted to crush opposition with harsh enforcement measures, including torture, exile, and mass imprisonments. These actions were criticized by international human rights organizations, which continue to monitor the situation of the Baharina.

See also BAHRAIN.

Bibliography

Bengio, Ofra, and Ben-Dor, Gabriel, eds. *Minorities and the State in the Arab World.* Boulder, CO: Lynne Rienner, 1999.

Scoville, Sheila A., ed. *Gazetteer of Arabia: A Geographical and Tribal History of the Arabian Peninsula,* Vol. 1. Graz, Austria: Akademische Druck, 1979.

EMILE A. NAKHLEH
UPDATED BY ANTHONY B. TOTH

BAHARIYA

A group of Egyptian oases in the Western Desert, located about 217 miles (350 km) southwest of Alexandria.

These oases in Egypt's Matruh governorate were known in the early history of Islam for their excellent dates and raisins. Cereals, rice, sugarcane, and indigo were also grown there. The fertility of the oases is due to hot springs containing various chemicals. Roman temples and Coptic (Christian) churches were built in the oases, and their ancient population probably exceeded today's estimated six thousand.

Bibliography

Fakhry, Ahmed. *The Oases of Egypt.* Cairo: American University in Cairo Press, 1974.

ARTHUR GOLDSCHMIDT

BAHAR, MOHAMMAD TAQI
[1886–1951]

Iran's last great qasideh *(ode) poet, also a literary scholar and politician.*

Mohammad Taqi Bahar was born in Mashhad. In response to a congratulatory *qasideh* he composed on the occasion of Mohammad Ali Qajar's accession to the throne, in 1907 Bahar was named *malek al-sho'ara* (king of poets, or poet laureate), the last Iranian poet to have that title. In 1906, when the constitution of Persia (now Iran) was granted, Bahar joined the constitutionalists in his hometown of Mashhad. For the next decade, he wielded his pen as poet, journalist, and editor for progressive causes and suffered incarceration and banishment.

In the 1920s he was elected to the parliament. A target for assassination, he turned from politics to literary scholarship and joined the faculty at Tehran University upon its founding in 1934. His *Divan* (Collected poems) appeared after his death, revealing Bahar as firmly traditionalist in terms of poetic form but modern in terms of poetic subjects. Among his many other books, his history of Persian literature called *Sabkshenasi* (1942) stands out.

See also LITERATURE: PERSIAN; MOHAMMAD ALI SHAH QAJAR.

Bibliography

Alavi, Bozorg. "The First Iranian Writers Congress, 1946." In *Critical Perspectives on Modern Persian Literature*, edited by Thomas M. Ricks. Washington, DC: Three Continents Press, 1984.

Loraine, M. "Bahar in the Context of the Persian Constitutional Revolution." *Iranian Studies* 5 (1972).

Loraine, M. "A Memoir on the Life and Poetic Works of Maliku'o-Shuʿara Bahar." *International Journal of Middle East Studies* 2 (1972): 140–168.

MICHAEL C. HILLMANN

BAHITHAT AL-LUBNANIYYAT, AL-

Nonpartisan women's organization.

The Association of Lebanese Women Researchers was officially registered in 1992, although a group of female scholars had been meeting informally since the early 1980s, during the Lebanese Civil War. These women increasingly felt the need for a space and a forum in which to share their opposition to the war, to political division, and to confessionalism within the Lebanese system. In 2003, the association had thirty-five members. Most were published scholars, professors at the various universities in Lebanon, who prided themselves on their religious and ideological diversity and on the democratic principles upon which the association was founded.

Since the mid-1990s, the association has held conferences, such as the 2001 conference on Arab women in the 1920s, and published proceedings. Its most visible publication is the annual *Bahithat*, a multilingual collection of essays on various themes, including "Women and Writing," "Women and Politics in Lebanon and the Arab World," and "The West in Arab Societies." The association regularly puts out scholarly books on subjects like television media, women and nongovernmental organzations in Lebanon, and Lebanese female writers. Further activities include monthly research workshops and seasonal retreats, as well as occasional outreach programs.

Bahithat fills a need in Lebanon. Although other women's organizations exist, the association remains nonpartisan and autonomous of institutional or financial dicta. However, because its focus has been on published research, and not on socio-political activism, its impact has not always been measurable.

See also GENDER: GENDER AND EDUCATION; LEBANON.

ELISE SALEM

BAHRAIN

An independent state comprising an archipelago of thirty-three islands in the heart of the Persian Gulf.

The Bahrain islands lie some 15 miles off the northeast coast of Saudi Arabia and 13 miles to the northwest of the Qatar peninsula. Connected by causeway to Saudi Arabia, al-Awal, the largest, is 27 miles by 10 miles. The total land area of the country, 213 square miles, in 2001 supported a population of 650,600. Manama is the capital and largest city. The ruling family, the Al Khalifa, is a branch of the

The King Fahd Causeway connects Bahrain with the mainland of Saudi Arabia. The cornerstone of the 26-kilometer bridge was placed in a 1982 ceremony by Saudi Arabia's King Fahd and Bahrain's Shaykh Isa bin Salman Al Khalifa, and the causeway was completed in 1986. © JACQUES LANGEVIN/CORBIS. REPRODUCED BY PERMISSION.

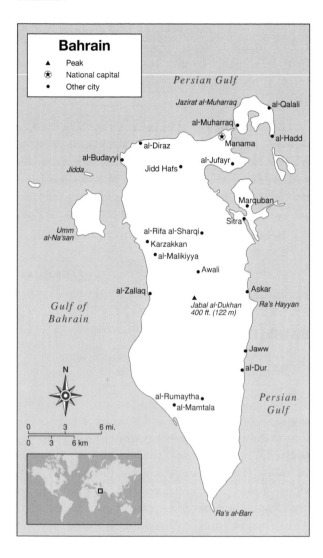

Bahrain
▲ Peak
✪ National capital
• Other city

Persian Gulf

Jazirat al-Muharraq • al-Qalali
al-Muharraq •
• al-Diraz ✪ Manama • al-Hadd
al-Budayyi • • al-Jufayr
Jidda Jidd Hafs •
Marquban
Sitra •
• al-Rifa al-Sharqi
Umm al-Na'san • Karzakkan
• al-Malikiyya
• Awali
al-Zallaq • • Askar
▲ *Ra's Hayyan*
Gulf of Bahrain *Jabal al-Dukhan 400 ft. (122 m)*

N

• Jaww
• al-Dur

al-Rumaytha • *Persian Gulf*
• al-Mamtala

0   3   6 mi.
0   3   6 km

Ra's al-Barr

MAP BY XNR PRODUCTIONS, INC. THE GALE GROUP.

Bani Utub confederation of the northern Gulf, which conquered the islands in 1782 and set up a commercial, estate-holding elite. Class distinctions between the new rulers and the indigenous population were reinforced by religious ones, since the Al Khalifa and their tribal allies were and remain adherents of Sunni Islam, while the local farmers, pearl divers, and fisherfolk remain Shiʿa. A British protectorate was imposed in 1880.

British Era: 1910s to 1973

Outbreaks of nationalist, labor, and religious unrest have been a recurrent feature of modern Bahraini politics. During the 1910s and 1920s, local merchants, tradespeople, and pearl divers rose in opposition to a number of innovative economic regulations

imposed by the government of British India, which took charge of the islands' affairs at the end of the nineteenth century. From the 1930s to the 1950s, a broad coalition of merchants, intellectuals, and oil workers (petroleum was discovered in 1932) demonstrated against continued British domination, against the presence of large numbers of foreign workers, in favor of allowing local labor to unionize, and in favor of establishing an elected legislature.

After the 1950s, outbreaks became increasingly localized and intermittent. Some episodes, such as the March 1972 general strike by the construction, shipyard, and aluminum-factory workers remained class based, while others took on sectarian overtones, as when Shiʿa openly demonstrated support for the Iranian Revolution during the late 1970s and early 1980s.

Shaykh Isa bin Sulman Al Khalifa became ruler of Bahrain in 1961, upon the death of his father, and took the title amir at independence in 1971. Since then, close relatives of the ruler have filled the most important posts in the country's cabinet. Ministers who are not members of the Khalifa family usually have been sons of the established wealthy merchant families and have received specialized training in Western universities. Bahrain's largest industrial concerns also are managed by this group of royal family members and influential civil servants.

Independent Bahrain: 1973 to Present

Political parties, like trade unions, were prohibited by the 1973 constitution. The constitution did, however, provide for an elected National Assembly, the first elections for which were held in December 1973. College-educated professionals, shopkeepers, middle-income merchants, and the country's intelligentsia were the strongest supporters of the electoral system. The commercial elite remained largely noncommittal and did not participate in the elections, either as candidates or as voters. Radical groups, most notably the local branch of the Popular Front for the Liberation of Oman and the Arab Gulf, tried to convince voters to boycott the proceedings and advocated more comprehensive freedoms of press and assembly, while agitating for the release of political prisoners and the adoption of laws permitting the formation of trade unions. Younger, comparatively radical delegates nevertheless emerged victorious from the balloting, although the government manipulated technicalities in the election law to block several newly elected delegates from taking their seats.

Although only empowered by the constitution to give advice and consent regarding laws initiated by the cabinet, the National Assembly began to debate three volatile issues during 1974. The first concerned a general labor law that would have authorized the formation of trade unions and reduced the number of expatriate workers in the country. The second was the renewal of the informal arrangement whereby the United States maintained a small naval facility at the port at al-Jufayr. The third was the continuation of the strict Public Security Law, which had been promulgated to suppress radical organizations during the early 1960s. By mid-1975, the two largest informal groupings of deputies, the People's Bloc and the Religious Bloc, could find no common ground on which to cooperate in overturning this statute. Consequently, the assembly became deadlocked and, in August 1975, the prime minister submitted the cabinet's resignation to the amir, who dissolved the assembly but reinstated the government, giving the cabinet "full legislative powers."

After the dissolution of the National Assembly, organized opposition to the regime came primarily from Bahrain's heterogeneous Islamist movement. Advocates of moderate reform could be found in the Sunni Social Reform Society and Supporters of the Call, as well as in the Shiʿite Party of the Islamic Call. Proponents of more profound social transformation belonged to the Islamic Action Organization (IAO) and the Islamic Guidance Society, both predominantly Shiʿite; demonstrations organized by these two associations erupted periodically during late 1979 and early 1980, culminating in a series of large marches in support of the new Islamic Republic of Iran during April and May of 1980. State security forces broke up these demonstrations by force, killing a number of marchers. In the wake of these events, underground groups, such as the IAO, changed tactics, abandoning mass popular demonstrations and turning instead to isolated acts of sabotage carried out by small groups of committed cadres. This shift was buttressed by the formation of the Islamic Front for the Liberation of

King Hamad bin Isa Al Khalifa assumed the throne upon the death of his father in 1999. The Al Khalifa family has ruled the country since 1782, the title generally passing from father to son. © BROOKS KRAFT/CORBIS. REPRODUCED BY PERMISSION.

Bahrain (IFLB) in Tehran, Iran, at the end of 1979; the clandestine operations envisaged by the leaders of this organization were epitomized by the alleged December 1981 plot to overthrow the Al Khalifa and set up an Islamic republic on the islands. Sizable caches of small arms belonging to clandestine groups of radical Shiʿa continued to be uncovered in rural districts as late as the fall and winter of 1983–84.

Concerted efforts on the part of the authorities to expose and destroy militant Shiʿite cells disrupted the IAO and IFLB during the late 1980s. Some one hundred people were charged in December 1987 with conspiring to assassinate the ruler and seize the country's main oil facilities, the radio and television studios, the international airport, and the U.S.

The al-Fatah Mosque near Juffayr is Bahrain's largest religious structure. The mosque can hold up to seven thousand worshippers and also houses the Religious Institute for Islamic Affairs. © ADAM WOOLFITT/CORBIS. REPRODUCED BY PERMISSION.

embassy; this group may have been affiliated with the IFLB, but Bahraini officials refused to implicate Iran in the plot. Nevertheless, the government imposed strict curfews on Shi'ite residential districts and prohibited Bahraini Shi'a from taking jobs in the armed forces. Police made further arrests in the days following the death of Iran's Ayatollah Ruhollah Khomeini in 1989.

In late 1994, simmering popular discontent erupted into a series of mass demonstrations calling for the reinstatement of the National Assembly and the constitution. The government responded by ordering the police and security service to break up the protests, prompting a wave of violence and sabotage that crested in 1996 and 1997. When Hamad bin Isa became amir after the death of his father in 1999, the uprising had already subsided. The new ruler introduced a series of reforms in an attempt to restore the regime's legitimacy. In a 2001 referendum, voters approved the transformation of the emirate into a "constitutional, hereditary monarchy." The draconian penal code and state security court were subsequently terminated, and in October 2002 elections took place for a reconstituted advisory council.

See also AL KHALIFA FAMILY; IRANIAN REVOLUTION (1979); KHOMEINI, RUHOLLAH; MANAMA; SHI'ISM; SUNNI ISLAM.

Bibliography

Herb, Michael. *All in the Family: Absolutism, Revolution, and Democracy in the Middle Eastern Monarchies.* Albany: State University of New York Press, 1999.

Khalaf, Abd al-Hadi. *Unfinished Business: Contentious Politics and State-Building in Bahrain.* Lund, Sweden: University of Lund, 2000.

Khuri, Fuad I. *Tribe and State in Bahrain: The Transformation of Social and Political Authority in an Arab State.* Chicago: University of Chicago Press, 1980.

Lawson, Fred H. *Bahrain: The Modernization of Autocracy.* Boulder, CO: Westview Press, 1989.

FRED H. LAWSON

BAHRAINI–QATARI WARS

A series of conflicts from the eighteenth through the twentieth centuries over disputed territory.

When it left Kuwait around 1760, the Al Khalifa clan landed at Zubara, on the northwestern coast of the Qatar peninsula. After capturing Bahrain in 1782, it kept Zubara until 1796. The Al Khalifa reoccupied Zubara in 1799, but by the early 1800s control of the area was contested by the Al Thani, based at Doha on the eastern coast of Qatar. Skirmishing persisted until 1880, when Britain imposed a truce. A 1913 treaty committed Britain to preventing the Al Khalifa from annexing any territory on the peninsula; a later pact promised British assistance to repel attacks against the Al Thani.

These agreements terminated Al Khalifa intervention at Zubara, but left indeterminate the status of the Hawar Islands and Fasht al-Dibal reef, situated just off the coast. In 1939, Britain put the sixteen islands under Bahrain's jurisdiction. Armed clashes erupted around the archipelago in 1978, 1982, 1986, and 1991. In 1992, Qatar asserted sovereignty over the islands, now thought to command a significant oil field, and rejected Bahrain's proposal to submit the dispute to the International Court of Justice. In 1994, Qatar changed tack and petitioned the court for a ruling, over the protests of Bahrain. In 1998, when proceedings lagged, Bahrain started work on a causeway and tourist facilities on the islands. Mediation attempts by Saudi Arabia and the United Arab Emirates failed to resolve the dispute, which threatened to polarize the Gulf Cooperation Council. Bahrain and Qatar set up a joint committee to deal with the matter in 2000, but it soon deadlocked. In 2001, the International Court of Justice awarded the Hawar Islands to Bahrain and Zubara and Fasht al-Dibal to Qatar.

See also AL KHALIFA FAMILY; AL THANI FAMILY; BAHRAIN; GULF COOPERATION COUNCIL; QATAR.

Bibliography

Kelly, J. B. *Britain and the Persian Gulf 1795–1880.* Oxford: Clarendon, 1968.

Lawson, Fred H. *Bahrain: The Modernization of Autocracy.* Boulder, CO: Westview, 1989.

FRED H. LAWSON

BAHRAIN NATIONALIST MOVEMENT

Bahrain's twentieth-century effort to gain autonomy from Britain.

Nationalism has a long history in Bahrain, because local notables persistently resisted British influence over the rulers in the years after 1880. When British officials deposed the ruler in 1923, Sunni Islamic notables opposed to overt British interference in the country's internal affairs organized a Bahrain National Congress to demand the ruler's restoration and the creation of an advisory council to assist him in governing the country. In 1934, Shi'ite leaders (of the petite bourgeoisie and working class) unsuccessfully petitioned the ruler to promulgate a basic law and institute proportional representation on the municipal and education councils. In 1938, Sunni reformers demanded the establishment of a popular assembly *(majlis)* and an end to administrative inefficiency. When students and oil workers (petroleum was found in 1932) threatened a general strike in support of the *majlis* movement in November 1938, the regime arrested some prominent reformers and deported them to British-controlled India. Several clandestine opposition groups—including the Representatives of the People, the Secret Labor Union, and the Society of Free Youth—remained active after the suppression of the reform movement, but none posed a serious challenge to the regime during the 1940s.

Unrest emerged in 1953 and 1954, culminating in a general strike in July 1954. Liberal reformers from both the Sunni and Shi'ite communities organized a Higher Executive Committee (HEC) that October to call for greater national autonomy, the convening of a legislature, the right to form trade unions, and the creation of an appellate court. Protracted negotiations between the ruler and the HEC led to formal recognition of a Committee of National Unity, in return for the HEC's agreeing to end its demands for a national assembly. Activists in the industrial labor force responded by forming the National Liberation Front-Bahrain, pressing for more fundamental changes in the country's political structure. Anti-British demonstrations at the time of the Suez (Sinai) War of 1956 precipitated restraints on all opposition forces and the declaration of a state of emergency, which effectively terminated the nationalist movements of the 1950s. Shaykh Isa ibn Sulman al-Khalifa succeeded to the throne in 1961; he announced Bahrain's independence on 14 August 1971.

See also BAHRAIN; NATIONAL LIBERATION FRONT (BAHRAIN); SUNNI ISLAM.

Bibliography

Halliday, Fred. *Arabia without Sultans: A Political Survey of Instability in the Arab World.* New York: Vintage, 1975.

Lawson, Fred H. *Bahrain: The Modernization of Autocracy.* Boulder, CO: Westview Press, 1989.

Nakhleh, Emile A. *Bahrain: Political Development in a Modernizing Society.* Lexington, MA: Lexington Books, 1976.

FRED H. LAWSON

BAHRAIN NATIONAL OIL COMPANY (BANOCO)

State-owned oil company.

The Bahrain National Oil Company was established in 1976, following the decision of the government of Bahrain to assume a direct 60 percent interest in Bahrain's petroleum business—which previously was totally owned by Bahrain Petroleum Company (BAPCO). By 1981, BANOCO took over the complete management and operation of offshore oil exploration, producing, and refining activities.

See also BAHRAIN.

Bibliography

Nyrop, Richard, ed. *Persian Gulf States: Country Studies.* Washington, DC: U.S. Government Printing Office, 1985.

EMILE A. NAKHLEH

BAHRAIN ORDER IN COUNCIL

Effort to establish Bahrain as a formal British protectorate, 1909–1913.

In response to active German interest in the Persian/Arabian Gulf during the first decade of the twentieth century, Britain became concerned with protecting its trade, position, and interests there. In 1909, Britain's Committee of Imperial Defense saw the necessity for better trade and port facilities, but it rejected the India Office suggestion to issue an Order in Council delineating the jurisdiction of the British resident agent in Bahrain—thus establishing a formal British protectorate (although Bahrain had been under British protection since 1820). It was concerned that the Order in Council might create unnecessary complications, since Persia (now Iran) and the Ottoman Empire both claimed the islands. An order was drawn in 1909 but was tabled in 1911 because of Anglo–Ottoman negotiations. The Bahrain Order was prepared in 1913, but it was withheld and never formally implemented; in that year, however, Bahrain was informally placed under a protectorate status.

See also PERSIAN (ARABIAN) GULF.

Bibliography

Busch, Briton Cooper. *Britain and the Persian Gulf, 1894–1914.* Berkeley: University of California Press, 1967.

EMILE A. NAKHLEH

BAHR AL-ABYAD

The White Nile.

Bahr al-Abyad rises in Lake No, from which it flows 625 miles (1,000 km) to Khartoum and its confluence with the Blue Nile. Flowing east, it receives significant water from its major tributary, the Sobat, which originates in Ethiopia, then swings north to contribute one-third of the total mean annual flow of the Nile. Along the reach of the White Nile the land becomes increasingly arid, and the river is dotted with clusters of water hyacinth and papyrus that become islands. It forms the reservoir behind the Jabal Awliya Dam 29 miles (47 km) south of Khartoum.

See also KHARTOUM; NILE RIVER.

ROBERT O. COLLINS

BAHR AL-ARAB

River separating southern Sudan from Darfur and Kordofan.

Bahr al-Arab is more important as the frontier between the Africans of Southern Sudan and the Arab Muslims of Darfur and Kordofan than as a hydrological entity. Rising on the watershed between Sudan and the Central African Republic, it flows sluggishly east in a great arc to its confluence with the Bahr al-Ghazal at Gabat al-Arab, by which point it has lost most of its water through evaporation. Its lower reaches are choked with aquatic vegetation.

See also BAHR AL-GHAZAL; KORDOFAN; SUDAN.

ROBERT O. COLLINS

BAHR AL-GHAZAL

Tributary of the Nile.

Bahr al-Ghazal (the Gazelle River) drains a basin the size of France, yet its contribution to the Nile is insignificant. Its tributaries, which come from the Congo–Nile watershed as well as from rivers of Darfur and Kordofan, are consumed by evaporation and transpiration in the great swamps along the river. The river should not be confused with the province in southern Sudan of the same name.

See also KORDOFAN; NILE RIVER.

ROBERT O. COLLINS

BAHR AL-JABAL

Tributary of the Nile.

Bahr al-Jabal (Mountain River) begins at the outlet of Lake Albert (Lake Mobutu Sese Seko); from there to the river port of Nimule, it is frequently called the Albert Nile. At Nimule, the river turns northwest and plunges through a narrow gorge 100 miles (160 km) long. At Bor the Bahr al-Jabal enters the Sudd, the world's largest swamp. It then flows 231 miles (370 km) to Lake No where it joins the Bahr al-Ghazal to form the Bahr al-Abyad.

See also BAHR AL-ABYAD; BAHR AL-GHAZAL; SUDD.

ROBERT O. COLLINS

BAIDA

City and administrative district (baladiyya) *of Cyrenaica, Libya.*

Baida (also called Zawiya al-Baidu) was the site of the first Sanusi *zawiya* (Islamic lodge) in Libya in 1843. In the 1960s it was developed as Libya's new administrative capital. The project was abandoned after the 1969 revolution, because of its impracticality, remoteness, and close association with the Sanusi monarchy (although much of the infrastructure, parliament house, and government buildings had been completed). The population of Baida in 2002 was 130,900.

See also SANUSI ORDER.

JOHN L. WRIGHT

BAKDASH, KHALID
[1912–1995]

Head of the Syrian Communist Party.

Khalid Bakdash, head of the Syrian Communist Party at the time of his death in 1995, was the longest serving secretary-general of any communist party in the Middle East region. He joined the Communist Party of Syria and Lebanon (CPSL) in 1930 when he was only eighteen and quickly rose in the ranks to become one of the most influential leaders of any Arab communist party.

Bakdash was of Kurdish origin and his father was either an army officer or a watchman who guarded olive orchards. He was recruited into the CPSL in Damascus by Armenian communists who had dominated the party structure in the late 1920s. In 1933 Bakdash was sent by a party decimated by arrests to study in Moscow at the Communist University of the Toilers of the East. Upon his return to Syria in 1936 to 1937 he undertook the role of secretary-general of the CPSL at a time when communist par-

ties everywhere were being ruthlessly purged of members whose loyalty to Stalinist orthodoxy was suspect and when the Comintern was trying to Arabize communist parties in the Middle East. Bakdash never wavered from the Stalinist style of leadership that he acquired in Moscow in the 1930s, and that eventually led to a split of the CPSL into Syrian and Lebanese branches in 1958 and then later, in the 1970s and 1980s, to the creation of multiple Syrian communist factions.

Bakdash played a significant role in Syrian politics during several periods of his life. After the Popular Front government came to power in France in 1936, Bakdash was part of a Syrian delegation that went to Paris to negotiate Syrian independence from the French Mandate. In 1954 Bakdash was elected to the Syrian Chamber of Deputies and was instrumental in leading the successful opposition to Syria's entry into the U.S.-led Baghdad Pact. In 1970 Bakdash supported Hafiz al-Asad's ascendancy to power and was rewarded by being allowed to appoint several ministers to the government. Because of Syria's strategic alliance with the Soviet Union until 1991, Bakdash and the Syrian Communist Party became permanent fixtures in political officialdom, including the Ba'ath-sponsored Progressive National Front, even though the party had been severely weakened by splits. Bakdash thrived in an overall environment of personality cult and dynastic politics. Shortly after his death on 15 July 1995 he was succeeded as secretary-general of the Syrian Communist Party by his wife, Wissal Farha.

See also ASAD, HAFIZ AL-; COMMUNISM IN THE MIDDLE EAST.

Bibliography

Batatu, Hanna. *The Old Social Classes and Revolutionary Movements in Iraq: A Study of Iraq's Old Landed and Commercial Classes and Its Communists, Baathists, and Free Officers.* Princeton, NJ: Princeton University Press, 1978.

Ismael, Tareq Y., and Ismael, Jacqueline S. *The Communist Movement in Syria and Lebanon.* Miami: University Press of Florida, 1998.

GARAY MENICUCCI

BAKER, JAMES A.
[1930–]

U.S. secretary of state, 1989–1992.

As secretary of state during most of the administration of U.S. president George H. W. Bush, James Baker played a crucial role in U.S.-sponsored negotiations to end the Arab–Israel conflict. In late 1989 he proposed the "Baker Plan," which dealt with Israel–Palestinian talks over the future of the West Bank. Israel rejected the plan in the spring of 1990.

In the wake of the Gulf War, Baker—known as a blunt and persistent negotiator willing to pressure and cajole Arabs and Israelis alike—exerted tremendous efforts in arranging for negotiations that included not only Israel and the Arab states but Palestinian representatives as well. In the spring of 1991, he traveled to Jerusalem and met with prominent Palestinians titularly independent of the Palestine Liberation Organization, which both the United States and Israel refused to include directly in the proposed negotiations.

In October 1991, face-to-face negotiations began in Madrid, under U.S. and Soviet involvement, within a framework established by Baker: Palestinian representatives would participate as part of a joint Jordanian–Palestinian delegation, and the various parties would engage both in bilateral talks aimed at producing peace treaties and in multilateral talks dealing with wider regional issues, such as refugee repatriation and water. Although not completely responsible for the successful Arab–Israel agreements that followed, the negotiations were the most significant diplomatic effort undertaken on behalf of a comprehensive settlement to the conflict.

See also BUSH, GEORGE HERBERT WALKER; GULF WAR (1991); PALESTINE LIBERATION ORGANIZATION (PLO); WEST BANK.

MICHAEL R. FISCHBACH

BAKHTAR-E EMRUZ

See NEWSPAPERS AND PRINT MEDIA: IRAN

BAKHTIARI

Luri-speaking tribal people of central Iran.

The Bakhtiari historically are members of several tribes claiming descent from a common ancestor and residing in the Bakhtiari region of the Zagros Mountains. The Bakhtiari primarily practiced pastoral nomadism. During the mid-nineteenth, Bakhtiari khans (leaders) organized the tribes into a large confederation that played an important role in Iran's national politics for fifty years. In particular, the khans were active supporters of the Constitutional Revolution between 1909 and 1911. Reza Shah Pahlavi's policy of forcible sedentarization of all nomadic tribes effectively destroyed the Bakhtiari confederation. Following his abdication in 1941 under Anglo-Soviet pressure, several thousand Bakhtiari villagers resumed pastoral nomadism, but the majority did not, and the sons of the former khans preferred urban life, where they were integrated with the political and social elite of the country. During the 1970s, an estimated 100,000 Bakhtiari—about 20 percent of the total—continued to carry out the twice-annual migrations. By the early 2000s, only 10 percent of Bakhtiari practiced pastoral nomadism, while an estimated 50 to 60 percent lived in cities.

See also CONSTITUTIONAL REVOLUTION; PAHLAVI, REZA.

Bibliography

Garthwaite, Gene R. *Khans and Shahs: A Documentary Analysis of the Bakhtiyari in Iran.* New York and Cambridge, U.K.: Cambridge University Press, 1983.

LOIS BECK
UPDATED BY ERIC HOOGLUND

BAKHTIARI, NAJAF QOLI KHAN SAMSAM AL-SOLTANEH
[1854–1930]

Prime minister of Iran, 1911–1913.

Born to a leading family of the Bakhtiari tribe, Najaf Qoli Khan Samsam al-Soltaneh was prime minister of Iran after Mohammad Ali Shah was deposed and the Constitutionalists assumed power in 1911. Samsam al-Soltaneh, with the aid of his tribal army, was instrumental in militarily defeating Mohammad Ali Shah, and thus he enjoyed significant mass support during his tenure in office. As a consequence, when the Russian legation in Tehran, together with the British, issued an ultimatum to the newly founded Iranian parliament asking for his resignation, popular uprisings ensued and he retained his position until 1913. He was made prime minister again, briefly, in 1918. During his premiership,

Swedish officers were charged with the founding of the pro-reform internal Iranian gendarmerie, which was modeled on the Ottoman Tanzimat. In 1921, Bakhtiari was named governor of Khorasan, but he refused the appointment because of his support for the rebellious Colonel Mohammad Taqi Khan Pesyan, who had set up government in Mashhad. Samsam al-Soltaneh died in the Bakhtiari region in 1930.

See also CONSTITUTIONAL REVOLUTION; KHORASAN; TANZIMAT.

Bibliography

Garthwaite, Gene R. *Khans and Shahs: A Documentary Analysis of the Bakhtiyari in Iran.* Cambridge, U.K., and New York: Cambridge University Press, 1983.

NEGUIN YAVARI

BAKHTIAR, SHAPUR
[1915–1991]

Last royalist prime minister of Iran, 1979.

Shapur Bakhtiar was born in the Bakhtiari region of Iran. He was brought up in a family of political influence that included his maternal grandfather, who was prime minister of Iran in 1912 and 1918. Bakhtiar was educated in France at the Sorbonne, from which he graduated in 1939 with a doctorate in political science and international law. He volunteered to serve in the French resistance to German occupation during World War II. Bakhtiar returned to Iran in 1946 and served as director of the labor department in the province of Esfahan, and in 1949 joined the National Front Party led by Mohammad Mossadegh. He served as deputy minister of labor in the Mossadegh government from 1951 to 1952.

After the coup that overthrew the Mossadegh government in August 1953, Bakhtiar opposed Shah Mohammad Reza Pahlavi's rule and devoted much of his time reorganizing the National Front. Consequently, he was arrested and briefly imprisoned in 1961. When antigovernment demonstrations intensified in December 1978, the shah tried to get support from the secular opposition. Bakhtiar agreed to become prime minister, a decision that prompted the National Front to expel him. Bakhtiar was overthrown within two months, when the Iran-

ian Revolution under the leadership of Ayatollah Ruhollah Khomeini triumphed. Shortly after, Bakhtiar fled to France where he formed and led the National Resistance Movement of Iran that opposed the Islamic Republic. In August 1991 three Iranians, believed to be agents of the Islamic Republic, killed Bakhtiar in his home near Paris.

See also IRANIAN REVOLUTION (1979); KHOMEINI, RUHOLLAH; MOSSADEGH, MOHAMMAD.

Bibliography

Ladjevardi, Habib, ed. *The Memoirs of Shapur Bakhtiar, Prime Minister of Iran.* Cambridge, MA: Harvard University Press, 1996.

AHMED H. IBRAHIM

BAKHTIAR, TIMUR
[1914–1970]

Iranian general.

The son of Sardar Mu'azzam Bakhtiari, Timur Bakhtiar attended the French military college at St. Cyr (1930–1935). During the premiership of Mohammad Mossadegh, he was commander of several provincial garrisons, but he enjoyed greater success after the fall of Mossadegh (1953), because he had the same tribal lineage as Soraya Esfandiari, who was then queen of Iran.

As military governor of Tehran, he was largely responsible for eradicating the opposition to the Pahlavi dynasty, whether the opposition stemmed from the leftist Tudeh Party, the liberal National Front, or the religious Feda'iyan-e Islam quarter. In 1958, he was appointed the first chief of SAVAK (Sazman-e Ettela'at va Zed-e Ettela'at-e Keshvar, or the National Intelligence and Counterintelligence Agency). Influenced by his premier, Ali Amini, who feared Bakhtiar's grasp on power and resented his reported meeting with U.S. president John F. Kennedy in Washington, D.C., Mohammad Reza Shah Pahlavi removed the general from his position. Bakhtiar joined the ranks of the opposition in exile, and he was active in Europe, Lebanon, and Iraq in contacting both Ayatollah Khomeini and remnants of the leftist Tudeh Party. In 1970, by instruction of the shah, Bakhtiar was murdered in Iraq, close to the Iranian border, by a SAVAK agent.

See also AMINI, ALI; FEDA'IYAN-E ISLAM; KHOMEINI, RUHOLLAH; MOSSADEGH, MO-HAMMAD; NATIONAL FRONT, IRAN; PAHLAVI, MOHAMMAD REZA; TUDEH PARTY.

Bibliography

Iranian Oral History Project. Cambridge, MA: Harvard University, Center for Middle Eastern Studies, 1988. Microform.

NEGUIN YAVARI

BAKIL TRIBAL CONFEDERATION

One of Yemen's two largest and most important tribal confederations.

The tribes of Yemen have traditionally been the basic unit of social, political, and military organization in the country. Until the reign of Imam Yahya (1918–1948), the vast majority of the tribes of Yemen belonged to one of four large confederations; the Bakil is one of the two largest and most important. Imam Yahya's campaign to subject the country, and more specifically the tribes, to his control, led him to undertake massive campaigns against their influence and power; in fact, his efforts succeeded in permanently eliminating all but two of the ancient confederations (the Hashid is the other one to survive).

Many writers have referred to the Hashid and Bakil confederations as the "two wings" of the Zaydi imamate; in the sense that many of the tribes that belong to these confederations are and were strongly committed to Zaydi Islam, the imams were recognized—to a greater or lesser degree—as the heads of the Zaydi community and could, therefore, count on a measure of support and loyalty. Not all the tribes, however, accepted the temporal and even legal role that the imams arrogated to themselves; consequently, many imams (Imam Yahya and Imam Ahmad in the twentieth century included) complained bitterly about the tribes' inordinate political power.

The member tribes of the Bakil Confederation are found primarily in the mountains of the west, northwest, and far north of the country; its leaders today are the Abu Luhum clan, of the Nihm tribe.

See also YAHYA IBN MUHAMMAD HAMID AL-DIN; ZAYDISM.

Bibliography

Dresch, Paul. *Tribes, Government, and History in Yemen.* New York: Oxford University Press, 1994.

MANFRED W. WENNER

BAKKAR, JALILLAH
[1952–]

Tunisian actress and playwright.

Born in Tunis in 1952, Jalillah Bakkar studied French literature at the Ecole Normale Supérieure before joining the Théâtre du Sud de Gafsa in 1972. With her husband Fadhel Jaïbi, Bakkar co-founded Tunisia's first independent theater troupe, the Nouveau Théâtre de Tunis (1975), and later the production company Familia (1994). Bakkar's film performances include *Les Magiciens* (The magicians; 1975), *Civilisées* (1988), *La Nuit Sacrée* (1992) based on Tahar Ben Jelloun's novel of that title, and *Chich Khan* (1992). In *al-Bahth an a'ida* (Looking for Aïda), Bakkar plays an actress going from theater to theater, from Tunis to Lebanon, to rendezvous with a Palestinian woman, Aïda, which means she who returns. Bakkar replicates the pain of the Palestinian diaspora in her monologue, talking continuously to an absent, displaced Aïda. Bakkar's 2001 play *Junun* (Madness) is based on psychotherapist Néjia Zemni's account of treating Nun, an illiterate psychotic youth at Hôpital Razi where Frantz Fanon once worked. Nun's flashes of lucidity and poetry illuminate how individual pathology mirrors social pathology. On stage, Bakkar plays the psychotherapist; off stage, she thinks of herself as a citizen-actress, using performance as critique, staging real acts to reveal the contingent nature of social and political truths.

See also ART; GENDER: GENDER AND EDUCATION; THEATER; TUNISIA: OVERVIEW.

Bibliography

Selaiha, Nehad. "Notes from Jordan." *Al-Ahram Weekly* 427 (29 April–5 May), 1999. Also available from: <http://weekly.ahram.org.eg/1999/427/cu1.htm>.

LAURA RICE

BAKLAVA

See FOOD: BAKLAVA

BAKR, AHMAD HASAN AL-

[1914–1982]

A senior Iraqi military officer and politician.

Ahmad Hasan al-Bakr (also called Abu Haytham) was born in Tikrit, Iraq, to a family of small landowners of the Begat tribe. Upon graduation from a teachers' training high school in Baghdad in 1932, he served as a primary school teacher. In search of a more promising career, in 1938 he joined the military academy that had recently been opened for cadets from middle- and lower-middle-class backgrounds. By 1958, he was a lieutenant colonel. In the mid-1950s, he became involved in political activity as a member of the Free Officers.

Simultaneously, al-Bakr became interested in the newly formed al-Ba'th party (although he did not officially join the party until 1960). After the republican revolution of 14 July 1958, he became associated with Abd al-Salam Arif and pan-Arabism, which demanded unification of Iraq and Egypt into the United Arab Republic under Gamal Abdel Nasser. As a result, when Arif lost power in October 1958, al-Bakr was dismissed from the army by the ruler, General Abd al-Karim Qasim. During the following years, al-Bakr became a central link between the two most potent pan-Arab opposition groups, which sought to bring down Qasim's "secessionist" regime: the civilian al-Ba'th Party and the Nasserite army officers—both retired and active—chief among whom was Arif.

Al-Bakr assisted in planning the first Ba'th coup d'état on 8 February 1963. Following this Ramadan revolution, he became a powerful prime minister, while Arif was made a ceremonial president. Throughout the nine months of Ba'th rule, al-Bakr served as a mediator between the civilian and military wings of the party as well as between its left and right factions. In September 1963, he became a member of the regional leadership of the Ba'th party and, a few months later, of the pan-Arab leadership.

On 18 November 1963, a severe rift between the party's left and right caused him to opt for a third solution: He supported President Arif and his Nasserite army officers in their coup d'état, which toppled the Ba'th from power. After a few months of cooperation, during which he served as deputy

Iraqi president Ahmed Hasan al-Bakr salutes during a military parade celebrating the first anniversary of Ba'thist Party rule in Iraq, 17 July 1969. © BETTMANN/CORBIS. REPRODUCED BY PERMISSION.

prime minister, Arif sacked him and his Ba'thi colleagues. In September 1964, most of the party leadership, including al-Bakr, were jailed for an attempted coup. Upon their release a few months later, they once again attempted to overthrow the Arif regime.

The Arab defeat in the Arab–Israel war of June 1967 presented al-Bakr and his conspirators with a golden opportunity to agitate against the regime for its failure to give adequate military support to the Arabs. On 17 July 1968, independent army officers joined the Ba'th to assume power in a bloodless coup d'état. Al-Bakr led one of the army units that participated in the takeover. He then became president of the republic and chairman of the all-powerful Revolutionary Command Council. By 30 July, the Ba'th rid themselves of their partners, with al-Bakr becoming prime minister and field marshal. He also held the positions of commander-in-chief of the armed forces, secretary-general of the regional leadership for the party, and deputy secretary-general of the pan-Arab leadership under Michel Aflaq as a figurehead. Between 1973 and 1977, al-Bakr also served as minister of defense.

Throughout these years, al-Bakr cooperated very closely with his young relative, the civilian party and internal-security apparatchik, Saddam Hussein. This cooperation stemmed from mutual interdependence. Al-Bakr needed Hussein as a watchdog against actual and potential enemies both inside and outside the party. Hussein, for his part, could not survive on his own even when he became the strongman in Baghdad in 1970 and 1971, because he lacked the necessary contacts with the military and sufficient support from the party old-timers—and because he was not yet known among the Iraqi public. Thus, while al-Bakr needed protection, Hussein needed time.

Throughout the 1970s, the two effectively purged the army of politically ambitious officers and turned it into a docile tool in the hands of the party, which sent its tentacles into every army unit. The relatives also shared their approach to politics—both were pragmatists, preferring Iraqi interests over those of Arabism, as interpreted by traditional party ideology. Yet, on a few occasions, al-Bakr showed more attachment to traditional party doctrine in terms of his commitment to Arab unity and the struggle against Israel. Differences, however, were minor, until the issue of Iraqi–Syrian relations came up in 1978 and 1979, after the Camp David Accords. Following a rapprochement, al-Bakr favored a loose federation with Hafiz al-Asad's Syria, while Hussein objected to it for fear of losing his position.

On 16 July 1979, Hussein—who by then had complete control of all internal-security branches and through them of the party and the army—staged a bloodless coup, forcing al-Bakr to announce his resignation, caused by ill health (Bakr's health was indeed somewhat shaky). A few days later, Hussein announced that he had uncovered a (Syrian-sponsored) plot to strip away his power, and he used this excuse to execute all his remaining opponents who, until then, could hide behind al-Bakr's back. Hussein also took advantage of this opportunity to sever ties with Damascus.

Between 1979 and 1982, when his death was reported, al-Bakr was living under house arrest and was not involved in matters of state. According to a widely believed rumor, al-Bakr was murdered by poisoning because in 1982, at a low point in the Iran–Iraq War, Hussein was afraid that the retired president might become a focus of opposition against him.

See also AFLAQ, MICHEL; ARIF, ABD AL-SALAM; ASAD, HAFIZ AL-; BA'TH, AL-; CAMP DAVID ACCORDS (1978); HUSSEIN, SADDAM; IRAN–IRAQ WAR (1980–1988); NASSER, GAMAL ABDEL; PAN-ARABISM; QASIM, ABD AL-KARIM.

Bibliography

Baram, Amatzia. "The Ruling Political Elite in Ba'thi Iraq, 1968–1986." *International Journal of Middle East Studies* 21 (1989): 447–493.

Batatu, Hanna. *The Old Social Classes and the Revolutionary Movements of Iraq: A Study of Iraq's Old Landed and Commercial Classes and of Its Communists, Ba'thists, and Free Officers.* Princeton, NJ: Princeton University Press, 1978.

Marr, Phebe. *The Modern History of Iraq.* Boulder, CO: Westview Press, 1985.

AMATZIA BARAM

BAKR, SALWA
[1949–]

Egyptian writer.

Salwa Bakr was born in 1949 to a lower-middle-class family in Matariyya, Egypt. The stories and rituals of her widowed and unschooled mother sparked Bakr's interest in the world views and speech styles of the poor or uneducated women who inhabit much of her fiction. Bakr was educated in the Cairo area, receiving a degree from the College of Business at Ayn Shams University in 1972 and a second degree in literary criticism in 1976. Her early stories explore the lives of women marginalized by poverty or social norms. In her collections *Zinat in the President's Funeral Procession* (1986) and *An al-ruh allati suriqat tadrijiyyan* (About the soul that gradually was stolen, 1989), Bakr focuses on portraying women's emotional worlds and the material circumstances of their lives through a language that claims a middle ground between standard and colloquial Arabic. Bakr received local and international critical attention for her satirical novel *The Golden Chariot* (1995), in which she makes use of circular and digressive narrative techniques, similar to those used in the *Thousand and One Nights,* to explore the lives and histories of inmates in a women's prison in Egypt. Bakr's experiments with narration and her focus on exploring women's private worlds have influenced writers of both her own and a younger generation. Bakr names Chekhov, Cervantes, and Isabel Allende among her literary influences.

See also AIN SHAMS UNIVERSITY; GENDER: GENDER AND EDUCATION; LITERATURE: ARABIC.

Bibliography

Bakr, Salwa. *The Golden Chariot.* Translated by Dinah Manisty. Reading, U.K.: Garnet Publishing, 1995.

Bakr, Salwa. *The Wiles of Men.* Translated by Denys Johnson-Davies. London: Quartet Books, 1992.

Booth, Marilyn. *My Grandmother's Cactus: Stories by Egyptian Women.* London: Quartet Books, 1991.

CAROLINE SEYMOUR-JORN

BALACLAVA, BATTLE OF

Battle that occurred during the Crimean War.

On 25 October 1854, a Russian field army under General Menshikov attempted to relieve Sevastopol, besieged by British, French, and Turkish forces, by driving a wedge among British units. The relative success of the attack netted some Turkish cannons, but a subsequent Russian cavalry attack was repulsed by the British Heavy Cavalry Brigade and the stubborn resistance of the 93rd Highlanders. The latter's success gave rise to the phrase "the thin red line," after their uniforms and signifying dedication against high odds.

The British Light Cavalry Brigade, in suicidal disregard for conventional military wisdom, then attacked the Russian field guns to their front. Whether Lord Lucan, commander of the cavalry division, or Lord Cardigan, commander of the Light Brigade, gave the order for the attack or whether it was the result of confusing dispatches has remained a mystery. The brigade's charge into the mile-long valley under murderous enemy crossfire from both flanks was immortalized by Alfred Tennyson's poem "The Charge of the Light Brigade." The brigade

reached the guns and rode beyond them to clash with Russian cavalry. Returning through the same crossfire, the survivors were assisted by the Fourth French Chasseurs d'Afrique. Of the 673 mounted officers and men entering the twenty-minute-long charge of the Light Brigade, 247 men and 497 horses were killed. A fitting epitaph was coined by French General Pierre-Jean-François Bosquet, who remarked: "It is magnificent, but it is not war." The Russians retained possession of the Vorontsov ridge commanding the Sevastopol–Balaclava road while the allies kept Balaclava and the approaches to Sevastopol. Neither the battle itself nor the charge of the Light Brigade had any effect on the outcome of the campaign.

See also CRIMEAN WAR.

Bibliography

Rich, Norman. *Why the Crimean War? A Cautionary Tale.* New York: McGraw-Hill, 1991.

JEAN-MARC R. OPPENHEIM

BALAFREJ, AHMED
[1908–1990]

Moroccan nationalist; prime minister in 1958.

Ahmed Balafrej earned degrees from Cairo University and the Sorbonne in Paris. Active in Rabat and Paris among student groups for reform and nationalism (Morocco was under French and Spanish protectorate from 1912), he founded the newspaper *Maghrib* in 1932. In 1943, he cofounded the Istiqlal political party. Following independence in 1956, and as secretary-general of Istiqlal, he was made foreign minister. In 1958, he became prime minister, a post from which he resigned in December of that year. By the late 1960s, Balafrej was largely inactive politically.

See also ISTIQLAL PARTY: MOROCCO.

Bibliography

Ashford, Douglas. *Political Change in Morocco.* Princeton, NJ: Princeton University Press, 1961.

Hahn, Lorna. *North Africa: Nationalism to Nationhood.* Washington, DC: Public Affairs Press, 1960.

Pennell, C. R. *Morocco since 1830: A History.* New York: New York University Press, 2000.

MATTHEW S. GORDON

BALBO, ITALO
[1896–1940]

Governor of Libya (by then the united Italian province of Libia), 1934–1939.

Italo Balbo was responsible for introducing state-aided settler colonization in Libya from 1938, which brought in 32,000 settlers before the outbreak of war under Italy's *Quarta Sponda* (Fourth Shore) program. This program replaced the previous scheme of allowing autonomous companies to organize sharecropping settler colonization alongside private colonization. By 1939, when Libya had been formally integrated into metropolitan Italy, there were approximately 110,000 Italians in Libya. Marshal Balbo was also an advocate of the Fascist Italianization program for Libya, in which Libyan Muslims were to become Muslim Italians. He was killed at Tobruk in June 1940.

See also TOBRUK.

Bibliography

Segre, Claudio G. "Italian Development Policy in Libya: Colonialism as a National Luxury." In *Social and Economic Development of Libya,* edited by E. G. H. Joffe and K. S. McLachlan. Wisbech, U.K.: Middle East and North African Studies Press, 1982.

GEORGE JOFFE

BALFOUR DECLARATION (1917)

A British declaration supporting the establishment of a Jewish national home in Palestine.

Few documents had such far-reaching consequences in the modern history of Middle East as did the Balfour Declaration of 2 November 1917. It was drafted by Zionist leaders, revised and approved by the British war cabinet, and forwarded by Lord Arthur Balfour, the British foreign secretary, to Lord Rothschild, a Zionist philanthropist and one of its drafters. It consisted of a single sixty-seven-word paragraph:

"His Majesty's Government view with favour the establishment in Palestine of a national home for the Jewish people, and will use their best endeavours to facilitate the achievement of this object, it being understood that nothing shall be done which may prejudice the civil and religious rights of the existing non-Jewish communities in Palestine, or the rights and political status enjoyed by Jews in any other country." (Hurewitz, 1979)

This was one of a number of contradictory promises Britain made during World War I. Needing Arab support against the Ottoman Empire, Britain promised in the Husayn–McMahon Correspondence (1915–1916) to support the establishment of an independent Arab nation, which Arabs understood to include Palestine (which Britain later denied); and needing French and Russian support, it promised in the Sykes–Picot Agreement (1916) to rule the region, including Palestine, with its allies. The cabinet issued the declaration for a number of reasons, both immediate and long term. It hoped to enlist American and Russian Jews help to bring America into the World War I and to keep Russia from abandoning it. In addition, the cabinet sought to preempt a similar German pro-Zionist declaration and needed Jewish money for Britain's own war effort.

The climate of opinion in England favored Zionist goals for Palestine. Fundamentalist Christians, some of whom were antisemites, considered it their duty to assist Jews to go to Palestine so that biblical prophesy could be fulfilled. Liberals such as Balfour and Prime Minister David Lloyd George believed that the West had committed a historical injustice against the Jewish people, one that must be atoned for. To this intellectual climate can be added the sociopolitical factor: Jewish contributions to British society were disproportionate to their numbers and were recognized and admired. Sir Herbert Louis Samuel, who later became the first high commissioner of Palestine, was a philosopher and a statesman who served in several cabinets; and Chaim Weizmann was a chemistry professor who assisted the British munitions industry. Both were persuasive advocates of a Jewish state. By 1917, the war cabinet accepted the view that postwar strategic advantages could be derived from a Jewish state or commonwealth allied to Great Britain.

The phraseology of the declaration was carefully chosen; even its ambiguity was deliberate. The phrase "national home" was new, with no precedence in international law; it was used in the declaration to pacify anti-Zionist Jews, who feared that creation of a state would jeopardize the rights of Jews in the diaspora. In private, however, British officials were clear about the objective. Lord Balfour and David Lloyd George explained to Weizmann in 1921 "that by Declaration they always meant an eventual Jewish State" (Ingrams, 1973).

Little thought was given to the indigenous Palestinian population, in large part because Europeans considered them inferior. The declaration referred to these Palestinians, who in 1917 constituted 90 percent of the population, as the "non-Jewish communities in Palestine," a phrase that conceals the identity of the majority. Yet the declaration contained a promise to guarantee the civil and religious rights of the "non-Jews," a promise that the British attempted to enforce even at the expense of Jewish religious rights. At the Wailing, or Western, Wall (in Hebrew, ha-Kotel ha-Maʿravi), the British, in order to protect Muslim property and religious rights to the wall, allowed the Palestinians to restrict Jewish visitation and prayer, even though the wall was the holiest shrine of Judaism.

But British political support for a Jewish national home worked against Palestinian national interests. The Balfour policy, which was incorporated in the League of Nations mandate for Palestine, was backed by the European powers and by the British military. It gave the Yishuv (Jewish community) time to grow through immigration, from about 50,000 in 1917 to more than 600,000 by 1947, and time to develop quasigovernmental and military institutions. Palestinians, fearing domination or expulsion, protested and resisted through political violence—in 1920, 1921, 1929, and 1933—that was put down by the British military. The Palestine Arab revolt of 1936 through 1939 was suppressed by both British and Zionist forces. The Palestinians were a weak, underdeveloped society, no match for the British and, after 1939, for the Zionists. Ultimately, the 1917 Balfour policy paved the way for the establishment in 1948 of the state of Israel and the exodus of some 726,000 Palestinians who left out of fear and panic or were expelled by the Israel Defense Force. The refugees were not allowed to return to their homes and their properties were confiscated.

See also DIASPORA; HUSAYN–MCMAHON CORRESPONDENCE (1915–1916); ISRAEL; LLOYD

The Balfour Declaration was issued in 1917 by Lord Arthur James Balfour. Balfour became the British prime minister in 1902, but resigned three years later due to dissention within his Unionist Party. Balfour remained active in politics, however, and was Britain's foreign secretary at the time the Balfour Declaration was drafted. © MICHAEL NICHOLSON/CORBIS. REPRODUCED BY PERMISSION.

GEORGE, DAVID; SAMUEL, HERBERT LOUIS; SYKES–PICOT AGREEMENT (1916); WEIZMANN, CHAIM; WESTERN WALL; YISHUV.

Bibliography

Hurewitz, J. C. *The Middle East and North Africa in World Politics: A Documentary Record,* 2d edition, revised and enlarged, Vol. 2: *British-French Supremacy, 1914–1945.* New Haven, CT: Yale University Press, 1979.

Hurewitz, J. C. *The Struggle for Palestine.* New York: Greenwood Press, 1968.

Ingrams, Doreen. *Palestine Papers, 1917–1922: Seeds of Conflict.* New York: George Braziller, 1973.

Jeffries, Joseph Mary Nagle. *Palestine: The Reality.* New York: Longmans, Green, 1939.

Khalidi, Walid, ed. *From Haven to Conquest: Readings in Zionism and the Palestine Problem until 1948*. Washington, DC: Institute for Palestine Studies, 1971.

Monroe, Elizabeth. *Britain's Moment in the Middle East, 1914–1971*. Baltimore, MD: Johns Hopkins Press, 1981.

Stein, Leonard. *The Balfour Declaration*. New York: Simon & Schuster, 1961.

Weizmann, Chaim. *Trial and Error*. New York: Harper, 1949.

PHILIP MATTAR

BALKAN CRISES (1870s)

Regional unrest led to independence for much of the peninsula but no permanent solutions.

As the Ottoman Empire decayed in the nineteenth century, various crises erupted in the empire's European regions as a result of the national awakening of its Christian subjects. Religious conflict and economic oppression led the Christian peasants of Herzegovina to revolt in July 1875, and despite Ottoman promises of reform, the uprising continued and soon spread into neighboring Bosnia. Despite diplomatic intervention by the Austro-Hungarians aimed at bringing an end to the conflict in the Ottoman Empire's two western-most provinces, fighting intensified, and within nine months approximately 156,000 refugees had fled to Austria-Hungary, Serbia, and Montenegro. Public opinion in the latter two states demanded intervention on behalf of their fellow Slavs, whose rebellion was joined in May 1876 by revolutionaries in Bulgaria. In that same month, the Russian, Austro-Hungarian, and German governments, associated in the Three Emperors' League, tried to mediate the conflict. The resulting Berlin Memorandum provided that refugees be repatriated, reforms enacted, and that the great powers supervise both. Nevertheless, the plan ran into opposition from the British government of Prime Minister Benjamin Disraeli, who was determined to introduce a new, more active foreign policy and unwilling to approve a plan that his government had not cosponsored. Collective mediation thus failed and the following month, Serbia declared war on the empire and Montenegro quickly followed suit.

Britain clung to its policy of nonintervention even after news of Ottoman mass killings in Bulgaria, the Bulgarian Horrors, provoked outrage throughout Western Europe. Public pressure for intervention eventually caused Czar Alexander II of Russia to issue an ultimatum to the Ottoman sultan demanding a six-week armistice for the Serbs. The Turks yielded and accepted the armistice on 30 October 1876, but Disraeli's refusal to accept a peace proposal that would have increased Russia's influence in the Balkans led the Turks to reject the settlement. Russia responded on 24 April 1877 by declaring war on the Ottoman Empire.

Russia's armies marched through Romania and into Bulgaria. Despite several months' delay caused by unexpectedly tenacious resistance by the Turkish garrison at Pleven (or Plevna), the Russians resumed their advance in January 1878. As Turkish defenses withered, armistice negotiations began, and Russian forces moved to within 10 miles (16 km) of Istanbul. Meanwhile, the British countered by sending their fleet to the Sea of Marmara as a show of support to the sultan and as a warning to the Russians. Negotiations between the Russians and the Turks ended in the Treaty of San Stefano, which was signed 3 March 1878. The treaty provided that reforms be enacted in Bosnia-Herzegovina and that Serbia and Montenegro become fully independent and receive more territory. Romania, which had entered the war against Turkey, was to receive part of the region of Dobruja, in return for giving southern Bessarabia back to Russia, which also was to receive Batum, Kars, Ardahan, and Bayazid in eastern Asia Minor. A Greater Bulgaria was to be created as an autonomous principality, with an elected prince.

The treaty, however, aroused the opposition of Britain and Austria-Hungary, who feared Russian access to the Aegean and control over Istanbul, and by Greece and Serbia, who could not accept the notion of a Greater Bulgaria that included areas that they coveted, especially Macedonia. The Russians recognized that the San Stefano settlement infringed upon the Peace of Paris (1856), which had, among other provisions, guaranteed Ottoman independence and territorial integrity, and the Russians now acknowledged the right of the signatories to the Paris treaty to consider the provisions of the new settlement. Meeting at the Congress of Berlin, those powers determined that Greater Bulgaria should be divided into three parts: an autonomous

Bulgaria, still under Turkish sovereignty but with its own elected prince; Eastern Rumelia, south of the Balkan mountains, which was to have a Christian governor appointed by the sultan but approved by the powers; and Macedonia, which was returned to direct Turkish rule. Serbia and Montenegro now became fully independent and were enlarged, while Romania did receive part of Dobruja in return for ceding southern Bessarabia to Russia. Bosnia-Herzegovina and the Sanjak of Novi Pazar were placed under the political administration of Austria-Hungary, and Russia received Batum, Kars, and Ardahan, while Cyprus came under British rule.

Signed on 13 July 1878, the Treaty of Berlin was the single most important agreement for the Balkan nations in the nineteenth century. While allowing the Ottoman Empire to maintain its presence in Albania, Macedonia, and Thrace, it left all of the Balkan peoples, with the exception of the Albanians, with independent or autonomous states. Its provisions, however, were an immediate source of frustration to them, and led to further strife and eventually World War I.

See also BERLIN, CONGRESS AND TREATY OF; BULGARIAN HORRORS; SAN STEFANO, TREATY OF (1878).

Bibliography

Jelavich, Charles, and Jelavich, Barbara. *The Establishment of the Balkan National States, 1804–1920.* Seattle: University of Washington Press, 1977.

Stavrianos, L. S. *The Balkans, 1815–1914.* New York: Holt Rinehart, 1963.

JOHN MICGIEL

BALKANS

While racially similar, the peoples of the Balkans diverge in language and religion.

Five peoples inhabit the Balkan Peninsula, an area in southeast Europe that is generally considered to be bounded by the Danube River plain to the north, the Black Sea to the east, the Aegean Sea to the south, and the Adriatic Sea to the west: South Slavs, Romanians, Greeks, Albanians, and Turks.

The most numerous group, the South Slavs, comprises five nations, settled in a broad band across the central Balkans from the Adriatic to the Black Seas: the Slovenes, northeast of the Adriatic; the Croats to the southeast; the Serbs farther east; the Macedonians to the south; and the Bulgarians along the Black Sea. The Slavs arrived in the sixth century and began assimilating and displacing the older inhabitants of the northern and central Balkan Peninsula—the Illyrians, Thracians, and Dacians. Some Illyrians and Thracians found refuge in isolated mountain areas, and their descendants eventually became Albanians and Vlachs, respectively. The latinized Dacians were pushed north and emerged as the modern Romanians. As the South Slavs settled down, some were conquered by the Bulgars, an Asiatic people few in number and so quickly assimilated that only their name survives.

Meanwhile, the ancient Greeks inhabited the peninsula farther south, as they do today. The arrival of the Ottoman Turks in the fifteenth century brought scattered Turkish settlements; with the exception of Eastern or Turkish Thrace (European Turkey), few Turks remain there at the end of the twentieth century. Germans came to the area as a result of Austrian defense policies that called for frontier colonization. Few, however, of the 1.5 million Germans in the area before World War II remain. Jews fleeing persecution in Spain and Portugal were given refuge by the Ottomans in the sixteenth century in what later became Bulgaria, Yugoslavia, and Greece, while many Jews arrived in Romania from Russia and Poland in the seventeenth and eighteenth centuries. Of the 1.2 million Jews in the Balkans before World War II, fewer than 50,000 remain. Gypsies arrived in the fifteenth century and more currently comprise a small and persecuted minority, particularly in Romania.

The Balkan peoples are predominantly Orthodox Christians. But the overwhelming majority of Slovenes and Croats are Roman Catholic, and Protestant communities exist in the northwest. Eastern Thrace is predominantly Muslim, as is 70 percent of Albania's population. Substantial Muslim minorities exist in Bosnia, Macedonia, and Bulgaria.

Bibliography

Stavrianos, L. S. *The Balkans, 1815–1914.* New York: Holt Rinehart, 1963.

Stoianovich, Traian. *A Study in Balkan Civilization.* New York: Knopf, 1967.

JOHN MICGIEL

BALKAN WARS (1912–1913)

Warfare among the states of the Balkan Peninsula that affected the balance-of-power politics in Europe and contributed to the outbreak of World War I.

In the first Balkan War (October 1912–March 1913), the Ottoman Empire fought against the Balkan League composed of Serbia, Bulgaria, Greece, and Montenegro. The second Balkan War (June–July 1913) pitted the former allies against each other and also involved Romania.

The Young Turk Revolution of 1908 in the Ottoman Empire precipitated changes in the Balkan status quo. Bulgaria declared independence, and Austria annexed Bosnia-Herzegovina, reducing Ottoman control in Europe to Thrace, Macedonia, and Albania. Fear of Austro-Hungarian expansion and the vulnerability of the Ottoman Empire, at war with Italy over Libya since 1911, prompted the formation of the Balkan League with Russia's blessing. The Christian Balkan states temporarily reconciled conflicting geopolitical ambitions and irredentist disputes over ethnically mixed Macedonia. They hoped for a more advantageous repartitioning of the region at the expense of the Ottoman state.

Montenegro opened hostilities against the empire over border disputes. At the same time, Bulgaria and Serbia, which had launched in March 1912 the series of alliances that led to the Balkan League, mobilized their armies. The Ottoman government hastily concluded peace with Italy and declared war against the Balkan allies on 17 October 1912. The Ottomans suffered defeats in both Macedonia and Thrace, as Albania declared its independence from the Ottoman Empire in November. On 16 December 1913, upon a ceasefire agreement and appeals from Anglophile Ottoman Grand Vizier Kamil Paşa, ambassadors convened at the London Conference. The Ottomans surrendered Macedonia and Western Thrace but refused to yield Edirne, which was besieged by Bulgaria. Failure to agree on revised borders led to a Bulgarian offensive in February 1913. This action forced the Ottomans to surrender the European territories to the west of the Enez–Midye Line, a situation formalized at the London Conference of 30 May.

Disagreement about the repartitioning of Macedonia revived old rivalries. Bulgaria, dissatisfied with its allotment, surprised former allies Serbia and Greece with an attack on 29 June. This led to an anti-Bulgarian realignment that also included Romania, which feared losing territory to its southern neighbor. The Ottomans exploited the disarray to recover Edirne from the Bulgarians in July. The Treaty of Bucharest of 10 August 1913, between Bulgaria and its former allies, was followed by the Istanbul Treaty between Bulgaria and the Ottoman Empire (29 September 1913), which left Edirne in Ottoman hands. The Ottomans concluded separate treaties with Greece (in Athens on 14 November) and Serbia (in Istanbul on 14 March 1914). Greece obtained the Aegean islands, except the Dodecanese, which went to Italy. The Muslims of ceded territories were given a choice of immigrating into the empire. The borders that emerged at the end of these treaties have changed remarkably little despite the shocks of World War I and later events.

In the Balkan wars, the Ottomans lost more than 80 percent of their European territory inhabited by 4 million people. The new demographic and geopolitical realities triggered domestic political and ideological change in the Ottoman Empire. On 23 January 1913, the Committee for Union and Progress implemented a coup against Kamil Paşa, ostensibly because he lost Edirne. At the end of the wars, with the Ottoman relinquishment of predominantly Christian territories, the empire was largely reduced to its Muslim-dominated Asian lands. This fact was reflected in the ideological reorientation toward a distinctly Islamic Ottomanism and in the proliferation of Turkish cultural activity.

See also COMMITTEE FOR UNION AND PROGRESS; EDIRNE.

Bibliography

Kiraly, Béla K., and Djordjevic, Dimitrije, eds. *East Central European Society and the Balkan Wars.* Boulder, CO: Social Science Monographs; Highland Lakes, NJ: Atlantic Research and Publications, 1987; distributed by Columbia University Press.

Stavrianos, L. S. *The Balkans, 1815–1914.* New York: Holt Rinehart, 1963.

HASAN KAYALI

BALTA LIMAN, CONVENTION OF (1838)

Agreement expanding British trade rights in Ottoman Empire.

Signed between Britain and the Ottoman Empire on 15 August 1838, the agreement reaffirmed and widened Britain's rights under the capitulations (privileges granted by the Ottoman government) that gave British subjects the right to trade freely in the Ottoman Empire. In a move designed to weaken the power of Muhammad Ali Pasha of Egypt, the convention also forbade the formation of commercial monopolies in the Ottoman domains.

See also MUHAMMAD ALI; OTTOMAN EMPIRE.

Bibliography

Anderson, M. S. *The Eastern Question, 1774–1923: A Study in International Relations.* London, Melbourne, and New York: St. Martin's, 1966.

Shaw, Stanford, and Shaw, Ezel Kural. *History of the Ottoman Empire and Modern Turkey.* Cambridge, U.K., and New York: Cambridge University Press, 1976–1977.

ZACHARY KARABELL

BALUCHI

See IRANIAN LANGUAGES

BALUCHIS

Ethnic group that lives in the border region where Afghanistan, Iran, and Pakistan meet.

The Baluchis are members of Baluchi-speaking tribes inhabiting the Pakistani provinces of Baluchistan and coastal Makran, adjoining southwestern Afghanistan, and southeastern Iran. Detribalized Baluchis have been migrating to the United Arab Emirates and Oman since at least the 1950s. Baluchi, an Indo-Iranian language, has five million speakers; the majority live in Pakistan. Traditionally Baluchis were nomadic sheep and goat herders and camel breeders; during the nineteenth century some became sedentary farmers (growing dates, almonds, apricots, and wheat) or fishers. The Baluchi tribal organization is hierarchical, with four social classes (aristocracy, nomads, farmers, and slaves); most tribes are led by a tribal chief (*sardar*) but sociopolitical organization is variable. Most Baluchis are Sunni Muslim. The area known as Pakistani Baluchistan was conquered by the British in 1887. In Iran and Pakistan, Baluchis have been migrating to non-Baluchi urban areas in search of employment since the 1950s. Most of the small Baluchi population of Afghanistan fled to Iran and Pakistan as refugees during the 1980s.

See also BALUCHISTAN.

Bibliography

Salzman, Philip Carl. *Black Tents of Baluchistan.* Washington, DC: Smithsonian Institution Press, 2000.

CHARLES C. KOLB

BALUCHISTAN

Literally "land of the Baluch"; the name given to the region of approximately half a million square miles that straddles southeastern Iran, southwestern Pakistan, and southern Afghanistan.

Although its precise boundaries are still undetermined, it is generally thought to stretch from the edge of the Iranian plateau (the Dasht-e Lut), including parts of the Kirman desert east of Bam and the Bashagird mountains, to the coastal lowlands of the Gulf of Oman, up to the rugged Sulaiman range in the East, at the edge of the western boundaries of the Pakistani provinces of Sind and Punjab. The volcano of Kuh-i Taftan (13,500 ft. [4,104 m]) located on the Iranian side is considered Baluchistan's most spectacular peak. Its most important cities are Iranshahr (formerly Fahraj), the capital of Iranian Baluchistan and Quetta, the capital of Pakistani Baluchistan.

Due to the nature of its divergent topography, Baluchistan appears to have been divided throughout its history between Iranian "highland" and Indian subcontinent "lowland" spheres of influence. Indeed, its hybrid population, comprising Baluch, Brahuis, Djats, and other South Asian elements, thought to amount to a little more than two million, reflects this. In particular, the region has been influenced greatly by the politics of the neighboring areas of Kerman, Sistan, Kandahar, Punjab, Sind, and Oman.

The Baluch are generally divided into two groups, the Sarawan and the Jahlawan, separated from each other by the Brahuis of the Kalat region.

The exact origins of the Baluch are unclear. It is generally thought that they migrated to the region either from the east, beyond Makran, or from north of Kerman sometime in the late medieval period. The earliest mention of them occurs in an eighth-century Pahlavi text, while a number of the medieval Muslim geographers mention a group called the "Balus," in the area between Kerman, Khorasan, Sistan, and Makran.

When they actually began to see themselves as a distinct cultural unit is another matter of debate. The idea of a single, politically unified Baluchistan seems to date back to the eighteenth century and the time of their only successful indigenous leader, the Brahui Nasir Khan, who attempted to consolidate all the Baluch into one unified nation. This idea of a single Baluchistan was further fueled by the British—who began to take a great interest in the area in the nineteenth century and formally incorporated large sections of it into their subcontinental empire as part of their divide-and-rule policy. Indeed, it was the British who first began extensive mapping of the area, promoted scholarship on the Baluchi tribes, and negotiated the formal international boundaries with Iran, Afghanistan, and Pakistan in 1947, ultimately spurring Iranian and Russian interests in the area.

Regardless of the debates, it can be said with certainty that a distinct ethnic and social entity, complete with an independent language, Baluchi, and a distinctive social and political structure based on a primarily nomadic way of life, emerged in the region known as Baluchistan.

Bibliography

Baloch, Mir Khudabux Bijarani Marri. *The Balochis through the Centuries: History versus Legend.* Quetta, Pakistan, 1965.

Embree, Ainslee T., ed. *Pakistan's Western Borderlands: The Transformation of a Political Order.* Durham, NC: Carolina Academic Press, 1977.

NEGUIN YAVARI

BALYAN FAMILY

Ottoman architects.

The Balyan (also Balian) family was composed of nine Ottoman architects: Meremetçi Bali Kalfa (d. 1803; after whom the family is named); his sons Krikor Amira (1767–1831) and Senekerim Amira (d. 1833); Krikor's son Garabet Amira (1800–1866); Garabet's sons Nikogos (1826–1858), Sarkis (1835–1899), Agop (1838–1875), Simon (1846–1894), and Levon (1855–1925). These architects were responsible, individually or in collaboration with each other, for the majority of the buildings for the Ottoman Empire in and near Constantinople (now Istanbul) during the nineteenth century.

Prominent among these works are the Nüsretiye (Tophane), Bezm-i Alem Valide Sultan (Dolmabahçe), Büyük Mecidiye (Ortaköy), Küçük Mecidiye (Ciragan), Pertevniyal Valide Sultan (Aksaray), Caglayan, Teşvikiye, Hamidiye (Yildiz) mosques; Mahmud II and Abdülmecit tombs; Dolmabahçe, Beylerbeyi, Ciragan, Yildiz, Küçüksu, Ihlamur, Baltalimani, Adile Sultan (Kandilli) palaces; Aynalikavak, Izmit, Mecidiyeköy, Zincirlikuyu, Ayazaga, Kalender royal pavilions; the Imperial College of Medicine (now Galatasaray Lycée); the Military School (Mekteb-i Harbiye); Selimiye, Davutpaşa, Rami, Gümüşsuyu, Maçka barracks and Taş Kişla near Taksim; Gümüşsuyu hospital; the Mint (Darphane); Bahçeköy Valide and Mahmud II dams; Terkos waterworks; Bayezid fire tower; Tophane, Dolmabahçe and Yildiz clock towers.

As leading figures of the Armenian Millet, members of the Balyan family were also responsible for the construction of Armenian churches, schools, and a hospital in Istanbul. They also were commissioned by other Armenian amiras to construct some of the earliest industrial plants around the capital. Their patronage of local Armenian talent made many of the official structures they raised almost entirely the work of Armenian artisans. Altogether they developed an art form described as Ottoman Baroque.

See also ARMENIAN MILLET.

Bibliography

Tuğlaci, Pars. *The Role of the Balian Family in Ottoman Architecture.* Istanbul: Yeni Cigir Bookstore, 1990.

APTULLAH KURAN
UPDATED BY ROUBEN P. ADALIAN

BAMYAN

Ancient Gandharan site; central Afghan province and city.

The modern province of Bamyan is located in the high mountains of central Afghanistan in Hazarajat. The population of 300,000 consists mostly of ethnic Hazara, a Persian-speaking ethnolinguistic group thought to be of Central Asian ancestry. The provincial capital is the city of Bamyan.

Bamyan was also an important Buddhist site of the Gandhara empire. In the Bamyan valley in central Bamyan Province there were several large statues of Buddha, the oldest dating from the second half of the third century, which were destroyed in 2001. During the rule of the Taliban government (1996–2001) the Bamyan valley became a major battlefield in the fighting between the Hazara political organization Hizb-e Wadat and Taliban forces. As the fighting spread north, thousands of refugees from other parts of Afghanistan took refuge in the valley. The Bamyan valley changed hands several times from September 1998 to the middle of May 1999. Taliban forces killed several hundred Hazaras citizens and many others starved to death.

In March 2001 the Taliban government declared that the Buddha statues were idolatrous and offensive to Islam, citing the Islamic stricture on representation of the human form. Despite condemnation from the international community, the Taliban government destroyed the statues with explosives on 8 and 9 March 2001.

See also HAZARA.

Bibliography

Dupree, Louis. *Afghanistan.* Princeton, NJ: Princeton University Press, 1980.

Mousavi, Sayad Askar. *The Hazaras of Afghanistan: An Historical, Cultural, Economic and Political Survey.* New York: St. Martin's, 1997.

GRANT FARR

BANDUNG CONFERENCE (1955)

Assembly of twenty-nine developing nations, including many from the Middle East, to discuss international relations, colonialism, and cooperation.

The conference was convened by prime ministers Muhammad Ali of Pakistan, Jawaharlal Nehru of India, U Nu of Burma, Sir John Kotelawala of Ceylon, and Ali Sastroamidjojo of Indonesia. Twenty-nine developing nations assembled in Bandung, Indonesia, in April 1955 to discuss their role in a world dominated by the superpowers. Major issues were colonialism, economic and cultural cooperation, the legitimacy of defense pacts such as the North Atlantic Treaty Organization (NATO) and Southeast Asia Treaty Organization (SEATO), and the viability of peaceful coexistence.

The Middle Eastern states were represented by such leaders as Dr. Charles Malik of Lebanon, Dr. Muhammad Fadhil al-Jamali of Iraq, Gamal Abdel Nasser of Egypt, and Prince Faisal ibn Abd al-Aziz of Saudi Arabia. The conference passed resolutions supporting the independence struggles of Algeria, Morocco, and Tunisia against France, and it called for a peaceful settlement of the issue of the Palestinians in accordance with United Nations resolutions.

The Bandung Conference saw Nasser emerge as an international leader. The ties that he established there with Nehru would lead in six years to the first Nonaligned Nations Conference in Belgrade, Yugoslavia.

See also FAISAL IBN ABD AL-AZIZ AL SA'UD; JAMALI, MUHAMMAD FADHIL AL-; MALIK, CHARLES HABIB; NASSER, GAMAL ABDEL; NORTH ATLANTIC TREATY ORGANIZATION (NATO).

Bibliography

Abdulgani, Roeslan. *The Bandung Connection,* translated by Molly Bondan. Singapore: Gunung Agung, 1981.

Bell, P. M. H. *The World since 1945: An International History.* London: Arnold; New York: Oxford University Press, 2001.

Jansen, G. F. *Afro–Asia and Non-Alignment.* London and New York: Praeger, 1966.

Wright, Richard. *The Color Curtain: A Report on the Bandung Conference.* Jackson: University Press of Mississippi, 1995.

ZACHARY KARABELL

BANI-ETEMAD, RAKHSAN
[1954–]

An Iranian filmmaker.

Rakhsan Bani-Etemad was born in Tehran in 1954 and is one of post-Revolutionary Iran's foremost film- and documentary-makers. Her career began in Iranian television after the revolution (1984–1987); she has made both documentaries and feature-length films, including *The Yellow Canary, Narges, The Blue Veil, The May Lady,* and *Under the Skin of the City.* Working in television and as a documentary filmmaker not only gave her full access and permission to film but also kept her close to the pulse of society, lending her feature films social import. Her style uniquely blends the documentary with the feature film to the degree that characters from her documentaries (most particularly Tuba, whose story she has followed and developed over sixteen years, resulting in her seminal feature film *Under the Skin of the City*) also appear in her feature films. While her most personal work, *The May Lady,* was the first to stray from her usual themes—social inequality, crime, blue-collar laborers, and strong female protagonists—and looks inward at the life of a female television documentary filmmaker from the upper middle class, it stays within the general themes that Bani-Etemad has developed over the course of her career: the struggle to survive emotionally and physically in postwar Iran, the particular strain the socioeconomic situation places on the mothers of young men, and a gendered perspective on the ever-changing role and responsibility of the documentarian, artist, and citizen.

See also ART; IRAN; MAKHMALBAF FAMILY; MI-LANI, TAHMINEH.

ROXANNE VARZI

BANI SADR, ABOLHASAN
[1933–]

First president of the Islamic Republic of Iran, 1980–1981.

Abolhasan Bani Sadr was born in Hamadan to a relatively wealthy, religious landowning family. He studied theology and law at Tehran University, where he played an active part in the Islamic branch of the National Front. He left Iran for France in the 1960s to pursue higher education after being exposed to the ideas of Paul Vieille, the French Marxist sociologist with whom he later coauthored a book (*Pétrole et violence,* Paris, 1974). While in opposition, he became convinced that Iran's only political solution was a return to a (reformed) Islamic ideology.

Bani Sadr met Ayatollah Ruhollah Khomeini in 1972 while in Iraq for his father's funeral, and the two kept in close contact. They were reunited in Paris in 1978, shortly before Khomeini's triumphant return to Iran.

After the Iranian Revolution of 1979, Bani Sadr served as foreign minister and minister of finance before becoming Iran's first elected president in 1980. The early stages of his presidency were fraught with conflicts with two pivotal members of the Islamic Republican Party (IRP), Ayatollah Mohammad Beheshti and Ali Akbar Hashemi Rafsanjani, although Bani Sadr still enjoyed the support of Ayatollah Khomeini. The tension between Bani Sadr and the IRP had become apparent after the seizure of the U.S. embassy in Tehran in November 1979 by a radical group of Muslim students, the so-called "Students following the Imam's Line." Bani Sadr opposed the takeover and tried in vain to secure the freedom of the hostages.

Khomeini appointed Bani Sadr commander in chief and chairman of the Revolutionary Council in February 1980. Under his influence the government sought to restore normalcy and order in the country. Bani Sadr's efforts to stabilize the country and curb revolutionary excesses did not bear fruit, however, and his influence was undermined by the IRP's sweeping victory in the first parliamentary election and the subsequent imposition of the IRP candidate, Mohammad Ali Raja'i, as prime minister. An attempted coup backed by part of the Iranian military in July 1980 was a further blow to his presidency. The armed forces were purged severely, and Bani Sadr's appointees to several key positions were executed.

After Iraq attacked Iran in September 1980, Bani Sadr was appointed by Khomeini as chairman of the Supreme Defense Council. Spending most of his time at the front and away from Tehran, he failed to exploit the opportunities provided by the war to bolster his power. From September 1980 until its closure by the IRP in June 1981, Bani Sadr used his newspaper, *Jomhuri-ye Eslami* (Islamic Republic), to criticize the IRP and other hard-line factions in the government. The IRP, for its part, criticized Iran's repeated defeats on the war front and Bani Sadr's policy of favoring the regular armed forces over the Revolutionary Guards in combat.

Further showdowns with the IRP drove Bani Sadr to seek support from various opposition groups active in Iran, including the National Front and the Mojahedin-e Khalq. Bani Sadr was dismissed as acting commander in chief of the armed forces on 10 June 1981. Following repeated failed attempts at reconciliation the parliament, with Ayatollah Khomeini's approval, proceeded to impeach him. Bani Sadr fled the country with the help of the Mojahedin-e Khalq and, once in Paris, joined the leadership of the National Resistance Council alongside Masud Rajavi, the head of the Mojahedin. It was a short-lived union, mainly owing to Rajavi's increasingly dictatorial and cultic personality, and Bani Sadr severed his ties with the National Resistance Council in 1984. In 1997 he was in the limelight once again, when he testified against Iran in a court in Berlin, where the Iranian government was accused of complicity in the murder of four of its opponents, including the leader of the Kurdish Democratic Party. The court ruled that the murder had been approved at the highest echelons of the Iranian government.

As of 2003, Bani Sadr continued to live in Paris, pursuing political activity mostly in the form of lectures and public statements on political developments in Iran, and signing his name always as the "elected President of the people of Iran." His many books include *L'espérance trahie* (Hope betrayed, 1982), *The Fundamental Principles and Precepts of Islamic Government* (1981), and *My Turn to Speak: Iran, the Revolution, and Secret Deals with the U.S.* (1991).

> *See also* BEHESHTI, MOHAMMAD; KHOMEINI, RUHOLLAH; RAFSANJANI, ALI AKBAR HASHEMI; RAJAVI, MASUD.

Bibliography

Chehabi, H. E. *Iranian Politics and Religious Modernism: The Liberation Movement of Iran under the Shah and Khomeini.* Ithaca, NY: Cornell University Press, 1990.

Milani, Mohsen M. *The Making of Iran's Islamic Revolution: From Monarchy to Islamic Republic,* 2d edition. Boulder, CO: Westview Press, 1994.

Rouleau, Eric. "The War and the Struggle for the State." In *Iran Two Years After, MERIP Report* 98 (July–August 1981): 8–11.

NEGUIN YAVARI

BANI SAKHR TRIBE

See TRIBES AND TRIBALISM

BANKING

Banking and finance issues in the context of the modern Middle East.

Commercial banks are especially strategic intermediaries between enterprises and investors in most countries of the Middle East and Africa, where alternative sources of private capital, such as stock markets, are relatively underdeveloped. In most of these countries, the banks are also important instruments of political control and patronage. Structural adjustment, undertaken on the advice of international financial institutions since the mid-1980s, has not significantly altered the patterns of political control discussed in this article.

History

Although the basic instruments of European finance were probably imported from Egypt to Italy (and from there to the rest of Europe) in the early Middle Ages, Britain, followed by France, Germany, and other European powers, introduced modern banking into the region in the nineteenth century. European trading houses founded banks in Alexandria, Egypt, as early as 1842, shortly after the British obliged Muhammad Ali to dismantle his state monopolies. The British opened a bank in İzmir, Turkey, in the same year. Moses Pariente, a Moroccan Jew operating under British consular protection out of Europe's trading entrepôt of Tangier, opened Morocco's first bank, a trading house tied to the Anglo-Egyptian Bank based in London and Gibraltar, in 1844.

Although Britain's İzmir venture failed, the Ottoman authorities took up the challenge to modernize their finances. The Porte (the Ottoman authorities) prevailed upon two *sarraflar* (money changers) to establish the Bank of Istanbul in 1847 to trade in *sehim kaimesi* (treasury bond documents), and Tunisia's infamous finance minister, Mahmud Bin Ayad, immediately followed suit with a central bank, Dar al-Mal, to issue treasury bills. But these experiments in central banking were short lived: Bin Ayad looted his bank and fled the country in 1852.

Virtually all of the other commercial banks founded in the nineteenth century were European, and they displaced the moneychangers or, like the National Bank of Egypt, subcontracted with them for business in the informal agricultural sector. The oldest survivor into the twenty-first century is the Osmanli Bankasi (Ottoman Bank), originally founded in London in response to the Ottoman decree of 1856, inspired by Her Majesty's Government, calling for "banks and other similar institutions" to promote and monitor overseas loans to the Ottoman treasury. The Ottoman Bank acquired a distinctly French look after 1863, when a consortium led by Crédit Mobilier doubled its shares and renamed it the Banque Impériale Ottomane (Ottoman Imperial Bank). As the result of a merger in 2001, it became Turkey's ninth largest bank but is wholly owned by an even larger Turkish private sector bank. The National Bank of Egypt, founded in 1898 and nationalized by Gamal Abdel Nasser in 1964, is one of Egypt's two most powerful state banks. The only other recognizable remnant of nineteenth-century European imperialism is the Banque Franco-Tunisienne, founded in 1878 but barely surviving in the twenty-first century after years of mismanagement by a leading Tunisian public sector bank.

National Banking Systems

Banking was too strategic an industry to escape the control of national governments once they achieved a degree of economic and political independence from their foreign sponsors. The patterns of control varied with the political and economic strategies of the respective regimes. The monarchies tended to prefer indirect family control through their business interests, whereas the single-party states, such as Turkey in the 1930s, and Algeria, Egypt, Iraq, Syria, and Tunisia in the 1960s, established public sectors for absorbing most or all of the banks, whether they were foreign or locally owned. Iran followed suit after the revolution of 1979. Israel had to bail out its big banks in 1983 but succeeded in selling off the government's share in some of them. The only republic in the region to support a privately owned banking system is Lebanon. Until the Civil War broke out in 1975, Lebanon was the financial center and trading entrepôt for much of the Middle East. Its Bank Control Commission regulates the eighty or so commercial banks on behalf of the Banque du Liban, the country's central

bank, and remains a model in the region for the professional supervision of banks.

Like Lebanon, the monarchies that survived the revolutions sweeping the Arab world in the 1950s and 1960s tended to conserve their banks as well as their ruling families, and they encouraged local businesspeople to gain control of the banks in the 1970s and 1980s, usually continuing a close association with their foreign founders. Until 2003, for instance, Citibank not only had a 30 percent interest in the Saudi American Bank but also a management contract. The leading Moroccan banks, despite the Moroccanization of commerce in 1973, have kept close ties with the French banks that founded them. In Jordan, the Arab Bank deserves special mention: Founded by Abd al-Hamid Shoman in Jerusalem in 1930, the bank survived the creation of Israel in 1948 and Jordan's subsequent takeover of the West Bank and East Jerusalem. It is not only the oldest locally owned bank but also one of the largest international ones to be based in an Arab country. The other large international players, such as Arab Banking Corporation, are based in the Persian Gulf states (see Table 1). Bahrain, a money-market center for offshore international banking since the mid 1970s, became the center for Islamic finance in the twenty-first century as well.

Market Penetration

Many Muslims tend to distrust banks, either out of a general distrust of public institutions or because they object to interest on religious grounds. The banking systems that preserved continuity with their foreign origins tended to be more in touch with local depositors than the public sector monopolies that broke with the foreign banks. The percentage of money held in banks, rather than as cash under people's mattresses, was high in the Gulf Cooperation Council (GCC) city states and also in Israel, Lebanon, Turkey, and Iran—countries that had delayed or never gotten around to nationalizing their respective banking systems.

The small size of a country may ease the penetration of banks into household finance, but the banks of large countries like Turkey and Iran also substantially outperformed those in all Arab countries except Lebanon. Lebanon had always encouraged commercial banking, which became its virtual

Top 100 Arab banks

Country	Bank	Capital (US $m)	Total assets (US $m)	Capital assets ratio (%)	Return on assets (%)
Syria	Commercial Bank of Syria	730	66,215	1.1	0.2
Bahrain	Arab Banking Corporation	2,110	26,586	7.94	0.6
Saudi Arabia	National Commercial Bank	2,275	26,569	8.56	na
Egypt	National Bank of Egypt	1,027	22,631	4.54	0.61
Jordan	Arab Bank	1,865	22,228	8.39	1.41
Saudi Arabia	Saudi American Bank	2,243	20,623	10.87	2.91
Saudi Arabia	Riyad Bank	2,139	17,933	11.93	2.01
Egypt	Banque Misr	528	16,130	3.27	0.44
Bahrain	Gulf International Bank	1,236	15,232	8.11	0.61
Kuwait	National Bank of Kuwait	1,421	14,551	9.77	2.52
Saudi Arabia	Al Rajhi Banking & Investment Corporation	1,794	13,816	12.99	2.98
Saudi Arabia	Saudi British Bank	1,055	11,194	9.42	1.98
Saudi Arabia	Arab National Bank	887	10,785	8.23	1.2
Saudi Arabia	Al Bank Al Saudi Al Fransi	1,075	10,683	10.06	2.11
Egypt	Banque du Caire	358	9,422	3.8	0.39
U.A.E.	National Bank of Dubai	1,133	8,893	12.74	1.38
U.A.E.	National Bank of Abu Dhabi	878	8,782	10	1.96
Libya	Libyan Arab Foreign Bank	445	8,769	5.08	1.52
Qatar	Qatar National Bank	1,294	7,797	16.6	1.86
Kuwait	Kuwait Finance House	685	7,674	8.93	2.26
U.A.E.	Abu Dhabi Commercial Bank	1,035	7,241	14.3	2.35
Algeria	Banque Extérieure d'Algérie	244	7,116	3.43	0.11
Saudi Arabia	Saudi Hollandi Bank	550	6,721	8.18	1.96
Morocco	Crédit Populaire du Maroc	536	6,716	7.99	1.63
U.A.E.	Emirates Bank International	1,075	6,406	16.78	2.38
Lebanon	Blom Bank	285	6,285	4.54	1.41
Egypt	Bank of Alexandria	322	6,225	5.18	0.55
U.A.E.	Mashreqbank	797	6,181	12.89	1.93
Kuwait	Gulf Bank	619	6,114	10.12	2.24
Algeria	Banque Nationale d'Algérie	312	5,944	5.25	0.6
Algeria	Crédit Populaire d'Algérie	273	5,557	4.91	0.02
Kuwait	Commercial Bank of Kuwait	618	5,503	11.22	2.12
Kuwait	Burgan Bank	530	4,839	10.95	1.46
Lebanon	Banque de la Méditerranée	470	4,659	10.09	0.64
Lebanon	Byblos Bank	271	4,651	5.83	1.14
Lebanon	Banque Audi	247	4,567	5.42	0.95
Morocco	Banque Commerciale du Maroc	441	4,313	10.23	2.14
Morocco	Banque Marocaine du Commerce Extérieur	449	4,199	10.7	1.11
U.A.E.	Dubai Islamic Bank	310	4,175	7.41	1.02
Egypt	Commercial International Bank (Egypt)	351	4,143	8.47	2.43
Bahrain	Ahli United Bank	542	4,103	13.22	1.34
Saudi Arabia	Saudi Investment Bank	594	4,073	14.59	1.99
Kuwait	Al-Ahli Bank of Kuwait	518	3,859	13.42	1.18
U.A.E.	Union National Bank	401	3,613	11.11	1.83
Kuwait	Bank of Kuwait & the Middle East	445	3,519	12.64	1.47
Oman	BankMuscat	318	3,502	9.08	0.68
Bahrain	Investcorp Bank	918	3,443	26.66	1.46
Lebanon	Banque Libano-Française	186	3,286	5.66	1.23
Morocco	Wafabank	317	3,253	9.73	1.6
Lebanon	Fransabank	218	3,108	7.03	1.3
Bahrain	Bank of Bahrain & Kuwait	299	2,929	10.21	1.52
Egypt	Misr International Bank	232	2,910	7.99	1.92
Bahrain	National Bank of Bahrain	330	2,868	11.5	1.68
Egypt	Arab International Bank	405	2,746	14.75	0.38
Tunisia	Société Tunisienne de Banque	235	2,668	8.8	1.17
Oman	National Bank of Oman	245	2,472	9.89	-0.64
Egypt	Suez Canal Bank	166	2,450	6.77	0.94
Jordan	The Housing Bank for Trade and Finance	362	2,410	15.01	1.76
Tunisia	Banque Nationale Agricole	243	2,242	10.84	0.97

[continued]

Top 100 Arab banks [CONTINUED]

Country	Bank	Capital (US $m)	Total assets (US $m)	Capital assets Ratio (%)	Return on assets (%)
Egypt	Faisal Islamic Bank of Egypt	77	2,221	3.45	0.39
Lebanon	Credit Libanais	108	2,123	5.1	0.92
U.A.E.	Commercial Bank of Dubai	333	2,002	16.63	2.94
Jordan	Jordan National Bank	98	1,910	5.12	-0.03
Tunisia	Banque Internationale Arabe de Tunisie	156	1,810	8.62	1.55
Qatar	Doha Bank	172	1,787	9.64	1.17
Oman	Oman International Bank	229	1,749	13.08	0.38
Lebanon	Bank of Beirut & the Arab Countries	78	1,682	4.64	0.79
U.A.E.	Arab Bank for Investment & Foreign Trade	336	1,573	21.35	0.7
Egypt	National Bank for Development	95	1,567	6.05	0.89
Egypt	Egyptian American Bank	116	1,537	7.56	1.06
Egypt	National Société Générale Bank	125	1,487	8.41	2.27
Libya	Sahara Bank	269	1,483	18.14	1.18
Qatar	Commercial Bank of Qatar	182	1,431	12.71	1.94
Morocco	Crédit du Maroc	128	1,417	9.04	1.13
Saudi Arabia	Bank Al-Jazira	185	1,365	13.53	1.12
Jordan	Jordan Islamic Bank for Finance & Investment	76	1,280	5.9	0.15
Bahrain	Shamil Bank of Bahrain	258	1,242	20.8	1.69
Qatar	Qatar Islamic Bank	102	1,213	8.4	1.52
Tunisia	Banque du Sud	101	1,079	9.35	1.55
Jordan	Bank of Jordan	75	1,040	7.18	2.52
Egypt	Arab African International Bank	142	1,029	13.84	1.01
Tunisia	Banque de Tunisie	116	945	12.28	2.59
U.A.E.	First Gulf Bank	141	938	15.08	1.79
Bahrain	United Gulf Bank	214	931	23.01	0.43
Bahrain	Bahrain International Bank	176	888	19.78	-5.29
Egypt	Cairo Barclays Bank	64	877	7.3	1.49
Oman	Oman Arab Bank	100	832	12.01	2.14
Jordan	Jordan Kuwait Bank	76	804	9.44	1.78
U.A.E.	National Bank of Fujairah	151	718	21.1	2.66
U.A.E.	Invest bank	135	700	19.31	3.11
U.A.E.	Rakbank	147	660	22.32	2.49
Bahrain	Bahraini Saudi Bank	88	595	14.82	2
U.A.E.	National Bank of Sharjah	188	557	33.8	3.73
Egypt	Delta International Bank	108	544	19.88	5.9
Bahrain	TAIB Bank	145	540	26.88	1.84
U.A.E.	Bank of Sharjah	93	525	17.78	2.6
Egypt	Société Arabe Internationale de Banque	85	500	16.89	2.1
U.A.E.	United Arab Bank	117	484	24.08	4.04
U.A.E.	National Bank of Umm Al-Qaiwain	126	466	27.04	3.45
Bahrain	Albaraka Islamic Bank	62	260	23.83	1.06

TABLE BY GGS INFORMATION SERVICES, THE GALE GROUP.

government during the anarchy of 1975 through 1990. Turkey systematically encouraged a Turkish private sector after 1924, and Iran delayed its revolutionary attack on privately owned banks until 1979, when the banks had already acquired substantial control over the country's money—a control that would be recovered in the 1990s (see Table 2).

Liberalization

Under the gun of international debt workouts after 1982 (but this time by international financial insti-

tutions rather than the nineteenth-century imperialists), most of the commercial banking systems in the region were partially liberalized in the 1990s. In the predominantly state-owned banking systems of Algeria, Egypt, and Tunisia, liberalization meant adding a satellite private sector, whereas reform in the monarchies tended to strengthen privately owned oligopolies in defense of their respective ruling families. The different regimes of the Middle East and North Africa were able to parry the international pressures for reform so as to reinforce rather than undermine their enduring authoritar-

The Saudi Arabia Bank in Riyadh. Banks in much of the Middle East and North Africa serve as important means of exercising political control and patronage, and many of them, particularly in countries with royal families, have maintained close ties to foreign founders or investment groups. © THOMAS HARTWELL/CORBIS. REPRODUCED BY PERMISSION.

Money in banks as percent of money supply

	1975	1980	1985	1989	1990	1995	1998
Algeria	62.2%	54.7%	65.8%	61.1%	60.6%	68.7%	69.7%
Bahrain	86.9%	88.9%	91.3%	91.9%	88.7%	92.6%	95.0%
Egypt	52.4%	67.2%	73.0%	82.9%	85.0%	86.0%	85.8%
Iran	85.9%	72.5%	76.1%	81.3%	82.7%	89.0%	90.1%
Iraq	46.5%	43.3%	n/a	n/a	n/a	n/a	n/a
Israel	85.0%	91.3%	98.2%	96.4%	96.2%	96.7%	n/a
Jordan	52.4%	64.1%	71.7%	73.1%	71.3%	78.1%	82.5%
Kuwait	88.6%	91.2%	92.6%	93.7%	n/a	95.2%	95.4%
Lebanon	79.0%	86.2%	91.4%	92.2%	91.3%	95.4%	96.9%
Libya	74.6%	83.3%	80.5%	78.1%	76.4%	77.7%	68.6%
Mauritania	69.5%	66.4%	66.1%	71.2%	73.8%	71.6%	n/a
Morocco	67.4%	67.3%	71.5%	73.7%	74.3%	76.8%	79.3%
Oman	67.4%	70.8%	80.9%	82.8%	81.7%	84.4%	88.5%
Qatar	86.3%	84.7%	90.1%	91.3%	90.1%	92.4%	93.6%
Saudi	62.4%	66.8%	75.7%	81.1%	76.1%	82.1%	84.1%
Sudan	61.0%	61.3%	n/a	n/a	59.4%	64.2%	60.0%
Syria	48.0%	44.1%	53.4%	48.5%	48.1%	53.4%	54.3%
Tunisia	75.6%	79.3%	80.0%	83.1%	82.0%	83.2%	84.4%
Turkey	77.9%	77.0%	88.2%	88.8%	87.9%	92.5%	95.0%
U.A.E.	92.9%	90.9%	93.7%	94.3%	92.4%	92.1%	91.7%
Yemen	n/a	n/a	n/a	54.9%	n/a	47.4%	57.6%
PRDY				52.9%			

TABLE BY GGS INFORMATION SERVICES, THE GALE GROUP.

ian traits. Neither in Egypt nor Tunisia, for example, were the patronage operations of their respective state banks seriously threatened, nor has the Moroccan private sector escaped a business oligopoly that is partly owned by the Makhzan (royal treasury). But foreign competition may pose new challenges under measures that break down national barriers to financial services.

Islamic Finance

One response to global economic pressures is Islamic finance, designed to attract the savings of people who distrust conventional banks. Islamic banking emerged officially for the first time in Dubai in 1974, and two Saudi entrepreneurs, Prince Muhammad al-Faisal (son of the late King Faisal ibn Abd al-Aziz Al Sa'ud) and Shaykh Salih Kamil, then projected such banks to over twenty countries, including the United Kingdom and Denmark, in the subsequent decade. In some of the less developed countries, such as Sudan and Yemen, the Islamic banking movement made important inroads. The Faisal Islamic Bank of Sudan enabled Hasan al-Turabi to cultivate new business networks that supported his seizure of power in 1989 (but then deserted him in 1999 when his military allies removed him). The wealthy Gulf countries, however, fuel most of the steady growth of these new institutions. In Saudi Arabia in particular, conventional banks have opened up Islamic windows to satisfy customers who reject interest as a matter of Islamic principle but who are eager to receive legitimate returns on investment. Most of the savings attracted by Islamic banks are just as likely, however, to be reinvested abroad, in the United States or Europe, as those of the conventional banks.

The international crackdown on money laundering after 11 September 2001 adversely affected Islamic banks because the Al-Baraka group of Shaykh Salih Kamil was confused with a company called Al-Baraka in Somalia, which transferred workers' remittances but was also suspected by the U.S. Treasury of being associated with international terrorists. The United States, however, has put only one very marginal Sudanese Islamic bank on its blacklist, and the Islamic banks not only recovered after the shock of 11 September but increased their share in the wealthy Gulf markets to well over 10 percent of their respective commercial banking assets.

See also FAISAL IBN ABD AL-AZIZ AL SA'UD; LEBANESE CIVIL WAR (1975–1990); NASSER, GAMAL ABDEL; TURABI, HASAN AL-.

Bibliography

Bistolfi, Robert. *Structures économiques et indépendance monétaire.* Paris: Editions Cujas, 1967.

Davison, Roderic H. *Essays in Ottoman and Turkish History, 1774–1923.* Austin: University of Texas Press, 1990.

Feis, Herbert. Europe: *The World's Banker, 1970–1914.* New Haven, CT: Yale University Press, 1930.

Fieldhouse, D. K. *Economics and Empire, 1830–1914.* London: Weidenfeld and Nicolson, 1973.

Henry, Clement M. *The Mediterranean Debt Crescent: Money and Power in Algeria, Egypt, Morocco, Tunisia, and Turkey.* Gainesville: University Press of Florida, 1996.

Henry, Clement M., and Wilson, Rodney, eds. *The Politics of Islamic Finance.* Edinburgh, U.K.: Edinburgh University Press, 2004.

Landes, David. *Bankers and Pashas: International Finance and Economic Imperialism in Egypt.* Cambridge, MA: Harvard University Press, 1958.

Snider, Lewis W. *Growth, Debt, and Politics: Economic Adjustment and the Political Performance of Developing Countries.* Boulder, CO: Westview, 1996.

Udovitch, Abraham L. *Partnership and Profit in Medieval Islam.* Princeton, NJ: Princeton University Press, 1970.

Warde, Ibrahim A. *Islamic Finance in the Global Economy.* Edinburgh, U.K.: Edinburgh University Press, 2000.

CLEMENT MOORE HENRY

BANKS

See BANKING

BANNA, HASAN AL-
[1906–1949]

Founder of the Muslim Brotherhood.

Hasan al-Banna was born in October 1906 in al-Buhayra, one of Egypt's northern Nile delta provinces, to a religious father. He was educated first at a traditional Islamic *kuttab* (religious school) and later, at the age of twelve, joined a primary school. During the early part of his life al-Banna became involved with Sufism and continued that association for most of his life. At the age of fourteen he joined a primary teachers' school and two years later enrolled in Dar al-Ulum College, from which he graduated as a teacher.

In Cairo during his student years, al-Banna joined religious societies involved in Islamic education. However, he soon realized that this type of religious activity was inadequate to bring the Islamic faith back to its status in the public life of Egypt. He felt that more activism was needed, so he organized students from al-Azhar University and Dar al-Ulum and started to preach in mosques and popular meeting places. During this period, al-Banna came to be influenced by the writings of Muhammad Abduh, Rashid Rida, and Ahmad Taymur Pasha.

When he graduated in 1927 he was appointed as a teacher of Arabic in a primary school in al-Isma'iliyya, a new small town in Egypt with a semi-European character. It hosted the headquarters of the Suez Canal Company and a sizable foreign community. In al-Isma'iliyya al-Banna started to preach his ideas to poor Muslim workers, small merchants, and civil servants, warning his audience against the liberal lifestyle of the Europeans in the town and the dangers of emulating it, thus cultivating fear and anxiety in them.

In March 1928 he founded the Muslim Brotherhood, or Muslim Brethren. In the first four years of its existence, al-Banna's primary goal was to recruit membership, establishing branches along the eastern and western edge of the delta. The quick and remarkable spread of the Brotherhood engendered governmental resistance, especially during the cabinet of Isma'il Sidqi.

In 1932 to 1933 al-Banna was transferred to Cairo and his group merged with the Society for Islamic Culture, forming the first branch of the Muslim Brothers, and Cairo became the headquarters of the society. During this period, the number of branches reached 1,500 to 2,000; most branches ran schools, clinics, and other welfare institutions. Branches also were established in Sudan, Syria, and Iraq, and the society's publications were distributed throughout Islamic countries.

At the beginning of his political career al-Banna did not have an elaborate program; his message focused on the centrality of Islam. Gradually, he developed the notion of Islam as a religion that embraces all aspects of human life and conduct. He declared that the objective of the Muslim Brother-

hood was to create a new generation capable of understanding the essence of Islam and of acting accordingly. He believed that Islam was the solution to the problem of Egypt and the Islamic world. Following World War II, al-Banna assumed a greater political role. He started to call for the replacement of secular institutions by Islamic-oriented ones and asked for major reforms. However, al-Banna did not advocate violent political action as the means toward achieving political goals; in fact, he and several members of his organization ran for parliamentary elections more than once and lost. Al-Banna accepted the legitimacy of the Egyptian regime and tried to work from within the system. His condemnation of Egyptian parties was not based on a rejection of the idea of multiparty systems but on the rejection of corruption and manipulation. This is why the Egyptian Brethren today have been able to embrace as legitmate theories pluralism, human rights, and democracy (respectively, *ikhtilaf, al-huquq al-shar'iyya,* and *shura*).

By the end of World War II al-Banna was an acknowledged political figure, and the Muslim Brethren had emerged as a strong force presenting itself as a political alternative. As was the case with other parties, the society established a military wing, which assassinated a number of its adversaries. The Brethren reached its apogee during the Arab-Israel War of 1948, in which the Muslim Brothers participated through their paramilitary organizations. However, the expansion of the society, its growing influence, and its development of a strong military force brought it into a clash with the government. In February 1949 al-Banna was assassinated by police agents. Today, his ideology still informs most of the moderate Islamic movements across all of the Islamic world, and his movement is still the leading ideological power behind the expansion of Islamism.

See also ABDUH, MUHAMMAD; KUTTAB; MUSLIM BROTHERHOOD; RIDA, RASHID.

Bibliography

Brynjar, Lia. *The Society of Muslim Brothers in Egypt.* Reading, U.K.: Garnet Publishers, 1998.

Moussalli, Ahmad S. *Moderate and Radical Islamic Fundamentalism: The Quest for Modernity, Legitimacy, and the Islamic State.* Gainesville: University of Florida Press, 1999.

ALI E. HILLAL DESSOUKI
UPDATED BY AHMAD S. MOUSSALLI

BANNA, SABRI AL-
[1937–2002]

*Palestinian militant who broke with the Palestine Liber-
ation Organization and formed his own group.*

Born in Jaffa, Sabri al-Banna (also called Abu Nidal)
fled Palestine as a refugee in 1948, joined the Baʿth
party in the 1950s, and later joined al-Fatah in 1967.
Al-Banna eventually headed the Palestine Liberation
Organization (PLO) office in Baghdad but also
worked with the Iraqi intelligence services. He opposed the PLO's move toward a two-state solution
in 1974, was expelled from al-Fatah, and formed his
own group, al-Fatah—Revolutionary Council. After
his eventual expulsion from Iraq, he based himself
in Syria and Libya.

Abu Nidal's radical group served the interests
of several Arab states, assassinating Arab and Israeli
diplomats as well as other Palestinians, including
moderates like Isam Sartawi in 1983. The group also
gained notoriety for terrorist attacks in nearly two
dozen countries, including the random killing of
passengers at the Rome and Vienna airports in
1985. In 1989, internal conflicts weakened his organization, which effectively ceased to function after 1996.

Abu Nidal died of gunshot wounds in Baghdad
in August 2002. Although Iraq claimed it was a suicide, al-Banna most likely was killed by Iraqi agents.

See also Baʿth, al-; Fatah, al-; Palestine
Liberation Organization (PLO); Sartawi,
Issam.

Bibliography
Seale, Patrick. *Abu Nidal: A Gun for Hire.* London: Hutchinson, 1992.

Shafritz, Jay M.; Gibbons, E. F., Jr.; and Scott, Gregory
E. J.; eds. *Almanac of Modern Terrorism.* New York: Facts
On File, 1991.

STEVE TAMARI
UPDATED BY MICHAEL R. FISCHBACH

BANNIS, MOHAMMAD
[1948–]

Moroccan poet and critic.

Mohammad Bannis was born in Fez, Morocco. He
received his Ph.D. in modern Arabic poetry from
the University of Rabat in 1989, and is a professor
of Arabic literature at Muhammad V University in
Rabat. He is director of the House of Poetry.

Bannis has published many books of literary
criticism and poetry, as well as an Arabic translation of Abdelkabir Khatibi's *La Blessure du Nom Propre*
(*al-Ism al-Arabi al-Jarih* [1980]). An avant-garde poet,
Bannis's interests extend from poetics to graphic
arts, and his writings are deeply rooted in Moroccan life and culture.

Bannis is closely involved in the political life of
Morocco, and favors the involvement of the individual in changing society; otherwise, the written
word is equivalent to a dead word, as he suggests in
his poem "Belonging to a New Family." He is among
the group of poets who changed the structure of the
poem and presented a new interpretation of reality, dynamic and optimistic. His collection of poetry, *Hibat al-Faragh* (1992; Gift of leisure), clearly
reflects these structural and thematic changes.
Another experimental technique is employed in
Mawasim al-Sharq (1986; Festivals of the east), in
which he combines poetic prose with free verse. The
poems adopt the shapes of the ideas they embody.
In *Kitab al-Hubb* (1995; Book of love) Bannis delves
into the world of dreams to understand the emotions of love, whereas in *al-Makan al-Wathaniyy* (1996;
Pagan place) the poet seeks a close connection with
nature.

See also Literature: Arabic, North African.

Bibliography
Jayyusi, Salma Khadra. *Modern Arabic Poetry.* New York:
Columbia University Press, 1987.

AIDA A. BAMIA

BANOCO

See Bahrain National Oil Company

BAQRI FAMILY

Prominent Jewish family in Algeria.

The Cohen—Baqri family (not related to the Arab
Bakri family) was one of three Livornese (Italy) Jew-
ish clans (the others were the Boucharas and the
Busnachs) that were prominent in Algerian com-

merce and politics throughout the eighteenth and early nineteenth centuries. Invariably it was a member of one of these three families who served as *muqaddam* (government-appointed head) of the Jewish community in Algiers.

In 1797, Joseph Baqri and his brother-in-law Naphtali Busnach went into partnership. Naphtali was the chief adviser of the newly elected Dey Mustafa, and all diplomatic and commercial contact with the regency had to go through the Baqri & Busnach firm. It was over a debt of 5 million French francs owed to the firm by the government of France since the 1780s that the Dey Husayn insulted France's consul in 1827. This touched off an international "incident" that ended with the French invasion of 1830. The last Baqri of importance was Jacob, who was reconfirmed as "Chef de la Nation Juive" by the French in November 1830 but moved to France shortly thereafter.

See also BUSNACH FAMILY.

Bibliography

Hirschberg, H. Z. *A History of the Jews in North Africa,* 2d edition. Leiden, Netherlands: Brill, 1974–1981.

NORMAN STILLMAN

BARAHENI, REZA
[1935–]

An Iranian poet, essayist, novelist, and literary critic.

Reza Baraheni was born in Tabriz and educated in his native city through college. He went to Turkey for graduate work, obtaining a Ph.D. in literature from Istanbul University in 1963. After returning to Iran, he became a professor of English at Tehran University. During the 1960s and 1970s, he produced several volumes of verse and essays and established literary criticism as a serious discipline. In 1972, government censors banned publication of his first novel, *The Infernal Days of Mr. Ayaz.* By this time, his essays were becoming increasingly critical of political and social life in Iran under the rule of Mohammad Reza Shah Pahlavi. In the fall of 1973, after returning from a one-year sabbatical in the United States, he was arrested by the secret police and detained under brutal conditions for 102 days. He described his prison experiences in *God's Shadow: Prison Poems.*

Baraheni left Iran in 1975 and settled in the United States but continued to be an outspoken critic of political repression in his native country. After the shah was deposed in the Iranian Revolution of 1979, Baraheni returned to Iran and resumed teaching at Tehran University. However, he was purged from the faculty in the cultural revolution of 1980 and was arrested briefly in 1981 and again in 1982. During the 1980s and early 1990s, he published numerous essays and several popular novels, but he also became critical of intellectual repression. In 1994, he was one of the signatories of an open letter to authorities condemning the lack of freedom of expression in Iran. In 1997, he decided for a second time to live in exile and moved to Canada, where he became a professor of comparative literature in Toronto. In June 2001, Baraheni was elected president of PEN Canada, an international organization of writers.

See also IRANIAN REVOLUTION (1979); PAHLAVI, MOHAMMAD REZA.

Bibliography

Baraheni, Reza. *God's Shadow: Prison Poems.* Bloomington: Indiana University Press, 1976.

Baraheni, Reza. *The Crowned Cannibals: Writings on Repression in Iran.* New York: Vintage Books, 1977.

MICHAEL C. HILLMAN
UPDATED BY ERIC HOOGLUND

BARAKA

See GLOSSARY

BARAKAT, HODA
[1952–]

A Lebanese novelist.

Hoda (also Huda) Barakat was born in Beirut in 1952 and grew up in a Maronite family. She studied French literature, married a Muslim, and in 1989 left Lebanon, with her two sons, for Paris, where she began to write and publish in Arabic. Although she had published a collection, *Al-Tha'irat* (The female rebels), in 1985, Barakat is best known for her powerful novels, set during or after the Lebanese Civil War (1975–1990). Her 1990 *Hajar al-Duhk* (Stone of laughter) won the prestigious Al-Naqid Award. It brilliantly investigates the distorting consequences of war. Her 1993 *Ahl al-Hawa* (People of the breeze) extends the Lebanese narrative to a postwar era in which war is clearly still playing itself out within the national psyche. The 1998 *Harith al-Miyah* (Tiller of waters) focuses on Beirut, a city Barakat admits to both loving and hating, a city totally altered by the war experience.

Although she lives and writes in France, Barakat is intent on writing in the language she worships, Arabic. All of her novels to date are first-person male narratives, complicating gender perceptions and revealing how entwined sex, violence, and identity are. Barakat has emerged as one of the more interesting literary voices from Lebanon, pushing the boundaries of narration by internalizing the war in fiction written in an idiosyncratic Arabic language.

See also GENDER: GENDER AND EDUCATION; LEBANESE CIVIL WAR (1958); LEBANESE CIVIL WAR (1975–1990); LEBANON; LITERATURE: ARABIC.

Bibliography

Rakha, Youssef. "Hoda Barakat: Starting Over." *Al-Ahram Weekly* 457 (Nov.–Dec. 1999).

Salem, Elise. *Constructing Lebanon: A Century of Literary Narratives.* Gainesville: University Press of Florida, 2003.

ELISE SALEM

BARAK, EHUD
[1942–]

Professional soldier and Israeli politician, prime minister (1999–2001).

Ehud Barak, a distinguished and decorated professional soldier, will likely be remembered as the Israeli prime minister who failed in a dramatic attempt to reach a peace agreement with Yasir Arafat. Barak was born in 1942 and educated in a kibbutz. He joined the Israeli Defense Force (IDF) in 1959, became a professional soldier and rose quickly through the ranks, holding positions such as commander of the prestigious central commando unit—a position in which he personally distinguished himself in a number of audacious commando raids. One such operation was the rescue of passengers of a Sabena airliner that was hijacked at Lod Airport, in which Barak and ten other commando fighters penetrated the plane dressed as mechanics. Barak, disguised as

an Arab woman, also led a squad to assassinate top-level Palestine Liberation Organization (PLO) officials in Beirut.

During the October 1973 Arab–Israel War, Barak distinguished himself as a tank battalion commander on the Sinai front. In 1976 he was a member of the team that planned the Entebbe operation, in which the passengers of an Air France plane hijacked to Uganda were rescued and brought back to Israel.

In 1982, as chief of operations at the General Staff, he rose to the rank of major general. During the 1982 war in Lebanon, he was the deputy commander of an army corps fighting against the Syrians in the Biqa Valley. In 1983 he was appointed chief of military intelligence, and in 1986 he served as the commander of the Central Command in charge of the West Bank and the Jordanian front. In 1987 he became deputy chief, and in 1991 chief, of the General Staff, reaching the rank of lieutenant general.

During his military service he gained the highest number of any soldier of medals and citations for bravery and courage in battle, among them the highest Exemplary Medal. Twice during his service he was sent by the IDF to take up academic studies, earning a bachelor's degree in physics and mathematics from the Hebrew University in Jerusalem and a master's degree in systems analysis from Stanford University in California.

As chief of staff he had reservations regarding the Oslo Accords but loyally implemented them and coordinated the military aspects of the first deployment of the PLO in the Gaza Strip and Jericho. He also participated in discussions with the Syrians led by Prime Minister Yitzhak Rabin and met twice with the Syrian chief of staff.

In 1995 Ehud Barak ended his term as chief of staff and brought to a close thirty-six years of service in the IDF. After the required "cooling-off period" of six months, he joined Rabin's government as minister of the interior. After the assassination of Rabin, Barak was elected in November 1996 to the 14th Knesset, after winning third place on the list in the Labor Party's primary elections. When Shimon Peres failed in his bid to be elected prime minister, Barak replaced him as the head of the Labor Party. For two years he led the opposition to

Prime Minister Benjamin Netanyahu in the Knesset and defeated him in the May 1999 elections by an impressive majority of 56 percent of the votes.

In July 1999 Barak became prime minister, heading a broad coalition. His first dramatic act was to order the final and total retreat of the IDF from the southern Lebanon "security zone," dismembering on this occasion the South Lebanese Army, which had been allied with the IDF. He also tried to arrive at an agreement with the Syrians but failed. He was ready to retreat only to the international border, and rejected the Syrian demand for a withdrawal to the lines of 4 June 1967, which would have permitted them to sit on the northeastern shore of the Sea of Galilee and to have some claim to its waters.

Barak then turned to the Palestinians and offered them the most far-reaching concessions ever offered by an Israeli prime minister. This included withdrawal from over 90 percent of the territories occupied in 1967, sovereignty over the Arab parts of Jerusalem, and recognition of a Palestinian state. But he rejected Palestinian sovereignty over the Temple Mount and was unyielding in his demand that the Palestinians publicly forgo the "right of return" of their refugees. While there is much dispute over the reasons for the collapse of the Camp David summit convened by U.S. president Bill Clinton in July 2000, Barak blamed Yasir Arafat for his refusal to accept his "generous" offer and to accede to Israel's conditions.

By late summer 2000, Barak's coalition was tottering and was given a death blow by the failure of Camp David and the outbreak of riots and other forms of violence that ushered in the second intifada (the al-Aqsa Intifada). Barak lost his majority in the Knesset and called for new elections, in which his party lost miserably to the Likud, led by Ariel Sharon. Barak resigned his position as Labor Party leader and also his Knesset seat. He began a new business career, but remained in the public eye, commenting frequently on issues of peace and security and leaving many with the feeling that Ehud Barak might one day return to politics.

Bibliography

Beilin, Yossi. *Touching Peace: From the Oslo Accord to a Final Agreement.* London: Weidenfeld & Nicolson, 1999.

Enderlin, Charles. *Shattered Dreams: The Failure of the Peace Process in the Middle East, 1995–2002,* translated by Susan Fairfield. New York: Other Press, 2003.

MORDECHAI BAR-ON

BARAKZAI, AFDAL

See BARAKZAI DYNASTY

BARAKZAI DYNASTY

Rulers of Afghanistan in the nineteenth and twentieth centuries.

The Barakzai dynasty of Afghanistan was created gradually. Although the Barakzai were Durrani Pushtuns, their advent marked a departure from the

Zahir Shah (photographed about 1950) was the king of Afghanistan from 1933 to 1973, but relatives serving in turn as prime minister wielded actual power until 1963. This was followed by a decade of emerging reforms under a new constitution, until the king's cousin overthrew him. © HULTON-DEUTSCH COLLECTION/CORBIS. REPRODUCED BY PERMISSION.

The former king, Zahir Shah (second from right), returned to Afghanistan in April 2002, after a 29-year exile in Italy. Days later, joined by Afghan interim leader Hamid Karzai (to his right), he prayed at the mausoleum of his royal father, Nadir Shah, in Kabul. © REUTERS NEWMEDIA INC./CORBIS. REPRODUCED BY PERMISSION.

imperial mode of government that characterized the Durrani dynasty and empire. Unable to preserve the empire, the Barakzai divided the country into a series of competing principalities, which fought one another. This competition eventually resulted in the creation of a centralized state and the concentration of power in the hands of the Mohammadzai lineage of the Barakzai clan. The Mohammadzais faced a number of domestic and foreign challenges to their power but held on until 1973.

The Barakzai brothers rose to prominence during the reign of Shah Mahmud Durrani (1809–1818), when Fateh Khan Barakzai became chief minister and appointed several of his brothers to important governorships. In 1818, the crown prince had Fateh Khan blinded; seeking revenge, his brothers overthrew Shah Mahmud and brought about the collapse of the Durrani dynasty. They were, however, unable to agree among themselves and ended up carving three principalities centered around Kabul, Peshawar, and Kandahar. Dost Mohammad, who gained control of Kabul in 1826, was ousted from power in 1838 in the course of the first Anglo–Afghan war. He returned in 1842 and extended his control to all the Afghan provinces. During the wars of succession that followed his death, the country again was divided. Sher Ali (r. 1863–1866; 1869–1879) succeeded in establishing a centralized state, but the second British

invasion of 1878–1880 shattered the political structure he had built.

Ceding control of the country's foreign relations to Great Britain, Abd al-Rahman Khan (r. 1880–1901) concentrated his efforts on consolidating yet again a centralized polity in Afghanistan. He also attended to the welfare of his Mohammadzai lineage by assigning both its male and female members a regular stipend disbursed by the state. During his reign, the country acquired its present boundaries, including the disputed Durand Line dividing the Pushtuns between Afghanistan and the North-West Frontier Province of British India. He was the last Barakzai ruler to die peacefully while still in power. His son and successor, Habibollah Khan (r. 1901–1919), was assassinated, and his grandson Amanollah Khan (r. 1919–1929) was overthrown.

The Barakzai briefly lost power in 1929 when a Tajik villager, Habibollah Khan, Bacha-e Saqqao, the son of a water carrier, became ruler for nine months. They regained control under the leadership of Nadir Shah (r. 1929–1933), a descendant of Dost Mohammad's brother. Nadir Shah derived most of the state's revenue from taxes on foreign trade. In return, he conceded many privileges to the merchant class, who established modern financial and industrial enterprises. Following his assassination by a student, his son Zahir Shah (r. 1933–1973) succeeded him.

Zahir Shah reigned but for the most part did not rule. In a first phase, his two uncles, Muhammad Hashem (prime minister 1929–1946) and Shah Mahmud (prime minister 1946–1953), managed the affairs of the state. Then for a decade his cousin and brother-in-law, Muhammad Daud, exercised power, also as prime minister. Daud, taking advantage of the polarization of world politics, welcomed offers of foreign aid from both the Soviet Union and the United States. The state's shift from relying on domestic revenue to relying on foreign aid reinforced the power of the Mohammadzai lineage at the expense of the merchant class. The Afghan bureaucracy expanded substantially. A number of state-sponsored projects in irrigation and road building were initiated.

Daud was forced to resign when his policy of confrontation with Pakistan backfired in 1963. Zahir Shah promulgated a new constitution and assumed actual power, selecting prime ministers from outside the lineage. During the following decade, the country witnessed the formation of political movements and the emergence of a free press. In 1973, Daud overthrew Zahir and proclaimed a republic, although he suppressed the political freedoms that had been implemented by Zahir Shah. His overthrow by an Afghan Marxist party in April 1978 marked the end of the Barakzai rule in Afghanistan.

See also ABD AL-RAHMAN KHAN; AMANOLLAH KHAN; DOST MOHAMMAD BARAKZAI; DURAND LINE; DURRANI DYNASTY; HABIBOLLAH KHAN; NADIR BARAKZAI, MOHAMMAD; PUSHTUN.

Bibliography

Dupree, Louis. *Afghanistan*. Princeton, NJ: Princeton University Press, 1980.

Gregorian, Vartan. *The Emergence of Modern Afghanistan: Politics of Reform and Modernization 1880–1946*. Stanford, CA: Stanford University Press, 1969.

ASHRAF GHANI
UPDATED BY ERIC HOOGLUND

BARBARY PIRATE

See CORSAIRS

BARBARY STATES

Sixteenth-century term for states of North Africa's Mediterranean shore.

Morocco and the Ottoman Empire provinces of Algiers, Tunis, and Tripoli, which ranged along the southern coast of the Mediterranean Sea, became known in the West as the Barbary states beginning in the sixteenth century. In the West, they became synonymous with Corsair raiding and the so-called Barbary pirates, who waged the Barbary wars against ships of Christian states until 1821.

See also BARBARY WARS; CORSAIRS.

JEROME BOOKIN-WIENER

BARBARY WARS

Naval battles from the sixteenth century until 1821 between European powers and corsairs of North Africa

who were attacking merchant shipping in the Mediterranean.

With the Christian reconquest of Spain from the Moors in the west and the rise of the Ottoman Empire in the east, the Mediterranean basin became the stage for a major, long-running confrontation between Christianity and Islam. Naval warriors (called the Barbary pirates, but more correctly corsairs) based in the North African port cities of Algiers, Tunis, Tripoli, and Rabat-Salé in Morocco were among the most important frontline participants in the conflict. They began in the sixteenth century and lasted until the Treaty of Aix-la-Chapelle (1821) outlawed their activity.

The corsairs seized the ships of the Christian states whose rulers did not have treaties with their political overlords, took their goods, and sold their passengers and crews into slavery. As a result, a series of wars was fought throughout the period between the Europeans (after 1800 the newly independent United States of America also became involved) and their North African corsair adversaries. Because the corsairs served the interests of some of the Europeans, and their depredations against commercial shipping served the interests of the mercantilist policies of the time, the Christian nations never formed a common front against them.

It was only with the rise of free trade as the dominant theory in international trade that the powers banded together to quash the corsairs following Napoléon Bonaparte's defeat in 1815. The final stand of the corsairs came in 1818, with the Treaty of Aix-la-Chapelle in 1821 putting an end to the era by banning piracy, privateering, and corsairing.

See also CORSAIRS.

JEROME BOOKIN-WIENER

BARDO, TREATY OF

See TUNISIA: OVERVIEW

BARGHUTHI FAMILY

Prominent Palestinian family from the Ramallah area, north of Jerusalem.

Since the latter years of the Ottoman Empire, members of the Barghuthi family have played prominent roles in Palestinian politics. Umar Salih (1894–1965), a lawyer, politician, and historian, was an active Arab nationalist during Ottoman rule in Palestine. He received a law degree from the Government Law School in Jerusalem in 1924 and taught there from 1933 to 1948. He was a founding member of the Palestinian Arab National Party in 1923. In 1952, he was appointed to the Jordanian senate and in 1954 was elected to the chamber of deputies. Bashir (1931–), the general secretary of the Palestinian People's Party (formerly the Palestine Communist Party), founded Jerusalem's Palestinian weekly *al-Tali'a* in 1978. In 1996, he was appointed minister without portfolio in the Palestinian Authority. Mustafa (1954–) is a physician and chairman of the Union of Palestinian Medical Relief Committees, one of the grassroots organizations that formed the social and political backbone of the first Intifada.

See also ARAB NATIONALISM; BARGHUTHI, MARWAN; INTIFADA (1987–1991); PALESTINIAN AUTHORITY.

Bibliography

Petterson, Matthew W. *Palestinians in Profile: A Guide to Leading Palestinians in the Occupied Territories.* Jerusalem: PANORAMA Center for Dissemination of Alternative Information, 1993.

Porath, Yehoshua. *The Emergence of the Palestinian-Arab National Movement, 1918–1929.* London: Frank Cass, 1974.

Smith, Pamela Ann. *Palestine and the Palestinians: 1876–1983.* New York: St. Martin's Press, 1984.

STEVE TAMARI
UPDATED BY MICHAEL R. FISCHBACH

BARGHUTHI, MARWAN

[1959–]

Palestinian activist and parliamentarian.

Born in the West Bank village of Kubar, Barghuthi joined al-Fatah at age fifteen and helped form Shabiba, its youth group in the West Bank. After six years of Israeli imprisonment, he was deported in May 1987. While in exile, he was elected to the Revolutionary Council of al-Fatah in August 1989. Exile also saw him finally finish the B.A. studies in history and political science he had begun at Bir Zeit University eleven years earlier, which had been in-

terrupted by his imprisonment and deportation. He later earned an M.A. in international relations from Bir Zeit in 1988.

As a result of the Israeli–Palestinian peace process, Barghuthi returned from exile in April 1994 and became secretary-general of al-Fatah's Higher Committee in the West Bank. He supported the peace process and tried to mobilize Palestinian support for it. In January 1996, he was elected to the Palestinian Council as an independent when Yasir Arafat, head of al-Fatah, refused to let him run as a candidate for the movement. Barghuthi grew vocally critical of the abuse of power in the Palestinian Authority over which Arafat presided, even presenting a no-confidence motion in the legislature in April 1997. He became one of the most popular and important political figures in the West Bank, and as a dynamic young West Bank insider was seen by some Palestinians as a possible replacement for the aging Arafat and the PLO outsiders who had returned with him from exile in 1994.

With the intense Israeli-Palestinian fighting of the al-Aqsa Intifada, which began in October 2000, Barghuthi broke with other al-Fatah figures and supported the Palestinians' use of arms against the Israelis. Israel accused him of leading both the Tanzim, a Fatah militia, and Fatah's al-Aqsa Martyrs Brigades, a militant movement implicated in terrorist attacks against Israelis. In April 2002, Barghuthi was arrested in Ramallah by Israeli forces and became the highest ranking Palestinian seized to date. He was put on trial in an Israel civil court, rather than the usual military tribunal, in June 2002 to face charges of murder. Barghuthi refused to recognize the court's standing and continued to call for change in the Palestinian Authority.

See also AQSA INTIFADA, AL-; ARAFAT, YASIR; BARGHUTHI FAMILY; FATAH, AL-; WEST BANK.

MICHAEL R. FISCHBACH

BAR-ILAN UNIVERSITY

University in Ramat Gan, Israel, that features Jewish studies.

The university was founded in 1955 as an institution of higher learning that would fulfill the basic aims of Judaic tradition. The curriculum for both men and women includes required courses in Jewish studies, which pursue the goals of integrating Judaism and present-day reality—cultivating a respect for Jewish principles and customs. Pinhas Churgin was the university's founder and first president. In 2003 it had 32,000 students, including those studying at five regional colleges. The university offers undergraduate and graduate degrees in liberal arts, social sciences, and natural sciences. There are faculties in Jewish studies, humanities, social sciences, natural sciences, and law.

In November 1995, Yigal Amir, a law student at Bar-Ilan, assassinated Prime Minister Yitzhak Rabin. The following day all classes were canceled and the university's president issued a statement expressing "deep shock, horror and utter condemnation." Bar-Ilan was subjected to massive criticism for fostering or allowing religious and political extremism. One of the most significant points made was that while students were exposed to the extreme religious politics of Jewish settlers on the West Bank and Gaza, no moderate alternative views were to be heard on campus. This derived, at least in part, from the fact that the university's founders decided to follow the pattern of Roman Catholic universities in the United States, rather than that of Yeshiva University in New York. Ironically, Bar-Ilan originally neglected direct religious education. This was changed in 1970 when a religious studies unit was established.

Bibliography

Fisch, Harold. "Bar-Ilan University." In *The Israel Yearbook, 1971.* Tel Aviv: Israel Yearbook Publications, 1971.

Klein, Menachem. *Bar Ilan University: Between Religion and Politics.* Jerusalem: Magnes Press, 1997.

MIRIAM SIMON
UPDATED BY PAUL RIVLIN

BARING, EVELYN
[1841–1917]

British consul general and Egypt's virtual ruler, 1883–1907.

One of Britain's most illustrious proconsular figures, Evelyn Baring, Lord Cromer, contributed profoundly through his policies in Egypt to the

Evelyn Baring (Lord Cromer) was consul general of Egypt for twenty-four years. During his tenure he reorganized its army, modernized its financial system, and extended its trade and communication along Western lines. PHOTOGRAPH BY ELLIOTT & FRY, LONDON. THE LIBRARY OF CONGRESS. REPRODUCED BY PERMISSION.

modern history of that country. As an administrator he stressed fiscal stability, hydraulic reform, and the cultivation and export of cotton. Critics charged him with neglecting industrialization and failing to fund vital social services, especially education. During his latter years in Egypt the nationalist movement revived, having been moribund since the Urabi revolt, and from then on became a vital force in Egyptian politics.

Lord Cromer was born Evelyn Baring on 26 February 1841 at Cromer Hall in Norfolk, England, a son of Henry Baring, a member of Parliament. His father died when Evelyn was seven, and the youngster was raised by his mother. In 1855 he entered the military academy at Woolwich and was commissioned as an artillery officer three years later. His first posting was to the Ionian Islands; it proved formative for him. Not only did he meet his future wife, Ethel Stanley, there but he also learned Greek and acquired an interest in ancient history—an intellectual avocation he pursued throughout his lifetime.

Upon returning to Britain he entered the military staff college, but instead of pursuing the military career for which his education had prepared him, Captain Baring in 1872 became private secretary to his cousin, Lord Northbrook, who was viceroy of India at the time. This decision cast his fate with Britain's overseas imperial interests. He quickly distinguished himself as a resourceful and skilled administrator and a person destined for high office. In 1877, at a time when the government of Egypt was endeavoring to stave off bankruptcy under the profligate rule of its viceroy, Khedive Isma'il ibn Ibrahim (1863–1879), Baring was selected as the British representative on a multinational financial body, the Caisse de la Dette Publique, or Egyptian Public Debt Commission, which protected the interests of the European creditors of the Egyptian government. In May 1879 Baring left Egypt, resigned his army commission, and planned to run for Parliament in 1880. Instead, he briefly returned to Egypt in October of that year as British comptroller on the Liquidation Commission. He was not involved directly in the decision of the European powers to replace Khedive Isma'il with his son, Tawfiq. In June 1880 Baring became the financial adviser to the viceroy of India's council under George Robinson, Lord Ripon.

Baring's absence from Egypt proved short-lived. Discontent had surfaced within the Egyptian army during the crisis of 1879. It welled up again in 1881. A group of young native-born Egyptian officers, led by Ahmad Urabi, galvanized a movement of opposition to Ottoman Turkish rule and the growing foreign influence over the country. In September 1882, the British invaded Egypt, defeated the Egyptian army at al-Tall al-Kabir, exiled Urabi and other nationalists, and restored Tawfiq to power in Cairo. The British promised a swift evacuation of Egypt, which remained legally part of the Ottoman Empire and in which several European powers, notably France, had substantial financial and cultural interests. The British hastened to reform Egypt's administration so as to facilitate their withdrawal.

In 1883 Baring was named Britain's consul-general in Egypt. Although his choice came as a surprise to many—he was only forty-two and had not previously held such a responsible position—he was in fact ideal for the job. He already had considerable knowledge of Egypt from having served on the Caisse de la Dette. He was familiar with the imperial administration from his duties in India, and he was a recognized expert on fiscal matters. Egypt's single most pressing administrative problem was financial. In 1880 the government's external debt had totaled 100 million pounds, the interest on which consumed nearly half of Egypt's tax revenues. To realize its goal of withdrawal—a goal enunciated repeatedly in official pronouncements—Britain would have to reform Egypt's budget.

Baring devoted his first decade as consul (1883–1892) to achieving fiscal solvency. He rightly judged that the only way Egyptian finances could be reformed was by increasing agricultural production and thereby raising the tax base. The key to agricultural development, in his estimation, was irrigation, since Egypt, as the gift of the Nile River, was totally reliant on irrigation waters for its agricultural success. Muhammad Ali, ruler of Egypt from 1805 until 1849, had first begun to transform Egyptian irrigation from a basin or flood system to what was called perennial irrigation. By digging deep canals and erecting dams and weirs along the Nile, he had enabled parts of Egypt to receive irrigation waters year-round instead of only during the flood season. As a result, Egyptian farmers had begun to cultivate cotton, which, as a summer crop, required irrigation waters when the Nile was at its lowest. Unfortunately, in the latter years of Isma'il's reign the hydraulic system of Egypt had fallen into disrepair. Bringing some of Britain's most talented irrigation engineers to Egypt, Baring put the old system in order and then embarked upon a vigorous program of hydraulic improvement. Critical in this first decade was the repair of the Delta Barrage—a wide dam at the bifurcation of the Nile, just north of Cairo—which had been built by French and Egyptian engineers in pre-British days but never rendered serviceable.

Even the dramatic events in the Sudan in the 1880s were tied to Egyptian finances. Egypt had expanded steadily into the Sudan in the nineteenth century. The Mahdist movement threatened Egypt's control. Because of financial pressures the British government compelled Egypt to withdraw its forces from the Sudan and to leave the fate of that territory to the Sudanese. Baring secured the evacuation of the Sudan but not before the Mahdists had killed one of Britain's war heroes, General Charles Gordon, slain while defending Anglo-Egyptian interests at Khartoum.

In 1892 Khedive Tawfiq died. He had worked closely with Baring to bring fiscal stability to the country and to improve agricultural productivity. His eldest son, Abbas Hilmi II, succeeded him. In the same year Baring was elevated to the peerage as Lord Cromer in recognition of his services to the British Empire. The political tranquillity that had characterized British rule to that point was shattered soon after Abbas came to the throne. In January 1893 the new khedive tried to replace his pro-British cabinet with a more nationalist one, and Cromer needed a letter from Foreign Secretary Archibald Primrose, Lord Rosebery, confirming the need for Egypt's viceroy to consult with the British representative about ministerial changes as long as British troops occupied Egypt. In the following January, Abbas publicly criticized the Egyptian army, which he was reviewing, and its commanding general, Sir Horatio Herbert Kitchener. Kitchener offered to resign, but Cromer, already worried by the nationalist advisers whom Abbas had brought together in his palace, moved with alacrity to defeat this challenge to British authority. A British battalion was diverted from its homeward journey and marched to Cairo in a show of strength. Abbas was compelled to back down. He reinstated Kitchener as commander. Although Cromer prevailed, these two incidents left a legacy of bitterness between the khedive and the consul. Although Abbas never again openly challenged British authority, the palace became a patron of various nationalist parties when they emerged during the early twentieth century.

During Cromer's second decade as consul, Britain extended its authority over Egypt's internal affairs and reconquered the Sudan. No longer was the prospect of evacuation imminent, although the British continued to proclaim their occupation a temporary one. Now British "advisers" were appointed in the ministries of justice, interior, and education. They sought to impose British cultural standards where previously Turkish, Egyptian, and French influences had predominated. Hydraulic reform continued apace, culminating in the construction of a massive dam at Aswan in 1902. Cotton accounted for more than 80 percent of the value of Egyptian exports at this time.

Cromer had hoped to postpone the military conquest of the Sudan until Egypt's finances were unshakable and the Aswan High Dam had been completed. The European scramble for African territory forced his hand. By the mid-1890s the Sudan was one of the few territories still independent of European colonial authority. The British deemed the upper Nile basin of vital importance to their African empire and feared that if a hostile power, like France, took control of the area, it would threaten British interests in Egypt. Hastily preparing the Egyptian army for action, Cromer sent troops into the Sudan in 1896. Khartoum fell to an Anglo-Egyptian force in 1898. A tense moment occurred on the upper White Nile at Fashoda (now Kodok) in 1898 when British and Egyptian forces under Kitchener met a small band of French soldiers under Jean-Baptiste Marchand. Both leaders claimed the territory for their countries, and war fever briefly stirred both the British and the French. Only after France had backed down and recognized Anglo-Egyptian preeminence in the Sudan did the Fashoda Incident end.

Once Cromer had engineered the military occupation of the Sudan, he set about creating its administrative system. Here he used considerable ingenuity to devise a way for Britain and Egypt to share in the governance of the Sudan. Seeking to spare the Sudan the tangle of international obligations that bedeviled Britain's rule over Egypt, he established the Anglo-Egyptian Condominium over the Sudan in 1899. By the terms of his anomalous political organization, the Sudan was exempted from the jurisdiction of the Capitulations and the Mixed Courts, while Egypt retained its formal suzerainty over the Sudan, and Britain became the effective sovereign power. Cromer's annual reports on the administration of Egypt and the Sudan were published, widely circulated, and sometimes even translated into Arabic to influence Egyptian opinion.

In the latter years of Cromer's administration, anti-British, nationalist sentiments gained in

The first Aswan Dam was constructed by the British to harness the Nile River and provide irrigation for cotton crops. Baring served as Britain's consul-general in Egypt at the time the dam's construction began. He initiated hydraulic system improvements as part of his plan for Egypt to achieve fiscal solvency. © HULTON-DEUTSCH COLLECTION. REPRODUCED BY PERMISSION.

strength. New political movements, like the National Party and the Umma Party, came into being, and new leaders, like Mustafa Kamil, attacked Cromer's autocratic rule. The nationalists castigated Cromer for failing to share power with Egyptians, neglecting parliamentary institutions, and starving the educational system of funds. A galvanizing nationalist event occurred in the village of Dinshaway in 1906 where the British hanged four villagers and imprisoned and publicly flogged several others for allegedly killing a British soldier while trying to protect their possessions. The severity of the sentences appalled many Egyptians (and Europeans) and came to symbolize the heavy-handedness of British rule in Egypt. Nine months after the Dinshaway Incident, Cromer submitted his resignation and left a country that he had dominated for a quarter of a century. He had never won the affection of the Egyptians, nor had he sought to do so.

In Britain Cromer did not completely cut his Egyptian ties. Always a prolific writer, with a marked scholarly bent, he published a two-volume account of Egyptian affairs before and during his time there. *Modern Egypt* (1908) was for many years the standard treatment of British rule in Egypt. It is read now, however, for its insights into the imperial mentality rather than for its descriptions of Egyptian society or its assessment of British rule. He also wrote *Ancient and Modern Imperialism* (1910) and *Abbas II* (1915) and collected his many essays on diverse subjects into three volumes, entitled *Political and Literary Essays* (1913).

A reassessment of Cromer's work in Egypt is long overdue.

See also ABBAS HILMI II; ASWAN HIGH DAM; CAPITULATIONS; DINSHAWAY INCIDENT (1906); FASHODA INCIDENT (1898); GORDON, CHARLES; ISMAʿIL IBN IBRAHIM; KAMIL, MUSTAFA; KITCHENER, HORATIO HERBERT; MAHDIST STATE; MIXED COURTS; MUHAMMAD ALI; NATIONAL PARTY (EGYPT); URABI, AHMAD.

Bibliography

Berque, Jacques. *Egypt: Imperialism and Revolution,* translated by Jean Stewart. New York: Praeger; London: Faber, 1972.

Marlowe, John. *Cromer in Egypt.* New York: Praeger; London: Elek, 1970.

Owen, E. R. J. *Cotton and the Egyptian Economy, 1820–1914: A Study in Trade and Development.* Oxford, U.K.: Clarendon, 1969.

Sayyid-Marsot, Afaf Lutfi. *Egypt and Cromer: A Study in Anglo-Egyptian Relations.* New York: Praeger; London: Murray, 1968.

Schölch, Alexander. *Egypt for the Egyptians! The Socio-Political Crisis in Egypt, 1878–1882.* London: Ithaca Press, 1981.

Tignor, Robert L. *Modernization and British Colonial Rule in Egypt, 1882–1914.* Princeton, NJ: Princeton University Press, 1966.

ROBERT L. TIGNOR
UPDATED BY ARTHUR GOLDSCHMIDT

BARKAN, ÖMER LUTFI

[1902–1979]

Turkish social and economic historian who pioneered the study of the Ottoman state and society based on archival documentation.

Born in Edirne in 1902, Ömer Lutfi Barkan studied philosophy at Istanbul University (1927) and social sciences at the University of Strasbourg (1931).

Barkan served briefly as lycée (secondary school) teacher in Eskişehir (1931–1933) before he joined the newly organized Istanbul University in 1933. He stayed there, first in the Faculty of Letters and from 1937 in the Faculty of Economics as docent, professor (1940), dean (1950–1952), and founder and director of the Institute of Turkish Economic History (from 1955) until his retirement in 1973. He married Süreyya Meriç in 1951 and had three sons. He was a member of the Turkish Historical Society and of various international organizations.

Barkan was the first historian in the Republic of Turkey to base his historiography entirely on the vast archives of the Ottoman Empire. His publication and analysis of Ottoman provincial regulations (*Kanunlar,* 1945), provincial population and production surveys (in many articles and *Hüdavendigar* [Bursa], published posthumously), and sixteenth-century Istanbul *waqfs* (1970), to name the truly seminal of his numerous important contributions, brought Ottoman historiography to the attention of non-Orientalist Western historians, especially Fernand Braudel and the Annales school. Facilitating this mutual respect must be considered his most significant legacy.

See also EDIRNE; ISTANBUL UNIVERSITY.

I. METIN KUNT

BAR-LEV, HAIM

[1924–1994]

Israeli general and politician.

Born in Vienna, Haim Bar-Lev grew up in Yugoslavia and immigrated to Mandatory Palestine in 1939. He joined the Palmah in 1942 and led many operations against British military installations. In the 1948 Arab–Israel War he commanded a battalion in the southern front. He remained in the army, and in 1954 and 1955 he commanded the Giʿvati Brigade. In the 1956 Arab–Israel War Bar-Lev commanded an armored brigade that came close to the Suez Canal, and in 1957 he became chief of the Armoured Corps. From 1961 to 1963 he studied economics and business at Columbia University in New York City.

Returning to Israel, Bar-Lev became chief of military operations in 1964, deputy chief of staff in 1967, and in 1968 succeeded Yitzhak Rabin as chief of staff. He led the Israel Defense Force (IDF) in the War of Attrition (1968–1970); Israel's line of defense along the Suez Canal, the Bar-Lev Line, was named after him. Retiring from the IDF in 1972, Bar-Lev joined Golda Meir's cabinet as minister of commerce and industry, a position he held until 1977. During the 1973 Arab–Israel War, in light of the initial debacle, he was sent to oversee the southern front and was the de facto commander of that theater.

Elected to the Knesset in 1973, Bar-Lev served as secretary-general of the Labor Party until 1984 when he was appointed minister of police in the Government of National Unity. He held this position until 1988. In 1992 he was appointed Israel's ambassador to the Russian Federation and served there until his death in 1994. Known as a tough and determined leader, he insisted on top performance and attention to details.

Bibliography

Rolef, Susan Hattis, ed. *Political Dictionary of the State of Israel.* New York: Macmillan; London: Collier Macmillan, 1987.

MARTIN MALIN
UPDATED BY MERON MEDZINI

BAR-LEV LINE

See BAR-LEV, HAIM

BARON, DVORA

[1887–1956]

Israeli writer.

Dvora Baron was born in a small Jewish town in Lithuania. From her father, who was the rabbi of that community, Baron learned Hebrew and became versed in traditional and sacred Hebrew texts, an education unavailable to women before that time. At age sixteen she began to publish short stories in Hebrew. Baron immigrated to Palestine in 1911 and served as the literary editor of a major Zionist periodical. Although she spent most of her life in the land of Israel, the thirteen volumes of her short stories describe life in the eastern European community of her childhood, particularly the plight of women under the yoke of traditional custom and law. Regeneration through family and community,

and individual victimization and human suffering, are the main themes of her work. Her style has been likened to that of Chekhov and Flaubert, authors whose works she translated into Hebrew.

See also LITERATURE: HEBREW.

Bibliography

Baron, Dvora. *The Thorny Path,* translated by Joseph Schachter, edited by Itzhak Hanoch. Jerusalem: Institute for the Translation of Hebrew Literature, 1969.

ZVIA GINOR

BARZANI FAMILY

Kurdish family of religious shaykhs and nationalist leaders.

This family is rooted in the village of Barzan, in what is today Iraqi Kurdistan (but was for centuries the Ottoman Empire). Unlike the Shemzini or the Barzinji shaykhs, the Barzanis do not claim any famous genealogy; they were uneducated and obscure mullahs until Taj ad-Din became the *khalifa* (deputy) of Mawlana Khalid (died 1826), who introduced the Naqshbandi *tariqa* (sufi order) to Kurdistan. Shaykh Muhammad (died 1903), his great-grandson, was himself a half-educated mullah but had nevertheless a considerable number of followers; after the disposition of his rival shaykh, Ubaydallah of Shemzinan, he marched on Mosul, to be captured by the Ottomans.

His sons continued the family tradition: Shaykh Abd al-Salam II (1885–1914), a nationalist leader and a religious shaykh revered by his followers, was hanged by the Ottomans. Shaykh Ahmad (died 1969), the second brother, led his first revolt in 1931 and gave up politics after the collapse of the Kurdish republic of Mahabad. Mullah Mustafa (1904–1979), the third brother, became famous under the name General Barzani. The family leadership was later split between Shaykh Muhammad Khalid, son of Shaykh Ahmad, and Mas'ud Barzani, son of the general, who, after the death of his brother Idris (1944–1987), claimed the political heritage of his father.

See also KURDISH AUTONOMOUS ZONE; KURDISH REVOLTS; KURDISTAN.

Bibliography

Chaliand, Gèrard, ed. *A People without a Country: The Kurds and Kurdistan,* translated by Michael Pallis. New York: Olive Branch Press, 1993.

CHRIS KUTSCHERA
UPDATED BY MICHAEL R. FISCHBACH

BARZANI, MAS'UD AL-

See BARZANI FAMILY

BARZANI, MUSTAFA

See BARZANI FAMILY

BASHIR

See CHEHAB, BASHIR

BASIC PEOPLE'S CONGRESSES

Part of the Libyan political structure.

The congresses provide the second level (above village and submunicipal congresses) of popular consultation and participation in the exercise of popular power in the Jamahiriyya (state of the masses) of Libya proclaimed in March 1977. Each of some two hundred basic people's congresses send three delegates to the chief debating and decision-making forum—the annual General People's Congress.

See also GENERAL PEOPLE'S CONGRESS (GPC); JAMAHIRIYYA.

JOHN L. WRIGHT

BAŞIRET

See NEWSPAPERS AND PRINT MEDIA: TURKEY

BAŞIRETCI, ALI

[1838–1912]

Ottoman Turkish journalist.

Ali Başiretci was educated at the Imperial Service school but did not enter palace service. In 1863, he began to work for the finance ministry, and in 1869, he began to publish the daily newspaper *Başiret* (In-sight), which popularized Jamal al-Din al-Afghani's ideas about Muslim unity. Accused of pro-Prussian activities during the Franco–Prussian war, Başiretci was forced into exile in Jerusalem. After being pardoned, he reentered government administration as a *qa'immaqam* in various districts. After 1908, he attempted to reestablish *Başiret,* but it was closed soon after.

See also AFGHANI, JAMAL AL-DIN AL-.

Bibliography

Shaw, Stanford, and Shaw, Ezel Kural. *History of the Ottoman Empire and Modern Turkey,* Vol. 2: *Reform, Revolution, and Republic: The Rise of Modern Turkey, 1808–1975.* Cambridge, U.K., and New York: Cambridge University Press, 1977.

DAVID WALDNER

BASMA BINT TALAL

[1951–]

Philanthropist and sister of Jordan's King Hussein ibn Talal (r. 1952–1999).

Princess Basma bint Talal was born into the Hashimite family as the sixth and final child of Jordan's King Talal ibn Abdullah. She was educated in Jordan and then at the Benenden School in Britain. She later studied languages at Oxford University, and in 2001 she was awarded a D.Ph. in development studies from Oxford. Noted for her work on issues of development and gender, she founded the Queen Alia Fund for Social Development in 1977 at King Hussein's request. Following his death in February 1999, the fund's name was changed to the Jordanian Hashemite Fund for Human Development (JHFHD). In 1992 Princess Basma founded the Jordanian National Commission for Women, part of the JHFHD, and in 1996 established the Princess Basma Women's Resource Center as part of the Queen Zein Al-Sharaf Institute for Development. From 1995 to 1997 she served as special advisor on sustainable development to UN Secretary-General Boutros Boutros-Ghali, and she has also worked with the United Nations Development Programme, the World Health Organization, and UNESCO.

See also BOUTROS-GHALI, BOUTROS; HASHIMITE HOUSE (HOUSE OF HASHIM); HUSSEIN IBN TALAL; TALAL IBN ABDULLAH.

Bibliography

Basma Bint al-Talal. *Rethinking an NGO: Development, Donors, and Civil Society in Jordan.* London: I. B. Tauris, 2003.

MICHAEL R. FISCHBACH

BASRA

City in Iraq; Iraq's only seaport, but situated some 75 miles (120 km) north of the Persian/Arabian Gulf, on the Shatt al-Arab.

Basra is an administrative and commercial center for Iraq, with a population of some 1.3 million (according to a 2002 estimate). It is linked to Baghdad, the capital, by railroad and is governed by the *muhafiz,* a chief of the administrative unit who is also the representative of the central government in Baghdad.

The seaport itself is actually situated at the head of the Shatt al-Arab, the confluence and the lower reach of the Tigris and Euphrates Rivers, which flows for some 112 miles (180 km) to empty into the Persian Gulf. Basra is bounded on the north by the

Basra Harbor, ca. 1955. Once called the Venice of the East, the Iraqi city of Basra has been a major center in the Arab sea trade for over 1,300 years. Today, it is an important source of oil refining and export. © HULTON-DEUTSCH COLLECTION/CORBIS. REPRODUCED BY PERMISSION.

governate of Maysan, on the east by Iran, and on the west by the Western Desert. Basra has a desert climate with great temperature variations between day and night, summer and winter. The high temperature reaches 106°F (50°C); the low is above frost. Annual relative humidity is 44 to 59 percent; annual rainfall ranges between 2 and 8 inches (50–200 mm). Winters are warm, with temperatures above freezing.

With its multitude of waterways, Basra has the right conditions for the successful cultivation of dates; the incoming and outgoing tides of some 635 rivers and channels that water approximately 14 million palm trees make the region one of the world's most fertile. Despite the devastation that occurred here during the Iran–Iraq War (1980–1988), the orchards are still farmed in quantity. Besides the 530 kinds of dates, other crops include maize (corn), citrus, apples, and many types of vegetables.

Petroleum has become the leading industry of Basra. The upstream operations are carried out by the Iraq National Oil Company, beyond the areas allotted to the British Petroleum Company, according to laws passed in 1961. In 1975, Iraq nationalized the Basra Petroleum Company, and the era of oil concessions ended. The oil refineries and the petrochemical and fertilizer plants were moved out of Basra during the Iran–Iraq War, but the paper, fishing, and date industries still operate. Through Basra as a port-of-entry come imports, such as sugar, timber, coffee, and tea. The main exports are crude oil and petroleum products, dates, leather, and wool.

Although historically Basra was a multiethnic city, because of the political changes in Iraq since 1958, Muslim Arabs form the majority: Armenians, Indians, and Iranians are, for the most part, gone, as are the Jews. Arabic is the language of the city, and Shiʿism is the predominant form of Islam—although some few Christians, Jews, and Sabaeans remain.

The University of Basra and a branch of the University of Technology are the schools of higher education; some 385 primary schools, 175 secondary schools, and 15 vocational schools exist. The Center for Arab Gulf Studies was located in Basra, but it was moved to Baghdad in 1985.

Basra was founded by Caliph Umar I in 638 C.E. It is the Bassorah of the *Arabian Nights* and Sinbad. In 1534, Basra was made part of the Ottoman Empire by Sultan Sulayman, who incorporated Iraq into his empire; along with Baghdad and Mosul, Basra was designated one of the *vilayets* (provinces) of Ottoman Iraq. Although the Mamluks ruled Iraq for several centuries, the Ottomans reestablished their authority in 1831, ousting the Mamluks and forcefully subjugating the tribal areas. British companies meanwhile established a sphere of influence, strengthening ties with tribal shaykhs and controlling the import–export market. The strategic position of Basra as a link in the overland route to Asia or the Mediterranean created a competition between the Ottomans, Germans, British, and Indians. The growth of the British and German presence in Basra during the eighteenth century awakened the Ottomans to its importance. They therefore attempted to reestablish their domination over Basra, Kuwait, and the surrounding region.

During World War I, Basra was the first Ottoman city to fall to a British–Indian occupation, on 23 November 1914, and a military governor was appointed. Britain was planning to keep Basra under permanent jurisdiction, perhaps linking it to the Indian administrative unit, but international events worked against this. Although Britain was granted a mandate over Iraq by the League of Nations in 1920, they recognized Faisal I ibn Hussein as king in 1922 and dissolved the mandate in 1932, when Iraq was admitted to the League of Nations.

One of the factors that led to the Iran–Iraq War was control of the Shatt al-Arab, the major waterway connecting the Gulf with Iraq's port of Basra and Iran's ports of Khorramshahr and Abadan. This had been the very issue between the Ottomans and Persia (now Iran) before World War I. Because of its location, then, Basra became central to the struggle, and the surrounding countryside suffered ecological damage, which was made worse by the destruction wrought by the Coalition forces during the Gulf Crisis of 1990–1991.

See also BAGHDAD; DATES; FAISAL I IBN HUSSEIN; GULF CRISIS (1990–1991); IRAN–IRAQ WAR (1980–1988); IRAQ; MAMLUKS; OTTOMAN EMPIRE; PERSIAN GULF; PETROLEUM, OIL, AND NATURAL GAS; SHATT AL-ARAB; TIGRIS AND EUPHRATES RIVERS.

Bibliography

Altimimi, Hamid. *Basra: Under British Occupation, 1914–1921.* London, 1973.

Atiyyah, Ghassan. *Iraq, 1908–1921: A Socio-Political Study.* Beirut: Arab Institute for Research, 1973.

Cordesman, Anthony H., and Wagner, Abraham R. *The Lessons of Modern War: The Iran–Iraq War.* London: Mansell; Boulder, CO: Westview, 1990.

Harris, George L. *Iraq: Its People, Its Society, Its Culture.* New Haven, CT: Yale University Press, 1958.

Longrigg, S. H. *Iraq, 1900 to 1950: A Political, Social, and Economic History.* London and New York: Oxford University Press, 1953.

NAZAR AL-KHALAF

BAST

Inviolable sanctuaries in Iran used to seek protection from political or religious persecution.

Bast means sanctuary or asylum. Mosques, holy shrines, and foreign embassy compounds have most frequently been used as *bast*. Although the period of the Constitutional Revolution (1905–1911) is when the most famous *bast* were taken, instances existed in early Islamic Iran. In April 1905, pro-constitutionalist merchants, bankers, and retailers took *bast* at the Shah Abd al-Azim shrine in Rayy. The most celebrated *bast* in Iranian history took place in July 1906, when between twelve thousand and sixteen thousand Tehrani demonstrators took *bast* at the British legation in Tehran, while about one thousand clergymen left the capital in protest for Qom. The *bast* at the British compound was instrumental in the granting of a constitution, and the creation of a national assembly by the monarch, Mozaffar al-Din Qajar. In turn, the anticonstitutionalist cleric Shaykh Fazlollah Nuri took *bast* at the Shah Abd al-Azim shrine with some followers for ninety days, to protest the granting of the constitution. At times, the inviolability of *bast* was breached, when for instance Sayyid Jamal al-Din Asadabadi was expelled from the Shah Abd al-Azim shrine during the reign of Naser al-Din Shah. After the constitutionalist period, the *majles* (national assembly) was also considered a *bast*. Mohammad Mossadegh took refuge there in 1953.

See also CONSTITUTIONAL REVOLUTION; MOSSADEGH, MOHAMMAD; MOZAFFAR al-Din Qajar; Naser al-Din Shah; Nuri, Fazlollah.

Bibliography

Algar, Hamid. *Religion and State in Iran, 1785–1906: The Role of the Ulama in the Qajar Period.* Berkeley: University of California Press, 1980.

Browne, Edward G. *The Persian Revolution of 1905–1909.* Cambridge, U.K.: Cambridge University Press, 1910.

Neguin Yavari

BA'TH, AL-

A pan-Arab political party.

The Arab Socialist Renaissance (Ba'th) party was founded in Syria in 1944. In one version of the foundation myth, it was established by two Damascus schoolteachers, Michel Aflaq, an Orthodox Christian, and Salah al-Din al-Bitar, a Sunni Muslim; in the other, it was started by an Alawite, Zaki al-Arsuzi. In both versions, the party advocated a mixture of national socialism, independence from foreign rule, and pan-Arabism (the creation of a unitary Arab state), and was to be the main instrument through which the goal of Arab unity would be achieved. Its main slogan was and is, "One Arab nation with an eternal mission." Ba'thist ideology is muddled and often contradictory: It advocates socialism yet at the same time stresses the sanctity of private property. The two countries in which Ba'thism has flourished, Syria and Iraq, either have been or still are dictatorships where any form of political pluralism is or has been either closely controlled or severely repressed.

Syria

During its early days in Syria, just after the departure of the French, the party drew support from radical secondary school and university students. Initially, the Ba'th did not enter formal politics, preferring to focus attention on developing its ideology rather than attempting to gain political power. Small party branches were established in Lebanon, Jordan, and Iraq in the late 1940s. Political instability in Syria and the crushing Arab defeat in the Arab-Israel War of 1948 led Aflaq and Bitar (al-Arsuzi had left the leadership by then) to merge their organization with Akram al-Hawrani's Arab Socialist Party in 1953, and as a result the group's membership increased from five hundred to two thousand members. The party ran candidates in the Syrian elections in 1954 and won sixteen seats.

By the middle 1950s, however, the dominant opposition force in Syria was the Syrian Communist Party, whose leader, Khalid Bakdash, had also been elected to parliament in 1954. The Communists' popularity was boosted by their association with a Czech arms deal in 1955, under which the Soviet Union and other Eastern European states agreed to sell arms to Syria and Egypt. Fearing eclipse by the Communists, Aflaq and Bitar approached Egyptian president Gamal Abdel Nasser with a scheme proposing Syrian-Egyptian unity, which resulted in the creation of the United Arab Republic (UAR). The Ba'th was taking a calculated risk; they knew that Nasser had dissolved the Egyptian Communist Party and would require the Syrian Communist Party to wind up its affairs, but they also knew that the Ba'th Party would be dissolved as well. The gamble did not pay off and the UAR gradually developed into a way for Egypt to exploit Syria, for which Aflaq and Bitar received much of the blame. In 1961, a military coup in Syria brought the UAR to an ignominious if unlamented end. The Ba'th leaders and Hawrani went their separate ways, leaving the party open for new leadership and young recruits, primarily from junior Alawi officers in the army.

In March 1963, a group of Ba'thist officers took control of Syria scarcely a month after a Ba'th-supported coup in Iraq. As the military began to dominate the Syrian party, disagreements began to develop between them and Aflaq and Bitar. On 23 February 1966, a neo-Ba'th coup led by Ghassan Jadid ousted a moderate government led by Bitar. Bitar retired from politics and went to France and Aflaq went into exile in Iraq, where he was appointed secretary-general of the Iraqi Ba'th Party in 1968, a position he held until his death in Iraq in 1989. The new and more radical Syrian government, with a strong Alawi support base, nationalized industry, implemented a land reform program, and vigorously supported the Palestinian struggle against Israel. Jadid aligned himself with the civilians in the party and was challenged for the leadership by his minister of defense, the former air force commander Hafiz al-Asad.

By 1970, Asad had gained control of the internal security apparatus and forced Jadid from power. Asad's principal support came from the Alawi minority in Syria (about 12% of the population) and from family members and trusted associates who held key positions in the security services and the military. By the middle 1980s, much of the more radical social and economic measures taken by the neo-Ba'th had been reversed or abandoned and the socialist sector of the economy no longer had much importance. In addition, a major rift had developed between Asad and the Palestinian leader Yasir Arafat. By the time of Asad's death in 2000, Ba'thism was devoid of whatever coherent ideological content it might once have had and the party was largely confined to applauding the actions of the leadership and eventually of endorsing the succession of Asad's son Bashar al-Asad.

Iraq

Ba'thist ideology was brought to Iraq by Iraqi students studying in Syria. The first Iraqi secretary-general was Fu'ad al-Rikabi, a Shi'ite engineer from Nasiriyya who collected a following of some one hundred to two hundred individuals, mostly recruited from among his own relatives and friends. Unlike the Syrian party, the Iraqi Ba'th remained at least nominally under civilian leadership. When Abd al-Karim Qasim and the Iraqi Free Officers overthrew the monarchy in July 1958, the Ba'th initially supported his coup but in 1959 ordered Qasim's assassination, fearing his left-leaning proclivities and the fact that he was dependent on the Communists. After the failure of the assassination attempt, the perpetrators, including Saddam Hussein, went into exile to Syria and Egypt.

In 1963, the Ba'th supported a military coup led by the Nasserist Abd al-Salam Arif, which overthrew Qasim and initiated a campaign of persecution of the left, but its initial success was short lived. A split between the militant pragmatists and the centrists led the centrists to appeal to Damascus for mediation, and in the ensuing confusion, Arif ousted the Ba'th from the government. While out of power, the Iraqi Ba'thists, led by General Ahmad Hasan al-Bakr and his young relative Saddam, reorganized themselves, deriving support increasingly from their kinsfolk from their home town, Tikrit, while seeking to maintain political legitimacy by remaining

Ba'th party leader Bashshar al-Asad was elected president of Syria by referendum in July 2000. Although the country has seen a relaxing of regulations since Bashshar assumed leadership, criticism of the government is still not permitted and the press is heavily censored. © REUTERS NEWMEDIA INC./CORBIS. REPRODUCED BY PERMISSION.

loyal to Aflaq. Now more politically astute and better organized, the Ba'th organized a coup on 17 July 1968, quickly purged their non-Ba'thist coconspirators, and took complete control of the Iraqi government on 31 July.

By 1970, the Iraqis had separated completely from the Syrian Ba'th. The new Iraqi constitution established a Revolutionary Command Council to operate as the supreme executive, legislative, and judicial institution of the state, separate from the regional command of the party. With Saddam in charge of security, al-Bakr was able to control the government, purging the party of military officers who opposed him. In 1972, in an extremely popular move, the government nationalized Iraqi oil. The boom that followed the oil price rise in 1973 created jobs, and improved health, educational and social welfare services, and the economic lot of

Iraqis, especially Ba'th party members, whose numbers increased substantially throughout the 1970s. Oil revenues went straight to the government, by then coterminous with Saddam and his circle, with no accountability as to how the money was spent.

At the same time, Saddam systematically purged his rivals from power and consolidated his position sufficiently to urge al-Bakr to retire in 1979. Between then and his fall in 2003, as head of both government and party, Saddam substituted personal for party rule. Relying more and more on family members for important positions, he repeatedly purged the party and the military and maintained the party structure purely for ceremonial purposes. His miscalculations in foreign policy during the war with Iran and during and after the invasion of Kuwait and the serious social and economic dislocations that followed resulted in the reversal of economic gains for most Iraqis, with the exception of a small coterie of loyalists. The U.S.-led coalition did not take the opportunity to remove him from power in 1991. Both Ba'thism and pan-Arab nationalism have been discredited by the activities of the Syrian and Iraqi regimes.

See also AFLAQ, MICHEL; ALAWI; ARAB–ISRAEL WAR (1948); ARAFAT, YASIR; ARIF, ABD AL-SALAM; ARSUZI, ZAKI AL-; ASAD, HAFIZ AL-; BAKDASH, KHALID; BITAR, SALAH AL-DIN AL-; HAWRANI, AKRAM AL-; HUSSEIN, SADDAM; NASSER, GAMAL ABDEL; QASIM, ABD AL-KARIM; TIKRIT; UNITED ARAB REPUBLIC (UAR).

Bibliography

Baram, Amatzia. *Culture, History, and Ideology in the Formation of Ba'thist Iraq, 1968–89.* New York: St. Martin's Press; Basingstoke, U.K.: Macmillan, 1991.

Batatu, Hanna. *The Old Social Classes and the Revolutionary Movements of Iraq: A Study of Iraq's Old Landed and Commercial Classes and of its Communists, Ba'thists, and Free Officers.* Princeton, NJ: Princeton University Press, 1978.

Batatu, Hanna. *Syria's Peasantry: The Descendants of Its Lesser Rural Notables, and Their Politics.* Princeton, NJ: Princeton University Press, 1999.

Farouk-Sluglett, Marion, and Sluglett, Peter. *Iraq since 1958: From Revolution to Dictatorship,* revised edition. New York; London: Tauris, 2001.

Hinnebusch, Raymond A. *Authoritarian Power and State Formation in Ba'thist Syria: Army, Party, and Peasant.* Boulder, CO: Westview, 1990.

Mufti, Malik. *Sovereign Creations: Pan-Arabism and Political Order in Syria and Iraq.* Ithaca, NY: Cornell University Press, 1996.

Tripp, Charles. *A History of Iraq.* Cambridge, U.K.: Cambridge University Press, 2000.

REEVA S. SIMON
UPDATED BY PETER SLUGLETT

BAYA
[1931–1998]

Algerian painter.

Baya Mahieddine was born in 1931 in Algeria. She was a self-taught painter whose work is notable in part because she did not study under colonial teachers at the early fine art schools in North Africa. Orphaned and illiterate, she never received a formal education in colonial Algeria. She worked as a servant for a French woman, who arranged Baya's first exhibition at the age of seventeen. The show was held in Paris, and both Spanish artist Pablo Picasso and French critic André Breton were impressed by her work. Picasso took her to his country home and watched in fascination as she molded clay animals. Breton tried to categorize her work as part of the Surrealist school; others, focusing on her Algerianness and lack of education, characterized her work, along with that of other self-taught Algerian artists of the time, as belonging to the naive tradition. She rejected both categories. Her work consists primarily of fanciful, colorful drawings of women, plants, insects, and animals, which some critics have linked to the decorative traditions of Islamic art and Algerian folk art.

Bibliography

Ali, Wijdan. *Modern Islamic Art: Development and Continuity.* Gainesville: University Press of Florida, 1997.

Nashashibi, Salwa Mikdadi, et. al. *Forces of Change: Artists of the Arab World.* Lafayette, CA: International Council for Women in the Arts; Washington, DC: National Museum of Women in the Arts, 1994.

JESSICA WINEGAR

BAYAR, CELAL
[1884–1986]

Turkish politician and statesman; Turkey's third president.

Celal Bayar was born in Umurbey, near Bursa, the son of a village teacher. Educated at the French school in Bursa, he worked as a clerk in a German bank there and rose rapidly in banking circles. In 1907, he joined the Union and Progress Society and became an important official in Bursa and Izmir; he was elected deputy for Saruhan (Manisa) in the last parliament of the Ottoman Empire. He was an active political leader during Turkey's war of independence, a member for Saruhan in the Turkish Grand National Assembly when it was first organized by Mustafa Kemal (Atatürk) in 1920; later he represented Izmir in all the republic's assemblies until 1960.

In 1920, he was made minister of economics. He was also founder and longtime head of the Türkiye Iş Bankasi (Turkish Labor Bank), and, by 1932, his vigorous advocacy of etatism (state economic enterprise) led to his being regarded as the leading promoter of state factories. He continued as minister of economics during much of the 1920s and 1930s. In 1937, Atatürk appointed him to replace Ismet İnönü as prime minister, continuing a bitter rivalry between the two men. His tenure in office lasted until shortly after Atatürk's death and İnönü's succession as president in 1938.

Until 1946, Turkey had a one-party political system under the aegis of the Republican People's Party (RPP); in that year Bayar became one of four RPP deputies who initiated Turkey's multiparty period by forming the opposition Democrat Party (DP). After only moderate success in the 1946 election, the Democrats came to power in 1950, and Bayar was elected the republic's third president. He presided over a decade that saw modifications to (but not basic reversal of) several of Atatürk's policies—which included the RPP's strong attitude of hostility toward the private sector and a relaxation of some aspects of secularism. In foreign affairs, Bayar and his associates continued a strong identification with the West, particularly the United States.

Convergence of several favorable factors enabled the Democrats to preside over a period of

Celal Bayar was the democratic president of Turkey from 1950 to 1960. Here Bayar is shown in Durham, North Carolina, visiting a Liggett and Myers' tobacco plant while on a tour of the United States. © Bettmann/Corbis. Reproduced by permission.

rapid economic growth, which together with more conservative social policies resulted in their electoral victory in 1954. Fear that the party's popularity would not continue, plus their intense dislike of the RPP and its leader Ismet İnönü, led to increasingly repressive measures. These included actions against the opposition party and the press, the partisan use of state funds, and eventually to accusations of serious election fraud in 1957, when they were returned to office but with a much reduced margin. In 1959, university students and others began violent demonstrations that led to the ouster of the DP government by the armed forces on 27 May

1960. Many Democrat officials, including all the party's assembly members, were arrested and brought to trial on the island of Yassiada, near Istanbul, on a long list of political and criminal charges. Bayar was one of four defendants sentenced to death, but he was spared due to his advanced age. He went to prison and was released in 1973. He was constitutionally barred from returning to active politics and so confined himself to occasional statements until his death at the age of 102.

> *See also* ATATÜRK, MUSTAFA KEMAL; DEMOCRAT PARTY; İNÖNÜ, İSMET; REPUBLICAN PEOPLE'S PARTY (RPP); TURKISH GRAND NATIONAL ASSEMBLY.

Bibliography

Karpat, Kemal. *Turkey's Politics: The Transition to a Multi-Party System.* Princeton, NJ: Princeton University Press, 1959.

Weiker, Walter F. *The Turkish Revolution, 1960–1961: Aspects of Military Politics.* Washington, DC: Brookings Institution, 1963.

WALTER F. WEIKER

BAYATI, ABD AL-WAHHAB AL-
[1926–]

A leading Iraqi and Arab poet from the late 1940s to the mid-1970s, who broke with traditional patterns of modern Arab poetry.

Born in Baghdad to a merchant family of the largely Sunni Arab Bayat tribe north of Baghdad, Abd al-Wahhab al-Bayati graduated in 1950 from the Higher Teachers' College and taught the Arabic language in Ramadi, western Iraq. In 1953, he returned to Baghdad, where he taught and edited a communist intellectual magazine *al-Thaqafa al-Jadida* (though he always claimed that he was an independent Marxist and never joined the party). Due to this political affiliation, in 1954 he lost his teaching job and in 1955 had to go to Syria, then to Egypt. Following the "Free Officers" coup d'état of 1958, Bayati returned to Baghdad to become one of the leading intellectuals in the regime of Abd al-Karim Qasim. But in 1959, following an estrangement between Qasim and the Communists, he was sent as a cultural adviser to Moscow. In 1964, he moved to Egypt, and in 1972 he returned to Baghdad, where Ba'th party officials made him cultural adviser for the ministry of information. A few years later, he was sent as a cultural attaché to Madrid, where he served in this capacity in the early 1990s.

His first *diwan*, *Mala'ika wa Shayatin* (1950), was written in a conventional romantic style. Following the example of two other Iraqi poets, Badr Shakir al-Sayyab and Nazik al-Mala'ika, in 1954 Bayati adopted the new style of free verse (al-Shi'r al-Hurr), in which the length of the line and the rhyming flow freely. Until the late 1970s, his poetry reflected most of the innovations that appeared in Arab poetry. Again, following al-Sayyab, since the mid-1960s his poetry is heavily loaded with surrealistic symbolism. Dominant among the various mythological symbols used were those borrowed from ancient Mesopotamia, chiefly Tammuz and Ishtar. Since the mid-1970s, the main tools in his poetry have been Sufi mystical motifs. In much of it, al-Bayati expresses the frustration and alienation of a secular revolutionary intellectual in a traditional society—a humanistic socialist under totalitarian revolutionary regimes that betrayed their human ideals.

> *See also* BA'TH, AL-; DIWAN; MALA'IKA, NAZIK AL-; QASIM, ABD AL-KARIM; SAYYAB, BADR SHAKIR AL-.

Bibliography

Baram, Amatzia. "Culture in the Service of Wataniyya: The Treatment of Mesopotamian-Inspired Art in Ba'thi Iraq." *Asian and African Studies* 17 (1983): 277–287.

Moreh, Shmuel. *Modern Arabic Poetry, 1800–1970: The Development of Its Forms and Themes under the Influence of Western Literature.* Leiden, Netherlands: Brill, 1976.

AMATZIA BARAM

BAYAT, MORTAZA QOLI
[1886–1958]

Iranian statesman.

Mortaza Qoli Bayat was the son of a wealthy landowner of Arak, a constitutionalist during the Revolution of 1906, and a member of the E'tedali (moderate) party. He was elected to the *majlis* (national assembly) in 1922 and was reelected nine times. In 1925, the fifth *majles* deposed the Qajar dynasty, voting in the Pahlavi dynasty, with Reza Shah

Pahlavi as monarch, and Bayat became minister of finance, then prime minister in 1945. He resigned in six months because he had to deal with the removal of Allied forces, especially the Soviets, who were entrenched in Azerbaijan. He also had to deal with the all-powerful Anglo–Iranian Oil Company and Soviet demands for oil concessions in the north.

In 1950, Bayat was elected senator and vice-president of the senate; after the nationalization of the petroleum industry by Dr. Mohammad Mossadegh, Bayat (who was related to him) was appointed head of the new Iranian oil company. From 1955 to 1958, he headed the newly formed oil consortium.

See also AZERBAIJAN; MOSSADEGH, MOHAMMAD; PAHLAVI, REZA; PETROLEUM, OIL, AND NATURAL GAS; QAJAR DYNASTY.

MANSOUREH ETTEHADIEH

BAYDH, ALI SALIM AL-
[ca. 1940–]

South Yemen revolutionary and republican leader.

Ali Salim al-Baydh was born into a family from the Hadramawt, with Yafi tribal origins. An early participant in the struggle against the British in South Yemen, al-Baydh (also al-Bid) survived intraparty struggles and rose from the second rank of party leaders and ministers to become head of the ruling Yemeni Socialist Party after an intraparty blood bath in Aden in January 1986. Over the next few years, he emerged as the most influential member of the new collective leadership of the People's Democratic Republic of Yemen (PDRY). In 1990 al-Baydh took the PDRY into merger with the Yemen Arab Republic, at which time he became vice president of the new Republic of Yemen (ROY). In 1994, at the peak of the political crisis in unified Yemen, he led the fight for southern secession from the ROY and announced the birth of the Democratic Republic of Yemen, with himself as president; he fled into exile in Oman when his forces were defeated in the short civil war that ended in July 1994. Except for a brief flurry of talk and activity in the late 1990s, when he was sentenced to death in absentia, al-Baydh has maintained a low political profile in exile. He has remained in Oman, despite being granted amnesty in 2003.

See also ADEN; PEOPLE'S DEMOCRATIC REPUBLIC OF YEMEN; YEMEN ARAB REPUBLIC; YEMENI SOCIALIST PARTY.

Bibliography

Dresch, Paul. *A History of Modern Yemen.* New York and Cambridge, U.K.: Cambridge University Press, 2000.

Lackner, Helen. *P.D.R. Yemen: Outpost of Socialist Development in Arabia.* London: Ithaca Press, 1985.

ROBERT D. BURROWES

BAYRAKDAR, MUSTAFA
[1775–1808]

Ottoman grand vizier.

The son of a Janissary, Bayrakdar was a notable of Ruschuk (or Ruse) in Bulgaria who served as a lieutenant in Tirsinikioğlu Ismail Ağa's large provincial army. He inherited command of the army in 1806 and used it in 1807 to restore order in Constantinople (now Istanbul) after the Janissaries deposed Selim III. But Bayrakdar was denied power in the new regime, and in 1808, in concert with the secret Ruschuk committee of Selim supporters, he and his army replaced the conservative new sultan Mustafa IV, with the reform-minded Mahmud II.

As Mahmud II's first grand vizier, Bayrakdar used his military standing to defy opposition and resume reform efforts. He invited all important local notables to Constantinople to negotiate new relations between the sultan and provinces, producing the October 1808 Sened-i Ittifak (Pact of Alliance). But the following month, Bayrakdar's planned military reforms produced another Janissary revolt, during which he was killed. Bayrakdar's defeat postponed military reform for nearly twenty years.

See also JANISSARIES; MAHMUD II; SELIM III.

Bibliography

Lewis, Bernard. *The Emergence of Modern Turkey,* 3d edition. New York: Oxford University Press, 2002.

Shaw, Stanford, and Shaw, Ezel Kural. *History of the Ottoman Empire and Modern Turkey.* Cambridge, U.K., and New York: Cambridge University Press, 1976–1977.

ELIZABETH THOMPSON

BAYRAM V, MUHAMMAD
[1840–1889]

Tunisian reformer, writer, administrator, and newspaper editor.

Muhammad Bayram V was born into an illustrious family of *ulama* in Tunis. His paternal uncle Muhammad Bayram III was *bash mufti* (chief jurisconsult) at the time of his birth. His mother was the daughter of Mahmud Khujah, a Mamluk official of Ahmad Bey; his father, Mustafa, was a farmer. His earliest recollections were of his father's laborers complaining of their situation. This, coupled with his maternal grandfather's political involvement, led him to consider a career in politics.

Upon completion of his studies at Zaytuna University, Bayram became a teacher of religion in a secondary school. When his uncle Bayram IV died in 1861, Bayram V was too young to succeed him as Shaykh al-Islam. (Apparently the designation "V" stemmed from the near assumption of this important religious office.)

The death of his uncle enabled Bayram V to establish a closer relationship with political reformers among the Mamluk class, especially Khayr al-Din al-Tunisi. When Khayr al-Din became prime minister in 1873, he appointed Bayram V editor of the official gazette, *Al-Ra'id al-Tunisi,* and head of the Hubus (*waqf*) Administration to regulate religious trusts. The *hubus* constituted an important economic base for the *ulama.* Bayram V regularized the *hubus,* eliminating corruption, improving efficiency, and maintaining accurate records of transactions. Bayram V also directed the state printing office, organized the new library at Zaytuna University, and regulated the curriculum at Sadiqi College.

After his ministry collapsed in 1877, Khayr al-Din left the country under a cloud of suspicion and failure. Bayram remained in government service until 1879. During these years, Bayram may have conspired with Khayr al-Din, who had become Ottoman prime minister, to seek French assistance in deposing Muhammad al-Sadiq Bey, ruler of Tunisia.

Bayram was allowed to go to Mecca in October 1879. He never returned to Tunisia but went to Constantinople for four years (where he reconciled with Khayr al-Din) and then to Egypt in 1884, where he spent the rest of his life. While in Egypt, Bayram launched an Arabic-language newspaper, *Al-I'lam* (The clarion), which became the most widely read and most influential Arabic newspaper of the 1880s. He also published a history of nineteenth-century Tunisia. He died 18 December 1889.

See also AHMAD BEY HUSAYN; KHAYR AL-DIN; MAMLUKS; MUHAMMAD AL-SADIQ; SADIQI COLLEGE; SHAYKH AL-ISLAM.

Bibliography

Barrie, Larry A. "A Family Odyssey: The Bayrams of Tunis, 1756–1861." Ph.D. diss., Boston University, 1987.

Green, Arnold H. *The Tunisian Ulama, 1873–1915: Social Structure and Response to Ideological Currents.* Leiden, Netherlands: Brill, 1978.

Perkins, Kenneth J. *Historical Dictionary of Tunisia,* 2d edition. Lanham, MD: Scarecrow, 1989.

LARRY A. BARRIE

BAZAARS AND BAZAAR MERCHANTS

Iranian traditional marketplaces.

The bazaar (Persian; Arabic, *suq*; Turkish, *çarşi*), traditional marketplace located in the old quarters in a Middle Eastern city, has long been the central marketplace and crafts center, the primary arena, together with the mosque, of extrafamilial sociability, and the embodiment of the traditional Islamic urban lifestyle. Merchants and commercial trade are esteemed in Islamic civilization. At the time of the rise of Islam, the society of Mecca, the birthplace of Islam, was already a major center of local, regional, and at times international trade. The city of Mecca itself was dominated by the merchant patricians. Friday congregational prayer, one of the most important Islamic institutions articulating the religious community and the state, coincided with the day on which the business activities of the weekly bazaar heightened because the people of the town and surrounding areas gathered in the marketplace for business transactions. The prophet Muhammad—whose first wife was among the city's prosperous merchants, as were many members of his clan—himself engaged in trade on behalf of his wife. In the pre-prophetic period of his life, he was called Muhammad al-Amin (trustworthy), an epithet bestowed upon him by the bazaar merchants with whom he did business.

The Traditional Bazaar

The traditional bazaar consists of shops in vaulted streets closed by doors at each end, usually with caravanserais connected into the middle of the bazaar. In small towns, the bazaar is made up of a covered street, whereas in large cities it can take up miles of passageways. Bazaars are divided into various parts, each specializing in a single trade or craft—carpet sellers, goldsmiths, shoemakers, and so forth. The social hierarchy of the bazaar includes the big merchants (*tujjar*) at the top of the pyramid; the master artisans and shopkeepers, loosely organized within over a hundred guildlike associations (*asnaf*), at the middle level; and apprentices and footboys, as well as such marginal elements as poor peddlers, dervishes, and beggars, at the lowest levels.

In premodern times, the bazaar served the governing notables as a source of tax revenues, custom dues, road tolls, credit, and unpaid labor. In return, the government provided the bazaars with internal protection and a system of justice. Although daily concerns such as the quality of the merchandise, the fairness of prices, and the accuracy of weights were supervised by local government, the state dealt with the bazaar's merchants, shopkeepers, and artisans collectively, through the chief of merchants and the guild masters.

The Modern Bazaar

Middle Eastern bazaars underwent drastic changes during the twentieth century. Rapid population growth, mass migration of villagers to the cities, modern urban planning, the development of modern quarters at the outskirts of old quarters, and the shift of the main economic activities from old bazaar to modern districts all led to the decline of Middle Eastern bazaars. In most cases, the bazaars have been reduced from their glory days as the commercial center of the city to their present function as retail centers of crafts, domestic commodities, and (often imported) industrial products. In Cairo, the most radical changes in the fabric of the old city began in the early nineteenth century, when Muhammad Ali Europeanized the city and developed modern commercial and residential areas on the outskirts of the old quarters. The old bazaar became the quarter of the poor in the twentieth century and the Khan al-Khalili, a more affluent section of the old bazaar, has remained to serve the tourist demand for Egyptian crafts. In Damascus, the western section of the grand bazaar, Suq al-Hamidiyya and its surrounding area, underwent extensive modernization during the later half of nineteenth century, and the modern quarters developed on the western outskirts of the town. Damascus still produces traditional handicrafts, such as high quality textiles, silk, leather goods, filigreed gold, and silver, inlaid wooden, copper, and brass articles. Although the bazaar remains as a center of exquisite craftsmanship, the center of economic activity has moved to the modern quarters of the city. The Grand Bazaar of Istanbul, Kapali Çarşi, once the center of economic life of the city, has in the twentieth century been adversely affected by rapid urbanization and construction of modern buildings and serves only as an important retail and crafts center.

Iranian Bazaars

The main exception is the Grand Bazaar of Tehran and the bazaars of major Iranian cities, which, in spite of Iran's rapid modernization during the latter half of the twentieth century, have shown remarkable economic resilience. Iran's bazaars have continued to serve as the financial and political power base of the Shiʿite religious establishment and a bastion of nearly all popular political protest movements in modern times, including the Tobacco Revolt (1890–1891), the Constitutional Revolution (1905–1911), the oil nationalization movement (1950–1953), the urban riots of 1963, and the Islamic revolution (1979). The commercial power and the political role played by the bazaar-mosque alliance remain unparalleled in the contemporary history of Middle Eastern cities. Compared to the bazaars of other major Middle Eastern cities, which experienced the consequences of modernization as early as the latter half of the nineteenth century, the bazaar of Tehran, founded in the early nineteenth century, developed as the bastion of the bazaar-mosque alliance, with a solid power base in the twentieth century.

Functionally, three major types of bazaars developed in modern Iran; (1) the unique bazaar of Tehran, functioning as a strategic center for local, national, and international trade; (2) the provincial bazaars, engaged in wholesale and retail trade for the central city and its hinterland; and (3) the local bazaars of small towns and large villages, in which retailers and peasant peddlers serve primarily the town and surrounding rural areas. The more significant provincial bazaars also played an important role in foreign trade. The bazaars of Isfahan, Kashan, Kerman, Kermanshah, Mashhad, Shiraz, Tabriz, and Yazd were in this category until the mid-twentieth century. The bazaar of Tehran, however, monopolized most of the foreign trade during the latter half of the twentieth century and became the main center of import, export, collection, and distribution of agricultural cash crops, modern manufactured consumer items, and Iran's most important handicraft product, Persian carpets.

The socioeconomic and morphological changes in urban Iran since the 1960s have reduced the traditional function of the bazaar as the sole urban marketplace, supplementing it with many new shopping centers in various parts of the city rather than replacing the bazaar's shops. In Tehran, for example, the bazaar underwent a rapid expansion as its surrounding residential areas were increasingly used for commercial and small-scale manufacturing establishments. The southern sections of the bazaar became a shopping area for the lower middle classes, the urban poor, and rural families, whereas its northern sections catered primarily to middle-class clients. As a result, in most cases, the shops' business price increased several times during the late 1970s, reaching as high as several hundred thousand dollars in the case of well-located shops.

Modernization and urban development created a socioeconomic and cultural duality in large urban areas of Iran, particularly in Tehran. This duality consists, on the one hand, of the religiously conservative merchants, master artisans, and shopkeepers who practice traditional urban lifestyles, living mainly around the bazaar and the old quarters of the town, and on the other, the elites and the new middle classes living in the more modern city quarters. The traditional bazaar lifestyle, shared with the *ulama,* includes such elements as sitting, eating, and sleeping on rugs or *kilims,* participating in prayer congregations in mosques, taking part in or organizing Shi'ite rituals of mourning for the martyrdom of Imam Husayn, and insisting on the veiling of women.

The main form of collective action of the bazaaris, from the Tobacco Revolt to the Iranian Revolution, was initially reactive, like bread riots, tax rebellions, and peasants' uprisings throughout history—responses caused by people being deprived of a privilege or by the imposition of oppressive measures. The novel feature of the Tobacco Revolt and the Constitutional Revolution was that they evolved from recurrent local riots to national movements. The national dimension was achieved by the increasing connection and cooperation among the bazaars of major cities in the latter half of nineteenth century. The coalition of the intelligentsia and the bazaar-mosque alliance burgeoned during the Constitutional Revolution and reemerged in the oil nationalization movement and the Iranian Revolution.

The bazaar's relationships with the state under the shah, Mohammad Reza Pahlavi (r. 1941–1979), were fraught with tensions and conflicts. Bazaaris made considerable material gains during the 1960s and 1970s, and the threats they faced were, more often than not, in the form of state intervention in commercial activities and the regime's repressive policies rather than the expansion of the new shopping areas. The government's arbitrary and discriminatory implementation of commercial regulations, its tax laws, and a campaign against price gouging were the major sources of the bazaaris' hostility toward the state. Another aggravating factor was the shah's and the elite's thinly disguised contempt for the "fanatic bazaaris [who] were highly resistant to change" (Pahlavi, p. 156). Bazaaris, along with the *ulama* and the young intelligentsia, constituted the major faction in the revolutionary coalition of 1977 through 1979. In the absence of labor unions, political parties, professional societies, and neighborhood associations, the bazaar-mosque alliance as well as schools and universities have proved to be the main vehicle for social protest.

The post-revolutionary period of the 1980s witnessed a bitter struggle between the rising young, radical, leftist elements within the new Islamic regime, on the one hand, and the merchants' and artisans' guilds and their old allies the conservative *ulama* on the other over such critical policies as nationalization of foreign trade, anti-price gouging measures, and state control over guild councils. By the early 1990s, with the normalization of the revolutionary situation, the government adopted a moderate approach to bazaar merchants and artisans.

See also CONSTITUTIONAL REVOLUTION; IRANIAN REVOLUTION (1979); MECCA; MOSSADEGH, MOHAMMAD; PAHLAVI, MOHAMMAD REZA; SHIʿISM; TOBACCO REVOLT; *ULAMA.*

Bibliography

Ashraf, Ahmad. "Bazaar-Mosque Alliance: The Social Basis of Revolts and Revolutions." *Politics, Culture, and Society* 1 (1988): 538–567.

Bonine, Michael. "Shops and Shopkeepers: Dynamics of an Iranian Provincial Bazaar." In *Modern Iran: The Dialectics of Continuity and Change,* edited by Michael E. Bonine and Nikki R. Keddie. Albany: State University of New York Press, 1981.

Pahlavi, Muhammad Reza. *Answer to History.* New York: Stein and Day, 1980.

Thaiss, Gustav. "The Bazaar as a Case Study of Religion and Social Change." In *Iran Faces the Seventies,* edited by Ehsan Yar-Shater. New York: Praeger, 1971.

Weiss, Walter M. *The Bazaar: Markets and Merchants of the Islamic World.* New York; London: Thames and Hudson, 1998.

AHMAD ASHRAF

BAZARGAN, MEHDI
[1907–1995]

Muslim intellectual and politician in Iran.

Mehdi Bazargan was born in Tehran. In 1931, he went to Paris to study engineering. Returning home in 1936, he taught at the college level. During the 1951 oil-nationalization movement, Bazargan worked with Prime Minister Mohammad Mossadegh and served as the director of the National Iranian Oil Company. After Mossadegh was deposed by the 1953 coup, Bazargan resumed teaching.

In the early 1960s, with the help of Ayatollah Mahmud Taleqani, Bazargan founded the Freedom Movement (Nehzat-e Azadi), which played an important role in the Iranian Revolution of 1979. After the revolution, Bazargan became the premier of the provisional government. With its fall, Bazargan lost much of his political influence but was elected, with a huge margin, as Tehran's representative to the parliament of the new Islamic Republic of Iran

in the 1980 election. Throughout his career, Bazargan was a leading advocate of democracy. He also was a prolific writer, publishing more than twenty books and articles.

See also FREEDOM MOVEMENT (NEZHAT-E AZADI IRAN); IRANIAN REVOLUTION (1979); MOSSADEGH, MOHAMMAD.

Bibliography

Chehabi, H. E. *Iranian Politics and Religious Modernism: The Liberation Movement of Iran under the Shah and Khomeini.* Ithaca, NY: Cornell University Press, 1990.

MANSOOR MOADDEL

BAZZAZ, ABD AL-RAHMAN AL-
[1913–1971]

Iraqi jurist, politician, and writer.

Abd al-Rahman al-Bazzaz was born in Baghdad to a Sunni Muslim family. He completed elementary school and high school in Baghdad and was graduated from Baghdad Law College in 1934. He completed his law studies in 1938 at King's College of London University. As a young man he was active politically. In the 1930s, he was a member of the Muthanna and Jawwal clubs, the intellectual focus of which was pan-Arabism and promotion of Arab nationalism. In 1941 he supported the Rashid Ali al-Kaylani uprising against the British. After the uprising's collapse and with the second British occupation of Iraq, he was interned during World War II. Shortly after the war ended, he was released from jail and appointed dean of the Baghdad Law College. In 1956 he was removed from his post for protesting the aggression against Egypt by England, France, and Israel. He and several educators signed a petition critical of Iraq's government's stand during the Suez crisis. He returned to his job as dean of the law college in the aftermath of the revolution of 14 July 1958.

Bazzaz's interest and activities in the pan-Arab movement again put him in conflict with the new government of Abd al-Karim Qasim. After the collapse of the Shawwaf uprising in 1959, he was arrested and tortured. Upon his release, he went to Egypt, where he assumed the deanship of the Institute of Arab Studies at the Arab League. He returned to Iraq after the military overthrow of the

Qasim regime in 1963. This coup marked a turning point in al-Bazzaz's political career. President Abd al-Salam Arif, a close friend, assigned al-Bazzaz to several government positions. He was appointed ambassador to the United Arab Republic (UAR), and later to England. In 1964–1965, he became the secretary-general of the Organization of Petroleum Exporting Countries. On 6 September 1965, he was named deputy prime minister. The prime minister then tried to unseat the president and seize power. The coup failed, however, and President Arif invited Bazzaz to form a new government on 21 September 1965. Al-Bazzaz was the first civilian prime minister since the collapse of the monarchy in 1958.

President Arif died unexpectedly on 13 April 1965 in a helicopter crash. A brief power struggle for the presidency ensued. In the first joint meeting of the Defense Council and cabinet to elect a president, al-Bazzaz held a plurality of one vote over the two military candidates. Nevertheless, he needed a two-thirds majority to win the presidency. A compromise candidate, Abd al-Rahman Arif, the brother of the late president, was chosen instead. The new president asked al-Bazzaz to form a new cabinet on 18 April 1966. Al-Bazzaz was forced to resign, however, on 6 August under pressure from various political groups. Chief among them was the group of politically minded senior officers who took for granted their right to govern the country. These officers resented al-Bazzaz's outspokenness concerning the proper role of the army and his intentions to reduce military salaries and privileges.

Furthermore, the officers opposed his attempts to solve the Kurdish problem peacefully. The leftist groups, including the Communists, denounced al-Bazzaz as an agent of the imperialists. The supporters of President Gamal Abdel Nasser of Egypt and Ba'thists accused him of being an enemy of Arab socialism and paying only lip service to the proposed union of Egypt and Iraq. On 24 January 1969, he was accused by the newly established Ba'thist government of involvement in clandestine activities against the government. He was tortured and imprisoned for fifteen months. In 1970, he was released because of illness and went to London for treatment, dying there in 1971.

Several features distinguished al-Bazzaz's eleven months as prime minister. First, he strongly advocated the rule of law and an end to the erratic behavior of military officers who had dominated Iraq's politics since the revolution of 14 July 1958. His government became increasingly civilianized. He replaced the Revolutionary Military Council with the National Defense Council and limited its function in regard to defense and internal security. The political system was open compared with previous regimes. As prime minister, al-Bazzaz held numerous news conferences and appeared on radio and television. Constructive criticism was encouraged, and he promised to restore parliamentary life and hold elections as soon as possible.

Second, in the field of economy, al-Bazzaz announced the First Five Year Plan (1965–1970). He advocated "prudent socialism," which attempted to strike a balance between the public and private sectors. He encouraged joint ventures between public and private sectors as well as between foreign and domestic investors. The doctrine of prudent socialism sought to increase production without abandoning the principle of equitable distribution. It was designed to lessen the impact of nationalization measures issued by the previous government.

A third distinguishing feature of al-Bazzaz's administration was the announcement of the twelve-point agreement in June 1966. Its purpose was to solve the Kurdish problem, the most unsettling difficulty of Iraq's government since 1960. The pact provided statutory recognition of the Kurdish nationality; recognized Kurdish as an official language, along with Arabic, in schools and local administration; and permitted the employment of Kurds in local administrative posts. The plan promised to hold a parliamentary election within the period stipulated in the provisional constitution of 1964. It provided for proportional representation of the Kurds in all branches of the government, including the cabinet, the Parliament, and the judiciary. It gave the Kurds the right to publish their own newspapers and to organize their own political parties. The plan provided general amnesty to all persons who had taken part in the Kurdish revolt and restored them to their previous posts and positions. It created a special Ministry for Rehabilitation and Reparation to pay damages incurred in Kurdish territory. It also endeavored to compensate Kurdish victims in northern Iraq. Unfortunately, al-Bazzaz was forced to resign in August 1966, and the agreement was never enacted.

In foreign policy, al-Bazzaz emphasized that Iraq needed to maintain a friendly relationship with its neighbors, including the non-Arab countries of Turkey and Iran. He visited both in order to improve relations, which had deteriorated since the 1958 revolution. As for the union with Egypt, he adhered to the pronouncement concerning the Iraqi–UAR Unified Political Command of 25 May 1965. He did little to advance the union, however, because of Iraq's internal affairs, including the Kurdish problem.

Al-Bazzaz was a prolific writer. He published more than twelve books on subjects including law, Iraq's history, Arab nationalism, and Islam. In his writings, he saw no apparent contradiction between Arab nationalism and Islam. Arab nationalism was not a movement based on race or solidarity of the blood. Rather, it was based on ties of language, history, spirituality, and basic interests in life. In addition to religious belief, Islam was viewed as a social system, a philosophy of life, a system of economics and of government. It belonged to the Arabs before becoming a world religion. The Prophet was an Arab. The language of the Qur'an is Arabic, and many of the Islamic rules and customs are Arabic. For example, the pilgrimage to the Ka'ba was an ancient Arab custom before its incorporation into Islamic tradition.

See also ARIF, ABD AL-RAHMAN; ARIF, ABD AL-SALAM; KA'BA; KAYLANI, RASHID ALI AL-; KURDS; NASSER, GAMAL ABDEL; ORGANIZATION OF PETROLEUM EXPORTING COUNTRIES; QASIM, ABD AL-KARIM; SUEZ CRISIS (1956–1957); UNITED ARAB REPUBLIC (UAR).

Bibliography

Bazzaz, Abd al-Rahman al-. *On Arab Nationalism,* translated by Edward Atiyah. London: Embassy of the Republic of Iraq; printed by S. Austin, 1965.

Khadduri, Majid. *Republican Iraq: A Study in Iraqi Politics since the Revolution of 1958.* London and New York: Oxford University Press, 1969.

Penrose, Edith, and Penrose, E. F. *Iraq: International Relations and National Development.* London: E. Benn; Boulder, CO: Westview Press, 1978.

AYAD AL-QAZZAZ

BEAUFORT, CHARLES-MARIE-NAPOLÉON D'HAUTPOUL DE
[1804–1890]

Commander of the French expeditionary force to Lebanon, 1860–1861.

Because of General Charles-Marie-Napoléon d'Hautpoul de Beaufort's past service in Syria, Italy, Algeria, and Morocco, Napoléon III sent him with seven thousand men to stymie the massacre of the Christians in Mount Lebanon. Chanting *"Partant pour la Syrie,"* they disembarked late, but their presence reassured the Christian population and foreshadowed the return of the French at the end of World War I. The expedition drew a geographic survey that later inspired proto–Lebanese nationalists in their quest for an enlarged and independent state.

See also LEBANON, MOUNT.

BASSAM NAMANI

BEDEL-I ASKERI

Tax paid by non-Muslims for exemption from Ottoman military service.

The *bedel-i askeri* essentially replaced the *jizya* (head tax) traditionally paid by non-Muslims, which was abolished with the 1856 Hatt-i Hümayun declaration that all subjects of the Ottoman Empire were equal and therefore obligated to serve in the military. The attempt to legislate equality among Muslims and non-Muslims, however, met opposition from all sides. In 1857, non-Muslims were once again allowed exemption from military duty. The *bedel-i askeri* tax of fifty liras was levied only on those theoretically required to serve, 1 out of 180 male subjects of age. It was much lower than the exemption tax paid by Muslims. In 1909 the *bedel-i askeri* and all other conscription-exemption taxes were abolished, and all male subjects regardless of religion were required to perform military duty.

See also JIZYA; TANZIMAT.

Bibliography

Davison, Roderic H. *Reform in the Ottoman Empire 1856–1876*. Princeton, NJ: Princeton University Press, 1963.

Shaw, Stanford, and Shaw, Ezel Kural. *History of the Ottoman Empire and Modern Turkey*, Vol. 2: *Reform, Revolution, and Republic: The Rise of Modern Turkey, 1808–1975*. Cambridge, U.K., and New York: Cambridge University Press, 1977.

ELIZABETH THOMPSON

BEERSHEBA

City in southern Israel.

Located in the northern Negev (Arabic, Naqab) desert, Beersheba (Hebrew, B'er Sheva; Arabic, Bir al-Sabi) is midway between the Dead Sea to the east and the Mediterranean to the west. It is one of the biggest cities in Israel, after the metropolitan centers of Tel Aviv-Jaffa, Jerusalem, and Haifa. Its principal industries are chemicals, porcelain, and textiles. Beersheba is the home of Ben-Gurion University of the Negev and the Negev Institute for Arid Zone Research.

Historically, the city has been an important trading center between a variety of ecological zones—the mountains to the east, the desert to the south, and the seacoast to the west. In biblical times, it marked the southern limit of Palestine. In 1901, the Ottoman Empire made Beersheba the administrative center for the bedouin tribes of the Negev. In 1917, it was the site of a British victory over the Turks that opened the way for the Allied conquest of Palestine and Syria. After Israel became a state in 1948, Beersheba was settled and enlarged by new immigrants. The population estimate in 2002 was about 182,000.

See also BEN-GURION UNIVERSITY OF THE NEGEV; DEAD SEA; MEDITERRANEAN SEA; NEGEV.

Bibliography

Fischback, Michael R. "Beersheba." In *Encyclopedia of the Palestinians*, edited by Philip Mattar. New York: Facts On File, 2000.

STEVE TAMARI

BEGIN, MENACHEM
[1913–1992]

Israeli statesman and sixth prime minister of Israel, 1977–1983.

Menachem (also Menahem) Begin was born on 16 August 1913 in Brest Litovsk, the third child of Ze'ev Dov and Hassia Begin, who were murdered by the Nazis. He studied law at Warsaw University. He joined the Zionist youth movement Betar in 1929. Ze'ev Dov—who had once struck a Polish sergeant who was cutting off a rabbi's beard and had come home bruised and bleeding—bequeathed his son a profound awareness of Jewish vulnerability as well as the courage to fight back. The Holocaust set it in steel. Vladimir Ze'ev Jabotinsky, the founder of Betar and radical prophet of Revisionist Zionism, added an ideological conviction that Jews must be soldiers before they could be farmers if they wanted a homeland. Between them, they made Begin proudly Jewish, stubborn, single-minded, and unbending. He could be gracious, but never ingratiating. In 1938 Begin was elected to head Betar in Poland. After the Germans invaded, he escaped to Vilna. Following the Soviet conquest, in September 1940, he was sentenced to hard labor in the Arctic region. He refused to be broken by the harsh conditions and interrogations. After he was released along with other Polish citizens, he joined General Władysław Anders's Free Polish Army at the end of 1941 and was posted to Palestine. A year later, he was released and took command of the Irgun Zva'i Le'umi (IZL), the National Military Organization. On 1 February 1944, Begin declared the opening of a revolt against British rule.

This campaign turned into a four-year underground struggle. Begin did not flinch from terrorism, believing that the fighting Jew had to be no less ruthless than his enemies. In hiding, Begin conducted the Irgun's military and political operations. Its first targets were British immigration, tax, and Criminal Investigation Department (CID) offices. The Irgun also robbed and extorted from Jewish banks and businessmen to fund its campaign. Begin kept it active in spite of the severe blows it suffered during the "saison" declared on it by the Haganah, the official Jewish defense force. Begin forbade the Irgun from retaliating against fellow Jews, but he was less scrupulous toward the British. In 1946 his men kidnapped six British officers to

Menachem Begin celebrates with fellow Likud Party members
after the May 1977 Knesset elections that brought them to
power. Begin served as prime minister of Israel from 1977–1983.
© AP/WIDE WORLD PHOTOS. REPRODUCED BY PERMISSION.

Irgun arms ship shelled by the Israeli army after he
had refused to hand over its cargo to the government.
In the same year, he founded the nationalist Herut
Party, which he led through three decades of opposition and eight electoral defeats. Begin's commitment to parliamentary government was ambivalent.
He argued for constitutional propriety and safe-
guards for the individual, but he incited a mob that
stormed the Knesset building in 1952 in protest at a
reparations agreement with West Germany. From
1965 onward, Begin strove to wrest Herut from its
isolation, first by establishing Gahal through a
merger of Herut and the Liberals and eight years later
by broadening it to form the Likud. In May 1967,
just before the Arab–Israel War of 1967, he was
named minister without portfolio in a National Unity
government. He resigned in 1970 to protest the government's acceptance of the United Nations framework for regional peace, Resolution 242, and the
Rogers Plan for a cease-fire between Israel and its
Arab neighbors. But it had been an apprenticeship
of power, an end to the inevitability of opposition.

In the "upheaval" of the elections of 17 May
1977, Begin became the head of Israel's first right-
wing coalition, and he won a second term in 1981.
Almost immediately after setting up his government,

secure a reprieve for two Irgun fighters on death
row. In July 1947 they hanged two sergeants in revenge for the execution of three Irgun men. Begin
felt the hanging had achieved its purpose: No more
Irgun prisoners went to the gallows.

At the end of 1945, Begin led the Irgun into the
umbrella Hebrew Resistance Movement with the
Haganah and LEHI (the "Stern Gang"). As its contribution, the Irgun destroyed twenty Royal Air
Force planes on the ground and caused £ 100,000
worth of damage to railway rolling stock. However,
Begin ignored a request from the mainstream Zionist leadership and sent the Irgun to blow up the King
David Hotel, the British headquarters in Jerusalem,
with the loss of ninety-one lives. The Irgun revolt
was not the only factor that propelled the British out
of Palestine, but it played its part.

In June 1948, a month after the declaration of
the Jewish state, Begin was on board the *Altalena*, an

Begin (right) with Egyptian president Anwar al-Sadat (left) and
President Jimmy Carter of the United States (center) sign the
Israel–Egypt Peace Treaty in 1979. The termination of war
between the two countries was the shining achievement of
Begin's prime ministry. © GETTY IMAGES. REPRODUCED BY
PERMISSION.

Before becoming Israel's prime minister, Begin was head of the organization Irgun Zva'i Le'umi, which protested British policy in Palestine. The organization was behind several terrorist attacks against British and Palestinian targets, including the bombing of the British headquarters in Jerusalem in 1945.
© HULTON-DEUTSCH COLLECTION. REPRODUCED BY PERMISSION.

Begin initiated secret negotiations with Egypt, which led to President Anwar al-Sadat's visit to Israel in November 1977, the Camp David summit in September 1978, and a peace treaty in March 1979. Begin, together with Sadat, was awarded the Nobel Peace Prize. The treaty was made possible by Begin's readiness to withdraw from Sinai. He also agreed to autonomy for the Palestinians, but he was determined to keep the "liberated territories" of the West Bank and the plan came to nothing. During his reign, Israel extended its law to East Jerusalem (June 1980) and the Golan Heights (December 1981), which was interpreted as de facto annexation. On 7 June 1981, Israeli planes destroyed Iraq's Osirak reactor, thus denying Saddam Hussein nuclear weapons for the rest of the century.

In June 1982, Israel invaded Lebanon. The war aimed to destroy the Palestine Liberation Organization's fighting capability, rid Lebanon of Syrian troops, and install Israel's Maronite allies in power. It succeeded only in the first objective. The mounting Israeli death toll, the massacre of Palestinians in the Sabra and Shatila refugee camps (for which an Israeli commission found his government indirectly responsible), a series of strokes, and the death of his wife Aliza all plunged Begin into a deep depression that culminated in his resignation on 19 September 1983. From that time until his death on 9 March 1992, he remained secluded in his Jerusalem home, played no part in politics, and rarely appeared in public.

Menachem Begin was asked during his six years as prime minister how he would like to be remembered. He replied: "As the man who set the borders of the Land of Israel for all eternity." When he resigned in 1983, he appeared to have succeeded. The number of Jewish settlements in the West Bank and Gaza Strip had grown fourfold from 24 to 117. The Jewish population living beyond the pre-1967 border had grown from 3,000 to 40,000. Under previous Labor governments, the emphasis had been on the Jordan valley, on populating the strategic frontier. Under Begin, most of the new settlements were planted among the Palestinian towns and villages. It seemed impossible to repartition Palestine. Yet within two decades, his successors as leaders of the Likud followed Labor in ceding territory to the Palestinian Authority and acknowledged that Begin's Greater Israel dream was no longer attainable. His other major achievement, the 1979 peace treaty with Egypt, proved more durable. It remained, however, a peace of the head rather than the heart. On the domestic front, he brought alienated Jews of Middle Eastern and North African origin into the centers of government. A decade after Begin's death, Israel had an Iranian-born defense minister and a Tunisian-born foreign minister.

See also ALTALENA; CAMP DAVID ACCORDS (1978); IRGUN ZVA'I LE'UMI (IZL); ISRAELI SETTLEMENTS; WEST GERMAN REPARATIONS AGREEMENT.

Bibliography

Begin, Menachem. *The Revolt.* New York: Nash, 1977.

Haber, Eithan. *Menahem Begin: The Legend and the Man,* translated by Louis Williams. New York: Delacorte Press, 1978.

Peleg, Ilan. *Begin's Foreign Policy, 1977–1983: Israel's Move to the Right.* New York: Greenwood Press, 1987.

Perlmutter, Amos. *The Life and Times of Menachem Begin.* Garden City, NY: Doubleday, 1987.

Silver, Eric. *Begin: The Haunted Prophet.* New York: Random House, 1984.

Sofer, Sasson. *Begin: An Anatomy of Leadership.* New York and Oxford, U.K.: Blackwell, 1988.

Temko, Ned. *To Win or to Die: A Personal Portrait of Menachem Begin.* New York: W. Morrow, 1987.

ERIC SILVER

BEHAR, NISSIM
[1848–1931]

Zionist and educator.

Born in Jerusalem, Nissim Behar has been called the founder of modern Hebrew education. After being taught the Hebrew language by Eliezer Ben-Yehuda, he became a teacher of modern Hebrew at the Alliance Israélite Universelle in Jerusalem and was the school's director from 1882 to 1887.

In 1901, Behar moved to New York City, where he directed the National Liberal Immigration League from 1906 to 1924. During his years in New York, he continued to develop his method for teaching Hebrew, which became known as Ivrit be Ivrit. At the same time, he was an active propagandist for Zionism, calling for the return of the Jews to Palestine, and along with Baron Edmond de Rothschild tried to regain the Western (Wailing) Wall for the Jewish community in Jerusalem. His methods were not always to the liking of U.S. Jewish leaders, some of whom were uncomfortable with the public meetings and protests that he organized to further the cause of the Jews of Palestine.

See also ALLIANCE ISRAÉLITE UNIVERSELLE (AIU); BEN-YEHUDA, ELIEZER; ROTHSCHILD, EDMOND DE; WESTERN WALL.

Bibliography

Rolef, Susan Hattis, ed. *Political Dictionary of the State of Israel*, 2d edition. New York: Macmillan, 1993.

ZACHARY KARABELL

BEHBEHANI, SIMIN
[1927–]

Iranian poet.

Simin Behbehani was born in Tehran. Her father, Abbas Khalili, was a writer and newspaper editor. Her mother, Fakhr Azami Arghoon, was a noted feminist, teacher, writer, newspaper editor, and poet. Behbehani began publishing poetry at the age of fourteen. She has become one of Iran's most important poets, using the traditional *ghazal* form—a set of couplets all with the same rhyme and usually dealing with themes of love and wine—in innovative ways. Influenced by modern writers like Nima Yushig, she has developed a unique style that has earned her a special place in the literary history of modern Iran. The honesty, openness, and passionate engagement of her poetry has allowed her work to serve as a social vehicle for her times, from mourning the Iran–Iraq War to voicing a strong cry for freedom of expression. She has become an important voice of post-Revolutionary Iran. Behbehani lives and works in Iran but has traveled widely, giving poetry readings and advocating freedom of expression.

See also GENDER: GENDER AND EDUCATION; LITERATURE: PERSIAN.

Bibliography

Iran Chamber. "Simin Behbehani." Available from <http://www.iranchamber.com/literature/sbehbahani>.

ROXANNE VARZI

BEHESHTI, MOHAMMAD
[1928–1981]

Iranian religious scholar and a principal figure in the founding of the Islamic Republic of Iran.

Receiving his early education in his birthplace of Isfahan, Mohammad Beheshti began his specialized studies in Islam in Qom (Qum) in 1946, studying under a series of prominent scholars that included Ayatollah Ruhollah Khomeini. He also obtained a doctorate from the Faculty of Theology at Tehran University and took pains to learn English and German. In the early 1960s, he contributed articles on the contemporary problems of the Muslim world to the numerous Islamic periodicals that were flourishing at the time. Despite his links to Khomeini, he escaped arrest in the aftermath of the June 1963 uprising in Iran and in 1965 was permitted to leave to become director of the Islamic Center in Hamburg,

Germany. He returned to Iran in 1970 and resumed his educational activities in Qom.

From 1975 on, Beheshti was active in mobilizing the religious scholars against the regime of Mohammad Reza Pahlavi. In 1978, he met with Khomeini to assist in the planning of the revolution; early in 1979 he was named to the Revolutionary Council that was intended to function as an interim legislature. After the success of the revolution, in 1979, he was appointed head of the Supreme Court and elected to the parliament as a leading figure in the Islamic Republican Party. In the latter capacity, he became the leading adversary of Abolhasan Bani Sadr, the first president of the Islamic Republic. Beheshti was killed on 28 June 1981 in an explosion that destroyed the Tehran headquarters of the Islamic Republican Party.

See also BANI SADR, ABOLHASAN; KHOMEINI, RUHOLLAH; PAHLAVI, MOHAMMAD REZA.

HAMID ALGAR

BEHRANGI, SAMAD
[1939–1968]

An Iranian teacher and short-story writer.

Samad Behrangi was born in Tabriz, capital of Iranian Azerbaijan, in 1939. He attended schools in the city and completed the two-year teachers' training program for elementary school teachers in 1957. He spent the next eleven years teaching in village schools in the Azar Shahr district, about 30 miles (50 kilometers) southwest of Tabriz. He early developed a fascination with Azeri Turkish folk tales. His first book, published in 1965, was a collection of several such stories that he had translated into Persian. That work brought him to the attention of literary circles in Tehran. The subsequent publication of an essay on educational problems, several original children's stories dealing realistically with social issues, and a second volume of Azeri folktales established his reputation as a rising star among a new generation of writers. Behrangi was drowned in a swimming accident in September 1968; he was only twenty-nine. At the time, his most famous children's stories, including "The Little Black Fish," were at the press; they were published posthumously. The popularity of Behrangi's work continued even after the 1979 revolution, with numerous editions of single stories, often illustrated by noted artists, appearing regularly throughout the 1980s and 1990s. His stories and folktales also were translated into Azeri Turkish.

Bibliography

Behrangi, Samad. *The Little Black Fish and Other Modern Persian Stories,* translated by Eric Hooglund and Mary Hoogland. Washington, DC: Three Continents Press, 1976.

ERIC HOOGLUND

BEHROUZI, MARYAM
[Unknown]

Political activist and representative in the Iranian parliament.

Maryam Behrouzi was a political activist prior to the Iranian Revolution and was imprisoned for her activities and beliefs.

As a veteran member of the majlis (the Iranian parliament), Behrouzi pushed through a bill allowing women to retire after twenty years of active service, instead of twenty-five. She was also instrumental in reforming Iran's divorce laws and providing national insurance for women and children. She is the head of Jame'e Zainab (Zainab Society), an organization that aims to enhance Iranian women's cultural and social relations by bringing together Muslim women under one umbrella. The organization's main activity is to provide courses on Islamic education, interpretation of the Qur'an, and the Arabic language. The organization is not politically active, although it is known to have supported the hard-line conservative speaker of the parliament, Ali Akbar Nateq Nuri, in the 1997 presidential elections.

Behrouzi has been labeled an "Islamic feminist," and as such, she is linked with Monireh Gorji, the female representative in the Assembly of Experts, who is responsible for nominating the national leader, and Faezeh Hashemi, among others. In their different capacities, these women have put forward new interpretations of Islamic texts in order to challenge laws and policies that are based on orthodox or literary interpretations.

See also GENDER: GENDER AND LAW; GENDER: GENDER AND POLITICS; HASHEMI, FAEZEH; IRANIAN REVOLUTION (1979).

CHERIE TARAGHI

BEIRUT

The capital of Lebanon.

Beirut, on the coast of the Mediterranean, is Lebanon's center of government and finance. It has been part of various empires through history, and its archaeological treasures attest to the multiplicity of its historic occupiers and rulers. The city has undergone substantial changes in its appearance, as devastating earthquakes have hit the city several times in the last two millennia. There are no reliable demographic statistics on the current inhabitants of Beirut. The city has over 1 million inhabitants, and Greater Beirut has around 1.5 million. The city has existed since the time of the Canaanites. The origin of its name is unknown, although it is often said to be *Ba'l Brit,* one of the deities of the Canaanites. A variation of the name in Hebrew, Syriac, and Phoenician means "a well," referring to its rich water sources. The city's name was given to a *vilayet* during the Ottoman Empire and was in a jurisdiction separate from Mount Lebanon.

The association of Beirut and Lebanon is a twentieth-century phenomenon. When the French formed Greater Lebanon in 1920, Beirut, along with other districts, was joined with the area of Mount Lebanon to compose a new political entity. Beirut was added for economic reasons: Mount Lebanon needed access to the sea, and the port of Beirut had had a crucial economic regional role since the nineteenth century. The people of Beirut at the time had a different demographic composition than Mount Lebanon, which was predominantly Druze and Maronite (Christian).

Beirut gradually grew in size and political significance. The centers of administration and government were located there, as were educational institutions such as the American University of Beirut and the Jesuit Saint Joseph University, both of which were founded in the nineteenth century. The centrality of Beirut increasingly marginalized other regions, including Mount Lebanon. This led to massive waves of migration into the city by people seeking education and jobs. This population movement changed the demographics of the city, which had been mainly Sunni and non-Maronite Christian: Maronites were increasingly present in the city, and Shi'a began settling in large numbers as early as the 1950s.

Soldiers walk the streets of war-torn Beirut, 3 February 1985. This photo was taken during the darkest days of the Israeli occupation of Lebanon, a period marked by intense Israeli shelling and frequent car-bomb explosions. © WEBISTAN/CORBIS. REPRODUCED BY PERMISSION.

Beirut was enlarged in the 1950s and 1960s as a result of the inflow of former rural residents who could not afford to live within the city boundaries. The "suburbs" of Beirut (as they came to be called) grew to include more than half a million migrants. Hundreds of thousands of Shi'a fleeing southern Lebanon, the center of the confrontation between the Palestine Liberation Organization (PLO) and Israel, resided in East Beirut and South Beirut, in what was later called the "poverty belt." Factories in East Beirut attracted Lebanese looking for work. During the period of prosperity and glamour before the Lebanese Civil War of 1958, Beirut was actually two cities: the old Beirut, where the rich and the middle class lived and prospered, and the old *suq* (market) attracted shoppers from around the region; and the suburbs, where poor Lebanese (mostly Shi'a, Armenians, Palestinians, and poor Christians) lived. The poor Lebanese came into contact with Palestinians in refugee camps in and around the city. This contact revolutionized the political situation in Lebanon for much of the 1960s and 1970s. The presence of a large student population in the capital helped the efforts of the PLO and its

A helicopter view of Beirut and the coastline of the Mediterranean Sea, 1967. © ROGER WOOD/CORBIS. REPRODUCED BY PERMISSION.

Lebanese allies who wanted to draw attention to the plight of the South and the poor in general.

The primacy of Beirut was shattered by the Lebanese Civil War of 1975 to 1990. The city that had symbolized prosperity and ostentation came to symbolize bloodshed and cruelty. The war began in Beirut, in the Maronite suburb of Ayn al-Rummana, where a bus carrying Palestinians was ambushed in April 1975 by gunmen belonging to the Phalange Party. The war sharpened sectarian divisions in the capital and produced the Green Line, a street that separated East Beirut (predominantly Christian) from West Beirut (predominantly Muslim, although it continued to house a substantial Christian population). The length of the war brought some degree of "sectarian purity" to the two sections, although Lebanese belonging to the "wrong sect" continued to live—at their peril—in their customary dwelling places. Attempts at "sectarian cleansing" were relatively successful in East Beirut, when forces loyal to the Phalange Party evicted hundreds of thousands

of Shiʿa and Palestinians from their homes. Refugee camps located in East Beirut were razed and demolished. There was no eviction of Christians from West Beirut, although some voluntarily left due to hightened sectarian tensions and the rise of Islamic fundamentalist parties in the 1980s.

In the course of the civil war, the downtown area (where the parliament and the financial district were located) was completely destroyed. Looting of shops in 1975 and 1976 forced businesses to relocate into sectarian enclaves. Local militiamen controlled the downtown area through much of the war. Although those Lebanese who could afford to emigrate did so, the city did not suffer from underpopulation because many were still coming to the capital seeking jobs and education: The instability of southern Lebanon continued to send waves of migrants into the southern suburbs of Beirut.

The end of the civil war was supposed to bring an end to the division of Beirut. Reference to the

Green Line is now politically unacceptable. The government of Rafiq al-Hariri has emphasized and showcased its reconstructed downtown Beirut, although critics complain about the purely commercial nature of the enterprise. Concerned economists warn that the reconstruction plans have only reinforced the service-sector bias of the prewar economy, which, according to critics, was responsible for the social injustices that were manifested in the civil war. War damage was repaired with great success, and new residential and office buildings have have been constructed, although only the rich can afford to occupy them: Residential apartments can sell for $1 million. The newly completed downtown area of Beirut attracts tourists and visitors from around the region, and some from Europe. The reconstruction plans undertaken by the government of Hariri have been largely responsible for the ballooning of the foreign debt of Lebanon, now exceeding $30 billion. Most of the downtown enterprises are restaurants and cafes; the office buildings have not yet been occupied.

See also AMERICAN UNIVERSITY OF BEIRUT (AUB); GREEN LINE; HARIRI, RAFIQ BAHA'UDDIN AL-; LEBANESE CIVIL WAR (1958); LEBANESE CIVIL WAR (1975–1990); LEBANON; LEBANON, MOUNT; PALESTINE LIBERATION ORGANIZATION (PLO); PHALANGE.

Bibliography

Fisk, Robert. *Pity the Nation: The Abduction of Lebanon.* New York: Thunder's Mouth Press/Nation Books, 2002.

Friedman, Robert. *From Beirut to Jerusalem.* London: Collins, 1990.

Gavin, Angus, and Maluf, Ramaz. *Beirut Reborn: The Restoration and Development of the Central Districts.* London: Academy Editions, 1996.

Makdisi, Jean Said. *Beirut Fragments: A War Memoir.* New York: Persea Books, 1990.

AS'AD ABUKHALIL

BEIRUT COLLEGE FOR WOMEN (BCW)

Four year college for the education of women in Lebanon, now a member college of the Lebanese American University of Beirut.

In 1914, the American Mission for Lebanon and Syria discussed developing a more demanding curriculum for its American School for Girls, founded in 1860, and drafted a plan for the American Junior Women's College. In 1924 the American Protestant mission received authorization to develop the junior college, and the Presbyterian Church of America in New York supplied the faculty and administration.

During its first year, the college enrolled eight students, five of whom continued on to the sophomore year. In June 1926, three of them graduated: Munira Barbir, Saniyya Habbub, and Armenouchic Megnodichian. Both Habbub and Megnodichian went on to become doctors. During 1936–1937 academic year, the junior college moved to larger accommodations in Ra's Beirut. Classes included history, sociology, psychology, chemistry, math, biology, religion, languages, and athletics. Students participated in sports, class trips, and various clubs. During the summers the college created a "village welfare camp," where student interns visited villages and taught girls and women various skills, such as literacy, childcare, and handicrafts.

After World War II, the junior college applied for four-year institutional status due to the high interest in developing education in the region. One of the most notable students to study at the college during that period was the young Princess Fatmeh, the shah of Iran's sister. On its twenty-fifth anniversary (1949–1950), the school was granted a provisional charter to award the degree of Bachelor of Arts as it graduated its first senior class. In March 1955, the college was granted an absolute charter as a four-year institution and changed its name to the Beirut College for Women. Soon after, the Lebanese government recognized the college's bachelor's degree and allowed its graduates to register for the examinations for major government appointments.

The college produced two newspapers. *Veils Up* was dedicated to the eradication of illiteracy and poverty, and to the promotion of mother-child healthcare. The *College Tribune* was the first attempt by young women to tackle such issues as the role of women in politics and the labor force.

In 1973, the college became coeducational and changed its name to Beirut University College. In the same year, it established the Institute for Women's Studies in the Arab World (IWSAW). The institute researches and documents women's status in the Arab world, publishing a quarterly journal called *al-Ra'ida* (The pioneer).

Improvements to the college came to a halt in 1975, when war broke out in Lebanon. From 1975 until 1990, very little quality education was available at any level. However, during that period, female enrollment rose while the number of male students declined. Also beginning in the mid-1970s, the college's administrators were Arab rather than American. During the civil war years IWSAW assumed an important, albeit informal, role as a research center and provider of services to widows and orphans, and it received significant financial support through grants from the Ford Foundation and several European governments. In 1978, Beirut University College decentralized its operations and opened a branch in the north, near Byblos, and one in the south of Lebanon, in Saida. After the war, developing and strengthening the university became a priority. In 1994, the New York Board of Regents approved another name change, to the Lebanese American University, reflecting its status as a full-fledged university. By the year 2002, it was a thriving coeducational institution and boasted more than 5,000 students, graduate as well as undergraduate.

See also GENDER: GENDER AND EDUCATION; LEBANESE CIVIL WAR (1958); LEBANESE CIVIL WAR (1975–1990); LEBANON.

Bibliography

Bashshur, Munir. "The Role of Education: A Mirror of a Fractured National Image." In *Toward a Viable Lebanon,* edited by Halim Barakat. Washington, DC: Center for Contemporary Arab Studies, 1988.

Dodge, Bayard. *The American University of Beirut: A Brief History of the University and the Lands Which It Serves.* Beirut: al-Khayat Publishing, 1958.

Khairallah, Shereen. *The Sisters of Men.* Beirut: IWSAW, Lebanese American University, 1996.

Lebanese American University. Available at <www.lau .edu.lb/general-info/historical-backg.html>.

Lebanese American University Academic Catalogue 1996. Beirut: Focus Press, 1996.

Roberts, Donald. *The Beirut College for Women: A Short History.* Beirut: Beirut College for Women, 1958.

MIRNA LATTOUF

BEITADDIN DECLARATION

A 1978 attempt by six Arab countries to end the Lebanese civil war of 1975–1990.

The Beitaddin Declaration was issued following a meeting (15–17 October 1978) in Lebanon, attended by the foreign ministers of the six Arab countries contributing troops to the Arab Deterrent Force (Syria, Saudi Arabia, Kuwait, United Arab Emirates, Qatar, and Sudan). The meeting took place during the Lebanese civil war, amid heightened tension. A national reconciliation document adopted by the Lebanese parliament (April 1978) had never been implemented. Further, Christian militias of the Lebanese forces and Syrian troops were involved in heavy clashes in east Beirut. In March 1978, Israel had invaded southern Lebanon. The resolutions adopted at Beitaddin (also Bayt al-Din, a famous residence of Lebanese amirs) included a recognition of Lebanon's independence, sovereignty, and territorial integrity; a call for the dissolution of all armed presences in the country; and the full implementation of the agreements adopted by Arab heads of state in Riyadh, Saudi Arabia, and Cairo, Egypt (1976), which involved the establishment of a phased program for the rebuilding of the Lebanese army and the creation of a follow-up committee with delegates from Saudi Arabia, Syria, and Kuwait.

See also LEBANESE CIVIL WAR (1975–1990); LEBANESE FORCES.

GEORGE E. IRANI

BEJA

A people of the eastern Sudan.

The indigenous people of eastern Sudan are a people of great antiquity who have had a variety of names; since medieval times they have been known as the Beja. They inhabit the hills and the coastal plain along the Red Sea. Much of their past is uncertain, but they were known to the pharaohs, and certainly to the British in the modern age. The British viewed them as a people who had survived the interest and the impact of more powerful nations without losing their character. They are composed of five clans: Ababda, Bisharin, Hadendowa, Amarar, and Beni Amir. They are nomadic, and are known for a mental and physical toughness that has helped them to overcome the harshness of their environment and blood feuds. Despite contact with the Egyptians, Greeks, and Romans, it was the Muslims who finally had a real and lasting impression on the Beja. The Beja Conference is a political and armed opposition to the central military government ruling Sudan since 1989.

There are a number of cultural markers of the Beja. Some of these are shared with neighboring people groups; others are uniquely Beja. The men wear a typical Sudanese white *jallabiya* (a long, loose-fitting shirt with baggy pants underneath), and a white turban. Usually they add a colored vest to the outfit. Men usually own a sword that can be used as a weapon or for special ceremonial dances at celebrations. Often, Beja men have a big bush of hair composed of large curls. It is common to see a carved wooden comb sticking out of the top of a man's head as a decoration. Beja women wrap a brightly colored cloth called a *tawb* around their dresses. Often, both Beja men and women have three decorative vertical scars on each cheek. The women often wear beaded jewelry and large nose rings.

The dominant Beja language in Sudan is the TaBedawie, which is a Cushitic language influenced by Semitic languages such as Tigre and Arabic. Until the early 1990s TaBedawie was an unwritten language, and therefore it has no literature. It is common for Beja to speak Arabic (Sudanese dialect) as a second language. The Beja like to sing and play musical instruments, in particular the *rababa,* which is similar to a guitar. Since they are renowned camel herders, camels are the most popular subject matter for songs, but many songs also describe the beauty of women or express a longing for a special place such as a village, a mountain, or good grazing lands.

The coffee ceremony is one of the most dominant elements of Beja life, because it is the main setting for socializing and sharing news. In the ceremony, first the beans are roasted and mixed with ginger root and pounded into a powder. Next, the

A Beja tribesman clutches his sword as he rests. The members of this nomadic tribe, composed of five clans in eastern Sudan, have endured their harsh environment since ancient times. © PENNY TWEEDIE/CORBIS. REPRODUCED BY PERMISSION.

powder is poured into a *jebana* or coffeepot, which is then filled with water. When the pot has boiled, the coffee is strained through a hair filter into small china cups the size of espresso cups, which are half-full of sugar. Once the pot has been emptied, more water is added, and the coffee is reboiled to produce a second, weaker round. This is usually repeated at least three times, and sometimes five or six. Coffee is very important to the Beja. The Beja, particularly the Hadendowa, spend 15 to 25 percent of their monthly incomes on coffee. It is a common saying in Sudan that a Hadendowa would rather starve than go without coffee.

See also SUDAN.

Bibliography

"The Beja of Sudan." Sudan 101. Available from <http://www.sudan101.com/beja.htm>.

Hjort, Anders. *Responsible Man: The Atmaan Beja of Northeastern Sudan.* Stockholm: Stockholm Studies in Social

Anthropology, in cooperation with Nordiska Afrikainstitutet, Uppsala, 1991.

Jacobsen, Frode F. *Theories of Sickness and Misfortune among the Hadandowa Beja of the Sudan: Narratives as Points of Entry into Beja Cultural Knowledge.* London and New York: Kegan Paul International, 1998.

Palmisano, Antonio. *Ethnicity: The Beja as Representation.* Berlin: Arabische Buch, 1991.

Paul, Andrew. *A History of the Beja Tribes of the Sudan.* Cambridge, U.K.: Cambridge University Press, 1954.

ROBERT O. COLLINS
UPDATED BY KHALID M. EL-HASSAN

BEJERANO, MAYA

[1949–]

Israeli poet.

Maya Bejerano was born in Haifa in 1949. She studied art, literature, philosophy, and music. In addition to writing poetry she works as a librarian. Bejerano won the Prime Minister's Prize and other literary awards.

Bejerano's poetry is concerned with the age-old journey of self-discovery, which, in her poems, takes place outside of the self. Bejerano makes frequent use of space-age terminology as metaphors for observation. In such books as *Ostrich* (1978) and *Song of Birds* (1985), she invokes technical imagery—computers, spaceships, laser light—in order to create the distance and the precision necessary for effective observation. Bejerano does not emphasize the existential emptiness and social detachment that is sometimes associated with modern scientific knowledge. Rather, she uses science to enhance and facilitate human communication. Unlike some of the somber and more iconoclastic Israeli poetry that preceded hers, Bejerano's poetic journeys emphasize the positive and humanistic. Humanity, according to Bejerano, is the center of meaning and it is only through humanity that the world around us can be intelligible. She is constantly aware of the very act of writing and uses that consciousness to infuse her poems with wit and irony. Bejerano does not promote a specific ethical or ideological message in her poems. To her, the very vacillation between conflicting choices is the basis of human existence. She muses freely in her poems without being afraid where that may take her. The focus of Berjerano's poetry is the journey itself and the inherent promise of change it holds.

See also LITERATURE: HEBREW.

Bibliography

Bejerano, Maya. *Retsef ha-Shirim 1972–1986* (Selected poems, 1972–1986). Tel Aviv: Am Oved, 1987.

Lahav, Avner. "A Wondrous Journey." *Achshav* 51–54 (1987): 562–569.

YAROM PELEG

BEKIR FAHRI

Ottoman Turkish writer.

Bekir Fahri was graduated from the Mülkiye and entered the civil service. A partisan of the Young Turks, he was forced to take refuge in Egypt, returning to Istanbul after the 1908 revolution. In 1910, his novel *Jönler* (The youngsters) was published, and he became literary editor of the journal *Piyano*. The last years of his life, like the early years, remain a mystery; all that is known is that in 1914, he sent some stories to the magazine *Ruhab* from Cairo. His naturalist style was heavily influenced by the French author Émile Zola.

See also LITERATURE: TURKISH; YOUNG TURKS.

DAVID WALDNER

BEKTASHIS

Members of a heterodox Sufi order that blends pre-Islamic, Christian, and Shi'ite elements.

Although different sources dispute the date of the appearance of the legendary Hajji Bektash, it is probable that he fled to Seljuk, Anatolia, around 1230 with Kharezmian Turkmen tribes of Central Asia seeking refuge after the Mongol conquests. He was welcomed into the Oghuz tribe of Çepni, where he was a healer and thaumaturge and led a life of meditation. After his death, Kadıncık Ana of the Çepni, who was either his adoptive daughter or spiritual wife, founded the order that today bears his name with the help of her disciple, Abdal Musa.

Unlike his contemporary Jalal al-Din Rumi, who fled to Anatolia near the same time, Bektash did not study Islam in a formal Sunni *madrasa*, but retained pre-Islamic practices of the Central Asian plains. There is some overlap in religious practices between Mevlevi and Bektashi dervishes, such as the semah, or whirling ceremony, although the former tends toward Sunnism. Bektashism incorporates elements of traditions of pre-Islamic Central Asia and Anatolia, including some Christian practices, and displays a distinctively intense veneration for the fourth caliph, Ali.

The Ottoman Empire recruited janissary soldiers from its Christian Balkan populations who found Bektashism easier to follow than Sunni Orthodox Islam. It is their adherence to Bektashism that helped it to spread during Ottoman times. Its characteristic liberalism, support for the oppressed, and support for political revolts attracted disfavor from the Sunni Ottoman establishment. In 1826 Sultan Mahmud II attempted to suppress the Bektashis by annihilating the janissaries. Devotees operated clandestinely, and their network of lodges (Tekkeler/Cem Evleri) helped the Young Turks before the revolution of 1908.

Bektashis welcomed Mustafa Kemal Atatürk's successful challenge to Ottoman rule because his secular policies curbed Sunni influence. They continued to support him despite his suppression in 1925 of all dervish orders, including their own. They survived in hiding in Turkey and openly in the Balkans—until the 1960s when some restrictions were lifted on religious groups. Their annual festival, held in mid-August in Hacibektaş, has become a significant national event publicly celebrating their mystical poetry, music, and dance as contributions to Turkish culture.

Estimated at between five and twenty million in Turkey in the 1990s, devotees are divided between those, commonly known as Alevis, whose leaders claim descent from their patron saint, and those who assert that he had no children. According to Alevis, one must be born Bektashi. Others claim that one becomes Bektashi by choice and can rise to the higher ranks of baba, halife, and dedebaba. However, all share a deep attachment to the trinity of Allah, Muhammad, and Ali, and the Twelve Imams, Fourteen Innocents, and Forty Saints of the spiritual hierarchy, and a conviction that their interpretation of Islam absolves them from the obligations observed by Sunni Muslims. Most practice in their own lodges instead of in mosques and do not make the pilgrimage to Mecca, but on visits to Hacibektaş they observe pre-Islamic and Meccan pilgrimage rituals. They are traditionally monogamous and proud of the equal participation of the women of their order. Their enjoyment of alcohol and nonadherence to the fast of Ramadan contributes to their popular image as irreligious and their famed satirical wit. Despite their differences regarding individual Bektashi membership entitlement, the terms Bektashi and Alevi are sometimes used interchangeably or hyphenated to indicate a blend of the two orientations.

Many Alevi Bektashis lost their lives when attacked by Sunni right-wing extremists at Kahramanmaraş in 1978, and at Sivas in 1993. Since the 1980s, Alevi Bektashi villagers come under growing pressure to improve their material lot by abandoning support for left-wing politicians and resistance to Sunni Islam. Though Alevi Bektashis trace their heritage to rural roots, they have become increasingly aware of the potential for tapping into urban discourses of democracy to strengthen their order. They run their own radio stations, print literature, and claim adherents in Western societies who come to them through the channels of Westernized Sufism.

See also ALEVI; ATATÜRK, MUSTAFA KEMAL; JANISSARIES; MAHMUD II; SHI'ISM; SUFISM AND THE SUFI ORDERS; SUNNI ISLAM; TEKKE; YOUNG TURKS.

Bibliography

Birge, John Kingsley. *The Bektashi Order of Dervishes.* London: Luzac and Company, 1937.

Mélikoff, Irène. "Bektashi/Kızılbaş: Historical Bipartition and Its Consequences." In *Swedish Research Institute in Istanbul Transactions: Alevi Identity: Cultural, Religious and Social Perspectives,* vol. 8, edited by Tord Olsson, Elisabeth Özdalga, and Catharina Raudvere. Istanbul: Numune Matbaası, 1998.

Trix, Frances. *Spiritual Discourse: Learning with an Islamic Master.* Philadelphia: University of Pennsylvania Press, 1993.

Webb, Gisela. "The Sufi Order (of the West)." In *Encyclopedia of Cults, Sects, and New Religions,* edited by James R. Lewis, 2d edition. Amherst, NY: Prometheus Books, 1998.

Yavuz, M. Hakan. "Media Identities for Alevis and Kurds in Turkey." In *New Media in the Muslim World: The Emerging Public Sphere*, edited by Dale F. Eickelman and Jon W. Anderson. Bloomington: Indiana University Press, 1999.

JOHN D. NORTON
UPDATED BY MARIA F. CURTIS

BELGRAVE, CHARLES DALRYMPLE
[1894–1969]

Adviser to the Bahraini ruling family, 1926–1957.

Born in England, Charles Dalrymple Belgrave was a junior officer in the British Colonial Office on leave from a tour of duty in Tanganyika when, in the summer of 1925, he answered a classified advertisement in the *Times* (London) for the position of permanent adviser to the ruler of Bahrain, a British protectorate since 1820. He arrived on the islands in March 1926 and took charge of all branches of the local administration, assisted by a small corps of British civil servants.

Under his supervision, petroleum was discovered in 1932 and the oil revenues accruing to the state were used to build the country's infrastructure and create a variety of new government departments, including those of education and public health. He gradually extended his influence over virtually all aspects of the country's fiscal and administrative affairs; by the mid-1950s, his identification with both the ruling family and British imperialism in the Persian/Arabian Gulf made him the focus of widespread popular discontent. At the urging of the ruler, Shaykh Sulman ibn Hamad al-Khalifa, he retired as adviser in April 1957 and returned to London, where he died on 28 February 1969. Bahrain announced its independence in 1971, under Sulman's successor, Shaykh Isa ibn Sulman al-Khalifa.

See also AL KHALIFA FAMILY; BAHRAIN; IMPERIALISM IN THE MIDDLE EAST.

Bibliography

Belgrave, Charles. *Personal Column.* London: Hutchinson, 1960.

FRED H. LAWSON

BELHADJ, ALI
[1956–]

Leader of Islamic Salvation Front in Algeria.

Born in 1956 in Tunis, Ali Belhaj is a popular figure, fiery preacher, and the second leader of the Islamic Salvation Front (Front Islamique du Salut; FIS), the main Islamic opposition party in Algeria. Belhaj's father died in the Algerian war of liberation, and his family originates from the desert city of Ourgal in the south of Algeria. He received an entirely Arabic education at Islamic schools in Algiers and became a secondary school Arabic teacher. He was educated by prominent Algerian religious figures such as Abdellatif Soltani (d. 1983), Ahmad Sahnoun (b. 1907), and Omar Araboui (d. 1984), and was influenced by the Salafi doctrines, particularly those of Ibn Taimiyya and Ibn Qayim al-Jauziyya, and the writings of Muslim Brothers' leaders such as Hassan al-Banna and Sayyid Qutb. Shaped by these influences, Belhadj represents the orthodox and uncompromising trend within the FIS.

Belhadj started his Islamic activities in the 1970s by delivering religious sermons and lectures. He was imprisoned from 1983 to 1987 for his association with the Mustapha Bouyali's armed group that sought to topple Chadli Bendjedid's socialist regime. After his release, he became a prayer leader in the mosques of al-Sunna and al-Qubba in Algiers. Belhadj's thorough religious knowledge, modest lifestyle, and remarkable oratory skills, particularly in addressing the depressed segments of society, enabled him to gain popularity and build a large constituency of followers. This popularity was asserted on several occasions when thousands of people responded to Belhadj's calls for peaceful marches in protest to certain policies of the state. Following a general strike that resulted in violent clashes with the military forces, Belhadj and the FIS's leader, Abbasi Madani, were arrested in June 1991, and Belhadj was later sentenced to twelve years in prison.

See also BENDJEDID, CHADLI; FRONT ISLAMIQUE DU SALUT (FIS); MADANI, ABASSI AL-.

Bibliography

Barazi, Tammam al-. "Interview with Ali Belhaj." *al-Watan al-Arabi* 176 (27 July 1990): 25.

Shahin, Emad Eldin. *Political Ascent: Contemporary Islamic Movements in North Africa.* Boulder, CO: Westview Press, 1998.

EMAD ELDIN SHAHIN

BELKACEM, CHERIF

[1930–]

Algerian officer and government minister.

Born in Morocco, Cherif Belkacem joined the Armée de Libération Nationale (ALN) in 1956. By the end of the Algerian War of Independence in 1962, he became a prominent general staff officer. As a member of the National Assembly, he influenced the passage of the Algerian constitution of 1963. He became minister of national orientation (1963) and then of education (1964) under Ahmed Ben Bella. After Colonel Houari Boumédienne's overthrow of Ben Bella in June 1965, Belkacem, then a member of the new Conseil de la Révolution, was charged with revitalizing the ruling one-party Front de Libération Nationale (FLN) and with coordinating its policies with those of the new government. He served as minister of finance from 1968 to 1970 and then as a minister without portfolio charged with the reorganization of the FLN. After this ministry was dissolved Belkacem left Algeria for Europe and did not return until after the October 1988 riots. He resurfaced prominently in 1991 as a leader of a faction composed of former Boumédienne government ministers and officials who opposed the policies of President Chadli Bendjedid. In 2000 he participated in a colloquium regarding torture and the War of Independence. Though a longtime friend of Abdelaziz Bouteflika, Belkacem questioned his administration and advocated the convening of representatives of Algerian civil society to regenerate the country. In 2001 he called upon the beleaguered Algerian president to resign. Belkacem remains a critic of the Pouvoir—the ruling military-civilian establishment.

See also BOUTEFLIKA, ABDELAZIZ; FRONT DE LIBÉRATION NATIONALE.

Bibliography

Algeria Interface. Available from <http://algeria-interface .com>.

Naylor, Phillip C. *The Historical Dictionary of Algeria,* 3d edition. Lanham, MD: Scarecrow Press, 2005.

Ottaway, David, and Ottaway, Marina. *Algeria: The Politics of a Socialist Revolution.* Berkeley: University of California Press, 1970.

PHILLIP C. NAYLOR

BELL, GERTRUDE

[1868–1926]

British explorer and orientalist.

A graduate of Oxford, Gertrude Bell traveled throughout the Middle East and wrote several popular books about her travels, including *The Desert and the Sown* (1907), about Syria, and *Amurath to Amurath* (1911), about Baghdad and Mosul.

Her skill as a linguist and her knowledge of the region brought her during World War I to Britain's Arab Bureau in Cairo, Egypt, where in 1915 she compiled information on the bedouin of Arabia. In 1916, at the request of Britain's viceroy of India, Lord Hardinge, she went to Basra in Mesopotamia (Iraq) to aid the Indian Expeditionary Force and gather military intelligence. She remained in Mesopotamia for much of the next ten years, as oriental secretary to both Sir Percy Cox and Sir Arnold Wilson, British administrators. In 1920 and 1921, she was an active partisan of Faisal I ibn Hussein and helped bring him to the throne of Iraq in July 1921. Aside from her political work, Bell was honorary director of antiquities in Iraq and took part in creating the national museum in Baghdad.

See also COX, PERCY; FAISAL I IBN HUSSEIN; WILSON, ARNOLD T.

Bibliography

Holland, Barbara. *They Went Whistling: Women Wayfarers, Warriors, Runaways, and Renegades.* New York: Pantheon Books, 2001.

Wallach, Janet. *Desert Queen: The Extraordinary Life of Gertrude Bell, Adventurer, Adviser to Kings, Ally of Lawrence of Arabia.* New York: Nan A. Talese/Doubleday, 1996.

ZACHARY KARABELL

BELL ORGANIZATION

See HUNCHAK PARTY

BELLOUNIS, MUHAMMAD

[1912–1958]

Algerian nationalist and Messalist.

Muhammad Bellounis was a staunch supporter of Messali al-Hadj and served in the Parti du Peuple Algérien (Party of the Algerian People, PPA), the Mouvement pour le Triomphe des Libertés Démocratiques (Movement for the Triumph of Democratic Liberties, MTLD), and particularly the Mouvement National Algérien (Algerian National Movement, MNA). The MNA (established in December 1954) disputed the claim of the Front de Libération Nationale (National Liberation Front, FLN) to be the only revolutionary voice of the Algerian people.

Bellounis was charged to organize a military MNA presence within Algeria. Instead of the French forces, the MNA targeted the FLN's military, the Armée de Libération Nationale (National Liberation Army, ALN). In the summer of 1955, the ALN, under the command of the fierce Colonel Amirouche (nom de guerre of Aït Hamouda), engaged Bellounis and 500 of his MNA fighters at Guenzetin, Kabylia. Bellounis and a small number of men survived the assault and escaped to the Mélouza region of Algeria, south of Kabylia, where there was still significant Messalist support. This provoked the fratricidal Mélouza massacre on 28 May 1957 by the ALN, where about 300 died, forcing Bellounis to turn to the French for logistical support.

With French assistance, Bellounis mustered 1,500 to 3,000 men by the summer of 1957 who were given their own uniforms and flag. Bellounis named this force, which Messali did not officially embrace, the Armée Nationale Populaire Algérienne (or du Peuple Algérien, ANPA) and styled himself as a two-star general. At first, Bellounis succeeded against the ALN, but his counterproductively severe treatment of civilians and of his own soldiers forced the French to terminate this collaboration (known as Operation Ollivier). The French army tracked down Bellounis in July 1958 and executed him. His death signaled the end of the MNA's military threat to the FLN.

See also ARMÉE DE LIBÉRATION NATIONALE (ALN); FRONT DE LIBÉRATION NATIONALE (FLN); HADJ, MESSALI AL-; MOUVEMENT NATIONAL ALGÉRIEN; MOUVEMENT POUR LE TRIOMPHE DES LIBERTÉS DÉMOCRATIQUES; PARTI DU PEUPLE ALGÉRIEN (PPA).

Bibliography

Horne, Alistair. *A Savage War of Peace: Algeria, 1954–1962.* New York: Penguin, 1987.

PHILLIP C. NAYLOR

BELLY DANCE

See DANCE

BEN-AHARON, YITZHAK
[1906–]

Israeli politician.

Yitzhak Ben-Aharon attended school in the Austro-Hungarian Empire and in Berlin, and emigrated to Palestine from Austria in 1928. He was active in the labor movement and was a founder of ha-Shomer ha-Tzaʿir (a Zionist socialist youth movement). During World War II he fought with the British and was taken prisoner by the Germans. After Israel's independence, he became a member of the Knesset (1949–1977); he helped found and led MAPAM, and was instrumental in creating the Labor Party in 1968. He served as secretary-general of Histadrut (1969–1973) and remained active in politics after his retirement from the Knesset in 1977. He has served on boards and committees, and has written two books, *Messianic Regime: The End of the Road* (1988, Hebrew) and *Pages from the Calendar* (1994, Hebrew). The April 2003 issue of *Executive Intelligence Review* carried an interview with him discussing Israel's present and future.

See also HA-SHOMER HA-TZAʿIR; HISTADRUT; ISRAEL: POLITICAL PARTIES IN; KNESSET; LABOR ZIONISM.

Bibliography

Ben-Gurion, David. *Israel: A Personal History.* New York: Funk and Wagnalls, 1971.

Sachar, Howard M. *A History of Israel: From the Rise of Zionism to Our Time.* New York: Alfred A. Knopf, 1981.

ZACHARY KARABELL
UPDATED BY GREGORY S. MAHLER

BEN ALI, ZAYN AL-ABIDINE
[1936–]

President General of Tunisia, replaced Habib Bourguiba in a bloodless six-day constitutional coup in November 1987.

A member of the Destour movement since his teens, Zayn al-Abidine Ben Ali pursued a military career, receiving training in France (St. Cyr Academy and Châlons-sur-Marne) and the United States (Ft. Bliss, Texas). He was the head of Tunisian military security from 1964 to 1974, when he became a military attaché in Morocco. Returning to Tunisia three years later, he became the head of national security, and ambassador to Poland in 1980. In 1984 he was appointed state secretary for national security and a cabinet minister in 1985. He suppressed riots in 1978 and 1984; in 1986, when he became minister of the interior, he set out to eliminate the Mouvement de Tendance Islamique (MTI; Islamic Tendency Movement), a group that opposed President Habib Bourguiba's secularist reforms. Despite two periods of disfavor between 1974 and 1984, Bourguiba appointed him prime minister in October 1987. He also served as secretary-general of the Parti Socialiste Destourien (PSD; Destour Socialist Party). Many considered Bourguiba, who had ruled Tunisia for thirty years since independence from France in 1956, unfit to govern; a month after Ben Ali became prime minister, he ousted Bourguiba in a peaceful coup.

Initially Ben Ali claimed he would ease some of Bourguiba's stern political measures concerning opposition movements, particularly the Mouvement des Démocrates Sociaux (MDS; Social Democrat Movement) and the MTI. His interest in a multiparty system led to the signing of a national pact with opposition leaders in 1988. Nevertheless, he maintained strong ties with the ruling party, the old PSD, renamed the Rassemblement Constitutionelle Démocratique (RCD; Constitutional Democratic Rally) in 1987. He pursued strong links with other North African states through the Arab Maghreb Union, founded in 1989. As head of the RCD, he won reelection in 1994 and 1999 with more than 99 percent of the vote. Although the constitution limits the president to three terms, it seemed it might be amended as the central committee of the governing RCD requested he run again in 2004.

In 1991 Ben Ali banned the Hizb En Nahda (Renaissance Party), an offshoot of the MTI that tried to legalize its party status, and severely restricted the actions of its leader, Rached Ghannouchi. On 12 July 1992 one of the harshest court cases in Tunisian

Tunisian president Zayn al-Abidine Ben Ali in 1999. In 1975 the National Assembly named Habib Bourguiba president for life, but he was deposed by a constitutional coup in 1987 on the grounds he was becoming senile. Ben Ali, then serving as prime minister, took over the presidency in November of that year. © AP/WIDE WORLD PHOTOS. REPRODUCED BY PERMISSION.

history was launched against Hizb En Nahda's members; 280 were accused of taking part in a plot and fifty were threatened with the death penalty. This case caught the attention of Western countries and international human rights groups, who exerted pressure to release the defendants. Thirty defendants were sentenced to life in prison.

Ben Ali's repression of Islamist and opposition leaders as well as human rights activists increased through the 1990s. In 1994 Moncef Marzouki, General of the League of Human Rights, was jailed for considering a run against Ben Ali, the only presidential candidate. When press agencies such as

Le Monde and Libération showed concern, they were banned. Despite Ben Ali's promise to improve human rights and his introduction of a more liberal press law, Human Rights Watch continued to denounce the government's human rights record. Tunisia had more than 1,000 political prisoners, was listed as one of the ten countries in the world most hostile to a free press, and is among the U.S. State Department's list of countries that use excessive "stress and duress" interrogation tactics. Ben Ali's government defends its policies. After the terrorist attacks in the United States on 11 September 2001, Foreign Minister Habib Ben Yahia visited London, where he spoke on the alleged danger of Tunisian Islamists abroad and called for the extradition of Hizb En Nahda leadership.

During the late 1980s and early 1990s, Tunisia faced serious economic problems, such as chronic unemployment, a balance of payment deficit, and an unwieldy state subsidy and price control system. Despite drought conditions, Tunisia's economy has improved, with gross domestic product up 6 percent in 2001, tourism up 3.5 percent in 2000, and direct foreign investment up 144 percent to $768 million. Despite the privatization of thirty-five of forty-one firms, with an average 5 percent improvement in their turnover, unemployment remains high at 15.6 percent.

> See also ARAB MAGHREB UNION; BOURGUIBA, HABIB; GHANNOUCHI, RACHED; MARZOUKI, MONCEF.

Bibliography

Alexander, Christopher. "Authoritarianism and Civil Society." *Middle East Research and Information Project* no. 205, vol. 27, no. 4 (1997): 34–38.

Burgat, François, and Dowell, William. *The Islamic Movement in North Africa,* 2d edition. Austin: University of Texas Press, 1997.

Shaikh, Farzana. "Tunisia." In *Islam and Islamic Groups: A Worldwide Reference Guide.* Essex, U.K.: Longman Group, 1992.

"Tunisia." *Human Rights Watch: Middle East and North Africa.* Available at <http://www.hrw.org/mideast/tunisia .php>.

MATTHEW S. GORDON
UPDATED BY MARIA F. CURTIS

BEN AMMAR, TAHAR
[?–1985]

Tunisian nationalist and diplomat.

A wealthy landowner, Ben (also ibn) Ammar served as president of the Tunisian section of the Grand Council in the early 1950s. In 1955, as premier, he signed a series of six conventions on internal autonomy for Tunisia with the French government of Premier Pierre Mendès-France. In March 1956, he was one of four Tunisian signatories to the official protocol granting independence to Tunisia. Ben Ammar died in 1985.

Bibliography

Hahn, Lorna. *North Africa: Nationalism to Nationhood.* Washington, DC: Public Affairs Press, 1960.

MATTHEW S. GORDON

BEN ARFA

See ARFA, MUHAMMAD IBN

BEN BADIS, ABD AL-HAMID
[1889–1940]

Algerian nationalist and founder of the Association of Algerian Muslim Ulama (AUMA).

Born to a traditional Muslim family in Constantine, northeast Algeria (although his father had served on France's colonial *conseil supérieur*), Abd al-Hamid Ben Badis received his higher education at Zaytuna mosque university in Tunis. There, he was influenced by the reformist Salafiyya Movement of Muhammad Abduh and Rashid Rida. Determined to apply Salafiyya principles to Algerian society, Ben Badis engaged in educating Algerians to proper Islamic practice and observance. Besides establishing schools, his ideas appeared in periodicals such as *al-Muntaqid* and *al-Shihab*. In 1931, he founded the Algerian Association of Reformist Ulama (Islamic scholars), known also as the Association of Algerian Muslim Ulama.

Although chiefly concerned with education, Ben Badis also entered the political arena by asserting that French assimilation was impossible. He declared: "This Algerian nation is not France, cannot be France, and does not wish to be France."

This complemented his famous conviction that "Islam is my religion, Arabic my language, Algeria my fatherland." These views inevitably brought him into contact with nationalists Ferhat Abbas and Messali al-Hadj. Ben Badis, however, preferred a cultural rather than a political role in Algerian history and nationalism. If later the Front de Libération Nationale (National Liberation Front, FLN) purposely ignored the contributions of other nationalist rivals, Ben Badis's legacy was recognized and respected.

See also ABBAS, FERHAT; ABDUH, MUHAMMAD; ASSOCIATION OF ALGERIAN MUSLIM ULAMA (AUMA); FRONT DE LIBÉRATION NATIONALE; HADJ, MESSALI AL-; NATIONALISM; RIDA, RASHID; SALAFIYYA MOVEMENT.

Bibliography

Naylor, Phillip C., and Heggoy, Alf A. *The Historical Dictionary of Algeria,* 2d ed. Metuchen, NJ: Scarecrow Press, 1994.

Quandt, William B. *Revolution and Political Leadership: Algeria, 1954–1968.* Cambridge, MA: MIT Press, 1969.

PHILLIP C. NAYLOR

BEN BARKA, MEHDI
[1920–1966]

Moroccan nationalist politician.

Mehdi Ben Barka, the son of a local Moroccan religious leader, was raised in a traditional milieu. He excelled in his studies, particularly in mathematics, entered the French system, and completed a baccalaureate. At twenty-one, he was graduated from the university in Algiers. Postponing graduate study in mathematics, he taught in Rabat, for a time at the imperial college, where Crown Prince Hassan was his student.

Drawn into nationalist, anticolonialist politics, he held a number of significant Istiqlal Party positions and various government posts following independence in 1956, culminating in King Muhammad V's appointing him president of the first National Consultative Assembly. Ben Barka devoted particular attention to party youth and the labor movement. As a second-generation Istiqlal leader, his policies of party reform often put him at odds with the senior leaders. He challenged the regime by calling for elections, a constitutional monarchy, and a greater role for labor and popular participation. Despite his progressive stance, he used party institutions to build a personal power base.

In 1959, Ben Barka announced the formation of a new political party, the National Union of Popular Forces (UNFP). In 1963, accused of participation in a reputed plot against King Hassan, he went into exile, where he continued to denounce the Moroccan monarchy. In October 1965, Ben Barka was abducted in Paris, possibly tortured, and killed by a conspiracy that involved the French secret service, Moroccan minister of the interior General Muhammad Oufkir, and Ahmed Dlimi, Moroccan chief of security. General Oufkir was brought to trial in absentia and found guilty. The refusal of the Moroccan government to extradite Oufkir generated a breach in Moroccan–French relations that lasted almost four years.

See also DLIMI, AHMED; ISTIQLAL PARTY: MOROCCO; OUFKIR, MUHAMMAD.

Bibliography

Ashford, Douglas E. *Political Change in Morocco.* Princeton, NJ: Princeton University Press, 1961.

Nyrop, Richard F., et al. *Area Handbook for Morocco,* 3d ed. Washington, DC: U.S. Government Printing Office, 1972.

Pennell, C. R. *Morocco since 1830: A History.* New York: New York University Press, 2000.

Waterbury, John. *Commander of the Faithful.* New York: Columbia University Press, 1970.

DONNA LEE BOWEN

BEN BELLA, AHMED
[1916–]

First premier (1962–1963) and president of Algeria (1963–1965).

Born in Marnia near Oran, Ahmed Ben Bella was decorated during World War II. Like other young Algerians, Ben Bella was deeply affected by the Setif Revolt (May 1945) and its bloody suppression. He joined Messali Hadj's Parti du Peuple Algérien (PPA) and later the paramilitary Organisation Spéciale (OS). He participated in an attack on the main post office in Oran in April 1949. He was later

Ahmed Ben Bella, Algeria's first president, was an organizer of the Front de Libération Nationale (FLN) during the country's battle for independence from France. Ben Bella was imprisoned by the French for six years and was elected president in 1963, a year after his release. © AP/WIDE WORLD PHOTOS. REPRODUCED BY PERMISSION.

captured by French police and imprisoned in 1950. He escaped to Egypt in 1952.

Along with other younger nationalists, Ben Bella planned an armed insurrection against the French. He is regarded as one of the nine historic chiefs of the Algerian War of Independence (1954–1962) who founded the Front de Libération Nationale (FLN). During the revolution Ben Bella sought assistance in foreign capitals for the Armée de Libération Nationale (ALN). He was viewed as the head of the external faction of the FLN, which competed with the internal group for leadership of the revolution. France's skyjacking in October 1956 of a plane carrying Ben Bella and three other historic FLN chiefs—Hocine Ait Ahmed, Mohamed Boudiaf, and Mohamed Khider—postponed an inevitable intra-

elite confrontation. Ben Bella was incarcerated in France until 1962.

After the war Ben Bella and Colonel Houari Boumédienne established the Bureau Politique in opposition to the Gouvernement Provisoire de la République Algérienne (GPRA) and seized power in August 1962. Ben Bella emerged as Algeria's first prime minister in 1962, then was elected president in 1963 and served until 1965. Criticized for his flamboyance and demagogy by detractors while projected as a political exemplar of the Third World by supporters, Ben Bella faced enormous problems. Nevertheless, he restored order in Algeria, steered his country toward a socialist economy highlighted by the self-management (*autogestion*) system, and allocated considerable sums toward education. In foreign policy, he supported wars of national liberation movements and espoused nonalignment. He also pursued close cooperation with France, because Algeria remained deeply dependent on the former *métropole*. Despite declarations of Maghrib (North African) unity, relations with Morocco deteriorated, as illustrated by the brief border conflict (the Moroccan–Algerian War) in late 1963.

Ben Bella became increasingly authoritarian in reaction to exacting political and military perils such as the Kabyle Revolt led by Ait Ahmad (1963) and the insurrection of Colonel Mohammed Chaabani (1964). Recognizing the competitive ambitions of Vice President Boumédienne, Ben Bella moved against his rival's supporters—notably, Interior Minister Ahmed Medeghri and Foreign Minister Abdelaziz Bouteflika. Boumédienne retaliated by deposing Ben Bella in a nonviolent military coup on 19 June 1965. He was placed in closely monitored and isolated house arrest. Ben Bella's disappearance incited considerable international concern. President Chadli Bendjedid freed Ben Bella in July 1979. He moved to France and organized an opposition party called the Mouvement pour la Démocratie en Algérie (MDA) in 1984. Ben Bella and Ait Ahmed reconciled in exile in 1985 and jointly called for constitutional reforms guaranteeing political rights in Algeria.

In 1990 the beleaguered Algerian government permitted Ben Bella to return to Algeria, where he continued his opposition to the Bendjedid government. For a brief period, observers believed that

Ben Bella could bridge secular and Islamist movements and promote political reconciliation, but Ben Bella discovered that he had no popular or political base. He strongly supported Iraq during the crisis leading to the Gulf War of 1991. The forced resignation of President Bendjedid by military and civilian elites and the inauguration of the Haut Comité d'Etat (HCE), briefly presided over by his old comrade Mohamed Boudiaf, still left Ben Bella consigned as a marginal political figure. He participated in opposition party discussions and signed the Sant Egidio Platform (National Contract) in January 1995. Given the constitutional referendum of 1996 that restricted political parties, the MDA was forced to disband. Ben Bella remains an important, historic figure determined to remain an active rather than anachronistic participant in Algerian affairs.

See also ALGERIA: POLITICAL PARTIES IN; ALGERIAN WAR OF INDEPENDENCE; ARMÉE DE LIBÉRATION NATIONALE (ALN); FRONT DE LIBÉRATION NATIONALE (FLN).

Bibliography

Gordon, David C. *The Passing of French Algeria.* London: Oxford University Press, 1966.

Merle, Robert. *Ahmed Ben Bella*, translated by Camilla Sykes. New York: Walker, 1967.

Naylor, Phillip C. *The Historical Dictionary of Algeria*, 3d edition. Lanham, MD: Scarecrow Press, 2005.

Ruedy, John. *Modern Algeria: The Origins and Development of a Nation.* Bloomington: Indiana University Press, 1992.

PHILLIP C. NAYLOR

BEN BOUALI, HASSIBA
[1938–1957]

Algerian nationalist.

Hassiba Ben Bouali was born in the city of El Asnam (today Chlef) and moved with her family to Algiers in 1947. She was studying at the University of Algiers when she became involved in the Algerian nationalist movement against French rule and participated in the student strikes of 1956. Ben Bouali quickly joined the National Liberation Front (FLN) and became the liaison officer of Ali La Pointe, deputy chief of military operations in the urban zone of Algiers. After a series of bombings in 1956 and 1957, the French army launched a security (offensive) operation often referred to as the Battle of Algiers. Hassiba Ben Bouali died on 8 October 1957, with Ali La Pointe, in the explosion of the house where she was surrounded by the French paratroopers in the oldest part of the Algerian capital (the Casbah). Along with some other young women, Ben Bouali is considered a key figure in the Algerian struggle against French colonialism. Her name was given to the university in her native town.

See also BOUHIRED, JAMILA; GENDER: GENDER AND LAW; GENDER: GENDER AND POLITICS.

RABIA BEKKAR

BEN BOULAID, MOUSTAFA
[1917–1957]

A historic chief of the Algerian revolution (1954–1962).

Moustafa Ben Boulaid (also Mostefa Ben Boulaïd) was born to a peasant family in the impoverished Aurès (Awras) mountain region. A Free French veteran, Ben Boulaid was an enterprising man who eventually owned a bus line. Colonial authorities terminated his business license due to his support of Messali al-Hadj. Like other young nationalists, Ben Boulaid grew impatient with Messali's leadership and demanded immediate action against colonialism. He played an important role in establishing the Comité Révolutionnaire d'Unité et d'Action (CRUA; Revolutionary Committee for Unity and Action), the parent organization of the Front de Libération Nationale (FLN; National Liberation Front), which earned him his reputation as one of the nine historic chiefs (*chefs historiques*) of the revolution. He unsuccessfully attempted to gain Messali's support for the FLN.

Guerrillas in the Aurès under his command opened the Algerian war of independence with attacks on 31 October and 1 November 1954. Ben Boulaid was captured by the French in February 1955, but he escaped in November. Resuming his guerrilla command, he died in March 1957 while examining a booby-trapped field radio.

See also ALGERIAN WAR OF INDEPENDENCE; COMITÉ RÉVOLUTIONNAIRE D'UNITÉ ET D'ACTION (CRUA); FRONT DE LIBÉRATION NATIONALE (FLN); HADJ, MESSALI AL-.

Bibliography

Horne, Alistair. *A Savage War of Peace: Algeria, 1954–1962,* 2d edition. New York: Penguin, 1987.

PHILLIP C. NAYLOR

BENDJEDID, CHADLI

[1929–]

Third president of Algeria, 1979–1992.

Chadli Bendjedid was born near Annaba, Algeria. His father was a small landholder. A veteran of the Algerian War of Independence (1954–1962), Bendjedid became a professional officer in the Armée Nationale Populaire (ANP). After his deposal of President Ahmed Ben Bella in 1965, Colonel Houari Boumédienne appointed Bendjedid to the Conseil Nationale de la Révolution Algérienne

Despite the institution of such reforms as opening up the economy, encouraging a free press, and providing for a multiparty government structure, Chadli Bendjedid's presidency was ultimately not a popular one, and he was forced to resign in 1992. © IMPRESS/GETTY IMAGES. REPRODUCED BY PERMISSION.

(CNRA). Bendjedid was entrusted with the command of strategic military regions—Constantine, then Oran. He also monitored French troop withdrawals, including from the strategic naval base at Mersel-Kébir in 1968. After Boumédienne's death in December 1978 Bendjedid emerged as a compromise presidential candidate within the Front de Libération Nationale (FLN) and the military. He was elected president of Algeria in February 1979.

Bendjedid was less ideological than his predecessors. Characterized as a pragmatic man, Bendjedid tempered Algeria's ambitious state-planning and foreign policy. His five-year plans emphasized more balanced sector development, with more attention to agriculture and services. He also reorganized the large state companies and encouraged smaller enterprises. In addition, he pursued tentative economic liberalization. Bendjedid also strove to realize Maghrib unity through amity treaties with Tunisia and Mauritania in 1983. Relations were restored with Morocco in 1988 after having been severed over the Western Sahara conflict. Though Western Sahara's future remained unresolved, the Arab Maghreb Union was proclaimed in February 1989. Bendjedid also was accorded a state visit to France in 1983.

Bendjedid consolidated his power internally by promoting military officers and removing Boumédiennist rivals such as Abdelaziz Bouteflika, a future president. He was reelected in 1985. The National Charter of 1976 was revised in 1986. The "enriched" charter included a section commemorating the historic struggle for independence and mentioned Messali Hadj and Ferhat Abbas, who had been previously proscribed. The revised document reaffirmed Algeria's Arab identity. This particularly dissatisfied restive Berbers, notably the Kabyles, who were fearful for the future of their distinct culture and language and had demonstrated in violent outbursts in 1980 and 1985. The continued official ideological attachment to secular socialism also alienated populist Muslims. Chronic unemployment exasperated the disillusioned younger generation. Furthermore, the collapse of oil prices, which were indexed to natural gas prices, crippled the economy. These variables contributed to widespread discontent that produced rioting in October 1988 resulting in hundreds killed and wounded and a state of siege.

Bendjedid quickly promised and delivered reforms—including political pluralism and civil rights—highlighted by the Constitution of February 1989. He was reelected president in 1989, but he failed to acquire political and popular support, as illustrated by a quick succession of prime ministers (Kasdi Merbah [1988–1989], Mouloud Hamrouche [1989–1991], and Ahmed Ghozali [1991–1992]). The rise of the Front Islamique du Salut (FIS) and its stunning success in regional elections in June 1990 astonished the ruling elite, but Bendjedid was determined to permit the democratic process to complete its imperfect course. Parliamentary elections in June 1991 had to be postponed, however, because of inflammatory protests and pronouncements by the FIS that were provoked by eleventh-hour gerrymandering by the FLN. The FIS's first-round electoral success in the rescheduled December 1991 elections incited a military and civilian coup in January 1992 that forced Bendjedid's resignation. He was kept under house arrest until October 1999. Since then, Bendjedid has criticized the policies of President Abdleaziz Bouteflika and has denounced the U.S.-led war against Iraq in 2003. Although Bendjedid's presidency is popularly discredited, he rehabilitated nationalists and helped restore Algeria's historical memory.

See also ARAB MAGHREB UNION; CONSEIL NATIONALE DE LA RÉVOLUTION ALGÉRIENNE (CNRA); FRONT DE LIBÉRATION NATIONALE (FLN); FRONT ISLAMIQUE DU SALUT (FIS).

Bibliography

Entelis, John. *Algeria: The Revolution Institutionalized.* Boulder, CO: Westview Press, 1985.

Mortimer, Robert A. "Algeria after the Explosion." *Current History* 89 (April 1990): 161–168.

Mortimer, Robert A. "Algeria's New Sultan." *Current History* 80 (December 1982): 428–431; 433–434.

Naylor, Phillip C. *The Historical Dictionary of Algeria,* Lanham, MD: Rowman & Littlefield, 2004.

PHILLIP C. NAYLOR

BENFLIS, ALI
[1945–]

Prime minister of Algeria; minister of justice.

Ali Benflis pursued a legal career before entering politics. His initial interest was in juvenile delin-

quency and in rehabilitation. He assisted in the founding of the state-sponsored Ligue Algérien des Droits de l'Homme (LADH) in 1987. He was appointed minister of justice in 1988 by Prime Minister Kasdi Merbah, and he maintained this portfolio in Mouloud Hamrouche's government from 1989 to 1991. He resigned, however, when Prime Minister Sid Ahmed Ghozali sought legislation for internment camps. After the deposal of President Chadli Bendjedid and the cancellation of the elections in January 1991, Benflis became increasingly involved within the Front de Libération Nationale (FLN) and was a rare successful party candidate in the first round of the parliamentary elections in December 1991. After the deposal of President Chadli Bendjedid and the cancellation of the elections in January 1992, Benflis devoted his political activities to the FLN. He managed Abdelaziz Bouteflika's successful presidential campaign in 1999, and served as interim general secretary to the president and the chief of staff. He opposed Prime Minister Ahmed Benbitour regarding privatization issues. In August 2000 Benbitour resigned and Benflis replaced him. As prime minister, Benflis has pursued prudent privatization and structural reform. He has also had to deal with Kabyle unrest since April 2001 as a consequence of police brutality and repression. Benflis was also selected as head of the FLN in September 2001. After the resounding success of the FLN in the parliamentary election of May 2002, President Bouteflika asked Benflis to continue as prime minister.

Bouteflika and Benflis reportedly disagreed over the speed of Algeria's economic liberalization. However, the rift that widened between them was primarily political. Bouteflika dismissed his prime minister in May 2003. Benflis remains one of the most significant members of Algeria's political elite.

See also ALGERIA: POLITICAL PARTIES IN; BOUTEFLIKA, ABDELAZIZ; FRONT DE LIBÉRATION NATIONALE (FLN).

Bibliography

Algeria Interface. Available from <http://algeria-interface.com>.

Naylor, Phillip C. *The Historical Dictionary of Algeria,* 3d edition. Lanham, MD: Scarecrow Press, 2005.

PHILLIP C. NAYLOR

BENGHAZI

Chief city and Mediterranean seaport of Cyrenaica (Barqa), second in Libya only to Tripoli.

Originally founded by the Greeks as Berenike on a small natural harbor on the gulf of Sidra, Benghazi (also Marsa ibn Ghazi) was refounded and renamed in the Middle Ages. Its importance was due to its position as the only port between Tripoli and Alexandria, as an outlet for the agricultural produce of northern Cyrenaica, and as a center of local administration. In the early nineteenth century, Benghazi was still an impoverished village of some five thousand people. Its prosperity and importance increased with the spread of the Sanusi order in Cyrenaica and, beginning in the 1840s, in the eastern Sahara and the Sudan. It became the main Mediterranean outlet for the newly opened, Sanusi-controlled trade route to the rising sultanate of Wadai in eastern Sudan (now Chad). In the later nineteenth century, despite being the local seat of Ottoman administration, it was one of the few remaining North African shipment markets for the trans-Saharan slave trade.

Benghazi was still largely undeveloped (with a cosmopolitan population of about 20,000) when Italy invaded in 1911. As in Tripoli, the Italians created a modern, European-style city outside the old Arab quarters, particularly after the defeat of the Cyrenaican rebellion in 1931 and 1932. By 1937, the population was fifty thousand, but expansion was constricted by its position between the sea and an inland saltwater lagoon.

During the North African campaigns of World War II (1940–1943), Benghazi changed hands five times and suffered some 2,000 air raids. Destruction was extensive and the British military administration, set up after the city's final capture by the British Eighth Army in November 1942, could not fund rebuilding. In 1949, Benghazi became the seat of the first Cyrenaican government and was later recognized as the joint capital—with Tripoli—of the independent United Kingdom of Libya (proclaimed December 1951). Over the next five years, the town and port were rebuilt, but rapid urban expansion and development started only with the oil boom of the 1950s and 1960s, with thousands of migrant families forced into shanty settlements. After the 1969 revolution, Benghazi was deprived of its joint-capital status, regaining its traditional role as chief port and city of Cyrenaica, a center of administration, industry, commerce, and education. It houses the University of Gar Younis and an international airport (at Benina). Benghazi is linked by road to Tripoli and Egypt and to the Saharan regions of eastern Libya. The 2002 population was some 708,000.

See also CYRENAICA; SANUSI ORDER; SLAVE TRADE.

Bibliography

Bulugma, Hadi M. *Benghazi through the Ages.* Benghazi, 1972.

Wright, John. *Libya.* New York: Praeger, 1969.

JOHN L. WRIGHT

BEN-GURION, DAVID
[1886–1973]

Labor-Zionist leader and a founder of the Histadrut; Israel's first prime minister and first minister of defense.

David Ben-Gurion was born David Gruen (later changed to David Green) in October 1886 in Plonsk, Poland. He was educated at an Orthodox Hebrew school. In 1903 he helped to organize the Polish branch of the Workers for Zion movement, known as Po'alei Zion. In 1906 he moved to Palestine, where he worked as a farmer in agricultural settlements and served as a guard against Palestinian attackers. He was an organizer of the Palestine Labor Party and became the editor of its newspaper, *Ahdut* (Unity), in 1910, which is when he Hebraized his surname to Ben-Gurion.

In 1913 he studied law at the University of Istanbul. When World War I began Ben-Gurion returned to Palestine, but was deported by the Turks in 1915 with his friend Yizhak Ben-Zvi, who later became the president of Israel. Both Ben-Gurion and Ben-Zvi left Palestine and moved to New York City, where Ben-Gurion met and married his wife, Paula.

In the United States Ben-Gurion helped to found the organization ha-Halutz (Young Pioneers) from 1915–1916 to support immigration to Palestine. Following the November 1917 British Balfour Declaration, he agreed with Zionist leader Chaim Weizmann that Zionist goals would be best served by supporting the British government. Accordingly, Ben-Gurion enlisted in the British army's Jewish Legion to fight the Ottoman regime. Ben-Gurion enlisted in Canada in 1918, and after training in Nova Scotia, England, and Cairo, he served with General Edmund Henry Allenby in fighting the Turks.

Back in Palestine in 1920, Ben-Gurion helped to create the Histadrut, the national labor federation, and was elected its first secretary-general in 1921. The Histadrut—referred to as a "state within a state," or a "government within a government"—was a major force in economic, social, and labor policy in the Jewish community in Palestine.

Mandatory Palestine

In 1923 the League of Nations mandate for Palestine passed to Great Britain. In 1929 the mandatory government recognized the Jewish Agency as the body representing Jewish interests in Palestine. The following year Ben-Gurion helped to found the Israel workers' party, Mifleget Po'alei Israel (MAPAI), and became its head.

In 1933 Ben-Gurion became a member of the executive board of the Jewish Agency for Palestine; in 1935 he became chairman of the Zionist executive. Ben-Gurion felt that the 1929 Arab riots against Jewish settlement required that the Jewish Agency push for the classic goals of Zionism: a Jewish majority in Palestine and Jewish self-defense. During this period Ben-Gurion published three books dealing with the labor movement, the Jewish working class, and Zionism. After the creation of the state of Israel, he took the position that real Zionism required migration to Israel. Jewish life outside of Israel, when migration was a possibility, was anathema to Zionism.

In 1936 a royal commission of inquiry—known by the name of its chairman, Lord Peel—arrived in Palestine to investigate Arab-Jewish tensions. Ben-Gurion testified before the Peel Commission. When the commission recommended the partition of Palestine in 1937, Ben-Gurion persuaded the Zionist Congress to accept the principle. In 1939 Britain changed its attitudes toward the Middle East, and adopted a strong pro-Palestinian line. Ben-Gurion called for the Jewish community to resist Britain and advocated "the fighting Zionist." The MacDonald

David Ben-Gurion served as prime minister and defense minister of Israel from 1948 to 1953, and then again from 1955 until he resigned in 1963. His paramount and partly successful political goal was to introduce stable majority rule to a disparate, divided Jewish society. PHOTOGRAPH BY HENRY GROSSMAN. PUBLIC DOMAIN.

White Paper on Palestine called for severely restricted Jewish immigration to Palestine over the five-year period starting in 1939; all immigration would end in 1944. At the outbreak of World War II, Ben-Gurion argued for Jewish forces to support Britain, despite the 1939 White Papers. He thought that Winston Churchill deserved the support of Zionists and that a solution to Zionist demands would be found at war's end. As late as 1940 he was still urging compromise.

In 1947, at the end of the war, Britain handed jurisdiction for the Palestine problem to the new United Nations. The United Nations formed a Special Committee on Palestine (UNSCOP) and in November 1947 voted to partition Palestine into Jewish and Arab states, maintaining control of a small area around Jerusalem. Ben-Gurion and the Jewish Agency executive council began to focus their attention on security for the Jewish population in

In 1956, shortly after becoming Israel's prime minister for the second time, David Ben-Gurion appointed Golda Meir as foreign minister. Meir replaced Moshe Sharett, whom Ben-Gurion had asked to resign due to political differences. © BETTMANN/CORBIS. REPRODUCED BY PERMISSION.

Palestine against Arab attacks during the transition period and defending the new state of Israel from neighboring nations once independence was declared.

Israeli Statehood

In April 1948 a people's council of thirty-seven members headed by Ben-Gurion was established as an unofficial provisional legislature and government after the departure of the British. On 14 May 1948 Ben-Gurion publicly read the declaration of independence of the state of Israel. The state was attacked by its Arab neighbors in what became known as the War of Independence. One of Ben-Gurion's priorities was access to Jerusalem; ultimately, access was achieved to only the western edge of the city. Another priority, access to the Red Sea, was achieved with conquest of the small city of Elat.

An armistice took effect in February 1949; soon thereafter a parliament, the Knesset, and other democratic institutions were formed. Ben-Gurion formed a coalition government that lasted until 1953, and again from 1955 to 1963. He served as both prime minister and minister of defense.

The first Knesset was to draft a new constitution, but decided not to adopt a draft authored by Leo Kohn, legal adviser to the Jewish Agency. Ben-Gurion argued against rushing into any constitution for fear of alienating any sector of Israel's heterogeneous population. Second, he argued that debate over constitutional structures would distract Israel from other issues including resolution of the war, immigration, housing, and finding jobs for new immigrants. Third, the role of religion in the new state needed to be resolved; the extent to which the new constitution would incorporate religious dogma was a contentious one that could not be ignored. (Indeed, many Orthodox Jewish leaders of the day argued that Israel already had a constitution in an assortment of Talmudic documents known to Israel's Jewish population.) Eventually an agreement was reached to respect the religious status quo while a constitution was worked on in piecemeal fashion.

Ben-Gurion had conflicts with his coalition partners over the years, primarily with Orthodox religious parties, the support of which was needed to maintain a majority of seats in the Knesset. His socialist background and secular beliefs often conflicted with the principles espoused by the religious parties, however. Each time his government fell, Ben-Gurion and his cabinet would stay in office as a caretaker government until a new coalition could be assembled. Typically, he would be able to construct a new coalition, usually with the same partners, with a majority in the Knesset.

In 1951 Ben-Gurion had to make a difficult decision concerning war reparations proffered by the West German government. There was an emotional outcry in Israel about whether this was "blood money." Ben-Gurion believed it was aid to help Israel absorb immigrants and survivors of the Nazi regime, not a gesture to allow Germany to forget its war crimes. Demonstrations and acts of violence bordering on civil war, led by opposition leader Menachem Begin, were unable to dissuade Ben-Gurion, and in 1952 an agreement was signed.

In 1953 Ben-Gurion resigned as prime minister for what he cited as health reasons, and Moshe Sharett became prime minister. Ben-Gurion moved to a kibbutz just outside Beersheba, Kibbutz Sde Boker. In 1955 he returned to political life as defense minister under Prime Minister Sharett. Later that year, following new elections, Ben-Gurion resumed the position of prime minister, with Sharett becoming foreign minister. In 1956 Ben-Gurion asked for Sharett's resignation when he felt he could not rely upon Sharett's unquestioning loyalty with regard to cooperation with Britain and France in a possible attack on Egypt. Sharett was replaced by the more supportive Golda Meir as foreign minister.

Ben-Gurion was a supporter of development in the sciences, especially atomic energy. As early as 1956, he decided to proceed vigorously to develop nuclear capability in Israel, primarily as a source of energy. The defense potential of the industry was not lost on him, however.

In 1963 Ben-Gurion again resigned from the government for "personal reasons," and was succeeded by Levi Eshkol. Ben-Gurion's base of power had been eroding for many years as a result of the Lavon Affair—an Israeli spy and sabotage operation in Egypt that had gone awry and embarrassed the Israeli government. Although he was officially out of power, he continued to be regarded as "the Old Man" and was kept informed of government decisions. Even the top-secret decision to launch preemptive strikes against Egypt, Syria, Jordan, and Iraq in June of 1967, which led to the Arab–Israeli War of 1967, was shared with Ben-Gurion before the fact; he gave it his blessing. In his later years Ben-Gurion tempered what were often militaristic views of Israel's security needs. Following the 1967 War he was a supporter of negotiating land for peace, arguing that Israel did not need the conquered territories, save those of Jerusalem and the Golan Heights.

Ben-Gurion retired from the Knesset in 1970 and moved back to his kibbutz. He died on 1 December 1973 in the aftermath of the Yom Kippur War.

See also ALLENBY, EDMUND HENRY; BALFOUR DECLARATION (1917); BEGIN, MENACHEM; BEN-ZVI, YIZHAK; HA-HALUTZ; HISTADRUT; ISRAEL: POLITICAL PARTIES IN; JEWISH AGENCY FOR PALESTINE; JEWISH LEGION; KNESSET; LABOR ZIONISM; LAVON AFFAIR; MEIR, GOLDA; PEEL COMMISSION REPORT (1937); UNITED NATIONS AND THE MIDDLE EAST; UNITED NATIONS SPECIAL COMMITTEE ON PALESTINE, 1947 (UNSCOP); WEIZMANN, CHAIM; WHITE PAPERS ON PALESTINE; ZIONISM.

Bibliography

Bar-Zohar, Michael. *Ben-Gurion: A Biography,* translated by Peretz Kidron. New York: Delacorte, 1978.

Ben-Gurion, David. *Israel: A Personal History.* New York: Funk and Wagnalls, 1971.

Gal, Allon. *David Ben-Gurion and the American Alignment for a Jewish State.* Bloomington: Indiana University Press, 1991.

Heller, Joseph. *The Birth of Israel, 1945–1949: Ben-Gurion and His Critics.* Gainesville: University Press of Florida, 2000.

Sachar, Howard M. *A History of Israel: From the Rise of Zionism to Our Time.* New York: Knopf, 1981.

Teveth, Shabtai. *Ben-Gurion and the Palestinian Arabs: From Peace to War.* New York: Oxford University Press, 1985.

Teveth, Shabtai. *Ben-Gurion: The Burning Ground, 1886–1948.* Boston: Houghton Mifflin, 1987.

Teveth, Shabtai. *Ben-Gurion's Spy: The Story of the Political Scandal that Shaped Modern Israel.* New York: Columbia University Press, 1996.

Zweig, Ronald, ed. *David Ben-Gurion: Politics and Leadership in Israel.* Portland, OR: Frank Cass, 1991.

GREGORY S. MAHLER

BEN-GURION UNIVERSITY OF THE NEGEV

Israeli university.

Ben-Gurion University of the Negev was established in 1969 by David Ben-Gurion, Israel's first prime minister, to develop the Negev desert (60 percent of Israel's land mass and 10 percent of its population). Originally called the University of the Negev, in 1973 it was renamed to honor Ben-Gurion. The center of education and research in the area, it focuses on desert research, high technology, medicine, and regional development. The university has campuses at Beersheba and Sde Boker.

Besides a medical school, there are four faculties: engineering sciences, natural sciences, health sciences, and humanities and social sciences. The student population in 2002 was 15,000.

See also BEERSHEBA; NEGEV.

MIRIAM SIMON

BEN JELLOUN, UMAR
[1933–1975]

Moroccan political activist.

Umar Ben Jelloun, born in Oujda, studied law and telecommunications in Paris, and was president of the Association of Muslim North African Students. In the late 1950s, he was among Mehdi Ben Barka's supporters within the Istiqlal Party, and joined him in the breakaway from it and the formation of the Union Nationale des Forces Populaires (UNFP). He was a member of the UNFP's national committee and political bureau and director of its newspaper, *al-Muharrir*. His duties led to clashes with trade union leaders over their alleged corruption and advancement of their personal interests. Ben Jelloun served several prison terms, underwent torture, and was sentenced to death in 1963 (pardoned in 1965). He was tried again in 1973 for plotting to overthrow the government and acquitted on 30 August, but was held and charged with another offense. In 1974 he received a limited pardon. Ben Jelloun was murdered by unknown assailants on 18 December 1975, in Casablanca. Clement Henry Moore described Ben Jelloun as a major casualty of a political system whose rules he rejected.

See also BEN BARKA, MEHDI; ISTIQLAL PARTY: MOROCCO; UNION NATIONALE DES FORCES POPULAIRES (UNFP).

BRUCE MADDY-WEITZMAN

BEN KHEDDA, BEN YOUSSEF
[1920–]

President of the Gouvernement Provisoire de la République Algérienne, 1961–1962.

Ben Youssef Ben Khedda, born in Berrouaghia, Algeria, worked as a pharmacist and was an active member of Messali al-Hadj's Parti du Peuple Algérien (People's Party). He rose to secretary-general of its successor organization, the Mouvement pour le Triomphe des Libertés Démocratiques (Movement for the Triumph of Democratic Liberties, MTLD), but he sided with the centralists in opposition to Messali.

Ben Khedda joined the revolutionary Front de Libération Nationale (National Liberation Front, FLN), earning a reputation as an ideologist. He co-drafted the Soummam Congress Platform and wrote for the FLN's newspaper, *al-Moudjahid*. In 1958, he was selected as minister for Social Affairs in the first Gouvernement Provisoire de la République Algérienne (Provisional Government of the Algerian Republic, GPRA) and also served as an FLN diplomat before replacing Ferhat Abbas as the GPRA's president (August 1961). Ben Khedda supported the conclusion of the Evian accords (March 1962), which gave Algeria its independence.

That summer, Ahmed Ben Bella and Houari Boumédienne, who had the support of a trained external army, took over the leadership of the government. Ben Khedda returned to private life until 1976 when he cosigned a manifesto criticizing the policies of Boumédienne. After the October 1988 riots and the constitutional reforms of 1989, Ben Khedda formed an Islamic party called Oumma.

See also ABBAS, FERHAT; BEN BELLA, AHMED; BOUMÉDIENNE, HOUARI; EVIAN ACCORDS (1962); FRONT DE LIBÉRATION NATIONALE (FLN); MOUVEMENT POUR LE TRIOMPHE DES LIBERTÉS DÉMOCRATIQUES; NEWSPAPERS AND PRINT MEDIA; PARTI DU PEUPLE ALGÉRIEN (PPA).

PHILLIP C. NAYLOR

BEN M'HIDI, MUHAMMAD LARBI
[1923–1957]

Algerian revolutionary leader.

Muhammad Larbi Ben M'hidi was born to a farming family in Ain M'Lila near Constantine. A follower of Messali al-Hadj, he joined the Parti du Peuple Algérien (PPA; Algerian People's Party) and the paramilitary Organisation Spéciale (OS; Special Organization), which was affiliated with the Mouvement pour le Triomphe des Libertés Démocratiques (MTLD; Movement for the Triumph of Democratic Liberties). Like other members of the younger elite, Ben M'hidi grew impatient with the venerable nationalist Messali and collaborated in the founding in 1954 of the Comité Révolutionnaire d'Unité et d'Action (CRUA; Revolutionary Committee for Unity and Action) and subsequently the Front de Libération Nationale (FLN; National Liberation Front). He is regarded as one of the nine historic chiefs (chefs historiques) of the Algerian revolution against French colonialism.

During the Algerian war of independence (1954–1962), Ben M'hidi initially commanded Wilaya I (the military district in the Oran region) and played an important role at the FLN's Soummam conference in August 1956. Ben M'hidi believed that the revolution should be directed by "internal" rather than "external" revolutionaries. During the Battle of Algiers (1956–1957), he headed FLN operations until his capture in February 1957. The French announced in March that Ben M'hidi had committed suicide in his cell. This account was disputed by others, who have contended that he was in fact tortured and murdered.

> See also ALGERIAN WAR OF INDEPENDENCE; COMITÉ RÉVOLUTIONNAIRE D'UNITÉ ET D'ACTION (CRUA); FRONT DE LIBÉRATION NATIONALE (FLN); HADJ, MESSALI AL-; MOUVEMENT POUR LE TRIOMPHE DES LIBERTÉS DÉMOCRATIQUES.

Bibliography

Naylor, Phillip C., and Heggoy, Alf A. *The Historical Dictionary of Algeria,* 2d edition. Metuchen, NJ: Scarecrow Press, 1994.

PHILLIP C. NAYLOR

BENNABI, MALEK

[1905–1973]

Algerian Islamic thinker.

Born in a poor family in Constantine, Malek Bennabi became a leader of modern Islamic thinking in independent Algeria. As a youth, he attended a Qu'ranic school in Tebessa. Abd al-Hamid Ben Badis, the influential leader of the Islamic Reformist Movement (ulama), persuaded Bennabi to pursue his studies in Paris. There he obtained a diploma in engineering. His writings began appearing during the 1940s. Among the most notable are *The Qur'anic Phenomenon* (1946, translated 2001), *Les conditions de la renaissance: Problème d'une civilisation* (The conditions of the [Islamic] renaissance: A problem of civilization, 1948), and *La vocation de l'Islam* (The vocation of Islam, 1954). Bennabi joined the Front de Libération Nationale (National Liberation Front, FLN) during the 1950s and served as one of its representatives abroad. While in Cairo in 1956, he wrote *L'Afro-Asiatisme* and began *Le problème des idées dans le monde musulman* (The problem of ideas in the Muslim world), which he gave up because of, in his words, "ideological struggles." The book was eventually published in 1970.

From 1963 to 1967, Bennabi served as director of superior studies at the ministry of education; he was removed because of suspicions that he belonged to al-Qiyam, an Islamist organization opposed to the regime. During the late 1960s, Bennabi's disciples established a mosque at the University of Algiers. Bennabi, who organized private discussions in his own home, attracted primarily French-speaking students enrolled in science departments. He and his disciples alienated Arab-speaking Islamists mainly because of Bennabi's criticism of the *salafists,* the followers of the so-called purist movement, who reject progress, urging Muslims to eschew modernity and go back to the "strictness" of the Prophet's epoch, which they view as the golden age of Islam. The Algerian *salafists* drew their inspiration from Egyptian and south Asian sources. During the 1990s a current within the Front Islamique du Salut (Islamic Salvation Front, FIS), known as the Jaz'ara, or Algerianists, formed an elitist Islamist group, purporting, implausibly, to be inspired by Bennabi's ideas. Nourredine Boukrouh, an opponent of the FIS and founder of the Algerian Party for Renewal, rejected that claim, insisting that he was Bennabi's true disciple. He edited a book, *Pour changer l'Algérie* (To change Algeria, 1991), which contained Bennabi's newspaper and magazine articles organized into sections on political, economic, cultural, and international themes. In view of Bennabi's enlightened approach, it is doubtful that he would have endorsed the radicalism of the Jaz'arists or any other violent Islamist group.

> See also FRONT DE LIBÉRATION NATIONALE (FLN); FRONT ISLAMIQUE DU SALUT (FIS).

Bibliography

Bariun, Fawzia. *Bennabi, Malik: His Life and Theory of Civilization.* Kuala Lumpur: Buaya Ilmu Sdn, 1993.

Christelow, Allan. "An Islamic Humanist in the Twentieth Century: Malek Bennabi." *Maghreb Review* 17, no. 1–2 (1992).

Zoubir, Yahia H. "Islam and Democracy in Malek Bennabi's Thought." *American Journal of Islamic Social Sciences* 15, no. 1 (spring 1998): 107–112.

YAHIA ZOUBIR

BEN-PORAT, MORDECHAI
[1923–]

Israeli politician and community leader.

A native of Baghdad, Mordechai (also Mordekhai) Ben-Porat joined the Halutz movement in 1942 and emigrated to Palestine in 1945. He joined the Haganah in 1947. During the 1948 Arab–Israel War he fought in the Latrun and Ramla-Lyddad battles. He studied political science at the Tel Aviv branch of the Hebrew University. He was sent to Iraq in 1949 to organize Jewish emigration and remained there until 1951, while mass emigration plans known as the Ezra and Nehemiah Operations were proceeding.

From 1955 to 1969 he was head of the Or Yehuda Local Council. In 1965 he was a founding member of the Rafi Party. He was deputy speaker of the Knesset in 1965; deputy secretary-general of the Labor Party from 1970 to 1972; and a member of Israel's United Nations mission in 1977. In 1982 he was reelected to the Knesset on the list of Telem, the party founded by Moshe Dayan. In 1983 he established the Movement for Social Zionist Renewal. He joined the Likud in 1988.

Ben-Porat founded the Tehiyah (revival) movement, the World Organization of Jews from Arab Countries, and the Babylonian Jewry Heritage Center, of which he is chairman.

See also EZRA AND NEHEMIAH OPERATIONS; ISRAEL: POLITICAL PARTIES IN.

Bibliography

Ben-Porat, Mordechai. *To Baghdad and Back: The Miraculous 2,000 Year Homecoming of the Iraqi Jews.* Hewlett, NY: Gefen Publishing House, 1998.

NISSIM REJWAN
UPDATED BY GREGORY S. MAHLER

BEN SALAH, AHMED
[1926–]

Tunisian political and labor leader.

Ahmed Ben Salah was born in Moknine, attended Sadiqi College in Tunis, and began his political career as a Destour student leader at the University of Paris. Neo-Destour was the Tunisian political party that led the nationalist struggle against French colonial control. Returning to Tunisia in 1948, he remained active in the party but became involved with the Union Generale des Travailleurs Tunisiens (General Union of Tunisian Workers, UGTT). From 1951 until 1954, he worked with the International Confederation of Free Trade Unions in Brussels. Following his election as general secretary of the UGTT in 1954, he advocated the introduction of socialist economic concepts.

In 1955 Tunisia was granted autonomy by France; Ben Salah's success in maintaining UGTT loyalty to Habib Bourguiba, leader of Destour and first president of the Republic of Tunisia (1957–1987), when he was threatened by a radical movement within the party headed by Salah Ben Youssuf, assured Ben Salah of an influential political role. Although Bourguiba initially rejected Ben Salah's socialist approach, the deterioration of the new republic and the economy led to Ben Salah's appointment as minister of planning in 1961.

Ben Salah, who was dubbed the economic czar, introduced a ten-year plan built around socialist development projects, intending to promote self-sufficiency and raise living standards. His ideas generally met with success in the industrial sector, but his insistence on organizing state-run agricultural cooperatives and his plan to bring all cultivable land under state management provoked widespread rural antagonism. Accusations of corruption and mismanagement followed and, in 1969, fearful that popular opposition to these policies would undermine the entire government, Bourguiba renounced Ben Salah, who was arrested and sentenced for ten years but escaped in 1973. In exile, he organized the opposition party Mouvement de l'Unite Populaire (MUP), embodying the socialist principles he had tried to introduce while in office. A group of dissidents led by Mohamed Bel Haj Omar later left the MUP and established a new party, the Parti de l'Union Populaire (PUP). In 1988 Ben Salah returned briefly to Tunisia, but left later for his European exile because of denial of his political rights. Ben Salah finally returned to Tunisia in September 2000 and did not assume an active political role.

See also BOURGUIBA, HABIB; MOUVEMENT DE L'UNITÉ POPULAIRE (MUP); TUNISIA.

Bibliography

Ben Salah, Ahmed. "Tunisia: Endogenous Development and Structural Transformation." In *Another Development: Approaches and Strategies,* edited by Marc Nerfin. Uppsala, Sweden: Dag Hammarskjöld Foundation, 1977.

Moore, Clement Henry. *Tunisia since Independence: The Dynamics of One-Party Government.* Berkeley: University of California Press, 1965.

Perkins, Kenneth J. *Tunisia: Crossroads of the Islamic and European Worlds.* Boulder, CO: Westview, 1986.

KENNETH J. PERKINS
UPDATED BY EMAD ELDIN SHAHIN

BEN SEDDIQ, MAHJOUB
[1925–]

Cofounder of the Moroccan Labor Union.

In 1955, after serving jail sentences for having organized a general strike, Mahjoub Ben Seddiq and Tayyib Bouazza founded the Union Marocaine du Travail (UMT). Ben Seddiq has been its secretary-general since 1960. The UMT, which initially was closely affiliated with the Istiqlal Party, was the first—and for a time the most important—all-Moroccan trade union. Ben Seddiq, one of the Istiqlal's "Young Turks" during the late 1950s, is also considered to be one of the founders of the Union Nationale des Forces Populaires (UNFP), which broke away from the Istiqlal in 1959. He formally disassociated himself from the UNFP in January 1963, while remaining associated for a time with "loyal opposition" politics. Ben Seddiq was sentenced to eighteen months' imprisonment in July 1967 for undermining the authority of the state after he sharply criticized the government's decision to block the firing of Jewish employees in state-owned firms in the aftermath of the Arab–Israel War of 1967, alleging that the government was colluding with Zionists.

In subsequent years the 700,000-member UMT was generally less confrontational, especially in comparison to the two other competing labor confederations—the Confédération Démocratique du Travail (CDT), which is affiliated with the Union Socialiste des Forces Populaires (USFP), and the Union Générale des Travailleurs Marocains (UGTM), which is affiliated with the Istiqlal Party. Ben Seddiq himself adopted a lower public profile, and assumed the post of secretary-general of Royal Air Maroc, the Moroccan national airline. In 1995 the heads of the three unions held an unprecedented joint meeting during which Ben Seddiq called for unity among the unions as a prerequisite to a social pact that would enable genuine democratic change. Although real unity remained out of reach, the unions did exhibit greater coordination.

See also ARAB–ISRAEL WAR (1967); CONFÉDÉRATION DÉMOCRATIQUE DU TRAVAIL (CDT); ISTIQLAL PARTY: MOROCCO; UNION GÉNÉRALE DES TRAVAILLEURS MAROCAINS (UGTM); UNION MAROCAINE DU TRAVAIL (UMT); UNION NATIONALE DES FORCES POPULAIRES (UNFP).

Bibliography

Waterbury, John. *The Commander of the Faithful.* London: Weidenfeld & Nicholson, 1970.

BRUCE MADDY-WEITZMAN

BEN SIMEON, RAPHAEL AARON
[1848–1928]

A leading Sephardic legal scholar and modernist.

Born in Rabat, Morocco, and raised in Jerusalem, Raphael Aaron Ben Simeon avidly studied foreign languages, read modern Hebrew literature, and kept abreast of scientific and technological developments in addition to learning traditional rabbinics. In 1891, Ben Simeon was appointed Hakham Bashi in Cairo. Together with his liberal colleague, Elijah Bekhor Hazzan, the chief rabbi of Alexandria, Ben Simeon made Egyptian Jewry the most progressive in the Middle East and the Maghrib (North Africa). His many *responsa* (writings and interpretations) show his openness to modernity, which he understood brought with it an unprecedented measure of freedom of choice to the individual.

He retired to Palestine in 1923 and lived his remaining years in Tel Aviv. His voluminous writings include *Nehar Mitzrayim* (Alexandria, 1908), a work on Egyptian Jewish customary legal practice; *Tuv Mitzrayim* (Jerusalem, 1908), a biographical dictionary of the Egyptian rabbinate; and *Umi-Zur Devash* (Jerusalem, 1911–1912), his collected *responsa*.

See also HAZZAN, ELIJAH BEKHOR; MAGHRIB.

Bibliography

Stillman, Norman A. *The Jews of Arab Lands in Modern Times.* Philadelphia: Jewish Publication Society, 1991.

NORMAN STILLMAN

BENTWICH, NORMAN
[1883–1971]

First British attorney general in mandatory Palestine; legal scholar and author.

An English Jew, Norman de Mattos Bentwich was born in London and educated at St. Paul's School and Trinity College, Cambridge, where he studied classics. After qualifying in law, he entered the Egyptian Ministry of Justice in 1912 as inspector of Native Courts. During World War I he served in the Camel Transport Corps of the British Army in Egypt. In 1918 he became senior judicial officer in the British military administration in Palestine and, after the establishment of a civil administration in 1920, legal secretary (later termed attorney general). A lifelong Zionist, Bentwich was close to the moderate wing of the movement. As the Arab-Jewish conflict in Palestine escalated, his presence in the mandatory government became an embarrassment to the British. In 1929 he was slightly wounded in an assassination attempt. In 1930 he went on leave to England and a year later his appointment was "terminated." In 1932 he became professor of international relations at the Hebrew University of Jerusalem. During the 1930s he played an active role in welfare efforts for German Jewish refugees. Bentwich was the author of more than thirty books on Judeo-Greek civilization, international law, and Israel.

Bibliography

Bentwich, Norman. *My Seventy-seven Years: An Account of My Life and Times, 1883–1960.* London: Routledge and Kegan Paul, 1962.

Bentwich, Norman, and Bentwich, Helen. *Mandate Memories.* London: Hogarth Press, 1965.

BERNARD WASSERSTEIN

BENVENISTI, MERON
[1934–]

Israeli reformer.

Formerly deputy mayor of Jerusalem (1967–1978) and Knesset member, Meron Benvenisti became head of the West Bank Data Project, a group formed to monitor and evaluate Arab–Israeli relations. He has been one of the most vocal critics of Israeli policy toward the Palestinians and the West Bank. In 1981, he put forth the "Benvenisti Prognosis," which foresaw a continued stalemate over the occupied territories (the West Bank and Gaza Strip) and predicted that inertia, religious beliefs, and Israeli "imperialism" would prevent the Israelis from withdrawing in the near future.

Bibliography

O'Brien, Conor Cruise. *The Siege: The Saga of Israel and Zionism.* New York: Simon and Schuster, 1986.

Rolef, Susan Hattis, ed. *Political Dictionary of the State of Israel,* 2d edition. New York: Macmillan, 1993.

Shipler, David. *Arab and Jew: Wounded Spirits in a Promised Land,* revised edition. New York: Penguin, 2002.

ZACHARY KARABELL

BEN-YEHUDA, ELIEZER
[1857–1922]

Author and editor; pioneer in the restoration of Hebrew as a living language.

Born in Lushky, Lithuania, where he received both a Jewish traditional and a secular education, Eliezer Ben-Yehuda was impressed by the nationalist struggles in the Balkans (1877–1878) against the Ottoman Empire and became interested in the restoration of a Jewish homeland in Palestine and the revival of the Hebrew language. In 1881, he settled in Palestine, working as an editor for various Hebrew periodicals and establishing his own, *Ha-Tzvi*, in 1884. In 1889, he established the Va'ad ha-Lashon (Hebrew Language Council), among whose tasks was the coining of new Hebrew words. He served as chairman of the council until his death.

Ben-Yehuda's greatest work was the compilation of a comprehensive dictionary of the Hebrew language, several volumes of which were published in his lifetime. The complete edition of seventeen volumes was published in 1959.

See also HEBREW.

Bibliography

Laqueur, Walter. *A History of Zionism.* New York: Holt, Rinehart and Winston, 1976.

MARTIN MALIN

BEN YOUSOUF, SALAH
[1910–1961]

Tunisian lawyer, political activist, and leader of a radical group within the anticolonial movement that challenged Neo-Destour party leader Habib Bourguiba on the eve of independence.

Born on the island of Djerba (Jerba), Salah Ben Yousouf was an early associate of Habib Bourguiba (who became president of Tunisia, 1957–1987) and was a member of the Neo-Destour political party, which was led by Bourguiba and which challenged French colonial control. The French had formed a protectorate in 1883, after the La Marsa Convention, and had suppressed first the Destour and then the Neo-Destour attempts to modify Tunisia's political status.

In 1937, Ben Yousouf was named to the Destour political bureau; in 1945, he became secretary-general of the party. At a congress of Tunisian opposition groups in 1946, he expressed the frustration of many politically conscious Tunisians by calling for immediate and unequivocal independence—a demand that Bourguiba had never voiced and one that invited a split between party radicals and moderates. Anxious to prevent the radicals from dominating the party, the French permitted Bourguiba to return from exile in 1949.

In 1950, Ben Yousouf accepted the post of minister of Tunisian justice in a government pledged to explore the possibility of internal autonomy. When French-settler protests caused the abandonment of political reforms in 1952, Ben Yousouf traveled to Paris to place the Tunisian case before the United Nations Security Council. Amid a campaign of re-pression of the Neo-Destour, the resident general ordered his return, but Ben Yousouf fled to Cairo. Influenced there by pan-Arabism, Ben Yousouf continued to insist on Tunisia's complete break with France and its establishment of ties with other Arab states.

In April 1955, Bourguiba negotiated an agreement with France granting Tunisia home rule, but allowing France to retain considerable influence in many important areas. Although this Franco–Tunisian convention enjoyed widespread support within the Neo-Destour, Ben Yousouf regarded it as a betrayal both of Tunisian national interests, by withholding the full sovereignty he sought, and of pan-Arabism, by allowing France to concentrate on the suppression of nationalist uprisings in Algeria and Morocco. Thus, he returned to Tunisia in September, determined to block the party's endorsement of the convention. Ousted from the political bureau because of his opposition, Ben Yousouf turned to the party membership for support. In addition to the backing of many small businessmen (especially fellow Djerbans who dominated the retail grocery trade), he also had the support of old aristocratic families and conservative religious leaders, both traditionally opposed to Bourguiba. But Ben Yousouf's efforts to mobilize a broader following were thwarted by Neo-Destour loyalists. In November, the party congress voted overwhelmingly to accept the convention.

Unwilling to admit defeat, Ben Yousouf and his aides set about creating rival Neo-Destour branches throughout the country. His most militant supporters resorted to a campaign of terrorism that resulted in a police crackdown in January 1956. Ben Yousouf fled to Egypt, but violence continued in his name until mid-1956. His denunciations continued even after Tunisian independence in March, with criticisms not only of Neo-Destour's undemocratic tendencies, but also of Bourguiba's decision to concentrate on resolving domestic problems before committing himself to pan-Arab concerns. In 1961, Ben Yousouf died at the hands of an unidentified assassin in Cairo.

The vehement opposition of this once-trusted colleague undoubtedly shaped Bourguiba's views on political dissent. For the rest of his career, Bourguiba refused to tolerate an opposition element, no matter how benign, within his party.

See also BOURGUIBA, HABIB; LA MARSA CONVENTION; PAN-ARABISM.

Bibliography

Moore, Clement Henry. *Tunisia since Independence: The Dynamics of One-Party Government.* Berkeley: University of California Press, 1965.

KENNETH J. PERKINS

BEN-ZVI, RAHEL YANAIT
[1886–1979]

Israeli labor leader and educator.

Born in Maline, Ukraine, Rahel Yanait Ben-Zvi (nee Lishansky) studied Hebrew in heder (a Hebrew day school), graduated from a Russian high school, and attended university for a year. An ardent Zionist-socialist from an early age, she was a founding member of the Zionist-Socialist Party (Po'alei Zion) of Russia in 1906. A year earlier, she had been a delegate to the 1905 Zionist Congress. In 1908, she immigrated to Palestine and embarked on a multifaceted career in politics, defense, and education. She joined the ha-Shomer Self-Defense Organization, was editor of *Achdut,* the organ of the Po'alei Zion Party of Palestine, and a founder of the Hebrew Gymnasium in Jerusalem, where she also taught. She studied agronomy in Nancy, France (1911–1914). During World War I, she supported Britain and helped create the Jewish Legion in 1918. In that year, she married Yizhak Ben-Zvi, well-known Labor leader and future president of Israel. In 1919, she was a founder of the Ahdut ha-Avoda party, which succeeded Poalei Zion and eventually became MAPAI in 1930. In 1920 she was one of the heads of the Haganah defense organization in Jerusalem. She was instrumental in developing agricultural training facilities for women and established a number of schools and farms. In 1927, she was an emissary to the United States for Pioneer Women. After the creation of Israel, she continued her work in agricultural training and in immigrant absorption into Israeli society. An outspoken woman who held intense convictions in many issues, she accompanied her husband on various missions during his term as president of Israel (1952–1963). She aspired to succeed him after his death, but Prime Minister David Ben-Gurion chose Zalman Shazar. The rest of her long life was devoted to her educa-

tional endeavors and writing her memoirs, *We are immigrating* (1962, in Hebrew).

See also ALIYAH; HAGANAH; HA-SHOMER; ZIONISM.

MERON MEDZINI

BEN-ZVI, YIZHAK
[1884–1963]

Journalist; Labor Zionist leader; second president of Israel, 1952–1963.

Born in Poltava, in the Ukraine, into a family active in Zionism, Yizhak Ben-Zvi served as second president of Israel until his death. He assumed the role of chief theoretician of Labor Zionism from his arrival in Palestine in 1907.

As a childhood friend of Ber Borochov, Ben-Zvi had attended the founding conference of the Po'alei Zion (Workers of Zion) movement in Russia in 1906. He lived near the center of Russian revolutionary activities and the site of major pogroms. Committed to socialism and Zionism, Ben-Zvi's intellectual and political activities had one overwhelming purpose—to bridge the gap between Labor Zionist theory and conditions in Palestine. One of the founders of the Po'alei Zion Party in Palestine, he also organized a clandestine Jewish defense society called Bar Giora (a name associated with one of the Jewish leaders fighting the Romans in 66–70 C.E.). Bar Giora's members aimed at replacing the Arab guards usually hired to secure outlying Jewish agricultural settlements. Hoping to raise class consciousness among Palestine's Jews, Ben-Zvi edited his party's newspaper and opened a small school in Jerusalem with a curriculum appropriate to the needs of a modern Jewish society.

With the restoration of the Ottoman Empire's constitution after the Young Turk revolution in 1908, Ben-Zvi and one of his closest friends and party comrades, David Ben-Gurion, traveled to Constantinople (now Istanbul) to study law as an avenue of entry into Ottoman politics. With the outbreak of World War I in Europe, he and Ben-Gurion returned to Palestine but were unable to remain. Exiled by Ottoman authorities as potential troublemakers, Ben-Zvi and Ben-Gurion lived and lectured, on behalf of the Po'alei Zion movement,

Born in the Ukraine, Yizhak Ben-Zvi was president of Israel from 1952 until 1963, succeeding Chaim Weizmann. Ben-Zvi died in office in 1963. © BETTMANN/CORBIS. REPRODUCED BY PERMISSION.

in the United States. Ben-Zvi returned to Palestine as a soldier in the Jewish Legion.

Ben-Zvi's commitment to the fundamental principles of Labor Zionism never wavered. The possibilities opened by the advent of British rule altered the perspective of many Labor Zionists and the positions adopted by the political parties and institutions. Ben-Zvi maintained his close personal friendship with Ben-Gurion despite the latter's departure from such Labor Zionist strictures as the inevitability of class struggle. As Ben-Zvi saw it, only a clear Labor Zionist ideology and program would unify Jews in Palestine and create the foundations for a humane society. Sensitivity to the differences between Zionist and Palestinian national interests led Ben-Zvi to devote considerable effort to uncov-

ering the history of Ottoman Palestine. As a prolific journalist, he also undertook research of ancient and remote Jewish communities.

Elected to the Jerusalem municipality several times, he established ties with the council's Arab representatives. He participated in the Vaʿad Leʾumi (National Council), first as a member and then later as its chair. He became a link between the British mandate government and the organized Labor Zionist leadership. He founded the Institute for the Study of Jewish Communities in the Middle East, later renamed the Ben-Zvi Institute. As president of Israel until his death in 1963, he lived in a simple house in a quiet Jerusalem neighborhood, personifying the original egalitarian impulse of Labor Zionism. He is the author of *The Jewish Yishuv in Peki'in Village* (1922), *Eretz-Israel under Ottoman Rule* (1955), *The Exile and the Redeemed* (1957), and *The Jewish Legion: Letters* (1969).

See also BEN-GURION, DAVID; JEWISH LEGION; LABOR ZIONISM; VAʿAD LEʾUMI; YOUNG TURKS.

Bibliography

Ben-Zvi, Yizhak. *Eretz-Israel under Ottoman Rule: Four Centuries of History.* Israel: Bialik Institute, 1955.

Ben-Zvi, Yizhak. *The Exile and the Redeemed,* translated by Isaac A. Abbady. Philadelphia: Jewish Publication Society of America, 1957.

Frankel, Jonathan. *Prophecy and Politics.* Cambridge, U.K., and New York: Cambridge University Press, 1981.

Halpern, Ben, and Reinharz, Jehuda. "The Cultural and Social Background of the Second Aliyah." *Middle Eastern Studies* 27 (July 1991): 487–517.

DONNA ROBINSON DIVINE

BERBER

Person(s), language(s), and culture of North African groups descended from the pre-Arab Mediterranean-type indigenous populations.

The term *Berber* was first applied centuries ago by foreign conquerors. Modern-day Berbers generally prefer their own designations—*amazigh* (male Berber) and *tamazight* (female Berber or Berber language/dialect)—or the local variants of these. Speakers of Berber languages, those who are now referred to as Berbers, are most numerous today in western North Africa, but they can be found as far east as eastern

Berber women, dressed in festive garb, attend the Douz Festival of the Sahara in Tunisia. Douz, an oasis at the edge of the Sahara, hosts the four-day international festival celebrating the arts and traditions of the desert people. © PATRICK WARD/CORBIS. REPRODUCED BY PERMISSION.

Libya and even western Egypt (Siwa) and as far south as the Sahara Desert, northern Saharan regions of Niger, Mali, and Burkina Faso. The nation of Senegal takes its name from a Berber-speaking group, the Zenaga, who live in an area of southwestern Mauritania.

No Berber race can be distinguished, rather the variety of features found throughout the Maghrib (North Africa) are essentially those associated with Mediterranean peoples generally. There seems always to have been a considerable mixture and, at present, one is confronted with Berbers having a wide spectrum of skin colors, statures, and cranial and facial proportions.

Several of the largest groups of Berbers that are characterized by linguistic and cultural distinctiveness are referred to using terms of non-Berber origin, usually from Arabic—the Kabyles in Kabylia (Djurdjura mountains, east southeast from Algiers); the Chawia (Aurès mountains in eastern Algeria, south of Constantine); the Tuareg (Saharan Algeria, Mali, Niger, Burkina Faso); the Chleuh (High Atlas and Anti-Atlas mountains, Sous valley in southern Morocco); and the Braber (also called simply *imazighen,* plural of *amazigh*) of the Middle Atlas mountains of Morocco. Virtually all other Berbers go by terms referring to the name of their place or region of origin: Nefusi, Djerbi, Mzabi, Rifi, and so on.

North African countries have not chosen to include native language data in their census process—but taking Berber speakers as constituting between 30 percent and the commonly cited 40 percent of Morocco's population, around 20 percent of Algeria's, adding several tens of thousands each from Tunisia, Libya, Niger, Burkina Faso, and Mauritania, one could very roughly assess the total to be somewhere around 12 million in the mid-1990s.

The overwhelming majority of Berbers have their homes in rural environments, far from the urban centers. In general, they can be found on the least productive lands—the mountains, the high plateaus, the pre-Saharan *hammada,* and in the Sahara Desert. Although the Tuareg—camel nomads of the central Sahara—more vividly capture our imagination by their fascinating aspect and institutions, their lifestyle is not particularly representative. Most Berbers are—and have been throughout recorded history—sedentary agriculturalists. Along the mountains bordering on the high plateaus and desert, some Berbers practice forms of seminomadism, or transhumance, during part of the year to maintain their flocks (especially in the Aurès mountains and the southern part of the Middle Atlas).

Sedentary Berbers typically live in villages and eke out a meager peasant existence from small irrigated gardens, dry cereal culture, arboriculture, and small flocks of sheep and goats, occasionally a cow or two. In today's world, it is necessary for many of the most able-bodied men to export, for a time, their most marketable asset, their labor. It is not uncommon to find villages largely devoid of men between the ages of sixteen and forty. They emigrate temporarily, usually without families, both to North African cities and to European industrial centers and, from there, send home the money that, by living frugally, they are able to accumulate. Without their support, these villages and areas simply could not survive.

In many instances, by virtue of a natural tendency of younger emigrants to follow their elder family members, a village or even a whole area becomes specialized in a particular vocational field to the extent that they hold a near monopoly on one or another activity or commercial enterprise. Interestingly, this has happened in the grocery trade in all three of the main Maghrib countries. In each case, Berbers from a specific area have come to dominate to such an extent that, in the towns and cities, one typically does not go to the grocer's: In Tunisia one goes to the Djerbi's (from the island of Djerba), in Algeria to the Mzabi's (pre-Sahara), in Morocco to the Sousi's (Sous river valley and Anti-Atlas mountains). It is a significant instance of very

successful adaptation to nontraditional ways, but it should be noted that its purpose, for the overwhelming majority, is precisely to permit the maintenance of the traditional homeland and lifestyle.

Art

The forms of Berber artistic expression, at least in the modern period, are primarily linked to utilitarian objects—pottery, weaving, and architecture—and to jewelry. All are characterized by predominantly geometrical, nonrepresentational patterns. Neither the forms and patterns nor the techniques appear to have changed significantly since ancient times, and they can be related directly to forms found in the Mediterranean basin from as early as the Iron Age. While they are not especially original or exclusive to Berbers, one is struck by the extraordinary persistence and continuity, in Berber country, of the tradition. Some of the most remarkable examples of Berber artistic expression are: (1) the fortified architecture of the southern Moroccan *ksars,* massive but majestic rammed earth and adobe-brick structures with intricate decorative patterns seemingly chiseled into their towers and facades; (2) Kabyle and Chawia pottery, extraordinary for the variety and elegance of its modeled forms as well as the composition and proportion of its applied patterns; (3) silver jewelry, embossed and inlaid with stones as well as with enameled cloisonné, especially—but by no means exclusively—that represented by the Kabyle tradition; (4) textiles throughout North Africa, but particularly in southern Tunisia and in central and southern Morocco.

Social Organization

Traditional social organization is family based and therefore quite segmentary. Relations between extended families—or, if need be, between clans or villages—have in the past been (and continue to some extent to be) mediated by an assembly of heads of family, or elders, called the Djema'a. In today's more centrally administered bureaucratic world, many of the traditional competencies of the assembly have been taken over by government agencies. Nonetheless, a number of issues—those concerning local resources of common interest and responsibility: Maintenance of paths, irrigation canals, mosques, and Qur'anic schools; hiring of the Qur'anic teacher; usage of forests and pastureland;

setting of plowing and harvest dates; protection of crops; cooperative support (usually in the form of labor) of disadvantaged families; collective meat purchasing; hospitality for outsiders; organizing local religious or secular celebrations; and so forth—continue to require consensus decisions and the shared provision of labor and material resources. While the term *democratic*, which has often been applied to Berber institutions, does not appear appropriate, one is struck by their profound egalitarianism, less as a moral imperative than one born of a distrust of power concentrated in the hands of one segment or another. This is often summarized in the terms *balance* and *opposition*: balance of power maintained by a constant resistance to the other segments' natural self-interest and by vigilance to assure that all segments bear burdens and reap benefits equally.

Berbers seem always to have had, and earned, a reputation of fierce independence, of inclination to rebellion, of resistance to any imposition of control over their lives. North African history is extremely fragmented, constantly jostled by new revolts, realignments, and alliances. Every schismatic movement seems to be welcomed against the previous orthodoxy, Donatism when the Berbers were being Christianized, Kharijism in the early years of Islamization. As often as not, the not yet entrenched conqueror is joined with to throw off the previous tyrant—whether either or both were Berber or not. Each time that a choice was to be made, it was seemingly made in the direction of greater local control and independence. Only on rare occasions in their history did the Berbers put together something like a Berber nation, uniting for a time over a vast territory to create a state or empire. In the two most important instances, the Almoravid and the Almohad dynasties of the eleventh and twelfth centuries, they were drawn together by the ideal of reform of the previously dominant regime(s), seen as having fallen into corrupt ways. This search for ever purer forms is, along with their deep cultural conservatism, one of the most constantly recurring themes throughout their history.

Religion

Virtually all Berbers by the twenty-first century were Muslims and, like most North Africans, are of Sunni Islam orthodoxy. In the Mzab and in Ouargla

in Algeria, on the island of Djerba in Tunisia, and in the Nefusa mountains of Libya, there subsist Ibadite communities—all essentially Berber-speaking—who trace their history back to the Kharijite schism of the seventh and eighth centuries.

Little reliable detail can be given as to the nature of the Berbers' pre-Islamic religious beliefs and practices. There is evidence from archaeology, from the remarks of observers in antiquity, and also from popular practices that have survived into the present in North Africa, of a generally animistic set of beliefs manifested in sacralization of promontories, outcroppings, caves, trees, and water sources. The usages seem to have been highly varied and local in their expression but widespread and reflective of the quasi-universal need to assuage the spirits to which the vicissitudes of everyday life can be—and are still—attributed. Much of the North African fondness for the veneration of local saints, so-called Maraboutism, tolerated by the central tradition of Islam as somewhat deviant and marginal, can be understood as deriving in large part from this substratum: Saints' "tombs" are often situated next to trees, caves, topographical features, or water sources that give evidence of cultic activity going back well before the life of the nominal vessel of *baraka* (blessedness, protection, God's power made present).

Language and Literature

Berber languages constitute together one branch of the Afro-Asiatic (or Hamito-Semitic) language family, whose other four branches are Semitic, Egyptian, Cushitic, and Chadic. Berber languages show a high degree of homogeneity in their grammar, somewhat less in their phonology. The differences that one notes between them are fewer and less considerable than those within the Semitic, Cushitic, or Chadic branches (Egyptian is manifested as essentially homogeneous at any historical moment). In a number of important respects, Berber bears a closer resemblance to Semitic languages than to the other branches: (1) the sound system employs contrasts of consonant "length" and pharyngealization (emphatics); (2) there are three basic vowels *a, i, u* with an archaic contrast of short versus long vowels found in the important set of Tuareg languages; (3) the morphological system is highly complex, characterized by a prevalence of tri-radical roots (less than Semitic, however), and

A Berber groom is introducing his bride to friends at this Muslim festival in Imilchil, Morocco. The festival, held in this small mountain village every year, allows the men and women to become engaged. The participants dress in their local costumes. © NIK WHEELER/CORBIS. REPRODUCED BY PERMISSION.

considerable use of both consonant length and intraradical vowel alternation to express grammatical categories such as verb aspect and noun number; (4) the verbal system is based on a fundamental contrast of perfective versus imperfective aspect, with tense being secondary; (5) word order is predominantly V(erb) S(ubject) O(bject), though SVO is very frequent in main clauses.

Some noteworthy features peculiar to Berber include the following: (1) as reflected in the words *amazigh, tamazight* (cf. supra), as well as many place names on maps, masculine nouns begin with a vowel and feminine nouns begin with t + vowel and most often end in t as well (the vowel is *a* in 80% of nouns); (2) a special form of the noun (the annexed or construct form), characterized by an alteration of the vowel of the first syllable (*amazigh* > *umazigh, tamazight* > *tmazight)*, is used for the subject noun after its verb, after prepositions, and as the second element in a noun-complement construction; (3) the subject markers of finite verb forms are both prefixed and suffixed to the stem (with the prefix elements being clearly identifiable with those of the Semitic prefix conjugation); (4) pronominal objects of the verb basically go immediately after the verb but must precede it in a number of conditions (essentially those of subordination); (5) particles can be used with the verb to "orient" the verbal action: *d* = "toward speaker" and *n* = "away from speaker."

Berber languages are generally only spoken, seldom written. Among the Tuareg, however, there subsists an alphabet, the *tifinagh,* which descends

Most Berbers live in rural areas, far from urban centers—in the mountains, on high plateaus, and in the Sahara Desert. The Tuareg, camel nomads of the central Sahara, represent a subset of nomaidic Berbers, while other groups are sedentary. © OWEN FRANKEN/CORBIS.

from the Libyan alphabet that is found in ancient inscriptions throughout much of North Africa (but principally present-day Tunisia and eastern Algeria). This alphabet, which like Arabic is essentially consonantal, can be written right to left or left to right, occasionally vertically. Among the Tuareg, it is used primarily for short inscriptions on rocks and for brief messages but does not seem to be employed for the recording of stories, documents, or history, those uses for which writing is basic in our Western cultures. Some efforts have been made by advocates of Berber cultural affirmation, to adapt the *tifinagh* to such functions and to broaden its use to other Berber-speaking groups, as in Kabylia and in Morocco. These efforts have had only very limited success and those publications (several in Algeria and in Morocco) written in the Berber language generally use the Latin-based transcription system employed by the French.

Berber literature is then essentially oral. It includes many traditional stories—tales of animals,

marvelous tales with ogres and monsters, tales of kings and princesses (à la *Thousand and One Nights*), hagiographic legends, and myriad other stories that hand down the moral and ethical base of Berber society. As for poetry, among the Berbers it goes with music and is—unlike the tales and stories—constantly regenerated around a wide spectrum of subjects. There are extremely traditional forms, such as the often bantering repartee in the context of celebratory line dances in Morocco. There are more lyrical forms, songs of the heart and its joys and pains. There are the elaborate and often quite lengthy commentaries by troubador-like itinerant singers who hold forth, often quite bitingly, on all subjects, including the political scene. And, of course, one cannot fail to mention Berber popular music, which constitutes the richest and most fertile field of Berber literary expression today.

Of the languages with which Berber has shared North Africa at different times and places—among them Phoenician, Latin, Germanic (German and

English), Turkish, Italian, Spanish, and French—none has had the profound effect that the Arabic dialects have had. Most Berber languages have a high percentage of borrowing from Arabic, as well as from other languages (these often indirectly through Arabic, however). Least influenced are the Tuareg languages; most influenced, those that are near urban centers and from whose areas there has traditionally been much temporary emigration for work.

Berber languages survive because children learn their first language from their mothers and it continues to be the language of the home, of the private world, long after they become adults and the men become bilingual. Berber women continue, in most areas, to have little education and little contact with the Arabic-speaking world around them, so their children will doubtless continue to learn and to perpetuate Berber languages. The movements to preserve Berber culture, most developed in Kabylia and somewhat in Morocco, will also doubtless have a conservative effect. Where Berber is spoken only in a village or two surrounded by Arabic speakers, it is disappearing. In the larger Berber-speaking regions, however, it is quite resistant, and the numbers of speakers are growing at nearly the same rate as that at which the population increases.

In postindependence North Africa, Berber languages and cultures have been neglected and even repressed by the agencies of the central governments. This seems to have been caused by a perceived need to discourage cultural differences in the building of the nation-state—cultural differences that, it was felt, had been exploited by the French colonial regimes to divide the colonized and impose their authority. On occasion, the reaction to this repression has been violent, as in 1980 in Kabylia. Not surprisingly, political movements have grown up around the issues of cultural expression and autonomy. In both Algeria and Morocco, there exist official political parties made up essentially of Berbers, with Berber cultural preservation as one of their highest priorities.

See also DJEMAʿA; MAGHRIB; MARABOUT; MAURITANIA; SUNNI ISLAM.

Bibliography

Brett, Michael, and Fentress, Elizabeth. *The Berbers.* Oxford, U.K., and Cambridge, MA: Blackwell, 1996.

Eickelman, Dale F. *Moroccan Islam: Tradition and Society in a Pilgrimage Center.* Austin: University of Texas Press, 1976.

Gellner, Ernest. *Saints of the Atlas.* London: Weidenfeld and Nicolson, 1969.

Gellner, Ernest, and Micaud, Charles, eds. *Arabs and Berbers: From Tribe to Nation in North Africa.* London: Duckworth, 1973.

Westermarck, Edward. *Ritual and Belief in Morocco.* London: Macmillan, 1926.

THOMAS G. PENCHOEN

BERBER DAHIR

The sultan's order that in 1930 removed Morocco's Berbers from the jurisdiction of Islamic law.

The Berber Dahir, a decree issued by Morocco's sultan at the instigation of French colonial authorities on 16 May 1930, created courts in Berber-speaking regions that decided cases by codified local custom (*urf*) instead of Islamic law (*shariʿa*). The mass urban protests against the decree served as a catalyst for Morocco's nationalist movement and drew support from Muslims worldwide.

See also SHARIʿA.

Bibliography

Pennell, C. R. *Morocco since 1830: A History.* New York: New York University Press, 2000.

DALE F. EICKELMAN

BERBER SPRING

An uprising, from March to June 1980, for linguistic and cultural rights in Berber-speaking Kabylia in northeastern Algeria.

Between March and June 1980, the northeastern Algerian provinces of Kabylia became the site of a violent social and political drama that would become known as the Berber Spring (*Printemps Berbère* in French, or *Tafsut n Imazighen* in Berber/Tamazight) and set the stage for the modern transnational Berber/Amazigh cultural movement. Kabylia has a history of resistance to state authority and since independence has been the center for advocacy of Berber cultural and linguistic rights in an officially Arab-speaking state.

On 10 March 1980 local authorities banned a lecture on ancient Berber poetry, which was to be given at the University of Tizi-Ouzou by the writer and ethnologist Mouloud Mammeri. In response, students went on strike, demonstrating across the country for an end to "cultural repression," and on 7 April they occupied the university. When on 20 April the military stormed the university, arresting and injuring hundreds of demonstrators, a series of violent confrontations between Kabyle youth and police broke out, which together with a four-day general strike shut down the region for nearly a week. Although calm was subsequently restored, antigovernment protests continued until the last of the arrested students was released on 26 June.

The Berber Spring made Berberism a political force in postcolonial Algeria and more broadly in North Africa. Commemorations of the events have become the indispensable activity of Berber cultural associations worldwide and have been moments for the elaboration of political programs and, in the case of the April 2001 Black Spring, for new confrontations with state authorities.

See also BLACK SPRING; KABYLIA; RASSEMBLEMENT POUR LA CULTURE ET LA DÉMOCRATIE (RCD).

Bibliography

Roberts, Hugh. "Towards an Understanding of the Kabyle Question in Contemporary Algeria." *The Maghreb Review* 5, nos. 5–6 (1980): 115–124.

PAUL SILVERSTEIN

BERIHAH

See BRICHAH

BERKOWITZ, YIZHAK

[1885–1967]

Hebrew and Yiddish writer and editor.

Born in Belorussia, Yizhak Berkowitz won a prize in a 1904 literary contest sponsored by the Warsaw Jewish newspaper *Ha-Zofeh* for his story "Moshkele Hazir." By 1905, his writings appeared in most of the contemporary Hebrew and Yiddish journals. From 1905 to 1928, Berkowitz served as editor of numerous Hebrew and Yiddish journals in Eastern Europe and the United States, among them *Ha-Zeman, Di Naye Velt, Ha-Toren,* and *Miklat.*

He reached Palestine in 1928 and became an editor of the weekly *Moznayim.* He translated into Hebrew and published the collected works of Sholem Aleichem, his father-in-law. Berkowitz is recognized as a master of the short story, many of which are set in Russia at the turn of the twentieth century. They deal with the social upheavals that confront Eastern European Jews.

See also LITERATURE: HEBREW.

ANN KAHN

BERLIN–BAGHDAD RAILWAY

Begun in the Ottoman Empire in 1903, it was to extend the existing Anatolian railway from Konya, in south-central Anatolia, to Baghdad and the Persian/Arabian Gulf.

In 1886, Sultan Abdülhamit II, desirous of greater economic control over his empire, proposed a railway from the Bosporus to the Persian/Arabian Gulf. It would extend Baron Maurice de Hirsch's Oriental Railway, which linked Berlin to Istanbul at its completion in 1888. In the same year, the Ottoman government granted the Anatolian Railway Company, a syndicate dominated by the Deutsche Bank, the concession to construct a railway from the Bosporus to Ankara, in order for Germany to pursue its economic penetration of the Ottoman Empire. This railway line, completed in 1893, was extended to Konya by 1896.

Developing Ottoman–German political and economic cooperation induced the Ottomans to grant the Anatolian Railway Company the concession to extend the railway from Konya to Baghdad and beyond. The Baghdad Railway Company, dominated by the Deutsche Bank and other German interests, was formed in 1903.

Construction was hampered by technical and financial difficulties, Anglo–French–Russian fears of German penetration of the region, and World War I. The Ottoman and German governments agreed to Britain's demand that the railway end in Basra, and not extend to the Gulf. The lines from Istanbul to Nusaybin, and from Baghdad to Samarra in the south, were not completed until 1917. Track laying and tunnel construction continued throughout the war, as late as September 1918. The Nusaybin–Mosul–Samarra gap was finally closed in 1939–1940, and the first train set out from Istanbul to Baghdad in 1940.

See also ABDÜLHAMIT II.

Bibliography

Earle, Edward M. *Turkey, the Great Powers, and the Baghdad Railway.* New York: Macmillan, 1923.

Wolf, John B. *The Diplomatic History of the Baghdad Railway.* Columbia: University of Missouri, 1936.

FRANCIS R. NICOSIA

BERLIN, CONGRESS AND TREATY OF

Treaty that ended the Russo–Turkish War, redividing the countries of southeastern Europe that had belonged to the Ottoman Empire.

In March 1878, following the Russian victory over the Ottoman Turks in the Russo–Turkish War of 1877–1878, the Treaty of San Stefano was imposed. The principal feature of that pact was the creation of a large Bulgarian state, possessing coastal territory on the Mediterranean as well as on the Black Sea. The new Bulgaria also included the bulk of Macedonia, denying Austria-Hungary any avenue for advancement south to the coveted Mediterranean coast. Britain disliked the treaty, because it could allow the Russians to become a naval power in the Middle East, using the Mediterranean ports of the newly created Bulgarian puppet state. A grave danger existed that Austria and Britain would make war rather than tolerate such Russian aggrandizement.

Prince Otto von Bismarck, chancellor of the new German Empire (1871–1890), realized that such a major war might provide France with allies and a chance to avenge Germany's 1871 conquest. He therefore proffered his services as an "honest broker" who sought peace disinterestedly, since Germany had no ambitions in the Balkans or Middle East. Thus, the Congress of Berlin was convened in June–July 1878, attended by the plenipotentiaries of Turkey and all the major powers. Benjamin Disraeli, prime minister of Great Britain (1874–1880), and Count Gyula Andrássy, foreign minister of Austria-Hungary (1871–1879), made their advance preparations carefully, offering African territory to France and Italy and slashing the size of Bulgaria by

returning most of it to the Ottomans, so that Russia's satellite would no longer claim Macedonia or a Mediterranean coast line. The Austrians gained a protectorate over Bosnia-Herzegovina and prepared for a future thrust southward to the Mediterranean by leaving their intended avenue of advance, the Sanjak of Novi Bazar, in Ottoman hands. Even Russia, deprived of a Mediterranean base, received compensations on the Asian Caucasus frontier. In a separate treaty, the Ottomans yielded the valuable island of Cyprus to Britain for ninety-nine years, in return for guaranteeing the Ottomans possession of their Asiatic lands for that period. Only afterward did the Ottomans realize that they had surrendered a valuable naval base in exchange for a British guarantee that neither could be nor would be fulfilled.

The Congress of Berlin is, therefore, the point at which Britain ceased to be Ottoman Turkey's great defender and Germany gradually took on that role. In the next generation, Germany, which had had no major Middle Eastern interests, was to become the principal protector of the Ottoman Empire and of Islam.

In the long term, by supporting Britain and Austria against Russian claims, Bismarck threatened that perfect harmony among the Great Powers—his chief instrument in keeping France isolated. To his credit, Bismarck "kept the telegraph lines open to St. Petersburg" as long as he held office. Nevertheless, Russian fears of an Austro–German alliance came to fulfillment in 1879, and those fears led to the Franco–Russian alliance, consummated from 1892 to 1894.

See also RUSSIAN–OTTOMAN WARS; SAN STEFANO, TREATY OF (1878).

Bibliography

Jászi, Oszkár. *The Dissolution of the Habsburg Monarchy.* Chicago: University of Chicago Press, 1961.

Jelavich, Barbara. *The Habsburg Empire in European Affairs, 1814–1918.* Chicago: Rand McNally, 1969.

ARNOLD BLUMBERG

BERNADOTTE, FOLKE
[1895–1948]

United Nations mediator in Palestine, 1948.

A scion of Sweden's royal family and chairman of Sweden's Red Cross, Folke Bernadotte was appointed mediator by the United Nations (UN) on 17 May 1948, at the termination of the British Mandate in Palestine. The Security Council reinforced his mandate by declaring an arms embargo. The terms Bernadotte proposed included the establishment and supervision of a truce between the forces of Israel and five Arab states, and "adjustment of the future situation." He established a truce, which was broken and restored several times and never properly supervised due to lack of personnel. Being a novice in the Middle East, Bernadotte received assistance from a UN team headed by the able African-American Ralph Bunche, who became the brains behind Bernadotte's mission and political plans. However, Bernadotte's design for a settlement of the Palestine issue was molded under Anglo-American pressure, motivated mainly by the Cold War policy of containing Soviet expansion in the Middle East.

The so-called Bernadotte Plan for Arab–Israeli settlement was sent out twice: in June as a trial balloon and in September as a proposal for UN action. The plan called for a modification of the partition recommended by the UN Assembly in November 1947. The boundaries he proposed reflected the status quo of the frontlines as of July, with Jerusalem in the first version allotted to Transjordan and in the second placed under UN auspices. Palestinians who had lost their homes in the war were to be given a choice between repatriation and receiving compensation and settling elsewhere. Implicit in the proposal was the abandonment of the UN Assembly's plan to establish a Palestinian Arab state beside Israel. Instead, Bernadotte proposed to cede the residual area to Transjordan.

Both the Arab states and Israelis rejected the proposals, the former because they entailed recognition of the Jewish state and the latter because the Israelis assumed they would not be able to retain their sovereignty within the boundaries proposed. Bernadotte expected the UN to enforce his proposals, as Britain and the United States initially seemed prepared to back the plan.

On 17 September 1948, before going to the UN General Assembly to submit his plan, Bernadotte was gunned down in Jerusalem by members of the LEHI (Lohamei Herut Yisrael [Freedom Fighters of Israel]), a diehard Israeli underground terrorist group, headed by a triumvirate, one of whose members, Yitzhak Shamir, would become Israel's prime minister forty years later. The assassination at first seemed to increase the chances of UN endorsement of Bernadotte's proposals, but the situation changed dramatically. This was in part because of Israel's military victories in October, which altered the front lines and broke the backbone of the military coalition of the Arab states, and in part because of a shift on the part of the U.S. administration during 1948 elections. A watered-down version of Bernadotte's proposals was endorsed on 11 December 1948 in UN Assembly Resolution 194, which created the Palestine Conciliation Commission and contained a declaration on the rights of Palestinian refugees to return to their homes. No one was ever punished for Bernadotte's assassination. Israel never exhausted all means to bring the culprits to justice and the Swedish government eventually accepted this lack of progress in bringing the culprits to justice.

Bernadotte's mediation mission was defeated by insufficient UN backing resulting from the Cold War; the utter rejection of his proposals by the rival parties. Ironically, it was also the result of the unforeseen impact of the UN embargo, which aimed to dry up the military resources of both warring parties but in fact increased Israel's military edge over the Arabs, resulting in an Arab defeat and an armistice based on lines more favorable to Israel than those Bernadotte had recommended earlier. In the end, those lines received international legitimacy.

See also LOHAMEI HERUT YISRAEL.

Bibliography

Bernadotte, Folke. *To Jerusalem.* London: Hodder and Stoughton, 1951.

Caplan, Neil. *Futile Diplomacy*, Vol. 3: *The United Nations, the Great Powers, and Middle East Peacemaking, 1948–1954.* London: Frank Cass, 1997.

Ilan, Amitzur. *Bernadotte in Palestine: A Study in Contemporary Humanitarian Knight-Errantry.* London: Macmillan, 1989.

AMITZUR ILAN

BERRADA, MOHAMMED
[1938–]

Moroccan novelist and literary critic.

Mohammed Berrada was born in Rabat, Morocco, studied in Rabat and Cairo, and received his Doctorat Troisième Cycle from the Sorbonne in 1973. Although he is bilingual, his creative writing is in Arabic; he also has translated books from French into Arabic. Berrada recently retired from his position as professor of Arabic literature at Muhammad V University in Rabat. He was editor in chief of the journal *Afaq* during his presidency of the Union of Moroccan Writers.

Berrada is an accomplished short-story writer who relies on symbols to convey his ideas. His short story "Qissat al-Ra's al-Maqtu'a" (The story of the cut-off head) is an excellent illustration of his technique; the absence of free expression in Morocco is portrayed through the surrealistic journey of a cut-off head. He also can be extremely realistic and direct, as in his short story "Dolarat" (Dollars). Berrada is concerned with the human quest for meaning in life and solutions to its dilemmas.

Berrada's novel *Lu'bat al-Nisyan* (1987; The game of forgetfulness) adopts a philosophical approach to human memory. While relating the childhood memories of the characters from different sources, the author demonstrates the workings of memory by sifting and discarding the events of the past. This process reveals the thin line that separates reality from imagination and casts doubt on a person's conscious recollection of the past. The only reality remains the city of Fez, a sign of immutable truth and a symbol of cherished souvenirs and elating emotions, regardless of their truth. A respect for reality is achieved through the dialogue of the various narrators of the novel, each of whom speaks the dialect that denotes his or her cultural level. Thus, Si Brahim, who is illiterate, speaks only colloquial Moroccan. A similar concern with the past is addressed in Berrada's second novel, *al-Daw al-Harib* (1993; The fugitive light). His semiautobiographical text *Mithla Sayfin lan yatakarrar* (1999; Like a summer that won't recur) sheds light on Moroccan students' lives in Egypt with a perceptive, in-depth look at Egyptian society from the perspective of narrator Hammad, who speaks for Barrada himself. The major event of the summer is the nationalization of the Suez Canal by Gamal Abdel Nasser.

The eye of the literary critic that Berrada revealed himself to be in *Muhammad Mandur wa Tandhir* *al-Naqd al-Arabi* (1975; Muhammad Mandur and the theorizing of Arabic literary criticism) is visible in the background of the creative writings but does not overwhelm them.

See also LITERATURE: ARABIC, NORTH AFRICAN.

Bibliography

Barakat, Halim, ed. *Contemporary North Africa: Issues of Development and Integration.* Washington, DC: Center for Contemporary Arab Studies, 1985.

Berrada, Mohammed. *La Mediterranée marocaine.* Paris: Maisonneuve and Larose, 2000.

AIDA A. BAMIA

BERRI, NABI
[1938–]

Politician in Lebanon.

Nabi Berri was born in Sierra Leone in 1938 and received his law degree from Lebanese University. He became a close associate of Imam Musa Sadr and came to prominence in the political life of Lebanon during the late 1970s after Musa Sadr disappeared in 1978, which thrust Berri, as a key leader of the AMAL movement, into the forefront of political activity. He assumed the presidency of AMAL in 1980. He has held several ministerial posts since 1984. His charismatic personality has helped his political fortunes, but it is his political deference to the government of Syria that has been primarily responsible for his ability to limit the influence of his rivals within the Shi'ite community. Berri transformed the AMAL movement from an organization loyal to the legacy of Musa Sadr into one under his political control. He headed the Liberation List in the 1992 election and formed the largest bloc in parliament, thereby becoming its speaker. Although Berri is not from a traditional political (*zu'ama*) family, he has not refrained from forming coalitions with traditional landowning families. His popularity has sunk since he took office as accusations of corruption and extravagance have surrounded him and his key associates. His movement almost lost the 2000 parliamentary election, but Syria forced the popular Hizbullah to form a joint ticket with AMAL. Berri was subsequently reelected, and he also was reelected speaker of the parliament. In 2000, his movement suffered a setback with the ouster of two key leaders, including the popular Muhammad Abd al-Hamid Baydun.

See also AMAL; HIZBULLAH; LEBANESE UNIVERSITY.

Bibliography

Norton, Richard Augustus. *Amal and the Shi'a Struggle for the Soul of Lebanon.* Austin: University of Texas Press, 1987.

AS'AD ABUKHALIL

BETHLEHEM

City in the West Bank.

This small city is a center of Christian pilgrimage to the birthplace of Jesus and to the site of the Church of the Nativity, built in the fourth century. Greek Orthodox, Armenian, and some Latin-rite churches also exist. In Judaism, it is the setting for most of the biblical Book of Ruth; King David lived there when it was called Judaea and was anointed king of Israel there by the prophet Samuel.

Bethlehem is 5 miles (8 km) southwest of Jerusalem. In addition to being a center of tourism and pilgrimage, Bethlehem is now an agricultural market and trade center, with a population of 21,673 Palestinian Arabs as of 1997. The town has long had a disproportionately high percentage of Christian residents, and it traditionally has a Christian mayor.

The city was part of the territory that brought the Crusaders to fight the Muslims; became part of the Ottoman Empire; then, with the dismemberment of the empire after World War I, became part of the British mandate territory of Palestine. During the Arab–Israel War of 1948, Jordan annexed the city, which became part of the West Bank. Israel controlled Bethlehem from 1967 to 1994, after which it passed into the control of the Palestinian Authority. Pope John Paul II visited the town in March 2000. In April and May of 2002, after the start of the Al-Aqsa Intifada that saw Israel reoccupy the city for some time, the Church of the Nativity was the scene of a five-week standoff between Israeli forces and armed Palestinians.

See also AQSA INTIFADA, AL-; ARAB–ISRAEL WAR (1948); PALESTINIAN AUTHORITY; WEST BANK.

BENJAMIN JOSEPH
UPDATED BY MICHAEL R. FISCHBACH

BEVIN, ERNEST
[1881–1951]

Foreign secretary of Great Britain (1945–1951).

Ernest Bevin was associated with the Bevin–Bidault agreement of December 1945, which provided for the evacuation of Britain's and France's troops from Syria and Lebanon. He was also responsible for the abortive Bevin–Sidqi agreement, signed between Britain and Egypt in October 1946, and the equally unsuccessful 1949 Bevin–Sforza Plan concerning Libya.

It was Bevin's involvement with the Palestine problem for which he is best known. When the affairs of the Palestine mandate came under the jurisdiction of the Foreign Office, Bevin took an active role in the formulation of British policy during the crucial years of the Arab–Jewish struggle for Palestine. In November 1945, Bevin announced the formation of the Anglo–American Committee of Inquiry on Palestine. Although he desired the United States to become involved in the resolution of the Palestine problem, he envisaged a dominant role for Britain in the Middle East.

Although Bevin pursued a policy that closely followed the aims of the British white paper of 1939—which restricted the number of Jewish immigrants from Europe to Palestine—it became clear that Britain could not resolve the differences between the Zionists and the Palestinians. In April 1947, Bevin decided to pass the Palestine problem to the United Nations. When the United Nations recommended partitioning Palestine into Arab and Jewish states, he refused to allow the British mandate authorities to participate in the implementation of the agreement. Instead, he ordered them to dismantle their administration and withdraw British forces by May 1948.

Many Zionists suspected Bevin opposed the creation of a Jewish state in Palestine, but recent revisionist scholarship has shown that he tacitly cooperated in implementing the partition plan. According to new accounts based on declassified documents from Israel's archives, Bevin met secretly with Transjordan officials in London and privately sanctioned King Abdullah ibn Hussein's plans to seize the West Bank. This plan had been arranged by Abdullah and Golda Meir, a prominent Zionist leader.

See also ABDULLAH I IBN HUSSEIN; BEVIN–SFORZA PLAN; MEIR, GOLDA.

Bibliography

Shimoni, Yaacov. *Political Dictionary of the Arab World.* New York: Macmillan, 1987.

Shlaim, Avi. *The Politics of Partition: King Abdullah, the Zionists and Palestine, 1921–1951.* New York: Columbia University Press, 1990.

LAWRENCE TAL

BEVIN–SFORZA PLAN

A post–World War II plan to administer former Italian colonies in North Africa.

After World War II, Italy was forced to relinquish its African colonies by the terms of its February 1947 peace treaty with the Allies. Libya was made the temporary responsibility of the United Nations, although Britain and France continued to administer it. Partly to protect their interest and partly to avoid Soviet interference, the British foreign secretary, Ernest Bevin, and the Italian foreign minister, Count Carlo Sforza, promulgated a joint plan on 10 May 1949, for the United Nations to grant trusteeships to Britain in Cyrenaica; Italy in Tripolitania; and France in the Fezzan, for a ten-year period, after which Libya would become independent. The plan, which met massive hostility in Libya itself, was rejected by the United Nations General Assembly eight days later.

See also BEVIN, ERNEST.

Bibliography

Wright, John. *Libya: A Modern History.* Baltimore, MD: Johns Hopkins University Press, 1982.

GEORGE JOFFE

BEY

See GLOSSARY

BEYOGLU PROTOCOL

Terms that reorganized the administrative structure of Lebanon as province of Ottoman Empire.

Following the massacres by the Druze of thousands of Lebanese and Syrian Christians in the summer of 1860, the Ottoman sultan, Abdülmecit I, sent Mehmed Fuat Paşa, foreign minister, to Syria to resolve the crisis. Fuat had two goals: to restore order and to prevent the European powers from intervening. Though France landed troops and Britain sent a fleet, Fuad was thorough and provided them with no excuse to intervene further. In June 1861 the French withdrew their forces, and on 9 June the sultan issued the Beyoglu Protocol, which reorganized the administrative structure of Lebanon. Under the terms of the protocol, Lebanon was given a new Organic Law that established Lebanon as a privileged province headed by a non-Lebanese, Ottoman Christian governor (*mutasarrif*) appointed by the sultan after consultation with European governments. The predominantly Christian mountain region was detached from the coastal district of Beirut and Tripoli as well as from the inland Biqa Valley. It was a smaller, more homogenous province, but it survived intact without major disruptions until World War I.

See also ABDÜLMECIT I; DRUZE.

Bibliography

Hurewitz, J. C., tr. and ed. *The Middle East and North Africa in World Politics,* 2d edition. New Haven, CT: Yale University Press, 1975.

Shaw, Stanford, and Shaw, Ezel Kural. *History of the Ottoman Empire and Modern Turkey.* 2 vols. Cambridge, U.K., and New York: Cambridge University Press, 1976–1977.

ZACHARY KARABELL

BEZALEL ACADEMY OF ARTS AND DESIGN

School located in Jerusalem.

The former Bezalel School of Arts and Crafts was founded in 1906 by the sculptor Boris Schatz and named for the biblical architect of the Tabernacle, Bezalel ben Uri. Within the Ottoman Empire, Schatz wanted to establish a cultural center and craft industry in Jerusalem's *yishuv* (Jewish settlement).

The Bezalel Museum was founded as part of the school.

From the outset, efforts were made to preserve a uniquely Jewish artistic style. Funding for the project was provided by wealthy Zionists in Germany. During World War I, the school was destroyed but later rebuilt. It closed in 1932 but soon reopened as Jewish refugees fled Hitler's Germany (1933–1945). The "new" Bezalel, independent of the museum, opened in 1935. In 1955, it began training teachers and, in 1970 became an academy, with its diploma recognized as a B.A. equivalent. Under the directorship of Dan Hoffner, it was modernized, emphasizing design.

ANN KAHN

BIALIK, HAYYIM NAHMAN
[1873–1934]

Acclaimed "national poet," formative influence on modern Hebrew poetry.

Hayyim Nahman Bialik grew up in Radi and then in nearby Zhitomir (Ukraine). His strict, pious, and scholarly grandfather placed him in a traditional religious school (cheder) before sending him to Volozhin Yeshiva, a leading Orthodox academy at which he and other students (including Abraham Isaac Kook) secretly pursued their interest in modern European literature, philosophy, and Zionism. The tension between the old faith and modernity, echoed later in poems such as "Levadi" (Alone) and "ha-Matmid" (The Talmud student), encouraged Bialik to embark on a literary career as a disciple of Ahad Ha'Am. During the First Zionist Congress (1897), Bialik supported Ahad Ha'Am's "spiritual Zionism" against Theodor Herzl's political Zionism. Ahad Ha'Am also influenced Bialik's attitude regarding the relationship between Jewish and European culture, ethics, and aesthetics (see "Megillat ha-Esh"; Scroll of fire).

His first anthology appeared in 1901 in Odessa, Bialik's home for the next twenty years. There he wrote his epic "Metei Midbar" (The dead of the desert, 1902), in which boundaries between self and nation are blurred, a hallmark of his poetics. The epic's failed rebels may symbolize unleashed psychic energies, cosmic powers, or a national uprising. The 1903 Kishinev pogrom prompted a less equiv-

ocal call for Jewish self-defense: "On the Slaughter" and "In the City of Slaughter" were the basis for his recognition as modern Jewry's "national poet."

Bialik then strove to revitalize Hebrew, creating a publishing house and translating classic rabbinic and European texts. He dominated the Hebrew literary scene, both as literary editor of *Ha-Shilo'ah* (1904–1909), *Keneset* (1917), and *Reshumot* (1918–1922) and through essays on the state of Hebrew culture (1907–1917).

In 1921 Maksim Gorky helped Bialik and other Hebrew writers leave Soviet Russia. Bialik resumed his literary activities in Berlin and, in 1924, settled in Tel Aviv. There he headed the Hebrew Writers Union, worked as a publisher and scholar of medieval poetry, and wrote the first children's poems in Hebrew.

Before Bialik, modern Hebrew poetry was conventional and collective, imitating biblical diction and old European models. Bialik, inspired by the themes and style of contemporary Russian literature in particular, subordinated linguistic and conceptual traditions to modern verse and to the conflicts of the individual and nation in crisis. Arabs appear infrequently in his work, living in an exemplary romantic harmony with the desert. Unlike Ahad Ha'Am, Bialik gave little attention to problems of coexistence—the spiritual and national revival he foresaw in "return to the East" would parallel Arab life, not conflict with it.

Bibliography

Aberbach, David. *Bialik.* New York: Grove Press; London: P. Halban, 1988.

Breslauer, S. Daniel. *The Hebrew Poetry of Hayyim Nahman Bialik (1873–1934) and a Modern Jewish Theology.* Lewiston, NY: Edwin Mellen Press, 1991.

NILI GOLD
UPDATED BY GEORGE R. WILKES

BIDONVILLE

One of many shantytown communities in French colonial North Africa, situated near cities and towns.

Bidonville is one of three forms of living space in colonial France's Maghrib possessions—the other two being the traditional Arab medina, which formed the nucleus of precolonial cities and towns, and the *villeneuve,* its Western counterpart that was designed by Europeans and built during colonial times. Bidonvilles in their original sense referred to the flimsy shacks and shantytowns that emerged in the nineteenth century at the margins of North African cities and towns—often built from *"bidons à pétrole,"* tin containers used to distribute kerosene.

The emergence of bidonvilles across North Africa was both directly and indirectly linked to the colonial presence. In several instances bidonvilles emerged as entire villages and populations were displaced, when in Algeria during so-called *cantonnements* and *regroupements*—policies that were aimed at either providing agricultural land to colonial settlers or to keep the local populations away from what were considered by the colonial authorities to be strategic areas.

What contributed to the physical growth of a population that could no longer be incorporated into the confines of the precolonial city or town included: the growth of the North African coastal cities, linked to their new and intermediary role in the French economy; the impoverishment of the rural areas either through neglect or their incorporation into wider economies; the burgeoning population as a result of the introduction of health, sanitary, and hygienic standards; and the creation of an urban salaried class employed by France. As a result of this uncontrolled and more often than not hasty growth, bidonvilles contrast sharply both with the planned *villeneuves* of North African towns and the carefully integrated design of the traditional medinas; as a result, they have often been described by French colonial observers as monotonous and unpleasing.

At the time of independence of the North African countries in the 1950s and 1960s, and in the two decades that followed, bidonvilles became firmly established features of the urban landscape. Often, they possess only rudimentary sanitary systems, water, or electricity. The conditions that had contributed to their creation or existence in the colonial period were continued and often exacerbated by the economic and development strategies of the new governments. In several cases, substantial portions of city populations—in some instances

up to 40 percent—found themselves temporarily but more often than not permanently in bidonvilles that often remained for years without the amenities enjoyed by other citizens. Perhaps not surprising, as bidonvilles became permanent fixtures throughout North Africa, they often were the focal points for riots and violent demonstrations against local governments—forcing them to devote considerable resources to upgrading and incorporating the bidonvilles into their towns and cities, providing water and electricity, sanitation and transportation. Despite this, one of the unavoidable and seemingly enduring sights of the Maghrib remains that of bidonvilles that physically, socially, and economically are literally at the margins of each country's society.

See also CANTONNEMENT/REFOULEMENT; MAGHRIB; MEDINA.

DIRK VANDEWALLE

BILAD, AL-

See NEWSPAPERS AND PRINT MEDIA: ARAB COUNTRIES

BILHAYR, ABD AL-NABI

[?–1930]

Local leader of the powerful Warfalla tribal group located to the south of Misurata during World War I.

Abd al-Nabi Bilhayr participated in the Council of Four, the ruling body of the short-lived Tripolitanian Republic, although, as the republic collapsed under Italian pressure, he also fell out with its most important leader, Ramadan al-Suwayhli. Eventually he retired to southern Tripolitania and Fazzan, where he continued to resist Italian occupation. In 1927 he retired to southern Algeria, where he died in 1930.

See also SUWAYHLI, RAMADAN AL-.

Bibliography

Anderson, Lisa S. "The Tripoli Republic, 1918–1922." In *Social and Economic Development of Libya,* edited by E. G. H. Joffe and K. S. McLachlan. Wisbech, U.K.: Middle East and North African Studies, 1982.

GEORGE JOFFE

BILKENT UNIVERSITY

Nonprofit private university in Ankara, Turkey.

Bilkent University was established in 1984 by a nonprofit foundation. Its founder, Professor Ihsan Doğramaci, who was serving as chairman of the Council of Higher Education at the time, received much criticism for being the benefactor of his own university.

Bilkent admitted its first students in 1986. In 2003, it had nine faculties (art, design, and architecture; administrative and social sciences; business administration; education; engineering; humanities and letters; law; natural sciences; and music and performing arts), five vocational schools (applied languages; applied technology and management; computer technology and management; English; tourism and hotel services), and six research institutes. Its language of instruction is English.

In 2002, Bilkent employed 1,230 faculty members (of whom 1,010 had full-time and 220 had part-time appointments) and had 10,086 students (of whom 2,274 held full scholarships and 110 were international).

Bilkent was the only private university in Turkey until 1993, when several other nonprofit universities were established. As a private university, it has higher tuition and fees than the state universities, but these charges are comparable to those of other private universities. Like its counterparts, the university receives financial support from the state. In 2003, its budget amounted to 97,100 billion Turkish liras, 4 percent of which came from the state.

Bibliography

Bilkent University. Available from <http://www.bilkent.edu.tr>.

I. METIN KUNT
UPDATED BY BURÇAK KESKIN-KOZAT

BILTMORE PROGRAM (1942)

Resolutions adopted at a Zionist conference held at the Biltmore Hotel in New York City, 9–11 May 1942.

About 600 U.S. Zionists were joined by a number of visiting Zionist leaders, including the Zionist Organization's president, Chaim Weizmann, and the Jewish Agency chairman, David Ben-Gurion, at the Biltmore Hotel to call for "the fulfillment of the original purpose of the Balfour Declaration and the Mandate."

One of the conference's eight resolutions strongly denounced the British White Paper of May 1939 as "cruel and indefensible in its denial of sanctuary to Jews fleeing from Nazi persecution." In its final resolutions, the Biltmore Program declared that "the new world order that will follow victory cannot be established on foundations of peace, justice and equality, unless the problem of Jewish homelessness is finally solved." To that end, the program was clearer and went further than any previous official Zionist statement in risking a breach with Britain and orienting the movement's fate toward U.S. sponsorship. The conference "urged that the gates of Palestine be opened; that the Jewish Agency be vested with control of immigration into Palestine and with the necessary authority for upbuilding the country, including the development of its unoccupied and uncultivated lands; and that Palestine be established as a Jewish Commonwealth integrated in the structure of the new democratic world."

The debates during and after the Biltmore conference were an important reflection of internal Zionist disputes between gradualists and radicals—a struggle characterized, somewhat simplistically, as one between Weizmann, the pro-British diplomat, and Ben-Gurion, the uncompromising activist. The Biltmore Program's call for the establishment of Palestine "as a Jewish Commonwealth" was interpreted by many as equivalent to the maximalist demand for a Jewish *state* in *all* of Palestine and, hence, aroused some internal controversy.

The Biltmore Program was endorsed by authoritative Zionist and Yishuv bodies, and remained official policy until late 1946, when a Jewish state in *part* of Palestine became the new operative goal of the movement's leadership.

Bibliography

Bauer, Yehuda. *From Diplomacy to Resistance: A History of Jewish Palestine, 1939–1945.* Philadelphia, PA: Jewish Publication Society, 1970.

Hurewitz, J. C. *The Struggle for Palestine.* New York: Norton, 1950. Reprint, 1968, 1976.

Laqueur, Walter, and Rubin, Barry, eds. *The Israel-Arab Reader: A Documentary History of the Middle East Conflict,* 6th edition. New York: Penguin Books, 2001.

NEIL CAPLAN

BILU

See ALIYAH

BINATIONALISM

Political theory for Palestine current during the British mandate, 1922–1948.

Binationalists asserted that Palestine belonged equally to Palestinian Arabs and Jews and that its ultimate political disposition should be based on this principle—that Palestinians and Jews are equally entitled to national self-determination within the full territory. Constitutional arrangements for any binational state should be based on parity, regardless of the relative numbers of each group, to assure equal representation for both in all the institutions of the national government.

The original supporters of binationalism formed a small but articulate minority within the political spectrum of the Yishuv (Palestine's Jewish community). Among the leading proponents of binationalism were idealists and humanists, rather than political tacticians: Judah I. Magnes, president and chancellor of the Hebrew University of Jerusalem; world-renowned philosopher Martin Buber; and land-purchase agent Chaim Kalvaryski. The most notable of the associations formed to advance binationalism during the mandate period were Brit Shalom (Covenant of Peace; founded in 1925), the League for Jewish-Arab Rapprochement and Co-operation (founded in 1939), and Ihud (Unity; founded in 1942). Two left-wing workers' parties, Po'alei-Zion Smol (Left Faction, Workers of Zion) and ha-Shomer ha-Tza'ir (the Young Watchman), also took an active part in advocating a binational solution.

Binationalism never became a strong force within the Zionist movement, within the Yishuv, or among any Palestinian political groups. The idea reached a high point in the year 1946, when the arguments advanced by Magnes and Buber before the Anglo-American Committee of Inquiry influenced the committee's report, which proposed that "Jew shall not dominate Arab and Arab shall not dominate Jew," and that "Palestine shall be neither a Jewish state nor an Arab state." But the committee's recommendations soon proved unworkable and, subsequently, the United Nations opted for the partition of mandatory Palestine (i.e., Palestine under British Mandate). Faced with the reality of the State of Israel after 14 May 1948, Magnes reluctantly abandoned binationalism and began advocating instead a confederation between the new Jewish state and a Palestinian Arab state-to-be-created. Thereafter, the concept of binationalism surfaced from time to time (e.g., following the 1967 Arab–Israel war), usually in academic discussions of alternative approaches to resolving the Arab-Israeli-Palestinian dispute.

Binationalists were opposed to the partition of Palestine into separate Arab and Jewish states on the grounds that it would fragment the integral unity of the small country and would give rise to irredentism (where a territory ethnically related to one political unit comes under the control of another). Likewise, they rejected as unjust and unworkable the mutually exclusive quests for either an Arab or a Jewish state, each with its recognized minority. Finally, binationalism—with its essential stress on the rights and status of Arabs and Jews as coequal but autonomous national communities living in a single state—should not be confused with either a "two-state" solution or Palestinian proposals for a nonsectarian, secular democratic state.

Bibliography

Cohen, Aharon. *Israel and the Arab World.* New York: Funk and Wagnalls, 1970.

Flapan, Simha. *Zionism and the Palestinians.* New York, 1979.

Goren, A. A., ed. *Dissenter in Zion: From the Writings of Judah L. Magnes.* Cambridge, MA: Harvard University Press, 1982.

Hattis, Susan Lee. *The Bi-National Idea in Palestine during Mandatory Times.* Haifa, Israel: Shikmona Publications, 1970.

Hurewitz, J. C. *The Struggle for Palestine,* reprint edition. New York: Shocken Books, 1976.

NEIL CAPLAN

BIN DIYAF, MUHSEN
[1932–]

Tunisian novelist and short-story writer.

Muhsen Bin Diyaf, born in Tunis, received a B.A. in Arabic language and literature. Although he is bilingual, he writes in Arabic. Bin Diyaf has published two novels, *al-Tahaddi* (1972; The defiance) and *Yawm min al-Umr* (1976; A certain day in a life), and a collection of short stories, *Kalimat ala Jidar al-Samt* (1977; Words on the wall of silence). His writings reflect a concern with human beings and the quality of life in political and social contexts. Bin Diyaf's latest novel, *al-Irtihal wa Zafir al-Mawj* (1996; Departure and the exhalation of the waves), is a detective novel, a genre that is slowly making its way in Maghribi literature.

See also LITERATURE: ARABIC, NORTH AFRICAN.

AIDA A. BAMIA

BIN LADIN, OSAMA
[1957–]

A Saudi militant; head of al-Qaʿida.

Osama bin Ladin was born in Riyadh to a Yemeni father who settled in Saudi Arabia in 1930. The father quickly rose in the construction business, built palaces for the senior members of the royal family, and died in a plane crash in 1970, leaving a fortune to his children. Osama was forty-third among the surviving siblings and twenty-first among the sons. His mother is believed to have been Syrian (his father married at least ten women). He had a childhood of privilege. No evidence exists of either a wild period or intense religiosity during his teen years. He most likely gravitated toward fundamentalism while studying public administration at King Abd al-Aziz University in Riyadh in the late 1970s. There he fell under the spell of a charismatic Palestinian Islamist, Abdullah Azzam, while the latter was on a speaking tour to raise funds for the Mojahedin (Islamic holy warriors) in Afghanistan. While at the university, bin Ladin is reported to have begun a study of the works of Egyptian Islamist Sayyid Qutb. One can still see the influence of Qutb's thought in bin Ladin's organization, especially his categorization of people into either believing Muslims or infidels, the latter group including Muslims who disagree with his interpretations of Islam.

Exiled Saudi dissident Osama bin Ladin, seen here in an April 1998 photograph in Afghanistan. Bin Ladin is the leader of the international terrorist organization al-Qaʿida, responsible for many terrorist activities, including the 11 September 2001 attacks on the United States. He is currently ranked by the F.B.I. as one of the ten most wanted fugitives in the world. © AP/WIDE WORLD PHOTOS. REPRODUCED BY PERMISSION.

After earning his degree, bin Ladin moved, with his sizable inheritance, into Pakistan, which was then the staging area for the Mojahedin struggle against the Soviet-backed government of Afghanistan. He did not distinguish himself in battle, although he carries an AK-47 that he claims to have captured from a Soviet soldier. His organizational skills, however, were impressive. He started a database to account for all the Arab volunteers who were passing through Afghanistan, and he used it as a nucleus for his later organization. During those years, bin Ladin was on excellent terms with the Saudi government, and he coordinated closely with Prince Turki al-Faysal, head of Saudi foreign intelligence. After the withdrawal of Soviet troops and the subsequent assassination of Abdullah Azzam, bin Ladin began to organize the Arab volunteers who had relocated to Afghanistan to fight the Soviet infidels, and those followers formed what became known as al-Qaʿida.

His troubles with the Saudi government did not begin until 1990, when Iraq invaded Kuwait. Bin Ladin was concerned about the U.S. desire to base troops in the kingdom, and he met with most of the Saudi senior princes, including the minister of defense, the head of foreign intelligence, and the crown prince. He proposed forming an army of Muslim volunteers to expel Saddam's army from Kuwait, but the royal family invited U.S. troops instead, and bin Ladin broke with the royal family and was expelled from the kingdom in 1991. He moved to Sudan, where he stayed until 1996. In Sudan, he was hosted by the powerful Sudanese Islamist politician Hasan al-Turabi, and the latter still claims that Bin Ladin was an entrepreneur while in the Sudan. It is not known what bin Ladin did in the Sudan, although he did use his construction experience to engage in business. The Saudi royal family stripped him of his citizenship in 1994, and under pressure from the United States and Saudi Arabia, the Sudanese government asked him to leave the country. He returned to Afghanistan, where his militancy grew and where he connected with the militant Egyptian Islamist Ayman al-Zawihiri. The Taliban came under the influence of bin Ladin (rather than vice versa), and bin Ladin and Zawahiri pooled their resources and skills to form, in February 1998, the Islamic Front for the Combat Against Jews and Crusaders. Bin Ladin's rhetoric was typically crude, and his agenda typically militant and violent. He came to world attention in August 1998, when he was blamed by the U.S. government for the suicide bombings of U.S. embassies in Kenya and Tanzania. Bin Laden was operating his global networks from bases in Afghanistan. He survived U.S. strikes on his bases there and managed to organize the 11 September 2001 attacks on targets within the United States. This led to the U.S. war on Afghanistan and the overthrow of the Taliban government. Bin Ladin managed to survive war and is believed to be in hiding somewhere between Pakistan and Afghanistan. He communicates with the outside world through carefully managed and produced video- and audiotapes. His group has been linked to acts of violence worldwide.

See also QAʿIDA, AL-; QUTB, SAYYID; TALIBAN; TURABI, HASAN AL-.

Bibliography

Asʿad AbuKhalil. *Bin Laden, Islam, and America's New "War on Terrorism."* New York: Seven Stories, 2002.

ASʿAD ABUKHALIL

BINT

See GLOSSARY

BINT AL-SHATI
[1913–1999]

Egyptian scholar and writer.

Aʾisha Abd al-Rahaman, known as Bint al-Shati, was born in Dumyat to a religious and conservative family. Her father sent her to a *kuttab*—a Qurʾanic school—to study the Qurʾan. With the help of her mother, Bint al-Shati was able to continue her education. She received her B.A. in Arabic Language and Literature from Cairo University. She got her Ph.D. in the same field under the supervision of the illustrious Taha Hussein in 1950.

Bint al-Shati held various academic posts in Egypt. She was the chairperson of the Department of Arabic and Islamic Studies at Ain Shams University, an academic inspector for the Egyptian Ministry of Education, and a visiting professor in several Arab universities such as Khartoum University in Sudan and Qarawiyyin University in Morocco. She also taught in Syria, Saudi Arabia, Iraq, and the United Arab Emirates.

Aisha Abd al-Rahman started writing articles for Egyptian women's magazines. When she began publishing in widely circulated journals and daily papers in 1933, she adopted her pen name Bint al-Shati ("daughter of the riverbank/beach") in order to hide her identity from her father, a well-known religious scholar at that time, Shaykh Mohammad Ali Abd al-Rahman. Her father, guessing her pen name—which refers to her birthplace, Dumyat, where the waters of the Nile and the Mediterranean meet—and recognizing her style, encouraged her later to keep writing. In addition to writing in academic and scholarly journals, she wrote for the prestigious newspaper *al-Ahram* until her death.

A prolific writer, Bint al-Shati had more than forty books and one hundred articles to her credit. Although she published some fiction and poetry, she is best known for her social, literary, and Islamic studies. Her first two books, which appeared in 1936 and 1938, deal with the difficulties facing Egyptian peasants. Her other books deal with Arabic literature (1961), contemporary Arab women poets (1963), Abu al-Ala al-Ma'arri (1968 and 1972), and a new reading of *Risalat al-Ghufran* (1972).

Bint al-Shati was a vehement defender of the rights of women. Some of the titles of her articles attest to the wide scope of her knowledge and interest: "The [woman] Loser," "The Lost Woman," "The [woman] Stranger," "The Rebellious," "The Dreamer," "The Innocent," "The Sad," "How Do Our [male] Literary Figures View Women?," "The Image of Women in our Literature," "We Are No More Evil than Men," and "Will a Woman Become a Shaykh in al-Azhar?" Her 1942 novel *Master of the Estate* depicts a peasant girl who is a victim of a patriarchal and feudal society.

Bint al-Shati excelled, however, in the field of Qur'anic studies, in which she published more than fifteen books, including *The Immutability of the Qur'an* (1971), *With the Chosen* (1972), *The Qur'an and Issues of Human Condition* (1972), and *Islamic Character* (1973). She published several biographies of early Muslim women, including *The Daughters of the Prophet* (1963), *The Mother of the Prophet* (1966), and *The Wives of the Prophet* (1959), which was translated into English.

Her autobiography, *On the Bridge* (1986), provides invaluable information about the different stages of her life.

See also AIN SHAMS UNIVERSITY; GENDER: GENDER AND EDUCATION; LITERATURE: ARABIC.

Bibliography

Zeidan, Joseph. *Arab Women Novelists: The Formative Years and Beyond.* Albany: State University of New York Press, 1995

SABAH GHANDOUR

BIQA VALLEY

Fertile region of eastern Lebanon.

Running parallel to the Mediterranean coast between the Lebanon and Anti-Lebanon mountain ranges, the Biqa valley throughout the eighteenth and nineteenth centuries enjoyed close ties to Damascus, whose populace constituted a ready market for its agricultural produce. Nevertheless, in August 1920, French mandatory authorities incorporated the Biqa into the newly created state of Lebanon. Thereafter, it served as the breadbasket for the rapidly expanding port city of Beirut.

After the outbreak of the Lebanese civil war in 1975, the towns of the Biqa provided strongholds for a number of militant Shi'ite organizations. These included not only Hizbullah and Islamic AMAL, headquartered around Ba'albak, but also a detachment of Revolutionary Guards seconded from the Islamic Republic of Iran. Neither Syrian troops, which controlled the Beirut-Damascus highway beginning in the summer of 1976, nor Israeli forces, which raided the area by air and land on numerous occasions, succeeded in dislodging the militants, who supported their activities by producing opium and other drugs for export. When the fighting stopped in 1989, Syrian military units maintained their positions in the area, and the local economy retained its wartime links to southern Syria.

See also BA'ALBAK; HIZBULLAH.

FRED H. LAWSON

BIRET, IDIL
[1942–]

Turkish pianist.

Born in Ankara in 1942, Idil Biret displayed an outstanding talent for music from the age of three. Her mother played the piano rather well and with other musical members of the family, there was always chamber music at home. Biret was sent to Paris with her parents by the Turkish government when she was seven. Trained at the Paris Conservatory by Nadia Boulanger, Biret performed Mozart's Concerto for Two Pianos with Wilhelm Kempff at Théâtre des Champs-Elysées under the baton of Joseph Keilberth in 1953 when she was only eleven. At age fifteen she graduated from the Paris Conservatory with three first prizes. Biret continued studying piano with Alfred Cortot and was a lifelong disciple of Wilhelm Kempff.

Even though Nadia Boulanger never encouraged her to enter competitions, Biret's concert career started very early. She was invited to the Soviet Union for an extensive concert tour when she was sixteen years old by recommendation of Emil Gilels.

Her debut in the United States, with the Boston Symphony Orchestra conducted by Erich Leisendorf, where she played Rachmaninov's Piano Concerto no. 3, unfortunately took place on the day of President John F. Kennedy's assassination in 1963. The following year she performed the same work with the London Symphony Orchestra conducted by Pierre Monteux.

In 1986 Biret launched a colossal project of recording all of Beethoven's nine symphonies' piano transcriptions by Liszt. In the same year she performed the nine symphonies in a series of four concerts at the Montpellier Festival in France. Since this outstanding event she has continued to record the complete solo piano works and piano concertos of Chopin, Brahms, and Rachmaninov. She was awarded the Grand prix du Disque Chopin prize in Poland in 1995. That same year her recording of the Pierre Boulez Sonatas won the annual Golden Diapason award and was selected among the best recordings of the year by the French newspaper *Le monde*.

Idil Biret has completed the recording of the Etudes of György Ligeti and the piano transcription of Stravinsky's *Firebird*. Her latest project is recording Beethoven's thirty-two Sonatas for the piano.

Biret has been a major influence on the musical life in Turkey. Generations of young people were encouraged by her example and chose music as their profession. Such younger Turkish pianists like Gulsin Onay, Huseyin Sermet, Fazil Say, Ozgur Aydin, and lately Emre Elivar followed the example of Biret toward international reputation.

See also GENDER: GENDER AND EDUCATION; MUSIC.

Bibliography

Idil Biret web site. Available from <http://www.idilbiret.org>.

FILIZ ALI

BIRTH CONTROL

Control or regulation of conception and birth, either to limit population growth, to increase births among particular populations, or to enable conception through medical intervention.

The terms *birth control* and *family planning* (in the sense of limiting births) and the concept of population reduction are controversial in the Middle East. Population, its growth, reduction, and control are at the heart of some of the region's most volatile political conflicts, such as the Arab–Israel conflict and the civil war in Lebanon, a country founded on the notion of proportional power-sharing between Christians and Muslims. Issues related to birth control and contraception also serve as lightning rods for some of the sharper social, cultural, and ideological controversies in the contemporary Middle East, particularly those centering on secular versus religious modes of organization and frames of meaning, women's rights, and the tension between individual and collective rights. In attempting to alter, influence, or control the literal and figurative reproduction of the family as the region's basic social institution and moral structure, birth-control policies straddle political, moral, and religious fault lines, highlighting contending sources of authority and revealing ongoing challenges of national integration and identity in the region.

Advocated by the state and international organizations, birth-reduction campaigns usually target impoverished, powerless, and marginalized groups, thus drawing attention to long-standing socioeconomic inequalities and class-based tensions in major cities such as Cairo, Tehran, and Istanbul. But birth control is not only imposed from above or beyond the contemporary Middle East—it is also chosen in increasing numbers by those living in the region as part of a larger trend toward claiming rights, taking control of personal health and the body, and domestic decision making and financial planning for families' futures. As a facet of projects designed to ensure women's increasing agency in and control over their own lives, birth control has drawn the attention and earned the censure of conservative religious authorities, be they Christian, Muslim, or Jewish.

Manipulating Population Growth

Population growth results from increased birth rates and falling mortality rates, as well as migration. In the major cities of the Middle East, rapid urbanization and dramatic population increases have been a common feature of the last sixty years. Most countries in the region have just attained, or soon will attain, the demographic transition—the stage at which birth rates slow down to replacement levels, death rates having dropped earlier. Rapid population increases in the Middle East have affected patterns of urbanization, labor, and immigration, and have often strained the provision of education, health, and social services in resource-poor countries. For many, state-sponsored policies encouraging birth control symbolize interference in family matters and the negation of such traditional values as the importance of marriage and family. Women's control over their own bodies and their own fertility, afforded by birth control, conflicts with some communities' values concerning the importance of women's chastity, their role in the home, and their status as mothers and nurturers. Others view contraceptive technology as an important tool in areas ranging from national development policy to a woman's safeguarding of her health.

Although the region shares a common culture and a dominant religion (Islam), variations of geography and resource allocation have generated different policy responses to population growth. Whereas some countries seek to limit their populations, others seek to increase theirs. Egypt, Iran, Turkey, Tunisia, Lebanon, and Morocco, lacking a sufficient resource base to support their growing and largely young populations, have supported national family-planning programs designed to reduce population growth. Saudi Arabia, Kuwait, Libya, Iraq, and the Gulf oil states, on the other hand, lack sufficient populations to supply their labor needs and have had pronatalist (probirth) policies. Israel also has a pronatalist policy for its Jewish population, and actively encourages Jewish women to have many children. This policy, however, does not extend to Israel's Arab citizens, who, representing 20 percent of Israel's population, have a higher birth rate and a younger median age than do Israeli Jews. Assisted conception and infertility treatments in Israel are the most advanced in the region, and state subsidies render these services affordable for all Israeli citizens, Arabs and Jews alike.

Overall, the rapid growth of population in the Middle East is a matter of concern within as well as beyond the region. In 1993 the population of the Middle East was approximately 360 million; by 2025 it is expected to reach 700 million. The region's population is young: 41 percent are under 15

years of age. Fears that resources, particularly water, may not stretch to support populations have prompted many governments to make contraceptive use an integral part of their public-health programs and to mount campaigns to encourage the use of family-planning techniques and mechanisms. Yet, women's fertility rates are often influenced more by educational levels and employment than by access to birth-control pills, intrauterine devices, or condoms. Women's status and life possibilities greatly shape their reproductive behavior; women who complete high school and college tend to marry later, and thus give birth to fewer children. Trends toward later marriage in most countries of the region (with the exception of the Occupied Palestinian territories, Yemen, and Oman) should translate into lower birth rates in the coming decades.

Demographic evidence suggests that disease, poverty, and warfare combined to keep population figures relatively even and stable until the beginning of the twentieth century. The population of the central Middle East (excluding North Africa) is estimated to have been around 40 million at the beginning of the twentieth century. By 1950 it had doubled to 80 million (1993, 265 million; 1999, 380 million). Explosive growth followed the end of World War II, when greater emphasis upon public sanitation and healthcare reduced the death rate while the birth rate remained high. In the early 1960s Gamal Abdel Nasser of Egypt and Habib Bourguiba of Tunisia were the first national leaders to appreciate the potentially negative relationship between unrestricted population growth and socioeconomic development, and they feared that the resulting pressure could spur political unrest. The family-planning programs they initiated encountered opposition, but since about 1970 their programs, along with those of Lebanon, Turkey, Morocco, and Iran, have achieved limited success.

Cultural, Political, and Religious Opposition to Family Planning

Opposition has come from political, military, religious, and cultural quarters. Both the culture of the Middle East and the religions of the area—Islam, Christianity, and Judaism—encourage marriage and family. The term *birth control (tahdid al-nasl)* is considered highly perjorative because it connotes preventing the birth of children. Less objectionable

Egyptian women wait to see a doctor at a birth control clinic in Cairo. Information is available on contraception, family planning, and other female health issues. © PETER TURNLEY/CORBIS. REPRODUCED BY PERMISSION.

terms are *tanzim al-usra* and *takhtit al-aʾila* (family planning), which connote organization and ordering rather than the outright limitation of progeny. Nations of the Middle East have historically sought to augment their strength against enemies by increasing their numbers. To many, birth control is suspect and assumed to be another facet of Western imperialism in disguise; family-planning programs are often considered Western impositions designed to weaken the Middle East.

Political parties and nationalist groups throughout the Middle East affirm that having children constitutes a national duty in order to supply a large population base for military endeavors. Following heavy military losses at the end of the Iran–Iraq War in 1988, both Iran and Iraq emphasized pronatalist policies. Competition among Middle Eastern nations for regional prominence has led them to discourage family planning and advocate high birth rates. National, ethnic, or religious factionalism of-

ten translates into lack of support for family planning as each group seeks to enlarge its numbers. European Community governments decided in the 1990s to attack root problems of immigration from the Middle East by initiating programs supporting family planning in North Africa.

Most of the major religious traditions of the area hold that contraception is permitted. Christians are divided on its permissibility. The traditions of Judaism differ, but largely consider it permissible. Islamic jurisprudence condemns a pre-Islamic form of birth control, *waʿd* (exposure of female infants), but, reasoning from *hadith* texts, Islam does permit contraceptive use as analogous to coitus interruptus (*azl*). This is a personal, mutual decision of the husband and wife. Muslim opponents of contraception see it as murdering a potential creation of God and as a denial of the will (*irada*) and sustaining power (*rizq*) of God. Furthermore, Islam acknowledges the importance of and the right to sexual fulfillment for both men and women, and thus does not teach that reproduction is the sole or primary justification for marital intercourse.

The continuing importance of family in the Middle East has proved to be the largest obstacle to family planning. Because the status of both spouses, particularly the wife, depends upon the birth of children, family-planning programs have had difficulty encouraging both men and women to consider contraceptive use. One important support has been the Qur'an's injunction to nurse children for two years, and most women appreciate the risks of becoming pregnant while nursing. The spacing of children as an important contributor to a mother's health is becoming better understood. Children have traditionally been seen as providing economic support for the family and, in the absence of social-security programs, are considered guarantors of parents' financial security in their old age. Finally, children are loved and valued as a true blessing and a gift from God in all the faith traditions and cultures of the region.

Contraception

The most common methods of contraception used by women in the Middle East are birth-control pills and intrauterine devices (IUDs). Concern over sexually transmitted diseases and AIDS has led to increased use and availability of condoms. Much interest has been shown in injectable or implantable contraceptives. Nonreversible sterilization for men or women is prohibited by Islam. Tubal ligations, however, are increasingly common, and because new medical technology makes the procedure reversible, they can be considered religiously permissible. Abortion is frowned upon but permitted in particular situations, mostly those in which the mother's life is threatened. The majority of states ban abortion except when the health of the mother is endangered, at which point responsibility devolves onto the woman's doctor. Tunisia permits abortion.

Family planning and contraception in the Middle East was the subject of worldwide attention and debate at the 1994 International Conference on Population and Development (ICPD) in Cairo. That gathering, as well as the other United Nations conferences held in the 1990s—the 1995 Beijing Conference, the 1999 five-year review of the ICPD (ICPD+5), and the 2000 five-year review of the Beijing Conference (Beijing+5)—witnessed an alliance of conservative Catholic and Muslim religious authorities joining forces to oppose and restrict Middle Eastern women's right to control their own bodies and sexuality.

See also GENDER: GENDER AND HEALTH; GENDER: GENDER AND LAW; MEDICINE AND PUBLIC HEALTH.

Bibliography

Ali, Kamram Asdar. *Planning the Family in Egypt: New Bodies, New Selves.* Austin: University of Texas Press, 2002.

Badran, Margot. *Feminists, Islam, and Nation: Gender and the Making of Modern Egypt.* Princeton, NJ: Princeton University Press, 1995.

Bayes, Jane H., and Tohidi, Nayrereh. "Introduction." In *Globalization, Gender, and Religion: The Politics of Women's Rights in Catholic and Muslim Contexts,* edited by Jane H. Bayes and Nayereh Tohidi. New York: Palgrave, 2001.

Ethelston, Sally. "Water and Women: The Middle East in Demographic Transition." *Middle East Report* 213 (Winter 1999): 6–10.

Inhorn, Marcia. *Infertility and Patriarchy: The Cultural Politics of Gender and Family Life in Egypt.* Philadelphia: University of Pennsylvania Press, 2002.

Inhorn, Marcia. *Quest for Conception: Gender, Infertility, and Egyptian Medical Traditions.* Philadelphia: University of Pennsylvania Press, 2002.

Kahn, Susan Martha. *Reproducing Jews: A Cultural Account of Assisted Conception in Israel.* Durham, NC: Duke University Press, 2000.

Kanaaneh, Rhoda A. *Birthing the Nation: Strategies of Palestinian Women in Israel.* Berkeley: University of California Press, 2002.

Musallam, Basim. *Sex and Society in Islam.* Cambridge, U.K.: Cambridge University Press, 1983.

Omran, Abdel-Rahim. "The Middle East Population Puzzle." *Population Bulletin* 48, no. 1 (July 1993): 1–40.

Omran, Abdel-Rahim. *Population Problems and Prospects in the Arab World.* New York: United Nations Fund for Population Activities, 1984.

Weeks, John R. "The Demography of Islamic Nations." *Population Bulletin* 43, no. 4 (December 1988): 1–54.

DONNA LEE BOWEN
UPDATED BY LAURIE KING-IRANI

BIR ZEIT UNIVERSITY

Palestinian university.

Founded in 1924 as a primary school on the West Bank, the school began to offer secondary education in 1930. In 1942, the institution became known as Bir Zeit College, and provided instruction above secondary level in the 1950s. In 1972, the name of the institution officially became Bir Zeit University. Students earn degrees in arts, commerce and economics, engineering sciences, and, since 1995, graduate degrees in fields such as Arabic studies and international studies.

Bir Zeit University became a center of anti-Israel activism in the 1970s and 1980s, with student groups becoming increasingly involved in Palestinian politics. Israeli authorities have viewed the university as a center for militancy. After the outbreak of the Intifada in December 1987, classes were disrupted, and the university closed during curfews imposed by Israel's military authorities. The university remained closed from 1988 to 1992. More than 5,000 students were enrolled in the 2001–2002 academic year, although closures and curfews have continued to disrupt classes.

See also INTIFADA (1987–1991); PALESTINE; PALESTINIANS; WEST BANK.

Bibliography

Fischbach, Michael R. "Bir Zeit University." In *Encyclopedia of the Palestinians*. New York: Facts On File, 2002.

Kimmerling, Baruch, and Migdal, Joel S. *Palestinians: The Making of a People*. New York: Free Press, 1993.

Morris, Benny. *1948 and After: Israel and the Palestinians*. Oxford: Oxford University Press, 1991.

LAWRENCE TAL

BISHARA, ABDULLAH

[1936–]

Kuwaiti diplomat, lecturer, and columnist.

Abdullah Bishara was born in Kuwait and educated in Cairo, Oxford, and New York. A diplomat since 1964, he was Kuwait's ambassador and permanent representative to the United Nations from 1971 to 1981, representing Kuwait on the Security Council in 1978 and 1979. From 1981 to 1993 he was the secretary-general of the Gulf Cooperation Council

and a member of its Supreme Advisory Assembly from 1998 to 2004. Beginning in April 1993, Bishara served as special adviser to the deputy prime minister and minister of foreign affairs in Kuwait, commenting frequently on current issues in the press. In 2003 he became a Commander of the British Empire and published his second book.

See also GULF COOPERATION COUNCIL; KUWAIT.

LES ORDEMAN
UPDATED BY MARY ANN TÉTREAULT

BISHARA, SUHA

[1968–]

Communist activist.

Born in the village of Dayr Mimas in South Lebanon, Suha Bishara joined the Lebanese Communist Party in her teens. She became famous in 1989 when she attempted to assassinate the Israeli-appointed head of the South Lebanon Army (a militia founded by Israel during its occupation of South Lebanon), Antoine Lahad. After the assassination attempt, which left Lahad seriously wounded, Bishara was incarcerated and tortured in the notorious Khiyam prison. She was kept in solitary confinement for six years and was released in 1998. Lebanese filmmaker Randa Shahhal Sabbagh made a documentary about Bishara's experience, titled *Suha: Surviving Hell*. Bishara settled in Paris, where she published her memoirs and took classes in Hebrew. Bishara became a folk heroine in Lebanon, and the communist movement took pride in her role. She, however, now avoids the limelight, living in Switzerland in 2003. Bishara has stressed the nationalistic dimensions of her political actions, and seems to have played down the role of communist ideology in her political motives.

See also LAHAD, ANTOINE.

Bibliography

Bechara, Soha. *Resistance: My Life for Lebanon*. Brooklyn, NY: Soft Skull Press, 2003.

AS'AD ABUKHALIL

BISITUN

Important archaeological site in western Iran (also Behistun; Bagestana; Bisutun).

On a limestone cliff in Lorestan province, Iran, is a ruined town and a monument to Darius the Great (550–486 B.C.E.), consisting of sculpture and cuneiform inscriptions that are considered the "Rosetta Stone of Asia" (its deciphering by Henry Rawlinson in 1846 led to our knowledge of Assyrian and Babylonian). Carved in 520 B.C.E., it shows Darius and two companions facing nine defeated rebels, accompanied by an inscription in Elamite, Old Persian, and Babylonian describing Darius's restoration of the Persian monarchy.

The site also contains remains of various epochs, notably Hellenistic and Parthian rock reliefs and a rock-cut terrace (called Teras-e Farhad) of Kosrow I and three capitals from his palace. A modern village of the same names exists at the base of the cliff.

See also IRAN.

Bibliography

Schmitt, Rüdiger. *The Bisitun Inscriptions of Darius the Great* (Old Persian text). London: School of Oriental and African Studies for Corpus Inscriptionum Iranicarum, 1991.

Voigtlander, Elizabeth N. von. *The Bisitun Inscription of Darius the Great* (Babylonian). London: Lund Humphries for Corpus Inscriptionum Iranicarum, 1978.

A. SHAPUR SHAHBAZI

BITAR, SALAH AL-DIN AL-
[1912–1980]

Syrian politician.

Born to a traditional and religious family from the Maydan quarter in Damascus, Salah al-Din al-Bitar studied physics at Damascus University and then in Paris. While studying in Paris from 1929 to 1934 he met Michel Aflaq and the two men became inseparable. Back to Damascus, Bitar started teaching physics at one of the city's most prestigious schools. In 1935 he coedited a left-wing weekly magazine, the *Vanguard*, which was known for its revolutionary views. He cofounded the Baʿth Party and was elected secretary-general during the first congress, which took place in a coffee shop in Damascus in 1947. He was elected to parliament for the first time in 1954 and served as foreign minister in 1957. In these capacities Bitar, along with Baʿthist colleagues, played a key role in the forging of the United Arab

Republic. He was appointed minister of state for Arab affairs and minister of national guidance in the United Arab Republic. After the coup that brought the Baʿthist, Nasserist, and independent officers to power in March 1963, Bitar served more than once as prime minister, but his influence was fading away until his arrest in the wake of the February 1966 coup in which the leftist/military faction of the Baʿth Party, best known as the Neo-Baʿth, seized power.

Exiled to Lebanon, Bitar distanced himself from the Iraqi faction of the Baʿth led by Aflaq, who also had been expelled from Syria by the Neo-Baʿthists. Bitar settled in Paris, where he started publishing a magazine called *Arab Resurrection*. Although he was sentenced to death by the Neo-Baʿthists in absentia in 1969, he was pardoned and was granted a visit to Syria in 1978 where he met then Syrian president Hafiz al-Asad. He was assassinated in Paris in 1980, presumably by the Syrian regime although the identity of his assassin has never been confirmed. Unlike Aflaq, Bitar was not an ideologue or philosopher and he did not leave any written work. He was known for his arid and reserved manner and did not enjoy the same popularity in the party as did Aflaq. He is mostly remembered for the editorial he wrote on the eve of his assassination in which he asked the Syrian people for forgiveness for all the mistakes the Baʿth Party had made.

See also AFLAQ, MICHEL; ASAD, HAFIZ AL-; BAʿTH, AL-; UNITED ARAB REPUBLIC (UAR).

Bibliography

Devlin, John. *The Baʿth Party: A History from Its Origins to 1966.* Stanford, CA: Stanford Hoover Institution Press, 1976.

Jaber, Kamel Abu. *The Arab Baʿth Socialist Party: History, Ideology, and Organization.* Syracuse, NY: Syracuse University Press, 1966.

BITAT, RABAH
[1927–2000]

Algerian revolutionary, government minister, and president of Assemblée Nationale Populaire (ANP).

Rabah Bitat was a founder of the Front de Libération Nationale (FLN) and is regarded as one of the nine historic chiefs of the Algerian revolution. The French captured Bitat and he remained in detention until the end of the Algerian war of independence in 1962.

Bitat first supported, then opposed, Ahmed Ben Bella. He held the transportation portfolio under Houari Boumédienne before becoming the first president of the ANP (by the constitution of 1976). Bitat served as acting president (December 1978–February 1979) after Boumédienne's death in December 1978. Bitat returned to the ANP following Chadli Bendjedid's election. After the October 1988 riots, Bendjedid's accelerated reforms compounded by a declining dinar alienated Bitat, who resigned in protest in 1990. He remained a critic within FLN circles. His wife was Zohra Drif, a heroine of the Battle of Algiers. Bitat died in 2000.

See also Algerian War of Independence; Algiers, Battle of (1956–1957); Ben Bella, Ahmed; Bendjedid, Chadli; Boumédienne, Houari; Front de Libération Nationale.

Bibliography

Naylor, Phillip C., and Heggoy, Alf A. *The Historical Dictionary of Algeria,* 2d edition. Metuchen, NJ: Scarecrow Press, 1994.

Phillip C. Naylor

BITTARI, ZOUBIDA
[1937–]

Pseudonym of Algerian novelist Louise Ali-Rachedi.

Zoubida Bittari, an Algerian, has written a single autobiographical novel. She was born in Algiers, to a Muslim family of modest means who withdrew her from school at age twelve in order to marry her to a man of their choice. After her divorce at age fourteen, she left Algeria to work for a French family in France. While there she wrote *O Mes Soeurs Musulmanes, Pleurez!* (1964; Oh! My Muslim sisters, weep!). The book relates the story of a young married woman at odds with her in-laws. She sees her dreams of freedom crushed as a result of her marriage. The highly melodramatic book analyzes the situation of women from the colonial position.

Bibliography

Badran, Margot, and Cooke, Miriam, eds. *Opening the Gates: A Century of Arab Feminist Writing.* Bloomington: University of Indiana Press, 1990.

Gordon, David C. *Women of Algeria: An Essay on Change.* Cambridge, MA: Harvard University Press, 1968.

Aida A. Bamia

BITTON, SIMONE
[1955–]

Moroccan-French-Israeli documentary film director, prominent in Arab-Jewish peace activities.

Born in Rabat, Morocco, Simone Bitton emigrated to Israel with her family at the age of twelve. At sixteen she became a supporter of the radical Mizrahi Black Panthers movement and the left-wing party Matzpen. After national service in the Israeli army, Bitton left for film school in Paris. The 1982 massacres at Sabra and Shatila provoked her into an activist career of making films, writing articles, and directing conferences that highlighted the plight of the Palestinians and Sephardim (Jews native to the Middle East, also known as Mizrahim), who are also, in her view, victims of Zionism. She founded the Mizrahi peace group Perspectives Judéo-Arabes, and was a key organizer of the historic 1989 meeting between Mizrahi Jews and Palestinians in Toledo, Spain. Her films include *Citizen Bishara; Ben Barka: The Moroccan Equation; The Bombing; Mahmoud Darwish: As the Land Is the Language; Arafat Daily; PLO: the Dialogue Desk; Daney/Sanbar: North-South Conversation; Palestine: Story of a Land; Great Voices of Arabic Music: Um Kulthum, Muhammad Abdel Wahab, and Farid al-Atrache; Chouf Le Look; Life Beyond Them; Between Two Wars* (in Hebrew, *Yoredet*); *Mothers; Nissim and Cherie;* and *Solange Giraud, Born Tache.*

See also Adot ha-Mizrah.

Bibliography

Elazar, Daniel. "A Sephardi Zionist in Wonderland." Jerusalem Center for Public Affairs. Available from <http://www.jcpa.org>.

George R. Wilkes

BIZERTE

Northern Tunisian seaport situated between a large inland lake and the Mediterranean Sea.

Although a settlement had existed on the site of Bizerte since Phoenician times, the town first attained significance in the sixteenth century when an influx of Moorish and Jewish refugees from Roman

Encyclopedia of THE MODERN MIDDLE EAST AND NORTH AFRICA 483

Catholic Andalusia (Spain) spurred both agricultural and artisanal development. Like other North African seaports, Bizerte served as a base for Barbary corsairs of the Barbary states and their raids against European ships. In retaliation, Spanish forces seized and fortified the city in 1535. Troops of the Ottoman Empire recaptured it briefly in 1572, but definitively only in 1574 when its garrison was sent to defend the more important Spanish positions at Tunis. Throughout the seventeenth century, Bizerte's economy continued to depend almost exclusively on the raiding of its corsairs.

France set up a trading post at Bizerte in 1738 as one of a string of such establishments along the Algerian and Tunisian coasts. Although poor relations between French merchants and the Tunisian government led to the post's temporary closing in 1741 and 1742, it operated until Ali Bey evicted the French in 1770. This, plus French anger over corsair forays staged from Bizerte, led to a naval bombardment that badly damaged the city. A similar attack by a Venetian fleet in 1785 all but destroyed Bizerte. Despite these hostilities, Marseilles merchants continued to import wheat from Bizerte, especially during the French Revolution and the Napoleonic Wars. In 1789, a French consulate opened there.

The Tunisian government's renunciation of corsair activity in 1819 hurt Bizerte, but the silting up of the port was an even more serious problem, causing a steady decline in commercial activity in the first half of the nineteenth century. At the same time, however, Tunisia was being drawn into a more extensive relationship with Europe. A telegraph line linking Tunisia with Algeria and France passed through Bizerte in the 1850s, and the city was the starting point for a submarine cable that opened communications with Italy in 1864.

Following the Treaty of Bardo (1881), which established a strong French presence in Tunisia, the canal connecting the lake with the sea was improved. This, and other extensive French public-works projects in Bizerte in the 1880s and 1890s, made its harbor and port facilities among the finest in the Mediterranean. Much of this work revolved around the creation of a French naval base and arsenal, which, by the turn of the twentieth century, were widely regarded as among the largest

and most powerful in the Mediterranean. During World War II, this base, and its proximity to the narrow channel between Sicily and Africa joining the eastern and western Mediterranean basins, gave Bizerte great strategic importance. The city was occupied by the Axis immediately following the Anglo–American landings in Morocco and Algeria in 1942. Allied air raids destroyed 70 percent of Bizerte prior to its liberation in the following year, but the canal remained intact and the base became a jumping-off point for the successful Allied invasion of Sicily.

France retained control of the naval facilities at Bizerte after Tunisian independence (1955–1956) and refused to accede to demands for their evacuation in 1961. France's attempts to break a blockade of the base led to violent confrontations with hastily mobilized Tunisian civilians and paramilitary units. Tunisia appealed to the United Nations, which called for negotiations on the base's future. Only after lengthy delays did France agree to abandon the installation in late 1963.

In the years since Tunisian independence, Bizerte and other cities around its lake have become major industrial centers, while the port remains the country's primary import–export terminal. The 2002 population was estimated at 527,400.

See also CORSAIRS; TUNIS; TUNISIA.

KENNETH J. PERKINS

BIZERTE CRISIS (1961)

Tunisian blockade of French naval base at Bizerte.

Tunisia imposed a blockade on France's naval base at Bizerte in July 1961, hoping to force its evacuation. French soldiers broke the blockade and gained control of most of the city in fierce fighting with hastily mobilized Tunisian civilians and paramilitary units. Tunisia appealed to the United Nations, which called for a negotiated settlement. French troops remained in occupation of the city until autumn, while the base itself was not abandoned until late in 1963, following the conclusion of the Algerian War.

See also ALGERIAN WAR OF INDEPENDENCE; BIZERTE.

Bibliography

Ruf, Werner. "The Bizerte Crisis: A Bourguibist Attempt to Resolve Tunisia's Border Problem." *Middle East Journal* 25 (1971): 201–211.

KENNETH J. PERKINS

BLACK PANTHERS

An Israeli protest movement of second-generation Middle Eastern immigrants, mostly Moroccan.

The Black Panthers aimed at improving material conditions in Israel in Middle Eastern Jewish communities *(adot ha-mizrah).* Erupting briefly as street demonstrations in Jerusalem and Tel Aviv, in 1971, the movement attracted publicity. The name, taken from the U.S. black-pride movement, was chosen to shock Israelis out of complacency. The movement led to improved community services and some activists began their political careers.

See also ISRAEL; MIZRAHI MOVEMENT.

SHLOMO DESHEN

BLACK SEA

Large inland saltwater sea between Turkey on the south and Ukraine on the north, connected to the Mediterranean Sea.

About 180,000 square miles (466,000 sq. km.), the Black Sea is connected to the Aegean Sea, the northeast arm of the Mediterranean Sea, by the Turkish Straits (the Dardanelles, the Sea of Marmara, and the Bosporus). Until the late eighteenth century, the Black Sea was controlled almost entirely by the Ottoman Empire, but the sea was opened to Russia in the Treaty of Kuçuk Kaynara (1774). Over the next century and a half, the Russians and the Ottoman Turks vied for control of the Black Sea. The Ottoman Empire attempted to keep Russia from establishing a military presence in the Black Sea, and the Russians attempted to push the Ottomans ever southward and prevent access to the Black Sea by the other European powers through the Turkish Straits. Control of the straits remained a live issue well into the twentieth century. After World War II, Josef Stalin, USSR premier, unsuccessfully pressured Turkey to revise the 1936 Montreux Convention, which barred belligerents from the straits and hence limited the ability of the USSR

to use the Black Sea as a naval base. The Black Sea is also a major commercial shipping region. It is thus a vital economic link between Eastern Europe, Russia and other states of the former USSR, Turkey, and the states of western Central Asia, as well as a link between these states and the countries of the Mediterranean and the world.

See also MONTREUX CONVENTION (1936); OTTOMAN EMPIRE; STRAITS, TURKISH.

Bibliography

Lenczowski, George. *The Middle East in World Affairs,* 4th edition. Ithaca, NY: Cornell University Press, 1980.

Shaw, Stanford, and Shaw, Ezel Kural. *History of the Ottoman Empire and Modern Turkey.* 2 vols. Cambridge, U.K., and New York: Cambridge University Press, 1976–1977.

ZACHARY KARABELL

BLACK SEPTEMBER

A Palestinian terrorist group that grew out of the defeat of the Palestinians in the September 1970 Jordanian civil war.

Black September is generally believed to have been established by elements of al-Fatah in the autumn of 1971 as a result of pressure from groups like the Popular Front for the Liberation of Palestine to wage a more radical war against the Palestinians' enemies. The group took its name from the term used by some Palestinians to describe their military defeat during the Jordanian Civil War of 1970. It is widely believed that Black September was the creation of al-Fatah's intelligence chief Salah Khalaf (a.k.a. Abu Iyad), who recruited Ali Hasan Salama as its operational mastermind. Al-Fatah always denied any connection with the organization, and many details about the group remain unclear. The shadowy group's first strikes were aimed against Jordanian targets; they included the assassination of Prime Minister Wasfi al-Tall in Cairo in November 1971.

Black September's most dramatic attack involved seizing eleven Israeli athletes as hostages at the September 1972 Olympic Games in Munich. All the athletes and five Black September operatives later died during a gun battle with the West German police. Black September was also at the forefront of an underground war of assassination between the Israelis and the Palestinians that was carried out in Europe and the Middle East. In March 1973, Black September terrorists seized guests at a diplomatic reception at the Saudi embassy in Sudan in March 1973, and later murdered the U.S. ambassador. No actions were carried out in Black September's name thereafter.

See also FATAH, AL-; JORDANIAN CIVIL WAR (1970–1971); KHALAF, SALAH; POPULAR FRONT FOR THE LIBERATION OF PALESTINE; TALL, WASFI AL-.

Bibliography

Bar Zohar, Michael, and Haber, Eitan. *The Quest for the Red Prince: Israel's Relentless Manhunt for One of the World's Deadliest and Most Wanted Arab Terrorists.* New York: The Lyon's Press, 2002.

Cooley, John K. *Green March, Black September: The Story of the Palestinian Arabs.* London: Frank Cass, 1973.

Reeve, Simon. *One Day in September: The Full Story of the 1972 Munich Olympics Massacre and the Israeli Revenge Operation "Wrath of God."* New York: Arcade Books, 2001.

Sayigh, Yezid. *Armed Struggle and the Search for State: The Palestinian National Movement, 1949–1993.* Oxford: Clarendon Press, 1997.

STEVE TAMARI
UPDATED BY MICHAEL R. FISCHBACH

BLACK SPRING

A violent uprising, from April to August 2001, against state security forces in the northeastern Algerian region of Kabylia.

Between April and August 2001, the Kabyle provinces in northeastern Algeria witnessed a violent uprising of local youth against national gendarmes that has become known as the Black Spring. On 18 April, high school student Massinissah Guermah died of gunshot wounds received while in police custody in the village of Beni Douala, on the outskirts of Tizi-Ouzou. Occurring on the eve of the twenty-first anniversary of the Berber Spring—the 1980 insurrection of Kabyle students for Berber cultural and linguistic rights—and in a civil war context of violence and socioeconomic marginalization, Guermah's death transformed a generalized sense of despair into one of explicit outrage against the state

and drew thousands of male youths into the streets throughout the region. "Refusing pardon" to Guermah's "assassins," they attacked state security forces and government buildings with rocks and homemade Molotov cocktails. The gendarmes responded with tear gas and live ammunition, launching a four-month cycle of protest and violent repression in which over one hundred local residents were killed and as many as five hundred injured.

The Black Spring brought about the emergence of a new political actor, the Coordination des Archs (CADC), which quickly became the principal Kabyle representative in the ongoing dialogue with the state. Whereas the institutionalized Kabyle political parties had failed to control the conflict, this informal committee of village and tribal assemblies succeeded in directing a series of general strikes and a 500,000-person Black March in Tizi-Ouzou on 21 May.

See also BERBER SPRING; COORDINATION DES ARCHS (ALGERIA); KABYLIA; RASSEMBLEMENT POUR LA CULTURE ET LA DÉMOCRATIE (RCD).

Bibliography

Silverstein, Paul. "'No Pardon': Rage and Revolt in Kabylia." *Middle East Insight* 16, no. 4 (2001): 61–65.

PAUL SILVERSTEIN

BLACK THURSDAY (1978)

Tunisian riots between government forces and striking workers over a sagging economy.

On 26 January 1978, demonstrations organized by the Union Générale des Travailleurs Tunisiens (UGTT; General Union of Tunisian Workers) in Tunis led to clashes between state security forces and striking workers. Scores of demonstrators were killed and injured, and hundreds of UGTT members, including its leadership under Habib Achour, were arrested. The demonstrations were organized to protest a worsening economic crisis in Tunisia brought on by state policies as framed in the Five-Year Plan of 1973–1977.

See also ACHOUR, HABIB; TUNISIA.

Bibliography

Perkins, Kenneth. *Tunisia: Crossroads of the Islamic and European Worlds.* Boulder, CO: Westview, 1986.

MATTHEW S. GORDON

BLED AL-SIBA/BLED AL-MAKHZAN

A theory recognizing the pragmatic governance of a multicultural society.

French colonial theorists developed the idea that pre-colonial Morocco consisted of two areas, *bled al-makhzan,* the land of government, where the sultan ruled over plains and cities and collected taxes more securely, and *bled al-siba,* the many Berber mountainous areas where the sultan was relatively powerless. The use of the term *makhzan* (treasury) for the government clearly showed the relationship between taxation and authority. The sultan's authority over *siba* areas, they said, was confined to his religious role. The *makhzan–siba* division laid the theoretical basis, under the protectorate, of a system of "indirect rule," under which the Berber areas would be administered separately from the Arab-speaking areas, supposedly in accordance with their customary law. Arabic-speaking nationalists saw this as an attempt to "divide and rule." Nationalist historians pictured the sultan not as a powerless figurehead but as an arbitrator who stepped in to settle disputes in the mountainous and Berber areas, but who was otherwise content to allow these more remote and poor areas to use local systems to maintain order.

Bibliography

Hoffman, Bernard G. *The Structure of Traditional Moroccan Rural Society.* The Hague and Paris: Mouton, 1967.

C. R. PENNELL

BLISS, DANIEL
[1823–1916]

The American University of Beirut's first president.

Born in the United States, the Reverend Daniel Bliss came to Beirut in 1856, as one of a group of American Protestant missionaries sent to what was then called Syria. When in 1862 the mission decided to create a college in Beirut, he was given responsibility for raising money for the project in England and the United States. His success in doing so was one of the factors that made possible the establishment in Beirut in 1866 of the Syrian Protestant College, which later was renamed the American University of Beirut. He became the college's first president and retained that position until 1902, when he retired and was succeeded by his son, Howard Bliss.

See also AMERICAN UNIVERSITY OF BEIRUT (AUB); BLISS, HOWARD.

Bibliography

Bliss, Daniel. *Letters from a New Campus.* Beirut: American University of Beirut, 1994.

Bliss, Frederick. *The Reminiscences of Daniel Bliss.* New York: Revell, 1920.

Salibi, Kamal S. *The Modern History of Lebanon.* New York: Praeger, 1965.

GUILAIN P. DENOEUX

BLISS, HOWARD
[1860–1920]

Missionary and educator.

Howard Bliss's claim to fame is the role that he played in continuing the Bliss family Protestant missionary legacy in Beirut—namely, the founding and administration of the American University of Beirut, then known as the Syrian Protestant College. Born in 1860 in Suq al-Gharb during the bloody Maronite-Druze riots, Bliss learned at a young age how to cope with conflict and rise above it. Growing up as the son of the first president and founder of the college provided him with the wherewithal to successfully negotiate with rich and influential people. It is said, for instance, that he and his brother, Frederick, were close boyhood friends with Theodore Roosevelt. Thus, Bliss was able to use his friendship with Roosevelt to shore up the status of the Syrian Protestant College in Beirut and secure its official recognition by the Ottoman government in 1903.

Bliss grew up on the campus in Beirut but returned to the United States for his higher education. There he earned degrees from Amherst College (1882) and Union Theological Seminary (1887). He also studied in Oxford and Berlin, then returned to the United States to be ordained in the Congregational ministry in 1890. Bliss was pastor of the

Christian Union Congregational Church in New Jersey until 1902, when he returned to Beirut to take over the reins of the college from his father to serve as its second president.

At his death in 1920 Bliss was credited with steering the college through its most precarious years, which were marked by World War I and the vacuum following the demise of the Ottoman Empire, and the political and financial pressures that the war unleashed. Although the college officially did not become the American University of Beirut during his lifetime, Bliss is credited with having paved the way by modernizing the college and increasing the size of its non-Christian student body. Upon his death, the eminent scholar Philip Hitti eulogized him as "one who brought relief during the disastrous experiences of war, . . . irradiating idealism and democracy . . . and love for his fellow men."

See also AMERICAN UNIVERSITY OF BEIRUT (AUB); BLISS, DANIEL; PROTESTANTISM AND PROTESTANT MISSIONS.

Bibliography

Penrose, Stephen B. L., Jr. *That They May Have Life: The Story of the American University of Beirut, 1866–1841.* New York: Trustees of the American University of Beirut, 1941.

Sayah, Edward Nassif. "The American University of Beirut and its Educational Activities in Lebanon, 1920–1967." Ph.D. diss., University of North Texas, 1988.

KAREN PINTO

BLOC D'ACTION NATIONALE

See GLOSSARY

BLOOD LIBEL

See ANTISEMISTIM

BLUDAN CONFERENCES (1937, 1946)

Inter-Arab conferences convened in response to proposals for the solution of the Palestine question.

A conference was held on 8 to 10 September 1937 at the Syrian summer resort of Bludan, attended by more than 400 delegates (none an official government representative) from Syria, Palestine, Lebanon, Transjordan, Iraq, Egypt, and Saudi Arabia.

Formally organized by the Damascus Committee for the Defense of Palestine, it was in fact the brainchild of the mufti of Jerusalem, Hajj Muhammad Amin al-Husayni. The conference members turned down the Peel Commission's recommendation to divide Palestine into an Arab and a Jewish state, and rejected the idea of a Jewish state. They called for a boycott of Jewish goods and threatened to take similar measures against British interests if the British government endorsed the Peel recommendation. The conference was considered a landmark in external Arab involvement in Palestine affairs and an achievement for the mufti, who had made great endeavors for its realization.

A second conference was convened in Bludan in June 1946, when the Council of the Arab League met to discuss the report of the Anglo-American Committee of Inquiry. The participants criticized U.S. interference in the Palestine question, recommended an economic boycott of the Jews, and pledged to assist the Arabs of Palestine. The conference also adopted secret resolutions regarding Arab military intervention in Palestine as well as steps against British and U.S. interests, including cancellation of oil concessions.

See also HUSAYNI, MUHAMMAD AMIN AL-.

Bibliography

Hurewitz, J. C. *The Struggle for Palestine* (1950). New York: Schocken Books, 1976.

Kedourie, Elie. "The Bludan Congress on Palestine, September, 1937." *Middle Eastern Studies* 17, 1 (January 1981): 107–125.

Khalaf, Issa. *Politics in Palestine: Arab Factionalism and Social Disintegration, 1939–1948.* Albany: State University of New York Press, 1991.

Mattar, Philip. *The Mufti of Jerusalem: Al-Hajj Amin al-Husayni and the Palestinian National Movement.* New York: Columbia University Press, 1992.

ELIZABETH THOMPSON
UPDATED BY JOSEPH NEVO

BLUE MOSQUE

See SULTAN AHMET MOSQUE

BLUE SHIRTS

See WAFD

BLUM–VIOLLETTE PLAN

French legislation that intended to give Algerian Muslims full citizenship rights.

Influenced by ex-Governor General and then Minister of State Maurice Viollette, Pierre Viénot, and historian Charles-André Julien, France's Premier Léon Blum submitted a bill to Parliament in 1936 that aimed at giving approximately 30,000 Muslims in Algeria full rights without the loss of their Muslim status. The Senate defeated it in 1938 and the legislation was never brought to the floor of the Chamber of Deputies. This was a terrible blow to the évolués (assimilated Algerians) and convinced many of them (including Ferhat Abbas) to pursue other directions of reform. It has been called a "lost opportunity" that might have prevented the savage Algerian War of Independence (1954–1962).

See also ABBAS, FERHAT; ALGERIAN WAR OF INDEPENDENCE.

Bibliography

Gordon, David C. *The Passing of French Algeria.* London and New York: Oxford University Press, 1966.

PHILLIP C. NAYLOR

B'NAI B'RITH

The world's oldest and largest international Jewish service organization.

B'nai B'rith (Hebrew, "sons of the covenant") was founded by twelve Jewish immigrants of German descent in New York on 13 October 1843 to respond to the needs of Jewish communities worldwide. The organization has since created three major institutions that have played a key role in contemporary Jewish life worldwide: the Anti-Defamation League (1913); Hillel (1923), the largest Jewish campus organization worldwide; and the B'nai B'rith Youth Organization (1924), concerned with the problems posed by the assimilation of Jewish youth in the diaspora and still operating an extensive network of summer camps.

B'nai B'rith lodges were established in the Middle East, starting with the Maimonides Lodge in Cairo (1887) and the Eliahu Hanabi Lodge in Alexandria (1891), followed by lodges in Istanbul, Edirne, and Beirut (1911). The organization's central concern was and is the promotion and implementation of programs that allow for the appreciation and maintenance of "Jewish unity, Jewish security, and Jewish continuity" worldwide.

The organization has five centers that develop and implement its programs: the Center for Community Action; the Center for Jewish Identity, devoted to "the transmission of Jewish values, ethics, and knowledge"; the Center for Human Rights and Public Policy (CHRPP), serving as the organization's research and advocacy arm; the Center for Senior Services, making B'nai B'rith the world's largest operator of affordable housing for seniors; and the World Center, established in 1980 to serve as the organization's official center in Jerusalem.

Within the United States, the organization acts as a powerful lobbying group, seeking the continuation of support for Israel. B'nai B'rith's CHRPP lists among its concerns "the security and welfare of Israel, rising Islamic militancy, resurgent anti-semitism, Jewish renewal in Eastern Europe and the former Soviet Union, [and] the security and welfare of Jewish communities worldwide." The organization has criticized human rights organizations that oppose the policies of the state of Israel, condemned the position of the European Union toward Israel, and consistently denounced what the organization calls "prejudiced reporting" about Israel by the foreign media.

B'nai B'rith is the only Jewish nongovernmental organization to be accepted as part of the Organization of American States, and it maintains a visible presence in South American countries. After the disintegration of the Soviet Union, it supported the attempts on the part of the United States to establish stronger ties with the republics of Azerbaijan, Kazakhstan, Kyrgyzstan, and Uzbekistan.

Bibliography

B'nai Brith International. Available from <http://www.bnaibrith.org/>.

Ivers, Gregg. *To Build a Wall: American Jews and the Separation of Church and State.* Charlottesville: University Press of Virginia, 1995.

VANESA CASANOVA-FERNANDEZ

BNEI AKIVAH

See GUSH EMUNIM

BODRUM

Town in southwestern Turkey on the Anatolian shore of the Aegean Sea on a peninsula of the same name at the northern end of the Gulf of Kerme, opposite the Greek island of Kos.

It is said that Bodrum (Turkish for "underground vault" or "cellar") gets its name from the vaultlike ancient ruins that abound in the area. Originally it was called Halicarnassos by its first settlers, the Dorians from the Peloponnese (1000 B.C.E.). Bodrum was the birthplace of many famous Greek intellectuals, notably Herodotus (ca. 484–ca. 420 B.C.E.), who chronicled the struggle for control of the city's fortunes between Greece and Persia in his *Histories.* In 1402 the Knights of St. John came from Rhodes and built one of its most famous landmarks, the Castle of St. Peter. The peninsula was brought back into Ottoman rule in 1523 when Süleyman the Magnificent ousted the Knights of St. John from Rhodes, and consequently from Bodrum.

Bodrum is part of the present-day Turkish Riviera and is known for its historic sites, clement weather, colorful jazz bars, idyllic whitewashed houses, marina and yachting facilities, and its resident artist community. Celebrated novelist Cevatsakir Kabaağaçlu immortalized the lore and legends of the local seafarers in a collection of short stories.

The 2000 Turkish government census listed the urban population as 32,227 and 65,599 in outlying rural areas (97,826). A favorite vacation spot, the population varies greatly in the summer, with an annual number of visitors totaling 1.5 million between June and August.

Bibliography

Encyclopaedia of Islam, 2d edition. Leiden: E.J. Brill, 1960.

Republic of Turkey. "Prime Ministry State Institute of Statistics (SIS)." Available from <http://www.die.gov.tr/nufus_sayimi/2000Nufus_Kesin.htm>.

KAREN PINTO
UPDATED BY MARIA F. CURTIS

BOĞAZIÇI (BOSPORUS) UNIVERSITY

Public university in Istanbul, Turkey.

Founded in 1863 as Robert College, an American missionary school, Boğaziçi (Bosporus) University maintains English as the language of instruction even though its administration was transferred to the Turkish state in 1971. It comprises four faculties (engineering; arts and sciences; economics and administrative sciences; and education), the School of Foreign Languages, the College of Vocational Education, and four research institutes (modern Turkish history; biomedical engineering; environmental sciences; and earthquake research). In the 2002–2003 academic year, it had 956 faculty members and 9,731 students (4,027 of whom were female). Its budget for the year amounted to 46,479 billion Turkish liras, 99 percent of which came directly from the state funds.

Robert College was founded by Dr. Cyrus Hamlin, a U.S. missionary, with the initial support of Christopher Rheinlander Robert, a wealthy merchant and philanthropist. The school was administered and financed by a U.S. board of trustees in New York. Being a missionary establishment, it was not allowed by the Ottoman state to admit any Muslim students, but a small number of Muslims was secretly enrolled in the school at the turn of the century.

The school had an academy, or lower, division in addition to the college. Its School of Engineering opened in 1912. As consequence of the financial problems during the Great Depression, it was merged with the American College for Girls in 1932. The college was substantially reorganized in 1958 in accordance with the changes in the Turkish educational system. The School of Business Administration and the School of Sciences and Languages were established in 1959. The Turkish state, which had strictly regulated foreign schools in the country, conceded to the college's enlargement primarily due to the increasing influence of the United

States after the World War II. The college responded favorably to the government's expectations: Its The School of Business Administration provided well-educated managers for the booming private sector, and its innovative curriculum set a high standard for its counterparts. Nevertheless, financial difficulties, even more than the campus militancy of the 1960s, compelled the American board of trustees to turn over the college division to the Turkish state in 1971. The trustees, however, retained the administration of the high school, which still operates under the name of Robert Lycée.

In the 1970s, Boğaziçi University grew steadily, becoming an academically prestigious institution. In the 1980s, however, it was forced to increase its student intake at an unrealistic rate, as were all other universities. It remains one of the major universities in the country, but faces escalating competition from the other state universities, including Middle East Technical University and Istanbul Technical University, and from the private universities, including Bilkent University and Sabanci University. Boğaziçi University has close ties with Turkish business circles, and many of its graduates have taken up academic positions throughout Turkey, as well as in the Middle East, Europe, and the United States.

See also BILKENT UNIVERSITY; ISTANBUL TECH-NICAL UNIVERSITY; MIDDLE EAST TECHNICAL UNIVERSITY.

Bibliography

Boğaziçi University. Available from <http://www.boun.edu.tr/about/history.html>.

I. METIN KUNT
UPDATED BY BURÇAK KESKIN-KOZAT

BOGAZKÖY

City in Turkey on the site of the probable Hittite capital in central Anatolia.

Known as Hattushash (or Pteria, in Greek), today's Bogazköy was built over a site first inhabited by Hittites in the third millennium B.C.E. It was a major trading town and became the Hittite capital in the second millennium B.C.E. Thousands of clay tablets impressed with cuneiform writing have been excavated. The Hittite kingdom was extended into Syria, where a famous battle was fought with the Egyptians at Qadesh (near today's Homs) in 1285 B.C.E. By 1200 B.C.E., the Hittite Empire was destroyed by migrating tribes known as the "sea peoples."

ELIZABETH THOMPSON

BONAPARTE, NAPOLÉON
[1769–1821]

French general and emperor.

The ascendancy of Egypt on the modern world stage can be traced to the period of French occupation, 1798 to 1801. French armies under the command of General Napoléon Bonaparte landed at Abuqir Bay on 1 July 1798, stormed Alexandria the next day, and proceeded to Cairo. On 21 July 1798, outside the city, the French, although less than 30,000 strong, defeated a Mamluk army twice their number and occupied the city. Bonaparte's initial reason for the Egyptian expedition was to threaten Britain's supply line to India. Once in Egypt, however, he realized the advantage to France that an occupation would ensure and set about structuring a system of local government to that end.

Suggesting that he himself was intent on becoming a Muslim, Bonaparte tried to convince the Egyptians of the sincerity of his intentions regarding their country. Among his claimed intentions were the liberation of Egypt from the stranglehold of the Mamluks, the introduction of enlightened government responsive to local needs, and respect for Egyptian religious traditions. Not surprisingly, the Egyptians were quite wary of his conversion, although given his intellectual makeup, he may very likely have found in Islam appealing characteristics.

He appointed *diwans*, or councils, composed of *ulama* (Muslim legal scholars), to stabilize local government by giving French policies the sanction of the country's notables. Having established relatively good relations with the local population, Bonaparte set about threatening the Ottoman Porte and Britain through an expedition to Palestine. Defeated and decimated by cholera, his troops returned to Egypt. Bonaparte, informed of the changes in the French political winds, left his army in Egypt in the care of General Jacques Menou and returned to France in August 1799. Menou was forced to capitulate to an Anglo–Ottoman force in 1801; he and the army returned to France.

Though historians considered it a failure from a military perspective, Bonaparte's occupation of Egypt had great impact on the world of learning. One member of the expedition was Jean-François Champollion, whose discovery of the Rosetta Stone in the Nile delta permitted the deciphering of hieroglyphics and the development of Egyptology. The expedition also included dozens of artists as well as hundreds of social and natural scientists representing most of the academic disciplines. Their task was to catalog all the flora, fauna, and architecture—ancient and contemporary—of Egypt as they discovered it. To that end, once he established himself in Cairo, Bonaparte founded the Institut d'Egypte, whose purpose was to store and structure the immense body of newly discovered information. Between 1808 and 1829, the institute published the *Description de l'Egypte* in twenty-three enormous volumes of narrative and accompanying plates.

Certain recent scholarship has credited Bonaparte's expedition to Egypt with a development of dubious honor: orientalism. Originally considered the study of the Orient, "orientalism," in the postmodernist view, represents the textual deconstruction of the non-Western cultural heritage. The *Description de l'Egypte,* for instance, in laying bare the structure of Egyptian culture, may be seen as making that structure "vulnerable" to what such critics call Western "imposition."

See also CHAMPOLLION, JEAN-FRANÇOIS; MAMLUKS; MENOU, JACQUES FRANÇOIS.

Bibliography

Herold, J. Christopher. *Bonaparte in Egypt.* London: Harper and Row. 1962.

Jabarti, Abd al-Rahman al-. *Napoleon in Egypt: Al-Jabarti's Chronicle of the French Occupation, 1798,* translated by Shmuel Moreh. Princeton, NJ: M. Wiener, 1993.

JEAN-MARC R. OPPENHEIM

BORATAV, PERTEV NAILI
[1907–1998]

Turkish scholar, folklorist, translator, and editor.

Pertev Naili Boratav was born in Gümülcine (now Ziotigrad, in Bulgaria). He received his elementary education in Istanbul, where the family had moved upon the outbreak of the Balkan Wars in 1912, and in various provincial towns of Turkey. After attending the Kumkapi French School in Istanbul, he graduated from the Istanbul Lycée in 1927. He continued his studies at the Istanbul Faculty of Letters and at the Teachers Training College (1927–1930). After his graduation he taught at these institutions and the Konya Lycée. In 1936 and 1937, Boratav studied in Germany on a government scholarship, but he was called back because of his liberal and anti-Nazi views. Upon his return, he first worked at the library of the School of Political Science of Ankara University and in 1938 he became an associate professor of Turkish folk literature at the same university. He was promoted to full professor in 1946 and folklore studies became an independent department at Ankara University under his leadership. Boratav encouraged popular interest in folklore by editing *Halk Bilgisi Haberleri* (News of folk culture) and turning it into a major instrument of research on social and religious groups, nomadic tribes, agricultural methods, and other matters of interest to the villages.

Boratav always spoke out for academic freedom, freedom of the press, and human rights at a time of transition to multiparty democracy. There were, however, certain limits to liberalism in Turkey of his time, especially when the fear of communism was rapidly escalating. In 1948, he was one of four professors at Ankara University who lost their posts for spreading Marxist views. Boratav spent the next two years directing the establishment of the Turkish collection at the Hoover Institute at Stanford University. In 1952, he joined the Centre National de la Recherche Scientifique (National center for scientific research) in Paris, where he remained until his retirement in 1974. He continued his research and writing in France until his death in 1998.

Boratav succeeded in attracting global attention to Turkish folklore and literature and became a highly respected figure among the international scholarly circles. He produced various books and translations on the general studies of folklore. He also published several collections on Turkish folk genres and individual figures. With Wolfram Eberhard, he compiled Typen Türkischer Volksmörchen (1953), a significant milestone in Turkology studies for its employment of Aarne and Thompson standards. His works in French included *Contes Turcs* (1955) and his contributions on folk literature in *Philologiae Tur-*

cicae Fundamenta, II, edited by Jean Deny, et al. (Wiesbaden, 1965). His publications in Turkish were on the other hand far more numerous: *Zaman Zaman İçinde* (Once upon a time; 1958); *Az Gittik Uz Gittik* (We went a little, we went afar; 1969); *100 Soruda Türk Halk edebiyati* (Turkish folk literature in 100 questions; 1969); *100 Soruda Türk Folkloru* (Turkish folklore in 100 questions; 1973); *Ağitlar, Türküler, Destanlar* (Eulogies, folk songs, legends; 1980); *I, Nasruddin Hoca, Never Shall Die* (1999).

See also BALKAN WARS (1912–1913).

Bibliography

Başgöz, İlhan, and Glazer, Mark, eds. *Studies in Turkish Folklore in Honor of Pertev N. Boratav.* Bloomington: Indiana University Press, 1978.

Birkalan, Hande Ayşen. "Pertev Naili Boratav, Turkish Politics, and the University Events." *The Turkish Studies Association Bulletin* XXV, no. 1 (spring 2001): 39–60.

KATHLEEN R. F. BURRILL
UPDATED BY BURÇAK KESKIN-KOZAT

BOREK

See FOOD: BOREK

BOROCHOV, BER
[1881–1917]

Ideologist of Marxist Zionism.

Ber (Dov) Borochov was born in the Ukraine. He had a formal high school education and subsequently was self-educated. As a young adult, Borochov was attracted to the Zionist Socialist Workers Union. He wrote numerous essays in which he developed a synthesis of class and nation, and argued that for Jews, nationalism was the most viable institution for conducting the class struggle. According to Borochov, once a Jewish society was reestablished, Jews would control their own economic infrastructure and would be integrated into the revolutionary process, and the Jewish economic structure would be reconstituted as a base for the class struggle of the Jewish proletariat. Zionism, Borochov asserted, would help to create "the new territory," Eretz Israel, and pioneer a new migration pattern among Jews that would culminate in the "stychic" (natural or automatic) migration of the Jewish masses to Eretz Israel, which is a precondition for Jewish national and economic liberation.

Borochov opposed Theodor Herzl on the Uganda Project, and at the Seventh Zionist Congress in 1905 he headed a faction of Po'alei Zion delegates who were against the plan. Several years later Borochov played a central role in the secession of the Russian Po'alei Zion, which had moved much further left, from the Congress and the World Zionist Organization. He left Russia in 1907, and from then until the beginning of World War I, he was a publicist for the World Union of Poalei Zion in Western and Central Europe. In 1914 Borochov went to the United States, where he continued his work as publicist for Po'alei Zion and also did publicity work for the American Jewish Congress. Borochov was in Kiev on behalf of Po'alei Zion when he contracted a fatal bout of pneumonia. He was buried in Russia, then reinterred in the cemetery of Kibbutz Kinneret in 1963, next to other founders of Labor Zionism.

See also AMERICAN JEWISH CONGRESS; HERZL, THEODOR; LABOR ZIONISM; UGANDA PROJECT.

Bibliography

Avineri, Shlomo. *The Making of Modern Zionism: The Intellectual Origins of the Jewish State.* New York: Basic Books, 1981.

Hertzberg, Arthur, ed. *The Zionist Idea: A Historical Analysis and Reader.* Philadelphia, PA: Jewish Publication Society, 1997.

Shimoni, Gideon. *The Zionist Ideology.* Hanover, NH: University Press of New England, 1995.

Sternhell, Zev. *The Founding Myths of Israel: Nationalism, Socialism, and the Making of the Jewish State,* translated by David Maisel. Princeton, NJ: Princeton University Press, 1998.

CHAIM I. WAXMAN

BORUJERDI, HOSAYN
[1865–1962]

Religious leader and teacher; director of the Feyziyeh in Qom, 1944–1962.

Ayatollah Hosayn Borujerdi was director of the religious teaching institution in Qom, the Feyziyeh, for seventeen years, and for fifteen years the most prominent *marja al-taqlid* (source of emulation) for

Shi'ite communities throughout the world. He was born in Borujerd, Iran, to a family of scholars; and at least five *marja al-taqlid* appear in his ancestry. He received his formal religious training in Isfahan and Najaf. In the early 1900s, Borujerdi moved to Najaf, to study with the famous Akhund Molla Mohammad Kazem Khorasani. In 1910 he returned to Iran. In 1944, he was appointed as head of the Feyziyeh religious seminary in Qom. The institution flourished considerably under his supervision, rivaling older such establishments of Najaf.

Borujerdi's tenure both as *marja al-taqlid* and head of the Feyziyeh was marked by his apolitical, compromising, and quietist stance. He actively pursued a Sunni–Shi'ite rapprochement and was in constant correspondence with the director of al-Azhar, his Sunni counterpart, in Egypt. In the 1950s, when the radical Islamic group Feda'iyan-e Islam (Devotees of Islam) embarked on a series of political assassinations, Borujerdi repeatedly denounced their actions, and he distanced himself and the Feyziyeh from any confrontation with the government of Mohammad Reza Pahlavi. He in fact expelled the Feda'iyan-e Islam from their headquarters at the Feyziyeh.

In 1955, Borujerdi involved himself with the anti-Baha'i campaign of another prominent cleric, Abu al-Qasem Falsafi, grounding his opposition in religious rather than political motivations. Borujerdi also denounced the land reform program of the shah, launched in 1951, on the grounds that it was contrary to Islamic law. Borujerdi's public denouncement of the bill was the first instance of open confrontation between the clergy and the government of Mohammad Reza Pahlavi. In 1953, when Mohammad Mossadegh, the prime minister of Iran, moved to nationalize the oil industry, Borujerdi distanced himself from the activist stance of Ayatollah Abu al-Qasem Kashani, who, together with the Feda'iyan-e Islam, opposed Mohammad Reza Pahlavi in support of Mossadegh. In that same period, he was steadfast in his conviction in the autonomy of Qom, and the unacceptability of any government interference in its religious and financial affairs. When the government tried to impose its representative in Qom's office for religious endowments, Borujerdi flatly denounced the move.

Borujerdi was closely associated with Ayatollah Ruhollah Khomeini, who had worked as Borujerdi's special assistant. But Borujerdi died in March 1962, before the clerical uprisings of 1963 led by Khomeini, along with several other clerics, his successor as *marja al-taqlid*. Borujerdi's death also paved the way for the coming to power of the more radical, reform-minded *ulama* in Qom, who sought to preserve Islam's sociocultural hegemony by direct participation in the political life of the country, and later criticized Borujerdi's conservative, apolitical policies. During his lifetime, Borujerdi was one of the few Iranian, Qom-based, *marja al-taqlid* who enjoyed considerable support and financial backing by Shi'ites outside Iran, notably in Najaf and Karbala, Iraqi centers of Shi'ite learning that tend to emulate their own clerical leadership.

See also FEDA'IYAN-E ISLAM; KASHANI, ABU AL-QASEM; KHOMEINI, RUHOLLAH; MOSSADEGH, MOHAMMAD; PAHLAVI, MOHAMMAD REZA; QOM.

Bibliography

Abrahamian, Ervand. *Iran between Two Revolutions.* Princeton, NJ: Princeton University Press, 1982.

Akhavi, Shahrough. *Religion and Politics in Contemporary Iran.* Albany: State University of New York Press, 1980.

Fischer, Michael M. J. *Iran from Religious Dispute to Revolution.* Cambridge, MA: Harvard University Press, 1980.

NEGUIN YAVARI

BOSPORUS

See STRAITS, TURKISH

BOST

Afghan city and ancient Ghaznavid site.

The city of Bost, later renamed Lashkar Gah, was once the site of a Ghaznavid palace and soldiers' bazaar near the confluence of the Helmand and Arghandab rivers in southeastern Afghanistan. Sultan Mahmud of Ghazni built Bost around the year 1000. The city is now the capital of Helmand province and has a population of about 20,000 inhabitants. In the 1950s and 1960s, Bost and its surroundings became part of the Helmand Valley Project, in which the Helmand River, which drains over half of the Afghan watershed, was dammed and a series of canal projects diverted water for irrigation. Afghan farmers were resettled from other areas of Afghanistan to farm this new agricultural area. Although many eventually left and the project was viewed by some as a failure because of the technical problems encountered and the salination of the soil, many thousand acres of arable land were reclaimed from the desert.

During the years of Afghan civil war (1980–2001) the area around Bost was ruled by a series of warlords. In addition, the drought of the late 1990s and early 2000s drastically reduced stream flows, restricting cultivation and leading to pockets of food shortages. The cultivation of opium poppies moved into this region by the early 1990s.

See also HELMAND RIVER.

Bibliography

Dupree, Louis. *Afghanistan.* Princeton, NJ: Princeton University Press, 1980.

Rubin, Barnett R. *The Fragmentation of Afghanistan: State Formation and Collapse in the International System.* New Haven, CT: Yale University Press, 2002.

GRANT FARR

BOUABID, ABDERRAHIM
[1920–1992]

Moroccan diplomat and opposition party leader.

Abderrahim Bouabid joined the movement for Moroccan nationalism, becoming a member of the Istiqlal Party in the 1950s. In 1956 France and Spain recognized the independence of Morocco, and Bouabid was placed in charge of economic planning in the first independent government. He played a leading part in the political crisis of 1958–1959, which led to a split in the Istiqlal. With Mehdi Ben Barka and others, he formed a new progressive party, the National Union of Popular Forces; in 1975 he helped form an offshoot party called the Socialist Union of Popular Forces (USFP), which emerged as the leading opposition to King Hassan II. In 1981, following riots in Casablanca, Bouabid and others were jailed, although he remained at the head of the party. In the early 1990s Bouadbid took a more moderate approach in view of the king's call for alteration in power, which promoted the inclusion of the left into the government. Upon Bouabid's

death in 1992, his succesor as USFP secretary-general was Abderrahmane Youssoufi.

See also BEN BARKA, MEHDI; YOUSSOUFI, ABDERRAHMANE.

Bibliography

Ashford, Douglas. *Political Change in Morocco.* Princeton, NJ: Princeton University Press, 1961.

Zartman, I. William, ed. *Man, State and Society in the Contemporary Maghrib.* New York: Praeger; London: Pall Mall Press, 1973.

MATTHEW S. GORDON
UPDATED BY ANA TORRES-GARCIA

BOUCETTA, MUHAMMAD
[1925–]

Moroccan lawyer and political figure.

Muhammad Boucetta was educated in Fez and at the law faculty at the Sorbonne in Paris. After joining the movement for nationalism in the 1940s, he became a leading member of the Istiqlal political party by the early 1950s. Morocco became independent of French colonialism in 1956; during the 1958–1959 split of Istiqlal, Boucetta remained in the more conservative wing, under Allal al-Fasi. As secretary-general of the party (1974; then 1978–present), Boucetta held a series of government posts, including minister of state for foreign affairs (1977; then 1981–1983).

See also FASI, ALLAL AL-; ISTIQLAL PARTY: MOROCCO.

Bibliography

Ashford, Douglas. *Political Change in Morocco.* Princeton, NJ: Princeton University Press, 1961.

Waterbury, John. *The Commander of the Faithful.* New York: Columbia University Press, 1970.

MATTHEW S. GORDON

BOUDIAF, MOHAMED
[1919–1992]

Algerian revolutionary; president of the Haut Comité d'Etat, 1992.

Born in M'Sila, Mohamed Boudiaf was drafted in 1943 into the French Army, where he tried to organize nationalist cells in the Algerian ranks. He supported the nationalist ideals of Messali Hadj and joined the paramilitary Organisation Spéciale (OS). He eluded French authorities and later became a party organizer for the Mouvement pour le Triomphe des Libertés Démocratiques (MTLD) in France. Aligning with the restive younger Messalist elite, Boudiaf played an important role in launching the Comité Révolutionnaire d'Unité et d'Action (CRUA), which led to the formation of the Front de Libération Nationale (FLN). He is regarded as one of the nine "historic chiefs" of the Algerian War of Independence. He served in the external faction of the FLN until a controversial French skyjacking in October 1956, when he was captured along with historic chiefs Ahmed Ben Bella, Hocine Ait Ahmed, and Mohamed Khider. Boudiaf spent the rest of the war in prison.

Boudiaf supported neither Ben Bella nor the Gouvernement Provisoire de la République Algérienne (GPRA) in the power struggle after the war. He founded instead an organization called the Parti de la Révolution Socialiste (PRS). Boudiaf was arrested in 1963 and condemned to death, but was later sent into exile. He supported a coalition of opposition groups known as the Comité National de Défense de la Révolution (CNDR), which was established in 1964. After President Ben Bella's deposal in June 1965 Boudiaf opposed the successor regime led by Colonel Houari Boumédienne.

Unlike his former FLN "brothers" Ben Bella and Ait Ahmed, Boudiaf did not return to Algeria right after the October 1988 riots that led to political liberalization. The crisis caused by the Front Islamique du Salut's resounding first-round victory in the parliamentary elections in December 1991 forced apprehensive civilian and military elites to depose President Chadli Bendjedid in January 1992. Then they inaugurated the Haut Comité d'Etat (HCE), a collective executive body, and persuaded Boudiaf to preside over it. His presence was viewed as historical and symbolic. Boudiaf claimed to serve no party except the Algerian nation. He inaugurated the advisory Conseil Consultatif National (CCN) in April. In an effort to mobilize and legitimize his authority, in the following month Boudiaf organized the Rassemblement Patriotique National (RPN).

Boudiaf's energetic engagement earned him respect and even popularity. Nevertheless, he also provoked important enemies. He was staunchly anti-Islamist and determined to address official corruption. His assassination in Annaba in June 1992 was a national tragedy that has been commemorated yearly. The reasons why a bodyguard shot him remain wrapped in mystery. It was reported that the assassin had Islamist tendencies, but clearly Boudiaf also threatened the privileges of members of the Pouvoir—the military and civilian power establishment. Fatiha Boudiaf, the president's widow, has appealed for the truth. She has earned an international reputation for her activism.

See also ALGERIA: POLITICAL PARTIES IN; ALGERIAN WAR OF INDEPENDENCE; COMITÉ RÉVOLUTIONNAIRE D'UNITÉ ET D'ACTION (CRUA); FRONT DE LIBÉRATION NATIONALE (FLN); MOUVEMENT POUR LE TRIOMPHE DES LIBERTÉS DÉMOCRATIQUES.

Bibliography

Gordon, David C. *The Passing of French Algeria.* London: Oxford University Press, 1966.

Ibrahim, Youssef M. "President of Algeria Assassinated; Officials Blame Muslim Fundamentalists." *New York Times,* 30 June 1992.

Willis, Michael. *The Islamist Challenge in Algeria: A Political History.* New York: New York University Press, 1996.

PHILLIP C. NAYLOR

BOUDJEDRA, RACHID
[1941–]

Algerian novelist.

Rachid Boudjedra was born in Aïn Beïda near Constantine and attended secondary school in Tunis. He was wounded while serving in the Armée de Libération Nationale (ALN), and then served as an overseas representative of the Front de Libération Nationale (FLN) during the Algerian Revolution. He earned a philosophy degree at the Sorbonne in Paris. Boudjedra's literary reputation stemmed from his novels *La répudiation* (1969; The repudiation) and *L'insolation* (1972; The sunstroke), which dramatically questioned contemporary social conventions and traditions through psychologically complex characters. Other novels include *Topogra-*

phie idéale pour une agression caractérisée (1975; Ideal topography for a characterized aggression), *L'escargot entêté* (1977; The stubborn snail), *Les 1001 années de la nostalgie* (1979; 1001 years of nostalgia), and *Le vainqueur de coupe* (1981; The cup winner). Boudjedra announced in June 1982 that he would no longer write in French. His Arabic novel *al-tafakkuk* (1982; The falling apart) appeared in French translation as *Le démantèlement* (1982; The dismantling). Other Arabic novels that have been translated into French are *al-mart/La macération* (1984/1985; The maceration), *Laylat imra'a Ariqa/Journal d'une femme insomniaque* (1985/1987; Nights of an insomniac woman), *Ma'arak zuqaq* (The battle of the alleys/La prise de Gibraltar (1986/1987: The taking of Gibraltar), and *Fawda al-Ashya/Le désordre des choses* (1990/1991; The disorder of things). He gradually returned to writing in French, in the novels *Timimoun* (1994; Timimoun), *La vie à l'endroit* (1997; The life at the place), and *Fascination* (2000; Fascination). He is also a poet (*Pour ne plus rêver* [1965; For not to dream] and *Greffe* [1985; Graft]) and a playwright (*Mines de rien* [1995; Mines of nothing]). His nonfiction includes *La vie quotidienne en Algérie* (1971; The daily life in Algeria), *Naissance du cinéma algérien* (1971; Birth of the Algerian cinema), *Journal Palestinien* (1973; Palestinian journal), *Lettres algériennes* (1995: Algerian letters), and *Peindre l'Orient* (1996; To paint the Orient). Boudjedra has opposed political Islamism, as illustrated by his *FIS de la haine* (1992; The Fis [Islamic Salvation Front] of Hatred).

See also LITERATURE: ARABIC, NORTH AFRICAN.

Bibliography

Naylor, Phillip C. *Historical Dictionary of Algeria,* 3d edition. Lanham, MD: 2005.

PHILLIP C. NAYLOR

BOUHIRED, JAMILA
[1935–]

Algerian nationalist.

Born to a middle-class family in 1935 and educated in a French school, Bouhired joined the Algerian Liberation Front (FLN) when she was a student activist, or *mujahida* like Hassiba Ben Bouali and many others. She was the liaison officer and personal assistant of the FLN commander of Algiers, Yusef Saadi, when she was wounded in a shootout and arrested by French troops in April 1957. Though tor-

tured, she did not speak and was sentenced to death in July on terrorism charges. The execution was postponed thanks to an international press campaign launched by her French lawyer, Jacques Verges (whom she later married). She was transferred to a prison in France in March 1958. In the film *Jamila the Algerian* (1958), Yusuf Chahine, the Egyptian filmmaker, depicted her courageous actions. Freed in 1962, Bouhired became a national heroine in Algeria.

Following Algeria's independence in 1962, she ran for a seat in the first National Assembly. Bouhired has worked then for many years with Verges for *Revolution africaine,* a French magazine devoted to nationalist struggles throughout Africa. In the beginning of the eighties, Bouhired was involved in the demonstrations by women in Algeria against the conservative Family Code, a set of laws finally adopted in 1984.

See also BEN BOUALI, HASSIBA; GENDER: GENDER AND LAW; GENDER: GENDER AND POLITICS.

RABIA BEKKAR

BOUIH, FATNA EL-
[1955–]

Activist, writer, and former political prisoner.

Fatna el-Bouih was born in Benahmed in Settat province. In 1971 she received a scholarship to a prestigious Casablanca girls' high school, Lycée Chawqi, where she became active in the national union of high school students (Syndicat National des Elèves). She was first arrested as a leader of the 24 January 1974 high school student strike. After her second arrest she was forcibly held from May to November 1977 in Derb Moulay Cherif in Casablanca with other women activists, including Latifa Jababdi, Ouidad Baouab, Khadija Boukhari, and Maria Zouini. They were later kept in Meknes Prison from 1977 to 1979 without trial. Bouih was charged with conspiracy against state security for membership in the illegal Marxist-Leninist group March 23 and for distributing political tracts and posters. She completed her sentence at Kenitra Civil Prison (1980–1982).

Bouih began to speak actively in 1991 as a member of the council for women's groups (al-Majlis al-Watani lil-Tansiq). These groups worked to change the *mudawana* with the Union d'Action Feminine (UAF), whose president is Latifa Jababdi, whom Bouih knew from March 23. Since 1995 Bouih has volunteered at Morocco's first center for battered women. She began writing about other women political prisoners, feeling that their stories should be part of Moroccan history. She wrote a book, *A Woman Named Rachid,* while in prison, but waited twenty years before publishing it. Her ability to publish this book in French and Arabic indicates a new openness since the end of the Hassan II era.

Bouih ran unsuccessfully in 1997 for councilor (*mustashara*) of Casablanca as a candidate of the Organization of Democratic and Popular Action (OADP), an official political party and successor to the March 23 group. She and her husband were founding members of the Moroccan Observatory of Prisons (OMP) in 1999. They work to help prisoners reintegrate into society. She finished a degree in sociology, and has been teaching Arabic since 1982 as part of her civil service.

> *See also* GENDER: GENDER AND LAW; GENDER: GENDER AND POLITICS; JABABDI, LATIFA; MOROCCO: POLITICAL PARTIES IN.

Bibliography

Slymovics, Susan. "This Time I Choose When to Leave: An Interview with Fatna El Bouih." *Morocco in Transition, Middle East Report* 218 (spring 2001): 42–43.

MARIA F. CURTIS

BOUMÉDIENNE, HOUARI
[1927?–1978]

First vice-president of Algeria, 1962; second president of Algeria, 1965–1978.

The son of a small farmer whose family originated in the Kabylia (Berber) region of Algeria, Houari Boumédienne was born Mohammed Ben Brahim Boukharouba at Clauzel (now al-Hussainiya), a small village near Guelma in the Constantinois region of the country. As a young man, he spent his school years attending both Qur'anic and French primary schools in Constantine and, at one point, a conservative *madrasa,* or religious school. After finishing his studies, he returned to his native village and became a teacher at the local school. Active early

on in student politics, Boukharouba, as many of his generation, became interested in the growing nationalist sentiments and the emerging struggle against the French. His early involvement culminated in his participation in the 1945 Setif Revolt and, later, in the Algerian War of Independence (1954–1962). In the aftermath of the insurrection, he joined the Parti du Peuple Algérien (PPA; Algerian People's Party), headed for a short while by Messali al-Hadj. To avoid forced enlistment in the French army, Boukharouba left Algeria in 1952.

During his years in exile in Cairo, he attended al-Azhar, the famous Islamic university. Although he remained a secularist throughout his years in power, he adhered to a secularism that was always tempered by respect for the Islamic/Arab heritage that Algeria had experienced. He infiltrated back into Algeria in 1955 and joined the *mujahidin* (fighters) of Wilaya V (the Oranie region) where he assumed his nom de guerre—Houari Boumédienne—a name he would keep after the Algerian War of Independence. As an assistant to Abd al-Hafid Boussouf, commander of Wilaya V at the time—the best organized and disciplined of the military apparatus in the interior of Algeria—Boumédienne was put in charge of the Moroccan wing of the Armée de Libération Nationale (ALN; National Liberation Army). He slowly rose to the top of the external army structure between 1957 and 1960 and became the chief of the western general staff in September 1958, then located in Oujda, Morocco, where most of the important army commanders of postindependence Algeria were gathered at one time or another.

In February 1960, he was again promoted—this time to chief of the united general staff, headquartered in Ghardimaou, Tunisia. His position as one of the most prominent officers and powerbrokers within the future Algerian army was confirmed in 1959 when Boumédienne was put in charge of a military court that prosecuted a number of ALN colonels in Tunisia who had plotted the overthrow of the Provisional Government of the Algerian Republic (GPRA).

In time, however, Boumédienne himself grew disenchanted with the GPRA and resigned as the second round of the Evian agreements (the negotiations between France and representatives of the Algerian leadership) limped to a halt. Although

Boumédienne cited disagreement with the Algerian participants at the Evian agreements on a number of issues, the real dispute centered on the power of the ALN versus the GPRA as independence grew nearer. At that point Boumédienne received the support of Ahmed Ben Bella, whose visibility, despite his incarceration in France, had steadily grown among Algerian participants in the struggle for independence. Ben Bella's help became crucial in 1961 and 1962 when Boumédienne wanted to remove a number of old-time revolutionaries and politicians from the GPRA. Boumédienne then returned to the provisional government, but the internal battle for power was far from settled and would resurface once independence was achieved.

After independence in 1962, Houari Boumédienne, as a key member of the Algerian military, became minister of defense and first vice-president of the republic under the presidency of Ben Bella. His primary task was to convert the internal and external units of the Algerian army that had emerged during the war of independence into a unified force. Disenchanted with the lack of direction of the newly independent government, faced with lingering internal political battles, and resentful of the foreign ideologues rather than local nationalists who helped determine Ben Bella's outlook on politics, Boumédienne deposed the first president of independent Algeria in June 1965 and assumed the presidency of the Council of the Revolution, the ruling body of the country, calling the coup a "historic rectification" of the Algerian revolution.

The 1965 coup, however, was not an indication of the personal power of the new president but reflected the political power of the armed forces whose independence Boumédienne had attempted to preserve. This would largely explain the collegial rule Boumédienne instituted after assuming power, a careful balancing act that he would be forced to maintain until his death.

Self-effacing, austere, pragmatic, and imbued with the ideals of the anticolonial struggle for which he had fought for almost two decades, Boumédienne after 1965 charted a political and economic future for his country that would slowly yield grudging admiration both abroad and at home. Its political and economic principles were described in detailed fashion in the 1976 national charter that

Algerian president Houari Boumédienne, 3 March 1975. Boumédienne was president of Algeria from 1965 until his death in 1978. Under his leadership, the country saw a period of steady economic growth and strong international presence. © BETTMANN/CORBIS. REPRODUCED BY PERMISSION.

became the guiding document for Algeria's socialist experiment.

The basis for his internal economic policies was a commitment to a socialist strategy that was simultaneously less draconian than that of his predecessor but still managed to put the Algerian state in charge of virtually all economic enterprises in the country. Boumédienne held the conviction that only coherent and centralized decision making would allow the country to overcome both the disastrous economic effects of the eight-year struggle for independence and the lingering factionalism within the country. Businesses were grouped into a number of state enterprises, forming the basis of what was called an "industrializing industry" strategy. This contained the notion that, with direct and consistent state intervention, Algeria would build a heavy industry base—fueled by the income from petroleum and natural gas—that would serve as a platform for creating intermediary and eventually consumer products. The ultimate aim, according to Boumédienne, was greater economic self-sufficiency.

In foreign policy, Boumédienne steered Algeria toward a policy of neutrality in international affairs while committing the country to increased solidarity with developing countries. Under Boumédienne, Algeria became one of the original sponsors of the New International Economic Order at the United Nations and remained one of the most vocal members of the nonaligned movement. Boumédienne's cautious approach in international politics paid off as Algeria became, in several instances, a valuable interlocutor in mediating conflicts, with a corps of skilled diplomatic representatives at its service. Internally, however, Boumédienne increasingly relied on a coalition of technical experts and professional military advisers, particularly after an attempted coup by a fellow officer, Colonel Tahar Zbiri, in 1967. The outcome was that the Front de Libération Nationale (FLN; National Liberation Front), the country's single party, lost much of the legitimacy and the mobilizing potential it had possessed. The long-term result of this increasingly technocratic/military alliance was a gradual loss of popular confidence in the single party and a further narrowing of the political base during the remainder of Boumédienne's tenure.

Boumédienne's economic strategy also was not as successful in the long run as he had hoped. The heavy state intervention had created an enormously inefficient public sector by the mid-1970s, exacerbated further by the easy borrowing privileges that Algeria enjoyed when oil prices rose after the Arab–Israel War (1973), and made worse by the one-party system where patronage and favoritism rather than personal capability provided criteria for recruitment. By the end of Boumédienne's life in December 1978, there was substantial disagreement over his economic strategy. This potential struggle had been kept in abeyance because of the personal respect Boumédienne enjoyed, and it reflected the crucial role he had played in Algeria's factional politics, which had never truly been resolved after independence.

After his death, the succession was not settled until 1980 at a special party congress but according to institutionalized procedures—a testimony in part to Boumédienne's political skills but also to the stranglehold the one-party system and the ALN, its most powerful defender, had on the country. The newly elected president, Chadli Bendjedid, abandoned his predecessor's economic strategy and embarked on a more market- and Western-oriented development that would have been anathema to Boumédienne and many of his advisers. Algerian socialism died along with its enigmatic second president.

> See also ALGERIAN WAR OF INDEPENDENCE; ARAB–ISRAEL WAR (1973); ARMÉE DE LIBÉRATION NATIONALE (ALN); BEN BELLA, AHMED; BENDJEDID, CHADLI; BERBER; FRONT DE LIBÉRATION NATIONALE (FLN); HADJ, MESSALI AL-; PARTI DU PEUPLE ALGÉRIEN (PPA); SÉTIF REVOLT (1945); ZBIRI, TAHAR.

Bibliography

Entelis, John. *Algeria: The Revolution Institutionalized.* Boulder, CO: Westview, 1986.

Ruedy, John. *Modern Algeria: The Origins and Development of a Nation.* Bloomington: Indiana University Press, 1992.

DIRK VANDEWALLE

BOURGUIBA, HABIB
[c. 1903–2000]

Leader of Tunisia's independence movement and first president of the Tunisian republic, 1957–1987.

The seventh child of a former army officer, Habib Bourguiba was born, according to some sources, on 3 August 1903, in Monastir, a small village in the Sahil, Tunisia's fertile coastal region. Other sources claim that Bourguiba was born in 1901. He was an intelligent youngster and won admission to Sadiqi College, a Tunis secondary school established before the imposition of the French protectorate in 1881. This institution provided the sons of the Tunisian elite with a superior education in both Arabic and French. He then went on to study law at the Sorbonne in Paris from 1924 to 1927, where he met and married a French woman, the mother of his only child, a son named Habib Bourguiba, Jr. (He later married Wassila Ben Ammar, the daughter of a powerful Tunis family.) In Paris, Bourguiba encountered other Maghrebi (Moroccan and Algerian) intellectuals as well as French liberals, and his interest in politics deepened. Upon his return to Tunisia, he opened a law office and became active in the Tunisian nationalist party, known as Destour (Constitution).

The Struggle for Independence

By the early 1930s, as the Great Depression deepened, Bourguiba grew impatient with the inability of the predominantly bourgeois Destour leaders to address the disproportionate burden of the economic crisis borne by Tunisian peasants and farmers while French settlers were being given special dispensations by protectorate authorities. He founded a French-language newspaper in 1932 to give voice to his demands on behalf of the predominantly rural Tunisian population, and in 1934 he led a secession from the Destour, establishing what became known as the Neo-Destour Party.

Openly agitating for independence with Bourguiba at its helm as secretary-general and later president, the Neo-Destour methodically organized a countrywide network of branches, turning the nationalist cause, previously an elite campaign, into a genuine mass movement. Moreover, although Bourguiba was clearly the principal figure in the movement, his willingness to encourage other leaders within the party ensured that his colleagues were able to sustain the momentum of the movement in the face of French repression. Many Neo-Destour leaders were repeatedly imprisoned or exiled, including Bourguiba himself, who was in detention for nearly ten years between 1934 and 1955.

In July 1954, facing rising local agitation, the French government (then headed by Pierre Mendès-France) decided to open negotiations with the Tunisian nationalists. In April 1955, the French granted Tunisia autonomy, reserving control of defense and foreign affairs, and within a year Bourguiba concluded a treaty granting the country full independence. On 25 June 1957, the Tunisian monarchy was abolished and Bourguiba was elected

Habib Bourguiba was one of Tunisia's prominent leaders during the country's struggle against France for independence. He became the country's first president in 1957—two years after Tunisia won the right of home rule—and worked to modernize his nation until his deposition in a bloodless coup in November 1987. © AFP/CORBIS. REPRODUCED BY PERMISSION.

president of the new republic. It was not until 1963, however, and at the cost of nearly a thousand Tunisian lives following a military showdown in the French naval base of Bizerte (July–September 1961), that the French evacuated their last military base.

Bourguiba's willingness to pursue a gradualist approach in negotiations with the French enhanced his reputation in the West as an artful, pragmatic leader, but it earned him enemies at home. In fact, the autonomy agreements nearly precipitated a civil war, as Bourguiba was opposed by other nationalist leaders, such as Salah Ben Youssouf, who argued that Bourguiba had conceded too much. Although Bourguiba won the war and eventually independence as well, he took the challenge very seriously. It was alleged that he ultimately arranged Ben Youssouf's assassination in 1961 at the latter's place of exile in Cairo.

Ideological Independence

Bourguiba's policies in the early years of independence demonstrated an independence of mind that only some of his fellow statesmen, both at home and abroad, appreciated. During the 1960s, like many Third World rulers, Bourguiba embraced socialism, declaring the Neo-Destour (later known as the Parti Socialiste Destourien) the sole political party, nationalizing much of Tunisia's trade and industry, and establishing cooperative farms. By the end of the decade, however, the policy was meeting increasing domestic resistance, particularly among the coastal farmers, who had been Bourguiba's most important supporters in his battles with the French and later with Ben Yusuf. In 1969, in a dramatic reversal, Bourguiba dismissed the prime minister associated with the policy, Ahmed Ben Salah (later to accuse him of treason), and became one of the Arab world's earliest proponents of economic liberalism as the surest path to development.

Bourguiba's ideological independence—the pragmatism that became known in Tunisia as *Bourguibisme*, contesting Egyptian Nasserism, which accentuated the importance of pan-Arabism—was also evident elsewhere. On 6 March 1965, during a visit to Jordan, he spoke in Jerusalem and at a Palestinian refugee camp at Jericho, openly urging Arab leaders to opt for a negotiated settlement with Israel to end the Arab–Israeli conflict. Bourguiba elaborated the reasons why the Arabs should recognize Israeli sovereignty: Military confrontation with Israel always ended in Arab defeat and this was bound to also be the outcome in the future; not only was war counterproductive, but the United States would never allow the Arab states to defeat or decimate Israel; prudence and wisdom had to prevail over emotionalism, for this only made Israel more powerful; Arabs needed to rid themselves of the feelings of humiliation that had resulted from past wars, and Israelis had to free themselves of the complex of embattlement; coexistence with Israel, even de facto recognition, would result in regional stability and prosperity for all parties involved in the conflict; and negotiations with Israel would mean direct Arab-Israeli contact, with Palestinian representatives leading the process from the Arab side. Bourguiba did not offer himself as a mediator and doubted that there would be a quick solution to the conflict.

At the time, such an initiative was virtually unimaginable. The Israelis followed his proposals closely, even though they would require Israel to accept U.N. Resolutions 181 (the 1947 Partition Plans) and 194 (repatriation of the 1948 Palestinian refugees). On the other hand, most Arab leaders opposed it outright.

This placed Tunisia on the fringes of inter-Arab politics. Similarly, although Tunisia was described in its constitution as an Islamic country, Bourguiba had little patience for what he viewed as the anachronisms of religious observance. Thus, he advocated abandoning the obligatory fast during the month of Ramadan, arguing that the consequent loss of worker productivity interfered with the country's development. He also engineered Tunisia's family code, one of the most far-reaching personal-status laws in the Muslim world, so that it outlawed polygamy and made access to divorce, support, child custody, and the like benefits that enabled women to be more equitable with men.

Weakening Influence

While many of these positions won him great esteem abroad, by 1975, when the national assembly declared him president for life (a position he had previously refused), Bourguiba's command of the Tunisian political scene had begun to weaken. Health problems that had appeared in 1967 recurred periodically, and although he proved not to be nearly as frail as many feared, his intellectual agility diminished. In the 1970s, his government was drawing increasing criticism for failing to accompany its economic liberalism with political reform. The architect of his economic policy, Prime Minister Hedi Nouira, was openly contemptuous of multiparty politics, but it was not until he suffered a stroke in 1980 that Bourguiba saw fit to replace him.

Nouira's successor, Mohammed Mzali, initially lived up to his more liberal reputation, authorizing a number of opposition parties and calling for contested elections, but he was soon consumed by the jockeying for position among the political elite that was precipitated by Bourguiba's increasingly erratic behavior. Bourguiba was said to be out of touch with most daily events, often preoccupied with plans for his own state funeral, yet unwilling to surrender any of his virtually absolute authority.

In the late 1970s, Bourguiba agreed to have the headquarters of the Arab League of States moved from Cairo to Tunis. At the time, the Arab world was boycotting Egypt for signing a peace agreement with Israel. Between 1958 and 1967, Bourguiba had regularly walked out of Arab League meetings, regarding it as an instrument of Nasser's involvement in inter-Arab politics. In 1982, Bourguiba allowed the Palestine Liberation Organization to establish its headquarters in Tunis after the Israel Defense Force ousted it from Lebanon.

By the middle of the 1980s, however, the country needed a strong hand; it faced serious economic problems, a growing Islamic political movement (al-Nahda, whose participation in Tunisian politics was anathema to the secularist Bourguiba), and a political elite divided by a preoccupation with its own political future. Although Bourguiba had designated Mzali his successor, he dismissed him in 1985, appointing in his place General Zayn al-Abidine Ben Ali, the first military officer ever to serve in a Tunisian cabinet.

As Bourguiba, long an advocate of a small and apolitical military establishment, might well have predicted, it was Ben Ali who ended Bourguiba's political career. After a Tunisian court failed to hand down death sentences to Islamists convicted on charges (real or trumped up) of seeking to overthrow the state, Bourguiba demanded that they be executed anyway. Instead, Ben Ali arranged to have several doctors certify that the president was too ill and too senile to govern effectively and Bourguiba was deposed in a coup on 7 November 1987. He retired to live in seclusion in the palace he had earlier built for himself in Monastir. He died on 6 April 2000.

See also BEN ALI, ZAYN AL-ABIDINE; BEN SALAH, AHMED; BEN YOUSOUF, SALAH; MZALI, MOHAMMED; PARTITION PLANS (PALESTINE); TUNISIA: OVERVIEW; TUNISIA: POLITICAL PARTIES IN.

Bibliography

Anderson, Lisa. *State and Social Transformation in Tunisia and Libya, 1830–1980.* Princeton, NJ: Princeton University Press, 1986.

Laskier, Michael M. *Israel and the Maghreb: From Statehood to Oslo.* Gainesville: University Press of Florida, 2004.

LISA ANDERSON
UPDATED BY MICHAEL M. LASKIER

BOUTEFLIKA, ABDELAZIZ
[1937–]

President of Algeria (1999–); foreign minister (1963–1979).

Born in Morocco, Abdelaziz Bouteflika was educated in his native Oujda and then at Tlemcen, Algeria. During the Algerian War of Independence (1954–1962) he served in the Armée de Libération Nationale (ALN) as a political officer and became a confidant of the powerful Colonel Houari Boumedienne. He served as minister for youth sports and tourism before being appointed foreign minister by President Ahmed Ben Bella after the assassination of Mohamed Khemisti in 1963. Apprehensive over Boumedienne's political ambitions, Ben Bella moved against the colonel's supporters, especially Bouteflika. This contributed to Boumedienne's June 1965 coup that deposed Ben Bella.

Bouteflika retained the foreign affairs portfolio during Boumedienne's rule. He continued Algeria's foreign policy of support for revolutionary movements and nonalignment. He especially championed the rights of the less developed countries, highlighted by his chairmanship of the United Nations special session on north-south relations in 1974. He negotiated the Algiers Accords of 1965 with France regarding hydrocarbons and industrial cooperation, and resumed difficult discussions with France in 1969 regarding the future of the hydrocarbons sector. This led to the nationalization of French hydrocarbons concessions in 1971. Having concluded conventions with Morocco regarding border disputes in 1972, Bouteflika misperceived Morocco's territorial intentions and ambitions concerning Western Sahara (the former Spanish Sahara). The tripartite Madrid Accords of November 1975 divided the territory between Morocco and Mauritania. An alienated Algeria gave POLISARIO—the Saharan liberation organization—substantial support and havens within its borders for guerrillas and refugees. Bouteflika subsequently lobbied with notable success for the international recognition of POLISARIO's Saharan Arab Democratic Republic (SADR).

Most observers viewed Bouteflika as the probable successor of President Boumedienne. He delivered the eulogy after Boumedienne's untimely death in December 1978. Nevertheless, the military and the Front de Libération Nationale (FLN) opted for

Abdelaziz Bouteflika (left) hosts French president Jacques Chirac (center) during an official visit to Algiers in December 2001. Chirac returned to the capital city in 2003 to sign a declaration promising increased cooperation between his country and Algeria. © AP/WIDE WORLD PHOTOS. REPRODUCED BY PERMISSION.

a compromise candidate, Chadli Bendjedid, who was elected president in February 1979. Bouteflika served as a minister without portfolio and as an adviser. In 1981 he was removed, however, from the FLN's political bureau and central committee. Bouteflika began a self-imposed exile the following year and was charged with corruption and embezzlement in 1983. His return to Algeria in 1987 was viewed as an effort for intra-FLN reconciliation. After the Third Extraordinary Congress of the FLN in 1989 that followed the destabilizing October 1988 riots, Bouteflika became a member of the expanded central committee. He campaigned for FLN candidates in the elections of June 1990 that were won by the increasingly popular Front Islamique du Salut (FIS).

Bouteflika kept a low profile after the January 1992 coup that forced Bendjedid to resign the presidency. As civil war raged, the Haut Comité d'Etat—a collective executive—urged Bouteflika to accept the restored presidency. He refused, and Liamine Zeroual was selected in 1994 and elected in November 1995—the first free multiparty election in Algeria's history (although the banned FIS could not participate). Zeroual's decision in late 1998 to

leave office before his term expired led to Bouteflika's candidacy. The April 1999 elections were tainted by charges of corruption that resulted in the withdrawal of six other candidates a day before the voting. Bouteflika—the favored candidate of the Pouvoir (the military and civilian "powerful" and influential establishment elite)—stood alone for election and was the inevitable winner.

Now as president, Bouteflika addressed the Algerian desire to end the civil war that had claimed an estimated 100,000 lives. He presented in September 1999 the Civil Concord Referendum, which was enthusiastically endorsed. The FIS's military wing—the Armée Islamique du Salut (AIS)—took advantage of the government's offer of amnesty and disbanded in 2000. Two other Islamist groups have continued their operations against the government—the Groupe Islamique Armée (GIA) and the Groupe Salafiste pour la Prédication et le Combat (GSPC)—but the violence has significantly decreased. The referendum also served to legitimize Bouteflika's presidency.

The April 2001 killing of a Kabyle (Berber) youth while in police custody incited widespread rioting in Kabylia, resulting in scores killed. Rumors circulated that Bouteflika intended to resign. The Kabyles' restlessness had important national ramifications; their appeal for political reform and economic development resonated sympathetically throughout Algeria. In an effort to mollify the Berbers, the Bouteflika government recognized Tamazight as an official, national language (with Arabic) in 2002, although institutionalizing this decision remains problematic.

Differences over the direction and pace of economic planning and privatization provoked other problems, and led to Bouteflika's sacking of prime ministers Ahmed Benbitour in 2000 and Ali Benflis in 2003. Furthermore, Bouteflika has aspired to exercise independence, although detractors have portrayed him as a puppet of the Pouvoir. This has created chronic tensions between the civilian president and the military.

Bouteflika's greatest achievement as president has been the restoration of a respectable international image of Algeria after years of strife and scorn. He helped mediate differences between

Ethiopia and Somalia in 2000. He also has sought a rapprochement with Morocco and a mutually satisfying resolution regarding Western Sahara. Relations with France improved markedly, resulting in Bouteflika's state visit in June 2003. Bouteflika reciprocated by hosting French president Jacques Chirac in March 2003. Furthermore, Algeria was among the first countries to offer support and assistance to the United States after the terrorist attacks of 11 September 2001. It is expected that Bouteflika will run for re-election in 2004.

See also BOUMEDIENNE, HOUARI; FRONT DE LIBÉRATION NATIONALE (FLN); POLISARIO; SAHARAN ARAB DEMOCRATIC REPUBLIC (SADR).

Bibliography

Khalfa, Rouala. "A Pyrrhic Victory: Algeria's New President Will Have a Hard Time Winning Popular Support after One-Horse Election." *Financial Times,* 17 April 1999.

Naylor, Phillip C. *Historical Dictionary of Algeria,* 3d edition. Lanham, MD: Scarecrow Press, 2005.

PHILLIP C. NAYLOR

BOUTROS-GHALI, BOUTROS
[1922–]

Egyptian politician and UN secretary-general, 1992–1996.

Boutros Boutros-Ghali was born in Egypt, the son of a former minister of finance and the grandson of Boutros Pasha Ghali, who served as prime minister from 1908 until he was assassinated in 1910.

Boutros-Ghali earned an LL.B. from Cairo University in 1946 and a Ph.D. in international law from the University of Paris in 1949. He was a Fulbright scholar at Columbia University from 1954 to 1955. He started his career as a professor of international law and international relations at Cairo University, where he also served as chair of the political science department and as head of the Center for Political and Strategic Studies. He was a founder of *Al-Siyasa al-Dawliyya* and the economic weekly *Al-Ahram al-Iqtisadi.*

When President Anwar Sadat decided to launch his peace initiative with Israel, Boutros-Ghali was appointed Sadat's minister of state for foreign affairs after Ismaʿil Fahmi, then foreign minister, resigned in protest to Sadat's peace moves. Boutros-Ghali accompanied Sadat on his historic trip to Jerusalem.

Throughout the negotiations with Israel that eventually led to the Camp David Accords (1978) and the subsequent Egyptian–Israeli peace treaty, Boutros-Ghali was one of the principal Egyptian negotiators. In 1991 he was appointed deputy prime minister for foreign affairs.

Javier Pérez de Cuéllar decided in 1991 to step down as secretary-general of the United Nations (UN) after two terms. Boutros-Ghali immediately began actively campaigning for the position, something that had never been done before. He was elected on the first ballot. During his term as secretary-general, the UN went through a transition from a world dominated by the U.S.–Soviet rivalry to a more multipolar political environment. This has meant a greater role for the world body in peacekeeping and peacemaking. Boutros-Ghali attempted to expand the mission of the UN to make it more relevant in solving ethnic conflicts and to redefine the use of UN forces in solving inter- and intranational conflicts. The transition was not easy, as the difficulties the UN faced in brokering peace in Somalia and the former Yugoslavia demonstrated. Nor was there consensus on what the role of the UN should be in the post–Cold War world. Moreover there were criticisms over waste and abuse in the UN bureaucracy. Principal among the critics was the United States, which regularly withheld financial contributions. During his tenure as secretary-general, Boutros-Ghali pleaded that without the necessary resources, the UN could not fulfill its historic mission. He was replaced by Kofi Annan.

See also ANNAN, KOFI A.; CAMP DAVID ACCORDS (1978); PÉREZ DE CUÉLLAR, JAVIER; SADAT, ANWAR AL-.

BRYAN DAVES

BOUYALI, MOUSTAFA
[1940–1987]

Leader of Mouvement Islamique Armé in Algeria.

Moustafa Bouyali was the first major Islamist insurgent of independent Algeria and the leader (*amir*) of the Mouvement Islamique Armé (MIA). Born in Draria, near Algiers, Bouyali joined the war for independence at a young age and fought alongside the armed groups of the Algiers region. Motivated by religious convictions, he was soon disappointed by the secular inclination of the new Algerian regime. His call for the implementation of Islamic law reached more adepts by the mid-1970s when he became preacher at the al-Achour mosque in Algiers. By 1979 Bouyali had gathered local Islamic groups under his leadership and gradually departed from the quietist Islamic current. His first organization, the Group for Defence Against the Illicit, carried out punitive interventions against behaviors that it regarded as un-Islamic, such as the selling of alcohol. Unable to secure the approval of other Islamic movements and prompted by the murder of his brother during a confrontation with the police in April 1982, Bouyali went underground, founded the MIA, and began to advocate revolutionary armed struggle against the state. Based upon the guerrilla tactics used by the National Liberation Front (FLN) during the colonial struggle, the MIA targeted state institutions and their representatives, with the intent of establishing an Islamic state. Bouyali pursued his clandestine struggle for five years until he was tracked down and killed by the secret services in 1987. He became the precursor of revolutionary Islamism in Algeria and many prominent members of the GIA (Armed Islamic Groups) and the Front Islamique du Salut (FIS), including Ali Belhadj, were among his followers.

See also BELHADJ, ALI; FRONT ISLAMIQUE DU SALUT (FIS); GIA (ARMED ISLAMIC GROUPS); MADANI, ABASSI AL-; SAHNOUN, AHMED; SOLTANI, ABDELLATIF.

Bibliography

Willis, Michael. *The Islamist Challenge in Algeria: A Political History.* New York: New York University Press, 1996.

HENRI LAUZIÈRE

BRAHIMI, ABDELHAMID

[1936–]

Algerian prime minister, 1984–1988.

After serving as an Armée de Libération Nationale (ALN) officer during the Algerian War of Inde-

pendence, Abdelhamid Brahimi became director of the Organisme de Coopération Industrielle, an institution established by the hydrocarbons Algiers Accords of 1965 to stimulate French-Algerian economic cooperation. He also represented the national hydrocarbon enterprise, SONATRACH, in the United States. President Chadli Bendjedid appointed Brahimi minister of planning and organization of the national territory in 1979. Brahimi then served as prime minister beginning in 1984 until he was replaced by Kasdi Merbah after the October 1988 riots. Brahimi favored conciliation between the ruling Front de Libération Nationale (FLN) and the Islamist Front Islamique du Salut (FIS). He was held responsible for the plummeting decline of the economy, and he became increasingly alienated. He charged that the cost of the corruption within the FLN amounted to $26 billion—coincidentally, the size of the foreign debt. This damaged the party's already tarnished image and consequently its performance during elections. Brahimi left the FLN and remains very critical of the Pouvoir—the military-civilian power establishment—and he believes that the military was responsible for the assassination of President Mohamed Boudiaf in June 1992. He remains an outspoken critic of the Algerian political establishment. Brahimi is the author of *Stratégies de développement pour l'Algerie: 1962–1991* (1992; Development strategies for Algeria) and *Justice sociale et développement en économie islamique* (1993; Transsocial justice and development in an Islamic economy).

See also FRONT DE LIBÉRATION NATIONALE (FLN).

Bibliography

Naylor, Phillip C. *Historical Dictionary of Algeria,* 3d edition. Lanham, MD: Scarecrow Press. 2005.

PHILLIP C. NAYLOR

BRENNER, YOSEF HAYYIM

[1881–1921]

Hebrew and Yiddish writer and editor.

Born in Novi Mlini (Ukraine), Yosef Hayyim Brenner's conversion to secular Zionism was accelerated by service in the Russian army (1901–1904) and exile to London and Lemberg. Editing, writing, translating, teaching and preaching socialism and the virtues of labor, he was recognized as one of the leading literary pioneers of the Second Aliyah. A contributor to the main Hebrew journals of the time, *ha-Po ʿel ha-Tza ʿir* and *ha-Ahdut*, Brenner also published the *Revivim* and *ha-Adamah* periodicals and cofounded the Histadrut in 1920. He was murdered by Arab rioters in Jaffa on 2 May 1921.

Brenner drew stylistic and ideological inspiration from Leo Tolstoy, Fyodor Dostoyevsky, M. J. Berdichevsky, Mendele Mokher Sefarim, and Hebrew writers close to the Hibbat Zion movement, and gave all his fiction a strong existential and autobiographical twist. The novel *Ba-Horef* (In winter, 1902) established Brenner's literary reputation, treating the experiences of a young boy who moved from yeshiva to the city, as Brenner had himself, becoming a secular intellectual. In *Shanah Ahat* (One year, 1908), Brenner wrote about military service, and in *Min ha-Metzar* (Out of the depths, 1908–1909) he dealt with Jewish workers in London. *Aggav Orha* (1909) describes the Second Aliyah, while *Ben Mayim le-Mayim* (Between water and water, 1910) depicts life in the settlements of Eretz Yisrael (mandatory Palestine). Throughout his stories, characters wander in the hope of ameliorating their unhappy destiny: from town to city (*Ba-Horef*); from eastern to western Europe (*Min ha-Mezar*); from Diaspora to Eretz Yisrael (*Aggav Orha, Azzabim*); and within Eretz Yisrael itself. He judged the foremost Hebrew writers—Perez Smolenskin (1910), Yehudah Leib Gordon (1913), Sefarim (1907, 1914)—by the same existential criteria, assessing how successfully they harmonized experience and expression and opposing pompous writing and the literary tendency to glorify life in Eretz Yisrael/Palestine. Brenner sought to capture spoken Hebrew, then in a state of flux and frequently dependent on Yiddish, German, or Russian words and phrases to compensate for words lacking in Hebrew. His existential preoccupations drew mixed reviews from contemporaries and pitched him against Ahad Haʿam's conception of a revived Jewish culture drawing on the traditions of the Diaspora, traditions deemed irrelevant to the secular Jewish intellectuals and workers of Brenner's generation. Later, critics reappraised the complexity of his characters and his simple style, and Brenner was a role model for many young Israeli writers who preferred his existential approach to the patriotic perspective espoused by many of his peers.

Bibliography

Hirschfeld, Ariel. "'My Peace unto You, My Friend': On Reading a Text by Yosef Haim Brenner concerning His Contacts with the Arabs." *Palestine-Israel Journal* 2 (1994): 112–118.

Holtzman, Avner. "Poetics, Ideology, Biography, Myth: The Scholarship on J. H. Brenner, 1971–1996." *Prooftexts* 18, no. 1 (1998): 82–94.

Sadan, Tsvi. "Will the Zionists Welcome the Prophet from Nazareth? Attitudes towards Jesus in 'The Brenner Event.'" *Mishkan* 33 (2000): 49–62.

ANN KAHN
UPDATED BY GEORGE R. WILKES

BREZHNEV, LEONID ILYICH
[1906–1982]

Soviet politician; president of the USSR, 1960–1964 and 1977–1982; premier, 1964–1982.

Son of a Russian metalworker in the Ukraine and a factory worker himself, Brezhnev went on to study land management and reclamation. He joined the Communist Party (CPSU) in 1931 and was appointed secretary of the Dnepropetrovsk (industrial center in Ukraine) regional party committee in 1939. After World War II, Brezhnev became first secretary of the Dnepropetrovsk Party organization and, subsequently, of the Moldavian Soviet Socialist Republic. In 1954, he was promoted to the leadership of the Kazakhstan party organization and placed in charge of Nikita Khrushchev's "virgin land" campaign. Recalled to Moscow in 1956, Brezhnev was appointed Central Committee secretary in charge of heavy industry and capital construction and, in 1957, was graduated to full membership in the Politburo. In 1964, having led the group that ousted Khrushchev, he became secretary-general of the CPSU, remaining in that position until his death in 1982.

In his foreign relations, Brezhnev adhered to many of the policies initiated by Khrushchev while introducing some changes of his own. Thus, he rejected the notion of superpower conflict and insisted that differences between Moscow and Washington be settled by peaceful means. Brezhnev did, however, allocate considerable resources to achieving relative nuclear parity with the United States. In this task he was successful. Like Khrushchev, Brezhnev insisted on superpower competition in developing countries.

Leonid Brezhnev (front left) meets with Egyptian president Gamal Abdel Nasser (front right) in August 1965. © BETTMANN/CORBIS. REPRODUCED BY PERMISSION.

While Khrushchev distributed Soviet largesse virtually for the asking, however, Brezhnev picked his clients with care. The determining factor was their ability to provide the USSR with tangible benefits (such as naval and air bases) or political advantages in its global competition with the United States. In the Middle East, in particular, the Soviets required naval and air bases to counter the U.S. Sixth Fleet and Polaris submarines. Khrushchev's efforts to obtain the bases failed. Brezhnev succeeded, but only temporarily. Gamal Abdel Nasser's "war of attrition," waged against the Israeli positions along the Suez Canal, led to Israeli deep-penetration raids against Egyptian targets. In desperation, Cairo asked Moscow for help. Brezhnev obliged but on the condition that Soviet naval and air bases be established on Egyptian territory. These important gains, made in 1970, did not last. In 1972, Anwar Sadat ordered the Soviet military advisers and the air force to leave Egypt; the navy followed in 1976. Nevertheless, the USSR had stood by its clients: Moscow backed the Arabs during the wars of 1967 and 1973. In the late 1970s, however, relations with Egypt and Iraq deteriorated sharply. Syria and South Yemen (or the PDRY) remained friendly but, by 1980, the Soviet position in the Middle East had grown much weaker than it had been a decade earlier.

In 1968, upset by the Communist reform movement in Prague, Brezhnev ordered Soviet troops into Czechoslovakia. The move was subsequently explained by Moscow's obligation to "protect socialism" in countries where it was being endangered by "anti-Communist elements." This Brezhnev Doctrine was invoked only once in the Middle East: In 1979, Soviet troops crossed into Afghanistan to back its Communist regime against powerful anti-government rebels (mujahidin). A quick victory did not materialize and, by 1982, Soviet forces were bogged down in a stalemated conflict with the anti-Communist opposition, finally withdrawing in 1989.

See also KHRUSHCHEV, NIKITA S.; NASSER, GAMAL ABDEL; SADAT, ANWAR AL-.

Bibliography

Dawisha, Karen. *Soviet Foreign Policy towards Egypt.* New York: St. Martin's, 1979.

Freedman, Robert O. *Soviet Policy toward the Middle East since 1970,* 3d edition. New York: Praeger, 1982.

OLES M. SMOLANSKY

BRICHAH

Underground movement, both organized and spontaneous, of Jewish Holocaust survivors fleeing Eastern Europe for Palestine.

Functioning from about 1944 through 1948, the Brichah (Hebrew for flight) organization was officially established in Lublin, Poland, in January 1945, under the leadership of Abba Kovner. Among the founders were Jewish resistance fighters, partisans, and Zionist underground groups, all of whom had had previous experience in smuggling Jews across hostile borders in Nazi-occupied Europe during the Holocaust. The key transit points were Czechoslovakia, Hungary, Yugoslavia, Italy, and U.S. army–controlled zones in Germany and Austria.

The height of Brichah activity was in 1945 and 1946, when about 180,000 Jews fled or migrated. In 1946 the USSR closed its borders; in early 1947 Poland halted its lenient policy of allowing Jews to cross freely; in April 1947 the U.S. army declared that it was no longer accepting Jews in D.P. (displaced persons) camps. By 1948 Brichah activity was winding down, although some crossing points remained on the borders of Eastern Europe.

From 1944 through 1948, Brichah helped approximately 200,000 Jews to flee Eastern Europe.

The organization's ideology was Zionism, and its importance lay not only in helping these Holocaust survivors flee lands of persecution, but, by bringing masses of Jews to Palestine, it also played a key role in the establishment of the State of Israel.

See also HOLOCAUST; ISRAEL; KOVNER, ABBA; ZIONISM.

Bibliography

Bauer, Yehuda. *Flight and Rescue: Brichah.* New York: Random House, 1970.

Rolef, Susan Hattis, ed. *Political Dictionary of the State of Israel,* 2d edition. New York: Macmillan, 1993.

ANN KAHN

BRITAIN AND THE MIDDLE EAST FROM 1914 TO THE PRESENT

Britain's short-lived Middle East empire was a product of economic interests and strategic imperatives.

British involvement in the region long antedated World War I, but Britain's "moment" in the Middle East, as it has been called—the period in which it was the dominant power in much of the area—lasted from 1914 to 1956. The axis of Britain's Middle Eastern empire stretched from the Suez Canal to the Persian Gulf. At its height between the two world wars, Britain's supremacy was almost unchallenged either by other powers or by indigenous forces. Yet after 1945, British dominance quickly crumbled, leaving few relics of any kind.

The initial impetus toward deeper British involvement in the Middle East arose from the entry of the Ottoman Empire into World War I on the side of the Central Powers at the end of October 1914. The British did not seek conflict with the Turks, seeing it as a diversion from the primary task of defeating Germany; they nevertheless moved quickly both to confront Turkey in the battlefield and to plan postwar dispensation in the Middle East. The "Eastern question" in its traditional form terminated abruptly, and a new phase began in which the Allied powers struggled over the postwar partition of the Ottoman Empire among themselves.

WWI and British Entry in the Region

The British cabinet decided on 2 November that "after what had happened we ought to take a vigorous offensive." In a public speech at Guildhall in London on 9 November, the prime minister, H. H. Asquith, declared: "It is the Ottoman government, and not we who have rung the death knell of Ottoman dominion not only in Europe but in Asia." The next month Britain severed the formal constitutional link between Egypt and the Ottoman Empire, declared a protectorate over the country, deposed the anti-British Khedive Abbas Hilmi II, and installed a successor, Husayn Kamil, as sultan.

Despite misgivings in the High Command, which favored concentration of Britain's limited military resources on the western front against Germany, an onslaught against the Ottoman Empire was launched on three fronts: at the Dardanelles, in Mesopotamia, and on the border between Egypt and Palestine; Russian forces, meanwhile, engaged Turkey from the north.

The attack on the Straits resulted in one of the great catastrophes of British military history. An initial naval attempt to force the Dardanelles was easily repulsed. Subsequent landings on the Gallipoli Peninsula by British and empire troops gained no significant military objective and led to a bloodbath. Turkish forces led by Mustafa Kemal (later known as Atatürk) repelled the invaders, causing many casualties. The reputation of Winston Churchill, then first lord of the admiralty, who had been the chief political patron of the operation, was damaged.

In Mesopotamia, too, the British were humiliated. An army was dispatched from India to invade the country, from the Persian Gulf. But in April 1916 General Charles Townshend's Sixth Division was forced to surrender at Kut al-Amara. The British nevertheless brought in new forces, which advanced to conquer Baghdad by March 1917.

On the Egypt–Palestine front, Turkish raids on the Suez Canal led to British occupation of the Sinai Peninsula. Thereafter, a stalemate developed, partly because of lackluster leadership but mainly because of British inability to commit large forces to a front that was regarded as peripheral to the outcome of the war. In 1917, however, the advance resumed under General Edmund Henry Allenby who entered Jerusalem in triumph in December 1917. He moved on the following autumn to win the battle of

After a single day's fighting in December 1917, Jerusalem fell to British forces under the command of General Edmund Allenby. Subsequent Turkish counterattacks failed to recapture the city, and its loss represented a serious blow to Ottoman pride. © HULTON-DEUTSCH COLLECTION/CORBIS. REPRODUCED BY PERMISSION.

Megiddo and to conquer Syria. This was the last great cavalry victory in the history of warfare. By the time of the Turkish armistice on 30 October 1918, British forces were thus in control of most of the Fertile Crescent.

Meanwhile, the British had sponsored and financed a revolt of tribesmen in the Arabian Peninsula against their Ottoman Turkish overlords. Organized by a Cairo-based group of British Middle East experts known as the Arab Bureau, the revolt began in June 1916. It engaged, in particular, the followers of the Hashimite ruler of the Hijaz, Sharif of Mecca (Husayn ibn Ali), and his sons. Among the British officers who advised the rebels was T. E. Lawrence, who fought with bands of Arab guerrillas against targets in Arabia. They blew up

Turkish installations along the Hijaz Railroad, captured Aqaba in 1917, and harassed the enemy on the eastern flank of Allenby's army as it advanced north toward Damascus. In recognition of their efforts, and as a sop to Arab nationalist feeling, Allenby stage-managed the capture of Damascus on 1 October 1918, allowing the Arab army to enter the city in triumph, though the victory had been chiefly the work of Australian cavalry commanded by General Sir Harry Chauvel.

The parade fitted into larger British schemes. During the war, the British had given benevolent but unspecific encouragement to Hashimite aspirations toward the creation of a unified Arab state under their leadership. Later Arab claims made much of alleged promises made in correspondence in

1915–1916 between the British high commissioner in Egypt, Sir Henry McMahon, and Sharif Husayn, though the exchanges were vague and inconclusive on both sides and never resulted in a formal treaty.

Carving Up the Ottoman Empire

Britain entered into more specific obligations to other allies. In April 1915, it signed a secret treaty promising Constantinople to Russia, thus explicitly jettisoning Britain's long-standing reservations about Russian control of the Straits. (In fact, British governments since the time of Lord Salisbury at the turn of the century had resigned themselves to eventual Russian control of Constantinople.) At the same time, as part of the price of persuading Italy to enter the war on the Allied side, Britain agreed in the Treaty of London that, in a postwar carve-up of the Ottoman dominions, Italy would receive southwest Anatolia. Under an agreement negotiated in 1916 between Sir Mark Sykes and François Georges-Picot, Britain promised France most of Syria, Cilicia, and the oil-bearing region around Mosul in northern Mesopotamia. Most fraught with evil consequence for the British was the Balfour Declaration of November 1917 in which Britain undertook to facilitate the establishment of a national home for the Jewish people in Palestine—with provisos protecting the "civil and religious rights of the existing non-Jewish communities" and the rights of Jews in other countries. All of these engagements were designed to serve urgent wartime objectives rather than long-term interests.

These overlapping (many said conflicting) claims came home to roost at the Paris Peace Settlements in 1919, at which all parties presented their claims. Both the Zionists and the Arabs were represented by pro-British leaders: the Zionists by Chaim Weizmann, the Arabs by a Hijazi delegation headed by Amir Faisal (Faisal I ibn Hussein). T. E. Lawrence acted at the conference as adviser to Amir Faisal, who conformed to British desires in all matters—even to the extent of making friendly gestures toward Zionism. The French, however, proved less amenable. They spoke darkly of "a new Fashoda" and vigorously asserted their territorial demands in the Levant and Anatolia.

In large measure, Britain, as the power in possession, was able to impose its own design on the region. Its forces, commanded by Allenby, were in

British solider and author T. E. Lawrence joined the British Expeditionary Force with the rank of major in 1917, and helped to coordinate the Arab revolt against the Turks. Better known as Lawrence of Arabia, he made friends with the Arabs, learned their language, wore their clothing, and ate their food.
© LIBRARY OF CONGRESS. REPRODUCED BY PERMISISON.

occupation of the Fertile Crescent and Egypt. Although Allenby's army included French, Italian, and other national units, these were too weak to form a counterweight to British military might. The Bolshevists had in the meantime published the text of the Constantinople convention and renounced their predecessors' claim to the city. The implosion of Russian power and the outbreak of the Russian civil war eliminated Britain's great historic fear of Russian movement south toward the Mediterranean, the Persian Gulf, and India.

Postwar Consolidation of British Influence

Overwhelming military power also enabled the British to dispose of indigenous challenges to their authority. Rebellion in Egypt in 1919 was repressed by Allenby with a dexterous mixture of force and diplomacy. Revolt in Iraq in 1920 was put down by General Arnold T. Wilson with an iron fist. Riots in Palestine in April 1920 and May 1921 were suppressed, in the latter case by bombarding villages from the air, and succeeded by political concessions.

The Paris Peace Conference did not, in fact, achieve a resolution of territorial issues in the Middle East. In August 1920, the Treaty of Sèvres, by which Turkey gave up all its non-Arab provinces as well as parts of Anatolia, was signed by the Allied powers and representatives of the Ottoman government, which by this time was little more than a diplomatic ghost. Simultaneous secret agreements among the Allies provided for an additional carve-up of much of what remained of Turkish Anatolia. The treaty never came into effect. As a result of the Kemalist revolt, it was disavowed by the Turks and fell into abeyance.

Following the peace conference, France continued to squabble with Britain over a division of the Middle East spoils. The British conceded control of Syria and Lebanon to their erstwhile ally. They were dismayed, however, when the French, in July 1920, unceremoniously ejected Faisal from Damascus, where his enthusiastic supporters had proclaimed him king of Syria. Faisal arrived in British-controlled Palestine as a refugee with a large entourage. A harried British governor of Haifa complained that they were "in and out like a swarm of bees" and warned that "they cannot stay here indefinitely." There was no disposition, however, on the part of his British patrons to seek to reinstall Faisal in Damascus. As a kind of consolation prize, the British arranged for his "election" by cooperative Mesopotamian notables as king of Iraq.

The British successfully resisted broader French territorial aspirations. The northern oil-bearing region of Mesopotamia, inhabited mainly by Kurds, was assigned to British-controlled Iraq. This departure from the wartime agreement had been informally agreed to at a meeting of the British prime minister, David Lloyd George, and the French prime minister, Georges Clemenceau, in November 1918, but the French continued for some time to grumble about the arrangement. French aspirations to a role in Palestine, where they saw them-

selves as historic protectors of Christian interests, were thrust aside by the British.

Meanwhile, in Transjordan, Faisal's brother, Abdullah I ibn Hussein, had suddenly appeared in October 1920 at the head of a motley army, threatening to attack the French in Syria and to reclaim his brother's "kingdom" there. The British government saw little advantage in taking over the unfertile hollow of the Fertile Crescent. On the other hand, they could not permit Abdullah to drag them into a war with the French. The foreign secretary, Lord George Nathaniel Curzon, reluctantly sanctioned the dispatch of some British officers to the territory, ostensibly to prevent its "relapse into anarchy"—in reality to restrain Abdullah from adventures against the French.

In March 1921, Churchill, then colonial secretary, convened a conference in Cairo of British officials in the region. This meeting set out broad lines of British administration in the Middle East that were to endure for the next decade. Under this arrangement, Abdullah was established as amir of Transjordan; the territory was to form part of the British mandate over Palestine without, however, being open to Jewish settlement. While Abdullah formally ruled the country, the British resident and a small number of other officials discreetly steered policy in directions compatible with British interests.

Reduction of Military Presence

Having established their paramountcy, the British rapidly reduced their military establishment in the Middle East. In the early 1920s, the conservative press in Britain, particularly newspapers owned by Lords Northcliffe and Beaverbrook, agitated against large military expenditures in the region and called for a British exit from recent acquisitions there. In a general climate of demobilization and budget cutting, the government felt obliged to withdraw the bulk of its troops. Henceforth, except in times of crisis, the British did not maintain a large standing army in any part of the Middle East except at the strategically vital Suez.

For the rest of the period between the wars, the British maintained security in the Middle East mainly with locally recruited forces financed by locally collected revenues. Riots, disturbances, and other challenges to British authority were suppressed by the new tactic of aerial bombardment, demonstrative shows of strength, and limited political concessions.

In the age of Gordon and Kitchener, Middle East empire building had a jingoistic tinge, but after 1914 this tendency disappeared. Unlike other parts of the empire—notably, regions of white settlement—Middle East imperialism had no significant popular constituency in Britain. (France, where there was a strong pressure group on behalf of Roman Catholic interests in Syria, was very different.)

At the same time, the legend of Lawrence of Arabia, stimulated first by public lantern shows in Britain and America and later by T. E. Lawrence's writings on the Arab revolt, encouraged the growth of public interest in Arabia. Although the Arab revolt had only minor military significance, it formed the basis of myth and countermyth. The myth was of a natural affinity between the British Empire and Arab desert warriors. The countermyth was of the betrayal of Arab nationalism by duplicitous British diplomacy. Both myths exercised a powerful subliminal influence on Anglo–Arab attitudes over the next generation. The Arab vogue was further encouraged by the writings of Middle Eastern explorers, travelers, and administrators, such as Freya Stark, Gertrude Bell, and Ronald Storrs. The great Victorian classics of Arabian exploration by writers such as Charles Doughty and Richard Francis Burton were revived and achieved a certain réclame.

The official mind of British imperialism, however, was shaped less by sentimental considerations than by hardheaded, realistic calculation of national interest. More than anything, official thinking was predicated on concern about India—specifically, about the security of routes to the subcontinent and the Far East and the possible effects of Middle East developments on internal security in India. With the growth of aviation as well as sea traffic, the need for a string of secure air bases was seen as vital. Indian priorities also lay behind British officials' anxiety about the inflammatory threat, as they saw it, of growing pan-Islamic feeling on the large Muslim minority in India. As it turned out, such fears proved exaggerated: Indian Muslims were not greatly preoccupied by Middle Eastern concerns.

Horatio Herbert Kitchener had a highly successful military career. Among his duties, he was sirdar (or commander) of the Anglo/Egyptian army in 1892, involved in the 1898 battle of Omdurman and Fashoda incident; governor-general of the Sudan in 1899; and commander in chief of British Forces in South Africa from 1900 to 1902. © HULTON-DEUTSCH COLLECTION/CORBIS. REPRODUCED BY PERMISSION.

The resurgence of Turkey under Atatürk caused some anxiety in Britain and led to a momentary crisis at Chanak (near Constantinople) in the autumn of 1922. As the revived Turkish army advanced on Constantinople, British and French forces, in occupation of the city, prepared to resist. Lloyd George, who had given encouragement to the disastrous Greek invasion of Anatolia, was at first inclined to order British forces to stand and fight. But there was no enthusiasm in Britain for such a war. The episode led to the withdrawal of Conservative support for Lloyd George and his fall from power. With the evacuation of British and French forces from Constantinople, the crisis passed. The new Turkish regime signed the Treaty of Lausanne in July 1923, giving up any claim to the Ottoman Empire's former Arab provinces—but holding on to the Turkish, Kurdish, and former Armenian regions of Anatolia.

With the settlement in 1923 of differences over the border between Palestine and Syria, British diplomatic conflict with the French diminished. Disputes with the United States over oil concessions were settled in 1925 with a division of interests in the northern Iraqi petroleum industry. For the next decade, Britain could control the region without worrying about any significant great-power competitor.

British policymaking in the Middle East was not centralized in any one government department. The foreign, colonial, India, and war offices all held responsibility at certain periods for different parts of the region. Broadly speaking, the foreign office was responsible for Egypt, the India office for the Persian Gulf, and the colonial office (from 1921) for the mandates in Palestine, Transjordan, and Iraq. Each of these departments refracted its specific angle of vision and concerns in its formulation of policy. Aden, for example, whose importance to Britain was primarily as a coaling station for ships en route to India, was ruled until 1932 directly from Bombay; after that, responsibility was taken over by the central government in Delhi, and, beginning in 1937, Aden became a crown colony. In some cases, diffusion of responsibility led to conflict between departments: Palestine, over which the colonial and foreign offices clashed repeatedly, was a case in point.

Indirect Rule and "Benevolent Paternalism"

Britain's favored method of rule in the Middle East was indirect and inexpensive: this was a limited liability empire. The model was not India but Egypt, where British advisers had guided government policy since the start of the British occupation. Hardly anywhere did direct rule by a British administration survive intact until after World War II. Typical of British attitudes throughout the region during the period was the comment of the colonial secretary, Lord Cranborne, in 1942: "We not only disclaim any intention of establishing direct rule, but also

quite sincerely and genuinely do not wish to do so." Warning against direct British administration of the tribal hinterland of Aden colony, Cranborne added: "We must keep steadily in front of us the aim of establishing in Aden protectorate a group of efficient Arab authorities who will conduct their own administration under the general guidance and protection of His Majesty's government." The characteristic tone of British governance was set by Sir Percy Cox in Iraq and by Allenby in Egypt: benevolent paternalism in time of peace; readiness to resort to brute force in reaction to civil unrest.

The British did not believe in large public investment in this new empire. They nevertheless greatly improved the primitive economic infrastructure bequeathed them by their Ottoman predecessors, established sound public finances, built solid judicial and (though slowly) educational systems, rooted out corruption, and protected minorities. Efficient government was not the primary purpose of imperial rule, but the British installed it almost by reflex.

The mandatory system in Palestine, Transjordan, and Iraq was a constitutional innovation. Formally, the British ruled these territories not as a colonial power but under the ultimate authority of the League of Nations. Mandatory government was to last for a limited period with the specific goal of preparing the countries for self-rule. All this, in the eyes of most observers, was merely a fig leaf to cover the nakedness of imperial acquisition. Although Britain was ultimately responsible to the league for its conduct of affairs in the mandated territories and was obliged to render account annually of its administration, the league exercised little influence over policy. In effect, Britain ruled the mandated territories as if they were colonies, though here too they sought to establish limited local self-government.

As in other parts of the empire, British power ultimately rested on a collaborative equation with local elements. Its exact form varied depending on local contingencies. In some places, the British practiced a variant of the politics of notables inherited from the Ottomans. In others, they established mutually beneficial alliances with minorities—as with the Jews in Palestine for a time. Elsewhere, they combined these policies with patronage of dynastic rulers, particularly with the family of Sharif Husayn.

Britain's patronage of the Hashimites was dealt a blow in 1925 when Sharif Husayn was driven out of the Hijaz by the resurgent Wahhabi army of Ibn Saʿud, ruler of Najd. Husayn escaped in a British ship bound for Cyprus. Although Ibn Saʿud had been granted a British subsidy in 1916, he had not joined in the Arab revolt and had remained jealous of his Hashimite neighbor. Compelled to accept realities, the British quickly came to terms with Ibn Saʿud. In 1927, they signed a treaty with him that recognized his sovereignty over the Hijaz and, as a result, his leading position among native rulers in the Arabian Peninsula.

Although Ibn Saʿud employed a freelance British adviser, Harry St. John Bridger Philby, a convert to Islam, the Saudi regime's relations with Britain were never intimate. In the kingdom of Saudi Arabia, which Ibn Saʿud proclaimed in 1932, U.S. rather than British companies were favored in the scramble for oil concessions. At the time, this seemed of minor importance; later, when vast oil reserves were discovered, the British regretted the failure. Oil production on a large scale, however, did not begin in the country until after World War II.

Until the late 1930s, the limited liability system survived more or less intact. The independence granted to Egypt in 1922 and Iraq in 1932 did not fundamentally affect Britain's paramountcy. In each case, Britain retained effective control over vital strategic and economic interests. The continuation of this "veiled protectorate," as it became known in the Egyptian case, exacerbated nationalist frustrations and resentments, but these posed no imminent threat to Britain. Independence in Iraq was followed by the mass killing of members of the Nestorian Christian community, known as Assyrians. Thousands fled overseas. Like other minorities, they had looked to the British for protection; the failure to assure their security left a dark stain on Britain's imperial record in the country.

Increasing Threats to British Control

From 1936 onward, Britain's dominance in the Middle East was increasingly threatened from within and without. Mussolini's determination to create an Italian empire around the Mediterranean and the Italian conquest of Ethiopia in 1935 posed a sudden danger to Britain. The powerful Italian broadcasting station on the island of Bari began broadcasting anti-British propaganda to the Middle East. The Italian dictator wooed Ibn Saʿud and other Middle Eastern rulers and gave covert support to anti-British elements in the region, including the anti-British leader of the Palestine Arab nationalist movement, Hajj Amin al-Husayni. The Palestine Arab Revolt between 1936 and 1939 tied down large numbers of British troops at a time when, with the Nazi threat looming in Europe, the British could ill afford such a diversion.

Conscious of their limited resources, particularly of military manpower, the British faced unpalatable policymaking dilemmas in the final months of the peace and felt compelled to subordinate all other considerations to the imperatives of imperial security: hence, the White Papers on Palestine of May 1939, which reversed the Balfour Declaration policy of support for a national home for the Jewish people and restricted Jewish immigration to Palestine at a time of mounting danger to Jews in Europe.

World War II

During World War II, the Middle East played a vital part in British strategic calculations. As prime minister from May 1940, Churchill placed a high priority on bolstering British power in the region. At a critical phase in the war, he insisted on dispatching large numbers of tanks and men to reinforce British forces confronting the Italians, and later the Germans, on the border between Egypt and Libya.

The British could no longer afford the luxury of a piecemeal bureaucratic approach to the Middle East. Economic planning and supply questions for the entire region were coordinated by the Middle East Supply Center in Cairo. A British minister resident was sent to Cairo to take charge of overall policy making. (One incumbent, Lord Moyne, a close friend of Churchill, was murdered in November 1944 by Zionist terrorists as a protest against British policy in Palestine.)

After Italian entry into the war in June 1940, the danger of attack in the Mediterranean precluded use of the Suez Canal by British ships carrying supplies to and from India and the Far East. Ships carrying reinforcements to British forces in Egypt had to take the Cape of Good Hope route before passing through the canal from south to north.

Except in Egypt, where they built up their forces to confront the Italians and later the Germans, the British could not afford to maintain more than a thin crust of military control in most of the region during the war. Yet by a mixture of diplomacy, guile, and occasional demonstrative concentrations of force, they succeeded in averting serious challenge from nationalist opponents. The two most dangerous threats came in Iraq and Egypt. A pro-Axis coup erupted in Iraq in April 1941, headed by Rashid Ali al-Kaylani, aided by Italian and Nazi agents and by the ex-mufti of Jerusalem, Hajj Amin al-Husayni. With pro-Vichy forces in control of Syria and Lebanon, British power throughout the Fertile Crescent seemed for a moment on the verge of toppling. But in May, a small British force from the Habbaniya air base moved into Baghdad. Al-Kaylani and the ex-mufti fled to Germany where they devoted themselves to anti-British propaganda. The following month, British and Free French forces, operating from Palestine, advanced into Syria and Lebanon and installed new French administrations sympathetic to the Allied cause.

The other threat appeared in Egypt, where nationalist elements, particularly in the Egyptian army, were impressed by Axis military successes and sought to take advantage of Britain's moment of weakness. The British reacted firmly. In February 1942, British tanks surrounded the royal palace as a weeping King Farouk was forced by ultimatum to appoint a prime minister acceptable to the British, Mustafa al-Nahhas, head of the Wafd party. From the British point of view, the Abdin palace coup, as the episode became known, gave a salutary demonstration of British resolve at a time of acute military pressure from the Germans in the western desert.

The battle in the western desert swung to and fro. In the initial phase, between June 1940 and February 1941, a British army under General Archibald Wavell beat back an offensive by Italian forces under Marshal Rodolfo Graziani and advanced into Cyrenaica. In the spring of 1941, however, Axis forces were bolstered by the arrival of the German Afrika Korps commanded by General Erwin Rommel, a brilliant strategist. The tide was reversed: the British were routed from Libya, and the British garrison at Tobruk was besieged and captured. By mid-1942, the Germans had advanced deep into Egypt. Government departments in Cairo began burning secret documents, and emergency evacuation plans were prepared.

In November 1942, the critical battle of the campaign was fought against Rommel at al-Alamayn by the British Eighth Army under General Bernard Montgomery. Months of careful planning coupled with imaginative mobile tactics, intelligent exploitation of ultra signals intelligence, as well as British superiority in numbers of men and machines, brought a decisive victory. This was, in Churchill's phrase, "the end of the beginning." Thereafter, the British strategic position in the region eased. Almost simultaneously in Morocco and Algeria, Operation Torch, the landing of U.S. and British forces commanded by General Eisenhower, had opened a new front against the Axis. By May 1943, the Germans and Italians had been cleared out of northern Africa.

Churchill's preoccupation with the Mediterranean led him up some blind alleys. He tried repeatedly to draw Turkey into the war on the Allied side but without success. Turkey remained neutral until early 1945, when it declared war on Germany at the last moment in order to qualify for membership in the United Nations (UN). The United States opposed Churchill's Mediterranean strategy both on military grounds and because the United States did not wish to give the appearance of propping up British imperial interests. Ibn Saʿud, too, remained neutral until the last moment, though he received handsome subsidies from the British and the United States and made some gestures of support for the Allied cause.

Britain did not seek territorial acquisition in the Middle East in World War II. It nevertheless found itself drawn into new responsibilities. Following the German attack on the Soviet Union in June 1941, Britain joined the USSR in occupying Iran. Arms and other supplies to the Soviet Union were sent by rail through Iran. With the expulsion of the last Axis forces from Libya in 1943, that country was placed under military administration—French in the Fezzan and British in Tripolitania and Cyrenaica. British forces also occupied the former Italian possessions of Eritrea, Abyssinia, and Italian Somaliland. Abyssinia was restored to its indigenous imperial ruler. Eritrea remained under British rule until 1952 when it was annexed by Abyssinia. Italian

Somaliland was returned to Italy as a UN trusteeship in 1950. Libya became independent in December 1951, though Britain was granted the right under the Anglo–Libyan Alliance Treaty of 1953 to maintain military installations there.

During the war, large reserves of oil in the Arabian Peninsula had come onstream. Because of the closure of the Mediterranean to British commercial shipping, British use of Middle East oil during the war was mainly restricted to the area east of the Suez. Elsewhere, Britain mainly relied on imports from the Americas. After the war, the balance changed. Over the next three decades, Britain became steadily more dependent on oil imports from the Middle East, especially Kuwait.

Postwar Loss of Empire and the Cold War

In the later stages of the war, the British government, seeing the nationalist mood in many Arab countries, tried to move toward a new relationship with the Arabs. Following a speech by the British foreign secretary, Anthony Eden, in which he indicated British sympathy for the idea of Arab unity, a conference of Arab states at Alexandria in October 1944 approved the foundation of the League of Arab States. The effort to ride the tiger, however, had only limited success; the British soon found that Arab nationalism turned strongly against them.

During the war, the Soviet Union had cautiously raised its diplomatic profile in the Middle East. After 1945, the region became a secondary arena of great-power conflict in the Cold War. In 1945 and 1946, the USSR signaled its newly aggressive posture by attempting to establish pro-Soviet administrations in northern Iran. Eventually British and American, as well as Russian, forces withdrew from Iran and a pro-Western regime was consolidated under Mohammad Reza Pahlavi.

Elsewhere, Soviet influence was exercised by propaganda and subversion rather than direct military intervention. Although Communist parties remained weak in the region, Soviet sponsorship of Arab nationalist movements posed a growing threat to Western interests in general and the British in particular.

The end of British rule in India in 1947 lessened the strategic argument for a major British military commitment in the Middle East. But oil—both investments and supply—and the security of the Suez Canal remained central British concerns. British policy now faced acute difficulties in the Middle East: on the one hand, Britain retained vital interests there; on the other, its postwar economic debilitation left it unable to muster the military forces required to meet any serious challenge to control those interests.

As a result, Britain was increasingly overshadowed by the United States in the Middle East. Under the Truman Doctrine, enunciated in 1947, the United States replaced Britain as the main provider of military and economic assistance to Greece and Turkey. The United States had already begun edging the British out of monopolistic control of oil concessions. Now, the United States became the dominant external diplomatic power, particularly in Saudi Arabia. It established a large air base in Saudi Arabia, built the Trans-Arabian Pipeline, and became the major external source of arms and other aid. Saudi relations with Britain were meanwhile clouded by the Buraymi Oasis Dispute (claimed by Abu Dhabi and Oman, which were both under British protection). The dispute flared into military conflict in 1952 and again in 1955; it led to a breach in Anglo–Saudi diplomatic relations between 1956 and 1963.

Palestine. British military and political weakness was damagingly demonstrated to the world by the collapse of the British mandate in Palestine. In spite of the presence of substantial British forces and the experience gained in crushing Arab insurgency between 1936 and 1939, the mandatory government proved unable to assert its authority in the face of a revolt by the half million Jews in the country.

The international ramifications of the Palestine conflict created serious difficulties for the British between 1945 and 1948. In the British-occupied zones of Germany and Austria, the military authorities were faced with growing numbers of Jewish displaced persons, the majority of whom demanded to be allowed to proceed to Palestine. In the United States, on which Britain depended for economic aid, the assertive and electorally significant Jewish community pressed Congress and President Harry Truman to secure a pro-Zionist outcome in Palestine. Meanwhile, British diplomats throughout the Arab Middle East reported that the Palestine question had become a central mobilizing issue for Arab nationalists and anti-British agitators.

Although the colonial office remained formally responsible for Palestine, these international complications led the foreign office to take effective control of British policymaking on the issue after 1945. The Labour Government's foreign secretary, Ernest Bevin, adopted an anti-Zionist position, which at times tipped over the edge into antisemitism; his undiplomatic outspokenness secured applause from frustrated officials but was bitterly resented by many Jews. In the final stages of the crisis (1947–1948), the British publicly washed their hands of the matter, professing to leave it to the decision of the United Nations. Yet, following the decision of the UN General Assembly on 29 November 1947 to partition Palestine into Jewish and Arab states, the British barely cooperated in implementing the decision. Privately, Bevin encouraged the government of Transjordan to reach a modus vivendi with the Zionists on the basis of a different kind of partition, one in which the Transjordanians would take over the Arab-inhabited hill regions of the country and coexist with a Jewish state in the rest of Palestine. In the end this was, broadly speaking, the outcome.

The Arab–Israeli War, which lasted from 1947 to 1949, tightened the British connection with Transjordan. Although the country had been granted independence in 1946, it remained under British tutelage. In March 1948, an alliance treaty was concluded in which the two countries promised each other military assistance and Transjordan agreed to the stationing of British forces in the country "until such a time . . . that the state of the world renders such measures unnecessary." Britain was the only country in the world to recognize the Jordanian annexation of the West Bank.

The Zionists' feat in driving the British out of Palestine in 1948 depressed British prestige throughout the region. The British government after 1945 made strenuous efforts to dissociate itself from Zionism; Arab nationalists for the next generation nevertheless attributed the creation of Israel in large measure to Britain's earlier support of a national home for the Jewish people.

British Influence in Decline

After Palestine, the second significant test of British political will in the Middle East came in Iran. In 1951, the Anglo–Iranian Oil Company, in which the British government owned 51 percent of the shares, was nationalized by legislation in the Iranian parliament. A nationalist government, headed by Mohammad Mossadegh, defied British attempts to secure a reversal of the nationalization. With the support of major international oil companies, the British government organized a boycott of Iranian oil. Diplomatic relations between the two countries were broken. The departure of foreign oil exports led to closure of the Abadan oil refinery. As the oil companies refused to process, ship, or purchase Iranian oil, the entire petroleum industry in the country ground to a halt. At the height of the crisis in 1953, the Shah, who strongly opposed Mossadegh, fled the country.

Meanwhile, in November 1952, the British had approached the United States about the possibility of organizing a joint covert operation to protect western interests in Iran. Shortly afterward, an Iranian army coup, engineered by the U.S. Central Intelligence Agency with British help, overthrew Mossadegh and brought about the return of the Shah. The Iranian oil industry was reorganized: The British granted formal recognition of Iranian ownership of the oil industry in exchange for the lease of its operations to a multinational consortium. The British share in this consortium was reduced to under a half, with the remainder held mainly by U.S. companies.

Of even greater concern to British governments was the deterioration of the British position in Egypt. Egyptian nationalists, chafing under what was seen as continued behind-the-scenes British influence, demanded the renegotiation of the Anglo–Egyptian treaty of 1936 and the closing of British bases. There was also conflict with Britain over the Sudan, which was ruled by Britain though it was formally an Anglo–Egyptian condominium; the Egyptian government now sought to annex the country to Egypt. In January 1952, anti-British riots broke out in Egypt and paved the way for the revolution of July 1952 in which a group of military officers, headed by Muhammad Naguib and Gamal Abdel Nasser, seized power, deposed the king, and declared a republic.

The British now began to consider moving the center of gravity of their Middle East operations to a more secure point. A first step was the decision in December 1952 to move the Middle East headquarters of the British armed forces from Egypt to Cyprus.

In the hope of constructing a bulwark against Soviet subversion and of limiting the growth of anti-Western influences in the region, Britain and the United States had proposed in October 1951 the creation of the Middle East Defense Organization. Turkey, which was concerned about Soviet pressure for a new regime at the Straits, expressed willingness to join such an alliance; but Egypt rejected it, and no other Middle Eastern state expressed interest, whereupon the scheme was abandoned.

Other such proposals met similar fates. The Baghdad Pact of 1955 represented a final attempt by the western powers, with the United States by this time playing the leading role, to create a regional framework under their auspices. The core of the scheme was a multilateral military aid treaty signed by Britain, Iraq, Turkey, Iran, and Pakistan, with the United States acting as an interested outside party. No Arab state apart from Iraq could be induced to join the pact, and Egypt, in particular, opposed it vigorously. The failure to attract Arab members was seen as a further sign of the decline of British authority in the region.

In Jordan, the young King Hussein ibn Talal, educated at Harrow and Sandhurst, became the most pro-British of postwar Middle East rulers. His cultural formation was as much British as Arab; he maintained a home in Britain and was the one Arab ruler who was a popular public figure in Britain (his second wife was British). Such personal predilections, however, could not overcome the larger forces shaping events. Hussein, whose long career was marked by frequent shifts of policy consummated with supreme maneuvering skill, found himself compelled to bend to the anti-British wind. In March 1956, responding to external and internal political pressures, he dismissed the British commander of his army, Sir John Bagot Glubb. Since the formation of the Transjordanian emirate in 1921, the state's army, the Arab Legion, had always been commanded by a British officer. In his ability to reconcile loyalties to the British and to his Arab

employer, Glubb had been characteristic of a fading type of British officer in the Middle East. While commanding the Arab Legion he had routinely supplied the British government with secret copies of Jordan's war plans. The dismissal of "Glubb Pasha" was generally regarded as the end of an era and a telling sign of the decline of British influence.

The Suez Canal

The supreme crisis of British power in the Middle East came later that year, appropriately at the focal point of Britain's interests in the region and the reason d'être of its presence there—the Suez Canal. In spite of its gradually diminishing economic position relative to other powers, Britain remained the world's foremost shipping nation, and the British merchant fleet was by far the largest user of the canal. With the growth of motor transport and the switch from coal to oil as the main industrial fuel, Britain had become overwhelmingly reliant on the importation of Middle East oil carried through the canal in tankers. Pressure from the Egyptian government for a British evacuation of the Suez Canal zone, therefore, encountered stiff resistance.

In October 1954, Britain had promised to withdraw all its force from the canal zone by mid-1956. The agreement, however, was hedged with several provisos reminiscent of the veiled protectorate, among them a stipulation that Egypt continue to offer Britain "such facilities as may be necessary to place the Base [in the canal zone] on a war footing and to operate it effectively" if any outside power attacked a member of the Arab League or Turkey. In November 1955, British troops withdrew from the Sudan as the country moved toward full independence in January 1956. The following July, in accordance with the 1954 agreement, Britain withdrew the last of its troops from the canal zone.

Nationalism and the Brink of War. Hardly had the last British soldiers packed their bags, however, than the Egyptian president afforded the British a pretext to return. On 26 July, Nasser, infuriated by the withdrawal of an offer by the United States, Britain, and the World Bank to finance the construction of a new dam at Aswan, announced the nationalization of the Suez Canal Company, which operated the canal. The British *locus standi* in the matter was doubtful. The British government owned a minority stake in the company, but nationalization in itself was no offense against international law, provided compensation was paid, and the Egyptians insisted that they would continue to operate the canal as before.

The nationalization was, nevertheless, regarded by the British prime minister, Anthony Eden, as an intolerable affront. When diplomacy failed to secure an Egyptian retreat, the British prepared for war. They were joined by France, which had its own reasons for opposing the Nasser regime on account of Egypt's support of Algerian rebels. Israel, which had suffered a series of border incursions from Egypt, was also drawn into military and diplomatic planning. Conspiratorial discussions among representatives of the three countries at a villa in the Paris suburb of Sèvres from 22 to 24 October culminated in a secret treaty. The agreement mapped out a scenario for war with Egypt. Israel would attack first across the Sinai peninsula. The British and French would then enter the conflict, ostensibly to secure the Suez Canal, in fact to destroy Nasser's regime.

The Israelis attacked on 29 October, and the British and French duly issued an ultimatum the next day calling on Israel and Egypt to withdraw to positions 10 miles east and west of the Suez Canal (the Israelis had not yet, in fact, reached the canal). In the absence of Egyptian acquiescence, British and French planes began bombing Egyptian military targets on 31 October. On 5 November, the two powers landed paratroops. The next day, however, British policy went into reverse as a result of U.S. opposition to the invasion and of growing market pressure on sterling. Britain and France were humiliatingly obliged to agree to a cease-fire, and by Christmas they had withdrawn their forces from Egypt.

Britain's collusion with France and Israel in the events leading to the Suez war became the subject of bitter controversy in Britain. The issue is said to have divided the nation more than any foreign-policy question since Munich. The Labour Party, a small part of the Conservative party, some foreign office officials, and most enlightened opinion were hostile to Eden's policy. For the British government, Suez was an unmitigated catastrophe—not least in the severe strains it placed on relations with the United States. Eden resigned a few weeks later, complaining of ill health.

Although Suez is generally regarded as a watershed in British history, heralding a wider imperial withdrawal, Britain continued for another decade to maintain a substantial military presence in the Middle East and to be ready on occasion to use it forcefully in defense of its interests.

Last Vestiges of Empire

The next flashpoint was Jordan. In March 1957, a nationalist government in Jordan abrogated the Anglo–Jordanian Treaty. In July 1958, the Jordanian regime was severely shaken by the revolution in Iraq, in which the Hashimite regime was ousted and the young King Faisal II ibn Ghazi and the pro-British Prime Minister Nuri al-Saʿid were both murdered. British paratroops were sent, at the request of King Hussein, to prevent a similar revolution in Jordan. Two aspects of this intervention, code-named Operation Fortitude, illustrated the changed political environment within which the British, perforce, now operated. First, the cabinet refused to commit British forces until the approval of the U.S. government had been secured. Second, the British requested and received permission from Israel to overfly Israeli territory in order to transport troops from bases on Cyprus. The British force succeeded in bolstering the Hashimite monarchy without firing a shot. The pro-British Jordanian monarchy survived, but Britain lost its bases in Iraq as well as its oil interests there.

In 1961, when Kuwait, hitherto a British protectorate, secured independence, the military regime in Iraq threatened a takeover of the oil-rich principality. As at the time of the intervention in Jordan in 1958, the British made sure that they had U.S. approval before taking military action. Eight thousand British troops were sent to Kuwait and remained there as a deterrent against Iraqi invasion until 1963.

In Aden in the mid-1960s, British forces conducted a miserable campaign against nationalist insurgents supported by Egypt. The British military headquarters at Aden were evacuated in November 1967 when the Federation of South Arabia achieved independence as the People's Democratic Republic of Yemen. Although the writing was on the wall for what remained of British power in the Middle East, there was no complete pullout yet. With the liquidation of the base at Aden, Britain expanded its military presence in Bahrain and other Gulf principalities.

In the crisis prior to the outbreak of the Arab–Israel War of 1967, the British government of Harold Wilson briefly considered participating in the dispatch of an international naval flotilla to assert the right of passage to Israel through the Strait of Tiran, which the Egyptian government had declared closed against Israeli and Israeli-bound ships. But no other country was prepared to join in the effort, and the idea was dropped. Although both Wilson and his foreign secretary, George Brown, were sympathetic to Israel, their attitude was not governed by any pro-Zionist altruism. The British remained vitally interested in free passage through the Suez Canal. Upon the outbreak of war with Israel in June 1967, Nasser closed the canal to all shipping; it did not open again until 1975. The closure severely affected the British balance of payments. The British economy was blown off course, and the government was compelled, against its wish, to devalue sterling in November of that year.

Only in 1968 did the Wilson government abandon pretensions to world-power status by dropping the east-of-Suez defense policy. In March 1970, the revolutionary government in Libya, headed by Colonel Muammar al-Qaddafi who had attended an officers' training school in Britain, ejected the British from their bases in the country. British forces withdrew from Bahrain in 1971, but retained naval facilities there. Also in 1971, British forces left Abu Dhabi, whereupon the seven Trucial Coast shaykhdoms formed the federation of the United Arab Emirates. The British retained troops in Oman, where they helped suppress a leftist rebellion in the Dhufar region. Although British forces were formally withdrawn in 1976, many senior British officers remained on individual contracts as commanders of the Omani army. Only in 1984 was the British commander in chief of the country's armed forces replaced by an Omani. After that, the sole remaining permanent British military presence in the Middle East was in the sovereign bases on Cyprus.

With the elimination of its military power in the region, Britain found itself relegated to a secondary role in Middle Eastern politics. More and more,

Militant Leila Khaled was one of the two hijackers who placed a time bomb on an American TWA plane and damaged the jet in Damascus, Syria, on 29 August 1969. Pictured with a machine gun, she rejoined her guerrilla unit in Amman, Jordan. © BETTMANN/CORBIS. REPRODUCED BY PERMISSION.

Britain was buffeted and unable to deflect ill political and economic winds blowing from the Middle East.

Oil, Terrorism, and the British Economy

During the 1970s, the exploits of Palestinian Arab terrorists and the anti-Western rhetoric of Middle East leaders like Qaddafi evoked some admiration on the radical left of the political spectrum in Britain as elsewhere in Europe. Episodes such as the hijacking by Palestinian terrorists of two planes to a desert aerodrome in Jordan—the episode that occasioned the Black September conflict between the Jordanian government and the Palestine Liberation organization in 1970—riveted television audiences in Britain. In that instance, the government of Prime Minister Edward Heath decided to give way to terrorist demands and released an imprisoned Palestinian, Leila Khaled, who became a folk hero of the revolutionary left.

The Arab–Israel War of 1973 and the ensuing international energy crisis had dramatic and damaging effects on the British economy. The sudden huge increase in the price of oil and the restriction of supply by the oil producers' cartel, the Organization of Petroleum Exporting Countries (OPEC), were the major causes of the stagflation that afflicted Britain in the mid-1970s. The coal miners' union attempted to seize the opportunity offered by the general rise in energy prices to secure a large increase in wages paid by the nationalized coal industry. The miners' strike ushered in a bitter confrontation with the Conservative government of Heath, which called a general election on the issue in February 1974 and narrowly lost to the Labour Party.

As a member of the European Economic Community (EEC) from 1973 onward, Britain generally sought to adjust her diplomacy in the Middle East to conform to a consensus of EEC members. In the aftermath of the 1973 and 1979 oil crises, this resulted in a suddenly humble attitude by former imperial powers to sometime protégés such as Iran and the Gulf emirates. A case in point was the Venice Declaration, issued by the EEC in June 1980, which marked a significant shift in diplomatic posture toward the Arab position in the conflict with Israel.

The power of OPEC enabled the producing states at last to seize effective control over their oil industries. During the 1970s and 1980s, they moved toward vertical integration of the industry, nationalizing the extraction installations, establishing refineries and petrochemical industries, investing in their own transportation of products by tanker or pipeline, and creating their own marketing mechanisms. The power of the international oil companies in the region consequently dwindled. The British government's direct interest in Middle East oil evaporated in the 1980s when the government of Prime Minister Margaret Thatcher sold off government share holdings in British Petroleum and Anglo–Dutch Shell.

Unlike most western industrial countries, however, Britain enjoyed fortuitous good fortune in the discovery and successful development of indigenous oil resources. Its dependence on Middle East oil imports ended after 1980 with the arrival onstream of large oil reserves from the North Sea. As Britain's oil production grew, it was able to play a major role in weakening and ultimately destroying the effectiveness of OPEC. Although oil production costs were much higher in the North Sea than in the Middle East, the British, in concert with other non-OPEC producers, proved able to undercut the floor prices set by OPEC. Several OPEC members, desperate for revenues to sustain their commitments to large expenditures on armaments or social programs, broke cartel discipline and secretly sold at lower prices. With demand flagging, this led in 1986 to a sudden collapse in oil prices.

In the 1980s, Middle Eastern politics spilled over onto the streets of London with a spate of terrorist incidents, including assassinations, bombings, and embassy seizures. In 1984, a British policewoman was murdered in the street during a demonstration in front of the Libyan People's Bureau in Saint James's Square in London. The gunshots were fired by a Libyan diplomat from within the embassy. There were also attacks on several Israeli and Zionist targets in Britain, as well as on Jewish institutions that had nothing to do with Israel. The most shocking terrorist incident was the midair explosion in 1988 aboard a Pan Am plane over Lockerbie, Scotland, in which all the passengers and crewmembers were killed. Scottish and U.S. prosecutors sought to secure the extradition of two Libyan citizens suspected of responsibility for planting the bomb. But the Libyan government long refused to yield up the men, in spite of the imposition of economic sanctions by the United Nations in 1992.

Perhaps the most bizarre of all these episodes was the *fatwa* (legal opinion) issued in 1989 by the leading Iranian cleric, Ayatollah Ruhollah Khomeini, pronouncing a death sentence against the British novelist Salman Rushdie, who is of Indian Muslim background. Rushdie's novel *The Satanic Verses* was held by some, but not all, devout Muslims to contain blasphemous libels against Islam. Rushdie was forced to live in hiding for several years, protected by the British security services. In spite of pressure, at first private and discreet, later public and emphatic, from the British and other western governments, the Iranian theocracy proclaimed itself unable to rescind the decree even after Khomeini's death in 1989.

By the 1990s, the Middle East occupied a relatively lower place in British diplomatic preoccupations than in any other decade since World War I. British economic interest in the region became focused primarily on trade rather than investment. But with their reduced purchasing power following the collapse of the oil cartel, the Middle East oil producers no longer offered such abundant markets. British arms and engineering exports to the Middle East assumed greater importance as the balance of oil imports decreased. During the long-drawn-out Iran–Iraq war between 1980 and 1988, Britain, like other western countries, sold arms to both sides.

This policy rebounded against the British government in 1990 when Iraq invaded and occupied Kuwait. The British joined the United States and twenty-six other countries in sending forces to the Gulf to eject the Iraqis from Kuwait in 1991. Although Britain played only a secondary role in the war, the crisis lit a slow-burning fuse in British internal politics in the shape of a scandal concerning the authorization of earlier British arms sales to Iraq. The Conservative government was gravely discredited by the affair and several senior politicians and civil servants were strongly criticized by a committee of inquiry in 1995.

Britain's Legacy in the Middle East

The cultural and social residue of Britain's Middle East empire was slight. Unlike France, Britain left behind no significant network of religious or educational institutions. Anglican Christianity had found few adherents in the region. Its mainly British clergy in the Middle East was gradually replaced at all levels by indigenous priests. The British Schools of Archaeology in Jerusalem, Ankara, and Baghdad continued to make a central contribution to excavations; but the one in Baghdad was defunct by the 1990s, and the Jerusalem school was largely inactive after the 1967 War (it later opened an Amman branch). In the Sudan, the Christian population in the south retained some links with the Church of England, but the University of Khartoum (formerly Gordon College) no longer looked to the English university system as a model. In Jordan, the royal court and the army maintained intimate links with Britain and copied British styles. Elsewhere, few relics of British cultural influence remained. Un-

like most other parts of the former British Empire, the imperial language did not survive into the postcolonial era in the Middle East as the primary means of communication. Insofar as English continued to be spoken, this was a reflection of new American, not old British, influence. Probably the most significant British cultural export was the World Service of the BBC: Its broadcasts in English, Arabic, and other languages commanded a wide audience in the region.

At no time in the twentieth century did the Middle East take priority over the rest of the world in British diplomatic or strategic preoccupations. Yet the most striking land victories of British arms in both world wars were won respectively at Megiddo in 1918 and at al-Alamayn in 1942; the resignations of three British prime ministers (Lloyd George, Eden, and Heath) were occasioned by Middle East conflicts; and Britain's most severe economic recession after the 1930s came about as a direct result of the interlinked political and energy crises in the Middle East in 1973. For all these reasons, the Middle East occupied a central position in the history of British external relations in the twentieth century.

See also ABBAS HILMI II; ABDULLAH I IBN HUSSEIN; ALAMAYN, AL-; ALLENBY, EDMUND HENRY; ANGLO–IRANIAN OIL COMPANY; ARAB–ISRAEL WAR (1948); ARAB LEGION; ARAB REVOLT (1916); ASSYRIANS; ATATÜRK, MUSTAFA KEMAL; BAGHDAD PACT (1955); BALFOUR DECLARATION (1917); BEVIN, ERNEST; CHURCHILL, WINSTON S.; EISENHOWER, DWIGHT DAVID; FAISAL I IBN HUSSEIN; FERTILE CRESCENT; HIJAZ; HUSAYNI, MUHAMMAD AMIN AL-; HUSSEIN IBN TALAL; KHOMEINI, RUHOLLAH; LAUSANNE, TREATY OF (1923); LAWRENCE, T. E.; LEAGUE OF ARAB STATES; MCMAHON, HENRY; MIDDLE EAST DEFENSE ORGANIZATION (MEDO); MIDDLE EAST SUPPLY CENTER (MESC); MOSSADEGH, MOHAMMAD; NASSER, GAMAL ABDEL; ORGANIZATION OF PETROLEUM EXPORTING COUNTRIES (OPEC); OTTOMAN EMPIRE; PAHLAVI, MOHAMMAD REZA; PALESTINE ARAB REVOLT (1936–1939); PARIS PEACE SETTLEMENTS (1918–1923); PHILBY, HARRY ST. JOHN; QADDAFI, MUAMMAR AL-; SÈVRES, TREATY OF (1920); SUEZ CANAL;

Bibliography

Antonius, George. *The Arab Awakening.* London: H. Hamilton, 1938.

Busch, Briton C. *Britain, India, and the Arabs, 1914–1921.* Berkeley: University of California Press, 1971.

Darwin, John. *Britain, Egypt, and the Middle East.* New York: St. Martin's, 1981.

Freedman, Lawrence, and Karsh, Efraim. *The Gulf Conflict, 1990–1991.* Princeton, NJ: Princeton University Press, 1993.

Hopwood, Derek. *Tales of Empire.* London: I. B. Tauris, 1989.

Hurewitz, J. C. *The Middle East and North Africa in World Politics,* 2d edition. New Haven, CT: Yale University Press, 1975).

Kedourie, Elie. *The Chatham House Version, and Other Middle Eastern Essays.* London: Weidenfeld & Nicolson, 1970.

Kedourie, Elie. *In the Anglo–Arab Labyrinth.* Cambridge, U.K., and New York: Cambridge University Press, 1976.

Kyle, Keith. *Suez.* New York: St. Martin's, 1991.

Lawrence, T. E. *Seven Pillars of Wisdom.* London: J. Cape, 1935.

Louis, William Roger. *The British Empire in the Middle East, 1945–1951.* Oxford: Clarendon Press, 1984.

Monroe, Elizabeth. *Britain's Moment in the Middle East,* 2d edition. Baltimore, MD: Johns Hopkins University Press, 1981.

Monroe, Elizabeth. *Philby of Arabia.* London: Faber and Faber, 1973.

Porath, Yehoshua. *In Search of Arab Unity.* London: Cass, 1986.

Searight, Sarah. *The British in the Middle East.* New York: Atheneum, 1970.

Storrs, Ronald. *Orientations.* London: I. Nicholson & Watson, 1937.

Tidrick, Kathryn. *Heart-Beguiling Araby.* Cambridge, U.K., and New York: Cambridge University Press, 1981.

Wilson, Mary. *King Abdullah, Britain, and the Making of Jordan.* Cambridge, and New York: Cambridge University Press, 1987.

BERNARD WASSERSTEIN

BRITAIN AND THE MIDDLE EAST UP TO 1914

Britain's engagement in Middle East affairs has a long and troubled history.

In the Middle East, Great Britain is remembered most for its interlude of paramountcy. The political-geographical concept of the Middle East was coined early in the twentieth century, several decades after Britain entered the region. In a review of Britain's relations with the region before then, and how it rose to the top, this must be kept in mind. Most of the territory that composed its Middle East empire from the end of World War I to the end of World War II had once been under Ottoman rule. Before the ratification in 1924 of the peace settlement with the Turkish Republic, the Ottoman Empire's lineal successor, the inspiration and rationale for adding each politically identifiable unit, with the arguable exception of Sudan in 1899, had come from the perceived need to defend British India.

On India's north (Afghanistan) and northwest (Persia—Iran after 1935—and the Ottoman Black Sea coastline and its interior), Russia's southward thrust stirred anxiety among Britain's empire builders. In the southern Mediterranean, France's tenacious pursuit of influence in Egypt made both Britain and India, as guardians of the imperial routes to the subcontinent, nervous. The anxiety dated from Napoléon's dramatic appearance in the self-governing Ottoman province of Egypt in 1798, through the opening in 1869 of the French-built Suez Canal, to the long-lived yet contested British presence that began in 1882.

In the first half of the twentieth century, to confirm its regional primacy, Britain served in effect as Europe's imperial coordinator in the Ottoman succession. Later, in the crisis of its global imperial mobilization in World War II, Britain was the region's unifier, after 1941 in close harmony with the United States. In retrospect, if the port of Aden (even including its insular appendages, it encompasses little more than 100 square miles [260 sq km]) is set aside, the rise and fall of Great Britain's regional preeminence lasted less than a century (1878–1971). This is not to suggest that the Ottoman sultan's Asian Arab and adjacent northeast African provinces were available earlier for easy European plucking. They were not.

The Levant and East India Companies

Napoléon's appearance in Egypt in 1798 with a massive armada and the declared aim of shortening the sea route to India, in order to reconquer the empire there that France had lost to Britain over the preceding half-century, marked a change in Britain's relations with the Sublime Porte from commercial to political imperialism and diplomacy. During Britain's monopoly of commerce under successively renewed royal charters (1581–1825), the Levant Company had cultivated trade with the Ottoman Empire's eastern Mediterranean territories from Greece to Egypt. As late as 1798 the company, at its own expense but in the name of Britain, handled all formal diplomatic and consular relations with the Ottoman Empire. It also paid the salaries of the British ambassador and the consul general in Constantinople (now Istanbul), and of other British consular officials in Aleppo and selected Ottoman ports. Beginning in the mid-eighteenth century, the ambassadors, though still on the company payroll, were gradually integrated into the regular diplomatic service. The Foreign Office did not begin paying their salaries until 1804 (five years after Britain entered into its first formal alliance with the Sublime Porte). The consuls remained employees of the Levant Company until just before its dissolution in 1825.

Once the industrial revolution had taken hold in Britain late in the eighteenth century, the Levant Company faced no serious competition from Western European rivals. With few exceptions, even during the French Revolution and the Napoleonic wars (1789–1815)—indeed, until 1825—the company enjoyed the most profitable phase of its 244 years of Anglo–Ottoman monopoly trade. Given the long head start before the industrial revolution crossed the English Channel, Britain captured and held first place in the external Ottoman trade until World War I. In the middle decades of the nineteenth century, the Ottoman Empire was Britain's third-best foreign customer.

Early on, the Levant Company yielded to the reality that the deep interior of its assigned zone lay beyond reach and released the privileges to the East India Company (1600–1858). The oldest charters of the two companies, both issued under authority of Queen Elizabeth I, were mirror images. But in the pursuit of monopoly commerce in the allotted areas, the prospects for each differed sharply. The East Indies titled not a fixed state, like the Ottoman Empire, but a zone in South Asia lacking precise geographic definition. At its height the Mogul Empire (1526–1857) ruled much, but not all, of the subcontinent and lacked diplomatic ties to Europe. Although the East India Company (EIC) trade centered on the Indian subcontinent, that sphere spread over more than a single suzerainty.

EIC agents moved freely, seizing commercial opportunities, including those in the Islamic empires (Ottoman, Persian, and Omani) and self-ruling shaykhdoms around the Gulf, with half the Gulf's littoral. Persia lay beyond the Levant Company's assured circuit. But in theory that circuit did embrace the Ottoman Gulf littoral, which varied in the seventeenth, eighteenth, and nineteenth centuries. Beyond Ottoman reach, and thus freely claimed for EIC trade, sprawled Oman (variously known as Muscat or as Muscat and Oman) and the "independent" shaykhdoms along the lower Gulf and the Arabian Sea as far as the entrance to the Red Sea.

Despite its exercise of Britain's diplomatic and consular duties, the Levant Company remained to the end a trading association. The EIC, by contrast, had become the primary instrument for conquering India and integrating it into the British Empire. In 1757 it rose from a decade-long war with its French rival as the governing agent for Britain. Within a dozen years the French company expired. After yet another war with France (1778–1783), the EIC absorbed the remaining Mogul provinces and districts until the Islamic empire passed out of existence in 1857. (By the 1780s French India had shriveled into the Union of Pondichéry, comprising four disconnected enclaves in the subcontinent's southeast with a total area of 143 square miles [372 sq km].)

Not until the shock of Napoléon's lightning entry into Egypt (July 1798) and his stealthy personal departure (August 1799), leaving behind for two years a large French military and civilian body of occupation, did British India begin building a durable political presence and strategy in the Gulf. At the EIC's request, the sultan of Oman signed a pledge—not honored by his successors—that nationals of France and the Netherlands, Britain's Gulf rivals in the preceding two centuries through their own East India companies, would be shut out of his realm. Oman was then more substantial than a shaykhdom yet less than a suzerain state (on European criteria). Thus, the true meaning of a second agreement, early in 1800, that looked like a provision for the Gulf's first permanent, if only quasi-diplomatic, mission, was that it reflected the dramatic structural transition of the EIC, which since 1757 had blossomed into the government of British India.

Parliament toughened its supervision of the EIC. In 1784, following the second and virtually complete rout of French rivals from the subcontinent, Parliament passed the Government of India Act, laying down strict rules of accountability. The president of the company court (board) of directors was given a nonvoting seat in the British cabinet, to serve as the channel for guiding the EIC's governance of India. To carry out the new duties of protecting and promoting British interests, the company began reorganizing its own administrative structure. Starting in the 1820s, the EIC changed its former commercial residencies into political residencies and agencies at key ports in the Gulf, broadly interpreted to include Basra and Baghdad, which could be reached by vessel via the Shatt al-Arab and the Tigris and Euphrates rivers.

Relations of Britain and British India with Persia in the eighteenth century had been the least satisfactory in the Gulf, because of the domestic political chaos in the decades between the effective end in 1722 of the Safavid dynasty and the rise of its Qajar successor, which in 1794 reunited the shahdom. As part of the strategy of defense in depth against Napoleonic France, in 1801 the EIC signed commercial and political agreements with the new dynasty designed to establish continuous diplomatic links. Fath Ali Shah (1797–1834), however, repudiated both agreements because British India had dallied for six years before returning the ratifications. The Foreign Office in London and the EIC unknowingly had separately framed plans in 1808 for fresh exchanges with Persia—the Foreign Office, out of anxiety about Russia; the EIC, about France. Their emissaries met for the first time in Tehran. In stages, from 1809 to 1814, a treaty of defensive alliance emerged, laying the base for Britain's permanent diplomatic relations with Persia. From then

on, Persia fell into the diplomatic jurisdiction of the Foreign Office, with only two lapses (1823–1835, 1858–1859) when the Asia-focused Political and Secret Department of the Bombay Presidency managed Britain's interests in Tehran.

Britain and the Arabian Peninsula

In 1858, after the last vestige of Mogul rule had vanished, the EIC charter was revoked. Responsibility for governing India passed from Calcutta—and for managing British affairs in the Gulf, from Bombay—to London. In London the secretary of state for India, with full voting rights in the cabinet but no longer attached to a nongovernmental company, presided over the India Office and thus over framing imperial policy. Even then, anxiety over India's defense colored all major decisions on the Middle East until World War II. By then, British India had to share the center of imperial concern with Britain's interest in Gulf oil, which at that time still came largely from Iran, with a modest supplement from Iraq.

Against this background it becomes possible to chart the origins, rise, and style of British Middle East imperialism east of the Red Sea and the complementary yet reactive diplomacy and imperialism in the Ottoman Empire. During the century-long conquest of the Mogul Empire, British India was distracted enough not to plan simultaneous expansion beyond the subcontinent. The distraction went far to explain India's nervous yet cautious reply to inflated fear of perils looming in and around the Gulf, reaching back to 1798. From time to time (1806, 1809, 1819), the EIC deployed in the lower Gulf, chiefly for service along the coast of the Arabian Peninsula, vessels of the Bombay Marine to suppress what the Anglo–Indian monitors labeled a rampant tribal piracy that "even preyed upon" vessels flying the Union Jack.

In 1820 the coastal shaykhs and their neighbors as far as the Bahrain archipelago were forced to sign a general treaty banning piracy and the slave trade. The pact was renewed semiannually until 1835 by all (except Bahrain), and then annually until 1843, when it was prolonged for a decade and finally hardened into a permanent maritime truce. By then the EIC had come to view the Persian Gulf as an Anglo–Indian lake. Upon authorization by

Tehran, the EIC named the British consul at Bushehr on the Persian coast as the EIC political resident, with the duty of observing the execution of the truce and guarding against piracy. He was assisted by the political agent for the Trucial Coast (at Sharja) and, at the turn of the century, by political agents named to the other pact signatories. In 1822, for the resident's service, British India deployed vessels of the Bombay Marine and, after 1879, of the Indian navy, berthed at the rented Basidu based on Persia's Qeshm Island, at the entrance to the Persian Gulf.

It was the port of Aden, however, lying outside the Gulf, that became Britain's first onshore presence in the Middle East. By the beginning of the second third of the nineteenth century, new anxieties had arisen. As seen in Britain and in India, the benefits of the dramatic shrinkage between the two of distance and time in transport and communication were risks when they served an imperial rival such as France. By the 1830s the EIC had developed a regular route between India and England via the Mediterranean and Red seas, with overland transfer in Egypt of passengers, goods, and mail between Alexandria and Suez in both directions.

In the Mediterranean, which had British bases at Gibraltar and Malta, there were no bunkering problems. East of Suez, the company chose Aden as the site for resupply of fuel and other needs of increasingly larger and more modern oceangoing ships. After six years of talks with the sultan of Lahij, punctuated by forcible occupancy, two treaties and a bond defined the terms of the Anglo–Indian use of the harbor at Aden, for an annual rent of £1,300 ($6,500). By handling its first onshore presence in the Middle East as a quasi-commercial station with a modest rental, British India minimized the likelihood of tribal hostility.

In 1854, the five virtually unpopulated Kuria Muria islets, east of Aden on the southwest coast of Oman, were given to Britain by the sultan of Oman for a telegraph station. The experiment (1859–1860) in the Red and Arabian seas with submarine cables to tie into the European lines failed. Britain finally built alternative routes to British India via the Ottoman Empire as well as Russia and Persia. Attached by conquest to Aden in 1857 was

the strategic islet of Perim, not quite in the center of the Bab al-Mandab Strait, then the only water entrance to the Red Sea. All the islands annexed by Britain were virtually uninhabited. Aden remained Britain's first and only dependency in the Middle East until 1878. Even with the port's enlargement by the addition of Little Aden in 1868 and its further enlargement by British India's purchase of the adjacent promontory belonging to Shaykh Uthman in 1862 and 1888, Aden's total area, islets and all, barely exceeded 100 square miles (260 sq km). Until 1937, it was administered as if it were the Bombay Presidency's private colony.

Britain and the Eastern Mediterranean

Also in the 1830s, Britain's primary Middle East attention, still inspired by India, moved from the Gulf and the periphery of the Arabian Peninsula to the eastern Mediterranean, and basic policymaking, from the Political and Secret Department in Bombay to the Foreign Office in London. With Viscount Palmerston as foreign minister (1830–1834, 1835–1841, 1846–1851) and as prime minister from 1855 until his death in 1865, Britain dug in its heels to deny France economic and strategic domination of the key link between Western Europe and South Asia. In 1840 and 1841 Palmerston framed a strategy that rested on an Anglo–Ottoman alliance and committed the major powers to preserve the European balance by upholding the territorial sovereignty and integrity of the Ottoman Empire. By consensual diplomacy the powers, with Britain serving as the balancer, prevented the overthrow of Muhammad Ali, the self-made governor of Egypt, by internal revolt (in 1839–1841); the shrinkage of the Ottoman Empire by European conquest (by Russia in 1854–1856 and by France in 1860–1861); and the unilateral revision of a concert agreement (by Russia of its 1856 Straits Convention with the Ottoman Empire, in 1871). In each European–Ottoman dispute, Britain kept France and Russia apart by forming temporary great-power coalitions that isolated the would-be offender.

Despite Palmerston's precautions, Anglo–French rivalry in and over Egypt deepened. In the 1840s French engineers began framing feasible designs for linking the Mediterranean and Red Seas by canal, to assure uninterrupted ocean travel from Britain and Western Europe to the African and

Asian rims of the Indian Ocean, as well as Australia and New Zealand. In the mid-1850s, once Ferdinand de Lesseps pocketed a ninety-nine year concession for building and running the waterway, French magnates and bankers promptly oversubscribed the operating company. But at the height of the Anglo–Ottoman alliance (from 1841 to 1879–1882), Palmerston's diplomacy had interrupted the canal's construction for more than a decade. At his urging, in order to escape an imperial contest for dominance in Egypt, British investors put their sterling into an Alexandria–Suez railroad via Cairo, completed in the 1850s.

In November 1869, four years after Palmerston's death, the French promoters finally opened the Suez Canal. As might have been expected, ships flying the Union Jack made up 70 percent or more of the traffic in the first years. The absence of British shareholders, however, denied British users a voice in canal policy. Even the secret purchase in 1875 of the 44 percent interest in the company owned by Egypt's khedive, making Britain the largest single shareholder, proved inadequate to modify rates and other rules of use. Nor did the boost to Egypt's treasury long delay Khedive Isma'il's fiscal collapse. In 1876 he accepted a Dual Control, the working title of the Anglo–French Public Debt Commission, to manage Egypt's finances. Two years later, after the dual controllers reported continuing breach of the commission's rules, the khedive installed a cabinet government, with the Briton as finance minister and the Frenchman as minister of public works. When Isma'il tried to restore direct rule by abolishing the cabinet in June 1879, British diplomacy in Constantinople brought his son Tawfiq to the governorship.

Occupation of Cyprus and Egypt

While Anglo–French rivalry in and over Egypt was turning explosive, a crisis in the north had led Russia to declare war against the Ottoman Empire in April 1877; eleven months later it imposed a humbling peace on the Sublime Porte that was promptly ratified. Britain saw its eastern Mediterranean interests squeezed yet again between renewed threats from Russia and continuing ones from France. Benjamin Disraeli's cabinet cobbled together a strategy of detaching Austria from its alliance with Russia, wooing France with an offer not to oppose

its conquest of Ottoman Tunisia, and coercing the reluctant sultan into allowing Britain to occupy Cyprus, purportedly to inhibit further intrusion by Russia into the Islamic realm.

After deliberate delay, with the secret deal on Cyprus in hand, Disraeli finally agreed to attend the Berlin Congress (13 June–13 July 1878), called by Chancellor Bismarck of Germany to cool the overheated diplomacy in Europe through top-level accord. Only toward the close of the congress did Disraeli divulge the text of the Cyprus convention for integration into the collection of approved actions. The congress modified Russia's crippling terms and sorted out the imperial rivalries, thus avoiding wider war in Europe. Nevertheless, the Ottoman Empire paid the price by having to make major land transfers to Russia in northeastern Anatolia and, to Russia and its Balkan allies, in southeastern Europe; placement of Cyprus under Britain's occupation without fixed time limit; and—unmentioned—Britain's promise to France of diplomatic support in assimilating Ottoman Tunisia. In the Ottoman view, the congress, by annulling the ban on European expansion into the Ottoman Empire, had erased the essence of its durable alliance with Britain. Britain's replacement by Germany came four years later.

Once on Cyprus, Britain added two other Ottoman provinces—Egypt and Sudan—to the western portion of its future Middle East empire. It is far from clear, however, that the island was originally meant to be the first such unit. Occupation by formal, if also forced, agreement without time limit was intended as notice that Cyprus had been taken over only temporarily. The island's administration, without transfer of ownership title, was simply handed to Britain for such use as might serve its immediate imperial interest and, it was claimed, that of the Sublime Porte, which received a British pledge to stop deeper penetration by Russia into Anatolia. Britain had already denied Russia possession of the Turkish Straits and Constantinople. Without the Turkish Straits, Russia could not become a Mediterranean power. To buttress the notion of a rental contract, the Disraeli government assured the Sublime Porte that all public revenue, beyond administrative needs, would revert to the sultan along with a fixed annual payment of £5,000 ($25,000).

More important, yet unmentioned in the convention, Britain saw Cyprus as a convenient military base to shore up its political and military stance in the eastern Mediterranean as a deterrent to both France and Russia. Within a fortnight of the outbreak of the Russian–Ottoman war in April 1877, Britain had warned Russia against blockading the Suez Canal and/or the Turkish Straits or occupying Egypt and/or Constantinople. The security planners in London felt a gnawing need for a nearby military presence to defend the Suez Canal, which they had come to see as the lifeline to India and to Britain's widening empire along the rim of the Indian Ocean and beyond. In this scheme, Cyprus "would enable us without any act of overt hostility and without disturbing the peace of Europe, to accumulate material of war and, if requisite, the troops necessary." This observation was embodied in Foreign Minister Salisbury's instructions to the British ambassador in Constantinople, charged in mid-May 1878 with imposing on the Sublime Porte the convention for Britain's open-ended occupation of Cyprus. (Egypt, though unmentioned, also was firmly in mind.)

Britain finally occupied Egypt in 1882 to quiet the long-standing fear of French conquest. The war in Europe that the British action threatened did not break out, even though the major powers withheld de facto recognition of the reality for nearly a quarter-century. After the British invasion, six years elapsed before the European maritime powers initialed a convention to assure free transit through the Suez Canal in peace and war, and seventeen more passed before its ratification. France kept goading Britain to fix a date for military withdrawal; Britain, no less stubbornly, insisted on recognition as the canal's sole defender for the duration of its military presence in Egypt.

Together with Russia, France did not stop condemning Britain for its occupation of Egypt, and particularly its refusal to share the Suez Canal's protection with the convention's signers. Nonstop collaboration against Britain in Egypt contributed to a Franco–Russian entente on European imperial issues in 1894. Ten years later, France and Britain finally signed their own Entente Cordiale in a trade-off: Britain's free hand in Egypt in return for France's free hand in Morocco. Within a year, the Suez Canal convention finally went into effect, carrying with it European de facto recognition of Britain's occupation of Egypt and, for its duration, as the waterway's exclusive guardian.

Conquest of Sudan

Lacking any document in its files to verify an unqualified Ottoman surrender of legal titles to Cyprus and to Egypt, Britain did not seriously seek the Sublime Porte's recognition of the conquest of Sudan in 1896 through 1898. Judged by the record, Britain seems to have concluded that without legal confirmation, it would be best to continue needed imperial expansion on the Mediterranean side of the Middle East by means of temporary tenancy. For this, given the Ottoman denial of legitimacy, the search for European recognition seemed the logical course of action.

The political status of Sudan had been complicated ever since 1885, when all British and Egyptian troops were pulled out after defeat by the self-proclaimed Mahdi (Messiah), Muhammad Ahmad, and his *mujahidin* (religious warriors). The mahdi did not long survive his declaration of Sudan's independence. But the independent Mahdiyya of Sudan survived under his dynastic *khalifa* (successor) for more than a decade, until Major General Horatio Herbert Kitchener, commanding a modest Egyptian force, reclaimed the province in the name of Egypt (1896–1898). The victory was capped by an Anglo–French standoff at Fashoda (19 September–3 November 1898), micromanaged by the Foreign Office in London and the Foreign Ministry in Paris.

Kitchener was pitted against Major Jean Baptiste Marchand, a desert explorer who for more than two years had trekked some 3,000 miles (4,800 km) from the Atlantic seaboard of French Equatorial Africa, with a small band of infantry volunteers, before arriving at the southern reaches of the White Nile. Fifteen months before Marchand and his commandos set out in June 1896, the undersecretary of state for foreign affairs, Sir Edward Grey, announced in Commons that the entire Nile (White and Blue) basin, from sources to mouth, formed a British sphere of influence. Any intrusion would be viewed as an unfriendly act. En route from the Atlantic to the White Nile, Marchand and company received little public notice, less the result of planned secrecy than of crude communications.

At Fashoda, one of the few rural towns along that stretch of the White Nile, Marchand subdued the *mudir,* who surrendered the patch of well-watered desert that made up his *mudiriyya* (municipality). On that basis, Marchand, as instructed, claimed for France all of southern Sudan, as yet without boundaries and thus undefined. The situation was formally resolved not by Marchand and Kitchener, on the bank of the White Nile, but by the foreign secretaries on the banks of the Thames and the Seine. Indeed, a confident Kitchener reached Dover on 27 October 1898 (before France had officially backed down) for weeks of national celebration.

The decision on how to factor Sudan into Britain's burgeoning Middle East empire was left to Lord Cromer, the British agent and consul general in Cairo. He rationalized a complex arrangement to establish Britain's right to rule Sudan at its pleasure, yet leave no more than a nominal role for Egypt, and to do so without seeking the Sublime Porte's approval. Cromer devised a formula to assure British supremacy while calming France and denying European powers capitulatory privileges.

The British claim to dominance in governing the Anglo–Egyptian condominium rested on the right of conquest, in the name not of the Ottoman sultan but of his viceroy, the Egyptian khedive, though the occupation had nullified the khedive's subordination to the sultan. In Cromer's scheme, except for the low-level civil and military service, Egypt had little more to show than its flag. Even that had to fly below the Union Jack. Though run as an undeclared British colony, Sudan was governed by the Foreign—not the Colonial—Office, which prided itself on installing a paternalistic regime. Until 1914, however, Sudan's public revenues came primarily not from local sources or Britain's Exchequer but from interest-free loans granted by Egypt.

In Sudan, as in Cyprus and Egypt, the Sublime Porte was infuriated by the denial of a policy voice or even of a nominal administrative role. In all three cases, the Foreign Office was pressed into an unaccustomed Colonial Office role by having to recruit and supervise senior administrative personnel. The makeshift handling of Cyprus had set the precedent for the later assimilation of Egypt and Sudan into the expanding western sector of Britain's Middle East empire. Named custodian of such borrowed territory was the Foreign Office, the branch of the British government best equipped to cope with problems of international law and diplomacy, but one of the most poorly equipped for colonial administration.

In Cyprus, Egypt, and Sudan, Britain did not stray from the fiction that the Foreign Office's exercise of Britain's de facto sovereignty had introduced neither legal nor political change into the former Ottoman provinces. The Ottoman Empire responded with an absolute refusal to surrender the title of ownership. Thus, the western sector of Britain's rising Middle East empire still lacked legal solidity at the outbreak of war in Europe in 1914—indeed, for a decade longer, until the peace settlement with the Turkish Republic.

Humbling the Gulf

In contrast with the political tenancies that Britain imposed on the Sublime Porte, British India continued to devise its own forms of British primacy along the periphery of the Arabian Peninsula. This activity must be seen in the context of India's progressive intrusion into the Gulf in the nineteenth century. The office of resident was a title that the EIC had used, ever since its arrival in South Asia, to identify its factors (merchants) at chosen commercial posts. The step-by-step politicization of the office traced back to the 1820 maritime truce and reflected the slow conversion after 1757 of the EIC from a merchants' monopoly into Britain's formally recognized empire-building and governing agency in the subcontinent. As early as 1822, the Bombay Presidency began appointing a "resident in the Persian Gulf" at Bushehr, on Persia's upper Gulf Coast, to oversee the truce, with instructions to take action against violators and advise on policy. Commonly a middle-level officer of the Indian army or navy, the resident was authorized to call upon the Indian navy (known as the Bombay Marine until 1830), which from 1822 deployed a token squadron at the rented base of Basidu on Qeshm Island, near the Gulf entrance. Soon after the EIC lost its charter in 1858, the Indian navy's facilities and manpower were folded into the Royal Navy.

The long-delayed 1841 British commercial treaty with Persia had reaffirmed the right of the resident to keep his office at Bushehr. Not much later, Persia grudgingly allowed Britain to confer on the incumbent a second and separate title of consul general for the coastal provinces, thus formally assuring that his jurisdiction embraced the Gulf's entire rim except for the Ottoman segment. Nominated through 1872 by the Bombay Presidency and thereafter by the governor-general and viceroy in Calcutta, the political resident, as he had been formally designated for some time, was still British India's senior official and policy coordinator in the Gulf. He also served as envoy at large to the Arab tribalities, shaykhdoms, and ministates on the coast of the Arabian Peninsula. As necessary, British India delegated political agents to selected shaykhdoms growing into ministates; and by the turn of the twentieth century, political officers were delegated to troublesome tribalities. Meanwhile, from the start of the truce, Indian naval officers who served on patrol duty at times doubled as surveyors to map the Gulf and its bed for navigation, pearl fisheries, and other marine sources of commercial value.

By 1880, British India's presence rested on a system of control by an experienced and informed bureaucracy that steadily deepened its knowledge of the Gulf and its rim's inhabitants. With such proved interests, British India was ready to fend off aspiring European rivals. The Anglo–Indian custodians of the British Empire then, and for some time to come, persisted in viewing the Persian/Arabian Gulf and the Arabian Peninsula not as part of the Middle East (a term not yet invented) but as a region that fell into the subcontinent's influence sphere. Still, British India's uncontestable presence remained offshore.

The Sublime Porte inadvertently sparked the growth of British India's onshore presence. On reabsorbing al-Hasa in 1871, the Ottoman Empire had reentered Gulf politics. Hasa's governor later gave asylum to a disgruntled faction of the Al Khalifa, the clan that ruled the Bahrain archipelago. To British India's political resident, the Sublime Porte appeared to be testing a rediscovered political option in 1879, when Hasa's governor and Isa ibn Ali, Bahrain's ruler, explored the rental of a coaling bunker on one of his islands. The action was seen as a likely Ottoman first step in claiming Bahrain, lying off Hasa's coast.

In December 1880, India undertook to protect Isa and his heirs as the shaykhdom's governing dynasty, assuring it full domestic sovereignty and a guaranteed safeguard against local opponents. In return, the ruler surrendered to Britain, and to India acting in Britain's behalf, the archipelago's external sovereignty. He agreed to an absolute ban on relations with other governments, the nearby shaykhdoms excepted, expressly disallowing the creation on his territory of "diplomatic or consular agencies or coaling depots . . . unless with the consent of the British Government." In March 1892, Shaykh Isa more explicitly reaffirmed his original surrender of external sovereignty by adding a general nonalienation clause that he would "on no account cede, sell, mortgage or otherwise give for occupation any part of my territory save to the British Government." Thus Bahrain became the model for what British India later called a system of independent states in special treaty relations with Great Britain.

In 1887 a first version of parallel exclusionary pacts with the shaykhs of the six tribalities of the Trucial Coast proved porous. Defying the Anglo–Indian ban, French agents appeared in 1891, seeking to open formal relations with the Trucial six by tempting them with such promises as the revival of slave trading under the French flag. India finally plugged the leak in 1892. In the next twenty-four years India, in Britain's name, absorbed the external sovereignty of Kuwait (1899) and, in World War I, of Najd (1915) and Qatar (1916). In the Trucial Coast, Fujayra broke away from Sharjah in 1902 but did not receive Britain's formal recognition until a half-century later. Between 1913 and 1932, starting with Kuwait's shaykh, British India won explicit pledges from the rulers of Bahrain and each Trucial shaykhdom never to grant an oil concession to anyone except an official British governmental nominee. In the accords with Najd and Qatar, such commitments were assumed in promises to issue no concessions whatsoever without British consent.

Meanwhile, in 1891, Sayyid Faysal ibn Turki of Oman also had placed himself in nonalienation bondage. Clearly, Oman still had not been reduced to the status of a shaykhdom. It persisted in styling itself a sultanate, and as such it remained larger than 80,000 square miles (208,000 sq km), nearly nine-tenths the size of Great Britain and Northern

Ireland. Oman still flaunted imperial pretensions with the residual possession of Gwadar, a port on the Baluchi coast with some 300 square miles inland that was not returned to Pakistan until 1958. Indeed, in earlier decades of the nineteenth century, Oman had held long-term leases on the island of Qeshm and the nearby port of Bandar Abbas, issued by Persia's Fath Ali Shah and renewed by his successor. Until 1856 it also comprised the African islands of Zanzibar and Pemba and the coastal towns of Mombasa and Dar es-Salaam, which collectively had served as the major conduit of the once thriving slave trade in the Gulf. For that commerce the realm's capital, Muscat, served as the entrepôt.

The key to understanding Oman's vague ties to the system of protected ministates was Britain's inability to gain full command over the sultanate's foreign relations. By the time British-India began moving to tighten its hold on the ministates, Oman had long since entered into capitulatory treaties with the United States (1833), France (1844), and the Netherlands (1877). Its ruler could not unilaterally cancel such instruments, even if he had wished to. Nor did Britain, in the exercise of its treaty rights in the sultanate, ever vigorously challenge the capitulatory powers, with the occasional exception of France.

Britain's management of its affairs in the Persian Gulf after 1858 was settling slowly and not always happily into the joint duty of the Foreign and India offices. Through World War I, the top administrator was recruited from the British officer cadre of the Anglo–Indian Army at the rank of lieutenant (or full colonel) and held appointments from both offices. In the overseas hierarchy of the Foreign Office he was the consul general at Bushehr, attending to Anglo–Indian and British interests in Persia's coastal provinces of Fars and Khuzistan and its islands in the Gulf. At the India Office and in India he was titled political resident in charge of Anglo–Indian affairs along the Gulf peninsular coast. Accountable to him in that role by 1914 were political agents for Bahrain and Kuwait, and political officers for the Trucial Coast and later also Qatar, all drawn from British India's political service. The political resident in the Persian/Arabian Gulf was thus responsible to the Anglo–Indian government and ultimately to the India Office in London for basic policy, at first with advice from the

Foreign Office, largely regarding interactive Gulf politics of Persia and the Arab ministates. But the Foreign Office's influence steadily increased as the Gulf was drawn, issue by issue, into European imperial politics after Britain's occupation of Cyprus and Egypt.

Sole Policeman in the Gulf

An immediate effect of abandoning the long-lived alliance with the Sublime Porte was that Britain lost its leverage in the European imperial rivalry over Ottoman territory. That loss promptly encouraged Russia and France to cooperate against Britain on Ottoman issues. No less important, it opened the way for Germany's belated entry into the competition. Germany, in fact, replaced Britain as the Porte's durable ally, a friendship that lasted until the armistice ending World War I in 1918. At first, Chancellor Bismarck still discouraged official promotion of German interests in the Ottoman Empire despite the Porte's receptivity. In 1881, when Germany sent its first military mission to Constantinople on Ottoman invitation, the chancellor cut the mission's formal national ties. By the time of Kaiser Wilhelm II's accession in 1888, the new friendship came into the open. German industry had made such striking advances after the nation's unification in 1870 that it sought new markets. Between 1886 and 1910, Germany vaulted from fifteenth to second place in Ottoman foreign trade, surpassed only by Britain.

Much of this upturn could be attributed to the kaiser's enthusiastic response to Sultan Abdülhamit II's national goal of building railroads across his Asian domains to underpin their economic expansion, unity, and defense. With official encouragement, investors in France centered their projects in Palestine, Syria, and the latter's adjacent zone in southern Anatolia. The sultan's chosen enterprise was a trans-Anatolian railroad linked to Europe via its international railway complex. The sultan coaxed the new kaiser, on his first visit to Constantinople, to arouse interest in the plan among German bankers and entrepreneurs. An initial segment was promptly begun that would link Constantinople to Europe's international railway complex. By 1896 the German-built segment (with limited French investment) had pierced western Anatolia as far as Eskişehir with a spur to Konya.

There the venture stalled. On a second visit to Constantinople in 1898, the kaiser's zeal was rehoned. But ahead, between Konya and Basra, lay the mountains of eastern Anatolia and Mosul province, where it would be far more expensive to build each kilometer of roadbed than it had been in the plains of west Anatolia. Also envisaged were four spurs along the way: to Aleppo, Urfa, and Khanaqin (on the Persian side of the Ottoman border, some 90 miles [154 km] north of Baghdad), and from Zubayr (9 miles [14.5 km] south of Basra) to a point on the Persian Gulf "to be agreed upon." Wilhelm II enlisted the aid of Georg von Siemens, director of the Deutsche Bank, to promote the project as a German national interest, and the sultan issued a preliminary concession in 1899. Limiting its concern largely to the venture's commercial side, the bank did not agree to the definitive concession until 1903, after having canvassed banks of other nations—notably France and Britain—to invest in the project. In March 1903 the Deutsche Bank finally signed a ninety-nine year concession for the Berlin–Baghdad Railway.

The quickening of European interest in the Persian/Arabian Gulf, especially the confirmation of the Berlin–Baghdad Railway concession on 5 March 1903, led Britain to update its defensive strategy. Precisely two months later, on 5 May 1903, Foreign Secretary Lord Lansdowne disclosed the commercial and strategic principles that would guide Britain's government in the future. Although high priority would be given to "protect and promote British trade" in the inland waters, Lansdowne ruled out the notion of excluding "the legitimate trade of other Powers." Yet he left no doubt that Britain would "regard the establishment of a naval base, or of a fortified port, in the Persian/Arabian Gulf by any other Power as a very grave menace to British interests and we should certainly resist it with all the means at our disposal."

The British strategy of depriving other European powers of a military presence in the Persian/Arabian Gulf, never seriously disputed, remained fixed through World War II and, with the exception (from 1949) of a modest U.S. naval station in Bahrain, lasted until Britain's final withdrawal in 1971.

Unlike the British-occupied Ottoman provinces, which European powers recognized but the Sublime Porte did not, the protected ministates in the Gulf won the approval of neither. Still, the European governments—not even Germany, the latest entrant into the contest—did not effectively dispute Britain's exercise of rights in the shaykhdoms. In the decade before the eruption of war in 1914 the Gulf's guardians, particularly in British India but also in Britain, perceived a mounting threat from Germany, which was enlarging its trade with Ottoman Asia and opening markets in the Gulf. In 1906 the Hamburg–Amerika Line began calling on a fixed monthly schedule at promising ports, offering lower rates and better banking services that those of the entrenched Anglo–Indian and British shipping firms.

In 1911, less concerned than British India, Britain finally responded to the persistent overtures of Germany and the Ottoman Empire to reconsider the differences over completing a railway with a terminal at the head of the Gulf. Britain felt the least pressure, since the Porte depended on British assent to increase the tariff rates, the only reliable funding source for Ottoman subsidies to the railway builders. Britain insisted on preserving its role as the Gulf's sole policeman to safeguard Anglo–Indian commercial and maritime primacy. On these terms Britain consented to pursue, with the Ottoman Empire and Germany, a multilateral settlement by weaving together three bilateral accords: British–Ottoman, British–German, and German–Ottoman.

From the outset the Sublime Porte had challenged the legality of Britain's protected ministate of Kuwait so as to reassert the sultan's suzerainty in the shaykhdom. Instead, the convention initialed in July 1913 gave the Porte only the symbols of political ownership. Although obliged to fly the Ottoman flag (with the inscription "Kuwait"), the shaykh was assured of "complete administrative autonomy." The Ottomans also conceded the validity of the shaykh's agreements with Britain. The purpose of the accord—whether, when, and under what terms the railroad might build its terminal in Kuwait—was described and the decision deferred. Beyond assuring Britain membership on the Berlin–Baghdad Railway directorate and guaranteed equal rates for all users, the British–German convention, initialed in June 1914, stated that the Baghdad–Basra extension would be built and run by a separate Ottoman company with an assured 40 percent British interest and a pledge of no extension to the Gulf without full prior approval by Britain, Germany, and the Ottoman Empire.

A fourth bilateral accord, framed by the Deutsche Bank and the French-dominated Imperial Ottoman Bank, was reached and initialed in February 1914. It was essentially designed to protect the special position of France's railroad entrepreneurs in Syria and Alexandretta, as well as their planned branches in western Anatolia, all to be linked to the German trunk line.

Ratification of the bilateral instruments awaited the drafting of the Ottoman–German convention. Preliminary talks, begun in June 1914 but interrupted by war in August, ended in a secret treaty of defensive alliance. The Sublime Porte became an active ally of Germany and Austria late in October. Early in November, Britain amplified the existing territorial guarantees to Shaykh Mubarak by declaring Kuwait, together with its islands and the ruler's date groves in the Faw district of the Basra *vilayet*, "an independent Government under British protection" as a reward for his pledged cooperation in the war effort.

Aden: Settlement and Protectorates

Reshaping the British protected shaykhdoms in the Gulf into potential ministates had run parallel with dividing Aden's upcountry, between 1880 and 1914, into projected tribalities that remained politically frozen in that condition until after World War II. The two imperial initiatives were sparked by perceived threats to Anglo–Indian security. Also, both Arabian coastal zones were recurrently infused with tribal migrants from the interior. Some tribal groups in each zone had passed in and out of the Ottoman Empire. This occurred for the last time in the early 1870s, when the sultan's troops reannexed Hasa, on the Gulf, and Yemen, on the Red Sea. In both retaken provinces, the Ottoman Empire did not simply seek recognition for its new international borders. The Sublime Porte clearly hoped to regain more of the land lost and to reintegrate tribal groups on the southern edges of Hasa and Yemen.

British India's imperial process in the southwestern Arabian Peninsula differed from that in the Gulf. Under the Gulf's enforced maritime truce, adjacent shaykhdoms gradually began to settle their common borders. Except for Aden itself, however, few upcountry tribalities had mutually defined borders before the eve of World War I. Instead, the process was essentially limited to those blending into unmarked edges of Yemen on the north. In this period British India had not yet negotiated Aden's upcountry periphery alongside Oman on the east or the suitably named Rub al-Khali (Empty Quarter) at the southern rim of the vast Arabian Desert. On neither of the two frontiers did the British face obstructions comparable with those in Ottoman Yemen.

Until January 1873, the Bombay Presidency had served as British India's ultimate custodian of the Gulf. Thereafter, it became accountable to the viceroy in Calcutta; beyond that, to the India Office; and, within the British cabinet after 1882, increasingly to the Foreign Office. Yet in regard to running Aden and its interior until 1932, the Bombay Presidency seems largely to have slipped through the net of accountability. From the outset, the Bombay Presidency treated the town of Aden as a private colonial trust. Even Aden's bureaucracy, below the top level, was almost wholly recruited in Bombay, joined in time by a swelling number of Indian settlers, mostly immigrant shopkeepers.

The presidency also kept watch on Aden town's hinterland, which widened eastward from slightly more than 30 miles (48 km) at the harbor to about 200 miles (320 km) and a total length close to 500 miles (800 km), for possible Ottoman or European intrusion. By 1902 Aden's administration in the interior covered some twenty-five to thirty local rulers with a wide range of titles—sultan, amir, sharif, *naqib*, shaykh. Even after agreements with the presidency, their number kept changing as a result of tribal fission and fusion in what finally compassed a thinly populated expanse of 112,000 square miles (291,200 sq km). Its eastern two-thirds was largely desert; its western sector, partly desert and partly hill country. Frequent regime changes reflected the absence of Anglo–Indian dynastic guarantees and stabilizing boundaries, and they revealed the rulers' loss of much domestic as well as all external sovereignty. They thus resembled less the Gulf's shaykhdoms than the contemporary European colonies on the nearby Horn of Africa.

In 1900 Aden town was renamed the Aden Settlement, to sharpen its distinction from the inland protected tribalities it administered. The resident was accordingly retitled governor. Nature roughly fixed the frontier with the Rub al-Khali. Like most boundary lines separating ownership claims to deserts that seem to have little or no commercial prospects, a straight line sufficed. That was also true, for the most part, of the eastern border with Oman.

From 1902 to 1905, when it came to marking the boundaries of Yemen, once again an Ottoman province after 236 years, the issue could not be resolved by British India in exchanges with Yemen. Only Britain could deal with the Sublime Porte. Because of Ottoman delays, the accord was not ratified until 1914, too close to the outbreak of war to take solid effect. Indeed, in 1915 Ottoman troops occupied a few adjacent British-protected tribalities and stayed for the duration of the war. The unresolved problem of legal title was thus left for renegotiation with the sovereign imamate of Yemen, which after World War I because an Ottoman successor state.

Persia and Afghanistan

The Anglo–Russian imperial rivalry over Persia, which traced back to the Napoleonic wars, grew menacing after the 1860s. It was then that Russia completed the conquest of Central Asia, thus extending its border with Persia to its full length (the formal line was not confirmed until 1885). Russia's territorial advance coincided with Britain's continuing effort to consolidate its strategic control of the Persian Gulf—in the case of Persia, by locking in its coast, the longest national segment on the Gulf's rim. Simultaneously, the tension roused by the imperial competition in and over Persia enveloped Afghanistan, which in the south looked to India, and in the north, to Russian Central Asia. The two Asian countries had thus become trapped between expansion by Russia and by British India. For the security planners in Britain and India at the turn of the century, Russia's designs on Persia appeared more threatening than those on Afghanistan.

To underpin eventual imperial claims to Persia, the contenders began laying the groundwork in the last quarter of the nineteenth century. They extracted military and fiscal privileges from the shah that trimmed his power. An 1879 agreement provided for a Persian Cossack Brigade, which enlisted Persians to serve under Russian officers chosen by Russia and paid by Persia. It remained a nominal brigade even after the murder of Naser al-Din Shah in 1896, when it was upgraded to an imperial guard for protecting the monarch and the dynasty, and even a decade later, when the Persian Cossacks, joined by a contingent of the regular Russian Army, failed to prevent adoption of the new constitution and the inauguration of a parliamentary regime— both realized with the implied blessings of Great Britain. (Only in 1916 did Russia finally transform the Cossacks into a fighting division and pay fully for its upkeep.) British India did not start responding until 1911, when it recruited and financed a gendarmerie or provincial police under Swedish officers. (In November 1916, the gendarmerie, without the Swedes, was integrated into the newly raised South Persia Rifles, trained and commanded by British officers.)

Less concealed and in most respects far more effective were the encroachments on the shah's fiscal sovereignty. In 1889, Baron Julius de Reuter, backed by the Foreign Office and the British legation in Tehran, procured a sixty-year concession to open the Imperial Bank of Persia, the first such institution in Persia. Its branches, in all the cities and larger towns, introduced the country to modern banking services. More significantly, the Imperial Bank received the exclusive right to serve as the fiscal agent of Persia and had the authority to issue banknotes. Two years later, Russian nationals, with active endorsement of their government, procured a parallel concession to launch the Banque de Prêts, originally designed to provide small-scale loans to Persians. Russia's Ministry of Finance bought the bank in 1894 and, under its new name, Banque d'Escompte de Perse, it pursued a deliberate policy of offering generous mortgages to rich landowners.

Russia's Foreign Ministry opened consulates not only in Mohammerah (present-day Khorramshahr), at the lower end of the Shatt al-Arab, but also in the major gulf ports of Bushehr and Bandar Abbas, where it sought to build coaling bunkers. In 1901 and 1902 the Banque d'Escompte issued personal loans to the shah totaling £3.4 million ($17 million). As surety, Russia's Finance Ministry won the pledge of customs, without explicitly omitting those collected in the Gulf ports. The Finance Ministry also lowered the customs rates on Russian imports while doubling them on those from Britain and British India, thereby violating their entitlement to most-favored-nation treatment under an 1841 commercial treaty. After briefly trying to soften Britain's rigid stance against such a meddlesome presence on the Gulf coast, Russia ended its discriminatory practice. Soon thereafter the customs service was transferred to Belgian officials employed by Persia.

Even more clearly in Afghanistan, Britain's imperial thrust was driven by strategic rather than economic concerns. Before 1747 Afghanistan had never formed a united independent state. It had passed back and forth, in whole or in part, between Persia and the Mogul Empire. From the mid-eighteenth century, the ruling dynasties came from tribesmen in the Kandahar area. Yet even after tearing itself away from the neighboring Asian empires, Afghanistan did not remain united. In the middle of the nineteenth century, rival khanates or principalities once again were struggling for supremacy.

While the outcome of the Russian–Ottoman War and the search for a renewed consensus in Europe at the Congress of Berlin in 1878 fully engrossed Britain, a small Russian force entered Afghanistan, seeking to round out Russia's recently captured Central Asian provinces. Anglo–India refused to tolerate such a prospect. In the early fall of 1878, the Russian mission and its Afghan puppet fled before advancing Anglo–Indian troops. Amir Shir Ali named his eldest son, Ya'qub, regent at Kabul. In the treaty of peace of May 1879, Ya'qub Khan surrendered Afghanistan's external sovereignty to Britain, accepted a resident Anglo–Indian mission at Kabul, and ceded the Khyber Pass and other strategic districts to British India. Ya'qub abdicated five months later.

Not until the midsummer of 1880 did British India finally inaugurate a new regime that took three years to put in place. The authority of Abd al-Rahman Khan, Ya'qub's cousin, at first did not reach beyond the district of Kabul. After demonstrating his ability to rule and his loyalty to British India, in 1883 he was finally allowed, with Anglo–Indian financial and military support, to take over the districts of Kandahar and Herat, thereby reuniting the

country. In June 1883, Abd al-Rahman reaffirmed the status of Afghanistan as a British protectorate, in return receiving assurance that he and his dynasty would be insured against external aggression and that he would receive a monthly subsidy of £10,000 ($50,000) to cover the costs of his troops and related expenses.

The border with British India was drawn in 1893 at a line, traced under the supervision of the foreign secretary in Calcutta, Sir Henry Mortimer Durand, that confirmed the cession to the British of the Khyber Pass and adjacent areas. Two years later, the Amu Darya River was accepted as Afghanistan's northeast boundary with Russia's Central Asian Tajik province.

Given the mutual fears aroused by the hardening rival positions, the European imperial strategies had been shaped to shut the adversary out. With boundaries fixed by the turn of the century, Afghanistan was removed temporarily from the zone of British–Russian contention. After the close of the Victorian era in 1901, Britain favored the division of Persia into mutually recognized spheres of imperial influence: Russia's in the north and Britain's in the south, with the two separated by a buffer. The Russian–Japanese war (1904–1906) interrupted exploratory talks that were resumed in the spring of 1906 and concluded in the summer of 1907. The convention divided Persia as originally agreed. Russia recognized Afghanistan as a British protectorate, won equal commercial opportunity, and gained the right to conduct local, nonpolitical frontier relations with Afghanistan.

The Coming of the Oil Age

Baron Julius de Reuter's 1889 bank concession in Persia included—as had his aborted railway concession more than a quarter-century earlier—the exclusive right to search for and develop mineral resources, including oil. To this end, he founded the Persian Bank Mining Rights Corporation, which never seriously pursued oil exploration. A decade later the Persian government canceled the mineral privileges. In 1901, William Knox D'Arcy, a wealthy British speculator with gold-mining experience in Australia, won the sole right to a sixty-year concession to explore for and extract oil across Persia except for the five northern provinces. The first commercial well in Persia was drilled in 1908, in the southern province of Khuzistan. A year later D'Arcy founded the Anglo–Persian Oil Company (APOC) to activate the concession. By 1912, on Abadan Island in the Shatt al-Arab, APOC put into operation the first units of its refinery to distill crude oil into fuel.

APOC's discovery of oil coincided with the British Admiralty's shift from coal to oil as the fuel for its war vessels. "In the year 1909," First Lord of the Admiralty Winston Churchill reported to the House of Commons on 17 July 1913, "the first flotilla of ocean-going destroyers wholly dependent upon oil was created, and since then, in each successive year, another flotilla of 'oil only' destroyers has been built. There are now built or building more than 100 [such] destroyers. . . . Similarly, during the last five years, oil has been employed in coal-burning battle-ships and cruisers, to enable them to realise their full powers in an emergency."

Churchill's statement prepared Parliament for the British government's partnership in APOC, so as to assure both British India and the Admiralty access to much of their oil needs at reduced cost. In an agreement of 20 May 1914, Britain bought 51 percent of APOC's shares and amended the company statutes to empower the government to veto any policy inconsistent with the national/imperial interest. As a further precaution, British India obtained explicit pledges from the shaykhs of Kuwait (1913) and Bahrain (1914) "never [to] give a[n oil] concession . . . to any one except a person appointed from the British Government."

Oil also figured prominently in the Anglo–German talks of 1913 and 1914. By then three groups were pursuing oil concessions in the Ottoman provinces of Mosul and Baghdad: the Deutsche Bank, APOC, and the Anglo–Saxon Oil Company (a subsidiary of Royal Dutch–Shell, an Anglo–Dutch combine). The Deutsche Bank's claim rested on a 1904 option that had been allowed to lapse; APOC's, on a series of appeals to the Sublime Porte after 1906, with the active backing of the British embassy in Constantinople; and that of Royal Dutch–Shell, on "the good offices of Mr. C. S. Gülbenkian, an Ottoman subject of considerable influence and ability, sometimes called the Talleyrand of oil diplomacy." Britain insisted that APOC be given

the largest share. When the two other groups acceded, a deal was framed at the Foreign Office in London on 19 March 1914. APOC procured a 47.5 percent interest in the Turkish Petroleum Company; the Deutsche Bank, 25 percent; the Anglo–Saxon Oil Company, 22.5 percent; and Gulbenkian, "a beneficiary five percent . . . without voting rights." On 28 June 1914, the Sublime Porte promised Britain and Germany that it would issue an oil concession in the Mosul and Baghdad *vilayets*.

The 1914 agreement etched the guidelines that, with appropriate adjustments to reflect the evolving postwar realities, assured Britain the largest share of the output of an international consortium that became operative in 1928, with a French company taking over the German allotment and a group of American companies, half of APOC's.

See also ABD AL-RAHMAN KHAN; AL KHALIFA FAMILY; BARING, EVELYN; BERLIN–BAGHDAD RAILWAY; BONAPARTE, NAPOLÉON; CHURCHILL, WINSTON S.; D'ARCY CONCESSION (1901); DUAL CONTROL; DURAND LINE; EAST INDIA COMPANY; FATH ALI SHAH QAJAR; ISMA'IL IBN IBRAHIM; KITCHENER, HORATIO HERBERT; LANSDOWNE, HENRY CHARLES KEITH PETTY FITZMAURICE; LESSEPS, FERDINAND DE; NASER AL-DIN SHAH; PALMERSTON, LORD HENRY JOHN TEMPLE; SUBLIME PORTE; SUEZ CANAL.

Bibliography

Bullard, Sir Reader. *Britain and the Middle East from Earliest Times to 1963.* London: Hutchinson, 1964.

Bush, Briton Cooper. *Britain and the Persian Gulf, 1894–1914.* Berkeley: University of California Press, 1967.

Hallberg, Charles William. *The Suez Canal: Its History and Diplomatic Importance.* New York: Columbia University Press, 1931.

Hurewitz, J. C. *The Middle East and North Africa in World Politics: A Documentary Record,* Vol. 1: *European Expansion: 1535–1914.* New Haven, CT: Yale University Press, 1975.

Kelly, J. B. *Britain and the Persian Gulf, 1795–1880.* Oxford: Clarendon Press, 1968.

Langer, William Leonard. *European Alliances and Alignments, 1871–1890.* New York: Knopf, 1931. Reprint, 1960.

Lee, Dwight Irwin. *Great Britain and the Cyprus Convention Policy of 1878.* Cambridge, MA: Harvard University Press, 1934.

Shibeika, Mekki. *British Policy in the Sudan.* London and New York: Oxford University Press, 1952.

Vatikiotis, P. J. *The Modern History of Egypt.* New York: Praeger, 1969.

Wilkinson, John C. *Arabia's Frontiers: The Story of Britain's Boundary Drawing in the Desert.* London and New York: I.B. Tauris, 1991.

Wood, A. C. *A History of the Levant Company.* London: Oxford University Press, 1935.

Yergin, Daniel. *The Prize: The Epic Quest for Oil, Money and Power.* New York: Simon and Schuster, 1991.

J. C. HUREWITZ

BRITISH EAST INDIA COMPANY

See EAST INDIA COMPANY

BRITISH–FRENCH OIL AGREEMENT

Agreement that placed Palestine and Iraq under British mandate and the newly partitioned Syria and Lebanon under French mandate.

The British–French Oil Agreement was announced on 5 May 1920 at the meeting of the Supreme Council of the League of Nations. It was held in San Remo, Italy in response to and in repudiation of the March 1920 Damascus resolution of the General Syrian Congress that proclaimed the independence of Syria. Under the agreement, Greater Syria was partitioned into Syria and Lebanon, which were placed under French mandate while Palestine was placed under British mandate. The British mandate for Palestine was charged with implementing the Balfour Declaration of 2 November 1917, which called for the establishment of a homeland for the Jewish people without having to "prejudice the civil and religious rights of existing non-Jewish communities in Palestine." Under the terms of British–French Agreement, Iraq in its entirety came under British mandate.

The agreement also gave the British permanent control over any entity exploiting Mesopotamian oil, including the Turkish Petroleum Company (TPC), which was established with the successful manipulation of the Armenian businessman Calouste Gulbenkian. Mesopotamia was strategically important to the British because of its military and commercial routes to India. With its decision before World War I to replace coal with oil as the main source of energy for its naval fleet, Britain planned to control the possible sources of the Iraqi oil even before the TPC was established in 1912. Even though Iraq became a British mandate in 1920, there was no guarantee that TPC was to be given a concession for oil exploration in Iraq. Complications arose from terms of the San Remo Agreement, which stipulated that Iraq could hold 20 percent interest in TPC if it invested. In spite of Iraq's objection, it was decided that Iraq would receive a flat fee as royalties per ton payable in British pounds, but with a gold clause, meaning in units of gold per pound on the day of the agreement. Iraq meant to safeguard the future payments it receives from royalties from possible devaluations of the pound. TPC won the oil exploration concession in Iraq in 1925, and the discovery of oil in the vicinity of Kirkuk occurred on 15 October 1927. TPC was renamed Iraq Petroleum Company (IPC) in 1929.

In its quest to have control over Iraq, the British–French Agreement—known also as the San Remo Agreement—was preceded by several relevant developments. The most important one was the conclusion of the secret 1916 Sykes-Picot Agreement by Britain, France, and Russia, which divided the spheres of influence over Syria and Iraq, the latter of which would be under the domain of the British. In fact, the French–British Agreement was simply a formulation of what had been secretly agreed. Following the communist revolution in 1917, terms of the Sykes-Picot Agreement were revealed by Moscow in order to embarrass both England and France and to give a push to Arab revolt and nationalism.

See also COMPAGNIE FRANÇAISE DES PÉTROLES (CFP); GÜLBENKIAN, CALOUSTE; IRAQ PETROLEUM COMPANY (IPC); PETROLEUM, OIL, AND NATURAL GAS; SAN REMO CONFERENCE (1920); SYKES-PICOT AGREEMENT (1916).

Bibliography

Hudson, Michael C. *Arab Politics Search for Legitimacy.* New Haven, CT: Yale University Press, 1977.

Hurewitz, J. C., ed. *The Middle East and North Africa in World Politics.* New Haven, CT: Yale University Press, 1979.

Lewis, Bernard. *The Middle East*. London: Phoenix Press, 1995

Mansfield, Peter. *The Arab World A Comprehensive History*. New York: Thomas Y. Cromwell, 1967.

Yergin, Daniel. *The Prize*. New York: Simon and Schuster, 1991.

ZACHARY KARABELL
UPDATED BY IBRAHIM M. OWEISS

BRIT SHALOM

See BINATIONALISM; MAGNES, JUDAH; RUPPIN, ARTHUR

BROOKINGS REPORT (1975)

Study that encouraged U.S. mediation in Arab–Israeli peace process.

In December 1975 a study group at the Brookings Institution, a liberal Washington, D.C., think tank, issued a report endorsing five principles for an Arab–Israeli peace. The intent of the report was to be more precise than the United Nations Security Council Resolution 242 had been in directing U.S. policymakers on the degree of mutual recognition that would be necessary, and it urged U.S. acceptance of Israel's 1967 borders and Palestinian national aspirations.

The sixteen-member Middle East Study Group met monthly from June 1974, particularly encouraged by Princeton University sociologist Morrow Berger and former diplomat Charles Yost, who argued that the outcome of the 1967 and 1973 Arab–Israel wars favored a U.S. peace initiative. The group balanced pro-Arab and pro-Israeli perspectives, and included academics and former U.S. officials and ambassadors from Republican and Democrat administrations, including Robert Bowie, Philip Klutznick, and Najeeb Halaby (father of the future Queen Noor of Jordan).

The report's deliberately general compromises were widely taken as an indication that solid grounds existed for a phased settlement between Israel and its neighbors. Moreover, two key study-group members—Zbigniew Brzezinski, Carter's National Security Adviser, and William Quandt, National Security Council Director for Middle Eastern Af-

fairs—subsequently helped to guide Jimmy Carter's administration to the Camp David Accords (1978). The report complemented Brzezinski's work with Carter on a wider security "architecture" at the Trilateral Commission (a non-governmental organization established in 1973 to promote coordination between North American, Western European, and Japanese foreign policies), encouraged the administration's inclusion of the 1967 borders and Palestinian autonomy in U.S. policy, and directly informed the Camp David discussions, at which Brzezinski and Quandt played active roles.

See also CAMP DAVID ACCORDS (1978); CARTER, JIMMY.

Bibliography

Brookings Institution. *Toward Peace in the Middle East: Report of a Study Group*. Washington, DC: Brookings Institution, 1975.

Brzezinski, Zbigniew. *Power and Principle: Memoirs of the National Security Adviser, 1977–1981*. New York: Farrar, Straus, and Giroux, 1983.

Quandt, William. *Decade of Decisions: American Foreign Policy Toward the Arab–Israeli Conflict, 1967–1976*. Berkeley: University of California Press, 1977.

GEORGE R. WILKES

BROWNE, EDWARD GRANVILLE
[1862–1926]

British Iranologist.

Born of a wealthy Gloucestershire family, E. G. Browne was educated at Eton and Cambridge, England, where he qualified as a physician. In 1877, his interest stimulated by the Russian–Ottoman War, he began a largely informal study of Turkish, followed by Persian and Arabic. Elected a fellow of Pembroke College at Cambridge, he spent the year 1887–1888 in Iran, which he described in *A Year amongst the Persians* (London, 1893, reprint 1926). On his return he was appointed university lecturer in Persian, then in 1902 Sir Thomas Adams Professor of Arabic. He married in 1906 and remained in Cambridge until his death.

As a rich man holding a virtual sinecure, Browne was able to direct his enormous energy and phenomenal memory into an almost virgin field. In

Britain, Middle East studies had formerly been concerned mainly with Arabic. Persian studies, a legacy via the "back door" from the Mogul Empire (of India, which had become part of the British Empire following the Sepoy mutiny of 1857), had been confined to the few literary classics used in examinations for the Indian Civil Service. Browne unlocked the "front door" to post-Islamic Persia (now Iran) and to the full range of New Persian studies—including the modern spoken and literary language, religious history, and politics.

His most important contribution is the four-volume *A Literary History of Persia* (1902, 1906, 1920, 1924), still a valuable resource for scholars. It quotes extensively from original sources and from information provided by his Iranian friends and correspondents, including major writers and scholars of the time such as Ali Akbar Dehkhoda and Mohammad Qazvini. Apart from his large scholarly output, Browne also promoted Oriental studies at Cambridge by attracting prospective diplomats and administrators to an academic training; these included later historians of the Middle East, such as Laurence Lockhart and Sir Reader Bullard.

Even before his journey to Iran, Browne had taken a sympathetic interest in the Babis movement (c. 1844–1853) and its successors, the Azali and Baha'i faiths. He wrote a detailed account of these for the Royal Asiatic Society in 1889, met with leading adherents of the sects (especially Azalis), and published some of their works. He is best remembered in Iran for his active support of the constitutional movement from 1905 to 1911, which was characteristic of his liberal sympathies with all aspirants to self-determination. In 1908 he helped found the Persia Committee, composed of prominent members of the British Parliament (MPs); through this pressure group, in lectures, and in letters to the press, Browne sharply criticized his own government's and Russia's machinations in Iran. His book *The Press and Poetry of Modern Persia* (1914) is not merely a supplement to his *Literary History* but an avowedly partisan promotion of the democratic ideals he saw in the vigorous free press of constitutionalist Iran.

Browne was awarded the Persian Order of the Lion and Sun and, on his sixtieth birthday, he received accolades from his Iranian admirers and his British colleagues. Both as a scholar and an activist, he did much to present a sympathetic picture of Iran's people and culture to a Western public, whose view of the Middle East was already being shaped chiefly by the dictates of geopolitics, and petroleum.

See also BABIS; BAHA'I FAITH; DEHKHODA, ALI AKBAR.

Bibliography

Arberry, A. J. *Oriental Essays.* London: Allen and Unwin, 1960.

JOHN R. PERRY

BUBER, MARTIN
[1878–1965]

Religious and social philosopher.

Martin Buber is most prominently known for his volume of 1923, *I and Thou (Ich und Du)*, in which he introduced his concept of dialogue, or an attentive and sympathetic listening to the Other, in which one suspends one's pre-established opinions and categories of perception and judgment, thus allowing the Other (*qua*, Thou, that is, an autonomous subject) to stand before oneself in the fullness of his or her existential reality. A life-long Zionist, Buber applied this principle to the "Arab Question," concluding that the land the Jews call *Eretz Yisrael* and the Arabs, Palestine, is "a land of two peoples." The fact that both Jew and Arab regard the land as their home and birthright must serve as the moral and political basis of a just and humane solution to the conflict between the two peoples. Accordingly, he supported binationalism, which envisioned shared political sovereignty over Palestine, with neither national community dominating the other.

In 1942, Buber joined Judah Magnes (1877–1948), then president of Hebrew University of Jerusalem, in founding the *Ichud* (or *Ihud,* i.e., Union), a political party that regarded "the Union between the Jewish and Arab peoples as essential for the upbuilding of Palestine." In a testimony before the Anglo-American Inquiry Committee, which convened in Jerusalem in March 1946 to explore solutions to the question of Palestine, Buber presented the vision of the *Ihud*: ". . .Jewish settlement [in

Palestine] must oust no Arab peasant, Jewish immigration must not cause the political status of the present inhabitants to deteriorate. . . A regenerated Jewish people in Palestine has not only to aim at living peacefully together with the Arab people, but also at a comprehensive cooperation with it in developing the country." Earlier, shortly after his emigration to Palestine in March 1938, in an open letter to Mohandas K. Gandhi, he set forth the presuppositions of this vision. It is the duty of the Jews, he explained, "to understand and to honor the claim which is opposed to ours" and to seek to reconcile the two claims that tragically divide Jew and Arab. For "we love this land and we believe in its future; and, seeing that such love and faith are surely present also on the other side, a union in the common service of the Land must be within the range of the possible." Although the political circumstances would radically change with the establishment of the state of Israel and, its wake, the displacement of hundreds of thousands of Arabs, this remained Buber's conviction.

See also MAGNES, JUDAH.

Bibliography

Mendes-Flohr, Paul R., ed. *A Land of Two Peoples: Martin Buber on Jews and Arabs.* New York: Oxford University Press, 1983.

PAUL MENDES-FLOHR

BUBIYAN ISLAND

Island at the head of the Persian/Arabian Gulf, off the north coast of Kuwait and west of the Shatt al-Arab.

Separated from Kuwait by a narrow waterway, Bubiyan is Kuwait's largest island. Along with al-Warba Island, it lies at the mouth of Iraq's Gulf port, Umm Qasr. Both islands have been the focus of Iraq's territorial claims. In 1990, before invading Kuwait and announcing an annexation of Kuwaiti territory, Iraq's President Saddam Hussein demanded that Kuwait cede its sovereignty over both islands. Following Iraq's defeat in spring of 1991 by a United Nations coalition of forces, and the restoration of Kuwait's ruling Al Sabah family, this boundary dispute cooled but has not been settled.

See also AL SABAH FAMILY; HUSSEIN, SADDAM; PERSIAN (ARABIAN) GULF.

Bibliography

Adams, Michael, ed. *The Middle East: A Handbook.* New York: Facts on File, 1988.

EMILE A. NAKHLEH

BUCHAREST, TREATY OF (1812)

Treaty ending the Ottoman–Russian war by which Russia returned territory to the empire.

After six years of war between the Ottoman Empire and Russia, the Treaty of Bucharest was concluded between 16 and 18 May 1812. With Napoléon Bonaparte, emperor of France, prepared to attack Russia, Tsar Alexander I renounced Russian rights to the Romanian principalities and evacuated most of the Black Sea coast territory that Russia had won during the war, excepting Bessarabia. The treaty also contained a provision for autonomy of the Serbs, who had rebelled against the Ottomans.

See also BONAPARTE, NAPOLÉON; RUSSIAN–OTTOMAN WARS.

Bibliography

Anderson, M. S. *The Eastern Question, 1774–1923.* London: Macmillan, 1966.

Shaw, Stanford, and Shaw, Ezel Kural. *History of the Ottoman Empire and Modern Turkey.* 2 vols. Cambridge, U.K., and New York: Cambridge University Press, 1976–1977.

ZACHARY KARABELL

BUDAPEST CONVENTION (1877)

Agreement between Austria and Russia regarding Russia's planned war against Ottoman Empire.

Determined to amend the decisions made by the 1876 Istanbul Conference, Russia made plans for war against the Ottoman Empire. By the Budapest Convention of 15 January 1877, Austria agreed to remain neutral in the coming war in return for the provinces of Bosnia and Herzegovina. Provision was also made for the partition of the Balkans in the event the Ottoman Empire collapsed.

Bibliography

Shaw, Stanford, and Shaw, Ezel Kural. *History of the Ottoman Empire and Modern Turkey.* 2 vols. Cambridge,

U.K., and New York: Cambridge University Press, 1976–1977.

ZACHARY KARABELL

BUGEAUD DE LA PICONNERIE, THOMAS-ROBERT
[1784–1849]

French military officer; governor-general of Algeria, 1841–1847.

In the early nineteenth century, North Africa was under the Ottoman Empire, but local rulers sponsored corsairs, pirates, and the slave trade in their coastal towns. The Europeans tried to salvage Mediterranean shipping from attack and end the taking of Christian sailors as slaves. In 1830, a French force took Algiers, but by 1832, local leader Abd al-Qadir of Mascara defeated the French and was recognized as dey of Mascara. Abd al-Qadir repeatedly defeated French forces from 1835 to 1837.

Marshal Thomas-Robert Bugeaud de la Piconnerie was sent to negotiate the Treaty of Tafna between France and Abd al-Qadir (30 May 1837), which abandoned most of Algeria to Abd al-Qadir. In 1839, the French broke the treaty, and in 1841 Bugeaud led a large force on the offensive against Abd al-Qadir. Bugeaud served as governor-general from 1841 to 1847. He was recalled to France and forced to resign in 1847 for disobeying orders; ironically that was the year that Abd al-Qadir surrendered to the French.

See also ABD AL-QADIR; CORSAIRS; SLAVE TRADE.

Bibliography

Sullivan, Anthony. *Thomas-Robert Bugeaud, France, and Algeria, 1784–1849: Politics, Power, and the Good Society.* Hamden, CT: Archon Books, 1983.

KENNETH J. PERKINS

BU HAMARA
[1865–1909]

The nickname of al-Jilali ibn Idris al-Zarhuni, a Moroccan pretender to the Alawi throne.

Initially a minor official in the Alawite dynasty in Morocco, Bu Hamara (Arabic, "the man with the she-ass") was imprisoned in 1894 on charges of forgery. Between 1901 and 1903, passing himself off as a brother of the sultan Abd al-Aziz, he rallied the forces of the Ghiyata tribal confederation in the middle Atlas mountains. His activity can be understood as one in a series of rural movements opposed to heavy-handed policies by the *makhzan* government. Bu Hamara effectively controlled northeastern Morocco until his defeat in 1908 and execution in 1909 by the new sultan, Mulay Hafid (Abd al-Hafiz).

See also ALAWITE DYNASTY; HAFID, MULAY.

Bibliography

Burke, Edmund, III. *Prelude to Protectorate in Morocco: Precolonial Protest and Resistance, 1860–1912.* Chicago: University of Chicago Press, 1976.

Pennell, C. R. *Morocco since 1830: A History.* New York: New York University, 2000.

MATTHEW S. GORDON

BUHAYRA

Egypt's westernmost delta province (governorate).

This province has existed as an administrative unit since Fatimid times. Nearest of Egypt's rural provinces to Alexandria, it was known while under the Mamluks and under the Ottoman Empire as a center of rebellious bedouin Arab tribes. Its capital is Damanhur. The estimated 1986 population of Buhayra was 1.8 million. Of its entire area, some 4,000 square miles (10,150 sq km) are in the Nile delta.

See also DAMANHUR; MAMLUKS.

ARTHUR GOLDSCHMIDT

BU JANAH FAMILY

See BUSNACH FAMILY

BULGARIAN HORRORS

Phrase coined by British politician Gladstone to describe the atrocities perpetrated by the Turks in putting down the revolt of the Bulgarians in 1876.

In 1875, a revolt began in Bosnia and Herzegovina that spread to neighboring Bulgaria the next year. Public opinion in Serbia and Montenegro soon caused them to declare war against the Ottoman

Empire in an effort to intervene on behalf of their fellow Slavs. Meanwhile, eyewitness reports revealing that more than 10,000 Christians had been slaughtered in Bulgaria by Turkish irregulars reached England, which had fought the Crimean War to preserve the Ottoman Empire and was intensely interested in the conflict. A wave of moral indignation swept over the country, fired by the revelations of the liberal press, the high point of which was an indictment by William Ewart Gladstone of Turkish rule in his pamphlet, "Bulgarian Horrors and the Question of the East." In it he argued passionately in favor of autonomy for the empire's Christian subjects, with little effect.

Although Gladstone was successful in rallying public opinion in Western Europe on behalf of the Bulgarians, the situation there was not resolved until after Russia attacked Turkey in 1877. In the following year, the treaties of San Stefano and Berlin established Bulgaria as an autonomous principality under Turkish sovereignty.

Bibliography

Harris, David. *Britain and the Bulgarian Horrors of 1876.* Chicago: University of Chicago Press, 1939.

JOHN MICGIEL

BULGUR

See FOOD: BULGUR

BUNCHE, RALPH J.

[1903–1971]

U.S. diplomat.

Ralph Bunche was born in Detroit, Michigan. His father was an itinerant barber. Orphaned at eleven, he was brought up by his grandmother in the Watts district of Los Angeles. Success at school both as student and athlete took him to the University of California, Los Angeles and, as a graduate student, to Harvard University. Colonialism was the subject of his Harvard doctoral thesis, and he did field work in Cameroon, French Togo, South Africa, Kenya, and Congo.

His writings on the race problem in the United States are part of the earliest literature of the Civil Rights movement. In *A World View of Race* (1936) he

made a spirited connection between the nature and causes of the race problem in United States and of the international phenomenon of colonialism. In 1935, with A. Philip Randolph, he founded the National Negro Congress to give a voice to wider spectrum of the black population. He was chief assistant and researcher to Gunnar Myrdal in writing the classic *An Ameran Dilemma: The Negro Problem and Modern Democracy,* eventually published in 1944.

During World War II Bunche worked in the Office of Strategic Services (OSS). In 1944 he moved to the State Department and was its first black official. There, and at the 1945 San Francisco Conference, he was the principal drafter of Chapters XI (Non-self-governing Territories) and XII (The International Trusteeship System) of the United Nations Charter.

In 1946 Bunche set up the Trusteeship Division of the United Nations Secretariat. In 1947 in Palestine, he wrote both the majority (partition) proposal and the minority (federation) proposal of the UN Special Committee on Palestine. In 1948, as chief assistant to the UN mediator, Count Folke Bernadotte, he set up the UN Truce Supervision Organization in Palestine. When Bernadotte was assassinated in Jerusalem by the Stern Gang in September 1948, Bunche took over as mediator and negotiated armistice agreements between Israel and its four Arab neighbors. For this feat he was awarded the Nobel Peace Prize. From 1953, as Under Secretary-General for Special Political Affairs, Bunche was the chief political adviser to Secretary-General Dag Hammarskjöld, and to Hammarskjöld's successor, U Thant. During the Suez Crisis in 1956, he set up the first UN peacekeeping force, the United Nations Emergency Force in Middle East (UNEF I) and organized and directed subsequent peacekeeping forces in Lebanon, the Congo, and Cyprus. He personally led the largest of these, in the Congo, in 1960.

Bunche's complete integrity and fair-mindedness were universally acknowledged and respected, and his intellectual grasp, ingenuity, and determination as a negotiator were widely admired. He turned down efforts by successive U.S. presidents to woo him away from the United Nations. At his death in 1971, U Thant hailed him as "an international institution in his own right."

See also BERNADOTTE, FOLKE; UNITED NATIONS SPECIAL COMMITTEE ON PALESTINE, 1947 (UNSCOP); UNITED NATIONS TRUCE SUPERVISION ORGANIZATION (UNTSO).

Bibliography

Henry, Charles P., ed. *Ralph J. Bunche: Selected Speeches and Writings.* Ann Arbor: University of Michigan Press, 1995.

Rivlin, Benjamin, ed. *Ralph Bunche: The Man and His Times.* New York: Holmes and Meir, 1990.

Urquhart, Brian. *Ralph Bunche: An American Life.* New York: W. W. Norton, 1993.

BRIAN URQUHART

BUND

Jewish socialist workers' association.

The Bund (full name in Yiddish: Algemeyner Yidisher Arbeiter-Bund in Rusland und Poylen, translated as "General association of Jewish workers in Russia and Poland") was founded in Vilna (now Vilnius, Lithuania) in 1897. It was opposed to the emigration of Jews from Eastern Europe and asserted that the survival and development of Jewish life was dependent, instead, on Jews joining the struggle for social change and social justice in their respective countries of origin. It was staunchly opposed to Zionism as well as to the Zionist emphasis on Hebrew as the Jewish national language. It promoted the value of Yiddish. It was originally neutral on the notion of a collective Jewish national identity, but in 1901 it endorsed the ethnicity of Russia's Jews, and in October 1905 it adopted the notion Jewish cultural autonomy.

After the Bolshevik Revolution (1917), government repression led to the Bund's demise in the Soviet Union. The Bund continued to play an influential role in Poland until the Nazi invasion in 1939 and the beginning of World War II. After the war, the remnants of the Bund in Europe and the United States continued to oppose vigorously the establishment of a Jewish state.

See also ZIONISM.

Bibliography

Jacobs, Jack. *On Socialists and the Jewish Question After Marx.* New York: New York University Press, 1993.

Jacobs, Jack, ed. *Jewish Politics in Eastern Europe: The Bund at 100.* New York: New York University Press, 2001.

Tobias, Henry J. *The Jewish Bund in Russia: From Its Origins to 1905.* Stanford, CA: Stanford University Press, 1972.

CHAIM I. WAXMAN

BURAYMI OASIS DISPUTE

Territorial dispute over the oasis villages in the Buraymi region, 1952–1974.

The oasis settlements of the Buraymi region have been coveted by regional powers for centuries. The principal contenders for sovereignty during the nineteenth century were the rulers of Muscat, Dubai, and Abu Dhabi, and the Al Saʿud. In the first half of the twentieth century there were nine villages in the Buraymi region, of which three were claimed by Oman, six by Abu Dhabi.

The scramble for oil helped to intensify territorial claims in the region after World War II, and the Buraymi dispute arose when the Saudis aggressively asserted their claim to the oasis region. In 1952, in support of claims by Abu Dhabi and Muscat, a British official established himself in the village of Buraymi. In opposition, a group of Saudi officials occupied the village of Khamasa. With military conflict looming, a standstill agreement was signed in 1952, and an international tribunal created in 1954. Disagreements among the parties precipitated the collapse of the tribunal in 1955. The rulers of Oman and Abu Dhabi subsequently sent a military force to occupy the Buraymi villages and expel the Saudis. In 1972 the United Arab Emirates and Oman divided the Buraymi oasis among themselves. In 1974 Abu Dhabi ceded to Saudi Arabia a territorial corridor to the Persian Gulf south and east of Qatar in exchange for recognition of the Abu Dhabi–Omani claim to Buraymi.

Bibliography

Henderson, Edward. *This Strange Eventful History: Memoirs of Earlier Days in the UAE and Oman,* 2d edition. Dubai, United Arab Emirates: Motivate Publishing, 1993.

Peck, Malcolm C. *The United Arab Emirates: A Venture in Unity.* Boulder, CO: Westview Press, 1986.

MALCOLM C. PECK
UPDATED BY ANTHONY B. TOTH

BURCKHARDT, JOHANN LUDWIG

[1784–1817]

Swiss explorer; known in the Arab world as Ibrahim ibn Abdullah.

Born in Switzerland to an Anglophile father, Burckhardt was educated at Leipzig University in Germany, then hired by the London-based Association for Promoting the Discovery of Africa. To perfect his disguise as a Muslim traveler, he gained their approval to study Islam in the Middle East. In this manner, he became the first European to produce detailed eyewitness accounts of Mecca and Medina and rediscovered Petra in 1812. Burckhardt wrote *Travels in Syria and the Holy Land* (1822), *Travels in Arabia* (1829), and *Notes on the Bedouins and Wahabys* (1830).

Bibliography

Sim, Katherine. *Desert Traveller: The Life of Jean Louis Burckhardt,* revised edition. London: Phoenix Press, 2000.

BENJAMIN BRAUDE

BUREAU OF TRANSLATION

Ottoman agency (Bab-i Ali Tercüme Odasi) that also served as a training ground for diplomats and government officials.

Having long employed Greeks as translators, in 1821 the Ottoman Empire reacted to the Greek war of independence (1821–1830) by dismissing the last Greek translator of the Imperial Divan, appointing a Bulgarian convert to Islam to replace him. In 1821, Mahmut II created the translation office, which led an obscure existence for the next twelve years—serving more as a school than as a translation bureau, because few Muslims then knew European languages well enough to translate. Upgraded during the Ottoman–Egyptian diplomatic crisis of 1832 and 1833 (during which Muhammad Ali of Egypt demanded all Syria as a reward for his aid in Greece), the translation office assumed an important role in preparing young men to serve abroad as embassy secretaries; some of these later became ambassadors, foreign ministers, even grand viziers. Primarily a diplomatic translation bureau, the office became part of the Foreign Ministry (Hariciye Nezareti) when it was organized in 1836.

For a generation, the translation office was one of the best sources of Western education in Istanbul, and men trained there dominated the ranks of reforming statesmen, Westernizing intellectuals, and opposition ideologues. Patterns of bureaucratic mobility changed within the Ottoman civil service, but this office kept its prestige as a place to begin a career, and it continued to function until the end of the empire (1922).

See also GREEK WAR OF INDEPENDENCE; MAHMUD II; MUHAMMAD ALI; OTTOMAN EMPIRE: CIVIL SERVICE.

Bibliography

Findley, Carter Vaughn. *Bureaucratic Reform in the Ottoman Empire: The Sublime Porte, 1789–1922.* Princeton, NJ: Princeton University Press, 1980.

Findley, Carter Vaughn. *Ottoman Civil Officialdom: A Social History.* Princeton, NJ: Princeton University Press, 1989.

CARTER V. FINDLEY

BUREAUX ARABES

French military administration in Algeria, 1830–1847.

The expansion of French power and influence in Algeria after the July 1830 conquest of Algiers necessitated intermediaries besides interpreters to deal with both Arab and Berber tribes. A systematic administration run by specially trained military officers was structured by Governor-General Thomas-Robert Bugeaud de la Piconnerie and established by decree in 1844 to execute this service. These *bureaux arabes* provided the governor-general with mediation and intelligence. The officers viewed their operations as a civilizing mission and were often paternalistic and protective of native rights. The civilian colons (European settlers in Algeria) resented this flaunted example of "rule by the sabre." After Bugeaud's departure (1847), the personnel and performance of the *bureaux arabes* declined. A French decree in October 1870 restructured the administration, which effectively ended the system though an analogous organization continued in south Algeria. The military resumed a similar political and social mission with the Sections Administratives Spécialisées (SAS) during the Algerian War of Independence (1954–1962).

See also ALGERIA; ALGERIAN WAR OF INDEPEN-
DENCE; ALGIERS; BUGEAUD DE LA PICON-
NERIE, THOMAS-ROBERT; COLONS.

PHILLIP C. NAYLOR

BURG, AVRAHAM
[1955–]

Israeli political leader.

Avraham Burg was born in Jerusalem in 1955, the
son of Yosef Burg, veteran and founder of the National Religious Party. After serving in the Paratroop Division of the Israel Defense Force, Burg
became a leader of the Yesh Gvul protest movement
against the war in Lebanon. In 1985, Prime Minister Shimon Peres appointed Burg to serve as his
adviser on Diaspora Affairs. Burg held that position
until 1988, when he was elected to the Knesset with
the Alignment Party. While in the Knesset Burg
served on several key committees, including the
Foreign Affairs and Defense Committee, the Finance Committee and the State Control Committee. He was reelected to the Knesset in 1992, and
continued to serve as chairman of the Knesset Education and Culture Committee.

In 1995 Burg was elected chairman of the executive of the Jewish Agency for Israel and the World
Zionist Organization and resigned from the Knesset. As chairman of the Jewish Agency for Israel he
led policy initiatives in restitution of Jewish property stolen during the Holocaust and religious pluralism and tolerance among Jews. He held that position
until 1999, when he once again ran for the Knesset on the One Israel list, a new political alignment
including the former Labor Party. After being reelected Burg was chosen in July 1999 to be speaker
of the Fifteenth Knesset.

See also BURG, YOSEF.

Bibliography
American-Israeli Cooperative Enterprise. "Avraham
Burg." In *Jewish Virtual Library*. Available from
<http://www.us-israel.org/jsource/biography>.

"Israel: Labor Party Leadership Election Disputed."
Facts On File, 4 September 2001. Accession number 2001227140.

State of Israel Ministry of Foreign Affairs. "Avraham
Burg, MK, Speaker of the Knesset." *Personalities.*
Available from <http://www.mfa.gov.il/mfa>.

GREGORY S. MAHLER

BURG, YOSEF
[1909–1999]

Israeli politician.

Born and educated in Germany, Burg received a
doctorate in philosophy from the University of
Leipzig and later was ordained as a rabbi at the Rabbinical Seminary in Berlin. Emigrating to Palestine
in 1939, he was a research fellow at the Hebrew University of Jerusalem. From 1945 to 1949, he worked
in Paris as director of the Religious Rescue Projects
in Europe, caring for Holocaust survivors.

He served in the Knesset from 1949 until 1988.
He helped found the National Religious Party
(NRP). From 1951 to 1986 Burg served in every Israeli government; he was minister of health (1951–
1952), posts (1952–1958), social welfare (1959–1970),
interior (1970–1984), and religious affairs (1984–
1986). He was relatively moderate on Arab-Israel
relations. As a member of Menachem Begin's 1977
Likud government, he participated in negotiations
with Egypt following the Camp David Accords. Burg
resigned from the government in October 1986, to
make way for younger leadership when Yitzhak
Shamir succeeded Shimon Peres as prime minister
in the rotation of the National Unity government.

In 1977 Burg was elected president of the World
Mizrahi Movement. He was selected as a member of
the Presidium of the Zionist Actions Committee in
1992. He died in October 1999.

Bibliography
Jewish Agency for Israel, Department for Jewish Zionist
Education. "Yosef Burg." Available from <http://
www.jafi.org.il/education>

Rolef, Susan Hattis, ed. *Political Dictionary of the State of Israel,*
2d edition. New York: Macmillan, 1993.

ZACHARY KARABELL
UPDATED BY GREGORY S. MAHLER

BURJ AL-BARAJNA
See HUMAN RIGHTS

BURLA, YEHUDA

[1886–1969]

First modern Hebrew writer of Middle Eastern Jewish descent.

Yehuda Burla was born in Jerusalem, the child of a family of Turkish rabbis and scholars who settled in Ottoman Palestine in the eighteenth century. He was educated at yeshivas (Hebrew schools) and at the Jerusalem Teachers' Seminary. He served as an interpreter for the Ottoman Empire during World War I. After the war, during the British mandate over Palestine, he directed and taught at various Hebrew schools. From 1930, he headed the Arab department of Histadrut, was envoy of Keren ha-Yesod to Latin America, was director of Arab affairs in the ministry of minorities, and served as president of the Hebrew Authors' Association.

After reading the works of modern Hebrew writers, Burla realized that they dealt exclusively with Ashkenazim. He was therefore determined to present the rich world of Middle Eastern Jewry. His first novella, *Lunah* (1918), is a love story among Sephardim in old Jerusalem. His first novel, *Ishto ha-Senu'ah* (1928, His hated wife), concerns a man who hates his wife but, fearing economic ruin, does not divorce her. He also wrote about bedouins in *Beli Kochav* (1937, Without a star). Burla was a realist; his style is narrative and the mood evoked is romantic.

See also ADOT HA-MIZRAH; HISTADRUT.

ANN KAHN

BURNOOSE

See CLOTHING

BURQAN OIL FIELD, AL-

See SUWAYDIYA OIL FIELDS

BURSA

Fourth largest city of Turkey, in northwest Anatolia.

Bursa was the first major conquest of the early Ottomans in 1324. A modest Byzantine provincial market town, it quickly developed as the first capital of the growing Ottoman Empire, featuring many of the finest examples of early Ottoman architecture. Positioned on the northern foothills of Uludağ (Bithynian Mount Olympus) close to the Sea of Marmara, with easy access to the Mediterranean and on the natural extension of Anatolian routes, it became a major international commercial center, where European, mainly Genoese, merchants bought silk and other Eastern goods. It was also widely known for its abundant hot springs and magnificent baths.

Even after the conquest of Constantinople (now Istanbul) in 1453, when it became the definitive capital of the empire, Bursa remained an imperial city and a thriving international market, with significant manufacture of cotton and silk textiles, in addition to its long-established role as terminus for long-distance Asian caravan trade. With a population of about 40,000 in the sixteenth century, it was the largest city in Anatolia. Bursa's growth was hampered in the seventeenth century as a result of the Ottoman policy of promoting İzmir as the major port for Asian and European trade, but the city retained its position as a prominent, if less prosperous, cultural, manufacturing, and commercial center. During the Tanzimat period of free trade, with competition from industrialized Europe, Bursa's silk and cotton textile manufacture suffered significantly, but both the Ottoman policy of industrialization and private investment in steam-powered plants allowed recovery of local production before the end of the century. Bursa became the seat of an enlarged province incorporating several northwest Anatolian districts. Abdülhamit II's efforts to glorify the early Ottoman heritage also contributed to the city's growing fortunes.

Bursa was occupied by the Greek army after World War I, and the city suffered during the ensuing Turkish War of Independence, especially with the destructive retreat of the Greek army in 1922 and the loss of its non-Muslim population. As a result of the state-led industrialization during the 1920s and 1930s, Bursa recovered its textile manufacturing prominence, but its real growth came in the 1960s, with the establishment by private enterprises first of large-scale canning and food processing and then of the automotive industry. In 2000, Bursa was the third largest contributor to Turkey's gross domestic product, with its population of 2,106,687, of whom 1,288,068 reside in the city center. It also ranked fifth among Turkish cities with respect to socioeconomic development. Even with this rapid industrial transformation, however, Bursa still maintains its role as a spa and a heritage center; Uludağ has recently become a favorite winter resort and its highland pastures have regained their early-Ottoman importance for summering. Uludağ University, opened in 1975, aims to foster the city's traditional position of cultural and intellectual prominence.

See also ABDÜLHAMIT II; ANATOLIA; ISTANBUL; İZMIR; OTTOMAN EMPIRE; TANZIMAT.

Bibliography

Özendeş, Engin. *The First Ottoman Capital, Bursa: A Photographic History.* Istanbul: Yapi-Endüstri Merkezi Yayinlari, 1999.

Turkish Ministry of Culture. Information found at <http://www.kultur.gov.tr/portal/default_en.asp?belgeno=1934>.

I. METIN KUNT
UPDATED BY BURÇAK KESKIN-KOZAT

BURTON, RICHARD FRANCIS
[1821–1890]

British explorer, orientalist, author, and consul.

Richard Francis Burton was born in England the son of a gentleman army officer and raised in Europe. He was expelled from Oxford University and became an intelligence officer in the army of the British East India Company, before being sent home after exposing the common resort of British soldiers to Indian brothels. During years of exploration and service to the British Empire, Burton learned forty languages and dialects, mostly by mixing with locals in India, the Middle East, Africa, the Americas, and Europe. A consistent admirer of Arab Islamic culture, in 1853 Burton posed as an Afghan doctor and joined the *hajj* (pilgrimage), gaining celebrity status in Britain after publishing his *Personal Narrative of a Pilgrimage to Al-Madinah and Meccah* (1855–1856). In 1856 he was sent to explore the Nile by the British Foreign Office. This led to a competition with John Speke over who could find the headwaters or source of the Nile; Speke won. Burton went on to serve as British consul in West Africa (1861), South America (1865–1868), and Damascus (1869–1871).

His last years were spent publishing acclaimed translations of Arabic and Indian literature on religion, society, and sexuality, notably the *Kama Sutra* (1883) and "The Arabian Nights," which was published as *The Thousand Nights and a Night* (1885). Burton also published much-noted works on Africa, encouraging a wave of British explorers to follow in his stead.

See also EAST INDIA COMPANY.

Bibliography

Brodie, Fawn M. *The Devil Drives: A Life of Sir Richard Burton.* New York: W. W. Norton, 1967.

Rice, Edward. *Captain Sir Richard Francis Burton.* New York: Harper Perennial, 1990.

Vincent, Andrew. "'The Jew, the Gipsy, and El-Islam: An Examination of Richard Burton's Consulship in Damascus and His Premature Recall, 1868–1871." *Journal of the Royal Asiatic Society* 2 (1985): 155–173.

BENJAMIN BRAUDE
UPDATED BY GEORGE R. WILKES

BUSH, GEORGE HERBERT WALKER
[1924–]

U.S. president (1989–1993).

George H. W. Bush was born in the state of Connecticut. He was a decorated naval combat pilot in the Pacific during the Second World War despite the fact that he was the youngest pilot in the U.S. Navy. After the war he graduated from Yale University, and moved to Texas to work as an oil executive. Bush later entered public life and served in the U.S. House of Representatives, and was director of the Central Intelligence Agency, American ambassador to the United Nations, and vice president of the United States, among other positions.

During Bush's presidency, the United States undertook several major initiatives in the Middle East. He continued the first official U.S. dialogue with the Palestine Liberation Organization, which had begun in December 1988, the month before Bush took office, and which lasted until June 1990. The U.S.-led military engagement that defeated Iraq's occupation forces in Kuwait during the Gulf Crisis of 1990–1991 marked the first major American military involvement in the Middle East. Following Iraq's defeat, Bush decided to take advantage of the new regional climate to convene the Madrid Conference in October 1991, the first face-to-face Arab–Israeli peace negotiations since the 1979 Israel–Egypt peace treaty. The United States and the Soviet Union presided over both bilateral and multilateral talks among Israeli and Arab delegations, including Palestinians for the first time as part of a joint Jordanian-Palestinian delegation.

See also BAKER, JAMES A.; GULF CRISIS (1990–1991); MADRID CONFERENCE (1991); PALESTINE LIBERATION ORGANIZATION (PLO).

Bibliography

Bose, Meena, and Perotti, Rosanna, eds. *From Cold War to New World Order: The Foreign Policy of George H. W. Bush.* Westport, CT: Greenwood, 2002.

Lesch, David W., ed. *The Middle East and the United States: A Historical and Political Reassessment,* 3d edition. Boulder, CO: Westview, 2003.

MICHAEL R. FISCHBACH

BUSH, GEORGE WALKER

[1946–]

U.S. president (2001–); dramatically increased America's role in the Middle East.

The son of President George H. W. Bush, George W. Bush earned a B.A. in history from Yale University in 1968 and an M.B.A. from Harvard in 1975. Like his father, he worked in the petroleum industry and he later served as governor of Texas (1995–2001). George W. Bush was elected president as a result of controversial elections of November 2000, in which his opponent, Albert Gore, actually received more popular votes than Bush but failed to win the presidency after the U.S. Supreme Court intervened in a disagreement over which candidate had carried the vote in Florida.

Attacks against targets in New York and Washington, D.C., mounted by the al-Qaʿida organization of Osama bin Ladin on 11 September 2001, profoundly changed the Bush presidency and America's role in the Middle East and southwest Asia. Bush's earlier disdain for involvement in the region's complexities gave way to his need to respond to the biggest terrorist attack in American history. He ordered the invasion of Afghanistan in October 2001, which succeeded in destroying the government of the Taliban and severely disrupting the al-Qaʿida network, which had used the country as a base for training and operations. The United States then worked with the United Nations in trying to rebuild the country around President Hamid Karzai. Beginning in 2002, Bush dramatically escalated pressure on Iraq and its president, Saddam Hussein. Claiming that Iraq still possessed weapons of mass destruction such as chemical and biological weapons, he argued that the country constituted a threat to U.S. security. Despite massive global opposition, even from traditional American allies like Germany and France, U.S. and British forces invaded the country in March 2003 and overthrew Saddam Hussein's government.

Bush also picked up the efforts of his predecessor, Bill Clinton, to forge peace between Israel and the Palestinians. He became the first U.S. president openly to call for the creation of a Palestinian state, although his administration refused to deal with Palestinian Authority leader Yasir Arafat and pressured Arafat to cede some of his powers to a newly created prime minister's position. On the other hand, Bush was willing to work with Israeli prime minister Ariel Sharon, whom he called a "man of peace." The Bush administration, along with the United Nations, Russia, and the European Union, developed a "Road Map" for peace between the two sides, which Bush tried to push in 2003.

See also ARAFAT, YASIR; BIN LADIN, OSAMA; HUSSEIN, SADDAM; KARZAI, HAMID; QAʿIDA, AL-; SHARON, ARIEL; TALIBAN.

Bibliography

Sifry, Micah L., and Serf, Christopher, eds. *The Iraq War Reader: History, Documents, Opinions.* New York: Touchstone Books, 2003.

MICHAEL R. FISCHBACH

BUSNACH FAMILY

Prominent Jewish family of Algeria.

The Busnach (in Arabic, Bu Janah) family was one of three Livornese (Italy) Jewish families (the others were the Boucharas and the Cohen-Baqris) that were prominent in Algerian commerce and politics throughout the eighteenth and early nineteenth centuries. The patriarch of the clan, Naphtali Busnach, established a shipping business in Algiers in the early 1720s. He was also involved in the ransoming of European captives of the corsairs (Barbary pirates).

His grandson Naphtali II was the right-hand man of Mustafa Bey of Constantine. When Mustafa was chosen dey in 1797, Naphtali became his chief courtier. At about the same time, Naphtali went into partnership with Joseph Baqri, with whom he was related by ties of marriage, and the firm of Baqri & Busnach came to hold a virtual monopoly on trade with the regency. Naphtali was appointed *muqaddam* (chief) of the Jewish community by the dey in 1800. Naphtali, who had survived one attempt on his life during a failed coup in 1801, was assassinated by a janissary in 1805. The incident touched off anti-Jewish riots among the Ottoman troops. Most of the Busnachs fled to Livorno at this time, although their relatives, the Baqris, remained in Algiers.

See also CORSAIRS.

Bibliography

Hirschberg, H. Z. *A History of the Jews in North Africa.* Leiden, Netherlands: Brill, 1981.

NORMAN STILLMAN

BUSTANI, SULAYMAN
[1856–1925]

Ottoman writer and government official.

Born to a Maronite Christian family in the village of Bkashtin in the Shuf region of Mount Lebanon, Sulayman Bustani was educated from 1863 to 1871 in the National School (al-Madrasa al-Wataniyya) in Beirut (founded by his relative Butrus al-Bustani). There he studied English and French in addition to Arabic and Turkish. He traveled extensively in the Arab provinces of the Ottoman Empire and beyond, to Persia and India. He assisted Butrus al-Bustani and his sons, Salim and Najib, in writing and editing the first Arabic encyclopedia, *Da'irat al-ma'arif,* and contributed to the periodical *al-Muqtataf,* published in Cairo, Egypt. In 1904, he published his most important contribution to the interaction between Arabic culture and Greek literature—the first Arabic translation of Homer's *Iliad.*

In 1908, after the coming of the Young Turks to power in Istanbul and the beginning of the second Ottoman constitutional period, Bustani published *Ibra wa Dhikra aw al-Dawla al-Uthmaniyya Qabla al-Dustur wa Ba'dahu* (A lesson and a memory, or the Ottoman state before the constitution and after it), which implicitly criticized the autocratic rule of Sultan Abdülhamit II and sang the praises of liberal policies in all aspects of political, social, economic, and religious life. He hammered away at the theme of allegiance to the Ottoman state and criticized Western educational institutions in the country, which undermined that allegiance. Bustani also believed that the best way to eradicate religious fanaticism was to make the Christians serve alongside the Muslims in the Ottoman army. Further, he thought the best way to eradicate ethnic conflict was to spread the Turkish language among the population by making it mandatory in all the empire's schools.

In 1908, Bustani was elected to serve as deputy for the province of Beirut in the lower chamber of deputies in Istanbul; in 1911, he became a member of the upper chamber. In 1913, he was appointed minister for commerce, agriculture, forests, and mines—he resigned, however, at the end of the following year when the Committee for Union and Progress, the effective Ottoman power, decided to enter World War I on the side of Germany. Bustani then belonged to a group of Ottoman officials who held that a policy of neutrality would serve the empire best.

See also ABDÜLHAMIT II; COMMITTEE FOR UNION AND PROGRESS; YOUNG TURKS.

Bibliography

Hourani, Albert. "Sulayman al-Bustani (1856–1925)." In *Quest for Understanding: Arabic and Islamic Studies in Memory of Malcolm H. Kerr,* edited by Samir Seikaly, et al. Beirut: American University of Beirut, 1991.

MAHMOUD HADDAD

BUTAYNA TRIBE

See TRIBES AND TRIBALISM: BUTAYNA TRIBE

BUYUK MILLET MECLISI

See TURKISH GRAND NATIONAL ASSEMBLY

CAIRO

The capital of Egypt, the largest city in the Middle East and Africa, and a major political, religious, and cultural hub for the Arab, Islamic, and African worlds.

A city with fertile hinterland and a crossroads location for river, sea, and land trade has flourished near the juncture of the Nile valley of Upper Egypt and the delta of Lower Egypt for five thousand years. In 640 C.E. the conquering Muslim Arabs founded al-Fustat (now *Old Cairo* to Westerners), which superseded the Babylon of the Romans and its predecessor across the river, the Memphis of the pharaohs. In 969 the invading Fatimids founded al-Qahira (the Victorious), and Cairo acquired its current name and resumed its ancient role as an imperial center. (In Arabic, *Misr* has long been used interchangeably for both Egypt and Cairo.) The Fatimids established the renowned mosque-university al-Azhar, and Salah al-Din (Saladin) of the Ayyubid dynasty built the hilltop Citadel, which remained the seat of power until the mid-nineteenth century.

Its population weakened by epidemics and the ruling Mamluks' internecine warfare, Cairo fell to the Ottomans in 1517. By the seventeenth century the Cape of Good Hope route had deprived Cairo (reduced once more to the status of a provincial city) of much of its spice trade. Europeans no longer spoke with awe of the city Egyptians called the Mother of the World. In 1798 the cartographers of Napoléon Bonaparte's military expedition found a city of a quarter of a million people, half of the population of Cairo at its fourteenth-century peak. The narrow, irregular streets of the preindustrial city served pedestrians, riders, and pack animals well enough, and balconies provided welcome shade. Gates that closed at night and dead-end alleys marked off city quarters, which were defined mainly along religious, ethnic, and occupational lines. Waqf endowments supported mosques, schools, Sufi lodges, baths, fountains, and hospitals.

The military, economic, administrative, and educational reforms introduced during Muhammad Ali's reign (1805–1848) left few external marks on Cairo, and the city's population, checked by epidemics and competition from burgeoning Alexan-

Cairo's famous al-Azhar mosque was built in 970 C.E. on the orders of the Fatimid caliph al-Mu'izz. Shortly after its completion, the mosque became known as a center of religious and secular learning, and the university which sprang up around it is generally considered to be the oldest in the world. © AP/WIDE WORLD PHOTOS. REPRODUCED BY PERMISSION.

dria, remained stagnant until the middle of the century. After 1850, however, the population grew because of lower mortality rates, an influx of people from the countryside, and the immigration of European and Levantine entrepreneurs. The Alexandria-Cairo Railroad and the Suez Canal, whose construction was completed respectively in 1855 and 1869, quickened the pace of life in Cairo. The city's share of Egypt's total population, which had dipped from 5.8 percent in 1800 to a low of 4.7 percent in 1865 (when Alexandria was in full bloom), rose to 6.9 percent in 1897. Today it accounts for over a quarter of the total population of Egypt.

Under Muhammad Ali's grandson Isma'il (r. 1863–1879) and the British occupation (1882–1922), the unused space between Cairo and its river ports Bulaq and Old Cairo was developed. Inspired by the municipal improvements effected in Paris by Baron Georges Haussmann and determined to impress the

Europeans at the ceremonies celebrating the Suez Canal's completion, Isma'il instructed engineer Ali Mubarak to equip the suburb Isma'iliyya with Parisian-style boulevards, traffic hubs, gardens, palaces, and even an opera house. Isma'il had two boulevards for vehicle traffic cut through the old city before the bankruptcy of Egypt intervened and cost him the throne. European connoisseurs of "Oriental Cairo" persuaded his successor to found the Comité de Preservation des Monuments de l'Art Arabe (1881), and preservationists still fight to save some monuments and neighborhoods in Cairo from relentless overpopulation, decay, and demolition for urban renewal.

Under the British, Cairo's European population (30,000, or 6 percent of the city's population in 1897) dominated big business and filled the fashionable new quarters of Heliopolis, Garden City, Ma'adi, and Zamalek with their Mediterranean-style villas. European concessionaires developed the

Boasting an ever-expanding population of seventeen million, Cairo, the largest city in the Middle East and Africa, lies at the center of all routes leading to and from the continents of Asia, Africa, and Europe. The city covers an area of more than 453 square kilometers and is located on both banks of the Nile River. © AP/WIDE WORLD PHOTOS. REPRODUCED BY PERMISSION.

water, gas, electricity, telephone, and tramway services, and built the bridges across the Nile. Bridges made accessible the first artery to the West Bank in 1872. By 1914 the access provided by additional bridges to more arteries to the West Bank and to the islands of Rawda and Gazira resulted in rapid development. Between 1896 and 1914 electric tramways (soon replaced by motor vehicles) revolutionized transportation within the city and made possible the swift development of suburbs to the northeast (Abbasiyya, Heliopolis), the north (Shubra), and the west (Rawda, Zamalik, Giza).

Between 1922 and 1952 the domination by Europeans of economic and political life in Egypt ebbed. In 1949 the closing of the Mixed Courts put an end to special privileges for Westerners, and Cairo belatedly acquired a municipal government that was distinct from the national ministries. Life in the old city deteriorated (see the masterful portrayal of this time by novelist Najib Mahfuz). Well-

to-do Egyptians left for the suburbs, Egyptians from rural parts of the country crowded in, and the overflow of tens of thousands of inhabitants spilled over into the cemeteries of the City of the Dead.

Cairo Population Estimates

1798:	264,000
1846:	257,000
1897:	590,000
1927:	1,065,000
1947:	2,048,000
1960:	3,416,000
1970:	7,000,000
2003:	9,600,000

Sources: Abu-Lughod, Janet. *Cairo: 1,001 Years of the City Victorious.* Princeton, NJ: Princeton University Press, 1971; *World Almanac 2004.* New York: World Almanac Education Group.

Under Gamal Abdel Nasser (r. 1952–1970) there was an acceleration of both planned and unplanned urban development. Private utility and transport concessions reverted to the state, *waqf* reform freed land for development, a new airport opened, and a revamped road network briefly alleviated some of the traffic congestion. The Corniche exposed Cairo to the river, and Maydan al-Tahrir became the city center. The Nile Hilton and the new Shepheard's were the first of many luxury hotels built to cater to the expanding tourist trade. Heavy industry was set up in suburban Hilwan and Shubra al-Khayma. The 1956 Master Plan for Cairo recommended that the city limit its population to 3.5 million (a maximum that had already been exceeded) and advocated planned satellite communities and development on desert rather than on agricultural land. The resulting Nasr City—with government offices, housing blocks, schools, a 100,000-seat stadium, and a new campus for al-Azhar—was a success, but Muqattam City, perched high on the desert cliffs, was not.

Since 1970 the Hilwan–al-Marj metro line has been opened in Cairo, sewer and telephone systems have been upgraded, and more satellite cities have been built in the desert (Sadat City, 10th Ramadan, 6th October, al-Ubur, 15th May). The population crush nevertheless threatens to dwarf such efforts. The runaway sprawl into agricultural lands in the delta and Giza continues while the problem-plagued desert satellite cities sit half empty and a purple cloud of polluted air regularly hangs over Cairo. Opportunities for jobs, schooling, housing, and healthcare are better in Cairo than in the teeming countryside, and people from rural areas keep pouring in. Shanty towns proliferate. One out of every four Egyptians lives in this Third-World megalopolis of seventeen million people.

Cairo remains the cultural capital of the Arab world. Its assets include al-Azhar and four modern universities, twenty-odd museums, a major movie industry and playhouses, a radio and television industry, bookshops and publishing houses, *al-Ahram* and other periodicals, a zoo, a new opera house, the headquarters of the Arab League, and the Academy of the Arabic Language.

See also AZHAR, AL-; BONAPARTE, NAPOLÉON; CAIRO UNIVERSITY; EGYPT; MAHFUZ, NAJIB; MAMLUKS; MIXED COURTS; MUHAMMAD ALI; NASSER, GAMAL ABDEL; SUEZ CANAL; WAQF.

Bibliography

Abu-Lughod, Janet. *Cairo: 1,001 Years of the City Victorious.* Princeton, NJ: Princeton University Press, 1971.

André, Raymond. *Cairo.* Cambridge, MA: Harvard University Press, 2000.

Francy, Claire E. *Cairo: The Practical Guide, 2003.* Cairo: American University in Cairo, 2002.

Rodenbeck, Max. *Cairo: The City Victorious.* New York: Knopf, 1999.

Seton-Williams, Veronica; Stocks, Peter; and Seton-Williams, M. V. *The Blue Guide Egypt,* 3d edition. New York: W. W. Norton, 1993.

Staffa, Susan Jane. *Conquest and Fusion: The Social Evolution of Cairo, A.D. 642–1850.* Leiden, Netherlands: Brill, 1977.

Stewart, Desmond. *Great Cairo: Mother of the World,* 3d edition. Cairo: American University in Cairo, 1996.

DONALD MALCOLM REID

CAIRO CONFERENCE (1921)

Meeting of Middle East experts to decide on administration of British mandates of Iraq and Transjordan.

The Cairo Conference was convened by Winston Churchill, then Britain's colonial secretary. With the mandates of Palestine and Iraq awarded to Britain at the San Remo Conference (1920), Churchill wished to consult with Middle East experts, and at his request, Gertrude Bell, Sir Percy Cox, T. E. Lawrence, Sir Kinahan Cornwallis, Sir Arnold T. Wilson, Iraqi minister of war Ja'far al-Askari, Iraqi minister of finance Sasun Effendi (Sasson Heskayl), and others gathered in Cairo, Egypt, in March 1921. The two most significant decisions of the conference were to offer the throne of Iraq to Amir Faisal ibn Hussein (who became Faisal I) and the emirate of Transjordan (now Jordan) to his brother Abdullah I ibn Hussein. Furthermore, the British garrison in Iraq would be substantially reduced and replaced by air force squadrons, with a major base at Habbaniyya. The conference provided the political blueprint for British administration in both Iraq and Transjordan, and in offering these two regions to the Hashimite sons of Sharif Husayn ibn Ali of the Hijaz, Churchill believed that the spirit, if not the letter, of Britain's wartime promises to the Arabs would be fulfilled.

See also Abdullah I ibn Hussein; Askari, Ja'far al-; Bell, Gertrude; Churchill, Winston S.; Cox, Percy; Faisal I ibn Hussein; Heskayl, Sasson; Lawrence, T. E.; San Remo Conference (1920); Wilson, Arnold T.

Bibliography

Fromkin, David. *A Peace to End All Peace.* New York: H. Holt, 1989.

Klieman, Aaron S. *Foundations of British Policy in the Arab World: The Cairo Conference of 1921.* London: Johns Hopkins, 1970.

ZACHARY KARABELL

CAIRO FAMILY PLANNING ASSOCIATION

Egyptian association to promote family planning.

In 1967, the Cairo Family Planning Association (CFPA) was established as a branch of the Egyptian Family Planning Association. Dedicated to the promotion of voluntary family planning, the CFPA advocates for the creation of comprehensive family planning services and health education. The CFPA is comprised of thirty-four associations and, in conjunction with the Ministry of Social Affairs, supervises forty-one health centers in Greater Cairo. The CFPA provides technical, administrative, and organizational support to member associations, directs two model reproductive health clinics, and has supervised the renovation of eighteen health centers in Cairo.

The activities of the CFPA are not limited to family planning. Conceptualizing family planning as a human right, the CFPA is also involved in direct service, research, and media campaigns on issues such as infertility, prenatal and pediatric care, and female circumcision. In 1979, the CFPA became a pioneer in the field of female circumcision, establishing the first seminar in Egypt on the subject. Dedicated to combating the practice, the CFPA has conducted studies, sponsored seminars and lectures, and trained health service providers to increase awareness about the detrimental health implications of female circumcision. The CFPA also documents and disseminates information about reproductive health through the production of a quarterly bulletin highlighting news, research findings, and recent publications.

See also Birth Control; Female Genital Mutilation; Gender: Gender and Education; Gender: Gender and Health; Gender: Gender and Law.

ANGEL M. FOSTER

CAIRO UNIVERSITY

Flagship modern university in Egypt.

Cairo University's early founding and location made it a model for later universities throughout the Arab world. Opened as the small, private Egyptian University in 1908 and taken over as a state university in 1925, it became Fu'ad I University in 1940 and Cairo University in 1954.

The retirement in 1907 of Britain's consul general, Lord Cromer (formerly Sir Evelyn Baring), who had opposed a university for fear of Egyptian nationalism, allowed the plan for the private university to proceed. Egypt's minister of education Sa'd Zaghlul, feminist judge Qasim Amin, and others insisted that Egypt needed a Western-style university to complement its state professional schools and the Islamic religious university of al-Azhar. Europe provided the models and a number of the professors when the university opened with Prince Ahmad Fu'ad as rector in 1908.

In 1925 Fu'ad, by then king, transformed the Egyptian University into a major state institution, with colleges of arts, science, law, and engineering—the latter two formed from existing higher schools. Other schools were introduced later: engineering, agriculture, commerce, veterinary science, and the teachers college of Dar al-Ulum. The university now has seventeen colleges and six institutes in Cairo and a number of branch colleges in Fayyum, Bani Suayf, and Khartoum. Alexandria (then Farouk I) University split off in 1942; today Egypt has a dozen state and several new private universities.

During the quarter-century after 1925, the British overtook the French in influence at the university, but slowly lost out themselves to pressures to Egyptianize the faculty. The battle for coeducation was won, with the first women graduating in 1933. In the 1930s Ahmad Lutfi al-Sayyid, rector, and Taha Husayn, dean of arts, fought for university autonomy from palace and cabinet interference, as the students were inevitably caught up in turbulent national politics.

At serious cost in quality, Gamal Abdel Nasser opened Cairo and other universities more widely to provincials and the poor. His purge of 1954 crushed student and professorial opposition until after the 1967 war. President Anwar al-Sadat initially encouraged Islamist groups on campus to counter the left, and campus Islamists remain a major challenge to the regime of Husni Mubarak. With about 155,000 students in 2003, Cairo University still has its pockets of excellence, but it is desperately underfunded and overcrowded and continues churning out thousands of poorly educated graduates onto a glutted job market.

See also ALEXANDRIA UNIVERSITY; AMIN, QASIM; DAR AL-ULUM; HUSAYN, TAHA; ZAGHLUL, SAʿD.

Bibliography

Cairo University web site. Available from <http://www.cairo.eun.eg>.

Reid, Donald Malcolm. *Cairo University and the Making of Modern Egypt.* Cambridge, U.K.: Cambridge University Press, 1990.

DONALD MALCOLM REID

CALAND, HUGUETTE
[1931–]

Lebanese artist and fashion designer.

Huguette Caland is an abstract painter and sculptor who has also worked in fashion design (notably for Pierre Cardin) and filmmaking. The daughter of a former president of Lebanon, she trained under Fernando Manetti and George Apostu and at the American University in Beirut. In Lebanon, she cofounded the Inʿash al-Mukhayyim art center. She lived in Paris for many years and participated in individual and group exhibitions, primarily in Europe and Lebanon. In her paintings, Caland has brought out the sensuous properties of color, the emotive qualities of line, and the tensions that can be created by the juxtaposition of different colors and lines in compositions that often involve the innov-

ative use of negative space. She has participated in major exhibitions in Europe, notably the Venice Biennial.

See also ART; GENDER: GENDER AND EDUCATION; LEBANESE CIVIL WAR (1975–1990); LEBANON.

Bibliography

Khal, Helen. *The Woman Artist in Lebanon.* Beirut: Institute for Women's Studies in the Arab World, 1987.

JESSICA WINEGAR

CALIPHATE

The caliph was the temporal and spiritual ruler of Islam until the office was abolished in 1924.

The Ottoman dynasty's claim to the office had been widely recognized in the Muslim world by the end of the nineteenth century, even though its historical basis was controversial. The claim was based on an alleged transfer of caliphal authority to the House of Osman after Ottoman armies conquered Mamluk Egypt. There an Abbasid caliph with descent from the Quraysh tribe of the Prophet Muhammad had been maintained as a dependent figurehead.

Nationalism and the Caliphate

The caliphate signified the ideal of pan-Islamic unity and solidarity and served as a psychological rallying point for Muslims against imperialist encroachments. The impending collapse of the Ottoman Empire at the end of World War I mobilized Muslims worldwide to campaign for the retention of the caliphate. The India Khilafat Congress was especially active in this cause during the peace negotiations of 1919, since Indian Muslims were seeking self-determination based on allegiance to the caliph.

After the Ottomans were defeated in the war, the Anglo-French occupation of Constantinople (now Istanbul), the seat of the caliphate, further compromised the authority of Sultan-Caliph Mehmet VI Vahidettin. Mustafa Kemal (Atatürk) and other leaders of the Anatolian independence movement declared that a principal objective was to liberate the sultanate and the caliphate from occupation forces. At the same time, Vahidettin denounced the resistance on Islamic grounds. Political and military circumstances, however, gradually transformed the nationalists' attitude toward the caliphate. In view of the successes of the independence struggle and the complicity of Vahidettin with the occupying powers, the rival Ankara government promulgated in January 1921 the Fundamental Law which established the nation's sovereignty. On 1 November 1922, it passed legislation to abolish the Ottoman monarchy, separating the sultanate from the caliphate and maintaining the caliphate as a vague spiritual and moral authority. On November 16, Vahidettin sought asylum with British authorities and left Constantinople for Malta and later the Hijaz.

A Caliphate without Political Authority

The new law authorized the Turkish Grand National Assembly to select a meritorious member of the Ottoman dynasty as caliph. As the Muslim world debated the legitimacy of a caliphate without political authority, the assembly conferred the title of caliph on Abdülmecit II (1868–1944), son of Sultan Abdülaziz. The separation of the caliphate from the defunct monarchy was a tactical step toward abolishing the House of Osman and soothing domestic and international Muslim public opinion.

Foreign reaction was apathetic as the Khilafat Congress recognized the new caliph. In Turkey, though, the caliph quickly became the focus around which the proponents of the constitutional monarchy rallied. In October 1923, Mustafa Kemal declared the Turkish republic. The designation of the president of the republic as the head of state further compromised the caliph's position.

In December 1923, Indian Muslim leaders Amir Ali and Aga Khan, the imam of the Isma'ili sect, wrote a letter to the Turkish prime minister Ismet İnönü urging retention of the caliphate. The Indian plea only accelerated the end. The Kemalists denounced the intervention of the two Muslim leaders as interference in the affairs of the new state and discredited them as Shi'ite British proxies. Indian religious scholars called for an international conference to determine the status of the caliphate. On 3 March 1924, the assembly passed legislation eliminating the office as part of a string of secularizing measures, including the abolition of religious education. The Kemalists argued that the caliphate was superfluous because the government of each Muslim country should administer both temporal and religious affairs.

Attempts to Create a New Caliphate

Abdülmecit left Turkey for Switzerland and later France. Since Turkey had emerged as the strongest independent country in the Muslim world, its abandonment of the caliphate elicited concern and disapproval from colonized Muslims, while in Turkey and other independent Muslim countries there was relative indifference. There was no Muslim consensus on how to respond to the Turkish fait accompli. The sharif of Mecca, now the king of the Hijaz, Husayn bin Ali, immediately put forward his claim, which was sanctioned by Vahidettin. King Fu'ad of Egypt and Imam Yahya of Yemen also emerged as possible candidates, as did the Moroccan and Afghan kings. Others advocated the continued recognition of Abdülmecit as the legitimate caliph. Husayn had a strong claim due to his prestige and descent from the Hashimite family of the Quraysh. Further, the British had revived the notion of a Meccan caliphate on the eve of the Arab Revolt. However, by 1924 Husayn lacked real political authority. In fact, Indian Muslims were inclined toward his rival, Abd al-Aziz ibn Sa'ud of Najd. Ibn Sa'ud, surrounded by Hashimite power in the Hijaz, Iraq, and Transjordan, felt even more threatened by Husayn's caliphal ambitions and invaded the Hijaz, forcing Husayn to exile.

There could be no agreement on a single candidate when no consensus existed on the continuation of the office. A Caliphate Congress (mu'tamar al-khilafa) convened in Cairo in May 1926 with the participation of ulama (clergy) from several Muslim countries. At this conference, King Fu'ad hoped to promote his claim, but the relative apathy toward the meeting and disagreement about eligibility requirements resulted in its adjournment with only the group's affirmation of the need to reinstitute a caliph. Yet the caliphate appeared as an ever-more-incongruent political institution in a Muslim world that was becoming increasingly fragmented. The issue of caliphal succession became embroiled in the nationalist rivalries and inward-looking struggles of the Muslim countries.

See also ABD AL-AZIZ IBN SA'UD AL SA'UD; ABDÜLMECIT II; ATATÜRK, MUSTAFA KEMAL; HASHIMITE HOUSE (HOUSE OF HASHIM);

İNÖNÜ, İSMET; ISMA'ILI SHI'ISM; OSMAN, HOUSE OF; SHARIF OF MECCA; *ULAMA*.

Bibliography

Arnold, Thomas W. *The Caliphate*. London: Routledge and Kegan Paul, 1965.

Teitelbaum, Joshua. *The Rise and Fall of the Hashemite Kingdom of Arabia*. London: Hurst, 2001.

Toynbee, Arnold J. "The Abolition of the Ottoman Caliphate by the Turkish Great National Assembly and the Progress of the Secularization Movement in the Islamic World.". In *Survey of International Affairs, 1925*, vol. I: *The Islamic World since the Peace Settlement*. London: Oxford University Press, 1927.

HASAN KAYALI

CALLIGRAPHY

Fine Islamic writing as an art form.

In the Islamic context, calligraphy refers to the artistic writing of the Arabic script, either in the Arabic

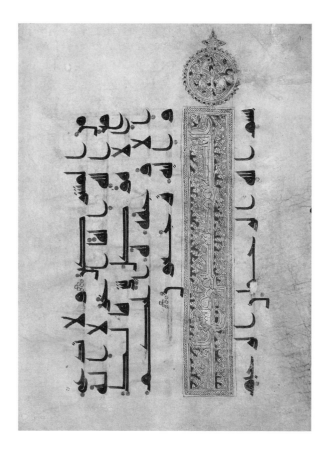

Qur'an leaf with heading of sura 29. Possibly dates from Iraq, before 911 C.E. © ART RESOURCE. REPRODUCED BY PERMISSION.

language or in other languages transcribed with the Arabic script. Originally, Islamic calligraphy was an expedient to ensure legibility. It soon became the primary visual art in the realms of Islamic religious influence and remained so at least until the nineteenth century.

Islamic calligraphy shares the characteristics of other fine arts: a long and well-documented history, an extensive roster of renowned practitioners, an elaborate educational protocol, a wide selection of acknowledged masterpieces, a variety of media that are peculiar to it, and a wide range of accepted techniques and styles. In addition, there are religious and cultural regulations that pertain to the teaching, production, and display of Islamic calligraphy. There are also ancillary professionals and amateurs who produce the tools and materials used in the production of the art works, such as inks, marble paper, and pens. Finally, a well-developed body of literature deals with the criticism and appreciation of Islamic calligraphy.

From the beginning of the Islamic period, and possibly substantially before it, two types of writing were used, according to occasion, in the Hijaz region of the Arabian peninsula. One was a simple, loose, and informal script for everyday use. The other—reserved for special purposes, especially religious uses that demanded a spectacular presentation—was the "dry" or stiff style of writing commonly, albeit incorrectly, called Kufic. In Islamic times, this became the favored style for Qur'anic transcriptions, due to its gravity, legibility, grace, and sheer visual impact.

By the tenth century, new scripts had taken shape from the earlier, informal writing and had gained in popularity. Because the shapes and sizes of the letters were calculated geometrically, these scripts were called "the proportioned scripts." They include the Thuluth, Naskh, and Muhaqqaq scripts. These are commonly referred to as Naskhi (supposedly meaning cursive), a name that has no basis in history.

Four important calligraphers, working in Baghdad during the Abbasid caliphate, founded the modern trend in Islamic calligraphy. These were Muhammad ibn Muqla (d. 940); his brother Abu Abdullah ibn Muqla (d. 939); Ali ibn Hilal, called Ibn al-Bawwab (d. 1022); and Yaqut al-Musta'simi (d. 1298). Through the works and teachings of these

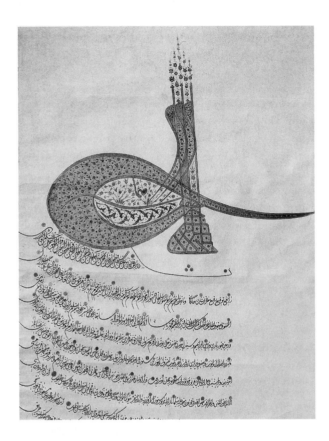

Monogram of Sultan Murat III. The monogram was created in 1575 for Murat III, who was sultan of the Ottoman Empire from 1574 until his death in 1595. © ARCHIVO ICONOGRAFICO, S.A./CORBIS. REPRODUCED BY PERMISSION.

masters, the art of calligraphy radiated to other important Islamic cultural centers.

By the sixteenth century, the center of Islamic calligraphy was to be found in Constantinople (now Istanbul) of the Ottoman Empire. There the pivotal Şeyh Hamdullah (1429–1520), a lifelong calligrapher, completely revised the structure of the basic scripts, of Thuluth and Naskh in particular, giving them a more precise, lighter, and more dynamic look. Since the life and teaching of this great master, the Ottoman Turkish method has been paramount. This method is distinguished by its special teaching protocols, its attention to detail, and its insistence on the highest standards.

Another Ottoman master, Mehmet Asat Yesari (d. 1798), took the Persian style Nasta'liq and, while maintaining its basic rules, transformed it into a powerful visual instrument, especially in its large (Celali) version.

Other trends in Islamic calligraphy of significant historical and artistic merit have existed continuously in the Maghrib-Andalusian orbit, in the Persian orbit, and in China. Although Islamic calligraphy reached its apogee in the late nineteenth century, it is experiencing a revival today, in particular due to the efforts of the Research Centre for Islamic History, Art, and Culture in Istanbul (IRCICA). The art continues to reign supreme in its ability to convey in the most emphatic way the written Islamic texts.

See also ARABIC SCRIPT.

Bibliography

Bayani, Manijeh; Contadini, Anna; and Stanley, Tim. *The Decorated Word: Qur'ans of the 17th to 19th Centuries.* New York: Oxford University Press, 1999.

Déroche, François. *The Abbasid Tradition: Qur'ans of the 8th to 10th Centuries.* New York: Oxford University Press, 1992.

Lings, Martin. *The Qur'anic Art of Calligraphy and Illumination.* London: World of Islam Festival Trust, 1976.

Safadi, Yasin Hamid. *Islamic Calligraphy.* London: Thames and Hudson, 1978.

Safwat, Nabil F. *The Art of the Pen: Calligraphy of the 14th to 20th Centuries.* London and New York: Oxford University Press, 1996.

Zakariya, Muhammad. "Islamic Calligraphy: A Technical Overview." In *Brocade of the Pen: The Art of Islamic Writing,* edited by Carol Garrett Fisher. East Lansing: Kresge Art Museum, Michigan State University, 1991.

MUHAMMAD ZAKARIYA

CAMBON–LANSDOWNE AGREEMENT (1904)

Pact between France and Great Britain affecting each country's activities in Egypt and Morocco.

After having been rivals for a long time, France and Great Britain mutually agreed to desist. According to the agreement, France had total freedom of action in Morocco; meanwhile France would stop interfering with English financial activities in Egypt, as it had since 1882. The English enjoyed immediate but limited advantages. As for the French, it meant getting potential interests and indicated the end of an obsessional opposition. The agreement took place on 8 April 1904 in a general atmosphere of mutual reconciliation, for the two countries were worried about Germany's growing power.

RÉMY LEVEAU

CAMELS

Domesticated ruminant of central Asia, Arabia, and North Africa.

A domesticated animal, with one or two humps, that is used as a mode of transportation in the Middle East, the camel is a survivor of an almost vanished group of ungulates (hoofed mammals) that once populated all the large land masses of the world except Australia. Its close relatives are the South American llama, alpaca, guanaco, and vicuña. The only camels existing today are two domesticated species: the Arabian dromedary, *Camelus dromedarius* (or *ibil*), which has one hump and is used for riding; and the two-humped Bactrian camel, *Camelus bactrianus,* which has shorter legs and is more heavily built. A few survive in the Gobi Desert.

Traditional belief has it that one-humped camels do not adapt well to cold or moist climates nor the two-humped camel to extremely hot climates. Both store fat in their humps, have long necks suitable for feeding on bushes and trees, and have padded feet suited for travel on sand but ill-suited for travel on mud. Both have the capacity to go long intervals without water. Camels do not store water as some folk stories allege. Rather, they conserve it through highly efficient kidneys that allow them to process water with a high concentration of impurities; they also have the capacity to absorb heat by allowing their blood temperature to rise, without ill effect. The horn of Africa constitutes the largest and most abundant camel territory in the world and today Somalia alone has a camel population exceeding four million. Camel milk is a dietary staple in Somalia. Camels exist as a form of wealth and nourishment and form part of the traditional bride-price.

Bibliography

Bulliet, Richard. *The Camel and the Wheel.* New York: Columbia University Press, 1990.

MIA BLOOM

CAMP DAVID ACCORDS (1978)

Agreements signed by Egypt, Israel, and the United States on 17 September 1978.

In November 1977, Egyptian president Anwar al-Sadat shocked the world by announcing his readiness to travel to Israel to resolve the Arab–Israel conflict, and Israeli prime minister Menachem Begin promptly issued an invitation. Sadat's visit to Israel on 19 and 20 November included an electrifying speech before the Knesset and inaugurated a series of unprecedented direct Egyptian–Israeli peace negotiations. The talks bogged down, however, over Israel's withdrawal from and Egypt's demilitarization of the Sinai and the future status of Gaza and the West Bank (all occupied by Israel in the June 1967 war), and over terms of normalization between Israel and Egypt. When it appeared that the negotiations would collapse, U.S. president Jimmy Carter invited Sadat and Begin to the presidential retreat at Camp David, Maryland.

The Camp David conference, 5 through 17 September 1978, ended with two accords signed by Egypt, Israel, and the United States: "A Framework for Peace in the Middle East" and "A Framework for Conclusion of a Peace Treaty between Egypt and Israel." Participants included the three leaders, their foreign and defense ministers, and teams of top civilian and military officials. Sadat and Begin's acrimonious relationship threatened to derail the conference, but President Carter's personal intervention saved it from failure. Sadat and Begin later received the Nobel Peace Prize.

The relatively straightforward framework for an Egypt–Israel peace embraced UN Security Council Resolution 242 and called for a treaty implementing the land-for-peace principle: Israel would return the Sinai to Egypt and Egypt would make peace with Israel. Also anticipated was the full normalization of diplomatic, economic, and cultural relations. The Egyptian–Israeli Peace Treaty of 26 March 1979 conformed to these September 1978 expectations.

With its complex and problematic formula for Palestinian self-rule, the framework for Middle East peace was crucial to Sadat's defense against Arab charges that he had sold the Palestinians short by making a separate peace with Israel. The other Arab states were invited to follow Sadat to the negotiating table. This framework envisioned Egypt, Israel, Jordan, and representatives of the Palestinians negotiating a five-year, three-stage plan for the future of Gaza and the West Bank, including full autonomy for the inhabitants of the West Bank and Gaza; the withdrawal of Israel's military government and civilian administration; the election of a self-governing Palestinian authority; and the redeployment of Israeli forces. Final-status negotiations during the five-year transitional period would resolve the disposition of the West Bank and Gaza, the refugee problem, and the entire Israeli–Palestinian conflict in a manner that would "recognize the legitimate rights of the Palestinian people and their just requirements."

The Camp David Accords were not without opposition. The Knesset ratified the agreements, but more members of the opposition than of the prime minister's coalition supported them. Those who abstained or voted against them scored Begin for accepting the precedent of territorial concessions for peace and for recognizing the Palestinian people as a negotiating partner. In Egypt, opposition elements, including Islamic, Nasserist, and other Arab nationalist groups, protested the peace negotiations with Israel. No Arab states supported the accords, and the Palestinians, aware of Begin's extremely narrow interpretation of "full autonomy," rejected them and demanded statehood. The refusal of the Palestinians and Jordan (the latter mentioned no less than fifteen times in the document) to cooperate with Egypt and Israel made the "Framework for Peace in the Middle East" a dead letter. Dependent only upon the actions of Egypt and Israel themselves, however, the second of Camp David's two frameworks—"For the Conclusion of a Peace Treaty Between Egypt and Israel"—came to fruition in the signing of the Egyptian–Israeli Peace Treaty of March 1979.

See also BEGIN, MENACHEM; CARTER, JIMMY; EGYPTIAN–ISRAELI PEACE TREATY (1979); GAZA STRIP; KNESSET; SADAT, ANWAR AL-; WEST BANK.

Bibliography

Bar-Siman-Tov, Yaacov. *Israel and the Peace Process, 1977–1982: In Search of Legitimacy for Peace.* Albany: State University of New York Press, 1994.

Carter, Jimmy. *Keeping Faith: Memoirs of a President.* New York: Bantam, 1982.

Dayan, Moshe. *Breakthrough: A Personal Account of the Egypt–Israel Peace Negotiations.* London: Weidenfeld and Nicolson, 1981.

Eisenberg, Laura Zittrain, and Caplan, Neil. *Negotiating Arab–Israeli Peace: Patterns, Problems, and Possibilities.* Bloomington: Indiana University Press, 1998.

Kamel, Mohammed Ibrahim. *The Camp David Accords: A Testimony.* London: Kegan Paul, 1986.

Quandt, William B. *Camp David: Peacemaking and Politics.* Washington, DC: Brookings Institution, 1986.

Telhami, Shibley. *Power and Leadership in International Bargaining: The Path to the Camp David Accords.* New York: Columbia University Press, 1990.

DON PERETZ
UPDATED BY LAURA Z. EISENBERG

CAMP DAVID SUMMIT (2000)

Failed Israeli–Palestinian negotiations, mediated by the United States (11 July–24 July 2000).

At the initiative of President Bill Clinton and Israeli prime minister Ehud Barak, an Israeli–Palestinian summit was convened at the U.S. presidential retreat at Camp David, Maryland, on 11 July 2000 to discuss the final-status issues foreshadowed by the 1993 Oslo Accords regarding such issues as Jerusalem, Jewish settlements, Palestinian refugees, and the borders of a Palestinian state. Because no official records or documents were exchanged, most public knowledge about the discussions comes from some of the participants and the media.

Regarding Jerusalem, Israel reportedly proposed turning some Palestinian villages and neighborhoods over to the Palestinian Authority (PA) and allowing Palestinian autonomy in the Muslim and Christian quarters within the Old City, with Israel retaining sovereignty over the rest of East Jerusalem and the Old City. The Palestinians reportedly proposed that East Jerusalem should be capital of the new Palestinian state and that Israel should withdraw to its pre-June 1967 borders, in accordance with UN Resolution 242.

On the issue of refugees, the Palestinians maintained the 3.7 million Palestinian refugees should have the right of return to their homes in what is now Israel or the right to receive compensation, in accordance with UN General Assembly Resolution 194 of December 1948. Israel rejected the right of return as a demographic threat to its Jewish character and denied that Israel had any legal or moral responsibility for the refugee problem. However, it would permit the return of a large but limited number of refugees to the state of Palestine under Israeli supervision and would allow some Palestinians to return to Israel as a family reunification measure.

Regarding Jewish settlements (of which there were in 1999 some 125, with about 200,000 settlers), Israel apparently proposed annexing some 10 percent of the West Bank territory, in which some 80 percent of the settlers lived, and ceding the remaining 90 percent to the Palestinians. The Palestinians disputed these figures because they did not include Jerusalem, parts of the Jordan Valley (which the Israelis wanted to lease for a long period), and other areas. The Palestinians were prepared to accept Israeli annexation of the largest West Bank settlement blocs, although they objected to the size, in exchange for an equal amount of territory in Israel of similar arable quality. After fourteen intense days of negotiations, the parties could not bridge their differences.

In the months and years following the summit, each side blamed the other for the failure. In a failed effort to ensure Barak's reelection, President Clinton publicly blamed Yasir Arafat, despite the fact that he had promised the Palestine Liberation Organization chairman—who had been reluctant to come to the summit because he said the parties were not prepared—that he would not be blamed if the discussions broke down. Barak also vigorously blamed Arafat, who he said was intent on the destruction of Israel, even though Arafat had championed the two-state solution embodied in the Oslo Accords in 1993 and had recognized Israel and endorsed UN Resolution 242 a dozen years before. The Palestinians blamed Barak, even though he was politically courageous in making far-reaching proposals, a number of which broke long-standing Israeli taboos, such as sharing Jerusalem, returning 90 percent of West Bank lands, and swapping territory.

The media and public of all sides accepted their governments' respective official versions, even though

each was a distortion of what happened at Camp David. In reality, all three sides contributed to the breakdown of the negotiations. Barak wasted several months negotiating with Syria; reneged on a third partial redeployment of troops from the West Bank and on handing over three villages near Jerusalem to the PA; continued to confiscate Palestinian land for Jewish settlements and access roads; and allowed for the increase of settlers in the territories, all of which raised suspicions among Palestinians about his sincerity. At Oslo, Barak's negotiating style— refusing to negotiate directly with Arafat, revising supposedly final offers, and presenting take-it-or-leave-it proposals—further alienated the Palestinians, who viewed him as arrogant. His demand for sovereignty over the Haram al-Sharif/Temple Mount was difficult for Arafat to accept for fear of Palestinian, Arab, and international Muslim reaction. In addition, Barak's offer, while generous from an Israeli point of view, would not have allowed for a contiguous and independent Palestinian state.

The Palestinians, on the other hand, in addition to being unprepared, seemed bereft of any strategy, were internally divided, and—most significantly—did not make serious, clear, and specific counteroffers to the Israeli side. Arafat—whose popularity was declining due to his inability to stop the settlement expansion and the obvious corruption in the PA, and who feared a trap by the Israelis and the Americans—was reluctant to make major concessions and seemed more interested in surviving the negotiations than in viewing them as a historic opportunity for peace.

The Americans ignored the extent to which settlement expansion had poisoned the peace process among the Palestinians and insisted on convening a meeting for which none of the parties was truly prepared. Although they were supposed to be honest brokers, their position—due to domestic pressure and the cultural and strategic relationship between the United States and Israel—was so close to the Israelis' that at times they presented Israeli positions. It was not until after Camp David that the United States presented its own position, called the Clinton proposals, on 23 December 2000. After the failure at Camp David, Palestinian and Israeli teams resumed negotiations in Taba, Egypt, and thanks to Clinton's suggestions, considerably narrowed their differences. The process begun at Camp

David might have thus ended successfully, but time ran out when—against the backdrop of the escalating violence of the al-Aqsa intifada—Clinton left office on 20 January 2001 and Barak was defeated by Ariel Sharon in the Israeli elections of 6 February 2001.

See also AQSA INTIFADA, AL-; ARAFAT, YASIR; BARAK, EHUD; CLINTON, WILLIAM JEFFERSON; HARAM AL-SHARIF; OSLO ACCORD (1993); PALESTINE LIBERATION ORGANIZATION (PLO); SHARON, ARIEL; UNITED NATIONS AND THE MIDDLE EAST.

Bibliography

Enderlin, Charles. *Shattered Dreams: The Failure of the Peace Process in the Middle East, 1995–2002.* New York: Other Press, 2003.

Malley, Robert, and Agha, Hussein. "Camp David: The Tragedy of Errors." *New York Review of Books*: 9 August 2001.

Pressman, Jeremy. "Visions in Collision: What Happened at Camp David and Taba?" *International Security,* 28, no. 2 (fall 2003), 5–43. Available from <http://bcsia.ksg.harvard.edu/BCSIA_content/documents/pressman.pdf>.

Sontag, Deborah. "Quest for Middle East Peace: How and Why It Failed." *New York Times*: 26 July 2001.

PHILIP MATTAR

CAMUS, ALBERT
[1913–1960]

French Algerian author.

Albert Camus was born in eastern Algeria at Mondovi near present-day Annaba. His father represented grape-growing and wine-making interests and also served as a Zouave, an Algerian member of a French infantry unit. He died in 1914 from wounds received at the Battle of the Marne in France. His mother was illiterate and of Spanish descent. Camus grew up with her and her extended family in the poor Belcourt neighborhood of Algiers. He received a degree in philosophy from the University of Algiers. During the 1930s, he publicized Kabyle deprivations and briefly joined the Algerian Communist Party. He distinguished himself in the Resistance by editing *Combat.* He associated with French existentialists Jean-Paul Sartre and Simone de Beauvoir. While his writings have "existentialist" themes, he claimed that he did not subscribe to that philosophy. His novels include *The Stranger* (1942), *The Plague* (1947), and *The Fall* (1957). His most important essays are *The Myth of Sisyphus* (1942) and *The Rebel* (1951). He also wrote short stories and plays. He received the Nobel Prize for literature in 1957. During the war of independence, Camus proposed a French–Algerian federation that was rejected by both sides. He died in an automobile accident.

Bibliography

Lottman, Herbert R. *Albert Camus: A Biography.* Garden City, NY: Doubleday, 1979.

PHILLIP C. NAYLOR

CANNING, STRATFORD
[1786–1880]

The most influential European diplomat in the Ottoman Empire during the first half of the nineteenth century.

While still an undergraduate at Cambridge, Stratford Canning (Viscount Stratford de Redcliffe) joined the British Foreign Office then headed by his cousin, George Canning. His first posting to Constantinople (now Istanbul) as secretary to the British mission occurred in 1808 in the midst of the Napoleonic wars. Upon his superior's departure, Stratford Canning became the acting chief. Despite his inexperience and with even less than the usual guidance from home, he secured the Treaty of Bucharest in 1812. By ending the war between the Russian and the Ottoman Empires, this treaty freed the Russians to repel the invasion of Napoléon Bonaparte. He then left for other assignments, but from 1825 to 1827, Canning returned to Constantinople to confront two problems: the Greek revolt and the deprivatization of the British consular service in the Levant (countries of the eastern Mediterranean).

Despite Canning's best efforts, he failed to mediate an end to the Greek conflict. As for the second, until the beginning of the nineteenth century, British affairs in the Ottoman Empire—commercial, consular, and diplomatic—had been managed by the Levant Company, which had been granted a monopoly to trade with the eastern Mediterranean by British royal charter in 1581. The transformation of

British interests in the East, particularly the growth of political and military concerns as a result of the Napoleonic wars, undermined the old arrangement. The British government took over direct responsibility for the embassy in 1804 and the consular posts in 1825; Canning's skill in overseeing this transition helped established Britain's diplomatic preeminence.

After his Ottoman tour had ended, Canning embarked upon an unremarkable parliamentary career, which quickly revealed that his skills were far greater as a diplomat than as a politician. Consequently, in 1831 and 1832 he returned to Constantinople on a successful mission to fix a more favorable frontier for the Kingdom of Greece, which was newly independent of Ottoman rule.

His last period of service in Constantinople was the most important and the longest, from 1842 to 1858, occasionally interrupted by efforts to resign. Canning played a key role in the major events of the era: Russian intervention in the region culminating in the Crimean War and the Tanzimat reforms—most notably the Islahat Fermani (Reform Decree) of 1856. He also succeeded in removing from the Ottoman realm to the British Museum such archaeological discoveries as the Bodrum frieze and the winged lions of Nineveh.

Although Canning began his career by promoting peace with Russia, he spent much of it as the Romanov Empire's implacable foe. Ottoman weakness in the face of the Russian threat forced ever greater dependence on Britain's diplomatic and military support, which Canning offered at a price—a program of internal reform that insisted upon the equality of the empire's Muslim and non-Muslim subjects. Canning's experience and personality backed by Britain's dominant position enabled him to secure Ottoman assent, at least on paper, to the effective annulment of Islamic law on this question.

Although he maintained close personal ties with the then-reigning sultan, Abdülmecit I, his deepest sympathies were reserved for the Christian subjects of the empire, whose improved status, he hoped, would maintain Ottoman integrity in the face of Russian ambition. Later in his life, when that hope proved false, he welcomed the end of Ottoman control in the Balkans.

See also ABDÜLMECIT I; BUCHAREST, TREATY OF (1812); CRIMEAN WAR; TANZIMAT.

Bibliography

Lane-Poole, Stanley. *The Life of the Right Honourable Stratford Canning, Viscount Stratford de Redcliffe.* 2 vols. 1888. Reprint, New York: AMS Press, 1976.

Temperley, Harold. *England and the Near East: The Crimea.* 1936. Hamden, CT: Archon Books, 1964.

BENJAMIN BRAUDE

CANTONNEMENT/REFOULEMENT

French colonial policies.

These French policies were meant—first in the mid-nineteenth century and then in the years just before independence—to confine sections of the Algerian population to areas that could be supervised by the colonial army. This was to prevent access to agricultural land by the local population or to areas judged strategically important by the French. By the independence of Algeria in 1962, an estimated 3 million rural Algerians had been displaced, thus adding considerably to the extremely high urbanization rates the new government faced as a result of these earlier cantonnement and refoulement policies.

Bibliography

Ruedy, John. *Modern Algeria: The Origins and Development of a Nation.* Bloomington: Indiana University Press, 1992.

DIRK VANDEWALLE

CAPITULATIONS

Term derived from capitula *(chapter or paragraph, in Italian) that refers to the clauses of an international treaty, particularly between a Muslim state and a European state.*

The term *capitulation* was originally a "privilege" given by a powerful Middle East government, such as the Ottoman Empire, to a weaker government in Europe. An early Ottoman treaty of this type was negotiated between Sultan Selim I and Venice in 1517. Formerly, Venice had enjoyed exclusive trade privileges with Mamluk Egypt in order to expedite the profitable spice trade. There is a similarity between this type of privilege (and the accompanying attitude) and the type of privileges the Chinese emperors accorded to lesser lands of Asia that wished to trade with China. The traditional attitude might be stated as follows: "Our realm is self-sufficient and superior; thus we have no need to trade with you. But because we are a civilized people, we show our beneficence in this manner."

Next consider the types of privileges accorded by such treaties. The most important clause dealt with mutual trade relations. Both governments agreed to provide, in their respective countries, a place for warehousing items to be traded; protection for those goods from theft or damage; and on the amount of tariff to be charged *ad valorem* for each item. Protection was also accorded to the vessels delivering the merchandise, and the flag under which these vessels could enter territorial waters was carefully controlled. For example, France obtained an *imtiyaz* (capitulation) early in the sixteenth century; thereafter, until Britain received its own *imtiyaz* about 1580, British ships entering Ottoman waters had to fly the flag of France (and doubtless pay for the privilege). In case of shipwreck, the capitulation provided for protection, docking, and repair.

To these general commercial clauses were gradually added legal clauses dealing with the right of extraterritoriality, protection of foreign personnel working in the trade facility, and specification of the court that held primary jurisdiction in case of a dispute. Generally speaking, if the trading company was established in a country where a diplomatic representative of its home country was in residence, the primary jurisdiction over, say, a foreign merchant committing a crime in the host country would be the merchant's own consular court. Often, however, in the case of a capital crime, such as the rape or murder of a Muslim subject, the primary jurisdiction would be the Muslim court.

These were provisions of what might be called the ordinary capitulation-type treaty. This arrangement underwent important changes in the eighteenth and nineteenth centuries as certain European countries, and the United States, grew much more powerful than their counterparts in the Middle East. First, foreign businesses selling their goods in the Middle East, as a means to save costs,

often sought out local Muslims, Christians, or Jews to assist in their transactions: interpreters and expediters to speed wares through customs, longshoremen, workers, secretaries, managers, agents, and sales personnel. Gradually these persons were placed officially under the protection of the company or the foreign government consular service by a device known as a *berat* (minor government decree). A bearer of such protection was known as *beratli* (bearer of a privilege). At first these *berats* were issued under the auspices of the grand vizier or his subordinates. Later, some embassies issued *berats* from their own chanceries.

Because the Muslim populations often were more interested in learning Arabic, Persian, or Turkish, it fell to the Christian and Jewish minorities to learn the languages of western Europe. Hence, many minority families came to be closely associated with Western firms and their governments. Often this relationship proved very advantageous financially. These subject people's *beratli* status extended to them, and often to their relatives and family, the privileges of extraterritoriality and the protection of a powerful foreign country; thus, in the nineteenth century, Muslim government officials began to harbor doubts about their loyalty. The *beratli* held a kind of dual citizenship. Thus, capitulations, originally straightforward trade agreements, became intertwined with issues of national sovereignty for Muslim governments, and for powerful governments of Europe, with the protection of their property, trade agreements, missionaries, and "*beratli* agents" for powerful governments of Europe. For some members of minority communities, the *berat* had become a cover for illegal activities. In the case of outright disagreement, the governments of Europe and the United States often resorted to gunboat diplomacy or "showing the flag" to coerce states of the Middle East. If this did not have the desired effect, such states as imperial Russia often resorted to open warfare. Thus, the Ottoman government and other states of the Middle East in the nineteenth century could not protect locally made crafts or manufactures from cheap imports because foreign powers blocked the raising of tariffs, nor could they directly punish violations of law within their own borders.

Various states of the Middle East, in the twentieth century, sought to abolish these trade treaties that had been turned into major tools of imperialist intervention and control by foreign powers. Ottoman Turkey, upon entering World War I on the side of Germany in 1914, announced the abolition of the capitulation agreements, a move that was not fully approved by Germany. The capitulations had become so burdensome that they constituted grounds for nations of the Middle East to join with a friendly power such as Germany against the exploiting states of Europe. True to their own attitudes toward weaker states, when the Allied powers of Europe won the war, they quickly declared the capitulations once again in full force. Only after Turkey's war of independence (1919–1922) were they forced to accept the end of these lopsided trade treaties under the terms of the Lausanne Treaty of 1923. At the Cairo Conference in 1921, establishing the semi-independence of Egypt from Britain, the powers of Europe agreed to lift most clauses of the capitulations, but the mixed courts, where foreign litigation had taken place, were left in place.

See also CAIRO CONFERENCE (1921); LAUSANNE, TREATY OF (1923).

C. MAX KORTEPETER

CARPETS, PERSIAN

Heavy woven floor coverings with traditional patterns; considered works of art today.

The twentieth century witnessed unparalleled expansion of Persian pile carpet weaving (*qalibafi*) in Iran. Gone were court manufactories and extensive weaving by nomadic tribal peoples. In their place came commercialization of the craft, the gradual introduction of quality controls and standards, and an unprecedented availability of a wide variety of Persian carpets of tribal, village, town, and city provenance for sale in the bazaars and abroad. Throughout the Iranian plateau, Persian carpets generally appear on the floor of all rooms except for the kitchen and bathroom. Often they constitute a room's main or only art, taking the place of a mural or large painting on the wall in Western homes.

Thus, Persian carpets achieved quite a high point in the twentieth century, although Persian pile carpet weaving is generally thought to have experienced its golden age with the curvilinear "city" designs of the Safavid period (1501–1736 C.E.) and with the rectilinear "tribal" carpets of the Qajar dynasty (1796–1925). Art historians, oriental carpet experts, and scholars generally think twentieth-century Persian carpets inferior because of their commercial production circumstances and less intricately designed patterns.

Early in the century, Isfahan and then Qom and other new production centers joined such famous traditional weaving centers as Kerman and Tabriz in producing carpets, almost all with traditional designs, but with synthetic dyes, mechanically spun yarn, and often the help of trained designers. Earlier Caucasus design traditions were continued in Ardabil and surrounding towns. Throughout Iran, classical medallion, garden, hunting, and prayer carpet designs continue to be produced, along with hybrid designs exhibiting the mutual influence of cartoon-prepared city patterns of the medallion sorts and the memory-produced repeat patterns typical of tribal weaving—Afshar, Bakhtiari, Qashqaʾi, and Turkmen.

All the major twentieth-century Persian carpet design types appear to pay tribute in a decorative or symbolic way to springtime or paradise gardens, important culture-specific images in Persian art since Persepolis (begun in 518 B.C.E.); they feature columns, representing a sacred, or paradisial, grove of trees. The existence of the Pazyryk Carpet (at the Hermitage Museum in St. Petersburg) is evidence that pile carpet weaving existed in Central Asia and on the Iranian plateau from at least the Achaemenid period (559–330 B.C.E.), although few Persian carpets or even fragments have survived from before the sixteenth century C.E.

In the 1960s and after, Iranian scholars began paying attention to Persian carpets from technical, sociological, and cultural perspectives, which resulted in the shifting of predominant scholarship in this field from Europe to Iran. In particular, as nomadic and seminomadic communities have dwindled in size, Iranian scholars have provided records of their textile traditions, especially for Turkmen, Qashqaʾi, Shahsavan, and Kurdish carpets.

In the Islamic republican era, beginning in 1979, carpet production continued unabated, although the U.S. embargo on Iranian goods in the 1980s changed the export market for Persian carpets. The same decade also witnessed a dramatic increase in the production of flat-weave products called *gelim* (Turkish, *kilim*) with their mostly uncomplicated geometric patterns. The Carpet Museum of Iran, inaugurated in 1979, the last year of the Pahlavi dynasty (1925–1979), remained the world's best showcase for carpets in the 1990s.

See also BAKHTIARI; QAJAR DYNASTY; TRIBES AND TRIBALISM.

Bibliography

Edwards, A. C. *The Persian Carpet: A Survey of the Carpet-Weaving Industry of Persia.* London: Duckworth, 1953.

Ford, P. R. J. *The Oriental Carpet: A History and Guide to Traditional Motifs, Patterns, and Symbols.* New York: Abrams, 1981.

Hillmann, Michael C. *Persian Carpets.* Austin: University of Texas Press, 1984.

MICHAEL C. HILLMANN

CARTER, JIMMY

[1924–]

U.S. president who mediated the Camp David Accords.

James Earl Carter, Jr., was born on 1 October 1924, in Plains, Georgia. After serving as governor of Georgia for one term (1971–1975) he rose from relative obscurity to win the Democratic nomination and defeat incumbent president Gerald Ford in 1976.

Carter came into office stressing the role of human rights in U.S. foreign policy and rejecting the Cold War perspective of previous administrations, particularly as embodied in the policies of former secretary of state Henry Kissinger. Carter argued that constructive engagement with the Soviet Union, rather than a hostile policy of containment, would advance U.S. interests by reducing Soviet inclinations to play the spoiler role in U.S. policy initiatives. Ironically, it was an early cooperative effort with the Soviets—a plan to cosponsor an Arab–Israeli peace conference in Geneva, announced in a joint communiqué on 1 October 1977—that contributed to Egyptian president Anwar al-Sadat's surprise decision to travel to Jerusalem in November 1977 for direct peace negotiations with Israel. Neither Sadat nor Israeli prime minister Menachem Begin wanted to harness the relatively straightforward Egyptian–Israeli issues (Israel's return of the Sinai to Egypt in exchange for a peace treaty) to the more difficult Palestinian and Syrian conflicts with Israel, and they effectively derailed Carter's Geneva idea by inaugurating bilateral Egyptian–Israeli talks.

When those negotiations threatened to break down, however, Carter invited Sadat and Begin to the presidential retreat at Camp David, Maryland. After thirteen days of intense discussions personally mediated by Carter, on 27 September 1978 the three heads of state signed the Camp David Accords, which in turn led to the Egypt–Israel Peace Treaty, signed on 26 March 1979 in Washington, D.C. The Egyptian–Israeli agreements constituted Carter's greatest foreign-policy triumph, though he later expressed regret that some aspects of the agreements went unfulfilled. The Egyptian–Israeli breakthrough made Israel and Egypt, respectively, the number one and two recipients of U.S. aid.

The Middle East brought success to Carter with Egypt and Israel, but it proved to be his undoing, with Iran. In January 1979 Islamic radicals inspired by the Ayatollah Ruhollah Khomeini overthrew the shah of Iran, a long-time ally of the United States. On 4 November 1979 militant Islamic students seized the U.S. embassy in Tehran, taking fifty-two Americans hostage. Carter's attempts to negotiate their release failed, and on 8 April 1980 the United States broke diplomatic relations with Iran and focused on a series of international legal and economic maneuvers designed to pressure Iran into letting the hostages go. On 24 April 1980 a commando attempt to free the hostages failed when U.S. helicopters crashed in a desert staging area 200 miles outside Tehran. The Iranian hostage crisis dominated the U.S. media and Carter's agenda throughout his failed reelection campaign against the Republican challenger, Ronald Reagan. Carter continued to work for the hostages' release until the very last day of his presidency, when Algerian mediation finally secured their freedom in exchange for the unfreezing of Iranian assets in the United States and a U.S. pledge of nonintervention in Iranian affairs. Carter received word that the hostages had been freed on 20 January 1981, several hours after Reagan took the presidential oath of office.

Despite losing the 1980 presidential election, Carter continued his career of public service. He published widely—memoirs, political observation and analysis, poetry, and fiction—and established the Carter Presidential Library at Emory University in Atlanta, Georgia. He has remained an active statesman, working through the Carter Center to help resolve international crises around the globe.

See also BEGIN, MENACHEM; CAMP DAVID AC-CORDS (1978); EGYPTIAN–ISRAELI PEACE TREATY (1979); HOSTAGE CRISES; HUMAN RIGHTS; KISSINGER, HENRY; REAGAN, RONALD; SADAT, ANWAR AL-.

Bibliography

Carter, Jimmy. *Blood of Abraham: Insights into the Middle East.* Fayetteville: University of Arkansas Press, 1993.

Carter, Jimmy. *Keeping Faith: Memoirs of a President.* New York: Bantam Books, 1982.

Carter Center web site. Available at <http://www.cartercenter.org>.

Jordan, Hamilton. *Jimmy Carter: A Comprehensive Biography from Plains to Post-Presidency.* New York: Scribner, 1997.

MIA BLOOM
UPDATED BY LAURA Z. EISENBERG

CASABLANCA

Largest city in Morocco.

As of 2002, Casablanca (al-Dar al-Bayda, in Arabic) had a population of 3,334,300. The *wilaya* (province) of Greater Casablanca, which covers 646 square miles (1,615 sq km), is composed of twenty-three urban districts and six prefectures. Situated on the Atlantic coast, the city is the principal maritime and air transport hub and the major industrial center of the country.

The site of modern Casablanca was occupied by Anfa, a commercial center in the thirteenth century. After being held briefly by the Portuguese, who called it Casa Branca (White House), it was abandoned in ruins about 1468. The village was rebuilt in 1770 by Sultan Muhammad III (1757–1790), who translated the name into Arabic as *al-Dar al-Bayda*. It was later retranslated into Spanish as Casablanca.

Muhammad III hoped to encourage trade with Europe through the port of Essaouira (Mogador); thus Casablanca remained small and inactive. When the tribes of the Shawiya district around Casablanca

revolted in the 1790s, Sultan Sulayman (1792–1822) closed Casablanca and several other ports to European commerce. It began to revive under Sultan Abd al-Rahman (1822–1859), who reopened it to commerce in 1831. Trade slowly grew from 3 percent of Moroccan maritime trade in 1836 to 10 percent in 1843. The port handled mainly agricultural produce: hides, wool, and grain. The population was estimated at 1,500 in the late 1850s and perhaps 4,000 a decade later as European merchants set up agencies, and steamship services started to call. By the late 1880s the population had increased to around 9,000. Although the port still had no proper wharves, it was important enough for French agents to take control of the customhouse following the Act of Algeciras (1906). European attempts to construct a modern port in 1907 led to an attack on

The Hassan II Mosque in Casablanca, Morocco. Completed in 1984, the mosque features a 22-acre prayer hall and the world's highest minaret, measuring 200 meters. © CHINCH GRYNIEWICZ; ECOSCENE/CORBIS. REPRODUCED BY PERMISISON.

the worksite by people from the surrounding countryside. A French warship bombarded the port, local people looted the town, and French and Spanish troops then occupied it.

The population grew quickly after the imposition of the French protectorate in 1912. It rose from perhaps 40,000 in 1914 to around 250,000 in 1930. The first French resident general, Louis-Hubert Gonzalve Lyautey, decided to make Casablanca the main port and the commercial center of Morocco; Rabat became the political capital. The port relied in particular on the export of phosphates, which became Morocco's largest and most valuable export.

European speculators quickly bought up land, and the city began to grow haphazardly. In 1914 Lyautey gave the French architect Henri Prost the task of designing the city. Prost developed an overall master plan for a European city surrounding the old Muslim *madina* and Jewish *mellah*. Public buildings were required to harmonize with traditional Moroccan styles; the post office, the city hall, and the Palais de Justice made particular use of Islamic architectural elements within a European-style structure. The commercial district was dominated by the kilometer-long Boulevard de la Gare (now Boulevard Muhammad V). The European suburbs spread quickly with little control. To the rapidly growing European population was added an explosive growth in the Moroccan population. This led to the emergence of shantytowns (bidonvilles) in the early 1930s. By the mid-1930s, some 70,000 to 80,000 Moroccans lived in bidonvilles.

European working-class immigrants brought French socialist politics with them, and Moroccan workers were soon involved. In June 1936 a series of strikes began in state enterprises and spread to commercial enterprises in Casablanca; both European and Moroccan workers took part.

After the Allied landings in North Africa in November 1942, Sultan Muhammad V had two meetings with U.S. President Franklin Roosevelt. This assured the sultan of American interest and support for Moroccan independence and raised his reputation in the eyes of the Moroccans. After the war, the political movements in Casablanca became increasingly militant for independence. This was reinforced by an incident on 7 April 1947, when

Two men walk along the stone pavers in the Casbah, the Old Medina section in Casablanca, Morocco. One man wears a business suit, while the other wears the jellaba, a long, loose hooded garment with full sleeves, commonly worn in Muslim countries, along with a fez, a box-shaped hat. © ROGER WOOD/CORBIS. REPRODUCED BY PERMISSION.

Senegalese troops in France's colonial army fired on a crowd in Casablanca, apparently after an argument over the molestation of a Moroccan woman. French officials did little to stop the massacre, in which several hundred people were reported killed.

Following Morocco's independence in 1956, Casablanca's population continued to grow and to become predominantly Moroccan as the Europeans left. By 1960 the population was nearly 1 million, and by 1970, 1.8 million. Although some attempt was made to house the new residents, most of whom moved in from the countryside, the apartment blocks that were built were woefully insufficient. This led to continued political radicalization in Casablanca, and there were riots in the poorer districts in 1965, in which large numbers of people were killed. A state of emergency was declared and remained in force for five years. Tension continued throughout the 1970s, and there were more, and very serious, riots in June 1981. In the 1980s and 1990s Ali Yata, the leader of the Party of Progress and Socialism (Parti du Progrés et Socialisme, the renamed Communist Party) repeatedly won election for a Casablanca constituency. There has been some Islamist activity as well. The importance of Casablanca politically was graphically shown when King Hassan II chose it as the site of the world's biggest mosque (the Hassan II Mosque), which was opened in 1993.

See also BIDONVILLE; COMMUNISM IN THE MIDDLE EAST; LYAUTEY, LOUIS-HUBERT GONZALVE; MUHAMMAD V; ROOSEVELT, FRANKLIN DELANO; YATA, ALI.

Bibliography

Issawi, Charles. *An Economic History of the Middle East and North Africa.* New York: Columbia University Press, 1982.

Wright, Gwendolyn. *The Politics of Design in French Colonial Urbanism.* Chicago: University of Chicago Press, 1991.

Zartman, I. William, ed. *The Political Economy of Morocco.* New York: Praeger, 1987.

C. R. PENNELL

CASABLANCA CONFERENCE

See TUNISIA: OVERVIEW

CASBAH

See GLOSSARY

CATHOLICS

See ROMAN CATHOLICISM AND ROMAN CATHOLIC MISSIONS

CATROUX, GEORGES
[1877–1969]

French general, governor-general, minister, and ambassador.

A graduate of the military college at Saint-Cyr, Georges Catroux served in Algeria, Indochina, and Morocco before he was wounded and imprisoned during World War I; after the war he was a political delegate of the high commissioner in Damascus and subsequently a military attaché in Turkey. He returned to Morocco in 1925 and held several commands there and then in Algeria. In 1940 he joined Charles de Gaulle in London and was dispatched to rally Syria and Lebanon to the Free French cause. He negotiated an agreement between Henri Giraud

and de Gaulle concerning the leadership of the Free French.

Catroux was governor-general of Algeria in 1943 and minister of North Africa in 1944. Catroux understood that France must ultimately heed the rising expectations of the colonized. He demonstrated this view in the delicate negotiations that returned Muhammad V to Morocco in 1955. His appointment as resident minister of Algeria in 1956 provoked the outrage of European settlers, forcing Catroux's resignation and his replacement with Robert Lacoste.

See also DE GAULLE, CHARLES; LACOSTE, ROBERT; MUHAMMAD V.

PHILLIP C. NAYLOR

CATTAN, HENRY
[1906–1992]

Palestinian lawyer and writer.

Henry Cattan was born in Jerusalem and educated at the University of Paris and the University of London. After becoming a licensed barrister, he was a lecturer at the Jerusalem Law School from 1932 to 1942, a practicing lawyer in Palestine and Syria, and a member of the Palestine Law Council until 1948. Cattan testified before the Anglo-American Committee of Inquiry on Palestine in 1946. On behalf of the Arab Higher Committee, he presented the Palestinian case to the UN General Assembly in 1947 and 1948. Cattan later negotiated with Count Folke Bernadotte, the UN mediator for Palestine. Cattan's best-known publications include *The Palestine Question* (1988); *The Jerusalem Question* (1981); *Palestine, the Arabs, and Israel* (1969); *Palestine: The Road to Peace*; and *Palestine and International Law.*

See also ANGLO–AMERICAN COMMITTEE OF INQUIRY (1946); ARAB HIGHER COMMITTEE (PALESTINE); BERNADOTTE, FOLKE.

LAWRENCE TAL
UPDATED BY PHILIP MATTAR

CAYLAK
[1843–1893]

Turkish Ottoman writer and journalist.

Born Mehmet Tevfik in Istanbul, Caylak was the son of an Ottoman official. After working as a civil servant and attempting poetry, Tevfik found fame as a journalist and folklorist; he was called Caylak after the newspaper in which he wrote humorous pieces. He also wrote for the newspapers *Geveze* and *Letaif-i Asar*. Worried that Turkish customs and traditions were vanishing, he devoted himself to gathering folk stories. Among his publications is a three-volume collection of the stories of Nasruddin Hoca.

See also NASRUDDIN HOCA.

DAVID WALDNER

CEM

See NEWSPAPERS AND PRINT MEDIA: TURKEY

CEMAL PAŞA
[1872–1922]

Ottoman general, statesman, and influential leader of the Committee for Union and Progress (CUP).

Ahmet Cemal Paşa was born on 6 May 1872 in Mytilene, Greece, the son of a military pharmacist. He graduated from the War Academy (Mekteb-I Harbiye) in 1895 as staff officer and was appointed to the General Staff in Constantinople (now Istanbul). He transferred to the Second Army unit of construction works stationed in Edirne and in 1898 to the Third Army in Salonika. As military inspector for railways, and later as staff officer in the Third Army headquarters, he contributed to the regional organization of the underground resistance movement to Abdülhamit II. He joined the Committee for Union and Progress (CUP), and during the Young Turk Revolution in July 1908 he emerged as a prominent committee leader. Cemal took part in the first delegation that the Salonika CUP dispatched to Constantinople and received promotion to lieutenant colonel.

After July 1908 Cemal went to Anatolia with a reform commission. When a counterrevolutionary uprising broke out in Constantinople in April 1909, he rejoined the Third Army units (the Army of Deliverance) that suppressed the uprising. Subsequently, he accepted the district governorship of Üsküdar, Istanbul-in-Asia (May 1909). The threat of foreign intervention in response to widespread massacres of Armenians in Adana Province led to his appointment as governor of Adana (August 1909). In 1911 he became governor of Baghdad. Upon the outbreak of the Balkan War in 1912 he went to Thrace as commander of reserve units and was promoted to colonel. Following the CUP's coup against the Kamil government (January 1913), which Cemal helped to engineer, he was made general and commander of the First Army in Constantinople as well as military governor of the capital. He consolidated the CUP's position in the capital by suppressing the Ottoman Liberty and Entente party's opposition and sending its leaders to the gallows. In the CUP-dominated cabinets of 1913 to 1914 he served first as minister of public works and later as minister of the navy. He is credited with the modernization of the Ottoman fleet.

As a senior and most versatile member of the Central Committee, Cemal had a strong following in the CUP. He was implicated in conspiring against the other two members of the Young Turk trio, Enver Pasa and Mehmet Talat, and even accused of attempting to establish a state in Syria as a base to supplant the leadership in Constantinople. His disagreements with other influential members notwithstanding, Cemal's political ambitions remained consistent with the broader goals of the CUP as a political organization.

Known for his pro-French proclivities, Cemal went to Paris in June 1914 to seek a wartime alliance with France. He returned empty-handed, except for the Legion of Honor. During World War I he served as the commander of the Fourth Army and governor of Syria while maintaining his portfolio as minister. He led the ill-fated expeditions against British military positions along the Suez Canal in February 1915 and August 1916. By virtue of the fact that he controlled Syria, Cemal had oversight of the last phase of the Armenian genocide. By mid-1915 Syria was dotted with concentration camps where the weakened population was starved to death while the still able-bodied were employed as slave laborers on construction projects including the Baghdad railroad. The infamous killing sites such as Raqqa, Ra's al-Ayn, and Dayr al-Zawr, at the end of the deportations routes where Armenians were exterminated en masse, were located in Cemal's jurisdiction.

As wartime governor in Syria Cemal gained notoriety for executing Arab leaders for their foreign sympathies and alleged nationalist aims and also for his draconian measures in the management of grain supplies. He also undertook construction and preservation projects designed to improve material conditions in Syria. He resigned in December 1917 and returned to Constantinople.

Together with other CUP leaders, Cemal fled abroad at the end of the war (November 1918). Along with Talat, Young Turk minister of the interior, and Enver, minister of war, Cemal was tried in absentia by a military tribunal convened in postwar Istanbul, was found guilty of war crimes, and was sentenced to death. Cemal went first to Berlin via Odessa, then to Switzerland. He also went to Russia and had contacts with the Bolshevik leaders. He entered the services of the Afghan king, Afdal Barakzai, to reorganize his army against the British. In 1922 he returned to Moscow and went to Tbilisi, where he hoped to monitor the independence movement led by Mustafa Kemal, possibly with an eye on returning to Anatolia. He was assassinated in Tbilisi on 21 July 1922 by two Armenians. He is buried in Erzurum, Turkey.

Cemal authored a tract to justify his stern policies in Syria, which was published in Turkish, Arabic, and French (*La vérité sur la question syrienne*; The truth about the Syrian question). His memoirs were published posthumously. He also commissioned a study of old monuments in greater Syria, *Alte Denkmäler aus Syrien, Palästina und West-Arabien* (Ancient Monuments of Syria, Palestine, and West Arabia).

See also ARMENIAN GENOCIDE; COMMITTEE FOR UNION AND PROGRESS; ENVER PAŞA; TALAT, MEHMET.

Bibliography

Erickson, Edward J. *Ordered to Die: A History of the Ottoman Army in the First World War.* Westport, CT: Greenwood, 2001.

Pasha, Djemal. *Memories of a Turkish Statesman, 1913–1919.* New York: Arno, 1973.

Zürcher, Erik J. *Turkey: A Modern History.* London and New York: I. B. Taurus, 1994.

HASAN KAYALI
UPDATED BY ROUBEN P. ADALIAN

CENSUS

See POPULATION

CENTRAL INTELLIGENCE AGENCY (CIA)

Principal U.S. agency responsible for collection and assessment of worldwide intelligence data.

The Central Intelligence Agency (CIA) was established in 1947. It is responsible directly to the president of the United States and carries out functions ordered by the president and the president's staff. The agency and its director (called the director of central intelligence, or DCI) are charged not only with collecting and analyzing intelligence data but also with coordinating the activities of other U.S. intelligence agencies, including those attached to the military services and those of the state and defense departments. The agency is divided into three principal directorates: for clandestine collection of foreign intelligence and the conduct of covert actions; for analysis of political, military, and economic developments outside the United States; and for collection and analysis of technical and scientific intelligence. It also maintains the DCI Counterterrorist Center. The CIA is headquartered just outside Washington, D.C., in Langley, Virginia.

In the Middle East, the CIA is best known for having organized the 1953 overthrow of Iranian prime minister Mohammad Mossadegh and having returned Reza Shah Pahlavi to Iran's Peacock Throne in a covert operation. Mossadegh, although widely seen in the Middle East as a nationalist, was viewed by the Eisenhower administration as a tool of the Soviet Union who threatened U.S. interests. The CIA has also been implicated in General Husni al-Za'im's 1949 coup in Syria, and the Free Officers' 1952 coup in Egypt. Other CIA covert actions in the Middle East have included providing arms and covert support to rebel groups, including the Iraqi Kurds in the early 1970s; the Afghan guerrillas following the Soviet invasion of Afghanistan in 1979; and Chad's forces opposing a Libyan invasion in 1980.

Lebanon was for some time the center of much CIA activity. According to newspaper accounts, during the 1970s and the early 1980s, the CIA and the Palestine Liberation Organization (PLO) had a cooperative arrangement, centered in Beirut, to ensure security against terrorist attacks to Americans. This occurred despite the U.S. government's official, public refusal to deal with the PLO. Apparently in the hope of gaining diplomatic advantage, the PLO warned of any impending attack on U.S. citizens and provided physical protection to U.S. diplomats and installations. The principal PLO contact person in this arrangement, Ali Hasan al-Salama (1940–1979), was killed in a 1979 car bombing believed to have been engineered by Israel, but the security cooperation continued until the PLO left Beirut in the aftermath of Israel's 1982 invasion of Lebanon. The following year saw a marked upsurge in attacks on U.S. installations and large numbers of American deaths. According to one account, following bombings of the American embassy and a U.S. Marine barracks in Beirut in 1983 and 1984—all believed to be the work of the Shiʿite group Hizbullah, whose spiritual leader was Shaykh Husayn Fadlallah—the CIA arranged to have Fadlallah stopped. A car bomb was detonated in March 1985 at his apartment building; Fadlallah, however, was not harmed. The CIA denied involvement, and the House Permanent Select Committee on Intelligence, following an investigation, concluded that no direct or indirect CIA involvement could be shown.

Although not responsible for maintaining diplomatic relationships with other countries, the CIA often provides a vehicle by which the U.S. government can solidify a relationship through unofficial contacts or cooperate with another country covertly on operations of joint interest. This often occurs through regular meetings between a CIA official and a foreign leader. Liaison between the CIA and the intelligence services of friendly nations provides another means of cooperation. This type of liaison—involving cooperation on counterterrorist operations, coordination on other specific operations, and the exchange of intelligence data—has been conducted with many Middle East countries, most particularly Israel. The CIA has also been involved as a diplomatic intermediary between nations, as was the case when senior CIA officials Kermit Roosevelt, James Jesus Angleton, and Miles Copeland provided a secret channel of communication between Egypt and Israel in 1954 and 1955. The CIA helped coordinate security arrangements made by Israel and the Palestinian Authority in the late 1990s, and DCI George Tenet even offered his own plan for resolving the Israel–Palestinian conflict in June 2001.

The CIA was actively involved in stepped-up counterterrorist activities in the wake of the 11 Sep-

tember 2001 attacks on New York and Washington that were engineered by the al-Qaʿida network. CIA operatives were active in Afghanistan during the American invasion of that country beginning in October 2001, and one became the first American to die there as a result of hostile activity. They were also present in Iraq during and after the U.S. invasion in the spring of 2003. The inability of the American forces to find the chemical and biological weapons the United States had claimed the Iraqi regime was stockpiling led to criticism of the CIA's and other U.S. intelligence agencies' prewar intelligence. In February 2004, President George W. Bush called for an investigation into U.S. intelligence failures prior to the invasion.

See also BUSH, GEORGE WALKER; FADLALLAH, SHAYKH HUSAYN; FREE OFFICERS, EGYPT; HIZBULLAH; MOSSADEGH, MOHAMMAD; PAHLAVI, REZA; PALESTINE LIBERATION ORGANIZATION (PLO); QAʿIDA, AL-; ROOSEVELT, KERMIT; ZAʿIM, HUSNI AL-.

Bibliography

Colby, William, and Forbath, Peter. *Honorable Men: My Life in the CIA.* New York: Bookthrift, 1978.

Marchetti, Victor, and Marks, John D. *The CIA and the Cult of Intelligence.* New York: Dell, 1989.

Turner, Stansfield. *Secrecy and Democracy: The CIA in Transition.* Boston: HarperCollins, 1986.

Woodward, Bob. *Veil: The Secret Wars of the CIA, 1981–1987.* New York: Simon and Schuster, 1987.

KATHLEEN M. CHRISTISON
UPDATED BY MICHAEL R. FISCHBACH

CENTRAL TREATY ORGANIZATION (CENTO)

Mutual-defense group of Middle Eastern countries and Britain, 1959–1979.

After the Iraqi revolution of July 1958, Iraq withdrew from the Baghdad Pact in March 1959. With its patronymic city now in a hostile country, the pact was renamed the Central Treaty Organization (CENTO). Its membership included Iran, Turkey, Pakistan, and Great Britain, with the United States as an associate member. CENTO, like its predecessor, was initially conceived as a defense organization on the lines of the North Atlantic Treaty

Organization (NATO); the northern tier of Middle Eastern countries that formed the southern boundary of the USSR were strategically important to the cold warriors of the West. While not officially part of CENTO, the United States was an active supporter, and it obtained the use of military bases and intelligence outposts in each of the northern-tier countries. By the late 1960s, CENTO had become more important as an economic bloc, though it remained a crux of American military planning. CENTO became defunct after the 1979 Iranian revolution.

See also BAGHDAD PACT (1955); NORTH ATLANTIC TREATY ORGANIZATION (NATO).

Bibliography

Bill, James A. *The Eagle and the Lion: The Tragedy of American–Iranian Relations.* New Haven, CT: Yale University Press, 1988.

Campbell, John Coert. *Defense of the Middle East,* 2d edition. New York: Council on Foreign Relations, Harper, 1960.

Hurewitz, J. C. *Middle East Politics: The Military Dimension.* New York: Council on Foreign Relations, Praeger, 1969.

Lenczowski, George. *The Middle East in World Affairs,* 4th edition. Ithaca, NY: Cornell University Press, 1980.

ZACHARY KARABELL

CENTRE DE RECHERCHES, D'ÉTUDES, DE DOCUMENTATION ET D'INFORMATION SUR LA FEMME (CREDIF)

Tunisian research center on matters concerning women, also known as CREDIF.

CREDIF, a public agency instituted on 7 August 1990 that performs research for the government, is now the scientific branch of the Tunisian Ministry of Women's, Children's, and Family Affairs, which was established in 1992. Its mission is to carry out research on women's rights and the status of women, to gather information, organize and maintain databases concerning gender, and produce reports on the evolution of women's condition in Tunisia. CREDIF has created a number of ways of intervening in the production of knowledge about women: by hosting forums for national and international exchange on women's issues; by creating an Observatory on Women's Condition, which allows for permanent, ongoing oversight and evaluation of women's condition through cross-disciplinary research, annual reports, and national and regional seminars on the changing condition of women; by establishing statistical databases disaggregated by gender; by disseminating information concerning bibliographic research, women's information networks, and nongovernmental development projects whose stakeholders are women; by extending outreach to women to increase their legal literacy concerning rights and obligations; by studying the representation of women in the mass media; by holding training seminars on gender analysis; and by publishing a bilingual (Arabic/French) magazine, *Info-CREDIF.*

See also GENDER: GENDER AND LAW; TUNISIA: OVERVIEW; TUNISIA: POLITICAL PARTIES IN.

Bibliography

Brand, Laurie A. *Women, the State, and Political Liberalization: Middle Eastern and North African Experiences.* New York: Columbia University Press, 1998.

Ministère des Affaires de la Femme, de la Famille, et de l'Enfance (MAFFE). Available at <http://www.ministeres.tn/html/ministeres/tutelle/femme.html>.

LAURA RICE

CERAMICS

A durable material with a history spanning 10,500 years that is significant to the study of archaeology and history.

Ceramic figurines and pottery vessels in Anatolia and the Iranian Plateau date to 8500 B.C.E.. The archaeological, ethnographic, and historic evidence for ceramic production in the Middle East and North Africa is complex and has a voluminous literature. The earliest Islamic potters (Umayyad dynasty, 661–750 C.E.) inherited extant traditions: Blue- and green-glazed wares had been produced in Egypt since Roman times; the alkaline-glazed ceramics of Syria, Iraq, and Iran had been made since Achaemenid times (seventh to fourth centuries B.C.E.); and the Roman lead-glazed ceramic tradition had been continued by the Byzantines. Chinese influences (Tang stoneware, ninth to eleventh centuries; Song whitewares, twelfth to fourteenth centuries, and Ming blue- and whiteware, fifteenth to nineteenth centuries) were significant. The spread of Islam correlates with the distribution of hybrid production methods (molds, tin glazes, underglazes, polychromy, and metallic pigments) and products (architectural tiles). Early Islamic wares included Umayyad (Mediterranean/Middle Eastern influence), Abbasid (Tang influence), Central Asian Samanid, Egyptian Fatimid, and Mesopotamian/Persian wares (twelfth to fifteenth centuries) from Rayy, Raqqah, and Kashan. Later Persian ceramics (fifteenth to nineteenth centuries) were made at Kubachi, Tabriz, and Kerman; Syrian artisans produced work at al-Fustat, Raqqa, and Damascus; Seljuk Turks fabricated wares at Iznik and Kütahya. Lusterware, Mina'i, Iznik, Gombroon, and Zillij are notable Islamic contributions to ceramic history.

The Museum of Islamic Ceramics in Cairo, the Ashmolean Museum in Oxford, and the Metropolitan Museum of Art in New York house specimens from different Islamic eras that span the region from Morocco in the west through Iran, Afghanistan, and Indonesia in the east. Although Iznik ceramics were prized by the Ottoman court into the early twentieth century, ceramic vessels and tiles produced from the earliest times to the present in Islamic lands, including Central Asia, are esteemed by museums, art historians, and collectors. With the availability of metal and plastic replacements, utilitarian production has diminished, but ceramic art and tile production remains strong.

Bibliography

Watson, Oliver. *Ceramics from Islamic Lands.* London: Thames and Hudson, 2003.

Whitehouse, David; Grube, Ernest J.; and Crowe, Yolande. "Ceramics: Islamic." In *Encyclopedia Iranica.* London; Boston: Routledge & Kegan Paul, 1995.

ELIZABETH THOMPSON
UPDATED BY CHARLES C. KOLB

CERIDE-I HAVADIS

See NEWSPAPERS AND PRINT MEDIA: TURKEY

ÇERKES HASAN INCIDENT

Assassination of Hüseyin Avni and Raşit Paşa.

Çerkes Hasan was a Circassian infantry captain, a brother-in-law of Ottoman Sultan Abdülaziz, and a member of the personal staff of Prince Yusuf Izzeddin. On 15 June 1876, he entered a meeting of cabinet ministers being held in the house of Midhat Paşa and assassinated Chief of Staff Hüseyin Avni and Foreign Minister Raşit Paşa, while wounding several others. Çerkes Hasan was swiftly tried and convicted, and on 18 June he was executed. Though Çerkes Hasan claimed that he was taking revenge against Hüseyin Avni for a personal affront and against Raşit Paşa for his supposed role in the death of Abdülaziz on 4 June 1876, conservative politicians viewed the incident as a plot manipulated by Midhat Paşa to remove the only rival minister in the cabinet, paving the way for cabinet approval of the new constitution. Sultan Murat V, who was already showing signs of mental unhealth, was so disturbed by the incident that he was unable to continue in his position.

See also ABDÜLAZIZ; MIDHAT PAŞA.

Bibliography

Lewis, Bernard. *The Emergence of Modern Turkey,* 3d edition. New York: Oxford University Press, 2002.

Shaw, Stanford, and Shaw, Ezel Kural. *History of the Ottoman Empire and Modern Turkey,* Vol. 2: *Reform, Revolution, and Republic: The Rise of Modern Turkey, 1808–1975.* Cambridge, U.K., and New York: Cambridge University Press, 1977.

DAVID WALDNER

CEUTA

Spanish enclave and port city on the Moroccan shore of the strait of Gibraltar.

Ceuta is a Spanish possession with a population in 2002 of 69,000 and an area of 7 square miles (18 sq km). It commands the strait of Gibraltar and was settled by Carthaginians, Romans, Vandals, and Byzantines. Taken by the Arabs in 711, it was the base for the invasion of the Iberian Peninsula. Under Muslim rule, Ceuta (Arabic, Sibta) was disputed by the various Spanish and Moroccan dynasties, interspersed with periods of autonomy. During the thirteenth century, Ceuta was a rich port, linking the trans-Saharan trade with the Mediterranean. In 1415, it was taken by Portuguese King John and abandoned by its Muslim inhabitants. After the union of the Spanish and Portuguese crowns in 1580, Ceuta became Spanish, which it has remained.

Until the mid-nineteenth century, it was frequently besieged by Moroccan government and tribal forces, and in 1860 this led to war between Spain and Morocco, following which the boundaries were expanded in favor of Spain. The independent Moroccan government has repeatedly demanded that Ceuta be handed over by Spain. Fishing and food processing are important economic activities.

C. R. PENNELL

CEVDET, ABDULLAH
[1869–1932]

Ottoman Kurdish writer, political activist, poet, and doctor.

Abdullah Cevdet was born in Arapkir, in eastern Ottoman Turkey, the son of an Islamic religious official and physician. After attending a provincial military school, he went to Istanbul at the age of fifteen to study at the army medical school. While at the medical school, Cevdet participated in a growing movement calling for liberal reform of the Ottoman Empire. In 1890 he and three colleagues, all non-Turks, formed a political society that, after a succession of name changes, became known as the Committee for Union and Progress (CUP).

Along with other members of the CUP, Cevdet was arrested in 1892. In 1896, he was sent into exile in Tripoli, where he served as the eye doctor for the military hospital. Continuing his political activities, he was forced to flee to Tunisia and from there to Europe. In 1900, Cevdet agreed to become the medical officer of the Ottoman Embassy in Geneva, Switzerland, in exchange for the release of political prisoners in Tripoli. For this compromise with Abdülhamit II, the sultan, Cevdet was branded a traitor and never attained high office once the CUP came to power.

Cevdet, however, never ceased his agitation for reform and, in 1905, was sentenced in absentia to life imprisonment. Between 1905 and 1911, he lived in Cairo, where he joined the Young Turks group that became the Decentralization Party. In 1911, following the abdication of Sultan Abdülhamit, he returned to Istanbul. There his freethinking ideas, especially his atheism, led to frequent clashes with the new government. Cevdet's opposition to the empire's entry into World War I also aggravated his relationship with the regime. Although after the war he was appointed director of public health, his writings on religion led to charges of heresy. His trial started during the empire and continued into the early period of the new Republic of Turkey. The case was finally dismissed in December 1926, but he was prohibited from publishing political works.

While in Geneva, Cevdet had founded the journal *Osmanli,* in which he published articles in French and Turkish opposing the absolute rule of Sultan Abdülhamit. After this journal was closed, the principal vehicle for Cevdet's political writings was the monthly newspaper he published and edited, *Ijtihad* (also known as *Içtihat;* The struggle). *Ijtihad* was founded in 1904 and continued until his death in 1932, although it was shut down several times, particularly during World War I. Alongside attacks on despotism, *Ijtihad* published articles attacking theocracy, tradition, and religion but advocating secular modernism.

In 1885, while a medical student, he met the poet Abdülhak Hamit Tarhan and began writing poetry. His four volumes of poetry, published in the 1890s, were influenced by Hamit and two other Ottoman Turkish poets, Namik Kemal and Mahmut Ekrem, as well as by French poets.

Two books strongly influenced Cevdet's intellectual orientation: Felix Isnards's *Spiritualisme et Matérialisme* (Paris, 1879), which presented a skeptical outlook toward religion, and Ludwig Buchner's *Force et Matière,* which provided the intellectual basis for a radical critique of religion. This orientation informed his political writings as well as his writings on sociology, psychology, science, and philosophy. Two important collections of his essays are *Science and Philosophy* (1906) and *An Examination of the World of Islam from a Historical and Philosophical Viewpoint* (1922). In addition, he translated into Turkish and wrote the preface to the mid-nineteenth-century book *Histoire des Musselmans* (History of the Muslims) by Reinhart Dozy—which created a furor on its publication.

See also ABDÜLHAMIT II; COMMITTEE FOR UNION AND PROGRESS; DECENTRALIZATION PARTY; LITERATURE: TURKISH; NAMIK KEMAL; NEWSPAPERS AND PRINT MEDIA: TURKEY; RECAIZADE MAHMUD EKREM; TARHAN, ABDÜLHAK HAMIT; YOUNG TURKS.

Bibliography

Mitler, Louis. *Ottoman Turkish Writers: A Bibliographical Dictionary of Significant Figures in Pre-Republican Turkish Literature.* New York: P. Lang, 1988.

DAVID WALDNER

CEVDET, AHMED

[1822–1895]

Ottoman Turkish scholar-statesman.

Born at Lofça (Lovech, Bulgaria) to an Ottoman Turkish family, Ahmed Cevdet, at the age of seventeen, went to Istanbul, capital of the Ottoman Empire. During seven or eight years of study in *medrese* (higher schools of religious studies), he also found ways to learn other subjects—Persian, astronomy, mathematics—that were not taught in these schools. Mixing with learned company in dervish (Sufi religious fraternity) halls and literary men's homes, he formed important contacts. He began writing verse, and one of his literary benefactors, the poet Süleyman Fehim Efendi, gave him the pen name Cevdet. In the 1840s, he took the examination required to become a *qadi,* thus beginning his career as a member of the *ulama* (Islamic religious scholars).

Cevdet's work in administration began with Mustafa Reşid Paş's first appointment as grand vizier in 1846. Seeking an expert on the *shariʿa* (law of Islam) to consult about laws and regulations he planned to issue, Reşid Paşa asked the Şeyh ül-Islam to send him a broadminded *alim* (singular of *ulama*), and Cevdet was assigned. He remained close to Reşid Paşa for the rest of the latter's life, settling into his household and tutoring his children. There, Cevdet came under the influence of Reşid Paşa's efforts to simplify the Ottoman Turkish language and make it an effective means of mass communication; he also began to study French. In 1850, Cevdet collaborated with the future grand vizier Keçecizade Fuʾat Paşa in writing an Ottoman grammar. In the same year, he became a member of the council on education (Meclis-i Maarif) and director of the teachers' college Dar ül-Maarif, founded in 1848, playing a major role in organizing the college. Serving the education council as its first secretary, he had an important role in founding the Encümen-i Daniş (Academy of Sciences, 1851), which published his coauthored grammar, the *Kavaid-i Osmaniye,* as its first publication. When the

Academy of Sciences decided to produce a history of the Ottoman Empire, Cevdet was asked in 1852 to write on the period from 1774 to 1826. So began the *Tarih-i Cevdet* (Cevdet's history).

Writing the first three volumes during the Crimean War, Cevdet was named official historian (*vakʿanevis*) in 1855. Over the next few years, he continued his *History* and studied the medieval Arab historian Ibn Khaldun, finishing the Ottoman translation of Ibn Khaldun's *Muqaddima* in 1860 (begun by Pirizade Sahib, 1674–1749). Based on European as well as Ottoman sources and emphasizing the importance for the empire of developments in Europe, Cevdet's twelve-volume *History* was completed over thirty years. The work distinguished Cevdet not as an old-style chronicler but as a standard-setter for later historians.

In the 1850s, Cevdet also began to work in legal reform. Following his appointment to the Meclis-i Ali-i Tanzimat (High Council of Reforms) in 1857, Cevdet presided over the commission that drew up the land law (*arazi kanunnamesi*) of 1858. He inaugurated the publishing of laws in a volume, subsequently a series, which continues still—the *Düstur.*

When Mustafa Reşid Paşa died in 1858, and Ali Paşa became grand vizier, Cevdet was offered the governorship of Vidin province. He was not yet ready to change from the religious to the civil service, a move he deferred until 1866. The incident indicates, however, Cevdet's emergence, following Mustafa Reşid's death, into the top bureaucratic echelons—where statesmen rotated among ministerial positions and provincial governorships. This Cevdet did for the rest of his career.

Although he held many high offices, the emphasis of Cevdet Paşa's career thereafter was on law and justice. He served as minister of justice five times. He had a critical part in developing the empire's civil (*nizamiye*) courts, especially in introducing—with the Divan-i Ahkam-i Adliye—an appeals instance in 1868. The Hukuk Mektebi (Ottoman Law School) opened in 1880, while he was minister, and he gave its first lecture. His greatest legal contribution, however, emerged from a controversy over whether the Ottoman Empire should adopt the French civil code. Cevdet Paşa successfully championed the opposing view that a compendium of *hanafi* jurisprudence should be adopted. In 1869, he chaired a committee of Islamic legal scholars that produced the *Mecelle-i Ahkam-i Adliye,* a pioneering attempt to codify Islamic law. He had a hand in preparing all the *Mecelle's* sixteen books, placed in effect by imperial decree between 1870 and 1876 as the civil code for both Islamic and secular courts. The *Mecelle* remained in force until the Turkish republic adopted the Swiss civil code in 1926; in some successor states of the Ottoman Empire, it served much longer. The *Mecelle* constitutes a unique case of successful resistance to the Ottoman tendency toward adopting European law.

Close to the palace and reluctant about the constitutional movement, Cevdet Paşa was politically very conservative. As his transfer from the *ulama* to the civil hierarchy and his close association with reformist statesmen suggest, however, he was intellectually broadminded. He also founded an extraordinary family. He took part personally, to an unusual degree, in educating his children, in addition to hiring private tutors. His son Ali Sedad (1859–1900) wrote several books on logic. His daughter Fatma Aliye (1862–1936) became the first Turkish woman novelist and a leading figure in the women's movement. His younger daughter, Emine Semiye (1864–1944), was allowed to study psychology and sociology in France and Switzerland, before returning to Turkey as an educator, writer, and political activist.

Cevdet Paşa's writings contributed to several fields. In history, he wrote not only his *History* (*Tarih-i Cevdet,* revised edition, Istanbul, 1891–1892) but two sets of historical "memoranda" (*tezakir, ma'ruzat*) that historians value as sources; he also completed the Ottoman Turkish translation of Ibn Khaldun's *Muqaddima.* In law, the *Mecelle* is largely his monument. He wrote, too, various pedagogical works, especially his multivolume *Kisas-i Enbiya ve Tevarih-i Hülefa,* presenting accounts of the prophets and Islamic rulers, down to Sultan Murad II.

See also MUSTAFA REŞID; NEWSPAPERS AND PRINT MEDIA: TURKEY; QADI; *SHARI'A;* SUFISM AND THE SUFI ORDERS; *ULAMA.*

Bibliography

Chambers, Richard L. "The Education of a Nineteenth Century Ottoman Alim, Ahmed Cevdet Paşa." *International Journal of Middle East Studies* 4 (1973): 440–464.

CARTER V. FINDLEY

CHADOR

See CLOTHING

CHALABI, AHMAD

[1945–]

Iraqi politician.

Ahmad Chalabi, a member of an oligarchic Shi'ite family with close ties to the Hashimite kingdom installed by the British imperial authorities in Baghdad after World War I, was born in 1945. He is a leading but controversial opponent of Saddam Hussein who in 1992 founded the Iraqi National Congress in London. His family, including his father, a member of the monarchy's Council of Ministers, fled Iraq during the 1958 coup d'état. Until Chalabi's Pentagon-staged return during the U.S. invasion of Iraq in 2003, he had lived in exile for forty-five years. He studied at the Massachusetts Institute of Technology and the University of Chicago, where he developed connections that would later serve his ambitions. He taught math at the American University of Beirut, and founded Petra Bank in Jordan in 1977. He turned to Iraqi politics after his bank collapsed in 1989. He had relative success lobbying the U.S. halls of power for "regime change" in Iraq. He claimed credit for the 1998 Iraqi Liberation Act passed by the U.S. Congress. His critics allege that he promised to privatize Iraqi oil and privilege U.S. companies in return for U.S. assistance in grabbing power in Baghdad. He continues to be dogged by accusations of fraud, including a 1992 conviction in absentia for embezzlement in Jordan, as well as by allegations of spying for the Mossad and the U.S. Central Intelligence Agency. After the 2003 U.S. invasion of Iraq, the U.S. appointed him to the Iraqi Governing Council that they formed. His support among the U.S. State Department and intelligence professionals waned after the invasion, when the Pentagon's predictions about Iraq, based mostly on intelligence provided by the Iraqi National Congress, turned out to be inaccurate. However, he continued to have the support of the Pentagon in early 2004.

See also AMERICAN UNIVERSITY OF BEIRUT (AUB); HUSSEIN, SADDAM; IRAQI NATIONAL CONGRESS.

KARIM HAMDY

CHALLE, MAURICE

[1905–1979]

French air force general and commander in chief of French forces in Algeria, 1958–1960.

Born in Le Pontet, Vaucluse, France, Maurice Challe was a Saint-Cyr graduate and, in 1953, was commandant of the École de Guerre Aérienne (School of Air War). In 1956, he assisted in the planning of France's operation to retake the Suez Canal after Egypt's nationalization of it. France's President Charles de Gaulle appointed Challe as commander in chief of the French forces in Algeria in December 1958. Challe responded by initiating highly effective aerial tactics (Challe Plan) against the nationalist Armée de Libération Nationale (National Liberation Army, ALN).

Although reassigned in 1960 to the North Atlantic Treaty Organization (NATO), Challe was deeply affected by his Algerian experience and had become disaffected with de Gaulle's policy of decolonization—especially with the plight of Algerian loyalists (Harkis). In February 1961, he resigned; in April, he and three other generals staged a revolt in Algiers against Paris, which failed to mobilize the anticipated support. Challe gave himself up and was interned until 1966 and then was granted amnesty in 1968. He wrote *Notre Révolte* (1968), which recollected his Algerian experiences and especially the April 1961 insurrection.

See also ARMÉE DE LIBÉRATION NATIONALE (ALN); HARKIS; NORTH ATLANTIC TREATY ORGANIZATION (NATO).

Bibliography

Horne, Alistair. *A Savage War of Peace: Algeria, 1954–1962*, revised edition. New York: Penguin, 1987.

PHILLIP C. NAYLOR

CHAMCHIAN, MIKAYEL

[1738–1823]

Armenian intellectual, regarded as the first modern Armenian historian.

Mikayel Chamchian was born in Istanbul to an Armenian family of the Roman Catholic faith. He was trained as a jeweler in the employ of the Armenian *amira* Mikayel Chelebi Diuzian, the imperial jeweler.

Abandoning secular life, Chamchian joined his brother in Venice at the monastery of the Armenian Mekhitarian order in 1762. Upon completion of his education and training, he was sent as a preacher among the Armenians of Aleppo and Basra. In 1774 he was appointed instructor of Armenian language and grammar at the monastery, and in 1795 he was assigned to Istanbul as the resident Mekhitarian representative. He died there, after a long and productive life.

Chamchian was more than a missionary and educator. As grammarian, theologian, and historian, he was the intellectual giant of his age. His *Kerakanutiun Haykazian Lezvi* (Grammar of the Armenian language, 1779) is a landmark in Armenian linguistic studies. It was the first descriptive grammar of the Armenian language, though still of classical Armenian. His theological studies were defenses of Roman Catholicism, which, however, did not pass the censor at Rome for their attempt to reconcile Roman Catholic theology with Armenian Orthodoxy.

He made his most important contribution, however, as a historian. He wrote *Patmutiun Hayots i Skzbane Ashkharhi Minchev tsam diarn 1784* (Armenian history from the beginning of the world to the year 1784). Writing a universal history, in these volumes Chamchian developed a continuous narrative depiction of the Armenian people from the Creation to his own time. Though grounded in the biblical framework of the origin of humankind and of nations, Chamchian nevertheless crossed a number of important thresholds from a medieval worldview. His interpretation of events suggests more modern practices of historiographic methodology: He familiarized himself with current scholarship; he contextualized Armenian history by studying the classical historians; he examined all the extant Armenian historical works; and he constructed a comprehensive history of the Armenians. As a result, Chamchian's *Patmutiun Hayots* is regarded as the first work in modern Armenian historical scholarship.

See also ARMENIAN MILLET.

Bibliography

Adalian, Rouben P. *From Humanism to Rationalism: Armenian Scholarship in the Nineteenth Century.* Atlanta, GA: Scholars Press, 1992.

ROUBEN P. ADALIAN

CHAMOUN, CAMILLE
[1900–1987]

President of Lebanon, 1952–1958; one of the most charismatic and influential Maronite politicians of the post–World War II period.

Born in Dayr al-Qamar, a predominantly Christian village located in the mixed Druze-Maronite district of the Shuf, in southern Mount Lebanon, Camille Chamoun (also Sham'un) was graduated from the Faculty of Law of Saint Joseph University in Beirut in 1925 and elected to Lebanon's parliament in 1934. A member of Bishara al-Khuri's Constitutional Bloc, he rapidly rose to political prominence and became minister of finance in 1938.

In the late 1930s and early 1940s, he developed a close connection with the British and American governments and repeatedly headed Lebanese missions overseas. It was then that he began to acquire the reputation of being one of Lebanon's most cosmopolitan and most sophisticated politicians. After playing an important role in the events that led up to the gaining of independence by Lebanon (1943), he was a minister in several of President al-Khuri's governments. He nevertheless broke with al-Khuri in May 1948, when the latter sought to have the constitution amended to allow for his reelection. In 1951, Chamoun created the so-called Socialist Front with Druze leader Kamal Jumblatt and Maronite leaders Pierre Jumayyil and Raymond Eddé. The members of the Socialist Front accused President al-Khuri of corruption, nepotism, and viola-

President Camille Chamoun (right) converses with King Hussein of Jordan in 1995. © BETTMANN/CORBIS. REPRODUCED BY PERMISSION.

tions of the law, and they sought to obtain his resignation. In the summer of 1952, they organized a successful countrywide general strike that forced al-Khuri to step down, and soon afterward, on 23 September 1952, Chamoun was elected president.

His presidency can be credited with several achievements. He increased the independence of the judiciary, induced Parliament to grant women the right to vote, and took measures to liberalize trade and industry that greatly contributed to the subsequent period of economic expansion and prosperity in Lebanon. He was criticized, however, for many of the very same practices he had accused his predecessor of fostering, particularly corruption and abuses of his authority. The political establishment distrusted his authoritarian leanings and his attempt to undercut the influence of traditional leaders. The Sunni Islam community especially felt alienated by his effort to undermine the authority of the premiership, which by convention was reserved for a Sunni, and by his unabashedly pro-Western foreign policy. During the 1956 crisis, for instance, he had refused to heed Muslim pressures to break off relations with France and Britain. As the pan-Arab rhetoric of Egyptian President Gamal Abdel Nasser became increasingly popular among the Sunni masses of Lebanon, he defiantly intensified the alignment of Lebanon with the United States, and, in 1957, he was the only Arab leader to publicly endorse the Eisenhower doctrine. Such open hostility to the rising tide of Arab nationalism in Lebanon made him very unpopular among Sunni Muslims. More generally, his heavy-handed, provocative style alienated many, including those within the Christian community. As a result, during his last two years in office, the people of Lebanon became increasingly polarized and discontented with his administration.

In 1957, Chamoun rigged the parliamentary elections to weaken his rivals and permit parliament to approve a constitutional amendment that would have enabled him to be reelected for a second term. Several of the country's most prominent political bosses thus failed to regain their seats in the Chamber of Deputies, which was then dominated by Chamoun loyalists. Such a blatantly illegal but effective maneuver to undermine their power led Chamoun's rivals to rise up against him during what came to be known as the 1958 Lebanese civil war.

Although Chamoun was allowed to remain in office until the end of his term, September 1958, he had to abandon any ambition of being reelected.

He never again exerted as much power as he had between 1952 and 1958, but he remained active in public life and continued to display his skills as a populist, pragmatic politician. In 1959, he founded the National Liberal Party (NLP), which, of all parties, became the most consistent advocate of free enterprise and close ties with Western countries. He also rapidly emerged as a determined opponent of President Chehab and his policies, and in 1967 he formed the so-called Tripartite Alliance with the other chief opponents of Chehab, Raymond Eddé of the National Bloc and Pierre Jumayyil of the Phalange Party. He thus was instrumental in electing Sulayman Franjiyya to the presidency in 1970 and remained a behind-the-scenes power broker in the years that followed.

As Lebanon slowly drifted toward civil war in the early 1970s, Chamoun proved himself to be one of the most hawkish voices within the Christian community. He was determined to maintain Christian domination over state institutions and to resist calls to end the confessionalism. During the first phase of the civil war, from 1975 to 1976, he was minister of the interior. In the course of the hostilities, he and his followers were rapidly overshadowed by Bashir Jumayyil and his Lebanese Forces. In July 1980, the Lebanese Forces destroyed the military infrastructure of the Tigers, NLP's small militia. Although Chamoun joined the Government of National Unity formed in 1984, he was then no longer in a position to influence the course of national politics. He died of a heart attack in August 1987.

See also EDDÉ, RAYMOND; FRANJIYYA, SULAYMAN; JUMAYYIL, BASHIR; JUMAYYIL, PIERRE; JUMBLATT, KAMAL; KHURI, BISHARA AL-; LEBANESE CIVIL WAR (1958); NATIONAL LIBERAL PARTY.

Bibliography

Cobban, Helena. *The Making of Modern Lebanon.* London: Hutchinson, 1985.

Hudson, Michael C. *The Precarious Republic: Political Modernization in Lebanon.* New York: Random House, 1968.

GUILAIN P. DENOEUX

CHAMOUN, DANY
[1934–1990]

Leader of Lebanon's National Liberal Party.

Son of former President Camille Chamoun, Dany Chamoun became active in Lebanese politics during the 1975 civil war, when he assumed the leadership of the Tigers, the small militia of his father's National Liberal Party (NLP). After the Tigers were thoroughly defeated by the Lebanese Forces in July 1980, Dany Chamoun was forced into exile in Paris. When his father died, in August 1987, he inherited the leadership of the NLP and returned to Beirut. From 1989 to 1990, he backed General Michel Aoun and opposed Syrian influence in Lebanon. He was assassinated in his Beirut apartment on 21 October 1990, together with his wife and two of their young children.

See also AOUN, MICHEL; CHAMOUN, CAMILLE; LEBANESE CIVIL WAR (1975–1990); NATIONAL LIBERAL PARTY.

Bibliography

Hiro, Dilip. *Lebanon: Fire and Embers: A History of the Lebanese Civil War.* New York: St. Martin's, 1993.

Randal, Jonathan C. *Going All the Way: Christian Warlords, Israeli Adventurers, and the War in Lebanon.* New York: Viking, 1983.

GUILAIN P. DENOEUX

CHAMPOLLION, JEAN-FRANÇOIS
[1790–1832]

French linguist and historian whose breakthrough in 1822 in deciphering hieroglyphics made him the founder of modern Egyptology.

The availability of the Rosetta Stone (uncovered in 1799) and other inscriptions, together with his mastery of Coptic, were the prerequisites to Jean-François Champollion's success. The Rosetta Stone's text was inscribed in two languages (Egyptian and Greek) and three writing systems—Greek, hieroglyphics, and demotic (a form of ancient Egyptian cursive writing). Having started studying Eastern languages as a child, Champollion recognized that the scriptural language of the Coptic Christian church was the latest form of ancient Egyptian.

As conservator of Egyptian antiquities at the Louvre museum in Paris, Champollion arranged the impressive Egyptian galleries, which opened in 1827. In 1828 and 1829, he and Ippolito Rosellini led a French–Tuscan expedition to Egypt to copy inscriptions from the ancient monuments. Champollion died at forty-two, leaving his elder brother Jacques-Joseph Champollion-Figeac to publish many of his manuscript works.

Bibliography

Dawson, Warren R., and Uphill, Eric P. *Who Was Who in Egyptology*, 2d edition. London: Egypt Exploration Society, 1972.

DONALD MALCOLM REID

CHAMRAN, MOSTAFA
[1931–1981]

Iranian political activist.

Born in Tehran, Mostafa Chamran was an engineer by training, having earned a Ph.D. in electromechanics from the University of California at Berkeley in 1962. While studying in the United States, he cofounded, with Sadeq Qotbzadeh and Ibrahim Yazdi, the Muslim Students Association, which opposed the shah. He entered political life during the days of the nationalization of the Iranian oil industry and the premiership of Mohammad Mossadegh (1951–1953) as a member of the National Resistance Movement, the more religiously inclined branch of Mossadegh's National Front. In the 1970s he moved to Lebanon and joined the AMAL group led by the Shi'ite cleric Imam Musa Sadr. After the Iranian Revolution of 1979, Chamran was assistant to the prime minister and a member of parliament, until his mysterious death on the frontline during the war between Iran and Iraq. In addition to being a political activist, Chamran was also the author of several collections of mystical poetry.

See also AMAL; IRANIAN REVOLUTION (1979); MOSSADEGH, MOHAMMAD; NATIONAL FRONT, IRAN.

NEGUIN YAVARI

CHAZAN, NAOMI
[1946–]

Member of the Knesset, political scientist, and prominent advocate of peace, dialogue, religious pluralism, and civil and women's rights.

Born in Jerusalem, Naomi Chazan received her B.A. at Columbia University and earned a Ph.D. at Hebrew University (1975). Director of the Truman Institute for Peace Studies at Hebrew University (1990–1992), then professor of political science and African studies (1994), Chazan has published widely on comparative politics, women's rights, and Israeli-Arab relations, and has occupied leading positions in the Israeli branches of the Society for International Development and the International Association of Political Science. She is better known, however, as an activist and politician.

As cofounder of a series of feminist organizations—the Israel Women's Network (1984), the Israel Women's Peace Net (1989), the Jerusalem Link/Engendering the Peace Process (1996–1998, with Hanan Ashrawi), and the Center for Women in Politics in Israel—Chazan has frequently focused public attention on the link between militarism and obstacles to women's rights, and on the unique contributions made by women peace activists. A member of the left-wing Zionist Meretz party executive, Chazan entered the Knesset in 1992, became deputy speaker in 1996, and has been one of the most active legislators, focusing on social issues, women's rights, and foreign affairs. She has been prominent in Peace Now, an active supporter of the unofficial Geneva Accord of 2003, and a leading campaigner for the rights of non-Orthodox Jews in Israel.

See also GENDER: GENDER AND LAW; GENDER: GENDER AND POLITICS; ISRAEL: POLITICAL PARTIES IN; KNESSET; PEACE NOW.

Bibliography

Swirski, Barbara, and Safir, Marilyn P., eds. *Calling the Equality Bluff: Women in Israel.* New York: Teachers College Press, 1993.

GEORGE R. WILKES

CHÉDID, ANDRÉE
[1920–]

One of the most prominent and prolific authors writing in French from the Middle East.

Andrée Chédid was born in Cairo, Egypt, in 1920 to a Lebanese family. After receiving her B.A. from the American University in Cairo and marrying, at twenty-one, Louis Chédid, she moved with her husband to Paris, where she has been living since 1946. Although her first collection of poems was written in English (*On the Trails of My Fancy,* 1943), most of Chédid's work is in French, and includes novels, short stories, plays, essays, and poetry, as well as children's books.

Like other francophone writers from the Middle East such as Amin Maalouf, Andrée Chédid is a product of both the Orient and the West. This hybrid aspect is reflected in her entire work, whose universality and humanity appeal to readers throughout the world. In most of her early novels, such as *Le sommeil délivré* (1952; *Sleep Unbound*), *Le sixième jour* (1960; *The Sixth Day*), *L'autre* (1969; *The Other*), and *Nefertiti et le rêve d'Akhnaton* (1974; *Nefertiti and Akhnaton's Dream*), Chédid used her native Middle East as the setting for her stories. Her poetry deals with nature, love and brotherhood, but is also an outcry against the violence and wars that constantly devastate not only the Middle East, but the entire world. Her plays, such as *The Goddess Lar* (1977), *Les nombres* (1965; *The Numbers*), and *Le montreur* (1967, *The Showman*), deal with the disenfranchisement of women in traditional societies. More recent works include the poems *Guerres* (1999; *Wars*); *Territoires du souffle* (1999; *Territories of Breath*), and *Le souffle des choses* (2000; *The Breath of Things*), and the novel *Le message* (2000; *The Message*).

Most of Chédid's writings have been translated into more than fifteen languages, and two of her novels, *L'autre (The Other)* and *Le sixième jour (The Sixth Day)* were made into films by, respectively, Bernard Giraudeau (1990) and Youssef Chahine (1996).

See also LITERATURE: ARABIC.

Bibliography

Knapp, Bettina. *Andrée Chédid.* Amsterdam: Rodopi, 1984.

NABIL BOUDRAA

CHEHAB, BASHIR
[1767–1850]

Early nineteenth-century ruler in Lebanon.

Bashir Chehab (sometimes Shihab) born in Ghazir, was converted to Christianity with the rest of his family. Growing up in poverty, he may have received some elementary education at home. He subse-

After consolidating his power in Lebanon, Bashir Cheheb built a lavish palace at Bayt al-Din. © ROGER WOOD/CORBIS. REPRODUCED BY PERMISSION.

quently went to Bayt al-Din, where land had been left to him by his father. Chehab's rise to power was not accidental. He first became wealthy by marrying the widow of a relative, and he cultivated good relations with al-Jazzar in Acre. When the rule of his relative Prince Yusuf became intolerable, Ahmad al-Jazzar chose him as his replacement in 1789 with the support of the Jumblatts. When Yusuf went to Acre to regain his throne, he was briefly reappointed ruler of Lebanon. Chehab, however, was able to persuade al-Jazzar to reverse his decision, and Yusuf was arrested and executed.

But Chehab's rule remained precarious, depending on the whims of al-Jazzar. In 1793, 1794, and 1798, al-Jazzar appointed Yusuf's sons as princes of Lebanon. The occupation of Egypt by Napoléon and his advance toward Palestine secured Chehab's position for a while. When the French besieged Acre, al-Jazzar asked for Chehab's help; Chehab declined, citing the instability of the situation. He also refused to aid the French, fearing the wrath of the Druzes if he did so, because the French were supported by the Maronites. When the French withdrew, al-Jazzar, intent on punishing Chehab, appointed five different people to challenge his authority. Chehab fled Lebanon and sought support from the Ottoman Empire. He remained in fear of al-Jazzar until the latter died in 1804.

Beginning in 1804, Chehab focused on consolidating his rule. Al-Jazzar had turned the Druze landlords against him, and he punished the latter by curtailing their economic and political power. Even members of his own family were not spared—many were killed and their holdings confiscated. By 1806, Chehab was promoting himself as the undisputed amir, and he built an opulent palace at Bayt al-Din that is now a tourist attraction. Chehab was secure in his position until 1819, when Abdullah Pasha took over as *wali* of Acre and demanded additional taxes from Chehab. The resulting protests and turmoil forced Chehab to abandon his emirate in 1820 and flee to Hawran. The resulting chaos alarmed Abdullah, who allowed Chehab to return in 1821. Chehab quickly reestablished order, for which he was rewarded with Abdullah's support of his claims against the *vilaye* of Damascus. When Abdullah was removed by the sultan, Chehab went to Egypt. There he befriended Muhammad Ali, who secured his reappointment.

Chehab's return to Lebanon marked the beginning of the disintegration of the emirate. Intoxicated with the backing of Muhammad Ali, Chehab assumed that a crackdown against Jumblatti Druzes would be safe; he had Bashir Jumblatt, the leader of the Druze community, killed. The Druzes never forgave him. The advance of Ibrahim Pasha to Acre in 1831 forced Chehab to provide help—against the wishes of the Druzes and to the delight of the Maronites. Fighting broke out between Druzes and Maronites. When Ottoman and European forces landed in Lebanon to expel Ibrahim Pasha from Syria, Chehab was evacuated on a British ship. He died in Istanbul.

See also AHMAD AL-JAZZAR; BONAPARTE, NAPOLÉON; IBRAHIM IBN MUHAMMAD ALI; JUMBLATT FAMILY; MUHAMMAD ALI.

Bibliography

Harik, Ilya F. *Politics and Change in a Traditional Society: Lebanon, 1711–1845.* Princeton, NJ: Princeton University Press, 1968.

Makdisi, Ussama. *The Culture of Sectarianism: Community, History, and Violence in Nineteenth-Century Ottoman Lebanon.* Berkeley: University of California Press, 2000.

AS'AD ABUKHALIL

CHEHAB FAMILY

A politically influential family in Lebanon.

The Chehab (also Shihab) family can be traced to Arab tribes from Hawran, Syria, who settled in southern Lebanon. The power of the family was established in 1697, when it inherited the leadership of the Mount Lebanon area from the last Ma'nid prince, who had no heirs. Originally a Sunni Muslim, Bashir II converted to Maronite Christianity, which displeased the Druze population in the mountains. Family members continued to occupy important positions in government and administration in the twentieth century. Its best-known member is General Fu'ad Chehab, one of the most powerful and popular presidents in twentieth-century Lebanon.

See also CHEHAB, BASHIR; CHEHAB, FU'AD; LEBANON, MOUNT.

AS'AD ABUKHALIL

CHEHAB, FU'AD
[1902–1975]

The most important Lebanese statesman of the twentieth century.

Fu'ad Chehab (sometimes Shihab) was born to a Maronite family. During the French Mandate, he served in the Special Forces of the Levant, established by the French government to legitimize their presence in Lebanon, and rose to the rank of lieutenant colonel. In 1946, with the official withdrawal of all French troops from Lebanon, Chehab was appointed the first commander in chief of the Lebanese army. He transformed the French-created force into a small national army, modernized the forces, and introduced Western-style military academies.

Chehab's name first appeared in a political context in 1952, when he refused to obey the orders of President Bishara al-Khuri to suppress demonstrators expressing their outrage at the corruption of Khuri's regime. Chehab strongly believed that the army should be kept out of internal political disputes. He also feared that any attempt to politicize the army would encourage a coup d'état. When al-Khuri resigned, Chehab was appointed prime minister (in effect, interim president) because the

Maronite establishment did not want to leave the country in the hands of a Sunni prime minister. Chehab led a smooth transition of power and oversaw the democratic election of Camille Chamoun as president.

When a civil war broke out in 1958, amid signs that Chamoun desired a second term (contrary to the provisions of the constitution and the wishes of the Lebanese) and wanted to use the army to crush the rebels, Chehab again refused to commit troops to support the president. His stance won him the backing of Lebanese Muslims. He feared that the deployment of troops would aggravate the social tensions in the country. His neutral position in those critical times made him the logical choice for the presidency, and with the support of Egypt (Nasserist) and the United States, Chehab was elected president in July 1958.

As president, Chehab initiated reforms to create an efficient and noncorrupt bureaucracy. He wanted to promote representatives of the professional middle class in order to end the monopolization of political power by traditional *zu'ama* (landholding elites). He also furthered social concord at home by transcending the sectarian interests of most politicians. Unlike other presidents of Lebanon, he was aware that political radicalism among Muslims was deeply rooted in socioeconomic dissatisfaction. He initiated a program of development in poor Muslim areas, although it did not, according to critics, go far enough. His presidency was not without problems. So disgusted was Chehab with the petty considerations and interests of the traditional political class that he tried to undermine their power by consolidating the security apparatus, which was accountable only to him. The rule of the Deuxième Bureau instilled fear and intimidation among civilians (especially Palestinians) and politicians.

The term *Chehabism* came to denote the political movement that pledged allegiance to the president. Unlike other political movements of the twentieth century, his power base cut across sectarian lines. Uninterested in power and politics, Chehab tried to resign before the end of his term, but was not allowed to do so by the deputies in parliament. He was succeeded in the presidency by his protégé Charles Hilu. Chehab shunned the limelight and rarely gave interviews. He died in seclusion.

See also CHAMOUN, CAMILLE; HILU, CHARLES; KHURI, BISHARA AL-.

Bibliography

Bangio, Ofra, and Ben-Dor, Gabriel, eds. *Minorities and the State in the Arab World.* Boulder, CO: Lynne Rienner Publishers, 1999.

El Khazen, Farid. *The Breakdown of the State in Lebanon, 1967–1976.* Cambridge, MA: Harvard University Press, 2000.

AS'AD ABUKHALIL

CHEHAB, KHALID
[1892–1978]

Lebanese prime minister (1937, 1952–1953), minister of finance (1927–1928), deputy, and speaker of parliament (1936–1937).

Born in Hasbeya, Lebanon, Khalid Chehab was first elected to the Lebanese parliament in 1922. A member of Bishara al-Khuri's Constitutional Bloc, he was minister of finance from 1927 to 1928. Following a short tenure as speaker of Parliament, he was appointed prime minister in 1937. Although he was one of the most influential Lebanese politicians under the French mandate, he is best remembered for the seven months during which he served as President Camille Chamoun's first prime minister (30 September 1952 to 30 April 1953). Chamoun, who had been elected with a mandate to modernize the administration, entrusted him with this important task. As head of a four-man cabinet, Chehab wielded emergency powers and issued several dozen decrees that consolidated the administration by defining much more clearly than before the responsibilities of civil servants and of the administrative departments. Other significant accomplishments of his cabinet included giving women the right to vote, changing the electoral system in a way that weakened the power of traditional patrons, substantially reforming the judiciary, and liberalizing the press law. Well-established persons who had been hurt by his policies acted in coordination with radical critics to force his resignation.

See also CHAMOUN, CAMILLE; CONSTITUTIONAL BLOC; KHURI, BISHARA AL-.

Bibliography

Hudson, Michael C. *The Precarious Republic: Political Modernization in Lebanon.* Boulder, CO: Westview Press, 1985.

Longrigg, Stephen H. *Syria and Lebanon under the French Mandate.* London and New York: Oxford University Press, 1958.

GUILAIN P. DENOEUX

CHELOW

See FOOD: CHELOW

CHENIK, MUHAMMAD

[1889–1976]

Tunisian businessman and political figure.

During World War II, as a member of Tunisia's Grand Council, Muhammad Chenik was chosen in 1942 by the bey, Muhammad al-Munsif, to lead a pro-nationalist government. The effort was suppressed by the Free French the following year. In 1950, with the campaign for the independence of Tunisia in full swing, Chenik was picked to head a new government that featured a Tunisian majority. In 1952, during a French repression of the nationalist movement, Chenik and his cabinet, along with Habib Bourguiba and other leading activists for nationalism, were arrested.

See also BOURGUIBA, HABIB.

Bibliography

Hahn, Lorna. *North Africa: Nationalism to Nationhood.* Washington, DC: Public Affairs Press, 1960.

MATTHEW S. GORDON

CHERKES

See CIRCASSIANS

CHINA AND THE MIDDLE EAST

Since the late 1980s, China's Middle East policy primarily revolves around its desire to maximize its economic interests without becoming entangled in political controversies.

Since the establishment of the People's Republic of China on 1 October 1949, China has had a roller-coaster relationship with the region. Periodic domestic upheavals and its long exclusion from the United Nations (UN) resulted in China oscillating from isolation and disengagement to active involvement with groups and movements hostile to Middle Eastern regimes. Even though the Bandung Conference (1955) opened the doors to the Middle East, Chinese diplomatic progress was slow and painful. Conservative Middle Eastern regimes that were apprehensive of atheist communist ideology were further threatened by China's identification with revolutionary regimes such as Egypt and Iraq and its support of radical movements. Likewise, some Middle Eastern countries maintained diplomatic relations with the breakaway Taiwanese republic, and this in turn raised concerns in Beijing.

China's admission to the UN in 1971 resulted in a nuanced foreign policy, and confident of its international recognition and acceptance, China toned down its criticism of the conservative monarchies and began adopting a friendlier posture with all the major countries. The emergence of pragmatic leadership of Deng Xiaoping in 1978 brought about significant shifts in China's Middle East policy.

As part of its four modernization processes, China commercialized its arms supplies and looked to the Middle East as a prime customer. The prolonged Iran–Iraq War in the 1980s and the U.S.–U.S.S.R. arms embargo upon the warring nations proved advantageous to China. As Iran and Iraq looked to Beijing for arms supplies, Chinese weapons were in action on both sides of the Shatt al-Arab waterway. Military modernization also compelled China to look to Israel as a possible ally, and military ties were established between the two long before the establishment of political relations.

In the 1980s China actively promoted proliferation of nonconventional weapons and helped countries such as Iran, Iraq, and Syria to acquire missile capabilities. The Saudi apprehension over the intensification of missile attacks during the Iran–Iraq War enabled China to conclude a multibillion-dollar deal for the supply of CSS-2 intermediate-range ballistic missiles to Riyadh, with whom China had not yet established normal relations.

Israel occupies an important position in China's Middle East policy. Even though the Jewish state was the first Middle Eastern country to recognize the People's Republic of China (in January 1950), it was the last country in the region to be recognized by China (in January 1992). Initial Israeli reluctance, owing to perceived pressure from the United States, was followed by Chinese recognition of the political value of and ideological affinity to the Palestinian cause. The Suez Crisis of 1956 alienated China further. Political rivalry with Moscow and ideological competition with Washington influenced China to become the staunchest supporter of the Palestinian cause, and in January 1965 it became the first non-Arab power to recognize the Palestine Liberation Organization (PLO). Besides political support, Beijing also provided military support and training to various Palestinian groups.

The 1990 Iraq invasion of Kuwait tested China's diplomatic skills and threatened its delicate relations with countries such as Saudi Arabia. Unwilling to join the U.S.-led coalition and unprepared to abandon Iraq, its political ally and economic market, during the critical UN Security Council vote authorizing the use of force to expel Iraqi forces from Kuwait (Resolution 678) China abstained. This tacit support endorsed the liberation of Kuwait without unduly damaging the Sino-Iraqi relations.

The resolution of the Kuwait crisis, coupled with the disintegration of the Soviet Union, the end of the Cold War, and the emergence of the United States as the preeminent global power, posed new challenges to China. Eager to participate in the Madrid peace process, in January 1992 China recognized and established diplomatic ties with Israel. Greater Chinese emphasis on economic relations is strengthened by increasing Chinese dependence upon Middle East for its hydrocarbon requirements. As China's economic growth continues, its energy needs shape its Middle East policy, especially towards countries such as Iraq and Iran, which were identified by U.S. president George W. Bush as part of an "Axis of Evil." During the Iraq war of 2003, China vehemently demanded Iraq to comply with the UN Security Council Resolution 1441 but opposed the use of force to secure Iraqi compliance. However, when the war broke out, China's Middle East policy reflected the traditional policy of seeking to maximize its economic interests without becoming entangled in political controversies.

Zhou Enlai, first premier of the People's Republic of China, attends the African Asian Conference with Egyptian president Nasser (third from left). It was during the later years of Zhou's reign that China's position towards the conservative Middle Eastern monarchies began to soften. © BETTMANN/CORBIS. REPRODUCED BY PERMISSION.

See also BANDUNG CONFERENCE (1955); IRAN–IRAQ WAR (1980–1988); WAR IN IRAQ (2003).

Bibliography

Bin-Huwaidin, Mohamed. *China's Relations with Arabia and the Gulf, 1949–1999.* London: RoutledgeCurzon, 2002.

Calabrese, John. *China's Changing Relations with the Middle East.* New York: Frances Pinter, 1991.

Gladney, Dru C. "Sino-Middle Eastern Perspective and Relations since the Gulf War: Views from Below." *International Journal of Middle Eastern Studies* 26 (1994): 677–691.

Harris, Lillian Craig. *China Considers the Middle East.* London: I. B. Tauris, 1992.

Kumaraswamy, P. R., ed. *China and the Middle East: The Quest for Influence.* New Delhi: Sage, 1999.

Shichor, Yitzhak. *The Middle East in Chinese Foreign Policy, 1949–1977.* New York: Cambridge University Press, 1979.

KAZUO TAKAHASKI
UPDATED BY P. R. KUMARASWAMY

CHOLERA

See DISEASES

CHRAIBI, DRISS
[1926–]

Moroccan novelist.

Born in al-Jadida to a Muslim Berber family, Driss Chraibi studied at the French lycée Lyautey in Casablanca. He received a college degree in chemistry in 1950 and went on to study neurology and psychiatry. Two months before qualifying for his doctorate in science, he gave up his studies and decided to travel in Europe while working at various jobs.

In his early novels, *Le passé simple* (1954; The simple past) and its sequel *Succession ouverte* (1962; Heirs to the past), Chraibi drew on his own experiences to depict the generational conflict and culture shock experienced by Moroccan youth. *Les Boucs* (1955; The Butts) describes the harsh living conditions of the Maghribi workers in France. In his next novels, *L'ane* (1956; The donkey) and *La foule* (1961), Chraibi conveys his views as a Muslim Maghribi vis-à-vis the West, whose civilization and philosophy he had acquired through education. A biting tone was set through the author's sense of cynical amusement in *La foule*, but much lighter humor was evident in *La civilisation, ma mère* (1971; Mother comes of age). In *De tous les horizons* (1958; From all horizons), a book described as narration *(récits)*, Chraibi again tapped into his personal experiences, with his parents and as a Maghribi in France.

The novel *Une enquête au pays* (1981; Flutes of death) marked a turning point for Chraibi: He embarked on a quest for his Berber identity, exploring pre-Islamic times and emphasizing the ties of Berbers with the land of the Maghrib and on the relatively recent Arabization and Islamization of North Africa. He continued the quest in *La mère du printemps (L'oum-er-Bia)* (1982; Mother spring). As a consequence, Chraibi found himself trying to dissociate himself from Arabic and the Arabs without rejecting the Islam brought to the Maghrib by the Arabs. A few of Chraibi's novels focus on more general topics—for example, the condition of the emancipated woman in *Un ami viendra vous voir* (1967; A

friend will come to see you) and the story of a man and woman's struggle to establish a relationship in *Mort au Canada* (1975; Death in Canada). More recent works include the novels *Naissance à l'aube* (1986; Birth at dawn) and *L'Inspecteur Ali* (1991; Inspector Ali), and the nonfiction work *Une place au soleil* (1993; A place in the sun).

In 1994 Chraibi published a fictionalized biography of the prophet Muhammad, *L'homme du livre* (1998; Muhammad), an account of the two days that preceded the Revelation. His latest work is an autobiography, *Vu, lu, entendu* (1998; Seen, read, heard).

See also MAGHRIB.

Bibliography

Abdel-Jaouad, Hédi. *Encyclopedia of African Literature,* edited by Simon Gikandi. London: Routledge, 2003.

Jack, Belinda. *Francophone Literatures. An Introductory Survey.* New York: Oxford University Press, 1996.

AIDA A. BAMIA

CHRAKIAN, ARTIN
[1804–1859]

An Armenian, minister of commerce and foreign affairs in Egypt, 1844–1850.

Artin Chrakian was born in Istanbul. His father, Sukias Chrakian, managed the commercial affairs of Tosun Pasha, one of the older sons of Muhammad Ali, the *vali* of Egypt. Sukias emigrated to Egypt in 1812, and two years later, his family followed him there. Artin Chrakian, his brother Khosrov, and a third Armenian, Aristakes Altunian, were allowed to attend school in the palace, where the young prince Abbas, later to inherit the governorship of Egypt, was one of their classmates. Sent to Paris, Artin Chrakian studied civil administration. His education completed, he returned to Egypt and began working at the war ministry at the mundane chore of translating French military manuals into Turkish. In succeeding years, however, Chrakian, along with other Armenian colleagues, was entrusted with the responsibility of reorganizing the educational system in the country. In May 1834, he opened the School of Engineering at Bulak, and in September of the same year, in conjunction with another Armenian, Stepan Demirjian, he opened the School of Translation in the citadel of Cairo. In 1836, he was appointed a member of the school council, which subsequently became the ministry of education.

By this time, Chrakian was a full-fledged member of the administrative machinery governing Egypt. His appointment as a member of the *majlis al-ali,* the council for civil affairs, brought him in direct contact with the viceroy. From then on, his promotion was rapid. Muhammad Ali chose him as his first secretary in 1839 and sent him as an envoy to Paris and London in 1841. Upon the death of Boghos Bey in 1844, Chrakian succeeded as minister of commerce and foreign affairs. He remained in that post during the regency of Ibrahim ibn Muhammad Ali. Along with many other Armenians in the employ of the Egyptian government, he fell out of favor after Abbas assumed the post of viceroy. He was removed from office in 1850 and went into exile in Europe. He returned after Sa'id, the succeeding viceroy, invited him back to Egypt. Chrakian may have been the first Armenian in Egypt to receive the hereditary title of pasha.

See also IBRAHIM IBN MUHAMMAD ALI.

Bibliography

Adalian, Rouben. "The Armenian Colony of Egypt during the Reign of Muhammad Ali (1805–1848)." *Armenian Review* 33, no. 2 (1980): 115–144.

ROUBEN P. ADALIAN

CHRISTIANS IN THE MIDDLE EAST

Originally a Jewish offshoot, Christianity has been present in the Middle East since the first century C.E.

Christianity is based on the spiritual and ethical teachings of Jesus of Nazareth, who lived and preached in Judea during the first century C.E. and was crucified by the Roman authorities; adherents of the faith believe he rose from the dead. To Christians, Jesus was the awaited Messiah of the Jewish people (*christos,* "the anointed one," is a Greek translation of "Messiah"). His teachings were compiled in the Gospels, which, together with the teachings of his earliest followers, the Apostles, form the corpus of the New Testament. These twenty-seven books, along with the Jewish Bible and the books of the Apocrypha, make up the Christian Bible.

History of Christians in the Middle East

Although the earliest Christians were all Jews, some time around 45 C.E. some of the Apostles—especially Paul and Barnabas—began to preach to the Gentiles throughout the Near East. Antioch, Edessa, and Alexandria emerged as early centers of Christianity. By the fourth century the spread and influence of Christianity were such that it had become the official religion of the Roman Empire, whose capital had been moved by the emperor Constantine from Rome to Constantinople. At that time, too, the religion underwent a series of theological disputes centered primarily on the relationship of the divine and human nature of Christ. At the Council of Chalcedon (451), those that stressed the unitary nature of Christ (the Monophysites) were deemed heretical. (They constituted the Oriental Orthodox family of churches.) The Eastern Orthodox (Greek) Church, centered at Constantinople, remained the official imperial church of the Byzantine Empire. With the expansion of the Latin-based, Western-rite church centered at Rome and looking west to Europe, the theologies, languages, and rituals of the two centers of Christianity—Constantinople and Rome—developed in their distinctive fashions, leading ultimately to the formal split of 1054. Throughout the formative period of Christianity, the Middle Eastern churches—Coptic, Armenian, Chaldean (centered in Iraq), Assyrian, and Syrian Orthodox (Jacobite)—drew their followers from the indigenous population, most of whom eventually converted to Islam after the invasions of the seventh century. The Western, Roman Catholic Church became interested in the region once again after the period of the Crusades (eleventh to fourteenth centuries). The churches of the Protestant Reformation (sixteenth century) were not yet in existence.

European economic and political penetration of the Ottoman Empire began in the sixteenth century with the issuance of capitulations to France; missionary work was initiated, as were attempts to reconcile the Eastern churches with Rome. The Catholic and Uniate churches in the Middle East (Syrian Catholic, Armenian Catholic, Chaldean Catholic, and Greek Catholic churches) that looked to Rome for authority date from the seventeenth and eighteenth century, except for the Maronite Church, whose union with Rome was initiated in the twelfth century. The Uniate churches, Eastern-rite churches that acknowledged the pope's authority, retained only a minority of Christianity's adherents. Protestantism came into the region through the efforts of, primarily, U.S. and British missionaries in the nineteenth century.

European strategic interests and the "Eastern Question" dovetailed with renewed religious interest in the Holy Land. Protection of Christian minorities by the European powers and the installation of Anglican and Roman Catholic institutions in Jerusalem were part of a growing European agenda to represent the interests of the various Christian minorities. Altercations over Christian holy sites led to the outbreak of the Crimean War. The fact that there are only four historical patriarchates and many contenders for their leadership has led to intercommunal acrimony. For example, Monophysite Copts, Catholic Copts, and Greek Orthodox Copts claimed the patriarchate of Alexandria; and Maronite, Greek, and Syrian Catholics, as well as the Greek Orthodox and the Jacobites, claimed the patriarchate of Antioch.

Christian communities were a part of the Millet system of the Ottoman Empire, which in turn was an elaboration of the *dhimmi* status given to Christians and Jews in early Islamic times. This system provided a measure of toleration, freedom of worship, and self-governance for the Christian communities, but always under the Islamic umbrella. Under this system Christians were barred from certain public offices and suffered certain legal disabilities vis-à-vis their Muslim neighbors. Proselytism was prohibited, as was conversion to Christianity from Islam.

Secular Nationalism and Christianity

It is therefore not surprising that Christians were among the more enthusiastic advocates of secular nationalist ideas at the turn of the twentieth century. They were also influenced by foreign mission schools, where such ideas were taught and discussed. Christians thus became prominent among the secular Palestinian and Lebanese leadership, and a Christian, Michel Aflaq, was one of the theorists of

the Ba'th movement that provided the ideology for modern Iraq and Syria. An important exception to this tendency has been a sector of Lebanon's Maronite population, which has favored the creation in Lebanon of a Christian enclave.

The challenge posed to secular nationalism by Islamist movements has led some Christians to reexamine their advocacy of secularism, but it remains the most attractive option for the majority of Christians in the region. Census figures for Middle Eastern countries, particularly as they reflect religious affiliation, are notoriously unreliable or, in some instances, nonexistent. An educated estimate, however, would put the number of Christians in the region at 8 to 12 million. Emigration, however, has been a growing trend in recent decades. The Christian population of Jerusalem, for example, has shrunk from 26,000 in 1948 to an estimated 6,000. The number of Syrian Orthodox people in southeast Turkey dwindled from about 30,000 in 1980 to 7,500 in 1992. There are no reliable figures for Christian emigration from Lebanon, but anecdotal evidence suggests that the proportion of Christians there has dropped from roughly 50 percent to 30 or 35 percent during the course of Lebanon's sixteen-year civil war. In 2001, out of a total population of 3,500,000 Lebanese, the number of Christians hovered between 1,300,000 and 1,500,000. There are a large number of Lebanese Christians who live in the diaspora. Reasons frequently cited for emigration are war, including the Gulf War (1991), poor economic prospects, and anxieties about the future. Despite the deteriorating situation of Christians in the Middle East—or perhaps in response to it—Christian churches in the region have reached a historically unparalleled degree of unity in recent years. In 1974 the Middle East Council of Churches, based in Beirut, brought together the two Orthodox families and the Protestants for common witness and service. In 1987 the Catholic family joined this council.

The Eastern (Greek) Orthodox Church

The Eastern Orthodox Church in the Middle East developed around the four patriarchates of the early church: Jerusalem, Antioch, Alexandria, and Constantinople. During the Ottoman period the Eastern Orthodox millet (community) was represented

Greek Orthodox Christians take part in a Christmas procession in Manger Square, Bethlehem. In the city of Jerusalem and elsewhere in the Middle East, there is a gulf between the Greek leadership of the Eastern Orthodox Church and its predominantly Arab parishioners; only the patriarch of Antioch is an Arab. © HANAN ISACHAR/CORBIS. REPRODUCED BY PERMISSION.

before the sultan by the patriarch of Constantinople, the ecumenical patriarch, who was considered *primus inter pares* among the patriarchs. Of the other patriarchates, which serve predominantly Arab parishioners, only one—that of Antioch—has an Arab serving as patriarch. The patriarchs of Alexandria and Jerusalem are Greeks who preside over Greek hierarchies. Particularly in the see of Jerusalem, this has created a gulf between Palestinian and Jordanian parishioners and their leadership. Of the four patriarchates the largest, both geographically and numerically (about 760,000), is Antioch. This patriarchate includes Syria, Israel, Iraq, Iran, and Kuwait, with a few parishes in southern Turkey. The smallest is Constantinople—the Greek Orthodox population in Turkey has dwindled to about 3,000. The ecumenical patriarchate, however, continues to exercise leadership for the Greek Orthodox diaspora outside the Middle East.

The Oriental Orthodox Churches

The Oriental Orthodox family in the Middle East includes three other churches: Coptic Orthodox, Armenian Apostolic Orthodox, and Syrian Orthodox (Jacobite). The largest of the three—indeed, the largest denomination in the Middle East—is the Coptic Orthodox, numbering perhaps 5.5 to 6 million. The Armenian Apostolic Orthodox Church includes four jurisdictions in the Middle East: the patriarchates of Jerusalem and Constantinople and the catholicates of Cilicia (based in Beirut) and Etchmiadzin, Armenia. The Syrian Orthodox Church—whose patriarch presides from Damascus, just a few buildings away from the Greek Orthodox patriarchate of Antioch—had its heartland in what is now southeastern Turkey, northern Iraq, and northern Syria. In recent years disturbances in Turkey (related both to the Kurdish question and to the Gulf War) have contributed to the emigration of many

Iraqi Christians gathered in the Chaldean Church of Saint Ephraim, in the northern city of Mosul, and in other churches on 20 April 2003 to celebrate the first Easter mass since the fall of Saddam Hussein. About 250,000 Christians in Iraq, or 75 percent of the total Christian population there, are Chaldean Catholics, whose head is the patriarch of Babylon. © AFP/Corbis. Reproduced by permission.

members of this community to Syria and Lebanon or to Europe and North America. The Syrian Orthodox people, locally called Suryanis, continue to speak their ancient Syriac dialect and use it in their liturgy.

Eastern Rite and Latin Catholics

The Eastern-rite Catholic churches owe their origins to Roman Catholic missionary activity in the sixteenth through the nineteenth centuries. These churches follow in general the rites of the orthodox churches from which their membership was drawn, but they acknowledge the primacy of the pope.

The Greek Catholic (or Melkite) church drew from Greek Orthodox membership. The patriarch of this church—the largest of the Middle East eastern-rite Catholic churches, at about 450,000 members—presides in Damascus. The largest concentrations of

Greek Catholics are found in Lebanon, Syria, Israel and the West Bank, and Jordan.

The Coptic Catholic, Armenian Catholic, and Syrian Catholic churches are related historically to the three corresponding Oriental Orthodox churches. The largest is the Coptic Catholic, with about 100,000 members. The patriarch of this church resides in Cairo. The Syrian Catholic Church was reorganized by the Ottoman authorities in the nineteenth century. The Syrian Catholics, unlike their Orthodox brethren, use the Latin liturgy instead of the Syriac. Today, Syrian Catholics number about 80,000. The patriarchal sees of both the Syrian and Armenian Catholic churches are located in Beirut.

The Chaldaean Catholic Church, whose head is the patriarch of Babylon, historically drew its membership primarily from the Assyrian church of the

East. Chaldaean Catholics constitute roughly 75 percent (250,000) of the Iraqi Christian population. In 2003 Patriarch Bidawid passed away in the midst of the U.S.-led war against the Iraqi regime.

The two other Middle Eastern Catholic churches are the Maronite and Latin Catholic churches. The early history of the Maronites is clouded in legend, but it is generally agreed that their origin had to do with the fifth-century dispute over the human and divine natures of Christ. The forerunners of the Maronites, seeking to find a compromise between the contending parties, proposed a "monothelite," or "one will," position. By the thirteenth century the Maronites, who four centuries earlier had sought refuge in the mountains of Lebanon, had concluded an agreement with the Church of Rome, whereby the primacy of the Pope was acknowledged. Like the Eastern Orthodox patriarch in Antioch and the Greek Catholic and Syrian Catholic primates, the Maronite patriarch bears the title Patriarch of Antioch and All the East. The Maronites remain the largest of Lebanon's recognized Christian sects. Given the vacuum in political leadership, the Maronite patriarch Nasrallah Sfeir has in recent years become both the spiritual and political leader of his community.

The Latin Catholic patriarchate was first established in Jerusalem in 1099 and subsequently moved to Acre. Effectively terminated in the latter part of the thirteenth century, it was reestablished in Jerusalem in 1847. The Latin Catholics in the Middle East are, for the most part, expatriates from Europe and North America—with the important exceptions of those in Israel and the occupied territories and Jordan, where the approximately 50,000 Latin Catholics are predominantly Palestinian. The election of Michel Sabbah, a Palestinian from Nazareth, as Latin patriarch in 1987 represented the first such election of an indigenous Middle Easterner. Since his election Patriarch Sabbah played a prominent role in supporting the Palestinians' right to self-determination as well as the Israeli people's need for security, reflecting the pope's often-stated policies regarding the Israeli–Palestinian conflict. During the two Palestinian intifadas Sabbah issued statements that were thought to be controversial by other Christian groups and by the Israeli government.

Protestants

Protestants make up a tiny minority within the overall Christian minority in the Middle East. Their influence has been substantial, however, both in the fostering of the ecumenical movement in the region and in the areas of education (secondary schools, colleges, and seminaries), medicine, and publishing.

See also AFLAQ, MICHEL; CONSTANTINOPLE; COPTS; EASTERN ORTHODOX CHURCH; MARONITES; MILLET SYSTEM; MISSIONARY SCHOOLS; PROTESTANTISM AND PROTESTANT MISSIONS; ROMAN CATHOLICISM AND ROMAN CATHOLIC MISSIONS; SFEIR, NASRALLAH.

Bibliography

Betts, Robert B. *Christians in the Arab East.* Atlanta, GA: John Knox Press, 1978.

Cragg, Kenneth. *The Arab Christian: A History in the Middle East.* Louisville, KY: Westminster/John Knox Press, 1991.

Haddad, Robert. *Syrian Christians in Muslim Society.* Westport, CT: Greenwood Press, 1981.

Horner, Norman. *A Guide to Christian Churches in the Middle East.* Elkhart, IN: Mission Focus, 1989.

DALE L. BISHOP
UPDATED BY GEORGE E. IRANI

CHUBAK, SADEQ
[1916–1998]

Iranian novelist, short-story writer, playwright.

Sadeq Chubak was born in Bushehr, the son of a wealthy merchant. Chubak published his first collection of short stories, *Khaymah shab bazi* (The puppet show) in 1945. His novel *Tangsir* (A man from Tangestan) was first published in 1963 and translated into English as *One Man with His Gun* together with four short stories and a play in *Sadeq Chubak: An Anthology.* This novel was later turned into a popular movie by Amir Naderi in 1974. Chubak's other major novel, *Sang-e sabur,* was also translated into English, as *The Patient Stone.* One of the most prominent "Southern" writers, Chubak resided in California at the time of his death in 1998.

See also LITERATURE: PERSIAN.

Bibliography

Chubak, Sadeq. *The Patient Stone,* translated by M. R. Ghanoonparvar. Costa Mesa, CA: Mazda, 1989.

Chubak, Sadeq. *Sadeq Chubak: An Anthology,* edited by F. R. C. Bagley. Delmar, NY: Caravan; New York: Center for Iranian Studies, Columbia University, 1981.

Moayyad, Heshmat, ed. *Stories from Iran: A Chicago Anthology, 1921–1991.* Washington, DC: Mage, 1991.

PARDIS MINUCHEHR

CHURCHILL WHITE PAPER (1922)

A 1922 British statement of policy regarding Palestine.

Drafted by the first high commissioner of Palestine, Sir Herbert Samuel, the white paper (also called the Churchill memorandum) was issued in the name of Colonial Secretary Winston Churchill in June 1922. A year earlier the Palestinians participated in political violence against the Jews, which a British commission found to have been caused by Arab hostility "connected with Jewish immigration and with their conception of Zionist policy." Samuel therefore urged Churchill to clarify to both communities the meaning of the Balfour Declaration of November 1917 and to reassure the Palestinians.

The Churchill statement reaffirmed British commitment to the Jewish national home. It declared that the Jews were in Palestine "as a right and not on sufferance" and defined the Jewish national home as "the further development of the existing Jewish community [Yishuv], with the assistance of Jews in other parts of the world, in order that it may become a centre in which the Jewish people as a whole may take, on grounds of religion and race [sic], an interest and a pride." In order to fulfill the Balfour policy, "it is necessary that the Jewish community in Palestine should be able to increase its numbers by immigration."

At the same time, the memorandum rejected Zionist statements "to the effect that the purpose in view is to create a wholly Jewish Palestine," which would become " 'as Jewish as England is English.' " His Majesty's Government regard any such expectations as impracticable and have no such aim in view." It assured the indigenous Palestinians that the British never considered "the disappearance or the subordination of the Arabic [sic] population, language, or culture in Palestine" or even "the imposition of Jewish nationality upon the inhabitants of Palestine as a whole." In addition, the allowable number of Jewish immigrants would be limited to the "economic capacity of the country."

The Zionist leaders regarded the memorandum as a whittling down of the Balfour Declaration but acquiesced, partly because of a veiled threat from the British government and partly because, off the record, the Zionists knew that there was nothing in the paper to preclude a Jewish state. (Churchill himself testified to the Peel Commission in 1936 that no such prohibition had been intended in his 1922 memorandum.) The Palestinians rejected the paper because it reaffirmed the Balfour policy. They were convinced that continued Jewish immigration would lead to a Jewish majority that would eventually dominate or dispossess them. Both Zionist and Palestinian interpretations of the memorandum were largely valid: The British did pare down their support for the Zionist program, but the Balfour policy remained intact long enough to allow extensive Jewish immigration and the establishment of semiautonomous Jewish governmental and military institutions.

See also BALFOUR DECLARATION (1917); CHURCHILL, WINSTON S.; SAMUEL, HERBERT LOUIS; YISHUV.

Bibliography

Caplan, Neil. *Palestine Jewry and the Arab Question, 1917–1925.* London and Totowa, NJ: Cass, 1978.

Hurewitz, J. C. *The Struggle for Palestine.* New York: Greenwood, 1968.

Lesch, Ann M. *Arab Politics in Palestine, 1917–1939: The Frustrations of a Nationalist Movement.* Ithaca, NY: Cornell University Press, 1979.

PHILIP MATTAR

CHURCHILL, WILLIAM

[?–1864]

Newspaper publisher.

An Englishman affiliated with the Tory Party, William Churchill went to Constantinople (now Istanbul) in 1832, where he worked for the British embassy as a merchant and as a newspaper correspondent, particularly for the *Morning Herald.* In

1840, he founded the first private Turkish-language newspaper in the Ottoman Empire, *Ceride-i Havadis* (Journal of events). This broke the monopoly of the Ottoman state's official paper, *Takvim-i Vekayi,* published since 1831. Churchill's lively coverage of the Crimean War (1854–1856) attracted a new audience to newspaper reading. *Ceride-i Havadis* was published irregularly, roughly every one or two weeks, until 1860, when it began daily publication. The paper closed when Churchill died in 1864, although his son Alfred revived it for one year.

See also CRIMEAN WAR; NEWSPAPERS AND PRINT MEDIA: TURKEY.

Bibliography

Lewis, Bernard. *The Emergence of Modern Turkey,* 3d edition. New York: Oxford University Press, 2002.

ELIZABETH THOMPSON

CHURCHILL, WINSTON S.

[1874–1965]

British statesman; prime minister, 1940–1945 and 1951–1955.

Winston S. Churchill's connections with the Middle East were based on two concepts—the national interest of Great Britain and what he called "the harmonious disposition of the world among its peoples." These concepts were not necessarily contradictory. Thus, in advocating British support for the establishment and maintenance of independent Arab states in Transjordan, Iraq, Saudi Arabia, and Syria after World War I and the breakup of the Ottoman Empire, his objective was to produce a satisfactory harmony of local Arab needs, in the hope of creating states that would be well-disposed toward Britain and its defense and petroleum needs.

As a young soldier serving in India at the turn of the twentieth century, Churchill had seen the importance of Egypt and the Suez Canal for the maintenance of Britain's sea link with India and Asia. He had participated in the reconquest of the Sudan, where he had been repelled by the cruel attitude of the British commander in chief toward wounded Sudanese soldiers, and he had expressed his disgust in a book published in 1900. While British control of Egypt was something he took for granted (although nationalist movements were already a prob-

lem for Britain), at the same time, he was insistent that the British connection should be beneficial for the well-being and advancement of the Egyptian people.

First Direct Interaction with the Middle East

At the time of the Young Turk revolution in 1909, Churchill not only supported the modernization efforts of the Young Turks for the Ottoman Empire, but met several of their leaders during a visit to Constantinople (now Istanbul) that same year and remained in contact with them. In August 1914 when World War I began, he appealed directly to the Turkish minister of war, Enver Paşa, to keep Turkey neutral and thereby preserve the integrity of the Ottoman Empire. Two months later, when Turkey committed itself to the Central Powers (against the Allies) and began the bombardment of Russia's Black Sea ports, it fell to Britain's First Lord of the Admiralty, Churchill, to direct naval operations against Turkey. These culminated in the attack on the Dardanelles (Turkish Straits), the failure of which led to Churchill's own temporary eclipse from politics.

In 1915, Churchill suggested that once the Ottoman Empire had been defeated, Palestine should be given in trust to Belgium, since Germany had violated Belgian neutrality and overrun most of the country. As compensation for this, Churchill wanted Belgium to be made the European overseer of the establishment of a Jewish national home.

Once the war ended in 1918, Churchill became secretary for war and air (1919–1921). In 1919, at a time when Britain herself had assumed the responsibility for Palestine, Churchill encouraged the Zionist leader Dr. Chaim Weizmann to consider the southern desert region of the Negev as an area of potential Jewish settlement (in 1949, David Ben-Gurion, Israel's first prime minister, was to urge this same policy on his fellow citizens). Churchill's own instinct was, at first, to keep Britain clear of all Palestine responsibilities and even to reject the League of Nations mandate for Palestine—on the grounds, he warned the cabinet in 1920, that "the Zionist movement will cause continued friction with the Arabs." Nor were his feelings entirely supportive of Zionism: Writing in a cabinet memorandum

British prime minister Winston Churchill joins his commander in chief of Middle East forces, General Sir Claude J(ohn) E(yre) Auchinleck, in Egypt, on 23 August 1942. © AP/WIDE WORLD PHOTOS. REPRODUCED BY PERMISSION.

in 1919 of those who stood to gain from the collapse of the Ottoman Empire, he declared: "Lastly there are the Jews, whom we are pledged to introduce into Palestine, and who take it for granted that the local population will be cleared out to suit their convenience."

Views on the Formation of a Jewish State

As colonial secretary in 1921 and 1922, it then fell to Churchill to fix the terms of the Palestine mandate. His attitude on Zionism had changed. In a public article in 1920, he stated: "If, as may well happen, there should be created in our own lifetime by the banks of the Jordan a Jewish State under the protection of the British Crown which might comprise three or four millions of Jews, an event will have occurred in the history of the world which would from every point of view be beneficial, and would be especially in harmony with the truest interests of the British Empire."

Having made the link of Jewish national aspirations and British interests, Churchill was also impressed by the ideological convictions of the Zionists and by their determination to create a flourishing world for themselves in a region that had been their home many centuries earlier. During a visit to Palestine in 1921, he was impressed by the Jews' success at cultivation and by the labor Zionist work ethic—the redemption of the land through toil. Henceforth, he encouraged the Jews to enter the region, stating in the terms of the mandate, as presented to the League of Nations in 1922, that the Jews were in Palestine "of right, and not on sufferance." He also gave the Zionists monopoly rights over the development of the hydroelectric power of the country.

During this same visit to Palestine, Churchill encouraged the development of a Jewish Agency for Palestine, through which the Jews would acquire virtual autonomy over health, education, and communal life, as well as participation in the political and diplomatic discussions concerning their future. At the same time, he urged the Palestinian Arabs to accept the fact of Jewish immigration and settlement and to recognize the economic benefits that the Jews would bring to the country.

When a Palestinian Arab delegation asked Churchill to suspend all future Jewish immigration, he replied (on 28 March 1921): "It is manifestly right that the Jews, who are scattered all over the world, should have a national centre and a National Home where some of them may be reunited. And where else could that be but in this land of Palestine, with which for more than 3,000 years they have been intimately and profoundly associated? We think it will be good for the world, good for the Jews and good for the British Empire. But we also think it will be good for the Arabs who dwell in Palestine, and we intend that it shall be good for them, and that they shall not be sufferers or supplanted in the country in which they dwell or denied their share in all that makes for its progress and prosperity."

At the Cairo Conference in 1921, Churchill agreed to the establishment of Arab self-government in Iraq and Transjordan and to the exclusion of Jewish settlement in Transjordan (now Jordan). He also argued in favor of a national home for Kurds in northern Iraq but was overruled by his officials.

During the 1930s, Churchill resented the pressure of the Arab states of the Middle East to curtail Jewish immigration into Palestine. He was an opponent of the white papers on Palestine (1939), by which the British government gave the Palestinian Arabs an effective veto over any eventual Jewish majority in Palestine. He also opposed the restrictions on Jewish land purchase in Palestine. These restrictions were introduced in 1940, shortly after Churchill had reentered the government as first lord of the admiralty, and as such he opposed the use of Royal Navy warships to intercept illegal Jewish immigrant ships heading for Palestine. As prime minister in 1940, he rejected Arab calls for the deportation of illegal Jewish immigrants.

During World War II, while he was prime minister (1940–1945), Churchill had to take steps to defend the Middle East from German encroachment. Although in 1942 he failed to persuade Turkey to enter the war on the side of the Allies, he did encourage Turkish neutrality. He also secured the basing of British military experts on Turkish soil, to immobilize oil pipelines and facilities crossing Turkey from Iraq, should German troops try to cross Asia Minor in any attack through Palestine to the Suez Canal. During the war, the pro-German revolt of Rashid Ali in Iraq was thwarted and the pro-German Vichy French government in Syria was ended by British initiatives. Throughout 1940, 1941, and the first half of 1942, Egypt and the Suez Canal were defended by Allied troops against continuous Italian and German military threats. Later in the war, Palestinian Jews were encouraged to volunteer not only for British military tasks, but for clandestine parachute missions behind German lines in Europe.

As wartime prime minister, Churchill watched sympathetically over Zionist aspirations. In 1942, he warned a personal friend "against drifting into the usual anti-Zionist and antisemitic channel which it is customary for British officers to follow." A year later, he told his cabinet that he would not accept any partition plan for Palestine between Jews and Arabs "which the Jews do not accept." Even the murder of his close friend Lord Moyne by Jewish terrorists did not deflect Churchill from his belief that a Jewish state should emerge after World War II, and he called upon the Jewish Agency for Palestine to take action against the terrorist minority in their midst.

In 1945, during a meeting in Egypt, Churchill tried to persuade King Ibn Saʿud of Saudi Arabia to become the leader of a Middle East federation of independent states, in which a Jewish state would form an integral part. Only Churchill's defeat in the general election five months later prevented him from setting up a Middle East peace conference and presiding over it, with a view to establishing such a federation. In 1946, as leader of the opposition, he told the House of Commons, after a Jewish-extremist bomb in Jerusalem had killed ninety people, including many Jews, at the King David Hotel: "Had I the opportunity of guiding the course of events after the war was won a year ago, I should have faithfully pursued the Zionist cause, and I have not abandoned it today, although this is not a very popular moment to espouse it." In 1948, Churchill pressed the Labour government to recognize the State of Israel. As prime minister for the second time, from 1951 to 1955, he argued in favor of allowing merchant ships bound for Israeli ports to be allowed to use the Suez Canal—which had been taken from British control by Egypt's military in 1952 during the revolt that ended in Farouk's abdication and the establishment of the republic.

Churchill's sympathies for Zionism were public and pronounced, alienating many Arabs. Yet he was not without understanding of Arab aspirations and of the vast potential of the Middle East. "The wonderful exertions which Israel is making in these times of difficulty are cheering for an old Zionist like me," he wrote to Weizmann, the first president of the State of Israel, in 1951, and he added: "I trust you may work with Jordan and the rest of the Moslem world. With true comradeship there will be enough for all."

See also ABD AL-AZIZ IBN SAʿUD AL SAʿUD; CAIRO CONFERENCE (1921); ENVER PAŞA; FAROUK; JEWISH AGENCY FOR PALESTINE; KING DAVID HOTEL; WEIZMANN, CHAIM; WHITE PAPERS ON PALESTINE; YOUNG TURKS.

Bibliography

Gilbert, Martin. *Winston Churchill*, Vol. 4: *The Stricken World*. London and Boston: Houghton Mifflin, 1980.

Gilbert, Martin. *Churchill: A Life*. New York: Holt, 1991.

MARTIN GILBERT

CILICIA

Valley in southern Turkey situated between the Taurus Mountains and the Mediterranean Sea, bordering Syria.

Cilicia is an important agricultural region. Adana is its largest city, and Alexandretta and Mersin are its major ports. In the late nineteenth century, Cilicia's growing cotton industry attracted large numbers of Muslim refugees from the Balkans and Russia. Cilicia's centuries-old Armenian population, descended from the eleventh century Kingdom of Little Armenia in Cilicia, was largely exiled or killed in the revolts and wars of the early twentieth century. The French occupied Cilicia from 1918 to 1921, when it was incorporated by the Franklin–Bouillon Agreement into the Turkish Republic.

See also ADANA; ALEXANDRETTA.

Bibliography

Shaw, Stanford, and Shaw, Ezel Kural. *History of the Ottoman Empire and Modern Turkey.* 2 vols. Cambridge, U.K., and New York: Cambridge University Press, 1976–1977.

ELIZABETH THOMPSON

ÇILLER, TANSU
[1944–]

Turkey's first female prime minister, 1993–1996.

Tansu Çiller was born in Istanbul. After getting her B.A. in economics from Boğaziçi (Bosporus) University in 1967, she went to the United States for graduate studies. She received her M.A. from the University of New Hampshire and her Ph.D. from the University of Connecticut. Having taught for a year at Franklin and Marshall College, she returned to work at Boğaziçi University. During her academic career, she also worked as a consultant to the Istanbul Chamber of Commerce, the Istanbul Chamber of Industry, and the Turkish Industry and Business Association.

Çiller became an economic adviser to Süleyman Demirel before joining his True Path Party (DYP). In 1991, she was elected vice president of the DYP and served as minister of economy in the coalition between the DYP and the Social Democratic Populist Party. When Demirel was elected Turkey's ninth president in 1993, Çiller became the chairperson of the party. Having opted to continue the DYP-SHP coalition, she announced her government's program, which focused on fighting the Kurdistan Workers Party (PKK), combating inflation and unemployment, and promoting democracy and human rights. It was with this program that she came to be known as Turkey's "iron lady."

After the 1995 elections, Çiller stepped down from the government and formed a coalition with Mesut Yilmaz's Motherland (Anavatan) Party. In 1996, however, the cabinet resigned due to insurmountable disagreements between the two leaders, and Çiller formed another coalition with Necmeddin Erbakan's pro-Islamist Refah Partisi (Welfare Party). She served as minister of foreign affairs in the new government until the military forced Erbakan to resign in 1997. Çiller continued her political career as the minority leader of the parliamentary opposition. After the DYP's electoral defeat in 2002, she resigned as chairperson and withdrew from active politics.

Çiller became a significant role model for many Turkish women, but her political failures and the scandals about her family's finances contributed to a widespread mistrust about female politicians as well. In July of 2003, there was a pending parliamentary investigation proposal about her misdeeds during the prime ministry.

See also BOĞAZIÇI (BOSPORUS) UNIVERSITY; DEMIREL, SÜLEYMAN; ERBAKAN, NECMEDDIN; KURDISTAN WORKERS PARTY (PKK); REFAH PARTISI; TRUE PATH PARTY.

Bibliography

Arat, Yeşim. "A Woman Prime Minister in Turkey: Did It Really Matter?" *Women and Politics* 19, no. 4 (1998): 1–23.

Cizre, Ümit. "Tansu Çiller: Lusting for Power and Undermining Democracy." In *Political Leaders and Democracy in Turkey,* edited by Metin Heper and Sabri Sayari. Lanham, MD: Lexington Books, 2002.

Reinart, Üstün. "Ambition for All Seasons: Tansu Çiller." *Middle East Review of International Affairs* 3, 1 (1999): 80–3. Available at <http://meria.idc.ac.il/journal/1999/issue1/reinart.pdf>.

NERMIN ABADAN-UNAT
UPDATED BY BURÇAK KESKIN-KOZAT

CIRCASSIANS

A term that includes several groups linked by language and culture.

Circassian refers to indigenous peoples of the north-western Caucasus who are found today as minority communities in Turkey, Syria, Jordan, Israel, and Egypt. The term encompasses several groups linked by language and culture who refer to themselves in their own languages by different ethnonyms; primary among them are the Adyge, Abaza, and Ubykh. The terms *Circassian* (English), *Çerkes* (Turkish), *Cherkess* (Russian), and *Sharkass* (Arabic) are used by outsiders loosely to include various north Caucasian peoples. In addition to the Russian Federation and the Middle Eastern countries mentioned above, migrations since the 1960s have led to a Circassian presence in Western Europe and the United States. One can thus speak of a widely dispersed Circassian diaspora that is linked through kinship, intermarriage, transnational social and political organizations, and cultural flows.

Russian and Ottoman Empires

The territories in which the Circassians lived were zones of contention between the Russian and Ottoman empires. After the Russian Empire consolidated its control over the region during the 1850s, Circassians and many other north Caucasian peoples began to migrate into the Ottoman Empire, and a mass migration ensued in 1864. At first they were settled by imperial agencies in the Balkans, although later most were settled in Anatolia and the Syrian Province.

Although this migration led to the current configuration of the Circassian population in the Middle East, there is a long history of linkages across the Black Sea and the Transcaucasus. A slave trade in men, women, and children was an important part of this and Circassians, like many others, fed imperial appetites for warriors, administrators, concubines, and servants. The presence of Circassians in Eygpt as well as some of the major cities of the former Ottoman empire is the complex result of this long history. Thus in Egypt, the Circassian presence goes back to the Circassian Mamluk dynasties of the thirteenth through sixteenth centuries, and Circassian identity persisted after the overthrow of the Mamluks and was augmented in the Ottoman period by a continuing inflow of administrators and slaves of Circassian origin.

In contrast, the mass migration during the second half of the nineteenth century led to the formation of farming communities in areas of Anatolia and along what is commonly referred to in the literature on pastoralism as the interface of the "desert and the sown" in the Syrian province. The new Circassian communities often came into conflict with indigenous inhabitants over resources, water, and government services but eventually arrived at various accommodations, as evidenced by intermarriage and mixed settlement.

The Circassian migration also led to a peak in the Circassian female (and to some extent, child) slave trade. Under pressure from the British Empire, black slavery via North Africa had ceased and the Balkans were no longer under Ottoman control, leaving the Caucasus as the main source of slaves for the Ottoman state. This trade was not without its contradictions and contestations, with the state attempting to close slave markets and limit or even sometimes forbid the slave trade while still maintaining the imperial privilege of purchasing women for the harem. Circassian slave and harem women became an integral part of Orientalist literature and arts.

Circassian Communities as Minorities

The breakup of the Ottoman Empire in the early twentieth century meant that the various Circassian communities became minorities within new nation states rather than part of a multiethnic empire. Colonial powers in Syria, Jordan, and Palestine had varying policies towards Circassians and other ethnic groups. Cultural, social, and political organization and patterns thus differ across countries, types of settlement, class, and other factors. However, Circassian identity does persist across time and space. The Circassian language, which is indigenous to the northwest Caucasus and unrelated to Semitic, Turkic, or Indo-European, continues to be spoken across these communities. In addition, Circassians speak the languages of the countries where they live and participate fully in economic, social, and political life. In none of the Middle Eastern countries are the Circassians legally designated as a minority, although some forms of recognition may exist. For example, in the Jordanian parliament a certain number of seats are designated for Circassian as well as for Chechen representatives (the Chechens are also a Caucasian group with a history and presence in Jordan similar to that of the Circassians).

No accurate count exists of the Circassians in the Middle East, as the censuses do not differentiate by ethnicity. Turkey has the largest Circassians' presence—well over 1 million, spread over rural and urban settlements all across the country. The wide variety of lifestyles and life conditions make it difficult to generalize, but Circassians in Turkey have been active in organizational and associational life and have been affected by the legal and political measures to limit ethnic self-expression that stem from the conflict between the state and the Kurdish population.

Syria is the next in terms of numbers, with possibly as many as 100,000. Although pan-Arab ideology is the basis of the Syrian state, Circassians have not suffered from assimilationist policies. However, almost half the Circassian settlements in Syria were originally in the Golan Heights around the city of al-Qunaytra, which was destroyed and captured by the Israelis during the Arab–Israel War of 1973. Almost all the Circassians of this region moved to Damascus and a good percentage then migrated to the United States, forming the core of a community in New Jersey.

In Jordan, the community of around 35,000 was historically influential in government, military, and the security apparatus, and was well represented in the cabinet and parliament. The community grew wealthy with the choice of Amman as the capital during the 1920s, since they were settled mainly in Amman and neighboring villages. Several ethnic associations and clubs, some established as early as the 1930s, form a focus of community activities and there is also a school (kindergarten through twelfth grade) that teaches Circassian language and history in addition to the regular government curriculum.

In Israel, there are two Circassian villages in the Galilee, Kufr Kama and Rihaniyya, with a population of around 3,400. Like the Druze, they serve in the Israeli military and are somewhat privileged over the Arab population. Circassian is taught in schools and folklore groups exist. Until the 1990s and the Oslo Accords, there was little interaction between the Circassians in Israel and those in Arab countries, but it is now increasing.

The most definitive recent change in terms of identity and self-perception has come about with the collapse of the Soviet Union. This has enabled Circassians to travel to their homeland for the first time in 150 years and has led many to question their history and identity. Some have chosen to settle in the Russian Federation and others have reaffirmed their ties to their Middle Eastern settlements and citizenship. For all, it has led to the formation of diasporic cultural, social, and economic networks, which may play transformative roles in the future.

See also ARAB–ISRAEL WAR (1973); BLACK SEA; GOLAN HEIGHTS; OSLO ACCORD (1993); OTTOMAN EMPIRE.

Bibliography

Jaimoukha, Amjad. *The Circassians: A Handbook.* New York: Palgrave, 2001.

Karpat, Kemal. "Ottoman Immigration Policies and Settlement in Palestine." In *Settler Regimes in Africa and the Arab World: The Illusion of Endurance,* edited by Ibrahim Abu-Lughod and Baha Abu-Laban. Wilmette, IL: Medina University Press International, 1974.

Lewis, Norman N. *Nomads and Settlers in Syria and Jordan, 1800–1980.* New York and Cambridge, U.K.: Cambridge University Press, 1987.

Shami, Seteney. "Nineteenth Century Circassian Settlements in Jordan." In *Studies in the History and Archaeology of Jordan IV,* edited by Adnan Hadidi. Amman, Jordan: Department of Antiquities, 1992.

Shami, Seteney. "Prehistories of Globalization: Circassian Identity in Motion." *Public Culture* 12, no. 1 (winter 2000): 177–204.

Toledano, Ehud R. *The Ottoman Slave Trade and Its Suppression, 1840–1890.* Princeton, NJ: Princeton University Press, 1982.

SETENEY SHAMI

CIRCUMCISION

For males, circumcision involves removal of the foreskin of the penis. For females, it is the excision of all or part of the external genitalia, and is commonly referred to as clitoridectomy or female genital mutilation.

When done as part of tradition, male circumcision often signifies a rite of passage—admission into group membership, or the achievement of a particular status. Jewish boys are circumcised on their eighth day of life (unless the procedure will complicate their health) in accordance with the biblical commandment symbolizing the covenant (brit) with God. The ritual, called brit milah in Hebrew, is also required of male proselytes. Male proselytes who were previously circumcised are required to have a drop of blood, called tipat dam in Hebrew, removed from the penis. Both rituals are to be performed by a mohel, a Jewish person trained in the ritual. Male circumcision is also widely prevalent in Muslim society. Deviation from this practice in both societies is related to an attenuated degree of observance of religious observance in general.

The practice of circumcising females may be attributable to an attempt to depress sexual desire and preserve the virginity of young girls, but the original motivation is unclear. (Major religions neither support the practice nor refer to it explicitly.) Female circumcision is often performed between five and twelve years of age, or after childbirth. It is widely criticized for medical and sexual reasons, and because of the pain, disfigurement, and mental anguish it may cause. The World Medical Association condemned the act in 1993, calling it "female genital mutilation." The practice is more widespread in African countries than it is in Western countries, despite criticism by African leaders.

Male circumcision has its medical proponents. About 60 percent of U.S. male infants undergo circumcision, but the practice is being increasingly challenged. Medical associations now render a more cautious appraisal of the medical benefits of male circumcision, and raise new questions about possible physiological, sexual, and psychological consequences.

See also FEMALE GENITAL MUTILATION.

Bibliography

Aldeeb Abu-Sahlieh, Sami Awad. *Male and Female Circumcision Among Jews, Christians and Muslims: Religious, Medical, Social, and Legal Debate.* Warren Center, PA: Shangri-La Publications, 2001.

Gollaher, David L. *Circumcision: A History of the World's Most Controversial Surgery.* New York: Basic Books, 2000.

Mark, Elizabeth, ed. *My Covenant in Your Flesh: Circumcision, Gender, and Culture Across Jewish History.* Boston: University Press of New England/Brandeis University Press, 2003.

EPHRAIM TABORY

CIVIL CODE OF 1926

Civil laws of the Republic of Turkey, a secular body of laws that covers all citizens—Muslims and non-Muslims.

Turkey's civil law was enacted in 1926; unlike the gradual evolution of European civil codes, the transition from the Ottoman Empire to the Republic of Turkey brought a new code that has undergone relatively few changes.

Prior to the foundation of the Turkish republic, from 1869 to 1926, Ottoman legislators promulgated private (civil) law—rules derived from the *shariʿa* (Islamic law), comprising 1,851 articles and called *Mecelle-i Ahkam-i Adliye* (Compilation of legal rules). It had no laws concerning family and inheritance matters. Near the end of World War I, in 1917, a decree on family law, *Hukuku Aile Kararnamesi*, was promulgated by the sultan. In 1919, the pressure of organized religious forces abrogated this decree.

The Ottomans had been allied with the losing Central Powers in World War I. With the dissolution of the Ottoman Empire, the founders of the Turkish republic committed themselves to Western institutions; and they decided to undertake, in the shortest possible time, radical changes in Turkey's legal system. For Mustafa Kemal (Atatürk) and his colleagues, the major tools of social change were education and legal reform. An additional factor forced them to act swiftly: According to the peace of Lausanne (of 24 July 1923), the Kemalist government was pledged to adopt—under the supervision of the League of Nations—a legal statute protecting their non-Muslim minorities. Turkey obliged by introducing a general code and juridical system that would be acceptable to all citizens—Muslim and non-Muslim. The secularization of the legal system became one of Mustafa Kemal's major goals.

Kemalism used a number of Swiss and other European codes with relatively few amendments as models. In 1926, the Kemalists produced the new civil code, the code of obligation, and the trade code; in 1927, the code of civil procedure; in 1929, the sea trade code. With these steps they realized very quickly two of Mustafa Kemal's goals while depriving the conservative Islamic clergy and others of time to organize resistance: (1) the domestic scene was free of all remnants of the Ottoman-Islamic legal system, and (2) their international relations had been freed from the obligations of the treaty of Lausanne.

The Swiss civil code was used as a model because it is based on twenty-five-year community studies of existing norms and mores in Swiss cantons where French, German, Italian, and Romansh were spoken. The Swiss code seemed best to accommodate the needs of a country with diverse cultural and linguistic groups. Turkey's Minister of Justice Mahmut Esat Bozkurt had studied law in Switzerland, and Swiss law professor G. Sausser-Hall was engaged to act as legal counsel to the government of Turkey. On 17 February 1926 the modified version was adopted in a single session of the Turkish Grand National Assembly; it entered into force on 4 October 1926. Some attempts to modify the code began in 1951—concerning human rights, family law, adoption, and divorce. Although the acceptance of the code has not been universal, and Islamic law is used in some remote rural regions, the civil code has served Turkey well.

See also ATATÜRK, MUSTAFA KEMAL; KEMALISM; LAUSANNE, TREATY OF (1923); OTTOMAN EMPIRE; *SHARIʿA*; TURKISH GRAND NATIONAL ASSEMBLY.

Bibliography

Ansay, Turgul, and Wallace, Don, Jr. *Introduction to Turkish Law.* The Hague and Boston: Kluwer Law International, 1996.

NERMIN ABADAN-UNAT

CIVIL SERVICE SCHOOL (OTTOMAN)

Established to train civil servants to administer the Ottoman state of the mid-nineteenth century.

Established on 12 February 1859, the Civil Service School (Turkish, Mektebi-i Mülkiye) of the Ottoman Empire trained administrators in accordance with the new Tanzimat reforms. (The term *mülkiye* refers to the civilian—the nonmilitary and nonreligious—branches of government.)

The school offered courses in humanities, social sciences, and foreign languages, as well as special courses on public administration. In 1877, the curriculum was expanded and modernized. The first graduating class had 33 members; by 1885, there were 393. Graduates often filled the provincial posts of *qaʾimmaqam* (district governor). In 1935, the name was changed to School of Political Science; as the Faculty of Political Science, it is now located in Turkey's capital, Ankara.

See also TANZIMAT.

Bibliography

Lewis, Bernard. *The Emergence of Modern Turkey,* 3d edition. New York: Oxford University Press, 2002.

Shaw, Stanford, and Shaw, Ezel Kural. *History of the Ottoman Empire and Modern Turkey.* 2 vols. Cambridge, U.K., and New York: Cambridge University Press, 1976–1977.

DAVID WALDNER

CLARK–DARLAN AGREEMENT (1942)

Armistice agreement ending Vichy French resistance to Allied invasion of French North Africa.

During World War II, after the Allies invaded North Africa in November 1942, the Vichy French commander in chief, Admiral Jean François Darlan, signed this agreement on 22 November with General Mark Clark of the United States in Algiers, capital of Algeria, then under French control. Darlan ordered an end to French resistance, was made high commissioner of French North Africa, and severed ties with Vichy France. Because of Darlan's reputation as a Fascist, the deal aroused intense criticism.

Bibliography

Ambrose, Stephen. *Eisenhower,* Vol. 1. New York: Simon and Schuster, 1983.

Hurewitz, J. C., ed. *The Middle East and North Africa in World Politics.* New Haven, CT: Yale University Press, 1979.

ZACHARY KARABELL

CLAYTON, GILBERT
[1875–1929]

British officer and administrator in Egypt, Palestine, and Iraq.

After serving under Lord Kitchener in the Sudan, Gilbert Clayton received a commission in the Royal Artillery (1895); he was subsequently private secretary (1908–1913) to Sir Francis Reginald Wingate, commander of Egypt's army and governor-general of the Sudan. He was the Sudan agent in Cairo and director of intelligence of Egypt's army from 1913 to October 1914, when he was promoted to head of all intelligence services in Egypt, a post in which he remained until 1917. Clayton rose to the rank of brigadier general in the General Staff, Hijaz Operations, in 1916, and became chief political officer to General Edmund Allenby of the Egyptian Expeditionary Force in 1917. He was adviser to the Ministry of the Interior in Egypt (1919–1922), replaced Wyndham Deedes as chief secretary in Palestine (April 1923–1925), and was high commissioner and commander in chief in Iraq (1929).

In September 1914, Clayton wrote a secret memorandum to Lord Kitchener suggesting that Arabs could be of service to Britain during World War I and that an Arab leader friendly to Britain should be made caliph in place of the Ottoman sultan. This sparked the Abdullah–Storrs correspondence, which led to the Husayn–McMahon correspondence. Clayton and his fellow officers convinced Sir Mark Sykes that the Arabs in the Ottoman Empire might split from the Turks and join the Allies.

Clayton, who had reservations about the Balfour Declaration, supported Zionism within a limited definition whereby the Yishuv would serve merely as a cultural center for Jews in a multinational Palestine under Britain's administration. He argued against giving Syria to France under the Sykes–Picot Agreement and wanted Britain to take control of both Syria and Palestine. Although he believed Britain ought to continue to govern the Arabs, he attempted to reconcile Britain's interests and Arab nationalist aspirations while chief secretary in Palestine. He allowed his political secretary, Ernest T. Richmond, to expand the authority of the Supreme Muslim Council and increased Palestinian Arab appointments to government positions. Clayton helped negotiate the borders between Transjordan, Najd, and Iraq in the Hadda Agreement, signed in November 1925.

See also ALLENBY, EDMUND HENRY; HUSAYN–McMAHON CORRESPONDENCE

(1915–1916); KITCHENER, HORATIO HERBERT; SUPREME MUSLIM COUNCIL; SYKES, MARK; SYKES–PICOT AGREEMENT (1916); WINGATE, REGINALD; YISHUV.

Bibliography

Clayton, Gilbert. *An Arabian Diary.* Berkeley: University of California Press, 1969.

JENAB TUTUNJI

CLEMENCEAU, GEORGES
[1841–1929]

French socialist journalist and statesman; French premier, 1906–1909 and 1917–1920.

In foreign policy, Georges Clemenceau pressed for military preparedness against German expansionism through closer strategic alliance with Great Britain and the expansion of military conscription among France's colonial populations. This brought Clemenceau into contact with the leaders of the Young Algeria movement: gallicized Muslims who were formed in the colonial educational system but found limited opportunities in the local administration or economy. Their proposals for military service in exchange for full civil rights found favor with Clemenceau and other liberal policymakers, especially after the armistice, when he led the effort to compensate Algerians for their payment of the "blood tax." The resulting Jonnart Law of 1919 was nevertheless greatly diluted by settler (*colon*) opposition to colonial reforms, and its failure to satisfy native demands may be considered a defining moment in the development of Algerian nationalism. Clemenceau headed the French delegation at the Paris Peace Conference, where he united with British prime minister Lloyd George to undermine the initiatives of U.S. president Woodrow Wilson and to realize the territorial provisions of the Sykes–Picot Agreement that pertained to the Arab provinces of the former Ottoman Empire. After his electoral defeat in 1920 Clemenceau retired from public life and devoted his remaining days to writing his memoirs.

See also SYKES–PICOT AGREEMENT (1916); YOUNG ALGERIANS.

Bibliography

Dallas, Gregor. *At the Heart of a Tiger: Clemenceau and His World, 1841–1929.* New York: Carroll and Graf, 1993.

ZACHARY KARABELL
UPDATED BY O. W. ABI-MERSHED

CLIMATE

Middle Eastern climatic conditions vary greatly, depending on the season and the geography.

The Middle East and North Africa are perceived as both homogeneous and intensely arid, but the region is best characterized by its climatic variation. Although the hot arid, or desert, climate predominates in the region, the well-watered highlands of Turkey and the mountains of Iran and Ethiopia are important as sources of the region's major rivers. Climatic variation finds further expression in the temperature regimes of the northern and southern parts of the area. Average July maxima for inland

North African Taghit Oasis sand dunes, located in the Sahara Desert—Grand Erg Occidental, Algeria. © JOSE FUSTE RAGA/CORBIS. REPRODUCED BY PERMISSION.

locations near 30° north latitude are as high as 108°F (42°C), while summer maximum temperatures in northern locations such as Ankara, Turkey, do not exceed 86°F (30°C). Black Sea coastal stations' (e.g., Trabzon, Turkey) average summer maxima may be as low as 79°F (26°C). January average minimum temperatures fall to 50°F (10°C) in Aswan, but reach 10°F (−12.5°C) in Erzurum on the Anatolian plateau.

Desert conditions are primarily the result of the subtropical zone of high pressure that coincides with 30° north latitude. In this area, cold, subsiding air warms as it approaches the earth, thus increasing its ability to hold moisture. This results in extreme evaporation from all surfaces, and under such conditions, very little rain falls. During the summer solstice, the sun is directly overhead at 23° 30′ at north latitude (e.g., at Aswan, Egypt). Annual periods of high sun in combination with clear skies through much of the year allow intense solar radiation with subsequent extreme evapotranspiration demands.

Evapotranspiration refers to the water needed by vegetation to withstand the energy of incoming solar radiation. This is accomplished through the mechanism of heat transfer by means of evaporation from inert surfaces and transpiration from stomata (pores) on leaf surfaces. Total demands made upon an individual plant are termed potential evapotranspiration (PE). Actual evapotranspiration (AE) is the amount of water actually available and used by the plant and reflects climatic conditions rather than optimal plant requirements. The difference between PE and AE defines the degree of aridity or drought and also the amount of irrigation water that would have to be applied for such vegetation to survive.

In the deserts of North Africa and Southwest Africa, total annual precipitation is between 2 inches (50 mm) and 14 inches (350 mm). The area from Aden to Baghdad receives from less than 2 inches (50 mm) annually to about 6 inches (150 mm). More than 39 inches (1 m) of water would be required in those places to sustain rain-fed agriculture. Under such conditions, sparse natural vegetation allows animals some seasonal grazing at best. Hyperarid areas, which seldom if ever receive rain, have no vegetation at all. Rainfall variability within the area of desert climate exceeds 40 percent, reducing to 20 percent on the moist margins of the semiarid zone, which forms a transition between the true desert to the south and the more humid areas farther north.

Precipitation on the semiarid margins of Middle Eastern deserts ranges from 14 inches (350 mm) to 30 inches (750 mm) annually. Dry farming of grains employing alternate years of fallow can be carried out with 16 inches (400 mm) or more of rain. It should be remembered that, while rainfall variability is greatest in the desert, this also means that aridity there has high predictability. Thus, the semiarid transition between regions of predictable aridity and predictable rainfall is one where rain-fed agriculture is possible but has a high chance of failure. This is biblical country—years of plenty followed by years of famine—and one to which pastoral nomadism was a practical adaptation.

The Black Sea coast of Turkey receives from 78 inches (2,000 mm) to 101 inches (2,600 mm) per year, although the transition from the windward, watered side of the Pontic range to the leeward, dry side can be very abrupt due to the topography. The Mediterranean climate, which is limited to a narrow coastal strip reaching from Gaza to Istanbul and from Tunis in the west to the Atlantic, is marked by mild winters with ample rain and long, hot summers when Sahara-like conditions prevail.

Precipitation results from three different processes. Orographic precipitation occurs on the Pontic and Taurus mountains of Turkey; the Elburz and Zagros mountains of Iran; the peaks of Lebanon and the hills of Israel, the West Bank, and Jordan; the highlands of Ethiopia; and the Atlas and Anti-Atlas mountains of northwest Africa. Such precipitation occurs as warm, moisture-bearing winds are forced to higher elevations over the mountains. When the air cools, it loses its ability to hold moisture, and rain or snow falls on the windward sides of those ranges.

The Anatolian plateau and the steppes of northern Syria experience small quantities of rain in the form of convectional summer showers from thunderstorms. Equatorial convectional rains provide the waters of the White Nile.

Overhead view of *feluccas* (sailboats) navigating near the Nile Delta's Elephantine Island and Aswan, Egypt. © JONATHAN BLAIR/CORBIS. REPRODUCED BY PERMISSION.

A third cause of precipitation, particularly in the wintertime, is the passage of frontal systems from west to east across the region bringing alternating high and low pressure cells with associated cold, clear, or moist warm air masses. Frontal systems are propelled eastward by the subtropical jet stream, the position of which varies latitudinally by as much as 15° from a winter position in the north to its summer position in the south. Summer months find the path of the jet stream located from central Turkey northeastward to central Asia. Six months later the jet stream is at its maximum along a path traced across the Gulf of Suez to the head of the Gulf of Aqaba and beyond. This shift accounts for the changes in temperature and precipitation noted above.

Surface winds in the Middle East have distinctive qualities and have received local names famous throughout the region. The cold northern wind blowing from the Anatolian plateau to the southern Turkish shore in the winter is the *Poyraz* (derived from the Greek: *bora,* i.e., north); the warm onshore wind in the same location is known as the *meltem.* Searing desert winds are infamous: The Egyptian *khamsin,* which blows in from the desert, is matched by the *ghibli* in Libya and the *simoon* in Iran.

Bibliography

Beaumont, Peter; Blake, Gerald H.; and Wagstaff, J. Malcolm. *The Middle East: A Geographical Study,* 2d edition. New York: Halsted Press, 1988.

Blake, Gerald; Dewdney, John; and Mitchell, Jonathan. *The Cambridge Atlas of the Middle East and North Africa.* Cambridge, U.K., and New York: Cambridge University Press, 1987.

Goudie, Andrew, and Wilkinson, Jon. *The Warm Desert Environment.* Cambridge, U.K., and New York: Cambridge University Press, 1977.

Grigg, David. *The Harsh Lands: A Study in Agricultural Development.* London: Macmillan; New York: St. Martin's, 1970.

JOHN F. KOLARS

CLINTON, WILLIAM JEFFERSON
[1946–]

U.S. president (1993–2001); closely involved in the Israeli–Palestinian peace process.

Bill Clinton received a B.A. from Georgetown University and a law degree from Yale University. Although he assumed the presidency of the United States in 1993 without a significant foreign policy background, Clinton almost immediately found himself thrust into Middle Eastern and South Asian issues. Attacks by Islamic militants against the World Trade Center in New York in 1993, and later against U.S. embassies in Africa in 1998, prompted Clinton to order bombing attacks against targets in Sudan and Afghanistan to disrupt the activities of Osama bin Ladin and his al-Qaʿida network. Clinton also focused considerable attention on Iraqi refusal to cooperate with United Nations (UN) weapons inspections and ordered that country bombed on several occasions.

Yet it was the Arab–Israeli peace process to which he devoted more personal attention and prestige than any other U.S. president. Clinton's administration was taken by surprise by the revelations in August 1993 that Israel and the Palestine Liberation Organization (PLO) had agreed to a framework on peace through secret talks in Norway. Although the United States had not been involved in the talks, the subsequent Oslo Accord was signed by Israel and the PLO in Washington on the White House lawn.

Clinton signed the accord as well, as a witness. When PLO chairman Yasir Arafat then reached out his hand to a hesitant Israeli prime minister Yitzhak Rabin, Clinton, known for his people skills, nudged the two men together for a handshake—the first public greeting ever between such high-level Israeli and Palestinian leaders. Given the long-standing U.S. refusal to deal with the PLO publicly, Clinton became the first sitting president ever to meet Arafat and to allow him to enter the country since he delivered a speech at the UN in 1974. In 1994, Clinton played host to Rabin and Jordan's King Hussein, who agreed to the second-ever peace treaty between Israel and an Arab state. Clinton later traveled to the Jordanian-Israeli border in October 1994 to witness the signing ceremony. In general, however, his administration allowed the various parties to the Arab–Israeli conflict to continue the pace of talks and negotiations themselves, removing the U.S. to a role of "honest broker."

Clinton's desire to keep the Israeli–Palestinian peace process alive was severely tried by the resumption of violence and the mutual recriminations between the two sides under Rabin's successor, Benjamin Netanyahu. In October 1998, Clinton invited Netanyahu and Arafat to Wye River, Maryland, where he persuaded them to negotiate a further set of Israeli redeployments from the West Bank. Two months later, he became the first U.S. president to visit the Palestinian Authority, addressing the Palestine National Council meeting in Gaza. In October 2000, Clinton traveled to Egypt for the Sharm al-Shaykh summit. His most significant effort to conclude a final Israeli–Palestinian peace treaty occurred in July 2001, when he hosted lengthy talks between Arafat and Israeli prime minister Ehud Barak at his presidential retreat at Camp David, Maryland. The talks ultimately failed and Clinton left the presidency having failed to see either a final peace settlement between Israel and the PLO or a resolution of the weapons inspections issue in Iraq.

See also ARAFAT, YASIR; BARAK, EHUD; BIN LADIN, OSAMA; CAMP DAVID SUMMIT (2000); HUSSEIN IBN TALAL; ISRAEL: OVERVIEW; NETANYAHU, BENJAMIN; OSLO ACCORD (1993); PALESTINE LIBERATION ORGANIZATION (PLO); PALESTINIAN AUTHORITY; QAʿIDA, AL-; RABIN, YITZHAK.

Bibliography

Enderlin, Charles. *Shattered Dreams: The Failure of the Peace Process in the Middle East, 1995–2002,* translated by Susan Fairfield. New York: Other Press, 2003.

Quandt, William B. *Peace Process: American Diplomacy and the Arab-Israeli Conflict Since 1967,* revised edition. Berkeley, CA: Brookings Institution Press, 2001.

MICHAEL R. FISCHBACH

CLOT, ANTOINE BARTHÉLÉMY

[?–1860]

French doctor who started first medical school in Egypt in 1827.

Known as Clot Bey, Dr. Antoine Barthélémy Clot was one of a group of European experts recruited by Muhammad Ali Pasha, viceroy of Egypt, to introduce European technology into Egypt. Clot Bey established the first medical school in Egypt in 1827, as well as Qasr al-Ayni hospital. The aim of the school was to train doctors and medical aides for the Egyptian army. Abbas I, who ruled from 1848 to 1854, dismissed Clot Bey along with most of Muhammad Ali's European advisers. Clot Bey returned to Egypt in 1856 and retired in 1857.

See also ABBAS HILMI I; MUHAMMAD ALI.

Bibliography

Vatikiotis, P. J. *The History of Modern Egypt: From Muhammad Ali to Mubarak,* 4th edition. Baltimore, MD: Johns Hopkins University Press, 1991.

DAVID WALDNER

CLOTHING

Overview of traditional and modern clothes in the Middle East.

Most contemporary Muslim societies reflect both old and the new realities. Resurgence of religion and nationalist attitudes of the postcolonial (twentieth-century) era are reflected in the modes of clothing. The traditional modes remain strongly defended and sometimes enforced by the governments of some Islamic nations. The great shift in political, social, and religious participation of women in many Muslim nations has affected clothing styles as well. In the twentieth century, there were two opposing models for Muslim women: the Westernized

A Bedouin man in Petra, Jordan, combines some modern clothing with traditional headgear. Headscarves and other coverings are among the most important items of clothing for men, and their size, colors, patterns, and other attributes can signify social or religious status, age, and tribal affiliation, among other things. © LINDSAY HEBBERD/CORBIS. REPRODUCED BY PERMISSION.

lifestyle prominent among minor upperclass and elites, and the more restrictive, traditional "Islamic" way of life for the majority of women. A third, alternative lifestyle that has attracted a large number of Muslim women is both Islamic and modern, the result of more education and an understanding of the difference between the patriarchal interpretation of Islam and the text of the Qur'an by the religious *ulama.*

Historical Background

Very little has been written regarding the dress of Arabs in classical historical literature. In terms of the Near Eastern people, more visual evidence survived

Israeli boys wearing decorated skullcaps called kippah, or yarmulke, study in a yeshiva, or Jewish day school, in the Galilee. The styles sometimes indicate political or religious affiliation. © ANNIE GRIFFITHS BELT/CORBIS. REPRODUCED BY PERMISSION.

in forms of stone carvings. The earliest evidence of Arab clothing from the first and second millennia B.C.E. shows that scant clothing was worn with a variety of headdresses. Men and women wore almost identical clothing in the early Islamic era of the seventh century and the time of *jahiliyya* (pre-Islamic era), as is still the case today among non-urban inhabitants of the Middle Eastern regions.

Arab material culture was influenced by contact with other great empires. Arab Muslim rulers influenced the clothing styles of the countries they ruled, while the fashion styles of the countries ruled influenced the rulers. Many customs regarding clothes have roots in ancient Near Eastern (Iranian plateau, Iraq) superstition found also in the Talmud, and still are practiced as they were during the *jahiliyya*. From the time of the Prophet (seventh century forward), early Islamic clothes fashions were an extension of the preceding period, with some modifications for new Islamic moral codes after the prophet Muhammad. The clothes of the villagers and bedouins of the Middle East are simpler, more functional, and more suitable to the climate and geography of the regions than those of urban dwellers, who are far more conscious of conservative modes of behavior.

In the urban Middle Eastern regions, Western styles of dress for the most part have replaced traditional clothing. Westernization of the Middle Eastern clothes styles is in itself unique and innovative at times and, importantly, accepted by the indigenous population. Traditional items of clothing mix with Western styles. For example, it is common to see Arab men of the Gulf region wearing the traditional long, ankle-length *jillaba*, or *dishdasha, kaffiya*, and *agal* along with a Western-style man's suit jacket and dress shoes.

Headgear

Among the most important items of clothing for men is the headgear, and the most common form of head dress for men is the *imama*, or turban. Historically, turbans were used for purposes other than merely covering the head—for example, for hiding objects, tying down a person, or using as a prayer rug. Turbans were wrapped in a variety of styles, as well. It was customary to leave a corner of the *imama* free to serve as a veil to protect the wearer against heat, dust, and the evil eye, and to conceal the wearer's identity. The locus of a man's honor and reputation was his head; therefore, to cover the head was proper and dignified and to leave it uncovered was considered shameful. In the book *Palestinian Costumes* Shelagh Weir notes: "Men swore oaths on their turbans, and the removal of a man's turban in anger was a slur and provocation and could necessitate material compensation."

The turban has long been worn by both Muslims and non-Muslims. The English word *turban* derives from the Persian *dulband* via the Turkish *turban* or *tulbent*. In Persian, the most common word for turban is *amama*, from the Arabic form of the word *imama*. Other less commonly known Persian terms for *imama* are *mandil* and *dastar-e-sar*.

The *imama* is usually wrapped around a small cap, which is placed at the crown of the head. This small cap is called *aragh chin* (Persian sweat collector), *tubior araqiyya* in Arabic. The early turban did not have the symbolic significance that it gained later, when it became associated with Islam and came to be referred to as "the badge of Islam" (*sima al-Islam*), "divider between unbelievers and believers" (*hadiza bayn al-kufr wa al-iman*), and "crowns of the Arabs" (*tidjan al-arab*).

According to an old Arab tradition, removal of a man's *imama* signified losing his manhood and abandoning his morals. Exceptions to this rule included removing the turban for prayer, to show before God, and for punishment, to show the public that the punished man is not respected. There are contradictory *hadiths* (Islamic traditions) regarding wearing or not wearing *imama*. In early Islamic times, the turban was forbidden to a person in a state of *ihram* (during the *Hajj* rituals). Turbans had to be removed before entering Mecca as a sign of humility and respect before God. The prophet Muhammad's turban was named *al-sihab*, "the cloud," and the prophet Muhammad was known as *sahib al-imama*, meaning "Master of the state turban," which is significant in terms of religious and community leadership. Numerous terms found in Arabic literature refer to different manners of wearing the turban: *al-sa'b, al-masaba, al-mikbar, al-mashwad,* and *al-khamar.*

In some Middle Eastern cultures, turbans were associated with sexual and social maturity. For example, in Palestinian culture, different types of headgear marked stages of maturity, and usually young boys were not allowed to wear a turban. The turban remained important even after the death of its wearer, and a traditional Muslim stone grave may have a mark with a turban. Non-Muslims who were ruled by Muslim Arab rulers were required to follow certain sumptuary laws regarding their garments. Among such obligations were the caliphs' orders to wear "the interchange," which referred to headgear, outerwear, shoes, and belts that would differentiate believers from nonbelievers in public. Non-Muslims were required to use special marks on their turbans to segregate them visually from Muslims.

In addition to marked turbans, the size and color of the turban was a badge of identification for certain classes and ages of people. The color associations have changed over time and place with various Muslim Arab rulers. For example, black turbans were associated with officials during the Abbasid period (ca. 750–950), and red was a sign of high rank. The Safavid court of Iran during the sixteenth and seventeenth centuries adopted a particular form of turban that contained a tall, red stick at its center. This red stick became a religious and political divider between the official Shi'ite court of

Female Iraqi students in traditional and modern—but modest—dress walk side by side at the University of Mustansiriyah in Baghdad. © Shepard Sherbell/Corbis Saba. Reproduced by permission.

Iran and its rival, the Ottoman Turks. Safavid soldiers wearing red-stick turbans were known as *qizel baş* ("red heads"), by the Turks. Religious and learned scholars wore smoothly wrapped flat, white turbans. Yellow was reserved for Jews, blue for Christians. Apparently, at various times the colors red and purple were also reserved mostly for Jews and Christians.

Men in the prime of life wore turbans in bright, warm colors; men of fifty exchanged their colored turbans for plain white ones. Until the early part of the twentieth century green turbans were worn by *hajjis* (men who have made the pilgrimage to Mecca) and by *sada* (men who claim descent from the house of the prophet Muhammad) to indicate a religious status with high social value. The extensive use of green turbans by illegitimate users led to the re-

A girl in Bahrain wears traditional clothing comprising an ornamental headdress and a chador extensively embellished with gold embroidery and sequins. © ADAM WOOLFITT/CORBIS. REPRODUCED BY PERMISSION.

placement of the green turban with the black turban, to distinguish the legitimate *sada*. In Iran after the Islamic Revolution of 1978, where separation of mosque and state is nonexistent, identification as a cleric denotes access to power, so it is significant that white turbans are associated with theologians and scholars, and black turbans indicate an association of the wearer to the house of the prophet Muhammad. There is no way to guarantee the legitimacy of the turban color vis à vis its intended meaning by its wearer. In general, the public trusts the wearer on this issue.

Because the turban originally was considered a part of a man's attire, traditionally, Arab men objected to women wearing this symbol of manhood. However, some literary references indicate that women at times in various parts of the Arab world wore turbans for certain occasions, perhaps in the privacy of the home. Young women sometimes wore turbans to appear more attractive, and when a woman gave birth to her first baby, she wore a turban comprised of six yards of material. After the second baby, she wore a turban with six additional yards. Northern Iraqi women wore turbans made of printed material and decorated with Ottoman Turkish gold coins. The practice of women wearing turbans is not unusual. and it is present even in the modern history of fashion, where there is an affinity for "exotic" headgear.

Another popular form of Arab headgear is the *agal*, which is a ringed cord or rope that goes over the headscarf worn by men in the Arabian Peninsula, Iraq, Syria, and Palestine. The head rope was originally a camel hobble (the word *agal* means "to hobble") that was carried on the head when not in use. Later, this rope came to distinguish the bedouins of north and central Arabia (and the ruling families descended from them) from other bedouins. The earliest reliable report on the *agal* dates back to the early eighteenth century, from a picture depicting the imam Abdullah Ibn Saʿud wearing an elaborate and highly decorative type of *agal* that is sometimes called *mugassab*.

Along with the *agal*, men wear the Arabic *kaffiya* (or *pocu*, pronounced *poshu* in Turkish and the dialect of the Turkish Kurds). The *kaffiya* (also *shamagh* or *hatta*) is a head cloth folded diagonally and secured on the head by the *agal*. Men from the Arabian Peninsula, Syria, Iraq, and Palestine wear the *kaffiya*. It comes in a variety of designs and colors that denote tribal affiliation. In modern history it has acquired another layer of meaning as a symbol of solidarity among Palestinians and their supporters in their quest for political and geographical autonomy. It is sometimes worn in defiance, as if a substitute for the long outlawed Palestinian flag. Like the black-and-white *kaffiya* of Yasir Arafat, chairman of the Palestinian Liberation Organization, which is worn by both Palestinian men and women as a sign of unity, the *pocu* has the same symbolic meaning for independence of the Kurds under the autonomy of the Turkish government. The *pocu* is also black and white, which are the colors associated with urban Kurdish intellectual men and women. It signifies political leftism, cultural freedom, and rights to an independent state. Both the *pocu* and *kaffiya* are draped over the shoulders by men and women, worn like a scarf on the head by women, or worn in the traditional manner with the *agal* by men only.

Another popular headdress for men is the fez, a word derived from Fez, a city in Morocco where it traditionally is manufactured. It is a brimless, cone-shaped, flat-crowned hat that usually has a tassel made of silk. The fez is made of red felt and is worn in Syria, Egypt, North Africa, and Palestine. Another name for the fez is *tarbush* or *tarboosh*. It was banned during the Tanzimat period in Turkey (beginning in 1839), when dress regulation took place. However, the *tarbush* also played a significant political role after the Young Turk Revolution of July 1908.

Also common among men in the Middle East region is the *sidara*, an Iraqi cap commonly made of black velvet, black lamb's wool, or black felt. The *sidara* is brimless, has a crown at the center, and folds like a pocket around the crown of the cap. It resembles the hat worn by the cadets in the U.S. military. This cap at one time was very popular with middle-class, upper-middle-class, and elite members of Iraqi society. The *sidara* lost its popularity after the 1958 deposition of the last king and the establishment of the Republic of Iraq. Muslim men of the subcontinent of India wear a similar hat in black as a sign of Muslim identity.

The *kippah,* commonly worn by Jewish men in the Middle East, is a skullcap that is also known in Yiddish as the yarmulke. Ashkenazic Jews wear the yarmulke at all times, and Sephardic Jewish men generally do not. In Israel, wearing a yarmulke also has social significance: Not wearing a yarmulke is like stating, "I'm not religious." The style of yarmulke in Israel can also indicate political and religious affiliation.

The most common headdress for Muslim women is some form of a veil. The generic term for veil, known by Muslims regardless of their cultural and linguistic heritage, is *hijab*. The *hijab* refers to a physical veil, a tangible item covering the hair and face of a woman. The word is of Arabic origin, from the verb *hajaba*, "to hide from the view, to conceal." *Hijab* also refers to the Muslim woman's dress code in accordance with interpretation of Islamic law. Muslim women around the world wear various forms of veils, each community according to its own cultural and religious interpretations, so there is no universal form of veiling among Muslim women. Other common interchangeable words for veil are *yashmek*, *purda*, *chador*, *paranja*, *burqa*, *bushia*, *niqab*, *pece* (pronounced *peeche* in Turkish), and *khimar*. Each represents some specific form of head or face veil commonly used by Muslims of various nationalities. The chador, which in Persian literally means "tent," is a form of *hijab* (head veil), consisting of a full-length semicircular piece of material. It is placed on top of the head and covers the entire body. It is held in place with one hand at all times. Sometimes a corner of it is pulled over the face to cover part of the mouth.

Other Clothing

Other important clothing for men and women are forms of long dress, wrap, outerwear gown, or caftan. The most common outerwear garment is the *aba* or *aba ʿa*, also known as *rida*, which is an ankle-length loose mantle or coat worn by Arab men over the shoulders. The *aba* opens at the front with no fastening device and has two openings for the arms to be pulled through. Piping sewn on the *aba* goes around the entire edge of the garment and around the sleeves. Customarily the *aba* is draped over the shoulders rather than worn as a coat. The fabric used for making the *aba* or *rida* identifies its region of origin, and a clear distinction is not made between fabric and garment. Traditional wraps or mantles are worn in most traditional Islamic societies, yet there is a considerable variety of draping styles from one region to another. Wearing an *aba* has religious associations in some regions of the Islamic world such as Iran or Egypt. In Iran, a man wearing an *aba* and turban is identified as a non-secular person associated with the mosque and theological schools.

Another form of wrap or cloak is the burnoose, which is a large, one-piece, hooded cloak worn by men throughout the Maghrib (Northern Africa). The burnoose is also used in religious ceremony as the chasuble of the Coptic priests in Egypt. Yet another common form of cloak or wrap is the *haik*, which is a large, voluminous outer wrap, usually white, worn by both sexes throughout the Maghrib. The *dishdasha* is a long, A-line, ankle-length, long-sleeved, light-colored shirt worn by Arab men in the Gulf region. A similar style of man's garment commonly worn by men in Egypt is the *jillaba*.

Bibliography

Esposito, John L., ed. *The Oxford History of Islam.* Oxford, U.K.: Oxford University Press. 1999.

Lindisfarne-Tapper, Nancy, and Ingham, Bruce, ed. *Languages of Dress in the Middle East.* Surrey, U.K.: Curzon Press, 1997.

Shirazi, Faegheh. *The Veil Unveiled: Hijab in Modern Culture.* Gainesville: University Press of Florida, 2001.

Shirazi-Mahajan, Faegheh. "The Semiotics of the Turban: The Safavid era in Iran." *Journal of the International Association of Costume* 9 (1992): 67–87.

Weir, Shelagh. *Palestinian Costumes.* Austin: The University of Texas Press, 1989.

FAEGHEH SHIRAZI

CLUB NATIONAL ISRAÉLITE

A Zionist association.

The Club National Israélite (Arabic, al-Nadi al-Qawmi al-Isra'ili) was founded in Syria in June 1924 by Tawfiq Mizrahi, a Jewish journalist and director of the Bureau de Presse et Publicité advertising agency in Damascus, and Dr. Sulayman Tagger, the chief rabbi of Beirut, together with seven other provisory committee members. The group's name was chosen in obvious imitation of the Arab Club, which was the focal point of Syrian and pan-Arab nationalism.

The Club National Israélite set out a nine-point program that, in addition to moderate Zionist goals, included working for friendly ties with other religious and ethnic communities in Syria. The club shifted its headquarters to Beirut in the late 1920s when the atmosphere in Damascus became increasingly hostile to any form of Zionism. It did not continue to be active for long, and most of its members joined other Jewish organizations with Zionist orientations.

See also ARAB CLUB; PAN-ARABISM.

Bibliography

Stillman, Norman A. *The Jews of Arab Lands in Modern Times.* Philadelphia: Jewish Publication Society, 1991.

NORMAN STILLMAN

CODE DE L'INDIGÉNAT

Law code in French colonial Algeria.

Imposed by France on the native Muslim population of Algeria in 1881, the Code de l'Indigénat (Code of the Indigenous People) was exercised summarily, covering a vast array of offenses. Its arbitrary application was tempered in 1914 and 1919 by the Clemenceau and Jonnart reforms. Nevertheless, the colonial lobby in France kept the intimidating code in effect until General Charles de Gaulle issued the ordinance of 7 March 1944 that gave Muslims French rights. Discrimination and prejudice, however, continued to prevent the full enjoyment of these new privileges. Summary rule resumed during the Algerian war of independence (1954–1962).

See also ALGERIAN WAR OF INDEPENDENCE; CLEMENCEAU, GEORGES; YOUNG ALGERIANS.

Bibliography

Naylor, Phillip C., and Heggoy, Alf A. *The Historical Dictionary of Algeria,* 2d edition. Metuchen, NJ: Scarecrow Press, 1994.

PHILLIP C. NAYLOR

COFFEE

See FOOD: COFFEE

COHEN, GE'ULA
[1925–]

LEHI radio announcer and politician.

Ge'ula Cohen was one of nineteen members of the Lohamei Herut Yisrael (LEHI) who were arrested when the British seized LEHI's radio transmitter on 19 February 1946 as part of a crackdown on Jewish terrorist groups. Cohen was a leading figure in the radio broadcasts of the LEHI underground led by Yitzhak Shamir. She was sentenced to nineteen years in prison but escaped and resumed the illegal broadcasts. As a journalist in Israel, she was an active participant in the militant struggle on behalf of Soviet Jewry.

In 1970 she joined the Likud party. She was first elected to the Knesset in 1973, and served through 1992, the Eighth through the Twelfth Knesset. She served first as a member of the Likud and then as a member of the Tehiya, a party she helped found that was to the right of the Likud. In the Twelfth Knesset she served as deputy minister of science and technology. After the defeat of the Tehiya party in the 1992 elections, she rejoined the Likud party. One of her most visible public roles was as a leading opponent of Israel's peace agreement with Egypt and its withdrawal from the Sinai; she is associated with the ideology of the hard-liners who espouse the vision of a Greater Israel, and she has consistently opposed concessions to any of Israel's Arab neighbors.

She was awarded the Israel Prize in 2001; the award cited her accomplishments as a LEHI fighter, writer, journalist, and member of Knesset, as well as her efforts to absorb immigrants from the former Soviet Union and Ethiopia. She has published her autobiography, *A Story of a Warrior* (Tel Aviv, 1962; in Hebrew), and she regularly writes articles for daily newspapers.

Bibliography

Haizly, Soormaira. "Correction: Setting the Record Straight." *Judea Electronic Magazine* 8, no.5 (Elul-Tishrei 5760–5761 [Sept.–Oct. 2000]). Available from <http://www.womeningreen.org/judea>.

Jewish Agency for Israel. "The Global Jewish Agenda." Available from <http://www.jafi.org.il/agenda>.

Polner, Murray, ed. *Jewish Profiles: Great Jewish Personalities and Institutions of the Twentieth Century.* Northvale, NJ: J. Aronson, 1991.

YAAKOV SHAVIT
UPDATED BY GREGORY S. MAHLER

COLE, USS

American destroyer attacked in 2000 while refueling in Yemen, focusing international attention on the developing conflict between the United States and terrorists in the region.

On 12 October 2000 two men exploded a small boat in the port of Aden alongside USS *Cole,* killing themselves and seventeen U.S. sailors and wounding thirty-nine. Despite suspicion that the bombing was sponsored by the al-Qaʿida network, initially no links were found and the U.S. administration decided against a retaliatory strike on al-Qaʿida camps

in Afghanistan. In a videotaped speech in January 2001, Osama bin Ladin praised the attack as a blow against American "injustice" but denied his own involvement, in an interview with the Kuwaiti newspaper *al-Raʾy al-Amm.* In June an al-Qaʿida recruitment tape that claimed responsibility for the bombing was brought to public attention by the newspaper; and in December, a letter was discovered ordering attacks on American ships in Yemen, purportedly written by bin Ladin in late 1997, before U.S. ships began to refuel in Aden. In the months following the attack, Yemen captured a number of mostly local suspects; in 2003 it revealed confessions had been made alleging that the attack was ordered by the prominent cleric Shaykh Zindani, a leader of the Islah Party. In 2002 U.S. forces killed one fugitive suspect and in 2003 indicted two of ten further suspects when they escaped from jail in Yemen.

GEORGE R. WILKES

COLONIALISM IN THE MIDDLE EAST

European control of Middle East areas beginning during the nineteenth century and continuing until World War II.

Between the mid-nineteenth century and World War I, most of the Middle East and North Africa either already was, or later came, under different forms of colonial rule. In North Africa, France began to conquer Algeria in 1830, conquered Tunisia in 1881, and (together with Spain) imposed a protectorate upon Morocco in 1912. All three were "colonial settler states" in that a substantial proportion of the population (12 percent in the case of Algeria in 1854) were Europeans, mostly French families, who came to live and work in North Africa, both on the land and in the cities. Some of their descendants remained there until forced out by the independence struggles of the 1950s and early 1960s. On a somewhat smaller scale, Libya was annexed by Italy in 1911 and attracted some 110,000 Italian settlers during the inter-war period.

Britain and France Take Leading Roles

In Egypt, following the rise of a nationalist movement that threatened to challenge the British and French administration of the public debt (put in place in 1876), British troops invaded in 1882 and occupied the country informally until the declaration of a British protectorate on the outbreak of World War I. Although large numbers of foreigners resided in Egypt, they were generally neither "settlers" nor *colons* in the French North African sense (since they lived mostly in the cities and engaged in commerce or in other service occupations) and a majority of them were not citizens of the occupying power.

On the coasts of the Arabian Peninsula, Britain's concern to keep the route to India safe and open led to the signing of a series of treaties with the rulers of Bahrain and of what are now the United Arab Emirates. In 1853 the rulers signed a Perpetual Maritime Truce; in 1892 Bahrain and the lower Gulf emirates, including Muscat and Oman, signed further agreements with Britain under which they agreed not to dispose of any part of their territories except to Britain, and to conduct their foreign relations exclusively through the British government. Britain concluded similar agreements with Kuwait in 1899 and Qatar in 1916. In 1839 Britain annexed Aden and turned it into a naval base; later, "exclusive" treaties were signed with the tribal rulers of the interior, and in 1937 the area was divided into the port and its immediate hinterland (Aden Colony) and the more remote rural/tribal areas (Aden Protectorate).

In the Levant, a form of colonialism of a rather different kind came into being after the defeat of the Ottoman Empire by Britain and France in 1918. The Ottoman Arab provinces were assigned to Britain and France as mandates from the newly created League of Nations, Britain taking responsibility for Iraq, Palestine, and Transjordan, and France taking responsibility for Lebanon and Syria. The guiding principle of the mandate system was that the states concerned should remain under the tutelage of the mandatory power, until such time as they were able to "stand alone," a period that, although unspecified, was viewed as not being of indefinite length.

Of the five states, Palestine was unique among its neighbors in that it was a settler state, since the text of the Palestine mandate included the terms of the Balfour Declaration (1917), in which Britain undertook to facilitate the setting up of a "national home for the Jewish people." European Jewish migration to Palestine had begun during the last decades of the nineteenth century with the rise of Zionism, whose objective was the creation of a Jewish state, although the specific details were not to be formulated until the early 1900s. By World War I there were some 65,000 Jews in Palestine, some 8 to 10 percent of the total population. In 1922 there were 93,000 Jews and about 700,000 Arabs; in 1936, three years after the Nazis had come to power in Germany, there were 380,000 Jews and 983,000 Arabs; and in 1946, about 600,000 Jews and 1.3 million Arabs. Thus the Jewish population had increased from 13 percent to 31 percent over a period of twenty-four years. Arab opposition to Jewish immigration was focused at least as much on the Jews' perceived character as European settlers (as in, say, Algeria) as on their religious affiliation.

The rest of the Middle East never experienced direct colonial control, although the Ottoman Empire's borrowings from European sources, and its mounting trade deficit, led it to declare bankruptcy in 1875 and then to the imposition of financial controls by the Ottoman Public Debt Administration, a committee representing the interests of the European bondholders. After the collapse of the empire at the end of World War I, Anatolia was occupied by the French, Greek, and Italian armies, but a national resistance movement formed around the Ottoman general Mustafa Kemal Atatürk, and an independent Turkish republic was declared in 1923. Iran had also been the object of external economic and political interest from the last decade of the eighteenth century; Britain wanted to control Iran because of its proximity to India, while Russia was expanding its empire in Central Asia and was also, or so Britain claimed, intent on gaining access to ports on the Persian Gulf. Iran achieved a certain degree of independence with the rise to power of Reza Khan, subsequently Reza Shah Pahlavi, who set up his own dynasty in 1925. Principally because of their remoteness and lack of major strategic importance, central Arabia and northern Yemen were never colonized. However, Ibn Saʿud, the ruler of central Arabia, gradually extended his rule over most of the rest of the Arabian Peninsula with substantial assistance from Britain, eventually establishing the Kingdom of Saudi Arabia in 1932.

Independence Movements

The states of North Africa were generally fairly quiescent until after 1945, although the colonial regimes, with their policies of widespread confiscation of tribal land for the benefit of the settler population, were deeply unpopular. In Morocco, the French generally were able to contain the movement for national independence, but they precipitated a major crisis by exiling the sultan, Muhammad V, to Madagascar in 1953. As a result, the rallying cry of the national movement became the return of the sultan from exile, which led to the sultan/king retaining his position as ruler after independence in October 1956. In Tunisia, Habib Bourguiba took over the leadership of the national movement after his release from prison in 1936; his Neo-Destour party had about 110,000 members in 1954 and was closely linked with the labor movement. After the war a guerrilla movement formed and attacked French farms and settlers. Probably because France could not take on anticolonial wars in both Tunisia and Algeria at the same time, Tunisian independence was negotiated fairly smoothly in April 1955.

Algeria's road to independence was far rockier than that of any other state in the region, largely because of the large numbers of French settlers in Algeria and of Algerian workers in France. Postwar French governments attempted to incorporate Algeria into France, a step that appealed to the settlers but was vigorously opposed by the great majority of the Arab population. In 1954 the Algerian resistance formed the Front de Libération Nationale under the leadership of Ahmed Ben Bella; after his capture in 1957, some of his colleagues set up an Algerian government in exile in Tunis. The "war of national liberation" lasted from 1954 until 1962; between a million and a million and a half Algerians were killed, and 27,000 French.

In Libya, Italian conquest and pacification between 1911 and 1932 had faced bitter resistance, involving major losses of life, but because of the country's sparse population, this general hostility did not produce a nationalist movement. The country's liberation in 1942 came about as part of the North Africa campaign; the British entered into a tentative alliance with the Amir Idris al-Sanusi, head of the Sanusi order, who was brought back from exile in 1944. After several years of negotiations, Libya became independent under United Nations auspices in 1952, and Idris became the new state's hereditary ruler.

Fearful of Jewish domination in their country, Palestinians rioted against unrestricted Jewish immigration in the 1920s and 1930s. British policy toward Jewish immigration into Palestine vacillated in the pre–World War II years, and by 1939 Britain again was restricting Jewish immigration to the area. © HULTON-DEUTSCH COLLECTION/CORBIS. REPRODUCED BY PERMISSION.

In Egypt, Iraq, Transjordan, Lebanon, and Syria—the situation in Palestine was of course unique—the British and French set up monarchies and constitutional republics, respectively. This new political order was widely contested, and the mandate regimes were generally unpopular, especially in Syria and Palestine. After having set up a compliant government in Iraq, the British felt able to make a formal withdrawal in 1932, although real independence was not obtained until 1958. In Lebanon the French were welcomed by the Maronites and the other Catholic Christians but by few others. In Syria there was a major national rising between 1925 and 1927, which the French had considerable difficulty in controlling, although a notable-dominated group, al-Kutla al-Wataniyya, emerged as the voice of moderate nationalism, with whom, it seemed, the French might be persuaded to work. Expectations were raised in 1936 with the victory of Léon Blum's Popular Front government in France in 1936, but negotiations for independence ceased when it fell a year later, and Syria remained under French control until 1945.

Egypt, already under British tutelage since the declaration of the protectorate in 1914, escaped the formal structures of the mandate system. Late in 1918, some Egyptian politicians asked the British authorities for permission to send a delegation (wafd) to the Paris peace conference. When permission was refused, a widespread national uprising broke out in March 1919. Eventually, Britain conceded limited Egyptian independence in 1922; further agitation during the 1920s and 1930s led to the signature of an Anglo-Egyptian treaty in 1936 that enabled Egypt to enter the League of Nations as an independent state. Nevertheless, a substantial British military presence remained in the country until Gamal Abdel Nasser's seizure of power in 1952.

Palestine and Zionism

In Palestine, the special situation created by Zionist settlement led to increasing hostility and resentment on the part of the Arab population. The British attempted to act in an even-handed fashion toward the two communities, but in general the Arab political leadership was disinclined, for example, to participate in any British constitutional proposals that would imply recognition of the Zionist presence. The Jewish National Fund gradually bought up land in Palestine from (mostly absentee) Arab landlords. It amassed about a quarter of the cultivable area between 1920 and 1948 and settled Jewish immigrants on it in farming cooperatives. Jewish immigrants also settled in the cities: Between 1911 and 1929 the population of Tel Aviv grew from 550 to 38,500. For this and other reasons, there were serious outbreaks of rioting in 1921 and 1929, and a more sustained Palestinian rebellion between 1936 and 1939.

During World War II there was a considerable amount of illegal immigration to Palestine, but in spite of their obvious discontent with Britain, many Zionists fought in, or in units attached to, the British army. After the war Britain decided that it could not solve the problems of Palestine on its own and re-

ferred the problem to the United Nations. In November 1947 the United Nations voted that Palestine should be divided into an Arab state and a Jewish state; the British began to evacuate and had left by May 1948. In January 1948 volunteer units from some of the surrounding Arab countries began to infiltrate into Palestine from Syria. The volunteers and the armies of the other Arab states proved no match for the Zionist forces, which outnumbered them about two to one. On 14 May 1948 the state of Israel was declared. Throughout 1948 large numbers of Arabs left Palestine, unaware that they would not be allowed to come back. By January 1949, there were some 730,000 Palestinian refugees, 280,000 in the West Bank (which became incorporated into Jordan in 1951), 200,000 in the Gaza Strip, and the rest in Lebanon, Syria, and Transjordan.

Bibliography

Abrahamian, Ervand. *Iran between Two Revolutions.* Princeton, NJ: Princeton University Press, 1982.

Anderson, Lisa. *The State and Social Transformation in Tunisia and Libya, 1830–1980.* Princeton, NJ: Princeton University Press, 1986.

Botman, Selma. *Egypt from Independence to Revolution, 1919–1952.* Syracuse, NY: Syracuse University Press, 1991.

Horne, Alistair. *A Savage War of Peace: Algeria, 1954–1962.* London: Macmillan, 1977.

Khoury, Philip S. *Syria and the French Mandate: The Politics of Arab Nationalism, 1920–1945.* Princeton, NJ: Princeton University Press, 1987.

Leatherdale, Clive. *Britain and Saudi Arabia, 1925–1939: The Imperial Oasis.* Totowa, NJ; London: Cass, 1983.

Louis, William Roger. *The British Empire in the Middle East, 1945–1951: Arab Nationalism, the United States, and Postwar Imperialism.* New York; Oxford, U.K.: Oxford University Press, 1984.

Meouchy, Nadine, and Sluglett, Peter, eds. *The British and French Mandates in Comparative Perspectives/Les mandats français et anglais dans une perspective comparative.* Boston: Brill, 2003.

Salibi, Kamal. *A House of Many Mansions: The History of Lebanon Reconsidered.* Berkeley: University of California Press; London: Tauris, 1988.

Sluglett, Peter. *Britain in Iraq, 1914–1932.* London: Ithaca Press, 1976.

Sluglett, Peter. "Formal and Informal Empire in the Middle East." In *The Oxford History of the British Empire,* vol. 5, *Historiography,* edited by Robin W. Winks. New York; Oxford, U.K.: Oxford University Press, 1999.

Wilson, Mary C. *King Abdullah, Britain, and the Making of Jordan.* New York; Cambridge, U.K.: Cambridge University Press, 1987.

Zürcher, Erik J. *Turkey: A Modern History.* New York; London: Tauris, 1998.

PETER SLUGLETT

COLONIAL OFFICE, GREAT BRITAIN

British government department responsible for administration of dependencies, including most of those in the Middle East.

Until 1854 the colonies of the British Empire were managed by the secretary of state for war and the colonies. As colonial affairs grew in importance, a separate Colonial Office with its own secretary was established, which was responsible for administration of Britain's colonies and for the recruitment of colonial civil servants (who comprised the Colonial Service). The lines of Colonial Office authority often overlapped and conflicted with those of the India Office and the Foreign Office. The India Office administered British territories around the Persian Gulf (including the Trucial Coast emirates Bahrain, Qatar, and those that later formed the United Arab Emirates) and the Indian Ocean (including Muscat, part of present-day Oman). The Foreign Office oversaw certain areas of informal British rule, such as Egypt. At the end of World War I, Palestine and Mesopotamia came under British military administration and were therefore the responsibility of the War Office. When civil administrations were established in 1920, the Foreign Office took over responsibility for these territories, designated mandated territories by the League of Nations. Under Winston Churchill, colonial secretary in 1921 to 1922, the Colonial Office took over responsibility for the mandates. At the Cairo Conference in March 1921 Churchill established the basic structure of British overlordship of the Middle East for the next generation. The Colonial Office remained responsible for the administration of Iraq until 1932, for Transjordan until 1946, for Palestine until 1948, and for Aden and its hinterland until 1967. After World War II the Colonial Office became the administrative organ for decolonization. In 1966 it merged with the Commonwealth Relations Office, which itself was later absorbed into the Foreign and Commonwealth Office.

See also FOREIGN OFFICE, GREAT BRITAIN.

Bibliography

Beloff, Max. *Imperial Sunset,* Vol. 1: *Britain's Liberal Empire, 1897–1921;* Vol. 2: *Dream of Commonwealth, 1921–1942.* Basingstoke, U.K.: Macmillan, 1987.

Fromkin, David. *A Peace to End All Peace: The Fall of the Ottoman Empire and the Creation of the Modern Middle East.* New York: Avon Books, 1989.

Porter, Bernard. *The Lion's Share: A Short History of British Imperialism, 1850–1995.* London: Longman, 1996.

BERNARD WASSERSTEIN

COLONS

European settlers (mostly French) who lived in Algeria during France's colonial rule.

When the Algerian war of independence broke out in 1954, the country's colon population stood at 984,000. Only 11 percent of the population, the colons dominated economic life, held a monopoly of political power, and comprised the majority of the professionals, managers, and technicians who kept the country functioning. Their per capita income was roughly seven times that of Muslim Algerians.

The first colons came to Algeria directly on the heels of the French invasion of 1830, mainly because the collapse of the Turkish power structure left large amounts of property available on attractive terms. By the 1840s, it became official French policy to encourage settlement on the land to ensure the permanence of French conquests and to provide a tax base that could put the colony on a self-supporting basis. Demographic pressures inside France, where population was growing more quickly than the economy, added momentum to the colonization movement. Similar pressures in Italy and particularly in Spain led to large immigration from these two countries as well.

Starting in the 1850s and the 1860s, Algeria also attracted significant amounts of French capital because large amounts of state land became available to corporate interests, and opportunities for investment in rails and other infrastructure were lucrative. The earliest colonial vision saw an Algeria peopled by thousands of small European freeholders. The outcome by the mid-twentieth century, however, was that most agricultural land was held by large landholders who mainly employed cheap native labor, while 80 percent of Europeans lived in cities and towns, employed in industry and, particularly, in services.

From the 1840s onward, colons realized that their ability to maintain and improve their economic status depended upon access to political power. In 1848 they won for the first time the right to elect municipal councils, and in these they were assured two-thirds majorities. Until the last years of colonial rule, the settlers were guaranteed two-thirds or three-fourths majorities in all municipal and departmental bodies. Legislation under the Second Empire in 1865 provided that Europeans were citizens of France, while Muslims were subjects. On numerous occasions during the nineteenth century, the Algerian government attempted to intervene in defense of indigenous rights, which were regularly threatened by expanding settler hegemony. Colons were usually able to foil such attempts by invoking republican principles and condemning what they called government authoritarianism. By the twentieth century, however, republican rhetoric quieted; most colons were increasingly out of tune with the more liberal political discourse of the *métropole*. In each decade of the century, they mounted vigorous movements to block native attempts at improving their status and sharing meaningfully in the political process.

When, during the Algerian war of independence, colons began to fear that the government might make unacceptable concessions to the revolutionaries, they allied increasingly with disillusioned elements of the military to challenge civil authority. While the Evian Agreement of 18 March 1962, which provided the framework for Algerian independence, also included specific guarantees of colon rights, many of them, in the last months of French rule, joined with the Organisation Armée Secrète (OAS; Secret Army Organization) in attacks upon Muslims and in systematic destruction of the country's infrastructure. At the same time, unable to countenance minority status, they packed bags

and trunks and headed for the ports and airports. By the end of 1962, not more than 30,000 colons remained in Algeria, mostly elderly, or among the minority who had favored the Algerian cause. Their numbers progressively declined in the years that followed.

See also ALGERIA; ALGERIAN WAR OF INDEPENDENCE; EVIAN ACCORDS (1962); ORGANISATION ARMÉE SECRÈTE (OAS).

JOHN RUEDY

COMITÉ D'ACTION MAROCAINE (CAM)

The first Moroccan nationalist party, established in 1933 and 1934, also known as the Bloc d'Action National, or simply kutla *(bloc).*

The Comité d'Action Marocaine (CAM) was the largest of three organizations created during the early 1930s by young urban nationalists to advance their aims; the two smaller bodies, the *zawiya* and the *taifa*, were clandestine. The most important of the initial cells of the *zawiya*, based in Fez, was led by Allal al-Fasi and Muhammad Hassan al-Wazzani (Ouezzani). Along with five others from the Fez cell, and Ahmed Balafrej and Ahmad Muhammad Lyazidi of the Rabat cell, they constituted the core leadership of the budding nationalist movement. Fasi was *primus inter pares* owing to his capabilities as a thinker and organizer, and to his personal charisma.

Their platform was disseminated through the Paris-based magazine *Maghrib*, and various Moroccan-based French and Arabic periodicals. Formally compiled and published in 1934 as the *Plan des réformes*, the CAM's program argued for comprehensive reform of the French protectorate—politically, administratively, judicially (mixing Western and Islamic legal codes), economically, and educationally—so as to achieve the protectorate's stated goal: the moral and material revival of Morocco with the aid of France. The plan was explicitly reformist. It did not contain any demand for discontinuing the protectorate or achieving independence.

The CAM made little headway from 1934 to 1935 in persuading the French authorities to respond to their demands. The ascent of Popular

Front governments in France and Spain in the first portion of 1936 temporarily gave them new hope; the subsequent lack of progress led the CAM leadership to convene a series of mass meetings in order to mobilize wider public support. In response, in November 1936, the French authorities arrested al-Fasi, al-Wazzani, Lyazidi, and others but released them a month later. The CAM then adopted a more vigorous strategy of broadening its ranks. By early 1937, it had expanded its official membership to about 6,500 (excluding the Spanish zone), had established thirty-two sections throughout the country, and was demonstrating mass appeal among urban workers, artisans, and unemployed rural migrants to the cities.

Alarmed by its success, the French authorities dissolved the CAM on 18 March 1937. The CAM leadership, however, quickly managed to reconstitute itself a month later as the Parti National (National Party for the Realization of the Plan of Reforms). Concurrently, a rupture occurred between a majority of the leadership, led by al-Fasi, and al-Wazzani, who formed the Parti Démocratique Constitutionnel.

See also BALAFREJ, AHMED; FASI, ALLAL AL-; PARTI DÉMOCRATIQUE CONSTITUTIONNEL (PDC); PARTI NATIONAL; POPULAR FRONT; WAZZANI, MUHAMMAD HASSAN AL-.

BRUCE MADDY-WEITZMAN

COMITÉ DE COORDINATION ET D'EXÉCUTION

The executive cabinet of Algeria's FLN, 1956–1958.

The Comité de Coordination et d'Exécution (CCE; Committee of Coordination and Implementation) was created by the Soummam Valley Congress of the Front de Libération Nationale (FLN; National Liberation Front) in September 1956. It was composed of five leaders of the spreading guerrilla movement in colonial Algeria. Revamped and enlarged in 1957, it lasted until September 1958, when it gave way to the new Gouvernement Provisional de la République Algérienne (GPRA; Provisional Government of the Algerian Republic).

See also FRONT DE LIBÉRATION NATIONALE.

Bibliography

Ruedy, John. *Modern Algeria: The Origins and Development of a Nation.* Bloomington: Indiana University Press, 1992.

JOHN RUEDY

COMITÉ JUIF ALGÉRIEN D'ÉTUDES SOCIALES

A Jewish antidefamation organization.

The Comité Juif Algérien d'Études Sociales (CESA; Algerian Jewish Committee for Social Studies) was founded in 1917 by Dr. Henri Aboulker to function as a kind of antidefamation league in the face of continued, virulent *pied noir* antisemitism in Algeria. CESA's expressed goal was "to be on the alert that the free exercise of the Jews' rights as citizens not be violated or ignored."

The group lobbied through French political channels to achieve fuller social and civil rights for Algerian Jews, not as Jews, but as Frenchmen. One of its first campaigns was to remove the barrier preventing Jews from being accepted into the Algerian General Association of Students. As part of its public relations, CESA published and distributed to French military and public figures the *Gold Book of Algerian Jewry*, which listed all Algerian Jews who were killed in action during World War I and all who received military decorations and citations.

Having achieved most of its goals, the group became inactive after several years but revived as the leading voice of Algerian Jewry during the late 1930s.

Bibliography

Stillman, Norman A. *The Jews of Arab Lands in Modern Times.* Philadelphia: Jewish Publication Society, 1991.

NORMAN STILLMAN

COMITÉ RÉVOLUTIONNAIRE D'UNITÉ ET D'ACTION (CRUA)

The body that planned the 1954 Algerian insurrection and gave birth to the FLN.

The Comité Révolutionnaire d'Unité et d'Action (CRUA; Revolutionary Committee of Unity and

Action) was a clandestine organization that kept few formal records. The details of its origins and development have been the subject of dispute among several participants and scholars.

During the early 1950s, frustration grew within the nationalist Mouvement pour le Triomphe des Libertés Démocratiques (MTLD; Movement for the Triumph of Democratic Liberties). That frustration resulted from the failure of political participation to produce tangible results for the Algerian people and also from the political infighting within the party leadership, particularly that which pitted the Central Committee against followers of Messali al-Hadj. In March 1954, Mohamed Boudiaf, an activist from M'Sila, called together a group of young militants, many of whom, like himself, had been members of the revolutionary Organisation Spéciale. Other founders identified with the MTLD Central Committee. It appears that the initial goal of the CRUA was to mediate between the Messalists and the centralists and bring about the reunification of the party. By the summer, when it became clear that the MTLD was irretrievably split, a Committee of Twenty-two decided that direct action was the only solution to Algeria's predicament and named an executive committee to take concrete steps toward armed action.

Boudiaf was to be the coordinator. The committee also included a leader for each of the *wilayas*, or military districts into which the national territory was divided. These were Moustafa Ben Boulaid of the Aurès and Nemencha, Mourad Didouche of the northern Constantine, Rabah Bitat of the Algiers region, and Larbi Ben M'hidi of the Oran. Later a Kabylia *wilaya* was recognized, and its leader, Belkacem Krim, became the sixth member of the executive committee. In October, three exiled militants, Hocine Ait Ahmed, Mohamed Khider, and Ahmed Ben Bella were also named part of the executive committee. These nine men were considered the historic chiefs *(chefs historiques)* of the Algerian revolution. But it was the six militants inside Algeria who made the critical decisions.

At an October meeting or meetings, the exact date or dates of which are debated by the participants, the internal CRUA leadership decided to create the Front de Libération Nationale (FLN; National Liberation Front) and drew up a proclama-

tion calling Algerians of all classes and political persuasions to join them in a war of national liberation. The insurrection broke out in the early morning hours of 1 November 1954.

See also AIT AHMED, HOCINE; BEN BELLA, AHMED; BEN BOULAID, MOUSTAFA; BEN M'HIDI, MUHAMMAD LARBI; BITAT, RABAH; BOUDIAF, MOHAMED; DIDOUCHE, MOURAD; FRONT DE LIBÉRATION NATIONALE (FLN); HADJ, MESSALI AL-; KHIDER, MOHAMED; KRIM, BELKACEM; MOUVEMENT POUR LE TRIOMPHE DES LIBERTÉS DÉMOCRATIQUES.

Bibliography

Horne, Alistair. *A Savage War of Peace: Algeria, 1954–1962,* revised edition. New York: Penguin, 1987.

JOHN RUEDY

COMMERCIAL AND NAVIGATION TREATIES

Allowed European merchants special privileges in trading with the Ottoman Empire; regulated passage of ships through the Dardanelles.

Beginning in 1352, the Ottoman Empire granted special privileges to the merchants of Genoa, Venice, and Florence. These privileges, known as the capitulations, placed European merchants under the direct jurisdiction of their own consular representatives—who judged the civil and criminal cases that involved their own citizens. In addition, the capitulations granted Europeans the right to travel and trade freely within the empire and to pay low customs duties on imports and exports. The capitulations allowed European merchants to organize almost all trade between the empire and Europe.

The first commercial treaty with a maritime state of western Europe, the Draft Treaty of Amity and Commerce, was negotiated with France in 1535. Based on the model of the earlier capitulations, this treaty, which was never confirmed by Sultan Süleyman (reigned 1520–1566), stated that French merchants would be permitted to move and trade freely within the empire and to pay only the taxes and duties paid by Turkish merchants. These privileges were eventually granted in 1569. In 1580, a similar treaty was concluded, granting these privileges to Britain, to English merchants who until this point had been required to conduct business with the empire under the French flag. In 1581, the English Levant company was chartered: All English consular and diplomatic officials became employees of the company, which supervised the execution of the capitulations.

These treaties governed commerce between the empire and western Europe until 1809, when the Treaty of Peace, Commerce, and Secret Alliance (the Dardanelles treaty) was signed between the empire and Great Britain. This treaty, which followed a brief period of British–Ottoman enmity, reaffirmed the capitulations while granting limited reciprocal privileges to Ottoman merchants. More importantly, the treaty granted the empire the right to close passage through the Bosporous and Dardanelles straits (the Turkish Straits) to foreign warships during times of war. The issue of free passage through the Straits would be a subject of diplomacy for the next 150 years. On 7 May 1830 the United States signed its first commercial and navigation treaty with the Ottoman Empire. This treaty extended to the United States the same privileges granted to European merchants.

Following British assistance to the sultan in defeating the army of Ibrahim ibn Muhammad Ali of Egypt, the Commercial Convention of Balta Liman was signed on 16 August 1838. This treaty, a renewal of the Commercial Convention of 1820, was a decisive defeat for the Ottoman government, which had sought to ease its fiscal constraints by raising the duties paid by British merchants. The negotiated increase from 3 to 5 percent *ad valorem* on imports was offset by a large reduction of duties paid on the internal movement of goods. The benefits accruing to Britain were strengthened by the 1861–1862 convention, which raised the external tariff to 8 percent in exchange for the gradual reduction of duties on exports to 1 percent; this convention transformed the empire into a virtually free-trading country. The 1838 and 1861 conventions expressed the political incapacity of the Ottoman government to substitute for the capitulations a new mode of organizing trade, and it signaled the continuing economic subordination of the empire to Western states.

After the dissolution of the Ottoman Empire in the aftermath of World War I, the Lausanne Treaty of Peace with Turkey and the accompanying Straits Convention was signed at the conclusion of the Turkish war of independence, dated 24 July 1923. It reestablished the principle of freedom of navigation through the Straits by demilitarizing the shores; it also established an international supervisory commission, under the permanent presidency of Turkey, to execute this agreement. In addition, the treaty bound the Republic of Turkey to maintain the prewar level of tariffs at their low rates.

Angered by the restrictive clauses of the treaty's Straits Convention, Turkey pushed for revisions, resulting in the Montreux Convention on the Turkish Straits, dated 20 July 1936. This conferred on Turkey all the duties and powers previously granted to an international commission, while permitting the remilitarization of the Straits. The passage through the Straits of warships that threatened Turkey was left to the discretion of the Turkish government, subject to ratification by the League of Nations.

In 1945, after World War II, the USSR demanded that unilateral Turkish control over the Straits granted by the Montreux Convention be replaced by joint Turkish–Soviet responsibility; the Soviets also demanded the right to establish military bases in Turkey for the defense of the Straits. These veiled threats were countered by the admission of Turkey into the North Atlantic Treaty Organization (NATO).

See also BALTA LIMAN, CONVENTION OF (1838); CAPITULATIONS; DARDANELLES, TREATY OF THE (1809); IBRAHIM IBN MUHAMMAD ALI; LAUSANNE, TREATY OF (1923); MONTREUX CONVENTION (1936); NORTH ATLANTIC TREATY ORGANIZATION (NATO); OTTOMAN EMPIRE; STRAITS, TURKISH.

Bibliography

Hurewitz, J. C. *The Middle East and North Africa in World Politics: A Documentary Record,* 2d edition. New Haven, CT: Yale University Press, 1975.

Owen, Roger. *The Middle East in the World Economy, 1800–1914.* London and New York: Methuen, 1981.

Puryear, Vernon John. *International Economics and Diplomacy in the Near East: A Study of British Commercial Policy in the Levant, 1834–1853.* Hamden, CT: Archon Books, 1969.

Shaw, Stanford, and Shaw, Ezel Kural. *History of the Ottoman Empire and Modern Turkey.* 2 vols. Cambridge, U.K., and New York: Cambridge University Press, 1976–1977.

DAVID WALDNER

COMMITTEE FOR DEFENSE OF FREEDOM AND HUMAN RIGHTS

The first independent human rights organization in Iran's history.

The Iranian Committee for the Defense of Freedom and Human Rights was established in Tehran in fall 1977. It was founded by twenty-nine members of the opposition to the government of Mohammad Reza Pahlavi, including Shahpur Bakhtiar and Mehdi Bazargan, both future prime ministers of Iran. Their first act was to draft a letter of protest to the secretary general of the United Nations, decrying human rights abuses in Iran. The committee's various activities contributed to the onset of the Iranian Revolution of 1979.

See also BAKHTIAR, SHAPUR; BAZARGAN, MEHDI; IRANIAN REVOLUTION (1979); PAHLAVI, MOHAMMAD REZA.

Bibliography

Abrahamian, Ervand. *Iran between Two Revolutions.* Princeton, NJ: Princeton University Press, 1982.

NEGUIN YAVARI

COMMITTEE FOR THE DEFENSE OF LEGITIMATE RIGHTS

Saudi dissident group established in 1993.

Founded in Riyadh by six Saudi scholars, the Committee for the Defense of Legitimate Rights (CDLR) had an agenda of political protest that was couched in a Sunni Islamic idiom that used the Qurʾan and hadith (sayings of the prophet Muhammad) to buttress its claims. The group's founding letter called for an end to injustice and the establishment of individual rights based on the precepts of *shariʿa,*

or Islamic jurisprudence. The Saudi government banned the organization, forcing its members to go underground or leave the country. In 1994 the CDLR established its headquarters in London under the leadership of Muhammad al-Masʿari, a former physics professor who had been imprisoned briefly in Saudi Arabia for his role in the committee. From London the group established a web site and used other forms of modern technology to promote a more strident program of opposition to the Saudi regime. Al-Masʿari criticized the profligacy and absolutism of the Al Saʿud ruling family and called for a government that was more open and a more equitable distribution of the country's vast wealth. He criticized religious authorities (*ulama*) who provided Islamic justifications for the Al Saʿud's policies, and he supported those who called for reform of the system.

See also SAUDI ARABIA.

Bibliography

Fandy, Mamoun. *Saudi Arabia and the Politics of Dissent.* New York: St. Martin's Press, 1999.

Al-Rasheed, Madawi. *A History of Saudi Arabia.* New York; Cambridge, U.K.: Cambridge University Press, 2002.

ANTHONY B. TOTH

COMMITTEE FOR UNION AND PROGRESS

The principal Young Turk organization that left its mark on the politics of the Ottoman state from the 1890s to 1918.

The Turkish name translates literally as the "Society for Union and Progress," although reference to it as *komite* is common in its conspiratorial phases. Its members are referred to as unionists. Its precursor was the Ottoman Union Society, a secret circle of liberal-minded students in the imperial military medical school in Constantinople (now Istanbul) who aspired to overthrow the autocratic regime of Sultan Abdülhamit II. The founders were Ibrahim Temo (Albanian); İshak Sükuti and Abdullah Cevdet (both Kurds); and Mehmet Reşid (Circassian). Despite its clandestine organization modeled along the Italian Carbonari, Abdülhamit's police discovered and suppressed the society as its cell spread among higher schools in Constantinople.

After 1895, the society established contact with Ottoman liberals in European exile. Its name changed to Committee for Union and Progress (CUP) under the influence of positivist Ahmet Riza, who became the president of the first European branch of the committee and represented the centralist camp in the Young Turk movement abroad. The first issue of Riza's *Meşveret* on 3 December 1895 publicized the CUP's program. The internal and external branches of the CUP differed on the appropriateness of use of force against the regime. Over this issue, the gradualist Ahmet Riza forfeited his leadership temporarily to Murat Bey (Mehmet Murat), a revolutionist exile from the Constantinople organization. After two unsuccessful coup attempts in 1896 and 1897, the domestic leadership, which now included high officials and officers, was imprisoned. In Europe, rivalries between Young Turk groups and within the branches weakened the committee.

After 1906, underground revolutionary activity intensified in the empire, particularly in Macedonia. Two groups, Patrie and Liberty and the Ottoman Liberty Society, merged in Salonika and contacted Ahmet Riza, who had reorganized with Bahattin Şakir the exile community under the name Progress and Union. The Macedonian and the external branches agreed to cooperate under the more familiar name of Committee for Union and Progress around the revised program of forcing Abdülhamit to submit to constitutionalist demands. The leadership of the domestic branch used the organizational tactics of Macedonian nationalist committees, masonic lodges, and Sufi brotherhoods to expand membership. Committee army officers had ready access to arms and disaffected men, whom they led in July 1908 to rebellious acts that triggered the revolutionary wave.

The 1908 revolution brought an end to the secrecy of the CUP. Its central committee, however, dominated by ethnic Turks and still in Salonika, remained exclusive and its proceedings clandestine. The administrative inexperience and social insecurity of its leaders (among them civilians Mehmet Talat, Bahattin Şakir, Midhat Şükrü; and officers Cemal Paça and Enver Paşa) kept the committee from taking charge of the government. After securing a decisive majority of approved candidates in

parliament, the CUP established a parliamentary group. It redefined itself as a political party only in 1913. The headquarters of the committee moved to Constantinople at this juncture, and decision making was broadened with the institution of a general assembly next to the central committee.

The society exercised more direct control over government after the counterrevolutionary attempt of April 1909 by placing its men in key cabinet positions. Its main objective was to unify all ethnic and religious groups around an Ottomanist allegiance. The CUP cultivated friendly relations with the great powers, while seeking the abolition of the capitulations. The centralist policies it imposed in the name of preserving the territorial integrity of the empire at a time when large territories were breaking away, strengthened the CUP's decentralist rivals. Its manipulation of the 1912 elections through its control over the state machinery gave the society a Pyrrhic victory. It was forced to give up power to the leaders of the old regime in 1912.

Alarmed by losses in the Balkan War and fearful of the government's suppression of their clubs, the unionists carried out a coup on 23 January 1913, to topple Kamil Paşa and replace him with Mahmut Şevket Paşa. The assassination of Mahmut Şevket later in 1913 gave the excuse to the society to crush its opposition and come to uncontested power. Wartime emergency after 1914 facilitated the establishment of single-party rule. The disastrous outcome of World War I discredited the unionist leadership. In November 1918, as the three strongmen—Talat, Enver, and Cemal—fled abroad, the Committee for Union and Progress dissolved itself.

Both as society and party, the Union and Progress had a diverse membership and grassroots political organization. Its clubs sponsored cultural and educational activities. It coopted the notables in the countryside, even though the latter did not always favor its policies. Its constituency included the officialdom, army officers, workers, and younger professionals and small merchants (especially in the Turkish provinces).

See also ABDÜLHAMIT II; AHMET RIZA; BALKAN WARS (1912–1913); CAPITULATIONS; CEMAL PAŞA; CEVDET, ABDULLAH; ENVER PAŞA;

KAMIL, KIBRISH MEHMET; ŞEVKET, MAHMUT;
TALAT, MEHMET; YOUNG TURKS.

Bibliography

Ahmad, Feroz. *The Young Turks: The Committee of Union and Progress in Turkish Politics, 1908–1914.* Oxford: Clarendon, 1969.

Ramsaur, Ernest E. *The Young Turks: Prelude to the Revolution of 1908.* Princeton, NJ: Princeton University Press, 1957.

HASAN KAYALI

COMMUNICATION

Because of the Middle East's central location and the relatively high percentage of its people who engage in commerce, ease and speed of information transmission have long been major concerns.

Early Muslim dynasties, including the Abbasids, the Zengids, and the Mamluks, used carrier pigeons to convey military intelligence or vital state information. Messengers mounted on camels or mules carried official information throughout the Umayyad and Abbasid realms. Although this service *(barid)* was unavailable for private or commercial use, unofficial couriers *(fuyuj)* carried mail on land and sea, and some merchants used private messengers. The Ottoman and Safavid states had postal and courier services. Modern postal service began in the Ottoman Empire as early as 1823 and was extended to most cities by 1856. Private courier services existed in Egypt by the 1830s; the government post office, founded in 1865, carried mail from the outset and money orders from 1868.

France's occupation of Egypt in 1798 and the spread of European commerce in the Middle East in the early nineteenth century led to the introduction of new courier services and communication devices, including semaphores and heliographs. The electric telegraph first came to Constantinople (now Istanbul) in 1839; Sultan Abdülmecit I authorized a telegraph line from the capital to Edirne in 1847 (it was not completed until 1855); and the first cable was laid under the Black Sea, from Varna to the Crimea, in 1854. Companies based in Britain vied to extend telegraph lines across the empire to Egypt and the Persian Gulf, but the Ottoman government undertook the task; the lines reached Baghdad by 1861. A telegraph line was built between Alexandria and Cairo in 1854, at the same time that Egypt's first railway was built. Under Saʿid Pasha (1854–1863) and Khedive Ismaʿil (1863–1879), telegraph lines were extended to all inhabited parts of Egypt.

The Sepoy Mutiny (1857), news of which took forty days to reach London, made Britain aware of its need for telegraphic communication with India. After an abortive attempt to lay an underwater cable from Aden to Bombay, Britain's government negotiated with the Ottomans and the government of Iran for the right to extend lines across their territories. The Indo-European Telegraph Department of the government of India began to string lines across Iran in 1863; two years later the telegraph was operational from Baghdad to Baluchistan, although problems arose, both from attacks by nomads and from official obstructionism. The Indo-European Telegraph Company, which was formed in 1867, built a more efficient line across Iran and Russia to Germany that began service in 1870. Telegraph operators, whether French-speaking Turks and Armenians in the Ottoman Empire or English-speaking Indian officers in Iran, soon became potent agents of Westernization and of tighter state control over provincial and local government.

The telephone was introduced to Constantinople and Alexandria in 1881. Used at first by European merchants, this new medium of communication was soon adopted by Egypt's government and later by businesses and households. The telephone's spread in the Ottoman Empire was upheld by Sultan Abdülhamit II (1876–1909), who was fearful of electricity, then accelerated by the Young Turks (1909–1914). Wireless telegraphy was introduced into the Ottoman Empire and Egypt in 1913.

World War I accelerated public familiarity with modern means of communication. After 1918, the governments of the states in the Middle East, new and old, set up ministries to manage the postal, telegraph, and telephone services for both official and private uses. Radio broadcasting began in Egypt in 1932 and soon spread to most other countries in the area, which established transmission facilities and radio stations under government auspices. During World War II and later, during regional conflicts such as the Arab–Israel War of 1948, extensive state censorship was imposed on all communications; this has been maintained in some

Palestine Telecommunications, developer of an intricate computerized network, helps rebuild part of the infrastructure of the Palestinian state, damaged by recent violent conflict with Israel. Severe damage and destruction by Israel to commercial and industrial projects, political institutions, water systems, etc., reversed the progress Palestinians built during seven years of peaceful co-existence with Israel. © RICKI ROSEN/CORBIS. REPRODUCED BY PERMISSION.

countries in the area. Television broadcasting began in Iraq in 1958 and soon spread to all other countries of the Middle East, generally under state control. In the last three decades of the twentieth century, governments expended large sums in updating their communications systems, replacing telegraphs with telex facilities and, later, augmenting telephones with fax machines.

The 1990s saw the region further revolutionized by the introduction of satellite dishes, mobile telephones, and the internet. Although some countries tried to regulate new technology—Iran and Iraq, for example, were among those banning satellite dishes, and Saudi Arabia and Syria tried to control internet access—such media allowed an unprecedented exchange of ideas, news and information, and entertainment to wide audiences in a region where censorship has reigned and the free exchange of ideas has been tightly controlled.

Bibliography

Davison, Roderic. "The Advent of the Electric Telegraph in the Ottoman Empire." In *Essays in Ottoman and Turkish History, 1774–1923: The Impact of the West*, edited by Roderic Davison. Austin: University of Texas Press, 2000.

Hershlag, Z. Y. *Introduction to the Modern Economic History of the Middle East*, 2d edition. Leiden, Netherlands: E. J. Brill, 1980.

Shaw, Stanford J., and Shaw, Ezel Kural. *History of the Ottoman Empire and Modern Turkey, Vol. 2*. Cambridge and New York: Cambridge University Press, 1977.

ARTHUR GOLDSCHMIDT
UPDATED BY MICHAEL R. FISCHBACH

COMMUNISM IN THE MIDDLE EAST

Origins of Middle Eastern Communism.

Communism reached the Middle East shortly after the 1917 Bolshevik revolution. Armenians, Azeris, Greeks, Jews, and Kurds were among the first to form trade unions and organize communist parties. But the transmission of Marxism was not purely an intellectual project of minorities, nor did minorities ultimately comprise the majority of communists in any country.

Formation of the Communist Parties in the Middle East

Turkish workers and students in Germany participated in the uprising of the Spartakusbund in January 1919. Some of them subsequently established the Workers' and Peasants' Party of Turkey. The first Iraqi Marxist, Husayn al-Rahhal, was a student in Berlin at the time and discussed the events with children of the participants. Iranian migrant workers became familiar with socialist ideas in Russia. The first communist parties in the Middle East were in Egypt, Palestine, Lebanon, and Iran.

Joseph Rosenthal, a Palestinian-born Jew, emigrated to Egypt around 1898 and became active in the trade union and socialist movement in Alexandria. Rosenthal, Mahmud Husni al-Urabi, and Anton Marun founded the Egyptian Socialist Party in 1921. Al-Urabi then traveled to Moscow for a course in Marxism. After returning he transformed the Socialist Party into the Communist Party of Egypt (CPE) in 1923 and expelled Rosenthal for "right-wing deviationism" in the first of many struggles between Jews and Muslims and Copts in the Egyptian communist movement. After leading an adventurous series of strikes in Alexandria in 1924, the CPE was destroyed by the newly installed nationalist government.

Communism in Palestine was born of the disaffection of a small number of Jewish immigrants from socialist Zionism. The Communist Party of Palestine (PCP) was officially recognized in 1924. Despite their anti-Zionist stand, the party's new-immigrant Jewish members were isolated from the country's Arab majority. Arabs began to join the PCP in the late 1920s. Radwan al-Hilu spent three years training in Moscow and upon his return in 1934 became party secretary general. As a result Al-Hilu's rise to the party leadership was due to the directive of the leadership of the Comintern, the international organization of communist parties, to Arabize the PCP. During the Arab Revolt of 1936 to 1939 the party suffered the first of several splits along ethnic lines. Another split in 1943 resulted in the establishment of the National Liberation League (NLL) in 1944 by young Arab intellectuals led by Bulus Farah and trade unionists of the Federation of Arab Trade Unions and Labor Societies. Jewish party members claiming to uphold internationalism reorganized the PCP in 1944 under the leadership of Shmu'el Mikunis. However, the post-1944 PCP was mostly a Jewish national communist group parallel to the NLL.

Palestinian Jewish communists encouraged the formation of the Communist Party of Syria and Lebanon. Fu'ad al-Shamali, a Maronite tobacco worker, led a Lebanese Workers' Party in Alexandria that was affiliated with the Egyptian Socialist Party from 1920 to 1922. He was deported in 1922 to Lebanon, where he joined forces with Yusuf Yazbak. In 1924 the Comintern dispatched PCP member Joseph Berger to meet with Shamali and Yazbak. The next year Elie Teper, a PCP member and Comintern emissary, connected the Shamali-Yazbak circle with a circle of Armenians. The two groups formed a Provisional Central Committee for the Communist Party of Syria and Lebanon.

The Communist Party of Iran was established in 1920. The next year the communists and the Jangalis—a guerrilla movement of small landowners led by a Muslim cleric—briefly established a Soviet Socialist Republic of Iran in Gilan. After their insurrection collapsed, the communists extended their activities to the interior of the country. Together with the Socialist Party they established a Central Council of Federated Trade Unions. Reza Shah Pahlavi destroyed the trade union federation and the Communist Party between 1927 and 1932. Party leaders in exile in Moscow were liquidated in the Stalinist purges.

The Growth of Middle Eastern Communism, 1930s to 1960s

From the mid-1930s on, continuing Anglo-French colonial and semicolonial rule, the Arab revolt in Palestine, the global challenge of communism and fascism to a capitalist world mired in protracted depression, and—after June 1941—the prominent role of the Soviet Union in the antifascist struggle enhanced the appeal of communism. The young intelligentsia and urban working classes—the principal social base of communism—grew substantially, while their standards of living declined. Unlike socially conservative nationalist leaders, the communists embraced the economic, social, and cultural changes in the region. In several countries they became the leading force for modern political organization and action, demanding both national independence and social justice. In the 1930s the Egyptian communist movement was revived and the Algerian communists became independent from the Communist Party of France, which equivocated on the question of Algerian independence. New parties were established in Tunisia (1934), Iraq (1938), and Morocco (1943). Communism became legal in Palestine in 1944, allowing both the NLL and the PCP to achieve some modest successes. In the same year the Communist Party of Syria separated from its Lebanese base. Its leader, the Kurdish figure Khalid Bakdash, became the most prominent orthodox Arab communist.

By the late 1930s, Iranian Marxism spread beyond its initial base among Armenians and Azeris to the Persian-speaking intelligentsia. They were the principal founders of the Tudeh (Masses) Party in 1941. The Tudeh became a mass movement after the deposition of Reza Shah Pahlavi, with some 100,000 members by 1946 and regional allies in the Democratic Parties of Kurdistan and Azerbaijan. It led a trade union federation of 355,000 members. The party was repressed between 1946 and 1950 but rose to prominence again during the oil nationalization movement of 1951 to 1953. It was all but destroyed after the CIA-sponsored coup in August 1953.

The Communist Party of Iraq (CPI) grew out of the Association against Imperialism established in 1935. Led by Salman Yusuf Salman (known by the *nom de guerre* Fahd), the CPI became a mass movement and the only truly national political force in Iraq from 1941 to 1949. Many Jews joined the party in the 1940s and three served briefly as secretary general in 1948 and 1949. The fortunes of the party declined sharply with the arrest of Fahd in 1948 and his execution the next year. It recovered and became a substantial force in the 1952 popular uprising and the 1958 coup that overthrew the pro-British monarchy.

The revival of Egyptian communism was fraught with factionalism and contention over the Jewish leadership of several of the organizations. Three Jews—Ahmad Sadiq Sa'd, Raymond Douek, and Yusuf Darwish—emerged from a circle of minorities and resident foreigners in Cairo to establish the New Dawn group (after the magazine they published in 1945 and 1946). In the 1950s their organization became the Workers' and Peasants' Communist Party. Darwish's work as legal counsel for many trade unions gave his comrades a foothold among textile workers and others in Cairo's northern suburbs.

Between 1940 and 1943 three other Jews established rival communist organizations: Marcel Israel (People's Liberation); Hillel Schwartz (Iskra); and Henri Curiel (the Egyptian Movement for National Liberation). From 1947 to 1948 the three factions united briefly under Curiel's leadership as the Democratic Movement for National Liberation (HADETU).

Curiel's unorthodox political style and his opposition to the open ideological confrontation with Zionism favored by Iskra and the New Dawn group made him suspect even before HADETU endorsed the UN partition plan for Palestine. The rebellion against Curiel's leadership in 1948 expressed both the desire of young Muslim and Coptic intellectuals to Egyptianize the movement and the tensions over Zionism that affected every Arab communist party. The Communist Party of Egypt was established in 1949 in opposition to the existing communist organizations and it excluded Jews from membership.

The nucleus of the future Communist Party of Sudan was formed in 1946 by Sudanese in Cairo under Curiel's patronage. In the 1950s and 1960s the party established a strong base among the intelligentsia, railway workers, and farmers in the Jazira—sectors of society that grew rapidly with capitalist development. Unlike in several other countries, foreigners and minorities were insignificant in the party. Hence, its national character was unassailable. It was nonetheless banned in 1965.

The Decline of Middle Eastern Communism, 1960s to the Present

Many assert that communist prospects in the Arab world were fatally undermined by support for the establishment of the state of Israel. Far more damaging in the long run was the ascendancy of authoritarian populist nationalist regimes favored by the Soviet Union. The Communist Party of Algeria dissolved itself in 1956 and directed its members to join the National Liberation Front, which became an ally of the Soviet Union after it came to power in 1962. The Egyptian communists enthusiastically supported Gamal Abdel Nasser's Arab Nationalism and Arab Socialism, even as they languished in jail. In 1964 the two principal Egyptian communist parties disbanded. The Soviet Union courted Iraq's Abd al-Karim Qasim even after he turned on his erstwhile communist allies. The CPI was decimated by a CIA-facilitated massacre during the Ba'th's brief rule in 1963. By the 1970s the Iraqi and Syrian communists became appendages of regimes allied to the Soviet Union. The failure of the 1971 coup led by the Communist Party of Sudan and supported by the Soviet Union marked the last serious possibility for communists to achieve significant power anywhere in the Middle East and North Africa.

The Communist Party of Israel split largely along national lines in 1965. The emergence of the New Communist List (RAKAH) ultimately allowed the Arab communists to establish an electoral front (HADASH) that became the leading force among Arab citizens of Israel in the 1970s and 1980s, in sharp contrast to the downward trajectory of communists elsewhere in the Arab world.

See also CURIEL FAMILY; LABOR AND LABOR UNIONS; NATIONAL PROGRESSIVE FRONT (SYRIA); QASIM, ABD AL-KARIM; TUBI, TAWFIQ; YUSUF, YUSUF SALMAN.

Bibliography

Abrahamian, Ervand. *Iran between Two Revolutions.* Princeton, NJ: Princeton University Press, 1982.

Bashear, Suliman. *Communism in the Arab East, 1918–1928.* London: Ithaca Press, 1980.

Batatu, Hanna. *The Old Social Classes and the Revolutionary Movements of Iraq: A Study of Iraq's Old Landed and Commercial Classes and of Its Communists, Baʿthists, and Free Officers.* Princeton, NJ: Princeton University Press, 1978.

Beinin, Joel. *Was the Red Flag Flying There?: Marxist Politics and the Arab–Israeli Conflict in Egypt and Israel, 1948–1965.* Berkeley: University of California Press, 1990.

Botman, Selma. *The Rise of Egyptian Communism, 1939–1970.* Syracuse, NY: Syracuse University Press, 1988.

Budeiri, Musa. *The Palestine Communist Party, 1919–1948: Arab and Jew in the Struggle for Internationalism.* London: Ithaca Press, 1979.

JOEL S. BEININ

COMMUNIST PARTIES IN THE MIDDLE EAST

See COMMUNISM IN THE MIDDLE EAST

COMMUNIST PARTY: EGYPT

See COMMUNISM IN THE MIDDLE EAST

COMMUNIST PARTY: IRAN

See TUDEH PARTY

COMMUNIST PARTY: IRAQ

See COMMUNISM IN THE MIDDLE EAST

COMMUNIST PARTY: ISRAEL

See COMMUNISM IN THE MIDDLE EAST

COMMUNIST PARTY: JORDAN

See COMMUNISM IN THE MIDDLE EAST

COMMUNIST PARTY: LEBANON

See COMMUNISM IN THE MIDDLE EAST

COMMUNIST PARTY: MOROCCO

See COMMUNISM IN THE MIDDLE EAST

COMMUNIST PARTY: PALESTINE

See COMMUNISM IN THE MIDDLE EAST

COMMUNIST PARTY: SYRIA

See COMMUNISM IN THE MIDDLE EAST

COMMUNIST PARTY: TURKEY

See COMMUNISM IN THE MIDDLE EAST

COMPAGNIE FRANÇAISE DES PÉTROLES (CFP)

A company, usually called CFP, formed to handle French share of Mesopotamian oil.

Formed in 1923–1924, the Compagnie Française des Pétroles (CFP) was organized to handle the 25 percent French share of the Turkish Petroleum Company. This percentage of oil from Mesopotamia (now Iraq) was stipulated by the Long–Berenger Agreement of 1919 and confirmed by the British–French Oil Agreement of 1920. Owned in part by the government of France, CFP cosponsored the 1928 Red Line Agreement, and after World War II, it was part of the Iranian oil consortium.

See also BRITISH–FRENCH OIL AGREEMENT; RED LINE AGREEMENT.

Bibliography

Hurewitz, J. C., ed. *The Middle East and North Africa in World Politics.* New Haven, CT: Yale University Press, 1979.

Yergin, Daniel. *The Prize: The Epic Quest for Oil, Money, and Power.* New York: Simon and Schuster, 1991.

ZACHARY KARABELL

CONDOMINIUM AGREEMENT (1899)

The 1899 pact that conferred and described joint British–Egyptian dominion over the Sudan.

The concept of condominium in international law refers to a joint dominion over a certain territory by two or more states, which jointly exercise their sovereignty over it. A unique feature of the condominium is that the territory in question belongs simultaneously to two or more states and is in this sense a part of the territory of each of them. Hence, each state is entitled to implement its authority in accordance with the condominium agreement.

In the context of Egyptian–Sudanese relations, the Condominium Agreement refers to the Anglo–Egyptian agreement on the Sudan signed 19 January 1899, by Lord Cromer, the British counsel-general in Egypt, and Boutros Ghali Pasha, the Egyptian minister of foreign affairs. Since Egypt itself was occupied by the British, the agreement legalized British control of the Sudan and framed it as an Anglo–Egyptian rule and administration. The Condominium Agreement was meant to offset potential Ottoman and European opposition to British expansionism.

The Condominium Agreement referred to "certain provinces in the Soudan [*sic*] which were in rebellion against the authority of the Khedive, but which had now been reconquered by the joint military and financial efforts of Britain and Egypt." The first two articles defined the Sudan by reference to territories south of the 22d parallel that had previously been administered by Egypt and had now been reconquered or that might in future be reconquered by Anglo–Egyptian forces or that had never been evacuated by Egyptian troops. Therefore, according to the agreement, the territories of the Sudan included both Wadi Halfa, a town in northern Sudan, and Suakin, a city on the Red Sea.

The third and fourth articles dealt with executive and legislative matters in the new joint administration. The supreme military and civil command of the Sudan was to be vested in one officer, termed the governor-general, who was appointed by a khedival decree on the recommendation of the British government and could be removed only by a khedival decree with the consent of the British government. The Condominium Agreement also dealt with judicial matters in the Sudan and stressed the independence of the Sudanese judicial system and the prohibition of slave trade. With the new arrangements, Lord Kitchener, who was the commander of the Anglo–Egyptian forces, was appointed as the first governor-general of the Sudan.

The Condominium Agreement lasted until 1954 when Sudan gained its independence.

See also KITCHENER, HORATIO HERBERT.

Bibliography

Holt, P. M. *A Modern History of the Sudan, from the Funj Sultanate to the Present Day.* London: Weidenfeld and Nicolson, 1961.

Shibeika, Mekki. *British Policy in the Sudan, 1882–1902.* London and New York: Oxford University Press, 1952.

ALI E. HILLAL DESSOUKI

CONFÉDÉRATION DÉMOCRATIQUE DU TRAVAIL (CDT)

Moroccan trade union confederation usually referred to as the CDT.

Affiliated with the Union Socialiste des Forces Populaires (USFP), the Confédération Démocratique du Travail (CDT) was organized in 1978 in opposition to the largest labor confederation, the Union Marocaine du Travail, whose leadership it accused of corruption and stagnation. Its membership in the mid-1990s was about 300,000, making it the smallest of the three trade unions (the third is the Istiqlal-affiliated Union Générale des Travailleurs Marocains [UGTM]). Following widespread riots and student unrest in 1981, the CDT was accused of helping to foment the troubles; all offices were closed, and many of its activists were imprisoned. It was allowed to reopen in April 1987.

During the early 1990s, the CDT and the other labor federations pressed the authorities for improved wages and working conditions. With the UGTM, the CDT led a one-day general strike in late December 1990 that resulted in a number of fatalities. The CDT's secretary-general, Noubir Amaoui, was sentenced to two years' imprisonment, in the spring of 1992, for "libel and insult" in his criticism of the government published in a Spanish newspaper. He was released in July 1993. The CDT received four seats in the 1993 indirect elections for parliament, an increase of one from the 1984 elections.

See also UNION GÉNÉRALE DES TRAVAILLEURS MAROCAINS (UGTM); UNION MAROCAINE DU TRAVAIL (UMT); UNION SOCIALISTE DES FORCES POPULAIRES (USFP).

Bibliography

Nelson, Harold D., ed. *Morocco: A Country Study,* 5th edition. Washington, DC: U.S. Government Printing Office, 1986.

BRUCE MADDY-WEITZMAN

CONFEDERATION OF IRANIAN STUDENTS

The most active organized opposition to the shah's regime during the two decades prior to the 1978–79 revolution.

Following the August 1953 coup, all activities against the Iranian government were brought to a halt. When opposition reemerged in the early 1960s, students in Iran and abroad were its leading force. Linking activists in France, Germany, and England, the Confederation of Iranian Students (CIS) was formed in April 1960. In the same year, the Iranian Students' Association in the United States (ISAUS), originally set up as a pro-government organization, was taken over by the opposition. The leaders of this new student movement were young National Front and Tudeh Party members and sympathizers.

Between 1960 and 1962, the National Front became the leading force in Iran and in the student movement abroad. In January 1962, the CIS and the ISAUS joined together and founded the Confederation of Iranian Students, National Union (CISNU), opposing Premier Ali Amini and Mohammad Reza Shah Pahlavi. The latter tried to combine unconstitutional rule with a reform project, the White Revolution, which included female en-

franchisement and the formation of a literacy corps, demands previously articulated by the CISNU.

When legal opposition in Iran was once again crushed in 1963, the CISNU survived and intensified its activities abroad. Its young National Front leaders moved leftward in cooperation with a splinter faction of the Tudeh Party. During the second half of the 1960s, while Marxist and Islamist revolutionaries in Iran clandestinely prepared for guerrilla armed struggle, the CISNU remained the country's only aboveground opposition organization. In 1965, some former CISNU leaders were arrested and tried in response to a failed attempt on the shah's life. This led to a direct confrontation with the government, pushing the CISNU toward further radicalization.

The CISNU also played an important role in the international youth and student protests of the 1960s and 1970s. The June 1967 demonstrations by Iranian and German students against the shah's visit to West Germany triggered militant student upheavals across that country and were in the forefront of the European-wide student protests of 1968 and 1969. The CISNU's U.S. branch became an active participant in the U.S. antiwar and radical student movement of the 1960s and 1970s. About half of Iran's university population was studying abroad, which made possible the CISNU's extraordinary growth and impact.

The second decade of CISNU activities saw its further radicalization and support for urban guerrilla operations in Iran. Already in 1971, the Iranian government had declared the CISNU illegal. By 1975, the CISNU had split into a number of independent, mainly Maoist and pro-guerrilla student organizations. However, both the effectiveness and numerical strength of the student opposition abroad continued to grow as these rival groups cooperated in a united front.

During the 1970s, in addition to being active in France, England, Germany, and the United States, the CISNU had spread its activities to Austria, Italy, Sweden, Holland, Turkey, Canada, and India. International attention to the shah's dictatorship and repression in Iran had increased considerably. Two decades of relentless activities by the CISNU may have been the most important factor in bringing about criticism of the shah's regime by international human rights groups, news media, political circles, and governments.

During the late 1970s, as a pre-revolutionary situation emerged in Iran, splinter CISNU factions gained even more publicity via events such as militant protests during the shah's 1977 official visit to the United States. By 1978, most student leaders and activists were returning home to join the revolution directly. A key chapter in the history of twentieth-century Iranian opposition had come to an end.

See also AMINI, ALI; PAHLAVI, MOHAMMAD REZA; TUDEH PARTY; WHITE REVOLUTION (1961–1963).

Bibliography

Matin-asgari, Afshin. *Iranian Student Opposition to the Shah.* Costa Mesa, CA: Mazda, 2002.

AFSHIN MATIN-ASGARI

CONFEDERATION OF TURKISH TRADE UNIONS

The largest labor confederation in Turkey.

The Confederation of Turkish Trade Unions, known as Türk Iş, was founded in 1952. Its history has reflected the increasing importance of industrial labor in a developing economy in which political regimes have been uneasy about voluntary associations whose appeal is bound to involve class interests. During the 1950s, the confederation played cat and mouse with the government, which sought to extend control over the organization, which, in turn, appealed to the opposition for support. The right to strike was finally legalized in 1963, opening the way for genuine trade unionism. The confederation's efforts to solidify its dominant position, however, were resisted by rival organizations. In 1966, the Revolutionary Confederation of Labor Unions (DISK) broke away and aligned itself with the socialist Turkish Workers Party. This split strengthened Türk Iş's relations with the ruling conservative Justice Party, which tried to solidify the confederation's dominance of labor through new legislation. The proliferation of often politically motivated strikes and lockouts, increasingly accompanied by violence, was a factor in bringing on the

military intervention of 1980. Ironically, the coup finally made possible the achievement of the confederation's goal of obtaining a monopoly in labor organization, since all other labor unions were simply banned by the military regime. This drastic measure was followed by a series of restrictive conditions written into the constitution that was adopted by popular referendum in November 1982.

See also JUSTICE PARTY; TURKISH WORKERS PARTY.

Bibliography

Bianchi, B. R. *Interest Groups and Political Development in Turkey.* Princeton, NJ: Princeton University Press, 1984.

Dodd, C. H. *The Crisis of Turkish Democracy,* 2d edition. Huntingdon, U.K.: Eothen Press, 1990.

FRANK TACHAU

CONFESSIONAL SYSTEM

See LEBANON

CONGRESS OF OTTOMAN LIBERALS (1902)

Forum for opposition groups.

Organized by Prince Sabahettin to reconcile differences among various groups opposed to the unconstitutional rule of Sultan Abdülhamit II, the first Congress of Ottoman Liberals was held in Paris between 4 and 9 February 1902. Participants included Young Turk liberals living in exile in Europe and representatives of minority national groups. A renewed attempt to coordinate opposition movements resulted in a second congress, held in Paris 27–29 December 1907, chaired by Sabahettin, Ahmet Riza, and K. Maloumian of the Armenian Revolutionary Federation (Dashnaks).

See also ABDÜLHAMIT II; AHMET RIZA; DASHNAK PARTY; YOUNG TURKS.

Bibliography

Shaw, Stanford, and Shaw, Ezel Kural. *History of the Ottoman Empire and Modern Turkey,* Vol. 2: *Reform, Revolution, and Republic: The Rise of Modern Turkey, 1808–1975.* Cambridge, U.K., and New York: Cambridge University Press, 1977.

DAVID WALDNER

CONSEIL NATIONAL DE LA RÉVOLUTION ALGÉRIENNE (CNRA)

The parliament of the Algerian revolution, September 1956 to July 1962.

The Conseil National de la Révolution Algérienne (CNRA; National Council of the Algerian Revolution) was created by the Soummam Valley Congress of the Front de Libération Nationale (National Liberation Front) to accommodate the broadening of the revolutionary movement that occurred during 1955 and 1956. The first CNRA, which for logistical reasons never formally met, included seventeen members of the founding Comité Révolutionnaire d'Unité et d'Action, members of the former Union Démocratique du Manifeste Algérien, the Mouvement pour le Triomphe des Libertés Démocratiques, and the Association of Algerian Muslim Ulama.

The first formal meeting of the CNRA took place in Cairo in July 1957 and formalized the growing authority of the external militants over the internal. The second and third meetings, held at Tripoli from December 1959 to January 1960 and during August 1961, reshuffled the membership of the Provisional Government, dealing with internal power struggles between civilian and military leaderships. The final session, held in Tripoli in May and June 1962, adopted the Tripoli Program, a statement of leftist ideological orientation. But, as Algeria faced independence, the CNRA was unable to agree on fundamental political arrangements.

See also ASSOCIATION OF ALGERIAN MUSLIM ULAMA (AUMA); COMITÉ RÉVOLUTIONNAIRE D'UNITÉ ET D'ACTION (CRUA); FRONT DE LIBÉRATION NATIONALE; MOUVEMENT POUR LE TRIOMPHE DES LIBERTÉS DÉMOCRATIQUES; TRIPOLI PROGRAMME (1962); UNION DÉMOCRATIQUE DU MANIFESTE ALGÉRIEN (UDMA).

Bibliography

Ruedy, John. *Modern Algeria: The Origins and Development of a Nation.* Bloomington: Indiana University Press, 1992.

JOHN RUEDY

CONSTANTINE

One of Algeria's major cities.

Constantine is located about 330 miles (530 km) east of the capital, Algiers, near the coast, with a population of 909,700 (2002). While known as a trading center, Constantine is best known for its association with the so-called Constantine plan, an attempt announced by the French in 1958 to tie Algeria economically to the *métropole* (the French nation) through a number of rural and industrial development plans. After independence in 1964, Constantine became an important educational center with the country's only Islamic university.

DIRK VANDEWALLE

CONSTANTINOPLE

Ancient Roman and Byzantine capital, now the city of Istanbul in modern Turkey.

The construction of the Roman city of Constantinople was begun in 324, after the final victory of the Roman emperor Constantine the Great (r. 306–337 C.E.) over his rivals for power. It was intended as a new, central capital, which would straddle the eastern and western portions of the Roman Empire. Originally known as New Rome, it came to be known as Konstantinoupolis, the City of Constantine.

The city was completed in May 330 on the site of the existing Greek settlement of Byzantium. It was set on a promontory extending eastward into the Sea of Marmara at the mouth of the Bosporus and was bordered on the north by a sheltered inlet known as the Golden Horn, which served as its harbor. In homage to the city of Rome, it was laid out on seven hills, with its own royal palace and square, senate, forum, and hippodrome. Lying at the crossroads of land routes through Europe and Asia and guarding the strategic and lucrative sea routes connecting the Mediterranean and Black Seas, it quickly assumed prominence as one of the wealthiest cities in the empire and benefited from both imperial patronage and intercontinental trade. The city's growth led it to extend toward the west and construct a new set of walls under Theodosius in 439.

A fire in the time of Justinian (r. 527–565) during the Nika Rebellion of 532 destroyed half the city. In its wake, Justinian embarked on an ambitious program of new building. This included a new hippodrome, which held up to 60,000 spectators, a new palace, and a massive church, the Cathedral of Hagia Sophia, dedicated to the wisdom of Christ. The latter stood on the site of the original church, which was built by Emperor Constantius in 360 and replaced after a fire in 404. Completed in 537 and rebuilt in 558 after an earthquake damaged it, the church is noted for its impressive, 110-foot-diameter domed vault, which dominates the city skyline to this day.

With the decline of Rome, Constantinople remained the capital of the Eastern (Byzantine) Roman Empire and the center of Eastern Christianity. A period of decline occurred during the eighth century, when losses to the early Muslim conquests threatened the empire. Yet Constantinople went on to become the wealthiest and largest city in medieval Europe, home of various nationalities and a transshipment center linking Europe with southwest and central Asia. It was venerated as the home of libraries and countless sacred relics. Its wealth and prestige made it the target of several invading armies. It was attacked and besieged variously by the Slavs (in 540, 559, and 581), the Persians and Avars (in 626), the Arabs (in 669–679 and 717–718), the Bulgarians (in 813, 913, and 924), and the Russians, who assaulted it four times in the period from 860 to 1043.

Following the schism of 1054, which divided Christianity between the Eastern and Western churches, Constantinople became a commercial rival to the Roman Catholic kingdoms in the western Mediterranean, especially Venice. The bishop of Constantinople came to be the ecumenical patriarch of the Eastern Orthodox Church, and the religious power of the city continued to be strengthened into the late Byzantine and Ottoman periods. The crusades of the late eleventh and twelfth centuries passed through Constantinople relatively peacefully. However, the common perception among the Crusaders that the Byzantine Empire sympathized with the Seljuk Turks allowed Venice to persuade the leaders of the fourth crusade to sack Constantinople. This established a Latin kingdom, centered on the city, that lasted until 1261, when the Byzantines restored their ancient capital. The city was greatly weakened and depopulated as a result and never reclaimed its earlier splendor. The weakness

of Constantinople led the Byzantines to ally with Genoa, which came to eclipse the Byzantine state.

In 1453, the Ottoman Turks under Mehmet II defeated the last Byzantine emperor of Constantinople, Constantine XI, who was killed in battle over the city. Turks resettled the city under the Ottomans, changing its cultural makeup over time, although Greeks remained an important part of the population until the early twentieth century. Ottoman building activity ushered in a new age of Islamic architecture, and the church of Hagia Sophia became a mosque, surrounded by four towering minarets. Over time, the Turkish corruption of the Greek phrase *eis teen polin* (into the city) led to the popular renaming of the city as Istanbul. The city became the administrative capital of the Ottoman Empire, and continued as the capital until it was moved to Ankara under the modern state of Turkey in 1923. It remains the largest city in Turkey, and that nation's most important commercial center. In the early twenty-first century it had a population of more than 12 million.

See also EASTERN ORTHODOX CHURCH; ISTANBUL; OTTOMAN EMPIRE.

Bibliography

Mango, Cyril. *Studies on Constantinople.* Aldershot, U.K.: Variorum, 1993.

Mansel, Philip. *Constantinople: City of the World's Desire, 1453–1924.* London: John Murray, 1995.

Sherrard, Philip. *Constantinople: Iconography of a Sacred City.* London: Oxford University Press, 1965.

PAUL S. ROWE

CONSTITUTIONAL BLOC

Twentieth-century parliamentary bloc in Lebanon.

The Constitutional Bloc was formed in 1936 to call for the restoration of the constitution in Lebanon after its suspension by French mandate authorities. It was headed by Bishara al-Khuri, who championed the cause of Lebanon's independence. Although the bloc cannot be considered a political party, it did not differ from other political organizations in Lebanon in terms of its personality-oriented structure. Its members were drawn from the commercial and political elite, who did not agree with the views of Emile Eddé, a supporter of French policies in Lebanon. It was most active in Mount Lebanon and Beirut, among Maronites and Druze. After 1941, the bloc became identified with British policy in the Middle East. The cohesiveness of the bloc, which was based on the shared goal of independence, quickly splintered after al-Khuri was elected president in 1943. He continued to use the bloc as a tool against his well-organized enemies. It continued to operate as a political force, with limited influence and appeal, into the 1960s. After al-Khuri retired, his son Khalil al-Khuri assumed leadership of the bloc. With the outbreak of the Lebanese civil war in 1975, the bloc ceased to exist, and Khalil retired to France.

See also EDDÉ, EMILE; KHURI, BISHARA AL-; LEBANESE CIVIL WAR (1975–1990).

AS'AD ABUKHALIL

CONSTITUTIONAL DEMOCRATIC RALLY

Tunisian government political party, formerly the Neo-Destour Party.

Tunisian nationalists formed the Destour Party in 1920. In 1934, the Ksar Hellal Congress consecrated the rupture between the Néo and Archéo sectors of the Destour under the leadership of Habib Bourguiba and Shaykh Abd al-Aziz Thaalbi respectively. Bourguiba and other younger members of the party formed the Neo-Destour Party, which would successfully lead the national struggle for independence. The French authorities made the party illegal in 1938. In 1964, the party changed its name to Parti Socialiste Destourien (Destourian Socialist Party, PSD). Between 1963 and 1981, the PSD was the only legal political formation in Tunisia. The presidency was held by Mahmoud Materi (1934–1938); Habib Thameur (1939–1948); and Bourguiba (1949–1987).

The structure of the PSD reflected a highly hierarchical division: The National Congress, comprising around a thousand members, met every five years. Below were the party's political bureau (the executive organ of the party), a central committee composed of eighty members, the regional coordinating committees, local circumscriptions, and cells. Bourguiba, heading the party in a highly personal fashion, transformed the Neo-Destour into a grass-roots populist party grounded in the Sahel middle class. Prior to independence, Neo-Destourians worked closely with Moroccan and Algerian nationalists. Following independence, the Neo-Destour won the first elections in 1956. A year later, the party won the first local elections in which Tunisian women were allowed to vote, with more than 90 percent of the vote.

The Neo-Destour worked closely with the Confédération Générale des Travailleurs Tunisiens (General Confederation of Tunisian Workers; later the Union Générale des Travailleurs Tunisiens, UGTT), staging numerous demonstrations, riots, and strikes. Salah Ben Yusuf, the Neo-Destour's secretary-general, fled to Egypt in 1952. Under the influence of Jamal Abd alNasir's pan-Arab nationalism, he opposed Bourguiba's gradualist, pragmatic approach toward independence. Ben Yusuf opposed the Paris agreements that had abrogated the Al Marsa Convention of 1883, and upon his return to Tunisia broke with Bourguiba and contested his authority within the Neo-Destour Party. He would eventually return to Cairo to lead a leftist opposition movement from exile until his assassination in 1961.

The introduction of Destourian socialism in 1961 consecrated the party's central role in the state policy of economic interventionism. Following independence, economic reforms led to a decline in the party's influence as a mass movement. Bourguiba's reorganization of the party in 1963 followed the proscription of the Parti Communiste Tunisien (Tunisian Communist Party, PCT; later known as Movement of Renewal). The 1964 congress endorsed centralized state planning, and the party was renamed the Parti Socialiste Destourien (Destourian Socialist Party, PSD). Single-party rule effectively consecrated the fusion of party and state in Tunisia. During the late 1960s and the 1970s, popular discontent with land collectivization and internal divisions within the party led to the expulsion of Ahmed Ben Salah, architect of the centralized state planning strategy and the decolonialization of the Tunisian economy.

The 1971 party congress signaled a new rift between the supporters of economic liberalization and the supporters political liberalization, headed by Ahmad Mestiri, while social unrest kept growing. In

1981, Islamist dissidents formed the Mouvement de Tendance Islamique (Islamic Tendency Movement), and student organizations in combination with workers' movements weakened the influence of the PSD. Other political organizations such as the Mouvement de l'Unité Populaire (Movement of Popular Unity) and the PCT remained very critical of PSD policies. During the extraordinary congress of 1981, the PSD approved a shift toward limited political pluralism while firmly excluding the Islamists from the political process.

On 7 November 1987, Zayn al-Abidine Ben Ali, then prime minister and secretary-general of the PSD, deposed President Bourguiba. In February 1988, the PSD was renamed Rassemblement Constitutionnel Démocratique (Constitutional Democratic Rally, RCD), and Ben Ali was elected president of the RCD during the party's first congress on July 1988. The second congress (1993) confirmed the shift toward complete economic liberalization. In the 1994 presidential elections, Ben Ali ran for office unopposed. In 1999, he was reelected for a third term with 99.4 percent of the vote, running against Mohamed Belhadj Amour and Abderrahmane Tlili. In accordance with changes made to the electoral code, the RCD currently holds 148 seats in the Tunisian parliament; the opposition parties hold 34 seats. The RCD maintains a strong grip on the political system, amidst increasing popular discontent. Hailed as a model of economic development and liberalization in the United States and the European Union, the government's continuous and often unreported human rights violations, its curtailment of freedom of the press, and its arbitrary imprisonment of members of leftist and Islamist organizations remain the source of harsh criticism.

See also BEN ALI, ZAYN AL-ABIDINE; BEN SALAH, AHMED; BOURGUIBA, HABIB; MESTIRI, AHMAD; MOVEMENT OF RENEWAL; THAALBI, ABD AL-AZIZ; UNION GÉNÉRALE DES TRAVAILLEURS TUNISIENS (UGTT).

Bibliography

Nelson, Harold D., ed. *Tunisia: A Country Study,* 3d edition. Washington, DC: U.S. Government Printing Office, 1988.

Perkins, Kenneth J. *Historical Dictionary of Tunisia.* Metuchen, NJ: Scarecrow Press, 1989.

Salem, Norma. *Habib Bourguiba, Islam, and the Creation of Tunisia,* 2d edition. Lanham, MD: Scarecrow Press, 1997.

Waltz, Susan E. *Human Rights and Reform: Changing the Face of North African Politics.* Berkeley: University of California Press, 1995.

Zartman, I. William, ed. *Tunisia: The Political Economy of Reform.* Boulder, CO: L. Rienner, 1991.

VANESA CASANOVA-FERNANDEZ

CONSTITUTIONAL REVOLUTION

Movement in opposition to the shah's rule that led to the convening of the majles.

Iran's Constitutional Revolution began in April 1905 when a group of merchants from Tehran sought sanctuary in the Abd al-Azim shrine south of the capital to protest against foreign control of the country's customs administration, the government's economic policies, and the repressive political regulations of the Qajar monarch Mozaffar al-Din Qajar (ruled 1896–1906). The merchants who led this demonstration belonged to a secret society that had formed several weeks earlier to oppose oppression and seek the establishment of a house of justice. Their protest—effectively a business strike—attracted the support of other secret societies with similar grievances. The demonstration was defused after two weeks when the shah agreed to discuss the complaints of the protesters, but he soon left for a prescheduled private tour of Europe and forgot about his promises. The secret society of merchants, as well as other clandestine political groups in Tehran and in Tabriz, the capital of Azerbaijan province and the official residence of the crown prince, circulated pamphlets calling for fulfillment of the shah's promises and the implementation of other reforms. By December 1905, when the shah had returned to the country and it seemed obvious that he would not honor his commitments, a much larger group of two thousand merchants, joined by two of the city's leading clergy and their theology students, again took sanctuary in the Abd al-Azim shrine and demanded, in addition to action on their earlier requests, that the government create a house of justice.

The second protest had been sparked by the arbitrary arrest and beating of two respected sugar merchants, whom the government tried to blame for the inflationary rise in sugar prices. Popular indignation over this incident was widespread. In addition to the merchants who sought sanctuary, artisans and laborers in the capital went on strike to register their sympathy with the merchants demanding justice. Unable to force an end to the general strike in Tehran, the shah agreed in January 1906 to dismiss the Belgian national who was director of customs and to establish a house of justice. In subsequent months, however, Mozaffar al-Din Qajar again failed to fulfill his promises, thus prompting a third round of demonstrations during the summer of 1906.

The demonstrations of 1906 were ignited by the arrest of a fiery Shi'ite preacher who had denounced the shah's government during religious ceremonies and the arrest of several other critics of the regime. A crowd gathered outside the police station to demand their release; in the ensuing confrontation, the police killed a protester. A huge crowd attended the funeral the next day, and demonstrators clashed with the Russian-officered Cossack Brigade; twenty-two persons were killed and more than one hundred injured. The incident transformed the antigovernment protests into a mass movement. In July 1906, most of Tehran's Shi'ite clergy demonstrated its disapproval of the government by departing in a group for Qom, a shrine city about 90 miles (145 km) south of the capital, thereby leaving Tehran without spiritual direction. In addition, more than ten thousand merchants took sanctuary in the British embassy's summer property in the mountains a few miles north of the city.

By mid-July 1906, most of the capital was on strike; even women organized demonstrations in front of the shah's palace. The growing opposition movement spread to several provincial centers, including Iran's second most important city, Tabriz; committees sent telegrams from all over the country to express sympathy with the protesters and their demands. The main intellectual ferment and negotiations took place among the ten thousand protesters who had camped out for three weeks in the British legation. Their most important decision was to change the former request for a house of justice to a new demand for an elected, constitutional assembly, or *majles*. The crisis forced the shah to accede to the popular demands, and on 5 August 1906 he signed a decree convening a constituent assembly.

The constituent assembly met immediately, drew up an electoral law, divided the country into electoral districts, and scheduled elections. The country's first elected *majles* met in October 1906. It drafted a fundamental law, based on the Belgian constitution, which provided for a parliamentary form of government. Special features that were incorporated into the constitution included articles authorizing the establishment of provincial assemblies and the creation of a body of senior Shi'ite clergymen to judge the conformity of legislation with Islamic law; these two provisions, however, were never implemented. Since the constitution limited the powers of the monarch, Mozaffar al-Din Shah indicated his opposition to the document by denouncing its main architects as religious heretics. His ploy not only failed, but, instead, incited mass demonstrations in favor of the constitution in the capital and several other cities, including Isfahan, Kermanshah, Mashhad, Rasht, Shiraz, and Tabriz. The disturbances climaxed with the assassination of the shah's prime minister, the public suicide of the assassin in front of the *majles* building, and a mass funeral procession for the assassin. Deeply distressed by these developments, the shah reluctantly signed the fundamental law in December 1906, a few days before his death. A supplementary fundamental law was signed by his son and successor, Mohammad Ali Qajar, in 1907. These two documents made up the Iranian constitution, which remained in force until 1979, when it was replaced by a new constitution.

To some historians, the Constitutional Revolution refers only to the events of 1905 to 1907, but other historians also view the struggles over the constitution during 1907 to 1909 as part of the Constitutional Revolution. Although Mohammad Ali (ruled 1906–1909) disliked the limits the constitution placed on his authority, the united opposition to the court within the *majles* initially forced him to abide by the new constraints. Factions of conservatives, moderates, liberals, and radicals soon emerged in the *majles,* however, and their differences over policies throughout 1907 provided the opportunity for the shah and his supporters to make political alliances with the conservatives and some moderates. By June 1908, the shah, feeling strong enough to mount a coup against the *majles,* ordered the Russian colonel of the Cossack Brigade to attack the volunteer militia defending the *majles* building and to arrest the deputies who had not escaped. After the bombardment, in which more than 250 persons lost their lives, the shah dissolved the *majles* and suspended the constitution.

Mohammad Ali's coup effectively put the capital under his control, but not the rest of the country. In Isfahan, Rasht, Tabriz, and other cities, volunteers took up arms to defend the constitution. For a year, constitutionalists and royalists waged a civil war for control of Iran's provincial centers, with the constitutionalists gradually gaining the upper hand. Constitutional forces finally advanced on Tehran from Rasht in the north and from Isfahan in the south. A mass uprising against the government opened the city to the constitutionalists in July 1909. Mohammad Ali, who had fled to the Russian embassy, was deposed; his twelve-year-old son, Ahmad (ruled 1909–1925), was installed as the new shah; the constitution was reinstated; and elections for a new *majles* were scheduled.

See also AHMAD QAJAR; MOHAMMAD ALI SHAH QAJAR; MOZAFFAR AL-DIN QAJAR.

Bibliography

Abrahamian, Ervand. *Iran between Two Revolutions.* Princeton, NJ: Princeton University Press, 1982.

Bayat, Mangol. *Iran's First Revolution: Shi'ism and the Constitutional Revolution of 1905–1909.* New York: Oxford University Press, 1991.

Lambton, Ann K. S. *Qajar Persia: Eleven Studies.* Austin: University of Texas Press, 1988.

ERIC HOOGLUND

CONSTITUTIONAL REVOLUTION, IMPACT ON WOMEN

The effect of Iran's Constitutional Revolution of the nineteenth century on the status of women in that country.

During the early stages of the revolution and during the entire period of the first *majles* (councils; 1906–1908), women's roles were minimal and their participation kept under control, restricted to staging street demonstrations in support of the constitutionalist religious and social welfare causes. But they also demanded the right for a public, and not just private, education, and many began to attend

what were then the only available institutions, the American and the French girls' schools. Here they won the intelligentsia's full support. Since the late nineteenth century, poets and journalists had championed this cause, arguing that it would benefit the fatherland to have educated women raise future generations of Iranians and, by the same token, pleading for the abolition of polygamy. Neither the *hijab* (wearing of the veil) nor the right to vote was addressed. Nonetheless, the *ulama* (community of learned men), led by Ayatollah Fazlollah Nuri, proclaimed their demands to be part of a Babi conspiracy to eradicate Islam in the country.

Following the royalist coup of June 1908, in the period of national resistance to the restored autocracy and throughout the second *majles* (1909–1912), small organizations of women, the close relatives of prominent secular constitutionalist leaders, began to express publicly their aspirations for the right to vote. A few even dared to manifest their revolt against the *hijab* in public. Fearful of the *ulama*'s onslaught, constitutionalist politicians and journalists dismissed these "extremists" as unrepresentative of women's constitutional interests. The Fundamental Law then guaranteed women's right to education, but nothing else. Nonetheless, women's organizations continued to play a role in support of the constitution, increasing pressure on court officials and *majles* deputies in their resistance to the Russian ultimatum that threatened the very existence of the constitutional government. By January 1912, the battle was lost, the *majles* suspended, and women gained no public recognition for their political participation.

See also GENDER: GENDER AND EDUCATION; GENDER: GENDER AND LAW; GENDER: GENDER AND POLITICS; IRAN; QAJAR DYNASTY; TOBACCO REVOLT.

Bibliography

Afary, Janet. *The Iranian Constitutional Revolution, 1906–1911: Grassroots Democracy, Social Democracy, and the Origins of Feminism.* New York: Columbia University Press, 1996.

Bayat-Philipp, Mangol. "Women and Revolution in Iran." In *Women in the Muslim World,* edited by Lois Beck and Nikki Keddie. Cambridge, MA: Harvard University Press, 1978.

MANGOL BAYAT

CONSTITUTIONAL UNION PARTY

See MOROCCO: POLITICAL PARTIES IN

COORDINATION DES ARCHS (ALGERIA)

A political grouping that grew out of disorders in the Kabylia region of Algeria during the spring of 2001.

On 18 April 2001, a high school student named Massinissa Guermah was killed in a police station in Beni Douala, a small town near Tizi Ouzou, the capital of the Berber region of Kabylia. Over the next several weeks, numerous protest demonstrations took place and violent riots broke out in several localities. Some fifty people were killed in the ensuing disorder.

Bypassing established political parties such as the Socialist Forces Front and the Rally for Culture and Democracy, local activists created a new organization, which was referred to as the Coordination des Archs, Dairas, et Communes (CADC; *archs* refers to the traditional Kabyle clans or tribes, *dairas* to the administrative subprefectures, and *communes* to the local village councils). The CADC organized a series of marches and boycotts while articulating a set of demands that expressed the long-simmering anger of Kabyle youth toward the military-dominated regime in Algiers. Among the grievances summed up in the El-Kseur Platform of June 2001, the new association called for criminal proceedings against the policemen guilty of armed violence, total withdrawal of the National Gendarmerie from Kabylia, and recognition of the Berber language, Tamazight, as a national language.

Initially organized at the departmental (*wilaya*) level of Tizi Ouzou, the CADC quickly expanded into the Interwilaya des Archs, bringing together delegates from seven of the country's forty-eight *wilayas*: Tizi Ouzou, Bejaia, Boumerdés, Bouira, Bordj Bouéridj, Setif, and Algiers. The most prominent figure in the movement was an economist and professor at the University of Tizi Ouzou, Belaid Abrika, a long-standing Berber cultural activist. The group led boycotts of the 2002 parliamentary and local elections, but by 2003 the organization was increasingly viewed as obstructionist and, despite a hunger strike by Abrika, was losing influence.

See also AIT AHMED, HOCINE; BERBER SPRING; BLACK SPRING; KABYLIA; RASSEMBLEMENT POUR LA CULTURE ET LA DÉMOCRATIE (RCD).

ROBERT MORTIMER

COPTIC MUSEUM

Cairo museum of antiquities from the Roman and Byzantine eras.

Founded in 1908 by Marcus Simaika, the Coptic Museum in Cairo has the world's greatest collection of antiquities reflecting the culture that flourished in Egypt after the introduction of Christianity in the first or second century. Many of the objects reflect the influence of pharaonic and Greco-Roman artistic styles on early Coptic art. Among the categories of approximately 14,000 antiquities are textiles, sculpture, relief, icons, woodwork, metalwork, glass, ceramics, ivories, and manuscripts. Perhaps the most famous works in the collection are the Coptic gnostic texts known as the Nag Hammadi Gospels, named after the town in southern Egypt near their site of discovery between 1945 and 1948.

Bibliography

Gabra, Gawdat, and Alcock, A. *Cairo: The Coptic Museum and Old Churches.* Cairo: Egyptian International Publishing Company, 1993.

Reid, Donald Malcolm. *Whose Pharaohs? Archaeology, Museums, and Egyptian National Identity from Napoleon to World War I.* Berkeley: University of California Press, 2002.

DONALD SPANEL
UPDATED BY DONALD MALCOLM REID

COPTS

Adherents of the Egyptian Orthodox Church

The Copts are the largest Christian community in the Middle East. Yet determining an exact number is extremely difficult. Population counts of the Copts made by the Egyptian government and by the Coptic Church are vastly divergent. In 1975 the Egyptian government placed the number of Copts at 2.3 million, but the Coptic Church suggested a figure of

6.6 million. A United Nations population estimate for Egypt in the year 2000 reckons the total inhabitants at 64,588,000; of this number, 3,128,000 persons are estimated to be Copts who openly acknowledge their faith. However, in addition to active members of the church, many more Copts are registered in church records (baptisms, marriages, deaths, etc.). Thus, a fair estimate of the actual number of all Copts as of 2000 is 9,817,000.

The term *Copt* comes directly from the Arabic *qbt,* which appears to derive from the Greek *aigyptos* (Egypt) and *aigyptioi* (Egyptians), a phonetic corruption of the ancient Egyptian word *Hikaptah,* one of the names of Memphis. The Greeks used the native name for the ancient metropolis Memphis as a term to describe the whole country. When the Arabs conquered Egypt between 641 and 643 C.E., they used a similar word to name the country's inhabitants *(qibt),* the vast majority of whom were Christian. Thus the word *Copt* began as a geographical and ethnic designation. Later the term *qibt* came to distinguish the native Christian inhabitants from the Arabs, who were Muslims. When the majority of Egyptians gradually converted to Islam, they naturally ceased to be Christians *(qibt).* In that sense, *Copt* and the adjective *Coptic* are relatively elastic in a historical, ethnic, religious, cultural, and social sense.

In theological terms, *Copt* describes an adherent of the Egyptian Orthodox church, which had become a national church after the Council of Chalcedon (451 C.E.). The patriarchs and bishops of several Eastern churches, particularly those of Alexandria in Egypt and Antioch in Syria, refused to accept what has been called the Chalcedonian Definition of Faith. By this exposition, Christ had two natures, human and divine, which coexisted but were not confused with each other. The Western church, with its two seats at Rome and Constantinople, favored this declaration of belief. The patriarchs of Alexandria and Antioch believed that this would divide the person of Christ and destroy his essential unity. Both the content of and the differences between Eastern and Western Christology are often exceedingly difficult to understand. The theology that slowly developed among the Eastern churches has been called *Monophysite,* from the Greek words for "single" and "nature." Notably, Anba Shenouda III, Pope of Alexandria and Patriarch of

Shenouda III, the current Coptic pope, joined the Coptic Orthodox Seminary after graduating from Cairo University. In the 1950s he devoted himself to monastic seclusion and lived for six years as a hermit in a cave he excavated himself. After serving as Bishop of Christian Education and president of the Coptic Orthodox Theological Seminary in the 1960s, Shenouda was proclaimed the 117th pope of Alexandria on 14 November 1971. © AP/WIDE WORLD PHOTOS. REPRODUCED BY PERMISSION.

the See of St. Mark the Evangelist (1971–), and other ecclesiastical officials of the Eastern churches rejected the term *Monophysite.*

Perceiving themselves as upholders of the true faith, Copts have always referred to themselves as "orthodox," as the name of their denomination—Coptic Orthodox—indicates. Because several other churches that are in communion with Rome also have "orthodox" as a part of their names, scholars use the phrase "Oriental Orthodox Churches" to designate the churches from Egypt, Armenia, Ethiopia, Syria, and India, which refused to acknowledge the Council of Chalcedon. The Ethiopic Orthodox Church is commonly called Coptic with some justification. Historically, it has shared close ties with the Coptic Orthodox Church of Egypt, especially in its recognition of the Coptic patriarch, but in modern times it came to exist as a separate entity. The liturgy of the Ethiopic Orthodox Church derives much from its Coptic counterpart, although significant differences give it a distinct identity. Nevertheless, many adherents of the Ethiopic Orthodox Church refer to themselves as Copts. Of the other Christian denominations in Egypt, at least two have the word Coptic in their names: the Coptic Catholic Church and the Coptic Evangelical Church. The former came into being during the late nineteenth century. The Coptic Evangelical Church was established in 1854 by U.S. Presbyterian missionaries. Communicants of both churches represent small minorities that had been drawn from Coptic parishes.

The word Coptic retains its original geographical and ethnic value as descriptive of the art and written language of Egypt in past centuries. The Coptic language is the last phase of the ancient Egyptian language. It is written in Greek letters except for six letters that were taken from Demotic writing. Coptic continued to be the spoken daily language among a considerable segment of the Egyptian population, perhaps as late as the eleventh century C.E., before its gradual replacement by Arabic. Today, Coptic is still used in the liturgy of the Coptic Church.

Coptic art is among the richest and most continuous of the Christian arts in the Middle East. As an independent form, it appeared toward the end of the third century C.E. and survived as late as the fourteenth century. Although Christian themes prevail in Coptic art, both pharaonic and especially classical themes and motifs are also prominent. Coptic art often reflects styles and fashions of the Byzantine world, adapted with originality and local individuality. In the absence of court patronage, it can perhaps be best characterized as folk art. Contemporary Coptic art reflects the deep roots of ancient Egyptian and Coptic theology, art, and culture, and uses several media, including icons, frescos, mosaics, and stained glass windows; icons are produced in the greatest number.

Historians speak of a Coptic Period of Egyptian history from the second century C.E.—the beginning of the formation of the Coptic language—or from 451 C.E.—the Council of Chalcedon—to the Arab conquest of Egypt in 643 C.E. However, although the Copts never ruled Egypt, they contributed and still contribute to all aspects of Egypt's culture, with their most important contribution to world civilization being monasticism.

The French expedition of 1798–1801 under Napoléon is considered a turning point toward Egypt's modernization. Muhammad Ali (1805–1849)

as well as most of his descendants, whose rule of Egypt dominated for decades following the French expedition, were relatively tolerant of the Copts. During the nineteenth century, the Coptic population began to flourish, as they became exempt in 1855 from the traditional poll tax imposed on Christians and Jews living under Muslim rule (the *jizya*). This revival was visible in the cultural movement within the Coptic Church sponsored by Patriarch Cyril IV the Reformer (1854–1861), who established many schools and patronized a revival of the Coptic language.

During the first half of the twentieth century a Coptic elite, educated in the West and in Egypt, came to play a crucial role in the economic and cultural development of the country and strove to establish a more democratic system in Coptic community affairs and in the management of church properties. Meanwhile, the Egyptian nationalist movement was gaining ground among the populace, characterized by its vocal opposition to British rule, which had begun in 1882. Mustafa Kamil (1874–1908) struggled to make the Egyptian question an international one and formed the Nationalist Party in 1907. Although some leading Copts joined his political movement, most Copts rejected the movement's religious aspect of pan-Islamism and Kamil's support of the Ottoman Empire. In 1910 a Muslim partisan of the National Party assassinated Prime Minister Boutros Ghali, who was a Copt. His assassination sparked serious quarrels between Copts and Muslims; concord and national unity were reached only in the revolution of 1919. In fact, the forced exile of the Egyptian leader Sa'd Zaghlul to Malta by the British government fueled the popular uprising and resulted in the formation of the largest political party, al-Wafd.

One of the most significant achievements of this revolution was national unity among all Egyptians. It was arguably the highest expression of harmony and understanding between Muslims and Copts in the modern history of Egypt. The emblem of this revolution was a crescent enclosing a cross. Zaghlul succeeded in unifying Muslims and Copts in the Wafd party. Muslims as well as Copts were exiled and put in jail in their struggle for independence. The establishment of a secular and liberal trend in Egyptian nationalism paved the way for the integra-

A Coptic monk studies in a monastery in Wadi al-Natrum in Egypt. Several monasteries were built in this area by monks fleeing persecution in their homelands of Iraq and Syria during the eighth century. One of the more famous is the Monastery of St. Macarius, from which many Coptic popes have been selected. © JOHANNES ARMINEH/CORBIS-SYGMA. REPRODUCED BY PERMISSION.

tion of the Copts into the national movement. The promulgation of a constitution in 1923 allowed the formation of a parliament by general election. Zaghlul and most Copts refused a proportional representation of the Copts in the parliament. Thus the number of elected Coptic representatives in the parliament was much higher than a special status would have allowed. In 1923 Copts comprised nearly 44 percent of the Wafd executive committee. In that sense, the "liberal period" between 1923 and 1952 is unique and is indeed a kind of honeymoon in the relationship between Muslims and Copts.

The second half of the twentieth century brought difficulties for the Copts. Although the Egyptian army did not lack Copts, none of the Free Officers of the military coup of 1952 was a Copt. Because of the wide popular support, this military coup is known as the 1952 Revolution. President Gamal Abdel Nasser's land reform in 1952 and his introduction of social measures during the 1960s fell

heavily on wealthy Coptic families, the Coptic patriarchate, and land-holding Coptic monasteries. The number of Copts in high government posts decreased dramatically. Nasser's interest in Arab nationalism led to a departure from Egyptian nationalism. During his tenure (1952–1970), a few Copts had been nominated to the parliament, often in consultation with the Coptic patriarch, so as to keep a formal Coptic representation in the political structure. This led to the gradual abolition of the influence of the Copts in political life and enhanced the role of religious institutions and church hierarchy.

Under President Anwar al-Sadat (1970–1981) the parliament adopted an amendment to the constitution stating that the Shariʿa (Islamic law) would be the principal source of legislation in Egypt. Sadat furthered the Islamization of national life and, at the expense of political leftists, favored extreme Islamists, whose influence increased dramatically in Egypt, particularly at universities. Muslim militants plundered and burned Coptic shops, especially jewelers and pharmacies at al-Minya and Asyut; some churches were attacked in villages throughout Upper Egypt. In 1981 bloody riots resulted in the burning of three churches at al-Zawiya al-Hamra in Cairo; these incidents affected the community to the extent that Pope Shenouda III canceled Easter celebrations. In September 1981 Sadat arrested eight bishops and four priests, and various Muslim clergy including Muslim Brothers were banned. About 2,500 individuals representing all political leanings were detained. Shenouda was forced to stay in the Monastery of St. Pschoi at Wadi al-Natrun under what was effectively house arrest. Ironically, a few weeks later, militant Muslims assassinated Sadat. In the years to follow, political prisoners were gradually released. Shenouda was not allowed to return to his patriarchate in Cairo until January 1985. However, Muslim militants reorganized themselves and targeted unarmed Christians, plundered shops, and burned churches. During the 1980s and the 1990s, those militants attempted to assassinate a number of ministers and slaughtered scores of foreign tourists in their insurgency against the Egyptian government under President Husni Mubarak. Most Muslim politicians and intellectuals strongly condemned the criminal activities of these militants.

Despite the guarantee of religious equality before the law contained in article 40 of the Egyptian constitution, Copts suffer discrimination, particularly concerning the appointment to governmental leadership positions such as provincial governors, city managers, police commissioners, university presidents, and directors of educational districts. Scarcely any Copts are appointed to posts in the judicial system, police ranks, or army. Copts are not proportionally represented in the People's Assembly: only 2 out of 444 are Copts. Restrictions on the building of churches often means that building projects take years or even decades. Still, the Coptic community, because of its relatively pacifist attitude, its economic success, and its members' profound attachment to their Christian faith and church, has sustained itself throughout 1,350 years under Islamic rule.

See also CYRIL IV; FREE OFFICERS, EGYPT; KAMIL, MUSTAFA; MUBARAK, HUSNI; NASSER, GAMAL ABDEL; SADAT, ANWAR AL-; SHENOUDA III; WAFD; ZAGHLUL, SA'D.

Bibliography

Atiya, Aziz S., ed. *The Coptic Encyclopedia,* 8 vols. New York: Macmillan, 1991. See esp. Bahr, Samira, "Modern Egypt, Copts in," vol. 5; Behrens-Abuseif, Doris, "British Occupation of Egypt," vol. 2; Boutros-Ghali, M., "Ethiopian Church Autocephaly," vol. 3; Du Bourguet, P. "Copt," vol. 2; Frend, W. H. C., "Monophysitism," vol. 5.

Atiya, Aziz S. *A History of Eastern Christianity,* rev. ed. Millwood, NY: Kraus Reprint, 1980.

Barrett, David B.; Kurian, George T.; Johnson, Todd M., eds. *World Christian Encyclopedia: A Comparative Survey of Churches and Religions in the Modern World,* 2 vols, 2d edition. New York and Oxford, U.K.: Oxford University Press, 2001.

Patrick, Theodore Hall. *Traditional Egyptian Christianity: A History of the Coptic Orthodox Church.* Greensboro, NC: Fisher Park Press, 1996.

Pennington, J. D. "The Copts in Modern Egypt." *Middle Eastern Studies* 2 (1982): 158–179.

Tagher, Jacques. *Christians in Muslim Egypt: An Historical Study of the Relations between Copts and Muslims from 640 to 1922.* Altenberge: Oros Verlag, 1998.

Tamura, A. "Ethnic Consciousness and Its Transformation in the Course of Nation-Building: The Muslim and the Copt in Egypt, 1906–1919." *Muslim World* 75 (1985): 102–114.

Watson, John H. *Among the Copts.* Portland, OR; Brighton, U.K.: Sussex Academic Press, 2000.

DONALD SPANEL
UPDATED BY MILAD HANNA AND GAWDAT GABRA

CORCOS FAMILY

A Jewish family of Morocco.

The Corcos family was one of the premier families of Morocco's Sephardim from the sixteenth through the twentieth centuries. They produced many rabbinical scholars.

Members of the Corcos family also held posts as court advisers, bankers, and *tujjar al-Sultan* (commercial agents of the ruler). Several acted as British and American consular representatives. Straddling the traditional and modern worlds, the Corcoses were a classic example of the Jewish comprador class.

Bibliography

Schroeter, Daniel J. *Merchants of Essaouira: Urban Society and Imperialism in Southwestern Morocco, 1844–1886.* Cambridge, U.K., and New York: Cambridge University Press, 1988.

NORMAN STILLMAN

CORSAIRS

Naval freebooters (often mistakenly called pirates) of many nations.

The corsairs sailed under the colors of the so-called Barbary states of North Africa from the early sixteenth century until the European naval powers suppressed their activity after the end of the Napoleonic wars. The North African corsairs attacked commercial ships sailing the Atlantic Ocean and Mediterranean Sea of those Christian powers that did not have treaty relations with their political masters, seized the vessels, cargoes, and crews, and sold them in their home ports—Algiers, Tunis, Tripoli, Rabat-Salé, and other smaller coastal towns. In Algiers, and to a lesser extent in Tunis and Tripoli, the corsairs came to control the (nominally) Ottoman Empire's political systems in the latter part of the sixteenth century, while in Morocco the Alawi (of the Alawite dynasty) sultans used them as a tool of their foreign policy after their rise to power in the 1660s. The corsairs were chief participants in the Barbary wars that ended in 1821.

See also ALAWITE DYNASTY; BARBARY STATES; BARBARY WARS.

JEROME BOOKIN-WEINER

COSSACK BRIGADE

Iranian cavalry unit that became the basis for the Iranian national army under Reza Shah.

Naser al-Din Shah established the Iranian Cossack Brigade in 1879. Hoping to emulate the ruthless reputation of Russia's Cossacks, he solicited the czar's assistance in contracting for a few Russian instructors to create a similar six-hundred-man mounted force. Reduced in its early years to two hundred, the so-called brigade (normally a 5,000-troop unit) was almost disbanded. In 1896, it helped maintain order in the streets after the shah's assassination; notoriety came when the shah used the unit to shell and intimidate the *majles* (parliament) in 1908.

With only Russians in command until 1920, the unit, which was reorganized as a division in 1916, served as a visible manifestation of Russian influence in northern Iran. The departure of all czarist officers in 1920 permitted Reza Khan, who had risen through the ranks, to take command of the division. In February 1921, his Cossacks supported the coup that led to the overthrow of the Qajar dynasty and transformed Reza Khan into Reza Shah Pahlavi by 1925. Under his control, the Cossack division became the nucleus of the forty-thousand-man national army he demanded as his first priority.

See also NASER AL-DIN SHAH; PAHLAVI, REZA; QAJAR DYNASTY.

Bibliography

Kazemzadeh, Firuz. "The Origin and Early Development of the Persian Cossack Brigade." *American Slavic and East European Review* 15 (October 1956): 351–363.

JACK BUBON

COTTON

A valued fiber crop.

An important fiber crop in the Middle East from the early Islamic period onward, cotton acquired new significance in the nineteenth century as the region's paramount export crop and most important raw material link to the world of European industrial capitalism. Egypt took pride of place in the development of the cotton industry as the earliest and long the largest producer of cotton for export. Traditionally, Egyptians had grown several different short-fiber varieties for domestic use, but under Muhammad Ali the government experimented with a locally discovered long-fiber variety of the sort preferred by European textile manufacturers. The first large harvest, overseen at every stage by experts from Syria and Anatolia, was realized in 1822. It brought a good price in Europe, where specialists appraised it as second in quality only to American Sea Island cotton from Georgia.

Poor agricultural practices and quality control, stemming partly from the Egyptian government monopoly's reluctance to reward peasant farmers

Young girls from poor villages in the Nile Delta pick cotton during the early fall harvest. Tens of thousands of children work the fields during Egypt's annual cotton harvest, which begins in September. © AP/WIDE WORLD PHOTOS. REPRODUCED BY PERMISSION.

for following the advice of the experts, led to a decline after initial success. After the mid-1830s, the frustration of Muhammad Ali's ambitious industrialization efforts, which had included textile factories for producing military uniforms, contributed to the decline. Recovery was unexpectedly prompted by the American Civil War, which made it difficult for European mill owners to acquire high-quality raw materials. Exports soared from 25,000 tons, the plateau reached in the 1850s, to 125,000 tons in 1865. After a postwar readjustment, exports resumed their increase, hitting a record 374,000 tons in 1910. By that time, cotton, to which almost a quarter of all cropped land was dedicated, accounted for 80.1 percent of Egypt's total exports, up from 66.6 percent in 1884. Later, nationalist critics charged the British, in control of Egypt since 1882, with turning the country into a giant cotton farm for the benefit of British manufacturers.

The American Civil War stimulated cotton exports from Syria and Anatolia, as well, but the postwar slump in prices drove production back down. Iran, too, shared in the wartime boom; but there the postwar fall in prices was eventually countered by a twelvefold expansion in general trade with Russia, particularly from the 1880s on. By World War I, Russia received 70 percent of Iranian exports, with cotton the most important product. Volume was 25,000 metric tons in 1913, amounting to some 95 percent of all cotton exports. In the 1930s, the

Iranian government entered on an industrialization drive that increasingly exploited cotton for domestic manufacturing. By the end of the decade, production had grown to 38,000 metric tons, of which only one-seventh was being exported; and Iranian mills were supplying half the domestic market for cotton cloth.

Cotton developed as the major cash crop of the Sudan from 1925 onward with the development of new irrigation projects. Turkish production expanded after World War I and boomed in the 1950s when the Korean War raised world commodity prices. The same circumstances turned cotton into Syria's biggest cash crop. Israeli and Afghan production expanded in the 1960s, much of the latter country's cotton being destined for export to the Soviet Union. By the late 1970s, 11.6 percent of the world's cotton production came from the Middle East, and the region encompassed 7 percent of the total world acreage devoted to cotton. The largest outputs, in thousands of metric tons, were those of Turkey (522), Iran (490), Egypt (413), Sudan (166), Syria (150), Israel (65), and Afghanistan (50). Much smaller amounts were produced in Morocco, Iraq, Jordan, and Yemen.

Cotton is the fabric of choice for clothing in much of the Middle East. Its lightness and absorbency particularly suit it to hot climates. Terms of Middle Eastern origin pertaining to types of cotton cloth—damask from Damascus, gauze from Gaza—testify to the long history of cotton textiles and are a reminder of a time when many cities of the area were known for their distinctive weaves and patterns. The transition from handwoven cotton fabrics to factory-made products initially favored the export of raw fiber and the import of inexpensive finished goods. This led, in turn, to disarray in the domestic textile industry, largely based on small workshops. Though tens of thousands of workers were still using handlooms at the end of World War I, and such distinctive local fabrics as the block-printed cottons of Iran and the embroidered tablecloths of Damascus survive to this day as choice products of national handicraft industries, most cotton textile production now takes place in modern spinning and weaving mills.

In 1977 the region produced 500,000 metric tons of cotton yarn, with the highest output from

Egypt, Turkey, and Syria. It also produced 2,640 million square meters of cotton fabric, with production concentrated most heavily in Egypt, Iran, and Syria. These figures represent approximately 5 percent of total world production from a region then comprising roughly the same proportion of the world's population.

See also MUHAMMAD ALI.

Bibliography

Issawi, Charles. *An Economic History of the Middle East and North Africa.* New York: Columbia University Press, 1982.

Owen, E. R. J. *Cotton and the Egyptian Economy, 1820–1914: A Study in Trade and Development.* Oxford: Clarendon, 1969.

Rivlin, Helen Anne B. *The Agricultural Policy of Muhammad Ali in Egypt.* Cambridge, MA: Harvard University Press, 1961.

Tignor, Robert L. *Modernization and British Colonial Rule in Egypt, 1882–1914.* Princeton, NJ: Princeton University Press, 1966.

RICHARD W. BULLIET

COUNCIL FOR DEVELOPMENT AND RECONSTRUCTION (CDR)

Council founded to design and supervise the reconstruction of Lebanon in 1977.

The Council for Development and Reconstruction (CDR) was founded to design and supervise the reconstruction of Lebanon in 1977 when the government falsely assumed that the civil war had ended. The CDR was supposed to receive and disburse foreign aid money to rebuild Lebanon, to assess the extent of damages resulting from Lebanon's civil war, and allocate international and Lebanese financial aid for reconstruction purposes.

The CDR enjoyed wide powers, often superior to those of the cabinet, and was directly accountable to the office of the prime minister. In 1978, $454 million was committed by the CDR for road repairs, housing, transportation, and the rebuilding of Beirut International Airport. In 1983, following Israel's invasion of southern Lebanon, which resulted in massive destruction and thousands of deaths, the CDR could raise only $571 million of the $15 billion necessary for the rebuilding of Lebanon's in-

frastructure. International and Arab pledges of financial support were never totally forthcoming; some countries did not make good on their pledges. Between 1985 and 1988, the activities of the CDR were undermined by government paralysis, rampant inflation, financial crisis, and the growing violence inside Lebanon.

In 1990, following the Ta'if Accord and the formation of a new government in Lebanon, the CDR was reinstated, and it became an arm of the political and economic apparatus of powerful prime minister Rafiq Baha'uddin al-Hariri.

See also HARIRI, RAFIQ BAHA'UDDIN AL-; TA'IF ACCORD.

Bibliography

American Task Force for Lebanon. *Working Paper: Conference on Lebanon.* Washington, DC: Author, 1991.

GEORGE E. IRANI
UPDATED BY AS'AD ABUKHALIL

COUSCOUS

See FOOD: COUSCOUS

COX, PERCY
[1864–1937]

British diplomat and colonial administrator.

After six years (1884–1890) in the British and Indian armies, Sir Percy Cox entered the Indian Political Department, where he was to spend most of the rest of his professional life. At this time, the government of India controlled British diplomatic relations with much of the coast of East Africa and with the shaykhdoms of the Persian (Arabian) Gulf. After postings at Zailaand and Berbera (Somalia), Cox was appointed British consul and political agent at Muscat (now a part of Oman), his first major post, in 1899. His knowledge of Arabic was crucial in enabling him to restore the relationship between the sultan, Faysal ibn Turki al Bu Sa'id, and the British and Indian governments, which had become strained as France attempted to replace British influence. By 1903 Faysal's subsidy had been restored, Faysal's son Taymur had attended the Delhi Durbar, and Lord Curzon, the viceroy of India, had visited Muscat and invested Faysal as Grand Commander of the Order of the Indian Empire (GCIE).

Cox spent most of the rest of the period before World War I in the Gulf, first as acting political resident and political resident, then as consul general (under the British minister in Tehran) for southwestern Persia (now Iran) including the Gulf islands, at a time when British trade with the area was rapidly increasing. In 1914 Cox, who had been knighted in 1911, was appointed secretary to the Foreign Department of the government of India. But a few months later, at the outbreak of World War I, he became chief political officer to Indian Expeditionary Force "D" that landed at Iraq's Fao Peninsula at the end of 1914. Apart from two years as acting British minister to Tehran (1918–1920), the rest of Cox's career was spent in Mesopotamia/Iraq. In the early part of the war, he also played a crucial role (although at a distance) in ensuring the neutrality of the Saudi ruler of Najd, Abd al-Aziz ibn Sa'ud al Sa'ud (Ibn Sa'ud), and postponing, if not ultimately preventing the differences between the former and Britain's other protégé, Husayn ibn Ali, Sharif of Mecca, from breaking out into open conflict.

Southern Mesopotamia was invaded in the last few weeks of 1914; British imperial troops reached Baghdad in March 1917 and Mosul a few days after the 1918 armistice that ended the war. One of the consequences of the fact that British authorities conducted the Mesopotamia campaign from India and the campaign in Egypt and Palestine from London and Cairo was that Cox, head of Iraq's civil administration, was not informed of the details of the Sykes-Picot Agreement until May 1917. As neither Cox nor his subordinates (notably Arnold Wilson) were kept abreast of London's thinking on possible future developments in the Middle East, they proceeded to set up an administration on the lines of the British Indian provinces with which they were familiar. When it became clear, toward the end of the war, that this kind of old-style colonialism was no longer acceptable (in the new international atmosphere that engendered the League of Nations), the result was a period of great uncertainty for British officials in the field.

Lord Curzon had asked Cox to go to Tehran to negotiate a new Anglo–Persian Agreement, but the turbulent political circumstances in Persia made this impossible. By June 1920, when he was appointed British high commissioner in Iraq, after spending nearly two years in Tehran, the situation had become extremely volatile, especially since the award of the Iraqi mandate to Britain at the San Remo Conference in April. During the summer, a rebellion broke out that threatened the whole future of the British connection with the country; Cox advised firmly against the lively "Quit Mesopotamia" campaign in the British press. He went to Iraq in the autumn and managed to secure the candidature of Faisal I ibn Hussein (whom the French had ousted from Syria) for the throne of Iraq. In October 1922, Cox forced through the signature of the Anglo–Iraqi Treaties (which replaced the mandate in form while maintaining its substance) and fixed the borders between Kuwait, Saudi Arabia, and Iraq over the next two months. After his retirement from Iraq in May 1923, he acted as British plenipotentiary in the negotiations over the Anglo–Iraqi frontier with Turkey in 1924.

See also ABD AL-AZIZ IBN SA'UD AL SA'UD; FAISAL I IBN HUSSEIN; HUSAYN IBN ALI; SAN REMO CONFERENCE (1920); SYKES–PICOT AGREEMENT (1916).

Bibliography

Graves, Philip. *The Life of Sir Percy Cox.* London and Melbourne: Hutchinson, 1941.

Sluglett, Peter. *Britain in Iraq, 1914–1932.* London: Ithaca Press, 1976.

PETER SLUGLETT
UPDATED BY MICHAEL R. FISCHBACH

CRANE, CHARLES R.

[1858–1939]

U.S. philanthropist, internationalist, and advocate for Arab independence.

Heir to a fortune from his father's plumbing-fixture business, Charles R. Crane was a major contributor to Woodrow Wilson's U.S. presidential campaigns. His experience as a member of the King-Crane Commission of 1919 turned him against Zionism and made him a passionate spokesman for the independence of the Arab states. Following a term as a U.S. minister to China (1921–1922),

Crane founded the New York–based Institute for Current World Affairs (ICWA) in 1925. The institute employed field representatives in Mexico, Jerusalem, and occasionally Moscow. The representatives compiled regular reports on developments in their regions and shared their expertise during ICWA-sponsored lecture tours to major U.S. universities. The reports were also made available to the U.S. State Department. From 1930 to 1941, the institute's Middle East representative was George Antonius, who researched and wrote his groundbreaking study *The Arab Awakening*; while in the employ of the ICWA. In the late 1920s Crane became so enamored of the rugged beauty of Yemen that he sponsored a team of engineers to develop that country's communications infrastructure.

See also ANTONIUS, GEORGE; KING–CRANE COMMISSION (1919).

Bibliography

Beecher, Frank W. *Reluctant Ally: United States Foreign Policy toward the Jews from Wilson to Roosevelt.* New York: Greenwood Press, 1991.

MIA BLOOM
UPDATED BY WILLIAM L. CLEVELAND

CREECH JONES, ARTHUR

[1891–1965]

British colonial secretary.

A member of the Labour Party and an expert on imperial issues, Arthur Creech Jones served as colonial secretary in Clement Attlee's government from 1946 to 1950. In this capacity, he was formally responsible for the British administration of Palestine, although the primary determinant of government policy there was the Foreign Office, headed by Ernest Bevin. Creech Jones was involved in discussions and negotiations over the report of the Anglo-American Committee of Inquiry into the Problems of European Jewry and Palestine (1946), the termination of the British mandate over Palestine, the transfer of responsibility to the United Nations, the partition of Palestine between Jews and Arabs, and the resettlement of European Jewish refugees in Palestine. Although mildly pro-Zionist, he presided over a British policy that incurred the violent opposition of the Zionist movement.

See also ANGLO–AMERICAN COMMITTEE OF INQUIRY (1946); BEVIN, ERNEST.

Bibliography

Louis, William Roger. *The British Empire in the Middle East 1945–1951: Arab Nationalism, the United States, and Post-war Imperialism.* Oxford, U.K.: Clarendon, 1984.

BERNARD WASSERSTEIN

CRÉMIEUX DECREE

French legislation that granted full French citizenship to the Jews of French colonial Algeria.

Named for Adolphe Crémieux, France's minister of justice, the Crémieux Decree was one of a series of acts affecting the political organization of Algeria that were issued by the French republic on 24 October 1870, shortly after it had come to power. Since the French occupation in 1830, Algerians had been French subjects but not French citizens. Only a handful had applied for naturalization, primarily because doing so necessitated acknowledging the primacy of French law and renouncing the right to be judged in accordance with religious statutes—a step almost no Muslims and very few Jews were prepared to take.

Because the Crémieux Decree accorded Jews—a religious minority in Algeria—a right denied to the country's religious majority, it angered Algerian Muslims. Further alienating Muslims was the decree's automatic application to the entire Jewish community, without conditions concerning their acceptance of the French legal system. Moreover, many of the European settlers in Algeria were opposed to the decree, because it permitted Algerian Jews to vote with them for local officials as well as for Algeria's seats in the French parliament.

Shortly after the passage of the Crémieux Decree, revolts erupted in the Algerian countryside, which threatened French settlers rendered especially vulnerable by the withdrawal of significant portions of the French army for service in the Franco–Prussian War. Asserting that Muslim anger over the Crémieux Decree had directly inspired these challenges to French authority, many settlers demanded its abrogation before it caused further troubles.

The settler reaction against the naturalization of the Jews was so vehement that the government did consider withdrawing the decree, but refrained from doing so to avoid antagonizing European Jewish financiers whose support it badly needed. It became clear in the light of subsequent evidence that the decree had played little, if any, role in sparking the rebellions. Rather, the rural Algerian Muslims involved in them had seized the opportunity presented by the decrease of French military power to challenge the newly constituted republican government—which, they were convinced, would sacrifice their interests while promoting those of the French settlers.

Settler opposition to the decree—and the deliberately deceptive attempt to tie it to the revolts—revealed a pervasive strain of antisemitism that continued to recur among lower-class Europeans in Algeria throughout the late nineteenth and early twentieth centuries. In 1940, during World War II, the German-sponsored French Vichy government abolished the Crémieux Decree when it took control of Algeria, but the provisions were reinstated after the war and remained in effect until the end of French rule in Algeria, in 1962.

Bibliography

Posener, S. *Adolphe Crémieux: A Biography*, translated by Eugene Golob. Philadelphia: Jewish Publication Society, 1940.

KENNETH J. PERKINS

CRIME

See LAW, MODERN

CRIMEAN WAR

The Crimean War developed out of a basic misunderstanding between Great Britain and imperial Russia over fundamental aims regarding the disposition of the territories of the greatly weakened Ottoman Empire.

About 1830, a Russian war against the Ottoman Empire had assured the independence of Greece. Until that time, the British, a close trade partner of Russia, had largely acquiesced to Russian acquisition of protector status over certain of the Ottoman Empire's Orthodox Christian territories, such as Serbia and the Romanian principalities.

There had always been Russophobes among British leaders, including William Pitt, the Younger, and George Canning. But it was only when Lord Palmerston was appointed secretary of state for external affairs that a clear British policy concerning the Middle East was conceived. The Treaty of Hunkar-Iskelesi, following Egypt's invasion of Asia Minor in 1833, appears to have been the catalyst. Apart from awarding to Muhammad Ali Pasha control of Syria and the island of Crete, a secret clause recognized Russia's right to intervene in Turkish affairs to "protect" the interests of Orthodox subjects. Palmerston made it clear to Parliament that this arrangement must be undone. He proposed that, to protect Britain's lifeline to India, Britain must either station soldiers in the Middle East at strategic points or energetically assist the Ottoman leadership to reform its armed forces and liberalize its system of government.

Britain chose the less expensive route of assisting such pro-British viziers as Mustafa Reşid Paşa and their protégés to reform the Ottoman system. Upon the accession of Sultan Abdülmecit I in 1839, the Ottoman government launched the so-called Tanzimat reform, which would culminate in the first Ottoman constitution of 1876. Also in 1839, the combined European powers forced Muhammad Ali, who was on the verge of usurping further powers from the Ottoman sultan, to withdraw his forces from Syria and the Sudan in exchange for the conciliatory gesture of receiving Egypt as his hereditary kingdom.

Despite this heightened British interest in the Mediterranean region, apparently Russia missed the message. When Czar Nicholas I (1825–1855) paid a state visit to Britain in 1842, he queried the British about the disposition of "the Sick Man of Europe." In typical British fashion, officials in London failed to give the czar a direct answer; consequently, he and his delegation concluded that if Russia strengthened its hold over Ottoman Turkey, Britain would not be upset.

A clash of interest and a cause célèbre was not long in developing. Sultan Abdülmecit, after consulting the powerful and popular British resident

Attendants during the Crimean War flank Ismail Pasha, mounted on horse. The photograph was taken in 1855 by the world's first war photojournalist, Roger Fenton. © HULTON-DEUTSCH COLLECTION/CORBIS. REPRODUCED BY PERMISSION.

ambassador, Stratford Canning, decided to award to France the traditional function and title of Protector of the Holy Sepulchre in Jerusalem. Imperial Russia, which annually sent thousands of pilgrims to the Holy Land and had recently invested sizable funds in Jerusalem for churches and pilgrim hostels, took grave offense at not receiving the honored designation. After long drawn-out bickering over the issue, Russia issued an ultimatum. With the Ottomans supported by the British ambassador, who now ordered the British fleet into the Black Sea, Russia declared war and marched on the Balkans, where the Turks put up a stiff resistance. Meanwhile, the British and French landed troops in the Crimea in 1853 and 1854 and besieged Russian fortifications at Inkerman and Sebastapol. Ill-equipped and ravaged by cholera, the Russians capitulated in 1855, and Czar Nicholas abdicated to be replaced by Czar Alexander II.

In the Peace of Paris (1856), Ottoman Turkey, France, Britain, and Austria—the latter not having been an active participant—forced upon Russia a humiliating settlement. Russia was to cease its meddling in Ottoman affairs, including Romania, and it was not permitted to fortify any point on the Black Sea. Her naval vessels also were placed under strict control of the allies.

This embarrassing result was an important factor in forcing Czar Alexander to declare the liber-

ation of the serfs in 1861. Moreover, the heavy commitment by Britain in the war and the great loss of life, in spite of heroic medical assistance by Florence Nightingale's field hospital in Istanbul, played a major role in Britain's decision twenty-five years later to occupy Cyprus and then Egypt to assure its lifeline to India without recourse to Ottoman Turkey.

See also ABDÜLMECIT I; CANNING, STRATFORD; HUNKAR-ISKELESI, TREATY OF (1833); MUHAMMAD ALI; MUSTAFA REŞID; OTTOMAN EMPIRE; PALMERSTON, LORD HENRY JOHN TEMPLE; TANZIMAT.

C. MAX KORTEPETER

CRIMES OF HONOR

Crimes, usually by men against women, committed in the name of honor.

The terms *crimes of honor* and *crimes committed in the name of honor* are commonly used to refer to violence with a claimed or imputed motivation related to honor. Recent regional and international attention to crimes of honor pays most attention to honor killings, which are documented across communities in different parts of the Middle East, including Jordan, Palestine, Israel, Lebanon, Egypt, Turkey, and Iraqi Kurdistan, as well as elsewhere in the world. The honor that is claimed or assumed to be behind the murder is family honor rather than the fidelity of a woman to her husband. The majority of victims are female and the majority of perpetrators are male. Family honor may be held to be impugned by sexual "misconduct" on the part of a woman—that is, intimate relationships with a man to whom she is not married. Honor killings thus typically involve the murder of a woman by a male blood relative who claims as motivation or defense her actual or suspected sexual activities outside marriage.

A number of civil organizations in the Middle East, particularly women's groups, conduct research, support, and advocacy activities related to crimes of honor. One target of their efforts is legislative and judicial policy. In some Arab states, there remains a partial defense in law (in Jordan, it is an absolute defense) in the event that a man surprises his wife or one of his close female relatives in the act of adultery and kills her and/or her partner in the act. Such provisions have antecedents in both French and Ottoman penal codes of the nineteenth century. Recent research shows that, in defending their actions, perpetrators rely on other partial defenses available in the law, notably that they acted in a "fit of fury" and in defense of their honor. Sentences may be substantially reduced in such cases. Research also shows that husbands as well as natal family members have recourse to arguments of honor in seeking reduced sentences for murder.

Among activists seeking to eliminate crimes of honor, there is deep discomfort over the apparent meaning of *honor* in the construction *crimes of honor*, since it implies that women embody the honor of males and seems to endorse violence against women. Using the term *honor killing* risks endorsing the description articulated by the perpetrator and obscuring (as may be the intention on the part of the perpetrator) the real motivation for the crime, which may be related to property disputes or other family or nonfamily matters.

Attention to crimes o f honor has increased in recent years across the region, enhanced by regional networking among women's organizations, and has been matched by growing attention among international organizations and at the United Nations.

See also GENDER: GENDER AND HEALTH; GENDER: GENDER AND LAW; GENDER: GENDER AND POLITICS; HAREM; *HIJAB;* HUSSEINI, RANA; KHADER, ASMA.

Bibliography

Abu Odeh, Lama. "Comparatively Speaking: The 'Honor' of the 'East' and the 'Passion' of the 'West.'" *Utah Law Review* no. 2 (1997): 287–307.

"Annotated Bibliography: 'Crimes of Honor.'" CIMEL/Interights. Available from <http://www.soas.ac.uk/honourcrimes>.

Moghaizel, Laure. "The Arab and Mediterranean World: Legislation towards Crimes of Honor." In *Empowerment and the Law: Strategies of Third World Women,* edited by Margaret Schuler. Washington, DC: OEF International, 1986.

Pervizat, Leyla. "'Honor Killings' in Turkey: Stories of Extra-Judicial Executions." *International Children's Rights Monitor* 15, no. 1 (2002): 18–21.

Shalhoub-Kevorkian, Nadera. "Femicide and the Palestinian Criminal Justice System: Seeds of Change in the Context of State-Building." *Law and Society Review* 36 (2002): 577–599.

LYNN WELCHMAN

CROMER, LORD

See BARING, EVELYN

CROSSMAN, RICHARD

[1907–1974]

British statesman and journalist.

The son of a judge, Richard Howard Stafford Crossman was an Oxford don, a journalist (long associated with the *New Statesman* and *Nation*), and a leading figure in the British Labour Party. During World War II he served in the Psychological Warfare Division of the British Army and in the spring of 1945 was one of the first British officers to enter the concentration camp at Dachau. A few weeks later he was elected to Parliament. Later that year the foreign secretary, Ernest Bevin, appointed Crossman to the Anglo-American Committee of Inquiry into the Problems of European Jewry and Palestine. The committee's report, submitted in April 1946, included a recommendation that 100,000 Jewish "displaced persons" be permitted to enter Palestine. The recommendation was rejected by the British government, deepening the Anglo-American rift over Palestine. Thereafter, Crossman strongly opposed British policy in Palestine, incurring the enmity of Bevin. Probably as a result, Crossman failed to secure a ministerial appointment before the fall of the Labour government in 1951. In 1955 to 1956 he served unproductively as a liaison in unofficial talks between Israel and President Gamal Abdel Nasser of Egypt. He held senior positions in Harold Wilson's government between 1964 and 1970. Toward the end of his life, Crossman was appointed official biographer of the Zionist leader Chaim Weizmann, whom he had known and greatly admired, but he completed only a fragment of the work before his death in 1974.

See also ANGLO–AMERICAN COMMITTEE OF INQUIRY (1946).

Bibliography

Crossman, Richard. *Palestine Mission: A Personal Record.* London: Hamish Hamilton, 1947.

BERNARD WASSERSTEIN

CUKUROVA

See CILICIA

CUMHURIYET

See NEWSPAPERS AND PRINT MEDIA: TURKEY

CURIEL FAMILY

Family of European Sephardim and Marranos who became active in Jewish life in Egypt in the nineteenth century. Most were Italian nationals who entered the banking profession.

The most noted family member was Henry Curiel (1914–1978), who joined Marxist groups during the years between the two world wars. In 1941, he opened a bookshop in Cairo, where Marxist and antifascist elements engaged in political discussions. As a fervent proponent of Egyptianization despite his communist leaning, Curiel was instrumental in creating the Egyptian Movement for National Liberation (al-Haraka al-Misriyya lil-Taharrur al-Watani; MELN) during World War II to promote the idea among Marxists. In 1946, Curiel's MELN and Hillel Schwartz's pro-communist ISKRA merged to become the Democratic Movement for National Liberation (al-Haraka al-Dimuqratiya lil-Taharrur al-Watani; HADITU), and membership quickly rose to several thousand.

HADITU enjoyed an ephemeral existence, for in May 1948, in the wake of the Palestine war, many of its activists were arrested along with the Zionists. HADITU was organized into sections of students, workers, women, and even army officers. Pursuing the Soviet line, HADITU advocated the creation of a secular democratic state in Palestine integrating Jews and Arabs. Subsequently, however, it advocated the two-separate-states solution—Arab and Jewish. In 1950, following the emergence of Egypt's Wafdist government, noted communists, either interned or under surveillance, were expelled from Egypt. Henry Curiel spent the rest of his life in Europe,

promoting revolutionary movements. In 1978, he was assassinated in France.

Bibliography

Botman, Selma. *The Rise of Egyptian Communism, 1939–1970.* Syracuse, NY: Syracuse University Press, 1988.

Krämer, Gudrun. *The Jews in Modern Egypt, 1914–1952.* Seattle: University of Washington Press, 1989.

Laskier, Michael M. *The Jews of Egypt, 1920–1970: In the Midst of Zionism, Anti-Semitism, and the Middle East Conflict.* New York: New York University Press, 1992.

MICHAEL M. LASKIER

CURZON, GEORGE NATHANIEL
[1859–1925]

English statesman who stressed Iran's strategic importance to Britain.

Born in Britain, George Nathaniel Curzon, the Viscount of Keddelston, was emerging as a British authority on the Middle East when he traveled to Iran in 1889 as a newspaper correspondent. During the six months he spent traveling throughout the country on horseback, he became impressed with Iran's importance to the strategic defense of British India. Russia had become Britain's principal imperial rival in central Asia, and Curzon perceived Russian interests in the region as being inimical to those of Britain. In his monumental work, *Persia and the Persian Question,* he argued that Britain should protect Iran, the gateway to India, from European (and especially Russian) encroachments. The book also contained insightful descriptions of Iran's politics and society at the end of the nineteenth century.

Following his tour of Iran, Curzon was appointed foreign office undersecretary for India and subsequently viceroy of India. As the de facto British ruler of India from 1899 to 1905, he played a major role in shaping policy toward Iran, which fell under the purview of the India office. In 1903, Curzon made a ceremonial naval visit to the Persian Gulf that he viewed as intended to convey to Russia the extent of British power in the area.

Curzon was appointed to the House of Lords after he returned home in 1905. He distrusted efforts by the government to establish an understanding with Russia and opposed the Anglo–Russian Agreement (1907), which he criticized for abandoning

British interests in Iran to Russia. After World War I, he was appointed foreign secretary. He was the architect of the Anglo–Iranian Agreement (1919), which would have made Iran a virtual British protectorate; much to his disappointment, the Iranian parliament failed to approve the controversial treaty.

See also ANGLO–IRANIAN AGREEMENT (1919); ANGLO–RUSSIAN AGREEMENT (1907).

Bibliography

Bennett, G. H. *British Foreign Policy during the Curzon Period, 1919–24.* New York: St. Martin's Press in association with King's College, London, 1995.

Curzon, G. N. *Persia and the Persian Question.* London: Longmans, Green & Co., 1892.

Gilmour, David. *Curzon: Imperial Statesman.* New York: Farrar, Straus and Giroux, 2003.

ERIC HOOGLUND

CYPRUS

The largest island in the eastern Mediterranean.

The Cyprus Republic was established as a sovereign independent state in 1960. It is a presidential republic in which the president is elected by popular vote to a five-year term and the legislature consists of the unicameral House of Representatives. Covering 3,700 square miles (9,251 sq km), Cyprus lies south of the Turkish mainland and east of Syria. Prior to 1960, Britain ruled Cyprus, after having annexed it from the Ottoman Empire in 1878.

Cyprus has been divided since 1974 when Turkey invaded and occupied the northern part of the island. Turkey's troops control this territory, which makes up about a third of the island. The Turkish occupation of 1974 caused 200,000 Greek Cypriots to move southward and 50,000 Turkish Cypriots to relocate to the occupied territories. In 1983, a Turkish Republic of Northern Cyprus was established, but has not been recognized by any country besides Turkey.

Population and Major Cities

The last census to survey the entire island, in 1973, recorded a population of 631,788, of whom about 80 percent were Greek-speaking Orthodox, 18 percent Turkish-speaking Muslims, and the remaining 2 percent Maronites and Armenians. A 1986 census found the population in nonoccupied Cyprus to be 677,200, whereas that in the north was estimated to be about 160,000 (not including about 65,000 people from mainland Turkey who had settled in northern Cyprus). An official estimate for the population of the entire island in 1991 came to 708,000.

The capital of Cyprus, Nicosia, was divided by a "green line" that separated the northern occupied part from the rest of the city and effectively closed the city's international airport. The other major cities are Larnaca (where the international airport was relocated), Limassol, and Paphos; in occupied Cyprus, the largest towns are Kerynia, virtually deserted since the invasion in 1974, and Famagusta. With the exception of Nicosia, all the major towns are seaports. Two mountain ranges on the island run east to west, one in the north and the higher Troödos range in the south.

Economy

After Cyprus gained independence in 1960, its economy changed dramatically. Within the next three decades, the formerly agrarian character of the island was transformed as domestic manufacturing and international trade were developed vigorously, in the process raising the per capita income from $350 in 1960 to $7,500 in 1986. The development of tourism was also a significant factor in this period.

The millet system, which operated in Cyprus during the period of Ottoman rule (1570–1878), allowed the Greek Orthodox church of Cyprus to play an important role in the affairs of the majority Greek-speaking population of the island. The leader of the church, Archbishop Kyprianos, and a group of notables who supported the Greek war of independence (1821) were executed by the authorities. The Tanzimat reforms of 1839 and especially the Hatt-i Hümayun reforms introduced in Cyprus in 1856 improved living conditions for the Greek Orthodox inhabitants and enhanced their commercial and educational opportunities.

British Rule

Cyprus was awarded to Britain at the Berlin Congress (1878), and Britain took over its administration. The island, however, remained formally part of the Ottoman Empire until 1914, when it was annexed by Britain as a consequence of the Ottoman Empire's siding with the Central Powers in World War I. British rule brought a greater degree of self-government for the population and a Western-based judicial system but also much higher taxation, imposed to finance the compensation Britain had undertaken to pay the Ottomans after 1878.

The disaffection of the local Greek Orthodox population with British rule served to encourage sentiment in favor of union with Greece. During an uprising in support of *enosis* (union with Greece) in Nicosia (1931), the British Government House was burned down. The authorities retaliated by suspending the island's legislative council. The pro-enosis movement grew again in the late 1940s after the referendum—organized by the all-party Ethnarchic Council under the new Greek Orthodox Archbishop Makarios III—that decided overwhelmingly in favor of union with Greece.

The Greek Cypriots took their case to the United Nations (UN) and Archbishop Makarios traveled to the United States to publicize the movement, but the UN assembly declined to take up the issue and more anti-British demonstrations occurred on Cyprus. On 1 April 1955 attacks on British installations signaled a new phase in the island's anticolonial struggle. The campaign was led by the Ethniki Organosis Kipriakou Agonos (EOKA; National Organization of Cypriot Fighters), a Greek Cypriot guerrilla organization headed by Georgios Theodoros Grivas, a colonel of the Greek army who used the nom de guerre Dighenis. In retaliation, Britain exiled Archbishop Makarios and his close collaborators to the Seychelles (1956). While diplomatic initiatives began to resolve the Cyprus crisis at the UN and in London (1957), the minority group of Turkish Cypriots on the island, fearing the consequences of enosis, declared themselves to be for either a federation or partition.

Independence and Internal Conflict

Diplomatic negotiations between the British, Greek, and Turkish governments led to the Zurich Agreement between Greece and Turkey and the London Agreement between Britain, Greece, Turkey, and the Greek and Turkish Cypriot leaderships. The se-

Makarios III (1913–1977), statesman and Orthodox Eastern archbishop (1950–1977). He supported the enosis movement, the political unification of Cyprus and Greece, and was the first president of independent Cyprus (1959–1977). © LIBRARY OF CONGRESS. REPRODUCED BY PERMISSION.

ries of arrangements brought about the establishment of an independent state, the Cyprus Republic, whose sovereignty was to be guaranteed by Britain, Greece, and Turkey. Small garrisons of Greek and Turkish forces were to be stationed on Cyprus, and the rights of the Turkish Cypriot minority were enshrined in the constitution, which provided for the office of a Turkish Cypriot vice president of the republic with extensive veto powers. In December 1959, Makarios was elected president and Fazil Kuçuk vice president. Elections for the legislative assembly were held in 1960, and in August of the same year the last British governor, Sir Hugh Foote, announced the end of British rule on the island (Britain retained two military bases under its sovereignty), thereby paving the way for the formal proclamation of the Cyprus Republic.

After a breakdown in Greek Cypriot and Turkish Cypriot relations led to intercommunal fighting in 1963, the areas populated by Turkish Cypriots were separated administratively by a so-called green line. When the situation continued to be tense in 1964, the Greek Cypriots began fearing a military invasion from mainland Turkey. Through a series of negotiations held under the aegis of the UN, diplomats sought a more practical resolution of the intercommunal conflict. Their proposals ranged from a reaffirmation of the original constitutional structure to either union with Greece or division of the island, but none of these measures was acceptable to both sides. The arrival of a UN peacekeeping force (1964), however, helped to reestablish peace. By remaining committed to preserving the Cyprus Republic, Makarios incurred the opposition of the Greek Cypriot nationalists and their leader, Colonel Grivas. Aided by the Greek dictatorship established in 1967, Grivas, working through an organization named EOKA-B, led a renewed struggle for enosis from 1971 till his death in 1974.

Growing conflict between Makarios and the Greek dictatorship culminated in the latter's support of Makarios's overthrow and the imposition of a dictatorship headed by Greek Cypriot nationalist Nikos Sampson (July 1974). Makarios survived an assassination attempt and left the island. Claiming to be exercising its rights as a guarantor of the sovereignty of Cyprus, Turkey launched a military invasion and eventually placed the northern third of the island under its control. The Greek dictatorship and the Sampson regime collapsed, and Glafkos Clerides was made acting president, pending the return of Makarios in December 1974.

After 1974, the two sides undertook numerous negotiations and held many meetings under the auspices of the UN, whose General Assembly called for the withdrawal of the Turkish occupying forces and the return of all the refugees to their homes. Several plans designed to resolve the crisis were submitted and although the Greek Cypriots agreed to a number of successive concessions, no overall arrangement has been acceptable to both sides.

Makarios died in 1977. His successor, Spyros Kyprianou, was president until 1988. As the candidate of the Democratic Party, he then lost the presidential elections to George Vasileiou, who was supported by, among others, the large Communist Party (AKEL). Vasileiou's tenure ended in 1993, when Glafkos Clerides won the presidential elections. In the meanwhile, Turkish Cypriot leader Rauf Denktash had declared the establishment of the Turkish Republic of Northern Cyprus (TRNC) in 1983. He was elected president of TRNC in 1985 and reelected in 1990.

See also BERLIN, CONGRESS AND TREATY OF; DENKTASH, RAUF; GRIVAS, GEORGIOS THEODOROS; MILLET SYSTEM; TANZIMAT.

Bibliography

Attalides, Michael A. *Cyprus, Nationalism and International Politics.* New York: St. Martin's, 1979.

Ioannides, Christos P., ed. *Cyprus: Domestic Dynamics, External Constraints.* New Rochelle, NY: Melissa Media, 1992.

Necatigil, Zaim M. *The Cyprus Question and the Turkish Position in International Law,* 2d edition. Oxford and New York: Oxford University Press, 1993.

ALEXANDER KITROEFF

CYPRUS CONVENTION (1878)

Agreement to let the British occupy Ottoman-held Cyprus in return for promise of military aid.

The Russian–Ottoman War of 1877 to 1878 ended with the Treaty of San Stefano, forced on the defeated Ottoman Empire by Russia's czar and his minister Nikolas Ignatiev. San Stefano, however, was not to the liking of Britain's prime minister, Benjamin Disraeli. He offered to support the Ottomans and seek a revision of the treaty. In return, he demanded the island of Cyprus. The British had been looking for a naval base in the eastern Mediterranean, and Cyprus was ideally situated. By the Cyprus Convention of June 1878, the Ottoman sultan allowed the British to occupy Cyprus in return for a British guarantee of military aid if Russia refused to withdraw from the eastern Anatolian provinces occupied during the war. It took some time for the details to be arranged to the satisfaction of both parties, and the final terms of the convention were not settled until 3 February 1879. With the tentative agreement in hand by 4 June 1878, however, Britain engineered a drastic revision of the San Stefano treaty in favor of the Ottoman Empire at the Congress of Berlin in July 1878.

See also BERLIN, CONGRESS AND TREATY OF; IGNATIEV, NIKOLAS PAVLOVICH; SAN STEFANO, TREATY OF (1878).

Bibliography

Hurewitz, J. C., trans. and ed. *The Middle East and North Africa in World Politics,* 2d edition. New Haven, CT: Yale University Press, 1975.

Shaw, Stanford, and Shaw, Ezel Kural. *History of the Ottoman Empire and Modern Turkey.* 2 vols. Cambridge, U.K., and New York: Cambridge University Press, 1976–1977.

ZACHARY KARABELL

CYRENAICA

Traditional region of Libya.

The three historic North African regions of Cyrenaica, Tripolitania, and the Fezzan combine to make up the modern state of Libya, officially known as the Great Socialist People's Libyan Arab Jamahiriya (Al Jumahiriyah al Arabiyah al Libiyah ash Shabiyah al Ishtirakiyah al Uzma). With an area of approximately 305,000 square miles (790,000 sq km), the boundaries of Cyrenaica stretch east from the Gulf of Sidra to the Egyptian border, west to Tripolitania, and south from the Mediterranean Sea to Chad and the Sudan. Geographically, Cyrenaica is divided into three distinct areas, consisting of the coastal plain, a mountainous area in the east, and the southern desert.

The city of Benghazi, the second-largest population center in Libya and the commercial center for the eastern half of the country, is located in Cyrenaica on the eastern side of the Gulf of Sidra. Five ancient Greek cities, known collectively as the *pentapolis,* are also located in Cyrenaica. Thought to have been founded around 631 B.C.E., the city of Cyrene is the best preserved of the five. After it became part of the Roman Empire, Cyrene was severely damaged during a Jewish revolt in 115 C.E. By the fourth century C.E., all five of the *pentapolis* cities lay virtually deserted.

Throughout history, Cyrenaica has looked eastward to the Mashriq, or eastern Islamic world, maintaining especially close ties with Egypt. When defeated in tribal wars, Cyrenaican Bedouins some-times migrated to Egypt, often eventually settling there. Other tribal members retained their nomadic way of life, crossing back and forth into Egypt with little concern for vague, unmarked borders. During the period of Italian occupation, which began in 1911, Cyrenaicans received arms and other supplies from Egypt in support of their struggle against the European invaders. Eventually, the Italian army built a barbed-wire fence the length of the Libya–Egypt border in an effort to stop the passage of military supplies to the insurgents.

The Sanusi Order, a Sufi religious movement dedicated to spreading religious enlightenment in areas where Islam was only lightly observed, was established in Cyrenaica in 1842 by Sayyid Muhammad ibn Ali al-Sanusi. Eighty years later, his successor, Sayyid Muhammad Idris al-Mahdi al-Sanusi, was forced by the Italians to seek refuge in Egypt, where he remained for almost three decades. He later returned to Libya as King Idris I to head the newly created United Kingdom of Libya in 1951.

With approximately 1 million people as of 2003, or almost 20 percent of the Libyan population, Cyrenaica is a vibrant economic and commercial center. The Jabal al-Akhdar, a high plateau in eastern Cyrenaica known as the Green Mountain, together with Kufrah and other irrigated areas in the south, are important centers of agricultural production. However, it is the petroleum sector that drives both the Cyrenaican and Libyan economies. Oil and gas from Cyrenaica, first discovered in commercial quantities in 1959, account for almost all of Libya's exports and approximately one-third of the national gross domestic product. The continued expansion of the petroleum industry into the twenty-first century led to the modernization of the port of Benghazi and the construction of many oil-exporting facilities along the coast of Cyrenaica.

See also BENGHAZI; IDRIS AL-SAYYID MUHAMMAD AL-SANUSI; LIBYA; SANUSI, MUHAMMAD IBN ALI AL-; SANUSI ORDER.

Bibliography

Nelson, Harold D., ed. *Libya: A Country Study,* 3d edition. Washington, DC: U.S. Government Printing Office, 1979.

St John, Ronald Bruce. *Historical Dictionary of Libya,* 3d edition. Lanham, MD: Scarecrow Press, 1998.

Wright, John. *Libya: A Modern History.* Baltimore, MD: Johns Hopkins University Press, 1982.

JOHN L. WRIGHT
UPDATED BY RONALD BRUCE ST JOHN

CYRIL IV
[1816–1861]

110th Coptic patriarch of Egypt, 1854–1861.

Despite his short tenure, Cyril IV was the father of reform in the Egyptian Coptic church, both in the laity and the clergy; he remains one of the greatest modern Coptic patriarchs. Concerned for education in its broadest sense, Cyril established many schools throughout Egypt, promoted basic literacy, advanced theological training, and published new editions of important Coptic documents. The most famous institutions founded by the patriarch were the Coptic Orthodox College for clerics and Egypt's first women's college, both in Cairo. Empowered by the tuition received at these new schools, Copts attained important governmental positions in unprecedented numbers. Cyril's aggressive reform of church administration, particularly in land management, made him unusually popular among the laity, which had long sought a more equitable balance of power with the clergy. Unfortunately, Cyril's successors had no interest in continuing the enfranchisement of the laity and thus created a tension that has been played out even in recent times. Cyril fostered Coptic nationalism through an aggressive campaign of restoring ancient churches and building new ones, his greatest achievements being the construction of Saint Mark's Basilica in Azbakiya. A skillful negotiator, Cyril successfully mediated a dispute between Egypt and Ethiopia from 1856 to 1858. His dream of closer ties with the Russian Orthodox Church and the Church of England led to a conflict with Saʿid Pasha, who feared foreign interference. Cyril's assassination (by poison) was rumored to have been ordered by the pasha.

See also COPTS.

Bibliography

Atiya, Aziz S. *A History of Eastern Christianity,* revised edition. Millwood, NY: Kraus Reprint, 1980.

Strothmann, R. *Die koptische Kirche in der Neuzeit.* Tübingen, Germany: J.C.B. Mohr, 1932.

DONALD SPANEL

CYRIL V
[1824–1927]

112th Coptic patriarch of Egypt, 1874–1927.

Cyril V enjoyed the longest tenure of any Coptic patriarch but had a relatively insipid career. Even his admirers commented upon his simple-minded disinterest in matters foreign to his conservative, clerical background. Like his predecessor, Demetrius II, Cyril supported education. In 1894, he established the Coptic Clerical College in Cairo. Nonetheless, Cyril lacked Demetrius's zeal, and he even closed some schools. To his credit, Cyril fostered Coptic nationalism by restoring ancient churches and building new ones, although he was unconcerned for the most crucial issue confronting his church, the sharing of power with the laity, which had enjoyed a promising but abortive start under Cyril IV.

The neglect by Cyril V further widened the gap between the progressive populace and the more conservative clergy. As a former monk, Cyril was solidly entrenched in that tradition. He especially infuriated the populace by reneging on his promise of cooperation in the administration of the *waqfs* (religious endowments). Worse still, he refused to attend the sessions of the Community Religious Council (Majlis Milli), which had come into existence shortly before his patriarchate, to empower the Coptic laity in the areas of church property, personal rights, and social welfare. Cyril's nonparticipation led to the suspension of the council and had serious consequences for the equitable adjudication of marriage, divorce, and inheritance, thus worsening the rift between ecclesiastical and secular factions within the church. Despite parliamentary restoration of the council in 1883 and 1891, Cyril's continued noncompliance left both assemblies powerless. The khedive acquiesced reluctantly to the council's petition for Cyril's banishment because he had enjoyed good relations with the patriarch. The action proved highly controversial; even many of Cyril's foes found his punishment unfair. Nevertheless, Cyril was exiled in 1892 and 1893 for his stubborn opposition to the council. Ironically, when restored, he enjoyed widespread support from friend and foe alike.

See also COPTS; DEMETRIUS II.

Bibliography

Atiya, Aziz S. *A History of Eastern Christianity,* revised edition. Millwood, NY: Kraus Reprint, 1980.

Wakin, Edward. *A Lonely Minority: The Modern Story of Egypt's Copts.* New York: Morrow, 1963.

DONALD SPANEL

CYRIL VI
[1902–1971]

116th Coptic patriarch of Egypt, 1959–1971.

Cyril became pope of the Coptic church amid a long and bitter controversy between the Holy Synod of bishops and the Coptic Community Council, which consisted of laypersons. At issue was the appropriate field of candidates for the office. Until the twentieth century, the patriarch had been chosen from the monks. Beginning with the tenure (1927–1942) of John XIX, however, the selection had shifted to provincial bishops. Yusab (Joseph) II, bishop of Girga in southern Egypt, served as acting patriarch from 1942 to 1944. After the brief tenure of another bishop, Makarius III, as pope (1944–1945), Yusab II was elected to the office and served from 1946 to 1956. Following his death, Athanasius, bishop of Buni Suwayf, became acting pope from 1956 to 1957. Because all four pontiffs had undistinguished and even disastrous (in the case of Yusab II) terms of office, both the government of Gamal Abdel Nasser and the populace generally favored a monk. In a confusing inversion of preference, however, the assembly of bishops favored a monk and the community council sought a monk. So divided was the church over the selection of a new pontiff that the government temporarily suspended the papal election in 1957. The choice of Cyril, a monk from Baramus in the Nile delta, represented a victory for the Nasser regime and the laity.

Cyril's name, adopted at the time of the papal election, honored several illustrious predecessors, particularly Cyril I (patriarch 412–444), a preeminent early Alexandrian theologian widely regarded as one of the fathers of the Coptic church. The true first name of Cyril VI was Mina. As a monk, he had enjoyed wide renown as an ascetic and a mystic. For many years he had sought unsuccessfully to rebuild the ancient monastery of his namesake, St. Menas (Mina), near Alexandria and lost no time as patriarch in realizing this project. At his behest, more than forty other churches and monasteries were excavated, restored, or built anew. These endeavors attracted criticism as well as praise. To many, Cyril was aloof, more interested in antiquarian and monastic concerns than with either the country's or the church's pressing needs. This complaint was repeated throughout Cyril's administration. Nonetheless, even Cyril's detractors admired his piety, which had been honed through his years as a monk.

Cyril's efforts at reform met with some success. He sought closer relations with the other Christian churches of the Near East. Coptic missionary activity flourished in many parts of Africa, and numerous African divinity students received scholarships to study at the Coptic Theological College and the Institute of Coptic Studies in Cairo. Of all African countries outside Egypt, Cyril was especially interested in Ethiopia because its primary Christian church had for centuries been under the jurisdiction of the Coptic patriarch and, in more recent years, had demanded autonomy. One of Cyril's first acts as patriarch was to convene a council that addressed the Ethiopians' demands. The historic accord of 1959 remains the foundation upon which the relations between the Coptic and Ethiopic orthodox churches are grounded. Although the Coptic pontiff retained his position as head of the Ethiopic church, the Ethiopians could henceforth participate in papal elections. Furthermore, the Ethiopians could now elect their own leader. Heretofore, the Ethiopians had had a metropolitan or archbishop but no patriarch. The new patriarch or *abuna* of the Ethiopian church was to be an Ethiopian, not an Egyptian. The *abuna* could consecrate his own clergy. Ethiopians could participate in all synods convened by the Coptic pope. Several other important privileges were granted to the Ethiopians.

In other areas, Cyril's achievements were more limited. In 1960, the government placed the handling of waqf property (endowments given to the church) under a special committee composed of

Copts. This move was hailed by some as an efficient administrative reform because the high clergy and the Coptic Community Council had clashed for decades over the handling of the waqfs, and it was condemned by others because the action took away much responsibility from both the clergy and the community council. The latter was left with responsibility for little more than administration of the Coptic centers for theological education and for building various projects.

Cyril's struggle to alleviate the discrimination toward and persecution of Copts tolerated by the Islamic regime was similarly inspired but fruitless. Believing that close cooperation with the Islamic government would foster better relations between Muslims and Copts, Cyril joined with Muslim leaders in denouncing Israel on several occasions. Furthermore, through wider participation in international religious conferences and meeting with leaders of other churches, Cyril reckoned that oppression of the Copts would abate if the rest of the world were watching. Although the plight of the Copts is now more widely recognized, unfortunately it has not improved.

See also COPTS; JOHN XIX; NASSER, GAMAL ABDEL; WAQF.

Bibliography

Atiya, Aziz S. *A History of Eastern Christianity,* revised edition. Millwood, NY: Kraus Reprint, 1980.

Meinardus, Otto F. A. *Christian Egypt: Faith and Life.* Cairo: American University in Cairo Press, 1970.

Wakin, Edward. *A Lonely Minority: The Modern Story of Egypt's Copts.* New York: Morrow, 1963.

DONALD SPANEL